Ted Morgan is the author of *Somerset Maugham* and *Churchill 1874–1915*. His articles in the *New York Times Magazine* have won numerous awards including two Front Page (Newspaper Guild) awards and the Pulitzer Prize. He lives in New York.

Reviewing *Somerset Maugham* Kingsley Amis said, 'As rich in detail as one of the master's novels,' and *Newsweek*, 'Morgan excels at succinct portraiture and pertinent anecdote.' Of *Churchill 1874–1915* Corelli Barnett wrote, 'A balanced, perceptive and very readable biography.'

Both titles are available in Triad/Grafton Paperbacks.

By the same author

On Becoming American
Rowing Towards Eden
Churchill: Young Man in a Hurry 1874–1915
Maugham

TED MORGAN

FDR

A Biography

GRAFTON BOOKS

A Division of the Collins Publishing Group

LONDON GLASGOW
TORONTO SYDNEY AUCKLAND

Grafton Books
A Division of the Collins Publishing Group
8 Grafton Street, London W1X 3LA

Published by Grafton Books 1987

First published in Great Britain by
Grafton Books 1986

Copyright © Ted Morgan 1985

ISBN 0-586-06926-7

Printed and bound in Great Britain by
Richard Clay Ltd, Bungay, Suffolk

Set in Times

THIS BOOK IS DEDICATED TO

JACQUES DE THIER

WHO, AT THE AGE OF 85,
HAS A CURIOSITY ABOUT LIFE
AND A LOVE OF SIMPLE PLEASURES
THAT FAR YOUNGER MEN MIGHT WISH FOR

"It must be borne in mind that my design is not to write histories but lives. And the most glorious exploits do not always furnish us with the clearest indications of virtue or vice in men; sometimes a matter of less moment, an expression or a jest, informs us better of their characters and inclinations than sieges, the greatest armaments, or the bloodiest battles. Therefore, as portrait-painters are more exact in the lines and features of the face, in which the character is seen, than in the other parts of the body, so I must be allowed to give my more particular attention to the marks and indications of the souls of men, and while I endeavor by these to portray their lives, may be free to leave more weighty matters and great battles to be treated by others."

—*Plutarch*, Lives of Nine Illustrious Greeks and Romans

CONTENTS

———

PROLOGUE

I N June 16, 1929, the Harvard class of 1904 gathered in Cambridge to hold its twenty-fifth reunion. Men who had been launched as ships are launched, by no means finished, returned to the Yard to take part in this mid-life ceremony and tell each other how skillfully they had navigated through the quarter century, men in their forties, established in their professions, the turns taken.

Exchanging banter at the scene of their undergraduate years ("remember the battle cry 'Oh Reinhart,' remember Forbes Robertson in *Hamlet*"), the members of the class of 1904 seemed as insulated from the world as gold bars in Fort Knox. Outside the Yard, Americans watched the months and years drag by, each one worse than the last. They would grow angry at the do-nothing Hoover administration. In North Dakota, wheat would drop to thirty cents a bushel. On Wall Street, speculators would push stocks to the breaking point. "In this republican country," Hawthorne had written, "amid the fluctuating waves of our social life, somebody is always at the drowning point."

Outside the Yard, in months to come, men in cloth caps will sell apples. Men huddled around bonfires will talk about where they used to work. Men will forage in city dumps. Men carrying burlap bags will walk along railroad tracks and pick up pieces of coal. Men will register in flophouses, give up their clothes for fumigation, and listen to sermons. Old men without hope will join young men losing hope. There will be despair in their faces. They will fade into the city grayness, they will be one with the fog and the pavement.

But on Thursday, June 20, all was bright good cheer as the alumni classes lined up for commencement. Normally, the quarter-mile procession from Harvard Hall to the quadrangle behind Sever Hall was led by the chief marshal, but this time tradition was ignored—for the chief marshal, the most distinguished member of his class, was a cripple. This time, the man who could not walk at the head of the procession was driven in a Ford runabout to Straus Hall to receive his baton and badge. With the help of his four sons, he was lifted from the car. Leg braces snapped shut, and he advanced with a stiff and awkward gait, his left hand holding a cane, his right hand gripping a son's arm for support, in his dark cutaway coat, white four-in-hand scarf, and silk hat. This man, who could not take a single step unassisted, was governor of New York and leader and hope of the Democratic party, which had not won a national election since 1916.

Throwing back his head and smiling, he greeted them one by one. There was his old roommate, Lathrop Brown, and C. B. Marshall, captain of the football team, who had once kicked a forty-yard field goal, now a stockbroker in Rhode Island, and Jim Burgess, who had been first marshal in 1904, now in insurance in Boston.

There was one of the old *Crimson* crowd, who hailed him with: "Frank, if only you'd stuck to the newspaper game, you might have gotten somewhere." And there was Arthur Ficke, the class poet who had read the "heroic part of considerable length" at class day ceremonies in 1904, and had later become the friend and lover of Edna St. Vincent Millay. Ficke could not understand how that nice, quiet, amiable young fellow he had known from 1900 to 1904 had developed into a leader, a generous idealist in the political life of his time. It was baffling. Frank was one kind of person, and he was another. Frank moved easily in the world of action, he prowled along in the world of moral reflection.

Sidney Gunn, who had nominated him for chief marshal, had worried that he might not get it, since there were so many Republican standpatters in the class. But they rallied round. Even Freddy Viaux, to whom a Democrat was about three degrees worse than an anarchist, had urged his election, and Roger Pierce, president of the New England Trust, had written him that "in my humble belief you have made far more of your life than any other member of our class."

Being governor was nothing in comparison, Franklin Delano Roosevelt wrote a friend. He had not made Phi Beta Kappa or Porcellian, or won his Harvard H or been elected one of three class marshals, so this was something of a vindication.

The day was cloudy and threatening, but it did not rain. At 1:30 P.M, Roosevelt went into the 1904 tent in front of Weld Hall for lunch, as the band broke into "Harvardiana":

> "O'er the stands in flaming crimson
> Harvard's banners fly."

Twenty-five years ago they had stood in Harvard Yard clutching their registration slips, as undifferentiated as oranges in a crate. How to explain the thousand elements that separated failure from success? It was like analyzing each grain of sand in an hourglass. Why had some done so much and others so little? In the triage of life, they had all advanced as far as Harvard, and some had continued their progress while others had stumbled. Why?

A photograph of the class of 1904 members of Signet, a literary society of good repute (several eminent members of the Harvard English faculty belonged) with a clubhouse on Mount Auburn Street, shows two men sitting on the steps: Franklin Roosevelt and Vincent Beede.

Beede became an Episcopalian minister and served as a chaplain in France in World War I, getting closer to the action than Roosevelt, who desperately wanted active service, ever did. As a stretcher-bearer in the La Chapelle district of Paris, he waited in the shabby freight station for the wounded to arrive. They weighed more and more heavily, until after several hours he thought that he could never lift another man as high as the upper deck of an ambulance. At three o'clock one morning he lay down on a stretcher and was awakened by a huge rat nibbling his lip. "You ass," he thought, "what have you done but witness what war has done to others."

After thirteen years in the ministry, he went through a spiritual crisis and converted to Catholicism. He took whatever work he could find, as a porter in a carpet house and as a house wrecker at two dollars a day, until a piece of ceiling fell on him. In 1928, at the age of forty-nine, he was nightman in a small hotel of the $1-and-up variety in Washington, D.C. His Armenian boss paid him $12 a week. He had no savings, and no pension or insurance.

When he learned that his classmate Frank Roosevelt had been elected governor of New York, Beede dropped him a congratulatory note. The years had realigned them: Beede was now among the wounded, a casualty of character and circumstance, while Roosevelt was the stretcher-bearer, his arms aching from the weight of those who had to be helped. In the connection that Vincent Beede formed with his more fortunate and powerful classmate, from his years at Harvard until his death in 1942, can be summed up the essential transaction between Franklin Delano Roosevelt and the American people: that of rescuer to rescued, of bringer of hope for the casualties of the system.

Maybe, Beede wrote on November 13, 1928, Roosevelt could find him a job as night watchman in some public building, or in a library, or as confidential secretary, or caring for an invalid in a private family, or for a backward child, or on a landed estate.

Roosevelt contacted the Department of Mental Hygiene and found a job for Beede at the Rockland State Hospital in Orangeburg, New York, a lunatic asylum with 900 employees and 5,000 inmates—those who could not cope in the "world" outside, the miserable, heart-wrenching world of the Great Depression. He copied commitment papers, filed patients' records, and kept the admissions, death, and discharge books up to date. Beede thought the asylum was a wonderful place. He liked the work so much that sometimes on Sundays he voluntarily put in nine hours.

Roosevelt wrote him on July 21, 1931: "I don't need to tell you how very happy I am that you like that interesting work and that all goes well with my old classmate."

Beede thought of Roosevelt as a father figure, a man of authority and compassion, the only person he could turn to. A civil service exam was coming up for medical statistical clerk, but Beede knew the superintendent had someone else in mind for the job, a newcomer, married, who was washed up as an accountant on Wall Street.

Again Roosevelt intervened, writing the superintendent on March 7, 1932: "This fellow Vincent Beede was my classmate and he has had a lot of hard luck in his life but he is perfectly sane. I do hope you can find some way to straighten him out and have him keep on at the Rockland State Hospital."

Beede got the job and loved the work. He was in charge of the patients' central files, and of the Kardex, the latest thing in card indexing, and he met visitors and issued them their passes.

Sometimes he thought that the asylum was a happier place than the depression-torn society outside. It was an asylum in the original sense of the word, a place offering safety. He had moved into a new dorm for the unmarried, and he had a front corner room that got the morning sun, away from the noise of the patients. It was wonderful to wake in the morning to the sound of the thrushes. He was thankful for the good meals in the hospital cafeteria, whose chef had once worked on a private yacht—one day outside St. Francis's Church near Penn Station, he had seen the breadline shuffling four abreast. He went to a meeting of New Thought devotees and the leader said: "Let us now surround with Beautiful Thoughts those living in the slums below 14th Street."

On the outside, Roosevelt was running for president. The supervisor of male nurses, who had named his son Franklin, told Beede: "I'll see to it that the boys help get him into the White House." They went into town and put up Roosevelt posters, and on election day the inmates were rounded up and taken to Orangeburg to vote. The supervisor was sure that, out of the 400, 350 would vote the straight Democratic ticket. Beede voted for Roosevelt and then stepped into St. Catherine's Church to pray for him.

That Christmas, the patients covered the hall lights with green and red tissue paper. The wards looked festive. There were Christmasy looks on people's faces, and the chuckles were pleasant rather than ironic. Beede wanted to give one of the men a box of candy, but the man wouldn't take it—he was afraid the candy was poisoned. Beede thought back to his days as a stretcher-bearer, carrying the wounded. Here the wounds were of a more subtle kind.

He walked to the village, the snow crunching under his feet, to mail a Christmas card to the man who would soon be inaugurated president, his benefactor, and reflected on the direction their lives had taken—he was beyond ambition, trying only to live a quiet life, to soft-pedal past and present, knowing how difficult he was to place in any job, and grateful to have three squares and a pleasant office in this plague of unemployment, while Franklin, who had risen to the highest office, represented the hopes of a nation in a time of catastrophe. By overcoming his own affliction through qualities of will and perseverance, he seemed to be setting an example for everyone. On the way back, it was dark. He saw something that seemed to personify the destiny of the classmate who had befriended him—a boy plodding up the long, gradual slope, pulling a sled. He would plod for a mile or two more, and be well repaid for the slow journey by the thrilling plunge through the dim night.

I

The First Fourteen Years

The family documents illuminated,
and night all round, extending far inside
the shelves. And he was consubstantiated
with his own kin . . .
He felt, the more he read, incorporated
in him their own, in all of them his pride.
. . .Down on the French clock gathered night was teeming,
and trembling from its golden mill was streaming
his own time, very finely ground.

Rainer Maria Rilke

I N 1882, with thirty-eight states and a population under 50 million, the nation was incomplete. Arizona and New Mexico, the Dakotas, Oklahoma and Utah and Idaho, Washington and Wyoming and Montana, were territories waiting to be homesteaded, where tribes of Indians pitched their tents outside growing towns. Half of America was on the move toward the setting sun. Look at the Lincolns, who had gone from Massachusetts to Pennsylvania, then to Kentucky and Indiana and Illinois, living the same as the Indians except they went to church. A migrant breed, who found it cheaper to clear a new acre than to manure an old one, traveled across roadless pastures and filed 640-acre donation claims. Whoever got there first could own the land for the signing of a paper and the building of a foundation! They could stop along the way where track was being laid and split rails at thirty-seven and a half cents a hundred. Immigrants who had fled the fought-over farmlets of Europe saw so much acreage to be had for the asking that an itching land-greed came over them, and they took up claims they didn't need and couldn't use. The uniqueness of America was that there were more places where nobody was than places where somebody was. The American experiment was a success, not because of the Founding Fathers and the Bill of Rights but because there was plenty of room.

In 1882, the nation was not far removed from the early years of the republic. There were men living who had known Thomas Jefferson and who had voted for Martin Van Buren. There was a sense of continuity that came from having known men connected with the nation's first events. It was an available form of collective memory. Franklin Roosevelt liked to say that he had known the son of John Tyler, the tenth president, born in 1790 and inaugurated in 1841. This seemed to cover an impossible stretch of time, but Tyler married twice and had a son when he was seventy, two years before he died, who was later president of the College of William and Mary. In a young country with a brief history, the past was represented by someone you knew, who was the son of someone.

In 1882, six years into its second century, America was still experimenting with a system known as free enterprise. There was a deeply held conviction that the economy was self-adjusting. Someone called it the free fox in the free henhouse, but that was not quite it, for there was both plunder and opportunity. It often seemed that the purpose of government was to provide favorable business conditions in the form of tariff advantages, land grants, subsidies, no income tax, and the exercise of that freedom somehow overlooked in the Bill of Rights, freedom from regulation.

In 1882, the Standard Oil trust, incorporated by John D. Rockefeller to circumvent state corporation laws, brought 95 percent of the U.S. petroleum industry under the control of a nine-man directorate. It was such a simple device—applying personal estate law to interstate commerce. In case there was anyone around who did not understand who ran things, William H. Vanderbilt made it clear on October 8, 1882, when a reporter asked him why the Chicago Limited extra-fare mail train was being eliminated. "Don't you run it for the public benefit?" the reporter asked. "The public be damned," Vanderbilt said. "I am working for my stockholders. If the public want the train, why don't they pay for it?"

On the mind of the Senate in 1882 was the welfare of the widows of assassinated presidents. A bill for the relief of Mrs. Lincoln, including a grant of $15,000 and an increase of pension of $5,000, was passed on January 24, and a $5,000 pension for Mrs. James A. Garfield was granted on February 16.

On January 25, Charles J. Guiteau was found guilty of shooting Garfield and was sentenced to hang that June, there being in those days no insanity plea.

Sara Delano Roosevelt went into labor Sunday evening, January 29, at 7:30. Pregnancy had begun while she and her husband, James, were on a ten-month tour of Europe. In Scotland she nearly fainted, giving James a little fright. But she did not dwell on her condition, except for a private remark written in French on the back of her list for the layette—diapers, crib sheets, nightslips—which shows not only that she kept careful count but that she was too modest to record such intimate details in English: *Pour compter, il faut 40 semaines ou 280 jours commençant plusieurs jours après l'indisposition* (in order to keep count, it takes 40 weeks or 280 days starting a few days after the time of the last period).

When they returned to their Hudson River estate of Springwood in September, a seamstress was brought in to alter Sara's dresses, and early in January a trained nurse arrived. Sunday was a cold and blustery day, with a high wind whistling through the pines. All that night, in the big mahogany bed in one of the upstairs bedrooms, Sara lay heaving as James went without sleep to comfort her. Monday morning Dr. Edward H. Parker arrived, an eminent practitioner from Poughkeepsie with a good bedside manner and a clientele of local gentry. All day Sara bore down as Dr. Parker instructed, but the baby did not come. By eight that evening, Sara had been in labor twenty-four hours and Dr. Parker decided to use chloroform. When a ten-pound baby was born three-quarters of an hour later, she was unconscious.

He would be her only child, she who was one of the eleven children of the China trader and sea captain Warren Delano, the name having been Anglicized not long after the arrival of a young Huguenot named Philippe de la Noye in Plymouth Colony in 1621.

Like his father and grandfather, Warren II, Sara's father, went to sea not to hunt whales but to bring tea from China. It was a profitable trade, if you had ships swift enough to get the tea to market before it lost its flavor, and in 1851, Warren Delano bought a sixty-acre farm on a point of land overlooking the Hudson near Newburgh (everyone said the view was equal to anything on Lake Geneva) and built a house, called Algonac, in the Hudson River bracketed style. Buddhist temple bells and teakwood screens indicated the origin of the family fortune.

In 1854, Sara was born, and someone later figured out that there converged in her thirteen bloodlines that went back to the *Mayflower*. Her mother was a Lyman, whose first American ancestor had landed in 1631.

In 1857, there occurred one of those cyclical financial panics that make capitalists wonder if the system named after them works. Businesses failed, banks closed, unemployment rose, the poor had the choice between starving or freezing, and the rich were ruined, among them Warren Delano, who went back to China in 1859 at the age of fifty to start from scratch. This time he dealt in a cargo no bulkier than tea but a hundred times more valuable: opium. His timing could not have been better, for when the Civil War erupted in 1861 opium became a vitally needed medical supply, and opium traders were upgraded from disreputable suppliers of addicts to patriotic savers of lives. Warren Delano was under orders from the government to ship this widely used anesthetic to the Medical Bureau of the War Department. He was also named the agent of the State Department in China for the war's duration.

The government was a good paymaster, and within three years Delano was able to charter a ship to transport his entire family from Algonac to

Hong Kong. All her long life Sara would remember the time when she was eight and embarked on a four-month trip to China aboard the *Surprise*. She spent two years in her father's fine house, Rose Hill, with her mother joking about how odd it felt to be a foreign devil again.

Home to Algonac she finally went, one of five surviving girls who came to be known as "the beautiful Delano sisters." Cassie was the practical joker, sending Sara boxes from Klunder, the fashionable florist, filled with fading flowers from the drawing-room vases. Their occupations were designed to fill up the time remaining before marriage. Singing and piano lessons, reading and discussing *Punch* and the *Illustrated London News*, visits to West Point, duly chaperoned, calico parties, tableaux at Mrs. Clarkson's: "The Roman Family" and "Moses in the Bulrushes." Formal debuts, and the appearance of young men who sat with awkward politeness as Annie played Beethoven or Dora sang French songs. A West Point cadet attentive to Sally (Sara's nickname) was dubbed the Pilgrim Father because of his pride of family, which he never stopped expressing; another beau was the brash young Stanford White, but that came to nothing because of her father's objections to "the red-haired trial."

The fading flowers were becoming less of a joke. Dora and Annie married young men in the tea trade. It was Sara's turn, but Sara did not marry. Each year a fresh crop of debutantes competed for the available men. She became the proverbial bridesmaid who was never a bride. Her father did not want to let her go and disapproved of her suitors. He wanted her to marry, like her sisters, into the family business. Also, there was about Sara something forbidding to men of her generation. In her early twenties, she already had a matronly dignity. She was not someone into whose ear you could whisper sweet nothings.

In the spring of 1880, Mrs. Theodore Roosevelt (the mother of the future president), a widow at forty-seven, gave a dinner party at her home, 6 West 57th Street in Manhattan. Her two sons were away, Theodore Jr. at Harvard and Elliott making ready for a hunting trip, but her two daughters, Anna (Bamie) and Corinne, were there, and so was Bamie's childhood friend, Sara Delano. Among the other guests were a Mr. Crowninshield from Boston and a fifty-two-year-old widower, James Roosevelt. Mr. Roosevelt might have been expected to be attentive to his hostess, widowed like himself, distantly related, and somewhat his junior, but instead he devoted his attention to Sara, who would be twenty-six that September and was facing a dismal future without matrimony. Trained in the admiration of her father, beside whom younger men seemed half-baked, Sara willingly responded to the interest of a man twice her age.

Discovering that they were neighbors, and hoping to see her again, James Roosevelt invited her to Springwood, but not wanting to seem forward, he invited also his hostess and her two daughters. They came on May 7, and Sara always remembered it as the day when she was rescued from spinsterhood, writing her son on May 8, 1932: "Just 51 years yesterday I came to visit [at Hyde Park]. . . . If I had not come then, I should now be 'old Miss Delano' after a rather sad life!" James asked Sara to arrange the flowers on the luncheon table, a mild but unmistakable expression of hoped-for domesticity.

When James began calling at Algonac, Warren Delano thought it was to see him. Set straight, he opposed the marriage, but for the first time Sara did not meekly obey. This, she sensed, was a suitable match and perhaps her last chance. Warren Delano came to realize that he could not forever keep his daughter as he kept his prize porcelain, under lock and key in a cupboard, and that the age difference was not that great a barrier, since he had married Catherine Lyman when she was eighteen and he was in his mid-thirties. He liked James, who was like himself tall and distinguished, blue-eyed and side-whiskered, and conceded that a Democrat might be a gentleman.

They were engaged that summer and married at Algonac on October 7, 1880—a perfect autumn day of bright sunshine and brilliant foliage. The transfer of the bride that afternoon from her father's estate to her husband's, from one Hudson River principality to another, was reminiscent of the transfer of Marie Antoinette from Austria to France on a neutral island in the middle of the Rhine when she married Louis XVI. The Delano victoria, drawn by the matched horses Meg and Pet and driven by the Delano coachman, took them north to Milton, the midway point, where Hutchins, the Roosevelt coachman, was waiting with a T-cart, a small vehicle with a high rumble seat. The bridegroom took the reins, and they crossed the river on the Highland-Poughkeepsie ferry and drove the remaining few miles up the Albany Post Road and into the tree-lined lane of their home.

On November 7 they sailed for a combination grand tour and honeymoon that lasted ten months. Sara liked traveling, for "one always meets people one knows." What she liked less was the physical side of marriage, but it had to be undergone, although she would, had it been within reach, preferred a virgin birth. In all likelihood, Franklin was conceived in April in Paris, a properly romantic time and place. Despite Sara's pregnancy, they lingered in Europe during the summer. In July, at Schaffhausen, they were dining on the terrace of their hotel when two Americans came out speaking excitedly—President Garfield had been shot but would probably recover. In September they came home to the quiet routine of boating on the river, calling on relatives and neighbors, piano and bezique.

Giving birth was the one achievement of Sara's life. She made Franklin and then, like the Creator, she rested, for she knew that what she had created was good. She wanted no more children, and indeed she had no more physical relations with her husband in the remaining eighteen years of their marriage. She was a good wife in every way but that one, devoted and companionable, attentive to his wishes, but her passion was reserved for her son.

All the rest of her days she fought a veiled but intense battle to retain possession of Franklin. This was her obsession, her purpose in life, her reason for being. This unique creature, this extension of his mother, who was (she asserted) so much more a Delano than a Roosevelt, would be memorialized from birth. She saved the Victorian wicker basket that swung rather than rocked. His baby clothes, the lace cap, the embroidered hood, the tiny slippers with black satin bows, were carefully wrapped, labeled, and stored. A foot-long golden tress was kept in a box with a satin lining when his shoulder-length hair was cut in 1886.

At a time when women in society hired wet nurses because feeding interfered with their social schedules, Sara breast-fed Franklin for nearly a year. Once, she sat at dinner next to the Nobel-prizewinning surgeon Alexis Carrel, who asked her what she fed her son. "Nature's own food," she replied.

Sara's character, now settled in its vocation, crystallized. Overwhelming in her devotion, she proclaimed her absolute knowledge and understanding of her son. When he was at Groton in 1897 she sent him a pair of shoes with the note: "You see a mother's eye can always see *inwardly* the size of her child's foot and everything about him."

Some great men when they were children suffered from parental neglect (Winston Churchill comes to mind), but Franklin suffered from parental overexposure, the unalleviated scrutiny of his mother, usually expressed in terms of do's and don'ts. He must cut his initials into his umbrella handle. He must use floss silk every night. He must be generous with the goodies she sent him from Park & Tilford. He must keep his nails nice and not travel without wearing gloves. He must take his cod-liver oil. He must not forget his silver clothes brush when invited to a lady's house. He must never cut the string on a wrapped package (thrift must be learned in small things). He must not cough, for coughing was nothing but a nervous habit or imitation.

Sara slotted all of life into categories, and from her lips and her pen came a stream of precepts. She was a woman of little intellect or perceptiveness, but she had a natural authority that came from knowing exactly her place in life. Operating from a base of social certainty, like one of those Edith Wharton dowagers who complain that people are not as particular as they used to be, she was able to intimidate and awe. As one of her friends said, she was not a woman but a Social Presence, the one who at dinner parties goes in with the host. She remained this way until her death, a doubt never crossing her mind, sure of the proper conduct in any situation. "I drove over to Hyde Park to see old Mrs. Roosevelt in 1940," said Herbert Claiborne Pell, "and she gave me iced tea, which I hate. I later told the President that she was the only woman who could make me take iced tea. I said 'you couldn't, for instance.' He said 'Yes, I was afraid of her too.' "

All that Sara asked of people was that they be well-bred and socially harmonious. But from these categories most of humanity was excluded. Whoever was not socially acceptable was "common" or "horrid." If someone looked common, she would say: "It is to be hoped that he *is* more than he looks." Politicians were "horrid," and she wrote Franklin at the time of the Democratic convention in San Francisco, on June 25, 1920: ". . . I can imagine that the time at San Francisco will be most interesting and I hope 'elevating,' as the old letters would say, but I fancy that the last epithet is not very likely in a crowd of every sort of politician."

Jews were "horrid"—anti-Semitism was a Delano trait, shared by her brother, Frederic. When she first met the Henry Morgenthaus in July 1918, she wrote: "The wife is very Jewish but appeared very well" (i.e., in spite of being Jewish). Once Franklin was married, one of Eleanor's mother-in-law problems was how to deal with Sara's offensive anti-Semitic remarks at the luncheon table. She would remind Sara that one of her ancestors was Jewish. Sara, indignantly: "Eleanor, how can you say such a thing?" and Eleanor would reply: "But mother, he was." Every religion but the Episcopalian was horrid, including what Sara called "the Dutch Deformed Church." "Natives" of every sort were "horrid." The poor were "horrid"; wasn't it Tennyson's farmer who had said, "The poor in a lump are bad"? But charity was therapeutic, and she wrote her son that "really nothing is so helpful to ourselves as doing for others and trying to sink all selfishness." She sent the needy baskets of food while complaining that "we are making beggars of the people up in the village."

Sara was a period piece, quite happily carrying out the duties of a wife and mother on a preindustrial estate, emblematic of the days when property and propriety were one (had not George Washington said that a good man was a landed man?), frozen in nineteenth-century conventions, like a series of Victorian tintypes: Sara telling the footman his duties, Sara hiring a maid to turn the mangle for the laundress, Sara looking for a new coachman (what a bother it was, it meant trips to New York and new liveries), Sara taking the silver to the bank before a European trip, Sara hoping that the new rector of St. James's would be the right sort. It was her assurance in all things that Eleanor could not take, writing Franklin after an evening with Sara and two of her sisters: "They all in their serene assurance and absolute judgements on people and affairs going on in the world make me want to squirm and turn bolshevik."

Sara was positively Machiavellian in her manipulation of her daughter-in-law and grandchildren. The simple aim of her efforts was to maintain a position of supremacy in the family. This she did by holding the purse strings. Hyde Park was hers after James died, and she sat at the head of the table, her daughter-in-law a guest. The twin houses she had built on 65th Street in Manhattan, with their communicating passages from Sara's house to Franklin's, were a tribute to invasion of privacy. To her grandchildren, she was the provider of expensive gifts. But she also had a punitive side, and when she felt neglected there were ominous references to her will. Betsy Cushing, who married Franklin's oldest son, James, remembers going to the wedding of one of Sara's grandnephews. On the way to church, Sara said, "I understand from Jimmy that it's your birthday. I have just the thing—some of my pearls." "No, grandma, that's too much," Betsy said. In church, Betsy and Jimmy somehow sat on the wrong side of the aisle, and Sara made emphatic beckoning gestures, but they stayed where they were. After the ceremony Sara told Betsy: "I've been thinking of what I could give you that would be more suitable and I know just the thing—paper napkins." Sara was the boss of her own political machine, dispensing patronage to deserving favor seekers and cutting off the wayward and the inattentive.

It was the power of her obsession that raised Sara above the level of convention. The outside world was filtered through the mother-son relationship. Eleanor and the grandchildren were adjuncts to this already-formed bond. In whatever she did and whoever she saw, there was always a connection to Franklin: "I met Dr. Wilmer the other day . . . he said *such* nice things about your being brave and having high standards and a constructive mind, and he was so pleased to see your 'ma.' " Or again, on March 23, 1928, "I had two charming old ladies to tea, Mrs. Morgan . . . and Mrs. Fairchild . . . both longing to vote for you! (of course for President). I said, 'when that happens I shall vote and then emigrate to foreign lands!' I suppose that sounds cowardly. . . ."

She was able to say with utter sincerity that she was not surprised when Franklin became president. She was convinced that he had come to greatness as a direct consequence of his upbringing. He was president because she had taught him proper rules of conduct, because he was well-bred and socially harmonious. When the country claimed him, she did not relinquish her claim. She remained his "Dear Ma" when he was president, and lived to within three years of his death.

When James Roosevelt was born in November 1828, John Quincy Adams was president. In the year of James's birth, Adams was defeated by Andrew Jackson, but did not consider it demeaning to serve in a lesser capacity and returned to Washington as a member of the House of Representatives, where he remained until his death. In 1848, when twenty-year-old James was touring Europe, his father, Isaac, wrote him on February 25: "As to political news . . . John Q. Adams died in the Cabinet of the Speaker of the House on the 23rd of February. He was attacked in his seat when the House was in session a day or two before by apoc. fit. His last words were—'This is the last of earth—I am content.' He was in his 81st year."

Going backward, as if reversing some biblical list of "begats," James was the son of Isaac, who was the son of James, who was the son of Isaac, who was the son of Jacobus (James), who was the son of Nicholas, who was the son of the first Roosevelt to step on America's shore, Claes Martensen Van Roosevelt. All that we know for sure is that he came from the Netherlands, at an unspecified date for an unspecified reason. Why leave a country in its golden age, the Netherlands of Rembrandt and Vermeer, of maritime supremacy and a far-flung empire? Those with good jobs and places in society stayed put, unless they were navigators. Those who felt the pull of the New World were often misfits, or dissenters, or no-goods. Was Claes a younger son seeking adventure, or was he one step ahead of the sheriff? We don't know, but we can imagine him around 1650 arriving full of wonder at the Dutch seaport of New Amsterdam, with its slant-roofed houses, busy piers, and a windmill or two. Perhaps, in a country where land was reclaimed from the sea, he had heard that the West India Company was offering as much free acreage as he and his family could cultivate.

We can't even be sure where in Holland he came from, the village of Vossemeer on the island of Tholen at the mouth of the Scheldt, where the Roosevelt coat of arms appears in the furnishings of the town hall, or the city of Haarlem, artistic and scientific center of northern Holland.

FDR preferred to believe that he was descended from the more prominent Haarlem Roosevelts rather than from the common Vossemeer Roosevelts, who produced nothing but clergymen and schoolmasters. In 1938, he told an interviewer, Virginia Pearce Delgado: "I don't believe a word about this Zeeland business [Zeeland was the province to which the island of Tholen belonged]. I think it's all a grand publicity stunt someone thought up to attract tourists off the beaten track. There's a tradition in our family that the Roosevelts came from somewhere near Haarlem. . . ."

In any case, Claes Van Roosevelt had enough money to buy a tract of land of about forty-eight acres near what today would be 29th Street on the east side of Manhattan. He was also a churchgoer, so that the birth of his son Nicholas in 1658 was recorded in the registry of the Dutch Reformed Church.

When Nicholas was six, he saw redcoats patrol the streets of New Amsterdam. In 1664 the mercantile Dutch had surrendered to the British without a fight, knowing that trade would continue whatever the flag. A practical fellow, and the first American-born Roosevelt, Nicholas anglicized his name but married within the Dutch community. With his wife, Heltje Kunst, a carpenter's daughter, he left for Esopus, the present-day city of Kingston, to make his fortune as a fur trapper. He was the first Roosevelt to go up the Hudson, a region with which the family would become identified, and saw the gray ramparts of the Palisades, and the three blue humps of the highest Catskills, and the barely fished rivers swarming with sturgeon and shad, and the land teeming with beaver and bear. Here was a provident nature and an almost mythical abundance.

After eight years upriver, trapping and trading with the Indians, Nicholas came back to New York and set up a small flour mill. A man of position, he was elected alderman in 1719. But his place in history is assured for another reason. His sons Johannes and Jacobus would each have as a direct descendant five generations later a president of the United States. Each branch prospered and multiplied, the Johannes branch settling in Oyster Bay and becoming Republican while the Jacobus branch became established on the Hudson and voted Democrat. But this they had in common: a president in the family.

There was nothing in the Roosevelt lineage to announce the arrival of two such remarkable men as Theodore and Franklin Delano. The two branches founded by Nicholas had the solid Dutch virtues of thrift and hard work and sound mercantile instincts. There was a patient accumulation of money, in contrast to the boom or bust pattern of the Delano fortune. The Roosevelts moved cautiously, avoiding flamboyance, and did not get involved in public affairs unless they had to.

It took them a while to catch on that the money wasn't in trapping or milling—it was in land. All of America was one vast real estate deal, and New York was no exception. Jacobus bought ten lots on Beekman's swamp that he converted into sites for tanneries. Friends in the right places gave him preferential treatment for land on the East River. He had eleven children, left the surviving ones well provided, and was the last of his branch to write his will in Dutch.

His sixth son, Isaac, was the first Roosevelt to gain distinction. Born in 1726, Isaac went into the sugar-refining business. From his office at the Old Sugar House on Wall Street, he saw business go downhill. There was a new king, George III, who thought the colonists were too well off and should pay more taxes. Parliament passed a Sugar Act in 1764, updating the old Molasses Act of 1733; Isaac couldn't import molasses or raw sugar from the French or Spanish West Indies unless he paid a huge tax. Across the ocean, some British lawmakers had voted to put him, Isaac Roosevelt, out of business. These acts in restraint of trade (to which was added the Stamp Act in 1765, taxing all documents used in commercial transactions) seemed directed particularly against the sugar refineries. How could Isaac make a profit unless he traded with the French and the Spanish? His first form of rebellion was to circumvent the acts.

From being restrained in trade, Isaac acquired a form of political consciousness. He departed from family tradition in another way, broadening the genetic line by marrying Cornelia Hoffman, the daughter of a Scandinavian soldier who had large landholdings on both sides of the Hudson. In 1775, he served as an elected member of the provincial congress, and when British troops occupied New York he moved his family to his father-in-law's estate near Rhinebeck. Isaac did not have a drop of English blood, he had never been to England, and he was a member of the Dutch Church. He had no reason to feel any loyalty to the crown. But many other New York merchants, the "business as usual" crowd, stayed on and took the oath to the king.

To FDR, Isaac's prominence came from having taken part in the state constitutional convention of 1788 in Poughkeepsie. In speeches and conversations, he often referred to the great struggle that had been fought in the old courthouse, a two-story stone structure with a cupola on top, in the steaming summer of 1788. The sixty-five delegates to the New York convention had arrived, some by sloop and some on horseback, to discuss the proposed Constitution. Seven other states had ratified it, only New York and Virginia held out. The situation was critical, for if New York did not ratify the United States would be geographically split, with New England on one side and Pennsylvania and the South on the other. The deadlock was over the question of ratifying the Constitution as it was laid down, without a bill of rights. Isaac was in favor of ratification, and that was the way the convention finally voted. The success of the federal venture was assured, and almost immediately after being formed, the new government submitted the first ten amendments to the states.

It was a source of intense pride to FDR that his great-great-grandfather had sat in that ancient courthouse through those hot days and cast his vote with the Federalists. Through family tradition, he was connected with the ratification of the Constitution, and understood by birthright what the framers were seeking. He thought the convention formula to accept the Constitution "in full faith and confidence" was a masterly way to achieve the compromise; it did not guarantee a bill of rights, but the wishes of the great state of New York could not be ignored, and it was appropriate that a new form of government should take some things on faith.

Issac became known in the family as "Isaac the Patriot" and had his portrait painted by Gilbert Stuart. When he came back to New York he got into banking (there was a lot of Dutch money behind the first New York banks), becoming the second president of the Bank of New York in 1786.

Isaac's son James, born in 1760, was the first of the Jacobus branch to obtain a college degree, from the New Jersey College at Princeton, where he graduated in 1780. He continued in the sugar trade, and was an officer but never president of the bank. In politics he was a Federalist like his father and served in the State Assembly. He missed the chance to make a great fortune when he bought a 400-acre tract in Manhattan in what is today an area bounded by Fifth Avenue, the East River, 110th Street, and 125th Street, about 120 city blocks. He wanted to farm it, but after cutting the timber he found that the soil was too poor and rocky, so he sold it to John Jacob Astor for $25,000. In later years, when he was shown an old map with one of the wharves on the East River marked "Roosevelt's," FDR reflected that "if my ancestors had held on to their land in New York City, lots of things might have happened."

James must have been fond of the Dutchess County area where he fled with his father from British-occupied Manhattan, for in 1819 he bought a tract of land there and built a big house called Mount Hope on a hill outside Poughkeepsie, overlooking the Albany Post Road and the Hudson. James was the first of the Jacobus branch to become a country squire. He was also the first to bring English blood into the family. By his first wife, Maria Eliza Walton, daughter of the notorious Tory Abram Walton, he had eight children. By his second wife, Catherine Barclay, he had eight children, and by the third, Harriet Howland, member of a rich shipping family that went back to the *Mayflower,* whom he married when he was sixty-one, he had none. "Thus the stock kept virile and abreast of the times," wrote FDR in a Harvard essay on his family.

By now, the Roosevelts were well enough off so that they didn't have to work. Sons of the industrious Dutch merchants could turn to scholarly pursuits and lead lives that were not obviously productive. James's oldest son, Isaac (FDR's grandfather), born in 1790, went to Princeton and to Columbia's College of Physicians and Surgeons, becoming a doctor. But he never practiced, preferring to continue studying on his own. When his father built Mount Hope, he moved to the country for good. Known as "Paddy," Isaac was a lover of nature and liked to go to St. Hubert's Inn in the Adirondacks in the summer. He seemed content to live in his father's house and to breed cattle and fine horses instead of children, for in his mid-thirties he was still a bachelor. But at the age of thirty-seven he married eighteen-year-old Mary Rebecca Aspinwall, a niece of his father's third wife, Harriet Howland. The Aspinwalls were a prosperous seafaring family with plenty of entrepreneurial spirit. Mary Rebecca's brother, William Henry Aspinwall, made millions by controlling the water-rail route through Panama from New York to the West Coast, which became heavily traveled after the discovery of gold in California.

Even though married, Isaac continued to live in his father's house. James was born there in 1828 and was baptized on December 2 in the Dutch Reformed Church in Poughkeepsie. It was not until James was four that his father bought land on the other side of the Post Road and built a gabled house with a good river view called Rosedale.

James grew up in the pleasant rural setting of a large estate and went to the Poughkeepsie Collegiate School with other "gentlemen's sons." He was an only child until the age of twelve, when his brother, John Aspinwall, was born. A year later, he was sent away to a "family school" in Lee, Massachusetts, run by Alexander Hyde, which was reputed to specialize in unruly boys. From Rosedale, Isaac wrote his son preachy letters such as this one on July 15, 1842: "How important my dear son that we should make it the great business of our lives to be prepared for another and a better world, where there is no sin or death or sorrow. Repent, believe in the Lord Jesus and lead a life of holy obedience to his commands. Strive to correct your faults—in your intercourse with your companions be gentle and mild—obtain the command of your temper. Be not discomposed by trifles." Isaac worried that his son was reading fiction, but wrote Mr. Hyde that "I have no objection to his reading *occasionally* a well-written and moral or religious work of fiction."

James's choice of New York University was another cause for concern. Isaac would have preferred a college in a country village, far from the temptations of the city. The only safeguard was that James would live in his grandfather's town house on Bleecker Street, surrounded by relatives. Isaac wrote James on May 14, 1843: "I trust you will never become a Dandy or an Idler. Your uncle G. Howland said to me—'Send James to the University of New York and he will become a Dandy and will walk Broadway with his cane.' You know you were created for better things. We live for God—for the good of our fellow man—for duty—for usefulness. You will not disappoint the expectations of your family."

Isaac wanted James to stay another year at Mr. Hyde's and enter the University of the City of New York (today's NYU) as a sophomore, instructing his son to "ask counsel of One who is wise to direct and kind to choose in all the difficulties of His weak shortsighted child." James kept his own counsel and entered as a freshman, although for reasons unknown he stayed only one semester. In those days it was not considered necessary to send a son to Harvard, and James in 1846 transferred to Union College in Schenectady, quite good enough for the river gentry. Isaac was sure that his son would be in good hands. Union's president, Dr. Eliphalet Nott, was an ordained Presbyterian minister, a professor of moral philosophy, and a leading advocate of temperance.

But college students have a way of escaping the surveillance of their elders, and a diary kept by one of James's classmates reveals that he was not the model of propriety his father would have wished. The classmate, Albert C. Ingham, wrote on June 15, 1846: "I was in Charley Nott's room and found him and Roosevelt drunk. They asked me to drink but were too drunk to hand me any liquor so I got none. Well I must say that I think the signs of the times bid fair to prosper the temperance cause—to bed."

James turned a deaf ear to his father's lectures and got into more hot water the following February. One of the features of Union College was a student government, with a college senate (of which James Roosevelt was vice president) and college courts for various undergraduate offenses. On February 26, 1847, Ingham reported in his diary that "this evening I was called to testify as a witness in Section Court . . . the case was Section vs. Murdock Nott Roosevelt and Paddock for attending a dancing school drunk and was pretty clearly sustained."

Of the three mentions of James Roosevelt in Ingham's diary, two have to do with drunkenness, so one can assume that he had a pleasant two years at Union, did his share of youthful carousing, and was not always the priggish and solemn squire that he later became. On August 13, the class of 1847 graduated with bachelor of arts degrees. Ingham wondered, "How many of the class now going forth into the world will succeed? We are going forth with the highest anticipation, there is no station however exalted to which we may not aspire, and yet experience has shown that out of a class numbering nearly a hundred only three or four rise above mediocrity."

Would James Roosevelt be one of the three or four? In any case, there was no hurry, for he left on a tour of Europe that lasted from November 1847 until May 1849. FDR later circulated the tale that his father had fought at Naples with Garibaldi. The only trouble with this story is that Garibaldi's siege of Naples with the Redshirts took place in 1860.

After Europe, it was Harvard Law School and admission to the New York bar. In 1851, he went to work as a law clerk for the distinguished New York

City firm of Benjamin D. Silliman, which provided him with the finest
training then available in business law. At first, he was a glorified errand
boy. One day, Silliman sent him to Washington to deliver some legal papers
to that legendary Texan, Senator Sam Houston. James went to his room at
one of the hotels on Pennsylvania Avenue and found him propped up in
bed, with a row of chairs extending from the door to the bed. When the
Senator completed his business with the caller next to the bed, the line
moved up one chair. When his turn came, James had a chat with the old
frontier fighter and was impressed by the splendid head and the force of his
personality. FDR doted on this story, which linked his father to one of the
great Americans of the early part of the nineteenth century.

In 1853, when he was twenty-five, James married Rebecca Brien Howland, a name frequently linked to the Roosevelts. His Roosevelt grandfather's third wife had been a Howland. His Aspinwall mother's mother had
been a Howland. Plump and pretty and humorous, Rebecca was a daughter
of his mother's first cousin. The pool of suitable young women among the
Hudson River gentry was limited. Like Hapsburgs, they often married their
cousins. Two years later, a son was born, James Roosevelt Roosevelt, who
became known as "Rosy."

In 1860, the Civil War inspired many patriotic young men to join the
Union Army. Others were picked at random in the first draft, and those who
did not wish to serve could hire substitutes. James either was not drafted or
hired a substitute. According to family tradition, he had something to do
with a precursor of the Red Cross called the Sanitary Commission. It was a
time when many New York Democrats broke ranks and joined the party of
Lincoln. The other Roosevelt branch, now settled in Oyster Bay, did exactly
that. But James, "independent as a hog on ice," refused to follow the clan,
stood by his belief in Jefferson and Jackson, and became a "Union Democrat." What his feelings were about slaves is not recorded, although his
grandfather James, the purchaser of Mount Hope, had kept three or four,
eventually manumitting them. Slavery was common among the estate families. When FDR was a boy there was a Negro sexton of St. James's Church
who had been born a slave to the Pendleton family.

By the time the war was over, James's father had died, and he inherited
Mount Hope, his brother John Aspinwall inheriting Rosedale. There was a
pleasing symmetry between the number of heirs and the number of family
estates. James had long since left the firm of Silliman, where he was doing
the legal work for some of the newly formed corporations, to strike out on
his own. Staid in appearance, cautious in manner, James in fact had a wild
plunger streak. In his heart of hearts, he wanted to match the Astors and the
Vanderbilts, whose families had arrived after the Roosevelts and amassed
greater fortunes in less time.

His two bold ventures took advantage of depressed economic conditions
in the postwar South. With his millionaire uncle, William Henry Aspinwall,
he formed the Consolidated Coal Company, which tried for a monopoly of

the coal mines in the Cumberlands of Kentucky and Tennessee. At the same time, through his appointment as a receiver and counsel for bankrupt southern railroads, he became an authority on the intricacies of railroad financing. With the Pennsylvania Railroad, he founded a holding company called the Southern Railway Security Company, which achieved a virtual railroad monopoly south of the Potomac. But the timing was bad, and the mirage of untold riches vanished in the financial panic of 1873, which put a stop to railroad construction and reduced the demand for coal. In 1875, a group of disgruntled stockholders threw James Roosevelt off the board of Consolidated Coal, and when the Southern Railway Security Company was liquidated, he lost the large sum he had invested.

James did not long enjoy the ownership of Mount Hope, for in the summer of 1865 it burned to the ground. He and Rebecca were in Europe and had rented it to a New York City family. Most of the Roosevelt papers were destroyed. A disgruntled butler was suspected. James sold the property for $45,000 to the state of New York, which built the Hudson River State Hospital, a lunatic asylum, and bought another for $40,000 on the bank of the Hudson, two miles north. Originally he had 110 acres, heavily wooded, sloping to the river. But he added other tracts until he owned about 900 acres.

This was Springwood, where FDR was born and grew up. It was his geographical and spiritual center, and he knew its history by heart. There was a direct link with the Indians through the fine old white oaks that grew on the property. When several of the oaks fell, the rings were counted and it was determined that they dated to about the year 1650. They had grown as field trees, spreading their branches out from the bottom to fifty or more feet on all sides, without hindrance from other trees. This to FDR was direct proof that the fields between the house and the road where the oaks grew had not been forest land but had been cultivated by the Indians. As added proof, they found Indian bone needles and arrowheads in these fields. There had been an Indian encampment or village right there, on the grounds.

James was less interested in the Indians (although he shared with them a tribal concept of society) than he was in copying the life of an English country gentleman.

Days at Springwood were a close emulation of English manor life, of supervising the servants, grooms, and farm hands, of daily rides through the property, of being served a dish of cream in which the spoon stood up that came from the Alderney herd. Someone said of James that "he tried to pattern himself on Lord Lansdowne [the Tory leader], but what he really looked like was Lansdowne's coachman." To James, breeding was important, not only in horses and cattle but in one's fellow humans. The Roosevelts were "unsnubbable," and James looked down his nose at more recent, though more prosperous, families. FDR remembered a conversation at the breakfast table when he was eight. The Vanderbilts lived in a fifty-four-room Renaissance mansion a few miles to the north, and Sara had received a cordial note from Mrs. Frederick Vanderbilt. "She has invited us to dinner," Sara said. "Sally," James said, "we cannot accept." "But she's a lovely woman, and I thought you liked Mr. Vanderbilt." That was true, James allowed, he had served on boards with Vanderbilt and did like him. "But if we accept we shall have to have them at our house." Breaking bread with the parvenu Vanderbilts was unthinkable to the squire of Springwood.

James was public-spirited in a mild way, maintaining a family tradition of involvement in the community. He was elected supervisor of the town of Hyde Park in 1871 for a two-year term. He was on the board of directors of the insane asylum that had been built on the grounds of Mount Hope. Having made the move from the Dutch Reformed to the more socially correct Episcopalian faith, he was a vestryman and senior warden of St. James's Church. He gave $25,000 to the St. Francis Hospital in Poughkeepsie and served on its board of trustees.

But beyond these local commitments he would not venture. A gentleman did not enter politics, which had become an occupation for those who were willing to deal with immigrants. Local elections were best left to the Irish bosses. It would have been unseemly for James to solicit the vote of people in the village, some of whom were his employees. Imagine having to ask his coachman for his vote! An entry in Sara's diary in July 1882 said: "James went to Hudson to a Democratic Convention to *prevent* their nominating him." In a handwritten summary of his life, James wrote: "I am a Democrat but have never taken any active part in political life; though repeatedly requested to accept the nomination for Congress, State Senate and Assembly I have always lived at Hyde Park . . . and am devoted to country life." In his *American Commonwealth*, Lord Bryce entitled a chapter "Why the Best Men Do Not Go into Politics," and noted "a certain apathy among the luxurious classes and fastidious minds who find themselves of no more account than the ordinary voter, and are disgusted by the superficial vulgarities of public life." Such was the case with James Roosevelt.

He did raise money for Grover Cleveland, who, when he was inaugurated in 1885, was the first Democratic president in twenty-four years. Sara wrote in her diary: "President Cleveland, Secretary Fairchild, Secretary Whitney and others told James they would any and all do *anything* for him and *begged* him to take a foreign appointment." His son Rosy, a conservative Republican who had bolted the party and contributed to the Cleveland campaign of 1884, was appointed first secretary of the Vienna legation. Rosy had by this time landed the catch of the season, Helen Astor, great-granddaughter of the original John Jacob, who had a $400,000 trust fund. After Cleveland, Rosy returned to staunch Republicanism, and wrote FDR on February 15, 1916, when Woodrow Wilson was president: "Your rotten administration will soon make us ashamed to live here!"

James would not accept a diplomatic post that would interfere with his routine: spring and autumn in Hyde Park, winter in his town house on Washington Square in Manhattan, summer in England and Germany, where he took the baths to treat a heart condition. He kept up his business interests and investments but in fact he came as close to being a member of the leisure class as America would produce.

James was a transitional figure between two eras. In the man of leisure, so protective of his pleasant way of life, his trips to Europe, his many-acred estates, in the speculator whose ventures went sour, there lay buried a dim sympathy for those less fortunate, for the plight of the common man, a trait that would be passed to his son.

Like her husband, Rebecca Roosevelt had a bad heart, and the German spas did not help, for she died in 1876. James mourned her vivacious presence and remembered her picking roses for the breakfast table as he sat alone in the big clapboard house. His married son, Rosy, had bought an estate next door and built a house painted red, called the Red House, but his presence did not fill the void. Four years later, James remarried, and two years after that Franklin was born.

FDR's understanding of America started with the land he was raised on, the land belonging to his father. His mind was a sponge that soaked up information, and he knew that the land along the Hudson was made up of three patents, the Pawling patent (Henry Pawling had bought land from the Indians in 1686), the Hyde Park patent (land granted to five men, one of whom was private secretary to then governor of New York Edward Hyde), and the Nine Partners patent (nine officers in the New York colony who bought a tract in 1697 that went from the Hudson River to Connecticut). He knew the names of the original Nine Partners.

The river frontage on the Hudson's eastern shore north and south of Poughkeepsie, wooded bluffs with clearings for houses, had been held since the Revolution by a few large estate owners, starting with the Livingstons and their tenant farmers. Then other prominent families such as the Bards and the Morgan Lewises had taken up farming. But before the Revolution there was no Hyde Park. There was a community that went by various names, such as De Cantillon's Landing and Stoutensburgh's Store, with, instead of a church, an occasional wandering Quaker preacher who came from Millbrook or Pine Plains and held a meeting once every three months or so on what would later be known as Quaker Lane.

The village grew around a church; when some of the people in the community decided in 1789 that they wanted a place to worship, they started the Stoutensburgh Religion Society and built a tiny church seating only forty-eight persons that afterward became Hyde Park Building. The interesting thing to FDR was that the first church, although Protestant, was nondenominational, open to every well-recommended preacher and to every Protestant faith, so that, for a generation, the entire community worshiped together. That changed, and as a boy he thought the Episcopal church was the only one in Hyde Park, until one day he passed a little home occupied by an elderly couple who invited him in for a piece of gingerbread, and it turned out that they were Mr. and Mrs. John Clay and that Reverend Clay was the Methodist minister, so that through a piece of gingerbread he had his first association with Methodism.

FDR absorbed the history of the place through the experiences of childhood, as when his father's old gardener, Sebastian Bauman, told the boy that he well remembered that back around 1840 the whole place was called Crum Elbow, or when some cannon balls were found in the garden of his brother Rosy's house. The cannon balls were British, and had been fired by warships sailing up the Hudson in 1777 to join General Burgoyne's army, which was marching south from Canada. This episode intrigued FDR greatly, and when he was president he instructed his ambassador to Great Britain, Robert W. Bingham, to ask the British Admiralty for the log books of the ships. The log entries arrived in 1934, and he was delighted to see that they explained the cannon balls in his brother's garden.

After the excitement of British men-of-war firing broadsides at the rebels, life along the Hudson settled into the cushioned immobility of the large estates. It was life on the latifundia, immune to change, with a gentry that maintained its privileges through inherited wealth, intermarriage, and education in exclusive schools. It was removed from the great events that shaped the nation, the Civil War, the waves of immigrants pouring into the cities, and the passing of the old West (ten years after Custer's massacre on the banks of the Little Big Horn, a rising politician from New York could capitalize on ranching in the Dakota country).

Secure in their private parks behind fieldstone walls, the Hudson River gentry practiced a life that had more in common with Queen Victoria's England than with the rest of America. They kept horses and cattle and farmed a little, and hired prominent architects to design not only the main houses but also the farm buildings, and landscape architects to do the grounds. The dairy farmer brought fresh milk to the farm each day. Hay was shipped to New York City for the bus horses. In the 1850s the railroad appeared, linking the estates where the money was spent to the city where the money was made. James Roosevelt had a private car, the *Monon*, which came to the border of his estate, a few hundred yards from his house. For those estate owners who had no private cars, the trains made unscheduled stops to let them off in front of their homes, as trains in czarist Russia stopped for grand dukes.

The village existed to fill the needs of the estate owners, providing a pool of labor. The farms employed herdsmen, dairymen, poultrymen, farmers, and teamsters (in a time when a teamster drove a team). The houses hired coachmen, grooms, chauffeurs, gardeners, maintenance men, butlers, maids, and cooks. Often the maids were French and the butlers were English. When Sara Roosevelt was hostess to the king and queen of England in 1939, her English butler, upon hearing that the White House staff of colored servants was coming to help out, refused to "serve my king" alongside the black help. The Hudson River gentry had its share of upstairs/downstairs problems.

It was pure paternalism, a perfect example of a class-bound society on the European model. The estate employees worked without vacations, social security, pensions, or unemployment and health benefits. No compensation was given to the widow of a man who died as a result of a fall while at work on the Vanderbilt estate, although he had been with the family for forty years. The villagers, who had not been told about the abuses of capitalism, saw no unfairness in the disparity of wealth. Their situation was not unlike that of their parents or grandparents who had come from Europe. The work was not demeaning, it was better than working in an office in Poughkeepsie or twelve hours a day in one of the canneries. The house servants, in close contact with their employers, often adopted their speech habits and mannerisms as well as their conservative political views. Mrs. Catherine Connel, whose grandfather had been Mr. Delano's coachman, recalled that "to be Republican in those days was a religion, a caste system. Many people who worked for the wealthy would become whatever their employers were."

The rich sponsored lectures and Punch and Judy shows. Once James hired a magician for the village boys. Each summer Mrs. Vanderbilt hired a barge for an all-day picnic and dance on the river. The Rogerses invited the men from the village to bowl in their private bowling alley. Archie Rogers, in addition, was known as a warm-hearted man who invested in the stock market for some of his employees.

James thought the boys in the village school should learn manual trades and the girls domestic skills. When FDR was a boy, James would take him to sit outside the schoolhouse and hold the horses while he attended board meetings. One day he came out saying, "Well, they beat me. They voted me down. You know I have tried to put a course in carpentry into this school for a long time." But a course in carpentry would not have brought any money in from the Board of Regents in Albany. So instead, the board voted a course of comparative anatomy. Then James said, "I wanted to have a course in the basement of the school for the girls, cooking and sewing." But that was voted down too. James felt that it was pointless to teach village children anatomy, since they would probably end up as carpenters and maids on the estates.

This way of life lasted well into the twentieth century. It was a combination of Woodrow Wilson's income tax and FDR's Social Security that did the estates in. They became too costly for the heirs to keep up, and the villagers found better things to do than work for the gentry. But as late as 1925, when the population of Hyde Park was 900, 175 were working on the estates, and if you counted four persons per family, that meant that 700 out of the 900 depended on the estates for employment.

Although his social programs sped the decline of the Hudson River gentry, FDR remained attached to the way of life of his childhood and managed to get the government to take over the Rogers and Vanderbilt estates. When he heard in 1940 that the 800-acre Rogers place was up for sale, it gave him nightmares that the grounds where he had spent so many happy hours might become a shopping center or be sold to Father Divine, who had a property across the river. One day after a cabinet meeting, FDR told Claude Wickard, his secretary of agriculture: "We've got to do something about this." Wickard was tearing his hair out trying to figure out what to do, and asked the Forest Service if they could buy it for a nursery, but they already had a nursery sixteen miles away. Then the United States got into the war, and FDR suggested that it could be bought as a convalescent center, but Wickard said, "We can't go to the Hill and get any money to do this, Mr. President. It's just out."

Eventually the government did buy it, but the people over at Agriculture felt that it was one of those ideas that had to be translated into action—one nod from the president was all it took to start the wheels spinning in all directions. It was like "something had to be done about the ticky deer," or about the water chestnuts that he had seen clogging the Potomac and wanted used for paper or fertilizer, thereby generating a year of fruitless research.

Above and beyond its physical setting, Hyde Park provided FDR with a set of values that were not necessarily in the mainstream of American life. Hyde Park stood for the rooted versus the uprooted, for the rural versus the urban, for the sedentary versus the migrant, for the old family versus the new arrival, for eastern gentility versus western crudeness, for tradition versus change. From these values, he took what he needed to project an image of himself, more mythical than real, as a farmer and country bumpkin and neighborly fellow who had a deep and abiding interest in the potato crop and apple barrels.

His attachment to the land was genuine. Hyde Park was his true home (even though after his father's death it belonged to his mother), the one unvarying part of his life, a source of inner strength, ritualized in the postelection ceremonies of receiving his neighbors there. This great maker of change wanted the land to stay as it was. When he was governor of New York, the Dutchess County engineer, James S. Bixby, wanted to straighten the curves of Violet Avenue (Route 9-G). Roosevelt told him not to touch a single tree or move a single stone in a wall. Every curve, originally laid out by cows making a path to the creek, was sacred.

His passion for trees was genuine. From Harvard, he wrote his mother that one reason for coming on Sunday was "to get home again before all the trees are bare." When he was away from home, and reports of bad storms in Dutchess County reached him, his first comment was always "I wonder what it did to the trees." In many a campaign speech he used the image of the tree—as it grew it produced rot and deadwood. The radicals said cut it down, the conservatives said don't touch it, the liberals said let's lose neither the old trunk nor the new branches. Below his father's house there was a lovely old virgin stand of hemlocks mixed with beech, birch, sugar maple, hickory, red cherry, yellow poplar, and an occasional butternut. He knew the qualities of each tree, the kind of wood each produced, whether they were slow- or fast-growing, whether they grew in the shade or needed full sunlight, and whether they could be used for lumber, fuel, crossties, or posts.

Over the years, FDR would plant 220,000 trees on the property. Planting trees made him feel good. It was a positive act, you could see the results, and it was something you could pass on to your children down the generations, so that you were, like nature, part of a continuing process rather than an isolated individual.

His dislike of the city was also genuine. The city represented a threat to the best values of American life, a threat made up of corrupt bosses, dirty streets, unwashed immigrants, congestion, and immorality. In one of his early letters he wrote his mother: "The less I have of New York the better." In an interview in the New York *Globe* on February 6, 1911, he said: "The lives of you city people are artificial. You don't breed exactly the same kind of people we do in the country. . . . I might almost say that the political salvation of the country lies with the country men and boys." When he was assistant secretary of the Navy he accepted a position as vice president of the State Forestry Association of New York and was listed on its letterhead as a resident of New York City, which prompted this letter to F. F. Moon, professor at the School of Forestry at Syracuse, on October 22, 1915: "By the way, I wish you would change my address on the Association's letter paper to Hyde Park, Dutchess County, New York, as I never have been and hope I never will be a resident of New York City."

Less genuine was his much-mentioned rapport with his neighbors. When he came back to Hyde Park after being nominated for the vice presidency at the 1920 Democratic convention in San Francisco, there was a demonstration outside his house, and he said: "I am moved more by this than anything else in my life. I am moved more than I was at San Francisco when the unexpected happened. . . . I want to tell you from the bottom of my heart that my success is due to my association with the good old stock of Dutchess County and the straight-thinking people I have been brought up among here."

In fact, his associations were mainly with the children of his millionaire neighbors. As a boy, he did not mingle with the village children. He was brought to the village for haircuts by his governess and told not to speak to anyone. His mother was known to be haughty. She treated people as if they were not there. The Roosevelts were not as rich as the Rogerses and the Vanderbilts, but they were snootier. In addition, Sara had a reputation as a tightwad. In August 1932, Arthur Smith, the son of the Roosevelt tenant farmer, Moses Smith, attended a Roosevelt Home Club meeting to discuss rumors that might prove harmful to FDR in his presidential campaign. Smith mentioned the rumor that FDR was taking advantage of the depression by cutting the wages of his employees to $1 or $1.25 a day. This was going around all over the county, but how could it be stopped? Smith wrote FDR to warn him, and received this reply on August 24: "As you know, I have nothing to do with the employees at my mother's place, however I am perfectly confident that she has no one to whom she is paying $1 a day. It is, of course, quite possible that she has reduced wages in order to avoid dismissing any employees, but I feel sure that if they were dissatisfied they would not stay with her. I know that you understand that it is not only people who are living on salaries who are feeling the depression, but that people who are living on incomes are really very much affected. I know my mother's income has been reduced to less than half of what it was. . . ." His neighbors, however, would sympathize with the underpaid employees rather than cry with Sara all the way to the bank.

In the 1932 election, as in every national election FDR ran in, his neighbors voted against him. He never carried his hometown or his county, which was downright unneighborly. People remembered the standoffishness of his parents and were not taken in by the son's geniality. They observed that when he came to campaign, someone behind him would whisper the name of the person he was greeting. And yet in hundreds of speeches he referred to his friends and neighbors in Hyde Park, and when he wrote a column in the *Beacon Standard* in 1928, the first one was called "Between Neighbors." But his "neighborliness" was in fact an adaptation of the gentry's patron-client relationship to the demands of state and national politics.

FDR liked to say that he was a farmer from a family of farmers. He wasn't, but had inherited the conceit from his father. Each spring, James bought a pair of oxen for field work and guessed their weight, coming within a few pounds. The farmers, eager to satisfy their employer's vanity at small expense, marveled at his expertise and said that only a genu-wine farmer like Mr. James could guess the weight so closely. Pleased, James laughed heartily. In fact, he was a capitalist with an office in New York, a private railroad car, and seats on the boards of various corporations.

FDR was a farmer the way Einstein was a violinist. He knew quite a bit about it, but he did it as a hobby. However, he liked to present himself as a farmer so he could benefit from the agrarian mystique that saw farmers as noble creatures, custodians of the land and of the rural virtues that made America great. The notion had sprung full-blown from the brow of Thomas Jefferson: "Those who labor in the earth are the chosen people of God, if ever he had a chosen people, whose breasts He has made the peculiar deposit for substantial and genuine virtue." Adopting the agrarian mystique gave FDR a connection with farmers all over the country and, extending outward from Hyde Park, with all of America as a land of tilled fields and rural folk. It connected him also to Jefferson, who had inherited Monticello—on a river like the Roosevelt place—from his father and had farmed there.

In his speeches and correspondence, FDR took pains to identify himself as a farmer. To Dudley Culver on February 24, 1911, when he was a New York State senator representing a rural constituency, he wrote: "I appreciate as a farmer myself, that it is impossible for milk producers to accept a lower price than they are getting now. . . ." To C. R. Van de Carr, he wrote on November 19, 1912: "I have heard many tales of methods used by some of our fellow farmers in packing apple barrels by means of stovepipes. . . ."

Often when addressing a rural audience, he would say that he was a "hayseed," and to establish rapport with his fellow hayseeds he would make fun of city slickers who knew nothing about rural life, as in this talk on May 14, 1935: "A few years ago in the countryside where I live, I was driving with a prominent city banker. Everything was brown. The leaves were off the trees. And all of a sudden we passed a beautiful green field. He asked me what it was. I told him it was winter wheat. He turned to me and said, 'That is very interesting. I have always wondered about winter wheat. What I don't understand is how they are able to cut it when it gets all covered up with snow.' "

FDR brought to farming the same enthusiasm that he brought to stamp collecting or naval history. It was one of his fields of expertise, absorbing only a small part of his life. He was a pretend farmer, who gave orders to the real farmer, Moses Smith. He loved to visit Moses and spend hours in earnest talk of pigs and fertilizer, and he would stop off and see another local farmer, Pete Rowen, and discuss the relative merits of Silver Queen and Country Gentleman. "Farmer" was one of FDR's many guises. A chameleonlike creature, if you placed him against a tree he turned the color of its bark.

Was there ever a stranger, less typically American childhood than Franklin Roosevelt's, the only son of an adoring mother and a doting father, who lived tradition-bound lives on their estate, leaving it only for the season in New York or trips to Europe? When Huck Finn was rafting down the Mississippi, Franklin was on an ocean liner to Liverpool. Behind his parents there was, on both sides, a long line of ancestors who had advanced the family to its present position. He saw life as a turnover of generations, in which he would take his appointed place. The idea that one is obliged to one's ancestors, that there is a debt to be repaid, was part of his upbringing. As his uncle Fred wrote him on July 31, 1899: "We are proud of our ancestors, but will our descendants be proud of us?" There were standards to be met, an estate to be inherited and managed, 200 years of consolidation to maintain.

FDR was one of the "once-born," as William James called those who painlessly fit in with their surroundings. His childhood was removed from the bustle and flux of mainstream America. While most children of his generation were determined by an undefined future, he was determined by an overdefined past. He was not a part of the decisive American experience of his time, the experience of the frontier. The call of the frontier, the temptation to move on, this was the uniquely American adventure. The gentry lived their static lives behind the hedges of their properties while the footloose man on the expanding frontier became an epic figure. Life on the frontier was made up as you went along, as against the life of antecedents.

While James Roosevelt watched over his herd of English cattle, tended to his duties as a vestryman, and took the cure in German spas, Walt Whitman wrote: "Talk as you like, he only suits these States whose manners favor the audacity and sublime turbulence of the States."

Franklin was far removed from audacity and sublime turbulence. In the country beyond Hyde Park, there was intermittent warfare, the Pullman strike, the McCormick plant riots, the battle at Homestead. In 1884, when he was two, the country was overrun with jobless tramps. When he was three, mobs stormed through Prairie Avenue in Chicago, demanding food. When he was four, a bomb was thrown into a crowd of workers assembled on Haymarket Square in Chicago by a provocateur hoping to break up the eight-hour-day movement. It was still true that any American had an alternative to despair, the country being open at both ends—there was free land in the West, with communities starting from scratch, while the immigrant goulash was strained through the eastern industrial colander. Iron workers arrived from Stockholm with only three words of English, "Charlie—Deere—Moline," Charlie being president of the John Deere Plow Company in Moline, Illinois.

Of all this Franklin had only an occasional glimmer. Once he went hunting in the town of Clinton and heard people talking about a section around Brown's Pond called "Kansas." Wondering why it was called that, he discovered that around 1850, when Kansas was still a territory opening up for settlement, an enterprising railroad agent had come up to Clinton with prospectuses and had persuaded six or eight families from Brown's Pond to get on a train to Kansas that was leaving from Poughkeepsie. They didn't see any future in Clinton, so they moved out to the new prairie land, disappearing from Dutchess County. In this way, through a place name, FDR acquired a sense of the expanding frontier. When he was seven, in 1889, he was thrilled by accounts of the first settlements in Oklahoma, the prospective settlers lining up at the border and, at the sound of a bugle, rushing forward to establish new homes and communities.

This experience of scrambling for land was the exact opposite of Franklin's own. He grew up with a sense of being at home in different family houses that were filled with mementos and photographs, reminders of past achievements. At Algonac, when he was two, one of his cousins dropped him into one of the huge Chinese vases. "Careful, children," said grandfather Warren Delano, "those vases were made in China years ago by great artists. If you broke one, there would never be another like it."

When he was four, Franklin was left at Algonac with his nurse, Helen McRorie, whom he called "Mamie," while James took Sara on his private car, the *Monon,* to inspect the various railroads he had interests in, mixing business with pleasure to tour Mexico. They returned with stories of the world "out there" that Franklin never forgot. In Salt Lake City, they saw two young ladies wheeling baby carriages with babies about a year old.

James asked if they were waiting for someone and they said, "Yes, we are waiting for our husband. He is the engineer of this train." Sara showed him on the colored globe the route they had taken to Laredo. They had changed cars because the Mexican tracks had a different gauge. James explained that the houses were built around patios because of the heat, and that the Mexican hero was Benito Juarez rather than George Washington.

Then there was the Homestead, the big gray house in Fairhaven where grandfather Warren had been born. Franklin knew it by heart, room by room: the vitrine in the middle parlor, the bookcase in the little west room, the ship model under glass in Grandpa's room upstairs, the sideboard on the west wall of the dining room, the model of the Chinese village, and the great wooden boxes up in the attic, bound in iron, lettered with the name of the ship. The boy would study the old log books of the whaling captains, with their accounts of the catch and of meetings with other ships. As an epic symbol, the whale ship was the equal of the prairie schooner, and it was an epic to which he was directly connected through his grandfather. On the old stringpiece of the Delano stone wharf, Franklin sat and gazed at the New Bedford shore, where a dozen tall spars overtopped the granite warehouses, and thought of the whalers that had sailed to the Falklands and Alaska.

Finally, there was Hyde Park itself and the experience of growing up rich. Of being made to wear dresses until he was five, and long blond curls, as if his mother wanted to delay his maleness. Of graduating from dresses to kilts of the Murray clan, with whom the Roosevelts had some distant connection, complete with a miniature sporran in his belt and a beribboned highlander cap.

Of not having to attend school until he was fourteen because it was the custom of the estate owners to have their children properly tutored, and because his parents wanted him to be physically present, a part of their landscape. Franklin studied with the Rogers boys next door, Archie and Edmund. They had German tutors, French tutors, and arithmetic tutors. The story was that one little boy climbed a tree with great skill and when he came down the other boys surrounded him and asked: "Who is your tree-climbing tutor?"

Of being a lord of the manor in training, following his long-striding father until his legs ached through furrowed fields and fruit-laden orchards, past a hemlock hedge three times his size, and into greenhouses smelling of damp earth and flowers. Learning the mystery of the threshing machines, their cleated tracks indenting the soft earth of the barnyards. Riding through the woods with his father in the winter with ropes tied to their saddles to tether their horses or to fell a dead tree. Getting a sense of the seasons: October and the faint smell of burning wood; November, the bright colors fading from the hills; Thanksgiving and Christmas—the head farmer and the farmhands and the gardeners and Buckle the English coachman and the stable boys all got turkeys; January, watching men in hip-high boots cutting eight-inch-thick ice on the river bank with huge saws, the ice cakes floating on the dark water, hooked to pulleys and loaded in sleighs to be stored in hay-and-saw-dust-filled ice houses.

Learning to own, being given a red setter named Marksman and a Welsh pony named Debby and having to take care of them. His father scolded him when he rode Debby too hard and the vet had to be called because he had committed the worst sin of all, the sin of being a careless owner. Learning to give a horse a lump of sugar, the chickens a handful of grain, a farmer a word of cheer. Going after birds' eggs, the loosely made nests of dry leaves with the crows' big white eggs, the compact rounded nests of brittle twigs with the light blue of robins' eggs. He did not have to carry the eggs away. They were his, as the woods were his and the scorching red of the autumn leaves. He was feeling his way, taking possession, digging in the woodchuck holes with his dogs, or going down to Thompson's Pond to hear the swamp birds as dawn broke.

Learning that one was not bound to the property, that there was a limit-less supply of places to visit. They were sources of wonder, and a way of amassing memories, one of the forms of acquisition that went with wealth. After every trip, there were photographic reminders of how pleasant life was.

In the fall of 1884, when Franklin was not quite three, he was taken on a six-month trip to Europe to try out spas. James believed devoutly in the benefits of mineral waters and spent many months of his life taking the cure, submitting to the regimen of places with "Wells" or "Bath" in their names. That year, he tried Tunbridge Wells, a fashionable watering place fre-quented by royalty, and Bad Kissingen, a Franconian health resort with sul-fur springs where an assassination attempt had been made against Bismarck. The pattern of Franklin's childhood was determined by his father's health. Between the ages of two and fourteen he made no less than eight transatlan-tic voyages, at a time when crossing the Atlantic was a serious business. Friends spoke of the trip as though it was a repetition of the performance of Columbus. There were no covered or enclosed decks. Passengers with cabins aft of the funnels were powdered with soot. Meals were served at long tables equipped with "fiddles," wooden compartments on top of the tablecloths where the plates and glasses fitted, and the chairs were screwed to the floors. On the return trip aboard the *Germanic* in April 1885, the ship was tossed in a storm, a bulkhead broke, and water leaked into the Roosevelt cabin. Un-afraid, Sara wrapped her fur coat around three-year-old Franklin and said, "Poor little boy, if he must go down he is going down warm."

After that near-shipwreck, there were no more European trips for a while, but in 1887 they took Franklin to spend the winter in Washington, for no special reason, to see friends, one of whom happened to be president. Sara saw a large man exhausted by the cares of office, writing letters in longhand because he did not have a secretary in the evening. He wanted James to take an appointment, perhaps ambassador to the Netherlands, but James demurred, although he was pleased that his son Rosy was in Vienna. On their farewell visit to the White House they took five-year-old Franklin. Grover Cleveland was worn down by his fight with Congress over pension bills and would lose his bid for reelection the following year. According to the oft-told story of this fabled meeting, he patted the child's blond head and said, "My little man, I am making a strange wish for you. It is that you may never be president of the United States." A wish like that suggested the myth that anyone can be president, whereas in fact almost no one can be president. Up to and including Cleveland there had been twenty-two. But it was the first time FDR was mentioned in connection with the presidency.

In 1891, Sara and James discovered the stodgy Hessian spa of Bad Nauheim, which they would faithfully attend until James's death in 1900. It was on the River Usa, near Frankfurt, and had a famous institute for cardiac diseases (James had suffered a severe heart attack in 1888, which made doctors shake their heads). Bad Nauheim attracted a large British and American clientele. People in the shops spoke English, and there was an Anglo-American church and a hotel called the Villa Britannia where James and Sara were always given the same rooms.

Each of the remaining six summers until he went away to school, they spent three or four months there with Franklin. Life revolved around the cure, which never ended, for one was never cured, and around people one knew. They mingled with the duke and duchess of Rutland, the Cholmeleys, Lord Clanwilliam, who was an admiral of the fleet, Sir Cameron Gull, who was a member of Parliament, Sir Cecil George Savile Foljambe, and Randal Thomas Mowbray Rawdon Berkeley, the future earl of Berkeley, one of the very few English families that could claim a pre-Norman pedigree. They exchanged symptoms, drank the waters, took the baths, had their pulses taken by Dr. Schott, went for walks of definitely prescribed lengths, ate the recommended diet with milk fresh from the cow, listened to concerts in the Kurgarten, and were under feathers by ten.

In his first year at Bad Nauheim, 1891, Franklin went to the local school, and caricatured Kaiser Wilhelm II, who had come to power three years before, drawing mustaches that went to the top of the paper. The teacher told him to write *Ich muss brave sein*—I must be good—300 times. During the five years that he attended the school, he saw a growing regimentation taking place under the kaiser's rule. They had to study *Heimatkunde*, an early version of the master-race theories, and each year the geography lesson expanded. At first it was about the village, then about neighboring towns, then about the province of Hesse-Darmstadt, then the following year they were taught what roads to take to get to the French border. In the geography lesson was contained the message of German expansion and the inevitable war with France. Schoolchildren and railway employees had to wear uniforms and were taught to march. The talk among the children was that the Reich would be built up into a world power. They were taught to have no respect for Englishmen and that Americans were barbarians, most of whom were millionaires.

Not surprisingly, Franklin adopted the social prejudices of his parents, who were contemptuous of Germans. James would write his son in 1897, when he was at Groton, that "Mama struck against feeding in company with the German swine so we have a separate table to ourselves at quite the other end of the dining room." In a similar vein, Franklin wrote his cousins Muriel and Warren Robbins (Aunt Cassie's children) on May 30, 1891, "I go to the public school with a lot of little mickies and we have German reading, German dictation, the history of Siegfried, and arithmetic in which I am 14×71, on paper, and I like it very much." He also wrote one of his aunts, who was visiting Bad Nauheim while he was in Campobello, on September 10, 1892: "I think of you being in the lovely baths just now or being rubbed by a filthy German woman...." If only they could have had Germany, with its restoring waters and splendid scenery, without the filthy German swine.

When he was home in Hyde Park, and not being tutored, Franklin put his energies into constructive play. Part of growing up rich was learning that it was better to build than to destroy, better to finish a task than to leave it. Early on, Franklin showed a healthy acquisitive streak, although there was never any danger that he would turn into a compulsive collector; his collections were part of his constructivist, builder side, as well as another way of connecting him with his family's past. Sara had collected stamps not long after the first stamps were put on letters, and she gave her collection to her brother Fred, who gave it to Franklin when he was ten. His cousin Helen (Rosy's daughter) had one too. She was strong on Austria and England, where her father had served, and they spent hours talking in the arcane language of the philatelist, of burelage and overprints and cachets. By 1890, he had 2,100 stamps, his rarest being the Formosa 1888. It was the same with naval mementos. His grandfather had given him an old sea chest and he began to store things in it—the cap his great-uncle had worn in the War of 1812, the button ripped off the coat of a naval officer in the same war, a miniature brass cannon, a tarnished bit of braid. This he continued, as he did his stamp collecting, into adult life, acquiring in the bargain an astounding knowledge of naval history. Dudley Knox, who was in charge of the Office of Naval Records and Library when FDR was president, said that "he had few if any peers" in the field. "His knowledge was exceptional.... Similarly his recollection of minor details was most unusual. This was borne out by his frequent reference to them in ordinary conversation." Once his naval aide, Admiral Wilson Brown, came in for his routine call and FDR said, "Hello, Moses Brown." "Did you say Moses?" Brown asked, thinking that Roosevelt had intimated that he looked Jewish. "Yes, I did say Moses," FDR said. "You go over and ask Dudley Knox." Brown hurried over to ask Knox, who said, "Yes, Moses Brown commanded a small man-of-war in the quasi-war with France. I have recently received a photograph of his portrait, sent by a descendant." "Do you see any resemblance to me?" Brown asked. "Was he Jewish?" Knox assured him that he was not, and reflected that only FDR would have made that particular connection and that he knew more about naval history than the navy men. A childhood pastime had become a lifelong area of expertise.

He was just as thorough in his collection of birds, although that activity ended with childhood. When he was eleven he was given a rifle and decided to collect one specimen of every kind of Dutchess County bird. He would shoot them and skin them and take a hand in the stuffing and mounting (perhaps he had been told that his cousin Theodore had wanted as a boy to be a taxidermist). More than an amusement, his collection would be a useful addition to the natural history of the region. For two years, Franklin could be found haunting berry patches where feeding birds gathered, or in heavily matted grass fields, or along the river bank, or standing long watches under tall trees waiting for the quick flash of red wings against a blue patch of sky. A shotgun leaping to his shoulder, a sharp report, and the flying bird fell to the ground, its feathers bloodied.

Most of the stuffing was done by a professional taxidermist, who mounted the birds on polished perches, alighting, springing to flight, drooping at rest. When he was fourteen, he offered a rare pine grosbeak skin to the Museum of Natural History in New York City. In exchange, the curator of ornithology, F. M. Chapman, offered him an associate membership in the American Ornithologists' Union, of which he must have been the youngest member.

When he was fourteen, his father gave him a twenty-one-foot knock-about, the *New Moon*, with a jib, mainsail, and spinnaker and a tiny cabin with two bunks and an oil stove. He cruised all over eastern Maine and the Bay of Fundy, and once had a rather Tom Sawyerish adventure. He was cruising around the southern end of Grand Manan Channel when fog started coming in and he anchored in a tiny harbor close to the lighthouse on White Head Island. At 11:00 P.M., in thick fog, he heard an anchor chain going overboard and realized that someone had come in who really knew the coast. At dawn, he saw a little black schooner that he recognized as belonging to a veteran Maine sea captain. Franklin rowed over in his dory to say hello and asked where he was going. From Digby to Machias with a load of potatoes, the captain gruffly replied.

"I never heard of carrying potatoes from Nova Scotia to Maine," Franklin said.

"Well, son, the market is ripe for it this year," the captain assured him.

Beyond the foremast, Franklin noticed that the forward hatch was propped up at one corner by a piece of kindling wood. He smelled a curious odor and said, "Captain, those are funny smelling potatoes." There was no reply. "You know," he went on, "my family was out in China for a great many years and those potatoes smell to me very much like Chinese potatoes."

Standing before him with his fists clenched, the captain said, "Young fellow, you're altogether too nosy. It is none of your damned business."

"How many of those Chinese potatoes have you got on board?" Franklin
persisted.

Having decided he couldn't throw the young fellow overboard, the captain suddenly grew affable and confided: "Sonny, I guess I can count on you.
I have eighteen of them below decks."

"What do you get apiece?" Franklin asked.

"One hundred per."

"Well, captain, I hope you have a good voyage and make Machias all
right," Franklin said, having obtained direct evidence of one aspect of the
immigration problem.

All in all, his was a peculiar childhood, at once cloistered and peripatetic,
its Little Lord Fauntleroy aspects alternating with healthy doses of outdoor
life. Franklin knew that he belonged to an exclusive and privileged class.
His family had a coat of arms and a Dutch bible that had belonged to them
since the seventeenth century. The family properties, at Hyde Park and
Campobello, were on the water, as the properties of the privileged should
be, and the sports practiced were the sports of his class, boating and golf.
The family homes were filled with evocative objects. Franklin was attached
to family things that could be passed on. Four years before he was born, his
father had a tweed suit made in Edinburgh. He wore the suit constantly until
his death, and Franklin inherited it and wore it steadily until 1926, when he
gave it to his son James, who was still wearing it in 1939.

Crossing the Atlantic repeatedly, speaking French and German, making
Europe his playground, all this was routine, a class prerogative. He learned
manners as the defense mechanism of a class that must keep others at bay. It
was not polite to speak with those one had not formally met, or to converse
except in a prescribed manner, or to get too friendly with the servants.
Manners were part of a code of behavior that excluded as well as included.
In the spring of 1896, Paul Rideout, a member of the American Historical
Society, came to Hyde Park to obtain a record of the Roosevelt and Delano
families for a history of the old Dutch settlers on the Hudson. He was at the
dining-room table with James and Sara when a fourteen-year-old boy came
in from playing with a dog out on the lawn and stood behind his chair until
James had introduced him and only then sat down.

From being raised in a privileged class, Franklin developed a sense of entitlement. He was entitled to what he had because his family had been in the
country from the start. Through his lines of descent, he absorbed American
history. Some of his ancestors had landed from the *Mayflower*, the first Delano had landed a year later, Isaac the Patriot had ratified the Constitution,
and the Delano sea captains had contributed to the prosperity of American
trade.

Franklin sifted what was best in his past, what he could use, and where
the past was wanting he filled in the gaps. In an essay on his family written

at Harvard in December 1901, he wrote: "Some of the famous Dutch families in New York have today nothing left but their names—they are few in numbers, they lack progressiveness and a true democratic spirit. One reason—perhaps the chief—of the virility of the Roosevelts is this very democratic spirit. They have never felt that because they were born in a good position they could put their hands in their pockets and succeed. They have felt, rather, that being born in a good position, there was no excuse for them if they did not do their duty by the community." This was a myth that Franklin created in order to live up to it. His grandfather Isaac had kept his hands in his pockets and lived on inherited money. His father cared less for the community than for his cures, and depleted the family fortune in misbegotten business ventures. His half brother Rosy was a reactionary and a fierce anti-Semite, who had written him from Aix-les-Bains on August 14, 1923, that there were "an awful lot of Jews, mostly of the detestable American variety. I am ashamed to hail from the U.S.A. . . . It's a relief to see a 'Gentile,' as the others call them," and from Bermuda on February 17, 1926, "The place is packed. Mostly an awful class of Jews, objectionable when sober, and worse when drunk." But Franklin preferred to see his father as a friend and adviser of President Cleveland, invited to the White House, and his half brother as a diplomat who had played a part in a foreign-policy crisis.

In 1895 there was a dispute over the boundaries of Venezuela and British Guiana, in an area where gold had been found. Lord Salisbury, the British prime minister, laid down an ultimatum that Venezuela should agree to the British point of view. The British stand was seen in Washington as a threat to the Monroe Doctrine. Grover Cleveland's secretary of state, Richard Olney, sent a stiff note telling Lord Salisbury that the United States considered Britain's presence in Venezuela "unnatural and inexpedient." As first secretary of the American legation in London, it fell upon Rosy Roosevelt to bring the note to the Foreign Office, where he was told it would mean immediate war. Rosy soothed the furious British, and the matter was submitted to arbitration and settled in 1899. It was an example of the enforcement of the Monroe Doctrine that came home to young Franklin through the participation of his brother. The United States would not tolerate, in North or South America, an invasion by foreign powers, or territorial conquest by a European power already established there, even if that power was England, with her great empire and naval might.

Franklin grew up with the feeling that the American past, thanks to the involvement of his forebears and, more recently, of his half brother, was a manual of personal instruction. He developed the ability to reconstruct history in such a way that it gave him an obligation to live up to.

As he made the past his own, he made the land his own, beginning with Hyde Park, understanding what it meant to own a large estate, to farm it, to plant trees, to remain on good terms with the help without being familiar. Above all, privilege was based on acreage. He was entitled to the land. And through the filter of the agrarian mystique, the idea that he was a farmer and that all farmers were kin, he could extend his sense of the land to the entire country. He understood the past, and he understood the land, and he made them his. Hyde Park was not his in fact—it belonged to his father and then to his mother—but he owned it through his appreciation and grasp of it, and this appreciation and grasp of a territorial base could be extended to a wider area.

"Don't you think Franklin is a remarkably good little boy?" Sara asked her mother, who had given birth to eleven children. "He can't help being good," Mrs. Warren Delano replied. "He has no brothers or sisters to bother him."

Franklin was an only child, and he was conscious of being an only child, which he saw as an auspicious circumstance. He wrote his Dutchess County friend Helen Reynolds on September 14, 1941: "You and I were only children; we received a love and devotion that were perfect in their forgetfulness of self and thought for us; and we experienced a companionship that was rare in quality between parent and child." Another advantage, unmentioned, was that he was not saddled with the scapegrace younger brother who has afflicted presidents from Theodore Roosevelt to Jimmy Carter.

Growing up, Franklin must have puzzled over the confusing web of family ties. His half brother, Rosy, was the same age as his mother. His father was close to the age of his maternal grandfather. His nephew, Rosy's son Taddy, was three years older than he was.

In neighboring families there was more than one child. There were three Ashton children and four Rogers children, two of them boys near his own age. Rosy had two, Taddy and Helen. They had to share the love and attention of their parents. He had his exclusively, and must have wondered why that was the case. It was natural for an only child to seek an explanation. The mother might say that giving birth had been such an ordeal that she wanted no more, and that had indeed been Sara's case, the overdose of chloroform nearly killing her. Or she might tell the child that he was hard enough to handle by himself. Or, and this would have been Sara's most likely reply, the mother might say, "All our love went to you and there was nothing left for another child."

To an only child, such explanations are unsatisfactory. The absence of siblings remains mysterious. He sees the advantages—never having to share, never having to quarrel, never having to compete, never having a parent say "Look at your brother, look at your sister," never being hurt by not being preferred, never being left behind while a brother is taken along, wondering why he has been excluded. He begins to wish that the status quo will be preserved. When the wish comes true, he may begin to believe that he is in some way responsible, that the power of his wish has denied life to potential brothers and sisters, that the magic of his thinking has won him a privileged situation.

In other families, the oldest child has to adjust to siblings, but the only child has to live with the fact that none ever come. This is his specific problem. One way of solving it is through an unstated transaction with the parents. He must pay them back for having deprived them of other children by meeting their expectations and by founding a large family and giving them lots of grandchildren.

Often, ambition in great men is spurred by the need to outdo their fathers. But James was no spur to ambition. With his unlucky investments and country life, he had achieved little. He had time and again refused to serve in an elected or appointed office. His was not an example Franklin could build upon. Since his father did not provide the necessary role model, his ambition had to come from elsewhere. Possibly it came from the dilemma of being an only child, the feeling that he had to pay back his parents for giving him their exclusive love and attention, that he had to excel because he had kept his favored position.

Being an only child gave Franklin a strong core of self-esteem and self-worth, the essential childhood traits that are the foundation for all others. He had dependable, caring parents, and he was the focus of their constant attention. He was the sun, his parents planets in orbit. The world he grew up in was a predictable and loving place. He had before him on a daily basis for the first fourteen years of his life the example of parents who did not quarrel, who never displayed emotion or anger. Sara had been taught to maintain her composure in front of the children. He was never the inwardly shrinking witness to conflicting interests or ill-tempered words. He never had to deal with parents transmitting derivatives of their own conflicts to their child. He was surrounded by caring adults, nurses and governesses and tutors, whose purpose was to attend to his needs and instruction.

To his father, Franklin's birth meant a renewal of youth. He was in his fifties and had a heart condition, but he was still physically active and did his best to be his son's companion.

When James went on his rounds—silk-hatted, always dignified and pleasant—Franklin accompanied him. To the post office for the mail, to the school to hear the children read, looking in on his gardener, William Plog: "Good morning, Plog. Have the seeds come from Thornburns?"

Whatever was going on, Franklin was included. When they went to Washington in 1887, Sara wrote: "Everyone has been charming to us, even Franklin knows everybody." When they were in Paris in 1890, James took Franklin to the top of the Eiffel Tower, completed the previous year. On election day in 1892, Grover Cleveland was running again, and James went to vote for his friend and got into a conversation with D. E. Howatt, the Hyde Park supervisor, and his neighbor Tom Newbold, and they wondered how they could get the election results that evening. Howatt said he would go into Poughkeepsie with a snare drummer and a piccolo player, and if Cleveland won he would drive his wagon into James's place and play "Yankee Doodle." And so he did, and James said, "Mr. Howatt, that was the sweetest music I have ever heard." More and more people arrived on their farm wagons, carrying torches. A ten-year-old boy, supposedly asleep in his room at the head of the stairs, was listening, and saw the queer light from his window, and wondered what was going on. He ventured down to the porch in his nightgown, and someone threw an old buffalo robe over him to protect him from the night's chill, and he attended his first election victory celebration.

Sara was ever doting and proud, certain that she had produced an exceptional human being. He was always her darling boy. He had good, kind instincts. He was easy to manage. When she did have to reprimand him, she did it out of earshot of the nurse and housekeeper, because in their eyes Franklin could do no wrong. Sara's diary is filled with examples of devotion, such as this entry on August 30, 1894, at Campobello: "We heard Frances lecture on 'Hydroid Colonies,' Betty Porter on 'Small Sea Life,' and Franklin on 'Ornithology.' They all did very well of course and our hearts beat for *our* special treasure."

Sara was convinced that she left her son a large measure of autonomy, that she and James never tried to influence him against his own tastes and inclinations. But the other side to being an only child, on a steady diet of exclusive maternal love, was that he began to feel smothered. He must have wondered whether he could ever exist outside the cocoon of parental devotion. Franklin instinctively understood the dual nature of possessive maternal love. He accepted its nurturing quality while protecting himself from its devouring aspect. There were in Sara elements of the mythical Mom, making it clear to her husband that she no longer wanted conjugal relations, preaching self-restraint while unable to restrict her intake of calories, and, where Franklin was concerned, doing her best to maintain the discontinuity between child and adult. He had to fight to get his locks trimmed and to graduate from dresses and kilts. He learned that there was a part of himself he could not reveal to his mother, and acquired an opaque core, a sort of inner armor. It was a matter of survival. He never rebelled openly but learned to be devious, to get around her. When he didn't want to go to church he said he had a headache, which became known to his parents as "Franklin's Sunday headache." When he wanted to get out of a drawing or piano lesson, he told his governess his hand hurt.

It was at his mother's knee that he learned the protective ambiguity that so many of his associates would later comment upon. As the brain truster Rexford Tugwell put it, "He was the kind of man to whom those who wanted him convinced of something—usually something in their own interest—could talk and argue and insist, and come away believing that they had succeeded, when all that happened was that he had been pleasantly present." Who could tell what FDR was really thinking? His flexible mind did cartwheels. He had learned as a child to mask his true intentions.

There are signs of this patiently acquired evasiveness in some of his early letters, in the transparent and jocular yet curious habit he developed of signing his name backward, as though concealing his identity. One letter to his "dear Mammy" on April 18, 1893, he signed "Tlevesoor D. Nilknarf." It does not occur to most children, even as a joke, to sign their names backward. In FDR, it may have corresponded to a need, announced to his parents in this easily decipherable manner, for keeping a part of himself hidden.

Aside from this mechanism of self-defense against adoring parents, Franklin was everything his mother said he was, outgoing, kind, and easy to manage. He was, said his Swiss governess, Jeanne Sandoz, "as cheerful as a finch." He had none of the introverted awkwardness that only children sometimes demonstrate among their peers, whom they consider substitute siblings and possible competitors. Indeed, there were children his age who met him once or twice and never forgot the encounter. In Bad Nauheim in the summer of 1891, when Franklin was nine, he went to see a little invalid English boy named John Percival Droop, who many years later would remember his kindness and the gift of a storybook inscribed "To Percy from his friend Franklin D. Roosevelt."

Another time at Bad Nauheim, he went to tea with a little English girl and her father. When the time came to pay, the girl's father beckoned for the check, but Franklin said, "No, this is my treat." The father was duly impressed, and the little girl, Eve Hulten, never forgot his largesse, and would write FDR during World War II that "I think that has been your line through your wonderful career." In 1944, she had a chance to pay him back for that tea in a German spa half a century before when her home was requisitioned for U.S. bomber crews.

Another young lady who remembered Franklin was Huibertje Pruyn of Albany. One winter day in 1892 her mother told her that Mr. and Mrs. James Roosevelt were coming to call with their ten-year-old son, Franklin, and she wanted Huibertje to take him coasting before dark. The fifteen-year-old girl mumbled that she wasn't interested, he would probably break her new sled. Going outside, she spied her chum Erastus Corning making snowballs across the street. "Ratty," she said, "there's a boy with a long name coming here this afternoon—mother says I must take him coasting—so you can come along too if you like. . . ." Ratty saw from her glum expression that she was not overjoyed at the prospect, and said, "I can settle him for you—I can trip him up so he won't know what happened and then wash his face [in snow]—he's probably a New York sissy."

When the Roosevelts drove up in their horse-drawn sleigh, Huibertje stood there next to her sled, in her red blanket coat and her red knitted cap and mittens, not looking cordial. Almost before the sleigh stopped, the boy in the backseat jumped out and came over with outstretched hand and said, "My name's Franklin, may I go coasting with you?" His eagerness and good fellowship were infectious, and Huibertje and Ratty Corning forgot their inhospitable plans and ran for the toboggan slide. Before the evening was over Huitbertje and Franklin were on the best of terms, stealing down the cellar stairs to loot some ice cream.

And yet Sara insisted that he was painfully self-conscious, and that only she appreciated the difficult time he had in speaking to anyone outside the immediate family. It was as if she wanted him to remain self-conscious as a way of keeping him dependent. Another child might have welcomed the comfort of his mother's skirts and become effeminate. But there was nothing sissy or prissy about Franklin. When he was nine, crossing to Europe on the *Teutonic,* he had a fight with an eleven-year-old who had cheated him in a game and beat him. Two years later, he didn't complain when friend Joe Lovering hit him in the mouth with a stick at Campobello, the stick having slipped while he was batting pebbles, and broke one of Franklin's teeth and chipped another. The following summer he got into trouble with some of his Campobello friends for releasing all of the horses in the hotel stable in the middle of the night.

He developed his own form of humor, based on comic exaggeration, very much in the American vein of the tall tale: when John Henry was born, the Mississippi ran upstream—that sort of thing. "Once I was hunting," he wrote when he was six, "and a buffalo took the trouble to cover his tracks and went into the mouth of a cave and when I got there I found he had disappeared in a hole at the top of the cave and so does my story." At the age of ten, he wrote his parents that he was dying of "school fever" and that his temperature was 150—in fact he had a cold and his nurse, Mlle Sandoz, was giving him five drops of camphor on a lump of sugar. A year later he wrote that he had only fallen three times from the top-story window.

He also liked to tease. Sharing a cabin with Mlle Sandoz on the boat to Europe, and having taken the upper berth, he awakened her in the morning by dangling the end of a string in her face. He thought it was funny when after one of their winter excursions in Hyde Park she fell off her sled and came back black and blue, and on one of his other governesses (the high-strung Fräulein Reinhardt, who would one day be confined to a mental institution) he played an offensive practical joke, managing to slip her a dose of Seidlitz powders, a then-popular laxative. His father called him in on that occasion and said: "Franklin, Fräulein is ill this morning and I think you know something about it. You can consider yourself spanked." In later years, FDR showed a mild fondness for toilet jokes, receiving his aides while shaving and saying, "Have a seat on the can, and remember your pants are up."

Mlle Sandoz tried to instill in her charge her concern for the humble masses, but Franklin took it with a grain of salt and treated serious subjects in a bantering tone, as if there was something humorous about human suffering. In a report on ancient Egypt when he was nine, he wrote: "The working people had nothing ... the kings made them work so hard and gave them so little that by wingo! they nearly starved and by jinks! they had hardly any clothes so they died in quadrillions." A social conscience came later, and he decided in retrospect that Mlle Sandoz had something to do with it, writing her in 1933: "I have often thought that it was you more than anyone else who laid the foundation for my education."

There was a bit of Rooseveltian flattery there, for surely his parents had been more responsible for laying the foundation, and with all Sara's coddling and James's leniency, it was a solid one. Freed of troublesome siblings and material want, FDR was able to turn his childhood into one continuous learning experience. One of the estate employees taught him how to use a saw and a chisel. His father taught him how to ride and to handle a boat. His mother taught him the pleasures of reading, and at a young age he was tackling, on his own, not for school, weighty tomes such as Mahan's *The Influence of Sea Power upon History* and Parkman's *Montcalm and Wolf.* He taught himself geography by looking up the countries his stamps came from, and naval history through his collection of mementos, and ornithology through the birds he shot. His was a childhood devoted to the development of skills and the acquiring of data. He had an uncannily retentive mind. Whatever he read remained forever on file in some compartment of his memory.

Those children who develop exceptional ability do so, we are told, because of instruction and attention, one-on-one tutoring being the ideal situation. Parental encouragement and the values stressed in the home are just as important. The source of human achievement is the satisfaction of excelling, and this too Franklin learned, for when his mother died in 1943 he wrote George Van Slyke of the New York *Sun:* "Those of us who enjoy the company of our mothers beyond the average number of years are indeed fortunate, for we know the good influence they exert and can appreciate the truth that the greatest pleasure we can get is to observe them rejoicing in our achievement, and conversely, our greatest source of regret is to disappoint those who have such abiding faith in us."

At the same time, traits acquired from his parents were a definite handicap to a political career. He inherited their priggishness, and Sara recalled him tearing himself away from the view in a railroad carriage "only long enough to wriggle with embarrassment and disapproval whenever he heard me talking to the nice strangers who from time to time shared compartments with us"; also some of the family prejudices, expressing his hope after one of her musical evenings that the piano was still intact, as "it might not stand the fine touch of a long-haired Polish Jew." He had no experience of struggle or confrontation, having been given everything he asked for. His parents always seemed to agree, and differences were amiably negotiated. All his life he would go to inordinate lengths to avoid confrontations. Often praised and seldom criticized as a child, he remained thin-skinned after years in office and would never admit to being wrong. If any positive traits could be singled out for future use, they were his capacity for learning and his healthy self-confidence, his parents never having diminished him, his limitations never having been tested.

Franklin did, however, carry within himself a sense of dual obligation: From being an only child, he owed it to his parents to excel. From being a Roosevelt, he owed it to his ancestors to meet the standards they had set. In this field of obligation, ambition could grow.

At an age when most boys had been in school for years, he still lived within the tight family triangle. Normally, he would have gone to Groton when he was twelve, when the other boys started, but still Sara clung to him. Ideally she would have kept him forever, but that was not possible. "In the end we realized," she said, "as we knew we would in the beginning, that the time had come when we could no longer allow our desire to keep him with us to limit his scope of experience. That it was only fair to the boy to send him out into a world whose boundaries were not limited by the barriers the very intensity of our devotion imposed."

September 14, 1896, was Franklin's last day at home. He and his mother dusted his birds, reminders of their life together and part of what he was leaving behind. He went for a swim in the river as Sara looked on with a heavy heart, thinking perhaps of earlier scenes that she still saw with perfect clarity: only a few months before, standing next to his camera, which was on a tripod almost as tall as himself, self-assured, hair parted in the middle, eyes closely set, she could never get over how like her he looked; and the birthday party when he was eleven, there had been a Jack Horner pie and presents for everyone; and that same year, at Campobello, when he had shot his first crow; and the time when they were crossing in May 1892 and he and his friend Babcock had thrown a bottle with a message in it off Queenstown, and the message was picked up on the beach and sent to the White Star Line office in Liverpool; and Franklin at seven, or was it eight, at the helm of his father's yacht, the *Half Moon,* in a stiff Bay of Fundy breeze, straining at the wheel; and Franklin in his sailor suit, riding his dock-tailed and curb-bitted Welsh pony; and Franklin at sixteen months, sitting on his father's shoulder in a long-sleeved white dress, his arm draped over his father's head and his fingers tickling his side-whiskers. Now he was going, but she had the memories to keep. On September 15, they took the 6:50 A.M. train to Albany, where James had his private car meet them and take them to Ayer junction, four miles from Groton. Even among the sons of the privileged who attended Groton, not many arrived at school in a private railroad car. Sara and James stayed at Groton on the sixteenth, leaving the following day. "It is hard to leave my darling boy," Sara wrote in her diary, "... James and I both feel this parting very much."

II

Groton

Groton school is perfectly incomprehensible to those who have not belonged to it.

William Amory Gardner

ALTHOUGH born in Salem, and a descendant of Massachusetts Bay Colony Governor John Endicott and of the Salem merchant Joseph Peabody, Endicott Peabody was a product of English schools. His father worked for the Morgan Bank in London, and he attended first Cheltenham, a public school of good repute (though a cut below Eton, Harrow, and Winchester), and then Trinity College, Cambridge.

An English education stays with you, and for the rest of his life Endicott Peabody would continue to spell in English (as in "honours") and speak in English (as in "sweets" rather than "candy"). But to this cultural Englishness, and to the religious vocation that brought him into the ministry, there was grafted an American entrepreneurial side. He was not afraid of bold ideas, or of starting from scratch. His idea, based on his own student years, was to adapt the traditions of the English public school to American education.

Endicott Peabody wanted to start a church school, with a strong emphasis on the sort of muscular Christianity he exemplified, for he was a broad-shouldered six-footer, blue of eye and square of jaw, with a soldierly manner and what the army calls "command presence."

In the spring of 1883, chatting with Peabody in her Groton home, Mrs. James Lawrence regretted that the nearest Episcopal service was at Fitchburg, fourteen miles away. She wished that someone would open a church school for boys in Groton, for that would bring the service closer. It was an omen. The Lawrences gave land, important men agreed to sit on the board, funds were found, children were signed up, the school was built, and on October 15, 1884, the first twenty-seven boys arrived, most of them from wealthy, socially registered families.

Largely on the strength of Endicott Peabody's personality, the right people started signing up their sons at birth, and sending them at the age of twelve to a village about thirty-five miles northwest of Boston, in the middle of a landscape that was like the New England character, tidy, uneffusive, a bit grim. The human landscape could be grim too, and unfathomable to outsiders, but Groton prided itself on its apartness, on the countless customs and regulations that made it distinct.

At Groton, the boys dressed for supper in white shirt and tie and black pumps. They spoke of Mr. Peabody as the rector. They were divided not in classes but in forms, one through six. They played the English game of "fives," a kind of handball, and the rector himself played doubles. In cheerleading they did not sound off with one two three but hip hip hurrah.

There was no duplication of fagging, the English custom of allowing the big boys to use the smaller ones as servants, but the rector kept the idea that the senior boys should discipline the junior ones. If a boy met an older boy on the narrow boardwalk between Brooks and Hundred House on a winter morning, he was expected to step off into the snow. If a boy was fresh, or did not have the Groton tone, he was boot boxed (crammed doubled up into a footlocker), or pumped (removed to a lavatory where water was poured over and into him). The pumpings were brutal—it happened that boys nearly drowned and had to be resuscitated. The rector saw a moral value in this sort of hazing. It also had the practical advantage of enforcing conventional behavior without his interference, by peer-group pressure.

The school's motto—*Cui servire est regnare* (To serve Him is to rule)—underscored its strongly religious character, with early-morning chapel, and evening prayers, and church on Sundays. The rector in white vestments delivering his sermons was a fearsome sight, as he warned the boys that the devil was a subtle spirit, and that his temptations were pride, irreverence, swearing, telling religious jokes, and praying only with their lips. Certain key phrases tended to recur, such as "the dyer's hand is subdued to what it is dipped in," and "his strength was as the strength of ten because his heart was pure."

If the rector's strength was as the strength of ten, it was partly due to his limitations. He saw life in unbending categories: there were gentlemen and bounders, madonnas and harlots, boys who conformed and boys who transgressed, whom he called "undesirable citizens." His faith protected him from doubt and his bland self-sufficiency colored his view of history and morals. He was ever vigilant for character defects, bad manners, betting, untruthfulness. One of the pleasures of his job was writing stern letters to parents about their sons' drawbacks. Another was greeting a boy with "The answer is no" before he had a chance to open his mouth.

But precisely because of his narrowness of vision, his authority came across all the more clearly. His strength was as the strength of ten because he actually made the boys covet his approval. He made them accept his assumption that the only basis for reward was performance. He made them want to excel. In the game against St. Mark's, the year that FDR was manager of the baseball team, a boy at bat named Fuller Potter did his best by reminding himself how important winning was to the rector.

Of course there were always a few introspective types who kicked their shoes at the dandelions on the lawn and wondered what it was all about, but for the most part the boys accepted their regimented lives, punctuated by gongs into periods of study, meals, and prayer. They slept in cubicles with no doors, washed up in cold water at long black sinks with hunks of yellow kitchen soap, obeyed rules they may not have understood (do not walk with your hands in your pockets, do not go for a walk with one other boy), and they did it to please the rector.

When they left Groton, the rector stayed in their lives. Often he married them, stuffing his six feet two into a Pullman berth and going off on a round of weddings. Each year, he took the trouble to send each graduate a handwritten birthday card, even though there came to be thousands of graduates. FDR wrote him on February 10, 1936: "If you had not sent me a birthday card I should have been really worried! Do you know that I have every one of them that you have sent me since the earliest days after I graduated?"

The rector *was* Groton. He made the school in his own image, and the boys came to consider him as the visible representation of everything it had meant to them. He gave his life to it, running it for fifty-six years until he retired in 1940 at the age of eighty-four, and dying four years later. One old boy who went to the funeral could not believe that the rector's body had been compressed into a narrow coffin. He remembered him as outsize, larger than life, a mighty warrior, a Hector. Only death could reduce him to human proportions. FDR sent this wire on November 1, 1944: "The whole tone of things is going to be a bit different from now on, for I have leaned on the Rector all these many years far more than most people know." The key word was *tone*—that indefinable but pervasive Groton tone.

Groton skimmed the cream of America's youth, so that its roster read like the board of a great corporation, with its Morgans, Harrimans, Whitneys, and Stillmans. Public service was held up to them as a noble goal. They should serve their country with the same dedication that they had played football and written daily themes.

Members of that estimable group known as Leaders of the Community came to Groton to lecture. In FDR's first year, Governor Wolcott of Massachusetts spoke "very interestingly" on the need for young men to go into public service, and in 1897 Dr. William S. Rainsford, the rector of St. George's Church in New York City, who had two sons at Groton, spoke on the Platt and Tammany political machines. Fifteen-year-old Franklin thought it was pretty strong stuff.

The rector's trump card was the rising young politician Theodore Roosevelt, a shining example of what he was trying to show his boys—that you could go into politics even though you came from a good family. Indeed, it was your duty to do so. Roosevelt was an enthusiastic backer of the school. He sent his two sons there and came often to speak.

Peabody felt that he had done all he could, and that "if some Groton boys do not enter political life and do something for our land it won't be because they have not been urged." The message was clear, but it was not heard. Out of all the Groton boys who had listened to Theodore Roosevelt, only a handful would do anything with their lives except make money. Why go into politics, there was no money in it. The highest position known to man was partner of Morgan. He was the equal of the president. And so the sons of the American elite flowed back into the family business, or Wall Street, or a New York or Boston law firm. It was a natural and accepted thing, practically an atavistic response, just as an Englishman will crawl on his stomach over heather all day long, wet and cold and uncomfortable, to take a shot at a deer.

For all the emphasis on God and country, most Grotties turned out to be stockbrokers and lawyers. In Louis Auchincloss's novel, the rector of Justin says of Endicott Peabody: "A man who considers that Theodore Roosevelt was America's greatest statesman and 'In Memoriam' England's finest poem is well equipped to train young men for the steam room of the Racquet Club."* That wasn't where FDR ended up, although 90 percent of the Grotties wished he had.

There were other exceptions, for Groton produced Senators Bronson Cutting and Frederick Hale, and Dean Acheson, Francis Biddle, Averell Harriman, and Sumner Welles. But the return on investment was meager. More typical was the career of FDR's classmate, Eugene Rensselaer Thayer, known as "Euey," who was senior prefect and captain of the football team, and who became president of Chase National Bank.

A puny boy, five feet three and not much more than a hundred pounds, arrived at Groton in the fall of 1896 and was placed in form IIIA. He and one other boy were new. The others had had two years to strengthen their adolescent cliques. How would Franklin fare? The answer is that he fared well. He had a deep need to conform, both to the demands of the school and the expectations of his parents. He threw himself eagerly into school life. On the day after their departure, he wrote that he was getting on fine, both mentally and physically.

There were some familiar faces. His childhood friend Edmund Rogers was in the form below. His nephew Taddy, Rosy Roosevelt's son, was in the form above, and they were soon nicknamed Nephew Rosy and Uncle Frank. They got along well, and hired a wagon for Thanksgiving. But Taddy was not an achiever. He would rather loaf than go to Mrs. Erving Winslow's reading of *The Merchant of Venice*. Everyone had to take foot-

---

* Louis Auchincloss won the lower school debating prize at Groton in 1933, and the prize, a book on modern English usage, was given by FDR.

ball, and there were eight teams, and Taddy was on the lowest team. Franklin was on the next to lowest, but that was because he was so slight. Taddy could have been on a much higher team if only he kept his wits about him, but Taddy was one of those boys who kicked their shoes into the dandelions and wondered what it was all about.

Franklin never wondered. He went ahead and did what he was expected to do, trying out for everything in sight. If he was teased as a new arrival, there was never a word of complaint (he was never boot boxed or pumped). In his twice-a-week letters to his parents, the barometer was always set at fair. James was the approving father, writing on September 28 that "I am glad to hear that you are in the choir, it will serve to keep up your music, which has always the effect of giving refinement to one's life," and on October 6, "I am glad to hear from you that you have no black mark yet and like Greek and are going in for a prize in punctuality." Sara was a bit mournful and apprehensive. The house was so quiet since he had gone. It made her miserable to go to his room and look at his clothes folded in their drawers. She was anxious to know how he was getting on with the boys. "It is a great change to be with so many," she wrote, "of all sorts, and a chance to exert all your good kind instincts." She was not sure what to think about her darling boy playing football. "I believe the game is good for teaching boys to control their tempers and not play fiercely," she wrote on October 4, "so I trust you will not have the misfortune of hurting anyone." Franklin reported several minor injuries, a dislocated finger, a small cut on the eyelid, a whack in the nose. My God, the Delano nose! Sara at once sent him a nose guard.

When he returned in January 1897 after the Christmas break, Franklin was pleased to see that he had been moved up from the kid table. The food was no better (sausage croquettes three days in a row and "sure-death" hash) but the change signified that he had arrived. He was learning the odd Groton customs and vocabulary—the boys who sorted the mail, for instance, were known as mail niggers, and the boys who helped in the chapel were chapel niggers.

Black marks were the lot of every Grottie, but it was only in May, in the ninth month of his first year, that Franklin got one, for talking in the classroom. He welcomed it, for it made him more of a regular fellow—up to then, he had been thought to have no school spirit.

In his first year, Franklin tried out for baseball and was put on a team called the Bum Baseball Boys, or BBB, made up of the worst players in the school. He tried for the reading prize with a reading from *Romeo and Juliet*, but was not one of the two readers chosen from his form. In winter sports, he put his name down for the high kick. This event was yet another Groton oddity, consisting of kicking a tin pan suspended from the ceiling of the gym. It did not require technique or skill, just the will to win, elevation, and not being afraid of bruises when landing. There were three classes, and Franklin won the class III kick, reaching seven feet and three and a half inches, two feet higher than he was. Each time he kicked he landed on his neck. His mother was not pleased, and thereafter referred to the event as "that awful high kicking."

Debating was another field where Franklin shone. He first spoke on the Nicaragua canal bill then being discussed in Congress. He had a personal interest in the matter, as his father was one of the investors in the Maritime Canal Company that had begun construction across the Nicaraguan isthmus before going bankrupt in 1893. At issue was whether Congress should appoint engineers to report on the cost of completion. Franklin's position was not hard to guess, but again his father had bet on the wrong horse (or the wrong canal), and in 1899 preference was given to the Panama scheme.

He had moved without visible pain from the routine of the estate to an active and competitive school life, and was now capable of asserting his independence, for even from across the Atlantic Sara continued to control his life. She turned down an invitation for him to go to Theodore Roosevelt's sister Anna (Bamie) in Oyster Bay on the Fourth of July. Franklin was annoyed. He knew it was going to be a large party and lots of fun. He decided to overrule his mother and wrote her on May 28: "Please don't make any more arrangements for my future happiness." There was a hint of sarcasm in his tone, putting Sara on notice.

On June 4, "Cousin Theodore" came to Groton to give a talk, and kept the boys in an uproar with his stories about the New York police. This was an important occasion for Franklin. It was at Groton that he came to know the two men who would become his role models, a position that had been abdicated by his ailing and inactive father. Endicott Peabody was an example of conduct while Theodore Roosevelt was a model of action. He had graduated from Harvard (where he had made Phi Beta Kappa and Porcellian), and joined the district Republican club in New York City, entering politics at the bottom of the ladder, while all the other Roosevelts, including Franklin's father, said that politics were dirty and party men were not gentlemen. Henry Adams in 1881 had told his Harvard pupil Henry Cabot Lodge that "I have never known a young man to go into politics who was not the worse for it." That same year Theodore Roosevelt was elected to the New York State Assembly. After that, he was civil service commissioner. When he came to Groton, he was about to become assistant secretary of the Navy. Not only that, but in the Assembly he had been a slashing critic of special interest groups, going after crooked judges and corrupt financiers like Jay Gould. Here was a man to admire, a man of strong convictions and limitless energy. There was nothing guarded or narrow or sectional about him.

Franklin was glad for the chance to get close to his cousin, and gladder yet when he was invited to Sagamore Hill for the Fourth of July weekend. This time there must be no parental meddling, and he wrote his mother on June 11: "I have accepted the Theodore's invitation and I hope you will not refuse that too." Franklin was moving away from his parents, into a wider circle of acquaintance. Cousin Teddy liked him, and once told Sara: "I'm so fond of the boy I'd be shot for him."

He returned to Groton that September of 1897, an old boy surveying new arrivals. His voice had changed, he could no longer sing soprano in the choir. He had graduated from the seventh football team to the sixth and was playing tackle. He had finished his first year fourth in a class of seventeen, but that October there was a crisis. He flunked a Greek exam, and wrote his parents on October 3 that it was "the most outrageous Greek exam which has ever been known in the history of education. Not only was the paper unfair but the marking was atrocious, and altho' I got about .50 the old idiot Abbott refused to pass me as is customary when one almost passes. . . . I intend to assassinate old Abbott if he does not pass me in my Greek this time, as I know the whole book by heart."

Sara prayed God that Franklin would pass. She believed in the power of prayer. "I also think," she wrote on October 6, "that this very unpleasant surprise of failing your Greek exam may do you good in more ways than one." After his sarcastic notes that June, she thought he needed a comeuppance. James was not pleased, and wrote him October 10: "We heard a rumor that if the delinquents did not pass on this occasion, they would all be put back in the third form. Fancy my son Franklin D. Roosevelt stepping down to a lower form." For the normally mild James, these were strong words. It would be a disgrace for Roosevelt to be put back. The crisis passed, the Greek was made up, and Franklin was not put back a form. In fact, he remained in the top half dozen of his class.

As an old boy, he was much less the goody-goody, and joined his classmates in hazing the new math teacher, Julian Coolidge. He was at a new table, sitting next to Lathrop (Jake) Brown, who would become his best friend at Groton and Harvard roommate. He was becoming more popular, and several boys asked if they could have his photograph. There were dissenting opinions, however, and James L. Goodwin, who had entered form III with Franklin in 1896, recalled that "as time went on and we proceeded into the fourth, fifth, and sixth forms and Franklin D. became better known by his classmates, he developed an independent, cocky manner and at times became very argumentative and sarcastic. In an argument he always liked to take the side opposite to that maintained by those with whom he was talking. This irritated the other boys considerably." The retroactive appraisals of former schoolmates in a highly competitive environment are open to review, and Goodwin's recollection should be balanced against that of George Biddle, who wrote that Franklin "was gray-eyed, cool, self-possessed, intelligent, and had the warmest, most friendly and understanding smile. Though he was not athletic . . . he seemed from my point of view to be all the more eminently successful."

That March of 1898, to his mother's dismay, Franklin tried the high kick again, but this time he was moved up a class, and came in second, with a kick of seven feet eleven and one quarter inches, better than last year. He had also been taking boxing lessons, and on March 5 he fought two three-minutes rounds in the lightweight division with Fuller Potter. Fuller was smaller than Franklin, but had been boxing longer and won the match, although both boys had bloody noses. Years later, when FDR was president and Fuller Potter was a Wall Street Republican, he would mutter: "I should have hit him one more time."

Groton was an ideal breeding ground for contagious diseases, and in April, when scarlet fever was going around, Franklin caught it, and his parents cut short their European trip to be at his side. One of his masters said that after his illness he looked a little like a *reconcentrado,* as the starving children of war-torn Cuba were called. But that summer Franklin was sufficiently recovered to win a golf prize at Campobello, and in the fall of 1898 he returned to Groton as a fifth former, which meant that he was entitled to a study. Banners and pennants were discouraged. Comfortable chairs were banned. His days were full: Roman history and German (thanks to the summers in Bad Nauheim, German was easy), daily themes (how hard it was to find a subject even for one page), visits to the dentist (the band was off and his teeth were now regular), items for the *Grotonian,* and football five days a week. "As your heart is a little weak you must be sure not to overdo," Sara warned on October 7. "It would be absolutely dangerous for you to play too hard or too long at football. I shall be glad when you begin golf instead."

Franklin was delighted by Cousin Theodore's election as governor of New York that November. His father, although a lifelong Democrat, had backed Teddy, who had carried New York State by 25,000, Dutchess County by 2,664, and Hyde Park by 81. It was one further proof that a Knickerbocker background was not a handicap to political success.

Sara, however, was less interested in the election results than in her darling boy's conduct and welfare. She could never thank God enough for giving her such a precious treasure as Franklin. No detail of the treasure's upkeep was overlooked, and on October 30 she wrote him: "I have been sorry since you left that I had not paid attention to your keeping your nails nice as they really looked badly and also I do not like you to travel without wearing gloves, as that always makes the nails horrid." When she did not have him to look after, she looked after his things. "I devoted the morning to the 'feathered tribe,' " she wrote on November 15. "I dusted each bird and used turpentine on a camel's hair brush, and locked up your bird closet with 80 birds in it. Then had all the drawers cleaned and fresh white paper put into the cabinets and replaced all the birdskins."

One school activity of Franklin's that she heartily approved of was the Missionary Society, a group that did good works in the community. Franklin was appointed to look after an eighty-four-year-old colored lady named Mrs. Freeman, the widow of a Civil War drummer, who lived alone. "We are to visit her a couple of times a week," Franklin wrote, "see that she has coal, water, etc., feed her hens if they need it, and in case of a snow-storm we are to dig her out, & put things ship-shape. It will be very pleasant as she is a dear old thing, and it will be a good occupation for us. I shall take her all my old 'Graphics' and any other papers I have." "I am glad you are in the Missionary Society," Sara wrote. "It will interest you in doing for others and the more we do, the more we feel that the need is woefully great and that really nothing is so helpful to ourselves as doing for others and trying to sink all selfishness." It was an age of private charity, when the government did nothing to help the indigent. Another assignment was playing the organ at various mission houses. His piano lessons came in handy, and he was able to manage about four hymns.

An important birthday was coming up, and on January 29, 1899, James wrote: "Tomorrow will be your seventeenth birthday, do you realize that you are approaching manhood and next year when you begin your university life you will be away from the safe ground of school and will have to withstand many temptations to which you will be exposed, but I always feel that your character is so well formed and established I have no fear as to your future career." There was a preachy tone reminiscent of the letters his father, Isaac, had written him when he was preparing to go to New York University. But there was also a pronounced degree of confidence in Franklin's ability to negotiate the next rung in the ladder as he had negotiated Groton.

Franklin himself was not so sure. He could hardly realize that he was seventeen. He felt more like fifteen. It was amazing to think that next year he would be at Harvard. For the moment, he applied himself to the task at hand. He was perfectly overrun with work—exams all in a bunch, the *Grotonian,* and a March debate, in which he argued against the United States and England guaranteeing the integrity of China.

Franklin's intention to try out in the one athletic event in which he shone, the high kick, was thwarted when the event was discontinued because of the physical danger involved. He loved baseball, but could not make the team. The next best thing was to manage it. In April, the manager, Dick Derby, asked Franklin to be his assistant. Derby, a year ahead of him, was a Hudson Valley friend and was president of the debating society (he would later marry Theodore Roosevelt's daughter Ethel). He was rowing that year, and Franklin knew that he would be the de facto manager. He threw himself into it, rolling the fields and getting out the players. He was out at eight working on the diamond, marking the base lines and returning to his room spotted with lime. After a game, he spent hours resodding where the grass was worn out. That June his efforts were rewarded and he was appointed manager, which, he informed his parents, was "a place of considerable responsibility."

An even greater responsibility was taking the prelims that June for Harvard. The system then was that if you passed the prelims (which were called "the Jacksons" after their originator, Edward Jackson), you were allowed to take the Harvard freshman courses in your last year of Groton. The students who did this could then finish Harvard in three years, taking courses freely chosen, as all the required ones were out of the way. The exams in Greek and Latin and algebra and geometry and English and history were awfully hard, but Franklin hoped he had scraped through "the dreaded Jacksons." He wanted to take fifteen hours worth of Harvard classes a week, the maximum allowed, but the rector put a spoke in his wheel. One of these was German, which he knew he could pass easily. But only Franklin and one other boy would be taking advanced German, and the rector balked at forming a special class for two boys. Franklin was furious at his "tyrannical ways."

As it turned out, he did well enough to qualify for fifteen Harvard hours. He thought it was a school record. For once, he was ahead of Ned Krumbhaar, who was always first in class but who was taking only fourteen Harvard hours. The school year ended with Franklin catching the mumps and having to take the regular Groton exams in early July all alone in the little room in the infirmary.

Returning that September 1899 to Groton for his fourth and final year in the sixth and last form, Franklin had reason to be pleased with himself. He was the record holder in Harvard hours. He was a dormitory prefect, and manager of the baseball team. He had worked his way up in football to the second eleven, which scrimmaged against the first team. He was one of the school's best debaters. And yet he had never made his mark as an athlete, and he was not one of the first five senior prefects. He had tried, oh how he had tried, but he had not quite been first-rate. At least he could lord it over the new boys, and reported to his parents on September 19 that "all is confusion and Babel; the new infants are like the sands of the sea."

On October 15, the school celebrated its fifteenth anniversary. In that short time, Groton had established itself as one of the best private schools in the country. The fifth formers sang the blue-bottle song, one verse for each year: fifteen blue-bottles a-hanging on the wall, take one blue-bottle from the bottles on the wall, and so on. One of the masters gave a violin solo. The high point was the poem by William Amory Gardner, a cofounder of the school, which had jokes on everyone, including a reference to Franklin's summer activities:

> "His maple-sugar kisses were
> The sweetest thing on earth.
> Like Roosevelt at the candy pull
> When maidens in their mirth
> Threw molasses at his face. . . ."

Franklin turned scarlet, and would not repeat the lines in his account of the evening to his parents, protesting that a mild summer incident had been "utterly perverted."

He was getting banged up in the scrimmages with the first eleven, but felt that the cracked head and the wrenched knees were worth it to get the team ready for the big game against St. Mark's in November. Groton lost the game when Euey Thayer slipped while trying to kick a field goal, and Franklin practically went into mourning.

In January 1900, the time came to pick his rooms at Harvard. He and Lathrop Brown went to Cambridge to look at the "Gold Coast" dormitories on Mount Auburn Street, which offered luxurious quarters to those who could afford not to stay in the Yard. Boys from the prep schools went there, maintaining their cliques, separate from the run-of-the-mill undergraduates. Franklin and Lathrop picked a first-floor corner in Westmorly, a vaguely Tudor building, with two bedrooms and a spacious sitting room, at $400 a year.

One of the benefits of Groton was that the boys, through the debates and their reading, were encouraged to keep up with current affairs. In the English magazines his mother sent him, Franklin read about the Boer War raging in distant South Africa. He had already expressed anticolonial convictions in a debate on Hawaii, and his reaction to the siege of British forces at Ladysmith was "Hurrah for the Boers! I entirely sympathize with them." Sara did not, she was a stout defender of Empire, and for the first time Franklin and his mother differed on a political issue. "I must say," Sara wrote on January 19, 1900, "I do not see how anyone can compare those treacherous Boers with our fine old colonists over a century ago! They even disregard a flag of truce *every time!* They killed a woman and child going under a white flag. Please study up both sides. I like you to form your own opinion of course."

Although increasingly assertive, Franklin was not prepared to battle his mother and beat a hasty retreat, writing her on January 21 that "I cannot help feeling convinced that the Boers had the side of right and that for the past ten years they have been *forced* into this war. I am sure you will feel this if you only read up on the Boer case. *However*, undoubtedly, now that the war is actually on, it will be best from the humanitarian standpoint for the British to win speedily and civilization will be hurried on, but I feel that the same result would have been surely obtained without war." Franklin held out the hand of compromise: the Boers were right, but should lose the war.

Sara finally revealed her true reason for disliking the Boers, who were "horrid" because they married natives. On January 23, she wrote: "I dare say you are right about the Boers and have looked into the causes etc. more than I have, but as things have reached the present terrible pass, I feel very strongly that the Boers are not a race to do good in the world. Perhaps I am a little bit influenced by meeting on a steamer and traveling with them for three weeks, some Dutch and half breeds. I was only a child of ten but I got a horror of the common Dutch men with their native and half native families! Then all one reads of their life in the colonies and in South Africa shows them to be 'boors.' Still, I like you to form your own opinions and to look into things more deeply than your mummy does." In fact, the Boers were more racist than Sara, and frowned on intermarriage.

A few days later, Franklin was eighteen, and Sara wrote: "Only 18 years ago and I had *no* child. What a difference in our lives you have made, and how I thank God daily for having given you to me!" But on the day of his birthday, Franklin lost his first debate, arguing that the Philippines, then under U.S. military government, should be given independence when they were ready to receive it. There was, however, good news to balance the bad. Each year, the sixth form put on a play for Washington's birthday, and Franklin desperately hoped for a good part in the 1900 production, a translation of a French farce by W. S. Gilbert called *The Wedding March—An Eccentricity in Three Acts.* Franklin was sure that Grafton Cushing, the master in charge of the production, was giving the best parts to his Boston friends. But on February 11, he announced: "Joyful news! I have a part in the play at last and entirely by accident. Jimmy Jackson had the part of the old hayseed countrified uncle of the bride. He is sick in Boston with rheumatic fever and water on the knee so he won't be back again this term. I suppose it is criminal to rejoice but I can't help it. I've got his part, and it's one of the best in the play!!!" Replacing someone who was out of commission was the American way to opportunity. It was the way his cousin Teddy would reach the presidency. Franklin had an added satisfaction that month when he tied Ned Krumbhaar in grades. They both had A's. One of his ambitions at Groton was to do better than Krumbhaar.

Three more prefects were being named in March, and Franklin hoped to be among them. On March 25, the names were announced: Harry Peabody, the rector's nephew; Jack Minturn, the boy whose shoes he had removed in evening study; and Harry Markoe, whose mother had given a tea for the fifth form the previous year. Franklin was disgusted. "Everyone is wild at the Rector for his favoritism to his nephew," he wrote his parents. He was glad not to have been made a prefect after such an unfair choice. The honor was no longer an honor.

There were frequent trips to Boston in his last months of school, to inspect his Harvard rooms and to have his eyes examined. He was nearsighted, and ordered his first pair of pince-nez, which would remain a distinctive feature for the rest of his life. It seemed so strange to be writing in "specks," he informed his parents on April 12.

In May, Franklin addressed himself to the Hyde Park servant problem. Sara could not keep servants, they were always leaving, and this time it was Todd, who was so clean and respectable, a real gentleman's gentleman, but who said the work was more than he could undertake with justice to himself. "I was awfully sorry to hear about Todd's leaving," Franklin wrote on May 13. "I quite realize what a great loss he will be to you and I only hope you can get another man who is equally clean and good at valeting & who is a little spryer & better at the table. Don't let Papa worry about it, after all there are plenty of good butlers in the world."

There are plenty of good butlers in the world: what a smug and narrow view of life was contained in that one sentence from the pen of an eighteen-year-old. Franklin at that time was still the product of a blinkered society, where it was natural to be waited on, and which was conveniently divided into servants and masters. He matched his parents for priggishness, his attitude toward his nephew Taddy provided a good example. Franklin had quickly adapted to Groton life, but Taddy was an outsider who did not get into the spirit of things, a shirker who had been on the lowest team in football, who had only had a small part in his sixth form play, and who had not even attended the lecture Teddy Roosevelt had given in October 1898 when he was campaigning for governor. Taddy had gone to Harvard in 1899 and been singled out at Bloody Monday, the freshman hazing, for rough treatment. It was reported to Franklin that he looked like a tramp with flowing hair. He was quoted as saying that he never wanted to see Groton again, which amounted to sacrilege. And then, in June 1900, at the end of his freshman year, he was put on probation. Franklin was not surprised, he had heard from *all* the Groton graduates that Taddy was not doing well. On June 13, knowing it would get to Taddy's father, Franklin snitched to his parents that he knew Taddy had been in New York several times without letting anyone know. Taddy had been Franklin's friend at Groton, but now he adopted a moralizing tone he had learned from his father, who had learned it from *his* father, writing that "if his last exam came June 7th he may be off on a bat now for ought (sic) I know. I think the very strictest measures sh'd be taken, but of course Papa must not worry in the least, as after all it is no affair of ours. Some measures should be taken to prevent him having his full allowance next year, as even this year he has had just *twice too much.*"

A week later, Franklin reported that Taddy had left college entirely. Asked to appear before the dean, he simply departed, and would not be allowed to return if he changed his mind. "I have never heard of such asininity," Franklin commented, "and everyone up here knows of it and thinks him a fool!" This sentence, so revealing of Franklin's judgmental mentality, was deleted from the published collection of his personal letters.

While Taddy ruined his college career, Franklin put the finishing touches on his years at Groton, trying for all three academic prizes, Greek, Latin, and English. On June 25, when the prizes were read out by the rector's father at the head table in the dining room, Krumbhaar won the form prize, Warren Motley won the English essay, Carrol Greenough won the Greek, and "then I was somewhat taken aback when my name was called for the Latin Prize. I was presented with 40 volumes, the Temple Shakespeare just like yours & you may imagine I feel rather tickled."

Franklin submitted unquestioningly to the code. He never wondered what was the point of kicking a pan suspended from the ceiling or playing a team sport for which he had no aptitude—he just did it. He never asked why a great American poet like Walt Whitman was proscribed. Some Grotties later felt they had been cheated, that they had been kept from entire areas of learning, but Franklin instinctively understood that Groton was a Darwinian training ground for power. You started at the bottom with small humiliations and you rose to a position of seniority and, in some cases, eminence.

Teenage boys attending all-male schools normally show curiosity, if not longing, for the opposite sex they see so little of. Franklin did not. He was disdainful and unflattering in his comments about girls. Faced with the prospect of having some of his girl cousins stay at Hyde Park over the Christmas holiday in 1897, he wrote his mother that "it will be a horrible nuisance having those *squaws* on our hands for such a long time."

The following year, when he was sixteen, he was invited to a number of "shindies"—among them the cotillion at the Orange Country Club in New Jersey and the Dodworth dances (Mr. and Mrs. Thomas George Dodworth ran a fashionable dancing school at 12 East 49th Street). Dancers stood on the diamond squares of the polished hardwood floors and learned the waltz and the polka as Mr. Dodworth, dapper and slim, kept the rhythm with what looked like a pair of castanets.

For the Orange dance, Franklin asked his cousin Laura, whose father, Warren Delano III, had a house there. For the New York dance, he asked his mother to help him think of a decent partner, "so that I can get somebody early, and not get palmed off on some ice-cart like the Hoyt girl" (the Hoyts were Hudson Valley neighbors with two daughters, Lydig and Julia).

Wondering whom to ask, "and not caring at all, I drew lots and the fateful die fell on Mary Newbold, so I wrote at once." When his next-door neighbor Mary said she could not go, Franklin wrote his mother that it was "just as well," adding that "I don't want to get left with the Solely girl as I did two years ago to my great and everlasting regret." There were two Solely girls, Mary and Una, the daughters of James Russel Solely, a professor at Annapolis and the author of naval books, who had married a Howland, making the girls Franklin's distant cousins. It was Mary that Franklin sought to avoid. A year later, asking his mother to invite one or two girls to Hyde Park for New Year's Eve, he specified "only not the Solely brat! Please!"

In the meantime, he asked his cousin Muriel Delano Robbins to the Dodworth dance, writing his mother a few days later that "the Robbins brat!!!" had accepted with thanks. It was with Muriel that he once went to a "baby party." One of the other guests wished she had taken a snapshot of the tall slender youth with the marvelous blond ringlets and the white dress that fell to his knees, and the ruffled pantalets peeping under the skirt. It was a sight to behold!

It was at this time that Franklin mentioned his future wife for the first time; fortunately she was neither a brat nor an ice-cart. On December 11, 1898, he wrote Sara that "I cannot think of anyone to get up here [to Hyde Park], as most of the boys are already engaged that I would like to have, so I hope you will be able to find someone else. How about Teddy Robinson [the son of Theodore Roosevelt's sister Corinne] and Eleanor Roosevelt? They would go well and help to fill out chinks." As events developed, Eleanor became quite a chink-filler in Franklin's life.

But other girls were spoken of disparagingly. On the afternoon of prize day in June 1900, he wrote his mother, girls were coming, but he didn't know any and would "probably be shelved with a pill."

One reason for this hostility was that he was still very much his mother's child. In January 1899 he asked for the picture of Sara in the little heart-shaped frame. He wanted to put it on his desk. In that privately arrogant Roosevelt tone, the same tone that called the Germans "filthy," Franklin spoke poorly of girls to prove his loyalty to his mother. They were pills and brats and ice-carts; why the Hoyt girl was elephantine. Sara must not worry about a rival. For Franklin to display any sign of sexual independence would have alarmed her. The transaction of the only child with his mother was based on exclusive devotion, which had to be reciprocated.

Women were a mystery he was not yet ready to explore. It was easier to dismiss them than to consider them honestly, as possible partners in love and sexual intimacy. He was reluctant to make a choice that would commit him even for a holiday dance, and asked his mother to choose for him. When she did not, he drew lots. But at the same time, he worried that he would be left with "the Solely brat," or shelved "with a pill." The comfort he derived from his mother was still more important than asserting his masculinity. He could not yet live by the words he had written in his English IV exam on October 19, 1897: "Duncan here tells Lady Macbeth his hostess, that because of love we are sometimes given much trouble but that we should thank it as love notwithstanding."

At the start of 1898, Taddy and Franklin went to confirmation lectures. Taddy did not go back after the first one, but Franklin persevered and was confirmed that March. He wrote his parents that Taddy "is as far from the Good Path as ever."

There was a pious strain on the Roosevelt side that Franklin inherited. His grandfather Isaac had looked upon this life as a preparation for the next and wrote preachy letters to his son, telling him to "repent, believe in the Lord Jesus, and lead a life of holy obedience to his commands." James in his mature years became the defender of Christian observance, writing Franklin on one occasion that "the village boys made Hyde Park a disgrace to a Christian community by their baseball matches on Sunday. Last Sunday morning there were 300 people on the grounds, men, women, and girls in wagons and on bicycles from all parts of the country. I am going to have it stopped."

At Groton, Franklin took religion seriously. In the rector's sacred studies class, he read the Bible. He listened to lectures by a succession of clergymen, reporting in May 1897 that he had heard a special address on "How to Pray."

Above all, the rector was a man of God. He may have saved his sermons for the select, but it was a substantial diet all the same. Franklin never suspected that religion was being used to promote conformity. He took at face value the sermons condemning adolescent impurity and castigating divorced parents. He believed the school motto, To Serve Him Is to Rule, and the words of the school hymn:

> "Oh! world all bright and brave and young
> With deed unwrought and songs unsung
> For all the strength Thy tasks will give
> We greet Thee, we about to live."

The Groton experience was indelible, and the attachment to Peabody was lasting. The rector married him, and when he wrote the directions for his funeral, it was Peabody he wanted to conduct the service. FDR was the first president to hold an intercessional service on inauguration day. He summoned the rector to Washington to assist the pastors of the other churches he attended in later life, and they gathered to pray two hours before he became president.

The rector approved, and wrote him on October 24, 1935 (the year of the school's fiftieth anniversary): "It is a great thing for our country to have before it the leadership of a man who cares primarily for spiritual things. At a time when the minds of men are distraught and their faith unsteady, a spiritual leader at the head of the nation brings fresh power to the individual and to the cause of Christ and His Church."

Franklin at Groton had been a true believer, accepting all the premises of the system—that reward was based on performance, that success came with effort, that competition was healthy, that one could serve God in every daily action, and that a basic moral cleanliness was indispensable to a productive life. He tried hard never to deviate from the Groton norm, and scorned those who, like Taddy, did not conform. The rector's ideal of a Christian gentleman devoting himself to public life was forgotten by most boys as soon as they left the school. But Franklin never forgot, and wrote the rector on April 25, 1940: "More than forty years ago you said, in a sermon in the Old Chapel, something about not losing boyhood ideals in later life. Those were Groton ideals—taught by you—I try not to forget—and your words are still with me and with hundreds of other of 'us boys.' "

As Franklin prepared to leave Groton in June 1900 he felt "very blue." He would have given anything to be dropped a form and stay one more year. He really loved the place, with its strange customs and demands. Never again would there be pancakes on Shrove Tuesday, and hot cross buns on Good Friday, and Uncle Billywag reading the annual poem on the school's birthday, and coasting on Joy's Hill, and afternoons on the Monadnock River, and study fires in the evening, and meetings in the library for a singsong, the hundred young voices rising in unison, and all the other activities that had made him feel that he belonged to something larger than his family. "What a joyful yet sad day this has been," he wrote on prize day, June 25. "Scarce a boy but wishes he were a 1st former again."

In the years to come, in the light of what he became, efforts were made to show that FDR had been forged in the smithy of Groton. George W. Martin, chairman of the Groton Alumni Association, wrote him on November 15, 1934: "The stuff you are made of was annealed while you were at school, for better or for worse; and you yet bear the scars of that process. If you amount to anything, if you will do certain things and refuse to do others; if you know the difference between cricket and non-cricket; the origins of these developments, these peculiar streaks, these inexplicable phases of strength and weakness, are found at school.... There was the stage you trod; there was the world you knew! There were your closest friends! There was the start of your Odyssey, and there you drank delight of battle with your peers, far on the ringing plains of windy Troy...."

There were prior claims, his mother's foremost, and there would be later ones, wanting to share the responsibility for his greatness. Surely Groton's claim was valid, for he had taken to heart its call to public service and religious observance. Now, for those about to live, it was time to move on. Most of them would go to Harvard, and then follow different paths. Ned Krumbhaar would become a respected doctor in Philadelphia. Jimmy Jackson, thanks to whose illness Franklin had won the part in the play, would one day be treasurer of the Commonwealth of Massachusetts. Edward Corning would be lieutenant governor of New York on a ticket with Al Smith. Lathrop Brown would be elected to Congress. Buell Hollister and George Clark and Fuller Potter would go to Wall Street. After the 1932 election, Fuller Potter, who had beaten FDR in boxing, commented: "I can't understand this thing about Frank. He never amounted to much in school."

III

Harvard

Resolved: that the Lord's anointed should inherit the earth. Resolved: that we are the Lord's anointed.

Hasty Pudding Club oath

On the pleasant morning of September 26, 1900, 451 freshmen assembled in front of Sever Hall to register as students. They strolled under the elms waiting for their turns, trying to feign the "tone" of Harvard indifference. Their pasture was Harvard Yard, framed by buildings of drab brick, in keeping with a tradition of Puritan simplicity that was centuries old—the first recorded use of the word "yard" as the open space of a college campus had been at Harvard in 1660.

Among the milling freshmen stood a lathy, narrow-shouldered young man, a shade over six feet, his darkening blond hair parted on the left, his eyes set a bit too close, his features almost overbred in their fineness, his expression reflective. He might have been a young guardsman waiting to be fitted for a uniform, or a young leading man waiting for an audition. Franklin recognized a number of Groton classmates, though most of the faces in the Yard were strange to him.

For a moment there was a semblance of true democracy, the democracy of the newcomer. Outwardly they were all at the same level, as yet unmeasured and undifferentiated. What they were remained for time to uncover. Any one of them might be president of his class, of the football team, of the *Crimson*. They were as alike as oranges in a crate. But on closer inspection some had a greenish tinge and others a golden glow. For they were entering an institution where family background and the school they had gone to mattered as much as personal merit. Some would go to bleak rooms in the Yard, others to spacious apartments on the Gold Coast. Some would be elected to "Dickey," others would join the Harvard Union, open to all. A few would wear the gold Porcellian pig on their watch chains, the rest would settle into the ranks of the ineligible. Classmates would cross in the Yard hundreds of times and sit next to each other in classes and never exchange a single word.

Clutching their registration cards (there were always a few jokers who put down Hindu or Confucian under the heading "Religion"), the freshmen scurried off to find their advisers and pick their courses. Planning to graduate in three years, Franklin had a heavy load of six courses, none of them the "snap" or "cinch" courses favored by social young men who coasted down their undergraduate years, content with a gentleman's "pass." Aside from History, he took French Prose and Poetry, Latin Literature, English Literature, Elementary Geology, and Constitutional Government. In his second year he took five courses, including one in public speaking "intended for students somewhat advanced in platform speaking"; an economics course; an American history course under Hiram Bingham, III, who would become a Republican senator from Connecticut and would in 1936 campaign against his former student. In his third and final undergraduate year he took six courses, among them English Letter Writers, taught by the celebrated Charles Townsend Copeland. Once when a boy arrived late and was tiptoeing about his classroom looking for a seat, "Copey" boomed out Hamlet's benediction on the ghost: "Rest, perturbed spirit." The oft-quoted couplet about him went:

"If wit and madness be as like as Pope and others tell
Then Copey by the nearest squeak escapes the padded cell."

Copey actually outlived FDR, dying in 1951.

Franklin also took Forms of Public Address under George Pierce Baker, who was famous for his play writing class, but withdrew after a few weeks because he disagreed with Baker's reading of the Gettysburg Address. Franklin had adopted a Lincolnesque slouch on the rostrum and spoke the classic phrases in a monotone, without a single gesture, but Baker wanted resonant periods and gestures and all the elocutionary tricks.

The elective system promoted by President Charles William Eliot offered a bewildering freedom of choice, leaving some graduates with the impression that they had nibbled at dozens of canapes of knowledge and never had their fill. Samuel Eliot Morison, the historian of Harvard, described it as "haphazard, illogical, postulated on too high an expectation of a young man's will and too low an estimate of the many attractive sideshows outside the main tent." But it suited Franklin, who was able to manage both the main tent and the sideshows. He was a C student, but considering his other activities, that was not a bad record. He went to his classes, took copious notes, and once turned down a weekend invitation to a privately owned island in Buzzards Bay because it would have meant taking three cuts.

Certainly, Franklin agreed with President Eliot, who in his address to the freshmen in Sanders Theater on October 1 said: "A course of study should be only long enough to win power; the sooner you begin to use it, the better.

Do not get in four years what you can get in three." Eliot had become president in 1869, and remained in that capacity for forty years, retiring in 1909. Out of his Puritan soul sprang the conviction that it was up to the undergraduate to waste or profit from his Harvard years. To impose required courses would have been to misconstrue the Harvard experience, which was founded on Emersonian self-reliance.

Eliot was an elitist who believed that "durable families" would supply the nation's leadership. By the time Franklin graduated, Harvard had given four presidents to the country—John Adams, John Quincy Adams, Rutherford B. Hayes, and Theodore Roosevelt. He was against free state universities that would educate the rabble, and approved of segregation in southern schools. Negroes, he felt, were recently removed from slavery. In every Harvard class, however, there were three or four token colored students, and the number slowly increased.

Harvard grew under Eliot, spilling beyond the fenced-in commune of the Yard. Housing was neglected, and private enterprise stepped in and built the Gold Coast residences. The gap between the "right sort" and the "greasy grinds" and Jews and scholarship students and other undesirables became geographical as well as social. The Gold Coast students housed and ate and played together in freshman year, but the real triage took place in sophomore year, when 100 students (about 25 percent of the student body) were chosen for the most important club (because it was a necessary way station for the other clubs), the Institute of 1770. They were elected in groups of ten in order of desirability, and the names of each "ten" were printed in the Boston newspapers and in the *Crimson*. The first six or seven tens also made Delta Kappa Epsilon, a fraternity known as "Dickey." These in turn were sure to be elected to the Hasty Pudding Club in their junior or senior year, and also to one of the "final" clubs, such as Porcellian, A.D., or Alpha Delta Phi (known as the "Fly").

Inside this rank-conscious Harvard world were elites within elites. Being in the right club meant that you were invited to the right dances and had access to the right young ladies, that you made the right friends, and, after graduation, that you would have the right employment opportunities and be admitted to the right clubs in Boston and New York.

As he had at Groton, Franklin threw himself into all sorts of activities, with more enthusiasm than success. At six feet one and 146 pounds, he was still too light for football, but he went out for the freshman team anyway. He stopped smoking to attain a peak of fitness, and went to Soldier's Field, lining up for short sprints of twenty yards, practicing falling on the ball, place kicks, drop kicks, and punts, and tackling a dummy suspended by a pulley from a wire stretched between two posts. The coach said, "That will be all for this morning," and Franklin knew he had not made the team. He did make the lightest of eight scrub teams, "The Missing Links," and proudly reported to his parents that he had been elected captain. He had a hunger for office, and was made secretary of the freshman glee club and captain of the second Newell crew (he failed to make the freshman crew, but there were two rowing clubs, Weld and Newell, each of which had four crews, and Franklin joined Newell). On October 19 he began heeling the *Crimson* and wrote home that "if I work hard for two years I may be made an editor. I have to make out notices and go to interviews."

That October, the contrast between Franklin and his nephew Taddy grew more pronounced. Franklin, the good Roosevelt, met the expectations of his parents and lived up to the family name. Taddy, the bad Roosevelt, deliberately failed at everything, and shamed his parents with his scandalous conduct. He was suspended from Harvard, and his furniture was attached for debt, even though in August 1900, having reached the age of twenty-one, he had come into an income of $40,000 a year. In New York, he met a girl of easy virtue named Sadie Meisinger, "Dutch Sadie," in the Haymarket Dance Hall, a well-known house of assignation where she was often to be found. Taddy ran off with Dutch Sadie to Florida and married her (the marriage was broken up by his father).

Sara reported that the news had seriously affected James's health, which was in decline in any event. "Your father cannot get it out of his mind," she wrote on October 20, "that his grandson has been leading a bad wicked life for months. His marrying the creature brings it before the public, but the sin came first and he disgraced his good name. Poor Papa suffered so much in the night for breath that he thought he could not live. He talked of you and said 'tell Franklin to be good and never be like Taddy. . . .' He says he never remembers a disgrace coming to his family before and it is dreadful to him."

Unwilling to excuse the marriage as a youthful fling, or to say a kind word for his former Groton friend, Franklin was ready to banish Taddy from the family fold, and replied on October 23: "The disgusting thing about Taddy did not come as a very great surprise to me or to anyone in Cambridge. I have heard the rumor ever since I have been here, but in the absence of facts the best course has been silence. I do not wonder that it has upset Papa, but although the disgrace to the name has been the worst part of the affair one can never again consider him a true Roosevelt. It will be well for him not only to go to parts unknown, but to stay there and begin life anew."

There was another Roosevelt in the news. Cousin Teddy was running as vice presidential candidate on the Republican ticket with McKinley. Mark Hanna, McKinley's sponsor and the power behind the Ohio Republican machine, had expressed his misgivings over Roosevelt by saying: "Don't you realize that there's only one life between this madman and the White House?" Teddy himself told William Lawrence, the Episcopal bishop of Boston, that "I should go wild rattling around in the chair of the President of the Senate with nothing to do," but changed his mind.

On October 30, 1900, Franklin in red cap and gown marched in the torchlight Republican parade that wended through the main streets of Boston. President Eliot had written an article in the *Outlook* discussing issues and candidates but not committing himself. His aversion to Theodore Roosevelt the imperialist, the man who wanted to annex Hawaii and go to war with England over the Venezuelan border dispute, was well known. Eliot had called Teddy "a degenerate son of Harvard" and "a ruffian and a bully." But a front-page story in the *Crimson* of October 29 appeared under the headline "President Eliot Declares for McKinley." "President Eliot gave the *Crimson* the following statement last night," the story said, "concerning his article in the *Outlook* about which there has been so much discussion: I intend to vote for President McKinley, Governor Roosevelt, and Representative McCall, and I have never had any other intention." The scoop was picked up by papers in Boston and elsewhere.

In later years, FDR took credit for the story, in an interview with a reporter from the New York *Telegraph* in 1913 and in another 1916 article by Theodore G. Joslin, in which he recalled: "I was connected with the *Crimson* while in college . . . nor have I ever forgotten my first scoop. I was still working on a permanent berth when the presidential campaign of 1900 . . . was raging. A week before the election I conceived the idea of asking President Eliot how he intended voting. He had not made known his intention and in New England, it was known that his opinion would be of value to whichever side he decided to support. Even in his silence the Democrats rejoiced in a tentative supporter. Not knowing that *Crimson* men were forbidden to interview the college president, I went to Dr. Eliot's home and was ushered in by a maid. I told her my name was Roosevelt, and, as T.R. was running for Vice-President, I guess that helped a bit, for I was taken into Dr. Eliot's presence. 'Well,' he questioned, to my discomfort. I stammered my question. 'Don't you know that the *Crimson* candidates cannot interview the President?' he asked sternly. I managed to say I didn't. 'Strange,' he remarked. 'There is a sign in the *Crimson* office to that effect. But I suppose I might as well tell you, I'm going to vote for President McKinley.' He then dictated a statement. When I got back to the *Crimson* office the managing editor was so elated he forgot to discipline me for breaking the rules."

This story was told so often it became part of the Roosevelt lore and entered the pages of many a biography. It was a bold-faced lie, a tall tale like the one FDR liked to tell about his father joining Garibaldi. FDR was a gifted and facile liar, fleshing out the story with convincing details—being brought into Eliot's presence because his name was Roosevelt. He finally admitted the truth in 1931, when a reporter for the Boston *Globe* named Michael E. Hennessy who was writing a feature story asked for a copy of his interview with Eliot. On October 22, FDR wrote: "In some way I was a number of years ago given credit for getting the scoop from President Eliot in regard to the way he was going to vote in the autumn of 1900. The real man who got that scoop was Albert W. De Roode, now a lawyer in New York City, and he should have the credit and not I. In the spring or autumn of 1901, I did get a scoop from President Eliot, but, to be perfectly frank, I have forgotten what it was about and the only way I could dig it up would be to go through the files of the *Crimson* for that year." "In some way" was a lovely evasion, for he knew perfectly well that he was the originator of the fable.

FDR could not resist the temptation to place himself in a favorable light. Other great men have had the same failing. Winston Churchill wrote an eyewitness account of British troops relieving the siege of Ladysmith, an event at which he was not present. Theodore Roosevelt as an assemblyman said he had been boxing lightweight champion at Harvard, a title he wanted but never won. Such are the insatiable achievers—when they have climbed to the top of the highest mountain, they still have to add a few feet to the altitude.

Franklin had a reputation for being two-faced among his fellow Harvardmen. James F. Curtis, who led a movement to make the clubs more democratic, drafted an agreement to that effect, which FDR signed on behalf of the "Fly" Club. "Who signed for Fly," another member of the reform group asked Curtis? "Frank Roosevelt," he said. "Oh, he did, did he," came the reply? "Have you looked to see what was written on the other side of the sheet?"

Now that he was at Harvard, there were more dances than ever during the Christmas holiday, and Franklin went through the usual indecision over whom to ask, writing his mother on December 3: "It is very good of you to bother so about my dances, I am writing Ellen & Laura, and as I don't like the awful Sedgwick pill & don't know the Cutting pill I shall ask either Alice Draper [sister of a Groton schoolmate] or Jean Reid [daughter of Whitelaw Reid, editor of the New York *Tribune*]."

But there would be no dances that year, for five days later his father died at the age of seventy-two. "All is over," Sara wrote in her diary. "At 2:20 he merely slept away. Dr. Ely was in the apartment and called, but it was too late. As I write these words I wonder how I lived when he left me." Franklin's letters were now black-bordered, and were no longer addressed to "My Dearest Mamma & Papa." There would be fewer jokes, and no more mock German, as in the 1897 letter when he had written "Blease expectorate me on ze dwendy ninse." Despite their considerable age difference, his father had been a cherished companion. They had done so many things together in the years before his bad heart made him sedentary. James had been warm and tolerant, as Franklin would be toward his own children. He died two months before Queen Victoria, and indeed he was a late Victorian in his narrow moral vision, the importance he attached to class distinctions, and the smug assumptions that came with lineage and inherited wealth. H. G. Wells said that Queen Victoria's death had removed a paperweight that had sat on men's minds for half a century. The paperweight had weighed on James, making him unreceptive to new ideas. Franklin had to find in others examples of political and civic involvement. The one thing James did that was useful for his son's future was to imbue him with a sense of responsibility toward the past.

In the spring of 1901, Franklin concentrated on heeling the *Crimson*. He had no journalistic talent, but he desperately wanted a berth. The demands were great, and the work had to be done in addition to courses and a heavy social schedule. On April 7 and again on April 20, weekend plans in Groton had to be canceled because of the pressure of *Crimson* work—three or four hours every day on assignments, and even longer hours on Sunday (his father would not have approved). As one of his fellow candidates, W. Russel Bowie, put it, the *Crimson* reporter was "the arrow that flieth by day, and the pestilence that walketh in darkness."

That April, Franklin got a legitimate scoop when newly inaugurated Vice President Theodore Roosevelt came to Cambridge. He called for an interview, and Cousin Teddy said they could meet the next morning after the lecture he was giving to Professor Abbott Lowell's class in government. A banner headline in the April 30 edition of the *Crimson* said: "Vice-President Roosevelt to lecture in Government I this morning at 9 in Sanders," and the brief story added that he would speak about his experiences as governor. Sanders was mobbed, and Lowell phoned the *Crimson* to protest. Franklin wrote his mother that he was working six hours a day for the paper and "last night I got a 'scoop' into it about Cousin Theodore's talk, about which I enclose a most amusing, highly colored and inaccurate piece from this evening's [Boston] paper."

Surviving the ruthless attrition among candidates, Franklin was elected to the *Crimson* the following fall. It was one place where Groton and family connections did not help; the editors were picked on hard work and ability. Walter E. Sachs, a Jewish student also elected to the *Crimson* (and later the founder of the Goldman Sachs investment company), measured the distance between himself and Roosevelt. Aside from being on the paper, they moved in different worlds. Franklin lived on the Gold Coast, went to dances in Boston, and ate at the Groton table in Westmorly. Sachs lived in Well Hall on the Yard, and ate at table 30 in Memorial Hall, which was co-op and nonprofit, with three meals a day costing $4.25 a week—none but the brave could eat the fare. At his table were Kendall Smith, who would become a professor of classics at Brown, and Arthur Ballantine, who would serve as undersecretary of the Treasury under Hoover. They would kid around, asking who in their class was most likely to become president of the United States—Ballantine was mentioned, but one name that never came up was Franklin Roosevelt. He was too much the preppy prince.

In preppy-prince fashion, Franklin went abroad that summer of 1901. In July, he and his mother sailed on the *Deutschland*. August found them aboard the *Prinzessin Victoria Luise*, on the way to Norway. Franklin wrote Albert De Roode, true author of the Eliot scoop, that he had found some classmates on board: "We intend to give three times three for Harvard and the *Crimson* while imbibing Bavarian beer at the most northern point of Europe. . . . It is nice here but it still doesn't beat America. How many As and Bs did you get? I have only heard from two courses. C and C+."

In Buffalo on September 5, President McKinley spoke at the Pan-American Exposition. The next day at a reception, he was shot by a demented anarchist, Leon Czolgosz. Doctors operated in time to save him, although the bullet was not found. Franklin heard the news in Paris, where he was visiting the house of Madame de Sévigné. He would always remember something his cousin Teddy had once told him: "The only real danger from an assassin is from one who does not care whether he loses his own life in the act or not. Most of the crazy ones can be spotted first." But no one had spotted Czolgosz, quietly standing in the reception line, his .32 revolver wrapped in a handkerchief.

In London, Franklin stayed at Brown's Hotel and had his hair cut at Truefitt's, a famous barbershop that went back to Regency days. Sailing home aboard the *Teutonic,* they passed the Nantucket Shoals lightship at 9:00 A.M. on September 18 and received the news by megaphone that President McKinley had died of his wounds. To Franklin it was a terrible shock that a president's life could be so foolishly ended.

When he returned to Harvard in September 1901, Cousin Teddy was president. This was a mixed blessing, for being related to the president put him in the limelight. He was frequently mentioned in the Boston papers as a cousin or a nephew. The papers stressed that despite his famous name he was "thoroughly democratic." Franklin's notoriety can only have hurt his position among his peers, for at Harvard conspicuousness was considered unattractive. There was a general dislike of "swelled heads." Anyone who was pompous or self-important became a target for deflation. Franklin was neither, he was unfailingly affable, but he was attributed faults that went with his name.

The first ten for the Institute of 1770 had been elected in the late spring of his freshman year, but Franklin was not among them. They in turn elected the second ten, who elected the third ten, and so on. Being in the first six or seven tens was crucial, for it meant election to the secret fraternity, Delta Kappa Epsilon, which in turn meant election to one of the final clubs. If Franklin didn't make it, he might just as well pack up and go home. The Dickey roll call was the Who's Who of the yard. All the fellows you wanted to know were in it, including practically the entire Groton contingent.

Through the fall of 1901 the tens were chosen. Concerned, Franklin wrote his mother on November 29 that "I have a ghost of a show for the D.K.E." His roommate, Lathrop Brown, however, made the ten that was elected in November, which improved his chances, for Brown could lobby on his behalf. On the morning of January 9, 1902, Franklin was told to stay in his room that evening, as he had been picked for the sixth ten. "I am about to be slaughtered, but quite happy nevertheless," he wrote his mother. Everyone knew that the week-long initiation, known as "running for Dickey," was a nightmare.

That evening, waiting in his room in Westmorly, Franklin heard the strange wordless chant of the Dickey song as the club members marched through the streets. It grew louder, "ta la, la la, la la, la la," and suddenly outside his door there was a cry of "pull him out, pull him out," and he was lifted in the air and dragged outside and rolled in the dirt and jerked upright and started down the street with a kick, roaring the Dickey song at the top of his lungs.

He was pushed and kicked down Mount Auburn Street with the other nine new members until they reached Claverly Hall, where their names were cheered in order of election. There was something ominous in the cheering, it was like a bunch of cannibals cheering a missionary. Then they were returned to their rooms, with vague threats of what was to come. Franklin was back at 8:30, finishing the letter he had been writing his mother: "My back is a bit raw, but I am through the first ordeal O.K. Feeling fine. Tomorrow night I begin running. L.B. is running me. . . ."

Lathrop Brown would make things easier, for it was a humbling initiation, one long mortification, the most wretched week of one's life. Accepted by the Harvard authorities in spite of the bodily harm that was sometimes inflicted, running for Dickey was a curiously primitive rite of passage that demanded perfect obedience and proved, if anything, the power of the institution over the individual, no matter how absurd its demands.

When asked his name, Franklin had to reply "Fool Roosevelt," until it became a habit. He was expected to do whatever a Dickey member asked, from a household chore to the performance of embarrassing practical jokes around Cambridge and Boston. Some of the favorites, annually repeated by successive contingents of Dickey candidates, included:

- Going to a Boston theater and rising after the final curtain and yelling repeatedly, until thrown out by the ushers, "This show is rotten and I want my money back";
- Kissing the occupants of baby carriages and exclaiming, "I am passionately fond of animals";
- Distributing cigars while delivering a lecture on the evils of smoking;
- Stopping an electric car, placing one's foot on the first step, tying one's shoestring, and then saying to the conductor, "Thank you, you may go on now."

Dickey led to membership in a senior club. Porcellian, with its succession of Cabots and Lodges and Saltonstalls and Warrens and Lymans, and its quaint pig figurines in various poses, was the top of the basket, the crème de la crème. No matter that President Eliot, as an undergraduate, had declined to join, sternly accusing them of being dissolute. Owen Wister said that not even the success of *The Virginian* had meant so much. Theodore Roosevelt had written his sister on October 13, 1878: "I went into the Porcellian Club formally. Nell can describe what it looks like to you. Of course, I am delighted to be in, and have great fun up there; there is a billiard table, magnificant library, punch-room etc., and my best friends are in it." When his daughter Alice married Nicholas Longworth, Teddy wrote Kaiser Wilhelm: "Nick and I are both members of the Porc, you know." Having been in the Porc was one of those things that gave a man invisible precedence.

In his sedulous imitation of his cousin (had he not taken boxing at Groton because Teddy was a boxer?) Franklin hoped for Porcellian. He may have felt that he had a family claim on it, that it was due to him by birthright, for his father had also been a member while at law school. But he tasted for the first time the bitterness of social rejection. Porcellian was a small club whose principal activity seemed to be competitive drinking. After business meetings, the clubroom was littered with empty bottles, and there was the notorious "Day by the Book" exercise, an all-day marathon of drinking—a quart of champagne for breakfast, drinks every hour until lunch and with lunch, afternoon same as morning, two predinner drinks, at dinner more fizz, then a scotch and soda an hour until midnight. Few were left standing as the clock struck twelve.

Perhaps the members felt that Franklin was too serious and purposeful to join such a merry, hard-drinking band. Effortlessness was admired in Harvard's clubby circles, and the oral history passed down to this day offers the reason that Franklin was "pushy." Perhaps his connection with Cousin Teddy hurt rather than helped. Perhaps he was perceived as wanting it too badly, whereas a more offhand attitude was prized. When he was assistant secretary of the Navy he told Sheffield Cowles, the son of Teddy Roosevelt's sister Anna (Bamie), that not making Porcellian had been the greatest disappointment of his life. Young Cowles thought it was odd for a man who rated a seventeen-gun salute to be dwelling on a Harvard fiasco.

It was not in Franklin's nature to dwell upon or even acknowledge failure. He moved on to the next event, which was membership in Alpha Delta Phi, the Fly Club. There he remained contentedly, attending drunken dinners, and singing "Harvard was old Harvard when Yale was but a pup." His bookish manner must have concealed a more boisterous side, for his Fly Club nickname was Crazy Kermit. He was made the club's librarian, and also the librarian of Hasty Pudding. "If all else fails," wrote Sara, "you can support yourself as a librarian in future years after so much training."

Whatever his fortunes at Harvard, Franklin was persona grata at the most exclusive club of all, the White House. On January 3, 1902, he went to the ball given by the president and his wife for their daughter Alice's debut. "From start to finish it was glorious," he reported. The next day he went to the White House again for tea, from four to six, which was "all most interesting." Not normally given to superlatives, Franklin found the White House ambience heady, and spent "one of the most interesting and enjoyable three days I have ever had."

Soon after the White House ball Sara arrived in Cambridge to be near her son, having taken an apartment at the Empire. The New York season without James would have been too sad to bear. She thought of attending Franklin's classes to improve her mind, and saw herself sitting next to her son and taking notes, but decided against it because when she saw the subjects she felt so ignorant.

That May, Franklin's interest in the Boer cause revived. One of his favorite teachers, Abram Piatt Andrew, had written an angry article in the *Crimson* denouncing the "unutterable criminality" of the British concentration camps. Two Boers came to Harvard and presented their case. Franklin collected money for the exhausted Dutch settlers, and a Boston paper reported: "Franklin D. Roosevelt, nephew of President Roosevelt, heads movement 'Harvard Fund for Boer Relief.' " On May 14 he cabled $336.50 to Capetown, but it was too late. A month later the war ended with the surrender of the Boers, whose republics became a British dominion.

For three years while he was at Harvard, Franklin kept a diary, in emulation of his mother. Like Sara's, his was in the main a perfunctory account of his activities. We learn that he went to many dances, often getting home at three or four in the morning; that he often had breakfast or dinner at the Touraine, then Boston's best-known hotel; that he played poker and vingt-et-un into the wee hours; that he drank too much and felt "like hell" the next morning; that in May 1902 a dentist cut off one of his front teeth, replacing it with a porcelain one; that in September 1903 he had his tonsils out; that he did his share of "doping," or studying, sometimes working "like a pup" all day; that he spent entire days "rummaging and resting," a recurring entry; and that one day of his Dickey initiation was spent with "Fool Brown" tobogganing with two girls.

Rarely are there any remarks of a personal nature, other than that one dance was "glorious" while another was "a kid affair." The tone is dry and matter-of-fact, usually listing in a sentence or two each day's events. The diary would be banal were it not for one curious feature: Franklin used a code of his own invention for three of the entries. It was a simple code, which substituted numbers one through five for vowels and deleted the tops or bottoms of consonants. But the use of any code expresses a need for concealment. Should anyone, and particularly his mother, who was inexhaustibly curious about her son, pick up the diary and start leafing through it, there were certain entries he did not want revealed.

Several of the coded comments concerned a seventeen-year-old girl, Alice Sohier, a Boston belle whose parents had a house in Beverly, a seaside resort fifteen miles northeast of Boston. Franklin probably met her at one of the holiday dances and went to see her in Beverly in the spring and summer. On July 8, 1902, he took the Sohiers sailing and had dinner at their house. His diary entry for that day reads as follows: "We all landed and played tennis. Took the Sohiers, T.P.B. and Swain out for a good long sail to Marblehead in p.m. All dine at Sohiers." Then comes a passage in code: "and spend evening on lawn. Alice confides in her Dr."

The next day's entry begins with a coded passage: "Worried over Alice all night," and continues uncoded: "Left Beverly at 6:30 a.m. Breeze as far as

Thatcher's island. Lay off it five hours. Started engine and got to Portsmouth harbor at 7."

Why would Franklin worry over Alice? And why did he need to conceal his worry? And what did "Alice confides in her Dr." mean? One explanation, provided by family members, was that Alice had been told by her doctor that for anatomical reasons she would have difficulty bearing children. Franklin, who thought of Alice as a possible wife, had told her that he wanted six children, a prospect to which she did not respond with much enthusiasm. Another reason for the coded entry that kept him from sleeping, one might speculate, was that Alice Sohier was pregnant.

The only further mention of the girl in Franklin's diary came three months later, on October 8: "See Alice Sohier off on the *Commonwealth* for Europe." The *Commonwealth* was a packet between Boston and New York that connected with Europe-bound ships. The relationship with Alice Sohier was obviously of some importance for him to have taken the time from his busy Harvard schedule to see her off. He does not mention anyone else being there. According to the family, Alice Sohier was sent abroad because her less beautiful sister was coming out that year and her parents were afraid that Alice would steal her thunder. That seems a frivolous reason for sending a young girl on what was then a long and inconvenient voyage. Her departure also fits the pregnancy thesis, for if an abortion had been decided upon, Europe was the place to do it, away from watchful parents and gossiping Boston society. But this is all conjecture, and we will probably never know what really happened between Alice and Franklin.

Alice Sohier boarded the *Commonwealth* and left for Europe. Franklin saw her occasionally when she got back, and commented on her poor health. In October 1903 she had her appendix removed. In March 1904, "poor Alice Sohier is layed up again—this time it is her hip—whether rheumatism or something out of joint they don't know. I saw her this afternoon on a sofa and quite unable to walk." Many years later, in July 1928, Franklin wrote a Boston lawyer friend, Robert M. Washburn: "Once upon a time when I was in Cambridge I had serious thoughts of marrying a Boston girl and settling down in the Back Bay to spend the rest of my days . . . it was a narrow escape."

The summer of 1902 was spent at Hyde Park and Campobello, and Franklin concentrated on golf and sailing. Back at Harvard in the fall, he "worked like a dog" on the *Crimson* and in October was made assistant managing editor, which meant that he ran the paper on Monday and Thursday nights. The other assistant managing editor was Walter Russel Bowie, later pastor of New York's Grace Church, who had this wonderful phrase about Franklin's days on the *Crimson:* "In his geniality there was a kind of frictionless command." Not everyone agreed. Robert W. Ruhl, one of the editors on the 1903 board that had elected Franklin, thought of him as a "bumptious, cocky, conceited chap, with a great name but nothing much else." However, the other 1903 editors liked him, and said he had a lot on the ball and the nerve of a brass baboon.

One of the fellows he had beat out for the job was Arthur Ballantine, and Franklin was convinced that Ballantine hated him ever after. He also beat out Bowie to become managing editor in February 1903, which meant that the following year he would be president of the newspaper. An election poster dated February 11, 1903, said: "For Managing Editor—Cousin Frank—The Fairest of the Roosevelts."

As president of the *Crimson,* Franklin was one of the leading members of his class. For instance, he would speak that fall to incoming first-year men, freshmen and law school, as the representative of all the student publications. Years later one of those first-year men, H. Maurice Darling, would remember him telling the group assembled in Phillips Brooks House that in Cambridge there was not only the *Lampoon,* which "tried to be funny," but another more serious journal, which "tried not to be funny."

It was not journalistic talent or writing skill that had won the top job for Franklin. It was tenacity and desire. He wanted it more badly than the others, and was willing to put in the time. There were three ways to shine at Harvard—through sports, academic honors, or leadership in some extracurricular activity. Franklin could not win his H or make Phi Beta Kappa, but he went out for the *Crimson* with complete single-mindedness. There was no task too lowly, no chore too time-consuming. Sara's reaction to his *Crimson* election was to advise him to get plenty of fresh air, for the air of the *Crimson* office was not the freshest.

Asserting his independence, Franklin left in the summer of 1903 for his first European trip without his mother. He had graduated on June 24 with the class of 1903, donning his cap and gown and marching in line to Sanders and receiving his A.B. parchment, but he would return to Harvard for his fourth year, taking graduate courses and serving out his term as *Crimson* president. "Of course I shall miss you," Sara wrote, "but I am not so silly and I have no intention of 'tying you to my apron strings.' " "Don't worry about me," Franklin said. "I always land on my feet—but wish you were with me." Here were examples of Sara and Franklin saying the opposite of what they meant. Sara had every intention of tying him to her apron strings. Franklin much preferred traveling alone, being free, white, and twenty-one, with letters of credit and introduction in his pocket.

He arrived in London on August 3 and took a room at the fashionable Burlington Hotel, but on the inexpensive Cork Street side, patronized mainly by army officers. It was a bank holiday—"damn it—nothing open," he wrote in his diary. He had to order suits at J. B. Johnstone's, and riding breeches at Thresher and Glenny, and custom-made riding boots at Peals. But after dinner at Claridge's, with a pint of Burgundy and a good "seegar," he felt better.

Two days later he went to Lincolnshire to visit friends of his parents, Lord and Lady Cholmeley, who lived in a stately home called Easton Hall. Lady

Cholmeley was not receiving, being in seclusion for a nervous condition, but her three daughters were there to greet him—May, who was rather better looking, though that was not saying a great deal; Winnie, who was quite stately; and Aline, who was really quite pretty and less large than the others. The house, however, was "a Dream of Nirvana," and Franklin liked it so much he took notes and measurements of everything.

On the afternoon of his arrival, he and Aline paired off on the tennis court against May and Winnie, and in the evening they played bridge. The next morning he went trout fishing with Aline, and was amazed to find a trout stream within a couple of hundred feet of the house. "Aline landed four for me," he noted in his diary. There were interesting discrepancies between the diary notes and the letters to his mother. Franklin wrote Sara on August 7: "I fished again—downstream—but it was too sunny & I only got two small ones." In his diary for that day, however, he wrote: "more fishing in a.m. with Aline. Not much luck for did not attend strictly to fishing." Franklin had been flirting with Aline on the trout stream, which he refrained from mentioning to his mother. The uncomplimentary remarks about the three sisters had been for her benefit.

Although he still felt the need to prove his loyalty to his mother by disparaging girls his own age, Franklin was adopting a far more relaxed and engaging manner with the opposite sex. The fear of women so apparent at Groton had vanished. A new Franklin appeared, eager to charm the ladies. On the afternoon of August 7, they went to visit the lord lieutenant of Lincoln County, Adelbert Wellington Brownlow, who lived at nearby Belton House. All the swells were having tea on the terrace, Franklin related to his mother in a newly confident tone, and he at once got separated from Aline and her father, "but I walked up to the best looking dame in the bunch and said 'howdy?' Things at once went like oil and I was soon having flirtations with three of the nobility at the same time. I had a walk with the hostesses' niece over the entire house which was really perfect in every way—I mean the house—although the walk wasn't bad—I will have to tell you about it in person—again I mean the house. Then I inspected the gardens with another 'chawmer' and ended up by jollying the hostess herself all by her lonesome for ten minutes while a uniformed Lord stood by and never got in anything except an occasional 'aw' or an 'I sy.' " The double entendres, and the picture of Franklin confidently flirting with every woman in sight and "jollying" the hostess in the presence of a tongue-tied English lord, show a new-found ease that must have been the fruit of experience—either with Alice Sohier or Aline Cholmeley or some unnamed young woman. We are a long way from the Franklin who would not pick a dance partner without consulting his mother and for whom so many girls were ice-carts and pills.

After touring the Alps, he came home on the *Kaiser Wilhelm*, confiding to his diary that there was "an awful crowd on board." This would be his last year at Harvard, the year of his eminence, when on the editorial page of the *Crimson* he wrote little sermons that combined Endicott Peabody's high-mindedness with Theodore Roosevelt's appeals to the strenuous life. The important thing was to try, to accomplish something, urged the *Crimson*'s new president. "Every man should have a wholesome horror of that happy-go-lucky state of doing nothing but enough classroom work to keep off probation." The college experience was not one of reflection and study, but a "career" where every young man had to try for "success." There were a great many editorials about football, perhaps because "Fool Brown" was manager of the team.

It was then the custom at Harvard to pick as cheerleaders men of prominence. Franklin was one of the three chosen for the Brown game in October, and he ran up and down the sidelines shouting, "Hit the line for Harvard, for Harvard wins today." He felt like a damn fool, waving his arms and legs before several thousand amused spectators.

That November, he cast his first vote, in an off-year state election for assemblyman, with Democrat Robert W. Chanler running against Republican Francis G. Landon. "I wouldn't have missed my first ballot for anything," he wrote his mother on November 6.

At Groton, the highest honor had been senior prefect, and Franklin felt he had been cheated out of it by the rector's favoritism. At Harvard, it was class marshal, of which there were three. The marshals led the class day parade to Appleton Chapel and then to Sanders Theater for the diplomas. Franklin was elated to learn in early December that he had been nominated for marshal, but added: "I don't stand a ghost of a show of being elected." He may have had inside information that his name did not appear on the slate made up by the final clubs. If that was the case, there was a self-serving tone to the editorial that appeared on December 15, election eve, which took the noble view that "there is a higher duty than to vote for one's personal friends, and that is to secure for the whole class, leaders who really deserve their positions." Can Franklin have meant himself, echoing Mark Twain's adage: "To do good is noble; to teach others to do good is nobler yet, and less trouble."

On election day, November 16, he wrote Sara that "I don't stand the least show—in fact will get less votes than any of the others for marshal." Three marshals were elected out of the six nominated, and Franklin came in fourth, and not by much, in an election that may have been weighted by the club-slate ballots. Two days later, he was elected, again by the entire class, as permanent chairman of the class committee. It was his first elective office.

He continued turning out editorials, some of a mildly reformist bent. He called for a boardwalk leading from the Harvard Union to Gore Hall, and for better fire protection in the Yard buildings, and for a better system of ventilation in Massachusetts Hall, where "the air is invariably hot and foul, and it is not to be wondered at that the men are listless and inattentive." Whenever he criticized, he proposed a remedy. One editorial, in the January 26, 1904, issue, was an accurate description of himself: "In looking back over the college careers of those who for various reasons have been prominent in undergraduate life in the University, one cannot help noticing that these men have nearly always shown from the start an interest in the lives of their fellow students. A large acquaintance means that many persons are dependent on a man and conversely that he himself is dependent on many. Success necessarily means larger responsibilities, and responsibilities means many friends." He might have been describing the essential transaction of politics, the mutual dependence of the voter and the officeholder.

The Harvard experience was coming to a close. On March 21, 1904, the senior class led the student body in the observance of President Eliot's seventieth birthday. The living room of Union filled up for the informal program, and in acknowledging the tribute Eliot said: "Yesterday, at a family gathering, a lady gave to me a note which she said that a lady in Boston had asked her to deliver. I opened it and there was not a word in it. Not one— only a leaf, but the leaf was laurel." Not one of those who had heard those words would ever forget them.

On June 29, although he had received his A.B. the year before, Franklin graduated with his class. There was the singing of "Johnny Harvard" by the glee club and of "Fair Harvard" by the entire class, and the delivery of the Ivy Oration by Fred Wayne Catlett, who spoke on "the millionaire in politics," and the exit of seniors amid the throwing of confetti and serpentines.

Although he had not, like his cousin Teddy, achieved the twin triumphs of Phi Beta Kappa and the Porcellian, Franklin had prospered at Harvard. The latitude of the place, the freedom to exert oneself or to coast, suited him. You could take the courses you wanted and try out for the activities you liked. At Harvard he experienced both a sense of possibilities and a sense of limitations. There were limits to his feeling of entitlement. He had been rejected by Porcellian, even though the club recruited among "his kind." He had learned to handle frustration, and not to let it contaminate other efforts. You had to try anyway. The meaning of the Harvard experience was that very American dictum, "The next step is up to you." Franklin took the step, showing an eagerness to assume responsibility and collaborate with others. He achieved ego integrity, realizing that healthy development was not achieved through self-love and narcissism but by becoming involved with others, by working toward common goals, by taking part in activities that gave you some sense of a larger order.

As a boy, insulated by the wealth and prominence of his family, with a strong sense of his position in the world, he seemed to have sidestepped all neurotic conflicts. He was an unself-consciously productive youth, who instinctively understood that self-generated activities would bring him into contact with the world outside the family circle. As an only child, without sibling rivals to divide love and attention, he felt the obligation of having to pay back his parents for not having had other children. In his dealings with his family, there was no autocracy or inequality. He was always consulted about decisions affecting him, even when he was very young, in the choice of nurses. There was no need, as in other families, to rebel or submit. Things could always be worked out, as in the argument with his mother over the

Boers, where it was natural for him to find a middle ground. His was the kind of upbringing that did not breed ideologues but undogmatic compromisers, always ready to drive a bargain.

Franklin found ways to protect himself against his mother's possessiveness, to dissemble and adapt without giving up his inner coherence. He knew how to flatter her need to be indispensable, as when he wrote that he wished he were traveling to Europe with her. He knew how to hide things from her, as he hid his relationship with the Sohier girl. By the time he graduated from Harvard, he had learned how to disguise his true feelings (as in the diary code) and how to give of himself (as in his devotion to the *Crimson*). In him there coexisted generosity and concealment.

At Christmas time in Hyde Park, there was always a big party at the Rogers estate, Crumwold Hall, complete with Santa, and a tree, and presents. Anne Rogers was seven in December 1901, and waited by the tree, the huge tree from their woods topped by a wax angel with gossamer wings, its branches covered with little glass trumpets that you could really blow, glass bells that really tinkled, hundreds of candles, French dolls, monkeys on sticks. Outside the room, she heard the sound of sleigh bells. When they ceased to jingle, Santa made his appearance, with long white beard and beetling eyebrows and a pillow stuffed in front of his red suit. He began handing out toys from his well-stuffed pack, calling all the children by name. How did Santa know their names, Anne wondered? When her turn came, she kissed Santa on the cheek and felt a mask and, peeking behind the mask, recognized a familiar face, who disappeared into the end room on the third floor, bidding a merry Christmas to all. Anne Rogers realized that Santa Clause did not exist. The man with the mask, the giver of gifts, was Franklin Roosevelt.

IV
Getting Married

Unless you can die when the dream is past—
Oh, never call it loving!
      Elizabeth Barrett Browning, "A Woman's Shortcomings"

THE sibling rivalry that Franklin escaped, with its character-shaping dangers, came out in full force between Theodore and Elliott Roosevelt. To be Teddy's younger brother was to be pulled constantly into the arena of competition. In 1862, when Teddy was four and Elliott not quite two, their mother wrote their father that "Elliott came into my bed and fell asleep while I was stroking his ears. Teedie was miserably jealous about his sleeping by me." Then "Teedie" would come into his mother's bed and stroke Ellie's ears "and say to me [in] the almost hysterical manner, 'Oh, do look Mamma, how he do obey me.'"

As they grew up, Teddy was always measuring himself against his brother. Elliott was three inches taller, a natural athlete, loaded with charm and social grace. But he did not have, and indeed did not want, Teddy's aggressive drive. He realized while still a boy that he would never equal his older brother, and adopted a tone of self-deprecation, writing his father on March 6, 1875: "Oh father will you ever think *me* a 'noble boy,' you are quite right about Tede he is one and no mistake a boy I could give a great deal to be like in many respects." But he could not be like him, and he knew that it was pointless to try, admitting that he lacked "that foolish grit of Theodore's." Teddy in the meantime wrote in his diary in 1879 that "as athletes we are about equal; he rows best; I run best; he can beat me sailing or swimming; I can beat him wrestling and boxing. I am best with the rifle, he with the shotgun, etc., etc." In addition, they were both sickly, but Teddy conquered his asthma, while Elliott's headaches and dizzy spells persisted, and contributed to his lack of self-worth. Because of his illness, he had to leave St. Paul's, and never went to college.

Elliott discovered that alcohol relieved the pain of his headaches. When he and Teddy were in Chicago in 1880 after a hunting trip in Iowa, Teddy reported that "as soon as we got here he took some ale to get the dust out of his throat; then a milkpunch because he was thirsty; a mint julep because it was hot; a brandy smash 'to keep the cold out of his stomach'; and then sherry and bitters to give him an appetite."

In 1882, Elliott married Anna Hall, one of six children of Mary (née Ludlow) and Valentine G. Hall, Jr., a wealthy member of the Hudson River gentry, and the son of an Irish immigrant who had settled in Brooklyn and made a fortune in real estate. Two years later, Eleanor was born.

It was as if Elliott had deliberately set out to become the exact opposite of his brother, dissolute where he was determined, weak where he was strong, apathetic where he was ambitious, ailing and accident-prone where he was fit. One subject upon which Teddy was particularly judgmental was sexual misconduct. Here again, Elliott was at the other end of the spectrum, impure and promiscuous. He seduced one of the maids on his Long Island estate, Katy Mann, and got her pregnant. She had a son, whom she named Elliott Roosevelt Mann, and the resemblance was striking, as Teddy learned when he sent one of his agents to see the child.

Katy Mann threatened to reveal the birth unless she was paid off. By this time, Elliott had taken his family to Europe, where he went through cycles of binge and remorse. That he had a child with a domestic was a "hideous revelation" to Teddy. "Of course he was insane when he did it," he wrote. He had reduced himself to a "flagrant man-swine." Teddy did not think much of Anna either, who "sweet though she is, is an impossible person to deal with. Her utterly frivolous life has, as was inevitable, eaten into her character like an acid." But this was too much, and Anna should leave him, "she ought not to have any more children, and those she had should be brought up away from him" (Eleanor by now had a baby brother, Elliott).

Theodore Roosevelt, by then a public service commissioner, became the go-between in a shabby paternity suit, intent on protecting his family and his own political reputation from scandal. Elliott committed himself to a sanitarium in Austria, then moved to Paris, where he had an American mistress, a Mrs. Evans. Instead of leaving her husband, Anna was pregnant again, and on June 28 another son, Hall, was born. "It is dreadful to think of the inheritance the poor little baby may have in him," Teddy commented.

Negotiations went on with Katy Mann. Teddy thought it was worth it to pay her three or four thousand dollars. If the suit came to trial, Elliott would make a poor witness, and every member of the family including himself would be splattered by the mud. But Katy Mann wanted $10,000, a large sum in those days. Eventually money changed hands and she vanished from the scene with her Roosevelt bastard.

In the meantime, Elliott was drying out in a sanitarium outside Paris, the Château Suresnes. Convinced that his brother was not competent to handle his estate, Teddy applied before the New York State Supreme Court to have him declared insane. It was a dreadful thing for one brother to do to another, and in a sense it was the tragic outcome of a rivalry that had begun when they were infants: "Oh do look Mama how he do obey me." Teddy still wanted to be obeyed.

The press got hold of it, which was an awful blow. The headline in the New York *Sun* on August 17, 1891, read: "Elliott Roosevelt Insane—His Brother Theodore Applies for a Writ in Lunacy." Elliott fought back, lodged a formal protest with the court, and published a denial in the Paris *Herald.* The suit bogged down as doctors disagreed.

In January 1892 Teddy went to Paris, found Elliott overwhelmed by guilt and remorse, and made him agree to sign over two-thirds of his property and to take a five-week cure at the Keeley Center in Dwight, Illinois. It was settled that after that he would go to Abingdon, Virginia, where he would manage his brother-in-law's landholdings.

Her health broken by years of torment, Anna died in December 1892 after catching diphtheria, and the children went to live with their grandmother, Mrs. Hall. Elliott, separated from his children, did not improve, and Teddy wrote his sister Bamie on July 22, 1894: "I do wish Corinne could get a little of my hard heart about Elliott; she can do, and ought to do, nothing for him. He can't be helped, and he must simply be let go his own gait. He is now laid up from a serious fall; while drunk he drove into a lamppost and went out on his head. Poor fellow! If only he could have died instead of Anna!" On another occasion, while reading with no clothes on, he upset a lamp and burned himself badly. On August 12, Teddy wrote to Bamie: "Elliott is up and about again; and I hear is already drinking heavily; if so he must break down soon. It has been as hideous a tragedy all through as one often sees." Two days later Elliott died after a bad fall, at the age of thirty-four. It was his frightful drinking, Teddy said; at the end he had been consuming whole bottles of anisette and green mint and raw brandy.

Elliott's death was a relief to his brother. It was as if his own dark side, all the defects and weaknesses he had fought so hard to suppress, were being buried. Teddy was able to banish the bad years from his mind and remember only the bright moments of their childhood.

Instead of trying to understand his brother, instead of seeing that his combativeness had smothered whatever flickering spark Elliott may have had, Teddy ruthlessly condemned him. Instead of showing fraternal feeling and compassion, he tried to have him committed and advised his sister to be hard on him. By Theodore's priggish and Victorian canons, Elliott's behavior was monstrous, but by any standards of humane conduct the real monster was Theodore Roosevelt. The tender but manly man, who did not want to compete, who did not want to follow his brother to Harvard or into politics, had been destroyed by the torment of not measuring up. The sibling rivalry had ended in death. The purposeful brother, freed from the threat of scandal and shameful publicity, could go on to become governor of New

York and president of the United States. Theodore was the success, the great man, while Elliott was the failure and nonentity—except in the eyes of his daughter.

Through the power of her love and the strength of her will, Eleanor was able to transform this wreck of a man into a noble figure. She created a fantasy father, not the promiscuous drunk who was rejected by his wife and shamed by his brother, but a man of generous instincts and kind deeds who enhanced the lives of those around him. Despite all evidence to the contrary, Eleanor maintained this vision of her father all her life. To do this was her mission, part of the secret transaction they had made to validate one another.

From her mother, she learned that she was unattractive and unlike other children. She would stand in the door with her finger in her mouth, and her mother would say, "Come in, Granny," and, turning to a visitor, explain, "She is such a funny child, so old-fashioned, that we always call her 'Granny.' " Eleanor wanted to sink through the floor in shame. She did not feel a part of the family circle; there was a barrier between her and her mother and two brothers.

She belonged to her father. Perhaps, as everyone said, she had been uglier and more wrinkled than other babies, but to Elliott she was his firstborn, a miracle from heaven. Her mother judged and compared her, there was something dutiful in her affection, but Elliott loved her without restraint, unconditionally.

Elliott "dominated my life as long as he lived, and was the love of my life for many years after he died. With my father I was perfectly happy. There is still a painting of a solemn child, a straight bang across her forehead, with an uplifted finger and an admonishing attitude, which he always enjoyed and referred to as 'Little Nell scolding Elliott.' " Little Nell was the character in Dickens's *Old Curiosity Shop* and Nell had also been Elliott's nickname.

Little Nell learned "Hiawatha" by heart to surprise her father. She called herself "Father's little Golden Hair" and came to his dressing room in the morning to help him dress and warn him that he would be late for breakfast.

She never doubted that she stood first in his heart. When they went to Italy in the winter of 1890, he took her on the canals of Venice in a gondola, taking over from the gondolier, joining in the songs of the other boatmen. At Vesuvius, they threw pennies into the volcano that were returned to them encased in lava.

But something was wrong with her wonderful father. She wasn't sure what, except that she knew in her heart that he was not at fault. She heard conversations and did not know what they meant. It was all garbled and strange. She woke up in the night and heard her mother and her sisters talking. When they traveled in Europe, he was often away, and then they came back to New York and he wasn't living with them anymore, and she didn't know why. The one certainty she had was their love, as strong as ever. On

October 9, 1892, Elliott wrote her for her eighth birthday: "Because father is not with you is not because he doesn't love you. For I love you tenderly and dearly."

Her mother was sick at that time, but still her father did not come. On December 7, her lovely mother died, and she felt no sense of loss. Her mother had been censorious, had made her feel that she was ugly, had made her conscious of her shortcomings. Now that she was gone, her father could return. To Eleanor, her mother's death meant only that she would see her father again.

She and her brothers were sent to live with their Grandmother Hall. One day she was told that her father was coming to see her. Each time the doorbell rang, she leaned over the bannister to hear the familiar voice. She went down to the dim, high-ceilinged library on the first floor of the house on West 37th Street. Elliott, sad-faced, dressed in black, held out his arms and embraced her. He explained that now he had only Eleanor and her brothers, but the boys were very young, so he and Eleanor must keep close together. Someday she would make a home for him, and they would travel together. There would be plenty of pleasant times to look forward to.

Eleanor was not sure what he meant. She felt somehow that in her father's eyes she was replacing her dead mother. Her two brothers would be their children, or else they would go away to school and be raised independently. Of one thing she was sure, that she and her father would someday have a life of their own together. They had a secret understanding. This intensification of the father-daughter relationship into a closer and more exclusive bond was a heavy emotional burden to pass onto an eight-year-old girl, but Eleanor saw only its promise.

The following year, both her brothers caught scarlet fever. As with her mother's death, Eleanor reacted to their illness in terms of how it would affect her relationship with her father. Because he was anxious over the little boys, he had less time for her. When Ellie died, that seemed to be in the nature of things. "We must remember Ellie is going to be safe in heaven and to be with mother who is waiting there and our Lord wants Ellie boy with him now," Eleanor wrote her father, whose prophecy that the two of them would have a life together was one step closer to being realized.

But in 1894 Elliott died. When word reached Eleanor, who was not quite ten, she refused to believe it. She went through the motions of crying, but her father's death did not seem real. Her grandmother did not let her go to the funeral, so she had no tangible evidence of it. On a rational level she knew he was dead, but on a deeper spiritual level he continued to live because of her devotion. He lived not as he had been, flawed and self-destructive, but as she wanted him to be.

The Elliott whose memory was perpetuated by Eleanor was almost saintly. At the age of seven he had gone out in winter in a new overcoat and returned without it—he had given it to a ragged urchin he had seen shivering in the cold. This incident was emblematic of a compulsive kindness.

"He never could learn to control his heart by his head," Eleanor wrote. "With him the heart always dominated." Instead of his brother's drive, Elliott had a talent for giving. "He loved to give and tried always to find just the thing which would rejoice the heart of the one receiving his gift. You always felt somehow surrounded by his thought and love.'

He was not grasping or self-seeking, and he had the common touch. Even in his last stages of delirium in Abingdon he was popular with the townspeople. It was not given to everyone to make a mark in the world, but perhaps a man could be great without being famous, simply by having rare human qualities that brightened the ordinary episodes of daily life. If Elliott had not done more, it was because of his illnesses—a fever in India that had undermined his constitution and probably had been a factor in his early death, and the bad break in his leg that had to be reset.

Such was the Elliott that Eleanor re-created, in repayment to her father for his gift of love. She carried his letters with her, reading and rereading them, content to have him at last to herself. Elliott had said that he wanted to be proud of her, and she grew up with the feeling that she must justify his pride, just as Franklin had grown up feeling that he had to maintain the standards of his Roosevelt ancestors. She was the custodian of her father's memory, which she sanitized and tried to redeem through her own actions. All her life she would identify with the proscribed, the defeated, the weak.

But certain realities of her childhood could not be dismissed. In two years, between the ages of eight and ten, she lost her father, mother, and a brother. It took an adaptive mind to be able to fit the death of both parents and a brother into the scheme of a sane and orderly world. Eleanor saw no injustice in it, she accepted it as God's will. She would not admit to herself that death was an irreversible deprivation.

Nor would she admit the ambiguity of her father's love. He was tender and loving, but also terribly unreliable. The price that had to be paid for his love was disappointment. He promised to take her for a drive and did not show up. He promised to write and forgot. He promised to come and see her but was delayed. She was constant, he was unavailable. He had promised that they would have a life together, and then abandoned her by dying.

She forgave her father, who could do no wrong. But in her marriage with Franklin she was unforgiving. She had a hunger for absolutes. When Franklin was unfaithful, the long-buried resentment at her father's inconstancy surfaced. Here again was an unreliable man who could not match her commitment.

After her father's death, Eleanor continued to live with Grandmother Hall, a stern and pious woman who, according to Eleanor, "really believed every word in the Bible. She believed the whale really swallowed Jonah." Her two sons were drunkards and her daughters lived strange lives, but that did not deter Grandmother Hall from the path of virtue. On Sunday Eleanor was not allowed to do anything but walk or read a Sunday book.

Having little control over her own children, Grandmother Hall was all the more strict with her grandchildren. Whenever Eleanor asked her anything the answer was always no. She must have been glad to leave when at the age of fifteen she was sent to school in Europe.

What Eleanor was lacking until she went away to school was an example. Her mother was a nagging and negative presence. Her father transmitted qualities of the heart but not standards of conduct. In Marie Souvestre, the headmistress of the boarding school outside London that she attended, Eleanor found an older woman she could admire and learn from, and also a nurturing presence under whose care she blossomed.

She was the daughter of Emile Souvestre, a distinguished French writer whose antimonarchist views during the 1848 revolution, when the readings he organized in working-class neighborhoods were banned, led to his exile in Switzerland. His daughter inherited his independence of mind, determination, and love of literature, and she too went into exile, for another reason.

Marie Souvestre was a lesbian who founded a school called Les Ruches (The Hives) in Fontainebleau with another woman, who was her lover. The story of the school's breakup was told by Dorothy Strachey, elder sister of the Edwardian author Lytton Strachey, in an autobiographical account called *Olivia*, which has taken its place in lesbian literature alongside *The Well of Loneliness*. It is an unpleasant story of the two founders picking favorites, of passions and jealousies, and finally of Mlle Souvestre's partner accusing her of having sexual relations with her "darlings." The charge that Mlle Souvestre was corrupting teenage girls entrusted to her care made it impossible for her to continue the partnership, and she closed the school and left France for England.

There she founded Allenswood in a little place near Wimbledon Commons called South Fields. Eleanor arrived in the fall of 1899 and remained for three years, which she said were the happiest of her life.

Mlle Souvestre, known as "Sou," was by then a woman of seventy, white-haired and stout, with a broad, fleshy face and intense gray eyes. She was a female version of Endicott Peabody, like him a figure of authority who had the same trick of seeming to know what was going on in the minds of her students. Like him, she made a supreme virtue of performance. She openly chose favorites on the basis of merit, while the rector had exercised favoritism by naming his nephew senior prefect. Unlike the rector, she had no interest in sports or public service, and was a professed atheist.

The mutual sympathy between Eleanor and Mlle Souvestre was immediate and strong. Once shy, she now chattered in French in the favored place across from Sou in the dining room. Once an outsider in her grandmother's house, she was surrounded by friends, and was assigned to help newcomers. Eleanor, whose self-confidence had been sapped by her mother, found in Sou a surrogate mother who admired her intelligence, her honesty, "the perfect quality of her soul."

Eleanor adapted well to a system of favorites that was as regulated as at Versailles. Certain girls were set apart and called "the clever ones." They were given the best seats when Sou read in the library. A girl would come to the dining room and search for her napkin ring, and her heart would skip a beat when she saw it in the place of honor, next to Sou's. A favorite would be hugged and kissed when Sou said good night. Eleanor too in later life would surround herself with favorites. A favorite was someone who had to deserve your love, who was always in some way on probation and could be replaced. Eleanor was comfortable in this type of relationship, having apprenticed at Allenswood.

From Mlle Souvestre, Eleanor learned to think for herself and to be wary of received ideas. She loved to listen to her read from the tragedies of Corneille and Racine. Mlle Souvestre would lift her hand and wave an ivory paper cutter to the beat of the verses, like a conductor. The girls were transported into the courts of legendary kings, where men and women were consumed by passion. The lesson of the tragedies was that the passion of love destroyed its victims. People were torn by conflicting emotions, and had to make terrible choices between love and duty. Eleanor was immersed in a world of passionate intensity expressed in iambic hexameters, and something of that combination of strong feelings and decorousness stuck.

She was so self-effacing, so incapable of haughtiness, that she made no enemies by being the favorite. Her cousin Corinne, who came to Allenswood during Eleanor's last year, said: "When I arrived she was 'everything' at the school. She was beloved by everybody. Saturdays we were allowed a sortie into Putney which had stores where you could buy books, flowers. Young girls have crushes and you bought violets or a book and left them in the room of the girl you were idolizing. Eleanor's room every Saturday would be full of flowers because she was so admired."

Imagine Eleanor, the clumsy, odd "Granny," being idolized. In spite of her popularity, and Sou's faith in her, she was still beset by feelings of worthlessness. She was poor at the piano, she could not draw, she could not act. Like her father, she saw herself as a person of few resources and moderate talents. Indeed, she did have drawbacks, the most obvious being a judicial solemnity of manner. As Mlle Souvestre wrote, "Totty [as Eleanor was known]—so intelligent, so charming, so good. *Mais elle n'est pas gaie"* (but she is not fun).

Sou asked her to travel to Europe with her during the Easter vacation in 1901. Together they went to Italy. Eleanor was a delightful companion, Sou wrote Mrs. Hall, never tired or out of sorts. Alone, Eleanor roamed the streets of Florence, Baedeker in hand. Always looking for motives that would reinforce her negative feelings, she believed the reason Mlle Souvestre had let her see Florence on her own was that she was not attractive enough to appeal to foreign men, and would be safe from their advances.

The three years at Allenswood went by quickly. Eleanor wanted to stay a fourth, but her grandmother insisted that she come home to be introduced to society. Eleanor learned from Sou that she was capable, and that women did not have to be victims, as her mother had been the victim of her father's excesses, and as her grandmother had been the victim of a patronizing husband and playboy sons. Women could make something of themselves, independently of men, as Mlle Souvestre had. Eleanor still believed that she was an ugly duckling, but the ugliest duckling can swim.

Everyone said that Eleanor was no beauty, but she was attractive to men, tall and willowy, with lovely eyes and skin, and a full-breasted, hourglass figure. Only her mouth lacked promise, and it was too bad that she was not taken to see the same Boston dentist who had fixed Franklin's teeth. But orphans don't get taken to the dentist. She was back at her grandmother's in July 1902, dreading her debut and her first winter in society.

Marriage was the true purpose of the social whirl. There seemed to be a need to hurry, to conform to expectations, Eleanor thought, but at the same time a girl had to be demure. Add to convention the propriety of a young woman who had just spent three years in a girls' school where the presence of a man was a rare occurrence, and one gets some idea of Eleanor's reserve. In spite of her feelings of inadequacy, her shame at being the first girl in her mother's family who was not a belle, Eleanor caught the eye of her cousin Franklin, in the fall of 1902 a handsome and debonair twenty, who could have had his pick of the prettiest girls. They were in his half brother Rosy's box at the Madison Square Garden Horse Show that November, and shortly after that they had lunch together.

On January 1, 1903, Franklin went to the New Year's reception at the White House and stood in the inner circle for three hours, watching hundreds of well-wishers file by and shake the hand of his cousin Theodore. Eleanor was there too and that evening at the theater he sat next to her.

She was one of the guests at the party that Rosy gave for Franklin on January 30 for his twenty-first birthday. She saw him come of age. That spring he visited the Rivington Street Settlement House, where she was doing volunteer work, and the children asked if he was her "feller." On June 21 there was this entry in Franklin's diary: "Eleanor at Hyde Park. All dine at Roger's and play blind man's bluff." In a game such as blindman's bluff, there were opportunities for physical contact between a young man and a young woman that were otherwise condemned by society. In July, at another Hyde Park house party attended by Eleanor and her maid, there was sailing, and a hay ride, and a cliff walk along the river, all good opportunities for increased intimacy. Franklin went to Europe on July 24, but invited Eleanor to Campobello at the end of August. On her last day there they read Stevenson's Christmas sermon together, and had a short sail in the afternoon before he took her to the train for Tivoli.

On September 24, Eleanor was again at Hyde Park, and they took a long ride through the woods. Franklin went to Groton to see how her brother, Hall, was doing, taking the time in spite of pressing duties bringing out his first edition of the *Crimson*.

Eleanor knew that Franklin was seeing other girls at Campobello and at various house parties, and when he sent her a "token from the sea," perhaps a seashell, she wrote on October 3 that he should have sent it to someone else. But at the same time she asked him to come and see her later that month. A few days later she wrote that his choice of graduate school over law school was wise and that *"Of course* you are going to get an A.M." (he never did get it). This letter she signed "Your Affectionate Cousin," a departure from her own standards that anything other than "Very sincerely yours" was an entirely inadmissible confession of feelings.

It was clear that romantic feelings were intruding in this cousinly relationship. Eleanor was offended when he took too long to reply to her letters. Despite busy social schedules, they managed to see each other about every other weekend. On November 14, they had lunch together at Sherry's in New York and then went up to spend Sunday on the Hudson River estate of ex-New York Governor Levi P. Morton. Franklin in his next letter sent her a poem, which Eleanor liked, commenting on November 18: ". . . but what ideals you have to live up to. I like 'fear nothing, be faithful unto death' but I must say I wonder how many of the poor mortals could act up to that."

The following weekend was the most important one of the year, the Harvard-Yale game, to which Franklin invited Eleanor. On the morning of November 21 they took a walk up Beacon Hill, and in the afternoon Franklin led the cheering during the game, which Harvard lost 16 to 0. Then he showed her his room and saw her off to Groton, where she was visiting her brother.

The next morning, November 22, Franklin followed her to Groton, arriving just in time for church. They had lunch with his mother's sister, Aunt Cassie. And then came the "never to be forgotten walk to the river with my darling" during which he proposed and she accepted.

There were things about Franklin that reminded Eleanor of her great and lasting love, her father—his easy charm, his ability to put her at ease and make her laugh, his thoughtfulness, as when he had gone to Groton to see her brother. She could be "Little Nell" again, and started signing some of her letters to him that way. Like her father, Franklin had gone to Europe as a boy and learned French and German. But he did not have her father's weaknesses. He was a prominent member of his Harvard class, hard working and responsible, who did not have an overpowering older brother to contend with.

But what, she wondered, did he see in her? Franklin was emotionally cautious, he had always found the love he needed within the family circle. The idea of marrying inside the larger circle of his extended family appealed to him. Eleanor's father had been his godfather, she was someone his mother could not dismiss as "horrid," and he would be closing the gap between the Hyde Park and Oyster Bay branches. She was also Teddy's favorite niece, and Franklin was eager for opportunities to increase his acquaintance with the president. Who knows what ambitions were already turning in his mind? His admiration for Cousin Teddy was such that a marriage bringing him into his orbit would be for that reason alone a success. Marrying Eleanor was a political decision, one his mother would accept that brought him closer to his role model. These were practical advantages, aside from the mutual attraction of the two young people, the quickening heartbeats and sighs of longing that could be diagnosed as love.

Love was there, even though (or because) Franklin and Eleanor were emotional opposites. The security of Franklin's upbringing had given him a strong sense of his identity and worth, a sense that nothing was beyond his reach. The price of this self-confidence and breadth of vision was a kind of emotional shallowness. He had not suffered, he had not had to make painful transactions of the heart to go on living. He took parental love for granted, never having been deprived of it.

But Eleanor, orphaned at ten, had gone through fire. All her life she would be drawn to those who had had painful childhoods—the first thing that drew her to the Associated Press correspondent Lorena Hickok was that she had been savagely beaten by her father. Eleanor was an emotionally wounded young woman, who to make her grief bearable invented the elaborate pretense of a noble father whose memory she kept alive. Franklin cannot have understood that by marrying Eleanor he was plunging into deeper emotional waters than any he had known. Her need for love was all the greater for her having lost her parents. She had the orphan mentality, which means never being sure of what you have, and always fearing that you are going to lose it.

She greeted the world from a base of insecurity, from which she made cautious sorties, testing the ground with every step. Franklin was never afraid to try, and usually thought he would succeed. She had made self-depreciation into a defense—if what you think about yourself is worse than what others think about you, you will not be hurt. She looked for reasons to be in the wrong, and for evidence of her own incompetence. Franklin was pleased with himself, sure of his skills, with a pride in success that bordered on smugness. He had always been told how wonderful he was. Franklin was the property owner who had a natural claim to whatever his eye took in. Eleanor was not sure she owned the space her body occupied. In terms of their temperaments, it was a marriage between a squire and a squatter.

In later years, after her marriage had failed, she wrote that "I know now that it was years later before I understood what being in love or what loving really meant." But that was the view of hindsight, and for the moment she loved with romantic intensity, sending Franklin two days after he had proposed a poem with the lines

> "Unless you can swear, *'For life, for death!'*
> Oh, fear to call it loving!"

"I wondered if it meant 'for life, for death' to you at first," she added, "but I know it does now. I do not know what to write. I cannot write what I want. I can only wait and long for Sunday when I shall tell you all I feel I cannot write."

Franklin in the meantime had told his mother, who wrote in her diary: "Franklin gave me quite a startling announcement." On Sunday, November 29, in New York he saw Eleanor and met her cousin, Mrs. Parish. Instead of going back to Cambridge on Monday he stayed in the city so he could introduce Eleanor to his mother. The meeting took place on the morning of Tuesday, December 1. Sara's diary entry read: "Franklin and I went out and soon he went to 76th street and brought Eleanor down to see me. I had a long talk with the dear child."

Franklin went back to Cambridge and Eleanor wrote him on the same day: "I love you dearest and I hope that I shall always prove worthy of the love which you have given me. I have never known before what it was like to be absolutely happy, nor have I ever longed for just the glimpse of a pair of eyes. . . . It seemed like a bad dream your having to go this morning and I wanted so to call you back. . . ."

During her "long talk with the dear child," Sara had expressed reservations. They were so young—Franklin twenty-one and Eleanor nineteen—wouldn't it be better to think it over? Her father Warren Delano had married at thirty-three, when he was settled in his profession and able to raise a family.

Sara meant to use every ounce of her authority to regulate the pace of her son's attachment. Perhaps if she could slow things down, and create obstacles, the marriage might be prevented. She objected to Franklin and Eleanor spending Sunday in New York. If they were seen together in church, it would be a serious breach of etiquette. She also wrote Eleanor that she was planning to take a house in Boston for the winter, and did not want Franklin to come to New York during that time, although Eleanor would be invited to stay once or twice.

To Eleanor it was like one of those tragedies by Corneille she had listened to at Allenswood. Should Franklin follow the inclinations of his heart or do his duty by obeying his mother? Not being in a strong enough position to disagree with Sara, Eleanor was ready to submit. But not Franklin, whom twenty years of dealing with his mother had made a natural tactician. He wrote Sara that he would come to New York, go with Eleanor to a small uptown church where no one knew them, and spend the rest of the day in the house. Of course he would go to Hyde Park if she insisted, knowing that by insisting she would appear unreasonable, but it seemed a little hard and unnecessary not to let them have one of their first Sundays together. Sara gave in.

Another way Franklin got around his mother was to present her with a fait accompli. On January 12, 1904, he wrote her that, having found himself nothing to do the previous Saturday, he had taken the 10:00 A.M. train to

New York and spent a quiet evening with Eleanor. On Sunday they had gone to church and lunched at the Parishes', and he had hopped on the 3:00 P.M. back to Cambridge, arriving at 10, just in time to write his editorial. "I positively couldn't help it," he wrote. "There was nothing to keep me here and I knew I should be in a much better humor for a short trip to N.Y.!"

The situation was slipping out of Sara's grasp. New tactics were required. She decided to take Franklin and Jake Brown on a five-week Caribbean cruise. That would at least give him a change of scene and take his mind off Eleanor.

"F. is tired and blue," Sara noted in her diary on February 6, the day of departure of the *Prinzessin Victoria Luise.* "I wonder if you know how I hated to let you go on Friday night, five weeks seems a long time and judging by the past two days they will be interminable," Eleanor wrote.

While Eleanor pined, Franklin had a jolly time. There were ports of call, and often a dance to amuse the passengers, to which young local women were invited, eager to meet the kind of Americans who could afford a cruise. At Trinidad there was a *bal costumé.* At some other port of call, Franklin had a flirtation with a French lady of thirty, to the great annoyance of his mother. He was pleased both by the lady's attentions and his mother's annoyance. At Caracas, he went to hear Caruso, who had made his debut nine years earlier. The cruise ended in Nassau, and on March 6 they reached Miami, where Sara complained that "crowds of overdressed vulgar people throng the hotel."

Sara made one last try to delay her son's marriage, going to see Joseph Choate, the American ambassador in London, who was in Washington for consultations, and asking him to take Franklin as his secretary. But he already had a secretary, and in any case Franklin was too young for the job.

Back at Hyde Park, putting away Franklin's stamp albums and fussing over them and placing the new volumes of *Punch* in their proper rows Sara realized that resistance was futile. The situation had to be accepted. Her son would soon be married. Eleanor would be her daughter-in-law, and from now on she would be the one taking trips with Franklin. She wondered whether she would ever take a trip with her dear boy again. "I must try to be unselfish and of course dear child I do rejoice in your happiness, and shall not put any stones or straws ever in the way of it," she wrote Franklin on black-bordered stationery in remembrance of her husband, which now seemed to be mourning the loss of her son. She was reassured by Eleanor's deference, by her willingness to share Franklin and to include her as much as possible.

Their engagement was announced in early December, but the news had got out lo. ̤ before, and congratulatory letters started arriving in July, many of them informing Franklin that he had chosen the very best. One of his Fly Club fellows wrote that "I didn't know Miss Roosevelt would have a Crazy Kermit," which had been his club nickname. A Harvard classmate wrote that "I suppose you think yourself fairly good size now that you are engaged to one of the most attractive girls in the bay. As a matter of fact I am twice the man you are and if we had had a week or so more at Isleboro last summer it would have gone hard with you old top." Franklin and some Harvard friends had appeared that summer at Isleboro in Dark Harbor, Maine, where Eleanor was staying. Since Eleanor had to pretend that there was nothing between herself and Franklin, some of the other young men expressed interest.

There were some broken hearts among the young women Franklin had flirted with. One of these he learned of only a year before his death, in 1944, when the girl's mother, Mrs. C. A. Lyman, sent him the following letter: "I have long wished to write to you to exonerate my daughter Minna [?] Lyman Housewell. To my surprise last winter she said she used to be crazy about you. One day she went to a tea at Harvard, on her return she said she was going to bed, did not wish to be disturbed or have any dinner. A few days afterwards she said that Walter Bradley who was at the tea had told her of your engagement. She did not marry for many years. When Walter Housewell asked her she refused him. . . . She said she did not know what was the matter with her, there was something that made her say no the first time. I may be mistaken, but I thought you cared for her. . . ."

The great man himself, Cousin Teddy, blessed the match, telling Franklin that he was as fond of Eleanor as if she had been his daughter, and that no other success in life, not even the presidency, compared with the love that never buried lover and sweetheart in man and wife. No one thought it was wrong for cousins to marry. Being five times removed, they had in common only one thirty-second of their genetic pool.

By this time Franklin had started at Columbia Law School, choosing it over Harvard so he could be in New York, near Eleanor. From Tivoli, she wrote: "I am anxious to hear about the first day, and whether you found any old acquaintances or had only Jew Gentlemen to work with." Eleanor at that time shared the anti-Semitism of her class.

The wedding was set for March 17, 1905, a date that suited Theodore Roosevelt, who agreed to give the bride away. There were several dates on which Cousin Teddy was busy, one of them being March 4, the day of his inauguration, for he had defeated Judge Alton Parker by 2.5 million votes, one of them Franklin's.

The wedding took place at the adjoining homes of Eleanor's cousin, Mrs. Henry Parish, Jr., and her mother, Mrs. E. Livingston Ludlow, on East 76th Street. Franklin designed stickpins for his ushers, three feathers set with diamonds, from the family crest. Endicott Peabody came down from Groton to officiate, Lathrop Brown was best man, and the bride's uncle gave her away, commenting afterward that "there's nothing like keeping the name in the family." In retrospect, it was an extraordinary moment, unique in the nation's history—one who was president transmitting not only his niece but, as it might seem, the secret of high office, or an eventual dynastic succession, to one who would be president. An exchange of vows, a ring placed on a finger, the bride kissed by both men, and the transmission was complete.

Among the messages, there was a one-word cable from Mlle Souvestre: "*Bonheur.*" Two days later she died. Franklin would never meet the woman who, more than anyone else, had formed his wife's character.

Sara seemed genuinely pleased. The day after the wedding she wrote the bride and groom in Hyde Park, where they were spending a week, that it was a delight to think of them there, where her own great happiness had begun. "You have a real spring day and I can just see the sun up there and feel how you two are resting and reveling in your quiet time together.... Everyone says it was the most perfect wedding so simple and yet so elegant and so refined.... The dearest and sweetest young couple in the world.... Eleanor dear you were a perfect bride and I was very proud of both my dear children." As a hint of things to come, for over the years she would pay a lot of bills, Sara promised to reimburse them for the admission to the riding club.

They were due to leave on a three-and-a-half-month European honeymoon, but Franklin was stuck in New York with law school exams. Considering the circumstances, it was not surprising that he flunked two courses, Contracts and Pleading. Eleanor was kept busy listing the more than three hundred wedding presents in a ledger, and writing thank-you notes.

On June 6, they left on the *Oceanic,* settling into cabin 22 on the upper deck, which was crowded with bon voyage baskets. In the next three months, they would examine England, France, Italy, Germany, and each other, for they had spent little time alone. As pleasant as the trip seemed, it was laden with anxieties. Eleanor had gone from a girls' boarding school where men were a proscribed subject into marriage, with only two chaperoned years in between. She came to the marriage bed with a rare degree of ignorance, even for those times. In addition, she felt that anything to do with the body or with sex was shameful. She was shocked by the women's bathing suits in Venice: "their upper garments could not be called a skirt, it was hardly a frill!" When her daughter Anna was three, Eleanor suspected her of masturbating, and subjected her to harsh preventive measures—her hands were tied above her head to the top bars of her crib when she went to bed. The little girl then graduated to a medieval torture device, aluminum mittens with air-holes and cloth bands to make them firm about the wrist. Nothing was said about it. It was one of those subjects that could not be discussed. Given her background and Puritan inclinations, it is not surprising that Eleanor fell back on the Victorian concept of sex as a duty. As she later told her daughter, it was not an enjoyable one.

As for Franklin, he may have had a fling with Alice Sohier, and flirted with one of the Cholmeley girls, but he was an ardent twenty-three-year-old rather than a man with experience of women. There came from him no indication of how the sexual side of marriage was progressing, nothing comparable to Churchill's letter to his mother-in-law on *his* honeymoon: "I find love-making a serious and delightful occupation." There were signs that Franklin was finding it an anxious-making occupation. One night aboard the *Oceanic* he started to sleepwalk. Walking away from the bedroom and his bride of less than three months in the middle of the night indicated a need to escape that was hardly auspicious. At Eleanor's suggestion, he returned quietly to bed. Then, in northern Scotland, where they were staying with friends, Eleanor was awakened by wild shrieks from the neighboring bed. Pointing at the ceiling, Franklin asked with irritation: "Don't you see the revolving beam?" She assured him that there was no beam and kept him from rising and awakening the household. The next morning, asked whether he remembered his dream, he said he remembered being very annoyed with her because she insisted on remaining in the path of the beam, which was threatening to fall on them. This dream of immediate physical menace may also have been sexual in origin.

There were other sleepwalking episodes in the early years of their marriage. Once Eleanor woke up to find Franklin standing at the foot of the bed, turning an imaginary crank as hard as he could and saying "The damn thing won't start." "Franklin, if you get into the car I'll help you start it," Eleanor said. Whereupon he got back into bed and held an imaginary steering wheel while she had to pretend to do the cranking. Finally he went back to sleep, and the next morning he remembered nothing about it. Another time she woke up and found him standing on a chair by the window, reaching upward with both hands. "Franklin, what are you doing?" Eleanor asked. "Leave me alone, can't you see I'm trying to get a book down?" he replied. "Why can't you get it down in the morning, dear?" "No, I want it now." "It will be much better if you get it in the morning," Eleanor persisted, at which point he turned around and angrily asked, "Why is it, when there is something I want to do, you always tell me that I can do it another time?" Eventually he came back to bed, mumbling and muttering to himself that he was never allowed to do what he wanted to do.

All this sounds rather charming and humorous, but in fact somnambulism is a psychological disorder taken seriously enough in the armed forces so that a sleepwalker is classified 4F. Studies done on sleepwalking indicate that it is an expression of emotional conflicts that are allowed to surface because a psychic barrier is lowered in sleep. But instead of staying in bed and working out the conflict in dreams, the sleepwalker acts them out in a trancelike state. One study was done by three Navy psychiatrists on fourteen cadets at the Naval School of Aviation Medicine who had been referred for psychiatric evaluation. The sleepwalking episodes, it was found, had often begun in response to stress—the divorce of parents, a change of school, being placed in an orphanage. The personality profiles of the cadets showed that many had protective and domineering mothers and an inadequate identification with a male figure.

Somnambulism was seen as a "psychopathological entity," a form of dissociation related to hysterical psychic symptoms. It was an acting out of unconscious wishes and impulses through locomotion rather than dream symbolism. It was like a hypnotic trance in that the sleepwalker was suggestible, he could answer questions and carry out orders.

It is not suggested that on the basis of a single study involving fourteen naval cadets an analogy should be made between these findings and the sleepwalking of the newly married Franklin Roosevelt. Psychiatric opinion is in fact divided as to whether somnambulism is an illness or simply an inconvenient form of behavior. But these episodes afford a rare glimpse behind FDR's facade of equanimity. He always seemed so controlled, so unflappable, so much a master of the situation. But in his repeated sleepwalking incidents, he revealed an odd compulsive manner, as if prey to secret anxieties and dimly perceived fears, that provides a clue to the inner turmoil he covered up so well.

For young couples who know one another only slightly, honeymoons are bound to be periods of mutual divulgence. As Eleanor discovered that her night's sleep might be interrupted by Franklin on the prowl, Franklin saw Eleanor struggling with her sense of inadequacy, afraid she would be seasick when he was such a good sailor, feeling shabby in her old black dress next to wonderfully dressed ladies, worrying that the caretaker at the hotel in Augsburg did not like her. Other sides of her character that came out during the trip were a nascent social conscience, as when she felt sorry for the steerage passengers, and exacting standards. The Royal Academy was "interesting as far as the Sargents went, but seemed to have a good deal of trash also." The Cholmeley girls had that "English artificial look." English women in general "look like frumps even when they're not," and "it is quite out of date over here to appear with your own face or hair." In Venice, Eleanor wrote Sara, Franklin had taken "a cunning photograph of a number of little naked babies in swimming at the mouth of the canal but I don't think it can go in our book!" Even the nudity of babies was improper. She was reading a novel by Anatole France "but he occasionally disgusts me so that I have to stop." Eleanor displayed a curious combination of traits, being on the one hand unsure of herself and on the other prim and superior in her judgments of others.

Franklin shared her priggishness. At the Hotel Albruck, he referred to the dining room with its German guests as "four long pigsties where the strange assortment of mortals (swine are mortal, *n'est-ce pas*) consume victuals." This was the arrogant Roosevelt tone that he had used before with his parents. The arrogance extended to compatriots. How comical and vulgar fellow Americans were when traveling abroad! At St. Blasien, they were much amused by an American couple (he of recent German vintage) who were trying to impress an English couple with their wealth: "After explaining that in America there was no such thing as a season for eatables, that strawberries were much better in January than in June and that of course the price was no consideration, they proceeded to discuss the government of the coun try and finally the negro question while Franklin and I pretended to do accounts and in reality nearly expired with suppressed laughter!"

For both of them, the trip awakened old memories. In Venice, Franklin took her in a gondola, as her dear father had, and the gondolier, charmed by her sweetness, gave her a volume of poems by the sixteenth-century bard Torquato Tasso. At St. Blasien they were indignant over German regulations, from which Franklin had suffered as a boy on his bicycle trip with his tutor. He was not even allowed to light a cigarette on the piazza after dinner, and when they saw the notice in the hotel that said *Türe Leise Zumachen* (close the door quietly), they made a point of slamming all the doors.

Coming home in the second week of September 1905, Eleanor was seasick every day. She worried that she was not a good sailor, but the feeling of nausea remained after the ship landed. Consulting a doctor, she learned she was pregnant. During the next five years, a period for Franklin of indifferently practicing law while waiting for his true calling, Eleanor had four children.

Anna's birth was difficult, and one of the consequences of carrying a ten-pound baby was a case of hemorrhoids serious enough to require surgery, which was performed at home by Dr. Albert N. Ely, who almost lost his patient by giving her too much ether. "Is she gone?" he asked. "Can you feel her pulse?"

Home was a gift from Sara, awaiting them when they returned from their honeymoon, furnished and equipped with three servants. It was at 125 East 36th Street, three blocks from her own house at 200 Madison. Sara may have been a meddler, but she was a *useful* meddler who allowed the young couple to live beyond their means, for Franklin was still going to law school—he had about $5,000 a year from a trust fund, and Eleanor had $7,500 a year, and Sara was the budget director, making up the deficits. She had no husband or absorbing activity; her time and money were at the service of her son and daughter-in-law and grandchildren.

Eleanor was grateful. It was so nice to come home and find that everything was ready. When Anna was born, she had a nurse, the short and stocky Blanche Spring. Eleanor did not have to do any cooking or cleaning, or take care of babies except on the nurse's day off. She gave up her social work because Sara told her it was risky to bring the diseases of the slums into her household.

Franklin's record at law school was unexceptional. His grades ranged from B to F, and his record contains a notation that in his first year he had seventy-three absences, forty-five of them excused on account of illness, and in his second year he had thirty-five, ten excused. He was eligible to complete the requirements for the LL.B. degree, but did not bother, although he passed his bar exam in the spring of 1907.

In June he was offered a job as an unpaid law clerk by the prestigious firm of Carter, Ledyard, and Milburn, 54 Wall Street, which dealt mainly in corporate and admiralty law. Edmund L. Baylies, the admiralty expert, wrote Franklin on June 10 that "the arrangements with you will be the same as we usually make in such cases, that is to say, you will come to us the first year without salary, and after you have been with us for a year we would expect, if you remain, to pay you a salary which, however, at the outset would necessarily be rather small." Clearly, he was expected to feel grateful to be allowed to work for nothing.

The summer of 1907 was spent in Campobello, without Sara, who may have decided that the young people needed some time to themselves and embarked for Europe, complaining that the passenger list was uninteresting.

Eleanor was pregnant again, she was so enormous she was sure it would be twins. It was a very active infant (or infants!) whom she was carrying very differently from Anna, very low down, and she was afraid she looked worse than she did the last time. She warned Sara not to buy her any pretty things in Paris, for she would not be "a graceful person" when Sara came back.

Carter, Ledyard, and Milburn specialized at that time in finding ways around the antitrust measures of the Theodore Roosevelt administration. Senior partner John G. Milburn was a counsel for Standard Oil of New Jersey in the antitrust suit that in 1911 dissolved the combine on paper but in reality kept it intact. Senior partner Lewis C. Ledyard performed the same highly paid service in the antitrust suit that ended in the apparent dissolution of the American Tobacco Company in 1911.

Franklin was far removed from these important cases. Like his father when he had first started with Silliman and was sent to Washington to deliver papers to Sam Houston, he ran errands. He had gone to Groton and Harvard and had a famous name and was in the social register, but now he walked around in the rain in his Brooks Brothers suits collecting witnesses, and entered the records of papers served and received in a large black ledger. "When I was a full-fledged lawyer," he would recall, ". . . I went to a big law office in New York, and somebody the day after I got there said, 'Go up and answer the calendar call in the Supreme Court tomorrow morning. We have such and such a case on.' I had never been in a court of law in my life, and yet I was a full-fledged lawyer. Perhaps I was lucky not to have been in a court before that. Then the next day somebody gave me a deed of transfer of some land. He said, 'Take it up to the County Clerk's office.' I had never been in a county clerk's office. . . . And there I was . . . a member of a so-called learned profession."

Franklin did the work with his customary good nature, but from the start he saw Carter, Ledyard, and Milburn as a place to escape from rather than rise in, and wrote doggerel about the partners:

> "Everyone loafs but Milburn
> He's at work all day.
> Gets down town at sunrise
> Gee! He earns his pay!"

His true feelings were expressed to another junior member who left the firm, John Lytle, to whom he wrote on October 6, 1913: "Apparently the noble firm of C.L. and M. have fallen on their feet as usual, for most of their millionaire clients have passed away within the last year or two and the pickings must be fat, indeed! All the same, confidentially, I never regret the determination to leave them and try some other line of attack. Do you?"

The legal profession as a whole he looked upon with detached amusement, as in his well-known mock self-advertisement: "I beg to call your attention to my unexcelled facilities for carrying on every description of legal business. Unpaid bills a specialty. [That much was true.] Briefs on the liquor question furnished free to ladies. [A reference to Eleanor's, and to his mother's, horror of drinking.] Race suicides cheerfully prosecuted. [A reference to Theodore Roosevelt's campaign against birth control.] Small dogs chloroformed without charge. [A reference to Sara's spitz, Toutou.] Babies raised under advice of expert grandmother etc. etc. etc."

After a year, Franklin started earning a salary, and he was eventually promoted to the admiralty division under Edmund Baylies, where he defended clients against petty claims. In 1909, for instance, he defended the Seamen's Institute against an ambulance chaser who had a client claiming he had been shot by the institute watchman.

His mind, however, was on bigger things, according to Grenville Clark, a Harvard classmate of Franklin's, who reported to the *Harvard Alumni Bulletin* of April 27, 1945, as follows:

"In 1907, when Franklin Roosevelt was 25, I happened to be a fellow clerk in the New York law office of Carter, Ledyard and Milburn. This was before the days of the 'law factories.' We were a small group with desks together in one large room, and in our leisure hours naturally fell into discussions of our hopes and ambitions. I remember him saying with engaging frankness that he wasn't going to practice law forever, that he intended to run for office at the first opportunity, and that he wanted to be and thought he had a real chance to be President. I remember that he described very accurately the steps which he thought could lead to this goal. They were: first, a seat in the State Assembly, then an appointment as Assistant Secretary of the Navy . . . and finally the Governorship of New York. 'Anyone who is governor of New York has a good chance to be President with any luck' are about his words that stick in my memory. . . . The only departure was in the first step of all. His initial office was as State Senator instead of Assemblyman. . . . I do not recall that even then, in 1907, any of us deprecated his ambition or even smiled at it as we might perhaps have done. It seemed proper and sincere and moreover, as he put it, entirely reasonable. The late President's career, should, therefore, I suggest, be judged against this background, as that of a man who not only made a profession of politics and government for thirty-five years (the interludes were accidental and short), but who adopted that profession deliberately and constantly enjoyed it, just as one enjoys a game that one has always liked and learned to play well."

The steps leading to the goal were those that his cousin Teddy had taken—New York State assemblyman, assistant secretary of the Navy, governor of New York, and president. But Teddy had also been a war hero, which had helped him bridge the gap between the second and third steps. Franklin identified with his cousin and wanted to follow his career, step by step. But Teddy had not hesitated to join the New York City Republican organization, even though it was corrupt and run by bosses, and was elected to the assembly from New York's twenty-first district. Franklin, however, had been anti-Tammany ever since hearing a talk about the bosses at Groton, and disliked the city in any case, seeing himself as an upstate rural Democrat who would represent farmers and other upstanding citizens rather than the urban dregs. Even though he worked in the city and lived in the city, he took no part in city politics but waited for his chance in Hyde Park.

In the meantime life went on for the young couple, pleasant and uneventful, with weekends in Hyde Park and summers in Campobello. Sara was always in the background, signing checks and dispensing advice. "Be careful," she wrote in September 1907, "one often hears of children beginning to walk and to use up their strength and it leads to trouble with the limbs and even to appendicitis."

For Christmas 1905 Sara had given them a drawing of a five-story house, complete with smoke curling from the chimney, adding "number and street not quite decided." The house turned out to be the symbol of their interlocking lives, for it was in fact two adjoining houses at 47 and 49 East 65th Street, connected so that Sara could move in and out of Franklin's and Eleanor's lives, with two dining rooms and two drawing rooms that could be joined with the sliding of some panels.

They moved in the fall of 1908. Eleanor had to pretend to be humbly grateful while resenting having to live in a house where her mother-in-law might appear at any moment of the day or night. It was still "Yes, Mama" and "No, Mama," although inside she was seething. Not until many years later did a member of the family dare to confront Sara about her habit of barging in unasked. Betsy Cushing, who had married Franklin's son James, was in her room calling Washington and saying "This is Mrs. James Roosevelt." Suddenly there was Sara standing before her and staring fiercely because of course *she* was Mrs. James Roosevelt. Betsy put down the phone and said, "I haven't invited you to come into my room," and Sara left.

Sara would have been surprised if someone had told her she was intrusive. She thought of herself as helpful. She gave dinners for Eleanor and Franklin on her side of the house. When the young people entertained, she arranged the flowers. She watched over Eleanor, who was pregnant for a third time. Franklin was out on the town, returning at 3:00 and 4:00 A.M., ostensibly from poker games at the Knickerbocker Club and Harvard Club dinners.

Franklin Jr. was born on March 18, 1909, the day after their fourth anniversary. But he had heart trouble, and the doctors were unable to help. On November 27 he died, at the age of seven months and nine days. It seemed to Eleanor that a tragic pattern was repeating itself: what you loved best was taken away from you.

"I was young and morbid," she later wrote, "and reproached myself bitterly for having done so little about the care of this baby. I felt he had been left too much to the nurse, and I knew too little about him, and that in some way I must be to blame. I even felt that I had not cared enough about him, and I made myself and all those around me most unhappy during that winter. I was even a little bitter against my poor young husband who occasionally tried to make me see how idiotically I was behaving."

To the outside world Eleanor was a model wife and mother. Her husband, however, found her mood swings and self-laceration baffling. His mother had given him the example of a woman who did not surrender to moods or self-doubt, and whose devotion was never in question. Taught by life that nothing is certain, Eleanor picked her way through the wreckage of her sorrows.

V

State Senate

... Observed his courtship to the common people
How he did seem to dive into their hearts
With humble and familiar courtesy ...

Shakespeare, *Henry V*

F RANKLIN wanted to enter politics, but not through the Tammany door. The trouble was that there was no such thing as a Democratic organization upstate. There were a few scattered groups with no state consciousness who confined their interest to local elections. Subservient to the Republicans, they were willing, in exchange for an occasional town supervisor or mayor, to refrain from any real effort for the state or national ticket, or even for assemblymen and state senators. Titular leadership was often in the hands of incompetent and demoralized party hacks. Their lack of success in election after election resulted in a spirit of complete discouragement—they did not feel they were part of a powerful and triumphant state organization, and they had lost so often they stopped trying.

In the land of the stone fence and Matthew Vassar's ale, that is to say Dutchess County, the situation was comparatively rosy. There was a Democratic mayor of Poughkeepsie, John K. Sague; a Democratic district attorney, John E. Mack; a Democratic sheriff, Robert Chanler; and a Democratic assemblyman for the district with Poughkeepsie as its hub, Robert's brother, Lewis Chanler. The Chanlers were Hudson River gentry whom the Democratic county chairman, Edward E. Perkins, also president of the First National Bank of Poughkeepsie, had lured into politics. One advantage of having affluent candidates was that they financed their own campaigns. One disadvantage was that they had so many other interests they got bored with politics.

Ed Perkins was always on the lookout for promising youngsters. One day toward the end of 1909, at a cattle fair in Poughkeepsie's Ruppert Park, Perkins ran into Thomas Jefferson Newbold, the Roosevelts' Hyde Park neighbor and the only Democrat to have won his district's State Senate seat since anyone could remember. Having both won livestock prizes, Perkins and Newbold were inclined to conviviality, and Newbold said: "Ed, there's that young Roosevelt of James's. Why don't you run him for supervisor?" "Mr. Newbold," Perkins said, "you know very well we never yet carried Hyde Park or North East. It would be money thrown away." "Well, keep Franklin in mind for something, anyway," Newbold said, "and don't tell his mother I suggested it." Sara was not eager to have Franklin associating with men who used bad language and wore loud clothes and had spittoons in their offices.

At about the same time Franklin was first mentioned as a possibility, John Mack went to see him in his New York law office with some papers for his mother to sign—Mack had a 100-acre farm in Clove Valley, where he had gained fame as a grower of peonies, and called himself "a Dutchess County farmer who does a little lawyering on the side." As district attorney, he vigorously prosecuted chicken thieves, there not being much crime in the county. Mack mentioned to Franklin that the Chanler boys were getting a bit tired of politics and might drop out of the 1910 election. Thinking that here before him was a splendid young man, Mack suggested that he come up and run for the Assembly in Lewis Chanler's place. Franklin thought that was a fine idea.

In the meantime, Lewis Chanler told Ed Perkins that he was bored with the Assembly and did not plan to run again. Perkins also thought of Franklin, and invited him one weekend when he was at Hyde Park to come along to a sale of high-grade Guernseys on the Reese place in Wappinger Falls. They could run down and pick up a couple of good ones. On the way home after inspecting the heifers, Perkins told Franklin that Lewis Chanler did not want to succeed himself. How would Franklin like to try? "I'd like to talk to my mother about it first," he said.

They rolled into Poughkeepsie and stopped in front of the bank where Perkins had the corner office. "Frank," he said, "the men that are looking out of that window are waiting for your answer. They won't like to hear that you had to ask your mother." "I'll take it," Franklin said.

When Lewis Chanler heard that an inexperienced youngster had been picked to succeed him, he changed his mind and decided to run. Disappointed, Franklin complained to Perkins, who said: "Frank, how would you like to look down on Lewis's flaxen curls from a balcony seat?"

"What do you mean?" Franklin asked.

"We'll make you state senator, with a larger district than he's got."

Franklin went to see John Mack, who told him that he had one chance out of five of being elected state senator in a district no Democrat had won in twenty-five years. Franklin asked how he could get the nomination. Mack told him he would be nominated by three committeemen, of which he was one. He was sure of one of the others and not quite sure of the third. "I'll take it," Franklin said without hesitation. He had not actively sought office, being inhibited by his mother's views and by the Boston-Harvard reflex that it was vulgar to be pushy. He subscribed to the "immaculate conception" theory of public office. You didn't go after it, you waited to be touched by an angel. But when the offer came, he jumped in.

The next scene is perhaps the most important one in Franklin's political career, comparable to the Russian czar's visit to Voltaire, when it dawned on the leader of that backward land that there was such a thing as the Enlightenment. It was Franklin's rite of passage from patrician to politician, which meant asking people who were your social inferiors to vote for you. It meant abolishing the natural distinction between squire and villager. It meant entering an arena where the privileges of birth could work against you. It meant being on familiar and friendly terms with every man who had a vote. It meant moving from the traditional master-servant order to a new and democratic order based on service, where the candidate was the voter's equal because he needed him. It meant moving from secure inherited advantages to a risky form of competition where your fate depended on mass appeal.

One of the three committeemen who held the key to Franklin's nomination was a Hyde Park housepainter named Thomas Leonard, who in August 1910 had been hired by Franklin's half brother Rosy to do some work on his house. At 3:00 P.M. on an August afternoon, Leonard was hard at it when he was interrupted by Rosy's housekeeper, who said, "There is a Mr. Franklin wants to see you." Leonard wondered who it was—he didn't know any Mr. Franklin. "All right, Mrs. Manning," he said, "I'll step out and see the gentleman." "Hello, Tom," Franklin said. "How do you do, Mr. Roosevelt," Leonard replied, a village employee, cap in hand, so to speak, before a member of the gentry. "No, call me Franklin," was the reply. "I'm going to call you Tom." With that phrase, he did something his father had been incapable of, placing himself on an equal footing with one of the villagers. He was paying obeisance to his new master, the voter, and serving notice that he was not to be considered as a squire (which, in fact, he wasn't, since his mother owned the property) but as a candidate. He had to court his brother's employee, one of the three men who would determine his future.

"I came to see you, in fact," Franklin went on. "I was advised by the county chairman, Mr. Perkins, to come to you. I want to enter politics, Tom, and he told me I'd have to see you."

"Now, Mr. Roosevelt," Leonard said, unable from long habit to call him by his first name, "he shouldn't have told you that. Perhaps what he wanted to tell you was that I could advance your interest politically, locally, being the committeeman? . . . I feel that the party would welcome you."

"Well, I'm ambitious to take an active interest in Democratic politics," Franklin said. "What advice would you give me?"

"Well, Mr. Roosevelt, we are having a town convention on next Wednesday night in the town hall in Hyde Park, and I think it would be fine if you could be there. Can you make it?"

"I'll be there, Tom," Franklin said. "I'll come up from New York."

It was not difficult for Franklin to expand his sense of belonging from the Hyde Park estate where he had been brought up to the county as a whole. He was eager to be liked, and fell quite naturally into shaking hands and talking about crops when John Mack took him to the policemen's clambake in Buckingham Woods. Mack thought he had made a definite hit.

It came as a matter of course at the Democratic convention in Poughkeepsie on October 6 that Franklin was nominated for state senator. There was only a month before the November 8 election, but the Democrats benefited from a series of disclosures about legislative graft in Albany. For years, the big New York insurance companies had been bribing committee chairmen and other key lawmakers in the Republican-controlled legislature with "firebug" funds to obtain favorable fire insurance bills. Nationally, the Republicans were also in trouble, for President William Howard Taft was unpopular.

Two delegates at the Poughkeepsie convention on October 6 drove home that afternoon to Matteawan, discussing the party's chances. One was Morgan Hoyt, owner of the Matteawan *Journal,* whose brother Ferd was running for the State Assembly. The other was James Forrestal, father of FDR's secretary of the Navy, who had been Matteawan postmaster under Grover Cleveland. They wondered what kind of candidate "that Roosevelt boy" would make. He had a pleasant personality, but they were skeptical about his chances. His opponent, John F. Schlosser of Fishkill Landing, a well-known lawyer with a nice turn of phrase, was a seasoned campaigner who had served one term in the State Senate and was president of the State Firemen's Association. He was popular in his district, which was made up of Putnam, Dutchess, and Columbia counties, an area of rolling farmland thirty miles wide and ninety miles long. Ed Perkins had a good organization in Dutchess, but in Putnam and Columbia they trailed badly. What chance would a twenty-eight-year-old who had never campaigned before have against Schlosser?

Franklin had the energy of youth. As the underdog, he decided that his only hope was to crisscross the district, holding as many meetings as possible. To do this he needed some form of quick transportation. With Morgan Hoyt, who was acting as unofficial campaign manager, he discussed getting an automobile. It might do more harm than good. You might have some accident on a dirt road and lose part of the farm vote. Farmers didn't like cars because they frightened the horses. A state law had been passed giving the right-of-way to horse-drawn vehicles. If a driver raised his whip, the car had to come to a complete stop and get off the road. Still, the only way to hold six or seven meetings a day was to have one.

Harry Hawkey, who sold and tuned pianos in western Connecticut, offered to rent them his red two-cylinder Maxwell for $20 a day. Franklin teamed up with Assembly candidate Ferdinand A. Hoyt and Richard E. Connell, candidate for the twenty-first U.S. congressional district. Connell was something of a laughingstock, having run often and always lost, but he knew the district. Together they chugged down country roads at twenty-two miles an hour, stopping and cutting the engine whenever they met a horse and team. The car had no top and no windshield, and they wore raincoats when it rained and dusters on dirt roads. They spoke at milk stations, grange halls, in village streets, they rang doorbells and shook hands, and they stopped to recuperate at cider mills with glasses of fresh cider.

Although he had spoken at Groton and Harvard, Franklin had never faced an audience of live voters before, and he was filled with trepidation. Watching him make his last speech in Poughkeepsie, Eleanor found him nervous and high-strung. He spoke slowly, with long pauses, hitting the theme of Republican bossism, and seemed terribly young, with his fair hair and gray-blue eyes and unlined face. At times, however, a set look of his jaw indicated that he was no cream puff.

Franklin learned from Dick Connell, who was quite a flamboyant speaker, with a set piece of patriotic oratory during which he waved a flag. He would rush up and down the stage at the big meetings, the tails of his Prince Albert coat flapping behind him, shouting, "The same old flag that waved at Lexington, the same old flag Sherman carried on his march to the sea. . . ." Franklin borrowed from Connell the habit of addressing the audience as "my friends."

He was an unknown quantity who could not be explained by his background. There was something else, which those who worked with him saw. Tom Pendell, a dairy farmer from Rock Tavern who was active in Democratic politics, had taken Franklin for a drive in his car one day during the campaign. When they approached a cedar gateway on the Roosevelt estate, Pendell started to jump out to open it, but Franklin said, "Sit still. You see that chain hanging down? Well, drive up and pull that chain." He did so and the gate swung back. "Now," said Franklin, "drive through and pull the other chain." The gate closed, and Pendell thought that Franklin looked as pleased as a boy with a new pair of boots. A moment later, however, he drove too close to a ditch and slid into it. "Well," Pendell said, "we'll have to walk over to the house and telephone for help." "Say, Tom," Franklin said, "I think we can get that car out ourselves—you jack up the rear wheels and we'll bring stones." About a hundred feet away there was a wall of big flat fieldstones. Pendell, who avoided manual labor when he could, busied himself with the jack, while Franklin lugged rocks as if he belonged to a chain gang. He moved enough stones to pave the ditch, while sweat covered his brow and dripped from his nose, and Pendell drove the car right out, thinking that it was a rare trait of human character to enjoy battling with and overcoming difficulties—such was life, and the winner took all. In this small incident the young Franklin Roosevelt was distilled—in his willingness to make the required effort, in his eagerness to take on a task undesirable to others, and in the satisfaction he derived from solving a problem.

Roosevelt may have been a household word, but Franklin was so little known to his opponents that on November 1 he received an appeal for funds from the Republican State Committeee chairman, Ezra P. Prentice, asking him to contribute $50 and warning that "Democratic success at this election . . . will inevitably give the vote of New York to the Democratic candidate for President in 1912. . . . It will enable the Democratic Party to re-district the Congressional Districts of this state so that for ten years 25 Democratic Congressmen will probably be elected in place of 12 as at present." (The state was about to be reapportioned after the census of 1910.)

When the results came in on November 8, it was a Republican rout. Dick Connell defeated Hamilton Fish, and Democrat John A. Dix won the governorship. The Democrats seized control of both houses in New York State, and the House of Representatives in Washington. In the twenty-sixth senatorial district of New York, a young man new to politics ended a quarter century of Republican rule. Franklin Roosevelt beat John Schlosser by 15,708 to 14,568, and carried Hyde Park by 406 to 258. On the day after the election, he wrote the Republican committee that he had used its appeal for funds "with great effect" in his campaign. On November 17, the Democratic State Committee wrote him, with gross hyperbole: "We had you scheduled as a winner."

In neighboring New Jersey, the 1910 election had brought in a reform governor, the Princeton professor, Woodrow Wilson. Joseph P. Guffey, who would one day serve as U.S. senator from Pennsylvania, and who had been one of Wilson's students, went to congratulate him, and as they chatted Wilson noted that several promising young Democrats had been brought into office. There was young Roosevelt, just elected to the New York State Senate. "Professor," Guffey said, "I thought the Roosevelts were all Republicans." "No," Wilson replied, "this one comes from the Democratic branch of the family. He'll bear watching. I think he has a political future."

"When I was beginning in the world and was nobody and nothing," wrote Samuel Johnson, "the joy of my life was to fire at all the established wits, and then everybody loved to hallow me on." The young rebel who breaks with party discipline and finds that the path of intransigent principle is also a shortcut to fame is a character often to be met in the lives of statesmen. Winston Churchill as a young member of Parliament made his reputation by attacking his own Tory party and joining the opposition Liberal party. As a freshman assemblyman, Theodore Roosevelt broke ranks and called for the investigation of a financial scandal involving highly placed Republicans. When "Big Tim" Sullivan, the Tammany stalwart who represented the Bowery in the Senate, heard that Teddy's cousin was going to be his colleague, he suggested that, having caught a Roosevelt, "we'd better take him down and drop him off the dock. The Roosevelts run true to form, and this kid is likely to do for us what the Colonel is going to do for the Republican Party, split it wide open."

Arriving in Albany on January 1, 1911, Franklin noted in a briefly kept diary: "We have rented the house of Mr. H. King Sturdee no. 248 State Street for four months at $400 a month. We moved James and Baby Elliott [born on September 23, 1910] here from New York on Wednesday last and after returning to Hyde Park brought up Anna with us yesterday, Mama accompanying us. This house seems palatial after New York, and it is a comfort to have only three stories instead of six."

It was indeed palatial, for most of the legislators, on salaries of $1,500 a year, lived at Keeler's Hotel, or the Kenmore, or the Tub, which had four floors of furnished rooms and a Turkish bath in the rear, commuting to their homes elsewhere in the state. By moving his family to Albany and taking a large house in the shadow of the state capitol, Franklin announced his intention of being a full-time senator.

He was already feeling rebellious. An important order of business was the election of a U.S. senator, for the term of the incumbent, Republican Chauncey M. Depew, was up on March 4. In most states, senators were still elected by the state legislatures, and the Democrats were sure to elect their man, since there were 114 Democrats out of the 50 senators and 150 assemblymen. The leading candidate was William F. Sheehan, known as "Blue-eyed Billy," a millionaire lawyer backed by Tammany who embodied the alliance between business interests and machine politics.

As counsel and director of a dozen public utility and railroad companies, Sheehan had organized a pool of utility contributions to Tammany's war chest in return for a promise of the senatorship. Half a dozen legislators, recipients of his largesse, were bubbling over with gratitude.

The other candidate, Edward M. Shepard of Brooklyn, counsel for the Pennsylvania Railroad, was for clean government in New York City and had no Tammany backing. In his January 1 diary entry, Franklin wrote that he was "without question the most competent to fill the position, but the Tammany crowd seems unable to forgive his occasional independence and Sheehan looks like their choice at this stage of the game. May the result prove that I am wrong! There is no question that the Democratic Party is on trial, and having been given the control of the government chiefly through up-State votes, cannot afford to surrender its control to the organization in New York City." The Senate contest would be a chance to challenge Tammany's control of the party.

On January 3, Franklin attended his first party caucus, which was instructive, if only he had been open to its lesson. Conducted by remote control by Tammany chief Charles F. Murphy, the caucus picked the Senate and Assembly majority leaders. Passing over senior Tammany men, Murphy reached down to his kindergarten and picked two able, respected, and reform-minded young legislators. Thirty-seven-year-old Alfred E. Smith, an assemblyman with an eighth-grade education, the son of an Irish mother and an Italian-German father (in spite of his name, which had doubtless been abbreviated by an immigration inspector from Smettina or somesuch), who had grown up poor on the East Side docks, was made majority leader of the Assembly. Thirty-three-year-old Robert F. Wagner, the son of a Wiesbaden printer, with whom he had landed at Castle Garden in 1886 at the age of nine, not speaking a word of English, was president pro tem of the Senate. The melting pot was at full boil. Franklin noted in his diary that Wagner would be "fairly good. He has good intentions; the only obstacle is the pressure of his own machine."

On January 4, Franklin arrived at the Senate chamber for the opening day of the legislative session, which normally lasted from January to April, presented his certificate of election to the presiding officer, took his oath of office, made his way up the carpeted aisle, and folded his six feet into a big leather chair behind a desk marked in white with the number of his district, 26.

The Democratic caucus to choose a candidate for U.S. senator was scheduled for January 16, and in the interval Franklin learned a few things about how it would be handled. The majority was binding on all those who attended. In other words, if Franklin went to the caucus and voted for Shepard, but Sheehan won, he was bound to vote for Sheehan in the joint session that would pick a senator. Since there were 114 Democrats, a majority in the caucus was 58, and since Murphy controlled that many votes and more, he had the power to appoint a senator.

Franklin found that he was not alone in his anti-Sheehan views. Edmund R. Terry of Brooklyn was gathering the pro-Shepard forces in the Assembly. When Franklin joined this group, Terry explained how by staying out of the caucus they could stop Sheehan.

At 9:00 P.M. on January 16, Sheehan went into the caucus so sure of his chances that he had already rented a house in Washington. Some legislators seemed to be absent, and the whips were sent to find them. In the meantime, the Republicans in their caucus named the incumbent, Chauncey Depew. At ten, the Democratic caucus was called to order, and the result was sixty-two votes for Sheehan, twenty-two for Shepard, and seven for another candidate named Merrick. All of those attending, that is ninety-one, were bound to Sheehan, but they were ten short of a majority in both houses.

Of the twenty-three missing Democratic legislators, twenty insurgents including Franklin were with Ed Terry in a hotel room preparing a manifesto for the next day's newspapers. The signers had refused to attend because "they believed the votes of those who represented the people should not be smothered . . . and that any majority secured for any candidate should be credited to the representatives in the Legislature and not someone outside the body."

In the joint session of the legislature that met on the morning of January 17, Sheehan had ninety-one votes; the eighty-six Republicans voted for Depew; the insurgents held the balance. In the Poughkeepsie *News-Press,* it was Franklin who made the headlines: "Sheehan Named: Roosevelt Bolts." He was identified as the leader and spokesman of the group. Even though he was one of the youngest and least experienced, he lived in a house where meetings could be held. In addition, he was not averse to being interviewed. In a profile in the magazine section of the January 22 Sunday *New York Times,* he was quoted as saying "There is nothing I love as much as a good fight. I never had as much fun in my life as I am having right now."

Franklin seemed to be treating the whole business as he would an undergraduate prank, with a light heart, but more experienced politicians shook their heads and wondered. What had happened to party discipline? Wasn't the main thing to elect a Democratic senator, with a presidential election coming up in two years? There was no quicker end to a promising career than to make an enemy of the Tammany boss. What were they, green kids, publicity seekers? What was so bad about Sheehan, how was he any different from Shepard, who also represented business interests—the Pennsylvania Railroad—and who originally had been supported by Boss McCooey of Brooklyn. Sheehan was Irish Catholic, and Shepard was a Protestant Yankee who had surface gentility and belonged to the right clubs.

Al Smith wrote Franklin off as a "damned fool," the sort of fellow who went chasing after a peripheral issue, missing the main point. He was tired of hearing about the corrupt city versus rustic virtues and idyllic villages where everybody knew his neighbor. Small-town farmers and merchants were no less corrupt than city dwellers, they had eyes and ears and hands like everybody else, and occasionally their hands were found in the till.

Franklin had joined the insurgents because, as an upstate Democrat, he did not want to be dictated to by the city machine, and also because he liked the attention-getting potential of insurgency. The insurgents would hold out for ten weeks, paralyzing the legislature, which met daily, cast a futile ballot for U.S. senator, and adjourned. But his antimachine stand made him a national figure, only weeks after taking office.

He was generally viewed as a hero, a David who had stood up to the big-city Goliath. In fact, he had no understanding whatever of the Tammany phenomenon. The battle over Sheehan was an episode of the deeper conflict between the patrician and the ethnic, between the old landed families who made America and the new immigrants who had won a share of political power.

Franklin saw Tammany as synonymous with corruption and bad government at a time when, under the leadership of Charles F. Murphy, the Tammany Tiger was in fact changing its stripes. Murphy had a cleansing influence, giving the political club that he ruled from 1902 until his death in 1924 an almost scrubbed appearance. The son of an Irish tenant farmer, he saved enough money driving a Blue Line horsecar to open a saloon and then three more, and, rising through Tammany ranks, became the most powerful of New York State's sixty-two Democratic leaders. He didn't say much—when you asked him the time he would pull out his watch for you to see—but he could and did make mayors and governors.

In the first decade of the new century, reform was in the air, and Murphy realized that Tammany had to move with the times. The only way not to be outflanked by citizens' groups was to adopt their programs. Reform was too serious a business to be left to the reformer, who in the words of Mr. Dooley was "a man who has to blow his nose ivry time he thinks iv the troubles iv others." Reform also happened to correspond to Murphy's political credo, a market-basket liberalism that supported practical measures to help the masses.

Tammany under Murphy became a potent force for implementing the new liberalism. The machine supported a Republican governor, Charles Evans Hughes, on the creation of a Public Utilities Commission. It supported laws regulating insurance, banking, and tenement housing. It backed laws for old-age pensions, workmen's compensation, and five-cent fares. In taking the position that government should play a more positive part in social welfare legislation and economic reform, Tammany was the daddy of the New Deal.

Murphy got rid of the looters who gave Tammany a bad name and promoted able men who would improve its image. He sent to Albany two men, Bob Wagner and Al Smith, who compiled a record of reforms that has not been surpassed in the history of the New York legislature.

Murphy realized that supporting social welfare measures was a more effective way to appeal to voters than ward picnics and ethnic parades. He backed men of integrity and promise, who were given pretty much of a free hand in Albany, as long as they remained loyal in party matters such as the Sheehan candidacy. Robert Wagner would later refer to Tammany as "the cradle of modern liberalism." By the time Murphy died in 1924, FDR's view of Tammany had changed, and he said that "in Mr. Murphy's death, the New York City Democratic organization has lost probably the strongest and wisest leader it has had in generations. . . . He was a genius who kept harmony, and at the same time recognized that the world moves on. It is well to remember that he had helped to accomplish much in the way of progressive legislation and social welfare in our state."

In 1910, Tammany men like Smith and Wagner were far more reform-minded than Franklin Roosevelt, who at this stage of his career was indifferent to social issues, had the upstater's scorn for the urban masses, and was animated by a simplistic hatred of machine politics. Sticking to the narrow interests of his rural constituency, and to his emulation of Cousin Teddy as a foe of the bosses, he failed to see that Murphy's Tammany was the greatest force for social change in the Democratic party.

On February 2, Mr. and Mrs. Sheehan came to lunch at 248 State Street. When Sheehan and Franklin repaired to the study after lunch, the two wives chatted about the weather. Had any agreement been reached, Eleanor asked when the Sheehans had left. "Certainly not," Franklin said.

Sheehan fought back. A whispering campaign that the insurgents were anti-Irish and anti-Catholic was brought into the open by the Catholic bishop of Syracuse, Patrick Ludden, who said on January 25 that the real meaning of the rebellion was "You are an Irishman, and that's agin you; you are a Catholic, and that's agin you." "Bishop Ludden's interference is uncalled for, unnecessary, and unfortunate," Franklin replied. "He does not seem to know what he is talking about or someone has deliberately misinformed him."

It was February, and the legislative session was still stuck on this one point, but the insurgents held fast. Indirectly, Theodore Roosevelt advised Franklin not to make Shepard the issue. "I had to see Coz. Theodore today about the Plant, Flower and Fruit Guild meeting," Sara wrote, "and he was so nice about you and said he knew how proud I must be etc. He said 'Franklin is going just right, there is only one thing I hope he will keep to, not to tie to one special man but to the good cause—not to say Shepard and no other.' Then he quoted from a novel and said 'I would be glad to play with the angels but the angels are not playing about just now'—he thinks you are splendid and as usual was dear and nice."

March followed February with no solution in sight. When the session met on March 17, St. Patrick's Day, Assemblyman Oliver used the occasion for a dig at the insurgents. Presenting Franklin with a green carnation, he said that "the curse of Ireland, the land of patriots and poets, has been its misrepresentation and attempted rule by the curse of an accursed minority," meaning Ulster. Franklin came right back with "and as for Ireland, who told my distinguished friend from New York that it was a minority that cursed Ireland? My reading is to the effect that it was the powerful majority which England held over Ireland that cursed that land, persecuted its brave people, and gave among the heroic minorities of history a shining place to the sons of St. Patrick." Behind their green-draped desks, Al Smith and others desperate to break the deadlock were not amused.

On March 29, a fire broke out on the west side of the capitol, doing several million dollars' damage. The fire seemed like a sign from on high that the insurgency must end. The legislature now had to meet in Albany's city hall, and everyone was testy. When Murphy on March 31 proposed a compromise candidate, Judge James A. O'Gorman, the insurgents were divided. O'Gorman was more of a Tammany man than Sheehan, he was a former Grand Sachem. But he had a good judicial record, and no embarrassing corporate ties, and he was the sort of liberal who would be favorable to Woodrow Wilson in 1912. Franklin and about eight others did not want to give in, but the rest were suffering from battle fatigue and found O'Gorman acceptable. Franklin finally promised to vote for O'Gorman at the joint session, but refused to go to the caucus.

At 5:15 P.M. on March 31, Al Smith ran into the Assembly room at City Hall and said, "Arrange everything for the caucus; it has all been fixed." O'Gorman won the caucus, and was elected at the joint session by 112 to 80 for Depew. One of the 112 votes was Franklin's, who said that he and his group "have followed the dictates of our consciences and have done our duty as we saw it. I believe that as a result the Democratic Party has taken an upward step. We are Democrats—not irregulars, but regulars. I take pleasure in casting my vote for the Hon. James A. O'Gorman."

Although his insurgency combined opportunism with an outdated view of machine politics, Franklin was seen as having fought the good fight. In the rest of the country, where Tammany was looked upon, to put it politely, as a bunch of corrupt immigrants, he was hailed as a hero. He had yet to vote on a single bill, but already he was described as a rising young statesman. As far away as North Carolina, the editor of the Raleigh *News and Observer*, Josephus Daniels, wrote an editorial praising his splendid stand, entitled "A Coming Democratic Leader."

Aside from Franklin's instant and rather spurious celebrity, the one important result of what he always referred to as "the Sheehan business" was to dramatize the case for the direct election of U.S. senators. The legislature recessed for two weeks to take stock and have the bills that had been burned in the fire reprinted, and when it reconvened in mid-April, Franklin introduced a resolution endorsing an amendment to the U.S. Constitution providing for direct election. After five hours of debate, the resolution was carried by 28 to 16, and four days later the Assembly adopted it, 105 to 30. The amendment was proposed, the U.S. Senate passed it, thirty-six states ratified it (New York being the third), and the Seventeenth Amendment became effective on May 31, 1913. Franklin could rightly claim that he had given an early push to the measure that put an end to the U.S. Senate as a "millionaire's club."

As the senator for three dairy and fruit counties, Franklin depended on the farm vote, but his first year in office was remarkable for its inactivity on farm legislation. He wrote folksy letters to dairy farmers, reminding them that he was a farmer himself and promising to try to keep milk prices above nine cents a quart. After the Sheehan fight, his mind was on other things. He wanted to form the insurgents into a permanent splinter group that would block Tammany legislation. But nearly all the insurgents were assemblymen, who served one-year terms, and when they came up for reelection in November 1911 Tammany sabotaged their campaigns and all but four were defeated. Franklin's hope for an antimachine power group with himself as leader was shattered. As one of the defeated assemblymen wrote him on December 5: "I assume you have heard that we got it in the neck. . . . Everyone else got it in the same location. . . . There were many reasons why the State reacted. The analysis is too lengthy to write, but may be summed up in the one word: 'Murphy.' "

Since he could not lead an anti-Tammany faction, Franklin was content to cultivate the image of a straight-arrow rural legislator with high moral standards, a foe of corrupt city machines responsible to church groups and clean-living farmers. He opposed a bill that would have allowed betting at the racetrack, and one that permitted baseball on Sunday, which might have kept thousands who had no other time to play out of saloons. He pushed his "Mr. Clean" image to an extreme rarely seen in the Senate. On June 7, when Al Smith introduced appropriation bill 1789, Franklin asked about the sum of $381.54 to improve a bridge over Wappinger's Creek. "Oh, that is to benefit your district," said James J. Frawley, chairman of the Finance Committee. "The money was not expended last year and this bill makes it available to carry on the work."

"Well," replied Franklin at his most sanctimonious, "I haven't heard that the money is actually needed and I'd like to have it returned to the state treasurer."

Senator Harvey D. Hinman was so astonished that he asked the stenographer to record the protest, which "will stand as a monument, greater than any that has been or will be erected, to perpetuate the achievements of his illustrious relative. The senator's remarks should be engrossed on parchment and handed down to his descendants."

"Well," Frawley interjected, "that's the limit!"

"Frank, you ought to have your head examined," added Big Tim Sullivan.

Behind the puritanical facade, however, there were some unheroic political realities that Franklin had to face. Sometimes principles had to be bent and deals had to be made. That fall there was a Tammany-sponsored charter for the city of New York that would have given more power to the machine, through the mayor's control of the principal boards. The mayor at that time was William J. Gaynor, a clubhouse hack, of whom a reporter had once written, in an account of some function: " 'Thank you,' said the Mayor, without referring to his notes."

At the same time as the charter bill, there was a reapportionment bill for congressional districts. Under the plan, Richard Connell's twenty-first district would lose Columbia County and gain Orange County, which would Republicanize it and prevent his reelection. Franklin wrote "Babs" on September 14, 1911, that "it seems pretty rough for poor old Connell."

At first he was against the charter and the reapportionment, but soon he began waffling on the charter. Lawrence Tanzer, an Albany lobbyist for civic organizations that opposed the charter, was counting noses, because he knew the fight would be close, and found that Franklin was an uncertain factor. His vote was in question. He seemed to be an opportunist, always ready to change his course.

The fact was that Tammany had made Franklin an offer he couldn't refuse. In exchange for his support on the charter, the Reapportionment Committee would tailor the twenty-first congressional district so that a Democrat was bound to win, and the machine would secure the congressional nomination for Franklin, who would replace his friend Dick Connell. Tammany would send the stormy petrel to Washington, just as Boss Platt had helped to propel Theodore Roosevelt from the New York governorship to the vice presidency.

One evening, Robert S. Binkerd, a lobbyist for the Citizens' Union, had dinner with Franklin at the Hotel Ten Eyck. They talked about the charter, and Franklin said that, after all, he wasn't a citizen of New York City, he was up in Hyde Park, why should he risk his political career trying to fight other people's battles? Binkerd looked up at him in amazement and said, "In the first place, your legal residence may be Hyde Park, but you and your family have been in New York City for a hundred years and the idea that you haven't any obligation to the people of New York is nuts." Franklin then told him that if he didn't buck Tammany he could get the nomination to Congress. They had two reapportionment bills in the hopper, one that added every Democratic vote they could find in the Hudson River territory, and the other that scattered Democratic strength through Republican districts. They had been pressuring him, telling him to "get smart. If you want to go someplace we can fix it. But if you haven't got the sense, we'll fix it so you don't go anywhere." Franklin was cold-bloodedly calculating his chances, Binkerd thought, and would not have hesitated to force out the man he had campaigned with in 1910, Richard Connell. (As it turned out, Connell died in office in 1912, so Franklin would not have had to replace him. Franklin arranged for a memorial, a children's playground in a park overlooking the Hudson.)

On September 30, when it was reported that Franklin now supported the charter, and that Connell's congressional district had been reapportioned to favor a Democrat, there was so much mail criticizing the change that he reversed himself again. Thomas Mott Osborne, leader of the anti-Tammany wing of the Democratic party, former mayor of Auburn, and an influential progressive, wired Franklin: "If you vote for it [the charter] I shall feel like retiring permanently from politics. For God's sake don't compromise." The Reapportionment Committee amended its report to favor a Republican. Franklin loudly denied any connection, but he had clearly been lured into a Tammany deal. On October 1, the reapportionment bill passed both houses and the charter bill was killed. Having lost his chance to run for Congress, Franklin promised Binkerd that he would continue to oppose Tammany.

He was not up for reelection in November 1911 (state senators had two-year terms) but he stumped the state, denouncing bossism. "Murphy and his kind must, like the noxious weed, be plucked root and branch," he said. "From the ruins of the political machines we will reconstruct something more nearly conforming to a Democratic conception of Government." He singled out Patrick E. McCabe, clerk of the Senate, and promised that he would be forced out of office in the spring.

McCabe's reply jarred Franklin out of his complacency. He said that Franklin's remarks were "bristling with the silly conceits of a political prig," and that "disloyalty and Party treachery is the political cult of a few snobs in our party who attain prominence through the exigencies of a turn-over in the politics of the state and who are simply political accidents." The party, McCabe went on, had "humored and coddled too much the . . . fops and cads who come as near being political leaders as a green pea does to a circus tent."

Harsh words to ponder on. Franklin had sought and found the limelight, but at the price of being unpopular among his peers. Frances Perkins, then lobbyist for the Consumers' League, remembered him as he was then, "going in and out of committee rooms, rarely talking with the members, who more or less avoided him, not particularly charming, artificially serious of face, rarely smiling, with an unfortunate habit—so natural that he was unaware of it—of throwing his head up. This, combined with his pince-nez and great height, gave him the appearance of looking down his nose at most people." Tammany men, of whom there was a large share of humbly born Irishmen, saw an idealism tinged with arrogance, a streak of self-righteousness, an indifference to human problems.

Life along the Hudson had equipped Franklin to deal with such issues as the fees of shad fishermen, the extent of the ruffed grouse season, and the size of apple barrels, but not to take part in the urgent issues of the day. On March 25, 1911, a fire had broken out in the Triangle Shirtwaist Company, which occupied the top three floors of a ten-story New York City loft building behind Washington Square. A cigarette ignited inflammable material, and the fire spread to the paper patterns from which the shirtwaists were cut, hanging in bunches on the walls between the windows, and leaped from one bunch of patterns to the other.

It was a Saturday afternoon, and most of the other factories in the building were closed. Frances Perkins, who had that January made her debut as an Albany lobbyist, was in the neighborhood visiting a friend, and heard the firemen shouting at trapped workers not to jump. She saw them hanging out the windows, their hands clutching ledges, faced with the choice of the flames or the void, and saw their grips loosen and their bodies fall. The door to the stairway had been locked to keep out possible thieves. Forty-seven employees fell to their deaths, and another hundred died inside. Firemen found skeletons bent over sewing machines. In the subsequent trial, the building's owners were not held criminally responsible, and collected $64,-925 in property damage insurance.

It was the worst industrial tragedy in New York's history, and there was a sense of outrage that such a thing could happen, that working conditions could be so hazardous, that employers could be so indifferent to safety. The Triangle fire was a powerful symbol of the evils of laissez-faire capitalism. It was such a clear-cut example of the horrors of unregulated industry that it served to mobilize reformers.

Obviously, if a fire in a garment maker's loft could snuff out 147 lives, new laws were needed and the government had to take a more active part in the protection of workers. On June 30, 1911, a New York State Factory Commission was created, consisting of two senators, three assemblymen, and four private citizens. Robert Wagner was chairman, Al Smith was vice chairman, and Frances Perkins was chief investigator. They visited mill towns and saw the unsafe machinery responsible for on-the-job accidents. They examined records that were doctored to dupe Labor Department inspectors. They went to upstate canneries where women, their children by their side, worked nineteen hours a day. In one factory, Robert Wagner crawled through a tiny hole in the wall leading to an ice-covered iron ladder that stopped twelve feet short of the ground—a fire escape. You could never tell Al Smith that children were not employed in New York factories because he had gotten up at 4:00 A.M. and made an unannounced visit to a sweatshop and seen them.

The Factory Commission investigation lasted more than three years. For Wagner and Smith, it was a transforming experience that brought them into direct contact with abuses that they had the power to correct. The work of the legislature during those years was improving safety, ending the exploitation of women and children, examining wage scales, enacting building codes and a workmen's compensation act. The result, a total of thirty-two epoch-making bills, made New York a pioneer and a model for other states and for the federal government. And all of it was sponsored by Tammany and pushed through by its two young legislative leaders.

Franklin Roosevelt, on the other hand, had practically nothing to do with this effort. He knew nothing about labor, and wasn't interested. As he had told Robert Binkerd, he represented a rural upstate district, why fight other people's battles? He had grown up on an estate where the labor problems were replacing a drunken coachman or hiring extra hands to bring in the crops. He saw labor matters in terms of the benevolent employer who handed out free turkeys at Christmas. When he visited a mill town during his 1910 campaign, he advised his audience "to communicate with working-men in Mr. Dix's mills and learn from them how highly they regard him as a wise, kindly and considerate employer."

Bent on positioning himself as an enemy of Tammany, he lined up with the insurgents, who in economic and labor matters represented the conservative wing of the party. He had won in 1910 because he had weaned a number of antilabor farmers and businessmen away from their normally Republican voting habits. Labor union support in his district would have done more harm than good. He thought that a strike was the same thing as a boycott, and when he was asked his position on a bill to legalize strikes and picketing, he wrote his friend G. H. Putnam on March 17, 1911, "There is no question in my mind that we cannot permit legislation which will legalize the practice of boycotting." He ignored union petitions against the use of prison labor, because he believed that putting convicts to work on state highways was good for their morale and for the economy.

When the Triangle fire called attention to the misery of the sweatshops, Franklin was sympathetic for humane reasons, not because he was prolabor, and consistently voted for the safety measures proposed by the Factory Commission—but he took no part in the commission's work. His priorities were dictated not only by his background and constituency, but by his committee assignments—in the 1912 session, he was chairman of the Agriculture Committee; ranking member of the old Forest, Fish, and Game Committee, now called the Conservation Committee; and a member of the Codes, Railroads, and Military Affairs Committee.

Since 1911, Frances Perkins had been lobbying for a fifty-four-hour bill for women and children, but the bill was stalled in committee. Its opponents argued, among other things, that women who worked nine hours a day six days a week would use their free time for immoral purposes. But the real reason the bill was stalled, Miss Perkins learned from Al Smith, was that the Huyler brothers, candy manufacturers who employed mostly women, were pals of Charles Murphy and solid contributors to the Democratic campaign fund. Miss Perkins hoped to win Franklin Roosevelt's support because they both came from the same side of the tracks. Like him, she was of respectable lineage; her people were early Maine settlers who had given their name to a landscape feature, Perkins Point. She had gone to Mount Holyoke, where she was class president, and then, having caught a bad case of social conscience, she had devoted herself to helping the less fortunate. Believing that men in political life associated women with their mothers, she wore black dresses with a bow of white at the throat and deliberately behaved in a manner that would remind them subconsciously of Mom.

But when she wrote asking Franklin to vote for the bill, saying that it appealed not only to the humanitarian interest but to the broad business sense of every member of the legislature, since it would protect women from fatigue and overwork, she got back a routine "I am giving this matter my most careful consideration" letter. And when she accosted him as he came off the floor of the Senate to ask for help in having the bill called up, he threw his nose up in the air, looked down, and said, "No, no. More important things. More important things. Can't do it now. Can't do it now. Much more important things." How absurd for him to be so superior, she thought. A good politician would have said, "Sure I'm with you," even if he wasn't.

The "more important things" included a bill that passed in January 1912 lowering the fee for shad fishermen from $25 to $5 and regulating the ruffed grouse season; backing a bill allowing suckers, a kind of lumpfish, to be hooked through the ice; and fighting bills that permitted certain birds to be caught for their plumage (for New York City milliners) and that extended the duck-shooting season on Long Island.

It would be unfair, however, to trivialize Franklin's intentions, for in his own way, coming from a different direction, he was tackling the same problem as the Factory Commission, which was, in fact, the basic dilemma of the twentieth-century American commonwealth: the degree of government intervention in private affairs. "They can't tell me how to run my business," said the entrepreneur. "They can't tell me how many acres to plant," said the farmer. And yet it was evident that unregulated capitalism was chaotic and harmful to the public interest, and that government had to step in.

Like the social reform legislators, Franklin was working out a theory of the common good within the framework of democratic capitalism and its rough mythologies of individualism and free competition, but instead of applying it to safety measures for workers, he was trying to pass the Roosevelt-Jones conservation bill. It was a tough bill, which called for state inspection of private forests, compulsory reforestation of denuded watershed lands, and state regulation of timber harvests to ensure permanent cover. The lumber lobby was up in arms, screaming that the bill was a denial of property rights. What right did the state have to tell a private individual how he should cut trees on his own land?

The timber men could not see farther than six inches in front of their noses, Franklin complained. They had destroyed the Adirondacks by overcutting, without giving back one quarter of what they had taken. To get his point of view across, he held committee hearings on February 20 and 21, 1912, in the Assembly chamber, and succeeded in getting a large number of senators to attend because he produced the legendary Gifford Pinchot, who had under Theodore Roosevelt created the U.S. Forest Service.

Pinchot projected two photographs on a screen. The first one showed a sixteenth-century painting of a Chinese walled town, with a stream flowing through the tilled valley, and mountains on each side covered to the top with spruce and pine. Running down one mountain, however, there was a streak, which turned out to be a logging chute. The Chinese were cutting the timber and chuting it down to the valley. The second photograph showed the same place in China as it now was, with not a tree, and not a blade of grass, just mountains covered with rocks, and a town in ruins.

Franklin was convinced that those two pictures had sold conservation to the New York legislature, and had enabled his bill to pass (it was signed that April). In fact, under pressure from the lumber lobby, many of its tough measures were amended. But through his love of trees, he came to the same conclusion as his colleagues on the Factory Commission—that the era of laissez-faire was over.

While he established the right of the state to regulate timber cutting on private land, Frances Perkins had succeeded in getting the fifty-four-hour bill before the Senate. Franklin had not helped her, had not pushed for it, had not gathered up votes, had not done any missionary work. The man who had done all that was Big Tim Sullivan, boss of the Bowery, symbol of the old Tammany and its lax ways.

The Senate bill passed 32 to 15, with even James A. Foley, who was Murphy's son-in-law and regarded as Murphy's proxy, voting for it. But Miss Perkins soon learned that she had been cruelly tricked. For the fifty-four-hour bill that the Assembly would vote on had an amendment exempting workers in canneries, on the grounds that their work was seasonal, and Murphy knew that Miss Perkins was under instructions from the Consumers' League not to accept the exemption.

Frances Perkins saw what was happening. The Assembly would not accept the Senate bill, since it had its own version, with the cannery exemption. The Senate, however, might accept the Assembly version, less stringent than its own. But it would do nothing unless she acted fast. It would be all too easy in an election year for each house to claim it had tried to do something for labor but had run out of time.

Going against her instructions, she decided that this was an occasion for the half-a-loaf approach—she had better take what she could get now and try for more later. Four hundred thousand women in factories would be affected by the bill, of whom only 10,000 worked in canneries.

Thanks to Big Tim Sullivan, who despite his Tammany affiliation was acting against Murphy's order to kill the bill because he had a soft spot "for them poor girls," she got the Assembly bill before the Senate in the last hours of the session's final day, March 29, 1912. On the first vote, 24 to 14, it failed to get a majority by two votes (there were fifty senators, but only thirty-eight voted, the others presumably having left before the session ended).

Tim Sullivan and his cousin, Christy Sullivan, had gone to catch the 8:00 P.M. boat to New York, and Miss Perkins sent someone to head them off as she asked for reconsideration of the Assembly bill. Under the parliamentary rules, this could be done as a matter of internal Senate action, needing a majority only of senators present and voting. On a motion to reconsider, each senator was allowed five minutes to explain his position, and a sort of mini-filibuster ensued as they waited for the Sullivans. When Big Tim burst through the door, shouting "Record me in the affirmative," the final vote was taken and the bill passed by 27 to 16. The following year it was broadened to include cannery workers.

In 1928, when FDR was campaigning for governor of New York and presenting himself as a longtime friend of labor, he said in an extemporaneous address in New York City on October 30: "I remember particularly one of the first things I got into awful hot water about up in my county district—and mind you, I came from an unfortunate district up there on the Hudson River where organized labor had mighty hard sledding. . . . And one of the first measures that we started in 1911 was the fifty-four-hour law for women and children in industry. In those days a fifty-four-hour law was considered the most radical thing that had ever been talked about. . . ."

This vague profession of involvement in prolabor legislation was to be repeated at other convenient times, such as November 4, 1938: "When we were in the legislature together more than a quarter of a century ago, Senator Wagner and I were called Communists and Socialists because we worked for a fifty-four-hour-a-week law for women and children in industry." In another account by Louis Howe, who had become FDR's chief adviser, Franklin was made the hero and architect of the hectic last-day passage of the bill. This was in an article in the *Saturday Evening Post*, published on February 25, 1933, shortly before FDR's inauguration, when he was about to launch the New Deal, and it was useful to portray him as a champion of the workingman. According to this account, "young Senator Roosevelt had been deeply interested in the passage of a 54-hour bill which by a single vote had failed to pass the Senate" (actually it was two votes). "Mr. Roosevelt would not acquiesce—'Make sure we have all the votes and I will start talking and move the passage of the bill.' . . . He rose and explaining that he wished to make a few remarks on the passage of the bill for the purposes of the record, launched into an entirely different subject. . . . Scouts reported that Tim Sullivan had gone down to the night boat . . . and had gone to bed. Get him up were the Roosevelt orders. . . . But he won't come, they objected. Yes, he will—tell him he has to and I said so. It was not until he had begun a long and interesting account of bird life in Dutchess County—a subject in which he was greatly interested—that Senator Brackett [Edgar T. Brackett, Republican leader of the Senate] suspected something wrong. . . . He protested to holding a weary Senate to listen to an ornithological dissertation—'the speaker should confine himself to the matter of shorter hours and bring his interesting lecture to a close.' 'Oh but I am, I am trying to prove that nature demands shorter working hours, more opportunity for rest for all the animal creation—and what better example can I use than the birds of the air, who go to their well-earned rest as soon as darkness falls?' . . . A sleepy Tim Sullivan appeared on the Senate floor. 'And now gentleman,' concluded the young Roosevelt, 'the time is late. I told you about the birds and I had in mind discussing the famous sleepers of history, including the five sleepers of Ephesus and the Sleeping Beauty, but I will not trespass on your patience any longer.' "

It was a good story, even though there was not a word of truth in it, because Franklin was not present on the evening of March 29 when the bill was passed. Frances Perkins, who was counting noses and buttonholing senators and desperately rallying support, and who had a vivid recollection of who was there and who was not, said categorically: "I knew he wasn't present the night [the vote] was taken."

In one of her oral-history interviews, Miss Perkins said: "I remember being considerably disappointed because Roosevelt wouldn't do anything about the 54-hour bill. He gave the bill lip service and was recorded in the Senate record as having voted for it. I always thought he hadn't. In my heart I believed that Roosevelt had not voted for the 54-hour bill and I knew he wasn't present the night it was taken. I asked him about it once and he said he did vote for it. What I think is that he probably was paired or something or other. Anyhow the record shows that he voted for it. I had it looked up once."

There were several ways that an absent senator could be recorded as having voted. One method, as Miss Perkins noted, was to pair off with a senator who was voting the other way, and those votes would be entered into the *Senate Journal.* Another was a short roll call, in which only those voting against a measure were asked to raise their hands and be tallied, all the others being entered as voting in the affirmative, whether they were there or not. A third way was to ask a friendly clerk to add your name to the majority. Procedure was fairly loose in Albany in 1912, and a small matter like a vote record was easy to arrange.

Louis Howe knew that his account of the ornithological filibuster could not be disproved by the *Senate Journal,* which recorded only votes and not speeches or speakers. But four New York City newspapers, three Albany papers, and one Poughkeepsie paper* published detailed accounts of the Senate session, and five of those eight papers mentioned the Sullivans being called back from the night boat. In none of the eight papers is there a single mention of Roosevelt taking part in the drama.

It was another example of FDR's utilitarian conception of the past, as when he had taken credit for the interview with President Eliot at Harvard. Sometimes the record had to be touched up to make the candidate more appealing.

On or about April 12, Franklin boarded the United Fruit Company's SS *Carrillo,* which was taking him to Panama to see the nearly completed canal. Eleanor would join him in New Orleans on his return trip. On April 14, as the ship passed the Bahamas, Franklin wrote his wife the closest thing we have to a love letter, for she destroyed the letters he wrote during their courtship. "I do wish you were here—it is hard enough to be away from the chicks, but with you away from me I feel too very much alone and lost. I hereby solemnly declare that I REFUSE to go away the next time without you.... I can't tell you how I long to see you again.... Give a great deal of love & kisses to sister [Anna] & Brud [James] and Snookums [Elliott]—I am just so crazy to see my four precious ones again that I am almost tempted to turn around in Kingston and sail straight back. Take good care of yourself dearest, and please don't overdo it in moving" (out of the house in Albany).

On April 19, while Franklin was heading out to the canal, Governor John A. Dix signed the fifty-four-hour bill, expressing his displeasure: "I don't think it's a good idea. I think it will put women out of work. I think they'll hire men instead. I think women will lose their jobs. Anyhow, it's not good for them not to be fully occupied."

On April 20, Franklin reached Colón, and was impressed by how clean and efficient everything was—it was a very different Panama than under the French. They even had an ice cream factory! Taking the train to Culebra, he saw the famous cut through the mountain and, from the top of it, the trains of dump cars, the locomotives, the steam shovels, all looking like gnats in the middle of the Great Cut. He inspected the locks of Pedro Miguel and Miraflores, which raised the vessels eighty-five feet to the level of the cut. It was all most impressive and so was the chief engineer, George Washington

* New York *Herald, New York Times,* New York *World,* New York *Tribune,* Albany *Knickerbocker Press,* Albany *Daily Argus,* Albany *Evening Journal,* Poughkeepsie *Daily Eagle.*

Goethals, who injected a patriotic note, telling him: "We like to have Americans come down, because they all say it makes them better Americans."

It was at this point that Louis Howe, author of the story on the dramatic, last-minute filibuster, entered Franklin's life. The connection between them reminds one of those organisms that Dr. Lewis Thomas describes, such as the medusa and the snail, which become bonded through mutual need. They set up a complex pattern of dependence based on biological function, and the organism that seems to be the parasite is nonetheless essential to the other's survival.

Alone, Louis Howe was a failure. He could only thrive once he fastened onto a larger and healthier organism. He looked like a child who had grown old without growing up, and described himself as "one of the four ugliest men, if what is left of me can be dignified by the name of man, in the State of New York. I am wizened in the Dickens manner. My eyes protrude because of so much looking. Children take one look at me and run from 'the man with the wicked kidnaping eyes.' "

Louis liked to think of himself as a walking corpse that the doctors had given up on. When you asked him how he felt, he said: "I feel as though I'd just lost three states." To aggravate his asthma, his chronic bronchitis, and his heart condition, he chain-smoked Sweet Caporal cigarettes and drank himself to sleep. Consistent with his poor health, he cultivated an "at death's door" appearance, slovenly and unwashed, with baggy clothes over which he flicked ashes. He was a sort of Pepys character: "Pissed in the chimney, and so to bed."

There was a strong element of self-dramatization in his "I only have three months to live" routine, for he lived into his sixties. It was part of a carefully rehearsed role, a disguise to be adopted behind enemy lines, for he was ever alert to slights or signs of dislike, and would abruptly turn to someone and say: "You don't like me so good, do you?"

Louis McHenry Howe was an only child, born eleven years before Franklin, in 1871, in Indiana. His father, Edward, known as "Captain Howe," had an insurance business, but was ruined in the panic of 1873 and moved to Saratoga Springs, where he bought a newspaper, the Saratoga *Sun,* and turned it into a Democratic organ. Instead of going to college, Louis worked for his father and married a Fall River girl named Grace Hartley, fathering a son and a daughter. When his father sold the business, Louis became a stringer for New York papers, covering Saratoga during the season, upstate elections, and Albany during the session.

Always broke, always pleading for salary advances, always hatching schemes, Louis latched onto Thomas Mott Osborne, the wealthy upstate reformer who wanted to build an anti-Tammany Democratic organization. For $40 a week, he drummed up grass-roots support, writing hundreds of letters from his Albany office. He became an anti-Tammany spy, using his access as a reporter to feed political gossip to Osborne, and slanting his news stories for the *Herald*. He was a born maneuverer, entirely at home with duplicity.

When Franklin came to Albany in 1911, Louis admired his anti-Sheehan stand, interviewed him, and became the insurgents' informal adviser. The friendship blossomed, each having recognized in the other qualities he needed. Franklin was green, and needed Louis's expertise and cynical appraisal of political realities. In Franklin, Louis saw what he was not—the Grand Young Man, overflowing with attractiveness and charm, the hero in the making.

In 1912, Franklin was up for reelection, and there were signs that the machine was trying to prevent his nomination. Tammany agents were going through his district stirring up the Sheehan business. He knew that the Columbia machine was against him because of patronage problems, but Putnam was for him. In his home county of Dutchess, he didn't trust the Poughkeepsie boss, Ed Perkins, who he thought was spineless and prone to listen to orders from 14th Street.

He spent the next three weeks doing a little repair work, driving up and down the district and seeing Democratic party "henchmen." The effort paid off, and on August 24 he sent this wire to Eleanor at Campobello: "Received designation by unanimous vote. Will wire Sunday if I can leave."

Franklin spent a few days with his family in Campobello. When they left for Hyde Park on the boat to Eastport, he and Eleanor brushed their teeth with water from a pitcher in their stateroom. When they reached their house at 47 East 65th Street, Franklin fell ill with a fever. His doctor could not identify it, and thought at first it was appendicitis. When Eleanor came down with it, her case was diagnosed as typhoid, and it followed that Franklin must have that too. He could not shake it off, and lay in bed, pale and haggard, looking, Eleanor thought, like Robert Louis Stevenson at Vailima.

The timing could not have been worse. This time, because Cousin Teddy was running on a third-party ticket, he had two opponents, Republican Jacob Southard of Cold Spring, banker and president of a light and power company, and the Progressive George A. Vossler. That might split the Republican vote, but it did not offset being bedridden. His success in 1910 had been due to the vigor and personality of his campaign, the seven meetings a day and the 2,000 miles traveled in the red Maxwell. Now he was sick in New York City, which would revive the nonresidency issue. This would be a Democratic year, with Woodrow Wilson running for president against a split Republican vote, and here he was unable to leave his room, staring at the walls. How could he possibly win? It could mean the end of his political career. If he was not elected, he might have to go back to the practice of law.

Because of his anti-Tammany stance, he would get no help from the party regulars. Indeed, Tammany would do its best to sabotage him, and Ed Perkins would look the other way. He needed someone he could trust to handle the campaign, someone in sympathy with his reputation as an independent. He thought of Louis Howe, who had recently written him to ask for employment. Louis, who knew everyone in state politics, Louis, the shrewd appraiser of local issues, Louis, who believed in his political future, who, indeed, had written him in June half jokingly, "Beloved and Revered Future President."

Franklin asked Eleanor to send a wire to his summer cottage at Horseneck Beach in southern Massachusetts, asking him to come at once to New York and discuss taking over the campaign. Thus was formed an alliance unique in American politics. From that moment until his death in 1936, Louis Howe gave his heart and soul to the promotion of Franklin's career. It was not a job, it was an obsession. He practically deserted his family, so that in later years his son Hartley would come to hate his father and the Roosevelts.

One evening at a dinner party in Washington, circa 1920, a place card was passed to Howe, with this message written in pencil on the back: "You don't know my face but I think you know my name (see on the other side of card). The counsellor of the French Embassy who sits at my left wants to meet you. He says you remind him of Marat." The name on the place card was that of journalist Arthur Krock.

The only thing Howe and Marat had in common was bad skin. Marat was largely responsible for the execution of Louis XVI, whereas Howe was a kingmaker. He was able to submerge his own ambition so that it was expressed through Franklin. He was like a boxer's second, who tapes his hands, closes his cuts, waves the ammonia under his nose, plans his round-by-round strategy, and whose greatest satisfaction is seeing his fighter win. With Franklin, Howe found his true vocation, which was working behind the scenes for the advancement of someone he believed in. He could continue to be scruffy, continue to be rude. Shaking hands and looking dapper and pleasant were the candidate's business.

Franklin found in Louis a second fiddle who did not aspire to become first violin. They were locked in a symbiotic embrace. Franklin represented Louis's last chance to escape the grubby backroom politics of Albany, the small-time newswriting at $25 a week, the seedy connection with second-rate politicians like Thomas Mott Osborne. Without Franklin, that is what he had to go back to. With Franklin, who knows how far he could go? Already in 1912 Louis saw him in the White House.

Franklin and Louis spoke to each other as equals. Their talk was full of ribbing and banter. Franklin loved to tease, and there were set pieces, such as the telegram Louis had once gotten from his missus, that said: "Love growing colder." There was the one about his brand of cigarettes: "I hear the Sweet Caporal factory is closing down since there is only one man in America who smokes their brand." And the one about his clothes: "When Louis gets a new suit it's news. I'm pretty sure he hasn't had a new suit in ages and certainly not new socks. Louis doesn't do any darning you know, so he just wears his socks till they don't cover his legs any more."

Nor did Louis mince his words when he spoke to Franklin. Here he is on the phone to Albany when Roosevelt was governor: "Franklin, you damned fool! You can't do that. You simply can't do it, I tell you! . . . But Franklin, if you do it you're a fool—just a damned, idiotic fool. And if you do it you will live to regret it. Mark my words, you'll live to regret it! All right, all right, pighead, go ahead and be a damned fool, if you insist. But don't say I didn't warn you. What's that, what's that? You're going for a swim? Well, go ahead, dammit, and I hope to God you drown." The telephone slammed on its cradle.

Louis was a tactician and maneuverer rather than a policymaker. His cynicism limited his usefulness. In his eyes, people were always ready to sell you out, they were disloyal until proven loyal, crooked until proven honest. In a talk at the Columbia School of Journalism on January 17, 1933, he said: "You can't adopt politics as a profession and remain honest. If you are going to make your living out of politics you can't do it honestly." His tone was invariably knowing and sardonic, implying that behind the facade he knew where the dirt was.

Unrelieved cynicism is as wishful a posture as naïveté, supposing on the part of others a consistency of behavior that does not exist. James P. Warburg, one of FDR's economic advisers in 1933, remembered Howe as "the fellow who was always saying to the President, 'Well, so and so made a big contribution and you've got to place him somewhere.' "

"I loathed Louis Howe," Warburg said. "I thought he was evil personified. He always came up with the really cynical political twist to an idea. He used to come into these meetings we had in the oval study in an old flannel nightshirt and sit there like a little elf of some sort. Just when we were getting somewhere, he would come in with something like 'well, I guess you'd better not do that.' He would give no reason and then we'd adjourn. A day or two later I would find that he had some political iron in the fire. I thought then that he was a dreadful person. . . . But I don't think Roosevelt would have been nearly as good a politician without Louis Howe. . . . He had very great political intuition."

When Howe arrived at 65th Street, Eleanor disliked him on sight, and showed her disapproval with a haughty reserve. Her husband was sick, and here this dirty little man was getting him worked up, and spoiling the fresh air he should have had in his bedroom with cigarette smoke. Together Franklin and Howe outlined a strategy for the campaign. In a presidential year, there would be a bigger farm vote, and Franklin had to dramatize his interest in the farmer. His record was not striking, for he had devoted much of his time to conservation. He was worried that, in the three-cornered race, the Bull Mooser would siphon off some of the independent Republicans who had voted for him in 1910.

The thing to do was bear down on the commission merchants. That was the issue the farmers were incensed about. The merchants must be made accountable through a system of bonds and state inspection. Now on the Roosevelt payroll at $50 a week, with headquarters at the Morgan House in Poughkeepsie, Howe sent out about 11,000 letters saying that if Roosevelt were elected he would be chairman of the Senate Agriculture Committee and would fight to protect the farmers from greedy commission merchants. The letters were backed up by full-page ads in the local papers, which no Hudson River candidate had ever tried before. "Here is your first ad," Howe wrote Franklin. "I plan to cut her loose Friday with the weekly edition of the *News-Press*. . . . As I have pledged you in it I thought you might like to know casually what kind of a mess I was getting you into. Please wire o.k. if it is all right. . . . I'm having more fun than a goat and Southard will know he's been to a horse-race before we're done. . . . Your slave and Servant."

"FARMERS! ATTENTION!" said the ad. "The time to put a stop to the ROBBERIES of dishonest commission merchants is NOW! . . . When Franklin D. Roosevelt says he will fight for a thing, it means he won't quit until he wins—you know that."

Howe was truly working like a slave, handling a huge volume of correspondence, traveling through the district to set up Roosevelt committees, going to Albany to find patronage jobs for key supporters, and sending daily reports to Franklin, always with a touch of humor: "Keep that temperature down, so that you can get on the job."

On October 30, six days away from the election, still sick in bed, Franklin worried about the turnout, writing a Putnam County supporter, Thomas M. Upp: "There is going to be more or less of the same old political methods in the way of trading, knifing, etc., between the circles and inner circles which seem to mean more than party to many voters. . . . The old Sheehan matter seems to be still alive in certain breasts, but this may be balanced in my case by an increased vote of Republicans or Bull Moosers whom I did not gather in two years ago."

On election night, November 5, he heard by telephone from Howe that he had won, receiving 15,590 votes to Southard's 13,889 and 2,628 for Progressive George Vossler (the combined votes of his two opponents would have defeated him by nearly a thousand votes). A supporter, Augustus A. Walker of the Methodist Parsonage in Philmont, wrote: "When a bull-moose and a G.O.P. elephant are both outrun by a man sick-a-bed it would seem 'Manifest Destiny.' " The real hero of the occasion was Louis Howe, who had won the election for a candidate who was not once present in his district during the entire campaign.

When the legislative session opened in Albany in January 1913, Franklin was fit and ready to tackle the commission merchants. He was named chairman of the Senate Committee on Agriculture, introduced five bills, and presided over public hearings. But by the time the bill licensing and bonding commission merchants was passed, he had left the Senate for greener pastures.

In the fall of 1911, after the end of the legislative session, which had dragged on into October because of the "Sheehan business," Franklin had made the pilgrimage to Trenton to meet the new governor of New Jersey, Woodrow Wilson. They had much in common, he thought—they had fought the political machines of their respective states, and they both wanted a reform in party nominating methods, a regulation of business abuses, and the conservation of natural resources. In his first year Wilson had done a spectacular job, apparently hypnotizing the legislature into voting through a bold program—a direct primary law, a public utilities commission with rate-setting powers, a corrupt-practices law, an employer's-liability law. It was a lesson in leadership that made him front-runner for the 1912 Democratic presidential nomination.

They spoke in Wilson's office, and then, along with his secretary, Joseph Tumulty, took the train from Trenton to Princeton Junction, sizing each other up during the short train ride—the man who would be the twenty-eighth president and the man who would be the thirty-second president, the two American presidents who would lead their country to victories in world wars. Franklin, twenty-nine years old, handsome and ebullient, glad to have found a Democratic leader he could follow, describing the situation in New York to the fifty-five-year-old Wilson, this dour son of the manse, this descendant of Scottish Covenanters, this dyed-in-the-wool Presbyterian who believed that God was ever-present, guiding his hand. This professor, this political scientist, this college president, who had left Princeton in defeat over an administrative quarrel, only to win the state's highest office. Did Franklin sense then, as he looked at the narrow face with the high forehead and the cold direct eyes, the inflexible principles, the belief that everything had a wrong side and a right side, the severe and unyielding temperament, uneasy of access, undramatic, disliking the masses? Whatever thought crossed Franklin's mind about the dangers of excessive virtue were set aside, for Wilson was the successful leader of the party's progressive wing, a probable antimachine candidate for 1912, and, in terms of education and intellect, perhaps the best-qualified man ever to seek the office of president.

Franklin had always thought of Cousin Teddy as his model, but here was another possible model, closer to Endicott Peabody in his righteousness and high principles. Cousin Teddy, who would run against him in 1912, would come to detest Wilson, calling him on one occasion a "Byzantine logothete," and saying that he looked too much like an apothecary's clerk to get elected. But Franklin was able to take from each example what he needed, and in 1935 would write the Wilson biographer, Ray Stannard Baker: "Theodore Roosevelt lacked Woodrow Wilson's appeal to the fundamental and failed to stir, as Wilson did, the truly profound moral and social convictions. Wilson, on the other hand, failed where Theodore Roosevelt succeeded in stirring people to enthusiasm over specific individual events, even though these specific events may have been superficial in comparison with the fundamentals."

Theodore Roosevelt and Woodrow Wilson were brothers in hubris, and both would be laid low by their presumptions, in one case that a third party could win a national election, in the other that the U.S. Senate could be forced to accept the League of Nations. This crippling character defect, known as standing on principle, was one that Franklin never suffered from—he knew from boyhood that to reach your goal you had to compromise. He was flexible where Wilson and Cousin Teddy were rigid. He was pragmatic where Wilson was visionary, although he thought of himself as an idealist in the Wilsonian mold and liked to quote Wilson's remark: "It is only once in a generation that a people can be lifted above material things. That is why conservative government is in the saddle two-thirds of the time."

For the moment, however, Franklin saw Wilson as a kindred spirit—they were united against machine politics—and when Wilson asked what support he would have in the New York delegation, he replied that probably thirty of the ninety delegates were leaning toward him, but that the delegation was controlled by Murphy and would vote under the unit rule.

Dim as Wilson's chances might seem, Franklin was eager to support him, not only because he liked what he stood for but because he was the only way around the Tammany roadblock. As an independent, he had to hitch his political wagon to the team of an antimachine candidate. With Thomas Mott Osborne and some other prominent Democrats, he founded the New York State Wilson Conference, which was intended to show the convention that there was plenty of pro-Wilson sentiment in New York even though the delegation voted otherwise. On April 12, 1912, the New York State Democratic convention picked a slate of ninety uninstructed delegates, and Franklin was pointedly excluded—he was not even an alternate.

In the meantime, the Republican party was a shambles. Theodore Roosevelt broke with Taft in February and announced: "My hat is in the ring." At the Republican convention in Chicago from June 18 to 22, Taft was renominated, and Teddy Roosevelt announced that he would run as a third-party candidate. His Progressive party was soon dubbed the Bull Moose party after his statement: "I am fit as a bull moose." Thus did Theodore Roosevelt guarantee the election of the man he detested, by splitting the Republican vote to ensure a Democratic victory.

Franklin went to the Democratic convention in Baltimore at the end of June with 150 Wilson supporters to circulate among the delegates and spread the message that, though the machine was opposed to him, he was popular with New York voters and would carry the state if nominated. With headquarters in room 214 of the Munsey Building, Franklin and Thomas

Mott Osborne and the others generally whooped it up for Wilson. He took Eleanor along, renting a house with two other couples.

This was Franklin's first taste of national politics, the first of many conventions he would attend. Caught by the excitement of the event, he lobbied for Wilson with manic energy. He met some of the leading Wilson Democrats, such as the antitrust New York businessman William Gibbs McAdoo, the Tennessee Congressman Cordell Hull, and the North Carolina newspaper proprietor Josephus Daniels, who was a national committeeman and was running Wilson's press office. Daniels, who had admired Roosevelt during the "Sheehan business," was in charge of distributing convention tickets to the press, and Roosevelt went to see him to ask for tickets for some upstate editors. Daniels saw a high-spirited, dashing young man burst into his office, saying that he was heart and soul for Wilson, even though he had no vote. It was, Daniels recalled, "a case of love at first sight—for when men are attracted to each other there is a born feeling that Mexicans call 'simpático'. . . ." Surely this was one of the most charming and handsome young men that he had ever seen.

The good impression Franklin made on Daniels would change his life, but for the moment he plunged into the convention fight, which opened on June 25. Wilson was going in as the underdog, with 248 pledged votes against 436 for Kentucky-born Missouri Congressman Champ Clark, a man with a fine record of public service, Speaker of the House, but in depth of intellect not Wilson's match.

A June breeze stirred the folds of gaudy battle flags as Franklin entered the convention hall, its floor littered with pamphlets and speech fragments. The Clark people were all over the place, singing the tag end of a song about hound dogs that had become their slogan:

> "I don't care if he is a houn'
> You gotta quit kicking my dawg aroun'."

The Wilson forces had nothing to equal that battle cry. If the nomination were to be decided by the decibel level, Champ Clark was in for sure. Franklin's pro-Wilson group had a block of seats in the gallery, where they could do little else than join in the applause. Franklin was not allowed on the floor, but watched with fascination as the week-long drama unfolded, with its strange rites, turnabouts, and shifting moods, and the final emergence of the collective will of the party.

There were 1,088 delegate votes, so that 545 was a majority, but the Democratic party had a two-thirds rule, which usually tied up the convention for days and often resulted in the elimination of strong candidates who could have led the party to victory and the selection of ineffective compromise candidates. It was felt that New York held the key, that Wilson could not be nominated without its ninety votes. But New York voted by the unit rule, another lamentable device. Hundreds of Wilson men were sewed up in delegations that would vote for Clark under the unit rule. Franklin could see the square red face of Tammany boss Charles F. Murphy, and sitting right behind him, the Wilson lieutenant, McAdoo, who was all over the floor rounding up Wilson votes, but who as a New York delegate could not vote for Wilson himself. It was absurd.

Franklin could see for the first time men he had only heard about, legendary Democrats like William Jennings Bryan, a stout balding man with long disorderly hair, who sat fanning himself in the Nebraska delegation. Bryan, the three-time loser who had led his wild agrarian following to the tune of free silver, had come to Baltimore with the future of "the other boys" on his mind—this might be a Democratic year. Of course if the other boys were divided it might be his duty to step in. He was supposed to be for Wilson, but under the unit rule Nebraska was voting for Clark. Bryan the teetotaler did not approve of the bibulous Clark and went around saying that he was a drunk.

As the balloting began, the New York delegation at first voted for Governor Judson Harmon of Ohio, a conservative backed by business interests. Murphy planned to throw the delegates to Clark at a moment of mounting strength, hoping to cause a stampede. When he switched to Clark on the tenth ballot, some of the Tammany men voted without enthusiasm. Al Smith had walked up to a Clark poster bearing the inscription "Don't he look like a President?" and had written underneath: "No, he do not."

The noise that followed the New York vote was deafening. Clark men seized the New York banner and marched around the hall with it, and Clark's attractive young daughter appeared in front of the speaker's platform bearing an American flag and was carried on the shoulders of her father's admirers. That was too much for Eleanor Roosevelt, who was so dismayed by the vulgarity and cheapness of it all that she left for Campobello with the chicks.

But Franklin had never seen anything so exciting, and knew that there was no place on earth he would rather be. When the dust had settled, Clark had 556 votes, one over a majority, but still far short of the 726 required for two-thirds, and Wilson had 350½. It was another peculiarity of Democratic conventions that some delegates had fraction votes.

On Saturday, June 29, with the Wilson forces so dejected that they were considering releasing their delegates, Bryan broke with his delegation and announced that he would withhold his vote for Clark as long as the New York delegation of "ninety wax figures" voted for him. This was a psychological turning point, and Wilson began to pick up votes.

On Monday, July 1, there was another moment that thrilled Franklin when McAdoo had the vote of the New York delegation challenged, which meant that each of the delegates would be polled in open convention. Would any of the ninety have the courage to defy Murphy and announce their preference for Wilson? Nine broke ranks, including McAdoo and Senator

O'Gorman, showing that the New York delegation still had a spark of independence.

It was at that moment that the Indiana delegation switched twenty-nine of its thirty votes from its favorite son, Governor Thomas R. Marshall, to Wilson. This was the first break from a large state, and Franklin watched Wilson's strength grow with each succeeding ballot. There was a feeling that Wilson would go over the top the next day, and he did. Illinois switched its fifty-eight votes from Clark to Wilson on the forty-third ballot, giving him 602 votes. After that, there was a scramble to board the bandwagon, and Wilson was nominated on the forty-sixth ballot.

Franklin's first convention had been one of the most stirring in the party's history, and ended with the nomination of Governor Marshall for vice president, as delegates yawned and stretched and examined railroad timetables. Marshall, the liberal governor of a midwestern state, would balance the ticket, and Indiana was rewarded for having made the key switch. Wilson owed nothing to the New York machine that had backed a loser, and took up the reins of the party leadership that had been held by Bryan with such disastrous results. He was a formidable candidate next to the lackluster Champ Clark. Franklin ran into Teddy's son, Kermit Roosevelt, who told him: "Pop was praying for Clark."

Franklin took it as a personal victory, although he had not voted and had not done any of the crucial missionary work on the convention floor. He had, however, led a highly visible and audible pro-Wilson group, and was now established as the leading Wilsonian in upstate New York. He seemed to sense that the nomination would affect him personally, for he wired Eleanor on July 2: "Wilson nominated this afternoon. All my plans vague. Splendid triumph." On July 3, Franklin went to see Wilson at his summer home in Sea Girt, New Jersey, to confer about New York State strategy, and found him surrounded by well-wishers and looking pained, as if he had been sentenced to sit in a store window.

In the event of success, Franklin intended to cash in on his early support of Wilson. He did not feel destined to remain in the state Senate, which he would always remember as an experience in frustration, writing Charles C. Burlingham in July 1928: "It is because of my three years in the state senate that I have already twice declined to be the party nominee for United States Senator. . . . I am not temperamentally fitted to serve in the United States Senate. I do not think I could endure the atmosphere of that verbose and eminently respectable club."

Woodrow Wilson, the first scholar-president, an exception to the tradition of lawyer-politicians and soldiers, was elected with a popular vote of 6,286,-214 to Theodore Roosevelt's 4,126,020 and Taft's 3,483,922. The Socialist candidate, Eugene V. Debs, made a strong showing with 897,011 votes. In the electoral college Wilson won by 435 to 88 for TR and 8 for Taft. He had polled almost 1.5 million fewer votes than the total of his two principal opponents, winning 41.8 percent of the popular vote, less than Bryan in any of his three campaigns. But he was not, as Lincoln had been, concerned over being a minority president, for he saw his victory as the will of God. He told his campaign manager, William F. McCombs, that "God ordained that I should be the next President of the United States." His mandate did not come from the people but from a higher authority.

For Franklin as well as Wilson, the four months between election and inauguration were an interregnum. While Wilson went on a Caribbean vacation and answered 15,000 letters of congratulations and free advice, Franklin took two rooms in the Hotel Ten Eyck for the 1913 legislative session, no longer needing the large house on State Street, as if knowing that he would not be in Albany for long. As he pressed his legislation on commission merchants, Wilson went through the agony of cabinet making.

On February 23, 1913, he offered Josephus Daniels the secretaryship of the Navy. Daniels was a landlubber Tarheel newspaper editor. His only connection with anything naval was that his father, a shipwright, had left him a chest of tools, and that his brother-in-law, Worth Bagley, had been the first naval officer killed in the war with Spain. Daniels wondered whether he should take it. He knew nothing about navigation, but then he had put out a newspaper without knowing how to run a linotype machine or a rotary press. He recalled the words of Nelson's biographer: "He was no seaman. All his energies were turned towards becoming a great Commander." He took it.

The inauguration was on March 4, and Franklin arrived in Washington three days early, renewing his acquaintance with men he had met during the convention, among them the new secretary of the Treasury, William Gibbs McAdoo, who asked him if he wanted to be assistant secretary or collector of the Port of New York. Finance had never been Franklin's forte, but the collectorship with its vast patronage was a power base from which to launch the anti-Tammany organization that he had long been dreaming of. His response was noncommittal; perhaps he knew that a better offer was coming.

On the morning of the inauguration, Franklin ran into Josephus Daniels in the lobby of the Willard Hotel and bubbled over with enthusiasm over his appointment, saying that it "made me happy. I congratulate you and the President and the country." Surely Franklin, whose interest in naval matters went back to the first log that a savage floated across a stream, knew that Daniels was a curious choice. He had always expressed contempt for landlubbers who professed to know about the sea, and had laughed over the Senate investigation of the sinking of the *Titanic,* when one senator had asked, "What is an iceberg made of?" and another had wondered why the passengers had not gone into the ship's watertight compartments to be saved. His effusive appreciation had an ulterior motive, to which Daniels immediately responded by asking: "How would you like to come to Washington as assistant secretary of the Navy?"

Franklin's response sounded rehearsed, and included the use of Cousin Teddy's favorite word, as if to underline that Teddy had held the same office, and that Franklin would be following in his footsteps: "How would I like it?" he asked. "I'd like it bully well. It would please me better than anything in the world. I'd be glad to be connected with the new administration. All my life I have loved ships and have been a student of the Navy, and the assistant secretaryship is the one place, above all others, I would love to hold." McAdoo had asked him to go to the Treasury, he said, "but nothing would please me so much as to be with you in the Navy."

After this chance encounter, which decided his fate for the next seven years, Franklin went to the inauguration, and saw President-elect Wilson arrive at the Capitol, glancing about at the dark-robed justices and the gathered congressmen, and move outside to the east facade, where a crowd of 50,000 waited to see him take the oath of office. Then he gave his speech and shook hands with former president Taft, porcine symbol of the party that had ruled for the last sixteen years.

Two days later, Daniels proposed Franklin to Wilson. "You are quick on the trigger," Wilson said. Daniels said it would be better to fill the position right away, and that "as I am from the South, I think the Assistant Secretary should come from another section, preferably from New York or New England."

"How well do you know Mr. Roosevelt, and how well is he equipped?" Wilson asked. Daniels made the case for the young man for whom he had felt a case of "love at first sight" in Baltimore, the state senator whose battle against the machine had lifted him into the "coming man" class, and Wilson approved.

Since Daniels planned to make good relations with Congress one of his strengths, he called in the two New York senators for their opinions. He was surprised when Senator O'Gorman, who was supposed to owe his office to the Roosevelt-led insurgents, said without enthusiasm that Franklin's appointment would be "acceptable." Then the respected Republican Senator Elihu Root arrived, who had been secretary of war in the McKinley cabinet and secretary of state under Theodore Roosevelt, and he said, speaking from experience, with a queer look in his eyes: "You know the Roosevelts, don't you? Whenever a Roosevelt rides, he rides in front." "A chief who fears that an assistant will outrank him is not fit to be chief," Daniels replied. He related the conversation to President Wilson, who expressed the same opinion. In his diary, Daniels wrote: "His distinguished cousin TR went from that place to the Presidency. May history repeat itself."

While waiting for confirmation, Franklin finished up pending business in Albany. He was glad to be leaving, but some of his mail accused him of being a quitter. C. Griffith, a Brewster businessman, wrote on March 12 that "during the last campaign, you made promises to push certain measures through the legislature which would be of inestimable benefit to all the farmers of our state. . . . You could not have accomplished this during your first term but now you are recognized as a leader in the upper branch of our legislature. Is it quite fair to those who took you at your word and elected you, to now leave them thus in the lurch?. . . . Please pardon my frankness but it is right from the heart."

On April 7, already in Washington, Franklin replied rather lamely that "conditions at Albany this year are in such a chaotic state that it is almost impossible for any one person to accomplish much. The lines are not, and cannot be, drawn in any definite way, and so far the conditions have resembled a free for all race and the devil take the hindermost."

Franklin had served in the State Senate for two legislative sessions and part of a third. It would be his only experience in the legislative branch. His bent was toward the managerial. He had gained quick notice by combating a political machine that was promoting young men of promise and a reform program. But Tammany was still seen in the rest of the country as an evil dragon, and Franklin's dragon-slayer image thrust him onto the national scene while his fellow insurgents saw their political careers ruined.

He was not popular with his colleagues. He still smelled of Groton and Harvard, and displayed the accent and mannerisms of the well-born. Al Smith made fun of his "pinchers" and was convinced that part of his opposition to Sheehan was the distaste of the Hudson River Episcopalian patrician for an Irish Catholic. He gravitated toward social equals, and his best friend in the Senate was the socially registered Westchester Republican, J. Mayhew Wainwright. Frances Perkins recalled that Franklin "stood out for being a little disagreeable." Why didn't he have more fun with the two Sullivans, Tim and Christy, she wondered? If she had been in his position, she would have gotten to know the Sullivans real well, she would have had a glass of beer with them and found out what life was like in a New York City slum. But Franklin was incapable of that, and they didn't like him. "What struck me about him," she said, "was that he wasn't being liked by his colleagues in the Senate. They just weren't getting warm to him."

Franklin was parochial in his outlook. He did not share the rage of urban legislators after the Triangle fire, and only gave lip service to the great wave of reform that was carried on that rage. Later, amending the past, he tried to make it seem that he had been a more active partisan of such measures as the fifty-four-hour bill. He was popular with his constituents, being twice elected in a normally Republican district, because he looked after their interests, whether standardizing apple barrels or regulating commission merchants. When he looked farther than his district, it was not for the improvement of conditions for workers but for the regulation of land use and the protection of fish and game.

There was a strain of opportunism in his character that made him adopt positions that would advance his career. He was quite ready at one point to back Tammany on the New York City charter because he had been offered a congressional seat, and it would not be long until he made his peace with Tammany once and for all, having realized that what he could not defeat he must join.

For the moment, he was leaving Albany for Washington, leaving state politics for an important post in the new administration. He had a curious double allegiance: one to his cousin, long an example of success in politics at the service of strong principle, but who had wrecked his career on vain third-party hopes and who was now no more than "an old cannon loose on the deck in a storm"; the other to Woodrow Wilson, who had brought the Democratic party to power and was not afraid to exercise strong leadership. It was the first time that a Democrat had been in the White House in the twentieth century. Franklin was a member of the crew, and was looking forward to the work of the ship. The weather was a little thick, as it was apt to be at the start of a long crossing, but the new pilot had the instinct for command.

His visit to the Panama Canal in April 1912 had opened his eyes to a larger scale of events than he was dealing with in Albany. When he saw the Great Cut, and the locks that moved ships vertically, he realized what the leader of a great power could do. In terms of the conquests of nature for the good of man, it rivaled anything that past civilizations had to offer. He saw that to each society was given the chance for great works, and wrote home that he had seen "this wonder of the world, greater than the Tower of Babel or the Pyramids." Perhaps in his mind's eye he saw projects, yet to be conceived, of equal magnitude.

VI

Assistant Secretary of the Navy

On the whole, a man must not complain of his "element," of his "time," or the like; it is thriftless work doing so. His time is bad: well then, he is there to make it better.

Thomas Carlyle

With one wave of the wand, Franklin had been transported from the blind alley of being a Democrat in a Republican district to stage center, Washington in a Democratic administration. He was young, barely thirty-one, half the age of many of the admirals with whom he would do business. He was a political novice, never having represented more than three rural counties in upstate New York. But the aura of Cousin Teddy's example clung to him, and several congratulatory letters reminded him that he was stepping on the same stones. Not that long ago, at that very desk, Cousin Teddy had planned the capture of Manila Bay, and four years later he was president.

For the moment, alone in Washington, Franklin stayed at the Powhatan Hotel, and on the afternoon of March 17, 1913, he went to his office for the first time, in the huge archaic pile of scrambled architecture on Pennsylvania Avenue flanking the White House that the Navy shared with the departments of State and War.

To his mother Franklin wrote, on his new letterhead with four stars around an anchor embossed in a corner, "I am baptized, confirmed, sworn in, vaccinated—and somewhat at sea! For over an hour I have been signing papers which had to be accepted on faith—but I hope luck will keep me out of jail. All well, but I will have to work like a new turbine to master this job."

Sara's reply had the same solicitous tone she had employed when he had first gone away to school: ". . . I just *knew* it was a *very* big job, and everything so new that it will take time to fit *into* it. Try not to write your signature too small, as it gets a cramped look and is not distinct. So many public men have such awful signatures and so unreadable."

Franklin kept his predecessor's secretary, Charles H. McCarthy, who knew the ropes, but also sent for Louis Howe: "Dear Ludwig . . . Here is the dope. Secretary—$2000—Expect you in April with a new uniform." "I am game but it's going to break me," Howe replied.

Two days later, on March 19, Daniels was away, and Franklin was acting secretary "and up to my ears. I must have signed three or four hundred papers today and am *beginning* to catch on," he wrote his "Dearest Babbie" (Eleanor).

On March 27, Franklin reported "a most interesting day. . . . I was suddenly called on by the President to make all the arrangements for sending surgeons, attendants, supplies etc. out to the flood district in Ohio—I had a hectic time getting the machinery going, but the force leaves tonight and I had some interesting work with the Sec. of War and Gen'l Wood" (General Leonard Wood was then Army chief of staff).

Franklin's satisfaction at working with the bigwigs was evident, but the man he would work most closely with in the next seven years, the man in the office next door, was his boss, Josephus Daniels. In a political career spanning thirty-five years, Daniels would be his only administrative superior, and Franklin could consider himself fortunate that his chief was fond of him and tolerant. On March 15, Daniels wrote in his diary that "it is singular that I never thought of any other man [than FDR] in that connection [assistant secretary]."

Daniels was a kind of American Franklin had not known before, a product of small-town life, the Bible Belt, and the South. He was at the same time an economic radical, a racist, a religious fundamentalist, a pacifist, and a defender of the common man against vested interests. It was a baffling mixture, a product of the contradictory forces at work in the postbellum South. His father, a ship's carpenter, had been killed by irregulars in the Civil War. His mother was postmistress of a small town in North Carolina, and when Daniels moved to Raleigh, it was with the fervent hope that he would never have to lick another stamp.

In the state capital, then the hub of a cotton-farming area, he founded a newspaper called the *News and Observer,* an organ for the Bryan wing of the Democratic party that inveighed against the Carolina rail and power and tobacco trusts. The "interests" tried to put him out of business with competing papers and, failing that, dubbed his sheet "The Nuisance and Disturber." Daniels was full of moral fervor, but he was also a traditional southern racist. The day had not yet come when the Democratic party courted the Negro vote, and in an editorial on October 1, 1912, a month before Wilson's election, he wrote that the South was solidly Democratic because of "the realization that the subjection of the negro, politically, and the separation of the negro, socially, are paramount to all other considerations in the South short of the preservation of the Republic itself. And we shall recognize no emancipation, nor shall we proclaim any deliverer, that falls short of these essentials to the peace and the welfare of our part of the country." Daniels was shocked when Eleanor brought white servants to Washington, and advised her to get some darkies.

With his string ties, pleated shirts, black broadcloth suits in winter and white linen suits in summer, Daniels was the cartoon southerner. "When I first knew him he was the funniest-looking hillbilly I'd ever seen," FDR later told his press secretary, William D. Hassett. Franklin used to mimic Daniels's folksy ways in front of his friends at the Metropolitan Club, and liked to tell Daniels-the-landlubber stories. Once, when they were visiting a naval base, they were sitting with an admiral after dinner when an aide came in and said: "I wish to report, sir, that all is secure." The admiral nodded a cue to Daniels, who, not knowing he could reply with a quiet "Very well," responded with boisterous cordiality: "Well, I declare! That's fine! I'm mighty glad to hear it!"

But Daniels was no cartoon character when it came to his job. He knew exactly what he wanted, and did not intend to rubber-stamp the suggestions of the admirals. He soon found himself in an adversary relationship with the Navy brass, for his priorities had nothing to do with war preparedness, naval construction, or increased personnel. As he sat in his office, gazing pensively at the chandelier with cut-glass pendants, the naval trophies in their cases, and the globe of the world, so much of it covered by seas where American ships might be called, he dreamed of making the Navy a great university. He did not want to hear about war—that was unthinkable—he wanted to hear about classrooms aboard ship, and the welfare of the enlisted men. He met defeat when he tried to get the sailors to wear pajamas, but succeeded in having laundries installed aboard ship.

Daniels saw himself as responsible for the moral fitness of the young Americans entrusted to his care. Accordingly, he banned the Navy issue of contraceptives. "The use of this packet," his directive read, "I believe to be immoral; it savors of the panderer. . . . It is equivalent to the government advising these boys that it is right and proper for them to indulge in an evil which perverts their morals."

As much against drink as he was against fornication, Daniels in April 1914 abolished the officers' wine mess. He had the backing of a letter from the surgeon general pointing out that there had been numerous court-martials of officers for drunkenness. The officers were outraged that they could not be trusted to have a glass of beer or wine aboard ship, but Daniels saw this pleasant custom in terms of the evils of grog.

Franklin was away from Washington when the wine-mess flap broke, but supported his chief, having a moralistic streak himself. He wrote Louis Howe that the "wine order is . . . on the whole absolutely right. It took nerve to do it, but tho the secy will be unpopular in a small circle for a while, it will pay in the end."

Daniels's other obsession, aside from morality, was thrift. "There is no waste of money as reckless or inexcusable as paying more for a thing than is necessary," he wrote. "To pay two dollars for something that can be bought for a dollar and a half is exactly as much a total loss as if the extra fifty cents had been thrown into the gutter." He carried to the Navy Department his hatred of vested interests and monopolies. Collusion among the big steel companies for Navy contracts had become a habit, and Daniels intended to put an end to it.

In May 1913, the big three, Carnegie, Bethlehem, and Midvale, brought in identical bids of $454 a ton for the armor plate for the battleship *Arizona*. Daniels obtained a lower bid from an English firm, which forced the American companies to cut their prices. Neither he nor his assistant had any qualms about awarding contracts to foreign firms. Turbine drums for the *Arizona* were bought from England, and a flag and bunting contract went to a Canadian company. What did the steel companies know about patriotism, Daniels huffed. They spelled it "paytriotism." They had sold armor plate cheaper to the Russians than to the U.S. Navy.

On July 18, 1913, having been on the job three months, Franklin spent a "hearty half hour" with President Wilson discussing "a nice point" concerning contracts with foreign firms. The lowest American bidder on large machines for the Navy Yard was slightly higher than a German firm, but other factors were involved. There was the cost of inspection of the German goods, which would offset the price difference. But there was also the 15 percent duty the Germans would have to pay the U.S. Treasury on the price. President Wilson argued that the national interest would be better served by awarding the bid to the American firm, in terms of jobs created and the boost to the economy. Therefore, the tariff should not enter into consideration. Franklin agreed, but half-heartedly, privately hoping that in some far-off day a global rather than a purely national view of economics could be taken.

What with meetings with the president, and appearances before congressional committees, Franklin felt that he was earning his salary. "I now find my vocation combined with my avocation in a delightful way," he wrote a friend. It was "real work," involving as it did a Navy and Marine Corps of 65,000 men, with an annual budget of $150 million. He delighted in the "fuss and feathers" of Navy ceremonial, the seventeen-gun salute when he visited a ship, four guns more than rear admirals with thirty years' service, and the sixteen-man guard standing at attention on the quarterdeck, and the officers in dress uniform gathered to greet him.

He designed his own flag, to be hoisted when he was aboard ship, which was often, for he was not bashful about using ships for personal excursions. He ordered the battleship *North Dakota* to Eastport, Maine, for the Fourth of July weekend of 1913. This was right across from Campobello, where Eleanor and the chicks were spending the summer. Eleanor was kept busy arranging teas and dinners for the senior officers. Three-year-old Elliott, in a blue sailor suit, boarded the huge ship, affecting a swaggering naval stride, and saluted the flag as his father had taught him.

On another occasion, a young Navy lieutenant, William F. Halsey, was ordered to take his destroyer to Campobello Island and report to FDR, who wanted to inspect the naval installations in Frenchman Bay, Maine. Halsey had been told that the assistant secretary had some experience with small boats, and when he offered to pilot the destroyer through the strait between Campobello and the mainland, Halsey gave him the conn (steering control) with misgivings and stood close by. The fact that a white-flanneled yachtsman could sail a catboat out to a buoy and back was no guarantee that he could handle a high-speed destroyer in narrow waters. A destroyer's bow might point directly down the channel, but she was not necessarily on a safe course. She pivoted around a point near her bridge structure, which meant that two-thirds of her length was behind the pivot, and that her stern would swing in twice the arc of her bow. As Franklin made his first turn, Halsey saw him look aft and check the swing of the stern. His worries were over. The assistant secretary knew his stuff.

Franklin and his family had settled into a red-brick house at 1733 N Street, on a tree-shaded street, with a postage stamp of a lawn and a little garden in the back. His New York house was rented to Thomas W. Lamont, the Morgan partner. Sara visited their new house and reported in her diary: "Dined at 1733 N Street. Moved chairs and tables and began to feel at home." Eleanor paid calls and left cards. She had it down to six minutes a call. Franklin was six blocks away from his office, walking down Connecticut Avenue and passing his clubs on the way, the Army and Navy and the Metropolitan. He worked late at the office, and Eleanor would call: "When are you coming home?" Then he would rush out the door, putting on his coat as he dashed down the steps three at a time, bobbing up and down like a man jumping rope.

It was a hectic life, for Franklin immediately had entree, through his job and his connection with Cousin Teddy, to the top of the basket in social Washington. There was an inner group of friends who formed an informal supper club that met every two weeks. The core members were the bald and paunchy secretary of the interior, Franklin K. Lane, a jolly man who loved Washington gossip; his economist friend, Adolph E. Miller, a consultant on pending Federal Reserve legislation; William Phillips, an assistant secretary of state; Franklin Roosevelt; and their wives.

Miller had first met Franklin one day in June 1913 when he was walking through Lafayette Park with Lane after lunch and spotted in the distance a tall erect young man with head tossed back. He was clearly not someone who had his eyes fixed on the pavement. They were introduced at the foot of the Jackson statue, and Miller sensed that here was a young man who combined an extroverted manner with courtesy and grace. Miller asked if he was related to Theodore, whom he knew, and Franklin said, "Yes, distantly," and then, "What is it about him that you admire most?" "His dynamic virility," Miller said. He had the feeling that Franklin was constantly appraising TR to guide his own conduct.

Franklin had known Bill Phillips since Harvard, where he had graduated summa cum laude in three years and made Porcellian. Phillips thought that Franklin was likable and attractive, but not a heavyweight. He could be brilliant, but he was not particularly steady in his views. He had tremendous vitality, an eagerness and interest in everything, and he was always the life of the party, but he did not seem fully mature. Eleanor nagged him about such things as answering a letter right away, as if he was not capable of doing it on his own. None of his friends then imagined that he would ever become a world figure. He was an efficient assistant secretary, of whom there were many, nothing more.

Of all the picturesque figures Franklin met in Washington, perhaps the most memorable was Henry Adams, the direct descendant of the second and sixth presidents, then seventy-five, a historian who had himself become a historical oddity. Sometimes Franklin and Eleanor received one of the much-coveted invitations to dine at his house overlooking Lafayette Square. He enjoyed sharp exchanges, and loved to tease people and draw them out. Franklin and Adams were like emissaries from different centuries, bearing dissimilar messages. Adams had made pessimism a rule of life. Having idealized the Middle Ages in *Mont-Saint-Michel and Chartres,* he felt that he was living in the ruins of a dissolved world, and dwelled without respite on the stagnation of his time—the earth was grimy and cheap; all statesmen were contemptible or incompetent or both; the middle class, all stomach and no brain, was taking over. He harped so on disintegration that in the eyes of many he had become a crank. One day after lunch, when Franklin mentioned some matter of current importance, Adams stared at him and said: "Young man, I have lived in this house many years and seen the occupants of the White House across the square come and go, and nothing that you minor officials or the occupant of that house can do will affect the history of the world for very long." Eleanor astutely observed that cynicism was Adams's defense against his own urge to be an active factor in politics, which he had stifled in his youth. Since he had no part in making decisions, he had to belittle their results.

Franklin was a living antidote to Adams's weltschmerz, radiating an incurable American optimism. He had a Boy Scoutish faith in the institutions he served, in the ability of the president, in the capacity of government to improve the lives of the people. He was a man absorbed in his time, without neurotic longings for past centuries and unifying symbols. He had a will to make things work, to resolve conflicts, to see the system hum. He was never, like Adams, "sicklied o'er with the pale cast of thought." As Adams waited for civilization to founder, his ear attuned to the cries of the drowning, Franklin was glad to be alive in the second decade of the twentieth century, and to have a small part in affairs of state.

Only four days in harness, he had told reporters on March 21: "There's another Roosevelt on the job today—you remember what happened the last time a Roosevelt occupied a similar position?" How could they not remember? In February 1898, after the blowing up of the armored cruiser *Maine* in Havana harbor, Secretary of the Navy John D. Long left Washington for the day, specifying to his assistant that he must not make any decisions without consulting him or the president. TR then sent the famous telegram ordering Admiral Dewey from Hong Kong to Manila Bay "in the event of declaration of war with Spain." His insubordination added to his fame, and four years later he was president.

Franklin seemed to be announcing that he too was prepared to be insubordinate. His dealings with Daniels were complicated and not always above-board. It was the classic situation of a young man destined for great things chafing with impatience at having to take orders rather than give them. Daniels forgot much, and overlooked even more of the sort of thing he would never have tolerated from his admirals. Franklin was the golden boy, and could always get back into his good graces through charm and a kind of easy give and take that comes out in some of their memos, such as this one concerning a function neither wished to attend:

"SECNAV—It would be unseemly for the ass. sec. to head the list. Ass. Sec.

"ASTNAV—I think this is one case in which the asst. secy. should take the lead. Go the limit! JD.

"SECNAV—I always obey orders worse luck. FDR."

At first Franklin did obey orders. He was in sympathy with Daniels's competitive-bidding crusade, and paid lip service to his Navy-as-university ideas. But gradually he started thinking of himself as the real power in the Navy Department, "the man who got things done," the advocate of preparedness and a big navy. He became a conduit for the lobbies and the congressmen who wanted more naval spending, and for the admirals who thought their ideas would get a hearing if they were presented by him. He showed a gift for duplicity in remaining on good terms with Daniels when he was sniping at him from hidden positions and consorting with his enemies. He was disloyal and affable at the same time, lavishing kind attention on Daniels, who confided to his diary on Christmas day, 1913, that his most prized present was a painting that Franklin had ordered for him of the USS *North Carolina*, the first American line-of-battle ship to cross the Atlantic.

The first thrust of Franklin's secret undermining of his chief was an attack on his competence. Not only was Daniels blissfully ignorant in naval matters, but he was dilatory and indecisive. Fortunately Franklin was there to save the poor dolt from blunders. In July 1913, he wrote his wife: "The Secy and I worked like niggers all day on all the things he *should* have decided before and as I expected *most* of them were turned over to me! The trouble is that the Secy has expressed half-baked opinions in these matters and I don't agree—I know that he would decide right if he'd only give the time to learn—however he has given me carte blanche and says he will abide by my decisions."

Daniels genuinely hoped that the day would come when large fleets would no longer be necessary. He was all for international talks to limit naval armaments, and agreed with Bryan, who wanted to build, instead of battleships, two great peace ships called the *Friendship* and the *Fellowship*. In addition, he found when he went on the Hill that whenever he mentioned preparedness he had to contend with the feeling among many congressmen that it was a plot hatched by suppliers of war matériel to obtain huge contracts at high prices. Franklin, however, made himself the spokesman for more ships, more men, more money.

Admiral Bradley A. Fiske, the aide for operations, and Admiral William F. Fullam, the aide for inspection, also favored a big shipbuilding program, and the prestigious General Board recommended four battleships a year, but Daniels cut that figure in half. Fullam, like Fiske, thought Daniels was wrecking the Navy with his plebeian ideas, such as opening the doors of the Naval Academy to enlisted men.

By the end of his first year in office, Daniels had been the butt of many brickbats. A typical remark was that of former president Taft in a letter to a friend on December 18: "I think Daniels is proving to be more kinds of an ass than any other member of the Cabinet." By comparison, Franklin was known as the "spark plug" who got things done.

In April 1914, all hell broke loose in Mexico. President Wilson having refused to recognize the dictator Victoriano Huerta, fleet units were sent into Mexican waters to protect American lives and property. This was the point of the policy of "watchful waiting," that is, waiting for a more acceptable regime.

On April 9, a seven-man party from the dispatch boat *Dolphin*, which Franklin had taken the previous October to inspect the fleet departing on its Mediterranean cruise, now stationed off Tampico, was sent on shore to load supplies. They were arrested, held for a few minutes, and released with apologies. Without notifying Daniels, Rear Admiral Henry T. Mayo demanded that the Mexicans raise and salute an American flag and deliver a formal apology. "I understand the State Department is yelling blue murder because Mayo on his own initiative commanded a salute," Louis Howe wrote Franklin, who was on the West Coast inspecting naval installations. "I am afraid Mayo is not a good 'watchful waiter.' "

Trifling as the incident was, Wilson seized on it and delivered two ultimatums to Huerta. Daniels sent the North Atlantic Fleet to Tampico. On April 19, when the second ultimatum expired, Franklin arrived in Portland and told reporters: "We're not looking for trouble, but we're ready for anything."

Two days later, the Navy and the Marines occupied Vera Cruz to prevent a German ship from landing machine guns and ammunition for Huerta. From Seattle, Franklin asked Daniels if the naval action could be extended to the west coast of Mexico. Here was a chance for combat experience, in Cousin Teddy's wake. But Daniels told Franklin to return to Washington as planned.

The bloodless occupation of Vera Cruz had not gone as expected. The Mexicans fought back, losing 125 killed and 195 wounded to the American losses of 19 killed and 71 wounded. Wilson was appalled that blood had been shed. The deaths of American sailors and marines shook him badly. He began to see that intervention had been a major blunder. American and international opinion was against him. He seemed to be making war over an absurd point of honor, like the war of the two kings to decide which end of the egg should be broken first. All over Latin America, the United States was seen as a bullying meddler. In Mexico, he succeeded in uniting the warring factions in their hatred of America, and three years of fratricidal war were forgotten in a single day. Wisely reconsidering, Wilson on April 25 accepted a mediation offer from Argentina, Brazil, and Chile, ending the crisis.

Returning to Washington by train, and not knowing the turn events had taken, Franklin was interviewed at every station, and sounded increasingly belligerent as he approached the capital. In Butte, Montana, on April 24, he said: "We are merely engaged in the occupation of a city, it is not a war." In Minneapolis on the following day, when asked by a reporter what the crisis meant, he said: "War! And we're ready." This was wishful thinking. Franklin *hoped* for war, seeing himself in the thick of it. In Milwaukee on April 26, he said: "I do not want war, but I do not see how we can avoid it." By this time, Wilson had accepted the mediation offer, but Franklin had not heard about it. He used the Mexican crisis to propound his big-navy views, this time, in the heat of the moment, announcing that the United States must have a navy second to none, which not even the most extreme big-navy men in Congress were advocating.

War was in the air, Franklin was right about that, though not necessarily in Mexico. On July 13, 1914, he was acting secretary when a critical situation arose in Haiti and Santo Domingo. Revolution swept the island, and both countries refused to accept treaties giving America a greater hand in their affairs. Franklin saw William Jennings Bryan and Bill Phillips and by 5:00 P.M. he had 700 marines and two ships en route for Guantanamo. It was just the kind of gunboat diplomacy à la Teddy that he relished.

That evening, there was a picnic in Rock Creek Park for the fiftieth birthday of Interior Secretary Franklin Lane. McAdoo was there, looking very correct and proper, and Bryan came up to him and said: "Guess what! Huerta's out!" To everyone's amazement, they began to do a sort of jig, with locked arms and high kicks, prancing around like a couple of chorus girls. Wilson's policy of steady pressure had been successful after all, and General Carranza would take over in August. Well, reflected Franklin, that brought to an end the timeworn cry of "Huerta must go," but he still regretted not having invaded, and wrote Eleanor that Huerta's departure "resulted entre nous in no *definite* policy of construction. We drift on from day to day as usual. . . ."

The spring had ended in Washington. The cherry blossoms were gone from the trees. The days were oppressively hot. One night Franklin took two cold baths and changed his sweat-drenched pajamas three times, and finally moved into the better ventilated middle room with a sheet and managed to get about four hours' sleep. He looked forward to spending a few days at the end of July with Eleanor and the chicks in Campobello.

Not since his inauguration, President Wilson felt, had he lived through such a difficult time. The crisis with Mexico was averted, but in Colorado there was a bloody conflict between mine owners and workers. His wife, Ellen, gravely ill, was not improving. Europe was a sputtering fuse, though no one in the United States realized it. The assassination of Archduke Franz Ferdinand in Sarajevo in June had not made the front page of the Atlanta *Journal,* but the fact that a man wore a sleeveless bathing suit did. America was unconcerned with the crisis in Europe. What was the matter with these people, the *Washington Post* asked; they had problems that a police court judge could adjust in a week.

Declarations of war began flying right and left. Austria-Hungary declared war on Serbia on July 28. Russia declared war on Austria-Hungary on July 29. Germany declared war on August 1. Franklin's vacation was interrupted by a telegram summoning him back to work. In the smoking room of the Bar Harbor Express, he ran into some friends from the New York banking and brokerage world. They were willing to bet that the bankers would stop the war within six months. Why, there wasn't enough money in all the world to carry on a European war longer than that. It was humanly and physically impossible. Franklin took the bets. He felt that a general war was inevitable.

But Daniels did not seem to grasp the seriousness of the situation. To Franklin's astonishment, nobody seemed the least excited about the European war: "Mr. Daniels feeling chiefly very sad that his faith in human nature and civilization and similar idealistic nonsense was receiving such a rude shock. So I started in alone to get things ready and prepare plans for what *ought* to be done by the Navy end of things. Friday I worked all day on these lines, and actually succeeded in getting one ship North from Mexico. These dear people like W.J.B. [Bryan] and J.D. have as much conception of what a general European war means as [his son] Elliott has of higher mathematics. They really believe that because we are neutral we can go about our business as usual. To my horror, *just for example,* J.D. told the newspapermen he thought favorably of sending our fleet to Europe to bring back marooned Americans! Aside from the fact that tourists (female etc.) couldn't sleep in hammocks and that battleships haven't got passenger accommodations, he totally fails to grasp the fact that this war between the other powers is going inevitably to give rise to a hundred different complications in which we shall have a direct interest. Questions of refugees, of neutrality, of commerce are even now appearing and we should unquestionably gather our fleet together and get it into the highest state of efficiency. We still have twelve battleships at Vera Cruz—their 'matériel' has suffered somewhat, their 'personnel' a great deal! The rest of the fleet is scattered to the four winds—they should be assembled and prepared. Some fine day the State Department will want the *moral* backing of a 'fleet in being' and it *won't be there.* All this sounds like borrowing trouble I know but it is *my* duty to keep the Navy in a position where no chances, even the most remote, are taken. Today we are taking chances and I nearly boil over when I see the cheery 'manana' way of doing business."

By the time Franklin wrote this indignant letter to his "own dearest," on August 2, Germany had invaded France. The best that could be expected, he felt, was a quick victory by one side, or a cessation of hostilities by mutual consent, but neither was likely. He hoped that England would join France and Russia and that their troops would invade Germany and force peace *at Berlin!*

On August 4, England declared war on Germany. Few Americans sensed that this was the end of the orderly nineteenth-century world, of Europe and its regulated societies, each the mirror image of the others, with the same conventions and values, with related families of rulers that kept the peace, with an accepted diplomatic system for smoothing out disturbances, with naval visits and court life and royal funerals. The machinery had broken down.

Americans would be affected, though they did not know it. The world of constant travel, cosmopolitan intercourse, secure comfort and culture, the world that Franklin had grown up in, would not be the same again. Americans would lose their easygoing confident way of looking at things, and the distinctness of the New World.

The general opinion at first was that the war would not last long. It would be over before the cotton season, said the Dallas *News.* The feeling was that Europe's mess was Europe's problem. "If Europe insists on committing suicide," wrote the New York *World,* "then Europe must furnish the corpse for Europe's funeral."

Alarmed at Daniels's "business as usual" attitude, Franklin felt that it was up to him to save the Navy. Daniels did not grasp the scope of the war. Nor did Bryan, as harmless as a cow, who sat in his messy office, his pockets filled with crumpled telegrams, piles of papers spilling from his desk onto the floor, as he signed his absurd peace covenants, and sent paperweights (made by the Navy yard) in the form of plowshares, with the familiar quotation on the blade, and on the plow his favorite saying: "Nothing is final between friends." Daniels was just as bad, he didn't understand that the battleships had to be brought back from Mexican waters and that the fleet must be kept in readiness on the Atlantic.

Daniels was less than useless. Franklin wrote his wife on August 5: "I am running the real work, although Josephus is here! He is bewildered by it all, very sweet but very sad!" Two days later he felt that "some order is coming out of the chaos," because Wilson had named him to sit on two boards, "as Mr. Daniels didn't seem anxious to do it himself." The first was the Neutrality Board. Following Wilson's strong proclamation committing the United States to complete neutrality, and making it a crime for anyone to be partial beyond the "free expression of opinion," it was the Navy's job to watch the coast, protect the neutrality of American ports, and prevent arms shipments to belligerents. The second was the Relief Board to help Americans stranded in Europe.

For Wilson, the nightmare of the world situation fused with his personal tragedy, the death of his wife on August 6. It was too terrible, Franklin thought. The president had been truly wonderful, but he dreaded a breakdown.

Once the conditions of neutrality had been established, there was nothing much to do but wait for infractions, and Franklin was able to leave the office after a morning's work on August 9 and get in a round of golf. He was also about to leave for Campobello, where his wife was about to give birth again. Blanche Spring, the nurse, had arrived on August 12, and Dr. Albert N. Ely, a leading gynecologist, was due to come up from New York for the delivery. Franklin was there on the sixteenth when she felt stirrings, and he sailed to Lubec on the *Half Moon* to get old Dr. Bennet. But the baby did not come and they sat around for a day, with Eleanor feeling guilty that she was keeping the doctor from his other patients. It was late on August 17 that Franklin Jr., all ten pounds of him, decided to make an appearance. Franklin's Poughkeepsie friend John Mack wrote that "it is apparent that while you believe in Woman's Suffrage you are not satisfied of its successful termination. It was rather selfish of you to insist on a boy with Woman's Suffrage in sight . . ."

Most of Franklin's work at the Navy Department had nothing to do with policy or large issues. He was responsible for the Navy's huge physical plant, and his time was spent on the nuts-and-bolts matters of the Navy yards and of the thousands of men employed there.

Another time-consuming aspect of the job was responding to requests from congressmen, who had to be kept in a friendly and open frame of mind. They were constantly calling on behalf of constituents who wanted to enlist, be discharged, come in from desertion, go to Annapolis, be promoted, take exams, be transferred or reassigned, go to sea, come ashore, or take compassionate leave.

When there was not prompt action, the congressmen came banging on his door. "Maher [Brooklyn Representative James P. Maher] was in here the other day and was madder than a wet hen because you had not answered his letter about Rockwell [an engineer threatened with transfer from the New York Navy Yard]," McCarthy wrote Howe on July 23, 1915. "Griffin [Daniel J. Griffin, a New York representative] was here at the same time and made his customary speech about what he was going to do if the Carson case was not settled soon!" (Samuel Carson was charged with operating a baseball pool in the New York Navy Yard.) When Congressman Tinkham of New York asked him to release from service a young sailor about to ship out to South America on the cruiser *Denver* because the boxing manager John Buckley thought he showed promise, Franklin managed to do it. The sailor was Jack Sharkey, who became world heavyweight champion.

Also sure to get a hearing was anyone on the Groton-Harvard-Hyde Park axis. Franklin was a sucker for classmates or anyone with wealth or social position. Lathrop Brown, his Harvard roommate, who had been elected in 1912 as Democratic representative from New York's first district, inquired on one occasion about a young man named Donald Clapham, who had gone astray with a beautiful woman, had been given a suspended sentence for stealing $38, and who now wanted to enlist in the Navy. Louis Howe wrote him about "your young friend Clapham, who appears to have nothing against him except that he has broken most of the Ten Commandments. I am willing to admit that if we bar from the Navy every gent who has become mixed up with a beautiful female we would have to put most of our ships out of commission and I am afraid might lose an admiral or two, but in this case the young man was unfortunately caught with the goods. You have run up against one of the Secretary's strongest antipathies. And while I know Mr. Roosevelt will speak to Mr. Daniels about the case again, I honestly do not think he has a chance on earth."

All the years he was in Washington, Franklin kept a watchful eye on New York, his power base. In all likelihood, when his term in the Navy was up, he would return to politics in his native state. He had to keep his bridges mended, and his office became a clearinghouse for every sort of request from New York contacts and members of his old State Senate constituency.

Franklin's sustained interest in New York State politics went far beyond doing favors for friends and constituents. He was still committed to building an upstate Democratic organization that could spearhead a frontal attack on Tammany. He soon discovered that he was in a better position to damage Tammany from the Navy Department than he had been as a state senator, through patronage. The Navy Department had very little patronage in New York, and most of the slices of the federal pie were already spoken for. McAdoo at the Treasury had a big slice, and was busy appointing independent Democrats as appraisers, collectors, U.S. marshals, internal revenue collectors, and census supervisors. Franklin's plate was empty, but he found some leftovers among the post office appointments.

Postmaster General Albert S. Burleson, an easygoing Texan, and his first assistant from South Carolina, Daniel C. Roper, had to fill postmasterships in every hamlet in America, 60,000 in all, and usually knew little or nothing about local conditions. Louis Howe offered to help pick the right men for upstate New York, and impressed Roper as being knowledgeable about state politics and apparently sincere about raising the quality of New York State postmasters. Through carefully cultivated connections, Franklin built his upstate machine, backing anti-Tammany men and holding up "unfit" candidates. Only a month after he had arrived in Washington, on April 16, 1913, Roper wrote: "Complying with your request of Monday I am sending you herewith a list of the Presidential post offices in New York where appointments are due by death, resignation, or where the commission of the postmaster has expired."

Soon Franklin was operating as a broker for federal jobs out of the Navy Department, and short-circuiting the Tammany regulars whenever he could. In some cases, Burleson agreed to name his candidate in spite of objections from Senator O'Gorman. Of course this meant keeping Burleson happy when he wanted a favor. A Burleson appointee to the Naval Academy, Ensign Stanley G. Womble, was stationed in San Francisco but wanted an assignment on the East Coast. Burleson's secretary, Ruskin McArdle, passed the request on to Franklin "in confidence, . . . knowing that it is against the established custom of the Department to permit any influence to be brought to bear by the officers who secure assignments." Franklin replied that although there was no precedent for bringing an ensign across the continent before his cruise was up, "I think it is probable that he could be transferred." In another case involving a gunner who wanted a shore assignment in the Boston Navy Yard, McArdle wrote: "I am writing this unofficially and beg that you will not permit this letter to become part of the files. . . . If you will secure for him this shore duty . . . I shall be very grateful and hold myself in readiness to reciprocate when opportunity offers."

This was influence peddling of the most blatant sort, but Franklin was willing to do it to build up his upstate power. If Franklin stopped short of the outright sale of offices, he sailed awfully close to the wind in his race after patronage. He had always been a stout defender of the civil service law, with competitive examinations and the office going to the best man, without favoritism or reference to party. In 1914, he gave a talk in Baltimore warning against abuses of the law and calling for its more widespread use. But in finding antimachine candidates for postmasterships, he routinely violated the spirit of the law by pressuring the Post Office Department to disqualify the top man on the list and take someone he approved of instead. Howe had gotten "chummy" with Dan Roper, who sent him lists of the first three men on the exams for each vacant office. He even gave Howe information on acceptable reasons for turning down the appointment of the top man on the list. This collusion between departments to deny the best-qualified candidates made a mockery of the civil service rules. As Franklin wrote a Rochester supporter, Louis M. Antisdale, on December 7, 1914: "The Post Office Department has made it very clear to us that if we want some other man they will take a pretty thin excuse provided it comes from us for the appointment." He crossed out "pretty thin," substituting "good," but the gesture did not cancel what was going on.

Franklin's triumph was the postmastership of his own city of Poughkeepsie, though it cost him the friendship of the Democratic leader, Ed Perkins, the man who had first suggested that he should get into politics. Perkins had his own Irish Catholic candidate, and as early as December 1913 urged that Franklin keep his hands off: "Hope you will try to keep out of the P.O. matter here. It will be a bitter fight and a good thing to leave alone for anyone looking forward to future success in the party, not only here, but in the state." Franklin ignored the threat, even though Perkins was backed by O'Gorman, and got his man named. Perkins was so angry that he resigned as treasurer of the Democratic State Committee, and in July 1914 attacked Franklin in the pages of the Poughkeepsie *News-Press,* reviving the old chestnut that he was anti-Irish. "Mr. Wilson is hearkening to the young and rash Roosevelt," he wrote. "The Old Guard here resents this action of Roosevelt's . . . NO IRISH NEED APPLY. They claim he is animated by racial and religious prejudice in the matter, rather than by actual hostility to Tammany."

Franklin swore revenge, writing his Poughkeepsie friend Tom Pendell: "For the present at least I think a dignified attitude of paying no more attention to their attack than I would to the obscene language of a drunken man is the best policy. But some day I am going to come back with a right hook that will catch not only the *News-Press,* but also some of the crooked old fossils of Poughkeepsie squarely between the eyes."

He saw nothing wrong with rewarding the party faithful. Why, President Wilson did the same thing. In 1916, the governor of Arizona, who had been elected and reelected without a break since Arizona became a state, was defeated. Henry Ashurst, one of the Arizona senators, went to see Wilson and said, "Our Governor has had such a continuous record that he ought to receive some recognition. Can you make him American Minister or Ambassador somewhere?" "Have you any suggestions as to what country?" Wilson asked. Ashurst got up without saying a word and walked to the other side of the room where there was a large revolving globe on a stand. He put his finger on Arizona, turned the globe around, placed another finger on the approximate point of the earth at the greatest possible distance from Arizona, and said, "Siam, Mr. President." And so it was that Siam got a new American ambassador. Was there any other way to do things in a two-party system?

In the meantime, Franklin was being mentioned as a candidate for governor in the 1914 election, and protested that he did not want it, which was the correct tactic while waiting to see if support built up. On January 24, 1914, he wrote to reassure the incumbent Democrat, Governor Martin H. Glynn: "By the way, if you happen to run across the inspiring idiot who started the report that I might be, or under any circumstances could be, a candidate for

Governor, you will do me a real favor by taking him into a quiet corner and firmly convincing him that he is absolutely mistaken."

He was quite ready to leave the Navy after a little more than a year in office, just as he had left the State Senate in the middle of a legislative session, although he had important bills pending. That was the name of the game. But the dream of being governor of New York State like Cousin Teddy, while still in his early thirties, soon evaporated. President Wilson was aloof when asked to support him. Nor did he have the backing of New York City Democrats, and he had alienated some upstate forces in the patronage struggle. On July 19, he wrote "Dearest Babs" that "I *might* declare myself a candidate for the U.S. Senator in the Democratic and Progressive Primaries. The Governorship is, thank God, out of the question."

Urged on by McAdoo, Franklin did declare in mid-August 1914 for the senatorial primary. The new direct-primary law invited defiance of the bosses, and he seems to have been told that Wilson wanted him to run. Daniels advised him against it. He had a hunch that Franklin could not win the primary and that even if he did the Republicans would carry the state in November. But Franklin, who had recently written a friend that "I am often too impetuous in seeking the accomplishment of results in too short a time," was off and running. His running mate was a flamboyant Irish reporter, John A. Hennessy, short of neck and thick of brogue, a sort of walking caricature of Mr. Dooley, who claimed to have proof of the misdeeds of the Glynn administration in a little black book.

The question was, who was Tammany going to run against him? An Albany newspaper on August 21 published a rumor that it might be William Randolph Hearst. Franklin sincerely hoped it would be, sure that he would win. Louis Howe felt that as a member of the administration, even if he did not have the declared backing of the president, Franklin was in a strong position. "The truth is that they haven't a thing to say against you," he wrote on August 24, "and no one is anxious to bell the cat—particularly when they have an idea that the President occasionally pats him on the back, calls him 'pretty pussy,' and gives him a nice saucer of warm patronage milk to drink."

Six days before the petitions had to be filed, Franklin still did not know who was running against him, which he saw as an element in his favor: "Of course the Murphy bunch may be going to spring some surprise, but whoever this surprise is this late announcement will stamp him even more indelibly with the Murphy stripes."

When Murphy did spring his surprise, it was a beauty: James W. Gerard, Woodrow Wilson's ambassador to Germany. Gerard had started out as a young lawyer for Tammany and was made a New York State Supreme Court justice with Murphy's blessing. In the patronage rivalries following the 1912 election, Wilson had to make some concessions to Tammany, and Gerard was sent to Berlin.

Franklin was outmaneuvered. He could not attack a prominent member of the administration who had the president's confidence and was the wartime emissary to one of the belligerents. He could not believe that Gerard would agree to run. If he did, he would be deserting his post at a critical time and increasing the president's difficulties. "If he is a fit man for senator, in other words, he will decline to run." Gerard announced that he would run but would not leave his post to campaign.

Franklin was in the ring, but could only shadowbox. "It's difficult to campaign against moles," he complained. "Murphy's candidates under his advice refuse to come out of their holes and declare their principles in accord with the spirit of the direct primary."

While Gerard, caught behind the British blockade, remained in Berlin, Franklin gamely toured the upstate counties, trying to present his opponent as Murphy's tool. He described himself as ready to work fulltime to help Wilson avoid war, which was the exact antithesis of his true sentiments. This was Franklin's second active campaign—in the 1912 State Senate campaign he had been laid low by typhoid—and he came across as green as grass. A September 23 editorial in the Walton *Chronicle*, a Republican paper, said that "the great personal force and magnetism necessary to push forward great national issues seem to be entirely lacking in him, and when compared to such a man as Elihu Root he cuts a sorry figure as a great statesman."

On September 27, the eve of the election, Franklin was still confident. "The result will be very surprising," he said, "to those who believe that the Democratic rank and file will, when voting a secret primary ballot, blindly carry out the orders of financially interested leaders."

These fine words were followed the next day, when Franklin voted in Hyde Park, by a crushing defeat: 76,888 for Roosevelt to 210,765 for Gerard. In the five boroughs of the city, Franklin trailed Gerard by 22,636 to 85,203. Louis Howe put the blame on the jovial Hennessy, who "ruined us and will sink any ship on which he is a passenger."

It was Franklin's nature to rationalize defeat into victory. He saw evidence in the results that "upstate autonomy" had been achieved. In fact, his defeat proved that the upstate independents were powerless against an entrenched statewide organization like Tammany. His patronage agitation had muddied the waters. He had not been a strong candidate. He was still widely viewed in party circles as an untested upstart, whose notoriety was based on having defied the machine over a senatorial appointment. He had never been elected from any district larger than three rural counties. His career was a fluke, a combination of a famous name and publicity seeking, and this setback would cut him down to size. Perhaps it would help him understand that his antimachine efforts were hurting the party all over the state. Perhaps he would learn that fighting Tammany did not pay off. The Republicans swept the November election. James Wadsworth defeated Gerard for the Senate; Charles S. Whitman defeated Glynn for governor. Daniels, refraining from saying "I told you so," felt that the primary defeat had hurt Franklin, in spite of his boasting. Back in Washington, he continued to use patronage to build an upstate organization, since under a Republican administration Murphy would get short shrift in Albany.

Franklin returned to the Navy Department in a more militant mood. In September, with German forces close to Paris, the French and British had beaten them back across the Marne. From a war of position, it was becoming a war of attrition, a long war, with miles of trenches facing each other across a no-man's land. American intervention could make the difference, and Franklin admired these martial lines of James Russell Lowell:

> "Better that all our ships and all their crews
> Should sink in Ocean's dreamless ooze,
> Each torn flag waving challenge as it went
> And each dumb gun a brave man's monument,
> Than seek such peace as only cowards crave,
> Give me the peace of dead men or of brave."

President Wilson, however, was still seeking peace through the secret mediation efforts of Colonel Edward M. House, and had told Daniels to order all his officers "to refrain from public comment of any kind upon the military or political situation on the other side of the water."

Franklin sided with those who spoke up for military preparedness. On October 16, Representative Augustus P. Gardner called for an investigation of national defense. Two days later, with Daniels away, Franklin gave the press a memo that supported "Gussie" Gardner's contention that the Navy was not ready. There was such a shortage of men, he said, that thirteen of the Navy's second-line battleships were out of commission. Eighteen thousand more men than the limit allowed by Congress were needed.

Worried about a reprimand, Franklin sent a copy of his memo to Eleanor, writing that "the enclosed is the truth and even if it gets me into trouble I am perfectly ready to stand by it. The country needs the truth about the Army and the Navy instead of a lot of soft mush about everlasting peace which so many statesmen are handing out to a gullible public." Less than a month later, however, and probably after a talk with Daniels, Franklin backtracked, releasing another memo that said: "I have not recommended 18,000 more men, nor would I consider it within my province to make any recommendations on the matter one way or the other."

The preparedness fight became an attack on the administration when Gardner in the House and Henry Cabot Lodge in the Senate introduced resolutions on December 7 and 8, 1914, for an investigation of national defense. Stung, Wilson hinted that business interests were behind the preparedness advocates. Although Wilson had the country behind him, isolated voices began warning about the nation's inadequate defenses.

Theodore Roosevelt, who had abandoned his support of neutrality, made a frontal attack on Daniels in December 1914: "During the last twenty months, ever since Secretary Meyer [Daniels's predecessor, George Von Lengerke Meyer] left the Navy Department," he said, "there has been in our Navy a great falling off relative to other nations. It was quite impossible to avoid this while our national affairs were handled as they have recently been handled. The President who entrusts the departments of State and the Navy to gentlemen like Messrs. Bryan and Daniels deliberately invites disaster in the event of serious complications with a formidable foreign opponent."

Wilson, who had told Daniels to hold the line on the 1915 building program, came to his defense at a White House lunch in January: "Daniels . . . is surrounded by a network of conspiracy and of lies," he said. "His enemies are determined to ruin him. I can't be sure who they are yet, but when I do get them—God help them."

Franklin, although in sympathy with Cousin Teddy's evaluation, was in no position to stand up and be counted among Daniels's enemies. When he differed from Daniels, as he did in the House Naval Affairs Committee hearing in December, it was in a cautious, muted, oblique manner. On December 9, Daniels and two friendly admirals, Frank L. Fletcher, commander of the Atlantic Fleet, and Charles J. Badger of the General Board, told the congressmen that the Navy was in tip-top shape. "Ship for ship . . . as good as the Navy of any other nation," Badger said.

When Franklin testified for five hours on December 16, he managed to convey a sense of the Navy's lack of preparedness without contradicting his chief. It was only natural, he declared, that the United States should be less prepared than warring nations, since it did not have the stimulus of war. As it was, he had no hesitation in saying that the United States had the world's third Navy, behind England and France. If submarines and destroyers were included, "Well then, the comparison would be less favorable to the United States," for the warring nations had greatly increased their submarine strength. He repeated that there was a shortage of between 30,000 and 50,000 men, and urged the adoption of a naval reserve, since in training men for a war emergency "it would take nine months to make an ordinary seaman of the average raw man. It would be rare to make a good gun pointer from raw material in a year." Under sharp questioning, Franklin shied away from policy and stuck to the facts, although his facts were not necessarily the ones that Daniels would have underlined.

Pleased with his performance, he wrote his mother on December 17 that the hearings had been "really great fun and not so much of a strain, as the members who tried to quiz me and put me in a hole did not know much about their subject and I was able not only to parry but to come back to them with thrusts that went home. Also, I was able to get in my own views without particular embarrassment to the Secretary." This was typical of Franklin's blowing his own horn and of his condescension toward congressmen who had made the Navy their first priority. Gardner used his testimony to attack Daniels, and said: "I admire the courage of Franklin Roosevelt."

Eager to see the war at first hand, Franklin in December 1914 asked to go to England to study the organization of the British Admiralty in wartime. The request, passed along from the American embassy in London to the Admiralty and curtly turned down, was of historic interest, for it marked the first contact between Franklin and Winston Churchill, then first lord of the Admiralty. Churchill, who would in years to come court FDR's friendship, at this point did not want him around. He had just suffered a severe naval setback. On December 16 some German cruisers shelled three coastal towns in northern England, and the British navy botched the pursuit. In addition, Churchill was angry at America for staying neutral. Prime Minister Herbert Asquith reported him in an August 19 letter as "in quite undefeated form, and the particular 'swine' at whom he would now like to have a fling are his kinsmen in the United States."

Under the circumstances, it was not surprising that on December 19 Sir William Graham Greene, permanent secretary of the Admiralty, wrote the American naval attaché in London, Commander Powers Symington: "I have asked the First Lord as to the possibility of affording facilities to Mr. F. D. Roosevelt and a staff of United States Naval Officers. . . . The First Lord desires me to express his regret that the present pressure of work in the Department would render it impossible to offer the assistance necessary for the accomplishment of the object of such a visit. . . . In the circumstances, he will not trouble you to call upon him."

Symington wrote Franklin on December 23: "I regret to tell you that the Admiralty would find it very inconvenient for you to come over here for the purpose of studying the war organization of the British Navy. . . . I am afraid that at this time it is hardly worthwhile to send any more officers over as observers. The lid is down tight and we get almost nothing."

Franklin did get to take a trip in March 1915, accompanying Vice President Thomas R. Marshall to San Francisco for the Panama Pacific Exposition. He and Bill Phillips were commissioners, and it was a pleasant occasion. The Lanes and the Millers decided to go too, and Franklin took Eleanor, who was with the crusty vice president on the back platform of their train when they crossed the Great Salt Lake. As everyone exclaimed on the beauty around them, he removed his cigar from his mouth and said: "I never did like scenery." At San Francisco, they reviewed the fleet, and the flagship, the USS *San Diego*, ran up a white flag with the presidential eagle and stars in the center, but without the four stars demonstrating command of rank, a flag that Franklin had designed for the vice president. When Marshall came aboard, he was so flustered that he shook hands with the enlisted men lined up to greet him, to Franklin's amusement. He and Bill Phillips went around in top hats and tailcoats dedicating pavilions.

In the arches of the pergola in front of the Fine Arts Building, examples of contemporary American sculpture had been placed. Franklin stopped in front of one of the statues and stared at it for a long time. It was called "Kneeling Girl," and it showed a nude young woman in a kneeling position, slender and graceful, her head bent, as if in an attitude of total submissiveness. For some reason, Franklin developed a fixation about the sculpture. Perhaps the girl represented an idealized vision of a woman ready to do a man's bidding, which he, with a strong-willed mother and a strong-willed wife, had never known. He talked about the statue for years, and in 1938 made inquiries about buying it from the sculptor, Ralph Stackpole. In 1943, Stackpole sent him a copy, but it was more an adaptation than a replica. The times had changed, and Stackpole was thinking of the great mass movements in politics and in labor, and of the great constructions, such as Boulder Dam, so that he made a heavier and stronger form, capable of carrying a heavier burden, made of domestic travertine and tipping the scales at over a ton. It must have been disappointing to have his longed-for vision so changed, as if the girl of 1915 had grown old and stout, but FDR placed the statue in the trees outside his Hyde Park bedroom window.

Back in Washington in April, Franklin was finding it increasingly difficult to subscribe to Wilsonian neutrality, and wrote Eleanor that "I just *know* I shall do some awful unneutral thing before I get through." Wilson seemed far too cautious. The illusion that the German submarine menace would not affect America had been shattered when on March 28 a German U-boat torpedoed a British liner, the *Falaba,* bound from Liverpool to West Africa. One of the passengers killed was a U.S. mining engineer on his way to his post on the Gold Coast. Wilson decided against sending a protest note. A cartoon in the Des Moines *Register and Leader* showed Uncle Sam with an ice pack on his head and a fan in his hand, with the caption: "Doin' His Darnedest to Keep Cool." On May 1, an American tanker, the *Gulflight,* was torpedoed in the Irish Sea, and three American lives were lost. Again Wilson did nothing, making it seem that he was submitting to a submarine campaign that sank neutral ships.

On May 7, the British passenger liner *Lusitania* was torpedoed in the Irish Sea and sank in eighteen minutes. True, it was carrying ammunition and was listed on the register of the Royal Navy as an auxiliary cruiser. But among the 1,200 casualties there were 124 Americans, and public opinion regarded the act as "wanton murder on the high seas." At a dinner in London given by American Ambassador Walter Hines Page, Colonel House predicted: "We shall be at war with Germany within a month."

Shaken from his torpor, Wilson sent a stern note to Germany. Bryan the die-hard pacifist signed it reluctantly, after an emotional outburst at the June 1 cabinet meeting, where he charged that "certain members" were unreasonably pro-Ally. Wilson sharply rebuked him, saying that his remarks were unfair and unjust. He had no right to say that anyone was pro-Ally or pro-German. Each one was merely trying to be a good American. A second note, promising to hold Germany to "strict accountability," was seen as a virtual demand that she abandon submarine warfare. Bryan was sure the note meant war. He had pledged on a hundred platforms that there would be no war while he was secretary of state. He could not sign it. Wilson and

Bryan were, as Daniels saw, two Presbyterian elders—neither would give way to the other.

On June 9, Bryan resigned. He had, reflected Daniels, entered the cabinet a young fifty-three, and was leaving it an old fifty-five. The next day, Franklin wrote "Dearest Babs": "These are hectic days all right! What d' y' think of W. Jay B.? It's all too long to write about, but I can only say I'm disgusted clear through. J.D. will *not* resign!" Franklin was disappointed that his chief had not followed in Bryan's footsteps, seeing him as an obstacle to naval expansion.

Two weeks later, Robert Lansing was appointed to succeed Bryan. Franklin was so annoyed at Bryan for quitting that, after attending an official dinner given by Lansing, he commented: "It was a delight to see a Secretary of State who is a gentleman and knows how to treat Ambassadors and Ministers from other civilized nations."

On June 23, he had a lunch date at the Shoreham Hotel with Daniels and Secretary of Commerce William C. Redfield. He was in an indignant frame of mind, for Secretary of War Lindley M. Garrison, who along with Franklin was in favor of compulsory military service, had the day before reported to him a discouraging conversation with Daniels, who had said: "I hope I shall never see the day when the schools of this country are used to give any form of military training—if that happens it will be proof positive that the American form of government is a failure."

As they walked from the Navy Department to the Shoreham, Daniels seemed worried and bewildered, wondering what could be done if Germany refused to give up her submarine warfare. "You know one or two men in the Cabinet spend a lot of time working things out to an ultimate conclusion," he told Franklin. "For instance, Garrison has kept on speculating about what we could do or should do in case Germany does not back down—of course he has that kind of a mind, the mind of a lawyer, and it makes him see a whole lot of unnecessary bogies. Why as a matter of fact we couldn't do anything against Germany except to withdraw Gerard, and what good would that do? If we broke off relations it would upset things terribly in this country—today the people are a unit behind the President but if we had to act, there would be all sorts of opposition and suggestions of course to pursue and the President would only become the leader of a faction."

"Do you think the people would stand for raising an army?" Franklin asked. "No," Daniels replied, "it would create terrible divisions of opinion."

"You know," Daniels went on, "it was just that that made Bryan resign— the fear of the next step if Germany does not give in. It is a mistake to look too far ahead, to cross the bridges before we get to them; it is sufficient to take up each step as it comes up."

Typical, Franklin thought. The president was not getting any real information because the Danielses and the Bryans did not want to discuss future steps—it was too disagreeable a subject. He knew for a fact that Wilson had not had the advice of a single Army or Navy officer. And yet there were military and economic steps to be taken to make the Germans realize America's determination. Of course they could go on negotiating by notes and more notes, but of that there was a limit—witness the War of 1812.

On July 1, 1915, Franklin told Louis Howe he had severe stomach pains. Louis thought it was indigestion and said, "Oh, take a pill, it's nothing but that cherry pie and glass of milk you had for lunch. I told you not to eat it." Realizing it was serious, Franklin went to the hospital, where his appendix was removed, and spent the rest of July and half of August convalescing. It gave him a chance to spend some time with his wife and four children, who were being raised under Sara's watchful eye. The situation had not changed. Eleanor was still on the defensive, still the obedient daughter-in-law. Sara's letters took note of her basic inadequacy. This one was typical: "I think in consequence of Eleanor's having had two hard days, and being up rather late, Baby is a little fussy and hungry."

While Franklin was laid up on the island off the coast of Maine, an important change was taking place in Washington. With a suddenness that bewildered friend and foe, President Wilson came out for preparedness. On July 21, he asked Garrison and Daniels to make plans for "an adequate national defense," which he could recommend to Congress when it convened in December. Wilson had finally come to realize, after the *Lusitania* and other incidents, that the vast majority of the American people were aroused.

When Franklin got back to work on August 15, Daniels was away and he was acting secretary. "That means that things will hum," he wrote Louis Howe. It was taken for granted that more got done in Daniels's absence. As Emory S. Land, who was in the Bureau of Construction and Repair for six of the eight years that Franklin was assistant secretary, recalled: "Daniels was a great procrastinator of matters in which he was in disagreement with the Navy. He had a tendency to pigeonhole those decisions. But when he left town, Roosevelt would go through Daniels' basket and pull out the things that were hanging fire, and he would make the necessary decisions. We in the service loved him for this. It would be wrong to say, though, that Roosevelt went behind Daniels' back when he did this. We always felt that Daniels knew what Roosevelt was doing or was about to do. In any case, he seemed invariably to ratify the decisions made in his absence."

On August 18 a German U-boat sank the White Star liner *Arabic*, outward bound from Liverpool with mail and 423 passengers, forty-four of whom died, including two Americans. Wilson at first did nothing. Franklin wrote Eleanor on August 21 that he would act "as soon as we can get the facts. But it seems very hard to wait until Germany tells us her version and I personally doubt if I should be quite so polite." It was becoming second nature for Franklin to imagine what *he* would do in the place of the secretary of the Navy or the president. A crisis was averted when the Germans said that the U-boat commander had acted contrary to instructions by sinking the *Arabic* without warning. They would indemnify the United States for the two lives lost.

ASSISTANT SECRETARY OF THE NAVY   *169*

As Franklin kept Eleanor abreast of war developments in Washington, she replied with accounts of the miniature wars inside the family. Elliott, nearly five and so bowlegged that he had to wear braces, had bit his older brother, James. Eleanor explained that no matter whose fault it was boys didn't bite. Elliott made such a long upper lip that he looked like a rabbit, and after Eleanor had spanked him with her slipper, he said, "It didn't hurt very much, Mother."

Although Daniels continued to hope that America would be, in Jefferson's words, "kindly separated by nature and a wide ocean" from Europe, he too was coming around to the idea of a bigger and better navy. He recruited inventors and scientists to serve without pay on a Naval Consulting Board under the presidency of Thomas A. Edison. This board, with its eminent members placing their time and talent at the service of the Navy, was later seen as one of the finest achievements of the Wilson administration. On October 6, the Edison board was received by the president, who said that defense was a matter "in which we must have the best minds and knowledge of the country." The phrase "best minds" would be invoked many times.

Franklin, who shared the cynical Navy view about "crackpot inventors," did not think much of the board, and wrote "Dearest Babs" on the eve of their arrival in Washington: "Tomorrow, the Inventors come in a force. . . . Most of these worthies are like Henry Ford, who until he saw a chance for publicity free of charge, thought a submarine was something to eat!" An ardent pacifist, Ford had recently set up a $1-million fund to combat preparedness. That December, he would sail for Europe with a band of cohorts aboard a chartered steamer, in order to promote peace negotiations that would get the soldiers "out of the trenches by Christmas." The mission was a total failure.

In February 1916, Franklin "got into a dispute with several million germs" and took to his bed with an infected throat. Daniels complained that although he seemed to be bursting with health and vitality, he caught every bug that came along. He was back in Washington in time for the birth of another son, the last child Eleanor would have, John Aspinwall, on March 13, 1916. Franklin had gone out for dinner, and by the time he was back, the baby was born.

Wilson on February 10 accepted the resignation of his irascible secretary of war, with whom he disagreed over compulsory military service. Franklin was mentioned in the press as Garrison's successor, but Wilson did not even consider him. From among those he did consider, he chose Newton D. Baker, who had played an important part in the 1912 convention, and had been mayor of Cleveland from 1912 to 1916. Baker's reaction was that he had "never even played with tin soldiers." But he accepted, even though he did not know the difference between a company of infantry and the crew of a fieldpiece. He was a very short man, who joked that he was always being mistaken for the office boy. But he was also a leading pro-Wilson progressive, and Wilson wanted loyalty over expertise. Only after his ap-

pointment had been announced did the press disclose that Baker was a pacifist who had opposed preparedness.

Because 1916 was an election year, Daniels was singled out for attack as a
liability in the Wilson camp. Some of those closest to the president wanted
to get rid of him, notably the president's second wife and Colonel House,
who wrote in an April 6 memo: "Mrs. Wilson and I . . . decided that the most
helpful thing that could be done for the president at this time, would be the
elimination of good Josephus Daniels and Joseph Tumulty. She undertakes
to eliminate Tumulty if I can manage the Daniels change."

Wilson hung on to Daniels because he liked him and needed him. Now
that Bryan was gone, Daniels was his link to the Bryan wing of the party;
and it was useful to have in the cabinet a nationally known pacifist who
backed his preparedness program. But Daniels's stock was so low that during the 1916 campaign there were billboards that said: "A Vote for Wilson Is
a Vote for Josephus Daniels."

In France that summer, place-names like Verdun and the Somme were
written in blood. The war had gone on nearly two years, and there was no
end in sight. In Chicago on June 10, the Republican convention, straining to
discern grass-roots sentiment, did not nominate the saber-rattling Theodore
Roosevelt, but Charles Evans Hughes, a moderate and a reformer and a
distinguished statesman—former governor of New York, associate justice of
the U.S. Supreme Court. What could Teddy do? The country was passing
through a thick streak of yellow. There would be no third party draining the
Republican vote this time, for he declined to run on the Progressive ticket.
In St. Louis five days later, Wilson and Marshall were nominated by acclamation. The Democratic platform included the words: "We commend to the
American people the splendid diplomatic victories of our great President,
who has preserved the vital interest of our Government and its Citizens, and
kept us out of the war." Those last six words would serve as the Democratic
campaign slogan.

It was in an election-year spirit that Franklin reconsidered his attitude toward Tammany. He had given up trying to control patronage in upstate
New York. Most of the post office jobs had been handed out, and he had
failed to found a rival organization. He had covered only a fraction of the
state and not even dented the major urban machines. Patronage, he was beginning to see, was a fickle bride, and he wrote his friend Louis Antisdale of
the Rochester *Herald* that "I realize perfectly that two-thirds of them would
slide back at the prospect of any loaves and fishes from the other side." It
was a time for reassessment. Tammany was a fact of life. Party unity was
important. His influence in Washington was slight. His war against the machine was doing him more harm than good.

Quietly working to gain the acceptance of his former enemies, he started
with the Brooklyn congressman and Tammany stalwart John F. Fitzgerald,
who happened to be chairman of the House Appropriations Committee.
When Fitzgerald asked for a favor from the Navy, Franklin acted on it.

Fitzgerald's constituency covered the Brooklyn Navy Yard, and his requests arrived with regularity.

"Louis Leow feels keenly the disgrace of undesirable discharge and would like one opportunity of re-entering the Navy. Promises exemplary and patriotic conduct in the future. Will you help to make a good citizen?"

"Hospital steward Edward McMillan attached to U.S.S. *Montana* desires to be assigned to the Lake Demarest Powder Magazine at Dover, N.J. Will you do it?"

Franklin would certainly try. When he appeared on July 19 before the Appropriations Committee to answer questions on the Navy bill, the chairman was more kindly disposed than on previous occasions. He reported to "Dearest Babs": "I am up here at the Capitol spending most of the day trying to get appropriations past Congressman Fitzgerald and Uncle Joe Cannon and will probably be at it again tomorrow. It is not cheerful work with the temperature at 94."

In August the bill was passed, an appropriation of $600 million over three years to build 256 ships and increase the number of enlisted men to 67,800. It was the largest appropriation ever devoted to naval expansion by any country.

Franklin had a rude shock on August 14 when he learned that his chauffeur, Henry Golden, had smashed up his Fiat landaulet and was in the hospital with a broken leg. He was "mad clear through," and got even madder when he discovered that Golden had been cheating him on the garage bills. He was pocketing part of the cash Franklin gave him each month, and arranging for the garage to send him only the monthly bill and not the arrears. In addition, Golden had wrecked his car while joyriding with friends, which meant he was not covered by insurance; Franklin would have to pay the repair bill, which looked to be at least $500—the car had gone off an embankment, turned completely over, and landed on its wheels. What a weak, miserable wretch Golden was! Franklin assigned Louis Howe to investigate his chauffeur's misdeeds. What Louis pieced together and sent to his boss was the old story—women and drink: "One woman in particular took a great liking to him at first, and he went joy riding . . . with the usual highballs needed to prove oneself 'a good fello,' then the skirt got her grip on him and he started to slide faster. . . . As he got in deeper and the girl demanded more he began to drink more. . . . Then the smash came and as soon as that happened the girl shook him. . . . His anxiety as to whether his wife knew about the girl is a good sign. No man is beyond redemption as long as he don't want his wife to find out."

In its small way, the incident was revealing. First, it showed Louis Howe's misogyny. Woman was the temptress who led a man astray and then dropped him. Louis urged that the chauffeur be given another chance, but Franklin fired him. For all his cynicism and hard-boiled exterior, Louis had a soft center. He was on familiar terms with temptation. Franklin, who was high-minded and seemingly generous, had a punitive streak inherited from his mother. He had learned how to deal with the servants from his parents. When the coachman drank, he went. Why make an exception of Golden? Franklin was still the product of his class and background, unwilling to make allowances for the help.

In the same way, as several of the naval officers he worked with noted, he was unusually receptive to anyone who came from his own background. On one occasion, for no other reason than a complaint from a Harvard classmate, he had a naval officer removed from an important assignment. The classmate was Edward Bell, known as "Nedski," who was second secretary at the American embassy in London, and who for some reason took a dislike to a member of the naval attaché's office, Captain W. D. McDougall. On May 3, 1917, Bell wrote Franklin that "This man is an object of ridicule and a figure of fun alike to the British navy . . . and his colleagues in the Embassy. . . . If by any possible excuse you could translate him to other spheres you would be doing a service to the government."

Without pausing to consider that this might be a private vendetta and that Bell might be exaggerating McDougall's shortcomings, Franklin arranged for his transfer, writing Bell that "everybody in this shop felt about him much as you did, but the usual attitude of careful consideration prevailed, and the result has been that I could obtain no action at all until the other day. I know you will be glad that he has gone. . . . Evidently, he is no gent." The class distinction of whether or not a man was a gentleman, a concern so much more English than American, still mattered to Franklin.

Another concern, the health of his children, absorbed him that summer. In June, cases of infantile paralysis were reported up and down the East Coast. Three out of four victims were children under five. Franklin had two children in that age group, and three others aged six, nine, and ten. No one knew what caused it. On June 27, the New York *Journal* wrote that "the strange epidemic which has caused fourteen deaths during the month is attributed by doctors to the prolonged damp weather of this spring and early summer. More than one hundred persons from Brooklyn are suffering from it, and it is said to be epidemic in Bridgeport and Philadelphia." "It is clear that in the eyes of most physicians," said a leading doctor, "that the trouble is endemic and that the germ is carried in the air, in the dust of the city or elsewhere. The germ has probably originated from the long period of damp weather and has spread rapidly, being infectious and not contagious." Another newspaper announced that "acting on the theory that the germs of the disease are spread by animals, the police of Brooklyn today arrested 215 cats from the infected districts of the borough." An editorial asked: "Cats and dogs carry disease, but what about doctors' beards?"

In July, Eleanor and the chicks went to Campobello. Would the disease reach that far north? Sara hoped not, writing Franklin on July 6 that "this awful disease infantile paralysis is spreading. I trust our island will be 'immune.' There is much excitement about it, and the state has taken the matter up." The whole thing was appalling, Franklin thought. In the Campobello house, there was a window overlooking the water where he trapped flies. There might be hundreds of live flies in the window, and for all he knew they might be carriers. On July 7, he wrote Eleanor: "Please kill all the flies I left."

In New York City that July, polio deaths reached epidemic proportions. On July 18, children sixteen and under were banned from leaving the city without a health certificate. Some suburban communities policed their railroad stations, and prevented out-of-town children from disembarking from trains. It was like London during the plague, with police breaking into people's homes and carrying off children to the hospital, and 4,000 arrested for violations of the health ordinances, and hucksters selling "remedies," such as boxes containing cedar shavings to be worn around the afflicted child's neck.

In that summer of suffering and despair, Franklin was grateful that the family was at Campobello. But the disease was gaining ground. Six cases had been reported in Poughkeepsie by August 5, and soon it infiltrated his mother's estate, striking down the three-year-old daughter of Sara's coachman, Westley Butler. Franklin began wondering what to do with his children once the summer was over. It was too dangerous to bring them to Washington. Maybe Hyde Park would be safe, but how to get them there? Trains were out of the question. There was too much IP in Boston and Springfield, and even in Rockland and other Maine points. He could not drive his car because of that wretch Golden. In any case, villages were keeping motorists with children out. The safest way was by ship, and he thought of Daniels's yacht, the *Dolphin*. He was in a position to requisition a U.S. Navy ship to ferry his children from Campobello to Hyde Park; they would escape any danger of contamination.

But worse luck, Daniels had just been accused in Congress of intending to use the *Dolphin* to campaign in Maine, which attracted leaders of both parties that summer because it voted early, on September 11. Daniels was scared blue, and Franklin knew that the *Dolphin* would not be allowed within 1,000 miles of Maine until after the election. On August 21, Daniels asked Franklin in writing not to use the yacht. "Don't you think it would be a mistake at this time," he asked, "to send the *Dolphin* into Maine upon anything but an official trip?"

Franklin waited out the election in Maine, which went Republican to no one's surprise. He was now so worried that he was thinking of keeping his family in Campobello until December. The disease had spread all over upstate New York. There were cases in almost every village in Dutchess County, and it didn't seem to be decreasing in New York City, where there were scenes of panic as families tried to flee, with long lines at railroad and ferry windows. It was like an exodus.

Finally, Daniels said he saw no reason why he could not have the *Dolphin*. Since his chief was off on a trip to the Middle West, Franklin said nothing further. That was the way to deal with Daniels—as soon as he left he would order the *Dolphin* to Eastport himself. There were no new cases in Hyde Park; it was less of a risk than a long autumn in Washington. If they waited until October 3 they wouldn't get to Hyde Park until October 6, and by that time Mildred, the coachman's daughter, might be out of quarantine and everything would be fumigated. But the children should not go into any of the cars or carriages where Mildred might have been.

On October 1, the *Dolphin* arrived off Campobello, and proceeded to embark the Roosevelt children and carry them up the Hudson to Hyde Park, to the annoyance of the commander, William D. Leahy, who wondered why his ship was being used to baby-sit five children, and who had to keep his mouth shut when they roamed all over the ship. By that time, the epidemic was over, and the ban on children leaving New York was lifted. In the city alone, there had been 9,000 cases and 2,448 dead, mostly children. Franklin saw at first hand a disease that attacked at random, children and adults alike, and that medical science knew almost nothing about.

In October, the campaign was in full swing. Wilson and Hughes were running neck and neck. It was the closest presidential race since the "Cross of Gold" campaign in 1896 between Bryan and McKinley. In New York, the odds were ten to seven against Wilson. On election day, November 7, with the returns from the eastern states coming in first, things looked bleak. That evening, the *New York Times* and the *World,* on the basis of his having carried all the big eastern states, announced a Hughes victory in banner headlines. Hughes was so sure he had won that his son replied to a late caller: "The president cannot be disturbed." Wilson was ready to concede, and worried that the result would be taken by Germany as a repudiation of his neutrality policy and that the country would be dragged into war. Yet he waited until the returns from the western states were in to send his telegram of congratulations.

Franklin left the gloomy Democratic headquarters at the Biltmore Hotel in New York at midnight with Franklin Lane, thinking that he would have to go back to the practice of law. Hughes had 247 electoral votes out of the 266 needed for election. Rationalizing defeats as he was apt to do, he saw a bright side—under a Republican administration, America would be more likely to enter the war, and he could get a Navy commission and see some action.

On November 8, the returns from the West started coming in and Wilson's fortunes rose. It looked as if the South and the West had banded against the East. By midnight, Wilson had pulled ahead of Hughes by 251 to 247, with California still unreported. An overjoyed Franklin wrote "Dearest Babs" that it was "the most extraordinary day of my life. After last night, Wilson may be elected after all. It looks hopeful at noon."

On November 9, he reported "another day of wild uncertainty. Returns, after conflicting, have been coming in every hour from Cal., N.M., N.D., Minn., and N.H. Without any of these Wilson seems to have 251 votes safe, 266 necessary to choice. This p.m. it appears we have N. Dakota 5 votes safe and in California (13) we are well ahead, though there are still 200 districts to hear from. Minn (12) looks less favorable, also N. Mexico (3), but N. Hamp. (4) is getting better and we may carry it."

In the final returns, Wilson won by 277 to 254 electoral votes. In the popular vote, he and Hughes were little more than half a million votes apart, 9,129,606 to 8,538,221. Wilson carried California by less than 4,000 votes, and New Hampshire by 56. By such slender threads were destinies pulled.

No sooner was he reelected than Wilson renewed his efforts for peace, appealing to the belligerents for a world system of collective security. Colonel House thought Wilson was incredibly clumsy in assimilating Allied and German war aims, as if both sides had equally valid reasons. Secretary of State Robert Lansing thought the peace initiative was wrong because it would alienate the Allies, and did his best to sabotage the president's efforts. Reaching London at the height of the Somme offensive, the peace note was regarded as close to an insult. Was there really no moral difference between the Allies and the Germans? Intervening after millions of lives had been lost, Wilson seemed to understand nothing.

Unable to sympathize with Wilson's foreign policy, Franklin had come to the conclusion that America must fight Germany. As a boy in Bad Nauheim with his parents, he had gained firsthand knowlege of German militarism, and had learned from his father to think of Germans as "swine." His friendship with the British and French ambassadors in Washington contributed to his favoring the Allied cause. In the fall of 1916, he began to come into Daniels's office and say: "We've got to get into this war," to which Daniels would invariably reply, "I hope not."

At a stormy cabinet meeting in January 1917, someone said that "people are demanding that we go to war against Germany and are accusing our administration of cowardice."

"I do not care what they say about us," Wilson replied tensely, "as long as we are seeking our goal without loss of life." That afternoon he confided to Daniels why he was resolved to keep America out of the war: "If we go to war thousands of young men will lose their lives. I could not sleep with myself if I do not go to the extreme limit to prevent such mourning in American homes. [Also] every reform we have won since 1912 will be lost. We have got new tariff, currency, shipping and trust legislation. These new policies are not thoroughly set. They will be imperiled or lost if we go to war. We will be dependent in war upon steel, oil, aluminum, ships, and war material. They are controlled by Big Business. . . . When the war is over . . . Big Business will be in the saddle. More than that—free speech and the other rights will be endangered. War is autocratic."

While the president had to defend neutrality in his own cabinet that January, Franklin was on an inspection tour of Haiti, which the Marines had occupied two years before to "restore order." In 1917, the island was in effect governed by the U.S. Navy. Smedley Butler, a Marine general of the "we have landed and have the situation well in hand" school, was commander of the Haitian gendarmerie. He presided over the inauguration of President Dartiguenave, the handpicked choice of the State Department. "I won't say we put him in," Butler said. "The State Department might object. Anyway, he was put in." Butler ran the Haitian customs, administered Haitian finances, and was in charge of Haitian public works, primarily road building. He had 6,000 men at work on the road systems, most of them forcibly recruited. He bragged that his roads cost only $250 a mile and once wrote Franklin that "it would not do to ask too many questions as to how we accomplished this work." Herbert J. Seligman, who went to Haiti for the *Nation* in 1920, reported that "the road program was used as an excuse for kidnapping thousands of Haitians from their homes" and "forcing them to live for months in camps, insufficiently fed, guarded by Marines, rifles in hand. . . . when Haitians attempted to escape . . . they were shot." Seligman charged that under the Marines, Haiti had become a police state. The Marines called the Haitians "gooks," treated them brutally, and in five years of occupation killed 3,000 of them.

Whether or not he had any detailed knowledge of these abuses, Daniels was against a policy that brought law and order on the point of a bayonet. He didn't like it one bit when the jocular Franklin Lane rose to greet him at cabinet meetings with "Hail the King of Haiti." He thought the State Department policies were high-handed and tinged with imperialism. He carried them out against his better instincts, and later admitted to Franklin that "the things we were forced to do in Haiti were a bitter pill to me, for I have always hated any foreign policy that even hinted at imperialistic control."

Franklin, however, saw the occupation as an example of American benevolence. When the Marines had arrived in 1915, the Haitians were primitive savages, living in mud and wattle huts concealed in the underbrush. They had to use force to bring the benefits of democracy to a primitive country. American investments would promote prosperity. Dictators would be overthrown and democratic principles would thrive. The stories of Marine atrocities were lies that came from the small group of educated Haitians who had previously been exploiting the rest of the population. Franklin admired the Marines' efficiency, their spirit of enterprise. He was delighted when Smedley Butler wrote him that "the Gendarmerie built 21 miles of roads in five weeks and five days, through the worst tropical wilderness I have ever seen." At Groton he had argued against the occupation of Hawaii and for the independence of the Philippines, but at this stage of his life he felt that America had an obligation to administer a backward and less fortunate nation. He also believed that in wartime there was a need for stability in the Caribbean, and that unfriendly nations must be prevented from using the islands as bases.

Franklin left on January 21, 1917, on what he called his jaunt into "Darkest Africa of the West Indies." In her customary tone, Sara wrote: "I hope you took dark glasses and a pith hat for I know how you feel the tropical sun." He took along the commander of the Marine Corps, Major General

George Barnett; John A. McIlhenny, the chairman of the Civil Service Commission; George Marvin, a former Groton master who was now Washington editor of *World's Work* magazine, who joined the party in Cuba; and his Harvard classmate and fellow sailor, Livingston Davis, who served as a sort of court jester. "I am your jolly boy on the trip to Haiti," Davis wrote, adding that he had heard tales of a very risqué theater in Havana, which if true should be too good to miss—"tell George Marvin to investigate, and procure tickets before our arrival. I will be host for the crowd." This was the celebrated show in which a well-endowed black couple copulated on stage. Franklin also tried to invite the mayor of New York City, John Purroy Mitchel, "especially as we shall have the opportunity of calling on their Excellencies, the Presidents of Cuba, Haiti and Santo Domingo. I am told only one of them is coal black." Althought not a racist in the Josephus Daniels sense, Franklin liked to make jocular remarks about Negroes, and routinely used the word "nigger," inherited from Groton with its "chapel niggers" and "mail niggers." He evidently thought blacks were inferior and that most Haitians were savages, but that was no reason to be uncivil. On January 27, when they were in the harbor of Port-au-Prince with the American fleet, they entertained President Dartiguenave and his cabinet for lunch aboard the flagship. Franklin noticed that McIlhenny, who was from New Orleans, was not eating, and after the Haitians had been piped over the side, asked why. "Did you see the Secretary of Agriculture who sat opposite me?" McIlhenny asked. "He was 6'6" and must have weighed 250 pounds. He ate with both hands—everything in sight—two helpings of every dish. I was fascinated—too fascinated to eat. I couldn't help saying to myself that the man would have brought $1,500 at an auction in New Orleans in 1860 for stud purposes." Franklin was amused at this comparison of a Haitian cabinet minister to a New Orleans slave. But although privately ready to joke about the "coal black" natives and their comical table manners, in public he was indifferent to the color line. When they were getting into a limousine, President Dartiguenave went first, and Smedley Butler grabbed his coat collar and started to pull him back, but Franklin insisted he go ahead.

In Haiti, Franklin saw what the Marines wanted him to see. His preconception that they had brought law and order and sanitation to the land was confirmed. He did not see the road gangs working in shocking conditions, or the 2,000 prisoners in grim lockups. He left Haiti convinced that the occupation was highly successful.

Boarding the collier *Neptune* on February 4, 1917, he was told that President Wilson had broken off relations in response to Germany's resuming unrestricted submarine warfare. But when he got to Washington, nothing was happening. Wilson said he could not move any faster than the great mass of people would permit. Hamletlike, he continued to agonize in February and March over what to do. What Franklin took for indecisiveness was a deeply felt conviction that war would corrupt America, that the spirit of ruthless brutality needed for its conduct would infect national life. It would infect Congress, the courts, the police. It would kill free speech and the right of assembly. Laws would be suspended, moral restraints would be relaxed, there would be a disregard for commercial integrity. The situation would be ripe for demagogues and profiteers. War was a debasing experience for a society, one to avoid at all costs.

In his avoidance of war, and to Franklin's growing disgust, Wilson was backed by Daniels, who was reluctant to commit the Navy to any form of action. At a February 23 cabinet meeting, there was a discussion on whether to send out merchant ships with guns or convoys. Daniels said he was against convoys—they were too dangerous. Imagine, thought Secretary of the Interior Franklin Lane, a secretary of the Navy worrying about danger.

But the Germans would not let America stay out of the conflict. On February 24, Wilson received a copy of a telegram that had been intercepted by British intelligence: the German foreign minister, Arthur Zimmermann, urged the German minister in Mexico to propose a deal—Mexico would join the war as a German ally and win back Texas, New Mexico, and Arizona. As he later explained it, Zimmermann wanted to "set new enemies on America's neck," to keep the Americans busy in their own hemisphere. The territories were the bait. This turned out to be one of the worst blunders in diplomatic history. It proved to Wilson that Germany had no respect for the integrity of a neutral power. He lost faith in German pronouncements. Further peace was out of the question. The publication of the telegram won over public opinion to the idea that America was forced to enter the war. On February 26, Wilson, in an address to Congress, asked for emergency powers and a policy of armed neutrality. The vote in the Senate was blocked by pacifist diehards, Wilson's "little group of willful men," who filibustered until the congressional session ended. Franklin was so disgusted with the way the administration was dragging its feet that he thought of leaving the Navy, writing his tenant, Thomas W. Lamont (the Morgan partner), on March 1 that he might need his New York house that winter. Lamont replied that "privately I was in hopes that Mr. Daniels might desire to retire to private life so that we could have the satisfaction of seeing you Secretary of the Navy!"

On March 5, 1917, Wilson was inaugurated. Washington was wet and cold, and a strong wind blew from the northwest, making him hard to understand. In the intermittent diary he kept, Franklin commented: "Too far away to hear the address—Little enthusiasm in the crowd." At six that evening, he saw Colonel House at the White House and spoke to him guardedly about the Navy's lack of preparedness. Franklin was turning against Wilson. The situation was so clear-cut. Why didn't he act? The White House statement on March 9 said that the president had the power to arm ships but only *inferred* that he would use it. Why didn't he say so without equivocation?

On Sunday, March 11, in New York, he saw Colonel House again, and complained about Daniels's procrastination. He was so damned slow!

House, who had been lobbying for some time to get rid of Daniels, was quick to agree.

Back in Washington after having visited the Boston and New York Navy yards, Franklin told Daniels that things there were not satisfactory. No one seemed to be in charge. They were supposed to start arming merchant ships on the twelfth, but no one knew what guns to use. Daniels, who was losing patience with his assistant's capacity for indignation, remained silent.

On March 13, Daniels signed the instructions for the officers who would be commanding the armed guards aboard the merchantmen, his heart sinking at the thought that he was fixing his name to a death warrant for young Americans.

On March 18, German submarines sank three American ships. Even after that provocation, Wilson refused to act. The following day, he went to see Daniels, who recorded in his diary: "He had been urged to call Congress and to declare war. He still hoped to avoid it and wished no cost and no effort spared to protect shipping."

The turning point came at the cabinet meeting of March 20. Composed and meticulous, Wilson asked each of his ten secretaries whether he should summon congress and ask for a declaration of war. In previous meetings, the cabinet had been divided. Burleson, the postmaster general, had an anti-British bias. Daniels and Newton Baker, the secretary of war, were pacifists. But this time, they spoke as one: they could wait no longer; America must go in. A great power could not submit to assaults on its sovereignty.

Querying them one by one, Wilson finally turned to Daniels, the lifelong pacifist, the close friend and follower of Bryan (who had resigned rather than risk war), the man who distrusted militarism and had wanted to turn the Navy into an educational experience for young men, and who had argued against convoys because they were *dangerous*. "Well, Daniels," Wilson said. In a low voice, his eyes brimming with tears, Daniels repudiated the convictions of a lifetime: he saw no other course but war. Lansing wondered whether Daniels spoke from conviction or because he lacked the strength of mind to stand out against the united opinion of his colleagues.

Whatever the reason, there was no alternative to war, and Congress was summoned for April 2. In addition, the Russian Revolution, occurring at that time, removed the last despot among the Allies, making it seem a clearcut conflict between democracy and autocracy. With the president's declaration only days away, the Navy Department moved into an active phase more to Franklin's liking. Rear Admiral William S. Sims, president of the Naval War College at Newport, an outspoken Anglophile and a personal friend of the commander in chief of the British First Fleet, Sir John Jellicoe, was sent to England as liaison officer, on Franklin's recommendation. Sims was startled when Admiral William S. Benson, the chief of naval operations, took him aside and said with bitterness: "Don't let the British pull the wool over your eyes. It is none of our business pulling their chestnuts out of the fire. We would as soon fight the British as the Germans." Good God, thought Sims, the secretary was a pacifist and his chief of naval operations was an Anglophobe.

Franklin, for some odd reason, pushed for fifty-foot harbor-patrol launches that the admirals considered worthless. He argued that the launches could be produced in a hurry, and could do useful work in harbors and inlets on both coasts. He pictured them going after enemy wireless stations, gunrunners, submarine repair bases, or even attacking submarines. Daniels and his advisers preferred to wait for 110-foot submarine chasers that would take longer to build. Daniels recorded on March 25: "F.D.R. and 50 foot boats—his hobby. Good in smooth water. I fear buying a lot of junk."

It was Franklin's nature to go off like a retriever in chase of any novel idea; once he had it in his teeth he did not let go. But in the case of the fifty-foot boats, there was an added reason, and that was his friendship with Arthur Patch "Pat" Homer, who was a vice president in the Boston office of Sterling Motors, a British builder of naval engines competing for Navy contracts. Pat Homer was a silver-tongued, glad-handing promoter, whom Franklin once described in a job recommendation as an "excellent salesman . . . [who] has aggressiveness and originality and is tireless in his efforts to further the interests of the business he is connected with." That may have been true, but it was also true that in Pat Homer the line between aggressiveness and dishonesty was blurred. "Pat Homer and his anchor to windward" was the nautical way a Bostonian described him.

Pat Homer courted Franklin, writing flattering letters to "my dear chief," sending him live lobsters and tickets to the National Motor Boat Show, and inviting him for trips aboard his boat, the *Remoh*, which was Homer spelled backward. On one occasion, in December 1915, he offered Franklin the presidency of an engine and boat company, which would have been a clear conflict of interest: "The proposition will be big enough, if it goes through, so that it will be well worth your while to accept the position." Franklin was not offended by this unethical suggestion, and replied that he was sorry he could not do it. Something in him was drawn to the "soldier of fortune" personality, bold, imaginative, and unscrupulous, like Pat Homer and Smedley Butler. They were big talkers, but they delivered the goods, although it was best not to ask too many questions how.

In fact, in an early illustration of sending private citizens on missions outside official channels, which he liked to do when he was president, Franklin twice sent Pat Homer to England in 1916, once to obtain a seaplane engine, and the next time to find a complete seaplane. On December 29, 1916, he wrote Captain W. D. McDougall of the naval attaché's staff in London (the same McDougall whom, a year later, he would with gross unfairness transfer on the say-so of his Harvard classmate Ned Bell) that Homer's trip was "something of a gamble. All on behalf of the Sterling Motor Company. . . .

What I want is the definite result of getting a seaplane over to this side and I do not care whether it is done officially, unofficially, or otherwise."

It was the same with the fifty-foot boats. If they were built, a Sterling engine would provide the power. Franklin favored Pat Homer against the recommendations of the Bureau of Engineering. One of their contracts came back from Louis Howe's office with Sterling Motors substituted for the firm they had picked. According to Pat Homer, he and Franklin were so close that they conspired to oust Daniels as secretary of the Navy. As he recalled it in a letter to FDR on January 4, 1940: "In 1917, you and I made a trip to New York to see Colonel House regarding certain changes in the Navy Department which would have promoted you to Secretary; I was to have the berth of Assistant Secretary. At that time, only Daniels' refusal to move blocked our being associated during the war."

In December 1917, Pat Homer abruptly left Sterling Motors. The reason was not disclosed, but C. A. Criqui, president of the American branch, informed Franklin that "a serious condition has arisen that has greatly interfered with our business relations. . . . It does seem that about every so often he does something to turn things upside down." Pat Homer would turn up again in Franklin's life, like a character in a picaresque novel, always hatching some new scheme. In 1919, it was a company that owned some Oklahoma oil fields, in which Franklin invested $5,000. In 1922, it was a heatless iron that could do everything from handkerchiefs to tablecloths four yards long. In 1923, it was potassium nitrate deposits in Brazil. In 1924, it was the Homer Oil Burner. Then there was the lobster-packing plant in Maine, to which Pat would refer as "the crustacean episode." Through all these business failures they remained friends, although FDR got annoyed with him once he was president and Pat shamelessly tried to exploit the connection. In 1938, he asked to be recommended as president of the New York Stock Exchange. In a sarcastic memo, Marvin McIntyre, one of FDR's assistants, said, "Neither Pat nor I can understand why he is overlooked when these important jobs are open for a mastermind." FDR replied: "I have an excellent job for Pat Homer—caretaker of Palmyra Island in the Pacific—companions, one Hawaiian boy and a Newfoundland dog; salary to be determined if he survives." Pat did not survive for long. The supersalesman whose schemes never panned out died of a stroke in October 1940.

Franklin saw himself as a man of action who got things done by cutting through red tape. Sometimes you had to sail close to the wind to get results. He was the opposite of the cautious and procrastinating Daniels, who let papers pile up on his desk for weeks. There was something vain and immature in his conviction that only his decisiveness and "let's get it done" mentality kept the Navy Department afloat. He wasn't shy about blowing his own horn, either. When James T. Williams, Jr., the editor of the Boston *Transcript,* went to see him in March 1917, Franklin told him: "This desk gets piled up at times with papers—important matters that the chief can't get through the Secretary. I wait until he's out of town, and then I go to the White House to get things done." Sometimes, as an admiral confided to Daniels, his bustling seemed ridiculous: "He'd come aboard a new ship and say to me, 'See that electric clock there? That takes exactly so much money and so much feet of wire and so many man hours to build and install. If that clock hadn't been put there, we could have had two more guns.'" What were they supposed to do, the admiral wondered, tell time by the sun?

His desire to go to war seemed self-serving compared to Wilson's soul-searching. Wilson had been reelected with a mandate to keep America out of the war. He had a baleful vision of what involvement in the affairs of Europe would lead to. The burden of having to order American young men into battle weighed heavily upon him. He had to consider the strong pacifist strain in America's heartland, as expressed by such men as Senators Robert La Follette and George Norris. With all the powers of his mind and heart, he was trying to find a way out of the maze. Franklin, on the other hand, seemed to want American involvement for self-advancement, so that he could run a wartime Navy, deploying ships and mobilizing men. He blindly copied Cousin Teddy's belligerent stand. When he had first come to the Navy Department, a newspaper article had described him as "a regular blown-in-the-bottle, antiseptic, non-corroding, self-cocking, dyed-in-the-wool Democrat." By now he had broken with administration policy, and was openly disloyal to his president and his immediate superiors.

Everyone wanted to attend the special session. Franklin managed to get a seat for Eleanor, and on the evening of April 2 they drove in a light spring rain to the Capitol, which was illuminated from below, white against a black sky. When Wilson arrived at 8:32, his pale face contrasting with his dark suit, there was a three-minute ovation. He spoke for thirty-six minutes, but these were the words that would make history:

"With a profound sense of the solemn and even tragical character of the step I am taking and of the grave responsibilities which it involves . . . I advise that the Congress declare the recent course of the Imperial German Government to be in fact nothing less than war against the Government and people of the United States; that it formally accept the status of belligerent which has been forced upon it."

Listening breathlessly, Eleanor went home half dazed by the sense of impending change. Back in the White House, Wilson seemed overcome by what he had done, and told Tumulty: "Think what it was they were applauding. My message today was a message of death for our young men. How strange it seems to applaud that."

By April 6, the resolution had passed both houses. Wilson was having lunch with his wife and a cousin when a messenger brought the document for him to sign. An usher went into the Executive Office to give the news to reporters. Then Daniels's naval aide, Lieutenant Commander Byron McCandless, ran out of the Executive Office and stood on the White House lawn with his arms raised in a prearranged signal. As he wigwagged the sig-

nal, Lieutenant Commander Royal Ingersoll, on the balcony, ran down the
Navy Department corridor to the communications office. Within minutes,
the news was flashed from the towers of Arlington to every ship and shore
installation. A message from Daniels went to every flagship: "Mobilize for
war in accordance with department's confidential mobilization plan of
March 21."

VII
The Navy at War

I will put in my poems that with you is heroism upon the land and sea,
And I will report all heroism from an American point of view.
                    Walt Whitman, *Leaves of Grass*

Once a nation unto itself, pursuing its private destiny, America was now catapulted into world affairs. For the first time in history, American soldiers fought in Europe. Once entangled, there could be no retreat. The comforting illusion that America could stay out of Europe's rivalries was forever destroyed. It would never be over "Over There." You could almost feel the process of change, you could see it unfolding the way corn grows when the season is right, you could actually hear it crackle.

It was the greatest national effort since the Civil War. Ending the casual voluntarism of the nineteenth century, Congress provided for conscription, over protests such as that of Champ Clark: "In the estimation of Missourians, there is precious little difference between a conscript and a convict." Military appropriations totaling $20 billion, many times the size of the federal budget, were passed for the Army and Navy and the Allies. General Pershing was in France by June 13, and by the end of the year was in the command of 176,665 soldiers, who went into battle early in 1918.

The government took on an economic role that would have been unthinkable in normal times in a private-enterprise system. In wartime, the military competed with the domestic market for goods, and had to exercise priority. War was the midwife of a hybrid, state-controlled capitalism. The Fuel Administration doled out coal and oil, the Emergency Fleet Corporation directed shipbuilding, the War Trade Board licensed foreign trade, the National War Labor Board guaranteed collective bargaining, Food Administrator Herbert Hoover bought the entire Cuban and American sugar crops, and War Industries Board Chairman Bernard Baruch fixed prices in the steel industry, a practice that would have been illegal in peacetime.

The mobilization of a nation's resources, and the carrot-and-stick methods used to bring private industry into line, were a dress rehearsal for the New Deal. President Wilson provided a model for government intervention in a crisis, whether foreign or domestic. All sorts of emergency actions were justified. On one occasion, troops were brought in to unload coal trains going through Baltimore. Another time, the Navy sent icebreakers to clear the way for some Anaconda Refinery cutters that were blocked in icebound rivers with vital copper.

The paradox of a democracy at war was that, for all its disorder and mismanagement, it functioned more efficiently than the authoritarian regimes of the Central Powers. President Hindenburg himself admitted that America's war industry had been "brilliant" compared to Germany's.

In 1918, Daniels would present impressive statistics to sum up the Navy's achievement. On the day war was declared, Navy enrollment was 65,777, and there were 197 ships in commission. On the day the armistice was signed, the enrollment was 497,030 and the number of ships in commission was 2,003. The first war service was sending destroyers to the other side. By May 4, 1917, the first destroyers were in European waters. By January 1, 1918, there were 113 American ships across, and by October, 338.

But the Navy's war readiness, which Franklin had harped on for years, was never tested. There was no naval war. By the time the United States came in, the German fleet, driven from the sea by the British, was bottled up in its North Sea harbors. The only American naval actions were the transport and protection of troops, the convoying of supply vessels, and the pursuit of U-boats. With the exception of a few engagements between U-boats and destroyers or merchantmen, not one American ship fired a single shot at a German ship. There was less naval fighting than there had been in the war with Spain.

"I get my fingers into about everything and there's no law against it," Franklin would say of his wartime service. He was willing to try anything. Once a man came in who said he had a substitute for gasoline that would cost two cents a gallon. "Chief, it is worth trying," Franklin told Daniels. "I say he should be given the opportunity to prove he can do what he says." Of course it came to nothing.

He became a sort of raging efficiency expert, who complained about the "outlying districts where men are sitting around twiddling their thumbs and doing no real duty." His favorite target was still Daniels, with whom he now disagreed about method rather than policy. Since the goal of the Navy was to win the war, Daniels with his indecision was letting down the side, while Franklin was the real team captain. Sputtering with impatience, he wrote Daniels that April in a tone that sounded like a superior addressing a subordinate: "Do *please* get through two vital things *today:* 1. Get that Interior Building or give it to War Dept. & let us take the latter's space. 2. Authorize calling out Naval Militia or Reserve—It is essential to get them if we are to get ahead. FDR." Across the top of this note, one of Daniels's aides had scribbled: "Do you always follow his advice?"

Franklin was a whirlwind of activity. On June 27, he saw a site for a cantonment in Brooklyn. On June 28, having sent his orders to the Bureau of Yards and Docks, he gave a contractor oral instructions to proceed with the work. On June 29, the drafting of the plans began, and on July 5, ground was broken. On August 4, the job was done, and on August 11, 6,800 men occupied the cantonment. The official contract went out sixty days after the cantonment was built. If there was a job no one wanted, Franklin took it gladly. There seemed to be no limit to the amount of work he could handle. When the Dallas lawyer Thomas R. Love was drafted by the Treasury to run the War Risk Insurance program, he discovered that hundreds of thousands of soldiers, sailors, and marines had to apply for the insurance within a few weeks. He called Daniels, who told him to take the matter to Franklin. He restated the facts to Franklin, who immediately replied: "I can take care of the Navy all right." Love was impressed, for the thousands of sailors and marines were scattered all over the globe. "How can you do it?" he asked. "I can arrange to speak by wireless to every sailor and marine in the service at the same time," Franklin replied, "and can arrange to have the men paraded to hear the address." That was a bit of an exaggeration, since there was no voice radio at the time, and the message was transmitted by Morse code to all ships and stations. More than 97 percent of the men received $10,000 each in life insurance, which gave Franklin, as Love pointed out, the world record as an underwriter of insurance written in a single day.

Always ready to see the light side of things, even of pain and suffering, Franklin collected humorous remarks inadvertently made by people asking about their insurance claims. Among them were:

"Both sides of our parents are old and poor."

"Please send me a wife's form."

"I have been in bed thirteen years with one doctor and intend to try another."

"I am a poor widow and all I have is in the front."

"I have not received my husband's pay and will be forced to lead an immortal life."

"Now you will have to keep me or who in the hell will if you don't?"

"Please correct my name as I could and would not go under a consumed name."

Among his many projects, the mine barrage across the North Sea was viewed as his finest achievement. A few days after America entered the war, he was studying a map of European waters. He measured the distance from the northern tip of Scotland to the Norwegian coast—it was about 240 miles—and examined the depth of the waters. It seemed to him that if the technical problems could be worked out, some kind of a barrier across that stretch of ocean would keep the U-boats out of the Atlantic. At that time the U-boats were destroying so many British and neutral merchant ships—875,-000 tons in April 1917 alone—that the commander in chief of the Grand

Fleet, Admiral David Beatty, said that "it looked as if the Germans might strangle us with their submarines before either our army or our blockade strangled them." The British and the French had the English Channel effectively sealed off. The long-cruising U-boats were reaching the Atlantic trade lanes from their North Sea bases in Kiel and Wilhelmshaven by taking the northern route east of Scotland.

Franklin pushed the idea in Operations and Ordnance, but it sounded like another of his wild schemes, such as the fifty-foot patrol boats. One man, however, Commander Simon T. Fullinwider, head of the mines section of the Bureau of Ordnance, saw the strategic possibilities—indeed, he was working on a similar plan. The problem was that they did not have the right kind of mine, one that did not require direct contact with a submarine to explode.

More than once, President Wilson had asked Daniels: "Why don't we shut the hornets up in their nests?" On April 16, Daniels inquired of Admiral Sims in London: "Is it not practicable to blockade the German coast efficiently and completely, thus making practically impossible the egress or ingress of submarines?" Sims replied that the idea would not work and recommended an increase in the number of patrol craft.

Unimpressed by Sims's objections, Franklin argued for the mining plan when Lord Balfour, who had been first lord of the Admiralty in 1916, arrived in Washington in mid-May as head of a British mission, with Admiral Dudley De Chair. He spent hours going over the project with De Chair, who expressed misgivings—what of the fog, and the current off the Orkney Islands, and the deep water off the Norwegian coast, and the difficulty of patrolling such a long stretch? Had not that great sailor, Jacky Fisher, once said: "Mine in haste and sweep at leisure"? Lord Balfour mentioned a diplomatic problem: how could they mine the territorial waters of a friendly neutral like Norway? Franklin responded that belligerent warships were restricted by international law from using the territorial waters of neutrals, "and if Norway fails to carry out her direct obligation to prevent the use of a narrow line along her coast as a means of . . . [passage] by German submarines it would seem perfectly fair to carry out this duty for her."

At the end of May, a technical breakthrough arrived on Franklin's doorstep in the form of Ralph C. Browne of Salem, Massachusetts. He looked up from his desk and saw a man "just like one of the thousands of crank inventors who pestered the Navy Department during the World War days." He was pushing a device called the Browne Submerged Gun for use against submarines. The gun, Franklin saw, had no practical value, but there was one intriguing feature: a long copper antenna, suspended from a buoy, caused the gun to fire when it came into contact with metal. This novel firing device could be adapted to set off rows of mines and would solve the major problem of the barrier.

Franklin went to see President Wilson on June 4 to urge that a commission be appointed to study the idea. He enlisted support where he could find it, while the months passed, but Sims, instead of bringing pressure to bear on the British, simply parroted their views. Daniels finally sent Admiral H. T. Mayo to London to bring them around, and he succeeded. A cable arrived from Sims in mid-October 1917: "Admiralty has approved mine barrier and now confirms approval."

Daniels had second thoughts, noting that it was "a stupendous undertaking. Perhaps not impossible, but to my mind of doubtful practicability. North Sea too rough and will necessitate withdrawing all our ships from other work and then can we destroy the hornet's nest or keep the hornets in?" But on October 20, Wilson and the cabinet approved the barrage.

Because of delays in the production of mines, laying operations in the North Sea did not begin until March 3, 1918. Great in scale and purpose, the northern barrage was a product of American drive and ingenuity that may have reminded Franklin of his first view of the Great Cut in the Panama Canal. A special fleet of twenty-four lake cargo carriers left Norfolk on February 1 with the mines, which were landed on the west coast of Scotland and brought overland to the final assembly bases at Inverness and Invergordon, where 2,200 men under Rear Admiral Joseph Strauss loaded them on mine-layers. Escorted by cruisers and destroyers, the minelaying squadron put down the barrage in thirteen expeditions of two days each. The Americans laid 56,000 mines along the 130 miles of the central section, and helped the British lay their 15,093 mines in the two wing sections. The mines were laid at 300-foot intervals in three tiers, the first at 45 feet, the second at 165 feet, and the third at 240 feet. Each mine contained 300 pounds of TNT that were discharged when metal brushed against the wire antenna suspended between the buoy and the mine. The barrier was many miles thick, so that it would take a U-boat from one to three hours to cross it.

Admiral Sims called it "one of the wonders of the war," and the U.S. Navy historian, Captain Dudley Knox, termed it "the most daring and original naval conception of the war." All of that it may have been, but how effective was it? The answer is: not very.

First of all, it had not been completed by the time of the armistice that November. Then it was open at both ends. Admiral Beatty insisted on a three-mile gap to the east of the Orkney Islands to allow a clear passage for British ships. On the far side of the barrage there was another gap, the three miles of Norway's territorial waters, which the Norwegians refused to mine, and which the U-boats routinely used to circumvent the barrage. The British submarine patrols had ocular evidence. Beatty received orders in August to mine the Norwegian waters, which was what Franklin had proposed to Balfour, but refused. It would be repugnant to the officers and men of the Grand Fleet, he said, to steam in overwhelming strength into Norwegian waters and coerce them, perhaps meeting resistance and shedding blood. That would constitute a crime as bad as any the Germans had committed. The British decided instead to use persuasion, and finally in October the

Norwegians agreed to close their waters, but the mines had not yet been laid when the war ended.

Aside from the gaps, there were problems with the mines, which in Franklin's haste had been insufficiently tested. Vice Admiral Andreas Michelsen, commander of the U-boat force, testified after the war that "for some unknown reason many of the mines detonated spontaneously. This tendency was well known to our U-boats.... Considering the number of mines lost in this way, one will readily appreciate that this barrage was far from being a complete seal to the North Sea's northern exit, and could have no more than a limited effectiveness.... In fact, it might be said that the barrage was more of a danger to the minelayers and minesweepers [after the war] than to the U-boats."

Was it then, as Admiral Beatty thought, a waste? In terms of U-boats sunk, the results were meager, particularly when compared with the expenditure of $80 million. According to the Admiralty's final postwar list of U-boats sunk, the barrage could account for three certain and three probable. Counting all six, that came to roughly $13 million per U-boat. It was impossible to close off the North Sea, not only because of the gaps and faulty mines, but because at its deepest spots the U-boats could go under the barrage.

"I dislike exaggeration," Franklin had written President Wilson, "but it is really true that the elimination of all submarines from the waters between the United States and Europe must of necessity be a vital factor in winning the war." It was not the North Sea barrage that ended the submarine menace in 1918 but the adoption of the convoy system, long resisted by the Admiralty. The convoys sank far more U-boats than the barrage, but that did not mean the barrage was useless. The Germans were apprehensive of its presence. It was too far from their bases for minesweeping operations or escorts. The officers and crews knew that they would have to pick their way through it on the way out and on the way home, and this contributed to the morale-sapping feeling that each cruise would be their last. At the very least, it made passage into Atlantic shipping lanes more time-consuming, which meant that the U-boats had less time to spend in operations. Captain Albert Gayer, an authority on U-boats, wrote: "It is not to be denied ... that the threat of this barrage was extremely unpleasant."

To call the barrage unpleasant is a long way from the claim later made by Franklin that it had helped end the war. In a memorandum written when he was president, he asserted: "There is no doubt in my judgment that the morale of the German submarine officers and men was badly shaken by the mere fact of the existence of the barrage.... It seems also to be a fact that discontent in the German submarine force became vocal by the early part of October 1918; that these mutterings spread from the submarine force to German battleships and cruisers and that it had great influence in what turned out, shortly thereafter, to be definite mutiny in the whole German navy. It may not be too farfetched, therefore, to say that the North Sea mine barrage initiated by the American navy and literally forced on the British navy had something definite to do with the German naval mutiny, the subsequent Army mutiny, and the ending of the World War."

Franklin clung to this version of the record for the rest of his life, writing Churchill on February 15, 1944, "Do you remember that in October 1918 it was the crews of the German submarines which cracked first?" In fact, the German naval mutiny at the end of October had nothing to do with the barrage and did not involve submarines. The mutiny erupted in response to a plan for one last suicidal sortie of the German High Seas Fleet, in keeping with the German naval code of "death with honor." It was confined to the larger ships, mainly the dreadnoughts and battle cruisers, leaving the U-boats totally unaffected. The North Sea barrage was a grandiose and costly conception that, aside from a modest deterrent effect, had no bearing on the war's outcome. It was the Navy's white elephant, for after the armistice was signed it had to be dismantled, at further risk and expense.

And yet surely it was worth trying, for who in 1917 was so clairvoyant as to prophesy that the war would be over in a year? Franklin believed in it and saw it through, with a decisiveness and drive that were, as usual, in contrast to the slow pace of his chief.

Some of those who had dealings with him in the Navy, having started out thinking he was a rich dilettante, had occasion to change their minds. One was a young man named Joseph Kennedy, the grandson of an Irish immigrant, who had gone to Harvard and into banking, and who was a bank president at the age of twenty-five. In the spring of 1917, he went to work for Charles Schwab, the chairman of Bethlehem Steel, as assistant manager of the Fore River shipyards in Quincy, Massachusetts, which had broken production records, building thirty-six destroyers in little more than two years. Kennedy's job was the housing, feeding, and transportation of thousands of workers.

Franklin had already had trouble with Fore River before Kennedy arrived on the job. In 1915, in a dispute over alterations, Bethlehem Steel had refused to deliver a ship to the Argentine navy. Interceding on behalf of a friendly power, Franklin had appealed to Schwab: "If the Argentine government can be made to feel secure in this country, I have no doubt that there will be many opportunities given us for increased business." The vessel was allowed to leave, and the Argentine navy ordered more ships.

Now in 1917, several of those ships were not paid for, and Schwab refused to release them. Franklin asked for an arbitration session, and Schwab sent over his assistant manager. It was a classic confrontation between the immigrant and the patrician, each approaching the other through the veil of his prejudice. To Franklin, Kennedy was a parvenu, only interested in making money, whereas he had to keep the goodwill of a Latin American neighbor. To Kennedy, Franklin was just another rich man's son who never had to work for a living and had nothing else to do but dabble in politics. He laughed and smiled and tried to get his way with charm.

"Don't worry about this matter," Franklin told Kennedy. "The State Department will collect the money for you."

"Sorry, Mr. Secretary, but Mr. Schwab refuses to let the ships go until they are paid for."

"Absurd."

"Not at all absurd, sir. Positively no ship will be delivered until it is paid for."

Franklin walked him to the door, an arm on his shoulder. It had been good to meet him, he hoped he would look in whenever he was in Washington. But this was wartime, and if the ships were not delivered at once, he would send a fleet of tugboats to Fore River to get them.

When Kennedy protested, Franklin smiled, warmly shook his hand, and said, "Hope to see you very soon again."

"A smiling four-flusher," was the way Kennedy described Franklin to his boss. Schwab decided to call "this youngster's bluff" and the battleships stayed in their berths.

Soon four Navy tugboats were puffing up the Fore River, with an escort of armed marines. The battleships were towed into harbor, where waiting Argentine crews boarded them. Kennedy was mortified. The charming dabbler had gotten the best of the tough East Boston immigrant's son. It had been a mistake to underrate him.

The toughness in Franklin was not readily apparent, but it was there. That June of 1917, to develop his physical toughness, he joined an exercise group conducted by the celebrated Yale coach Walter Camp, with Franklin Lane, William McAdoo, and other cabinet secretaries and undersecretaries. It became known as the most exclusive club in Washington. Four times a week between 7:30 and 8:30 A.M., these busy men did calisthenics in Potomac Park. They called themselves the Campers, and one of them wrote the following verse:

> "He's better made the best of us,
> And much improved the rest of us,
> He's raised each sinking chest of us,
> And much reduced the vest of us."

The odd thing was that, in spite of his splendid appearance and vitality, Franklin was always getting sick. His susceptibility to germs was extreme. On June 5, he wrote his mother to discourage her from coming to Washington: "My cold is gone and you mustn't worry one second—if I get another tummy ache I will wire you to come, but I really feel that you would not get any satisfaction in a visit unless I am laid up, as I leave the home at 7:15 a.m. for physical exercise, breakfast with the other exercisers and get to the Dept.

at 9. I rarely am able to leave for lunch and don't get home until just in time for dinner."

All through 1917, it seemed that Franklin was in a permanent state of outrage because not enough was being done to help the Allies. When the Germans captured Riga, the capital of Latvia, he told Daniels: "We ought to have sent TR over to Russia with 100,000 men and this would not have happened." On May 9, he wrote Henry Van Cleff, who was in Paris with the Red Cross: "Here we are a month after getting into war with all sorts of magnificent plans for the future and, between ourselves, mighty little done to get concrete assistance over to the other side." The Atlantic Fleet had not been brought from Cuban waters until the end of March. The first six destroyers had not left for England until April 23. The surgeon general was begging for tents and hospital supplies. Daniels spent his time magnifying ridiculous details.

In his attacks on the secretary, he tried a flanking movement, bringing in the well-known historical novelist Winston Churchill, who was a friend of the president and a graduate of Annapolis, to serve as a sort of independent auditor of the Navy who would report directly to Wilson. On April 18, Franklin wrote Churchill to express the hope that he would do more than "turn out mere write-ups or recruiting posters of Navy life." Churchill did a thorough job, coming across widespread complaints and low morale. On June 30, he wrote Franklin that the Navy Department was "suffering from hookworm—certainly not through any fault of yours." On July 25, he saw the president, to whom he gave his confidential report, which was not kind to Daniels. The secretary "spends much of his time and energy in signing unimportant letters," he wrote, "and wastes also the time and energy of officers in discussing small matters that should be left to the bureaus. . . . The chief comment concerning him . . . has been of his dilatoriness, of his unwillingness in matters great and small, the result of which has been to delay and at times almost to paralyze the activities of the naval service. . . . Bureau chiefs have had to wait on him for days, to bring upon him the utmost pressure before the affairs of the most ordinary routine could be got through."

Franklin was sure the report had done some good, and saw the president himself in mid-August, writing "Dearest Babs" on August 17: "The more I think over the talk with the President, the more I am encouraged to think that he has *begun* to catch on, but then it will take lots more of the Churchill type of attack."

Daniels displayed the patience of an Old Testament elder in putting up with his assistant's sniping. His reserve of fondness was never exhausted. He truly loved Franklin. He was not turning the other cheek, for Daniels was a fighter—he had fought the flag-waving profiteers, and the companies that brought in collusive bids, and the officer corps, and the liquor interests, and the oil companies who wanted drilling rights on the Navy's California oil reserves, and the Navy League. Franklin got away with more than all of them combined. Daniels took no action when Franklin was mentioned in a crackdown on crooked Navy contracts. A Boston influence peddler named Eugene Sullivan was indicted for promising the Quaker City Raincoat Company a lucrative Navy contract in return for a fee. He bribed a clerk in the Bureau of Construction and Repair, who admitted that he had secured contracts for Sullivan at higher prices "by using much bull on the Assistant Secretary." For Franklin, who was so proud of always getting the best deal, this was a comeuppance.

Nineteen eighteen was an election year, and on February 11 the New York *Tribune* announced that Franklin Delano Roosevelt was the Tammany candidate for governor against the Republican incumbent, Charles S. Whitman. They liked him because he could get the upstate vote, while Tammany could take care of New York City. They liked the sound of his name. Tammany district captains could tell the voters that he was Teddy's son, returned from the front loaded with honors and turned Democrat, as when Henry Goldfogle had run in the Irish districts and the voters had been told that his name was Guilfoyle.

How had Franklin, the archfoe of the machine, who had tried through patronage to build a rival organization, and who had lost no occasion to denounce Charles Murphy and his minions, suddenly found favor with Tammany? The reversal had come about through the slow process of realizing that fighting Tammany did not pay. The 1914 senatorial primary had shown him that, and so had the weak reed of patronage. Why should he burn himself out in anti-Tammany tirades that only served to isolate him in his own state?

Franklin cultivated Tammany congressmen, doing favors for those who had Navy yards in their districts. At the end of June 1917, Daniel J. Riordan, representative for Staten Island and lower Manhattan, came to his office and asked him to "give the long talk" at Tammany's most sacred ceremony, the July 4 celebration. Franklin accepted. He could have found no more dramatic way to announce a new alliance. "I guess if we can stand having you, you can stand coming," Riordan said.

And so it was that on July 4, 1917, Franklin found himself at the 14th Street Wigwam, honoring the 128th year of Tammany's existence. The Sixty-ninth Regiment band furnished the music, the Tammany Glee Club sang "Tammany Forever," with the audience joining in, and Franklin mingled and joked with his former enemies, and was observed in animated conversation with Charles F. Murphy.

It was in the aftermath of his reconciliation with Tammany that he was mentioned as a candidate for governor. He called the idea "utterly wild" and said he would stay on the job in the Navy. When support began to build, he was noncommittal. That June, the German offensive was in full stride, and he desperately wanted to go to Europe and see the war for himself. He was getting mail from Dutchess County young men in France, such as soldiers' cards that said "I have arrived safely overseas," or this June 28 letter from Albert Ornsteen, Jr., of Poughkeepsie: "Most of the men have had the 'cooties' but as yet I've to experience their effects. In our sector, things are particularly quiet, and I guess Jerry realizes he'd better keep away from American forces for his own good." He had been badgering Daniels for weeks to go as either a naval officer or on an official inspection tour. The trip was discussed at the June 18 cabinet meeting, and President Wilson said that "he ought not to decline to run for Governor of New York if it is tendered to him."

Alarmed, Franklin wrote the president that he was not interested in being governor, which "is frankly very much of a local political office in these times," and would only leave his present job for active service. He hoped that Wilson would not listen to any appeal to make him run. As it turned out, the Democrats nominated Al Smith for governor, and he was elected that fall.

Franklin sailed on July 9 on the USS *Dyer,* one of the Fore River destroyers, just out of the builder's hands, which was part of a fast convoy carrying 20,000 troops to France. He loved the life at sea, the rough weather and the danger of submarines. Responding to a 4:00 A.M. alert, he came on the bridge in his pajamas, barefoot, and the captain cautioned him about hitting a ringbolt. When not in pajamas, he wore a traveling-at-sea costume of his own devising—khaki riding trousers, golf stockings, a flannel shirt, and a leather coat.

When they reached England on July 21, 1918, he was welcomed with great fanfare, for he was the first official of subcabinet rank to make the trip since America had entered the war more than a year before. Sir Eric Geddes, the first lord of the Admiralty, a large and forceful man who had been an engineer on the India railways, and who reminded Franklin of a successful American businessman, briefed him on July 22. Their most urgent problem was the Italian fleet, which was sitting in its harbor at Taranto, refused to go after the Austrians, and would not agree to a unified command under the British.

The next day, he was supposed to have lunch with Rudyard Kipling, but Geddes whisked him to Pembroke, at the tip of Wales, where they inspected the dockyards and then crossed the Irish Sea to Queenstown (today's Cobh), where a large Anglo-American destroyer force was stationed.

"I do so wish you could see all this in war time," Franklin wrote Eleanor on July 26. "In spite of all people say, one feels much closer to the actual fighting here. The counter attack in the Rheims salient has heartened everybody enormously, our men had undoubtedly done well. One of my Marine regiments has lost 1200 and another 800 men."

Doing the rounds of the Admiralty, Franklin went to see the head of Naval Intelligence, Admiral Sir William Reginald Hall, who ran an outstanding service and loved to startle his visitors with his latest feat. As they talked about possible German fleet movements, Hall suddenly said, "I am going to ask that youngster at the other end of the room to come over here. I will not introduce him by name. I want you to ask him where he was exactly twenty-four hours ago. Franklin asked him and he said: "I was in Kiel, sir." Franklin was mystified. How had he gotten to Kiel, and back to the Admiralty, where he now sat looking clean and composed, inside twenty-four hours?

On Saturday the twenty-seventh, Franklin went out to the country for a weekend with the millionaire Waldorf Astor and his Virginia-born wife, Nancy, the first woman to be elected to the House of Commons. They had turned some of the outbuildings of their vast estate, Cliveden, into a 110-bed hospital, and the Italian garden into a cemetery for those who died of their wounds. Nancy was the same lively chatterbox. That evening, his hosts briefed him on all the terrible hardships people in England had gone through. They hadn't had this to eat or that to drink, they had no butter, no sugar, no bacon, they had really had to tighten their belts enormously. The next morning, late for breakfast, he went over to the sideboard, and the first hot dish he removed the cover from was piled high with bacon. He filled his plate and sat down. When Nancy looked in, she said, "What! Only bacon?" "Yes," Franklin replied. "You know, at home I have gone without bacon for a year and a half, in order that you good people might have it!"

Monday morning, July 29, he drove into London for a 10:30 appointment at Buckingham Palace with the sailor king, George V. They exchanged reminiscences of Germany, and the king said: "You know, I have a number of relations in Germany, but I can tell you frankly that in all my life, I have never seen a German gentleman." The king's jaws almost snapped when he described German atrocities in Belgium and northern France. They got going so well that they both talked at the same time, and Franklin stayed half an hour longer than the allotted fifteen minutes. The *New York Times* carried a story on Franklin's visit to the king, and ten-year-old James proudly told Sara: "It is on the first page, Grandma!"

That night, he attended a dinner at Gray's Inn, one of the four legal societies that in England have the exclusive right to admit men to the bar, in honor of the war ministers. He sat next to the lord chief justice, who insisted that he take vast quantities of vintage pepper. Years later, when Gray's Inn was bombed, in May 1941, Franklin thought of the dinner, and hoped that some of the pepper had escaped destruction. Churchill, then minister of munitions, was self-absorbed as usual, so that Franklin made no impression on him. Asked to say a few words, Franklin was able to announce the landing of 200,000 American troops in France during the previous week.

The next evening, Franklin was asked to dinner at the House of Commons with Lord Balfour and other distinguished parliamentarians. Once again, he wondered at the hardship stories when he saw the menu: *sole meunière, jambon au chablis, omelette soufflée aux pêches, croûtes à l'écossaise, fromage et beurre.* Balfour, perhaps the craftiest English politician of his time, poured on the flattery—everyone knew that it was the U.S. Second Division with the brigade of Marines who had stopped the German rush at Château-Thierry and opened the counteroffensive at Soissons.

It was Balfour's aim to gull Franklin into pulling a British chestnut out of the fire. Something had to be done about the Italian naval situation. Would Franklin go to Italy and try to get them to agree to put their fleet under British command? He was delighted to be of use, although such a mission went beyond his instructions. He was leaving the next day for France, but perhaps he could go on to Rome after that.

Eighteen years later, in a memorable speech, FDR would say: "I have seen war. I have seen war on land and sea. I have seen blood running from the wounded. I have seen men coughing out their gassed lungs. I have seen the dead in the mud. I have seen cities destroyed. I have seen two hundred limping, exhausted men come out of line—the survivors of a regiment of one thousand that went forward forty-eight hours before. I have seen children starving. I have seen the agony of mothers and wives. I hate war."

He may have hated war in 1936, but he loved it in 1918, and could not get enough of it. He was like the kid in the circus who wants to touch the elephant's trunk; indeed there was something juvenile in his insistence on being in the thick of the action. War cast a seductive spell. Rather than being revolted at its horror, he was drawn to its every aspect. In fact, he had told William Castle, a friend at the State Department, as they were walking home from the office one day, "It would be wonderful to be a war President of the United States."

A tireless sightseer and questioner, Franklin was fascinated by the technical details—the size of the bombs, the methods of night bombing, the number of horses lost in Channel crossings. He noted the strange blend of the normal and the uncommon. In the Channel, French fishing boats went about their business, but Dunkirk was so badly bombed not a pane of glass was intact. And yet the population took the nightly raids "as we would a thunder-storm." He watched the faces of the French troops, and the expressions of those going into battle, and of those coming out. He marveled at the sight of the antiaircraft guns at Calais at night, the shells bursting in tiny starpoints. He was disappointed when a Navy night-bombing squadron at Saint Inglebert did not take off because of ground mist. During the night there was a German air attack in nearby Calais. Evidently, Franklin reflected, the Boche did not think the mist was too heavy.

He was thrilled when, on August 2, he met the seventy-seven-year-old "Tiger" himself, Premier Georges Clemenceau, whom the war kept youthful. Every Saturday, he drove to the front, visited a corps commander, spent Sunday inspecting the battle lines, and was back at his desk on Monday morning. Recently he had seen a *poilu* and a *Boche* standing partly buried in a shell hole, locked in a grotesque embrace. They had dropped their rifles, and had been trying to bite each other to death when a shell killed them both. Clemenceau grabbed Franklin by both shoulders, shook him with a grip of steel, and made as if to bite his neck. Truly he was a wonderful old man, Franklin thought, the greatest civilian in France.

Longing to see action, he left on August 4 for a four-day tour of the front lines. But the naval attaché, R. H. Jackson, who was responsible for his safety, tried to keep him away from the fighting. Franklin lost his temper, berating Jackson for taking them to villages where the battles had ended days ago. He did not want late risings, easy trips, and bombed houses thirty miles from the front. He would take over the travel arrangements himself. Franklin later had Jackson removed from his Paris assignment, and in 1919 tried to have him ousted from his next station, writing Daniels on April 3: "The only thing which has rather appalled me, and which I have only just heard today, is the appointment of Captain R. H. Jackson to command the base at the Azores. . . . Frankly, I am rather upset, because I saw Jackson in Paris on my first trip, and he is decidedly the last man in the world to send to a place like the Azores, or to any other spot where tact and good manners are desirable. . . . I cannot help feeling, in view of my knowledge of the case, often expressed, that he should be relieved of the Azores and sent somewhere else immediately." It was a petty retaliation, since Jackson had been following orders to protect an important naval person.

Franklin caught up with the Franco-American offensive at Château-Thierry, and was soon threading his way through Belleau Wood, where the Marine brigade had distinguished itself, past the debris of war: water-filled shell holes, improvised shelters, rusty bayonets, broken guns, empty ration tins, rain-stained love letters, and unmarked mounds with rifles stuck bayonet down in the ground or whittled crosses etched with crudely carved American names. Franklin wondered whether he was really in the battle. At 5:00 P.M., when they reached the village of Mareuil, a few miles from the Vesle River, his "sensitive naval nose" told him that he was. He could smell dead horses and soon began passing their carcasses. The cleaning-up outfit had not yet sprinkled them with lime. The Boche had held the village the night before, and their corpses were piled up, awaiting burial. An American gun battery was shelling German lines seven kilometers away. Franklin fired one of the 155s at a railroad junction twelve kilometers north, and a spotter plane reported that he had hit the mark. Pleased with himself at this gesture, which was about as significant as tossing a coin into Rome's Trevi Fountain, he later said, "I will never know how many, if any, Huns I killed."

That evening, they were back at French army headquarters at Château-Thierry, for a delightful dinner with the commander, General Degoutte. "The members of my staff," Franklin observed, "have begun to realize what campaigning, or rather sight-seeing, with the Assistant Secretary means, and Captain Jackson is still visibly annoyed because I upset his comfortable plans for an inspection of regions fought over a month ago." It had been a thoroughly successful day.

The next morning, August 5, Franklin went looking for the Marine brigade, which he found at Nancy. He was proud that they had seen more continuous fighting than any other American unit. The men were exhausted, but there were no complaints. That evening, with assorted generals, he had dinner in a "delightful" restaurant in Nancy's famous Place Stanislas, a gem of seventeenth-century architecture undamaged by the fighting. Franklin felt the companionship of war, the exhilaration of dangers and difficulties shared and overcome, and the sense of being part of a noble undertaking. These were happy hours. "There was no scarcity of good things," he wrote, "and we sat at table talking over war until one o'clock in the morning. It was a most interesting evening."

On August 6, he toured Verdun, where the French had lost 300,000 men, and saw the famous sign at the entrance to the citadel: *Ils ne passeront pas* (They shall not pass). The town was a scene of colossal destruction, although miraculously the bridges across the Meuse had not been hit. After a very good lunch, he saw one of the battle cemeteries, where thousands and thousands of graves were tightly packed together, and the battlefield—mile upon mile of shell-churned brown earth—and the Valley of Death below Fort Douaumont. How was it possible that 100,000 men had been killed in that little stretch? The French colonel taking them around pointed out the village of Fleury. Not even a brick on the tumbled earth could verify his statement. On the way to the fort they were shelled. The German trenches were a mile away. The rest of Franklin's party sometimes grew impatient with his zest. "I was so much interested in going through [the] narrow winding tunnels [of the fort]," he wrote, "that the rest of the party failed to appreciate my enthusiasm." The scenes of carnage did not spoil his appetite, and he was so excited that he forgot his briefcase full of secret papers on the running board of the car. It fell off and was picked up by a *poilu*.

On August 7, he drove back to Paris, arriving just in time to hear the last few shots fired by the German long-range gun, Big Bertha, one of which exploded near the Louvre, killing some people in a restaurant. A letter from his mother informed him that Eleanor was well, but Sara hoped she would add a little layer of fat to her frame before he got back. That evening, he left for Rome, where he read with amusement accounts in the papers of how well the Italian soldiers were fighting, having seen the Italian deserters doing road work in France after running away from the Austrians at the Piave River. On August 10, he saw the minister of marine, Admiral del Bono, and his chief of staff, Admiral Thaon di Revel. Franklin knew that the Italians had no intention of risking their capital ships in offensive operations, wanting to keep their navy intact until the end of the war. He pointed out that they had not gone outside Taranto harbor for over a year. They had had no fleet drill or target practice. Leaning forward, as if to confide a telling point, Admiral Thaon di Revel replied: "Ah, but my dear Mr. Minister, you must not forget that the Austrian Fleet have not had any either." That was a classic, thought Franklin, hard to beat—if one side did nothing, the other side did nothing. If he could not prod the Italians into fighting, at least they might agree to a unified command. Prime Minister Orlando seemed receptive when Franklin approached him on August 11 with a plan for a general staff in the Mediterranean: a British chairman, perhaps Admiral Jellicoe, and French, Italian, American, and Japanese members. Feeling that the problem was solved, he reported to Daniels that the Italians had "finally agreed to the proposition of a commander-in-chief for the naval force in the Mediterranean."

Franklin soon found himself at the center of a diplomatic tempest. The way he had sold the British plan to the Italians angered the French and embarrassed Daniels in Washington. On September 3, Secretary of State Lansing asked Daniels whether Franklin was authorized to tell Italy that the United States favored the British plan. Daniels said he was not—on the contrary, Daniels had written to him that the United States had no preferred choice for the command. The French ambassador, Jusserand, complained that Franklin was promoting a plan detrimental to his government. Prompted by Balfour and Geddes, Franklin had overstepped himself, incurring the president's displeasure. On September 10, Wilson asked Daniels to let him know in advance the name and mission of any civilian going to Europe, because "too many men go over there assuming to speak for the government."

By this time, Franklin had decided that when he got back to Washington he would resign and ask for a commission. Back home, Eleanor knew how eager Franklin was for active duty, but Louis Howe reassured her on August 23 that "it had practically been decided to accept no volunteers whatever under the new draft, and also that married men with children are not going to be called. I feel that he will have a somewhat strenuous time getting the President to waive the regulations, particularly as I feel the President has sufficient judgement to know that things would go badly here if he should leave."

At the end of August Franklin returned to the front, and visited La Panne, one of the few Belgian coastal towns held by the Allies. He had lunch with King Albert, and afterward they drove inland a few miles and came to a very old and recently bombed village. A German shell had taken out one side of the town hall. On the second floor, the wooden pigeonhole cases were exposed, but the bundles of old records had not been hurt. Franklin and the king looked through them and found some old Flemish documents written by the captains of fishing boats who had visited the Grand Banks around 1580. As he stood in the bombed-out rubble of the building, a few miles from the German lines, he was suddenly transported to the time of the first ocean voyages to America. The archivist in him hunted for clues. He had always claimed that there must have been hundreds of unheralded voyages to America in the sixteenth century. It was inconceivable that the Spaniards had never gone north of Florida, or that the Cabot discoveries in Newfoundland had not been followed by other trips down the eastern seaboard. And now here he was with the Belgian king looking through the log books of sixteenth-century Flemish fishing captains. He was sure that some of them had not stopped at the fishing banks but had kept going as far as the New England coast. A German shell had almost destroyed the evidence. Armies had no more respect for Gothic churches, or ancient town halls where the records of a community were kept, than the 1911 Albany fire that had destroyed the library in the state capitol. This was the true meaning of war— not only a destroyer of lives, but a destroyer of history and civilization.

Franklin had a compulsion to cram each hour with activity. With only a few days left, he inspected all the American aviation and antisubmarine bases on the Bay of Biscay from the Spanish border to Brest; he then inspected the Grand Fleet in the Firth of Forth and the American battleship squadron, and the North Sea mine barrage. When he recrossed the Channel, in weather so rough that a man was swept overboard, and a trip that normally took five hours took fifteen, he was running a fever of 102. His body ached, and his head roared, but he refused to go to bed. On September 8, he boarded the *Leviathan,* America-bound, and collapsed in his bunk, seriously ill. He had influenza, which would, that year, reach epidemic proportions, claiming 20 million lives. The *Leviathan* was like a floating hospital. Men and officers died on the way home and were buried at sea. He also came down with double pneumonia, and was so weak when the ship docked on September 19 that he had to be carried off in a stretcher. An ambulance drove him to his mother's house, and four Navy orderlies carried him inside.

It took Franklin a month to recover, but he was still bent on returning to Europe as a naval officer. On October 13, from Hyde Park, he wrote to his former secretary, Charles McCarthy: "I am up here getting over the attack of pneumonia which I contracted at Brest before leaving France, and am nearly all right again. . . . You are quite right in guessing that I am probably going to get into the fighting end of the game, but if I do so I suppose it will be the Navy and not the Army."

But when he went to see President Wilson at the end of October to request reassignment, his hopes were dashed. Wilson had already received a peace proposal from the new German chancellor, Prince Max of Baden. Franklin did not give up. On October 31, a story appeared in the papers attributed to "intimate friends" (Louis Howe?) that he planned to enlist as an ordinary seaman. He wanted so badly to take part in the war that he actually hoped the negotiations would break down and the conflict would be prolonged. On November 9, the day the Kaiser's abdication was proclaimed, he wrote his Harvard roommate, Lathrop Brown, that "the consensus of opinion seems to be that the Boche is in a bad way and will take anything, but I personally am not so dead sure as some others. If the terms are turned down and the war continues, I think I shall get into the Navy without question."

Two days later, at 5:00 A.M. on November 11, in Marshal Foch's train in the forest of Compiègne, the armistice documents were signed. As an eyewitness recalled, there was no triumph in the faces of the victors. Orders went out to all military units to end all fighting on the eleventh hour of that eleventh day of the eleventh month of the year. At noon, after four years and 10 million dead, all was quiet on the western front.

On that day, an Austrian-born corporal lay weeping on a hospital bed, not because he had missed the war but because Germany was prostrate. In Franklin there were two conflicting emotions, elation and disappointment. The elation was contagious when he heard Wilson address Congress, and when at the mention of the evacuation of Alsace-Lorraine everyone rose and cheered. How could he not feel relief and gratitude that the horror was over? The disappointment was that he had not seen action. There was a lot of luck in the game. An outstanding officer might be placed in an inactive area, while a mediocre officer might be in the right place at the right time. This was what made field marshals and presidents. His usual good fortune had not been with him, and thereafter he would take pains to describe himself as having seen active service, which in the strict sense he had not. He wrote an alumnus of Groton who was preparing a World War I tablet for the school that "I believe that my name should go in the first division of those who were 'in the service,' especially as I saw service on the other side, and was missed by torpedoes and shells." On September 8, the young Poughkeepsie man who had written him about the "cootie" problem in France was killed in action. Franklin wrote his parents, Dutchess County constituents: "I am greatly shocked to receive your letter telling of your son's death." It may have crossed his mind that although he had not fought, at least he had returned safely, unlike so many others. Did not the Bible say, better a live dog than a dead lion?

As Franklin lay abed in September 1918 with a high fever and double pneumonia, Eleanor while unpacking his things discovered and read some letters that proved beyond a doubt that he had been having an affair with her social secretary, Lucy Mercer.

It was early 1914, when she was pregnant again, and overwhelmed by invitations and calling cards and letters to write, that Eleanor hired the tall and lovely twenty-two-year-old to assist her three mornings a week. Lucy Page Mercer had breeding but no money. Her handsome father, Carroll Mercer, belonged to a prominent Maryland family but conformed to the hard-drinking wastrel type. In the Marines, he had been court-martialed for drunkenness on duty. Her mother, Minnie, was a Washington beauty who married Mercer in 1888, after a divorce from a first husband at a time when divorce was scandalous. Lucy's parents separated but never divorced because Carroll Mercer was Catholic. Minnie went to New York and became an interior decorator, finding rich patrons upon whom she was said to bestow her favors. In the meantime, Lucy attended a strict convent school in Austria, where she had relatives. She had recently returned to Washington with her mother when she went to work for Eleanor.

Franklin first mentioned Lucy in the spring of 1914 when he returned to

Washington from a trip to the West Coast, in a letter to "Dearest Babs": "Arrived safely and came to house and Albert [the chauffeur] telephoned Miss Mercer who later came and cleaned up." A social secretary was expected to perform all sorts of tasks, from filling in as an extra woman at a dinner party to walking the dog and washing the baby. Lucy had charm and poise and good manners; everyone liked her, even the hard-to-please Sara, who, while visiting Washington in March 1915, wrote: "Miss Mercer is here, she is *so* sweet and attractive and adores you, Eleanor."

It was the custom for the wives and children of Washington officials to spend the summer in some cooler place, as Eleanor and the chicks went to Campobello. These long absences were open doors to temptation, and it was not unusual for summer bachelors to conduct discreet liaisons. This seems to be the way Franklin's affair with Lucy Mercer began. She was present, while Eleanor was absent; she was available, while Eleanor was unavailable; she was interested, while Eleanor was impassive. Eleanor's last baby, John, was born on March 13, 1916. She had been bearing children with wearisome regularity since 1905, six in all. She wanted no more, but was not knowledgeable enough about such matters to suggest the use of contraceptives. There was only one sure way, and that was abstinence. When the new wing was built in Hyde Park in 1915, they had separate bedrooms, and one of the reasons why they moved into a larger house in Washington was so they could each have their own room. As her son Elliott wrote, Eleanor's "blank ignorance about how to ward off pregnancy left her no choice other than abstinence. Her shyness and stubborn pride would keep her from seeking advice from a doctor or woman friend. She said as much to her only daughter when Sis [Anna] grew up. It quickly became the most tightly held secret that we five children ever shared and kept."

Then in his early thirties, Franklin was blessed with great vitality and physical attractiveness. A newspaper description of the period makes him sound like a matinee idol: "His face is long, firmly shaped and set with marks of confidence. There are faint wrinkles on a high straight forehead. Intensely blue eyes rest in light shadow. A firm, thin mouth breaks quickly to laugh, openly and freely. His voice is pitched well, goes forward without tripping. . . . He recalls Conrad's description of the young Malay 'war comrade' in *Lord Jim:* 'Unobscured vision, tenacity of purpose.' In the mocking humor of the Capital, he is called 'a he man.' "

Naturally enough, this he-man was attractive to ladies, and would not long remain content with enforced celibacy. The doughty Admiral Cowles, who had married Cousin Teddy's sister Anna (Bamie or Auntie Bye), whose Washington house Eleanor and Franklin had rented, wrote him on August 18, 1917, that Bamie "speaks of you as her debonair young cousin, so brave and so charming, but the girls will spoil you soon enough, Franklin, and I leave you to them." The tone was critical and informed, as if the admiral had been told about a dalliance of Franklin's by his wife. According to Livingston Davis, the Harvard friend whom Franklin brought to the Navy

Department in 1917 as "my second pair of legs," but who in fact served as his cover when he wanted to step out without Eleanor, Franklin was an ardent ladies' man, a man of many affairs. Davis was the "jolly boy," Franklin's partner in amusement, who had recommended that they visit the sex show in Havana. No wonder Eleanor disliked him, and thought he was "lazy, selfish and self-seeking to an extraordinary degree, with the outward appearance of being quite different."

After Franklin had been stricken with polio, Davis suggested, on September 15, 1921, that now he would have time to write books, and offered the following topics:

- "The Ladies of Washington: or Thirty Days and Evenings as a Bachelor;
- "Frivolities of a Capital: On the Trail of Roosevelt, or 29 Concussive Nights in a Different Place and Bed."

The tone of belabored mirth aside, Davis strongly suggested that Franklin had repeatedly been involved in sexual escapades, and that Lucy Mercer was not his only mistress.

In the summer of 1916, when Eleanor was nursing her latest-born in Campobello, her suspicions may have been aroused, for when Franklin wrote her that his chauffeur Golden had wrecked his car, she replied with what could have been a double entendre: "Isn't it horrid to be disappointed in someone, it makes one so suspicious?"

That summer she and the children stayed in Campobello longer than usual, because of the infantile paralysis scare, which gave Franklin three months of bachelor life. Eleanor wondered when he would come up, and he promised on August 14: "I will get that holiday in *somehow,*" and a week later wrote: "I have had a bad three weeks. I long to get to you all." He spent about ten days in Campobello, and came back at the end of September to take his family to Hyde Park aboard the *Dolphin.*

It was not until the following summer, however, that Eleanor sensed the indefinable pulling away that signals another woman. In July 1917, Lucy, while continuing her work as social secretary, joined the Navy as a female yeoman third class, attached to the Navy Department, where there were daily opportunities to see Franklin. She was described in her application as five feet nine, blue-eyed, brown-haired, with a small scar on her left arm and a scar on her right leg. When the time came in mid-July to take the children to Campobello, Eleanor resisted going. She accused Franklin of trying to get rid of her and wanting to stay alone in Washington. Weighed down by the burden of work in the first months of America's entry in the war, as well as by the tensions of his personal life, Franklin was unreasonable and touchy. But he tried to soothe his wife, telling her she was "a goosy girl" to think she wasn't wanted. She ought to have six weeks straight at Campo, just as he ought to, only she could and he couldn't. A summer in Washington was hell on his nerves, and if he didn't get a change or some cold weather, he would be like a bear with a sore head. After her departure he wrote on July 16 that he hated the house all alone without her, and that he had had a vile day, unable to read or work, or even play his favorite game of solitaire, Miss Millikin. He sent her many many kisses. The next day he wrote that "it seems years since you left and I miss you horribly and hate the thought of the empty house."

But on July 18, his tone changed to annoyance after reading an article in the *New York Times* with the headline "How to Save in Big Homes," describing Eleanor's food-saving program for her family of seven and her ten servants, which had been adopted as a model by the Food Administration. The Roosevelts did not eat bacon, had only two courses for lunch and three for dinner, and made good use of leftovers. "Making the ten servants help me do my saving has not only been possible, but highly profitable," Eleanor was quoted as saying. "Since I have started following the home-card instructions, prices have risen, but my bills are no larger."

This was the sort of publicity Franklin could do without, for it made him out to be a rich man with more servants than family members, who considered a three-course dinner a hardship. In a sarcastic letter on July 18 that omitted the usual "Dearest Babs," Franklin wrote: "All I can say is that your latest newspaper campaign is a corker and I am proud to be the husband of the Originator, Discoverer, and Inventor of the New Household Economy for Millionaires! Please have a photo taken showing the family, the ten cooperating servants, the scraps saved from the table and the hand book. I will have it published in the *Sunday Times*." A contrite Eleanor wrote her husband on July 20: "I do think it was horrid of that woman to use my name in that way, and I feel dreadfully about it because so much is not true and yet some of it I did say. I never will be caught again that's sure and I'd like to crawl away for shame."

Letters asking for more information about the food plan arrived from many parts of the country, and Lucy Mercer forwarded them to Eleanor with the answers that Franklin had asked Lucy to provide. "Why," Eleanor asked on July 23, "did you make her waste all that time answering those fool notes? I tore them and the answers up and please tear any other results of my idiocy up at once. She tells me you are going off for Sunday and I hope you all had a pleasant trip but I'm so glad I'm here and not on the Potomac!"

One can imagine Franklin complaining about Eleanor and her newfound fame to his guests aboard the presidential yacht *Sylph* when they started down the Potomac on Sunday July 22: Charlie Munn, a Harvard connection, and his wife, Mary, who helped Eleanor with her "wool Saturdays" for the Navy League; Cary T. Grayson, President Wilson's doctor, and his wife; Lucy Mercer; and Nigel Law, the British third secretary, a bachelor who was invited so it did not look as if Franklin and Lucy were pairing off.

They went down to Hampton Roads and visited the fleet in a destroyer and had lunch on the battleship *Arkansas* with Admiral Tommy Rodgers. Things were not right, Franklin thought, due to indecision and too many old lady officers. That afternoon, they went up the James River to Richmond, stopping to swim and visit old houses. That night, they slept aboard the yacht. It seemed like a funny group, but it had worked out *wonderfully,* Franklin reported. Obviously, he was getting on quite nicely, in spite of his vile days, and his inability to play Miss Millikin, and Eleanor replied: "I'm glad you are so gay but you know I predicted it."

Feeling neglected, Eleanor wrote on July 24: "I wish you could come here but I want no one else!" Who else did she expect? Did she think he was going to bring Lucy Mercer to Campobello? "I don't think you read my letters," she went on, "for you never answer a question, and nothing I ask for appears!" Franklin had promised to come and see her at the end of the month, but reneged on July 26: "I do miss you so *very* much, but I am getting busier and busier and fear my hoped-for dash to Campobello next week for two days will not materialize."

A few days later, he came down with a bad throat infection and was hospitalized. Eleanor made the long trip from Maine to be with him, and stayed until August 14, having extracted a promise that he would come to Campobello at the end of August. "I hated to leave yesterday," she wrote on August 15. "Please go to a doctor twice a week, eat well and sleep well and remember I *count* on seeing you the 26th. My threat was no idle one." What can the threat have been? Possibly that she would return to Washington with the children unless he came to visit.

No sooner had Franklin recovered than he went on another Sunday outing with Lucy Mercer, on August 19, this time to a farm near Harper's Ferry, about an hour outside Washington. They were chaperoned by the Graysons, but there was no Nigel Law along this time to act as Lucy's escort. Franklin reported these activities to his wife, apparently thinking himself above suspicion.

He did go to Campobello, but Eleanor was getting just a bit fed up with Miss Mercer, whom everyone was charmed by, and who seemed to be rather often in her husband's company. Her irritation came out in a minor practical matter, a check sent to Lucy for handling her "wool Saturdays," to remind her that their relationship was from employer to employee. Lucy returned the check but Eleanor insisted. This small test of wills took on a symbolic importance, and Eleanor informed Franklin on September 8: "I've written Miss Mercer and returned the check saying I knew she had done far more work than I could pay for. She is evidently quite cross with me!" Franklin replied on September 9 that Daniels, in his quarrel with the Navy League, had disbanded the Comforts Committee and was forming a rival knitting group under the Red Cross. As a result, *"you* are entirely disconnected and Lucy Mercer and Mrs. Dunn are closing up the loose ends."

There were other occasions when Franklin and Lucy were seen together. Alice Roosevelt, Teddy's daughter, who had married Nicholas Longworth, called Franklin to say that she had seen them in a car. "I saw you 20 miles out in the country," she said. "You didn't see me. Your hands were on the wheel, but your eyes were on the perfectly lovely lady." That was better than the reverse, Franklin could have rejoined, but instead replied: "Isn't she perfectly lovely?" Alice, who disliked Eleanor and was a gossip and trouble-maker ("If you can't say something nice about a person, sit right here by me," she used to say), encouraged the romance by giving a dinner party to which she invited them both. "He deserved a good time," she later said. "He was married to Eleanor."

That October, with Lucy's father dying of heart disease in Sibley Hospi-tal, she was discharged from the Navy "by special order of Secretary of the Navy," but continued to work for Eleanor. Soon after her father's death, there was an item in *Town Topics* that referred to Lucy's supposed romance with Nigel Law: "The gossip in Washington [concerns] a charming young girl highly placed in the official world and an equally delightful young man, a close kin to the loftiest of British nobility. . . . As the girl has recently gone into retirement because of family bereavement, the affair may reach a cul-mination sooner than expected." Nigel had played his part convincingly, but at about that time was called back to England.

Franklin was on edge. He had to comfort Lucy after her father's death, and he was torn between his duties as a father and husband and the pull of passion. On October 14, during a Sunday visit to Hyde Park, he quarreled with his mother. There seems to have been a confrontation between Sara's view of society, based on tradition and permanent values and noblesse oblige, and Franklin's belief, reinforced by his romantic involvement, that personal happiness might consist in freedom from the restraints of tradition and permanence. Whatever the particular issue that caused the dispute, Sara took it as an occasion to remind her son of what she stood for: family life and simple home pleasures. She could not believe that her precious Franklin really felt as he had expressed himself. She hoped that while she lived she would continue to feel that *home* was the best and happiest place and that her son and daughter and their children would live in peace and keep from the tarnish that seemed to affect so many.

Sara's words may have been an appeal to her "dearest children" to hold their marriage together. Eleanor saw in her a strong ally, and wrote her that winter almost every day, as though enlisting her support in advance for the crisis to come. It came when Franklin returned from Europe in September 1918, and she read the letters that told her unmistakably that her husband was in love with another woman.

Was that love ever consummated? The Roosevelt children themselves disagreed on this point. James said that the register of a hotel in Virginia Beach showed that Franklin and Lucy had checked in as man and wife and spent the night together. Anna, however, thought that they were so Victo-rian that if they spent an afternoon together it was driving in the country, and having tea and holding hands and perhaps kissing. She doubted that either of them would have tried to go to a hotel. Too much was at stake. That, according to Anna, was Eleanor's feeling—that they were very much in love, but that it was not a consummated kind of thing, because they were wary of what people would think. Each had responsibilities and family pride, and Franklin was a public figure.

According to Lucy Mercer herself, the love affair was consummated. Soon after FDR's death in 1945, Betsy Cushing, who had divorced James Roosevelt and married John Hay Whitney, went to stay with friends in Aiken, South Carolina. One day, Lucy Mercer, who had married Winthrop Rutherfurd and spent part of the year in Aiken, asked her to tea. They sat across from the portrait of the president that had been commissioned by Lucy and painted by the Russian-born portraitist Elizabeth ("Mopsy") Shoumatoff, who had hardly begun when FDR died during a sitting. The Navy cape had only been outlined, half the crimson Harvard tie was unpainted, and there was some loose gray wash behind the head. What there was showed a man aged by world cares, who seemed to be fading away.

Betsy thought at first that Mrs. Rutherfurd was awfully ladylike—she wore white gloves at teatime. But Lucy began to ask embarrassingly personal questions. She wanted to know whether any other woman had had the same physical claim on Franklin, whether there had ever been, after her departure from the scene, a rival for Franklin's physical love. Betsy found herself unable to respond to Lucy's inquiries, and was relieved when suddenly all the lights in the house went out. It must be Franklin, she thought, annoyed at the line of questioning.

When Eleanor learned of her husband's infidelity, the bottom dropped out of her world. It was a horrible confirmation of what she had always known—nothing was yours, nothing lasted. What you loved most was taken away from you. Men were unreliable and abandoned you, as her father had by dying, after promising that they would have a life together. Her fears of inadequacy were realized. How could ugly, shrill-voiced, stodgy Eleanor compete with this ravishing, dreamlike, velvet-voiced creature? How could she, who had given birth to six children without being awakened physically, stand a chance next to feminine, seductive, geishalike Lucy Mercer? Surely Franklin found in her arms a pleasure and comfort she was unable to give him.

Eleanor had been betrayed, not only by Franklin but by Lucy as well. Lucy worked with her, spent many hours in her home, was almost a part of the family, endearing herself to her children and her mother-in-law. How could this young woman, so proper and well-bred, have gone behind her back and claimed her husband? Such a venture demanded continuous, day-by-day pretense, the concealment of true feelings, an attitude of feigned friendliness toward a woman whose marriage she was destroying. How furtive they both had been, arranging their meetings with Livy Davis or Nigel Law to cover up. How effortlessly Franklin had lied, telling her that Washington was awful without her, when he had arranged to spend the day, and probably the night, with Lucy. Eleanor had been made a fool of in her own home. Lucy had helped her with the travel arrangements, impatient for the time when she would be gone and Lucy and Franklin could be together, while she, gullible fool, waited in Campobello for her husband's visits. Eleanor could echo Elizabeth Barrett Browning: "You have not half the power to do me harm as I have to be hurt." Franklin had broken the bond of trust, and it could never be mended.

Eleanor confronted him, they discussed divorce, which in those days was a grave matter. Josephus Daniels had fired his brother-in-law from a management job on his newspaper because he got divorced. The only ground in New York State was adultery, which would have badly damaged if not ruined Franklin's political hopes. It was unthinkable to Sara that her son should be divorced. If the memory of his dear father was not enough, firmer pressure could be applied, for she held the purse strings. In addition, Lucy was Catholic, and would have to go outside the church to marry a divorced man. The whole thing was too messy, and would attract unpleasant publicity. Daniels, who had refused to condone the fornication of sailors, would never forgive him. He would probably have to resign from the Navy Department. Even if Franklin was willing to leave Eleanor and give up custody of his children and lose his job, he was incapable of openly defying his mother and of causing her pain that would have affected her physically, as his nephew Taddy's misbehavior had affected his father. Sara was the unifying force that kept the marriage together.

Louis Howe was the broker who managed a sort of reconciliation between Franklin and Eleanor. According to Elliott, "It wasn't just Sara, it was Louis Howe going back and forth and just reasoning, convincing father that he had no political future if he did this. Lucy would not marry a divorced man, she was an ardent Catholic. Louis did a selling job. Father wanted to give it up and mother felt betrayed and had a primitive outlook on it, but she came around because Louis convinced her. He said she could not destroy Franklin's goal and he convinced her that she too would have a great role to play. He convinced her it was better for the children."

From then on, it was less a marriage than a limited partnership. Eleanor told Franklin that marital relations would never be resumed, which protected her from the risk of further childbearing and freed her to lead her own life as long as she did what was required to further Franklin's career. Franklin's affair was the price of Eleanor's emancipation. The price to Franklin was in atonement. Often his children saw him hold out his arms, and saw Eleanor ignore him. In the currency of tenderness withheld, Franklin paid dearly. And yet, through one of those odd after-the-event conversions, he became a loyal husband, not in a physical sense, for he had other women, but in the way he supported Eleanor and would not accept criticism of her. Once, after he was president, he and Eleanor were on a train leaving Pittsburgh, with Betsy Cushing Roosevelt in an adjoining compartment. Betsy could hear Eleanor's high-pitched and high-powered voice wake Franklin at 3:30 A.M. to tell him that she had run into her brother, Hall, in Pittsburgh. Betsy was upset that Eleanor had disturbed the president's much-needed rest with news that could have waited until morning, but FDR said, "Bets, you don't understand her at all—she has no concept of time."

On February 14, 1920, Eleanor ended a long chatty letter to Sara with this noncommittal query: "Did you know that Lucy Mercer married Mr. Wintie Rutherfurd two days ago?" Lucy would be twenty-nine in April, and Winthrop Rutherfurd was a fifty-six-year-old widower with six children (the eldest died just before the wedding). A wealthy horseman and breeder of fox terriers, whose mother was a direct descendant of Peter Stuyvesant, Rutherfurd was so distinguished and handsome that Edith Wharton used him as a prototype in her first novels. He had been in love with Consuelo Vanderbilt, who was forced into marriage with the duke of Marlborough. "Six-foot-two in his golf stockings," a newspaper account said, "he was no match for five-foot-six and a coronet." Winty married Alice Morton, the daughter of Levi Morton, a Hudson River neighbor of Franklin's. She died in 1917, after she and her husband had converted to Catholicism, and he married Lucy three years later. They divided their time between an estate called Tranquility near Allamuchy in western New Jersey, and a plantation estate in Aiken, and had a daughter named Barbara.

Franklin and Lucy continued to see each other and correspond, as friends whose brief intimacy it would have been pointless to recall. On April 16, 1927, during the period when polio prevented him from seeking office, Lucy wrote from Aiken: "I hear that you are a grandfather [his daughter Anna had given birth to a daughter in March] and though I do not know exactly just what one's feelings are on that question—still I am sure—in your case—it is a subject of congratulation—for all concerned. . . . I was interested to hear a little about your projects from Livy Davis who was here. I have had a miserable winter, but am much better and we have at last decided to go abroad this summer—sailing in June—11 strong of us—it seems quite an undertaking as the time approaches—but it has to be faced sooner or later and the children are keen to go—and I feel sure that with one season they will get it out of their system for several years to come. I hope you and Eleanor and the children are all very well—and that Warm Springs [where Franklin had gone to treat his polio] is booming. Aiken is, which has its advantages and disadvantages. V sincerely yours, Lucy Rutherfurd."

On July 2, she wrote again, while crossing the Atlantic on board the SS *Belgenland*: "You see we are off on our first extended family jaunt—so far it has been a great success. The children have all enjoyed it every second—and it has been a great pleasure for me to find them all entertained without having to lift a finger for the accomplishment—or trying to figure out how they can be transported simultaneously to six different engagements at the same time. I should think you and Eleanor would try it sometime—of course the worst is yet to come and the score in trunks is difficult to keep. . . . But it is rather fun not to know what is going to happen tomorrow. Bessie Kittredge's sister who cannot walk [as Franklin could not, being crippled by polio] went abroad last year—they had a special chair made that would fit easily in the French trains—I am not sure it was collapsible—it simplified things a good deal—I could find out about it more definitely if you ever wanted to know. I hope you have a happy summer and that I shan't go home to find you President—Nor Secretary of State—nor yet a physical wreck from too much work for Al Smith or any potentates!! Ever yrs sincerely Lucy R."

One gets the picture of a woman absorbed by the task of raising five step-children and a daughter of her own, but wanting to maintain contact with a cherished friend, and continuing to see the friends they had in common who could bring her recent news of Franklin, like Livy Davis. They did see each other, particularly toward the end of Franklin's life. Once in 1944, he visited Bernard Baruch's South Carolina plantation, Hobcaw, and Lucy came to visit from nearby Aiken. Again in 1944, when Anna was acting as hostess at the White House in Eleanor's absence, Lucy came several times to dinner, always with other guests. It seemed a shame to Anna that two people who had loved each other couldn't even have a meal together and spend an hour or two talking, and she arranged it, although when Eleanor found out she was hurt that her daughter had acted as go-between with her husband's former mistress. It was yet another deception, but not the final one, for Lucy was with Franklin in Warm Springs when he died.

They were lovers only briefly, but Lucy thought of FDR as the love of her life. As he became great, she cherished her link to greatness. She wrote Anna a month after his death, on May 9, 1945, recalling "the strength of his beloved presence—so filled with loving understanding—so ready to guide and to help—I love to think of his very great pride in you and can still hear his voice speaking on a different note when he would say 'Hello, Girl—how is Johnny' [her youngest child by her second husband, John Boettinger]. He was so distressed about his little grandson and so concerned about you and your terrible anxiety. . . . And through it all one hears his ringing laugh and one thinks of all the ridiculous things he used to say and do and enjoy—the picture of him sitting waiting for you that night with the Rabbi's Cap on his extraordinarily beautiful head is still vivid [this may have been at Hobcaw when he was visiting Baruch]. The world had lost one of the greatest men that ever lived—to me—the greatest—He towers above them all. . . . It is a sad inescapable truth that you will now suffer in the sum and measure of your love which was so great. . . ." The idea that the intensity of one's suffering was commensurate with the intensity of one's love was one that Lucy applied also to herself.

The affair changed Franklin. All his life, first at Groton, then at Harvard, then as a family man, he had lived up to the standards set by his parents. He was conscious that he had an obligation to the family name. He tried hard to do the right thing, to be a model student, a model *Crimson* editor, a model father. In his striving to conform he had become priggish and judgmental. When his nephew Taddy had married beneath him, Franklin thought it was "disgusting," and wrote his mother that "the disgrace to the name has been the worst part of the affair . . . one can never again consider him a true Roosevelt."

There was a certain amount of hypocrisy in this stance, for Franklin was able to stray from the path of morality without letting it affect his self-righteousness, as when he lied about the scoop at Harvard, or when he lived the bachelor life during Washington summers and, according to Livy Davis, spent "29 concussive nights in a different place and bed." But the affair with Lucy Mercer was a crisis that he could not so easily shrug off. Could he call himself a true Roosevelt now that he had betrayed his wife, committed adultery, and contemplated divorce? What would Cousin Teddy think, whom he so admired, and who was so intolerant when it came to any deviation in marital conduct? After Lucy Mercer, much of Franklin's moral superiority went out the window, and he joined the mass of sinners. His conduct had been just as "disgusting" as Taddy's. A divorce would have stained the Roosevelt name, and he would have had to follow his own advice to his nephew: "It will be well for him not only to go to parts unknown, but to stay there and begin life anew." Franklin had made a conventional marriage; lover and sweetheart had been buried in man and wife. With Lucy Mercer he discovered emotions so powerful that he was willing to throw away everything he had patiently achieved, family, public office, political future. He found in the commitment of passionate love an alternative to the dutiful life, and he was tempted. He pulled back, but only after a humbling experience, in which his own humanity and vulnerability were revealed. Franklin, the good Roosevelt, was not so different under the skin from the wayward Taddy, the bad Roosevelt.

With the war over before he could get overseas, and his affair with Lucy Mercer ended, Franklin was in a rotten mood, and vented his spleen on Daniels. There were all sorts of postwar problems, such as storage for the war matériel being brought home from Europe. But on November 12, the day after the armistice, Daniels blocked the construction of a storage plant in New Jersey. "When will the shortage become so acute that it secures *action* by the Sec'y?" Franklin wondered in a memo for his files.

Restless and out of sorts, he longed to return to Europe to preside over the dismantling of the huge naval establishment there—54 shore bases, 20 port offices, 359 ships, 80,000 men, and warehouses packed with millions of dollars' worth of supplies and munitions. He knew he could do a better job than Admiral Sims, and save the Navy a lot of money—why, on the one small item of buying shellac direct from Calcutta and shipping it in a naval collier he was saving $21,000 a year.

Daniels did not encourage the trip, but finally let him go. He too had his doubts about Sims, who had so slavishly followed the English line. Franklin, who was being the model husband, giving up his Sunday morning golf to accompany his wife to church, decided to take Eleanor. It would be their first European trip since their honeymoon fourteen years before. Perhaps some of the goodwill and affection of that time so full of promise could be rekindled.

On January 1, 1919, they left on the USS *George Washington,* which was carrying seven tons of silver bars and $1.6 million in cash for the AEF, as well as dignitaries on their way to the Paris Peace Conference, where President Wilson would present his new order to European leaders. Always ready to hop on a podium, Franklin on January 5 gave a little talk on the ship's good name, following a minstrel show. The sea was so rough the crew lashed heavy ropes around the lifeboats, fearing they would be washed away. The next day, a radio message brought news that Theodore Roosevelt was dead at the age of sixty-one. Franklin was glad that he had been spared a lingering illness, while Eleanor saw "another big figure gone from our nation and I fear the last years were for him full of disappointment." In Paris, President Wilson remarked to his intimates that Roosevelt had not one constructive policy to his record, but Vice President Marshall was closer to the popular view when he said that "death had to take him in his sleep, for if Roosevelt had been awake, there would have been a fight."

When they had dropped anchor at Brest on January 10, Franklin had to dispose of naval installations in France in a climate of mistrust. The story was going around that the French were charging rent for graveyards in which American troops were buried. Admiral Benson, who was representing the Navy at the Peace Conference, wrote Daniels that "due to the peculiar ideas of our French friends, who in my opinion can give the worst kind of Yankee points and then beat him on a bargain, it is difficult to settle any of the financial questions involved. It may be uncharitable to say so, but I cannot escape the feeling that they are trying to force us to leave as much of our equipment in France as possible, and give it to them." There were hundreds of buildings, piers, hangars, and hospitals, as well as ships and trucks and lumber, that had to be sold. The biggest item was the Lafayette radio system near Bordeaux, intended for use in case the cable system broke down. Franklin had to act fast, before the Army came in and started bringing prices down. The word got around that "Franklin knows how to handle the French." He was able to bluff André Tardieu, the minister for liberated regions, into buying the Bordeaux station for $4 million, and jubilantly wrote Daniels on January 28: "The most successful thing I pulled off in Paris was the sale of the radio station to the French Government. They had backed and filled for over six weeks, and I finally put it up to Tardieu and told him that if they did not wish to keep it themselves, I would have to take the material down and ship it home for use at the new Monroe station. They agreed to take it the next day."

On a visit to the Allied-occupied Rhineland, Franklin drove up to the south bank toward Koblenz, looking forward to the thrill of his life—the great fortress of Ehrenbreitstein, the largest masonry fort in the world, rising on the hill overlooking Koblenz, which he had passed as a boy on his bicycle, would be flying the Stars and Stripes. As they rounded a bend in the river, the fortress came into view, but the flagstaff was bare. Furious that his expected thrill was spoiled, he strode into the commanding general's office and demanded to know why the hell wasn't the American flag floating over Ehrenbreitstein. The general replied that he had orders to take no action that would disturb the peace of mind of the German population. Returning to Paris, Franklin went straight to General Pershing's hotel and asked him to rectify "what I think is a very grave error. The German people ought to know for all time that Ehrenbreitstein flew the American flag during the occupation." "You are right," Pershing said, "it will be hoisted within the hour." It was, and stayed there until the last American soldier was gone.

President Wilson was aboard on the *George Washington*'s return voyage, bringing back the covenant of the new League of Nations. He had a messianic sense of mission about the ratification. When Wilson said of the League that "the United States must go in or it will break the heart of the world, for she is the only nation that all feel is disinterested and all trust," Franklin agreed, and stored the quote for use in future speeches.

Back in Washington on March 2, he told the Washington *Star* one of the Negro dialect jokes he was fond of to illustrate Germany's plight: "Germany is going to feel like Rastus Rosin, who was convicted of stealing a hog. 'Rastus, the judge said, you are fined $5.' 'Jedge,' said Rastus, 'Ah'm obleeged to ye. Ah got dat five-spot right here in mah left-hand vest pocket.' 'Well,' continued the judge, 'just dig down in your right-hand pocket, Rastus, and see if you can find thirty days.' "

It was Daniels's turn to leave for Europe on a two-month inspection tour, leaving Franklin in charge as acting secretary. "You ought to see the change in carrying on of the Department work," Franklin wrote Livy Davis. "I see civilians at the old building from 9 a.m. to 10:30, then I see the press, and then dash down to the new building in a high-powered car, and from that time on—11 a.m.—see no outsiders, Congressmen, Senators, or anybody else. The department mail is signed at regular hours, and absolutely cleaned up every day, with the result that nothing is taken home, mislaid, lost, et cetera, et cetera!"

Franklin may have kept a clean desk and worked hard (once he kept at it until midnight, signing 4,000 commissions), but there were no startling innovations during his tenure. When workers at the Key West Navy Yard struck because Negroes had been hired, Louis Howe advised the commandant of the seventh naval district, Rear Admiral Benton C. Decker, that perhaps "their services will eventually be dispensed with without any official action on our part."

When Daniels got back on May 17, Franklin was mightily pleased with himself, writing John McIlhenny on May 23 that "I have had a perfectly delightful two months, running things with a high hand and getting things done that were never done before. Last Saturday the Secretary got back and now I shall have a little leisure."

But it was not a leisurely summer. It seemed as if the war had been brought home. Leftist agitation and bombings led to a retaliation that became known as the red scare, initiated by the new attorney general, A. Mitchell Palmer, who lived across the street from the Roosevelts. Shortly before midnight on June 2, a powerful bomb exploded in front of the Palmer home, blowing up the anarchist who had planted it and showering debris on the Roosevelt front steps. Franklin ran across the street to see if the Palmers were all right, and returned saying: "What do you know, he's a Quaker, he says thou and thee."

On July 20, a mob of several hundred white servicemen and a thousand civilians, whipped up by reports that Negroes had raped some white women, started attacking blacks in the streets. This developed into a full-fledged race riot, and the Army Reserve was called in. "The riots seem to be about over today," Franklin wrote "Dearest Babs" on July 23, "only one man was killed last night. Luckily the trouble hasn't spread to R Street and though I have troubled to keep out of harm's way I have heard occasional shots during the evening and night. It has been a nasty episode and I only wish *quicker* action had been taken to stop it."

Franklin was no red-baiter, indeed he upbraided Rear Admiral S. S. Robinson, commandant of the Boston Navy Yard, for discharging three machinists because they were Socialists, at a time when Congress and the New York State legislature were expelling Socialists from their ranks. "Now, my dear Admiral," he wrote, "neither you nor I can fire a man because he happens to be a Socialist. It so happens that the Socialist party has a place on the official ballot in almost every state in the union . . . now these men were not themselves called before the hearing; were not examined in any way on this question of Socialism, and there was, therefore, no real justification for discharging them on that ground."

When an old grad tried to enlist his support to have a twenty-five-year-old instructor named Harold Laski, who was Jewish, foreign, and "radical," dismissed from his Harvard teaching job, Franklin showed no desire to do so. Paul Tuckerman (class of '78, Wall Street) had been told that Laski was advocating the taking of power by a proletarian minority as a remedy for existing social conditions. He urged Harvard President A. Lawrence Lowell to fire Laski, adding that the matter would have a bearing on subscriptions to the endowment fund. Lowell, although he disliked Laski's public posturing, replied that he was a stimulating teacher and that academic freedom was essential to Harvard. "If Mr. Laski were teaching mathematics," Tuckerman responded, "the argument of academic freedom would have some force . . . but he teaches our sons, not mathematics, but government, and what reverence for our government and institutions can a professed Bolshevik teach? Is it not, Mr. President, like selecting an atheist to teach our boys religion?" Lowell would not budge, so Tuckerman appealed to the Harvard overseers, among them Franklin, to whom he wrote: "Why not clean house and get rid of this foreign propagandist?" Franklin, who had no more sympathy for witch-hunts at Harvard than in the Navy yard, replied that he would be glad to take the matter up at the meeting of the overseers the following Monday, where it was decided that a committee should interview Laski at a downtown club. The chairman, an old fellow named George Wigglesworth, asked: "Mr. Laski, do you believe in bloody revolution?" "Mr. Wigglesworth, do I look as if I did?" the dapper and urbane Laski replied. At that, the overseers laughed and took Laski off to dinner. But he left in the summer of 1920 to teach at the London School of Economics, convinced by the continuing pressure on Lowell and by a series of virulent editorials in the *Lampoon* ("From the firstski to the laski he's a Red!") that he had no future at Harvard. Laski would go on to become a noted political economist, chairman of the British Labour party, and a friend of President Franklin D. Roosevelt.

Although an early supporter of the League of Nations, Franklin was not involved in the political battle that led President Wilson to take the case to the country. He was concerned with other matters, as he wrote to his Harvard classmate Joseph R. Hamlen on August 21, in the facetious tone he sometimes adopted with social equals: "I expect to be making a series of speeches welcoming the returning heroes from the front and telling of the great and glorious future of the honest and horny-fisted laboring man." On September 3, 1919, Wilson started a national speaking tour, traveling 8,000 miles. The strain was too great, and on September 25 he collapsed aboard his train, and the rest of his tour was canceled. A few days later, in the White House, a cerebral thrombosis felled him. He was bedridden, helpless, unable to function, his left side paralyzed. Until December, when he began to resume his duties, the country had no president. He could consider no legislation, make no appointments, issue no pronouncements. The cabinet met without legal status, for only the president had the authority to convene it.

Congress and the public were not told the truth. Not even those of cabinet rank seemed to know how gravely the president was stricken. On October 17, Franklin wrote his cousin, Warren Delano Robbins, who was serving in the embassy in Santiago, Chile: "We have had, of course, a good deal of labor trouble and the President, as you know, has been very ill. Also, there is this interminable row over the League of Nations in the Senate. Everybody is heartily sick of it and would give anything to have some action taken one way or the other. I think the League and the Treaty will go through without any question."

How wrong he was. The president insisted on unconditional ratification, which was defeated in the Senate that November. Senator Lodge led the fight, insisting that the League would plunge the United States "into every controversy and conflict on the face of the globe."

The president's illness was a milestone in Franklin's career. He began to be mentioned in the press as a presidential hopeful. A Boston newspaper said that "some of Massachusetts' most clever Democratic politicians have been whispering around the name of Franklin D. Roosevelt as possibly, quite possibly if you will, the most available man the Democrats will have to put forward for the great prize next summer."

Whether the article came to the sick president's attention was doubtful, but for other reasons the new year began inauspiciously for Franklin. Truly, trouble did not come as single spies but in battalions. James had appendicitis, and several other children had chicken pox. Franklin himself had tonsilitis. He had money problems, from which he was rescued by a large birthday check from his mother (he was thirty-eight on January 30, and Eleanor gave a party to which the guests came as characters from books, and Franklin might have gone as Mr. Micawber, who spent more than he earned). The check came at a critical moment, he wrote Sara, it wasn't a matter of doctors' bills, but of paying the gas man and the butcher, "lest the infants starve to death."

Then there was the Sims business. Admiral Sims had returned from London to resume the presidency of the Naval War College at Newport, but still felt bitter about Daniels—a mixture of personal pique at not having been allowed to accept the title of honorary sea lord in the British Admiralty, and the conviction that Daniels had prolonged the war by his inaction. In December, when the list of medals for heroism and meritorious service in wartime was published as an appendix to the secretary's annual report, Sims's wrath exploded, for many of his recommendations had not been approved. Sims turned down his medal, and made sure that news of his protest was published in the *Army and Navy Journal,* where it would be noticed by Senate Republicans eager to discredit the Wilson administration. Franklin, who was fond of medals and flags and all Navy ritual, sympathized with Sims, writing his wife on December 24: "Strictly between ourselves, I should like to shake the Admiral warmly by the hand."

A subcommittee of the Senate Naval Affairs Committee was formed to investigate the awarding of medals, with Sims due to testify on January 16. But on January 7, Sims sent Daniels a memorandum entitled "Certain Naval Lessons of the Great War," in which he charged that the "failure of the Navy Department to immediately send its full force of destroyers and anti-submarine craft prolonged the war four months, and occasioned the loss to the Allies of 2,500,000 tons of shipping, 500,000 lives, and $15,000,-000." This attack of a distinguished admiral on the secretary of the Navy made front-page news when it was leaked to the press. The *Washington Post* on January 14 called it "a frank and fearless expose of the hopeless . . . maladministration, mistakes and blunders into which the American Navy has fallen as a result of Mr. Daniels' policies."

On January 23, Franklin wrote Livy Davis: "It does seem a pity, does it not, that really fine, interesting men seem so often to lose their heads completely. The net result of all this will be, of course, to hurt the Navy. . . . The hurting of a Secretary or an Assistant Secretary, who are, after all, but birds of passage, is very incidental and very unimportant, but the Navy has gone on for nearly 150 years, and, we hope, will always go on; therefore its reputation is of importance."

It is a measure of the deviousness of Franklin's mind that he was able to sincerely deplore Sims's action, while a few weeks later he delivered a speech that backed up many of Sims's allegations. At the Brooklyn Academy of Music, on February 1, 1920, before an audience of 1,500, Franklin said that, in trying to get the Navy ready for war, he had "committed enough illegal acts to put him in jail for 999 years," and that he would have been impeached if he had made "wrong guesses."

"Two months after the war was declared," he said, "I saw that the Navy was still unprepared and I spent $40,000 for guns before Congress gave me or anyone permission to spend any money." He added that he had been "opposed by the President, who said that he did not want to commit any overt act of war, but who added that he was following a definite course in an effort to avert a war." In addition, Franklin took credit for picking Sims to go to London.

In seven years at the Department of the Navy, Franklin had never been more self-serving, more disingenuous, more disloyal. According to him, he had fought both Daniels and the president to arm the Navy. Only he, the knight in shining armor, had stood between the Navy and the slow beast of inaction. It was he who had raised Sims from obscurity to a post of distinction, which he was now using as a platform to attack Daniels. It was he who now parroted Sims at a time when Daniels was under fire, providing ammunition for the secretary's enemies.

Deeply hurt, Daniels wondered what bug had bitten his assistant. Franklin's remarks were not even accurate. Daniels sent for Rear Admiral Ralph Earle, chief of Navy ordnance, who confirmed that the order for guns for merchant ships had been made by Daniels early in 1917, while Franklin was on a mission to Haiti. All the orders for matériel had been made "after conference by me," Daniels recorded in his diary, and not by Franklin.

When he returned to the Navy Department on February 2, he got a frosty reception. Daniels demanded a public apology, which was released to the press and published on February 3. Franklin tried to heal the rift by inviting Daniels to dinner. But Daniels felt betrayed, and recorded in his diary on February 17: "Dinner 17. To go or not to go?" There was also Wilson, whom Franklin had infuriated by saying that he was opposed to preparedness. As Daniels recorded on February 21, "FDR persona non grata with W."

Why had Franklin deliberately alienated Daniels and Wilson? His best friends were mystified. Livy Davis wrote him on February 5: "What in the world is the matter with you for telling the public that you in your tenure of office committed enough illegal acts to keep you in jail for 900 years?" Franklin knew that the speech would be widely reported, that Daniels would be hurt, that the president would be angered, that he would be jeopardizing his career in the Navy Department. But he went ahead, because he was thinking beyond the Navy. His time there was coming to a close. It looked like a Republican year, and there would be no room for him in Washington under a Republican administration. He would have to go back to New York and practice law. Unless . . . he could find a place on the Democratic ticket. After all, in seven years in Washington, he had made friends with congressmen and party leaders, and had won a national reputation. He was no longer a beginner, to be confused with his cousin Teddy.

Three weeks before his Brooklyn Academy speech, on January 10, Franklin had received a visit from an old friend, Louis B. Wehle, with whom he had worked on war labor problems, for Wehle was general counsel of the War Finance Corporation. Wehle had been talking to some leading Democrats, and they had come up with a winning ticket—Herbert Hoover of California for president and Franklin D. Roosevelt of New York for vice president. "Frank," Wehle said, "you would have everything to gain and nothing to lose through being a candidate for Vice-President. Whether you win or lose, you would suffer the stigma of mediocrity that seems to attach to the Vice-Presidency or to one who tries for it. But you are young and you could live it down for several reasons: first, you bear the name Roosevelt; second, you have a first-rate record of public service in your state and in the nation; and third, in your campaign tours you would make a great number of key acquaintances in every state. If afterward you would methodically build on them you would come to have such a personal following in the Democratic party that it would probably lead you eventually to the Presidency."

The idea of running in a presidential campaign, even with a high risk of losing, in order to become better known nationally, appealed to Franklin, who told Wehle: "You can go to it so far as I am concerned. Good Luck! And it will certainly be interesting to hear what the Colonel [House] says about it." The colonel, who was estranged from Wilson because of his jealously suspicious wife, thought it was a wonderful idea, and the Democrats' only chance, but would Hoover run as a Democrat?

On January 16, Wehle called on Hoover at the office on lower Broadway where he managed postwar relief to Europe. Hoover sat there doodling with a pencil, his head bent over his desk blotter, and finally said, "I don't believe that I want to get into a situation where I have to deal with a lot of political bosses."

"Let me tell you," Wehle replied, "that if you expect ever to get into American political life you'll have to take it as you find it. You can't make it over first from the outside. You'll have to get into the middle of it and take care of your own soul afterward if you expect ever to do any big public service in America in peacetime." Courted by both parties, Hoover kept his counsel.

Wehle's visit had kindled hope in Franklin. Perhaps he could have a place on the ticket—he could carry New York, which was crucial. He admired Hoover, who had emerged from the Food Administration as something of a hero, and wrote the career diplomat Hugh Gibson on February 2: "I had some nice talks with Herbert Hoover before he went West for Christmas. He is certainly a wonder and I wish we could make him President of the United States. There could not be a better one." It was with these thoughts in mind that he made his Brooklyn speech on February 1, dissociating himself from the politics of Daniels and Wilson, which would come under attack during the campaign. The speech was a signal that he was available, even if it meant treachery toward his chief and his president. At the same time, Franklin was canny enough not to make any announcement or solicit support, believing as he did in the "bad luck of the early worm, rather than the good luck of the early bird." To those who wrote asking him to run for this or that office, he replied that "I do not personally intend to make an early Christian martyr of myself this fall if it is going to be a strongly Republican year." He was sending out two contrary messages, one to Wehle and his friends that he was available for the ticket, another to his supporters that he was "not running for Senator or Governor or dog catcher." The Democratic convention in San Francisco was not till June—there was plenty of time.

Meanwhile Franklin was embroiled that January in a dispute over policies at the naval prison in Portsmouth, New Hampshire. He had a friend and political ally named Thomas Mott Osborne, with whom he had fought Tammany during his years in the State Senate, who had gone on to become warden of Sing Sing prison in Ossining, New York. Osborne had masqueraded as a convict to learn what prison life was like from the inside. He was a difficult, quixotic man, always quarreling with his superiors, always on the edge of a breakdown, but he was also a courageous prison reformer, who believed that convicts should be rehabilitated and restored to society as law-abiding citizens.

Osborne's ideas dovetailed with Josephus Daniels's aim to make the Navy an educational training ground for young men. When Daniels visited Portsmouth prison, he was shocked to see that there were more marine guards than prisoners. The system promised "to break a man instead of making him." Franklin liked to tell the story of an officer giving a grammar lesson and asking, "What are the two principal parts of a sentence?" A sailor replied: "Bread and water, and solitary confinement."

Osborne was appointed to run the prison in July 1917, with the rank of lieutenant commander in the Naval Reserve, over the objection of many naval officers who did not want a civilian in charge. His aim was to have the prisoners return to the fleet after they had served their sentences rather than leave with dishonorable discharges. "Is this ex-convict morally unfit to fight the savage Huns?" he asked. To many officers, fearing the contamination of ex-convicts, the answer was yes. But Daniels and Roosevelt backed him up, and he returned about two-thirds of his 6,000 prisoners to active service. The *Army and Navy Register* complained that the Navy was being turned into a "refuge for criminals."

On January 3, 1920, the *Army and Navy Journal* published an article based on information provided by the assistant secretary of the Navy, stating that "the younger Navy officers, particularly the commanders of destroyers, have taken the view that every chance should be given to those guilty of infractions to expiate in a Navy atmosphere their derelictions and have an opportunity of coming back into the service. They have held that every way should be open to the enlisted man to come back to the ship a better man for having learned his lesson."

Captain J. K. Taussig knew this to be false. He had asked to be transferred from the Bureau of Navigation, where he was in charge of the Enlisted Personnel Division, to the Naval War College in Newport, because his warnings about the demoralizing effect of returning criminals to the Navy had been ignored. He had commanded the USS *Little* from January until September 1918, and had heard from other destroyer commanders what they really thought—how they shuddered when they received prison "graduates" aboard their ships, how they were unalterably opposed to Osborne's policy. Unable to contain himself, he wrote the *Army and Navy Journal* a stern letter, repudiating Franklin's assertion that destroyer commanders welcomed the chance to rehabilitate ex-convicts. "The good men of the ships," he said, "must of necessity, owing to the intimate way of living on board and the requirement of working in the same confined spaces, associate to a more or less extent with these moral perverts, and thereby be exposed to contamination. . . . In the redemption of an individual we should not permit the degradation of the Navy."

Stung, Franklin replied on January 24, belittling Taussig's objections. Since Osborne had been in charge of Portsmouth prison, he said, two men convicted of sodomy had been returned to service. "This over a period of more than two years, proved to be the shocking condition of the Naval Service outlined by Captain Taussig." He insisted that those who committed minor offenses should be given another chance. "Anyone who, like Captain Taussig, attempts to give the wrong impression, deliberately or otherwise, can only harm the service itself." Franklin hoped that Taussig had, "merely through lack of knowledge, made a false statement."

As ambitious as he was hotheaded, and feeling that Franklin's rejoinder had publicly discredited him and endangered his career, Taussig on February 4 asked for a court of inquiry. He added that on or about April 12, 1919, Franklin as acting secretary had personally restored to the service ten men convicted of immoral acts, including one sentenced to ten years for sodomy.

A court of inquiry was the last thing Franklin wanted at a time when his political future hung in the balance. He prevailed upon Daniels to lean on Taussig a little. In spite of his wounded feelings over the Brooklyn speech, Daniels on February 14 wrote Taussig that no court of inquiry was necessary and that the whole incident would have been avoided had not Taussig disobeyed the spirit of Article 1535 of the Navy regulations stating that no person belonging to the Navy could act as a correspondent of a newspaper or periodical without the express permission of the department. That was enough to calm Taussig down and get Franklin off the hook.

Having weathered the fallout of the Brooklyn speech on one side and Taussig's broadside on the other, Franklin turned his attention back to the national scene. The convention in San Francisco was only months away, but the Democratic party seemed unable to promote a candidate. The sick president threw a long shadow. Would he be well enough to run, and would he violate the third-term tradition? At the Jackson Day dinner in January, the traditional warm-up in an election year, Wilson disappointed party leaders by not mentioning a third term. His silence could be read as a clue that he wanted to run again. There was a sense of pessimism in the party—it was a no-win situation.

Franklin did not share the pessimism, for he was still thinking in terms of a Hoover-Roosevelt ticket. On March 15, he wrote his Harvard classmate Joseph R. Hamlen: "People are more and more seeming to get away from the old political stuff, and to be insisting upon a practical business administration of their government affairs. Of course, Hoover, of all the candidates, is more ideally fitted for this particular line of administrative work than any other, and I am especially gratified to see the apparent interest in Hoover's candidacy in the solid South."

The Sims hearings opened in March and continued until May 28, providing a forum for a flock of disgruntled admirals. With three Republicans and two Democrats on the committee, the investigation turned into a political tribunal, bent on ruining Daniels's reputation for partisan reasons. If Franklin was asked to testify, his past disloyalty might be brought out. The Republicans would have a field day citing the chapter and verse of his disagreements with his chief, including his February speech. The wide publicity the hearings were getting could do a lot of damage nationally.

Franklin had to line up with Daniels against the admirals. By proclaiming his allegiance to the secretary, he might save himself an embarrassing appearance before the committee. At a Democratic dinner on March 26, he said that "in spite of ninety-seven investigations, costing more than $2,000,-000, they have still to unearth an embalmed beef or paper shoe scandal," such as those that had surfaced under Republican rule. Senator Frederick Hale, the Republican chairman of the committee, had planned to call him, but Franklin bluffed him by boasting that he would make Hale sorry he had ever been summoned to the stand, and that he was sick of "three-to-two" history.

Franklin was not called, and instead was asked to submit his ideas for reorganizing the Navy Department. He wrote Livy Davis on May 15 that he was "somewhat lucky," and that "I think I shall drop a bomb into the committee by saying that nobody in the Navy, either in Washington, or London, was in any way to blame for anything at any time, but that the whole blame for anything and everything that went wrong rests squarely on the shoulders of the Senate and House of Representatives. I think this would make a hit besides being largely true." But his bomb was a dud. All he said was that "what is the most serious trouble with the Navy now, as it has been in the past, is Congress."

The hearings ended in June, and with them Franklin's long service in the Navy, for after the Democratic convention, he would be caught up in the 1920 campaign, although he would not formally resign until August. He served seven and a half years in the Navy, at a time of world crisis. He was the assistant head of a service department during America's first involvement in a European war. He saw how a democracy, removed from the theater of battle, and slow to abandon neutrality, was able to mobilize its massive resources and end the war in less than two years.

In his grasp of naval affairs, in his limitless energy, in his knack for getting things done and cutting through red tape, Franklin showed himself to be a superb administrator, equal to any task. Whether it was a labor dispute in a Navy yard, a negotiation for armor plate with steel companies, or the demobilization of naval installations in Europe, Daniels knew that Franklin could handle it. His mind was pragmatic, always oriented to finding a solution. On the basis of sustained performance, he had to be given high marks.

And yet his tenure at the Navy Department was flawed because he came to be viewed as untrustworthy by his chief and his president. Convinced that America should enter the war, he tried to commit the administration prematurely. It also seemed sometimes that his energy was unfocused, that he went off in too many different directions. Why, after only a year on the job, had he run in the New York State Democratic primary, suffering a humiliating defeat? Why had he used the power of his office to meddle in New York State patronage battles? It showed poor judgment, a bent for rash action.

In a long political career, Franklin's only administrative superior was Josephus Daniels. It was his good fortune that Daniels was a patient and fond boss, ready to forgive in his assistant the kind of insubordination that would have cost the head of any admiral. Franklin made fun of the pudgy Methodist teetotaler, the plebeian editor with the red clay of North Carolina still on his shoes. He bragged that only when Daniels went away and he was acting secretary did things get done. He pictured himself as a martyr who had to put up with Daniels's ignorance and indecision. He criticized him publicly and sided with his enemies.

Daniels's tolerance of the young man he described as "a twentieth century Apollo," for whom he had felt "love at first sight," was truly wondrous. Daniels thought of firing him more than once, but in the end they were reconciled, and Daniels recorded in his diary, on the occasion of Franklin's resignation on August 6, 1920: "I spoke of only two compensations for men in public office—consciousness of giving one's best to the public weal & appreciation & friendship of co-workers. FDR had both. He left in the afternoon, but before leaving wrote me a letter most friendly & almost loving wh. made me glad I had never acted upon my impulse when he seemed to be taking side with my critics."

President Wilson, who did not have a forgiving nature, came to dislike Franklin, and when Daniels on August 3 approached him about a replacement, he launched into a tirade about how much he resented Franklin's disloyalty.

Franklin would maintain a close friendship with Daniels, whom he would send to Mexico as American ambassador when he was elected president. On the train carrying him to the inaugural in Washington in 1933, Franklin was with the brain truster Rex Tugwell when he suddenly spotted Daniels. Tugwell saw him fondly take the hand of this surviving Democratic patriarch of the Bryan era in both of his, as he said: "Rex, this is a man who taught me a lot that I needed to know."

VIII

On the National Ticket

Once there were two brothers. One ran away to sea, the other was elected vice president, and nothing was ever heard of either of them again.

Anonymous

As the convention approached, Franklin began to be mentioned as a possible vice-presidential candidate, although not on a ticket with Hoover, who had finally decided that he was a Republican. On June 4, a Washington union leader wrote a friend at the Mare Island Navy Yard: "There is every indication that the Hon. Franklin D. Roosevelt will be on the National Ticket." A demure Franklin wrote his law partner, Langdon Marvin, on June 17: "I am wondering who started this fool Vice-President boom. I have seen nothing about it in the papers and I am not at all sure that I care for it."

While Franklin tested the water, the Democratic party was stuck in a Wilson-created quagmire. On April 13, Wilson attended his first cabinet meeting since his breakdown. Secretary of Agriculture David F. Houston noted in his diary: "The President looked old, worn and haggard. It was enough to make one weep to look at him. One of his arms was useless. In repose, his face looked very much as usual, but, when he tried to speak, there were marked evidences of his trouble. His jaw tended to drop to one side. . . . His voice was very weak and strained."

And yet on June 18, ten days before the convention, Wilson in an interview in the New York *World* said he could not support other candidates and did not think the convention would "permit themselves to be led astray in order to gratify the vanity or promote the uncharitable or selfish impulses of any individual." Coupled with the picture showing him working at his desk, this had to be viewed as a statement of availability. Wilson was like a dead Saracen general who was strapped on his horse to lead his army into battle. He also continued to wed the party to the League of Nations, so that Democrats had the choice of taking up a limping cause or risk splitting the party. As Barbara Leahy wrote Franklin on June 9: "I fear ... that the Wilson League of Nations is about the most effective millstone that any party, bent on suicide, has tied about its neck to date."

The Republicans nominated Warren Harding, who had served two terms in the Ohio State Senate and a term as lieutenant governor before being elected to the U.S. Senate. Harding could run on a "I-am-none-of-the-things-Wilson-is" platform; he was not a stubborn ideologue, he did not want to save the world, he had no lofty principles or high intellectual standards, he was not headstrong and arrogant. Calvin Coolidge, the governor of Massachusetts, was his running mate.

The Republicans were united against Wilson, whereas the Democrats were in disarray when they gathered in San Francisco, a pleasant city for a convention, with good weather and good restaurants. Daniels had ordered ships from the Pacific Fleet there for the occasion, and stayed aboard the flagship *New Mexico,* while Franklin, still assistant secretary, made the battleship *New York* his headquarters. As a goodwill gesture, he invited the New York delegation to visit the ship.

At his first convention in 1912, Franklin had not even been a delegate. Now, only eight years later, he was mentioned for a spot on the ticket. This was a very different convention. For one thing, women now had the vote, and there were 300 women delegates. Another change was Prohibition. The Eighteenth Amendment had been passed on January 15 over President Wilson's veto, dividing candidates into "drys" and "wets."

Adding to the confusion was the attitude of the sick man in the White House, surrounded by his wife, his doctor, and his secretary, powerless except as the spoiler of his own party, lost in pointless brooding over the League defeat. Did he want the nomination? If not, why did he not indicate the man best suited to succeed him?

That was William Gibbs McAdoo, Wilson's son-in-law as well as his secretary of the Treasury. There was also Mitchell Palmer, who had a bloc of delegates but was unpopular with labor and progressives, and James Cox, the three-term governor of Ohio, a pro-League progressive who also had support from the urban bosses because he was wet and wasn't linked to Wilson. He had been divorced in 1911 and remarried in 1917, which some said was an insurmountable obstacle.

When the convention opened on June 28 in the Exposition Auditorium, the lights were turned out and searchlight beams focused on a curtain, which was slowly drawn, revealing a huge oil portrait of Wilson. This resulted in a twenty-minute ovation, with delegates parading around the hall carrying their state standards. In the midst of the acclamation, the Wilson men missed the chance to stampede the convention. Fueled by the bosses of New York, Illinois, and Ohio, the Cox drive was gaining momentum. To the tune of "The Battle Hymn of the Republic," anti-McAdoo forces sang "Every Vote Is on the Payroll." Cox had a majority on the forty-third ballot, and defections from the McAdoo camp put him over the needed two-thirds on the forty-fourth, in the small hours of July 5.

Cox was in his newspaper office in Dayton at dawn on July 5 when the manager of his forces, Ohio delegate Edmond H. Moore, called to remind him that when the convention reassembled it would want to know his choice for vice president. "Naturally, I've been thinking about this a good deal," said Cox, "and my choice is young Roosevelt. His name is good, he's right geographically, and he's anti-Tammany. But since we need a united front, go see Charlie Murphy and say we won't nominate Roosevelt if he objects. He can suggest other names—maybe Ed Meredith" (Edwin T. Meredith of Iowa, secretary of agriculture). Moore asked whether Cox knew Roosevelt. He did not, Cox replied, he was picking him sight unseen, which was quite a compliment.

Moore consulted Murphy, who said: "I don't like Roosevelt. He is not well known in the country, but, Ed, this is the first time a Democratic nominee for the Presidency has shown me courtesy. That's why I would vote for the devil himself if Cox wanted me to. Tell him we will nominate Roosevelt on the first ballot as soon as we assemble." Murphy had emerged as the kingmaker of the convention, whose seventy New York votes had given Cox the needed momentum, and who could exercise a veto over the vice-presidential nomination. But why block Franklin, when Murphy could export him to Washington, out of New York State politics, make the upstate independents happy, put a New Yorker on the ticket, and win over an insurgent leader by promoting his chances in a national campaign?

There were scattered nominations, and then Judge Timothy T. Ansberry came to the platform and said: "The young man whose name I am going to suggest is but three years over the age of thirty-five prescribed by the Constitution . . . but he has crowded into that short period of time a very large experience as a public official. . . . [He is] an able experienced campaigner, full of virility and the optimism of youth, yet sobered by service as Assistant Secretary of the Navy. . . . His is a name to conjure with in American politics . . . Franklin D. Roosevelt." Kansas and Indiana seconded the nomination. Al Smith spoke for New York. Former governor of Missouri David R. Francis moved that the rules be suspended, and Franklin was nominated by acclamation.

Among the many messages of congratulation, one might contrast a serious one from a rising young journalist with a facetious one from a Harvard classmate. Walter Lippmann of the *New Republic* wrote that "your nomination is the best news in many a long day. When cynics ask what is the use we can answer that when parties can pick a man like Franklin Roosevelt there is a decent future in politics." From the American embassy in Tokyo, Ned Bell adopted the "we are the lord's anointed" tone to tell Franklin that he was "in a fair way to become *M. le vice-président,* which, let us hope, is only a preliminary canter and that the day will come when you will be our Father which art in the White House *tout simplement,* without any 'Vice'—When that happy moment arrives I shall *not* ask you to send me as Ambassador to the Court of St. James's unless they have raised the pay in the meantime."

Franklin later told the biographer Emil Ludwig: "They chose me because my name had become known during the war. It was also intended that as an official I should be the connecting link between Wilson and Cox, who had not been a member of the federal administration, especially the war part of it. Of course, I was delighted. I was only 38, and only one other vice-president had been younger. Theodore Roosevelt had been 42."

In the steeplechase to the presidency, he was four years ahead of his cousin. Franklin saw himself as TR's heir, who could in Bull Moose fashion capture the votes of independents and progressive Republicans. Indeed, he campaigned as TR's clone, even stopping off on the way home from San Francisco for a bear hunt in Colorado at a place where Cousin Teddy had hunted. He was full of TR stories, of his hatred for Taft: when Whitelaw Reid died in 1912, and both Taft and TR turned up at the funeral, and the pallbearers hesitated as to whether they should start leaving the church before the president, TR had said in a stage whisper, "I did not know that there was any rule of precedence between corpses." What the British statesman John Morley had once said of TR could now apply equally well to Franklin: "As I watched his remarkable energy I could not help suspecting that his opinions sprang rather from physical than from mental exertion."

The prospect of the vice presidency, however, was a mixed blessing. Here was a man elected as fully capable of being president, but his only official work was to preside over the Senate. It was a grotesque predicament. It usually took an assassin's bullet to raise a vice president to the highest office. Andrew Johnson had hoped to fill the Great Emancipator's shoes and had gotten impeached for it; Garfield's death had raised Chester Arthur; and Cousin Teddy had become president after McKinley was shot. There were newspaper articles saying that both tickets would improve if the candidates were reversed, if Coolidge and Roosevelt were in first place. Franklin didn't know about that, but he did know, as he wrote James J. Montague of the Bell Syndicate, that if the ticket was elected, "the old idea about the Vice-Presidency is going to be knocked into a cocked hat. . . . There is plenty of opportunity in that position for the use of brains and energy, and . . . four years from now the Vice-Presidency is going to be a highly respected and live-wire office."

When Franklin stopped in Columbus, Ohio, to meet his running mate, Cox found him alert to the conditions of the campaign, but was startled when Franklin suggested that the vice president sit with the cabinet. That would never do, Cox said. He wanted to get on with Congress, and if the vice president sat with the cabinet he would be regarded as a White House snoop.

On July 18, Franklin and Cox went to the White House to see the invalid Wilson, an object of sympathy and reverence, even though his ambiguity about a third term, his refusal to endorse the candidates, and his insistence on turning the election into a referendum over the League, would hobble the Democratic campaign. Cox wept when he saw Wilson in a wheelchair, a shawl concealing his paralyzed left arm, and said, "Mr. President, we are going to be a million per cent with you, and your administration, and that means the League of Nations." "I am very grateful," Wilson said in a voice that was barely above a whisper. Cox went to the Executive Office, asked Tumulty for paper and a pencil, and wrote the statement that would bind the candidates to the League's creaky mast. Cox felt that the banner of Woodrow Wilson had been placed in his hand, to wave in exaltation of the dying leader. Franklin was equally moved. It was one of the most impressive scenes he had ever witnessed.

There were, however, other issues besides the League, among them inflation, labor strife, unemployment, and the plight of the farmer. The scandal of divorce was also in the air. Ellery Sedgwick, editor of the *Atlantic,* was urging Charles W. Eliot, retired president of Harvard and America's Grand Old Man, to come out for Cox, but Eliot was balking because of his divorce. Sedgwick asked Franklin to set Eliot's mind at ease. "You undoubtedly know that there has been divorce trouble in the Harding family also," Franklin replied on July 31. "Mrs. Harding was divorced by her first husband, and almost immediately afterwards married Mr. Harding. I hate, of course, to have this sort of thing enter into the campaign at all, but if the Cox divorce is made a factor by the opposition, you may be sure that the Harding divorce will be brought out also." In other words, if the Republicans played dirty, the Democrats would play dirty too.

There was another skeleton in Harding's closet—that he had Negro blood. Harding himself had once told a newspaper friend: "How do I know, Jim? One of my ancestors may have jumped the fence." Franklin fanned the "touch of tarbrush" rumors by spreading the story that in 1854 a man named Butler had killed a man named Smith for calling his wife a Negro, and that the governor of Ohio, at the request of Harding's grandfather, had pardoned the murderer.

As for Eliot's doubts, Franklin went on in his letter to Sedgwick, "He need not be in the least worried about the family record of Governor Cox. I hate, of course, to have this kind of thing enter into the campaign one way or the other, and I would not want to have my name used in any way. . . . His first wife was a really impossible sort of person, and everyone, including her own family, knows conclusively that the divorce was in no way his fault. As a matter of fact, the custody of the children was given to him." It may have occurred to Franklin that if he had gone ahead and divorced Eleanor, he would probably not have been nominated, as two divorced men on the ticket would have been one too many.

On August 10, Franklin hit the campaign trail, as eager as a boy in a pie-eating contest. Heading west, he crossed twenty states in the next eighteen days, averaging seven speeches a day, traveling in his private car, the *West-*

boro. The campaign was a discovery of America. He was able for the first time to extend the sense of entitlement he had felt as a boy about the past and about the land. He seemed to devour and digest the country, making it his. He understood both its vastness and its limits, and would later recall that "during three months in the year 1920 I got to know the country as only a candidate for office or a traveling salesman can get to know it. I became impressed with the fact that in these latter days we had come, to a certain extent, to the end of that limitless opportunity of new places to go to and new sources of wealth to tap. . . . I realized that the time was ripe, even overripe, for the beginning of planning . . . to meet certain obvious economic and social needs of the nation."

Already he was thinking of the country as an extension of Hyde Park, a property to be managed. History also had to be managed, and he rummaged through the past looking for a campaign theme. He found it in the manipulation of the Theodore Roosevelt image, and followed the strategy proposed by a correspondent, J. W. Holcombe: "It is for you to show how completely the Republican party has become reactionary, to the extent of flouting and ignoring the Roosevelt tradition. Broadly proclaim that you are the political and spiritual heir of Theodore Roosevelt, that he was an essential and fundamental democrat, the exponent of liberalism and progress, that the Democratic party inspired by Wilson now stands for everything the great Roosevelt represented."

This took some doing, for had TR lived he would have been opposed to the League of Nations, which was Franklin's central issue. He fudged the issue by declaring that the same blind and reactionary Republicans who had once opposed Teddy were now opposing the League: "I do not profess to know what Theodore Roosevelt would say were he alive today, but I cannot help but think that the man who invented the word 'pussy-footer' could not have resisted the temptation to apply it to Mr. Harding."

Presenting himself as the heir to TR in an effort to snare what remained of the Bull Moose vote, Franklin made sure to let his listeners know they were related, and used TR buzzwords such as "bully" and "square deal." He described Harding as one of those who had driven TR to form a third party and who had then called him a Benedict Arnold and an Aaron Burr in his Ohio newspaper, the Marion *Star*. "As a Roosevelt," Franklin said, as if Harding's editorial had been a personal affront, "I can never forget that in 1912, when another Roosevelt was working with his coat off to save the Republican party from that same old gang that now has it by the throat, it was Mr. Harding of Ohio" who had libeled TR.

On August 13, the Chicago *Tribune* called Franklin "the one-half of one percent Roosevelt. . . . Franklin is as much like Theodore as a clam is like a bear-cat. . . . If he is Theodore Roosevelt, Elihu Root is Gene Debs, and Bryan is a brewer."

The antidote was to send out a loyal Republican relative to recapture the stolen TR image. Theodore Roosevelt, Jr., was picked for the job, and infuriated Franklin when he said in Maine that the Republican party had won the war, and that the Democrats had 60,000 useless clerks in Washington. On September 16, Teddy Jr. told a group of Rough Riders who had met him at the station in Sheridan, Wyoming, that Franklin "is a maverick—he does not have the brand of our family."

But Teddy Jr. could not do anywhere near the damage to Franklin that he did to himself by overdoing the imitation of TR and his swaggering imperialism. On August 18, in Butte, Montana, he sought to refute the charge that, in the League of Nations, Great Britain and her colonies would have six votes to the United States' one.

"The United States has a lot more than six votes," he said, "which will stick with us through thick and thin through any controversy. For instance, does anybody suppose that the votes of Cuba, Haiti, San Domingo, Panama, Nicaragua and of the other Central American States would be cast differently from the vote of the United States? We are in a very true sense the big brother of these little republics."

Digressing from his text, Franklin could not resist an "I took Panama" TR-type remark, and said: "You know I have had something to do with the running of a couple of little republics. The facts are that I wrote Haiti's Constitution myself, and, if I do say it, I think it a pretty good constitution."

M. J. English, a Butte lawyer who was sitting on the platform as part of Franklin's welcoming committee, found this statement so absurd that he could not resist making an embarrassing audible comment. When newspapers across the country picked up the Associated Press dispatch, Franklin issued emphatic denials, and accused the AP of spreading a false story. When the influential Boston magazine, the *Outlook,* printed an editorial entitled "A Vice-Presidential Disappointment," Franklin wrote its editor, Lawrence F. Abbott: "Please let me assure you that I was wholly erroneously reported and that a complete and full denial of this erroneous report was made by me on the Pacific coast as soon as the misquotation appeared in print. I should have hoped that it would be obvious to you that, after experience in Washington during a period of nearly eight years, I could not say anything so unjustifiable as the statement put in my mouth by some ingenious but inaccurate reporter."

Despite this holier-than-thou denial, Franklin *had* said it, not only in Butte but in Billings, which prompted a Spokane paper to comment: "To have misquotations follow a candidate from one city to another in this fashion must be annoying, to say the least." Backing up the AP correspondent, whose job Franklin's denial had jeopardized, thirty-one Butte citizens signed the following statement: "I heard Franklin D. Roosevelt's speech delivered in Butte on August 18, 1920. I heard Mr. Roosevelt discuss the League of Nations. I heard him say that he had the votes of Haiti and San Domingo in his pocket·and that he had turned them over to Secretary Daniels, and I heard him say that he wrote the constitution of Haiti and heard him add 'and if I do say it myself it was a pretty good little constitution.' I have read the Associated Press dispatch in which the speech was reported, and in my opinion, it is in all essential particulars fair and correct." Franklin's gaffe would be used against him for years to come. At a labor meeting on April 18, 1933, a month after his inauguration as president, the speaker, William L. Patterson of the International Labor Defense, said: "Even now in the White House sits a man who drafted the constitution that enslaved Haiti."

He was willing to go to any length to give his audience what they wished to hear. In Centralia, Washington, there had been labor violence instigated by the Wobblies. Some American Legionnaires were killed in a gun battle. But the Legionnaires captured Wobbly leader Esley Everest, castrated him, and roped his naked body to a bridge over the Chehalis River. Speaking in Centralia that August, Franklin, who had never approved of red-baiting, made a speech that could have been written by A. Mitchell Palmer: "I particularly wanted to make this visit to Centralia. I regard it as a pilgrimage to the very graves of the martyred members of the American Legion who here gave their lives in the sacred cause of Americanism. Their sacrifice challenged the attention of the Nation to the insidious danger to American institutions in our very midst. Their death was not in vain for it aroused the patriotic people of our great nation to the task of ridding this land of the alien anarchist, the criminal syndicalist and all similar anti-Americans."

The biggest mistake of his campaign, however, was his commitment to the League. Having sworn to carry on Wilson's program, he and Cox were stuck with it. The League issue backfired, particularly when, on October 3, President Wilson issued a public appeal to vote for the League that did not even mention the candidates.

Also, Franklin's use of Cousin Teddy, although it may have won some "Bull Mice," struck other voters as an obvious ploy. An Alabama lumberman told him the story of two brothers who had to divide some goats. The older brother put all the healthy goats in one pen, and all the one-eyed and mangy and skinny goats in the other pen with the younger brother's pet goat, Billy. The younger brother had first pick and put his arms around his pet goat and said: "Billy, you have been my constant companion since you were born; I have loved you, fed you, and led you to where the pasture was the greenest; your fights have been my fights, where I went you went. . . . It breaks my heart to have to give you up, but I can't stand the company you are in. . . . I'll take the other pen." "That is just how I feel," said the lumberman. "For the first time I shall cast my vote against a Roosevelt . . . and oh how I wish you were in the other pen."

Halfway through the campaign, Franklin told the financial manager of his campaign and old friend, Tom Lynch, that he wanted him to come to Washington the following March. "Listen, Frank," Lynch said, "you're not going to Washington."

"Why not?" Franklin asked.

"While you've been speaking, I've been getting around in the crowds. They'll vote for you, but they won't vote for Cox and the League."

A cold rain fell on Hyde Park when Franklin voted at the town hall on November 2. He knew that his chances were poor, but his buoyant nature still hoped for victory as he went back to his mother's house to await the returns. It was a landslide for Harding and Coolidge, who won 61 percent of the popular vote (16,152,200 to 9,147,353), and carried the electoral college by 404 to 127. In New York State, Franklin's home base, the fulcrum of his political future, the Democrats had not carried a single county or won a single state office. Running on Wilson's coattails had proved a disaster. Making the League the main issue had been a serious misjudgment of the national mood. Harding's campaign was right on target, with its appeal for a "return to normalcy." After the wartime years of sacrifice and rationing, and the thousands of families who had lost a son or a brother, the American people did not want high-minded thoughts about international cooperation but a chance to improve their lives.

Franklin said he was not disappointed, and professed to be grateful to be going back to a law practice that would be more lucrative than government work, writing his friend George Marvin, the editor of *World's Work:* "You are mighty lucky to be away from all the pettiness of New York and Washington at the present time. Washington this year will be quite disgusting to live in, and I am thankful that I am to be back in New York trying to practice law and make up for a government salary all these years. The election after all was not much of a surprise. The country not only returned to provincialism, but the victory of Harding has brought under one tent everybody with a grouch in the whole United States. The result will be the finest little cat-fight you ever saw."

In later years, Franklin would say that it had been a privilege to run and lose. He had spent about sixty days in a sleeping car and had campaigned in thirty-two states, addressing every manner of audience. He had dealt with hecklers (like the fellow who asked him what Teddy Roosevelt thought of Wilson), shaken thousands of hands, flashed his smile when he was dead tired, talked about cattle in Wyoming and wheat in Kansas, grabbed a few minutes of sleep between whistle stops, and learned something about the average voter. You could not start out with an idea like the League of Nations and impose it on people. Favorable sentiment for a policy had to come from the grass-roots level. Voters had ethnic and regional roots that could not be ignored. One of his mother's gardeners had voted for Harding because he was of German origin and had received a letter from the old country telling him of food shortages there—he blamed Wilson, who had brought America into the war. "Are you not an American citizen?" Franklin asked. "Yes," the gardener replied, "but if America joins with England and France against Germany, I am a German."

Franklin had no immediate future in national politics, but he now had a reputation of his own, distinct from Wilson and the Navy Department.

There was a big job to do in rebuilding the Democratic party in New York State. Tammany, which had concentrated on Al Smith's gubernatorial campaign at the expense of the national ticket, had been unable to get Smith reelected. It was in a cheerful frame of mind that Franklin went off to Louisiana on a hunting trip with his brother-in-law, Hall Roosevelt, describing himself in a letter to a friend as "Franklin D. Roosevelt, Ex. V.P., Canned (Erroneously reported dead)."

IX

The Newport Scandal

The dyer's hand is subdued to what it is dipped in.

Endicott Peabody

IN 1919, reports began to come into the Navy Department about conditions at the Naval Training Station in Newport, Rhode Island. Apparently, there was a group of homosexuals among the sailors who called themselves the "Ladies of Newport" and who attended the socials at the Army and Navy YMCA. The Newport military chaplain, Episcopalian minister Samuel N. Kent, was often at the socials. Dressed in his officer's khaki uniform with a cross on the cap, the forty-six-year-old Kent was reported to pick up sailors, tell them they looked lonesome, and invite them back to the parish house on Spring Street, where he had a spare room.

Ervin Arnold, a forty-four-year-old chief machinist's mate stationed in Newport, who had once worked as a detective for the state of Connecticut, reported on the situation on February 27 to the training station's welfare officer, Lieutenant Erastus Mead Hudson, Medical Corps.

Together, they took the matter to the station commander, Captain Edward H. Campbell, who had recently been instructed by Josephus Daniels to "clean the place up." Campbell asked Arnold how he would proceed, and Arnold said that conditions in Newport were so rotten that the only way would be to recruit a vice squad of enlisted men and send them out to be solicited. They might have to commit homosexual acts in order to obtain evidence, but there was no other way.

On March 15, 1919, a four-man court of inquiry was appointed to investigate the immoral conditions in Newport, with Lieutenant Commander Murphy J. Foster as president and Lieutenant Hudson as one of its members. The court asked Arnold to form a squad to help secure evidence. He recruited thirteen newly enlisted sailors, and was given office space in the Newport Red Cross headquarters.

Arnold told his men to go to Newport bars and other hangouts and mingle with homosexuals. "You people will be on the field of operation," he said. "You will have to use your judgment whether or not a full act is completed. If that being the fact, it might lead into something greater. You have got to form that judgment at the time you are on that field with that party."

Arnold was very insistent that his men be legally protected when they allowed immoral acts to be performed on them. He was told by Stewart Davis, the aide for information in the second naval district, that they would be protected provided they did not take the leading part. The volunteers were warned that they might be placed in embarrassing positions, and that the work was of a very nasty nature.

On March 22, 1919, Franklin, who was acting secretary in Daniels's absence, was informed about the conditions in Newport, and at once wrote Attorney General A. Mitchell Palmer a confidential letter: "The Navy Department has become convinced that such conditions of vice and depravity exist in and around Newport, R.I., as to require a most searching and rigid investigation with a view to finally prosecuting and clearing out those people responsible for it. This department, through its local representatives, can indicate certain persons in the Army, Navy, and Marine Corps, and others who are civilians, who, our information leads us to believe, are not only engaged in traffic in drugs, but also are fostering dens where perverted practices are carried on. In view of the fact that the conditions involve others than those in the naval service, and of the further fact that the practices are carried on outside the places under the jurisdiction of the Navy Department, it is impossible for this department through its own efforts to handle the situation. As the facts so far indicate that the combination is working beyond the limits of Newport, even to Providence, New York and Boston, it is evident that the situation is one that is even above the state authorities to handle. Newport is the home of several naval activities, one of which is a training station where thousands of young men are under training for the Navy. It is also one of the bases from which the Atlantic Fleet operates. This department, eager for the protection of its young men from such contaminating influences, desires to have the horrible practices stopped, and therefore requests that the Department of Justice put its most skilled investigators to work."

While waiting for the Justice Department to root out this sinister network with its tentacles stretching up and down the eastern seaboard, Arnold's Newport squad was busily catching "perverts." As Lieutenant Commander Foster remarked to Lieutenant Hudson: "If they don't stop Arnold right away he will hang the whole state of Rhode Island." The "Ladies of Newport" ring was broken up. Eighteen sailors were arrested between April 8 and April 14, fourteen of whom were court-martialed in August (two deserted and two were given dishonorable discharges). In its report, the Foster court of inquiry named the Arnold squad operatives upon whom completed homosexual acts had been performed, and recommended that a notation be entered in their service records "in recognition of their interest and zeal in their work in assisting the Judge Advocate, and in the best interests of the naval service." Surely this was the first time in the history of the U.S. Navy that sailors were officially commended for committing homosexual acts.

In the meantime, Franklin was called by his old friend, Governor R. Livingston Beekman of Rhode Island, who told him he was sending the Reverend Charles P. Hall, field director of the Newport Red Cross, to tell him what was going on. Hall said conditions were worse than ever. "What do you mean by that?" Franklin asked. "Everything," Hall said, "drugs, prostitution and perversion."

"What do you think we ought to do?"

"I think you should start a new investigation."

"Why can't we go ahead with the Court of Inquiry that is already sitting in Newport?"

"Because all the people they have got working for them are thoroughly well known in Newport."

"Why can't we employ civilians?"

"Because a civilian coming to a little bit of a place like Newport is spotted before he leaves the station platform."

Hall suggested that Franklin send for Lieutenant Hudson, who was familiar with conditions and could suggest ways to proceed with the investigation.

On May 1, Hudson and Arnold were summoned to Washington for temporary duty under the office of the assistant secretary of the Navy. Franklin was pleased to see that Hudson was from Plattsburgh in upstate New York and had gone to Harvard (class of 1913). Arnold handed him a detailed report on the completed homosexual acts performed by his operatives. Included in the report were accounts of homosexual acts with the Reverend Kent.

On May 5, Franklin sent a confidential memo to the director of Naval Intelligence, Rear Admiral Albert P. Niblack: "The conditions in and around one of our naval training stations is very serious indeed, insofar as moral perversion and drugs are concerned. . . . I wish Lieut. E. M. Hudson . . . and Chief Machinist Mate Ervin Arnold . . . be placed in your office for work in connection with suppressing these practices. . . . It is requested that this be the only written communication in regard to this affair, as it is thought wise to keep this matter wholly secret."

Niblack did not like the idea of a vice squad. You couldn't handle pitch without getting some on your hands. It would be extremely difficult for a young man in a U.S. Navy uniform, without any experience as a detective, to engage in work of this character without subjecting himself to the danger of suspicion as to his real motives, and as to the method which he would necessarily have to adopt to get evidence that would hold up in a court of law and lead to conviction. He told Franklin that the suppression of vice was outside the jurisdiction of Naval Intelligence.

Since the Justice Department was dragging its feet and Naval Intelligence wasn't interested, Franklin decided to take the Hudson-Arnold unit under his wing. On May 9, he signed the order detaching Lieutenant Hudson to new duty. On May 15, he gave Hudson a "To whom it may concern" letter, a highly unusual procedure in the Navy, which said: "Lieutenant E. M. Hudson, Medical Corps, U.S. Navy, is engaged on important work in which I am interested, and any assistance you can render him will be appreciated."

On June 6, Hudson was back in Washington, complaining that nothing had been done because no orders had been issued and they still couldn't figure out where to attach him. Someone suggested the naval district in Hawaii, but that seemed ridiculous, so Franklin attached him directly to his own office. The order that he signed on June 11 read: "You are hereby designated as Commanding Officer of a group of officers and enlisted (or enrolled) men and women who have been assigned or may be assigned certain confidential special duties as agents of the Assistant Secretary of the Navy. This group, or unit, will bear the name: 'Section A—Office of the Assistant Secretary,' or simply: 'Section A—OASN.' "

As commanding officer of the mysterious Section A, Hudson was given the authority to promote his men, which as a lieutenant he would not normally have had. Since the Bureau of Navigation leaked like a sieve, all the orders and the correspondence would go out through Franklin's confidential stenographer. All the orders, including the "Transfer of Personnel to Special Duty," were signed by Franklin. In all he signed at least twenty orders relating to Section A, including one on June 9 attaching Arnold to the assistant secretary's office for "duty of such a nature that he does not have written orders and will be out of the district most of the time." Thanks to Franklin, both Hudson and Arnold were given Naval Intelligence cards as special agents. Section A was financed out of the Contingent Navy Fund, with which the secretary of the Navy paid for unforeseen needs, such as banquets for distinguished foreigners or oil paintings of war actions.

When he had been in Washington on June 6 and 7, Lieutenant Hudson had expressed his concern to Franklin about the legal status of the operatives, whose unusual methods of investigation might make them vulnerable to criminal charges. Franklin directed Hudson to seek the advice of Assistant U.S. Attorney General Porter, whom he saw on June 10, and Assistant U.S. District Attorney Harvey D. Baker of Providence, whom he saw on June 25. He was told that the methods he proposed to use constituted no criminal offense under the law, although Porter did raise the moral question of whether the end justified the means. Section A recruited a total of forty-one enlisted men, ten of them between the ages of sixteen and nineteen. They were quite active in July, obtaining cases against sixteen Newport residents.

One of the sixteen was the Reverend Kent, who on July 30 was arrested, handcuffed, thrown into prison, and charged with being a lewd and wanton person. One of his fellow ministers put up the $400 for his bail. At his trial in Newport district court on August 22 and 23, before Judge Hugh Baker, two members of Section A testified that Kent had performed homosexual acts upon them. Thus it came out in open court that young men, some of them still in their teens, confided by their parents to the care of the U.S. Navy, had been ordered to submit to immoral acts in order to obtain evidence. This caused great indignation among the citizens of Newport. It was felt that Kent's possible guilt was less odious than the methods used by the Navy Department.

It was in this climate of wrought-up public opinion that Kent was acquitted, to the consternation of Franklin, who was informed by Hudson that Baker was a crooked judge who had been pressured by the Newport political and religious establishment.

On September 3, two Newport clergymen, Hamilton Fish Webster and Stanley C. Hughes, came to Washington to complain to Franklin about the methods of entrapment used by the Hudson squad. They presented him with a transcript of part of the trial testimony and asked that the Navy Department make a statement exonerating Kent. Professing to be greatly surprised that such orders had been given to enlisted men, Franklin said: "If anyone has given orders to commit immoral acts, someone will swing for it."

Then he added that "Newport has always been a very bad or immoral place."

"Why then do you arrest a clergyman from Massachusetts?" asked Reverend Hughes.

"Well, your courts are corrupt and untrustworthy," replied Franklin, "and I am informed that the judge who presided in this trial is accustomed to give his decisions for political reasons."

Reverend Webster rejoined that he knew the judge to be a man of the highest rectitude and character.

"I haven't time to go through all this matter that you have brought here," Franklin said. "Please lay it before Captain Leigh and I will give you a note to him and let him consider what ought to be done."

The two ministers went to see Captain Richard H. Leigh, acting chief of the Bureau of Navigation, who felt that the Hudson operatives had gone too far, that it could be embarrassing for the Navy, and that Section A should immediately cease its activities. The order to that effect, confirmed by Franklin, went out on September 4. Captain John D. Wainwright was chosen to conduct an internal investigation of Section A. He interviewed the operatives and found that most of them had either been sodomized or had committed acts of sodomy in the course of their work.

On September 22, James De Wolf Perry, the Episcopal bishop of Rhode Island, came to Washington to see Josephus Daniels, who passed him on to Admiral Niblack of Naval Intelligence. Niblack, who had been opposed to Section A from the start, said: "Bishop, I know these facts very intimately and have been following the thing very closely. We placed these investigators in Newport and gave them wide range and I have reason now to investigate the investigators and to disapprove of the whole proceeding, and I have decided that it should come to an end, and I am making that recommendation."

That afternoon, Niblack spoke to Captain Leigh, who expressed his distress and disgust that methods had been used that would discredit the personnel of the Navy and adversely affect recruiting. When Niblack questioned Hudson and Arnold and read some of their reports, however, he felt that he had done them an injustice in having doubted the sincerity and merit of Section A. It seemed outrageous to him that the YMCA had been used as a recruiting ground for homosexuals. He was so convinced of the Reverend Kent's guilt that he took Hudson and Arnold to see Daniels on September 25. Daniels was horrified by their disclosures and agreed with Niblack that the Navy should press for a retrial. All the evidence the Navy had collected was turned over to the Justice Department, which decided to try Kent before the U.S. district court in Providence.

When the federal trial opened in Providence on January 5, 1920, Kent claimed entrapment. Four days later, he was again acquitted. The trial had somehow shifted from the issue of Kent's guilt to whether the sailors of Section A were right in obeying Hudson's orders. As Judge Arthur L. Brown put it: "There is no provision of law in the United States which compels any man to receive orders from any government official through the whole length of executive, judicial, military or naval authorities, which compels him to subject his person to indignity."

Indignity was what the Newport clergy felt it had been subjected to after the Reverend Kent's two acquittals. On January 10, Bishop Perry and twelve other clergymen took their grievance to the highest authority, writing President Wilson that ". . . a score of youths enlisted in and wearing the uniform of the United States Navy [had been] instructed in the details of a nameless vice and sent through the community to practice the same in general and in particular to entrap certain designated individuals; and this in spite of the fact that prominent citizens of Rhode Island made in person strong and continuous protest directly to the Secretary and Assistant Secretary of the Navy against this iniquitous procedure." The clergymen asked the president to take "such measures as will eliminate from the Navy all officials, however highly placed, who are responsible for the employment of such execrable methods."

At a time when Franklin was being mentioned as a possible vice-presidential candidate, the Section A mess was turning into a dangerous political scandal. Acting quickly to keep the situation under control, Daniels appointed a court of inquiry on January 17, 1920. Heading it was Admiral Herbert O. Dunn, commandant of the first naval district, with whom Franklin was on particularly cordial terms, having just done him a favor. He had written Representative Henry D. Flood of Virginia to recommend a nephew of Dunn's wife for a Naval Academy appointment, which the young man obtained.

On January 22, the Senate Naval Affairs Committee appointed Senators L. Heisler Ball (R., Del.), Henry W. Keyes (R., N.H.), and William H. King (D., Utah) to determine whether the Newport matter should be investigated.

When Hamilton Fish Webster, one of the two clergymen who had come to see Franklin in September, wrote to ask "in view of this second acquittal do you still feel that the evidence given in the Newport Court did not warrant acquittal, that the Chaplain was guilty, and that an apology was not due him by your Department?" Franklin replied angrily that "I did not feel that the Chaplain was guilty or not guilty. . . . Now, my dear Mr. Webster, I want to keep my temper, just as long as I possibly can, but I will not stand idly by and have rotten statements made, as they have been made in Newport, by people who cannot prove them, by people who know them to be false, and I shall not only welcome just as much publicity as you may want to give to it, but I will go just as far, and probably farther, than you will in seeing that the Navy gets a square deal."

The Dunn court of inquiry convened in Washington on January 26, and met for eighty-six days, collecting 4,800 pages of testimony. By the time Franklin was called to testify, on May 20, the Senate Naval Affairs Subcommittee had also launched its investigation.

Questioned by Judge Advocate Henry L. Hyneman, Franklin denied all knowledge of the Arnold squad's activities before it had been turned into Section A.

Q. "Mr. Secretary, did you know that in nine instances, between the 18th of March and the 14th of April, that certain naval operators had permitted sexual perverts in the naval service to suck their penis for the purpose of obtaining evidence to be used before the court of inquiry, which evidence resulted in a recommendation by that court to try by general court-martial sixteen enlisted men and to give two men undesirable discharges?"

A. "The answer is no. I knew absolutely nothing about the court or its methods or its personnel. . . . In view of the fact that the Acting Secretary is called upon each day to pass on anywhere from 20 to 100 court-martials, courts of inquiry, and boards of investigation cases, to go into details would require ten lives instead of one day."

Franklin further denied all responsibility for or knowledge of the methods of the secret section he had organized and led.

Q. "Who would be responsible for the acts of the men in an organization so constituted?"

A. "The officer in command."

Q. "Did you give them [the men] any instructions or orders as to how the details should be carried out?"

A. "Naturally not."

Q. "Would that not have been your duty, since these men were attached to your office?"

A. "Absolutely not."

Q. "Whose duty would that have been?"

A. "The commanding officer."

Q. "Did not Hudson report to you from time to time what progress he was making?"

A. "Several times during the summer Dr. Hudson either telephoned me or came to my office and told me, in general terms, that the investigation was proceeding very satisfactorily."

Q. "And on none of these occasions you asked him what methods he was using?"

A. "Absolutely not."

Q. "Why not?"

A. "Because I was interested merely in getting results. I was not concerned any more in finding out about their methods than I am concerned in finding out how the commanding officer of a fleet takes the fleet from New York to Newport. What I want to know is that he gets the fleet over to Newport."

Ervin Arnold, however, testified that on May 1 he had given Franklin the operatives' report in the Kent case, that he had seen the report in Franklin's hands, and that Franklin had taken it and other reports to his office and "went over them in a rough way."

Franklin was then cross-examined by Mr. Branch, a Newport lawyer representing the clergymen, who asked whether he had said that the judge in Kent's Newport trial was incompetent: "You are aware, are you not, that mere repetition of this serious charge, is often as serious as the original statement?"

A. "That is impossible to answer any more than this: Have you stopped beating your wife? And you cannot answer it either way, yes or no."

Q. "You were aware of the fact that one of the subjects of investigation was unnatural crime?"

A. "One. Sodomy was one of four or five other vices which were to be investigated."

Q. "As a lawyer, how did you suppose that evidence of such a crime could be obtained?"

A. "As a lawyer I had no idea. That is not within the average lawyer's education."

Q. "Did you give that matter any thought whatsoever?"

A. "Not any more than how they were going to close the whore houses or the sale of drugs."

Q. "Did you realize as a lawyer ... that investigations in such matters often lead to improper actions on the part of the investigators?"

A. "I never had such an idea. Never entered my head. No, sir."

Q. "Were you aware that unnatural crimes are not commonly committed in the open?"

A. "Neither is prostitution nor the selling of drugs committed in the open."

Q. "How did you think evidence of these things could be obtained?"

A. "I didn't think. If I had I would have supposed they had someone under the bed or looking over the transom."

The Dunn court was a whitewash. The one man who could have testified that he had kept Franklin informed about the methods of Section A, Lieutenant Hudson, was excused from appearing on account of illness.

Franklin had repeatedly said that if immoral methods had been used "someone should swing for it," but Hudson was let off with a letter of censure. A court-martial would have implicated the secretary and assistant secretary of the Navy. Hudson was allowed to resign from the Navy in January 1921.

The Dunn court report, released in March 1921, said: "This court is of the opinion that it was unfortunate and ill-advised that Franklin D. Roosevelt, Assistant Secretary of the Navy, either directed or permitted the use of enlisted personnel to investigate perversion."

"Unfortunate and ill-advised" was pretty mild, hardly even a slap on the wrist. There the matter would have ended had it not been for the Senate investigation. When the subcommittee released its report in July 1921, a strong case was made that Franklin had known about the methods used by Section A from the start, and had lied to the Dunn court under oath, committing perjury.

As the Senate report said, "It is not reasonable to believe that a man of the wide experience of Assistant Secretary Franklin D. Roosevelt should have discussed an investigation for several days (in May and June) without any mention being made of the methods by which evidence had been and was to be obtained. Prior to the conference there had been many completed acts performed upon the men under Hudson and Arnold and it is unbelievable that such acts should not have been referred to by one or both of them. It is impossible for the committee to conceive of discussion lasting this length of time concerning a subject of such unusual gravity without some mention of the methods Hudson had in mind for the rounding up of the sexual perverts in Newport. It is incredible that at no stage of the discussion Franklin D. Roosevelt or anyone else present asked Hudson or Arnold how he intended to proceed and what duties he had in mind for the men under his command to perform. If the 'ways and means' for rounding up sexual perverts in Newport were discussed at all during the two days' conference, it is beyond the comprehension of this committee how the methods to be used could have been entirely eliminated and apparently forgotten. The committee . . . believes that at this time Franklin D. Roosevelt and the others present had knowledge that enlisted personnel had been and were to be used to investigate perversion and must have realized that in previous investigations under charge of Hudson and Arnold men had allowed lewd and immoral acts to be performed upon them and that a similar plan was being adopted. If, during the conferences of May 1 and June 6 and 7, Assistant Secretary Franklin D. Roosevelt did not inquire and was not informed as to the proposed method theretofore used and to be used by the men attached directly to his offices and under his supervision, then it is the opinion of this committee that Assistant Secretary Franklin D. Roosevelt was most derelict in the performance of his duty. The committee, however, cannot believe so. Franklin D. Roosevelt was a man of unusual intelligence and attainments, and after three days of conversation on the subject must have known the methods used and to be used to secure evidence."

In addition, the committee report said, when Hudson had come to see Franklin in June to ask about the legal status of the operatives, and Franklin told him to obtain legal advice from two U.S. attorneys, he "realized that the operations to be conducted were out of the ordinary and were fraught with legal danger for the men who actually performed the acts. It is probable that any man with ordinary intelligence, and who had not previously known what procedure was contemplated, would have advised the visit of Hudson to the attorneys without knowing why such legal advice was necessary."

Another damning bit of evidence was Franklin's request in his confidential letter of May 5, 1919, to Admiral Niblack that the matter be kept secret, which "would seem to indicate knowledge on Roosevelt's part of the seriousness of the situation and of its astonishingly unusual character, as otherwise he would not have gone to such extreme and unusual length to keep it 'wholly secret' and have no written communications regarding it."

Franklin had lied to the Dunn court, the Senate report went on, which itself was a mockery of justice, having waved aside all recognized rules of evidence. Lieutenant Hudson, who had shown "an utter lack of moral responsibility . . . should have been ordered before a general court-martial." Ervin Arnold should have his "name stricken from the roster of the Navy." His moral perspective was "entirely warped . . . he was perfectly willing to sacrifice young men morally to gain his ambitious end, which was apparently to be known as a great detective, a modern Sherlock Holmes."

This was as shocking a matter as had ever been found in the annals of the U.S. Navy. It was shocking to the American standard of morality, and flagrantly at variance with the example that should be set by a military department. Young boys, immature and inexperienced, who because of their patriotism and the patriotism of their parents had responded to the call of their country to defend their flag and their homes, had been sent out to have their bodies polluted, which they would remember and regret to their dying day. It was particularly shocking that Josephus Daniels, who was such a Bible-thumping moralist, who had banned wine from officers' messes and condoms for the enlisted men, was the ultimate authority who had permitted young men under his care to commit sordid acts with homosexuals.

The man directly responsible for this "most deplorable, disgraceful and unnatural proceeding," the man who had set up Section A, signed the orders, and condoned the entrapment of homosexuals by enlisted men, was the assistant secretary of the Navy, Franklin D. Roosevelt.

The Senate subcommittee report concluded: "That such orders, instructions, or suggestions could have been given . . . is most reprehensible and beyond comprehension. . . . The committee is of the opinion that Secretary Daniels and Assistant Secretary Franklin D. Roosevelt showed an utter lack of moral perspective when they allowed men in the uniform of the United States Navy . . . to publicly testify to the beastly acts that had been performed on them. . . . That Franklin D. Roosevelt, Assistant Secretary of the Navy, ever permitted or directed as he did, according to the opinion of both the Dunn court of inquiry and of this committee, the use of enlisted personnel for the purpose of investigating perversion, is thoroughly condemned as immoral and an abuse of the authority of his high office."

This was the majority report drafted by the two Republican senators, Ball of Delaware and Keyes of New Hampshire. A minority report written by the subcommittee's only Democrat, King of Utah, said that "the attacks upon Mr. Roosevelt I consider unjust, entirely unwarranted and not supported by the record."

But the majority report, with its scandalous revelations, would get press coverage, and Franklin would be branded as guilty of gross abuse of high office. All the years he had spent in the Navy Department, guiding its fortunes through a world war, trying to infuse energy and decision into his vacillating chief, were culminating in public censure. His political career, already at a standstill after the 1920 campaign, would receive a terrible, perhaps fatal blow. In the Senate report, he was described in nauseating terms, not as a distinguished public servant, but as the mastermind of one of the most shameful episodes in the history of the U.S. Navy. The Grand Young Man had stumbled, and might not rise again.

On July 21, 1921, having learned that the majority report was about to be released to the newspapers, Franklin was in Washington, in a Navy Department office with his friend Steve Early, going through the 6,000 pages of testimony. It was like emptying the sea with a child's pail. They went through volume after volume as a fan buzzed overhead, working on the statement that Franklin would give to the press.

"Damn it, Steve," he said, "this whole business is nothing but dirty politics. That's the point we've got to emphasize."

"We'll make that subcommittee look sick," Early said.

At four that afternoon, reporters called to say that the majority report had been released. Senator Ball had declined to hold it back. That alone proved the futility of trying to get any fair treatment. Well, he would make his statement anyway, and he would ask for an open hearing before the full Senate Committee on Naval Affairs.

The statement was finished by eight, and Early took it across the street to the Senate Office Building.

It was a spirited defense, but the *New York Times*, on July 23, told the real story: "Lay Navy Scandal to F. D. Roosevelt—Details Are Unprintable."

Refusing to concede that there was any validity to the report, Franklin felt that he had been smeared. He seemed to have convinced himself that he really hadn't "officially" known about the methods until September, that his "unofficial" knowledge didn't count, that there was a difference between the "official" knowledge of an assistant secretary and knowledge in the accepted sense, as the ordinary person has it.

Franklin was hurt as he had never been before. All his life he had succeeded, as president of the *Crimson,* as state senator, as assistant secretary—even his defeat on the Cox ticket was a disguised success, for he had run on a national ticket before he was forty and secured a national reputation. With his charm and good looks and trenchant intellect, he had until now escaped wounding criticism. He was accustomed to praise, a habit formed at his mother's knee.

Now for the first time there was an attack to which he could not respond, because it was largely true. The Senate subcommittee's majority report described his conduct as dishonorable, and said flatly that he had abused the authority of high office. As in the Lucy Mercer incident, he had strayed from the model of the "good Roosevelt." He had done something that was truly disgraceful, which he could only excuse by claiming that the majority report was a partisan hatchet job.

Publicly, Franklin said he was the innocent victim of Republican calumny. He pretended not to be bothered by the report, and wrote Daniels: "In the long run neither you nor I have been hurt by this mud-slinging . . . what is the use of fooling any longer with a bunch who have made up their minds that they do not care for the truth and are willing to say anything which they think will help them politically?"

Privately, he was in pain, the pain of someone who has been tried and convicted, for whom there was no appeal, and whose sentence was the besmirching of his good name. The extent of that pain could be measured in a letter he wrote on the day after the first newspaper stories appeared, July 21, to Republican Senator Henry Keyes, coauthor of the majority report and an alumnus of Harvard. "I have had the privilege of knowing many thousands of Harvard Graduates," Franklin wrote. "Of the whole number I did not personally know one whom I believed to be personally and willfully dishonorable. I regret that because of your recent despicable action I can no longer say that. My only hope is that you will live long enough to appreciate that you have violated decency and truth and that you will pray your Maker for forgiveness." On the back of the envelope were a few scrawled words: "Not sent—what was the use? FDR."

X

The Stricken Prince

Courage and hope both teaching him the practice.
Shakespeare, *Measure for Measure*

AFTER the 1920 campaign, Franklin returned to New York to practice law with his two partners, Langdon P. Marvin and Grenville T.
Emmet. He didn't bring in much business, but his name and reputation were
assets. In addition, Van-Lear Black, a wealthy Maryland businessman
whom Franklin had met and charmed at the 1912 convention in Baltimore,
had made him vice president in charge of the New York office of the Fidelity & Deposit Company, at a salary of $25,000 a year. He was a Harvard
overseer, the chairman of committees to raise funds for Lighthouses for the
Blind, and president of the Navy Club and the Greater New York Boy
Scouts Council. He was, in sum, a prominent and still public man with a
bright future.

On July 27, 1921, a few days after the crushing blow of the Senate report,
Franklin visited a Boy Scout camp in Palisades Interstate Park, and seemed
to have regained his high spirits. One of the officials passed around a hollow
cane filled with booze. When the police commissioner took a swig, Franklin
and the others arrested him for violating the Volstead Act. Declaring himself to be "prosecuting attorney," Franklin sampled the stuff, and said:
"May it please the court, I find that the liquid in this container is nothing
more than vanilla extract, and I move that the case be dismissed."

The photograph of him marching in the Boy Scout parade was the last
one taken that showed him walking unassisted. The day was hot, and perhaps he took a dip in the Scout camp's lake.

He was looking forward to spending the entire summer with his family in
Campobello, for the first time since he had joined the Navy Department in
1913. Waiting for him there, Eleanor on July 30 was glad to hear that he was
coming up on Van-Lear Black's yacht, the *Sabalo,* avoiding the long, hot
train ride.

On August 5 they sailed. Marguerite A. ("Missy") LeHand, Franklin's new secretary, wrote Eleanor: "I thought he looked tired when he left." Franklin navigated the yacht through fog and currents, spending hours at the wheel, and brought it safely into Welchpool Harbor on the seventh. He had promised his boss some deep-sea fishing in the Bay of Fundy.

The last morning of the *Sabalo*'s visit was bright and clear, perfect for cod. Franklin baited the hooks, alternating between the fore and aft cockpits of the motor tender, crossing beside the hot engine on a three-inch-wide varnished plank. He slipped and fell over the side into the icy Maine water, still holding onto the tender, so that he hardly wet his head, but the water was so cold it seemed paralyzing.

On August 10, he took some of the children sailing on his twenty-four-foot boat, the *Vireo*. On the way back, they noticed a blue haze over a stretch of shore on one of the islands, and a breeze carried a pungent odor their way. "Burning spruce," Franklin said. Making for the shore and beaching the boat, he cut wands of evergreen, and he and the children beat back the flames curling around a grove of spruce, flailing away, calling encouragement to each other, brushing away the sparks that flew against their arms, until only a few wisps of smoke rose from the charred trees. The ground was covered with rotting logs, inside which the fire would smolder for hours. Grimy and exhausted, they set sail for home, the smell of wood-smoke clinging to their clothes.

"I think the remedy for this condition is a nice cool swim at Glen Severn," Franklin said when they got back to Campo. They swam for an hour in the fresh-water lagoon on the other side of the island and dogtrotted the two miles home on the dusty roads in their wet bathing suits. Franklin took a quick dip in the frigid Bay of Fundy, but did not feel the usual glow. He came in and sat reading the paper for a while, too tired even to dress, scanning it for reports of his bout with Congress. At supper, he excused himself and went to bed. He thought he had a slight attack of lumbago.

The next morning when he swung out of bed, his left leg lagged. He was able to get up and shave, and convinced himself that the trouble with his leg would disappear as he used it. But presently the left leg refused to work, and then the right leg collapsed, and he dragged himself back to bed. When Eleanor took his temperature, it was 102.

There was no telephone in the house, so Eleanor sent an islander to Lubec with a message for their family doctor, E. H. Bennett, who diagnosed a common cold, ignoring Franklin's pain and the loss of feeling in one of his legs.

The next day, August 12, Franklin could not move his legs at all. He was partly paralyzed from the chest down. His thumb muscles were so weak he could not hold a pen. A second opinion was in order. Louis Howe canvassed the nearby resorts and located an elderly surgeon who had once operated on Grover Cleveland, W. W. Keen, vacationing in Bar Harbor. Dr. Keen promptly diagnosed a blood clot from a bladder congestion that had settled in the lower spinal cord, temporarily removing the power to move though not to feel. He later changed his diagnosis to a lesion of the spinal cord, prescribed heavy massage, and sent a bill for $600. As Thomas Jefferson once said: "When I see two doctors in conversation, I scan the sky for an approaching buzzard."

Immobilized, Franklin kept up his good humor, writing a friend on August 17: "Thanks to a severe chill which I lay to the vagaries of the Bay of Fundy climate, which has more tide and more kinds of weather than any other place on the globe, I am spending a considerably longer vacation than I intended under the stern eye of a doctor who refuses to allow me to more than look at my mail and sign a few letters each day."

Eleanor slept on a coach in his room and devoted herself to his care until a nurse arrived from New York. He had lost the use of his bladder, and she had to insert a catheter in his urethra to help him urinate. "You have been a rare wife," Dr. Keen told her, "and have borne your heavy burden most bravely. You will surely break down if you do not have immediate relief. Even then when the catheter has to be used your sleep must be broken at least once in the night."

On August 18, Eleanor wrote Franklin's half brother, Rosy: "Yesterday, today his temperature has been normal and I think he's getting back his grip and a better mental attitude though he has of course times of great discouragement."

Franklin's uncle, Frederic A. Delano, dissatisfied with Doctors Bennett and Keen, set off for Boston to talk to the doctors at the Harvard Infantile Paralysis Commission office. They were on vacation, but he found a young internist at the Peter Bent Brigham Hospital, Dr. Samuel A. Levine, who, after being told the symptoms—paralysis, pains in the limbs, moderate fever, which were consistent with hundreds of cases he had treated in the 1916 epidemic—diagnosed infantile paralysis. Frederic Delano wrote Eleanor on August 20: "He [Levine] said at once, as did Dr. Parker in Washington, that it was unquestionably infantile paralysis. Secondly, he said that you should stop the manipulations and massage as unwise so early in the game."

Franklin had poliomyelitis, an inflammation (itis) of the gray (polios) anterior matter of the spinal column (myelos). The virus lodged in the anterior horn cells of his spinal cord, which controlled the lower extremities. Those cells were destroyed and could not regenerate themselves. He lost and never regained the use of his legs.

Polio, or infantile paralysis, as it was then called, was perhaps the most dreaded disease in America, a mysterious and disabling blight that struck mainly children in overcrowded urban areas with poor hygiene. It was feared as the plague had been feared in medieval times, with terrified parents going to extraordinary lengths to protect their children, as Franklin in 1916 had sent a Navy ship to bring his five from Campobello to Hyde Park. Doctors knew it was a virus, but did not know how it reached the spinal cord and why some of those who caught it became paralyzed and others did not. The only treatment then being tried, a serum administered after the disease had been identified, was totally ineffective. The only cure, a vaccine, was thirty years away.

How had Franklin caught it? You could not pinpoint the date of exposure or trace the source of infection, because the incubation period varied from three to thirty-five days. Water was the likeliest source, not the clean and changing tidal waters around Campobello, but stagnant water like the Boy Scout lake, the swimming pool of a Washington club, or even a contaminated clam or oyster.

It would be years before it was understood that the submicroscopic polio virus entered the body by way of the mouth, established itself in the intestine, and then moved on in the bloodstream to invade the spinal cord and cause paralysis. Usually, the immune system of a healthy person could stop the virus in the intestine, before it did permanent damage.

But Franklin had not stopped it, which indicates a possible deficiency in his immune system. How could a thirty-nine-year-old man, proud of his physical prowess, evaluated as a remarkable athlete by Walter Camp, have been felled by a particle that was not even visible under a microscope? In fact, Franklin had a long history of illness. He was an athlete with clay feet. As Josephus Daniels observed, he picked up every bug around.

His illnesses seemed to come at times of stress. Just before he was due to start on an arduous three-cornered campaign for the State Senate in 1912, he came down with typhoid. In the summer of 1917, when he had started his affair with Lucy Mercer and had to go through the repertoire of adulterous deceit, he was hospitalized with a bad throat infection. In September 1918, when he was in Europe and Lucy Mercer was writing him love letters, and he was coming home to face the wrenching decision of whether or not to leave his wife, he was stricken with influenza and pneumonia. Twenty-two days after the publication of the Senate report that caused him such anguish, right in the middle of the incubation period, he lost the use of both legs.

Franklin was the target of a known viral agent that struck healthy children as well as men and women in the prime of life. Catching the disease was a matter of exposure to the transmitter. Today, however, it may be worthwhile to reexamine his polio in the light of a relatively new field of medicine with the multisyllabic name of psychoneuroimmunology, which raises the possibility that stress, through the mediation of the immune system, can lead to a diminished resistance to infection.

That stress has a bearing on illness is part of our common experience. A mother says to her child, "If you don't get some rest, you are going to get sick." So-called psychosomatic illnesses, such as asthma and ulcers, have long been linked to stress. But today's researchers are trying to show that infectious diseases as well may be stress-related. The "germ" is a necessary but not a sufficient determinant of disease, for the simple reason that when two persons are exposed to the same germ, one will catch the disease and the other will not, because one is "ill" and the other is "well." But what is "illness" and what is "wellness"?

It may be in part the ability to handle stress and keep the immune system in good working order. Stress, the new research shows, affects immune responses and other functions. If we use the analogy of war, with the germ the surprise attacker, some bodies are poorly defended, their borders poorly guarded, their troops not mobilized, their armaments not deployed, while others are fortresses. Stress can destabilize the chemistry factory that is the body in ways that can be tracked and measured. It can remove protective lymphocytes from the bloodstream and reduce the number of antibodies that help fight the invader. With the stress-affected brain sending signals to the central nervous system, it can set off chain reactions: chemical agents cause the kidneys to raise the blood pressure; the pituitary gland releases corticosteroids that suppress immune responses to infection.

A few studies have already linked infectious diseases with psychological factors. There is, it appears, an enormously complex interaction in stressful situations from the brain to neurotransmitters, hormones and enzymes, and elements of the immune system. So that even diseases with known viral agents, such as cancer and polio, may be multifactoral in cause, involving genetic, behavioral, nervous, glandular, and immune-system interrelationships.

In sum, the new studies show that virtually every illness can be influenced by the body's mental state. Terms such as immunological competence and immunological responsibility are ways of describing how we raise or drop our guard against germs.

The way Franklin contracted polio fits right into this scheme of things. There was a strong stress factor when he learned on July 21, 1921, that the Senate subcommittee majority report had accused him of gross abuse of office. He took it badly. It seemed to him that he had been unjustly attacked, that his reputation and political career were at stake. It was the worst thing that had ever happened to him. With the exception of the Lucy Mercer episode, he had pretty much managed to avoid emotionally stressful situations in his thirty-nine years. Everything had come easily, and he was accustomed to being showered with praise and affection by significant figures from his mother to his boss at the Navy Department. He had not developed the protective psychological hardiness that comes from being hurt. As one of the doctors who treated his polio put it, he had "an extraordinarily sensitive emotional mechanism." The revelation that he was the Navy official responsible for sending young men to entice homosexuals was literally a crippling blow. He was so wrought up that he wrote an angrily accusing letter to a U.S. senator, which, had he sent it, would have led its recipient to conclude that he must be temporarily deranged. The letter was written on July 22, and twenty days later, well within the parameters of polio incubation, he lost the use of his legs.

Why was a man in the prime of life, radiating vitality and fond of many forms of physical exercise, struck down by polio at the low point in his life, when his career was threatened and his ambitions were frustrated? The link between his dilemma and the polio, although speculative, should not be dismissed.

On August 25, Dr. Robert W. Lovett, the austere and aristocratic Boston polio specialist, arrived in Campobello and found Franklin paralyzed from the waist down, running a moderate fever of 100 degrees. His back muscles were also affected, and he could not sit up without help. There was some facial involvement, and weakness in the arms. A major danger was a paralyzed bladder, and since Franklin was unable to urinate by himself, Eleanor had to draw urine every few hours to prevent bladder and kidney infection.

Dr. Lovett discontinued the massages prescribed by Dr. Keen, believing that overtiring weak muscles would impair their function even further. But although harmful, the massages were the only tangible treatment Franklin was getting, the only evidence that something was being done, and their discontinuance caused him great anxiety. At the end of August, he went into a depression so serious that the alarmed Lubec physician in attendance, Dr. Bennett, wired Dr. Lovett: "Can you recommend anything to keep up his courage and make him feel the best is being done or tell him those changes are unavoidable? His wife anxious to avoid worry on his part."

On September 1, Bennett wrote: "Mr. Roosevelt seemed a little unnerved yesterday. The last few days have shown some falling off, which has disturbed him somewhat. Is still unable to urinate—bowels the same—Is less motion in feet, especially the left. The muscles are more flabby . . . he attributes the loss in muscular tone to discontinuance of massage or rather he wonders if that is the real cause. . . . He seems to feel that perhaps something more might be going on. It is easy to imagine how he feels. When you stated that the improvement in two weeks would be considerable, did you mean above or below the waistline? If the former it is working out correctly, if the latter, not so. Will it be better to tell him frankly that these changes must come and not to be so discouraged?"

Sara, who had been vacationing in Europe, knew nothing about her son's illness, and heard the bad news on her arrival at the dock on August 31. She went at once to Campobello and did her best to copy the cheerful attitude of poor Franklin, who lay there unable to move his legs. When the doctor came, they laughed and joked, with Eleanor in the lead. Dr. Bennett told Sara: "This boy is going to get well all right."

Behind the brave front, Franklin was going through mental agony. He could not come to grips with the hard fact that nothing could be done to treat his paralysis. Dr. Lovett wrote Dr. Bennett on September 3: "There is nothing that can be added to the treatment, and this is one of the hardest things to make the family understand. . . . There is likely to be mental depression and sometimes irritability in adults, as you heard me say to Mrs. R. I would have the patient sit up in a chair as soon as it can be done without discomfort."

In mid-September, it was decided to bring Franklin back to New York, where he was treated at Presbyterian Hospital by Dr. George Draper, a friend from Harvard and an authority on infantile paralysis.

Franklin had been hospitalized for over a week when Dr. Draper wrote Lovett that he was much concerned "at the very slow recovery both as regards the disappearance of pain ... and as to the recovery of even light power to twitch the muscles. There is marked falling away of the muscle masses on either side of the spine in the lower lumbar region, likewise the buttocks. There is marked weakness of the right triceps; and an unusual amount of gross muscular twitching in the muscles of both forearms. He coordinates on the fine motion of his hands very well now so that he can sign his name and write a little better than before. The lower extremities present a most depressing picture. There is little motion in the long extensors of the toes of each foot. . . . He is very cheerful and hopeful and has made up his mind that he is going out of the hospital in the course of two or three weeks on crutches. What I fear more than anything else is that we shall find a much more extensive involvement of the great back muscles than we have suspected and that when we attempt to sit him up he will be faced with the frightfully depressing knowledge that he cannot hold himself erect. . . . I feel so strongly after watching him now for over a week that the psychological factor in his management is paramount. He has such courage, such ambition, and yet at the same time such an extraordinarily sensitive emotional mechanism that it will take all the skill which we can muster to lead him successfully to a recognition of what he really faces without utterly crushing him."

In other words, Franklin was getting worse instead of better, but persisted in believing that he would soon regain the use of his legs and that Eleanor and the doctors were conspiring to keep him bedridden longer than necessary. This unfounded optimism came out in a letter to Josephus Daniels: "I am sure you will be glad to learn that the doctors are most encouraging and express great pleasure at the speed I am making toward complete recovery, but it is rather tedious to a young man who is not fond of sitting still, and your surmise regarding the stern determination of my 'missus' not to let me proceed too rapidly, is absolutely correct. In fact, I already suspect that she has entered into an alliance with the doctors to keep me in the idle class long after it is really necessary."

Dr. Lovett suggested immersing Franklin in a strong saline bath, and Dr. Draper reported on October 11: "We have had him in the hot tub every other day for the past week and a half with very definite benefits I believe, and great comfort to the patient. He still has a little tenderness in his hamstrings. I was delighted to find that he had much more power in the back muscles than I had thought, but I must say that the pelvic girdle and thighs, and indeed most of the leg muscles are in very poor shape." Lovett came to New York to see him on October 15 and found him in "good spirits—just able to sit up."

Franklin was discharged on October 28 and started learning to use a wheelchair at home. On November 19, Dr. Draper reported that "the patient is doing very well . . . navigates about successfully in a wheel chair. He is exceedingly ambitious and anxious to get to the point where he can try the crutches, but I am not encouraging him."

In December he began to work with a physiotherapist, Kathleen Lake, to retrain idle muscles. The tendons behind his knees had tightened so that it was unbearably painful to stretch his legs. Mrs. Lake had him exercise on a board, and reported to Dr. Lovett on December 17: "He told me today that he marked a very definite change at the end of each week and feels his legs growing stronger all the time. . . . He is perfectly satisfied also to remain as he is now and not get up yet on crutches as he says he has plenty of occupations for his mind, everything is going well in the city, and he would rather strengthen his legs this way than try to get up too soon. . . . He is a wonderful patient, very cheerful, and works awfully hard and tries every suggestion one makes to help him. He has certainly improved since he started the board which he insists on calling 'the morgue'!"

But in mid-January 1922 he suffered a setback. His ankles and calves were swollen, and his knees locked painfully underneath him. Mrs. Lake could have done a great deal more stretching but Franklin could not stand the pain. It was "really getting on his nerves," she wrote Dr. Lovett. ". . . The fact that he sits every afternoon in his wheelchair with his knees flexed rather counteracts the stretching in the morning." He seemed to be getting worse, the stretching was getting to him, the contractions tired him out. In February, to solve the hamstring problem, his left leg was placed in a plaster cast into which four wedges were driven. When the cast came off on February 13, he was relieved to see his leg straighten without pain.

In March, Franklin was fitted with steel braces weighing seven pounds each that covered his legs from feet to hips. With the braces and crutches, he learned to stand up and walk, even though he had no power in his legs. Dr. Draper reported that "Mrs. R. is pretty much at the end of her tether," and commented on "the intense and devastating influence of the interplay of these high voltage personalities one upon another." The mother and the wife fought for control of Franklin's crippled being. Sara was sure she knew better than the doctors what was best for her boy, and there were bitter arguments that left Eleanor trembling with rage and Sara in high dudgeon. Sara came and went through the connecting doors until Eleanor moved a big breakfront against the entrance that linked the twin dining rooms. Sara saw in Franklin's invalidism a chance to restore her ascendancy, urging him to retire to Hyde Park under her care.

Eleanor, who slept on a cot in one of her sons' rooms, later said it had been the most difficult winter of her life. She was trying to do too much, as Mrs. Lake observed: "If only his wife could be persuaded that he does not need urging on all day and entertaining all evening, he would not be so tired and would do better physically. . . . He is too surrounded with family, all giving him advice and ordering him round, and he gets quite desperate."

Unable to move without a wheelchair or crutches, dependent on nurses and therapists, his body functions exposed to the view of women, Franklin was helpless as a baby. Mrs. Lake thought he had come to depend too much on Edna Rockey, the night nurse, and herself, and that "a little shake-up would do him no harm at all."

In June, he was moved to Hyde Park, and Dr. Draper reported that "Mr. R. . . . seems to be cheerful, and I should say he has gained considerably in the tricks of handling himself. The new braces are, of course, infinitely better than the others, which I must say were an absolute failure. There is still some discomfort about the foot-plates . . . but I think this can be adjusted very easily. There is no question but that the change of scene has had a very beneficial effect on everybody concerned, and I look forward to the continued stretch of quiet at Hyde Park with great hopefulness."

He was now able with slight assistance to sit up from a prone position and was hoisted onto a horse, keeping it at a walk. He swam in Vincent Astor's heated pool in Rhinebeck, and exercised with parallel bars on the lawn. But Eleanor told Dr. Lovett that he was not using his crutches enough, and Lovett reminded him on August 14: "I think it is very important for you to do all the walking that you can within your limit of fatigue. . . . Walking on crutches is not a gift, but an art, acquired by constant practice just as any other game, and you will have to put in quite a little time before you get about satisfactorily." Thereafter, Franklin could be seen on the gravel drive in front of the house, pushing his braces one in front of the other, his hips swiveling awkwardly, his crutches working, his brow damp with perspiration, as he inched ahead, a little farther each day, between the double row of maples, until he reached the brownstone gateposts more than a quarter of a mile away. At the end of the summer he reported to Lovett: "I have faithfully followed out the walking and am really getting so that both legs take it quite naturally, and I can stay on my feet for an hour without feeling tired. I think the balance is coming back also, and though I can negotiate stairs if I have a hand rail I cannot get up steps with only the crutches, and I doubt if this feat can be accomplished for a long time."

Of course he knew that braces would not restore his muscles. Only exercise might help, even though well-wishers offered a variety of cures, including the Coué method ("Day by day in every way I am getting better and better"), an electric belt, a miraculous elixir, and magnetic healing. "It may be monkey glands or perhaps it is made out of the dried eyes of the extinct three-toed rhinoceros," Franklin wrote Dr. Draper in February 1923. "You doctors have sure got imaginations! Have any of your people thought of distilling the remains of King Tut-Ankh-Amen? The serum might put new life into some of our mutual friends. In the meantime, I am going to Florida to let nature take its course—nothing like Old Mother Nature anyway!"

Old Mother Nature was preferable to his natural mother and another captive winter with Sara and Eleanor. He seemed to be in better spirits when he was away from home; it was the only way for a severely disabled man to escape from the humiliation of dependence. He chartered a houseboat, the *Weona II,* for $1,500, and spent six happy weeks in the Florida Keys catching jewfish and groupers, with Louis Howe, Missy LeHand, and three friends—Lewis Cass Ledyard, Jr., a member of his first law firm; John S. Lawrence, a Harvard friend; and Henry C. de Rham, a Harvard classmate—and their wives. When "Mr. Cass" (Ledyard) caught a forty-two-pound jewfish, Franklin found an anti-Semitic remark amusing enough to include in the log: "And I thought we left N.Y. to get away from the Jews, quickly ejaculated friend's wife."

After the Florida trip, he had a falling out with Dr. Lovett, who demanded complete control of his patients, while Franklin wanted to go his own way. He made one final visit to Boston, and this was his condition when Lovett examined him on May 28, 1923.

- His arms and face and neck were normal.
- His bowel, bladder and sexual functions were normal.
- His abdominal muscles were weak.
- His ability to flex from the hips was poor.
- From the waist down, he remained paralyzed.
- There was no motion in his hamstrings.
- His toes showed no more than a trace of motion.

Nearly two years after catching the disease, he had made no real progress, except in learning to adapt to his disability. This is the way he would be for the rest of his life, despite the years of exercise and swimming. It was a permanent condition, as Dr. Draper confirmed on February 11, 1924: "I saw F.D.R. a day or two ago before he went south and I am very much disheartened about his ultimate recovery. I cannot help feeling that he has almost reached the limit of his possibilities. I only hope I may be wrong on this."

When Franklin was first stricken, he fell back on the defense of denial. The only way to cushion the psychic blow was to convince himself that his paralysis was temporary. If he repeated it often enough he would believe it, and so he wrote his friends that there was no question he would get the use of his legs back after several months of treatment. Within a month or two, he would discard his crutches. Within a year or two, he would be playing golf.

He spent the next seven years of his life trying to regain the power in his legs. Instead, he proved conclusively that the damage done by the polio virus was irreversible. Franklin was the most mobile of men. As a boy, his one athletic feat had been to kick his leg in the air higher than anyone. On his walks through Hyde Park, he would leap over a rail rather than open a gate. On an inspection tour in the Navy, he had climbed the rigging of a ship. In Europe in 1918, he walked through so many battlefields that he exhausted the rest of his party. Even in slumber he sleepwalked. Shoes were an important item, bought from Peals in London ("By Special Appointment to

King George V"), as in this order on March 18, 1913: "Will you please order for me one pair of low tan shoes with rubber soles, one pair of low black shoes, and one pair of evening slippers?" He never threw a pair away, and had a closetful.

Whether on the job or on vacation, he displayed a basic incapacity to sit still. Now, like a pianist with damaged hands, he was deprived of this key element of his nature. Never again would he take the chicks on cliff walks, or stroll through the woods behind the house at Hyde Park, or bound down the stairs three at a time on his way home after a late day at the office. Never again would he hit a golf ball and follow it down the fairway, or hold a woman in his arms on a dance floor, or climb a fence, or burrow his toes in the sand, or march in a parade. Dependent on a helping hand for every common daily activity, he could not dress or undress himself, or get in and out of a car, or on and off a train, or up and down stairs.

It was like a return to infancy to have to be carried about, to always need the assistance of another person, to have to devise complicated stratagems to get from his bed to the bathroom. The loss of his manhood would have been total had his potency not been spared. Dr. Lovett specifically stated that his sexual function was "undiminished." He had fathered six children before the attack and could continue to have sex, except that his wife touched him only as a nurse touches a patient. Now that he was a cripple, his need to affirm his manhood was greater than ever, and those who knew him at the Warm Springs retreat, where he spent so many months of convalescence, confirmed that he had "girlfriends."

When Dorothy Schiff, who was close to Franklin in the thirties but never had an affair with him, went to see him in Warm Springs, she asked the doctor in charge, Leroy W. Hubbard: "Is he able to make love?" "Oh, yes," the doctor said. "How does he do it?" Mrs. Schiff asked. "The French way," the doctor replied, which she took to mean the only position for a man who could not use his legs, lying on his back.

His son Elliott said that he had an affair with his secretary, Missy Le-Hand, though others, including his son James, dispute this. The daughter of a Massachusetts gardener, Missy was delicately attractive, with a pale oval face and large blue eyes, and became a sort of surrogate wife while Eleanor pursued her own activities. She was by his side from 1920 until 1941, when she suffered a stroke that led to her death from a cerebral embolism in 1944, first at Warm Springs, then in the governor's mansion, and finally in the White House.

As Felix Frankfurter wrote on January 18, 1943, "Sam [Rosenman, one of FDR's key advisers] said he always regarded her as one of the five most important people in the U.S. during the Roosevelt Administration. . . . She was one of the very, very few people who was not a yes-man, who crossed the President in the sense that she told him not what she knew to be his view of what he wanted to hear, but what were, in fact, her true views and convictions. That she did all this with uncommon charm and persistence gives some indication of what her absence from the scene has withdrawn."

Missy saw more of Franklin than Eleanor did, and treated him with wife-like familiarity. Henry Morgenthau, Jr., recorded in his diary that when he, as secretary of the Treasury, was in conference with FDR in April 1935, Missy came in with a small amateur moving picture camera and a light meter. She stood in front of the president, pointing the camera at him. After a minute or two, FDR stopped talking and just waited. Missy disagreeably said, "Why don't you go ahead with your work?" and he said, "I can't work with that damn thing pointed at me." "Oh, if that is the way you feel about it," said Missy like a spoiled child, and walked out.

This example of peevishness, related to show the many facets of their association, is trivial alongside the quarter century of absolute devotion she gave Franklin. She served him so long and studied his habits so thoroughly that he had no need to ask for what he wanted or needed, since she knew and supplied it without being asked. Her commitment was a form of the deepest love. She never married, and ruined her health in his service. In 1927 she had a heart attack in Warm Springs. Franklin was away, and Helen T. Mahoney, the physical therapist, wired him that "she says she is dying . . . she is lonely for you." In 1941, she had a stroke that left her partly paralyzed and was sent to stay with relatives in Somerville, Massachusetts, where she pined for Franklin. She was expecting him to call on Christmas day, but he did not. When she sat down to dinner, she lifted her glass and said, "A toast to the president's health," and her eyes filled with tears. On New Year's Eve, shortly before midnight, she started crying and no one could stop her, and she began calling, "F.D., come, please come, oh, F.D. . . ." The others in attendance, including FDR's daughter, Anna, thought it was the saddest thing they had ever seen. She was important enough to Franklin so that when he made out his will the interest on his estate was left half to Eleanor and half to Missy (she died before he did, but he did not change it). "If it embarrasses mother," he told his son James, "I'm sorry. It shouldn't, but it may."

More than the loss of mobility, polio caused a spiritual crisis. There was a strong psychic temptation, reinforced by his mother, to retreat from life into invalidism, to become a "back parlor" case, one of those people whom doctors told that nothing could be done for them and who spent the rest of their lives sitting at home in rocking chairs with shawls over their shoulders. Or he might have sunk into pettiness and bad temper, as Wilson did after his stroke. His political goals for the moment were abandoned. Who had ever heard of a man in a wheelchair winning high office? The vocabulary of politics was one of mobility. You "ran" for office (in England you "stood" for office), you were "in the running," you were a "front-runner," or if you didn't have a chance "you didn't have a leg to stand on." If you were nominated, the other fellow on the ticket was your "running mate." The campaign was a "race," after it "kicked off" you were "in the lead" or you "trailed," or you were "neck and neck," and in the last days of the campaign you were "in the home stretch." Until the winner took office, the defeated incumbent was a "lame duck."

In the eyes of many, he was through.

Franklin was not through. He was locked in struggle with a powerful enemy, and although his legs remained withered, his spirit triumphed. It was this spiritual battle, this passage from despair to hope, this refusal to accept defeat, this ability to learn from adversity, that transformed him from a shallow, untested, selfishly ambitious and sometimes unscrupulous young man into the mature figure we know as FDR.

An Englishman who lost a leg in World War II climbed the Matterhorn with a wooden leg. Asked why he had done it, he said: "I did it to save my soul." In his Hyde Park library, Roosevelt was visited by a clergyman. As they discussed a book, he slipped out of his wheelchair, crawled crablike across the floor, pulled the book out of the shelf, wedged it between his teeth, and crawled back. "What did you do that for?" the clergyman asked. "I felt I had to do it to show that I could," Roosevelt replied.

He could not do otherwise. From within the deepest reaches of his being, the signal came that, no matter what your fate was, you endured and did not give in. He could not join the ranks of the passive and dependent and those who are overwhelmed by misfortune. He could not become an example of defeat.

Polio was the dividing point of his life, like Luther's fit in the choir when he fell to the ground raving because he was unable to believe. There were two Franklin D. Roosevelts, before and after polio. Before polio, he walked along flower-strewn paths. Men came to him offering valuable prizes: Would he like to be state senator, or assistant secretary of the Navy? Would he like to run for vice president? There was an embarrassment of riches. It all came to you if you had the right name, the right appearance, and a cheerleader's vision of the world. But it did not quite ring true. There was something fraudulent in his early successes—in the way he led the insurgents in the State Senate for personal glory; in his flattery of Daniels and later in his insubordination; in his use of patronage to build an upstate anti-Tammany network, and in his later reconciliation with Tammany; in his haste to leapfrog to bigger jobs; in the way he chose expediency over principle, as when he wanted to mine neutral Norway's waters, which Admiral Beatty refused to do; in his exploitation of Theodore Roosevelt's memory in the 1920 campaign; in the colossal blunder of Section A—in all of these, Franklin seemed to have no goal beyond self-advancement. He was charming and gifted, but he was opportunistic. Disloyal to his superiors, he could be vindictive toward those beneath him, as he was with the naval officer who escorted him to the World War I battlefields. He lacked the essential quality of the statesman—the fusion of one's own interest with the national interest.

On his fortieth birthday, as he lay in his Campobello bedroom overlooking Passamaquoddy Bay, thinking that a little more than a year before he had campaigned across the country and now he couldn't even move his big toe, he wondered what lay ahead, and asked himself Job's question: "Why me, O God?"

There was no adequate answer. The next step, however faltering, was up to him. It was a private decision, although he was supported by those around him. Louis Howe, who had various offers, did not abandon him. The sour and cynical Louis kept the faith. Still believing in his future, he remained at Roosevelt's side during the years when he devoted most of his time to physical recovery. In his loyalty, there was an example from which his crippled boss could draw strength.

For years, Roosevelt continued to believe that he could not run for office until he walked again. As he wrote his friend Louis Wehle on October 23, 1925: "I must give principal consideration for at least two years more to getting back the use of my legs. Up to now I have been able to walk only with great difficulty with steel braces and crutches, having to be carried up and down steps, in and out of cars etc. Such a situation is, of course, impossible in a candidate. I am, however, gaining greatly and hope, within a year, to be walking without the braces, with the further hope of then discarding the crutches in favor of canes and eventually possibly getting rid of the latter also."

It was all wishful thinking. The years of effort ended in having to accept that the damage was irreparable. The hope that he could walk again turned into longing for the time when he had walked. Once, in the White House after an exhausting Gridiron dinner, Betsy Cushing Roosevelt asked him: "Pa, how do you ever get to sleep after this kind of an evening?" "It's very easy," Roosevelt said. "I coast down the hills at Hyde Park in the snow, and then I walk slowly up ... and I know every curve." As other people have flying dreams, expressing the need for escape and freedom, Roosevelt had walking dreams.

He changed during those years in the wilderness. He changed physically, from a slender, narrow-shouldered, long-limbed young man with a long thin face, to a middle-aged man whose strength was in his upper body, with a massive torso, bulging arms, and a face that filled out to twice its former size. He liked to show off his strength with arm wrestling, and once landed a 237-pound shark after a two-hour fight.

His character changed too. Once during a lecture in Akron, Ohio, Eleanor read aloud a written question: "Do you think your husband's illness has affected his mentality?" Eleanor paused a moment, then said: "Yes, I am glad that question was asked. The answer is Yes. Anyone who has gone through great suffering is bound to have a greater sympathy and understanding of the problems of mankind." Eleanor also felt that his years of convalescence had taught him patience. Freud said that the capacity for postponement of gratification was the hallmark of maturity, and this too Franklin learned. He had always wanted to see instant results. With polio he waited years for results that did not come. He learned to wait, to let situations ripen. There were some events you could not control. As he learned balance and leverage walking with crutches and braces, he learned also their political equivalents. He came to know where the fulcrum of a situation was, when to act, and when to give his enemies enough rope. What was called his procrastination was in fact an uncanny sense of timing that his illness taught him. "Polio did that for Franklin," Eleanor said. "Once he'd made up his mind, he knew you had to wait to see results, and there was no use worrying. . . . You had to wait and see what happened."

He learned also to be more reflective. Herbert Lehman, who was his lieutenant governor, said: "After he was stricken he had a great amount of time for contemplation and for several years he felt there was no use having political ambitions because he wasn't going to be able to satisfy them. It mellowed him, and it certainly added to his spiritual stature and his willingness to listen to other people's views." Steve Early, Roosevelt's advance man in 1920, told Harold Ickes: "If it hadn't been for his affliction, he never would have been President of the United States. In those earlier years, he was just a playboy. . . . He couldn't be made to prepare his speeches in advance, preferring to play cards instead. During his long illness, he began to read deeply and study public questions."

Frances Perkins saw him only once between 1921 and 1924, but was instantly struck by the change. He was crippled and physically weak, but he had a firmer grip on life than before. It wasn't a game anymore. He had become conscious of human frailty. Never again, she thought, would he be harsh in his judgment of the less fortunate and the less gifted, or even of wrongdoers. Now at last the "good Roosevelt," who could be so scornful of weakness in others, had learned that good and evil, hope and fear, wisdom and ignorance, selfishness and sacrifice, are inseparably mixed in human beings.

Once, when he was governor and she was his industrial commissioner, she was with him in Utica and realized that because of his immobility he had lost all traces of his youthful impatience and arrogance. In the State Senate he had cut off conversations and walked away when he wasn't interested. Now he could not walk away, he had to listen to the often inconsequential chatter of the Democratic rank and file. When they came with their tedious reports, he sat and nodded and smiled and said, "That's fine." He listened, and out of it he learned that everybody wanted a sense of belonging, of being on the inside, and that, as he would put it years later in a speech in Columbus, Ohio, "no one wants to be left out."

The heart of the matter, Miss Perkins believed, was pride going before a fall: "I would like to think that he would have done the things he did even without his paralysis, but knowing the streak of vanity and insincerity that there was in him, I don't think he would have unless somebody had dealt him a blow between the eyes. . . . An old priest whom I know once said to me, 'Well, you know, humility is the first and greatest of the virtues. If we

don't learn it of our own accord, the Lord will surely teach it to us by humiliation, because there's no other way to live.' . . . I think the personal adversity
that was torturing Roosevelt brought out this completely humane sympathy,
which he perhaps could never have even imagined otherwise."

Just before the 1932 convention, Adolph C. Miller, the economist who
had been a part of the little group of Washington friends that included
Franklin Lane and Bill Phillips, came to Hyde Park to see Roosevelt, whom
he found on the terrace having his hair cut. How would it go, Miller asked.
"You know as well as I do that our party is only a minority party," Roosevelt said, "and it's only as fate arranges it that we elect a President. That's
the way it was with Cleveland and that's the way it was with Wilson."

But what about his eligibility, Miller asked. "I suppose if I am nominated
I'll accept. But my heart is in Warm Springs. That's what I really care
about." Miller was astonished. He really meant what he said about the
higher value he placed on his work with the polio victims. He thought of the
self-centered young man he had first met in Lafayette Park in June 1913—
he had grown enormously in humanitarian impulses. It was as if he had
made a transaction with God, accepting misfortune in exchange for missing
qualities.

Roosevelt's transformation through debilitating illness was analogous to
the situation of the country. In the twelve years of Republican rule that just
about coincided with the period of his illness and attempted rehabilitation,
the country went from health and prosperity to illness and breakdown. His
predicament seemed to be a private expression of the state of the nation,
crippled by depression and unemployment, its motor cells destroyed.

Out of his pain came personal renewal, greater understanding, and surprising reserves of strength. Out of the nation's pain would also come renewal, and the making of a more compassionate society. The transformation
of America through economic collapse, and the transformation of Roosevelt
through illness, bear out Freud's remark about the superego, the division of
the psyche that absorbs the moral standards of the community: "The community, too, develops a superego, under whose influence cultural evolution
proceeds. The superego of any given epoch of civilization originates in the
same way as that of an individual; it is based on the impression left behind
them by great leading personalities, men of outstanding force of mind, or
men in whom some one human tendency has developed in unusual strength
and purity. . . . In many instances, the analogy goes even further, in that
during their lives—often enough, even if not always—such persons are ridiculed by others, ill-used or even cruelly done to death. . . . Ethics must be
regarded therefore as a therapeutic effect; as an endeavor to achieve something through the standards imposed by the superego which had not been
attained by the works of civilization in other ways."

Although polio transformed Roosevelt's character, he had a solid foundation to build on. He rarely gave in to the psychology of the invalid, trading
on helplessness to wheedle pity and favors, and becoming a nuisance to ev-

eryone. Rarely complaining, concealing his frustration, he remained as buoyant as the magnesium-laced waters of Warm Springs, where he went for rehabilitation. As Anna said, he "removed the sadness by showing us his legs. He gave us the names of each of the muscles, then told us which ones he was working hardest on at that moment." Rather than retreat into brooding and introspection, he became even more expansive—"an unconscious habit formed when he realized he could not make an excuse and leave people because he was sedentary; and it was, therefore, his responsibility to give them as good a time as possible while they were with him." It was also a defense against what he did not wish to hear, a personal filibuster. Many were those who had an appointment with President Roosevelt and found that they could not get a word in. For an immobile man, a mobile tongue was a form of protection.

In Hyde Park, Sara had a deaf maid named Fabienne Pellerin. Fabienne didn't mind hard work, although she wished her duties were more varied than dusting and mopping all the time. But nobody thought a deaf person had any intelligence. When Roosevelt arrived in his wheelchair she was amazed at how cheerful he was. Even she, deaf as she was, could hear his laughter ringing through the house. His high spirits gave her courage, for he knew what it was to be physically different from others.

Roosevelt never conquered polio, but he managed so well to conceal his disability that he gave the impression he had. Perfecting his movements to hide the true condition of his crippled limbs, adopting various stratagems for public appearances, giving his chin a confident tilt as he rode in big open cars, he conveyed to the public the image of a man in full control of his faculties. He received many letters that said "I admire you because you overcame a physical enemy" or something similar. His battle with polio gave him a heroic dimension.

One morning after breakfast, when he was visiting Roosevelt in Hyde Park in 1923, Adolph Miller joined him in the living room on the second floor. Sitting in a chair with two little tables flanking him, he was working on the hull of a model boat for a regatta on the Hudson. As Miller watched him at work, he was amazed at how skillfully he handled his tools and carried on a conversation at the same time. Suddenly, his cutting instrument slipped, ripping off the hull he was modeling. The pout of a frustrated child darkened his face for a moment, but a split second later he was beaming. "That's all right," he said, "I have a new idea. I always wanted to try a new experiment and I can do it now on this hull."

Miller would often think of that incident. It reminded him of what Tacitus had said about the Gauls: "Always studious of new things." Instead of accepting the destruction of his ship hull, he had used the mishap to improve the design.

XI

The Seven Lean Years

His very crutches have helped him to the stature of the Gods!
Jedediah Tingle

In the years following his illness, Roosevelt led a triple life. He spent much of his time in Warm Springs, a resort near Columbus, Georgia, that he bought in 1926 for the treatment of polio patients. He remained active in Democratic politics. And, by one of those ironies that enrich the lives of great men, he became a Wall Street businessman.

The surety bond business he had joined was a specialized form of insurance. Unions bonded their secretaries and treasurers. Banks, stock brokerage houses, construction firms, and city governments bonded employees who handled money. Bonds were also required on government and corporate contracts against the risk of noncompliance. Fidelity & Deposit was the fourth largest company engaged in this lucrative field. Why did Van-Lear Black hire a novice like Roosevelt as vice president of the important New York office? Because one surety bond company was very much like another, and getting the business depended on whom you knew. Political influence was a greater asset than insurance expertise. Roosevelt knew everyone in New York politics. He could call the mayor or the governor and his calls would be returned.

Appeals for sympathy were one way of drumming up business. On October 27, 1921, he wrote a prospect: "I had hardly become identified with the bonding business before my illness put me out of the game for some months to come, and, as you can easily imagine, it has been very hard to lie idle and do nothing to increase the company's business."

Unions were a special target because of friendships formed during the Navy years. Louis Howe got his friend, A. J. Berres, the secretary-treasurer of the Metal Trades Department of the AFL, to write his colleagues on Roosevelt's behalf. The Granite Cutters' International and the Boiler Makers promised to throw some business his way.

In the best "you scratch my back and I'll scratch yours" tradition, Roosevelt did a favor for Berres, writing Governor Al Smith in October 1924 to ask for a pardon for a patternmaker named Rheinhold Lippstein, in jail for robbery. The pardon was refused, but he continued to get union business because he was willing to put himself out.

To Brooklyn Congressman J. A. Maher he wrote on March 2, 1922: "I am going to take advantage of our old friendship and ask you if you can help me out any in an effort to get fidelity and contract bonds from the powers that be in Brooklyn. There are a large number of bonds needed in connection with the city government work, besides the personal bonds which every city official has to give, and I am in hopes that some of my old friends will be willing to remember me. . . . I assure you the favor will not soon be forgotten."* Thanks to Maher's help, he wrote a Brooklyn subway bond with a premium of $25,000 a year.

In doing business with city agencies, kickbacks were the order of the day, as John Griffin, in charge of the New York contract division, explained to Roosevelt on September 23, 1925, after Jimmy Walker had become mayor of New York: "The big victory of Walker over Hylan will of course make a new set-up in the bond broker situation. . . . As I see it, our strongest connection will be through Al Smith. . . . I know all these people pretty well and favorably, but mere personal friendship will not be sufficient."

By 1924, and presumably in part because of Roosevelt's contacts, Fidelity & Deposit had moved from fourth to third place among surety companies, showing a gain of nearly $4 million in business. He boasted to Van-Lear Black that "things in the office are going exceedingly well and we are really getting a lot of new business through my political connections."

Aside from Fidelity & Deposit, Roosevelt was always on the lookout for investments, preferring highly speculative and gimmicky ventures. Profits were uppermost in his mind, and he was quite prepared to make money from other people's misfortunes, such as land foreclosures. On March 21, 1921, he wrote Hall Roosevelt: "I met a man yesterday who made a killing in Louisiana in 1912 and 1913 by picking up sugar lands in the alluvial soil for from ten to fifteen dollars an acre. This, of course, was when sugar was down around four or five cents. He got out again when sugar came back during the war and made a good many hundred percent. He is now waiting for a chance to do the same thing. He believes that a couple of really bad years in sugar and in rice will throw a lot of fundamentally good land on the market at a sacrifice. Therefore it seems to me that you and I ought to keep in touch with things down there for we both believe that the land has possibilities, and some day we may be able to pick up something at a real bargain."

Those were days when new millionaires were being hatched every day. Between 1924 and 1927, the number of Americans who paid taxes on in-

---

* The favor was not forgotten. In 1937, when medical bills left Maher broke, FDR asked Frances Perkins to find him a job as a labor conciliator.

comes of more than $1 million grew from 75 to 283. Roosevelt was hungry to make a killing, but in scheme after scheme the pot of gold eluded him. He became part owner of a business that sold a coffee substitute from South America called "Yerba Mate." He tried to market Warm Springs water as a table water called "Cherokee." In another misguided venture, based on his conviction that the dirigible had a brighter future than the airplane, he organized a blimp service between New York and Chicago. This company needed German patents embargoed by the Navy, which he got thanks to his contacts, but the blimp was made obsolete by the passenger plane.

Some of his ventures came back to haunt him when he was president. The Sanitary Postal Service Company, based on the idea that the stamps in post offices were germridden, produced a machine with a crank that sold two two-cent stamps for a nickel. "Laboratory tests" confirmed that stamps were contaminated with disease-causing bacteria. Ads in drugstores said: "Scientific investigation has shown that the practice of selling loose stamps is unsanitary and is a menace to public health." By 1927, there were 18,000 sanitary postage machines in operation, and a year later the company merged into CAMCO, the Consolidated Automatic Merchandising Corporation, which aimed to replace salespeople and introduce the Age of the Robot.

CAMCO, with Roosevelt as a director, operated three clerkless stores in New York City. Their walls were lined with machines that said "Thank you" after every sale (because of complaints that they were too dehumanized) and dispensed razor blades and cigarettes and other articles. Every year the company lost money while predicting high earnings, because the machines took slugs and jammed. When the depression struck, CAMCO was attacked for causing "technological unemployment."

Roosevelt had chased unearned riches with the best of the "roaring twenties" speculators. He was a director of no less than three separate companies formed to speculate on the German mark, which had collapsed in the hyperinflation of 1922–23. Two of them never got off the ground because of legal problems, but United European Investors, which invested billions of German marks held by Americans in German companies, was a moderately successful venture. When the mark became valueless, the equity was sold at a profit and the American investors were saved from holding a worthless currency.

A less commercial venture was the American Construction Council, a trade association of the building industry, which had been investigated in 1920 in New York and found ridden with criminal practices—many contractors and labor leaders had been indicted and jailed. The ACC was a cosmetic to cover the industry's black eye, and Roosevelt was made president in June 1922. In this unsalaried role, he was the sworn enemy of government interference, saying "Government regulation is not feasible. It is unwieldy, expensive, it means employment of men to carry on this phase of the work; it means higher taxes. The public doesn't want it; the industry doesn't want it."

But after this brave stand, he went to Herbert Hoover, secretary of commerce in the Harding administration, and asked him to persuade several construction company leaders to cooperate with the ACC. Hoover replied on June 12, 1923: "I am somewhat in a quandary about your telegram of June 7. I had hoped that the Construction Council would be solely originated from the industries without pressure from the Administration. Otherwise it will soon take on the same opposition that all Governmental touches to this problem immediately accrue. The vast sentiment of the business community against Government interference tends to destroy even a voluntary effort if it is thought to be carried on at Government inspiration."

You had to be consistent. If you headed a council devoted to voluntary self-regulation, you couldn't ask the federal government for help. But the ACC never worked very well, and Roosevelt complained at a board of governors' meeting that "frankly, it has not done one darned thing except collect dues from some 115 different organizations, I think." Did they want to go on as before, "build all we can, paying any old price as long as we get the orders?" If that was the case, "we might as well adjourn." It sometimes seemed that the ACC's reason for being was to keep Roosevelt's name before the public.

In September 1924, his time taken up by rehabilitation and investments, he ended his law partnership with Grenville Emmet and Langdon Marvin. The reason he gave was that he could nct get up the stone steps of his office at 52 Wall Street. In fact, as he wrote Van-Lear Black, "their type of law business . . . is mostly estates, wills, etc., all of which bore me to death." Marvin and Emmet were probably glad to see him go, for according to Albert W. DeRoode, a junior partner in Roosevelt's previous firm, Marvin, Hooker, and Roosevelt, he was a poor lawyer. DeRoode, the Harvard classmate who had gotten the Eliot scoop that Roosevelt for years boasted was his, told Frances Perkins that "we can never make a lawyer out of Roosevelt. He hasn't got the right kind of mind. He comes to conclusions. He hasn't got the patience to work things out." In December, he formed another partnership with D. Basil "Doc" O'Connor, the son of a Massachusetts tinsmith, who had paid his way through Dartmouth by playing the violin in a band. Voted most likely to succeed, he had gone to Harvard Law School and opened a one-man New York firm that specialized in contracts between oil producers and refiners.

O'Connor became a trusted confidant and liaison man. On October 29, 1929, for instance, when Roosevelt was governor of New York, he asked Tammany boss John F. Curry to communicate with him via O'Connor "on subjects which had better not go through political circles!"

Roosevelt was looking for a way to get back into politics. He could not run himself, but he could be of assistance. He was a man in search of a bandwagon. In Al Smith, he found the one Democratic leader who could bring him back from oblivion. They had seen something of each other at the

1920 convention, when Smith was a favorite son and FDR was picked for vice president. There was mutual respect but little warmth.

Smith had run for governor in 1920 and was submerged in the Republican tide. In 1922, having gone into the trucking business, he was pretending that he was not a candidate. On August 13, shortly before the nomination papers had to be filed, Roosevelt wrote Smith a letter that was issued to the press: "I have been in touch with men and women voters from almost every up-state county and there is no question that the rank and file of Democrats want you to run. . . . We realize that years of public service make it most desirable that you think now for a while of your family's needs—I am in the same boat myself—yet this call to further service must come first." Two days later, Smith replied that even his family would be dissatisfied if he did not answer the call. When the convention nominated Smith, Eleanor, appearing as her husband's surrogate, led the Dutchess County delegation.

Thanks to Al Smith, Roosevelt was able to show that he could still take a leading role in New York State politics. He sent Eleanor on the campaign trail, and played the part of the admiring young disciple. In November, Smith was elected by a margin of 400,000 votes, and Roosevelt was restored as a factor in the Democratic party. Smith settled in for six years in the governor's mansion, with his trusted aide Belle Moskowitz as a more buxom version of Colonel House. In her dreams, she saw a wet Roman Catholic as chief executive of a dry Protestant country.

The country, however, was doing fine under Harding. After eight years on the thin air of Wilson idealism, everyone was breathing easier. "Return to normalcy" meant a return to normally functioning government, after the bizarre interregnum of Wilson's bedroom circle. Instead of a sick and resentful recluse, the country had a gregarious president who enjoyed the ceremonial aspects of the office. In counterpoint to his predecessor, he did not demand sacrifices or make an enemy of Congress. Things almost seemed to be running themselves.

A deliberate pursuit of policies favorable to business interests—tax cuts for the rich, antilabor decisions from the Supreme Court—created a climate where the spoils system became acceptable. Under Harding, there blossomed a fill-your-pockets kind of laissez-faire.

How could Harding have known, when he stepped aboard the presidential car *Superb* on June 20, 1923, for a transcontinental journey that would take him as far as Alaska, that he would return to Washington in a flag-draped box, lie for a few hours in the East Room of the White House, for a few hours in the rotunda of the Capitol, and then be turned over to the hanging judge of history? Harding wasn't so bad. He had governed two and a half years, suiting the national mood, at a time of peace and prosperity. His vices were those of conviviality—poker, golf, tobacco, drink, women, and trusting his friends.

Calvin Coolidge, the hatchet-faced Vermonter who derived his philosophy from McGuffey's *Reader,* took office, showing once more the importance of accident in American politics. He had made a national reputation as governor of Massachusetts during the Boston police strike with one remark: "There is no right to strike against the public safety by anybody, anywhere, anytime."

On August 20, Roosevelt wrote his friend and fellow paralytic, Abram I. Elkus: "I cannot help feeling that Harding's unfortunate taking off has helped rather than hurt the Republican Party. Coolidge, as you know, is not a world beater, but in his past career he has been clever enough to take advantage of situations after the other fellow has done all the work—witness the Boston Police Strike, where Andrew Peters [mayor of Boston and a good friend of Roosevelt's] practically settled things before Coolidge made any move. It looks now to me as if he would be nominated next year."

Democratic prospects seemed brighter, however, at the start of 1924, with the revelation of the Harding scandals. The secretary of the interior, Albert B. Fall, had secretly leased government oil lands to private companies that gave him payoffs—those same lands that Josephus Daniels had so jealously guarded when they had been under the Navy's jurisdiction.

But corruption is bipartisan, and one of the Democratic front-runners, William Gibbs McAdoo, was splashed with some of the Teapot Dome oil. He had served as legal counsel, at a $25,000-a-year retainer, for one of the oilmen who had leased government land, the California multimillionaire Edward L. Doheny. McAdoo was also unacceptable because he had the backing of the Ku Klux Klan.

Al Smith was not tainted by Teapot Dome. "There ain't no oil on Al," his supporters said. On the other hand, there was the smell of whiskey, four to eight highballs a day, some said. The Anti-Saloon League was aligned with the Protestant churches against any wet candidate, and a drinker's reputation cost votes.

With rum went Romanism, and objections to Smith's Catholicism started crossing Roosevelt's desk. To one he replied: "After all, it is not a man's religious belief but how much that religious belief influences his official acts that counts, isn't it? For instance, there are many tenets of the Swedenborgen [sic] faith to which I am unalterably and violently opposed, but, frankly, I would not think of voting against a Swedenborgen unless I felt that if elected he would make some of those principles his guiding star in matters of government and legislation."

Others objected to Al because of his Tammany affiliation and his obese, vulgar wife. "How can you abuse your mind with the idea that Tammany Al is the man for the Democratic nomination?" one of Roosevelt's anti-Smith letters asked. "Why, my dear sir, do you not realize that he is not presidential timber? . . . What sort of a First Lady do you think the consort of Oliver Street Al would be?"

His mail told Roosevelt that Smith didn't stand a chance. He was an Irish Catholic immigrant's son whose career had been sponsored by Tammany and who was the recognized leader of the anti-Prohibition forces. He was a stalking-horse for the wet city bosses. His New York parochialism, as when he had said that he would rather be a lamppost on Park Row than governor of California, would work against him. How could he speak with authority on national issues, on the soldiers' bonus, on the Mellon tax politics, on farm relief? On the other hand, three New York governors—Martin Van Buren, Grover Cleveland, and Theodore Roosevelt—had vaulted to the presidency and, with the convention being held in New York City, Tammany might be able to stampede it.

In mid-April, back in his New York town house after a winter in Florida, Roosevelt received a visit from his old enemy, Charles F. Murphy, who was affable, even deferential, for he wanted help in rounding up delegates for Smith. "I remember telling C.F. (with his complete agreement)," Roosevelt later recalled, "that with hard work and good luck we might be able to get 300 delegates in the National Convention for Al, but that in all probability we could not nominate him; that, however, it would be a good thing to do and we might be able to get him the nomination in 1928."

With the convention coming up in June, someone had to take charge of the Citizens' Committee for Smith, someone who was not wet, not Catholic, not connected with Tammany, someone who could serve as liaison to the rural-dry-Protestant wing of the party. Belle Moskowitz and Joseph Proskauer, who had ably managed Smith's 1922 campaign and was now a State Supreme Court justice, asked Roosevelt to take the job. By running the Smith campaign, he could share the limelight and reemerge as a national figure in the party. But his physical condition would severely restrict his mobility. That didn't matter, Moskowitz and Proskauer told him, they would do the work—they saw Roosevelt mainly as an eye-catching piece of window dressing. Proskauer thought he was untested. He had a way of sitting back and smoking that long cigarette of his and believing profoundly that he could smile anybody into his hands.

Roosevelt learned that selling Smith outside the Northeast wasn't easy. The Democratic party was polarized between urban and rural, wets and drys, Catholics and Protestants. So he formed committees and wrote letters. "Your life beginning as it did in humble surroundings and your long, steady upward climb to the splendid success you have attained in baseball leads me to think that the record and achievement of Governor Alfred E. Smith must strike a responsive chord in your heart," he wrote to Babe Ruth on May 9. Ruth replied: "Sure, I'm for Al Smith. There is one thing about your letter, Mr. Roosevelt, that went across with me good and strong—that was the take about the humble beginning of Governor Smith. Maybe you know I wasn't fed with a gold spoon when I was a kid. No poor boy can go any too high in this world to suit me."

The convention was opening on June 24, and no one had been picked to place Smith in nomination. Bourke Cockran, Tammany's silver-tongued orator, who had spoken for Smith in 1920, was dead. One day in June, Al Smith asked Judge Proskauer who should be given the job. "Frank Roosevelt," Proskauer said. "For God's sake, why?" Smith asked. "Because you're a Bowery mick and he's a Protestant patrician and he'd take some of the curse off you." They went to see him in his office across from the Biltmore Hotel. "Joe and I have been talking this over and I've come here to ask you to make the nominating speech," Smith said.

"Oh, Al, I'd love to do it, but I'm so busy here working with delegates I have no time to write a speech," Roosevelt said. "Joe, will you write a speech for me?"

He didn't know it, but Proskauer had already written a speech, which ended with Wordsworth's lines:

> "This is the Happy Warrior; this is he
> Whom every man in arms should wish to be."

Roosevelt didn't like Proskauer's draft and wrote his own over the weekend in Hyde Park. When he saw Proskauer again, he said: "Joe, I can't make that speech. It's too poetic. You can't get across Wordsworth's poem to a gang of degenerates. I wrote another speech," handing him the draft.

"Frank," Proskauer said, "there's no use you and me debating the merits of our brainchildren. Let's get somebody who has good publicity sense and he can tell us which is better. . . . I'm thinking of someone like Herbert Swope" (then managing editor of the *World*).

Swope was a friend of Roosevelt's. They exchanged humorous letters. "What could be better?" he asked. That evening they met at the Roosevelt house (one advantage of his disability was that people had to come to him). Swope read the Roosevelt draft and said, "This speech is lousy." Then he read Proskauer's and said, "This is the greatest nominating speech since Cleveland was nominated by Bryan. This is historic." Roosevelt kept arguing. Around midnight, Proskauer said, "Frank, the time has come for a showdown. I wrote this 'Happy Warrior' speech for Smith and its purpose is right. I have just enough authority to tell you that you're either going to make that speech or you're not going to make any." "All right," Roosevelt said. "I'll make the goddamned speech and it'll be a flop."

On June 24, delegates showed tickets that were like miniature dollar bills, with Jefferson's picture and "1924" in the upper left- and right-hand corners, at the doors of Madison Square Garden, a red-brick structure built by Stanford White on the block bounded by 26th and 27th streets and Madison and Fourth avenues. The circus had just moved out, and it had taken seven tons of chemicals to get rid of the animal smells. The circus atmosphere continued, with the bands and the songs, and the "Mc'll Do" hatbands, and the gallery taunts of "Ku Ku McAdoo." Because of the two-thirds rule, which Roosevelt in this case supported, for it could block a fast start, 732 votes were required, but there were twice that many delegates because some of them shared votes.

Roosevelt sat with the New York delegation on the crowded floor. Determined not to be wheeled in, he had his sixteen-year-old son Jimmy help him get in early, on crutches, before the floor got clogged. As he held his father's arm, matching his stride to his father's ponderous gait, Jimmy thought of San Francisco and Pa jumping up and grabbing the state standard. Now, just getting into his seat was an ordeal. Jimmy supported him and took his crutches as he lowered himself slowly into place, his legs stiffly extended until the knee joints of the braces were unlocked. Only then could he bend his legs and adjust his sitting position. When he wanted to stand, he had to lock them again.

On June 26, Roosevelt made his first political speech since being stricken. This was the start of his comeback, when he showed that a cripple could take an active part in a national convention. Leaning on his son's arm, he made his way to the rear of the speaker's platform. He appeared smiling and unconcerned, but Jimmy knew that the sweat on his brow was due to more than the heat, and could feel his fingers digging into his arm like pincers.

Then came the moment when he had to walk alone. Releasing Jimmy's arm, he took the second crutch and moved across the stage, the crowd almost holding its breath as it watched. Putting aside his crutches, he grabbed the lectern, threw back his head and smiled into the spotlight's glare.

Here was a man of American ancestry older than the nation itself, a man with a background of Cambridge Square, bearing a famous name, who had dragged his crippled body into the steaming convention hall to make a bid for a second-generation American born and bred in the East Side slums— surely this was what the framers of the Constitution had had in mind. He spoke for thirty-four minutes, and when he concluded with the Wordsworth lines, at 12:33 A.M., there was a pitch of excitement the convention would not reach again. For forty minutes, state delegations marched and cheered and sang "The Sidewalks of New York."

Roosevelt emerged as the hero of an otherwise pathetic gathering. He was the one figure who could be admired without reservation. In little more than half an hour, he had done more to enhance his national reputation than in seven years in the Navy, awakening the Democratic party to his availability for high office and his inherent appeal. Tom Pendergast, the skeptical boss of the Kansas City machine, told a supporter: "You know I am seldom carried away . . . but I want to tell you that had Mr. Roosevelt . . . been physically able to have withstood the campaign, he would have been named by acclamation in the first few days of the Convention. He has the most magnetic personality of any individual I have ever met, and I predict he will be the candidate on the Democratic ticket in 1928."

The lesson for Roosevelt was that his political future did not depend on walking again. Indeed, his condition could be turned into an advantage. Because he could not walk, his public appearances were small dramas. Would he make it? How courageous he was!

Jedediah Tingle, the pseudonym of a New York banker who liked to reward good deeds with cash gifts, wrote him that "when I listened to your scholarly measured words at Madison Square Garden, your character took on a new glory—the glory that can only come through the soul's conquest of pain and mental suffering, and I said—'His very crutches have helped him to the stature of the Gods.' ... That day's work established you in the respect, admiration and affection of all America."

The only dissenting voice amid the acclaim was that of the man who had written the nominating speech, who was annoyed that Roosevelt routinely claimed that Proskauer's only contribution had been the "happy warrior" phrase. Proskauer saw him as shallow and tricky, with a genius for self-deception.

The convention was deadlocked. On the thirty-eighth ballot it voted 444 for McAdoo to 321 for Smith. The days grew hotter, and the delegates were concerned about spending July 4 in the Garden. Some of them turned over their badges to their alternates and went home. Roosevelt's state of mind can be judged from an angry letter he wrote McAdoo on July 4, after the sixty-fourth ballot, but never sent: "I have no idea of how many days or weeks or months you intend to hold us in futile session by refusing to release unwilling votes. ... It is incredible that you would be willing to ruin your party by any such dog-in-the-manger tactics." Roosevelt saw McAdoo as a tool of the Klan, which was seeking through him to capture the nomination, as it had captured the Republican primaries in Indiana and nominated its man for governor.

At the same time, he had second thoughts about Al Smith. One day the Kansas delegates came to see Roosevelt. They were stocky, round-faced men with square-toed shoes, who looked like farmers. Roosevelt sent word out to get Al, who had been to an Irish wedding, and came in with a shiny silk hat on the corner of his head, and spats and a cane and a flower in his buttonhole, talking in his broadest "Irishese." "Hello boys," he said, shaking hands. "Glad to see you. Y'know, the other day some boys were in from Wisconsin and I learned somethin'. I always thought Wisconsin was on this side of the lake. It's on the other side. Glad to know more about the place where the good beer comes from." Roosevelt winced, Kanses being a strong Prohibition state. He watched the Kansas boys freeze up and kissed Kansas good-bye right then and there.

Finally Smith and McAdoo released their delegates and there was a movement toward John W. Davis, who won with 844 votes on the 103rd ballot. Davis chose William Jennings Bryan's lackluster brother, Charles, as his running mate. As Arthur Krock put it: "When the debris began to fall, somebody looked underneath the pile and dragged out John W. Davis, who then showed that he was not in his right mind by extricating Charles W. Bryan ... and, with the bland smile of a Chinese angel, went forth among the electorate for incredible slaughter."

Davis was a textbook example of party disunity leading to the selection of a mediocre and inappropriate candidate. Born in West Virginia, he was a lawyer who had served as congressman and as solicitor general before being sent to London as ambassador. The English admired his propriety and reserve.

Returning to the law, he joined the firm of Stetson, Jennings, and Russell, who served as counsel to J. P. Morgan & Co. His firm numbered more than a dozen of the country's largest corporations among its clients, and he was a director of several. He once argued before the U.S. Supreme Court that a Pennsylvania law to protect small property owners from cave-ins beneath their homes deprived mineowners who held the subsurface rights of due process. His views opposed to welfare and supporting reduced taxes in the upper brackets would have found a warmer welcome in the rival party. William Jennings Bryan said there was no difference between Davis and Coolidge, and pointed out that only the nomination of a progressive could prevent Robert M. La Follette's third party from drawing more votes from the Democrats than the Republicans.

Davis was doomed and knew it, long before the aura of granitelike integrity had settled on Coolidge. The returns in November gave him 8,385,586 votes to 15,725,016 for Coolidge and 4,822,856 for La Follette. Even adding the third-party vote, Davis would have lost.

"There is something wrong with the Democratic Party," Charles McCarthy wrote Roosevelt on December 2. "It needs a dose of salts, even an emetic at the same time and then the so-called Bosses will be on the shelf and there will be no more trading."

There was more to it than the party's failure, as Roosevelt, who had taken little part in the campaign, explained on December 9 to Willard Saulsbury, a Wilmington lawyer: "In 1920, after the poke we got that year, I remarked to a number of my friends that I did not think the nation would elect a Democrat again until the Republicans had led us into a serious period of depression and unemployment. I still think that forecast holds true, for much as we Democrats may be the party of honesty and progress, the people will not turn out the Republicans while wages are good and the markets are booming. Every war brings after it a period of materialism and conservatism; people tire quickly of ideals and are but now repeating history."

This feeling was echoed by E. T. Meredith, who wrote Roosevelt from Des Moines, Iowa: "We had, of course, one tremendous handicap from the start and that is the characteristic of the American people so long as they are reasonably comfortable and prosperous to let well enough alone and vote for the party in power."

To which Roosevelt replied that there was another factor: "It is hopeless for the Democrats to try and wear the livery of the conservative."

Water, Roosevelt was fond of saying, had gotten him into this mess, and water would get him out. He believed in its curative powers. The warmth and good fishing in Florida at first attracted him, and after his first stay aboard the *Weona II* in 1923, he returned for winter cruises the next three years. With John S. Lawrence, the son of the Lawrences who had recommended Groton to his father, who now ran a dry goods commission house in Boston and was also crippled in the legs, he bought a houseboat for $3,750, which they called the *Larooco,* reflecting their partnership.

He called it "the floating tenement," and spent lazy days fishing in the bayous of the Ten Thousand Islands, with Missy LeHand, Livy Davis, and an ornithologist friend from Rhinebeck, Maunsell Crosby. With his wrestler's torso, Roosevelt could land any fish he hooked, while Crosby spotted ninety-eight varieties of birds. In the afternoon they played bridge or "Ma and Pa Cheesy." Roosevelt ate hearty fish chowders and indulged his penchant for puns such as "Birthington's Washday." On February 5, 1924, they saw flags at half-mast. Woodrow Wilson had died two days before. They would keep their own ensign at half-mast for thirty days.

Roosevelt, who had no false modesty about showing his wasted legs, was prudish about other matters, and berated Livy Davis in the log for his lack of propriety: "L.D. went to the R.R. bridge to fish and came back minus his trousers—to the disgust of the two ladies. Earlier he had exercised on the top deck à la nature. Why do people who *must* take off their clothes go anywhere where the other sex is present? Capt. Morris remarked that some men got shot for less."

Roosevelt wrote Lawrence that "poor old Livy was with me for over two weeks. I think there is something seriously the matter with him. He was upset the whole time—magnified everything, got in wrong with everybody and got everybody in wrong with everybody else."

In 1926, he was back for his third and final cruise. In mid-February Oswald and Cynthia Mosley came aboard for four days (she was the daughter of the British statesman Lord Curzon, who had a Polish border line named after him; he would gain notoriety as the leader of the British Union of Fascists). Roosevelt thought they were a delightful couple. Mosley shot a seventy-nine-pound hammerhead shark after it had been hooked. On March 16, Elliott arrived, looking pale. He admired his father's absolute lack of embarrassment about his condition, and observed the open affection he showed Missy LeHand. In the main stateroom, Franklin sat in a wicker chair with Missy on his lap, embracing her in his sun-browned arms. He had a right, Elliott felt, to the love and physical affection that Eleanor denied him.

Roosevelt decided that Florida was not the right place for rehabilitation. The sharks made it impossible to swim in deep water, and the sand beaches were few and far between. After the 1924 convention, he heard from a wealthy friend, George Foster Peabody, who had an interest in a run-down resort in Georgia known for its beneficial springs. A young polio victim named Louis Joseph had taught himself to use his legs in the water and found that he could walk on dry land. It may have sounded like Lourdes, but Roosevelt was ready for a miracle and went down there that October and stayed six weeks.

There was a forty-six-room hotel called the Meriwether Inn, fifteen cabins, and the warm-water pool. The only people there were Tom Loyless, a newspaperman down on his luck who ran the place, his wife, and old Mr. Watts, the mailman who read everybody's postcards. Roosevelt moved into a cottage and started spending hours each day in the pool. Soon he was able to move his right leg for the first time in three years.

He had been there two weeks when a reporter from the Atlanta *Journal* turned up. The article led to inquiries, and when he returned to Warm Springs in April 1925 six polio victims were there for the cure. The manager in Roosevelt emerged, and he took charge of their exercise program. After all, he was an expert on polio, having had it for almost four years. The patients called him "Dr. Roosevelt," and morale was good. Males and females of all ages and weights did their exercises under his leadership. It felt good to be in command of something again, even if it was only half a dozen cripples. Pleased with himself, he wrote Livy Davis on April 25, 1925: "I sometimes wish I could find some spot on the globe where it was not essential and necessary for me to start something new—a sand bar in the ocean might answer, but I would probably start building a sea wall around it and digging for pirate treasure in the middle."

Tom Loyless was improving the place, but Roosevelt told him he looked run-down and ought to take a rest. He would look after the road work for him; he was "a shark" at road building.

Loyless wrote a column for the Macon *Daily Telegraph*. "Do my stuff on the *Telegraph* for a few days," he said, "and heaven, as well as I and the general public, will bless you."

The first of nine "Roosevelt Says" columns came out on April 16. The columns were bland and mildly reformist, like the stuff he had written for the *Crimson*. Roosevelt was for civil service reform and reforestation. One column, on immigration, revealed his suspicion of the ethnic masses that had poured into the country in the last half century: "Taking it by and large, I agree that for a good many years to come, European immigration should remain greatly restricted. We have, unfortunately, a great many thousand foreigners who got in here and who must be digested. For fifty years the United States ate a meal altogether too large—much of the food was digestible, but some of it was almost poisonous. The United States must, for a short time at least, stop eating."

Heading the list of toxic immigrants were the Japanese, as he explained in another column of April 30, which gives added relevance to his World War II decision to intern thousands of Japanese-Americans. Clearly, Roosevelt did not consider them true Americans, and had a deep-rooted racist view of Orientals: "It is undoubtedly true," he wrote, "that in the past many thousands of Japanese have legally or otherwise got into the United States, settled here and raised children who became American citizens. Californians have properly objected on the sound basic ground that Japanese immigrants are not capable of assimilation into the American population. . . . Anyone who has traveled in the Far East knows that the mingling of Asiatic blood with European or American blood produces, in nine cases out of ten, the most unfortunate results. Eurasians—men and women and children partly of Asiatic blood and partly of European or American blood. These Eurasians are, as a common thing, looked down on and despised, both by the Europeans and Americans who reside there, and by the pure Asiatic who lives there. . . . In this question, then, of Japanese exclusion from the United States, it is necessary only to advance the true reason—the undesirability of mixing the blood of the two peoples."

Roosevelt continued to believe that he would walk again, and wrote Al Smith on May 7: "The old legs are improving a lot. If I could only drop my business and stay here for a whole year, I am convinced that I would be able to get around without crutches."

Returning to Warm Springs at the end of March 1926, Roosevelt found that Tom Loyless had died of cancer. Feeling a strong commitment to the place and to the thirty-odd "parals" who were there seeking treatment, he decided to buy it. To own a center for rehabilitation and help other polio victims gave him the sense that he had some measure of control over his condition, even though in fact there was no dramatic improvement. George Foster Peabody, who had an option to buy Warm Springs at $100,000, sold it to Roosevelt for twice that. Known as a philanthropist, he wasn't doing his old friend any favors. Doc O'Connor, who handled the deal, commented: "Something tells me he's doing all right." Roosevelt bought Warm Springs for $201,667.83 on April 29.

In lieu of political office, Warm Springs gave him a mission. He brought in the cherubic Leroy W. Hubbard, an orthopedic surgeon, and the forceful Helen Mahoney and her corps of "physios." He built a second pool, raised funds, and responded to inquiries. "Our rate," he wrote Paul Hasbrouck of Poughkeepsie, "as Dr. Hubbard has probably told you, is $42 a week, this including board, lodging, medical and therapeutic treatment, pool charges, etc.—in fact, everything except your traveling expenses and cigarette money."

In 1927, Roosevelt formed the Georgia Warm Springs Foundation. He asked his wealthy friends for contributions, and got $25,000 from Edsel Ford. The foundation was a success, and Roosevelt was justified in thinking that he knew more about polio than any other layman and than many doctors, writing his mother on November 19, 1927, that "we have so many cases here that come to us from the so-called leading doctors where the treatment has been *criminal* and left permanently bad results that could with knowledge have been avoided. We don't, of course, take any cases till all soreness is gone, but we know from the history of dozens of cases what awful mistakes are made."

He was an example to the others, always cheerful, never visibly irritated, sensitive to the needs of the patients. The small community in western Georgia formed an odd subculture, with its paralyzed citizens trying to lead lives as normal as possible. There were picnics at Flat Shoals, past some of the finest peach orchards in Georgia, and trips to Manchester, a cotton-mill town of 5,000, and softball games between the polios, most of them in wheelchairs, and the physios, who played on crutches with their ankles tied. There was a newspaper, the *Polio Chronicle,* with a cartoon character called the Old Paral. "Do you take them off when you go to bed?" someone asks the Old Paral, pointing at his braces. "There are a lot of cases of polio between the ears," the Old Paral replies.

There were, of course, limits to FDR's concern. Warm Springs was segregated. In 1936, Walter White of the NAACP complained that black polio patients were not admitted. Although they contributed to the foundation through attending the president's charity birthday balls, they were barred from treatment. Eleanor wrote a memo for her husband: "They should have a cottage. What is the answer?" Missy LeHand replied that the answer was separate facilities in some other location. FDR asked Doc O'Connor, "Will you let me know what chance there is of having a cottage for negroes at Warm Springs?" No chance at all, so long as he needed the support of southern committee chairmen for the passage of New Deal legislation. It was a different world then. His Warm Springs property tax return was labeled "White Taxpayer" in big letters at the top of the page.

Roosevelt realized the linkage with Al Smith was the key to his political future, but it was a marriage of convenience. Smith still thought of him as a lightweight with no practical knowledge of politics, who was useful because of his name and his contacts. Although increasingly drawn to big money, Smith still acted like a man of the people. He liked to have a glass in his hand and make picturesque remarks—bureaucratic jargon was referred to as baskets of doorknobs or fur coats for elephants.

Roosevelt also had misgivings about Smith, and Louis Howe openly ridiculed both Al and his portly wife, writing on April 15, 1925: "Mrs. Smith is back from Europe and complains to your 'Missus' that there were too many ruins in Rome. She is talking too much for Al's good, describing with much gusto and detail their special audience with the Pope and how he referred to Al as his son and the great knowledge he showed in the political campaign. One of her stories is particularly delicious. She says that the Pope turned to McCooey, was was with them, and said, 'I know you have worked for my beloved son, Governor Smith, but next time you must work even harder.' She also is announcing she brought back a photograph of the Pope, personally inscribed 'To my beloved son, Alfred E. Smith.' Can you imagine the joy amongst the ranks of the Ku Klux Klan if she ever repeats this where it will come to their ears, and from what your 'Missus' says I judge she is spreading it just as fast as she can see her old friends."

But it was important for Roosevelt to stay in Smith's good graces, and he regularly sent him friendly little notes, such as this one on April 7, 1925: "Some time I hope to have a chance to see you and let you know what is going on in the national situation. If McAdoo's fool friends will only continue their idiotic policy of perpetually pressing his claims as a candidate for 1928, he will be entirely and automatically eliminated very soon."

He still saw Smith as the only hope for the Democrats in the 1928 national election, and wrote his union friend, A. J. Berres, on November 22, 1927: "We Democrats have no chance of electing a president unless the nominee be Smith. We may go through the empty gesture of nominating another respectable person who will be defeated by a large majority. On the other hand if Smith is nominated and actually gets into the campaign he stands some chance of the election—in other words, he can carry possibly most of the Eastern states and will get a big vote in nearly all the larger cities. Personally I think the South will hold its nose and vote for him. . . . Don't worry about McAdoo. He is through as far as being a serious candidate."

Grateful for any crumb from Smith's table, Roosevelt had accepted in 1925, in return for services rendered during the convention, the chairmanship of the Taconic State Park Commission, which was laying out a parkway running north from Westchester County through the three counties of Roosevelt's old senate district, Putnam, Dutchess, and Columbia, and eventually connecting with the Berkshire extension of the Massachusetts Turnpike.

In this unpaid job, which placed him under the authority of the president of the New York State Council of Parks, Robert Moses, Roosevelt formed one of the lasting enmities of his life. There were few men he hated more tenaciously than Bob Moses, the difficult, arrogant head of the state parks system, who in his brief career in state government had already acquired a reputation for needlessly offending his colleagues. Moses was a new breed of public official. He hated politics, logrolling, and patronage. He wouldn't give jobs to deserving party men. He exercised power behind the scenes, with inhuman efficiency, and learned that he could get things done as long as he let the elected officials take the credit.

Their first collision was over Louis Howe, already known in Al Smith's circles as "lousy Louie," whom Roosevelt wanted to appoint as secretary of the Taconic Commission at $5,000 a year. According to Moses, Howe ambled into his office one day and tossed a blank Taconic progress chart on the desk of Henry F. Lutz, the overworked executive director of the State Council of Parks, and told him: "I'll have a look at the record every month or so because I've got more important things to do for Mr. Roosevelt." Moses told Howe that if that was his attitude his services would not be needed. Roosevelt asked to see Moses and said, "I want Howe employed." "You can, as regional chairman, employ Howe," Moses responded, "but when the next budget comes around I'll throw him off if he isn't going to work."

Howe did in fact work for the commission for three months, starting in September 1926, and was then dismissed. Roosevelt tried to get Al Smith to intervene on Howe's behalf, but Al wrote him that "the man you employed did not give full time service and I believe there has been considerable objection on other grounds."

Moses felt that Howe never forgave him for separating him from a state park sinecure, and found devious ways of communicating his grudge to his chief. But Roosevelt did not need any help from Louis to hate Moses. He had enough reasons of his own. The Taconic Commission, the first government job he had been given since 1920, meant a lot. He saw the parkway as another example of public good versus private greed.

But in his efforts to get the parkway moving, he was frustrated by Moses at every turn. In the allocation of funds, Moses naturally gave priority to projects closer to New York City, where the population was concentrated. To Roosevelt this was one more chapter in the continuing battle between the corrupt city and the virtuous but deprived upstaters. In October 1925, submitting his budget request for 1926, he asked for $300,000 for surveying and land acquisition. Moses offered $175,000. In addition, Moses did not think Roosevelt was doing a good job. He was always in Warm Springs or Florida.

That November, when Roosevelt submitted his budget request for 1927, asking for funds for engineering plans, for right-of-way surveys, and for staff salaries, he was awarded the paltry sum of $15,000 for the maintenance of existing parks, on the grounds that he had not spent all the money allocated the previous year. After a stormy confrontation with Moses, he went over his head to Smith, writing the governor on December 3: "It is an absurd and humiliating position to be put in, to be informed that we could have no money because through lack of an Executive we have not been able to properly expend the money we had and then to be informed that we cannot have an Executive because we have not been given more money." But the governor backed Moses on park matters.

Roosevelt was sure that Moses was acting from personal spite, and wrote Alexander MacDonald of the Conservation Commission on February 3, 1927: "I am quite certain that somebody has been deliberately misrepresenting and balling up the purpose and work of the Taconic State Park Commission." That November, he was humiliated once again, when all his fund requests were cut except those for maintenance. Furious, he wrote Smith on December 14: "I know all about the need of cutting appropriations. Try just for once making the cut on somebody else—I decline the honor." When he threatened to resign unless the cuts were restored, Smith replied sternly on January 23, 1928: "I do not believe that our park allocations should be made on the basis of regional logrolling. Money ought to be put where it is most needed." There was a priority for Long Island, which took care of the recreational needs of the city and had so much shorefront and salt water.

In a reply to Smith on January 30, Roosevelt accused Moses of sabotaging his work: "When all is said and done, I wasn't born yesterday! You see I have been in the game so long that I now realize the mistake I made with this Taconic State Park Commission was in not playing the kind of politics that our friend Bob Moses has used. I am sorry to say it is a fact that Bob Moses has played fast and loose with the Taconic State Park Commission since the beginning. . . . You know, just as well as I do, that Bob has skinned us alive this year—has worked things so beautifully that his baby on Long Island is plentifully taken care of and that *all* the other Park Commissions, upstate, except ours, are getting practically what was approved by the State Council of Parks. When the State Council of Parks approved appropriations to the Taconic State Park Commission of nearly $200,000 Bob knew perfectly well that it would not go through and had his tongue in his cheek when he tried to tell us that he was trying to get it through."

Roosevelt's anger was powerless against the combined wills of Al Smith and Bob Moses. He could have built a beautiful scenic highway that would have relieved the congestion on the Albany Post Road, but the dirty politics of Bob Moses, a New York City Jew, had him stymied. Moses had won the first round, but there would be others. Roosevelt was willing to wait. Vengeance, as someone said, is a dish best eaten cold.

During the years when Roosevelt concentrated on physical recovery, Eleanor went her own way, slowly emerging from her husband's shadow, with her circle of friends and activities. Amended by the Lucy Mercer affair, their marriage had become a limited partnership, with long separations. The possessiveness that Eleanor had displayed in the early years was now a benign tolerance. Missy LeHand was in attendance, and that was fine with her, for she was relieved of the nursemaid role. It was Missy who stayed with Roosevelt in Warm Springs, a place that Eleanor did not take to. She did not like the racist society, the poverty, or the slow and slovenly southern style, and wrote her friend Marion Dickerman: "I think what I hate down here is the untidiness and the pressure all about one, the hotel, cottages, woods, porch, everything untidy and everyone apparently oblivious to the cans and dirt!"

Marion Dickerman, a tall and solemn schoolteacher, lived with Nancy Cook, who had grown up on a cattle farm in upstate New York. Nancy Cook's curly hair was cropped, she wore mannish suits and flat shoes, and had a deep voice. Nancy and Marion had met at Syracuse University, sharing a passion for social reform. Marion ran for the State Assembly in Oswego and lost. She went to see Al Smith, who told her to be sure and report her campaign funds, except for the yellow dog fund. What was that, she asked. "Oh, that's what's paid for votes," Al replied.

Nancy Cook became active in the women's division of the Democratic State Committee, and invited Eleanor to speak at a lunch. Soon, the three were inseparable. There were professions of love. "Darling," Eleanor wrote Nancy Cook on August 14, 1925, "don't be unhappy because you've grown to care for me. I have the power of disassociating myself from things, because I've had to do it so often, and I'm not unhappy that way, you should cultivate it, you won't be happy but you won't be unhappy."

As her son Elliott put it, Eleanor "had a sort of compulsion to associate with fellow sufferers in frustration, women like herself who had found it impossible to get along with the opposite sex. . . . Her sensibilities were not tuned to sexual attraction of any kind, whether it existed between a man and a woman or between members of the same sex. On the strength of their appearance and knowledge of their living patterns, I suspected that some of the women, all dead now, who flattered my unwitting mother with their attention were active lesbians."

According to Dorothy Schiff, who saw Nancy Cook often in the thirties, "Nancy was an obvious lesbian who told me, 'I've only liked two men in my life and one is F.D.R. and the other is your husband.' " (Mrs. Schiff was then married to a man-about-town, George Backer.)

Another lesbian couple that Eleanor grew close to was Elizabeth F. Read, who became her personal lawyer, and Esther Lape, a teacher who was active in the League of Women Voters. While in Paris, Esther Lape sent Eleanor a copy of André Gide's *Les Faux-Monnayeurs,* the story of a homosexual relationship, which she thought of as a sensitive treatment of a delicate subject. Eleanor was shocked, Esther Lape later told Joseph Lash. "She couldn't even bring herself to consider homosexuality. Generally, her reaction was not so final, but in this case it was."

Eleanor was too naive to see that side of what Elliott called "the she-men," and was overjoyed to have found friends who appreciated her and sought her out, to whom she could confide her private thoughts and her sense of inadequacy. Marion and Nancy also provided an escape from her mother-in-law's criticism. Eleanor was fed up with Sara and her little snide slaps, and wrote her husband on August 4, 1925: "I wish you could read Mama's last letter to me. She is afraid of everything in it! Afraid of your going over bad and infrequented roads, afraid I'll let the children dive in the shallow water and break their necks, afraid they'll get more cuts! She must suffer more than we dream is possible!"

With his usual geniality, Roosevelt welcomed Marion and Nancy into his extended family. He was genuinely fond of them, and made it possible for Eleanor to build a cottage where she and her friends could have the privacy that was lacking in Hyde Park. The cottage went up on Sara's property, across the Albany Post Road, beside the Val-Kill brook. Roosevelt also encouraged Nancy Cook's plan (she had taught woodworking) to produce copies of American antiques, which they would sell to department stores. The Val-Kill cottage would have a cottage industry!

As Eleanor went her way, the chicks also began leaving the nest, sometimes with relief. Anna had grown up thinking of her as a cold-hearted disciplinarian. When Anna interrupted, she would say in a chilling voice: "What do you want, dear?" Anna felt that she had to ask her mother for an appointment to approach her with a subject she wanted to discuss. She developed into a tall and lovely blonde, but felt rejected at Chapin, where she was known as "Anna Banana." After her graduation, her grandmother took her on a tour of Italy. She saw the pope in the morning and Mussolini in the afternoon. Her mind was not on either of these gentlemen, but on the suitors she had left behind, three in number. "You can't imagine how many letters I've been getting from Robert," she wrote her mother on February 11, 1925, from Rome, "It is something fierce. . . . I wrote him the letter which I told you I was going to write him, telling him a few things which I'm afraid he won't appreciate much. . . . I've also had loads of letters from Sidney and several from Curt, and they all seem to take for granted that they are the one and only in my thoughts! I don't suppose I can help that but honestly Ma I'm perfectly certain that when I get home I won't be anymore anxious to be engaged than I was when I left. . . . I have so much fun with other people that I'm not in the least ready to say I'm sure I like one person more than any other on earth."

Curt was Curtis Dall, a tall stockbroker with a receding hairline ten years her senior, who "gave her the biz" when she got back from Europe. The trouble with Anna was that she couldn't make up her mind. Did she want to get engaged? Did she want to go to college? Did she want to take an agricultural course at Cornell? Anna had a tendency to sullenness, to clamming up the way her mother used to do in her Griselda moods. She felt her parents were trying to manage her life—she was nineteen and old enough to think for herself. "Poor old Sis [Anna]!" Roosevelt wrote Eleanor in July 1925. "She has got my letter by now in which I do some philosophizing! Even tho' she won't admit it she *has* gone through at least three changes of point of view in three years—I still think Cornell will do more good than anything and I hope she will see more clearly this summer. . . . She will work out of this nonsense. It is because she is 19."

Anna did go to Cornell, to take what she called her "short-horn course." Fifteen-year-old Elliott, a natural gossip, reported from Groton that he had heard from several Yale boys that she would probably flunk out because she never went to class.

In the fall, her engagement to Dall was announced. The future son-in-law went for inspection to Roosevelt's Fidelity & Deposit office, which was entirely covered with naval pictures. They had lunch on trays. Dall had gone to Princeton, and Roosevelt fell back on Ivy League banter. "Curt, just where is that college located?" he asked. "You must have heard of it," Dall replied, "because we send our junior varsity football team to Cambridge every other November to play Harvard." Having tested each other with this bit of chaff, they parted on the best of terms.

Anna was married in June 1926, marriage being the logical avenue of escape from the family. Sara's wedding gift was an apartment. Eleanor was furious that she had not been consulted on so lavish an expense. It was all she could do to keep her self-control!

Eleanor turned out to be the same kind of interfering mother-in-law that Sara had been. In the summer of 1929, Anna's brother James asked Curt Dall to invest $1,000 that Granny had given him for a European trip in the stock market. Curt bought blue chips, Du Pont and National Dairy Products, but the October crash wiped out Jimmy's account. One Monday morning in November, when Curt was having breakfast with his mother-in-law, she lowered her coffee cup and said, "Curt, I've just been talking with Jim." Her voice rose in pitch in that familiar way. "Yes, I've been talking with Jimmy, and he tells me that you have lost his $1,000 for him, which he gave you some time ago, to invest." "Yes, he has about lost it," Curt said, "much to my regret, and the market is still moving lower, Mama. I did just what he insisted upon my doing. He wished to gamble in the stock market, hoping to make some money. I bought a few shares of two leading common stocks for him, on margin, and the Panic has put his account in bad shape."

"Well!" Eleanor said. "You certainly knew that he planned to go abroad next June, so I think you ought to *return* his money to him!"

Curt was stunned. "Do you really think *I* ought to return the $1,000?"

"Yes," she replied firmly. "I do."

"All right, Mama, I will." But Jimmy took his loss like a man, telling Curt he knew stocks played no favorites, and if the money wasn't there, it wasn't Curt's fault.

Jimmy was surprised that his mother had stood up for him, for usually she gave him no sympathy. Once as a boy, when he was suffering from a bad case of poison ivy, she had said: "You silly boy, you ought to know better than to get near poison ivy." Eleanor did not know what to do about Jimmy, who did so poorly in his studies. When he was ten, and going to St. Albans in Washington, she wrote Sara: "James stands 13th in a class of 19 with a dreadful mark in arithmetic. . . . I think James is much ashamed but it is all his careless way of working & liking to have a good time so much that he neglects his work." Eleanor would scold James and James would weep and then the cycle would begin anew.

When he failed his Groton entrance exam, he wrote his father that his low marks—mathematics 21, English 30, Latin 15, and French 16 (out of 100)—"were all dew [*sic*] to careless and thoughtless work." It was, however, axiomatic that a Roosevelt got into Groton whatever his grades, and eventually Jimmy piled up a respectable record.

When James went to Harvard, his father worried that he had too much of a love of social good times. Roosevelt's fears were justified, for at the start of his sophomore year, in November 1927, James was threatened with probation. "The great part of the difficulty in his case has been, I am very certain, this impossible club procedure," Roosevelt wrote the assistant dean, "which seems to be even worse than it was when I ran for the 'Dickey' and was 'joining' various other social organizations in the autumn of my sophomore year. I hope and expect that now the worst part of this social business is out of the way, he will do better next term." James brooded about the high cost of keeping up with father, and decided it was hopeless. He never graduated from Harvard, having flunked German.

James planned to go to law school, but took his time about it. In the meantime, he fell in love with Betsy Cushing, lovely daughter of the distinguished Boston surgeon, Harvey Cushing. In January 1929, by which time his father was governor of New York, James was in Albany, bedridden with pneumonia. Betsy got a call from Eleanor: "Jimmie is desperately sick and is calling for you—will you come?" Flattered, she went, and soon they were engaged. When Betsy was introduced to Sara, she said: "I understand your father is a surgeon—surgeons always remind me of my butcher."

They were married on June 6, 1930, and FDR prodded James to continue his studies: "I do very much hope you will make law school this autumn. After being out a whole year you would find it fifty percent harder. Take the advice of an old and experienced bird." James did go back, but only for a year, and then went into insurance. This was a reaction against his over-bearing grandmother, who came to see him in Boston and said: "You're only in law school because of the allowance I give you." "I won't take your allowance," James said, and went to work for a Russian immigrant named Victor De Gerard, who had the Shell Oil account. FDR warned Jimmy that now that he was governor there were sound reasons "for the great willing-ness of some people to be awfully nice to you. Incidentally, and confiden-tially, I wish you would impress upon Mr. De Gerard, politely but firmly, that he must not use your name in seeking business." This was the first ap-pearance of a problem that would plague Roosevelt in his presidential years—people trying to get to him through his children.

Elliott, the next in line, was frail as a child, and had to wear braces to cor-rect bowlegs. Rebellious, he announced that he would go to the public school in Hyde Park rather than Groton. Forced to go to Groton, he hated it, and each year there was a scene when he had to go back. In 1926, when FDR had the sixteen-year-old boy aboard the *Larooco,* he wrote Endicott Peabody that "he is a much more individual boy than James—less cast in the common mold, and I am convinced that he has a perfectly good mind, but he is going through a not unusual period of wondering why he has to study things like Latin which he sees no future use for."

Elliott by now was a big strapping lad with a fierce streak that disturbed the rector. In the game against Milton in December 1927, he went downfield under a punt and landed with both knees on the receiver, who suffered a kidney injury. Elliott was benched for the rest of the game. "It is a fact that he gets over-excited and allows himself to go on blindly, so that in a way he was responsible for the offense," Peabody wrote FDR. "I could see this last year when I coached him in rowing. If he was criticized he would seem to become angry with himself, he would explain, but it made him an unpleas-ant person to coach and one felt that there was something wrong with him."

The rector was practically calling his son a pathological case. FDR rose to his defense in a letter arguing that perhaps Groton rather than Elliott was at fault: "Elliott tells me that not only was the 'kneeing' episode in the Milton game entirely accidental, but was so recognized by the coach & after the game by the referee and umpire—I don't see why, if this was the fact, it can in any way be charged to lack of self-control. . . . Now I am not making an excuse for a quick temper, which at times he shows & which we have recognized for many years, but I am a little surprised that it is being discovered at School in his 5th form year. He is extremely sensitive to praise or blame. The first four years he struggled at or near the bottom of his Form. This year he has done really better in his scholastic work—but apparently no one has given him an encouraging word. It is the feeling of never being patted on the back that has brought him today to a personal feeling of complete discouragement. . . . If you could all try the experiment of encouraging him when he does well in studies or sport . . . and if anything goes badly to talk it over with him—give him a chance to explain, instead of assuming that it is an 'angry spirit,' it might work out vastly better. . . . An inferiority complex at Elliott's age is an unfortunate and dangerous thing for after life—Even at a cost of an occasional bit of over-praise it is worth it if it shall bring back a degree of self-confidence with which to face life. In my judgment any lack of self-control cannot be corrected while there is such a lack of self-confidence."

Peabody responded that Elliott had bragged to his teammates that he wished he had hit his opponent harder: "My point is that his conduct has been such as to give him the reputation of being a fierce player who does not care particularly whether he hurts people or not." But Peabody tried to give Elliott the guidance he so obviously needed, and had two talks with him in February 1928. He wrote FDR on February 24 that Elliott "wanted to leave school, had made a failure of it, nobody cared for him. I pointed out to him that he would carry elsewhere the same personality: that the real trouble was that he referred everything to himself, that he could change completely if he would accept for himself the principle of love—of doing what he could for others. . . . He has tried what was suggested and finds that it works."

But the damage had been done. Feeling that he had failed at Groton, Elliott turned in a blank college-entrance exam so that he would not be accepted at Harvard. Nothing his parents said could make him change his mind. He was determined not to follow in his father's footsteps but to make his own tracks. That did not imply a refusal to use his father's influence when it came in handy. He went into advertising and in 1930 proposed a plan for flying produce from upstate to New York City to feed families ruined by the depression, the emergency aid to be publicized by his firm, Albert Frank & Company. FDR replied that the plan was impractical and expensive. "The only reason why I suggested it at all," Elliott explained, "was that I thought there might be something in the idea which you could make use of. . . . I found that Jimmie has now become a full-fledged member of an insurance company in Boston. More power to him! He certainly draws down a handsome salary for a beginner in the business." There was a trace of envy in Elliott's appraisal of his older brother, who had gone to Harvard and law school and was now established in a respectable profession.

For FDR, the Roosevelt name was something to live up to. For his children, it was an ambiguous legacy; sometimes they could take advantage of it; sometimes they were taken advantage of; the one thing they could not do was lead normal lives.

Roosevelt's priorities were as follows: first he would regain the use of his legs, then he would run for office. From this plan he did not waver. His friend Louis Wehle, who had dreamed up the Hoover-Roosevelt ticket in 1920, wrote him on October 10, 1925: "It seems to me fairly clear that you are the logical Democratic nominee for President in the next election. . . . Smith cannot possibly have the nomination. If anything so inconceivable could happen as his obtaining it, it would be at the cost of a practical paralysis of the Party for some time to come; certainly its complete disorganization."

"I must give principal consideration for at least 2 years more to getting back the use of my legs," Roosevelt replied. "Up to now I have been able to walk only with great difficulty with steel braces and crutches, having to be carried up and down steps, in and out of cars, etc. etc. Such a situation is, of course, impossible to a candidate. I am, however, gaining greatly and hope, within a year, to be walking without the braces, with the further hope of then discarding the crutches in favor of canes and eventually possibly getting rid of the latter also."

In 1926, Al Smith was reelected by the largest margin in the history of New York State, enhancing his prospects for the 1928 nomination. Roosevelt was solidly behind him, writing his reporter friend, Stanley Prenosil, on May 24, 1927: "Quite aside from my loyalty to him, I honestly have no desire either to run for the Presidency or to be President. I have seen much of Presidents and administrations. Even though it may sound selfish, I would rather do my bit as a private in the ranks." It sounded improbable rather than selfish, particularly in the light of the legitimate doubts being raised concerning Al Smith's capacity for the job. The office was supposed to make the man, and even a hack like Harding could get elected. But Smith's flaws became more glaring once he transferred his talents to the national scene. His personality, which was an asset in New York State, became a handicap in the rest of the country. His speech mannerisms were objects of mockery.

Roosevelt knew the extent of anti-Smith feeling from the mail he was getting. It wasn't just the anti-Catholics and the drys; there was a widespread populist resistance to Smith throughout rural America as the embodiment of detested values. C. H. Kimball, a Brooklyn salesman who met all sorts of people, reported what they were saying about Al. One fellow said he would give the breaks to the church schools. Another fellow said he had seen him kiss the ring of a visiting cardinal. "I suppose he did kiss the ring," Roosevelt replied. "That is a century-old custom of the Catholic church—I don't think it means any more than if I, as an Episcopalian, were to place Bishop Manning at my right at a dinner party."

As in 1924, Roosevelt was asked to deliver the nominating speech for Al at the convention in Houston. On June 27, he made his way to the speaker's platform in Sam Houston Hall, and nominated Al Smith for the second time. The convention was being broadcast nationally to an estimated 15 million listeners, and as Roosevelt wrote Walter Lippmann, "I tried the definite experiment this year of writing and delivering my speech wholly for the benefit of the radio audience and press rather than for any forensic effect it might have on the delegates and audience in the convention hall. Smith had the votes anyway and it seemed to me more important to reach out for the Republicans and Independents throughout the country." Eleven minutes after the speech was over, Roosevelt had in his hands the first telegram from a well-wisher, Thomas J. Gallagher of Rochester: "Nomination speech masterly every word distinctly heard here congratulations." Radio worked!

With the specter of the 103 ballots of the 1924 convention hovering over them, the delegates nominated Smith on the first ballot, with 849½ of the 1,-100 votes. Senator Joseph T. Robinson of Arkansas was picked as his running mate. In Kansas City, in the wake of Coolidge's "I do not choose to run," the Republicans nominated Herbert Hoover, who had served for seven years as secretary of commerce.

Roosevelt expected to be a member of Al Smith's inner circle during the campaign, but that was not to be. On July 10, Smith appointed John J. Raskob as chairman of the Democratic National Committee. Roosevelt was stunned, writing a friend that Al "said he wanted an organizer and a man who would bring the Democratic Party into favor with the business interests of the country. My first judgment is that it is a grave mistake as he is a Catholic; secondly, he is even wetter than Smith, seeking the repeal of the Eighteenth Amendment; third, he is the head of the largest business organization in the world. I fear that it will permanently drive away a host of people in the south and west, and rural east who are not particularly favorable to Smith but who up to today have been seeping back into the party."

The Raskob appointment was nothing less than the sellout of Al Smith to big business interests who wanted to use the Democratic party for their own ends. John J. Raskob believed that a political party could be bought like a corporation. The son of a cigar maker of Alsatian descent and an Irish mother who ran a boardinghouse in Lockport, New York, near Niagara Falls, and a devout Catholic, he helped put himself through school as a newspaper boy and a candy butcher on the train to Buffalo. In 1900, Pierre S. du Pont, president of E. I. du Pont de Nemours, hired him as a bookkeeper. Raskob had a quick and ingenious mind and soon became Du Pont's right-hand man. It was said that "P. S. du Pont is the one who breathes in and John Raskob is the one who breathes out."

In vain, Pierre du Pont had fought Woodrow Wilson's efforts to levy high taxes on corporations and income. During Prohibition, he became convinced that the solution to high taxes was the legalization of beer. A tax on beer, he asserted, would yield $1.85 billion a year and permit the total abolition of personal and corporate income taxes. The burden of taxation would shift from the productive entrepreneurs to the beer-guzzling peons. Bent on his quixotic crusade with his henchman Raskob, Du Pont backed an organization founded by a former naval officer, the Association Against the Prohibition Amendment. Starting in 1927, he contributed $500,000 a year to its efforts to bring about repeal.

The association was not enough. Political clout was needed. After the 1924 convention, Du Pont and Raskob had their eyes on Al Smith, the "wettest" of the candidates, whose election would guarantee repeal. All those years in the executive mansion had changed Al, who had gotten the Fulton Fish Market out of his nostrils and now liked the company of millionaires. He met Raskob during the 1926 reelection campaign, and the attraction was so great that Raskob contributed $50,000 to his campaign chest. Raskob's message to Wall Street was that business had nothing to fear from Al Smith. He was against government regulation and the Volstead Act. In July 1928, when he took over the National Committee, Raskob saw himself as the next secretary of the Treasury, with Pierre du Pont as the next secretary of state. Smith saw him as a welcome recruit, even though he was a lifelong Republican. He would bring big business, or at least part of it, into the Democratic camp. The Democratic national headquarters was installed in the General Motors Building at Broadway and 57th Street.

With the campaign under way, the prospects were not bright. The antiCatholicism, although often couched in vicious terms, rested on honest doubts. In much of America, Catholicism was seen as antidemocratic, with its papal figure of infallible authority and its insistence on religious education. Its very name, the Roman Catholic church, its seat of temporal power in the Vatican, and its Irish-dominated priesthood, suggested alien influences. Corrupt elements of society, such as political bosses and labor leaders, were Catholic. The church could exert influence over its members through the secret confessional and papal edicts, making it seem like a rival to the state. There were occasional examples of meddling. In Massachusetts in the spring of 1928, several Catholics were excommunicated for daring to bring a civil suit against a bishop who had misused a charity fund.

Al Smith made no concessions to the feelings of Protestant America. An autographed picture of the pope was prominently displayed in his Albany office. A worried Louis Howe wrote Roosevelt: "Al's youngest daughter is to be married on June 10 in Albany and insists on having the Cardinal himself with his full Cardinal's court perform the ceremony. Won't the newsreels in the morning look nice in the Southland on this. . . . I hope the young couple won't have to kiss the Cardinal's toe as part of the ceremony."

Smith seemed to cultivate parochialism. When reporters asked him about the needs of the states west of the Mississippi, he replied: "What are the states west of the Mississippi?" Traveling from Colorado to Wyoming, he saw a horse in the middle of nowhere and asked the conductor: "How does that horse get home?" He had never heard that there were wild horses in the

American West. As H. L. Mencken said, Smith's world "begins at Coney Island and ends at Buffalo."

As Smith campaigned, Roosevelt spent the summer in Hyde Park and Warm Springs, carrying on an active correspondence on Al's behalf. He did his best to counter what he called "the meanest and dirtiest kind of attacks, some in the open, but most of them of the whispering variety." He pointed out that of Governor Smith's thirteen cabinet members, nine were Protestant, two were Catholic, and two were Jews. He noted the absurdity of the Prohibition laws. He defended Tammany as "a pretty clean political organization."

In late September, Al Smith interrupted his campaign to go to Rochester where the state Democratic leaders were meeting to pick a candidate for governor. He knew he had to carry New York's electoral votes to win in November, and there were grave doubts that he could without Roosevelt to bring in the upstate vote. But Roosevelt would not run. He still had hopes that with a few more years of rehabilitation he would regain the use of his legs. In addition, he and Louis Howe agreed that 1928 was a bad year. Al Smith would be beaten and would drag Roosevelt down with him. Howe wanted him to wait for the Hoover tide to pass, to run for governor in 1932 and president in 1936.

Louis was in New York, fending off the Democratic leaders and the press. "Please let me know," he wired on September 26, "if your decision not to run is still final so I can make some definite reply to newspapers and politicians who have been after me all day.... It has even been seriously urged that [your condition] could be overcome by nominating a lieutenant governor with the understanding he would act during the legislative session. I have replied you are not the kind of man who would take a job and leave it to an understudy.... If they are looking for a goat why don't Wagner sacrifice himself?... They seem to think that sufficient coaxing will change your mind."

Two days later, Howe reported that Herbert Lehman "would gladly run as Lieutenant Governor if you would head the ticket so that you can feel you could go away each winter and leave a competent person in charge."

On September 29, Smith called Roosevelt in Warm Springs and asked him to reconsider. Roosevelt was adamant. Smith said: "Well, you're the doctor," and hung up. For emphasis, Roosevelt wired a confirmation of his refusal: "The continued improvement in my condition is dependent on my avoidance of cold climate and on taking exercises here at Warm Springs during the cold winter months."

"I have had a difficult time turning down the Governorship," Roosevelt wrote his mother on September 30, "letters and telegrams by the dozen begging me to save the situation by running, but I have been perfectly firm. I only hope they don't try to stampede the Convention tomorrow and nominate me and then adjourn!"

Smith found Roosevelt's telegram when he arrived at the Hotel Seneca in Rochester on October 1 and was ready to look for someone else. There was Justice Townsend Scudder of the State Supreme Court, but he was too austere. There was Herbert Lehman, but the upstate bosses didn't want him. Smith was worried because the Republicans had nominated Albert Ottinger, a crusading attorney general who had fought loan sharks and stock frauds, and who could get the New York City vote because he was Jewish. Already, there was talk of ticket-splitting, of voting for "Al and Al."

When Smith tried to reach Roosevelt on October 1, he would not take the call. That night, Howe wired: *"World* man reported Al still hoped to draft you. Jim [Farley] tells me confidentially that real pressure comes from leaders and jobholders who feel you will be elected Governor and patronage made secure and that Governor does not really consider your nomination vital to his personal success."

Smith finally reached Roosevelt at the Warm Springs Hotel. First John Raskob got on the line and pleaded with him to take the nomination. Roosevelt said he had a responsibility toward the Warm Springs Foundation. "Damn the foundation," Raskob said, "we'll take care of it."

"You take the nomination," Smith said. "You can make a couple of radio speeches and you'll be elected. Then you can go back to Warm Springs. After you have made your inaugural speech and sent your message to the Legislature, you can go back there again for a couple of months. You know the Legislature doesn't do very much during the first two months. Then you can come back again and get your thirty days' bills out and go back for the rest of the summer."

"Don't hand me that baloney," Roosevelt replied.

"Frank, I told you I wasn't going to put this on a personal basis, but I've got to," Smith said. Roosevelt replied that things were not as bad as he made them sound, having heard from Howe that Smith did not consider his nomination as vital.

"I just want to ask you one more question," Smith said. "If those fellows nominate you tomorrow and adjourn, will you refuse to run?"

Roosevelt said he didn't know. "All right," Smith said. "I won't ask you any more questions."

The next morning, Louis Howe came into the office of Adolphus Ragan, who was on the staff of the Democratic National Committee. He was holding a telegram and looked woebegone. The telegram said: "The Governor has just telephoned me that I will be nominated whether I accept or not. Isn't that a mess?" Howe was weeping. The tears were rolling down his wrinkled face.

"Ragan," Howe said, "they are killing the best friend I ever had in the world."

Ragan put his arm around Louis and said, "Perhaps not. It might be the very best thing for his health. Who knows?"

Certain that running would mean another defeat, like the 1920 vice-presidential race, Howe wired back: "Mess is no word for it. For once I have no advice to give."

That afternoon, Mayor Jimmy Walker of New York City entered Roosevelt's name, and he was nominated by acclamation.

Eleanor wired: "Regret that you had to accept but know that you felt it obligatory."

Sara wrote: "Eleanor telephoned me before I got my paper that you have to 'run' for the Governorship. Well, I am sorry if you do not feel that you can do it without too much *self* sacrifice, and yet if you run I do not want you to be defeated: Now what follows is *really private.* In case of your election, I know your salary is smaller than the one you get now. I am prepared to make up the difference to you."

The health issue came out at once, when the *Herald Tribune* said the nomination was unfair both for Roosevelt and the people of the state, and the *Evening Post* called it "pathetic and pitiless." At a press conference the next day, Al Smith made this sensible reply: "A governor does not have to be an acrobat. We do not elect him for his ability to do a double back-flip or a handspring. The work of the Governorship is brainwork. Ninety-nine per cent of it is accomplished at a desk."

Why did Roosevelt give up the treatment he had pursued for seven years to run in an election in which the Republicans were favored? He was forty-six years old and a grandfather, his daughter, Anna, having given birth to a daughter. He had not held elective office since 1912, sixteen years before. He felt the call and the excitement of another campaign, and the satisfaction of being needed by his party. Smith and the others had come to him on bended knee. He was practically obliged to accept. How could he remain in public life if he never ran for anything? It was well and good to wait until 1932, but the political context might make it impossible for him to secure the nomination then. Wasn't it better to run than to stagnate as an invalid in Warm Springs? In all the years of treatment, improvement had been slight. He had to face the hard fact that he would never be completely well. He had seen at two national conventions that his condition, far from hurting his popularity, actually enhanced it. If he won, he would make a tremendous leap from years of enforced political exile to governor of the nation's most important state. If he lost, he could go back to Warm Springs and swim in the pool. He didn't have to worry about the foundation, Raskob had promised to fund it and in late October made the first payment of $25,000. The temptation to get back in the game he knew and loved won over the slim chance of mending his legs. As one of his admirers wrote, "It is better to go foaming over the precipice than waste your life in sandy deltas."

As for Al Smith, he seemed to think that once again he could use the Roosevelt name as window dressing with Herbert Lehman doing the real work. Returning from Rochester in a private car with some of the New York City delegates, he unburdened himself to the Tammany district leader Daniel E. Finn. They were discussing Roosevelt, and Finn asked: "Al, aren't you afraid that you are raising up a rival who will some day cause you trouble?" In his rasping voice, Smith replied: "No, Dan, he won't live a year."

Years later, when Smith's callous remark was repeated to him, Roosevelt commented: "At headquarters in the General Motors Building in 1928, I was treated by Raskob and Mrs. Moskowitz all the time I was there in July, August and the first part of September as though I was one of those pieces of window-dressing that had to be borne with because of a certain political value in non-New York City areas. That remark of Al Smith's was I know sincere. Just as, I think, he was sincere when he told me over the telephone at Warm Springs that if I were elected Governor I could be sworn in and then go South for January and February, leaving the Governorship to Herbert Lehman in the meantime, and returning a few days before the close of the legislative session."

In the Smith camp, Roosevelt was still viewed as a lightweight. When he was nominated by acclamation, Robert Moses shouted above the uproar to Al Smith's daughter, Emily: "He'll make a good candidate but a lousy Governor." Moses told Frances Perkins that his only asset was a smile. "It's a pity to have him and that Al has set his heart on him," he said. "It's undoubtedly a good name to carry the ticket with ... but of course, he isn't quite bright." During the campaign, Moses continued to belittle Roosevelt, saying "I don't like him, I don't believe in him, I don't trust him." His attacks became personal, and he told Miss Perkins: "He's a pretty poor excuse for a man." He also made fun of Eleanor's buck teeth and shrill voice.

On the morning of October 17, 1928, Samuel Rosenman, the son of immigrant Jews from Poland, born in San Antonio, Texas, took a taxi from his home to a Hudson River pier in lower Manhattan. Rosenman, a thirty-two-year-old lawyer, had been in the New York State Assembly for five years and was a member of the Bill Drafting Commission. He knew about pending legislation, and had been asked to accompany the Democratic candidate for governor on his upstate swing and feed him information and help him with his speeches.

Rosenman had several suitcases full of material, divided by subject matter in manila envelopes. He knew little about the candidate, except that he belonged to the Hudson River gentry. He wondered why someone from that background would go into politics. He felt detached, almost indifferent about the trip—it was just a chore.

The man he met at the pier was in a wheelchair, but had a kind of contagious ebullience. His legs might be useless, but his handshake was bone-crushing. They boarded the ferry to Hoboken and took the Erie Railroad in the direction of those strongly Republican counties north of Pennsylvania.

In Buffalo, Roosevelt decided to deliver a speech on labor. "Sam," he said, "I've got to run now and meet some of the local political brethren. I'm afraid I'll be busy most of the evening. Suppose you knock out a draft of what you think I ought to say tomorrow night, and let me have it in the morning." Calling for his valet to wheel him into his bedroom, he added: "Don't stay up all night."

"Any particular line you want me to follow?" Rosenman asked nervously.

"No, just put something together so we can look at it in the morning."

Rosenman thought it was odd that a man in a wheelchair would use the expression "I've got to run now." He was also surprised that a stranger would place such confidence in him. At breakfast the next morning, Roosevelt said: "You've got all the stuff in there we need, and it's pretty good but a little on the dull side." He called in a stenographer and began to dictate corrections, and as he listened, Rosenman got his first lesson in how to make statistics come to life: "And so tonight I am going to tell you all about it, tell you the facts, go back in my own mind and in your mind into the history of this state. Somewhere in a pigeon-hole in a desk of the Republican leaders of New York State is a large envelope, soiled, worn, bearing a date that goes back twenty-five or thirty years. Printed in large letters on this old envelope are the words 'promises to labor.' Inside the envelope are a series of sheets dated two years apart and representing the best thought of the best minds of the Republican leaders. . . . Nowhere in that envelope is there a single page bearing the title 'Promises kept.' "

Almost apologetically, Roosevelt added: "I'm going to take one more crack at religious bigotry. If Al is licked that's what will do it. I know some of the boys at my campaign headquarters won't like it, but I'm more interested in electing Al than anything else." And he dictated the passage that said if anyone voted from religious intolerance, "may God have mercy on your miserable souls."

When Roosevelt gave that speech, Rosenman was standing in the back of the hall, silently mouthing the words he had helped write, feeling the excitement of a playwright on opening night. He no longer felt detached. He felt committed to the candidate. He had to admire the man's courage as he saw what an ordeal it was for him simply to get up and sit down, locking and unlocking his braces, and to get in and out of cars and hotels, and to be carried up back stairs to the place where he was speaking. He always remained smiling and cheerful. It was as though being crippled gave him an equanimity that his fellow beings did not possess. He had a great gift for putting people at ease, for making them feel that he was interested in them and their families. He also had an amazingly retentive mind. Rosenman had never met anyone who could grasp the facts of a complicated problem as quickly and as thoroughly.

Roosevelt was enjoying himself, writing his childhood friend Mrs. Charles Hamlin that "it is rare good fun to be back in action again. I had almost forgotten the thrill of it." To a cousin who expressed concern about his health, Archie Roosevelt, he replied that "if I get elected I don't think a winter in Albany will do me any harm—some of my friends there are already planning to turn the greenhouse into a swimming pool! In any event, I shall be able to go to Warm Springs in May for a few weeks and again in the early autumn. Eleanor and I are taking this new situation very calmly—if I am elected she will be at least sixty per cent of the Governor—I shall insist on that even though at the present time she thinks she can go on teaching school in New York during the middle of the week!" But Eleanor was not sure she wanted her husband to run, and spent most of the campaign working for the Smith organization in New York.

Joining him upstate to introduce him to local labor leaders, Frances Perkins was impressed by his stamina and good humor. When things went wrong and the scheduled stop at Oriskany Falls had to be canceled, he discarded the prepared speech with its paragraph on the battle monument, pulled into the center of Skaneateles, and greeted the people with a few impromptu remarks. It was a valuable talent, which she felt he had developed since his illness. He had learned flexibility, the art of the possible. "If you can't use your legs and they bring you milk when you wanted orange juice," he told her, "you learn to say 'that's all right' and drink it."

Roosevelt thought things were going well. In many places he visited, the audiences were twice as large as the number of registered Democrats. Even Louis Howe brightened, saying; "I am horribly afraid you are going to be elected." He established himself as a vigorous candidate, who could stand the strain of an active campaign—he traveled 1,300 miles and made fifty speeches—and as the heir to Al Smith's record on welfare legislation, aid to agriculture and labor, and power policy. He continued to campaign for Smith, sending out thousands of letters on October 20 that described him as the heir to Wilsonian ideals.

On the morning of November 6, Roosevelt voted in Hyde Park, then went to campaign headquarters in the Biltmore Hotel in New York City to hear the returns. As the hours passed, it became clear that Smith was beaten. In New York State, he was trailing by 100,000 votes. Al and his wife, Katie, were in the Seventy-first Regiment Armory. Al was glassy-eyed, his face set in a permanent smile. You could see that he and Katie were crushed and hurt. Almost crying, Katie said to Frances Perkins: "People have been so mean." Miss Perkins nodded, having been told that even some of the campaign workers had complained that she was cheap stuff. By 9:30, Al knew that he had lost and wondered whether his concept of Americanism was at fault, whether he had misread the lesson of his own life. The time just hadn't come when a man could say his beads in the White House.

Would Roosevelt be buried in the landslide? Looking over some bad upstate returns, he told Sam Rosenman: "We'll stay until it is over. I have an idea that some of the boys upstate are up to their old tricks of delaying the vote and stealing as many as they can from us." Roosevelt called the sheriffs in several upstate counties and said: "The returns from your county are coming in mighty slowly, and I don't like it. I shall look to you, if they are unduly delayed, and I want you personally to see that the ballots are not tampered with." If they needed help, he would ask Governor Smith to call out the state troopers. He would have a hundred lawyers sent into the fifty-seven counties to watch over the official canvass.

About half past one or two in the morning there were funny little reports, tiny returns. A village in Cattaraugus County had given a plurality of six to Roosevelt. He joked that such remote places were under the misapprehension that they were voting for Teddy. At 4:00 A.M., someone said: "Roosevelt is elected. It seems incredible, but he is." He had won by 25,000 votes out of 4,200,000 cast, and joked that he was "the one-half of one per cent Governor." Voters had split their tickets, voting for Hoover for president and Roosevelt for governor. Some upstate Protestants probably did not vote for Ottinger because he was Jewish. Catholics voted for Roosevelt because he was behind Al Smith. Jews voted for him because Herbert Lehman would be his lieutenant governor. Protestants voted for him because he was a prominent Episcopalian who had headed the fund-raising drive for the Cathedral of St. John the Divine.

It took a while for Ottinger to concede, and FDR wrote his friend Bruce Kremer in Butte, Montana, on November 22 that "it was only this week that my friend Ottinger finally conceded my election, so I am apparently definitely in for a difficult two years in Albany. Of course I shall be the target of the concentrated batteries of the Republican Party, both state and national."

The morning after the election, Louis Howe was having breakfast at the Biltmore with Jim Farley, Jimmy Walker, and Eddie Dowling. They'd been up all night, and the returns were in, and Roosevelt had won, and Louis broke a roll in half and looked at it, and tore it into quarters, and took a bite, and with a mischievous grin, asked: "Who's going to say it?"

"We've got the next president," Eddie Dowling said.

"Don't you know it, Eddie! Don't you know it?" Louis agreed. "How do you feel about it, Jim?" It was a vindication for Howe, who had stuck by Roosevelt through his years of illness and shared his enforced inactivity.

Not sharing in the euphoria was Al Smith, the Unhappy Warrior. The slaughter had been terrible throughout the nation. It was the Democratic party's worst defeat since the Civil War. Al's home state, which had elected him governor four times, had repudiated him. He was finished on the national scene, and would not hold public office again. He blamed his defeat on religious bigotry, not realizing that he had been rejected for other reasons. As Mrs. F. B. Long of Statesville, North Carolina, wrote Roosevelt: "There were vast numbers who did not regard him as a fit man, either by birth, culture, dignity, or breadth of vision, to fill the great office of President of the United States. One who had never until middle life traveled beyond the counties of his native state could not possibly have other than a provincial viewpoint. His superficial knowledge of nationwide affairs, hastily acquired, could not give him the understanding or sympathetic outlook necessary in dealing with great national and international problems."

Smith was through, but the man who had campaigned as his disciple had survived the wreckage. Smith and Roosevelt were like two long-distance runners, the one unwittingly taking the early lead and setting the pace for the other, and then falling back, having sacrificed himself. It was thanks to Al Smith that Roosevelt had survived politically in the long years of his rehabilitation, by nominating him at two conventions. And now Roosevelt was in the office that Al had held so long, and Al was a defeated, embittered man. Illness had made Roosevelt aware of the common man and his plight, and he had grown in vision and understanding, at the same time that Al Smith had become identified with John Raskob, who saw the Democratic party as an instrument for the Du Pont and other interests. The man of humble origins, the alumnus of the Fulton Fish Market, respected money. The Hyde Park patrician, who had been around it all his life, did not. Al Smith's vision narrowed, and he came to represent sectarianism, as a Catholic, as a wet, and as the front man for Raskob and his millionaire friends. Roosevelt's vision broadened, and he came to represent a process of unification, in the party and in the nation.

From Marietta, Ohio, George White wrote him that he was now "the logical leader of the party. I pray that you may have the physical strength to meet the responsibilities that fall upon your shoulders."

XII

Governor Roosevelt

————

*If personality is an unbroken series of successful gestures, then there
was something gorgeous about him, some heightened sensitivity to the
promises of life, as if he were related to one of those intricate machines
that register earthquakes ten thousand miles away.*

F. Scott Fitzgerald, *The Great Gatsby*

Roosevelt wanted an outdoor inauguration, in the dead of the Albany
winter. It would be a display of his stamina and good health and
would symbolize the qualities he hoped to bring to his administration—
open for all to see, with the spaciousness of a progressive program.

In this he was opposed by the secretary of state, Robert Moses, who, disgruntled by his victory, was telling everyone that the executive mansion
would now be occupied by a very charming gentleman of mediocre abilities.
Moses wanted as little to do with the inauguration as possible, writing Roosevelt on November 20: "I think you should ask the retiring Governor to introduce you instead of having this done by the Secretary of State." He
advised Roosevelt that an outdoor inauguration "will not work.... It is
bound to be very cold, and of all the cold places in the State there is none
that is chillier than State Street on the front steps of the Capitol.... I am
afraid we shall have a lot of pneumonia patients as a result."

Another, more serious problem was Al Smith and his entourage. Smith
had been governor so long he thought it was a tenured position. Now he
hoped to be governor emeritus, working behind the scenes to keep the pleasant but untried fellow who had the job on track. A week before Christmas
he told Roosevelt that Belle Moskowitz was preparing his inaugural address
and message to the legislature. It was a way of announcing that Al and Belle
and Bob Moses would continue to run things. Roosevelt told him that he
had already prepared his inaugural address, and that his message to the legislature was nearly finished. He would be glad to show them to Mrs. Mos-

kowitz before he went to Albany on January 1, he said. Somehow he never got around to it.

Smith urged Roosevelt to retain Mrs. Moskowitz as his secretary. "You see, Mrs. Moskowitz knows all about everything," he said. "She knows all the plans. She knows all the people. She knows all the different characters and quirks that are involved in everything. She knows who can and who will do this or that." Roosevelt was noncommittal. Then there was Bob Moses. It would be a real tragedy to lose him as secretary of state. He did the work of twelve men. Roosevelt tilted his head back, drew on his cigarette, and said: "No. He rubs me the wrong way."

On January 1, 1929, a cold wet day, with streets slushy from snow followed by rain, the inauguration was held in the Assembly chamber of the capitol. Roosevelt took the oath on the Dutch bible that had been in his family for 200 years, an oath administered by Robert Moses, who left immediately afterward, not waiting to hear the address. Roosevelt thought of the very first inauguration he had ever been to—Cousin Teddy's—and of the very similar scene in the same Assembly chamber. Eleanor was in black velvet, her thick long hair tied in a bun, her hat slightly askew. She was buttonholing people, asking: "Would you like to have a little chat with the governor?" Al was shaking hands all around, he had not quite said goodbye, in fact, he had reserved a large suite at the De Witt Clinton Hotel so he could continue to be of use.

Then there was the charade at the executive mansion. Smith in front of the reporters saying "A thousand welcomes. We've got the home fires burning and you'll find this a fine place to live." Roosevelt responding in kind: "I only wish Al were going to be right here for the next two years." In the cloakroom the maids were crying. The Smiths' luggage and personal belongings lined the hallways. After supper, Smith and Roosevelt went off into one of the little parlors. Smith pulled up close to Roosevelt's chair, leaning forward. Roosevelt assumed his "I'm listening but" expression, with his lips pulled down. Smith started lecturing on what had to be done, the various programs, the hospitals, the parks. He would continue to be available, why he'd be glad to come to Albany two days a week if he was wanted. He could come up Sunday night and be there Monday and Tuesday, the big legislative days, and provide counsel. Again, he urged that Roosevelt keep Mrs. Moskowitz. Roosevelt felt funny about it, but thought it might be all right. He had nothing against Belle. Once, during the campaign, she had arrived at Hyde Park, and Eleanor had pleaded with Sara to ask her to stay for lunch, but Sara would not have "that fat Jewess" at her table. Roosevelt overruled her, and she stayed.

But when he discussed Mrs. Moskowitz with Eleanor, she said: "Franklin, Mrs. Moskowitz is a very fine woman. . . . But you have to decide now whether you are going to be governor of this state, or whether Mrs. Moskowitz is going to be governor of this state. If Mrs. Moskowitz is your secretary, she will run you . . . in such a way that you don't know that you're being run a good deal of the time. Everything will have been arranged so subtly that when the matter comes to you it will be natural to decide the thing that Mrs. Moskowitz has already decided should be done. That's the way she works. That is the kind of person she is." Eleanor knew that her husband could be manipulated. If you didn't oppose him outright, he was easy to manage. If eight or ten persons gave him the same line he'd begin to think he'd heard the vox populi.

Roosevelt got rid of Mrs. Moskowitz, who complained bitterly. "It's going to be terrible," she said. "He's got that dreadful Louis Howe up there. Louis Howe will poison his mind about everything. Howe hates Smith. He's that kind of sour person. It's going to be very bad." In fact, Louis Howe was suffering from a case of answered prayers. As his ambitions for Roosevelt were realized, he had to share his beloved boss. Howe still saw himself as steering Roosevelt's thinking, sitting on the edge of his bed at breakfast and planning his day. But he no longer controlled access. Other voices had the governor's ear. Louis fought jealously for priority, confusing threats to his position with dangers to his chief. As if to emphasize the one area where he had no rival, he sometimes railed at Roosevelt so that a disbelieving hush fell over the office as the sunken-cheeked gnome shouted "Pighead!" and "Dumb Dutchman!"

Moses went too, although Roosevelt kept him as chairman of the State Council of Parks and president of the Long Island Park Commission. He brought in Edward J. Flynn, boss of the Bronx, as secretary of state. Smith didn't like Flynn because he wasn't loyal to Tammany and gave himself airs, speaking in a scholarly way about population shifts, as if he'd graduated from Harvard, whereas in fact he'd gone to Fordham.

What hurt Moses was that Roosevelt, in a spirit of continuity, reappointed sixteen of Smith's eighteen department heads, all but Moses and Dr. James A. Hamilton, the state industrial commissioner, who Moses suspected was a "throw-in," so it would not look as if he had been the only one fired. Hamilton wasn't a throw-in. Roosevelt wanted Frances Perkins in the job. Sam Rosenman came aboard as counsel, and another adviser, mainly on farm matters, was Roosevelt's Dutchess County neighbor, editor of the *American Agriculturalist,* Henry Morgenthau, Jr. Frances Perkins did not think highly of Henry. He never stuck to anything. Miss Perkins had given him a job as a factory inspector, but he lasted only two months. Then he went to agriculture school. It was his uncle who had bought him a controlling interest in the newspaper.

Then there was the bald and bushy-browed lieutenant governor, Herbert Lehman, who filled in when Roosevelt was away; he usually spent between two or three months a year in Warm Springs. Lehman, the banker turned politician, was loyal and able, and Roosevelt called him "my good right arm."

With the changing of the palace guard, Smith did not long remain in Albany. When he visited the state capital in mid-January, he complained to

Frances Perkins: "I only had an hour with Frank all the time I was there." Nothing was more tiresome than a predecessor hanging about in anterooms and offering advice and serving as a conduit for the grumbling of malcontents. The 1928 defeat, as Robert Moses put it, was his Gethsemane. His resentment, instead of being aimed at the man who had defeated him, focused on Roosevelt. He had befriended Franklin Roosevelt. He had reached down into this sick man's life and said, "Now you can run for governor. I'll show you how." He had rescued Frank from political oblivion, and now he was ignored.

Al Smith had turned over to Roosevelt a state in good working order. He had reduced the 187 state agencies to eighteen departments, all but two of them responsible to the governor. He had pushed through a constitutional amendment establishing the executive budget. He had cut taxes while supporting bond issues for public works.

But Republican-controlled legislatures often frustrated the plans of reform governors. They routinely opposed increases in government spending that would benefit the urban masses at the expense of the rural folk and the wealthy. The only advances came out of bipartisan coalitions of urban legislators.

Roosevelt saw his first task as regaining control over lump-sum appropriations in the budget. Under the previous governors, the practice had developed of giving the legislature the right to approve how the money was spent. To Roosevelt, this was a clear case of the legislature taking over executive functions. How could a legislature frame an efficient budget, with all its special interests and logrolling? But the Republican leaders saw Roosevelt making the budget into a political weapon, giving raises to the 40,000 state employees, who were numerous enough to turn an election, or favoring districts where votes were needed.

On March 13, Roosevelt sent back the budget bill with all the lump-sum items vetoed—fourteen pages of them amounting to $54 million.

The legislature sent back an identical budget bill, along with about 900 other bills, in the frantic rush before the session's adjournment at the end of March. Roosevelt had thirty days to decide which to sign and which to veto. It was a depressing task, when you saw that the legislature had killed all the progressive bills, and that two-thirds of the 900 bills they did bring in were trivial—one of them would legalize five hooks on a line instead of three for a certain kind of fishing.

Far from being discouraged, Roosevelt enjoyed the fight, writing a friend: "This family is going through the usual tribulations. James is getting over pneumonia; Elliott is about to have an operation; Franklin, Jr., has a doubly broken nose and John has just had a cartilage taken out of his knee! Anna and her husband, Curtis Dall, are taking a short holiday in Europe and their baby is parked with us at the Executive Mansion. Eleanor is teaching school

two and a half days a week in New York, and I am in one continuous glorious fight with the Republican legislative leaders. So you can see that it is a
somewhat hectic life."

On April 12, he once again vetoed the lump-sum items, which would force
a court test. In the meantime, arrangements were made so the state could
continue to spend funds without a budget. The Republican attorney general,
Hamilton Ward, decided that he would plead for the legislature, so Roosevelt had to hire a well-known constitutional lawyer of the day, William D.
Guthrie.

When the Appellate Division of the State Supreme Court delivered its
decision on June 21, it sided with the legislature. Roosevelt took the case to
the Court of Appeals, but in the meantime had to work with the Republican
chairmen of the Senate Finance and the Assembly Ways and Means committees. "The difficulty which I constantly feel," Roosevelt wrote a friendly
Republican assemblyman on August 3, "is that the moment I make any recommendation or even try to get together with them, they take the angle that
to accede or even meet me half way would be to hand me some kind of political credit, and that in order to avoid this, the only method is to turn down
every proposal which emanates from the Executive Chamber!"

Everything depended on the oral argument before the Court of Appeals,
which in November reversed the Appellate Division in a unanimous decision written by a Republican, Judge Cuthbert W. Pound, who ruled that it
was unconstitutional for the legislators to share in the segregation of lump-
sum items.

It was a striking victory for Roosevelt, who had successfully warded off
the encroachment of the legislature. Letters from all over the country arrived telling him that the decision would go down in history as one of the
most far-reaching on the fundamentals of government in his generation.
"That is what I call batting one hundred percent," applauded the Democratic Assembly leader, Maurice Bloch. Roosevelt emerged as a strong governor, who refused to give in where Al Smith had temporized, and who was
willing to go to the mat for a principle.

Felix Frankfurter, the Harvard Law School professor who liked to hover
on the edge of power, and who acted as a conduit for the political aims of
U.S. Supreme Court Justice Louis D. Brandeis, had been on friendly terms
with Roosevelt since the early twenties, and had written him a few days after
his election as governor: "You have, as Smith has, the conception of government which seems to be indispensable to the vitality of a democratic government, namely, the realization that the processes of government are
essentially educational processes."

Nowhere was this so true as in the antiquated prison system he had inherited. It seemed as if the convicts had waited for Roosevelt to be installed
in office to express their discontent. In July at Dannemora, 1,300 inmates at
Clinton State Prison, known as the "Siberia of New York," rioted for five

hours, set fire to buildings, and stormed the walls. Three were killed and twenty were wounded as they were driven back into their cells. Six days later at Auburn, an overcrowded prison built in 1916, 1,700 convicts fought guards for five hours and caused damage totaling $250,000 before they were turned back with two killed and eleven wounded.

Joseph A. McGinnies, the Republican Speaker of the Assembly, wrote Roosevelt that, although the prison situation was a bit annoying, "these things did happen." Republicans seemed to feel that the trouble was due, as one of them put it, "entirely to the misguided, ill-starred idiosyncracies of Thomas Mott Osborne and his theories with regard to the coddling and pampering of inmates of State prisons. . . . Going to prison has been a vacation in Auburn."

Others pointed to the harsh law named after State Senator Caleb H. Baumes, under which criminals convicted of four felonies were given mandatory life sentences, without hope of parole. For these men, there were only two ways to leave prison: death or escape. If a few men with nothing to lose started trouble, nervous tension and mob psychology did the rest.

Roosevelt believed that the root of the problem was the Baumes Law, as he wrote Felix Frankfurter on August 5 in response to a suggestion that a commission of inquiry be named: "There have been inquiries of this nature almost every year for the last twenty or twenty-five years. We have volumes of reports from expert penologists. . . . My present inclination is to appoint no new commission but to ask the existing Baumes Commission to reopen the whole subject of life sentences for fourth offenders, especially when the offenses are committed against property and not against persons. . . . Our chief immediate problem in the state is a physical one—the building of more prisons to take care of the overcrowding and to eliminate the use of present antiquated cell accommodations."

The new prison was Attica, which when it was completed in 1930 at a cost of $12 million was hailed in the *New York Times* as a "convict's paradise." There was a cafeteria, and recreation rooms, and beds with springs and mattresses, and every prisoner had his own radio. The village of Attica, it was said, took as much pride in the prison and its 200 inmates as Niagara did in its cataract.

Roosevelt changed the Baumes Law so that fourth offenders would get from fifteen years to life instead of mandatory life, and reorganized the parole system. He restored time off for good behavior, and started construction camps for certain types of offenders, who were allowed to do outside work. If he had been able to, he would have had the entire convict force out doing road work like Smedley Butler's Haitians. He hated to see men wasting away in the "eternal autumn" of prison. He wanted everyone to have a useful place in society.

In the commutation of sentences, Roosevelt had power over life and death. Executions were always held on Thursday night, with an open telephone line between the governor's mansion and Sing Sing Prison in Ossining. On those nights, Roosevelt was tense and dispirited, and Missy LeHand would try to find someone he could play cards with.

Earle Looker, a reporter who was given considerable access to Roosevelt in the preparation of a book, was a witness at one of the evenings when the governor and Rosenman dealt with commutations and pardons, in his bedroom at the executive mansion. It was like a "bed of justice" under one of the kings of the ancien régime.

"This man is to be released immediately," Roosevelt said. "This shortens his sentence by thirty days."

"A thief," Rosenman whispered to Looker. "But a man who was very greatly tempted by circumstances. He showed real courage at the prison riots, helped the guards at the risk of his life; he shows every sign of wishing to become a good citizen."

Rosenman blotted the governor's signature, and another case was presented. "Denied," Roosevelt said. "Impossible," Rosenman explained. "To let him out would be like freeing a leper to walk down Fifth Avenue, indiscriminately touching people."

On one bundle where the photographs lay uppermost, Roosevelt flung the file down as if he had burned his fingers. "I saw him," he said, almost angrily. He did not want to connect a face with a case, a face that might provoke sympathy or antagonism.

In one case, Roosevelt commuted to life imprisonment the death sentence of a man who had been convicted of first-degree murder. The man, Ernest Duane, was an epileptic, and Roosevelt, who suffered from another crippling disease, felt sympathy for him. "This man was discharged from the United States Army during the World War on the ground of epilepsy (grand mal)," he said. "I cannot bring myself to believe that the state would visit the extreme penalty of death upon a man whom the government rejected for service because he was suffering from a mental disorder."

Roosevelt's attitude was humane and sensible. When there were extenuating circumstances, he studied them closely, knowing how unfair a literal reading of the law could sometimes be. As Frankfurter wrote him on one occasion, "There are various ways of doing the right thing, and your statement setting forth the reason for the commutation of this sentence will have an honored place in the history of the exercise of the pardoning power."

On labor matters, Roosevelt had come a long way since the days in the State Senate when he concerned himself with the length of the ruffed grouse season. His years in the Navy, when he had been the employer of thousands of men in the yards, had made him conscious of labor's legitimate demands. He no longer represented a three-county rural constituency but the entire state. Power broadened the spectrum of his interests. He believed in the "safety net" role of government, to catch the casualties of the free-enterprise system. Only three months after his inauguration, he urged a law providing for security against want for the aged, and a bill was passed in the 1929 session of the legislature providing for the appointment of a commission to study the condition of elderly men and women.

At the Department of Labor, Frances Perkins was absorbed in workmen's compensation cases. Half a million industrial accidents were reported a year, and in 1929 nearly 200,000 compensation cases were adjudicated. She was dealing directly with human suffering. Also with corporate greed, indifference to the misery of longtime employees, and the willingness to resort to dirty tricks to avoid the payment of claims. Roosevelt got hundreds of letters from persons who felt their cases had not been settled fairly, and passed the complaints on to Miss Perkins. The insurance companies had stables of doctors who would testify that you were not disabled or that the disability was not due to an industrial accident. The compensation boards were forums for perjury. The doctors who did the diagnoses were not civil to the workingmen. There were long delays—you filled out a form and three months later you got a postcard.

Miss Perkins kept a file that she showed Roosevelt on the horrors of industry: men who were polishing the insides of glass milk tanks were getting silicosis; girls painting luminous dials on clock faces and pointing the fine brushes with their lips had contracted radium poisoning; an old carpenter who had lost an arm and settled his compensation claim without a hearing had been cheated out of $5,000 by his employer. When the carpenter was asked why he had settled for so little, he said, "Well, the men in the office were all educated men, and I supposed they knew the law. I never thought that educated men would cheat me."

In some ways as naive as the old carpenter, Roosevelt was shocked by Miss Perkins's accounts of shyster doctors and phony compensation cases. "Wouldn't you think that a man who has been through our medical schools would be honest?" he asked. "Don't the medical schools teach them anything about their duties to society?"

"Well, they all take the famous oath," Miss Perkins said. "They sign that."

"But do they know what it means? What do they get besides surgery, materia medica, and anatomy?"

The law was changed so that workers had the right to choose their own doctors, and the process was speeded up. By such small pragmatic measures thousands of lives were affected.

The crash of '29 brought unemployment, and solutions had to be found. But it was one thing to recognize the gravity of unemployment and quite another to find remedies for it. Roosevelt gradually came around to the idea of unemployment insurance. At the governors' conference in December 1930, in Salt Lake City, he announced that "unemployment insurance we shall come to in this country, just as certainly as we have come to workmen's compensation for industrial injury, just as certainly as we are today in the midst of a national wave of insuring against old age want." And yet he had misgivings about it. He hated the idea of a dole, and wrote his brother-in-law, Hall Roosevelt, on February 24, 1931, that he wanted to "work into it gradually instead of starting any wholesale plan like that in England." But in Buffalo that August 28, at the New York Federation of Labor convention, he became the first chief executive of any state to favor state-controlled unemployment insurance, in which the employer, employee, and state would jointly pay the premium.

Unemployment insurance was not a cure for unemployment but arose from the economic organization of society, which had to offer some protection for the wage earner. Thus, by observing the situation in his own state, and by relying on the judgment of trusted aides such as Frances Perkins, whom he sent on a six-week trip to England to see how their system worked, Roosevelt's opinions were evolving.

In January 1929, the president of the City Trust Company died, and it soon became apparent that the bank had been involved in a number of illegal practices, such as forgery and juggling account books. The scandal touched the state government through the superintendent of banks, Frank Warder, who was somehow implicated, and who resigned in April. Roosevelt was in Warm Springs. Upon learning that Warder was planning to leave the country, Acting Governor Herbert Lehman, without consulting Roosevelt, appointed Robert Moses to investigate.

With his usual thoroughness, Moses found criminal evidence against Warder, who was arrested in June and later found guilty of accepting a $10,-000 bribe and was sentenced to five to ten years in Sing Sing. On July 10, Moses submitted his report, which made banking sound like a legal form of piracy. Probably the worst abuse was that commercial banks were allowed to sell stocks to their customers. The banks also loaned them money so they could buy the stocks. In addition, although savings accounts were protected, so-called thrift accounts in commercial banks were not. If one of these banks failed, the depositor had no way of getting his money back. Finally, there were completely unregulated private banks that were no better than first-class bucket shops. When their depositors bought stocks on margin, often their orders were not fully executed. Clark Bros. on Nassau Street in New York City, which filed for bankruptcy in June, advertised as "rendering a complete banking service" but did not have the word "bank" on their window and did not come under the banking law.

Thousands of small depositors were hurt by the Clark Bros. closing on June 29 and had no recourse. One of these, a lawyer named Samuel Burstein, wrote Roosevelt on July 2: "As late as 3:40 p.m. on Friday afternoon, June 28, 1929, I personally made a deposit of $242.50 in the regular way at the teller's window, while one of the Clark brothers looked on in silence. There seemed to be nothing unusual; but nevertheless, the bank closed at 5 p.m. that day and failed to open up again for business. . . . I don't believe that any sane-minded person can for one moment be made to think that the members of the firm did not know within one hour before closing that the bank was insolvent or unable to meet the demands of depositors."

Roosevelt was unaffected by Moses's report and the letters he received from angry depositors. His personal dislike for Moses may have influenced him to disregard the crying need for reform. More than that, he had a residual faith in the banking community stemming from his years on Wall Street. He had himself been the apostle of business self-regulation as head of the American Construction Council. The banks could work out their own problems. Roosevelt appointed a commission of his own, which did not include Moses but did include a former state senator who was counsel to the Bank of the United States, which was on the verge of failure.

He also named Joseph A. Broderick, a respected figure in the banking community, as superintendent of banks. Broderick agreed that the banks should reform themselves, and was opposed to such radical schemes as insuring depositors against losses, which he called "vicious in principle." Roosevelt's commission did recommend the regulation of private banks, which the 1930 legislative session put into law. "The new legislation is wonderful," Broderick wrote the governor, "it gives us even greater responsibility than we dreamed of."

It was not all that wonderful, for it did not give Broderick the responsibility to deal with the wobbly Bank of the United States, which had fifty-eight branches and 450,000 depositors. This was a bank that people had faith in because of its name—they thought there was something official about it. It was a little people's bank, known on Wall Street as the "pants pressers' bank" because it did a lot of garment-trade business.

In October 1930, Roosevelt held a secret meeting in his home with some of the city's leading bankers to negotiate a merger that would save the bank. As he later told a friend, "I reached out. I sent for Morgan and I sent for several of the other great bankers in this state and city. I told them, in the privacy of my own room, that this would be a frightful thing, that this was little people. I wanted them to come to the rescue of that bank. At that time my commissioner was ready to move in and close that bank, but each time he proposed it I got a statement that these men were considering saving the bank. . . . After a considerable delay, these men, Morgan and his cohorts, sent back word that they could do nothing about it and that if it had to fail let it fail."

Fail it did. It was the worst bank failure in the nation's history. On December 10, there was a run on the bank, with 15,000 depositors lined up in the rain, and the next day Broderick closed it. Not only were the depositors' assets frozen, but those who held Bank of the United States stock were assessed $25 a share, under a state law that bank stock was assessable at its par value in the event there were insufficient funds to pay depositors. The widow of an Episcopal clergyman wrote Roosevelt: "I was told, and believed, that stock of a large New York bank such as that was a safe investment for widows and orphans. . . . I had invested money that we have saved for the boys' education."

It belatedly dawned on Roosevelt that the bankers were incapable of self-regulation. But when a thrift-account bill was introduced in the State Senate that March it died, and in 1932, by which time banks were failing right and left, the legislature again refused to act. A Republican legislature had its uses. Roosevelt could make public pronouncements on issues he only half-heartedly supported, such as bank reform, and then the legislature could kill the bills and take the blame.

By this time, a scapegoat had been found in Broderick, who was indicted in 1931 for not acting fast enough to close the Bank of the United States. Roosevelt testified on his behalf, in April 1932, saying "This man, Broderick, is my appointee. I knew everything that he did. The reason he didn't move in sooner on the bank was mainly my responsibility. . . . Mr. Broderick shouldn't be on trial, I'm the one who should be on trial." Broderick was acquitted.

Of course, Robert Moses thought this soft-pedaling of the banks was just another example of Roosevelt's shallow and vacillating nature. In later years, he liked to say that if Albert Ottinger had been elected governor, Roosevelt would never have been heard from again and the history of the world would have been different.

Roosevelt and Moses offered an interesting contrast in methods of governing. Moses held politicians in contempt, distinguishing between the grandstanders who took the credit and the anonymous toilers who really got the job done. Insulated from the necessity of having to ingratiate himself with voters and politicians, he could indulge an abrasive and insulting manner. He had his fiefdom, the parks system, by virtue of his expertise, hard work, and honesty, and conducted his business in a dogmatic and authoritarian manner.

Roosevelt, however, was ingratiating by nature and profession. He depended on the goodwill of voters and fellow politicians. Government in a democratic society was a system of alliances; it served no purpose to alienate potential allies. Compromise and conciliation were his tools.

Being cordial and charming did not mean cronyism, and Roosevelt was quite prepared to support people he did not like against people he did like on the merit of the issue. This was what occurred in the battle of the Northern State Parkway, which pitted Moses against Roosevelt's Harvard classmate and former law associate, Grenville Clark. Moses was trying to put the parkway through some of the big Long Island estates in Wheatley Hills, north of Garden City. The estate owners retained Grenville Clark to represent them. Clark wrote Roosevelt proposing an alternate route that would dip southward and avoid Wheatley Hills before it got to Old Westbury.

Moses wrote Roosevelt on December 3, 1928, before his inauguration, that locations other than the one he had decided on "involve torturing the parkway down toward the middle of the island where the landscaping problem is almost insuperable and where small houses and lots are affected. . . . The remaining opposition comes from people of large wealth who have always been able to buy what they wanted or to get what they wanted by influence and pressure. It is difficult for these people to believe there is anyone they cannot reach in some way. They live in a kind of sound-proof vacuum and have no idea what is going on outside."

Roosevelt knew all about those people. He was one of them. He had grown up on a large estate. His father would have had apoplexy if they had tried to put a road through his Hyde Park property. But he rose above the vested interests of his class. The landed gentry of Wheatley Hills would have to make sacrifices for the ultimate benefit of the tens of thousands of New Yorkers who would use the parkway. It was unconscionable that less than ten property owners were holding up appropriations in the legislature and had attempted to prevent Nassau County from acquiring land and dedicating it to the state.

When Clark complained that anyone who disagreed with Moses was treated with contempt, Roosevelt replied on April 9, 1929: "I have had some experience in the acquisitions of rights of way. It is a very difficult procedure, especially when there are local interests pulling one way or another, and I am ready to say from my park experience that the acquisition of so much right of way with little or no cost to the state is an extraordinary achievement especially when there has been so much opposition. . . . It is simply absurd to imply that hundreds of acres of land of great value have been dedicated without full knowledge and approval of those who made the dedications."

Roosevelt backed Moses, even though he thought Moses was his own worst enemy. Instead of trying to win people over, he had an almost compulsive need to humiliate them. In one case, a New York stockbroker named A. E. Walbridge, who had a home in Roslyn, Long Island, wrote Moses a polite letter about a planned viaduct that would close the view of the harbor to the village. The people of the community, he said, were not so selfish as to disregard the necessity of traffic relief in the vicinity but hoped that some alternate plan might be found. Moses replied: "I am most skeptical as to any genuine interest which your family may have as to State public improvement on Long Island. Your father's . . . sole desire has been to have the public pay for any cheap construction which will enable him to exploit his property without regard to preservation of natural beauty and the interests of people generally."

Where Moses dealt in personalities, Roosevelt dealt in issues. Writing to soothe the irate Walbridge, he said: "Personally, I had hoped that a route could be found further inland than the village, but the engineers assure me that this is not possible. Therefore, by a sort of process of elimination the viaduct seems to be the only thing left. I can tell you quite frankly that I do not think that Commissioner Moses' letter to you was either called for or polite. I do not understand what his long tirade about your family had to do with the merits or demerits of the viaduct!" That type of personal attack was not only crude, it was unproductive.

In October 1929, when the struggle over the Northern State Parkway was at its height, Roosevelt received a report that gave him further cause for concern about his quarrelsome parks commissioner. It seems that the American Scenic and Historic Preservation Society, a private group of nature lovers, opposed the Northern State Parkway because it would spoil the North Shore glacial moraine. The society was represented on the State Parks Council, which Moses had formed in 1924 and which he completely dominated, by the $6,000-a-year secretary, a pudgy little man named Raymond H. Torrey. Moses found out that Torrey had been leaking information on council proceedings to Grenville Clark, who showed a knowledge of the council's budget preparations that he could have obtained only from a privileged source.

On the morning of Thursday, September 12, Moses was meeting in the Parks Council office at 302 Broadway with Jay Downer, chief engineer of the Westchester County Park Commission, and D. Hart Ames, the executive secretary of the Allegheny State Park Commission. Torrey was called in, and Moses began to berate him for passing information to Grenville Clark. Torrey said he had only given him information that anyone was entitled to. Moses then berated him for publishing an article opposing the Northern Parkway in the Scenic and Historic Preservation Society's bulletin. Torrey said the article had been reprinted from the *New York Times* as a news item.

Livid with rage, Moses shouted: "Goddamn you, what do you mean by doing anything like that?"

For years, Torrey had endured Moses's verbal assaults in silence. He was a meek man, a bird-watcher, a lover of the deep woods who spent weekends building lean-tos on Adirondack trails. But this time Moses's manner and his cursing provoked Torrey beyond restraint, and he replied, "You big noisy kike, you can't talk to me like that."

Moses leaped on him, grabbed his throat with both hands, and began to strangle him. Jay Downer stepped in and pried his hands away, saying "Stop that, Bob, this is a public meeting, and you can't act that way."

"You goddamned son of a bitch," Moses shouted as he tried to free himself from Downer's grasp. Downer urged Torrey to get out of the office, and as he started to leave, Moses picked up a heavy glass ashtray, but Ames deflected his arm as he threw it, and it fell short. "Get to hell out of here," Moses yelled as Torrey departed, rubbing his sore neck.

Reporting the incident to Roosevelt on October 5, Torrey asked: "Is not this example of Mr. Moses' truculence and violence against anyone who opposes him evidence that he is unfitted to hold a public office?"

Unrepentant, and ever on the attack, Moses responded to Roosevelt's inquiry on October 11 by saying that Torrey was "lazy, incompetent and disloyal. . . . He used an epithet which has never been addressed to me in all my life and I think he deserved much more of a thrashing than he got and I guess pretty nearly anyone will agree with me as to this. There is a good deal of picturesque exaggeration in Torrey's reference to my language and conduct and I see no reason to refer to this at length nor to the silly rubbish about the functioning of the Parks Council. . . . Like all other human institutions, however, the Council suffers because of the presence of one or two crackpots."

By this time, Roosevelt was wondering whether he should number Moses among the crackpots, and advised his secretary, James T. Mahoney, on October 14: "I should regret it as unfortunate if this dirty linen had to be washed in public, but if this has to be done I propose that we have a thorough washday."

In the end, the Torrey incident was hushed up, but Moses lost the Northern Parkway battle through his own doing. Grenville Clark discovered that Moses had made a deal with his relative, the estate owner Otto Kahn, to shift the parkway around Kahn's private golf course in exchange for a $10,000 gift to the Long Island Park Commission. Moses was prepared to oblige a millionaire and use his gift to buy farmers off their land. When the legislature found out, Moses protested to Roosevelt that "the idea that we shifted our route to please one man because he gave us some money is too absurd to entertain. There were many other dedications involved in the shift." But the harm was done, and Grenville Clark told Roosevelt that there would be a full-scale battle on the parkway's route in the 1930 legislative session. That was a year in which Roosevelt was running for reelection and the Moses-Kahn deal might prove embarrassing. A compromise was worked out so that the parkway avoided the Wheatley estates. For Moses, the victim of his own arrogance, it was an abject surrender.

There was another odd thing about Moses. He loved to be the master builder, but disliked the people who benefited from his projects. Jones Beach had been called by H. G. Wells one of the wonders of America, but Moses resented the hordes who invaded the park on weekends, littering and soiling his magnificent creation. He tried to segregate blacks to distant beaches through bus permits. When Roosevelt investigated, one of his aides confirmed that "Bob Moses is seeking to discourage large Negro parties from picnicking at Jones Beach, attempting to divert them to some other of the state parks."

Moses further restricted the use of Jones Beach by charging a fifty-cent parking fee. "I was a good deal impressed the other day by the complaint of one man in regard to the parking space at Jones Beach," Roosevelt wrote him on August 19, 1929. "He put it this way: that the people who can come to Jones Beach on Saturdays and Sundays are charged fifty cents for parking cars [while] in the middle of the week people who are on an average better off financially are only charged twenty-five cents for parking. I also think fifty cents for a parking charge is too high. It is out of line with the prices charged at private popular resorts. Frankly, I think the people have a legitimate kick. Won't you seriously take up the question of reducing the Jones Beach charge to twenty-five cents at all times?"

Moses argued that the average car on Saturday and Sunday carried five people, which came to ten cents per person. Most of them came in their bathing suits. You couldn't find a cheaper day at the beach on the entire Atlantic seaboard. People had a greater respect for what they paid for. Jones Beach needed more lifeguards and more attendants to keep it clean. The parking fee was their greatest source of revenue, and the easiest to collect. Why give in to a handful of people who wanted everything free? In the end it would mean they couldn't charge for anything, which would result in staggering appropriations. Under this barrage of reasons, Roosevelt gave in. When the legislature passed a bill prohibiting fees in state parks, he vetoed it.

When Roosevelt wanted a favor from Moses, however, he was brusquely rejected. His son Jimmy had a friend named Francis J. Buckley who had been dropped from the parks engineering staff to a $5-a-day job as parking attendant at Jones Beach. Buckley was the son of a retired Massachusetts Democratic state senator and Roosevelt supporter, and was recommended by such Bay State political powers as Frank Hurley. Accordingly, Roosevelt asked Moses on April 12, 1932: "Is it possible for you to consider Francis J. Buckley, one of the engineers in the employ of the Long Island Park Commission, who has been let go because of failure of appropriations? I am personally rather interested in the young man."

On April 19, Moses replied: "I think the efforts of this young man to get himself some kind of special preference through political channels in Massachusetts is wholly improper. . . . The best thing this young man can do is to take his medicine and be glad he has a job of any kind."

There was no give to Moses. He alone among state officials insisted on continuing to call Roosevelt "Frank" rather than "Governor," to let him know that in his eyes they were equals. On one occasion, someone sitting in the anteroom of Roosevelt's office heard Moses shouting at him as he shouted at everyone: "Frank Roosevelt, you're a goddamned liar and this time I can prove it!" Roosevelt did not take offense. He smiled and played the waiting game. He did not tell Moses that he was about to slash the parks budget, knowing that Moses would only run to the newspapers to raise support.

The feud with Moses continued when FDR was president. When Mayor Fiorello H. La Guardia appointed Moses to the Triborough Bridge Authority in February 1934, FDR tried to get him fired. The bridge was being funded with PWA money, and FDR told Harold Ickes, the PWA administrator, to send for La Guardia and tell him to get rid of Moses. La Guardia hemmed and hawed and Ickes told him he would not honor any more requests for PWA funds until the Moses case was settled. Finally, on December 26, 1934, Ickes issued an order that seemed general in application but was in fact aimed at Moses, to the effect that the PWA would not advance funds to any authority that had a member who also held public office— Moses, of course, was a member of the Triborough Bridge Authority and also chairman of the New York State Council of Parks. But the order back-fired when Moses leaked it to the press and the PWA was charged with being used for political purposes. Ickes had to back down, and Moses stayed on in his dual capacity. In fact, on July 11, 1936, FDR attended the cere-mony for the opening of the bridge, presided over by Moses.

Biding his time, FDR made up for the Triborough fiasco in 1939 when Moses proposed a bridge from the Battery to Brooklyn, a mile and a quarter below the Brooklyn Bridge. Ickes thought it would improve the waterfront and said so at a cabinet meeting, but Roosevelt pulled down his lip and said, "Well, I don't know, we want to think about that and look into it, Harold. We'll have to consult the military. That's a very important channel." "That's all right, Mr. President," Ickes said. "We've figured out everything. It will not interfere with the operation of ships."

The next thing you knew the Army Engineers were involved—they had charge of all navigable waters for the country's defense. "The President is going to kill this wonderful project," Ickes told Frances Perkins. "He's get-ting the military to condemn it by saying it interferes with the navigable streams, and it doesn't. . . . It's just that he so hates Moses."

Miss Perkins took the matter up with Roosevelt, who said, "It's no good, Frances. It's just a no good idea. They'll ruin the looks of it. They'll ruin its park possibilities. They'll just make it into a great traffic highway. Besides, I'm reliably informed, though the engineers haven't finished, that they think it's a very great hazard to navigation. In case of a war we can't have any bridges around there. They'll drop bombs and so forth." Miss Perkins knew the real reason, and no one was surprised when the War Department in May rejected the proposal. That was one way to handle Bob Moses, and in Roo-sevelt's book the man he couldn't handle was not yet born.

The public regulation of electric utilities was a matter dear to Roosevelt's heart. It was a national issue, one upon which he could take a position of leadership. In New York State, it was an issue that cut across party lines, appealing to upstate Republicans vexed by high electricity bills as well as to urban Democrats. It was a way of bringing out into the open the sinister connection between high rates and political corruption. Everybody knew that the utilities controlled the State Assembly and ran the New York State Republican party. As in the matter of the highway going through the estates, Roosevelt could be the spokesman for the many against the few.

In short, this was an issue on which he couldn't go wrong, and a source of embarrassment to the Republicans if they obstructed change. Public power was the pivot of political debate. The important thing was to keep the debate open. Even if he was stalemated by the legislature, he could arouse public sentiment and use the issue to political advantage.

Felix Frankfurter spurred him on, writing that "hydroelectric power raises without a doubt the most far-reaching social and economic issues before the American people certainly for the next decade."

Roosevelt boned up on it, consulting experts and reading books, and felt that "the whole question, in my mind, is as to whether a public utility has the right to make any old profit that it can or not, in other words, as to whether there is any real distinction between a public utility company and a purely private business."

The Public Service Commission, under its Republican chairman, William A. Prendergast, was not doing its job of setting fair rates. Under attack for his pro-utility bias, Prendergast resigned in a huff in February 1931. Roosevelt appointed Milo Maltbie, a utilities expert known as "the people's champion." But that was about the extent of what he could do, for the legislature continued to kill all bills that would have brought him closer to his goal—power that was developed by the state but transmitted and distributed by private companies.

Beaten in the legislature, Roosevelt went to the people, arguing his case in a radio talk on April 24. There was a great distinction between private industrial companies dealing in steel or shoes or clothing or groceries or automobiles and semipublic corporations dealing in service to the public such as gas, electricity, and street cars. The state had the absolute right not only to regulate those utilities but also to give or deny them the rights to charters except on terms laid down by the state. The Public Service Commission had been created to supervise the utilities, but gradually it began to see itself more as a court and the utilities as normal corporations.

The root of the problem was whether the utility companies were rendering regulation ineffective by insisting that they were entitled to profits based on inflated valuation of their properties and by initiating litigation in the courts when they did not like the rates set by the commission. The U.S. Supreme Court had gradually allowed large additional amounts to the rates, based on what it would cost to reproduce the plant anew after many years. But that was a wholly illogical depreciation, and Roosevelt was insisting that New York State should return to the theory of granting only a reasonable return on investment.

Roosevelt came to see the utilities magnates as selfish and unprincipled men. His suspicions were confirmed when an important businessman told him candidly that as long as the cost of labor and materials went up the utility companies would favor the reproduction-cost theory, but as soon as it looked as if the cost of labor and materials would go down over a period of years, they would abandon reproduction-cost theory altogether and demand the substitution of the prudent-investment theory. "In other words," Roosevelt reflected, "we don't give a damn which theory is right but we will be for whichever theory will give us the largest capital increase."

It took him two years just to get the legislature to agree to the appointment of a five-man Power Authority, which would study the feasibility of harnessing the waters of the St. Lawrence River for electric power. Water from the Great Lakes flowed into the St. Lawrence and escaped into Canada and emptied into the Gulf of St. Lawrence and the Atlantic Ocean. The thought of all this vast untapped and wasted power chafed at his constructivist side. It was a grandiose scheme. A dam would have to be built in the international section of the St. Lawrence River, and a treaty would have to be signed with Canada and ratified by Congress. But President Hoover was not going to be rushed into a project that would benefit his chief political rival.

A quarter century would pass before the waters of the St. Lawrence were harnessed, but even though Roosevelt could not get much done in this area while he was governor, he created a climate of opinion that his successors could build on, and he succeeded in projecting himself nationally as the champion of government regulation of power companies. When James I. Wendell, a student at the Hill School in Pottstown, Pennsylvania, asked Roosevelt to name a topic for the annual debate with Lawrenceville, he suggested the following: Resolved, that regulation of privately owned electric utilities by public service commissions has failed to provide adequate protection for the consuming public.

Roosevelt had a talent for governing. Whatever the office, he filled it with natural ease. By training and instinct, he knew how to handle the controls. He had the right mix of leadership and responsiveness. He knew how to make half a loaf sound like a feast. He had a "feel" for things that could not be rationally explained, in the same way that it was said of Henry Ford that he could pick among six carburetors the one that wasn't working by holding them in his hand.

Part of it was that he saw his own life as history. It was a life devoted to public service, and meant to be inserted into the life of the nation. As he drew on the past for lessons, he could now draw on his own life. "When I was first in the legislature," "when I was in the Navy," "when I visited the front in 1918"—these were recurring themes. History was always in the making, and he was part of it, and he had absorbed the American past and made it his own. He had an intuitive sense of the nation's character, of the sources of its energy and equilibrium. Like Walt Whitman, he assumed all the attributes of his country.

As Frances Perkins observed, "Roosevelt was a walking American history book. He had the kind of historical understanding and grasp that came from having heard about the events from people who had either seen them or heard about them from their grandparents. He knew exactly how the troops went here and there, and exactly where the Indian massacres were and why." He knew that George Washington's motto *Exitus act probat* meant "The end justifies the means," but also that it was a quotation from Ovid, which in context might mean "The event justifies the deed." What was important was whether the Washingtons adopted the motto before they left

England or after they got here. In the monk Latin of the fifteenth or sixteenth century, it might be possible to translate the word *exitus* as "departure," with the implication that the emigration of the first Washington
justified his deeds after he got here.

There were no isolated events for Roosevelt. Everything that happened in
the state and the nation, every crisis, every decision taken, was part of a
larger context of America fulfilling its destiny, of an experiment in government still being worked out.

He had the dual vision necessary for leadership, seeing the grand design
of the tapestry but capable also of attending to a single stitch. Was there an
item in the budget to cover the pests that were causing great losses to the
growers of daffodil bulbs on Long Island? What about another janitor for
the State Normal School in New Paltz? One man could not take care of a
unit of 500 rooms and a two-acre lawn.

The worst part of the job had nothing to do with running the departments.
It was that the governor was seen as a savior, and that people constantly
wrote him asking to be saved, from unemployment, from injustice, from deportation or jail or discharge, from all the disappointments of life. It was
frustrating to have to admit over and over to these people in misery that
there was nothing he could do. To the hundreds of requests for jobs a form
letter replied that they could not be dealt with individually. For begging letters there was also a standard reply.

People were suffering, but that was outside his jurisdiction. When the wife
of a man in Buffalo who had been electrocuted by a coil of wire left by
workmen on his back gate asked for help, she was told that "the matter on
which you write is one entirely without his jurisdiction." When a passenger
on the excursion steamboat that circled Manhattan drowned, the crew doing
nothing to save him, that was outside his jurisdiction as well, because the
waters surrounding the island were tidal waters and came under the responsibility of the Bureau of Navigation in Washington.

And what to do about messages from madmen, such as this wire from one
Adolph Bay: "I am subjected to the most cruel torture by means of nightly
diseasing electric ray overexposures by state police and local men help
today"?

It was all part of being in the public eye. If he was photographed without
his Legion button in his buttonhole, a Legion post would complain that the
69,000 Legionnaires in the state, who were proud that he was the first among
them to be elected governor of New York, wanted him to wear it.

There was a unique atmosphere in Albany under Roosevelt, an élan, a
sense of largeness and potentiality. It radiated so strongly from his buoyant
personality that it cast a kind of glow. People were affected by a man who
was performing well in his position and also proceeding with seeming effortlessness toward a larger destiny. Roosevelt had the knack that all true
artists have of making what they do—the brush stroke, the touch on the
keyboard—look easy. He was invincibly cheerful, as if he had decided that

the whole thing was a game, and should be played according to the standards of good sportsmanship. You didn't gloat when you won, or whine when you lost, or blame the weather. He never gave in to anger or name-calling, like Bob Moses. He stayed on good terms with the press, even though he was misquoted five or six times a day: he joked about it—why, one paper had written about the bottle-scarred veterans. He didn't mind being the butt of a joke. At the 1929 legislative correspondents' dinner, when the state budget had risen to the unprecedented sum of $311 million, he was crowned "King of the Budget-Makers" and clad in a regal robe of red bespangled with dollar signs, and handed some fireplace tongs as a royal scepter. Even the quarrels with the legislature were good-tempered. He emitted amiability and optimism, inviting reciprocity, as if keeping always in a corner of his mind the words of one of Endicott Peabody's favorite prayers: "O God, author of the world's joy, bearer of the world's pain, make us glad that we have inherited the world's burden, deliver us from the luxury of cheap melancholy, and at the heart of all our trouble and sorrow, let unconquerable gladness dwell."

Who knew what was behind the genial exterior? Miss Perkins sensed loneliness—so many people around him, and so few close friends. He was friends with church people, for instance, but shared nothing with them except their interest in the church. He had friendships of this character and friendships of that character, all on a convivial but fragmentary level. He had a kind of reserve that prevented the sharing of deeply felt emotions. Eleanor taught three days a week at the Todhunter School and had the furniture factory at Val-Kill, and a weaving business in Hyde Park, and political responsibilities of her own, although she tried to be in Albany four days a week. Louis Howe, to whom Roosevelt revealed himself most fully, was in New York, acting as political chief of staff. The children were far-flung. Where could Roosevelt turn for emotional intimacy? More and more, he relied on Missy LeHand, who lived with him in the executive mansion, although recollections differ as to whether she had an adjoining bedroom.

Sam Rosenman also lived there during the second term, and recalled that "the Roosevelt family life was not of the best. I often think that's one of the reasons that his children didn't turn out as well as they should have. . . . Eleanor loved to mother people, but sometimes the people she picked to mother were not the kind of people that I would pick even to be a brother to, much less a mother. . . . But so far as close family life goes, which exists where a man and his wife and his children are always there, that couldn't be true at the Mansion, because the children were away and only came back for the beginning of the summer and then usually disappeared into various parts of the country."

Was he happy? With Roosevelt you never knew, because he rarely revealed his true feelings. That was a trait rooted in his childhood, when he had to conceal parts of his life from his parents, to keep from being smothered. The first rule was never to let anyone know that something had hurt you or made you mad. The second rule was not to give away what you were really thinking. In his public life as governor, this was translated into shiftiness. Roosevelt had a reputation for being misleading. Legislators would ask him his intentions on a bill and he would mislead them. Al Smith had said, "When I give my word, it sticks." But Roosevelt's word sometimes became unstuck. There were men who, after dealing with him, uttered what amounted to the worst insult that could be given in Albany: "From now on, we deal in writing."

On balance, however, many would have agreed that Roosevelt conformed to the definition that Helen Keller, who like him had learned to master a crippling handicap, proposed in a letter on February 10, 1931: "If I were asked to define the characteristics of a great Governor, using the term in its widest sense, I would reply, the will to put himself in the place of others; the desire to help others out of positions from which he himself would recoil; and the wisdom to recognize constructive effort that is worthy of encouragement."

On December 1, 1929, from Warm Springs where he was spending a few weeks, Roosevelt asked Louis Howe to bid on some items in an estate sale at the Anderson Galleries in New York. "It is just possible," he said, "that the recent little flurry downtown will make the prices comparatively low."

This was his reaction to the stock market crash, during which nearly 55 million shares had changed hands, and which signaled the end of prosperity and business rule. But it did not seem so at the time.

After nine years of Republican rule, prosperity seemed like a permanent condition rather than the upswing of an economic cycle. America was the spoiled child of history, with the greatest privileged class the world had ever seen. The number of shares on the New York Stock Exchange had grown from 25 million in 1923 to 1,125 million in 1928. Every clerk and every postman knew what a margin account was. John J. Raskob wrote an article in the *Ladies' Home Journal* entitled "Everybody Ought to Be Rich." But after the crash, the value of stocks was down by 50 percent and those depreciated stocks were the collateral for bank loans. The borrowers couldn't pay and the banks couldn't collect and the depositors withdrew their money. On December 2, Jackson E. Reynolds, a friend of Herbert Hoover and a New York banker, went to the White House to tell the president what was happening.

Hoover was scornful and asked: "What makes you so yellow, Jack?" "I'm glad you feel that way," Reynolds replied, "because you are going to have something bust right in your face in a few days, and it will just smear you with garbage. And that's the Bank of the United States."

The country weathered 1929 because the number of bank failures was small and widely scattered, so the total impact was diffused. The new year opened without serious alarm. The financial community said the depression would be highly beneficial, although no one suggested that it should be prolonged so that its benefits might continue to be enjoyed.

In June 1930, Hoover received a delegation that had come to Washington to plead for a program of federal public works. "Gentlemen," he said, "you have come sixty days too late. The depression is over." But in Kansas, wheat was thirty cents a bushel; and in North Dakota, handbills tacked to the walls of public buildings announced "Farms for Sale"; and in Chicago, the public libraries had never been so crowded, having become a refuge for the unemployed.

In September, England went off the gold standard, which was like doomsday to the financial community—it was unthinkable. Every foreign investor who owned American securities sold them and took the gold home. The native-born sheep did the same. The flight of gold continued until $5 billion had left the country. As deposits shrank, more banks closed. Real estate lost value and the equity in mortgages disappeared. The new Empire State Building could not rent its offices and cut off elevator service between the forty-second and sixty-seventh floors. Construction stagnated because builders could not get loans.

New York State was not exempt from the crisis, and Roosevelt wrote Robert F. Wagner, who with other Senate progressives backed federal spending for public works and direct unemployment relief, on September 9, 1930: "On the matter of the serious unemployment situation, I regret to say that my trips to practically every part of the state this summer confirm the fear that the depression exists not only in a few of the larger cities but extends to all of the smaller cities and even to the villages and rural districts."

In the congressional elections that November, Hoover lost control of the House, where the Republicans and Democrats each had 217 seats, with one Farmer-Labor member holding the balance, and kept only nominal control of the Senate, which had forty-eight Republicans and forty-seven Democrats and one Farmer-Labor member.

What was wrong with society, when the richest land on earth had gone broke? How could people go hungry in a country that produced so much wheat? As Will Rogers put it, the United States was "the first nation to go to the poorhouse in an automobile."

Where were Work and Thrift and Sound Principles and the American Way of Life and Go West Young Man and the Land of Opportunity and Everybody Ought to Be Rich? They had been replaced by tighten your belt, breadlines, soup kitchens, grown men working as caddies, panhandling, and riding blind baggage. Through freight trains often included two or three empty boxcars with open doors so that hoboes wouldn't break open the loaded cars.

The depression destroyed the myth of self-reliance, which had been appropriated by the corporate world to justify noninterference by government. An American was a man who did not need help. Like the pioneers who had made the continent habitable, he went his own way and solved his own problems. "An American was a man who knew which way to take to reach tomorrow," wrote Archibald MacLeish. "An American was a man who could let himself in and let himself out and nobody asking him 'please,' not even the President. An American was a man who never asked anyone any-thing—who he was or where he came from or what he did—because it was answer enough to be a man. At least in America." This was a splendid ratio-nale for all the excesses of laissez-faire capitalism. It was a noble thing for General Motors to believe it and make sure it was applied in every govern-ment department. But for the farmer who lost his farm and the worker who lost his job in the unregulated misery of those depression years, self-reliance was cold comfort.

Self-reliance was an ideology that perfectly suited Herbert Hoover's cir-cumstances. Orphaned at the age of ten, he had been farmed out among rel-atives and had worked his way through Stanford. As a mining engineer and promotor, he became a millionaire by buying and selling his interests in mines. "If a man has not made a million dollars by the time he is forty," he said, "he is not worth much."

Having done it unassisted, Hoover found it hard to grasp why others could not. He honestly believed that federal government interference would destroy American individualism. When a drought killed cattle and crops in the Southwest in 1930, he asked Congress to make provisions for federal loans to farmers to help them buy seed, fertilizer, and cattle feed. But when he was asked to allow the Farm Board to give away the surplus wheat it had bought to the unemployed, he refused. He was willing to feed starving cattle but not starving people.

And yet many agreed with him. The myth of self-reliance had deep roots. George W. Shafer, the governor of North Dakota, said: "These people out here are farmers, and farmers don't starve. Things get tight, but they always manage. These things have happened before and they got out of it without becoming public charges. They never went down to Washington to be put on the public teat and by God if it's left up to me they ain't going down now."

It was a vision of society that was hard to reconcile with widespread suf-fering. To say as Hoover did that the depression could not be cured by laws or executive action, and that state government and private charity would take care of the unemployed, and that the situation would redress itself, was fine as long as you were not in a breadline. As Anatole France once put it: "The law in its fairness prohibits the rich as well as the poor from sleeping under bridges." Hoover's beliefs, however sincere, seemed inadequate when unemployment in the winter of 1931 was climbing to 25 percent. And be-hind Hoover there was his secretary of the Treasury, Andrew Mellon, the champion of big business and dribble-from-the-top prosperity, who feared that federal relief would lead to a soak-the-rich policy and that the years of shielding the big fortunes at the expense of everyone else would be over.

Hoover, the great humanitarian of World War I, when he had fed the Belgians, was now seen as indifferent to the suffering of his own people. His name became a generic term. The newspapers that covered sleeping men on park benches were Hoover blankets. A pocket turned inside out was a Hoover flag. A community of shacks with walls made from grocery cartons smoothed flat, roofs of hammered-out tin cans, and door hinges cut from worn-out tires, rising in the excavations of unbuilt apartment houses, was a Hooverville.

The doctrine of self-reliance that Hoover as an orphan, a self-made millionaire, a Quaker, and a Republican was so comfortable with and so bent on defending was one that did not fit Roosevelt's experience. Roosevelt had had every advantage—birth, education, inherited wealth, the support of a devoted mother; a member of the landed gentry, he had been invited to enter local politics much as a young English lord might have been offered a safe seat by the Tory party. At every obstacle, he had been given a leg up—Josephus Daniels had wanted him as his assistant, and Al Smith had asked him to run for governor. His illness had made him dependent on others on a daily, even hourly basis. A man who did not have the use of his legs could hardly proclaim the virtues of self-reliance, when he could not even get dressed or get out of a car by himself. Roosevelt's existence was a testimonial to helping hands.

Hoover's position that the federal government could not solve the depression or directly assist its millions of casualties provided a clear-cut view of the role of the state with which Roosevelt found it natural to disagree. Not only for humanitarian reasons, or because helping those in distress was an impulse originating in his personal situation. He saw it as the latest chapter in the ongoing struggle between the heirs of Thomas Jefferson and Alexander Hamilton. The Hamiltonian idea of a strong central government directed by a small group of citizens, Roosevelt thought, would lead in the long run to government by selfishness, and that was what was happening now, with Hoover acting in the interests of big business and forgetting the people.

That big business should be regulated also had a strong historical buttress, and here Roosevelt drew on *The Federalist,* in which James Madison had written: "A landed interest, a manufacturing interest, a moneyed interest, with many lesser interests, grow up of necessity in civilized nations and divide them into different classes, actuated by different sentiments and views. The regulation of the various and interfering interests form the principal task of modern legislation."

Big business was always on the Republican side, and it was always under Republican administrations that gifts of oil lands to favored individuals and similar scandals took place, and that men such as Andrew Mellon came to power. Mellon believed that the laws were meant to be obeyed by the weak and not by the strong. The business of the church bells, Roosevelt thought, was a perfect example. To protect a small and favored industry, a very high tariff had been levied on imported bells. Some of Mellon's rich friends, who wanted to donate fine bells to their favorite churches, objected to paying the heavy import duty. To accommodate them, Mellon made the belfries where the bells would be installed bonded warehouses in which they could be kept duty-free, as long as they were not removed and sold. It was a small matter, but to Roosevelt it illustrated an utter disregard for the law, and a perversion of the functions of the state.

"What is the state?" Roosevelt asked in his 1931 message to an extraordinary session of the legislature. "It is the duly constituted representation of an organized society of human beings, created by them for their mutual protection and well-being. 'The State' or 'the Government' is but the machinery through which such mutual aid and protection are achieved." If mutual aid required the expansion of government functions, that went hand in hand with the concept of social responsibility. "In broad terms," Roosevelt went on, "I assert that modern society, acting through its government, owes the definite obligation to prevent the starvation or the dire want of any of its fellow men and women who try to maintain themselves but cannot."

The question was, what to do. There was no government machinery for dealing with problems such as unemployment relief. They were still in the days of the poorhouse and private charity. Roosevelt's measures were tentative and fragmentary, but he thought of what Lord Bryce had once told him—that the states were laboratories. He was willing to experiment.

He authorized the use of National Guard armories to house the homeless. He set up a commission to study unemployment insurance—that was as far as the legislature would go in 1931. Another commission, on stabilization of industry, studied ways to keep workers from being laid off. One method was the eight-hour day and the five-day week, which won him applause from an unexpected quarter. The poet Ezra Pound, an admirer of Mussolini then living in Rome, who would later be arrested and charged with treason for his pro-Axis broadcasts during World War II, wrote him on April 11, 1931: "Respected Gov: go to it. Is there *any* public man honest enough to say that the readiest remedy for unemployment and the one needing no special increase in bureaucracy and bureaucratic blah is the shortening of the working day? (The objections being cut and dried quibbles.)"

But even such a timid measure as shortening the work week met with resistance. Merwin K. Hart, a Harvard classmate of Roosevelt's and president of the New York State Economy Council, wired him: "You have before you bills providing for rigid five day week on all state contracts and extension of eight hour day and prevailing rate of wages to highway work stop if these bills become law you will do injustice to the taxpayers from whom all money spent must come . . . the philosophy back of such bills is false and militates against revival of private business."

"If you were not an old friend and classmate I would tell you that you were all wet!" Roosevelt replied. "Honestly, my dear fellow, I cannot at all see the point of your telegram about the five-day week. It will undoubtedly raise to a very small amount the cost of certain types of contract, but on the other hand it will result in the actual employment of a great many more individual human beings, and that after all is what we are seeking."

Roosevelt could not get over how shortsighted and thickheaded the business community was, writing a friend on August 20 that "many of the so-called business men and financiers, even now, after two years of depression, have not the foggiest idea of what happened. . . . As to the suggestion that 'the great silent body of American people' believe that any . . . minor regulations of certain business by government has been responsible for our troubles I am inclined to think that the contrary is true. Most average citizens with whom I talk are impressed with the rather serious failure of business to prevent present conditions when they had a chance to do so."

On August 25, Roosevelt convened a special session of the legislature to consider unemployment relief. He went in person to the capitol to deliver his request for a new state agency, the Temporary Emergency Relief Administration, which would distribute $25 million and would be financed by a 50-percent increase in the state income tax. "It is clear to me," he said, "that it is the duty of those who have benefited by our industrial and economic system to come to the front in such a grave emergency and assist in relieving those who under the same industrial and economic order are the losers and sufferers."

Roosevelt was carrying out President Hoover's wishes that state and local government should be responsible for relief. The special session stayed in Albany until September 19 as the Republican-controlled legislature quibbled, and finally agreed on a $20 million compromise bill. Half the money would be returned to the communities and the other half would be spent on public works. The money was not a dole, it was to be paid out for work, a dollar's worth of relief for a dollar's worth of labor.

Jesse Straus, the president of Macy's, was picked to run the TERA, while Roosevelt went to Warm Springs for a vacation. Straus brought in the bright young man who had been working for the New York Tuberculosis and Health Association, Harry L. Hopkins, and by February 1932 he had 75,000 people on work relief and 82,000 on home relief.

This was the first concrete plan by any state in the nation to alleviate unemployment distress by direct government action, and it received much national attention, dramatizing the difference between Hoover, still waiting for the depression to correct itself, and Roosevelt, who was willing to experiment. A forward-looking state program could serve as a vehicle to enhance presidential prospects.

In the bitter winter of 1931, when the depression seemed invincible, a young man named Samuel Beer was taking the bus back to college in Ann Arbor from his home in Ohio. As they drove through Toledo, devastated by unemployment, they came through an industrial section and saw, on both sides of the street, stretching endlessly, crowds of men standing on the sidewalk. What were they doing? They were not waiting for a handout or a soup kitchen. They were not rioting or picketing. They were doing very much the same thing that Mr. Hoover was doing, which was exactly nothing and for the same reasons. They did not expect government to do anything for them. They did not think that government could or should do anything for them. Underlying the depression was a vast national passivity, which Roosevelt, by temperament and conviction, was unprepared to accept.

The shortest distance between a candidate and the White House was a very crooked line that zigzagged between professed denials and backstage maneuvering. It was an art in itself, making it seem that the office was seeking you, and it was also quite time-consuming, as it required writing letter after letter, such as this one to Miss Wyona Dashwood: "I am really concerned by talk about 1932, for two very good reasons. The first is that I am honestly not in any sense, manner or form a candidate for the Presidential nomination, for many reasons—the chief being that I have seen so many Presidents at close hand in the White House that I have come more and more to the conclusion that the task is the most trying and most ungrateful of any in America. The second reason is much more important—I am honestly trying to devote myself wholly to the purely state task of being Governor."

He knew of course that whatever he did as governor did not go unnoticed in the rest of the country. By readjusting the tax burden on the farmer, for instance, by providing state aid for rural education, by using the gasoline tax to finance the construction of farm-to-market roads, he identified himself as a sympathetic spokesman for the rural voter, a position he could project on the national scene as the farmer's friend.

A few days after his inauguration as governor in January 1929, his friend Louis Wehle had dropped in on him in Albany. Roosevelt pulled out some long open pasteboard boxes containing white and yellow index cards and tabs, and said: "I've been wanting to show you these. You remember in January, 1920, you said that if I built up on the acquaintances I'd made on my campaign for Vice-President it might lead to the Presidency. Well, Louis Howe and I took that seriously. See these yellow cards: Louis and I put down on these the names, connections, and addresses of the men I met all over the country on our 1920 swings. Ever since, we have followed them up and kept in touch with them. They are the nucleus of my personal organization today. The white cards are names that have been added since."

Roosevelt mailed 5,000 letters to Democratic leaders shortly after his election, asking for suggestions on how to strengthen and unify the party. Louis Howe tabulated the results. What were the reasons given for Smith's defeat? How many "Raskob must go" letters were there? How many proposed Roosevelt in '32? Quite a few, as it turned out, so that under the guise of sounding out the party hierarchy, he conducted a popularity poll. A typical reply came from a county chairman in New Hampshire: "You are the only Democrat that can be elected in 1932. You would hold all of Alfred E.

Smith's friends and would gain millions of votes that he did not get on account of his religion. (I am a Catholic.)"

Another typical reply came from the mayor of Chicago, Anton J. Cermak, calling for a full-time national organization: "There is distress in the pitting of an untrained donkey against the year-round trained elephant.... The reason the Democratic Party loses so many national elections is because it functions nationally only every four years and then we find there are so many holes in the old blanket that we cannot hold the strength we should.... As old Joe Cannon used to say, the same sun that brings out the snakes brings out the lilies."

In fact, a permanent national organization had been announced in April by the chairman of the Democratic National Committee and Du Pont front man, John J. Raskob, still trying to force-feed the Democratic donkey with repeal. He appointed a former Kansas City congressman, Jouett Shouse, as chairman of the executive committee, which would run party affairs on a day-to-day basis. Roosevelt urged a strategy that would emphasize Republican mishandling of the economy—it "should bring out very forcibly the fact that Republican political leaders even up to the Secretary of the Treasury himself have joined with Republican bankers and Republican industrial and power company presidents for many months past in telling the country that everything was sound and that the speed of prosperity could not possibly slacken. They deliberately led the country to believe that it could pull itself up by the bootstraps, doubling its wealth and earning power every two or three years by simply pouring more money into new stock issues and mergers. During this period anyone who dared to call a halt, to criticize, or to warn, was set down as a pessimist, a spoil-joy, or of being short of the mark. The point to be made is that the Republican leaders themselves are the people responsible for inflating the general prosperity bubble until like the Florida land boom it burst with a loud report."

In July 1929, Roosevelt attended his first governors' conference, in New London, Connecticut. The main thing was to get to know them and to oil the wheels of compatibility with small favors. William Tudor Gardner, the governor of Maine, was interested in a friend of his who was up for promotion as a New York City detective. Roosevelt took the matter up with the police commissioner, who promised to do all he could. Governor George H. Dern of Utah wanted to help a young man from Salt Lake City to obtain a scholarship at New York University. Roosevelt said he would see to it. Governor George W. P. Hunt of Arizona, which had voted Republican in the last four elections, expressed his concern that Hoover was grabbing millions of acres for national parks and Indian reservations. Roosevelt displayed a keen understanding of western problems, saying that the solution should be state home rule rather than federal administration. Hunt predicted that in 1932 Arizona would vote Democratic. When Roosevelt learned that Governor George White of Ohio had broken his collarbone in a car accident, he wrote to say that he was sorry to hear about it, it was a pretty painful thing, but it wouldn't keep a good man down. Governor Lamartine G. Hardman of Georgia was a student of dactyloscopy, and wrote an article in the Columbus *Ledger-Enquirer* affirming that criminals and idiots could be recognized through their abnormal fingerprints. Roosevelt applauded this preposterous theory. He wished the article could be printed in one of the big weeklies with a circulation in the millions like the *Saturday Evening Post* because "people have done very little thinking along these lines . . . they fail to realize that the study of heredity or mentality is still in its infancy and that the steps that will be taken in the next twenty years will surprise us all." In 1930, Hardman was one of the first governors to come out for a Roosevelt ticket.

Roosevelt reminded all the governors that the latchstring was out if they were passing through Albany. This went for other politicians too. When Senator Clarence Dill of Washington came through Schenectady in January 1931 to visit the General Electric plant there, Roosevelt invited him to dinner. They talked for three hours and Dill came away a devoted booster. Back in Washington, Dill was having lunch with some other senators, one of whom, Henry Ashurst, announced: "Gentlemen, you may not believe in what I am about to say. Roosevelt is a Man of Destiny! . . . He will lift this country out of the depression and go down in history as one of our greatest Americans." Dill asked him where he had gotten that idea. "When he was elected Governor of New York," Ashurst said, "and couldn't walk. Providence doesn't drag a man back from the grave unless it has a great purpose to be served."

In a hundred ways, Roosevelt was making friends among influential Democrats and attracting national attention as a candidate, while denying that he was one, on the theory that premature bloom invites frostbite. It was pointless to declare when his chances hinged on winning reelection for governor in 1930. But how to protect himself from his friends, eager to announce their support?

One of these was Senator Burton K. Wheeler of Montana, the first important Democrat to come out publicly for Roosevelt, in April 1930, which upset the plans of Raskob and Shouse, who thought the nomination should go to Owen D. Young, then head of General Electric, or Myron C. Taylor, then president of U.S. Steel. It was clear to Wheeler that Raskob and Shouse were Democratic clones of Hoover Republicans, just as subservient to big business, with the difference that they were also wringing "wets."

The Republicans wanted to head Roosevelt off at the pass. If they could beat him in 1930, they wouldn't have to worry about him in 1932. He had to patch his weak spots, one of which was Prohibition. James B. Cooke, editor of the Babylon *Leader,* asked him on June 25 to come out in favor of repeal: "Your silence is extremely embarrassing to your friends and is jeopardizing your chances of re-election. New York State has always favored the repeal of this obnoxious amendment and you can lose nothing by coming out. It is a year that no one can afford to straddle."

On September 9, in an open letter to Senator Wagner that was published in the *New York Times,* Roosevelt came out for repeal of the Eighteenth Amendment, which would be replaced by another amendment returning control over the sale of liquor to the states. This short-circuited Republican attacks that he was waffling but also brought mail from out of state charging him with having sold out to the brewers, distillers, and saloon keepers.

Barring Prohibition, the Republicans found another issue—corruption in New York City. With Al Smith's retirement, the city was in control of Tammany boss John F. Curry, a throwback to pre-Murphy days. He was, Sam Rosenman thought, the most stupid and obstinate of all the Tammany leaders. Graft was once again in the open. You could take your pick of scandals—judgeships for sale, sewer graft, unsolved murders, payroll padding in the Street Cleaning Department. Corruption was growing like sunflowers in Kansas, said Norman Thomas.

Roosevelt was trapped between past and present positions. Having made his reputation by railing against the wickedness of Tammany, he now was accused of whitewashing it, for he took the position that the governor had no authority to interfere in the affairs of the city.

That summer the Republicans nominated the racket-busting New York City district attorney, Charles H. Tuttle, to run against him, with Caleb H. Baumes of mandatory-life-sentence fame as his running mate. It was a law-and-order ticket. "Tiger Tamer" Tuttle had won headlines by indicting crooked judges.

Roosevelt was in a bind. If he investigated Tammany and New York City Mayor Jimmy Walker, he would build up the kind of ill will that could hurt him at the polls: Tammany might drag its feet about getting the vote out. If he didn't investigate, he was leaving himself open to charges that he condoned Tammany corruption, which would badly cut his New York City plurality.

Roosevelt acted, asking the Appellate Division of the State Supreme Court to start an inquiry of the city magistrates' courts, and convening a blue-ribbon grand jury to hear evidence on the sale of a judgeship, which he assigned his Republican attorney general, Hamilton Ward, to present.

With that out of the way, he was nominated at the Democratic convention in Syracuse that September, and outlined his strategy to his advisers, Sam Rosenman and Jim Farley. The important thing was not to be apologetic or defensive. He had nothing to be ashamed of. He had done everything the law allowed to uncover graft in the city of New York. This had nothing to do with state issues. The number one problem was still the depression. What had happened to the full dinner pail?

Tuttle ran a single-issue campaign. Everywhere he went he harped on city corruption. This was the wrong pitch upstate, where people were worried about farm prices and wanted to know what had happened to Hoover prosperity. The candidate was dubbed "Tittle-Tattle-Tuttle." In addition, upstate drys did not approve of Tuttle's switch to a wet position after having been a prosecutor enforcing Prohibition, and nominated their own candidate, who split the Republican vote.

Tuttle was such a lackluster campaigner that in October the Republicans brought in the first team: three cabinet members came to stump—Secretary of State Henry L. Stimson, Under Secretary of the Treasury Ogden L. Mills, and Secretary of War Patrick Hurley. This too backfired, for it made the Republicans vulnerable to charges of carpetbagging, which Roosevelt made the most of in his last New York City speech, at Carnegie Hall on November 1:

"Of these three estimable gentlemen, one comes from that great state of Oklahoma [Hurley]. . . . He has never lived in New York State, he knows nothing of the situation in New York State. . . . Well may the people of New York State resent this, as would the people of Oklahoma if the tables were turned. . . . The other two gentlemen of this triumvirate . . . are both citizens of this state. . . . Both of them have run for Governor. . . . Both of them were defeated at the polls by the people of this State. . . . I say to these gentlemen: we shall be grateful if you will return to your posts in Washington, and bend your efforts and spend your time solving the problems which the whole Nation is bearing under your Administration. Rest assured that we of the Empire State can and will take care of ourselves and our problems."

Farley predicted that Roosevelt would win by 350,000 votes. In fact he won by 725,000, carrying New York City by 557,217 and the rest of the state by 167,784. He had been favored by several factors. The dry candidate had siphoned off 181,000 votes, most of them Republican. Herbert Lehman had helped with the Jewish vote. Tuttle had made a poor impression. Hoover was unpopular, and sending in his emissaries had boomeranged. Tammany had made a tremendous effort, getting out 91 percent of registered voters. But the fact remained that Roosevelt was a formidable vote getter, with a broad appeal that ranged from the upstate apple farmer to the New York City immigrant.

Winning the 1930 election made him an obvious and visible presidential candidate. But in public he continued to demur, writing E. L. Riley of Ironton, Ohio, on December 4: "I really mean it, however, when I said after election that I was in no sense a candidate for the Presidency and I cannot give any consideration or thought to it. I have my hands full with the job of being Governor of the State of New York with its twelve million people and its many problems."

First among Roosevelt's hurdles was the National Committee of his own party, which was firmly in the hands of John J. Raskob, whose fixation was still repeal, even though insisting on it in the platform would lose the South. Raskob maneuvered to make sure that whoever the nominee was he would have to run on a repeal platform and choose the urban over the rural wing of the party. He called for a meeting of the Democratic National Committee on March 5, 1931, the day after Congress adjourned, hoping to pass a resolution that would commit the 1932 Democratic convention to repeal.

To counter the maneuver, Roosevelt allied himself with influential southerners and westerners. Men like Senator-elect Cordell Hull of Tennessee and Senator Tom Connally of Texas saw Raskob as a menace who would divide the Democratic party and maintain the Republicans in power. What was the point of a convention if Raskob was imposing a platform ahead of time?

Roosevelt found himself leading the stop-Raskob fight, and wrote Al Smith on February 28: "I have been trying to get you on the telephone. I do not know what the plans for next Thursday's meeting of the National Committee are, but the more I hear from different parts of the country, the more certain I am that it would be very contrary to the established power and precedents of the National Committee, were they to pass resolutions *of any kind* affecting party policies at this time."

On March 2, the New York State Democratic Committee in Albany backed Roosevelt's position that the National Committee had no authority to determine policy. The remaining days before the March 5 meeting were spent on the telephone, lining up the proxies of committeemen who would not be present. When Jim Farley took the train to Washington, he had more than enough proxies to defeat Raskob's motions. At the meeting Senator Joseph T. Robinson of Arkansas angrily proclaimed: "You cannot write on the banner of the Democratic party . . . the skull and crossbones emblematic of an outlawed trade." Seeing that he was outnumbered, Raskob backtracked.

"Things here are getting fairly exciting," Roosevelt wrote a friend on March 24. "I had to have a row with the National Chairman about two weeks ago because our friend Raskob wanted to put through various resolutions committing the party on tariff, business mergers, prohibition, etc. I got our State Committee to come out in opposition to resolutions on the ground that they are not a function of the National Committee. By the time the meeting was held the proposal for resolutions was dropped. Everything would have gone well but for the fact that Joe Robinson made a somewhat inflammatory speech and of course was answered in kind."

This behind-the-scenes struggle showed that Raskob did not control the party, and it rallied southern leaders behind Roosevelt, who was seen as the man who could deliver them from the repeal-obsessed and city-controlled Raskob-Smith menace. At the same time, the March skirmish made it clear to Raskob that the price of repeal was stopping Roosevelt. In this he was in agreement with President Hoover, who had awakened to the Roosevelt threat. "I got it on very good authority," Roosevelt wrote a newspaper editor on March 2, "that he [Hoover] told a very distinguished New York Republican leader the other day that 'at all cost you have got to destroy Roosevelt.' As the innocent victim, I don't understand!"

In June, Roosevelt went to French Lick, Indiana, to attend the governors' conference, and heard some favorable noises from the Indiana organization. On his way back through Ohio, he saw Governor George White and his 1920 running mate, James Cox. The meeting with Cox was to have unforeseen consequences, for Cox asked him, now that he had been governor for two years, for an estimate of Al Smith's administration. Roosevelt replied that it had been first rate in many ways, but that in two ways he had been able to improve it—he had cut the overhead on state buildings from 7 percent to 4 percent; and as for power legislation, Smith had recommended a program at the start of each legislative session, and sent fiery messages asking why nothing had been done, while in reality he had an understanding with upstate leaders that his fiery messages were for public consumption only. Cox later repeated all of this to Smith (apologizing to Roosevelt afterward), and Smith took it as a wholesale condemnation of his administration and broke off relations. The rumor circulated that Roosevelt had said: "Smith was a rotten Governor. I didn't know it until I got into the governorship myself." This was published in the January 16, 1932, issue of *Collier's*, by someone who signed himself "The Gentleman at the Keyhole," and Roosevelt responded with the anger he reserved when he knew he had been caught out, saying: "Any man who circulates a story of that kind is not only a liar but a contemptible liar."

As Louis Howe was Roosevelt's inside man, sending out thousands of letters, but too ugly and disheveled to go on the road, the genial Jim Farley was his outside man. Farley had made a political career out of being obliging. He was the one who always remembered names and sent follow-up notes with the familiar signature in green ink. Born in a small town on the Hudson, he had become a salesman and gone into local politics. As town clerk of Stony Point, he built up goodwill, not accepting the ten-cent fee from hunters and fishermen so that they remembered him on election day. Under Al Smith, he was boxing commissioner, and Roosevelt made him head of the State Democratic Committee, recognizing his talent for organization and an affability that exceeded his own. Loyalty was another trait, and Farley liked to say: "I have never held a card in the Disloyal Brotherhood of Political Switchmen."

In late June, Roosevelt sent Farley on a delegate hunt. He went to Hyde Park on June 21 with a Rand-McNally map, a flock of train schedules, and a list of Democratic National Committee members and state chairmen. On June 29, he left, ostensibly to attend an Elks convention in Seattle, on a journey covering eighteen states in nineteen days, feeling that he had graduated from the minor leagues. Roosevelt was conceded a convention majority, but could he muster the necessary two-thirds by overcoming the combination of favorite sons and pro-Smith following in the urban Catholic states? Billing himself as "a traveling Elk on a tour," Farley used the line that there were three outstanding candidates, Roosevelt, Al Smith, and Owen D. Young, to sound out what people thought.

On a roasting hot July day in Aberdeen, South Dakota, he sat in a lunchroom with National Committeeman William H. Howes, who banged his heavy fist on the table and growled: "Farley, I'm damned tired of backing losers. In my opinion, Roosevelt can sweep the country, and I'm going to support him."

That was it, Farley thought, the world loves a winner. He also reassured those who were concerned about Roosevelt's fitness to run: "I stood with him in a Cincinnati hotel four weeks ago," he said, "and he shook hands with 1500 persons." From Seattle on July 6, he reported: "Since I left New York, I have visited Indiana, Wisconsin, Minnesota, North and South Dakota, and Montana. . . . There is apparently an almost unanimous sentiment for you in every one of these states. . . . The consensus of opinion among the leaders is that you are the one man who can win. The . . . sentiment is so general that, to be frank with you, Governor, it is almost unbelievable."

There was in Farley a desire to please that blurred political judgment. In Indiana, he reported that the pro-Roosevelt group would have "absolute control of the delegation," whereas in fact the Indiana delegation was split. He thought Roosevelt had a lead in California, but Roosevelt would be beaten in the California primary. Farley's trip was a mixed blessing. He accurately reported the groundswell for Roosevelt, but failed to head off uninstructed and favorite-son candidacies in two key states, and brought his boss pleasant but unfounded predictions of a first-ballot victory.

While things looked promising out west, in New York Al Smith was nursing his resentment. Nineteen twenty-eight had been a Republican year, and now when for the first time since 1916 the Democrats could win, he felt that he should be given another chance. Before, when friends had told him that he ought to run in '32, he had laughed and said: "What do you think I am, another William Jennings Bryan?" But the more he thought of it, the more he felt that he had as much if not more of a right to the nomination as Roosevelt, whom he had brought back from oblivion.

When Clark Howell of the Atlanta *Constitution* told him that he could not do otherwise than support Roosevelt, Smith replied: "The hell I can't!"

"Governor," Howell asked, "is there any ground for personal hostility on your part against Roosevelt?"

"No," Smith said, "socially we are friends. He has always been kind to me and my family, and has gone out of his way to be agreeable with us at the Mansion at Albany, but"—he rose and stamped his foot—"do you know, by God, that he has never consulted me about a damn thing since he has been Governor? He has taken bad advice and from sources not friendly to me. He has *ignored* me!" Slamming his fist on the table, he added: "By God, he invited me to his house before he went to Georgia, and did not even mention to me the subject of his candidacy."

While Smith still saw himself in the race, Raskob and Shouse cast about for another alternative to Roosevelt. They promoted Melvin Traylor, president of the First National Bank of Chicago, and Governor Albert Ritchie of Maryland, who was wet and conservative and distinguished-looking.

On November 12, Bernard Baruch, the financial and political speculator and former chairman of the War Industries Board, praised Ritchie at a banquet as the man at "whom the finger of fate seems to point as being perhaps destined to move" into the White House. Earlier that year, Baruch had attended a meeting of the finance committee of the Woodrow Wilson Foundation, held in the office of Raymond Fosdick, with Henry Morgenthau, Sr. Morgenthau went up to a photograph on Fosdick's wall of Roosevelt in 1920 and said, "That's my candidate for president." "Uncle Henry," Baruch said, "if Frank is nominated, I won't give one cent to the Democratic party." "But Bernie, hasn't he been a good governor?" Morgenthau asked. "Yes," Baruch said, "but he's so wishy-washy."

Baruch was sure of a Democratic victory in '32. Why, the 12 million people who held securities—each representing no less than two votes—would cinch the election. Covering all the bases, he wrote Roosevelt on December 8: "I resented very much a statement by Mr. Lindley . . . in which he tried to make it appear . . . that I had entered into a combine with Raskob and Smith to head you off. . . . The only thing he had to which he could pin his statement was a kindly reference I made regarding Ritchie. . . . I want you to know—and I am sure you do—that I would not engage in any surreptitious, underhand methods affecting anything that interests you. . . . Sometimes one's friends injure him more than one's enemies."

"I do not need to tell you," Roosevelt responded on December 19, "that I know you yourself would not engage in any surreptitious methods because you, too, realize that the situation from the national and party viewpoint is too serious to engage in such tactics—and also because you personally are above them. But I cannot, of course, help knowing of the conversations of some people who profess friendship but nevertheless emit innuendos and false statements behind my back with the blissful assumption that they will never be repeated to me." Roosevelt's informants told him that Baruch was backing Ritchie and contributing funds to Raskob's stop-Roosevelt movement.

There were also reports that Raskob was in touch with Newton D. Baker of Ohio, Wilson's pacifist secretary of war, who had told Walter Lippmann in 1917: "What a country we are! Do you know that I have a petition about a mile long asking me not to move supplies on Sunday?" Baker, who had once advocated public ownership of electric power, was now a lawyer for Electric Bond and Share, challenging the constitutionality of the Federal Power Act. He was conservative enough for Raskob, and had support among old Wilsonians. Lippmann, editor of the influential New York *World*, supported him, writing him in November that Roosevelt "just doesn't happen to have a very good mind, he never really comes to grips with a problem which has any large dimensions, and above all the controlling element in almost every case is political advantage." He had coddled Tammany and shown petty jealousy toward Al Smith. He was really little more than a "kind of amiable boy scout."

Roosevelt knew perfectly well that Raskob and Shouse were traveling around the country rounding up unpledged anti-Roosevelt delegates. When Shouse protested that he was only doing his duty without regard to any candidacy, Roosevelt replied on December 9: "I think that these situations arise in large part because a great many people who are very enthusiastic friends of mine have jumped to the conclusion that while you and John have very properly not come out in favor of any candidate for nomination next year you are going into different states seeking to 'block Roosevelt' by encouraging uninstructed delegations or favorite sons. They feel that this of course would be just as unethical as if you and John were to come out definitely for an individual, and, of course, they are right in this point of view."

The irony was that bright Democratic prospects encouraged favorite-son candidacies. People were saying that the Democrats could win with a black or a Jew in 1932. One of the jokes going around was that if Hoover won, Mahatma Gandhi would make the best-dressed list. Aware of the problem, Louis Howe advised Roosevelt on December 4 that "oddly enough what is hurting us more than anything else is the propaganda that Shouse is spreading that we can win with anybody this year and it is not necessary to consider the relative vote-getting ability of the different candidates. If it looked like a desperate fight I do not think you would have an adverse vote on the first ballot but all these favorite sons are kidding themselves that Hoover is so unpopular as to make certain that they would be elected if nominated."

It began to seem that beating Hoover would be simple compared with wresting control of the party from Raskob and his crowd. Raskob literally owned the party and its machinery at the national level, and had plenty of money from the Du Pont and General Motors millionaires. Roosevelt wrote Josephus Daniels that "Raskob is apparently so angry with me that he does not even want to discuss matters. I do not particularly care but I do want to avoid a row this November or December."

The row was unavoidable. Raskob announced at the end of November that he was polling the 90,000 contributors to the 1928 campaign on what the party platform should be on Prohibition, and called another meeting of the Democratic National Committee for January 9, 1932. It was a reenactment of the March 5 battle, with Farley scurrying for proxies and forcing Raskob once again to back down. But the choice of Chicago as convention site was a blow. The wringing wet mayor, Anton Cermak, in league with Raskob, could pack the galleries with anti-Roosevelt crowds. Farley did not leave the meeting empty-handed, however, having won for Robert H. Jackson of New Hampshire, a stalwart Roosevelt man, the position of committee secretary.

As 1931 ended, the Christmas day issue of the *New York Times* showed that, while many were suffering from the depression, life went on as usual for those who were not. For every man who was unemployed, three were employed, who could buy the goods the newspaper advertised—mink coats were on sale at Franklin Simon, knocked down from $1,650 to $850. There was pleasure seeking side by side with despair. Liners were leaving on Caribbean cruises, while the Salvation Army gave 8,000 dinners. All over town, fathers at great expense launched their daughters into society with debutante balls. At the Ritz-Carlton, the main ballroom had been transformed into an Italian terraced garden. In Middletown, New York, a jobless couple was found starving in a vacation cottage they had broken into.

At his estate in Glen Cove, Matinecock, J. P. Morgan held his annual Christmas party, surrounded by sixteen grandchildren. In Virginia, an organizer for the Communist party was jailed for distributing incendiary propaganda.

Walter Bowie, Roosevelt's classmate and fellow *Crimson* editor, now rector of Grace Church, had a new book out, an excellent depression nourishment called *On Being Alive,* which argued that the sheer fact of existence was so rich a heritage that it went far beyond material gain and business conditions. The *Times* also reported three suicides: K. L. Ames, owner of the *Journal of Commerce* and a great Princeton back, shot himself in his parked car. An army officer threw himself from the eleventh floor of the Hotel St. George in Brooklyn. A World War veteran left a Christmas party, went to his furnished room, put a shotgun to his head, and fired both barrels.

The International Labor Organization in Geneva reported that there were 25 million unemployed worldwide. The United States led with 6 million, followed by Germany with 5, Great Britain with 2.5, and France with 1.5, while the Soviet Union admitted to none. Pope Pius XI in his Christmas message said the world presented "a terrifying spectacle."

But on Broadway, theatergoers could choose among thirty-nine productions, including Cornelia Otis Skinner in *The Wives of Henry VIII,* Paul Muni in Elmer Rice's *Counsellor-at-Law,* Helen Hayes in Molnar's *The Good Fairy,* George White's *Scandals,* Earl Carroll's *Vanities,* and a new musical called *Of Thee I Sing,* about a presidential candidate named John P. Wintergreen. Roosevelt saw the show in April 1932 and laughed straight through. The song "Wintergreen for President" became popular among Roosevelt supporters, with the appropriate substitution.

Roosevelt spent most of Christmas day working on his tax program with the director of the budget, Mark Graves. Owing to the emergency aid, the state had to raise an additional $140 million in taxes. More than $6 million had already been allotted for public works. Harry Hopkins announced that 50,000 men had been placed in jobs through work bureaus. It was mostly manual labor, sewer construction, brush cutting, water mains, street widening, airports, and playgrounds.

The Lord & Taylor advertisement in the *Times* showed a sleeping child, with the caption: "A child asleep with a stocking beside the bed, is not so asleep as those who have grown up and have lost their illusions."

A nineteen-year-old boy, still believing in the importance of Christmas, and determined to find a tree for his younger brother and sister, stole one from a street stand, and was shot and killed by a police officer while running from the scene with the tree in his arms.

XIII

Who Are You Indeed Who Would Talk or Sing to America?

Who are you indeed who would talk or sing to America?
Have you studied out the land, its idioms and men?
Have you learned the physiology, phrenology, politics, geography?
Pride, freedom, friendship of the land? Its substratums and objects?
Have you consider'd the organic compact of the first day of the
First year of Independence, sign'd by the Commissioners,
Ratified by the States, and read by Washington as the head of the
Army? Have you possess'd yourself of the Federal Constitution?
Do you see who have left all feudal processes and poems behind
Them, and assumed the poems and processes of Democracy?
                                        Walt Whitman, *Leaves of Grass*

Under state law, candidates for the North Dakota primary on March 15 had to announce their availability. Roosevelt took this occasion to declare that he was running, writing F. W. McLean, the secretary of the State Central Democratic Committee in Grand Forks on January 22, 1932: "If it is the desire of our party leaders in your state that my name be presented at your coming primaries as a candidate for the Democratic nomination for the Presidency, I willingly give my consent, with full appreciation of the honor that has been done me. It is the simple duty of any American to serve in public position if called upon."

Three days later, he confided to his cousin Nicholas Roosevelt, now minister to Hungary: "You know me well enough to understand that I am perfectly truthful when I tell you that I don't give a continental as to whether I am nominated or not, because the thought of returning to books and trees and a bit of traveling is, from the personal point of view, a good deal more alluring than the possibility of holding down the most difficult and thoroughly annoying job in the world. Still, like all others of our tribe, if I get projected into a fight, I like to win it."

On January 30, Roosevelt was fifty. Al Smith sent him a telegram: "Hearty congratulations on the half century." Helen B. Coutts, an astrologer, sent him his chart, pointing out that he was an Aquarian, the man of the New Age, symbolized by the Water Bearer holding to his heart an urn from which the water of life poured out for the refreshment of the spiritually thirsty. Other noted Aquarians were Abraham Lincoln, Thomas Edison, and Charles Lindbergh. Fifty was the age decided upon by Plato as correct for a man to take over the guardianship of the state.

At a surprise birthday party in Hyde Park, guests representing various periods of his life reviewed his career, as they partook of soup and turkey and sausages and Virginia ham and sweet potatoes with marshmallows and vanilla ice cream with chocolate sauce and birthday cake. They included his Harvard roommate, Lathrop Brown, and his law partner, Langdon Marvin, who spoke on "The Budding Lawyer as I Knew Him," and Admiral Christian J. Peoples, representing the Navy days, and Henry Morgenthau, Jr., on "The Senator from Dutchess," and Jim Farley on "How I Made Him Governor," and Herbert Lehman on "The Man Who Goes to Warm Springs Just Before the Tough Breaks Come."

It was a festive and high-spirited occasion, with Roosevelt reciting rhymes about those present, including his mother and wife:

> "Delegates from many states
> Favor local candidates
> But there always will be one
> Place where I'm the favorite son.

> "Did my Eleanor relate
> All the sad and awful fate
> Of the miserable lives
> Lived by politicians' wives?"

There was a shadow over the proceedings, however, for one of Roosevelt's dearest friends, the uncritically admiring Livingston Davis, had committed suicide that month, shooting himself in the woodshed of his Brookline estate. He and Roosevelt had cruised the waters of eastern Maine and the Bay of Fundy, and had gone on hunting and camping trips together. Roosevelt had brought him to Washington to act as his second pair of legs. Eleanor had never liked him, suspecting that he had helped Franklin conceal his affair with Lucy Mercer. He had been Roosevelt's "jolly boy" on many occasions, and represented carefree aspects of Roosevelt's life that were now fond memories. The great comic phrase between the two sailors had been "slack off the peak halyards," and when Livy had been made honorary Belgian consul in Boston two years before, Roosevelt had sent him this referral: "The said Davis, while proficient in Choctaw and nautical profanity, does not speak English. . . . Said Davis is not a Belgian but is of direct Turkish descent, and his true first name is not Livingston but Lirvinstein." Davis left his friend $1,000 "in grateful remembrance of joyful comradeship."

It was baffling to Roosevelt that the friend with whom he had shared so many happy times had taken his own life. He had gone through a messy divorce and been burned in the crash, but he still had wealth and social position and friends. Here was someone he felt he knew well who had acted in a completely uncharacteristic manner. It made him ponder the mysteries of the human heart and the climate of the times. Perhaps one factor was that Livy Davis had measured the distance between himself and the man he had always admired, so purposeful and buoyant, and had found himself wanting. "Livy's death certainly was a great shock," Roosevelt wrote a mutual friend, "and I shall miss him dreadfully. I cannot understand it. He seemed to me the last person in the world who would brood, because he always talked things over with his friends."

However tragic Livy's death was, he did not have time to dwell on it. There were too many hurdles on the road to Chicago, and failing to clear one could mean losing the race. There was the question of his health, which was being used to make him appear unfit to be president. The lengths to which his enemies were willing to go became apparent in October 1930, when someone with access to a list of delegates and alternates to the 1928 convention sent out across the nation an anonymous circular claiming that Roosevelt had syphilis. "In the home office of every life insurance company in the United States," it said, "there is on file the health examination report of every person holding a life insurance policy, no matter in what company it is held. If you will examine the health examination report of Governor Franklin D. Roosevelt you will find that he is suffering from locomotor ataxia produced by syphilis. For almost ten years, however, Governor Roosevelt has been parading himself before the public as a victim of infantile paralysis in order to gain sympathy and to hide his real affliction. Carrying on this deception further, Governor Roosevelt has induced some men of wealth to establish at Warm Springs, Georgia, a sanitarium for the treatment of the real victims of infantile paralysis. The most disgusting, vicious and really dangerous thing about this matter is the fact that Governor Roosevelt (with his loathsome and infectious venereal disease) bathes in the same pool with these poor innocent children at the sanitarium at Warm Springs, Georgia, when he himself visits there for months at a time."

James J. Mahoney, Roosevelt's assistant secretary, passed the circular along to Louis Howe with the comment: "Honestly, I could murder for much less." The need arose to obtain an accurate medical report, and on October 18 Roosevelt took out $560,000 worth of life insurance with twenty-two companies, who picked a group of doctors to examine him. His heart and blood pressure were normal, and his weight of 182 was normal for his height of six feet one and a half inches. Dr. Edgar W. Beckwith, medical director of the Equitable Life Assurance Company, pronounced him "a splendid physical specimen."

But he had to keep reminding the public that he was physically fit, for the whispering continued that he could not stand the strain of high office. In 1931, he accepted the challenge of the Republican writer Earle Looker to be examined by a panel of three doctors chosen by the director of the New York Academy of Medicine, the psychiatrist Foster Kennedy, the cardiologist Evan Evans, and the internist Samuel Lambert, who disapproved of Roosevelt's policies. As the other two prepared the statement that April stating that "his health and powers of endurance are such as to allow him to meet any demands of private and public life," Lambert stood looking out the window. "Come on, Sam, sign up and let's get through," the others said. "All right," Lambert replied, "but remember, so far as I am concerned this doesn't go for above the neck!"

A more immediate threat was Al Smith's decision to run. On January 26, he had summoned Bob Jackson, Roosevelt's man in New Hampshire, to his Empire State Building office to ask him what his chances would be in the New Hampshire primary should he decide to enter. Jackson said he would be beaten. "You say so. You're for Roosevelt," Smith shouted angrily. He spoke harshly of old friends like Jim Farley. "Why doesn't he be a man?" he asked. "He crosses to the other side of the street to avoid meeting me."

Smith declared on February 6. He felt that everyone else, including Roosevelt, should stand aside to let him have the nomination. Felix Frankfurter wired Al Smith's supporter, Joseph Proskauer: "Out of a great public figure you fellows are making a small office seeker."

Kansas City boss Tom Pendergast saw Smith on February 23 in New York and reported to his friend, Ike Dunlap: "I have never known a man so ravingly mad with ego insanity. Smith said, 'I control two thirds of Pennsylvania, all of Rhode Island, New Jersey, New Hampshire, Massachusetts and Vermont, and more than likely I will have the entire Garner delegation from Texas.' "

John Nance Garner, the hard-drinking, poker-playing Texan, had been named Speaker of the House in December 1931 after serving in that body twenty-eight years. There was a Garner boomlet. He was backed by Hearst, and won the Texas and California primaries. But Garner said there was no presidential bee buzzing in his bonnet. He had worked a long time to be Speaker, and if the Democrats won he would have a comfortable majority in the House.

Waiting in the wings in case a compromise candidate was wanted was Newton D. Baker. Walter Lippmann was promoting Baker, and tried to recruit Felix Frankfurter, describing Roosevelt as a "dangerous man." "Walter," Frankfurter replied, "a fellow who has your command of adjectives I should think could use a more felicitous one to describe Franklin than dangerous. I can understand anything that might be said about him, but to say that he's a dangerous man is straining the word dangerous."

On January 8, Lippmann came out with his well-known broadside: "Franklin D. Roosevelt is no crusader. He is no tribune of the people. He is no enemy of entrenched privilege. He is a pleasant man, who, without any important qualifications for the office, would very much like to be President." By any yardstick it was a sour and unfair judgment, particularly if Roosevelt was compared to Lippmann's candidate, Newton Baker, who had held no office since World War I, and whose Wilsonian liberalism was tarnished by the business interests he represented as a lawyer, whereas Roosevelt, as governor of New York, had gone farther than any public official, state or national, in fighting the depression. In later years, when the January 8 column was brought up to plague him, Lippmann insisted: "I will maintain to my dying day that this was true of the Franklin Roosevelt of '32. As a matter of fact, as everyone knows, he started his regime by trying to balance the budget for three months and then deliberately threw it out of balance under the Keynes thinking. He was always starting one line and taking another. It was experimental and ad hoc."

When Roosevelt read the article in his morning paper, he grinned and turned over a page, noting the headline: "Ubangi Natives Arriving Today." "All have wooden discs in their lips," he read aloud, "and will fill a vaudeville engagement here." "I could suggest one political writer for the same circuit," he added. "His comments have about the same relation to actuality—interesting and perhaps pleasing to some, but just as distorted as the faces of those savages." To his lawyer, Basil "Doc" O'Connor, he wrote: "If Mr. O'Connor wishes to have Mr. Lippmann appointed to some important post in the State Government, all Mr. O'Conner has to do is suggest the post. The only vacancy at the present time is a lamppost with which goes a hemp rope."

Roosevelt discovered the scrutiny with which the press punishes presidential hopefuls. The utility interests he had been fighting were spreading reports that he was eccentric and unreliable, and that he wasn't suffering from polio but from paresis. The Philadelphia *Record* sent its top reporter, J. David Stern, to Albany. Stern bluntly announced: "I'd like to find out how much there is to the utility propaganda that you're not right in the head." Roosevelt threw back his head and laughed, saying "Why not stick around and find out?" There came to lunch that day the president and general counsel of the New York Central, and the conversation turned on the bonded indebtedness per mile of railroads throughout the United States. Roosevelt shot statistics at them, he had the president turning to his counsel and asking if the figures were right, and the counsel kept nodding and saying "I'm afraid they are." Stern was impressed and his paper came out for Roosevelt.

It was amazing when you were running for the highest office the number of things that could be found to use against you. Old positions, such as his 1920 campaign for the League of Nations, came under attack. The Hearst press went after him days after he entered the North Dakota primary. "This is bad ball," Howe wrote on January 20. "You may have to make a public statement before we get through, if this thing gets any more violent."

Roosevelt unloaded the League albatross at a February 2 meeting of the New York State Grange, where he admitted that he had been a leading spokesman for American participation but that the world organization had not developed according to the lines laid down by Wilson and "therefore, I do not favor American participation." This was the age-old political ploy—I haven't changed, but what I believed in has. It was pointless to back a League that America had never joined. Nonetheless, Roosevelt was viewed as selling out his Wilsonian heritage. He had, as Colonel House wrote Jim Farley, "created something akin to panic among the devoted Wilson followers." Of course, he also picked up some anti-League Republican votes and silenced Hearst.

Another albatross was the Tammany situation. Roosevelt could not afford to lose the New York delegation with its ninety-six votes, or force Tammany into an anti-Roosevelt urban alliance with the machines of New Jersey, Indiana, and Illinois. Nor could he appear to be soft-pedaling the corruption issue. The investigation he had launched under Samuel Seabury was uncovering new offenders, among them the New York County sheriff, Thomas M. Farley, who was collecting graft. Roosevelt had him removed in February. Seabury's probe eventually implicated Mayor Jimmy Walker, who was called to testify in May. It was all highly embarrassing to Roosevelt, who complained to Colonel House that "this fellow Seabury is merely trying to perpetuate another political play." When Seabury sent Roosevelt a transcript of the hearings and a list of fifteen accusations against Walker, Roosevelt passed them on requesting a reply. Walker said he would reply when the convention was over. The day of reckoning was delayed, and Seabury's political ambitions were for the moment stalled.

The news wasn't all bad, for by April 1 seven states had fallen into the Roosevelt camp: Maine, New Hampshire, Georgia, Iowa, Minnesota, North Dakota, and Washington. Roosevelt decided to force a test of strength with Raskob and Shouse at the normally serene session of the Democratic National Committee's subcommittee on arrangements, which was picking Jouett Shouse as temporary chairman of the convention. He realized that rulings from an unfriendly gavel in the opening stages of the convention would damage his cause. "I am doing everything possible," he wrote Josephus Daniels, "to prevent Jouett Shouse from being made Temporary Chairman of the Convention." Through his man at the meeting, Robert Jackson of New Hampshire, who was secretary of the National Committee, Roosevelt backed Senator Alben Barkley of Kentucky.

When Shouse on April 4 nominated himself for the temporary chairmanship, arguing past services, Jackson moved for an adjournment and telephoned Albany for instructions. Roosevelt proposed a solution that displayed typical sleight-of-hand cleverness. In exchange for Barkley's being named temporary chairman, Shouse could be "commended" rather than "recommended" for consideration as permanent chairman of the convention. To fracture an aphorism, this would be trading off a bird in the hand for a pie in the sky. It was a devious way of tricking Shouse into giving up the temporary chairmanship by seeming to offer him the permanent chairmanship. Shouse took the bait, and when the subcommittee on arrangements reconvened at 4:40 P.M., Jackson said: "When I sit down, Governor Byrd of Virginia will move that Mr. Barkley can be recommended Temporary Chairman of the convention by acclamation, and when that resolution is adopted, I shall offer the following resolution, which has been read to Governor Roosevelt over the telephone and which meets with his approval: 'This committee commends to the Permanent Committee on Organization the consideration as Permanent Chairman of the National Convention of Honorable Jouett Shouse of Kansas.'"

Political mastery or sneaky tactics? You could take your pick. Shouse of course yelled dirty pool when Roosevelt supporters started promoting Senator Thomas J. Walsh of Montana, who had chaired the 103-ballot 1924 convention, as permanent chairman. On June 5, Roosevelt held a crucial strategy meeting in Hyde Park. Gathered in the large living room, with the high windows overlooking the Hudson, were Louis Howe, Jim Farley, Ed Flynn, Homer Cummings (former chairman of the Democratic National Committee), Dan Roper (who had once helped Roosevelt with post office patronage and was now a Washington lawyer), Bob Jackson, and Senators Cordell Hull of Tennessee, Clarence Dill of Washington, Tom Walsh and Burton K. Wheeler of Montana, and Joseph Guffey of Pennsylvania.

Louis Howe's latest delegate count showed a clear majority, though he was still a long way from the required two-thirds. In his own state of New York, as well as in Pennsylvania, he split the delegates with Al Smith, who was showing strength in the urban East, winning the primaries in Massachusetts, Connecticut, Rhode Island, and New Jersey. The unkindest cut was California, where "Cactus Jack" Garner, supported by Hearst and McAdoo, won in a three-cornered primary against Smith and Roosevelt.

But Roosevelt had the delegate strength to control the convention machinery, and appointed various committee chairmen and aggressive Arthur Mullen of Nebraska as floor leader. He agreed to back Walsh against Shouse as permanent chairman. The matter of the two-thirds rule came up. It was tempting to try and abolish it and then nominate him. But would his majority, dependent as it was on southern delegations, hold together to end a practice that was widely viewed as a southern veto? It was better to wait and see.

For the nominating speech, Roosevelt settled on his old friend and Dutchess County neighbor, Judge John E. Mack. Some saw it as a curious choice, for Mack was unknown outside New York. But Roosevelt was pay-ing a long-standing debt, for it was Mack who had brought him into politics in the first place, suggesting that he run for the state legislature. And it was Mack who, on October 6, 1910, at the Democratic state convention in Poughkeepsie, had nominated an inexperienced youth still in his twenties, giving as one of his qualifications that he spoke at least two languages.

In 1931, Roosevelt had given his most loyal aide a formal certificate of appointment that said: "Louis McHenry Howe, General Goat." Howe still looked as though he hadn't had a bath in months and might blow away at any moment, and still practiced rudeness as a way of influencing people. When he was dubbed "medieval gnome" in the Boston *American*, he started answering the phone that way.

He still thought of himself as the only person standing between Roosevelt and catastrophe. When Jim Farley proclaimed "Roosevelt on the first bal-lot," he thought that was one of Jim's fairy stories, for he trusted no one. That was why he piled up data and lists—he had lists of state committee-women, of people who should be given seats in the galleries, of the arrival times of delegates in Chicago and of the trains to be met, of "those we have relied on to conduct the fight for delegates." He had confidential memos giving a state-by-state breakdown of prospects:

Nevada: "There are five million people in the west who do not know T.R. is dead and who will vote for your Governor."

Maryland: "Our Governor [Ritchie] is standing pat, he will go to the con-vention committed only to himself. . . . His strategy is to remain a fourth contender with a view of moving up in the deadlock."

On the three-by-five pink cards in his file, political leaders of each state were skewered in a single sentence. For Texas, as an example, there were these entries:

Amon G. Carter, Fort Worth: "Non-committal, powerful, king-maker type, loud, breaks with everyone."

A. S. Burleson (who had helped Roosevelt when he was postmaster gen-eral under Wilson), Austin: "Disgusted, tired, ready to die."

Tom Connally, Marlin: "U.S. Senator, politician, no convictions, friendly but non-committal . . . *Tremendous* influence, key man."

Jesse H. Jones, Houston: "Money, *Houston Chronicle*, owner of, for him-self first, last and all time. Ambitious. Promises everybody everything. Dou-ble-crosser."

The trouble with Louis, as Herbert Lehman pointed out, was that he thought of himself as a strategist, but he was really a maneuverer, a one-idea man, the idea being that Roosevelt ought to be president. When politics had to be formulated on national issues in depression America, he was out of his depth. His thinking was on the level of the little book he liked to pass out, *Everybody's Political Primer.* Louis's favorite page showed Hoover, dressed in rompers, with a round hat set back on his head, busily driving nails into the head of a little wooden man labeled "Depression," while splinters flew in all directions. The caption read:

> At what is Her-bert working?
> Her-bert is working to abol-ish pov-er-ty.
> Did he abol-ish it?
> Not pre-cisely. Her-bert just broke it up and scattered it all over the country.

Roosevelt was still governor, absorbed in state matters, with 800 bills to sign at the end of the legislative session, and had to run his campaign as well. He didn't have time to study the national issues. He couldn't simply apply his knowledge of the state to the nation. His mail told him there was a breakdown in the system, and that old approaches were futile. But as to how to fix it, he was no economist. His competence on every topic of national concern was going to be tested in the campaign, and he wasn't ready. He had to rise above the Lippmann view that he was no more than an amiable fellow who wanted to be president. He needed tutoring, but the men around him, aside from Sam Rosenman, weren't much help. Howe and Farley and Ed Flynn were tacticians, and he was about to lose Rosenman, who was filling a vacancy on the State Supreme Court.

Rosenman brought it up one evening in March: "If you were to be nominated tomorrow and had to start a campaign trip within ten days, we'd be in an awful fix. You would be without a well-defined and thought-out affirmative program. It would be pretty hard to get up intelligent speeches overnight on the many subjects you would have to discuss.... My thought is that if we can get a small group together willing to give some time, they can prepare memoranda about such things as the relief of agriculture, tariffs, railroads, government debts, private credit, money, gold standard—all the things you will have to take a definite stand on.... The first one I thought I would talk with is Ray Moley. He believes in your social philosophy and objectives, and he has a clear and forceful style of writing. Being a university professor himself, he can suggest different university people in different fields. Is that all right with you?"

Moley, the first member of what came to be known as the "brain trust," had already done some work for Roosevelt. In February, he had written the removal order for Sheriff Farley. His hostility toward international bankers and "fat cat" Republicans came from his Ohio background. Born in 1886 in Berea, where his father had a "gents' furnishings" store, he grew up a passionate admirer of William Jennings Bryan and of Cleveland's progressive mayor, Tom L. Johnson. His bible was single-tax advocate Henry George's *Progress and Poverty*. A professor at Columbia, Moley was eager for public service and served on a commission to revise the parole laws under Roosevelt. Moley at first thought Roosevelt's amiability was "be good to the peasants" stuff, but came to realize that he genuinely enjoyed being open and friendly—he was conscious of his ability to send callers away happy and glowing, often having forgotten what they had come to ask. A typical approach to big problems was "so and so was telling me today"—there was complete freedom from dogmatism, a case-by-case approach, a fluid mind. The frightening aspect was his grand receptivity; he made no attempt to check up on anything anyone told him.

Moley had a gift for putting into words Roosevelt's half-formulated ideas, and carved out a position of eminence, which Rosenman resented. Rosenman came to see Moley as "a very ambitious man, very devious in some of his dealings." He was offended by Moley's remark that it was because of Rosenman's "boyish love" of Columbia that all the members of the brain trust came from there. The fact was he had little love of Columbia, having spent unhappy years there when Jews were social outcasts. The reason he wanted Columbia men was purely practical: Roosevelt had no funds to pay the expenses of a professor from the University of California or even from Yale. He had to draw on men living in the city who could come to meetings on a nickel subway fare.

James P. Warburg, who was assistant secretary of the Treasury in the first Roosevelt administration, believed that Moley's attraction to Roosevelt was almost physical. "He was a man in whom homo and heterosexuality was curiously in balance," Warburg said. "He 'fell for' men the way a man falls for a woman. He seemed to have a great need to make a series of friendships with men. I don't mean by this that he was or is an overt homosexual at all. The pattern seemed to be one of making these friendships and being betrayed by one after another. . . . It always seemed to end up with the favorite of today becoming the disloyal betrayer of tomorrow. . . . He idealized Roosevelt and Roosevelt, in a psychological sense, was his 'dream girl.' And thus Moley became his very humble worshiper and servant."

On a blustery March morning, Moley ran into economics professor Rexford Guy Tugwell on Morningside Heights, near Columbia University. Moley thought Tugwell was politically naive, but he was an expert on agriculture. He liked Tugwell, who was handsome and brilliant—his conversation was like a cocktail, it picked you up and made your brain race along. He asked Rex if he would be willing to advise Roosevelt. Tugwell, who could see the Hooverville spreading across the tracks from Columbia, had formed the habit of indulging immoderate remarks about the president. This was a chance to do something, to be an insider, to influence policy, to have the words he had written spoken before a large audience. "I was just a fellow who was pretty mad and thought he saw some things that could be done," he recalled.

Then forty-one, Tugwell came from Sinclairsville in western New York, where his father owned a farm and a cannery. He graduated from the Wharton School of Finance and Commerce at the University of Pennsylvania, and mingled with the socialists of the League of Industrial Democracy. In 1927, he spent two months in Soviet Russia with a delegation of trade unionists and intellectuals. Impressed by the renewal of Soviet agriculture, he wondered whether there might be an alternative to the boom-and-bust cycle of laissez-faire capitalism. "How shall we settle our irrepressible agricultural problem except by some such series of devices as the Soviets use?" he asked. He rejected Soviet political doctrine, but wanted to adapt some of their economic practices, such as long-range centralized planning and crop limitations. He commented that "if Communism is a religion, capitalism is a fetish." But he made this distinction between liberals and radicals: "Liberals would like to rebuild the station while the trains are running; radicals prefer to blow up the station and forgo service until the new structure is built."

Moley had been impressed by a young colleague at meetings devoted to curriculum revisions at the Columbia University Law School. He was sharp and clever and knew a lot about finance—indeed, he was coauthoring a book on the nature of the modern corporation. He would fit right in. But when approached, the colleague, Adolf A. Berle, Jr., told Moley that he supported Newton D. Baker. That was all right, Moley said, it was his technical expertise that was wanted, not his political support, which did not carry the slightest weight in any case. Berle laughed and signed on, although he continued to work for Baker as well.

Berle was born in the Boston suburb of Brighton in 1895. His grandfather was a German immigrant, his father was a Congregational minister, and his mother was the daughter of another Congregationalist minister who had done missionary work with the Sioux in South Dakota. From his father and his maternal grandfather, he had examples of religious vocations combined with social activism. His father was a reformer, preaching the social gospel, the rights of children to finish high school and not be sent to work when they were fourteen, the need for a basic economic reorganization. Berle grew up believing that with proper guidance the system could be made to work. Tutored at home, he entered Harvard when he was fourteen, and graduated in three years with honors. He had his Harvard Law School degree by the time he was twenty-one. In the World War he was a pacifist, seeing no reason why the United States should put its energies into deciding whether the Hohenzollerns or the French controlled Europe. But in 1917 he enlisted in the Signal Corps. After that, he taught law at Harvard and Columbia, becoming an expert on large corporations and how they challenged the power of the state.

Berle was delighted by Roosevelt because he was not hidebound or orthodox. He was prepared to look at an idea on its merits and adopt it. But you had to present it in a way that he could use. Once they brought in the economist James W. Angell, who knew more about money than anyone. Roosevelt asked him if they should change the gold content of the dollar. Angell said the question was too complicated to answer off the bat. "Well, we obviously aren't going to have any huge amount of time for research," Roosevelt said. "These problems are going to be presented right quick."

"Well, to estimate the effects of what would happen is going to be very difficult," Angell cautioned.

"Listen, Jim," Roosevelt said, "I'm a ham and eggs politician, and you're an authority on monetary matters. Forget about your academic reputation . . . just tell me, if you had to guess what it would be."

"You know, I really don't think I could take the responsibility of making a guess," Angell said.

That was the end of him, Berle recalled. But Berle made the grade, although Moley sometimes regretted bringing him in because he was so arrogant and self-centered. It was Moley who said that he may have been an infant prodigy, but he continued to be an infant long after he had ceased to be a prodigy. Rex Tugwell said that Berle was a "walking mind," but not a modest one.

Despite the personality clashes, the brain trust worked. Roosevelt liked to gather the professors around him and pick their brains. They were young and intense world changers, smelling the heady aroma of power for the first time, plucked from the classroom and given a golden opportunity to implement their ideas. Tugwell felt that they were turning weakness into competence, leading an agile mind to higher levels of discussion. They were tailors conducting fittings, cutting the cloth to the pattern, trying it on, letting it out here and tucking it in there.

The first major collaboration was a ten-minute speech Roosevelt was due to deliver on April 7 over network radio on the "Lucky Strike Hour," sponsored by the American Tobacco Company. Moley wrote it, remembering the phrase "forgotten man" from an essay by the Yale economist William Graham Sumner, who had used it to designate the middle class. But Moley applied it to the disadvantaged lower third of the population. Roosevelt compared the depression to the World War, when the nation had mobilized its resources to win. The same mobilization was needed now. Public works were not enough. The government must not only lend money at the top, as it was doing through Hoover's Reconstruction Finance Corporation, but should prevent mortgage foreclosures on farmers and homeowners. It must put its faith once more in "the forgotten man at the bottom of the economic pyramid." This was hardly earthshaking, but it announced a new direction.

On April 13, at the Democratic party's Jefferson Day dinner in Washington, Al Smith, flushed with anger, charged that Roosevelt was stirring up class against class, poor against rich. "I will take off my coat and fight to the end any candidate who persists in a demagogical appeal to the masses of the working people of the country to destroy themselves," he said.

Here was the poor kid from the sidewalks of New York siding with the rich men, while the patrician with inherited wealth was identifying with the underdog. It was a prince-and-pauper reversal, the most bizarre twist of the campaign. Smith now derived his support from wealthy reactionaries whose only goal was "anyone but Roosevelt." What a pathetic last act for a man who had been a great reform legislator and a great governor!

The split between the party's two wings was now in the open, but Roosevelt knew that to win in Chicago he must have support from all sides; the others were the spoilers, but he had to unify diverging interests. His next important speech was in St. Paul on April 18. Colonel House, who was still peppering him with suggestions, even though his outmoded Wilsonian views were generally ignored, wrote: "I am clear on one thing, and that is that you should strike a conservative note in your St. Paul speech." Howe warned Moley that "the Minnesota people are just as anxious as our Eastern friends that the Governor's speech should not be treated as radical."

Again with Moley's help, Roosevelt prepared a speech that was thoughtful rather than inflammatory. "I am not speaking of an economic life completely planned and regimented," he said. "I plead not for a class control but for a true concert of interests." He confided to Senator Walsh that he had decided to keep his temper after Al Smith's outburst, "and at the same time I took back nothing!"

After the St. Paul speech, Roosevelt was due to attend the governors' conference in Richmond, Virginia, from April 24 to 28, and then head south to Warm Springs for a rest. In Richmond, the governors were invited to visit the White House. Herded into line in the East Room by naval aides, they stood waiting for half an hour before Hoover came down to shake hands. For Roosevelt, with his braces and crutches, it was an ordeal. He declined offers of a chair, not wanting to endorse in front of his fellow governors the whispering campaign that he was not physically fit. Eleanor resented Hoover's tardiness, as she resented it when the musicians who had come to play—artists of great reputation—were dismissed from the company when they had finished.

In Warm Springs, Roosevelt kept in touch with developments, while the brain trust continued to hatch policies. When California went to Garner on May 3, he wrote Herbert Lehman that "I am not in the least disturbed . . . because Garner will, I am sure, not join any mere 'block movement.' " Yet the block movement existed, and he did not discount it, writing a friend a few days before the convention: "The drive against me seems to be on. All I can hope is that it will not develop into the kind of a row which will mean the re-election of Brother Hoover."

As both parties prepared to hold their conventions that June in Chicago, the black cloud of depression hung over the land. The weakened economy was collapsing. Tar paper slums rose on the outskirts of cities. There was reverse immigration, people leaving the United States to seek a better life in Europe. With 12 million unemployed, thousands rode the rails looking for work. The crack of the auctioneer's gavel was heard across the land. Farmers rioted, and in three farm states, Idaho, Minnesota, and North Dakota, further foreclosures were barred to keep the peace.

Roosevelt's mail brought him daily cries for help. Charles Kroll of Antioch, Tennessee, wrote: "There are millions of others who like myself are sinking. It seems at times almost a physical sensation. There is nothing to stand on, nothing to grasp and no direction to turn toward anything tangible or stable. On every hand the word of those who are getting by is 'I'm sorry, but.' " For every unit in a statistic, there was a tale of human misery.

The Republican convention from June 14 to 16 in Chicago's vast new stadium was, H. L. Mencken said, "the stupidest and most horrisome ever heard of . . . a convention of country postmasters, Federal marshals and receivers in bankruptcy." The party mascot should have been the ostrich, for the depression was virtually ignored. "An eavesdropper would seldom guess," wrote Raymond Daniell in the *New York Times,* "that the country was passing through a serious economic crisis. Unemployment and the Depression are seldom mentioned, except by the serious-minded elder statesmen."

And yet, outside the stadium, where panhandlers accosted delegates under the bunting-draped streetlights of Michigan Avenue, the depression was hard to ignore. Bands played "Over There" to recall the heroic days of the Belgian War Relief, but the present problems were "Over Here." The Hoover administration had shown that voluntarism and appeals to the business community could not end the depression, and yet the convention had to renominate him, for his rejection would make the defeat of not only the national but also the state and local tickets a certainty. He was nominated for a second term by 1,126½ to 23½. As Arthur Krock put it, "To all this the national assembly of the Democrats will provide the contrast of scarlet to dull gray."

Jim Farley and his staff arrived in Chicago on June 20 and set up the Roosevelt headquarters at the Congress Hotel, where he had reserved sixty-two rooms, most of them on the second floor, known as President's Row. Farley lost no time holding a press conference at which he predicted a first-ballot victory, hoping to create a bandwagon psychology. A large map of the United States on one wall showed the states "committed to Roosevelt" in red. The map looked convincing, even though Roosevelt's home state was left a neutral white.

In the meantime, the stop-Roosevelt forces prepared their counterattack. On June 26, Bernard Baruch arranged a lunch meeting at the Blackstone Hotel between the two foes of the deadlocked 1924 convention, Al Smith and William McAdoo, now united against a common rival.

Greeting each other with forced cordiality in Baruch's suite, McAdoo recalled 1924, saying: "Well, we both got licked."

"Yes, we both got licked," Smith replied, "but it was better for me to beat you and you to beat me than for either of us to take a fall from Coolidge."

"I'm going to level with you," Smith said during lunch. "We're both against Roosevelt or you wouldn't be here. . . . If we get together we can bust this feller. . . . If we go to the fifth ballot, we've got him licked. All right. Then my candidacy is out the window. I can't be nominated, but we can then sit around a table and get together on a candidate."

"When you sit around the table," McAdoo asked, "will I be there?"

"If you're not there I won't be either," Al said.

Smith left the lunch thinking that he and McAdoo had an understanding to use their respective delegations to block Roosevelt.

In the hall but lately vacated by the Republicans, wrote Mencken, the Democrats were gathering on June 27 "to carry on their quadrennial suicide pact." The principal reason for this appraisal was the two-thirds rule, a glaring anomaly in the party's history. Why should a party whose very existence was based on majority rule cling to a century-old tradition requiring a candidate to win by two-thirds in a national convention? It was one of the reasons why, in the sixty-four years between the end of the Civil War and the start of the depression, out of fourteen presidents, only two had been Democrats, Grover Cleveland and Woodrow Wilson, and even Wilson in 1912 had almost been brought down by the rule.

It was one thing to prepare the ground, however, and educate the delegates, and make sure there was enough support, and quite another to launch a last-minute effort on the floor of the convention. which would be like changing the rules after the opening whistle of the game.

But Farley was a general who could not control his troops. At a pep rally at Roosevelt headquarters just before midnight on the eve of the opening session, he introduced Bruce Kremer of Montana, the Roosevelt choice for chairman of the rules committee, who suggested doing away with the two-thirds majority. In the ensuing discussion, Louisiana's governor, the leather-lunged Huey Long, took the floor and proposed a resolution to that effect, which Kremer promised to recommend to the convention. Farley had lost control of the meeting; in the words of the Democratic organizer, Mollie Dewson, he "looked bewildered, confused and pathetic, like a terrier pup who is being reproached for knocking over a vase of flowers."

When presented with this fait accompli in Albany, Roosevelt had no choice but to go along. It proved to be the worst mistake of the convention, providing his enemies with a handy club to beat him with. There was a chorus of indignation about poor sportsmanship and moral flaws. Speakers at the opening ceremonies on June 27 were ignored as delegates huddled to discuss the two-thirds rule. Farley began to see some slippage, particularly among the southern states that had always used the rule to veto undesirable candidates. The carefully tailored Roosevelt majority was coming apart at the seams.

There were only a few hours left before the convention voted on the rules committee's recommendation. If Roosevelt lost that vote by simple majority, how could he hope to be nominated by two-thirds? In a telegram released from the governor's office, he beat a strategic retreat: "I am accordingly asking my friends in Chicago to cease their activities to secure the adoption of a majority nominating rule at the opening of the permanent organization."

Telegram in hand, Farley burst into the rules committee conference and said: "Look here, just so there won't be any misunderstanding, I want to tell you what our position is. We are for the rules as they now stand and we're for them 1,000 percent—the two-thirds rule all the way through, and not ending on the sixth ballot or any other ballot."

In the meantime, the convention was under way, and one of the reasons the opposition to Roosevelt was so vocal was the feeling that any respectable Democratic nominee could be elected. Didn't some of the buttons say "Anybody but Hoover?"

On Monday, June 27, the curtain rose on this uniquely American spectacle, with the 3,210 delegates casting 1,154 votes settling into their red-upholstered seats, which filled two acres of floor space. The galleries were packed with 30,000 spectators, and the early summer light, filtered through the bunting, was softened as if by stained glass. Opening the convention, John J. Raskob made one last effort to promote Jouett Shouse as permanent chairman, but it was clearly his swan song. As Mencken noted, it had cost him a million dollars to become chairman of the Democratic National Committee, but now he had to bow out, and the money would have been better invested if he had put it in Kreuger & Toll. Then the curly-haired Kentuckian, Alben Barkley, in white linen suit and vest, gave his two-hour keynote address, which was delivered with such vigor that his pince-nez bounced off his nose five times. "As a history of the United States in modern times it left little untold," observed reporter Elmer Davis.

On June 29 came Roosevelt's first test of strength, the vote for convention chairman. The speeches for Shouse were listless, and Tom Walsh of Montana won by 626 to 528. Walking across the ramp to the platform, Walsh paused to shake hands with Jouett Shouse before accepting the gavel from Barkley. That handshake was less a greeting than a farewell to a group of well-funded and reactionary men who had tried to place the Democratic party at the service of big business.

June 29 was devoted to the platform, and it was not until June 30 that the delegates cast their first vote for a nominee. The convention floor that afternoon was like a stock exchange, bid and ask, everyone trading. The roll of the states was called out, and for five hours the delegates were subjected to full-blown rhetoric for candidates who had little or no hope of winning.

When John E. Mack rose to nominate Roosevelt, a scowling Al Smith said, "Hell, I can listen to that at the hotel over the rad-dio," and left the stadium. "Country born and country living, this man's whole life is an open book," Mack said, as boos from the pro-Smith claque installed by Chicago Mayor Anton Cermak drowned him out.

It was not until after four o'clock on the morning of July 1 that the first ballot was taken. The delegates were exhausted. The stadium hospital reported twenty-two patients suffering from stomach disorders and heat prostration. In spite of this, Farley wanted a vote, hoping for a first-ballot victory. At 4:28, the clerk began to call the roll, and that alone took nearly three hours.

Tom Walsh announced the result at 7:15—666½ for Roosevelt, 203¾ for

Smith, 90¼ for Garner, the rest scattered among the other six candidates. It was a strong showing, with Roosevelt claiming the South, the Farm Belt, the Rocky Mountain states, and the Pacific Northwest, but still 104 votes shy of the needed two-thirds. New York had split with 28½ for Roosevelt and 65½ for Smith. While the tellers were making their check, Farley sat hoping that some state would make a last-minute switch—normally, if a man received such a huge vote on the first ballot, he was nominated without delay. Were two years of heartbreaking labor about to go down the drain?

In Albany, Roosevelt sat by the radio in his shirt-sleeves, chain-smoking, as Sam Rosenman munched frankfurters and worked on the acceptance speech, wondering if it would ever be delivered. In Chicago, Farley knew that Roosevelt's total had to keep rising with each ballot, or a landslide could start in the wrong direction. Would a delegation break on the second ballot and start the bandwagon rolling? He hunted around, but there were no takers. Only the faithful Boss Pendergast of Missouri had a few reserve votes to dole out to maintain momentum. The official count on the second ballot showed a gain of eleven votes for Roosevelt, to 677¼. The Oklahoma delegation, having deserted "Alfalfa Bill" Murray, but unwilling to switch to Roosevelt, cast twenty-two votes for Will Rogers.

By now, it was 8:00 A.M., but the yawning clerk called the roll again. This time, Roosevelt's gain was slightly less, up to 682. The engine wasn't stalled, but it was sputtering. Oklahoma switched to Garner, a lead that others might follow if the convention was deadlocked.

When they adjourned at 9:00 A.M., and the thousands of rumpled and stubbled-chinned delegates shuffled off to their hotels, blinking in the bright July morning, Jim Farley was a desperate man, unsure of being able to hold his delegates through a fourth ballot, and in urgent need of eighty-nine votes, with only hours to find them. California and Texas would fill the bill, and Farley looked to those two states, wrote Arthur Krock, "as the sisters of Bluebeard's wife looked to the highway for the help which alone could avert tragedy." Farley had been leaning on Garner's campaign manager in Chicago, Sam Rayburn, who was friendly but noncommittal.

In the hours on the first of July before the convention was to reconvene, there were three separate efforts to corral the Garner delegation. The first was Farley's, who again met briefly with Rayburn, who simply said: "We'll see what we can do."

In the meantime, Joseph Kennedy, the young businessman who had fought over the Argentine ships with the assistant secretary of the Navy in 1917, now a millionaire and a Roosevelt supporter, reached William Randolph Hearst at his ranch in San Simeon. "W.R., do you want Baker?" Kennedy asked. Hearst loathed Baker, the foremost Wilsonian internationalist. "If you don't want Baker," Kennedy said, "you'd better take Roosevelt, because if you don't you're going to take Baker." "Could I get Ritchie?" Hearst asked. "No, I don't think so," Kennedy said. "I think if Roosevelt cracks on the next ballot, it'll be Baker."

Hearst dictated a message for his Washington correspondent, George Rothwell Brown, who had written a flattering biography of Garner, to pass on to the Speaker: "Mr. Hearst is fearful that when Roosevelt's strength crumbles it will bring about either the election of Smith or Baker. Either would be disastrous. Tell Garner that the Chief believes nothing can now save the country but for him to throw his votes to Governor Roosevelt." Garner was handed the message at 11:00 A.M. in the Speaker's room at the Capitol, and replied: "Say to Mr. Hearst that I fully agree with him. He is right. Tell him I will carry out his suggestion and release my delegates to Roosevelt."

Daniel C. Roper, who had been commissioner of internal revenue in the Wilson administration, was working on his old friend, McAdoo, who should have been aware of the dangers of deadlock, having been the victim of one in 1924. Late that afternoon, they retired to a private room in the stadium. McAdoo said the Garner forces did not want to switch until the seventh or eighth ballot. That would be too late, Roper replied, by that time Newton Baker would have emerged as second choice. McAdoo named his price: Garner as vice president, control over California patronage, and a veto over the choices for the secretaries of state and Treasury. After relaying the offer to Roosevelt, Roper gave McAdoo what he wanted. McAdoo promised to caucus the California delegation.

In Washington, Garner studied the three ballots state by state. Al Smith tried to reach him, but he would not take the call. Garner knew that if he released his delegation he would end up on the ticket with Roosevelt. He wasn't keen on the vice presidency, which he told a friend was "not worth a pitcher of warm piss." But he didn't want another Madison Square Garden. The party had defeated itself in the convention hall in 1924 and had taken another licking in 1928. At 3:00 P.M., he called Rayburn and said, "Sam, I think it is time to break this thing up. Roosevelt is the choice of the convention. He has had a majority on three ballots. We don't want to be responsible for wrecking the party's chance. The nomination ought to be made on the next roll call." Rayburn, who knew the stubbornly pro-Garner mood of the Texas delegation, asked him to think it over.

By 6:00 P.M., when the California and Texas delegations were caucusing in the lobbies of the Hotel Sherman, Mississippi had switched to Newton Baker, and Arkansas, fourth in the roll call, was crumbling. Farley was frantic.

There were 184 Texas delegates, each with a one-fourth vote, but Rayburn could round up only 105. The others were scattered all over the city recruiting Garner delegates after his third-ballot increase. Under the unit rule, a majority of the quorum present could vote for the entire delegation. The caucus had just rejected a request from seventeen delegates to let them vote for Roosevelt when Rayburn was told that Garner was on the line. On the way to the phone, Rayburn ran into McAdoo, heading for the California caucus. "Sam, we'll vote for Jack Garner until Hell freezes over, if you say so," McAdoo said, not mentioning the deal he had made with Roper. Rayburn told him he was about to get Garner's release, and advised him to do the same.

"All right," Garner told Sam Rayburn, "release my delegates and see what you can do. Hell, I'll do anything to see the Democrats win one more national election."

But Rayburn had to convince an angry group of Texans, who did not want to abandon Garner. Texas was a Wilson state, a League of Nations state, where Roosevelt's reversal on the League was not admired. It was not until 8:00 P.M., after hours of wrangling, that Rayburn brought the meeting to order, and the delegation voted to support Roosevelt by 54 to 51. Things might have been rather different if the seventy-nine absent delegates, most of them Garner diehards, had taken part in the vote. It was on flukes such as these that national destinies depended.

McAdoo was also having problems controlling the divided California delegation, which finally agreed to elect a steering committee of three to decide where the votes would go. The steering committee secretly agreed to pledge the delegation's forty-four votes to Roosevelt.

Notified of the switches in the Garner camp, Farley was too nervous to finish his dinner and grabbed a taxi to the stadium, where the delegates, all in clean collars and pressed suits and auras of bay rum, were taking their seats.

The roll call for the fourth ballot began, and when California's turn came, William Gibbs McAdoo asked for permission to speak from the platform, which tipped off the convention that something important was about to happen.

He strode to the speakers' stand, tall and lanky, his gray hair parted in the middle, his high collar giving him the air of a Sunday school teacher, his hooded eyes gazing at the world with amused skepticism. Eight years before, he had come close to the nomination that he was now about to bestow on another.

"California came here to nominate a president of the United States," he said. "She did not come here to deadlock this convention, or to engage in another desolating contest like that of 1924. . . . California should take a stand here tonight . . . a stand prompted by the fact that when any man comes into this convention with the popular will behind him to the extent of almost seven hundred votes. . . ."

At that moment, the Roosevelt delegations rose and cheered. The spotlights picked out the figures of dancing delegates, the Texans let out a rebel yell, and one delegate ran down the aisle to present the Lone Star flag to McAdoo. Walsh beat his gavel in vain, and Mayor Cermak had to intervene to restore order, for the pro-Smith galleries were unloosing their boos.

Raising his hands over his head, McAdoo yelled into the microphone: "And so, my friends, California casts forty-four votes for Franklin Delano Roosevelt."

"Good old McAdoo," Roosevelt exclaimed, unaware of how tortuous his itinerary had been.

By the time he had finished speaking, leaders of dissident delegations were at the back of the rostrum, waiting for their chance to climb aboard the Roosevelt bandwagon. Mayor Cermak released Illinois's fifty-eight votes, and one by one the other states fell into line, except New York and four other eastern states.

At 10:32, Tom Walsh announced the results: 942 votes for Roosevelt, 201½ against. "I proclaim him the nominee of this convention for president of the United States," Walsh said.

After it was all done, there were many who claimed they had been instrumental in putting over Roosevelt. As Doc O'Connor put it, "Of the 55,000 Democrats alleged to have been in Chicago for the recent convention, unquestionable 62,000 of them arranged the McAdoo shift."

Garner of course had been the key figure, willing to put the interests of the party above his own. He would have preferred to remain Speaker of the House, but was catapulted to vice-presidential candidate so that Roosevelt could head the ticket.

Along with securing the nomination, he had cleaned up the party, ridding it of the Smith-Raskob wing. Smith was finished as a political force, although he received 200 telegrams urging him to form a third party. Raskob mourned the power shift, writing Jouett Shouse on July 7 that "it takes all one's courage and faith not to lose hope completely."

Roosevelt's running mate was sure that all he had to do to win was stay alive until election day. People would vote against the depression and against Hoover. Ward Smith, a lifelong Republican who was voting Democratic for the first time, reflected widespread voter sentiment when he wrote Roosevelt that Hoover had handed the American public a rubber check on prosperity from which it would take a lifetime to recover. He had promised a chicken in every pot and now they didn't even have the pot, and two cars in every garage, but the garage had been foreclosed. Hoover was as spineless as a chair cushion always bearing the impression of the last ass that sat on it. He had reduced the country to such a condition of abject poverty that the peanut vendors and the fruit vendors were exchanging their fruit and their nuts as they passed one another on the street.

Roosevelt announced that he would fly to Chicago and deliver his acceptance speech before the convention rather than wait several weeks as was the custom. It was a signal to the nation that this man, crippled though he was, could move swiftly and was willing to break with precedent. Louis Howe was against it, he was afraid of a smashup that would give Garner first place on the ticket.

Commercial aviation was in its infancy, and his flight refueled in Buffalo and Cleveland and fought headwinds and took nine hours to get to Chicago. In Louis Howe's rooms at the Congress Hotel, Howe and Moley were working on their draft of the acceptance speech. Jesse Straus, the chairman of Macy's who had headed the TERA, tapped Moley on the shoulder and said: "Can we let Baruch see the acceptance speech? We want to be nice to him because he can contribute a good deal to the campaign."

Moley didn't trust Baruch, who represented Wall Street and had worked against Roosevelt's nomination. He yanked the speech out of his pocket and flung it at Straus, saying "Please do! It wouldn't be a regulation campaign, would it, if the nominee didn't tack and trim? This happens to be what Franklin Roosevelt believes and wants to say. But I'm sure he wouldn't be the first man to cave in under pressure." Straus was baffled. What was all this about tacking and trimming? But Rex Tugwell shared Moley's indignation. Asking to see the acceptance speech when he wasn't even in the Roosevelt camp was the greatest piece of effrontery he'd ever seen.

When Roosevelt landed and Howe saw Rosenman's acceptance speech, he hit the roof: "Good God," he told Moley, "do I have to do everything myself? I see Sam Rosenman in every paragraph of this mess." "Damn it, Louis, *I'm* the nominee," Roosevelt said, when Howe urged him to use his version. Howe had lost his position of eminence. He was now one among many advisers. As Roosevelt came closer to his goal, the man who had pulled him toward it for so many years was relegated to the position of office manager, while the college professors did the thinking.

Arriving at the stadium at 6:00 P.M., Roosevelt was met with a standing ovation. The Smith forces had left. "I pledge you, I pledge myself," Roosevelt said, "to a new deal for the American people." That had been written by Rosenman, and it was not a new or original phrase, but it seemed to fit the candidate's program and it stuck.

The brain trusters were alarmed by the realities of the campaign. Baruch offered a $50,000 contribution as a peace offering, which was accepted. He foisted upon them, with Roosevelt's blessing, one of his economic sharpshooters, Brigadier General Hugh S. Johnson, a colorful figure who had fought in the Spanish-American War. Johnson was the spokesman for Baruch's thesis that the depression would end when businessmen got back their confidence, which depended on a balanced budget and a tax reduction.

Distressed by this infusion of the Wall Street mentality, Moley wrote in a note: "So it goes—first the radicals will be betrayed, then the conservatives. So everyone is ultimately sold out.... The Republicans, of course, are selling out just the same."

As for Tugwell, he was so troubled by Roosevelt's apparent shift to the right, and the sudden entry on the scene of one of the party's foremost reactionaries, that he retreated for a few days to the quiet of his family home on the shore of Lake Ontario. He wanted a commitment to planning for agriculture and industry, a program of institutional change, but Roosevelt was willing to make all sorts of compromises in order to win in November. He and Moley and Berle were political novices, clinging to principles. They had to learn that politics was never simple or straightforward. A balance had to be struck. Stray sheep as well as less tractable breeds had to be brought back into the fold.

Although he meandered, Tugwell realized, Roosevelt was pointed in the right direction, which could not be said for the other fellow. Look how he had handled the bonus marchers! In 1924, Congress had passed the Adjusted Compensation Act, to pay servicemen for the time they had spent away from home—they would be given an insurance policy that they could cash twenty years after its issue in 1925, an average sum of $500 plus interest. But in the thick of the depression, the veterans did not want to wait until 1945—they wanted their bonus now. In May 1932, a bill in the House to give it to them was shelved. The administration was against it because it was inflationary and would unbalance the budget.

On May 10, 250 men in Portland, Oregon, decided to go to Washington by freight train and protest. Their number swelled along the way until they became the Bonus Army. The men who had marched behind Pershing now encamped in the capital, waiting for their handout. A shantytown mushroomed on the banks of the Anacostia River in Maryland. Hoover at first provided them with free beds, tents, food, and medical supplies.

Disapproving of the early payment of the bonus, Roosevelt offered the New York State veterans transportation home and guaranteed employment. Most of them stayed in Washington, however, and when the House voted to pay the bonus on June 13, 8,000 veterans massed in front of the Capitol to await the outcome of the Senate vote. Their last hope vanished when the Senate voted against the measure 62 to 18, but half of them stayed in the camps, an embarrassment to the administration and a health hazard to the city, in spite of the president's offer to pay their train fares home.

Hoover ordered the camps evacuated on July 28. Chief of Staff Douglas MacArthur led the troops, assisted by, among other officers, Major Dwight D. Eisenhower and Captain George S. Patton. Tanks rumbled down Pennsylvania Avenue, cavalrymen attacked the tent dwellings with drawn sabers, and infantry fired tear gas. In the ensuing battle two men died, the shacks and tents were set on fire, and the veterans were dispersed. "That . . . was a bad looking mob," MacArthur said. "It was animated by the essence of revolution."

At 7:30 on the morning of July 29, Rex Tugwell went to Roosevelt's bedroom in the executive mansion and found him looking at a page of pictures in the *New York Times*. He pointed to soldiers stamping through smoking debris and dragging off resisters weeping from tear gas. The victorious general, one of the few in American history to have led armed troops against American civilians, resplendent in field uniform and medals, surveyed the scene of battle with a smile.

Roosevelt said he had to apologize for suggesting Hoover as a candidate in 1920. From the crash of 1929 until yesterday, when he had set Douglas MacArthur on those harmless vets, he had depended altogether on his business friends. Now look where he was, surrounded by guards to keep away the revolutionaries. There was nothing left inside the man but jelly. At least now he knew that Hoover could not be reelected.

What about all those registered Republicans, Tugwell asked, wouldn't they vote the party ticket anyway?

No, Roosevelt said, this went too deep. In his four years as governor, in a state troubled by depression, he had never called out the National Guard. He had always said that suppression would not be effective when there were real grievances.

But wouldn't people sympathize with the president, and consider him justified in using force?

What Hoover should have done when those 200 veterans marched up to the White House gate, Roosevelt said, was to send out for coffee and sandwiches and invite a delegation in. Instead, he had let Doug MacArthur do his stuff. He might even feel sorry for Hoover if he did not feel sorrier for those people, 11,000 of them, the paper said. They must be camping right now along the roads leading out of Washington. It was a wonder that there was not more resentment and radicalism when people were treated that way. Roosevelt lit a cigarette. Anyway, he said, it would make a theme for the campaign. After that day, Rex Tugwell had no doubt about the outcome.

When Huey Long called one day while he was eating lunch with Tugwell to complain that he was moving too far to the right, Roosevelt did his best to calm him, and after getting him off the line, said: "That is one of the two most dangerous men in America." Tugwell asked who the other was. "Douglas MacArthur," Roosevelt said.

At that point in the campaign, however, the most dangerous man to Roosevelt was the fun-loving mayor of New York, Jimmy Walker. The son of an Irish immigrant carpenter, Jimmy was a product of the city streets and parochial schools, where he had been dubbed "Jimmy the Talker." He joined Tammany and was sent to Albany as an assemblyman in 1910, the same year that Roosevelt was elected to the State Senate. But as Walker confided to Gene Fowler, "I was unable at that time to envision him as a prospective pal. He then seemed . . . engaged in a slumming expedition. I suppose this mannerism suggested an aloof son-and-heir conceit to my sidewalks of New York mind. . . . When he tried to exercise his charm upon me in those days, I mistook it to mean that he was patronizing me."

Elected mayor in 1925, Walker had the carefree spirit of the age. He was dapper and amusing and tolerant. He drank and gambled and chased chorus girls, and the voters shook their heads and said "Good old Jimmy" and reelected him. They liked him because he had style, and in New York City style is an accepted form of atonement for character defects. Why, he even wrote songs—"After the Hayride" and "There's Music in the Rustle of a Skirt." He had perfect pitch, in music and human relations.

In Samuel Seabury, direct descendant of the first bishop of the Episcopal church in America, State Supreme Court judge at thirty-three, and Court of Appeals judge at forty-one, Jimmy Walker found his grand inquisitor. Investigating municipal malfeasance under the orders of Governor Roosevelt, Seabury had followed the trail of hands in the till until it reached the mayor's office. His charges had been sent to Roosevelt in June, but the dénouement had been averted until after the convention. It was transparent to Roosevelt that Seabury had his eye on the nomination.

By delaying the Walker investigation, Roosevelt had bottled up Seabury's mischief-making potential, but now that the convention was over the mayor's fate was a campaign issue. His mail told Roosevelt that many voters would judge him on how he handled Tammany. A man from Easthampton, Massachusetts, wired: "I am a Republican but will vote for you provided you avail yourself of the opportunity to dismiss Mayor Walker, and there are millions more who will do exactly the same thing."

Seabury had turned up three major instances of mayoral payola. With the aid of a mysterious brokerage account in the name of his financial agent, Russell T. Sherwood, Walker had amassed more than $1 million. He had used his influence to push a bus franchise through the Board of Estimate for the Equitable Bus Company, receiving a $3,000 payoff. He had pocketed $26,500 in bonds from J. A. Sisto, the owner of a taxi fleet who wanted to limit the number of city taxis through the establishment of a Taxi Control Board.

Wondering what to do next, Roosevelt asked Moley: "How would it be if I let the little mayor off with a hell of a reprimand?" Then, answering his own question, he added: "No. That would be weak." He wasn't really the Torquemada type, and, what was more, he liked Walker. But the little mayor had to walk the plank. Millions of undecided voters were waiting to see what he would do. He had to appear strong and decisive. In a way, Walker was a heaven-sent opportunity for a demonstration of personal leadership. When he sent Roosevelt an evasive reply to Seabury's charges, the governor summoned him to appear in the executive chamber on August 11 for removal hearings.

It had been nearly a quarter of a century since Roosevelt had practiced law, and now he was in effect both prosecutor and judge in a courtroom drama pitting the governor of the state against the mayor of its greatest city. Moley recommended a lawyer to assist him, Martin Conboy, and they worked long hours preparing the case.

Walker knew that his political life was at stake when he arrived on August 11 in the executive chamber known as the Hall of Governors, a room off the governor's private office on the second floor of the statehouse, but he radiated confidence, telling reporters: "I have no fear of removal." At 1:30 P.M., Roosevelt came in, ponderously walking to his desk on his secretary's arm, the creak of his braces audible to all. He sat at the high-backed leather chair before the great mahogany desk, with two state troopers standing behind him. To his left was the table where Walker sat with his defense counsel, John Curtin. To his right were Samuel Seabury and his six assistants.

Roosevelt was courteous but firm, denying Walker's request that the hundreds of witnesses who had previously testified before Seabury be recalled.

Walker had warned his lawyer not to get "Frank's Dutch up," but Curtin did exactly that by patronizing Roosevelt on his knowledge of the law. When he tried to explain what was admissible as evidence, Roosevelt broke in: "Mr. Curtin, I happened to be a good lawyer, and remarks of that kind are wholly unnecessary to the Governor of this state."

"I assume you do know that," Curtin said. "Still, when a lawyer makes a statement as to what the. . . ."

"All right," Roosevelt interrupted. "Don't try to instruct me about the difference between putting a thing into evidence and marking it for identification."

Roosevelt had done his homework, plodding through thousands of pages of testimony, and was able to steer the hearings through Walker's evasions and theatrics, and the obstructions of his lawyers. When Walker retold the story of receiving $26,500 in bonds without looking at them, thinking they were his share in a stock pool, Roosevelt seized on the incongruity. How then did he know how many shares there were?

"I didn't know. . . ," Walker stammered, "if I didn't know . . . my understanding was . . . there were no questions asked . . . if I never heard of [the shares] again it would have been all right with me."

Time and time again, Walker was cornered into amnesia and incoherence. When he had to explain the accounts deposited by Sherwood, who had fled to Mexico, Roosevelt said pensively: "I wish he were here."

"So do I wish he were here," Walker replied.

"Did you do anything about it, then, when you found he was in Mexico City?"

"I had no reason to believe that the subpoena would not bring him back."

"Isn't that a curious thing for you, when a man with whom you had a safe-deposit box and who looked after your personal affairs, disappears, and the whole town is looking for him, and he turns up, not to communicate with him?"

Day after day the hearing continued. It took time from active campaigning, but Roosevelt did not want to give Walker grounds for claiming that he had been railroaded, and in any case the publicity was highly favorable, for the chamber in Albany had become an arena watched by the nation, where the gladiator-candidate had the detested Tammany beast caught in his net.

On August 17, Roosevelt took up the matter of the mayor's brother, Dr. William H. Walker, who served as a medical examiner to the Department of Education and the City Pensions Retirement Board, and who had made a fortune splitting fees with a small band of doctors who monopolized workmen's compensation cases.

"Do you consider that a proper, ethical practice?" Roosevelt asked.

"I don't know of itself that fee splitting is wrong," Walker said. "I have done it. I don't know whether Your Excellency has done it in your law practice or not, but most lawyers have." Roosevelt, who had with Frances

Perkins striven to reform workmen's compensation practices, did not appreciate the implication.

"If the city was not defrauded," Walker went on, "and the doctors—because of some arrangement they had between them—were paid off by splitting the check, or as many checks as there were—I don't see anything unethical about that."

"Let me put it this way," Roosevelt said. "If you were a doctor and had to give half your fees to somebody else, wouldn't you try to get more money out of the city?"

To this Walker had no reply. The second week of hearings recessed and were to resume on Monday, August 29, but the death of another brother, George, a tubercular, intervened. The mayor's doctor said he was suffering from nervous exhaustion and needed a week of rest. Roosevelt put off the hearings until Friday, September 2, the day after the funeral. In the meantime, Walker's lawyer applied to the New York State Supreme Court for a stay, which was denied.

Attending the funeral at St. Patrick's on the first of September, Farley observed that "Jim looks worse than George." That evening in Albany a group of advisers including Rosenman and Farley and Doc O'Connor warned Roosevelt that removing the mayor would cost him the support of Tammany in November and might lose him New York State and possibly the election. As the discussion heated and fists pounded on the table, O'Connor lit a cigarette and flicked the match at Roosevelt, with the sneering remark: "So you'd rather be right than be president!" "Well, there may be something in what you say," Roosevelt conceded. It was a hard decision, but he did not have to make it, for at that moment the phone rang with the news of Walker's resignation. The hearings were closed.

Jimmy Walker's trial without jury turned out to be the bonanza of the campaign. It was a focused and compact little drama with a hero and a villain, acted out in daily headlines, which showed the candidate to be forceful and statesmanlike, and ended with the removal of a popular but corrupt mayor.

It completely reversed the opinion of Roosevelt's most powerful critic in the press, Walter Lippmann, who now wrote: "On the score of his own abilities my own judgment has been greatly modified by the manner in which he conducted the Walker hearings. They were a very severe test. . . . He was exposed on all sides and nothing could have saved him except his own capacity to master an exceedingly intricate mass of evidence. That he did master it, that he revealed a most unusual power of seeing what mattered, that he showed poise and judgment and tact, no one would deny. Now the ability to conduct successfully a semi-judicial proceeding of this sort is not final proof of statesmanlike ability, but a man cannot put on a first-rate performance of this sort and not have more intrinsic capacity than many of us had previously believed was his. . . . Having become convinced that the Governor's abilities have either been underrated or, as is more likely, that he has been young enough to develop and mature impressively . . . I shall vote cheerfully for Governor Roosevelt."

There was, however, a kangaroo court flavor to the Walker proceedings. As someone said, "They sent an ice wagon to catch a weasel." Although far from blameless, Walker was a victim of the presidential campaign. The Tammany leaders were sore, but what could they do, switch to Hoover? Boss Curry's moment of spite came when he denied Sam Rosenman's renomination for his Supreme Court seat. Roosevelt reassured him, wiring: "I have a long memory and a long arm for my friends." Within a year, Curry was ousted and Rosenman was back on the bench.

The Walker hearings over, Roosevelt had to explode the rumors that he could not stand strenuous campaigning. On September 12, he boarded the "Roosevelt Special" in Albany for a 9,000-mile western tour. Under the scorching sun in Topeka, he spoke to farmers about crop control. At the Mormon Tabernacle in Salt Lake City, sitting in the Mormon Apostle's chair, he promised more government aid to railroads. In Sioux City, he castigated the Hoover administration for spending—sometimes the campaign speeches read like a misprint, with each candidate speaking the other's lines. When he was not speaking, he sat and gazed at the countryside as the train rolled along. He saw shacks made of packing cases near the tracks, warmed by coal tossed from passing freights by sympathetic brakemen. In the rich Corn Belt of Indiana and Illinois, he saw unpainted farmhouses, crumbling fences, and food rotting in fields. In the cool autumn of Seattle on September 20, he spoke "in the name of a stricken America and a stricken world."

As Roosevelt built up support, there was one disaffected enclave made up largely of people of his own background, including relatives. One of his cousins living in Paris, Mary W. Roosevelt, wrote him on September 26: "I shall not sail under any false colors, but tell you that because of your running mate, and your silly attitude about the 'forgotten man' and all the rest that you have said about the President in your very bad political strategy, and in attacking him, a thing that has always been considered bad form in politics, I am unreservedly against you—James who saw hundreds of men a week in his work, said there were no 'forgotten men' but plenty of them who thought they were owed something for *nothing,* and James was dead set against such ideas of socialistic patting them on the back as you are handing out. You have only belittled yourself by talking like that, and I know many people who, because of it, have decided they will *not* vote for you."

"I am sorry that you feel as you do," Roosevelt replied, "but I must tell you quite frankly that it really never occurred to me that you would vote for me."

In the meantime, Hoover derived small comfort from incumbency. His supporters were engulfed in pessimism. His distaste for the herd made him a poor campaigner. He had created the Reconstruction Finance Company, which had $1.5 billion out in loans, mostly to banks and railroads, and would remain the key finance agency of the New Deal; he authorized the

RFC to lend $300 million for relief and spend another $1.5 billion on public works; but he was perceived as a failure, and some of his statements came back to haunt him: "Many people have left their jobs for the more profitable one of selling apples," he had said.

His campaign was based on personal hurt, a sense of having been wronged, which found its pathetic expression in a speech in Fort Wayne on October 5: "I shall say now the only harsh word that I have uttered in public office. I hope it will be the last I shall have to say. When you are told that the President of the United States, who by the most sacred trust of our nation is the President of all the people, a man of your own blood and upbringing, has sat in the White House for the last three years of your misfortune without troubling to know your burdens, without heartaches over your miseries and casualties, without summoning every avenue of skillful assistance irrespective of party or view, without using every ounce of his strength and straining his every nerve to protect and help, without putting aside personal ambition and humbling his pride of opinion, if that would serve—then I say to you that such statements are deliberate, intolerable falsehoods." Those were the words of a beaten man.

The main difference between the two candidates was that Hoover wanted to use the government's powers sparingly, while Roosevelt was ready to intervene directly to redress the situation. Other differences came not from political philosophies but from the circumstance of being in office or out of office. The paradox of the 1932 campaign was that Roosevelt spoke out against spending, against unbalanced budgets and a bloated bureaucracy, while Hoover defended deficit spending and experimental measures—it was as if the speeches had gotten mixed up.

Such was the message of Roosevelt's Pittsburgh speech on October 19, drafted by Baruch's sidekick, Hugh Johnson, which would later be used to plague him. It was a "making both ends meet" speech, a "let's cut government spending" speech. The Hoover administration was running a billion-dollar-a-year deficit. This was reckless and extravagant. Roosevelt promised to cut the cost of government operations by 25 percent. He would pay no bonus to the veterans until there was a balanced budget with surplus cash in the Treasury. Roosevelt would later explain that the great increase in spending under *his* administration came from agencies created to reduce unemployment, and that he had kept his promise to reduce *normal* government expenses.

His two-faced admirer, Felix Frankfurter, wired after the speech that "your bonus treatment could not have been better done," while writing Walter Lippmann: "If Roosevelt is elected, I think he will often do the right things, as it were, on inadequate and not wholly sturdy grounds. That's what I feel about his bonus statement. . . . I don't expect heroic action from him."

With two weeks left in the campaign, the polls had Roosevelt winning forty-four out of forty-eight states. Senator Thomas P. Gore of Oklahoma wired him: "If every Democrat in Iowa should be put in jail on election day you would carry President Hoover's native state anyway."

Jackson E. Reynolds, who had been a professor at Columbia Law School when Roosevelt was going there, went to Hyde Park on October 14 and noted that Eleanor never said "If you are elected" but "When you are elected."

On October 25, Roosevelt gave his "four horsemen" speech in Baltimore—"Destruction, Delay, Deceit, and Despair" were the horsemen of the Republican leadership. This goaded Hoover into retaliation. Roosevelt was in his hotel suite in Boston with Moley and Joe Kennedy and Felix Frankfurter when he heard from Louis Howe that Hoover was about to come on the the air with some unpleasant references to the boss. Roosevelt said he had no intention of listening and went into his bedroom, but did hear snatches through the half-open door. "I simply will not let Hoover question my Americanism," he raged, preparing a retort, which Moley convinced him not to use.

Hoover was so unpopular that it was unsafe for him to campaign. In Detroit, mounted police had to be deployed to disperse an angry mob. Traveling in a fleet of limousines provided by Henry Ford, the presidential party drove down streets lined with glum and silent men.

He had foreseen the disturbances. When the Senate Appropriations Committee had considered the first economy bill, they had proposed reducing the salaries in the armed forces by 10 percent. Hoover urged the committee to make an exception in the case of enlisted men. If there were riots, he did not want to have to rely on soldiers who were disgruntled because their pay was less. Where, he may have wondered, was the America of his youth, the America that had allowed a poor orphan to become a millionaire and reach the highest office. Alas, it had closed its heart to him, and once again he was friendless and alone.

On election eve at Hyde Park, Roosevelt and Moley sat before an open fire and talked quietly of the campaign and of the gathering economic clouds, the tumbling prices and the mounting unemployment. Moley felt that his job was over, but Roosevelt had glimpses of the terrifying responsibility that would soon be his.

On November 8, the Roosevelts voted in the Hyde Park town hall, and that evening Eleanor prepared a buffet supper at the house on 65th Street for the Rosenmans and a few intimates before going to the Biltmore Hotel to wait for the returns. Despite Louis Howe's chronic pessimism, early returns indicated a Roosevelt sweep.

Roosevelt carried forty-two states, and won in the electoral college by 472 to 59. His popular vote was 22,809,638 to 15,758,901 for Hoover, who wired his congratulations. Appearing in the grand ballroom, Roosevelt said: "There are two people in the United States more than anybody else who are responsible for this great victory. One is my old friend and associate, Colonel Louis McHenry Howe, and the other is that splendid American, Jim Farley."

To Ray Moley, it was more than a victory, it was the creation of a new party that would hold power for twenty-five years. The Democrats were no longer dependent on the South and three or four pivotal states; as in the early days of the republic, they were *the* dominant party in the country.

Deeply troubled, Eleanor saw the election as the end of any personal life of her own. She had seen in Mrs. Theodore Roosevelt what it meant to be the president's wife, and the prospect did not please her. She had recently achieved a measure of independence and had been able to pursue activities that she found rewarding. All that was being taken away from her. The turmoil in her heart was great on the night of the election.

The next morning, the police guard around the house had doubled, and the family was shadowed by Secret Service men. The president belonged to the people, who were quick to let you know it in a hundred different ways. Margaret Blodgett offered to repair the bindings and lubricate the leather of his books, so that his library would be ready to move to the White House. Elizabeth Boykin told him to add suction rubber tips to his crutches for greater comfort. Porter Browne said that America was a land of confidence men and suckers, and the only way to do business with crooks was to be crooked. Homer Brett, the American consul in Milan, said that he should take Mussolini as an example of leadership. Frank L. Boud sent his name in for an anagram contest—Never to Fall or Sink (omitting the D.). One man wrote to ask if he could be the fish warden of the Painted Desert.

Of all the messages of congratulation, from the obscure and the famous, perhaps the most moving was the one that came from his old friend Helen Wilkinson Reynolds, the historian of Dutchess County houses. "You stand at a threshold, or a parting of the ways, with an old outworn world order receding and a new world in the birth. Washington, Lincoln, Wilson . . . are they not the only other Presidents in whose fields of service were possibilities and opportunities comparable to those in yours? With that in mind I hope . . . that you may be known to the generations that come after as a President who, in troubled days, wrought helpfully for a confused and suffering humanity."

Roosevelt was president, and would remain president for the rest of his life. He would serve in the highest office for twelve years and two and a half months, which was as long as the combined terms of all the other offices he had held—two years in the State Senate, seven years in the Navy, and four years as governor.

Primarily, he had won because he was not Herbert Hoover. The hardest-fought victory had been inside his own party. His Democratic rivals were still rubbing their eyes in disbelief. He had always been underrated, ever since the days in the State Senate when he had struck Al Smith and some of the others as a rich dilettante. From each level of achievement he had climbed to the next through layers of assumption that he was not quite capable. He had been picked for governor for that precise reason, in the fond hope that Al Smith and his cohorts would pull the puppet's strings.

But from the days when, as a young lawyer, Roosevelt had blithely forecast a bright future for himself, the presidency had been a plausible goal. The White House was a familiar place, where his cousin had been domiciled. He had an example to follow, and a loyal aide devoted to the purpose. The reason he often gave for *not* running was that he had seen so much of presidents and the presidency that he wanted no part of it. In fact, he felt he had been groomed for the job. It was the natural conclusion to having been taken to meet Grover Cleveland as a child, to having been a frequent guest of Cousin Teddy's, to having worked with Wilson during his two terms.

Drawing on the usable past, Roosevelt identified with former presidents—they were all links in the same chain now, and at the same time they were tutors like his boyhood tutors at Hyde Park. From George Washington he took the personal knowledge of the country—in his case, on horseback, covering a smaller surface, but deciding that it was one of the duties of his station to visit every part of the United States. From Washington, too, governing in a time of crisis, the hard succession of tasks, the seemingly endless difficulties to overcome.

Lincoln was another president who had saved the republic from destruction, and Roosevelt was indignant that he belonged to the rival party, writing the journalist and historian Claude Bowers on April 3, 1929: "I think it is time to claim Lincoln as one of our own. The Republican party has certainly repudiated, first and last, everything that he stood for. That period from 1865 to 1876 should be known as America's Dark Ages. I am not sure that we are not headed for the same type of era again."

And then of course there was Jefferson, a man of many gifts and disguises, of chameleonlike powers of adaptation to new situations, who saw America as a land of shining newness, a land of limitless and blessed future, and who had told his daughter, Martha: "It is part of the American character to consider nothing as desperate; to surmount every difficulty by resolution and contrivance. Remote from all other aid, we are obliged to invent and to execute; to find means within ourselves and not lean on others." These were not words stored between the covers of dusty books, but instructions for the present.

In Roosevelt's New Deal, there was a Jeffersonian hope for renewal. Experience had taught him to entertain no private purpose, to speak and act, not for a class, but for a people. In the Navy, he learned from Josephus Daniels how to defend the aims of a large department against special interests. His disillusionment with the business community began with the collusive bids of the steel companies, and continued when he was governor with the corrupt practices of the bankers and their inability to regulate themselves, and with the greed and bad faith of the utilities. And it was also as governor, hamstrung by the legislature, that Roosevelt saw the Republican party at the service of big business. He learned these things not in a doctrinaire way but through the practical day-by-day work of government. And so his break with his own class came about quite naturally, and members of his family wrote him that they could not vote for him. One of the men he most admired, Endicott Peabody, voted for Hoover in 1932, and Mrs. Peabody sent a letter of apology.

In speaking and acting for a people, Roosevelt learned to hold the middle ground, and to shun dogma and sectarianism. Again, he had the lesson of the past—his ancestor Isaac had attended the New York convention at which a compromise formula had been found, "in full faith and confidence," to ratify the Constitution. The first church in Hyde Park had been nondenominational, open for worship to the entire community. He saw the growth of the nation as the growth of a tree, and said let's lose neither the old trunk nor the new branches. Roosevelt's greatest asset in the office of president was not his talent or his courage, but his capaciousness of spirit, which absorbed the inconsistencies of a nation the size of a continent. If something didn't work, you tried something else. If you were attacked, that came with the territory. If there were delays, that was inherent in a democracy. It took a long time to get the Congress to pass laws, and then the courts could declare them unconstitutional. Look how long it had taken to get an income tax. It wasn't because of the inefficiency of the departments, it was because of the necessary compromise among the three branches of government. And what were laws in any case but the crystallization of public opinion? It was pointless to blow the bugle for the charge and find that no one was following.

This capaciousness of spirit was intact in a crippled body. The psychiatrist Erik Erikson, arriving for the first time in America, recalled that "the earliest memory I have of the mood of this country, in the days of my immigration, the early thirties, was the time of the New Deal. Here was a great and wealthy country having undergone a traumatic economic depression which, as I can now see, must have seemed to paralyze that very self-made identity and put into question its eternal renewal. At that lowest period, a leader appeared who himself could not stand on his own feet because, alas, he was paralyzed from the waist down. But on the arm of a son or an aide, he appeared always erect; and as his mood seemed to belie the catastrophe that had befallen him, and as his voice ringingly rose above any emotional depression, he was able to lift the spirit of the masses, and they marched—behind the man in the wheelchair."

The nation was self-made, and after his polio, the man was self-made.

XIV

The Peaceful Revolution

---

*Dear sheeps—I ain't only go'ner give you a New Deal—I yam go'ner
give ya a whole blasted new game!*

Popeye

There took place, on March 4, 1933, the quadrennial transformation of
man into president. Until now, Franklin Delano Roosevelt had been
someone whose life you could follow. You could trace every step of his rise,
from the days when his mother had him wearing dresses. But now the man
would lose himself in the office. He would appear briefly behind a microphone, or on the platform of a campaign train. Most Americans saw the
components of an image—a smile, a tilt of the head, a cigarette holder, the
intonations of a voice made familiar by radio. The man behind the image
was hidden, screened. In its day-to-day routine, his life was like anyone
else's. He got up in the morning and brushed his teeth and played with his
grandchildren and read the paper and complained about the White House
food and played poker and mixed martinis. Unlike anyone else's was the
degree of power he exercised as the disposer of the national fate. He called
everyone by their first names and everyone called him "Mr. President."

Such was the paradox of leadership in America. The president was raised
to an exalted elevation and yet had to maintain the common touch. He had
to preside and he had to respond. He had to see the nation whole, composing
policy from multiple pressure points, and conveying the impression that he
was without prejudice or vested interest. He had to accept into himself the
collective personality of the American people, as the white oak on the family
property, planted by the Indians, accepted the arrangement of nature.

And yet, in the worst of times—the five-month interregnum between his
election and his inauguration was the most desperate period of the depression—he maintained a surprising cheerfulness. How, Rex Tugwell wondered, could he be so confident when a third of the work force was
unemployed and millions of families were in need? There was a kind of na-

tional melancholia in the air, like swamp gas. You could not identify the enemy, so you blamed "conditions." If you believed, as so many Americans who had learned the cathechism of Darwinism did, that failures were meant to fail, what did it signify when the planet's most prosperous society failed? It was like a biblical vengeance, like the flooding of the earth or the destruction of Sodom.

You would not have known there was anything amiss from contemplating Roosevelt, who, shortly after his election, was ribbing Ray Moley about what to wear when they went to see President Hoover: "Ray, have you got any striped pants? As a matter of fact, he will need a top hat too. I'll bet he doesn't have one of those. You know, Rex, they say Hoover is very formal. We could not afford to have our expert dressed wrong."

That Hoover wanted to see him was odd in itself. It was not the practice for an outgoing president to ask his successor for help. But Hoover was worried about war debts. The British and the French were not paying and had no intention of paying. If Germany wasn't paying its reparations, why should they pay their debts? Hoover wanted to reconstitute the Debt Commission and Roosevelt's support would help him with the Congress, which had not budged from Coolidge's laconic "They hired the money, didn't they?" But why should Roosevelt pull Hoover's chestnuts out of the fire? Why should he risk the contamination of a discredited administration?

It was a measure both of Hoover's wishful thinking and of Roosevelt's evasiveness that after the White House meeting on November 22 the president was sure that his proposal had been accepted and the president-elect was equally sure that it had not. When there was no follow-up, Hoover, mistaking affability for agreement, thought that this very ignorant young man had acted in bad faith, while Roosevelt was content to let the lame-duck president finish his term in solitary unproductiveness.

At that point, Secretary of State Henry L. Stimson thought that Hoover "made it look as if he were trying to hang on to Roosevelt's coattails when Roosevelt didn't want to be hung on to." But Felix Frankfurter, the eternal go-between, plugged away at Stimson, countering the poor impression he and Hoover had formed. Frankfurter spoke of FDR's shrunken legs and of the elaborate harness he had to wear and of the uncomplaining way he had to put it on and take it off at least four times a day. On January 3, 1933, the president told Stimson that Roosevelt was a very dangerous and contrary man, and he would never talk to him alone again. Of course if Stimson wanted to go see him at Hyde Park that was all right, though he was very jumpy about it.

And so it was that on January 9, 1933, rain turning to sleet as the train took him up the Hudson, Stimson visited Roosevelt, and they had a talk that lasted through the day. Stimson explained his policy of not recognizing the Japanese conquest of Manchuria, and Roosevelt agreed, though again with more affability than conviction. Stimson came away with a better opinion of the man, although he was alarmed at the way he ran down the Foreign Service, whose members, he said, "were wealthy young men who got entirely out of touch with American affairs in the course of their permanent service away from this country."

Thanks to the Stimson connection, Roosevelt agreed to another White House meeting, on January 20. Again they got nowhere, and Stimson felt that Moley had reversed the position he had taken privately the day before. It was now abundantly clear that Hoover would have to manage by himself until March 4.

As if to underline that fact, Roosevelt sailed on February 4 for an eleven-day Florida cruise on Vincent Astor's yacht. In the meantime, a number of Democratic politicians who had been less than enthusiastic about his candidacy were wondering how to come in from the cold. One of these was the mayor of Chicago, Anton "Pushcart Tony" Cermak, who had filled the convention hall with an anti-Roosevelt claque. The Chicago alderman Paddy Bauler urged Cermak to wave the olive branch. "I don't like the sonofabitch," Cermak stubbornly proclaimed. "Listen," Bauler argued, "for crissakes, you ain't got any money for the Chicago schoolteachers and this Roosevelt is the only one who can get it for you. You better go over there and kiss his ass or whatever you got to do. Only you better get the goddamn money for them teachers, or we ain't goin' to have a city that's worth runnin'."

Roosevelt was due to arrive in Miami on February 15 at the end of his cruise, and Cermak went down there to make his pitch. That evening, Roosevelt drove from the harbor to the public park where 20,000 American Legionnaires were convening and spoke to them briefly about the fish he had caught, perched on the back of the open car. Cermak came up to wish him well. Thirty-five feet away, a man jumped on a bench in the second row of the park bandstand and fired five shots from a .32. Cermak fell over. Roosevelt took the wounded mayor into the backseat, and put his left arm around him and his right hand on his pulse, but he couldn't find any pulse. "Tony, keep quiet," he said, "it won't hurt if you keep quiet." They got him to the hospital, but he died in early March, having lost his life for Chicago patronage, and also having taken the bullet that was meant for Roosevelt. The killer, an Italian bricklayer named Joseph Zangara, wanted to destroy the visible presence of a system he detested. "I just went there to kill the president," he told the judge. "The capitalists killed my life. I suffer, always suffer. I make it 50-50—someone else must suffer." Ray Moley, who was in the car holding the belt of a cop on the running board, marveled at Roosevelt's calm. He had lived the moment in his mind. Cousin Teddy had told him it might happen. There was not so much as the twitching of a muscle or the mopping of his brow.

Zangara went to the chair, and Roosevelt went to the White House. But before the inaugural, there was the delicate process of mixing the cabinet cocktail, the political equivalent of the perfect martini. They had to be people with whom, in Ray Moley's phrase, he could "put on his mental carpet slippers." They also had to add strength to the administration through their affiliations and geographical origins.

The pleas of self-seeking friends had to be resisted. The brain trusters were all disgusted with Henry Morgenthau, Jr.'s embarrassing campaign to be named secretary of agriculture. He enlisted Eleanor to lobby on his behalf, and she wrote her husband in January: "Henry Morgenthau came to see me the other day and told me he could serve really well as Sec. of Ag. & all the big farm organizations were for him. . . . Please at least talk to him—I have transmitted my message!"

Roosevelt had other plans, having summoned Henry Wallace to Warm Springs the previous month. An expert on plant genetics, Wallace was himself a hybrid of sorts. A gen-u-wine farmer, with the good soil of Iowa on his shoes, he was also an intellectual who could talk economics and history. He inherited the newspaper *Wallace's Farmer* (a strategic listening post for farmers' grievances) from his father, who had been secretary of agriculture under Harding and Coolidge. It would be an understatement to say that he was not a natural politician. As the journalist George Creel put it, "Henry's the sort who keeps you guessing as to whether he's going to deliver a sermon or wet the bed."

Roosevelt wanted him because he was a respected leader of the midwestern agricultural movement, had ideas on crop curtailment that jibed with own, and was a link with the other Republicans who had voted for him. When Wallace went to Warm Springs, he was a bit put off by Roosevelt and his entourage. Moley kept going on about how he'd disgraced himself with Cissy Patterson (publisher of the Washington *Times-Herald*) at a party on her private train. He'd gone into the men's room and discovered that the toilet had a gold-plated handle, which he had detached and come back waving and flourishing and saying "No wonder people in the United States are so upset when the wealthy travel with gold-plated toilet handles." FDR had rambled for an hour and a half about some buried treasure on an island off Nova Scotia. What kind of a man was this, he wondered, who could go on at such length about buried treasure that was never found. Wallace had doubts about his seriousness of purpose, but decided to take the job.

For Treasury, FDR wanted Carter Glass, the irascible seventy-four-year-old Virginia senator who had been Woodrow Wilson's secretary of the Treasury and the architect of the Federal Reserve Act, but Glass elected to stay in the Senate, and FDR settled on William H. Woodin, president of the American Car & Foundry Company and one of the "Friends of Roosevelt" who had contributed $10,000 each to the preconvention campaign. Woodin, a delicate, birdlike little man, had no banking experience, and his real love was music, for he was a composer of popular songs. But he was loyal and tractable, and could serve as Roosevelt's link to big business. Woodin accepted, and on February 14 Louis Howe wired FDR: "Prefer a wooden roof to a glass roof over swimming pool."

Another wire had gone out three days earlier, this one from Moley: "Further conference on Tennessee project indicates possibility adoption provided some other food supplying and consuming means can be found." This referred to sixty-two-year-old Cordell Hull, the senator from Tennessee, whom FDR had tapped for secretary of state, but who was hesitating because of the expense of social obligations.

Cordell Hull's was an authentic American "up from humble origins" story. This man who in his twelve years as secretary of state would meet as an equal most of the world leaders of his time was born in a log cabin in the haze-hung Tennessee mountains, the son of a farmer whose only ambition was to move from the ridge to the rich bottomland. The way out of that life was through law and politics, and he went from a law practice to the state legislature to the House, and from the House to the Senate—politically, like his father, from the ridge to the bottomland. From 1921 to 1923, with the Democratic party out of power and bankrupt, he held the unrewarding job of national chairman, and this was the way he came to know FDR.

Hull liked to illustrate points with Tennessee stories, like the one about the man who came to a little town and asked directions for another town, and was told to take a shortcut over the mountains. At nightfall, he found himself back in the first town. "At least," he said, "I am holding my own." That about summed up his career in the State Department. He was slow, he was plodding, but he held his own. When someone asked FDR why he kept Hull in the cabinet, he replied: "You must realize that Cordell Hull is the only member of the Cabinet who brings me any political strength that I don't have in my own right." The unavowed reason was that he wanted to be his own secretary of state.

As secretary of labor, Roosevelt chose Frances Perkins. Her gender didn't hurt now that women voted, and he knew he could work with her. The joke was that he had put Frances in labor. Still uncomfortable with union bosses, he did not want one in the cabinet. Miss Perkins had known him longer than anyone else in the cabinet, had seen him mature from a supercilious state senator, who had shrugged off her appeal for help on the fifty-four-hour bill with an abrupt "more important things," to a figure of real stature. She knew the way his mind worked, by intuitive processes, the way an artist works, not with a pattern in his mind, not saying "I will paint a landscape in Holland" or "I will now paint a figure composition of Cupid and Psyche," but taking out his brushes before he knew what he was going to paint, and putting on the paint, and seeing the pattern gradually evolve as he followed the rhythm of his instincts.

For War, he picked George H. Dern, one of the few non-Mormons who had risen to high position in Utah. Dern had run in 1924 against the Republican governor, Charles R. Mabey, with the slogan "We want a Dern good governor, and we don't mean Mabey." He didn't know much about the Army, but that mattered less in peacetime than having a westerner in the cabinet. Picked for the Navy, the handsome Senator Claude Swanson of

Virginia did know something about it, having been chairman of the Senate Naval Affairs Committee during the World War, but he was seventy-one and feeble.

Who else was there? Well, there was thirty-nine-year-old Lewis Douglas, plucked from the House of Representatives to be director of the budget, a position now raised to cabinet rank. His father had moved to Arizona, where he discovered a mountain of solid copper and founded the Phelps-Dodge Company. Douglas was out of step with the New Deal, for his single obsession was a balanced budget. He had the philosophy of a Taft Republican and did indeed join the Republican party in 1936. There was Jim Farley, the new postmaster general, dispenser of 100,000 jobs, and the South Carolinian Daniel C. Roper at Commerce, who as assistant postmaster general had in the early days of the Wilson administration steered some New York State patronage in Roosevelt's direction. There was Harold Ickes, who had managed Theodore Roosevelt's Chicago campaign in 1912 and was FDR's link with the Bull Moosers. When Ickes was summoned to New York, he thought he was going to be offered commissioner of Indian affairs and was stunned when he got Interior, which had been turned down by two influential senators, Hiram Johnson and Bronson Cutting. "Well," Louis Howe commented, "that's the first break the Indians have had in 100 years."

The last appointment was the result of an untimely death. Roosevelt had wanted as attorney-general Montana Senator Thomas J. Walsh, who had devoted much of his career to investigating big business. His presence in the cabinet would be a message that special interests were no longer immune. At seventy-four, Walsh was still romantically inclined, and he went to Cuba in February to court the widow of a sugar planter, Señora de Truffin. They were married in Havana, but the honeymoon proved to be too taxing, and Walsh died of a heart attack on March 2, on the train taking him to Washington for the inauguration. Roosevelt recruited Homer S. Cummings, the tall, deep-voiced prosecutor from Connecticut who had been chairman of the Democratic National Committee in 1919 and a floor leader at the 1932 convention.

It was not a brilliant cabinet, indeed it had its share of timeservers, but it was balanced politically, with lines out in all directions—to the Senate and the South via Hull and Swanson, to the House and the Southwest via Douglas, to the governors and the West via Dern, to the farm bloc and the Midwest via Wallace, to the eastern financial community via Woodin, to the party via three present and former national chairmen, Farley, Cummings, and Hull, to the workingmen and women via Perkins, and to Republicans and progressives via Wallace and Ickes.

On March 3, aboard the train that was carrying the president-elect and about fifty members of the future administration family to Washington, Rex Tugwell thought that the first priority was to save the banks. A newspaper headline said "Thirty States Now on Bank Holiday." Those that remained open were on a "restricted withdrawal basis," with soft-voiced tellers handing depositors their passbooks and saying "Everything is all right" when it wasn't. People had lost their faith in banks and had put their money into postal savings, which had grown from $150 million in 1928 to $1 billion in 1933. On March 2 and 3, there had been runs on banks in Chicago and Detroit, with armored trucks feeding the branches cash. Ray Moley and Will Woodin had been tearing their hair out over the closed banks and the millions in gold that European banks were withdrawing as a hedge against devaluation of the dollar, but FDR was serene in his conviction that it was Hoover's baby.

Saturday, March 4, was a cold, dreary day. The Capitol looked like polished granite. The trees were leafless. Flags were at half-mast, honoring the late Senator Walsh. The Washington Hotel Association had posted notices at hotel counters: "Members find it necessary that, due to unsettled banking conditions throughout the country, checks on out-of-town banks cannot be accepted." Eleanor Roosevelt wondered how they would pay their bill at the Mayflower.

The outgoing Republican administration was bitter, hating to give up power. Frances Perkins had never heard from her predecessor in the Labor Department. For him, she didn't exist (when she first went to her office, it hadn't even been cleaned, and she found huge cockroaches in her desk drawers). At the Willard Hotel, she found a note on her door to call Mr. Early at once, and she didn't know who Mr. Early was. He was the new press secretary, and he told her to be at St. John's Episcopal Church, diagonally across Lafayette Square from the White House, at ten sharp.

She was there in time to see Roosevelt and his family come in the side door. Then the church rector arrived with Endicott Peabody, who conducted the service. It was the order of morning prayer with special psalms and hymns. In the tone of a prayer for a newly baptized child, Peabody asked for "Thy blessing upon Thy servant, Franklin." In his true and sonorous voice, Roosevelt sang "Faith of Our Fathers" and "O God, Our Help in Ages Past." He remained in prayer long after the clergy had retired, making his compact with the Almighty.

The cabinet members milled around outside the church. No one had been introduced, but Miss Perkins recognized them from their photographs—Hull tall and white-haired, Wallace with his country-bumpkin awkwardness, Ickes with one of those good Saxon faces, you could see him standing with Robin Hood's men rather than with the Norman lords. The inauguration was at 12:30 p.m. and the streets were jammed. Miss Perkins shared a cab with the Wallaces and they reached the Statuary Hall and went out through the rotunda, showing their blue tickets, and came to the platform where everybody was, the outgoing Hoover people, the Supreme Court, the diplomatic corps with white plumes in their hats.

A little before eleven, Roosevelt in striped pants and silk hat arrived at the porticoed north entrance to the White House, as Army trucks were removing the Hoovers' belongings. Seven cars framed by a hollow square of cavalry riding at a trot started up the mile-long ribbon of red, white, and blue bunting that was Pennsylvania Avenue. At the top of an empty grandstand across from the White House sat Roosevelt's Harvard classmate Aymar Johnson, who studied the two faces in the lead car, FDR's full of cheer and confidence, while Hoover's round face looked like a lump of dough before it goes into the oven, puffy and expressionless.

They arrived at the Senate wing of the Capitol at 11:20, and Hoover went to the president's room to perform his final presidential duty, the signing of bills, while Roosevelt waited in the Military Affairs Committee room. In the Senate chamber, Vice President Charles Curtis swore in his successor. The Republican Senate leader, Jim Watson, was heard to say that he was "going home with the almost unanimous consent of the people of Indiana." This was a comment on the new Congress. Roosevelt had a majority in both houses. There had been a complete change in party control.

As he waited on the inaugural stand, Roosevelt's old friend Herbert Pell reflected on the circumstances that had brought about the change. He remembered the 1921 inauguration, when Harding had said, "We need more business in government and less government in business." That day the business leaders were handed the richest country in the world and dominance was theirs if they would only deign to keep it. They could have continued forever taking for themselves one egg out of three. It took them less than twelve years to ruin their magnificent gift and bring the country to the edge of ruin. With every court card in the pack they had managed to lose the game. Now the capitalists had to be saved from themselves, like the drowning Frenchman in the rhetoric book who shouted, "I will drown, no one will help me."

When the ceremony in the Senate chamber was over there was a rush for the exit to the ramp leading from the east doors of the Capitol to the inaugural stand. There was Garner in the southwest corner in formal morning clothes, suffering from the chill wind that went straight to the bone. There was Curtis in a fur coat, lost in ruminations on a forty-year career in Congress. There was Eleanor and her tall sons, and Chief Justice Charles Evans Hughes in his long black silk robe and his black silk skullcap. There was Hoover, motionless in a leather-upholstered armchair to the left of the metal lectern that Roosevelt would use, his face set in a permanent expression of resentment.

The ancient Dutch bible that had recorded Roosevelt births and deaths for 263 years was brought up. In the windswept forty acres in front of the Capitol, 100,000 pairs of eyes focused on the ramp where Roosevelt appeared, advancing slowly on the arm of his eldest son, approaching the stand on his useless legs, braces supporting six feet of height. It occurred to radio broadcaster Ed Hill, as it must have to many others, that if this man had the courage to lift himself by the sheer power of his spirit from the bed of invalidism, had the determination and patience to make himself walk, then he must have within him the qualities to lead a nation to recovery.

A smile crossed his face as he shook Hughes's hand, and the Marine band in its scarlet jackets and blue trousers finished the last bars of "Hail to the Chief." Down in front, from their places on the yellow pine benches, men and women, many of them worthy of a chapter or a page in their country's recent history, were stirred by the moment. Mrs. Woodrow Wilson waved a handkerchief and Bernard Baruch swung his top hat. Was it the bitter northwest wind blowing across the open stands that brought tears to the eyes of Josephus Daniels, or the memory of a long and close association with the man about to take the oath?

His hand rested on the thirteenth chapter of St. Paul's Epistle to the Corinthians, that chapter beginning with the words "Though I speak with the tongues of men and of angels, and have not charity . . . I am nothing." Hughes read the oath with dramatic effect, and Roosevelt repeated it like a bridegroom at the altar: "I, Franklin Delano Roosevelt, do solemnly swear that I will faithfully execute the office of President of the United States and will, to the best of my ability, preserve, protect and defend the Constitution of the United States, so help me God."

And then, standing bareheaded as the raw wind ruffled his gray hair, and as the apostles of the old order scattered around him drew their coats tighter, Roosevelt gripped the sides of the reading stand and began his inaugural address: "This is a day of national consecration. . . ."

Was it the words alone, or the sense of a man meeting his fate, or the collective understanding that a turning point in history had been reached? Whatever it was, you could sense a galvanic response in the crowd.

"So first of all, let me assert my firm belief that the only thing we have to fear is fear itself—nameless, unreasoning, unjustified terror which paralyzes needed efforts to convert retreat into advance." To Frances Perkins, it was like a revival meeting. Roosevelt had seen and understood the spiritual need of all the people who had to be given purpose and direction. Despair was the greatest of sins, the contrary of hope, and Roosevelt was asking "Do you believe?" You could see tears streaming down people's faces. Sitting next to her, mousy-faced Ray Moley said, "Well, he's taken the ship of state and turned it right around."

Not everyone was so strongly affected. The writer Edmund Wilson saw Roosevelt as a less forceful heir of Woodrow Wilson's liberalism, smiling an inhuman Boy Scout smile that made one's flesh creep. His ideas on currency were derived from the Boy Scout handbook: "All the things you can do with a dollar." He had the old pulpit vagueness, in phrases such as "in every dark hour of our national life. . . . And yet our distress comes from no failure of substance. . . . Where there is no vision the people perish. . . . "

But to many of his listeners, and there were millions on the radio hookup, Roosevelt's words were inspiring, and to some they were alarming. In Toledo, a young British lecturer named Harold Nicolson, giving a talk to a woman's club in a department store, was competing with a broadcast of the inaugural that brayed out across the ceramic daffodils in the kitchenware department.

His talk over, the woman next to him was describing a peristyle of pure white marble, one of the wonders of Toledo, as he tried to hear the inaugural address. These words came through: "In the event that Congress should fail to take one of these two courses, and in the event that the national emergency is still critical, I shall not then evade the clear course of my duty. . . ."

"You see, Mr. Nicolson," the woman was saying, "our peristyle is a dream in stone. . . .'

"Mrs. Strachey," Nicolson blurted out, "do you realize that your new President has just proclaimed that he will, if need be, institute a dictatorship?"

"My now, isn't that interesting?"

Another impression was that of the actress Lillian Gish, who wrote Roosevelt that he seemed "to have been dipped in phosphorus"—he had a kind of incandescence. Whatever it was, it was a welcome contrast to the dour and uncharismatic Hoover, the scapegoat from central casting.

The inaugural address was over, and Tom Beck, the president of the Crowell-Collier Publishing Company, watched Roosevelt come down from the ramp on his son's arm, with his cane and top hat in the other hand. Beck noticed that he had picked up his hat in such a way that if he put it on his head it would have the wrong side forward. He could not free both hands to make the adjustment, or give it to Jimmy to right its position, so as he moved down the ramp his left hand worked laboriously on the brim until he had it moved around so he could put it on front forward. This small observation gave Beck an insight into Roosevelt's tenacity.

The inaugural stand was bare, and from the distance came the high clear notes of cavalry bugles as horsemen wheeled into line around the motorcar of the thirty-second president. Four times in the nation's brief history a president had overthrown the pride of existing power and made himself the herald of a new era, giving us names indelible in memory: in 1801, Jefferson; in 1829, Jackson; in 1861, Lincoln; and in 1913, Wilson. Roosevelt was gone, but people lingered in the plaza, gazing at the empty stand, kept there by something beyond reason and comprehension.

Normally a day of rest, Sunday, March 5, the first day of the Roosevelt administration, was a working day. FDR convened the cabinet and decided on measures to stop the run on banks and the hoarding of gold. He proclaimed a three-day bank holiday and called for a special session of Congress to open March 9. There was so much activity that Harold Ickes confided to his diary that evening that he was "dog tired."

On March 8, FDR gave his first press conference. One hundred and twenty-five newsmen crowded into the Oval Office and were pleased to find a talking president. He talked about reopening the banks and managing the currency. Gone were Coolidge's White House spokesman and Hoover's written questions. Newsmen could recall only one president who had talked as freely—Theodore Roosevelt.

That afternoon, breaking with protocol (had not Hoover told him, "My dear Governor, after you have been here awhile, you will learn that the President of the United States never calls on anyone!"), the president paid a social call. He went to see retired Supreme Court Justice Oliver Wendell Holmes at his home, 1720 I Street, on the occasion of his ninety-second birthday. Holmes showed FDR a pair of swords that his grandfather, Charles Jackson, had fought with in the French-Indian wars. "I remember," Holmes said, "that my governor [father] told me that he was having lunch as a young student and his father came home for lunch with a friend. And the friend said, 'You know, I saw that little West Indian bastard downtown today,' referring to Alexander Hamilton." Such was the brevity of American history that Holmes's father had been a contemporary of one of the authors of *The Federalist*. "Well," said FDR, who for once could not match the tale, "my grandmother goes back as far as the Revolutionary War, but not as far as the Indian Wars."

When it was time to leave, FDR asked, "Have you got any final advice to give me?" "No, Mr. President," said Holmes, who had fought in the Civil War. "The time I was in retreat, the Army was in retreat in disaster, the thing to do was to stop the retreat, blow your trumpet, have them give the order to charge. And that's exactly what you are doing." When FDR had gone, Holmes told his secretary, Donald Hiss, "You know, I haven't seen Frank Roosevelt for years, but this ordeal of his with polio, and also the governorship and the presidency, have made his face much stronger than it was when I knew him." Holmes also made the oft-repeated remark that the president had a second-class intellect but a first-class temperament, which might more truly have been said of Eleanor than of FDR. Those who worked closely with him recalled that he had an intellect of outstanding range, retentiveness, and subtlety. His mind had the intricate balance of a gyroscope.

On March 9, Congress convened in special session, and that period of machine-gun legislation known as the "Hundred Days" began. For a time, FDR had a Congress that did his bidding. He sent the legislation over and they rubber-stamped it. Roosevelt had a mandate for action. He had majority support in both houses. Of 435 members of the House, 150 were impressionable freshmen congressmen, washed in on the tide. The House elected as Speaker the first northern Democrat in more than fifty years, seventy-four-year-old Henry T. Rainey of Illinois.

When the Emergency Banking Act was introduced in the House on the first day of the session, rules of procedure had not yet been adopted; committees had not yet been named; the printed bill was not available. There was one copy, which was read by the clerk. Majority Floor Leader Joseph W. Byrns, Jr., introduced the bill, asking that the total time of debate be limited to forty minutes. Minority Floor Leader Bertrand H. Snell asked for Republican support, saying "The house is burning down, and the President of the United States says this is the way to put out the fire." The bill, a conservative document that gave various forms of government assistance to banks, was passed by House and Senate that day and was sent to the White House and signed that evening.

It was an atmosphere of hysteria, thought House Republican James W. Wadsworth. The bill had not been referred to a standing committee. There had been no minority strategy, and no caucus. Banking was so technical that most of those who voted for the bill did not understand it, not having been given the chance to read it. And this bill, put forth as an emergency measure, would become established as permanent policy. In effect, it took the United States off the gold standard, since the dollar would not be redeemable in gold—holders of gold were ordered to turn it in at Federal Reserve banks at $20.67 an ounce, and the export of gold was forbidden.

Hysteria it may have been, but it worked. There were no new runs on banks, and depositors brought back their money. The Treasury licensed the solvent banks and closed the weak ones. Within a month, seven out of every ten banks were open, with deposits of $31 billion.

Next on the agenda was an economy bill drafted by Budget Director Lewis Douglas, reducing the salaries of federal employees by $100 million and veterans' benefits by $400 million. This seems curious on the part of an administration whose policy would later be described as "tax and tax, spend and spend, and elect and elect." But in FDR's double-entry mind, there would be savings on the ordinary expenses of running the government while millions were spent on emergency measures.

In his message, which reached the House on March 10, FDR warned of the terrifying prospect of a deficit that "will probably exceed one billion dollars unless immediate action is taken." Since standing committees had not been formed, a special Economy Committee was created to act on the president's message. This was truly the red-carpet treatment: creating a congressional committee for the passage of a single bill. Floor Leader Byrns introduced a resolution limiting debate to two hours and ruling out amendments. The bill passed in spite of opposition from the veterans' lobby.

One of its features was a cut in the defense budget from $752 million in 1932 to $531 million in fiscal year 1934. The Army would bear the brunt of the measure, for its appropriation would be cut by about half. Secretary of War George Dern was so alarmed that he went to see the president with Army Chief of Staff Douglas MacArthur.

Dern could make no headway, he was no match for the president. MacArthur broke in, saying that "the country's safety is at stake." FDR replied with sarcasm about the need for a large army in peacetime. MacArthur felt the familiar nausea that overcame him in moments of crisis, when he got so wrought up that he could not control the words that came out of his mouth. "When we lose the next war," he found himself saying, "and an American boy, lying in the mud with an enemy bayonet through his belly and an enemy foot on his dying throat, spits out his last curse, I want the name not to be MacArthur but Roosevelt."

FDR rarely lost his temper, but this was intolerable. "You must not talk that way to the President," he roared.

MacArthur apologized, sure that his career was over. Insulting the commander in chief was worthy of a court-martial. He offered his resignation. As he reached the door, he heard a calm voice say: "Don't be foolish, Douglas; you and the budget must get together on this." As they left the White House, Dern told MacArthur happily: "You've saved the Army." Perhaps, but MacArthur had suffered the worst humiliation of his life. He had lost his self-control in front of the president of the United States. He felt like vomiting on the White House steps.

In the meantime, bills originating in the White House were passed almost daily. This was presidential power without precedent—FDR could dream up an idea, something that had never been tried, and set the huge machinery of government in motion to implement it. For instance, he wanted to take the unemployed out into the woods and give them forestry work. Frances Perkins thought that was a pipe dream. What did Roosevelt know about the unemployed? "An awful lot of these people have heart trouble, varicose veins and everything else," she told him. "Just because they're unemployed doesn't mean that they're natural-born lumbermen." And who was going to take care of them once they got to the forests? You couldn't just take men off the breadline and turn them loose in the Adirondacks.

Miss Perkins suggested the use of the Army, which had plenty of trucks, tents, and blankets. George Dern said yes, they had all the equipment, from cots to field kitchens, and they also had a lot of unemployed reserve officers who could be put in charge. Since the program would be operated by the military, it was a bit of Rooseveltian logic to call it the Civilian Conservation Corps.

Poured through the congressional funnel, the bill was signed on the last day of March. It was the New Deal's first attempt at unemployment relief, with the federal government giving each corpsman a dollar a day plus room and board and clothing.

More than that, it illustrated the first law of the New Deal, the Law of Unintended Consequences. You could not initiate large-scale national programs without shaking up the society in ways that no one had planned.

In this case, you had four different departments working together. The Department of Labor enrolled the men. The Department of War equipped, sheltered, and supervised them. The Department of the Interior had charge of fieldwork in national parks, and the Department of Agriculture directed fieldwork in national forests. It was an example of what government could do, in the spirit of Grover Cleveland and his civil service reforms, of TR and the Square Deal, of Wilson's wartime truce on partisan politics. It gave the lie to Hoover's "scarlet fever" solution—allowing the illness to run its course. FDR had the faculty that Dr. Johnson recognized in "The Great Commoner," William Pitt, first earl of Chatham, "the faculty of putting the state in motion."

With $25 million allotted to the purchase of forest lands, the CCC increased the public domain.

It employed the peacetime army in socially productive work on an unprecedented scale.

It took uneducated and unemployed young men, turned them into wage earners, and gave them a start in life.

It reduced the drain on states that had been paying them relief.

It encouraged the social promotion of blacks.

On the debit side, there was the exploitation of the program for political and patronage ends. In Indiana, CCC members were asked to donate 2 percent of their salaries to so-called 2 percent clubs to build up Democratic campaign chests. In Mississippi, CCC men were given the day off so they could vote in the Democratic primary, although some of them came from out of state.

All in all, however, it was an auspicious venture. By June 16 there were 239,644 men enrolled, all of them sons of families on welfare rolls or World War veterans. They were split up in 1,330 work camps located in all the states except Delaware. For many of them it was their first job. They built lookout towers and telephone lines and truck trails and ranger stations. They planted millions of trees. In Wyoming they put out a coal-mine fire that had been burning for seventy years. Some of them lost their lives fighting forest fires. Tens of thousands were taught to read and write, and thousands went on to college. Many passed civil service exams and joined the forest and national parks services.

Of course, some of the camps were mismanaged and some of the work was ill-planned. You could not expect Napoleonic leadership from every reserve officer and Horatio Alger initiative from every corpsman. When you sent city boys to places that could only be reached by canoe and pack train, some of them couldn't make it. Some camp managers were drunks, and others were crooks, diluting the milk with water. One was reprimanded for using camp personnel to salvage his sunken motor boat. Harold Ickes had to laugh when an officious Army officer briefed him on the splendid instruction the boys were getting in a camp in Virginia: "There won't be none of these boys leave these camps illiterate."

The CCC code stipulated that "no discrimination shall be made on account of race, color, or creed." In fact, strict segregation was enforced. There were white camps and colored camps. Most of the colored camps were on military reservations because white communities objected to having them in their midst. In the South, they were not wanted at all. It was only when the CCC threatened Georgia's Governor Eugene Talmadge with terminating the program entirely that blacks were at last enrolled, over the objections of county committees who wondered what on earth black families would do with the $22 a month in cash money that the corpsmen were allowed to send home.

Despite the segregation, Roosevelt saw the CCC as an opportunity for the discreet promotion of blacks that would not agitate southern senators. "Find out," he wrote Steve Early on May 8, 1935, "if they are going to use, in the CCC camps, any Negro reserve officers. Even if they only use half a dozen I think it would be good ball." Early replied that to place white workers under the command of Negro reserve officers would make trouble. But FDR went ahead and authorized thirty-nine Negro reserve officers. He also issued an executive order for Negro educational advisers, of which, by 1937, there were 152 out of 2,000, and he asked CCC Director Robert Fechner for more Negro chaplains: "I understand we have over two hundred camps for colored boys but that there are only six colored chaplains in these camps and only eleven medical officers. Can you increase this percentage?"

In its nine-year existence from 1933 to 1942 (it was disbanded because of the war), the CCC enrolled about 2.5 million men, including about 200,000 blacks, not far from the national percentage of blacks in the population (although there were more poor blacks than poor whites). Thousands of black youths were given their first chance in life, and FDR tried to place as many blacks as he could in positions of responsibility.

The Triple C was also the setting for the first scandal of the Roosevelt administration, in which a modest $1.40 toilet kit for the corpsmen was carried to the highest reaches of government. The slipup was Louis Howe's, who, having achieved his dream of making Franklin president, had been shunted aside from the important work and was assigned odds and ends such as negotiations with Chile over nitrate. He was FDR's errand boy on the CCC, and on May 11, 1933, he was visited by a contractor recommended by his old friend (and Roosevelt's lawyer) Basil "Doc" O'Connor, who was eager to tell him how to save money on toilet kits. The contractor, Richard B. BeVier, presented Louis with two kits, one of which was furnished by the Army, while the other one, produced by his firm, would cost less, he said, even though it contained such additional items as shaving cream and toothpaste.

Impressed by the obvious superiority of the BeVier kit, Louis wrote CCC Director Fechner: "It has come to my attention that toilet articles for the men of the conservation corps . . . can be purchased in the form of a kit containing more items and of a much higher quality at a considerably less price than they would cost if purchased singly or if procured through the Navy Department. . . . I have seen the inferior articles referred to, and I have seen the kits of superior articles. . . . If you feel that you are in need of specific authority for taking this matter into your own hands, this letter will serve the purpose." Acting on Howe's letter, Fechner contracted for 200,000 BeVier kits at $1.40 each.

It developed from a War Department study that kits identical to the BeVier kit could have been bought from the Quartermaster Corps for $1.15.

The War Department was concerned with Howe's interference in the regular government purchasing machinery set up to prevent favoritism and graft, and on June 1 the Senate Military Affairs Committee held its toilet-kit investigation.

According to Louis Howe's crony, the actor and producer and Democratic stalwart Eddie Dowling, one of the senators on the committee gave Dowling the evidence against Louis to pass on to him so he could study it and be prepared when he testified. Louis was touched, explaining to Eddie: "I gave it to this one firm because of their reputation that they would keep faith with the contract, and in some respects it's a far better kit. The little case that this was all done up in was of much better quality. It's as simple as that."

Howe testified that a man had come to see him "and I do not know to this day who sent him," which was less than candid, for the contractor would not have gained admittance without the blessing of Doc O'Connor, who over the years was earning a reputation for using his friendship with Roosevelt for personal gain. The committee exonerated Louis from corruption but not from negligence. Its chairman, Morris Sheppard, wrote, "There is no foundation for any criticism of you."

The trouble with the first months of the New Deal was that so many things were going on at once you could not keep track of them. As Supreme Court Justice Harlan Fiske Stone wrote in May, "To judge by the rapidity of changing events, as many decades might have passed" as months. And yet, no matter how many things there were under the circus tent, the ringmaster kept his aplomb. His Republican cousin, Nicholas Roosevelt, invited to the White House to swim in the new pool, found him cheerful and full of inquiries about relatives. "Vigorous, plausible, charming, he was full of the fun of life. As I watched his handsome head over the waters of the pool and listened to his genial comments, I kept saying to myself: 'It's not possible. This delightful, youthful-looking man in this pool cannot be President of the United States!' " He thought of the German word *Leichtsinnigkeit*—a light-hearted nimbleness, a mercurial capacity to react to surface indications.

On April 18, in the Red Room with Ray Moley and Cordell Hull and Bill Woodin and Lew Douglas, FDR announced with a chuckle that he was going off the gold standard. The dollar would no longer be redeemable in gold. The flight of gold made the measure imperative. When Key Pittman came in, FDR said, "Congratulate me. We are off the gold standard." Hull was paralyzed and Douglas wanted to resign. He had wild pictures of inflation going through his mind and said, "This is the end of Western civilization." Someone suggested that they change the inscription on bills from "In God We Trust" to "I Hope that My Redeemer Liveth."

The British screamed stinking fish, which was a fine example of hypocrisy, since they had been off the gold standard since 1931, letting the pound fluctuate, regaining their trade position and making competition harder for the United States.

On May 12, Congress passed the Agricultural Adjustment Act, which proposed paying farmers who reduced acreage or production of the major staple crops of wheat, cotton, hogs, and tobacco. It was an effort to bring agriculture into balance with the rest of the economy. For years, farmers had been subsidizing everyone's living standards by providing the nation's food supply at low cost. AAA brought relief, and soon farmers who had trained their mules not to step on cotton plants were whipping them over the rows. At a cabinet meeting, FDR asked Henry Wallace what Triple A would cost. "A billion dollars a year, Mr. President," Wallace said. "Lew, remember that figure," FDR declared. "I will, Mr. President," Douglas replied. "It's a very easy figure to remember."

James W. Wadsworth, a Republican congressman and a farmer in western New York, called the Department of Agriculture from the House cloakroom and told an official there that he was in possession of 800 bushels of surplus wheat that he could not sell according to Triple A crop restrictions. What could he do with it?

He could feed it to his chickens, the official said, but he could not sell the eggs laid by the chickens. The whole thing was laughable, Wadsworth thought. Under the Potato Control Act you couldn't raise more than five bushels of potatoes without a license from the federal government. And as for all the little pigs they were slaughtering, they could not be processed in the packing plants equipped for large hogs and had to be put in stalls and killed with baseball bats. They were dumped in fields after the fat had been boiled out of them.

Wadsworth represented the ingrained American resistance to planning. A certain amount of regimentation was the price for helping large groups of people. The payments were flowing out to the farmers, who knew that the money they would receive did not depend on the weather. But again, in keeping with the Law of Unintended Consequences, the Triple A ended up favoring big farmers. When the farmers had enough cash to buy tractors, they laid off sharecroppers. As an Oklahoma farmer put it, "I had I reckon four renters and I didn't make anything. I bought tractors on the money the government give me and got shet o' my renters." The combination of mechanization and acreage control pushed the Negro sharecropper and the tenant farmer off the land.

With all these agencies sprouting up, there was a tremendous demand for lawyers. The agency heads were so busy they were interviewing them in pairs, young men a few years out of law school. Anyone with ability could create his own job. The yeast was rising, and there seemed to be little resistance to forward motion. All sorts of ideas were floating around. A proposal that the government build factories and put the unemployed to work in its own factories was seriously considered. Not even the war had squeezed the last ounce of strength out of people the way these New Deal programs did. One of the young lawyers who joined the Triple A that July was Adlai Stevenson, whose first job was drafting a marketing agreement for the California deciduous tree fruit industry. Stevenson did not even know what deciduous meant. A few days of intense heat, however, decimated the pear crop, eliminating the need for government intervention that year.

Also on May 12, Congress created the Federal Emergency Relief Administration, which was responsible for distributing half a billion dollars through state and local agencies. To run the new agency, FDR picked Harry Hopkins, who had been giving away other people's money for more than twenty years, having gone into social work right out of Iowa's Grinnell College in 1912. The fourth of five children, Hopkins was born in 1890 in Sioux City, the son of a harness maker and not very successful businessman who moved around a lot. A product of midwestern isolationism, he registered as a Socialist in the New York City election of 1916 because he wanted to keep the United States out of the World War.

But Harry Hopkins was hard to pin down with labels. He was the social worker as cynic and bon vivant, the registered Socialist who liked the company of the rich, the friend of the poor who played the ponies and drank champagne. His personal life was complicated. After marrying Ethel Gross and fathering three sons and a daughter, he fell in love with a coworker named Barbara Duncan and went into Freudian analysis to try and get over the attachment. In vain, for by the time he joined the New Deal he had divorced Ethel and married Barbara and was behind in his support payments. Hopkins had no fondness for politicians, having fought the New York City Council when he wanted to set up a bureau for transients because they only wanted to put up money for residents who voted.

He had run the relief operation for New York State under Governor Roosevelt, who recognized a self-starter; Harry didn't need his hand held. The core of Hopkins's thinking was the relation of the government to the individual. Hadn't the government given away the national domain in free land to settlers and veterans? Hadn't it given away vast lands to railroad companies? Hadn't it subsidized infant industries with a protective tariff? It was in the same tradition that wages could be paid to the unemployed to improve America. Hopkins was a problem solver in the pure and volatile state. You didn't start with a panel of experts or a study group, you gave the states the money and you let them handle it. His first day on the job, he gave away $5 million to seven states. "Money Flies," a *Washington Post* headline read.

On May 18, another vast social experiment was launched when Congress created the Tennessee Valley Authority. The Tennessee River basin made a great curving loop through seven states—Virginia, North Carolina, Tennessee, Georgia, Alabama, Mississippi, and Kentucky—and the floods were disastrous. The land had been stripped of its timber after the Civil War. It was an area of dire poverty, America's *mezzogiórno,* where a million families lived on cornmeal and salt pork. If you didn't believe that children went hungry during the depression, you could go to towns like Decatur, Alabama, and see them, undernourished and vacant-eyed. Land sold for the amount of the tax owed. In some areas, 30 percent of the population had malaria. They had tuberculosis and pellagra and trachoma. Half the valley's population lived on farms, and 97 percent of the farms had no electricity.

During the World War, the federal government had built a large hydroelectric plant on the Tennessee River at Muscle Shoals, Alabama. Senator George Norris of Nebraska, a Republican progressive, had for years fought for government operation of the plant but had been frustrated by the Coolidge and Hoover administrations.

FDR had been in favor of public power as governor of New York. He read an article on a unified river system by Dr. Arthur E. Morgan, president of Antioch College, and decided to act on it. He would set up a regional authority that would build dams to control floods and generate cheap power. Its rates would be a yardstick for the private power companies. It would make fertilizer and dig a 540-mile navigation channel from Knoxville to Paducah. Flood control would save the cities and the farmland. Malaria, the scourge of the valley, would disappear. The valley forests would be replanted.

There were so many advantages it seemed like an obvious thing to do, but cries of socialism rang out. The *New York Times* called it "Congressional folly," and Representative Joe Martin of Massachusetts said it was "patterned closely after one of the Soviet dreams." Nonetheless it was passed in the euphoria of the Hundred Days, although no one knew quite what it was, since it did not fit any previous category—was it a planning agency, a public corporation, or a government department? Suffering from an identity crisis, the three members of the executive board asked FDR what TVA was supposed to be. It was a *regional* agency, the president explained. It wasn't just providing navigation and flood control and power, it was reclaiming land and human beings.

One of the more interesting sideshows that spring was the investigation of the stock market being conducted by the Senate Committee on Banking and Currency. Ferdinand Pecora, a hard-driving prosecutor who had already investigated Wall Street under Hoover, subpoenaed the leading bankers in the country as if they were ordinary mortals. He brought in J. P. Morgan himself, whose bank at 23 Wall Street on the corner of Broad, just opposite the New York Stock Exchange on one side and the U.S. Subtreasury Building on the other, was known as "The House on the Corner," for there was no sign on the door. Heavy-lidded, mustachioed, and Olympian, Morgan toyed with the heavy gold chain across his paunch like an Arab with his worry beads as Pecora asked questions that no one had dared ask before. Why had he paid no income tax for 1930, 1931, or 1932? Morgan did not know—that was a matter for accountants. And who was this immigrant from Sicily, homeland of the Mafia, this upstart just off the boat, to inquire into the affairs of a man who had acted as America's central banker, Morgan's manner seemed to say. But this time the roles were reversed, and the bankers were the mafiosi, claiming *omerta*, and the capo was J. P. Morgan, claiming that he did not know what his minions were up to. Pecora brought out that the Morgan bank, which floated stock issues for the companies it loaned money to, had a "preferred list" of clients to which it offered stock below the market price. It was as good as a cash gift. As Morgan partner George Whitney explained it, "They take a risk of profit; they take a risk of loss." Would that we could all share in that sublime "risk of profit," Pecora reflected. At last the banks' dirty little secrets were being aired.

One of the names on Morgan's "preferred list" was that of William Woodin, secretary of the treasury, who had in February 1929 been offered some stock for $20 a share that was selling on the market for $35 to $37 a share. Woodin had been brave enough to take "the risk of profit." On May 26, 1933, a full hour of the cabinet meeting was devoted to the Woodin matter. Woodin wanted an expression of opinion from the members of the family. Ickes pointed out that at the time he bought the stock he was not in public life. But Vice President Garner, whose passionate hatred of the eastern establishment was matched only by his own eagerness to turn a dollar, said that people had the impression Morgan ran the country. Did Garner think that he should resign? Woodin asked. Yes, he did, the blunt Texan replied. But FDR did not think so, telling the cabinet that many of them had done things prior to 1929 that they wouldn't think of doing now. Their code of ethics had radically changed. Woodin stayed on.

It was in the context of the Pecora investigation that the Securities Act was passed in May, requiring new stock issues to be registered with the Federal Trade Commission. The Glass-Steagall Banking Act also passed in May, separating investment from commercial banking and creating the Federal Deposit Insurance Corporation, one of the more successful and enduring New Deal measures—FDR had finally come around to insuring bank deposits.

In his first three months in office, FDR had shored up the banks and helped the farmers and the jobless. Something had to be done to put business back on its feet, but what? Alabama Senator Hugo Black had introduced a bill prohibiting the shipment in interstate commerce of any goods produced by men working more than a six-hour day or a five-day week. The idea was that available work should be shared. Black said his thirty-hour bill would create 6 million jobs, and he had the backing of the AFL. But Roosevelt thought it was unworkable. "There have to be hours adapted to the rhythm of a cow," he said.

On April 6, however, the Senate passed the Black bill 56 to 30, and FDR had to hustle to find a substitute. He sent Frances Perkins to testify before the House Committee on Labor that it wasn't enough to limit the number of working hours, you needed a minimum wage and some sort of industrial recovery program. The House bill was buried while Congress waited to see what FDR would pull out of the hat.

The subsequent making of the National Industrial Recovery Act was not unlike the cooking of a stew by a number of different cooks, each throwing in his ingredients. You could only hope that it would be reasonably nutritious and not give those who tasted it stomach pains. Two bodies of thought—that of trade associations to benefit industry, and that of collective bargaining to protect the worker—joined (some might say collided) in the act. It was not a single program but a veritable cornucopia of programs, designed to satisfy conflicting pressure groups, to which was grafted a $3.3 billion public works program.

Roosevelt's method was a bit like sending out bids to different contractors and seeing who came in with the best bid. From one group under the leadership of Senator Wagner and Leon Keyserling came the public works program and the part about collective bargaining, known as Section 7(a). This unassuming paragraph, slipped into an act setting up industrial codes, was in fact a Trojan horse of monumental proportions. It placed the federal government behind the right of workers to organize and bargain collectively, free from restraint or coercion. It eliminated company unions and yellow-dog contracts. It was a mandate from on high to the labor movement, telling them that they could organize the big union-busting industries like steel and coal and automobiles. Section 7(a) was the birth certificate of big labor. Union membership multiplied, and dues made the unions rich. Big labor became a political force. Section 7(a) was responsible for a major political realignment, the alliance between the labor movement and the Democratic party that kept the Democrats in power from 1933 to 1953. This was the Law of Unintended Consequences at its most dizzying, for FDR did not have a clue as to what the results of Section 7(a) would be. Casually, almost unknowingly, he committed himself to a policy of government protection of collective bargaining. It did not occur to him at the time, nor to anyone else, that it would make the Democratic party the majority party.

The actual bill was stitched together from the input of different groups, although there was considerable wrangling. At a May 10 meeting, FDR told them to lock themselves in a room until they reached an agreement, which struck Leon Keyserling as leadership by default. Roosevelt did not seem interested in the provisions of the bill so long as he had something that was acceptable to both industry and labor. In the next week, the omnibus bill, the National Industrial Recovery Act, was put in its final form. Title I would set up trade codes and Title II would be the public works part. FDR would deliver a message to Congress on May 17, and on the same day Wagner would introduce it in the Senate.

But on Friday, May 12, Frances Perkins discovered that Lewis Douglas, with his obsession about balancing income with outgo, had prevailed on FDR to drop the public works part of the bill. She informed Wagner, who, still having in mind the Roosevelt of State Senate days, told Keyserling, "Frank doesn't understand these things, he's too busy going to Hyde Park and sailing boats."

Miss Perkins called FDR and asked for a Saturday appointment, making sure that she saw him after he had seen Douglas. She took along the Labor Department solicitor, Charles E. Wyzanski, another twenty-five-year-old New Deal whiz kid. When they were shown in at 2:00 P.M., she urged FDR to restore public works. "We've got to lock the presses *now,*" she said. "If Douglas hears about this before the bill goes in on Monday morning he will do all he can to upset it."

FDR questioned Wyzanski about some of the Title II provisions, and finally said, "All right, put it in the bill and tell Wagner." As they left the White House, Wyzanski told Perkins, "This really is a most revealing thing. I've studied law. I've studied political science. I never could have conceived that important matters were settled like this, but this is the way government operates apparently." It all seemed to depend on who was the last person to see the president.

The House passed the bill quickly, 326 to 76, in a spirit of loyalty to the president, and despite awareness of its doubtful constitutionality. "He is the Moses who is leading us out of the wilderness," one congressman said. But the Senate was not so obliging. Progressive senators like Norris and La Follette who had followed FDR down other uncharted New Deal paths were suspicious of a bill that seemed to suspend the antitrust laws and sanction cartels. Senator Clark of Missouri wanted to strike out the entire industrial recovery section. "Shades of Stalin," exclaimed the old Idaho antitruster, Senator William Borah. "Stabilization, what crimes are to be committed in thy name?"

While the senators debated, FDR had to decide whom to appoint to head the National Recovery Administration. It was a position of great power, with a voice in the affairs of industry and labor, and billions of dollars to spend. He was leaning toward Hugh Johnson, the one-time cavalry general who had worked under Baruch in the World War industrial board, where, as he put it, "We did not repeal the Anti-Trust Acts. We simply ignored them."

To Johnson, all of life was a saber charge. You cut through red tape, through committee meetings, through congressional obstruction, and *you got it done.* He was in the Smedley Butler "the Marines have landed" tradition that FDR admired, and he had Butler's gift for pungent expression. "It will be red fire at first and dead cats afterward," he said when Moley brought him in. "This is just like mounting the guillotine on the infinitesimal gamble that the ax won't work."

Frances Perkins, who considered him "an erratic person, but with strokes of genius," had an early warning when Baruch tried to block his appointment, telling her that Johnson was not fit to head the NRA. She passed that on to FDR, who said, "That's astonishing. We got Hugh from Baruch. He lent him to us. . . . Have you seen anything wrong with Hugh?"

"He *is* excitable," Miss Perkins said, "and he has got certain elements of instability. . . . I know that Wagner's been ready to tear his eyes out several times because he's gruff. . . ."

"Well," said FDR, "I'll have to handle him myself." That was one of his fondest illusions, Miss Perkins reflected, that he could handle anybody.

She began hearing complaints from all sides about Johnson's tyrannical ways, megalomania, and inefficiency. He was drunk a good deal and was conducting an affair with his secretary, Frances "Robbie" Robinson. Miss Perkins wondered whether he could handle the public works side of the bill, with those thousands of contracts. Would he have the patience to check the accountants' figures? His genius was for splurging enthusiasm, not for detail.

She finally told FDR it would be a mistake to put Johnson in charge of the public works section of the bill. "Hugh'll be wild," he said.

"I know he will," Miss Perkins replied. "Ask somebody else. . . . Ask [Marvin] McIntyre [FDR's appointments secretary], he's seen a lot of Hugh."

"She's absolutely right, boss," McIntyre chimed in. "Hugh is just an easy mark for any grafter in the U.S.A. He doesn't know the difference. . . . He would throw those public works around to please anybody and get him off his back. I think it would be terrible."

"Oh Lord," FDR moaned, "how will I break this to Hugh?" He also wondered who could take his place. Miss Perkins suggested Ickes: "I have been very well impressed with his kind of punctilious, fussy scrutiny of detail. . . . That's exactly what you want, I think, in a public works administration."

"Well," FDR said, "it's very irregular, but I think you're right in your estimate of Harold. . . . I don't know why it's so terrible to have a cabinet officer take on another duty."

But by the time the Senate had passed the bill, on June 15, FDR had still not told Johnson that he was half-fired. Miss Perkins, who saw the president the next day, before the 2:00 P.M. cabinet meeting, was incredulous. "I thought it would be better and he would be less hurt if we did it in an atmosphere of glory and praise," FDR said. The way to do it was to invite Johnson to the closing minutes of the cabinet meeting that afternoon.

And so it was that Johnson was brought into the cabinet that afternoon, introduced, seated at the right hand of the president, and showered with praise for his fine work. Then FDR told him that he had just discussed the administrator's job with his cabinet colleagues (which he had), and that "we" had come to the conclusion that the NRA part would be "so enormous" and take so much of his time that "he ought to be relieved of any responsibility for public works," which was "just an ordinary, routine" program.

As Roosevelt cheerfully rattled on, terrific physical changes came over Johnson's face. Under the pressure of emotion, he turned red, then dark red, then purple when FDR announced that he was going to appoint "that fellow

down there," pointing at Ickes. A laugh went round the table, Ickes registered the appropriate surprise (he had been tipped off by Perkins), and FDR
declared the meeting over. As he was wheeled out, and the other cabinet
members left the room, Johnson remained slumped in his chair as if shot,
muttering "I don't know why, I don't know why."

Miss Perkins caught up with FDR and said, "Hugh is about crazy." "Stick
with him," the president replied. "Don't let him talk to the press. Get him
over it."

She took Johnson for a two-hour drive while he cursed and carried on.
Then he fell into deep melancholy, saying "The President has disgraced me.
If he doesn't believe in me, why doesn't he get somebody else?" "He does
believe in you," Miss Perkins kept repeating, "public works is nothing."
"Why did he give it to somebody else?" Johnson wailed. "I need it. I want it.
I've got to have it." Finally, she drove him to the airport, for he was due in
Chicago to announce the birth of the NRA to a convention of businessmen.
Bad weather forced him down in Pittsburgh, so he addressed the group by
radio. It was not one of Hugh Johnson's better days.

As it turned out, the program given to Ickes by default would make his
reputation. The Public Works Administration was not a relief measure but a
gigantic construction program providing bridges and dams and buildings
and roads. With hindsight, turning over public works to the Department of
the Interior seemed like a brilliant stroke. All his life, Ickes had fought the
domination of the public interest by business. Now he was given a mandate
to turn the Department of the Interior into a center for reform. It would
provide a counterbalance to government support of private industry. Ickes's
nit-picking honesty was a form of insurance against the fear that public
works might turn into a scandal far surpassing those in the Grant and
Harding administrations. At the same time, the division allowed Congress to
keep its finger in the public works pie through the committees that had tra-
ditionally investigated the affairs of the department. The rivers and harbors
bloc would maintain its influence, as would the national parks bloc. The
route of public works from the Department of the Interior to the vast and
greedy jumble of state and city agencies would continue to follow the well-
worn path of patronage and logrolling, past the public troughs and pork
barrels. All this and more might be said to explain the decision, but in fact it
was seat-of-the-pants thinking on FDR's part, forced upon him by the erratic personality of Hugh Johnson.

It has often been said that FDR did not have the courage to fire anyone,
but here is one example (and there are others) where he did exactly that. He
did not like to do it, and put it off as long as he could, and would have preferred delegating the task, but when the knife finally slipped between the
ribs there was no less pain. This was not so much weakness of character as it
was a method of governing. it was better to govern by accommodation than
confrontation. You could not keep having showdowns with people and

making enemies of them. It was often better to kick somebody upstairs than fire him. It was often better to wait, even though people said you waited too long, than to act hastily.

The Hundred Days were over, and the congressmen went home to their constituencies, having passed more legislation than any previous session of Congress. Some of what they had done they had barely understood. It was like the placekicker who kicks a forty-yard field goal against the wind. The coach says: "That's very good if it was meant." What it boiled down to was the government stepping in to help the casualties of the system and to make business and labor less vulnerable to economic cycles.

There was a new spirit in the land, born of the feeling that anything was possible. In a hundred corridors in Washington office buildings, the young and intense world-changer types gathered and talked of what they were accomplishing. They were designing homesteads in Appalachia, they were lending money to farmers to pay off their mortgages, they were funding artists to paint murals in post offices. The New Deal was a laboratory for ideas, not all of them sound. One New Dealer told the story of the man who was buying a mule and just as he settled the price with the owner the mule took off at a fast clip and went straight up against a stone wall. "I'm not buying that mule," the man said, "that mule is blind." "It's not blind," the owner said, "It just doesn't give a good goddamn." That was the New Deal.

Roosevelt was modest about his achievements. Over lunch with Henry Stimson, he said that he had had the good fortune to come in just when the crisis had peaked. The people of the United States had thrown up their hands and said, "Please lead us—tell us what to do!" He had therefore pushed ahead as far as he could and gotten his measures through the House, which then folded its hands and said, "See what we have done, all of the delay comes from that wretched ole Senate." Then, with the pressure of the people that was brought upon the Senate, he had gotten the main part of his program passed into law.

The theme of FDR as savior, however, was already finding expression. It was reported to the president that a Dutch Amish woman in Lancaster County, Pennsylvania, had said of the NIRA: "I believe it's a-goin' to work out. . . . You may not have took notice, but them letters was used in the Bible. Let's see, what was it Ma said? Oh, I call it to mind now. It was them letters they wrote above Jesus when he hung on the cross."

With the special session over, Roosevelt turned his attention to foreign affairs. Ray Moley had been sent to the State Department in one of those parallel assignments FDR favored. He liked to go outside normal channels, feeling that the departments weren't doing their jobs. "Why consult a doctor who let the patient die," was his attitude. It did seem that Hull lacked a firm hand on the tiller. All he was interested in was what he called, with his funny little lisp, "fwee twade." Bill Phillips, FDR's friend from World War days, had asked Hull for his list of choices for embassies, but Hull said he didn't have a list. Phillips was flabbergasted and told him to think of some people. All Hull could come up with was one Tennesseean as minister to Finland.

Ready and willing to step into the vacuum was Ray Moley, who saw himself as the President's Emissary for Everything in General. He was constantly going behind Hull's back, telling an aide something and then saying "You mustn't repeat this to the secretary." The State Department was completely demoralized because the routine had been shot to pieces. Here was Moley, who had come in from the outside, running across the street to the White House ten times a day.

Moley seemed torn between wanting to live up to the expectations that Roosevelt had placed in him and resentment for having been given an impossible job. He was always doing several things at once, studying a draft on unemployment while discussing foreign debt with the British ambassador. The job was getting to him, and he was a mass of suspicions, seeing enemies under the bed and protecting his privileged access to the president. He was furious when FDR paid attention to anyone else, and flew into irrational rages.

In May, when it was decided that an economic conference would be held in London, Moley did not want to be a member of the delegation. An entry for May 16 in the diary kept by his secretary, Celeste Jedel, explains why: "If he comes over later as the personal representative of the President he will come with definitely more prestige and will serve a much more useful purpose."

The conference opened on June 12, and the American delegation distinguished itself with its colorful behavior. Senator Key Pittman went on monumental drunks during which he shot out street lights. William C. Bullitt, who had been Roosevelt's foreign policy adviser during the 1932 campaign, took Ramsay MacDonald's secretary out to dinner, and MacDonald complained that it was a low way to gain the secrets of 10 Downing Street.

Against the backdrop of these shenanigans the conference played out its forlorn hopes. Everyone wanted something different. The French and the British wanted a way out of paying their debts and wanted to tie the dollar to European currencies. In other words, thought delegation member James Warburg, they wanted to go out in the rain without getting wet and without buying an umbrella. The Americans weren't sure what they wanted, reflecting conflicting trends in Roosevelt's thinking. On one hand, he wanted to cooperate with the Europeans to make an orderly world, and on the other there was the temptation to say "Let's fix things at home and to hell with Europe."

With the conference stalled, Moley flew to Nantucket in mid-June to see the president, who was vacationing aboard the yacht *Amberjack*. According to Moley, FDR insisted that he go to London and obtain an agreement on stabilization, saying: "You know, if nothing else can be worked out, I'd even consider stabilizing at a middle point of $4.15, with a high and low of $4.25

and $4.05 [dollars to the pound]. I'm not crazy about it, but I think I'd go that far."

At 8:30 on the morning of June 28, Moley was shaking hands with Hull in his rooms at Claridge's Hotel, confident that he had brought with him the solution to the conference. Pained at being upstaged, Hull told Moley that the press had featured him as being the savior of the situation and the only authentic representative of the president, while he (Hull) had no authority over major questions and had had no hand in the selection of the delegates, who were leaking information to the press.

Courted by prime ministers, and acting as if he were in entire charge of the U.S. government, Moley single-handedly negotiated an agreement to stabilize currencies, which he cabled to FDR.

On July 3, FDR cabled back that he did not want stabilization. Moley was dumbfounded. He had been launched and now he had been scuttled. Pleased to see arrogance humbled, Hull told him: "You had better get back home. You had no business over here in the first place." Moley later explained the change in FDR's thinking this way: Louis Howe had gotten to him. They had both been drinking and got high, and FDR was worried about his son Elliott's upcoming divorce. Therefore he was not himself when he repudiated Moley. In fact, FDR had simply decided that since things were improving at home there was no need to tie the dollar in with foreign currencies. It was his first isolationist reflex. He effectively torpedoed the conference, which limped along for a few more weeks and then died. It was the last of the great conferences of the period, a test case for internationalism, and its failure demonstrated the futility of collective action. When, Europeans wondered, would the United States look beyond its borders again? The British press blamed FDR for being erratic and offensive in tone, although the *New Statesman* admired his "cut-the-cackle-I-won't-argue-anymore" style.

It was not only the end of the conference, it was the end of Moley. He had made the mistake of sending FDR an evaluation report on the American delegation, which said: "On personal side Pittman is only member of delegation able intellectually and aggressively to present your ideas to Conference." This cable was sent through the embassy code room with the designation "From Moley to the President alone and exclusively, with no distribution to the Department."

But the cable found its way into Hull's hands thanks to the American ambassador, Bob Bingham, who had been outraged by Moley's high-handed manner—he had insisted on staying at the embassy and made demands on everyone.

That first-class sonofabitch Bingham, thought Moley when he found out, whom he'd helped during his confirmation hearings when it was rumored that he'd poisoned his second wife (who was the widow of Flagler of Standard Oil), inheriting $5 million with which he bought the Louisville *Courier*. That was the thanks he got!

Hull was beside himself. He showed the cable to Warburg, saying: "That pissant Moley, here he curled up at mah feet and let me stroke his head like a huntin' dog and then he goes and bites me in the ass."

From then on, Hull had his squirrel gun out. He cabled FDR on July 11 that Moley's attitude had been "utterly dumbfounding." Stories were leaked that he had left a trail of unpaid bills. Realizing that the Hull-Moley relationship was poisoned, FDR confided to Henry Morgenthau, Jr., "that it was absolutely necessary for him to get Moley out of Washington before Hull returned as Hull would kick up such a terrible fuss. FDR said that after Moley was in London two days, he started dealing direct with some of the countries which, naturally, made Hull furious."

On July 29, Louis Howe told Moley that the situation in Hawaii was very bad and the police department was shot through with Jap spies and Moley should go there and write up a report. That afternoon, Moley went to see FDR and said he would consider it if it was made clear that this was not a voyage to St. Helena.

But of course it was, and a few weeks later Moley resigned as assistant secretary of state. He became the editor of a weekly magazine, *Today,* which in 1937 became *Newsweek,* and gradually drifted into the conservative opposition, a betrayed loyalist. He had not realized that one of the duties a close aide of the president might be called upon to perform was walking the plank. The inner workings of New Deal government required scapegoats to shield the president, and Moley was the first of a distinguished line. He had been the chief brain truster, the one who put the "organ roll" in FDR's speeches, but his brains had gone to his head. One day he was the assistant president, and the next day he was nothing.

Back from London, Hull went to Hyde Park to see FDR, who told him he had never intended to give Moley any special powers, he had only meant for him to go to London as a liaison man, and the great blare of trumpets had surprised him greatly. Chatting with friends on the drive back, Hull suddenly pulled his forefinger across his own throat and said of Moley: "I cut the sonofabitch's throat from ear to ear." Hull had a grim tenacity. It was in his blood. His father, as a captured Confederate soldier, had been mistreated by a Union captain in an Illinois prison camp. It took him three years to find the man, and when he did he shot him dead.

For the moment, FDR had a hands-off policy toward Europe, and this extended to the regimes in Germany and Italy. Hitler had come to power at about the same time he had, and was already blaming Germany's woes on the Jews. FDR was looking for a suitable ambassador to Berlin, and settled in June on William E. Dodd, a sixty-three-year-old historian of the American South who taught at the University of Chicago and had once studied in Germany.

Over lunch on June 16, FDR told Dodd that his first glimpse of the Nazi regime had been via the overbearing Dr. Hjalmar Schacht, who had as head of the German Reichsbank threatened to stop paying debts owed to American creditors. FDR had told Hull to receive Schacht but to pretend to be deeply engaged in looking for certain papers, leaving him standing awkwardly for a few minutes. Then Hull would discover a note from FDR indicating serious opposition to any defaults, hand it to him, and watch his face turn color. Another way to humiliate him was to say that he could not receive him because he had to receive the Japanese ambassador.

They discussed the Jews, and FDR told Dodd that "the German authorities are treating the Jews shamefully and the Jews in this country are greatly excited. But this is also not a governmental affair. We can do nothing except for American citizens who happen to be made victims. We must protect them and whatever we can do to moderate the general persecution by unofficial and personal influence ought to be done."

Once in Berlin, Dodd reported that Jewish professors were dismissed without pensions and Jews were beaten in the street when they did not salute SA troops. Madness and nihilism were closing in, and Dodd wrote FDR on November 27 that "the Hitler regime is composed of three rather inexperienced and very dogmatic persons, all of whom have been more or less connected with murderous undertakings in the last eight or ten years. . . . Hitler's devices are the devices which men set up in ancient Rome, namely, his flag and salute. He has definitely said on a number of occasions that a people survives by fighting and dies through peaceful policies. His influence has been wholly belligerent. . . . In the back of his mind is the old German idea of dominating Europe through warfare. . . . You have a unique triumvirate here. Hitler, less educated, more romantic, with a semi-criminal record; Goebbels and Goering, both Doctors of Philosophy, both animated by intense class and foreign hatreds and both willing to resort to ruthless arbitrary methods."

From another ambassador, the Wisconsin millionaire John Cudahy, who had visited Germany on his way to his post in Warsaw, FDR received a report that the Nazis were harmless. "There is a unity in Germany," wrote Cudahy on December 27, 1933, "an intense feeling of national solidarity and patriotic buoyancy, which strikes one almost immediately, and the allegiance to Hitler borders on fanaticism. But the reports of training large bodies of troops for war, and assembling huge supplies of war materials are in my opinion entirely baseless." As for the Brownshirts, the Blackshirts, and the Hitler Youth, they were really only "an outlet for the peculiar social need of a country which loves display and pageantry. Half of the Brownshirts are unemployed and the organization provides relief and cheap meals for needy members. These marching clubs are essentially social. The German feels important and distinguished in a uniform and what has been taken for a blatant display of militarism is merely an expression of the unique German gregarious instinct, accountable on the same grounds that our Elks . . . are accountable."

That the Brownshirts and Blackshirts, who were assaulting Jews on sight in the street, were merely the German version of an American fraternal order was a view that FDR had some trouble accepting. He hoped Cudahy was right, he replied on January 8, 1934, but "the chief problem is whether the marching of the general spirit of things is heading consciously or subconsciously toward an idea of extension of boundaries."

It was a year of misconceptions. Just as Cudahy described the Nazis as inoffensive patriots, FDR at this time saw much good in Mussolini, whom he called "the admirable Italian gentleman." After all, the Duce maintained a semblance of parliamentary government. Roosevelt wrote his ambassador in Rome, Breckinridge Long, on June 16: "I am much interested and deeply impressed by what he has accomplished and by his evidenced honest purpose of restoring Italy and seeking to prevent general European trouble."

Another misconception, widespread in England and France, was that the New Deal was an American analogue of National Socialism. The programs of Hitler and FDR seemed on the surface to be similar ventures in state capitalism, based on government regulation of industry and agriculture. In both countries there were youth camps, vast public works schemes, and monetary experiments. To some British observers, "the FDR dictatorship" could be lumped with the antidemocratic movements of the times. Just as the Nazis wore colored shirts and had a distinctive emblem and salute, the CCC was run by the Army and the NRA had its Blue Eagle, of which more were in evidence than swastikas in Germany. Roosevelt himself was tempted by the analogy, telling Ickes on October 5 that "what we are doing in this country are some of the things . . . that are being done under Hitler in Germany. But we are doing them in an orderly way."

In 1933, the expansionist threat did not come from Germany or Italy but from Japan, whose record in international relations was that of a highway robber. Japan had fought China in 1904 to grab Korea, and had tried to annex Siberia during the Russian Revolution. In 1931, it had invaded Manchuria, the first open violation of treaties since Versailles, and seemed bent on gobbling up China. American policy was restrained. There was a $50 million gift to China, so it could buy American cotton and wheat, and an announcement that the U.S. fleet would be kept in the Pacific, which the Japanese protested. In April, FDR saw the Japanese foreign minister, Yosuka Matsuoka, and commented afterward that "his suggestion to us in regard to where we should keep our own fleet has brought me thousands of protests. I am wondering if he said this in order to ingratiate himself against assassination by the Junker crowd when he gets home."

FDR's first venture into personal diplomacy was the recognition of Russia. Here in embryo form was a style of negotiation that would affect the course of World War II and the postwar world. It was based on the conviction that if he simply bypassed official channels and talked to his opposite number, everything could be worked out. As he put it on this occasion, "If I could only, myself, talk to some one man representing the Russians, I could straighten out this whole question.'

The desirability of the move seems to have originated with Ray Moley, who wrote FDR on May 19 that "the old shibboleths as to whether Russia is a democratic government or not, should not weigh in the discussion. In other words, we should apply to Russia at this time the policy of recognizing a de facto government, without attempting to force it into the form of our own conception of what a government *should be.*"

FDR saw the advantages of such a step. This was, after all, the established government of Russia, recognized by every other major power. It was a potential ally against Japan, and a potential buyer of American goods.

To Cordell Hull, it was an ironic reversal of the situation in 1781 when Congress had sent Francis Dana as envoy to Russia, with John Quincy Adams as his private secretary, and the autocratic Catherine the Great had refused to receive the representatives of a dangerous revolutionary government. They were unable to obtain recognition. Hull was against recognizing a regime where religious freedom was denied and where foreign nationals were thrown in jail on slight pretexts, a regime that did not pay its war debts and that spread hostile propaganda through the Communist International. Another foe of recognition was Jack Garner, who said: "If this outfit has kept its word to anyone or done anything in good faith I have not heard about it."

FDR at first used back channels, going through Henry Morgenthau, Jr., governor of the Farm Credit Administration, who opened negotiations with the Soviet trade organization, Amtorg. In October, there was a greater urgency for recognition because Hitler withdrew from the League of Nations; the Soviet Union was seen as a valuable ally in case of German expansion. FDR brought in the State Department, using Assistant Secretary of State Bill Bullitt to conduct the negotiations.

On October 10 the president broke the logjam with a personal letter to Soviet President Mikhail Kalinin, telling him that he had "contemplated the desirability of an effort to end the present abnormal relations between the hundred and twenty-five million people of the United States and the hundred and sixty million people of Russia."

The Soviets, fearing an attack from Japan, were eager for recognition, and sent over their portly foreign minister, Maxim Litvinov, in November. After a week of talks with Hull and Bullitt, Litvinov saw FDR on November 15 and gave him the assurances he was seeking: that the Soviet Union would not permit subversion or propaganda in the United States, and that Americans in the Soviet Union would be guaranteed freedom of worship.

With a bonhomie that ignored recent Russian history, FDR sought to convert Litvinov to Western notions of freedom of religion. "Now you know, Max," he told the Bolshevik envoy, "your good old father and mother, pious Jewish people, always said their prayers. I know they must have taught you to say prayers. You must know all the good old Jewish psalms and prayers."

By this time Litvinov was blushing with embarrassment. "Now you may think you're an atheist," FDR went on. "You may think you don't have any religion, but I tell you, Max, when you come to die do you know what you're going to think of? You're going to be thinking about what your father and mother taught you. That's what you'll think of when you're dying." Litvinov blustered and puffed and laughed nervously, thinking perhaps that merely by listening to this Sunday school talk he was committing a crime against the state, but FDR went right ahead: "In America nobody can understand this idea that people shouldn't have access to religion—any kind they want. That's all I ask, Max—to have Russia recognize freedom of religion."

Russia did, but only for Americans, not for their own people. As for the promise that the Soviet Union would not export Bolshevism, it was broken in July 1935 when the Third International, meeting in Moscow, targeted the United States in particular for agitation and propaganda. No agreement was reached on the war debt, a relatively minor (compared to the British and French debts) $300 million, which the Soviets refused to pay, saying they were not responsible for debts run up by the Kerensky government. On November 17, 1933, FDR announced the resumption of diplomatic relations with the Soviet Union, a decision he could make without going to Congress.

Bullitt was sent to Moscow as the first American ambassador, full of high hopes that he would be the architect of a lasting friendship. Stalin greeted him with a kiss when he arrived in December, telling him that FDR was one of the most popular men in the Soviet Union. Three years later, when he left, he was thoroughly disillusioned. The Russians had reneged on every promise. Once they were sure Japan would not attack they dropped all pretense of cooperation. Bullitt could not even get them to make good on the site that Stalin had personally pledged for the American embassy. He was shocked by the brutality of the regime, the purge trials and the murder of Stalin's rivals, such as Sergey Kirov, head of the Communist party in Leningrad. In his letters to FDR, Bullitt reported the climate of paranoia—Stalin received his meals from the kitchen of the Kremlin hospital in sealed containers to protect him from poison, and there were six OGPU agents watching the cooks.

And yet you could not say on balance that resuming relations with the Soviets was a mistake. Although it produced aggravation instead of entente, it was instructive. Sometimes, even if a policy hurt in certain ways (as when the American Communists were made the stars of the Third International), it was worth trying. The strength of Roosevelt's leadership was his willingness to venture down blind alleys.

He did so again in his gold-buying policy, in the mistaken belief that by raising the price of gold and devaluing the dollar you could raise farm prices. Gold had been at $20.67 an ounce since 1900. FDR wanted to set up a government agency to buy it at a higher price. Secretary of the Treasury Woodin was seriously ill, and the acting secretary was a principled young man named Dean Acheson, son of the Episcopal bishop of Connecticut and onetime private secretary to Supreme Court Justice Louis D. Brandeis. To

Acheson, the gold-buying plan was a shoddy trick. He was in the process of selling government securities to the public. How could he in good conscience do that when he knew that the securities would be worth less when the gold buying devalued the dollar.

FDR complained to Morgenthau that he had tried for six weeks to get the Treasury to buy gold but it was "like punching your fist into a pillow." Finally, in October, Attorney General Cummings ruled that the secretary of the Treasury had the power to buy gold on the open market.

Each morning in the president's bedroom, starting on October 25, there took place a strange rite called "setting the price of gold." As FDR breakfasted on soft-boiled eggs in his solid mahogany bed, he and Morgenthau and Jesse Jones, the chairman of the Reconstruction Finance Corporation, set the price of gold slightly higher than the London and Paris prices. One day they decided on a rise of twenty-one cents and FDR said, "It's a lucky number because it's three times seven."

Acheson was a reluctant party to these transactions. When Morgenthau on one occasion asked him where his statement on the price of gold was, Acheson asked: "Why don't you move into Mr. Woodin's office?" "Dean," Morgenthau replied, ". . . I live each day for itself. . . . I am neither a schemer nor a plotter."

Morgenthau did however move into Woodin's office on November 13, when Woodin went on a leave of absence, and became acting secretary of the Treasury. FDR had asked Jim Warburg what he thought about giving Morgenthau the job, and Warburg said, "If you want a good guard on a football team, who'll charge straight ahead on every play and get the signals mixed about every tenth play, he'll be fine." By that time, Acheson had resigned, leaving, as he put it, the alchemists to turn gold into rising prices.

Acheson was sure the gold buying was illegal, and furthermore he disapproved of what might be called the "Roosevelt style." He thought there was something condescending in the way FDR called everyone by their first name—it was "not gratifying to receive the easy greeting which milord might give a promising stable boy and pull one's forelock in return."

The early bedside appointments reminded him of a seventeenth-century *levée* at Versailles, at the mercy of undignified interruptions, such as the entrance of FDR's grandchildren, Sistie and Buzzy, who galloped across the room and climbed on the bed. "Then began a game not designed to improve communications between President and caller. The child, leaning innocently against her grandfather, would suddenly clap her hand over his mouth in the middle of a sentence, smothering the rest of it. The President's counterattack, a vigorous tickling of her ribs, brought her hand down in defense and produced joint hilarity. Conversation became intermittent. . . ."

FDR kept raising the price of gold through 1933, but it did not produce the hoped-for rise in farm prices. Lord Keynes, the theorist of countercyclical spending, described his currency management as "a gold standard on the booze," and the British ambassador to Washington, Sir Ronald Lindsay, sent this gruff appraisal to Winston Churchill, who had in 1929 resigned as chancellor of the Exchequer: "For two months Roosevelt has been giving us pure hocus pocus and a continent has watched him agape. Now he has got to produce something out of his hat and pretty quick too. Let's hope it won't be the mixture of murder and suicide which the rest of the world dreads so much" (murder and suicide was a favorite phrase of the London *Times* to describe FDR's monetary policies). The tinkering with gold stopped in January 1934, when Congress passed the Gold Reserve Act, setting the price at $35 an ounce and the gold content of the dollar at about 60 percent of its pre-1933 content.

It's surprising how virulent the criticism of Roosevelt already was at this time, when he had been in office less than a year, not only on the part of the British, who could be forgiven their long habit of obtuseness when it came to American affairs, but also on the part of affluent Americans, who did not seem to grasp the simple fact that he was only trying to save the capitalist system. In Rome that November, Mrs. Camilla Lippincott, widow of a former Republican senator from Rhode Island, traveling with the Washington hostess Mrs. Truxton Beale, said at a dinner given for her by the counselor of the American embassy, Mr. Kirk: "I wonder how the members of the Roosevelt family will juggle their income tax reports to conceal all the money they have been making through their official position." The counselor asked her to leave at once, and the ambassador, Breck Long, reporting the incident to FDR, commented that it was intolerable for Americans abroad to express such views.

Americans at home expressed them too, and FDR told his Groton classmate George Biddle that he did not understand why he was so hated. "In chemistry," Biddle said, "a drop will precipitate the contents of a jar and separate the liquid into its component parts." "Yes, but the stupidity of it," FDR said. "Not entirely," Biddle replied. "They know or fear that what they want in life—irresponsible power—is gone. They hate the symbol of those impersonal forces." "Our friend X told me he was so disgusted by the language in the Rittenhouse Club last month that he swore he would never enter it again," Roosevelt said.

FDR knew from his study of history that the more a president tried to do, the more people went on about his commissions and omissions. He liked to tell the story of Lincoln listening patiently to complaints and then saying: "Gentlemen, suppose all the property you were worth was in gold, and you had put it in the hands of Blondin [the French tightrope walker] to carry across the Niagara River on a rope. Would you shake the cable, or keep shouting out to him, 'Blondin, stand up a little straighter—Blondin, stoop a little more—go a little faster—lean a little more to the north—lean a little more to the south'? No, you would hold your breath as well as your tongue and keep your hands off until he was safe over."

As the year ended, FDR did not think things were going as badly as all that. His devaluation of the dollar had helped people pay their debts. In nine months, he had seen cotton go from four and a half to nine and a half cents. Cotton farmers would get $350 million more than they had gotten last year. Writing Colonel House from Warm Springs on November 21, he said: "Now let me tell you something cheerful. This Southland has a smile on its face. Ten cent cotton has stopped foreclosures, saved banks and started people definitely on the upgrade. That means all the way from Virginia to Texas. Sears-Roebuck sales in Georgia are 100 per cent above 1932. Another angle: Hugh Johnson has just telephoned me to be sure to read the latest Dun & Bradstreet report. He says every section of the country is showing a definite gain."

And whom was the recovery helping? Not Mrs. Camilla Lippincott or Mrs. Truxton Beale, but the millions of working people and farmers who even in so-called prosperous times never got much of a break. They were the ones who since 1929 had been in deep trouble. Other Americans had their investments cropped and their salaries cut, but they never had to face the tragedy of hunger, unemployment, and the constant fear of being dispossessed.

Under its dynamic leader, Hugh Johnson, the NRA seemed to be the very spirit of the New Deal, with labor, industry, and government sitting down together to work out agreements. Johnson saw himself as the marquess of Queensberry of industry. In laissez-faire there were no rules, you fought without gloves, and by pickling your hands in brine or alum you could mar your opponent for life. That was what codes were—they eliminated eye gouging and ear chewing and below-the-belt blows.

The Blue Eagle became the symbol of the New Deal. Only industries that agreed to a code (including a minimum wage of $12 for a forty-hour week) had the right to display it. It was a sort of licensing device that enhanced the product. There were parades in various cities celebrating the bird that Senator Carter Glass referred to as "the Blue Buzzard."

Hugh Johnson rapidly achieved the status of national hero, the man who was bringing equity to business. Talking to reporters on July 13, he said he had no political ambitions even though he was getting more publicity than Roosevelt. All he wanted, he asserted with becoming modesty, "was to be down between Brownsville and Matamoras where the owls fucked the chickens," which was evidently an old army expression.

In the first euphoric months, Johnson had a resounding success. At the textile code hearing, the room burst into applause when cotton magnate George Sloan announced that the mills would abolish child labor. By August, Johnson had these notches on his gun: steel, lumber, shipbuilding, woolens, electricals, the garment industry, and the automobile industry with the exception of Henry Ford, who made one car out of four. While Chevrolet and Chrysler said they were proud to have the Blue Eagle on their windshields, Ford refused to submit to collective bargaining, saying "I wouldn't put that Roosevelt buzzard on my cars." The only nationally known businessman to stand up to the NRA, Ford won a good deal of public sympathy as the champion of individualism who paid good wages without government interference, and in 1934 he increased his share of the market to 28 percent. Eleanor Roosevelt said that he had done more than any other man to wreck the NRA.

In September, the soft-coal operators signed the code after a dramatic White House meeting on September 6 where we can observe FDR in action as the Honest Broker. "Come along and sit ye down, let's make it a family party," said the president to the four coal operators and their archenemy, United Mine Workers President John L. Lewis, setting a tone of cordiality. At issue was a clause the operators wanted telling the workers they did not have to join the UMW. FDR said the wording was unclear—"... I don't know what it means. I tried hard for ten minutes to make it out and if I, as a lawyer, can't figure it out—well, that language is obscure. Why not let me, as President, put it plainer, what you want to say is that a man shall have the right to work without being a member of a union. Neither Johnson nor I are happy about these weasel words that were put into the auto codes. They will always add difficulties and finally land us in an endless mess."

Both sides agreed that FDR should draft a preamble to the code. At this point, in his first meeting with Roosevelt, the fearsome brawler John L. Lewis was lamblike in his meekness. When the president asked him whether he agreed that there were too many miners and that 100,000 miners had to be moved into other occupations, Lewis, who did not agree at all, said, "Yes, Mr. President."

It was also part of the president's technique to give those assembled a little lecture, to show that he knew as much as they did about the matters under discussion. "Remember," he said, "quite a lot of that country was farm country in 1810, but the top soil has been running off it since the mines opened and it's all in the creek bottoms and that land will have to go back to forest. There used to be 20,000 farm families in Harlan County. It dropped to 10,000 and coal jumped it up to 50,000. They came in from the valleys and have been getting poorer and poorer. It is a very difficult problem. . . . The move out is a lot slower in coal. You know the saying 'once a miner, always a miner,' and it's darned hard to get a miner to do anything else or to change his point of view. . . . Look at Lewis!" This brought a round of laughter.

In the meantime, Hugh Johnson had been drafting FDR's preamble to the code. "Well," said FDR, "can we write out something to suit everybody?"

"This is it," said Johnson, handing him a slip of paper, which he read.

Feeling they were being bulldozed, one of the operators said, in a last-ditch attempt at resistance: "They may ask you, Mr. President, to explain what it means."

"Oh," said another with sarcasm, "he'll call in Mr. Richberg [the NRA counsel]. Mr. Richberg can explain anything."

"Can you sign up for General Johnson tonight?" FDR asked.

"No," said an operator, "we've got 100 other generals to deal with, but we might get through with it in the morning."

"You get that contract written up tomorrow, and if you've anything else on your minds, just let me know," FDR said.

The code was written up and signed, thanks to FDR's willingness to use the prestige of his office to exert a little discreet arm-twisting.

It was also noteworthy that labor was treated as an equal partner in the discussions, reflecting an unforeseen result of the NRA, the boom in union recruiting. John L. Lewis saw the passage of Section 7(a) as a golden opportunity and sent 100 organizers into the coal towns with posters showing a picture of FDR with the caption: "The President Wants You to Join the Union." He fixed a day for a rally, and the miners came out of the mountains like an army on the march. By the end of June the UMW had enrolled 128,000 new members among Pennsylvania soft-coal miners. Thanks to the NRA, Lewis had become a national figure, invited to the White House.

What was supposed to be business's big chance turned out to be labor's big chance. FDR sided with Lewis when the captive mines (the coal mines owned by steel companies) refused to accept the coal code. He wrote Myron C. Taylor, the head of U.S. Steel, a man of the world who shot grouse in Scotland and had autographed portraits of Mussolini and FDR in his office, that "the old doctrine of 'pigs is pigs' applies. Coal mining is coal mining, whether the coal is sold to some commercial plant . . . or whether the coal goes to run a steel plant." FDR told Taylor that October that union dues should be deducted from pay envelopes, but U.S. Steel would not comply.

"I am getting a bit fed up," FDR said, "and if I am I guess the coal miners are." The miners were fed up to the extent that 35,000 of them went on strike in Pennsylvania. FDR summoned the steel men to the White House as he had summoned the coal men, and a few days later the captive-mine owners agreed to recognize checkoffs and allow the miners to choose their union. The miners went back to work. The United Mine Workers had breached the walls of the steel industry.

Behind the facade of early success, however, the NRA rested on shaky foundations. The part of the code concerning trade practices regulated such things as price reporting, advertising, and sales below cost. One-cent sales and ads that said Macy's sold at 6 percent below other stores were prohibited. The codes covered a wide area of business practices and tended to be in restraint of trade. The big firms, with their louder voice, could co-opt the code and control the industry.

That was one danger; another was noncompliance. Johnson had trouble enforcing the codes. A small group within an industry would start price-cutting, and soon the others would follow. There was also, lurking in the background, the danger that the entire act was unconstitutional. Finally, there was the collective-bargaining provision, which industry fought with various forms of noncompliance, such as setting up company unions.

Soon the NRA, the act that had something for everyone, became the act that was hated by everyone. Harry Hopkins told Johnson: "Hugh, your codes stink." Seven Cleveland grocers wired the president: "NRA is the worst law ever passed by Congress." Strikers on a Baltimore picket line carried a sign that said: "NRA Means National Run Around."

Johnson aggravated the situation with his manic faith that codes would solve all the nation's ills; there was a code for the hog ring industry and a code for the fishhook industry. George Creel, head of the NRA in California, said there were "scores of new agencies, boards, and commissions, headed by campus experts and pink-pill theorists. . . . The spread of the bureaucratic mania had the sweep of pestilence. . . . The manufacturers of egg-beaters and bird cages were not put under the Wire Code, but had separate codes of their own."

Johnson, who was going at full throttle all the time, had begun to drink heavily. He would arrive at the office incoherent, or go off on bats and not show up for a week. In October, he checked into Ward 8 of the Walter Reed Hospital with delirium tremens. He could not have functioned without Robbie Robinson, his secretary and mistress, to cover up for him.

But in September, when Johnson was due to talk at a big NRA rally in New York, the leader of a women's group called the White House and told Marvin McIntyre that no one wanted "that Robinson woman."

FDR was trying to get the country back on its feet, and now he had to deal with the adulterous conduct of one of his agency heads. He sent for Frances Perkins and said, "What am I going to do, Frances? They're up in arms in New York. They don't want this Robinson girl there with Johnson."

"The only thing she does is keep him from drinking," Miss Perkins said.

"Does he drink too much?" FDR asked.

Is the pope in Rome, Miss Perkins might have replied, but she didn't have time, because the president ordered her to drive to the airport and make sure Miss Robinson did not go to New York.

By the start of 1934 the NRA was a big muddle. Antitrusters on the Senate floor blasted away that Johnson was promoting cartels in the interest of scarcity profits. Employers herded their workers into company unions. Businesses that wanted no part of the codes sued to stay out of it, while companies found in violation of the codes, such as Firestone and Goodrich, sued to enjoin the NRA from taking away their Blue Eagles. To all critics, Johnson replied with disdain that they knew as much about industry as he knew about "the queer ichthyology of the great Pacific deep."

Responding to the criticism, FDR created on March 7 by executive order a National Recovery Review Board headed by the famed criminal lawyer Clarence Darrow to hold hearings on some 3,000 complaints. Darrow's report, published on May 20, found that most of the codes favored the big companies and encouraged monopolistic practices. For instance, the motion-picture distributors' code had been written by the chain houses, though 13,571 of the 18,321 theaters were independent.

Darrow's conclusions were highly dubious, for in fact there was no corporate strategy to co-opt the codes. Big business did not step in and take over; indeed it was loudest in its denunciation of the program, and one of the biggest industrialists in the country, Henry Ford, had stayed out of it rather than use it to increase his share of the market. A more accurate complaint was that the codes had fragmented industry. There were now 750 codes, including the dog food code, the shoulder pad code, and the burlesque theatrical industry code, which determined the number of strippers in each production.

FDR's thinking on the NRA was as confused as the average man's. He admired the Brandeisan philosophy of smallness, but he was also drawn to the idea of agreements that could eliminate market gluts and increase employment. Above all, the NRA was a constant headache, with litigants lined up in front of the White House to state their case. In March, when he announced the creation of an Automobile Labor Board favoring no particular union, FDR seemed to be giving legal sanction to company unions. The unions felt they had been sold out and concluded that they would win bargaining rights not by invoking Section 7(a) but by going on strike.

By this time, Senator Robert Wagner had realized that there had to be legislation to implement collective bargaining. The National Labor Board that FDR had set up in August 1933 to mediate NRA labor disputes was being flouted by employers. Wagner and his aide, Leon Keyserling, drafted a bill that would create a National Labor Board with teeth, armed with subpoena powers and the authority to enforce its orders through the federal district courts. This labor dispute bill was introduced in the Senate on March 1.

FDR did not back the Wagner bill. He seemed to fear that it would alarm industry, saddle the country with widespread strikes, and split his congressional majority. Rather than accept the implication of Section 7(a) as a mandate for all workers to choose the union they wanted, he preferred to use the machinery of the codes to deal separately with each labor crisis as it arose. Thus, at a press conference on March 23, 1934, when he was asked his position on the Wagner bill, he said, "You are a little previous on that."

On April 14, he effectively killed the bill's chances in that session of Congress when he told a group of influential senators, "We can get by without legislation, if Bob could be persuaded to take his Bill and say 'I would like to have ⅞ths of this studied until the next session."

"This might just as well be made absolutely clear once and for all," FDR told the press on June 15. "About 120,000,000 people out of 125,000,000 understand plain English; there seems to be a very, very small minority that does not. . . . Section 7(a) says that the workers can choose representatives. Now if they want to choose the Ahkoond of Swat they have a perfect right to do so. If they want to choose the Royal Geographic Society they can do that. If they want to choose a union of any kind, they can do that. They have a free choice of representation and that means not merely an individual or a worker, but it means a corporation or a union or anybody."

Senator Wagner had to settle for a mild presidential resolution, signed on June 19 as Congress adjourned, setting up a National Labor Relations Board for one year.

By this time, FDR was receiving various reports on Johnson's conduct. On one occasion he had done something obscene while drunk in a public place. He was an embarrassment to the administration in an election year. What if it got out that he spent weeks in Walter Reed drying out and that he kept a mistress at the taxpayers' expense? Hugh had to go.

FDR suggested that he go to Europe to study the economic recovery, but he wouldn't bite. He was then summoned to see the president, and they talked for an hour and a half, and there was some pretty loud talk, according to Marvin McIntyre. When he left, and reporters asked him if he was resigning, he said: "The President told me to stay right here with my feet nailed to the floor. That's what I'm going to do."

Roosevelt was frantic. He could not get rid of the fellow. Finally, on August 20, he summoned Johnson to the Blue Room, along with Donald Richberg and Frances Perkins. When Johnson arrived, puffy but sober, FDR did not have his usual quip and friendly greeting.

"General Johnson," he began, grave and unsmiling, ". . . . I asked you to go on a mission to Europe. . . . I believed that was a good solution of what has frankly become a problem. . . . I want to ask you once more, General Johnson, if you are willing to go."

"No, I told you, Mr. President, I would not go. I will stay here and do my duty by NRA."

"Well, then, we must move on to the second item. I think you have misunderstood me, General Johnson, although I tried to make myself clear the other day. If you don't wish to go to Europe, I think you should resign at once. Frankly, you have become a problem. I can't discuss it much further, but I think you should resign immediately."

Miss Perkins and Donald Richberg were looking firmly at their feet. To do this in their presence was a terrible reproach.

Johnson stood up and said: "Very well, Mr. President, I understand what you say. I'm a good soldier. I do what I'm asked to do by my Commander-in-Chief. That's all there is to it."

When Johnson had gone, Frances Perkins asked FDR: "What in the world did you send for me and Richberg for?"

"I had to have witnesses," he said. ". . . . You can testify that I did tell him to resign. . . . I expect he'll be confused again by tonight and not know whether he's been told to stay with his feet nailed down or go."

FDR looked exhausted. He wiped his brow and said, "Gee, that was awful. Thanks for coming."

When the second session of the Seventy-third Congress opened on January 3, 1934, FDR, back from a fishing holiday, said he would apply some of the lessons he had learned from the barracuda and the shark. This at first seemed unnecessary, for with the entire House and one-third of the Senate coming up for reelection in November, accommodation was in the air.

There was not the same sense of urgency, but he was still able to get his measures through by the use of parliamentary devices. When an appropriation bill was passed with forty minutes for debate and no amendments, Republican Minority Leader Snell objected that it was "the most unfair, the most ruthless decision" he had seen in twenty years in the House. Appropriations passed during the session, which lasted until June 18, exceeded $7.5 billion. Once again the ringmaster was putting Congress through the hoops, and it passed the Emergency Farm Credit Act, which earmarked $3 billion in bonds to refinance farm mortgages, and the National Housing Act, which created a $200 million Home Credit Insurance Corporation. The argument that Lincoln had built his own log cabin without federal aid was of no avail.

Just as everything was going so well, FDR suffered his first serious setback from the supposedly tame Congress. Perhaps it was a reaction to the tyranny of the Rules Committee, the phone calls from the White House, the party lash. FDR wanted to reduce the veterans' budget as part of his ongoing economy program for normal expenses, even as emergency expenses were spiraling. For Congress to go along with this was bad politics in an election year. Congressmen had to weigh whether loyalty to the president would cause them to lose the soldier vote. There were poignant outcries that FDR was only adding a new group of sufferers to the country in a time of crisis. Huey Long objected to "authorizing some little 2-by-4, two-bit, job-hunting politician" in the Veterans Administration to decide the amount of compensation.

In response, Congress included a large appropriation for the veterans in an Independent Offices Appropriation Bill. FDR vetoed the bill, but in late March his Democratic majorities divided and Congress overrode the veto. In the House, wrote Harold Ickes, "man after man, like so many scared rabbits, ran to cover out of fear of the soldier vote." Thus, even at the height of his power, the president was vulnerable when congressmen were asked to support a measure that would cost them votes back home.

At about this same time, FDR suffered another setback that provided ammunition to those of his enemies who accused him of being dictatorial. A Senate committee headed by Hugo Black had found inequities in the Post Office Department's awarding of air mail contracts to commercial companies. Without conducting hearings, FDR canceled all the existing contracts in February. Charles Lindbergh, who had been an air mail pilot before his flight to Paris in 1927, sent FDR a telegram on February 11, which he released to the press, charging that he had condemned the airlines without a fair trial.

Within two months, the Army Air Corps, which was flying the mail, suffered twelve fatalities in a series of crashes, and the mail routes were quickly returned to private lines. FDR learned that Lindbergh's legal adviser, Henry

Breckinridge, who had been Wilson's assistant secretary of war but was now a declared foe of the New Deal, had put the Lone Eagle up to sending the wire, and expressed the hope that "he will begin to cut loose from some of his associates."

But the harm had been done, and the air mail contracts offered a convenient focus for anti-Roosevelt feelings. One of FDR's correspondents, W. R. Hutchinson, said he was lunching in a New York City downtown club with a prominent jurist, a staunch Democrat, who said, "The President's actions in declaring air mail carriers guilty of misdoings without giving them the privilege of a hearing upsets the fundamentals of jurisprudence and smacks of Hitlerism; and the government, in hiding behind its prerogative of refusing permission to be sued, has placed itself in the position of being afraid to allow a just tribunal to decide."

Sometimes it seemed as though trouble did not come as single spies but in battalions, and FDR summed up the situation to Felix Frankfurter on March 24: "The scattered forces of the opposition seized on the loss of life among the Army flyers to come together and make a concerted driving. For the last three weeks we have been under very heavy bombardment. The steel crowd have shown their teeth, the aviation companies have been shrieking to high heaven, using Chambers of Commerce and every small community with a flying field to demand the return of their contracts, the automobile companies are, at this writing, still trying to flaunt the provisions for collective bargaining, the bigger bankers are still withholding credit at every possible opportunity, the Republican politicians like Fess and Robinson and Fish are denouncing me as a murderer, and the old line press harps increasingly on state socialism and demands the return to the good old days. . . . I am by no means discouraged, though the work during the past month has been just as difficult and the hours just as long as in the days of March and April 1933."

There were more blows to come. In May, Bill Woodin died, the first fatality of the New Deal. He had been hospitalized in January with throat abscesses. While getting his blood transfusions, he thought of FDR, who had been down into the blackest deepest Valley of the Shadows and had emerged with the happiest of souls. His example would pull him out. But it did not, and FDR grieved for a man of generous instincts who had done his duty with loyalty and modesty.

Another loss was Budget Director Lewis Douglas, who resigned on August 30 over government spending. The fact that Roosevelt was running a deficit of $6 billion caused him intolerable pain. He saw Communism or Fascism taking over in America unless the monstrous spending stopped. FDR was sorry to lose him, he was useful to have around to check the spenders, but he could not give up relief programs just yet.

In spite of the clotting opposition and the losses due to death and resignation, there were some bright spots. Harry Hopkins's emergency relief program, the Civil Works Administration, had been a miracle of quick action.

Over lunch in October 1933, Hopkins had told FDR that he wanted to put 4 million men to work because Ickes with his public works program was so slow getting started. Hopkins knew that fast action was needed, even if there was some spillage. It was better to move with the nonwasted 90 percent than to avoid the wasted 10 percent. "Let's see," said FDR, "four million people—that means roughly four hundred million dollars." The money was siphoned away from Ickes, and by January 1934 Hopkins had employed 4,230,000 men on every conceivable kind of project. He had workers building roads and schools, but he also had rabbis on relief rolls writing a Hebrew dictionary.

It had to be done, but FDR was ambivalent about it. He didn't want to create a class of reliefers and told the National Emergency Council on January 24: "You know, we are getting requests practically to finance the entire United States. There are individuals who want $500 to start raising chickens, and from there up to the corporation that wants to borrow money to meet its payroll; from there on to the railroad that has to refund its bonds coming due; from there up to the municipality that says the wicked banks won't let us have any money; and from there down to the individual who says he is entitled to work. . . . There is the general feeling that it is up to the Government to take care of everybody, financially or otherwise . . . the artists, musicians, painters and brass bands. One brass band asked to be financed on a trip around the country." Dan Roper, the secretary of commerce, said that a group of scientists were claiming they could cure cancer "provided they can get sufficient ray power developed. We are asked to laboratory these tests which will cost . . . probably as much as $250,000."

FDR told Hopkins to wind down the program, and it ended its brief life in April 1934. "Nobody is going to starve during the warm weather," he cheerfully predicted. He later told the cabinet that he would not undertake such a program again because the country was not satisfied with it. It made a bad impression on taxpayers to see men raking leaves or mowing grass along the roadside. He wanted the states and localities to take care of their unemployables.

Another bright spot was the enactment of the Securities Exchange Act on June 6. The Securities Act of 1933, passed during the Hundred Days, required new stock issues to be registered with the Federal Trade Commission. This new act provided for federal regulation of the stock market. It established the Securities and Exchange Commission, which could license stock exchanges and make rules, many of which were designed to protect the rights of shareholders. If the company was asking for a proxy for a slate of directors, for instance, it had to show the stockholders whether they were voting for a management that had made or lost money.

Looking for a commission chairman, FDR brought together at the White House on the evening of June 28 Ray Moley, Bernard Baruch, and Joseph P. Kennedy, who had made a fortune on Wall Street. When they started to talk about the commission, Baruch pointed at Kennedy and said, "What's the

matter with that redhead over there?" FDR agreed, giving him the chairmanship and a five-year appointment. Moley was annoyed when Baruch
later took credit for the appointment—it was, he thought, like Michelangelo
getting some squirt to polish toes who then claimed he had built the statue.

Harold Ickes wasn't pleased when he heard the post had gone to a stock
market plunger. "The President has great confidence in him," Ickes wrote in
his diary, "because he has made his pile, has invested all his money in Government securities, and knows all the tricks of the trade. Apparently he is
going on the assumption that Kennedy would now like to make a name for
himself for the sake of his family, but I have never known any of these cases
to work out as expected."

In this case it did. FDR had "set a thief to catch a thief," and Kennedy
became the tough cop with his former cronies, once telling SEC lawyer Milton Katz: "You know, Milt, when you deal with those fellows you know
what you've gotta do? You've got to force their mouths open and go in with
a pair of pincers and just take all the gold out of their teeth." The president
liked Kennedy but complained to Morgenthau that "the trouble with Kennedy is you always have to hold his hand. . . . He calls up and says he is hurt
because I have not seen him."

It was slow and patient work, setting in motion these new agencies, hoping you had picked the best men and anticipated some of the foul-ups, and it
was in marked contrast to the panacea brigade led by fellows like Huey
Long, who had urged FDR in March to correct the maldistribution of
wealth through legislation. "Can you suggest," the president replied, "any
equitable way of segregating the great fortunes owned in this country and
gained through the abuse of social ethics, from those which were gleaned by
inventive ingenuity or as compensation for honest toil plus good management?"

And yet you could not always help those who needed it most. The prolif-
eration of agencies and bureaucracies sometimes seemed to be setting up
barriers. One example that came home to FDR was that of his Poughkeepsie
neighbor, the florist and nurseryman Alfred E. Bahret, who wrote the president that he was about to lose his property. He had applied to the Federal
Land Bank for relief from mortgage indebtedness but was turned down. He
went to the Farm Credit Administration, who advised him to go to the
Home Owners Loan Corporation, who said that since he was deriving his
living from the soil he should go to the Farm Loan Association. Truly, it was
a nightmare. "We are wondering," Bahret wrote, "whether we are going to
be bounced from one department to another until it is too late, as we do not
think it is the intention of our government to punish a person and not give
him assistance just because he owns a valuable piece of property."

FDR asked Governor Myer of the Farm Credit Administration to do
something for his Dutchess County neighbor. Myer passed the buck to the
Federal Land Bank, where Bahret had first applied, which pointed out that
its loans were limited to the agricultural value of the land, whereas Bahret's

place had a high real estate value. Nonetheless, since the word had come from on high, Bahret got a $7,000, twenty-year loan.

The lesson was that it was better to do something imperfect than to do nothing. FDR was always getting reports on how to reform this and how to improve that. His uncle Fred Delano sent him a report on the "Perfect Union." FDR knew there was no such thing. A democracy was the most complicated form of government there was, where decisions were reached through the slow distillation of interests and wills, through the convoluted interplay of three branches of government, where effective leadership was a matter of not getting too far ahead of the pack. He was not an idealogue, and he told his uncle: "I am a bumblebee. I am going to keep on bumbling."

You could not be an idealogue and govern when within the New Deal itself there were so many conflicting philosophies. The New Deal was more like a series of collisions than a smoothly flowing current. There was the collision between Lewis Douglas, who wanted to balance the budget, and Harry Hopkins, who wanted to spend and didn't care where the money came from. There was the collision between Hopkins, who set up quick make-work programs, and Harold Ickes, who patiently funded lasting public works projects.

But beyond that, in a hundred different ways, government was reaching out a helping hand to the have-nots. With the midterm congressional election of 1934 coming up, there were many people of modest means who had pictures of FDR in their homes like icons. Not because they liked his looks or admired his voice in the fireside chats, although the benevolent physical projection was not to be neglected, but because millions had been directly assisted by his administration. Leroy Westervelt of Hackensack, New Jersey, a laid-off carpenter about to lose his home, applied under the Home Loan Act and had his mortgage taken over with a two-year exemption on principal so that he paid only interest. He got a job in a local hospital at $18 a week and the following year resumed payment on the principal. He had been on relief only four days, doing roadwork with a pick and shovel. He knew who to thank for having a job and keeping his home.

Small wonder then that the election turned into a plebiscite and that the voters upset the tradition that the party in power is bound to lose seats in an off year. Jim Farley predicted that the Democrats would "hold their own." Instead, they gained in the House, from 313 to 322. Only once since Martin Van Buren had a president gained support in the lower house in the middle of a presidential term, and that had been under Theodore Roosevelt. In the Senate, where only one-third (or thirty-two) were up for reelection, the Democrats went from fifty-nine to sixty-nine—one of the new senators was Harry S. Truman of Missouri, who recalled the prediction of a friend: at first he would wonder how he got there, but after six months he would wonder how the others had got there.

The percentage of Republicans had never been so low (one-fourth of the House and one-third of the Senate), but out of the ashes of a demoralized party a bitter opposition was already crystallizing, made up of business leaders and newspaper publishers, and joined by disgruntled Democrats. That August the American Liberty League was chartered. And out of the woodwork came the same cast of characters that had tried to prevent FDR's nomination in 1932—Pierre du Pont, Jouett Shouse, Al Smith, and the Morgan lawyer and 1924 Democratic candidate, John W. Davis.

The growing anti-Roosevelt sentiment took various and at times bizarre forms. At the 1934 outing of the New York Bond Club, held at the Sleepy Hollow Club in Tarrytown, the dart game target was a caricature of FDR. In the galleries of the Westchester Institute of Fine Arts, also in Tarrytown, there was a painting on exhibit called "The Nightmare of 1934." Eight by four feet, it showed FDR speaking into a row of microphones, a smile on his face and a small crown on his head, with his right hand holding the stand of microphones and his left a fishing line from which dangled a large fish. Eleanor was in an evening gown, waving a paper crown, a mass of papers dropping from her left hand. On the table in front of FDR were scattered playing cards, all of them deuces. Secretary of the Treasury Henry Morgenthau, Jr., sat in the foreground, clad in a clown suit, juggling money, while below him hands reached out beggingly from a pool of water.

On August 31, a housepainter of Latvian descent named John Smiukese flung the contents of a bottle of varnish remover at the painting and touched a match to it. As the canvas burst into flames he ripped it from the wall and completed its demolition. Attracted by the screams of women visitors, police arrested Smiukese and at first charged him with arson, which was later reduced to malicious mischief. Pleading guilty, he was sentenced to six months in the Westchester County jail. Here was a working-class immigrant who had entered one of the lairs of the Republican establishment to protest against a painting that was offensive to the president and the first lady, and who had gone to jail for it. In America, class warfare had some farcical aspects.

XV

Stumbling in the Right Direction

When someone criticized his administration for stumbling along, Abraham Lincoln replied: "It may be true, but please God, I think we are stumbling in the right direction."

A T the start of 1935, FDR seemed to be in a strong position, having reversed the slippage of off-year elections, but a strong mandate from the people was not enough to protect him from attacks on three different fronts.

Two years before, he had called a special session of Congress, and the "must" legislation had rolled off the assembly line, almost without dissent and without anyone asking whether it was constitutional. Aloof from the events of the Hundred Days, the nine elderly gentlemen of the Supreme Court read their newspapers and waited. They knew that some of the legislation had been hastily drafted, and that the administration was delaying legal tests. They also knew that what de Tocqueville had written was still true: "Hardly any political question arises in the United States that is not resolved sooner or later into a judicial question."

The first decisions, based on challenges to state laws, were favorable to the New Deal. The court upheld a Minnesota law delaying the foreclosure of mortgages and a New York law fixing minimum prices for milk.

The federal cases started coming in toward the end of 1934, and the first swing of the ax came on January 7, 1935, when the court by a vote of 8 to 1 invalidated the section of the NIRA that regulated the interstate shipment of oil. It was a jolt to the administration, for it became apparent that the court could destroy New Deal legislation with rulings from which there was no appeal, no matter how many votes Roosevelt got or how many fireside chats he made.

Just as there seemed to be nothing he could do about Supreme Court decisions, FDR learned that he could not count on automatic party loyalty, even though many of the Democrats in the House and Senate owed their seats to campaign pledges that they would back the New Deal. He wanted the United States to join the Court of International Justice at The Hague, a largely symbolic gesture supported by two Republican presidents, Coolidge and Hoover. This required a two-thirds vote of the Senate, and there were sixty-nine Democratic senators, five more than two-thirds.

But the isolationist reflex was stronger than party loyalty. There was a commonsense appeal in the notion that America should stay out of Europe's affairs. "I am a believer in democracy," said Senator Homer T. Bone of Washington, "and will have nothing to do with the poisonous European mess."

On January 30, 1935, the day after the vote, which Ickes described as "a major defeat of the Administration," FDR wrote Arkansas Senator Joe Robinson: "As to the 36 senators who placed themselves on record against the principle of a World Court, I am inclined to think that if they ever get to Heaven they will be doing a great deal of apologizing for a very long time— that is if God is against war—and I think he is." This was FDR at his most self-righteous, invoking a pro-administration deity. From time to time, when he was really irked—as after the "Section A" report in 1921—he had reminded his foes that God was on his side. This was not done in the Woodrow Wilson Presbyterian manner of believing that God was speaking and acting through him. It was more a stance that no one but himself could recognize the complexity of the problems before the nation and thus see the common good. "If only you could be at my desk and see what I see" was the theme of many letters. It was just as valid a theme as the one that made many Americans want to stay clear of Europe's mess.

When ambassador to Germany William Dodd visited Washington that February, he was startled by the neo-fascist strain in some of the isolationist talk. Dodd had come to hate Hitler, whom he had met in March 1934, when the Führer kept saying "Damn the Jews!" and "Ach, that is all Jewish lies," and swore that he would get rid of all the Jews in Germany. "He is such a horror to me," Dodd confided to a fellow diplomat, "I cannot endure his presence."

At a dinner with Rex Tugwell and some congressional leaders, Dodd was sickened to hear Senator Burton K. Wheeler of Montana spout what sounded like National Socialist talk. "We shall soon be shooting up people here, like Hitler does," Wheeler said. His plan for the world favored American domination of the Western Hemisphere, German domination of Europe, and Japanese domination of the Far East.

When Dodd reported Wheeler's remarks to FDR, the president said it sounded like him, and predicted that Huey Long would be a candidate of the Hitler type in 1936.

One of the by-products of the New Deal was a bunch of radical movements that raised the specter of a third party in 1936. They could have sprouted only in the fertile climate of New Deal reform, and were trying to outflank FDR with wild promises. There was Floyd B. Olson, Minnesota's militant Farmer-Labor governor, who had won a third term on a platform of state ownership of key industries. There was the La Follette brothers' Progressive party, organized in Wisconsin along similar lines. There was the California doctor, Francis E. Townsend, who wanted to give $200 a month to everyone over sixty. There was Father Charles E. Coughlin in Detroit, clamoring for a guaranteed annual wage. And there was Huey Long, the Louisiana "Kingfish," who had his own murky Share-Our-Wealth program.

There was no doubt that Huey had his eye on the White House. He wanted to put a third party in the field in 1936, carry eight or nine states, and throw the election to the Republicans. Then his chance would come in 1940. "I can take him," he said of FDR. "He's a phoney. . . . He's scared of me. I can outpromise him, and he knows it. People will believe me and they won't believe him. His mother's watchin' him, and she won't let him go too far, but I ain't got no mother left. . . . He's livin' on an inherited income. I got nothin, so I don't have to bother about that."

Something had to be done about Huey Long, and at a February 5 meeting of the National Emergency Council, a body that coordinated the work of the New Deal agencies, FDR urged that the jobs be given to those who were loyal to his administration: "Nobody wants to put all these agencies into Administration politics, but we must prevent them from being anti-Administration. If they are not in sympathy with what we are doing, we do not need to use them. . . ."

"In a delicate situation like Louisiana we may have to ask for your advice," Henry Wallace said.

"You won't have to do that," FDR replied. "Don't put anybody in and don't keep anybody that is working for Huey Long or his crowd! That is a hundred per cent!"

"That goes for everybody," Vice President Garner chimed in.

"Everybody and every agency," FDR said. "Anybody working for Huey Long is not working for us."

Of course it was being said that in 1936 Huey Long would do to FDR what Theodore Roosevelt had done to Taft in 1912. FDR knew the Republicans were flirting with Long and probably financing him. "There is no question that it is all a dangerous situation," he wrote Colonel House on February 16, "but when it comes to a show-down these fellows cannot all lie in the same bed and will fight among themselves with almost absolute certainty. They represent every shade."

There were ways of dealing with Father Coughlin too, and FDR said he would "send for the three Cardinals and the Apostolic Delegate and show them the attacks that Father Coughlin had made on the Sovereign of the United States, namely the President, and ask them how that jibes with their theory that the church should have an ambassador in each country."

In March 1935, FDR learned that one of his own brain trusters, a man who had been his close adviser since before the Chicago convention, was flirting with a third-party movement. This was Rex Tugwell, now known as

"Rex the Red" because of his inflammatory antibusiness speeches, whose early association with FDR still gave him a kind of precedence. He had barged into the president's office on March 14 to tell him that his handling of unemployment was all wrong, that his insistence on putting men back to work was all wrong, that public works should be something in which the profit motive played no part.

When FDR said he wanted to put even more men back to work by using more hand labor and less machinery, Tugwell said that reminded him of the story of two jobless men watching a steam shovel. "If they did not have those damn machines we would have a job," one said. "Yes, and if they did it with spoons a lot more people would have jobs," the other replied.

FDR was not amused and said Rex was just trying to be clever and reduce the thing to an absurdity. Tugwell replied that FDR evidently shared the same theory as the AFL, whose conception was that there was only so much work to be done and that their members ought to do it, whereas in fact there was no limit on the amount of work that could be done to improve the community.

Very few people could talk to the president like that. Four days later, Morgenthau, who was always ready to run down anyone close to the boss, informed him that Tugwell had told some people in Chicago that he was going to support Governor Olson of Minnesota, feeling that he was the man of the hour. Olson's unsavory private life had been pointed out to Tugwell, who said that would just add romantic charm to his candidacy for president.

"Knowing that Tugwell is disloyal to you," Morgenthau asked, "do you think you should appoint him to a new position of responsibility?"

"You know," FDR replied, "when Napoleon had a Marshal in whom he did not have complete confidence he would put him in a position of the greatest responsibility and test him. That is what I am going to do with Tugwell. . . . If I put Tugwell out today what would he do? He would start writing a few articles, lecturing, saying that he tried as long as he could to be loyal to the administration but he just could not possibly continue to go along with this policy of restricting production and that he was for the policy of plenty, and gradually he would work up a following. If I put Tugwell out today there would be another big hullabaloo that I turned to the right. They would magnify it tremendously and the thing for me to do is not to give these people a chance to go out and work against me now. . . . I consider Tugwell one of the most ambitious and clever people here in Washington."

And so it was that Tugwell, who had been in the Department of Agriculture, was handed the Resettlement Administration, which included Subsistence Homesteads, in order to keep him from defecting to a third-party movement. Tugwell came under his share of criticism. It was said that with a staff of 12,000 he had created 5,000 relief jobs. Which was unfair, for his main task was not to create jobs but to lend money to destitute farm families and buy up submarginal farmland. He also built three greenbelt cities (known as Tugwell Towns), which were early prototypes for suburban com-

Holding hands at age 11 with his mother, with whom he shares the Delano nose; her face is beautiful but unsmiling, making her seem severe and unyielding. Two years later, his hair neatly parted in the middle, Franklin posed with his mutton-chopped father, the picture of Victorian rectitude.

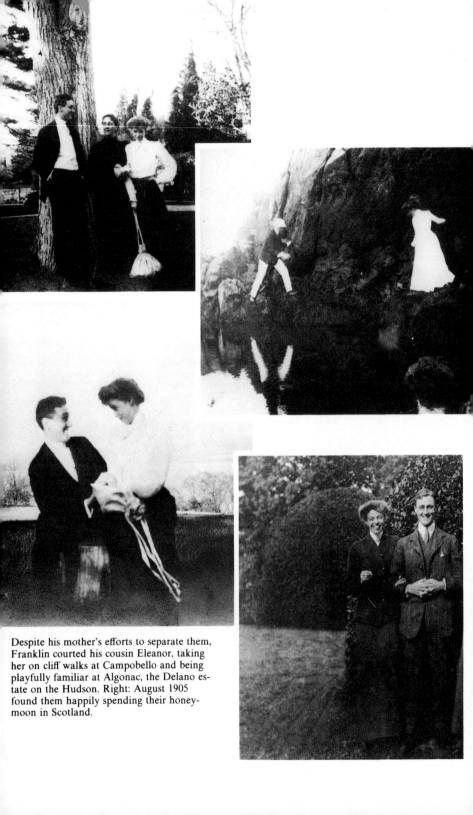

Despite his mother's efforts to separate them, Franklin courted his cousin Eleanor, taking her on cliff walks at Campobello and being playfully familiar at Algonac, the Delano estate on the Hudson. Right: August 1905 found them happily spending their honeymoon in Scotland.

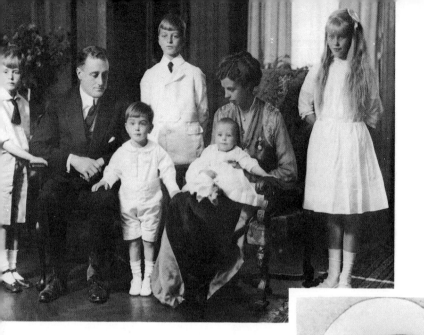

By 1916, the Franklin Roosevelts had five children: (left to right) Elliott, Franklin Jr., James, John, and Anna. But the marriage was threatened by Lucy Mercer, and Franklin had to be persuaded not to break up his family. His close friend and "jolly boy" on various Washington escapades was Livingston Davis, a Harvard classmate and Boston broker who later committed suicide, shown below with Franklin at Hyde Park in 1913.

Between one day and the next, an exuberantly healthy and athletic man of 39 became a polio victim who tried in vain to recover the use of his wasted legs at the Georgia spa of Warm Springs. In the midst of calamity, he maintained his sense of fun, inventing comic rituals while on a yachting trip to Florida in 1926 with his guest Oswald Mosley (at right), later head of the fascist party in England.

Franklin played no part in the election of 1924, apart from greeting (on crutches) the Democratic candidate John W. Davis at Hyde Park that August.

Having won the Democratic nomination in 1932, Roosevelt flew to Chicago to make his acceptance speech. During the campaign, he met one of the "forgotten men" and was photographed as he was lifted from his car in Hollywood. The story that Herbert Hoover sat stony-faced and silent on the drive to the first inaugural on March 4, 1933, is shown here to be mistaken.

The Presidential mood swung from the jovial . . . at a 1934 "Roman orgy" birthday party, with FDR as Caesar, encircled by vestal virgins (standing) Nancy Cook, Eleanor, Marion Dickerman, and Malvina Thompson; and, kneeling, Grace Tully, Missy LeHand, daughter Anna, and Marguerite Durand . . . to the stern, at the second inaugural, January 20, 1937, facing Chief Justice Charles Evans Hughes, a few weeks before the announcement of his court-packing plan.

Three Presidents-to-be: A youthful Lyndon Johnson in 1937, four-star general Dwight D. Eisenhower in 1943, and Harry S. Truman in 1944, sharing a laugh with the man he had replaced as Vice-President, Henry A. Wallace.

Left: As the isolationists, led by Charles A. Lindbergh (shown here on a 1937 visit to Germany), tried to keep America out of the war, FDR invited the King and Queen of England to Hyde Park in June 1939. In October 1940, Secretary of War Henry L. Stimson drew the first capsule in the national lottery for Selective Service registration.

Below: FDR and Churchill held their first conference in Newfoundland's Placentia Bay in August 1941. Looking over FDR's shoulder is Admiral Ernest J. King, while behind him, Harry Hopkins is watching the scene with a bemused expression.

With America in the war, FDR presented Jimmy Doolittle with the Congressional Medal of Honor for his raid on Japan on May 19, 1942, as Mrs. Doolittle and generals Hap Arnold and George C. Marshall looked on. The war healed the rift between big business and the Roosevelt administration, and on September 18, 1942, FDR toured the Ford bomber assembly plant at Willow Run, Michigan, with Henry Ford, who had long hated everything the President stood for.

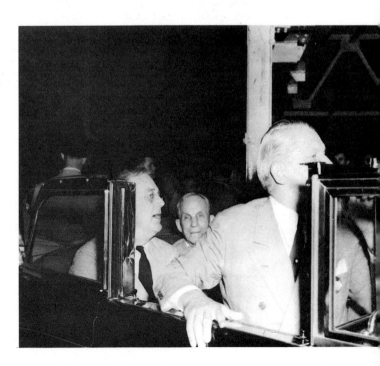

As coalition leader, FDR logged many thousands of wearying miles. In Egypt in November 1943 (above), he and Churchill drove out to see the Sphinx, who gave up none of her secrets. In July 1944 (below), he was in Hawaii, conferring on Pacific strategy with General Douglas MacArthur and Admiral Chester Nimitz.

The Allied leader FDR was least fond of was General Charles de Gaulle, whom he referred to as "a nut." But when the prickly general came to call at the White House on July 6, 1944, the President turned on the charm, and is shown here with Cordell Hull and daughter, Anna.

On his way to the Yalta Conference, FDR relaxed for a few hours on February 2, 1945, aboard an American warship in the harbor of Valletta, Malta, in the company of Churchill and their respective daughters, Anna and Sarah. At Yalta, FDR met Joseph Stalin for the first time, sitting next to him at dinner. The "Big Three" photograph shows Secretary of State Edward R. Stettinius bent over to exchange a few words with FDR. Lord Moran, Churchill's doctor, was struck by the President's loss of weight and haggard appearance.

Intent on dismantling Europe's
colonial empires, FDR met leaders of what would become known
as the Third World on his way
back from the Yalta Conference,
in February 1945. They came in
succession aboard the U.S.S.
Quincy: King Farouk of Egypt
(above), Emperor Haile Selassie
of Ethiopia (below), and King Ibn
Saud of Saudi Arabia (right).

A few days before his death, FDR sat at his work table in Warm Springs, his crippled legs stretched on a wicker stool.

On April 14, 1945, the President's coffin was pulled by six white horses through the streets of Washington. The following day he was buried in Hyde Park.

munities, and he was saddled with projects such as Arthurdale, in Reedsville, West Virginia, where the first ready-built houses did not fit their foundations. Arthurdale failed, and Tugwell was tagged as being in charge of the administration's Department of Utopia.

If anyone had more bricks thrown at him than Rex the Red it was Harry Hopkins. In theory, it was a simple matter to help millions of unemployed by creating federal jobs for them. In fact, it opened a Pandora's box. In April 1935, Congress passed the Emergency Relief Appropriation Act, which gave FDR $4.8 billion for work programs, the largest peacetime appropriation in American history.

Ickes and Hopkins fought over control of the program, and Hopkins confided to his diary on May 13: "All day planning the work program—which would be a great deal easier if Ickes would play ball—but he is stubborn and righteous which is a hard combination—he is also the 'great resigner'—anything doesn't go his way, he threatens to quit. He bores me."

In the end, Ickes continued to run his Public Works Administration, while Hopkins was put in charge of the Works Progress Administration. Most Americans didn't know the difference or why there were two agencies with the same initials. It was the difference between Ickes the master builder and contractor, priming the pump by subsidizing private enterprise, and Hopkins the social worker who wanted people to have jobs, fast. Ickes was proud of the huge amounts he spent on materials to build his New Deal monuments like the Bonneville Dam, while Hopkins boasted of the small slice of the WPA dollar that went toward materials, so that most of it went into the pockets of the jobless.

FDR recognized the need for both when he dedicated Boulder Dam, begun by Herbert Hoover and finished by Ickes: "But can we say that a five-foot brushwood dam across the head waters of an arroyo, and costing only a millionth part of Boulder Dam, is an undesirable project or a waste of money? Can we say that the great brick high school, costing $2,000,000, is a useful expenditure but that a little wooden schoolhouse project, costing $10,000, is a wasteful extravagance?"

What the president did *not* want was more leaf-raking projects, which led to allegations that relief workers were lazy bums. Jim Farley sent him a clipping that said a worker had fallen while resting on his shovel and fractured his wrist, and suggested "a nonskid shovel handle."

Thus Hopkins got into building, competing with Ickes on such projects as the Atlanta sewage system. As William E. Leuchtenberg writes, WPA "restored the Dock Street Theater in Charleston; erected a magnificent ski lodge atop Oregon's Mount Hood; conducted art classes for the insane in a Cincinnati hospital; drew a Braille map for the blind at Watertown, Massachusetts; and ran a pack-horse library in the Kentucky hills."

WPA was also responsible for a minor social revolution through its side effects. For one thing, it weakened the city and state political machines. Patronage that had once originated locally now came from the federal treasury. Mayors and governors seeking projects that would help them win the next election had to pass loyalty tests.

Another side effect was to raise wages in chronically underpaid sectors because employers had to match the WPA wage. Governor Charles H. Martin of Oregon complained to FDR that "you can imagine how bitter it must make a farmer who is desperately in need of help to get in his crops but who is unable to pay more than 25 cents an hour to see relief workers lazily 'manicuring' the road in front of his place at 50 cents an hour."

Governor Eugene Talmadge of Georgia forwarded to FDR a letter from a "good, honest, hard-working farmer in Lee County," R. L. Andrews, who reported that "all our negro farm labor that we used to farm with are sitting around town, waiting for a ditch job at $1.30 a day. They prefer this to working for a farmer at farm wages, the general price of which seems to be 40 to 50 cents a day with house, wood, and water furnished free. . . . I can't blame them. I wouldn't plow nobody's mule from sunrise to sunset for 50 cents a day when I could get $1.30 for pretending to work on a ditch."

FDR wrote this reply to Governor Talmadge but did not send it—why antagonize the governor of the state where his Warm Springs Foundation was located? "I take it . . . that you approve of farm labor at forty to fifty cents a day. Your correspondent does not mention the hours of work per day, but I assume that the forty or fifty cents is paid for working at least ten and possibly twelve hours. If one of these farm laborers were employed three hundred days a year, which means six days a week excluding Sundays and holidays, he would make, at forty cents a day, one hundred and twenty dollars a year. . . . In view of the fact, however, that this type of employment is generally seasonal, I take it that the man described would actually have to live on from sixty to seventy-five dollars a year. Somehow I cannot get it into my head that wages on such a scale make possible a reasonable American standard of living."

In this manner relief became an instrument of social justice, and the farmers who complained they could not find help were often identified as harsh or unfair employers. Relief programs also made dents in Jim Crowism. For the first time in the South, blacks were paid the same as whites, and became visible in the work force in jobs that were not demeaning. Oklahoma Congressman Wesley D. Disney damned Harold Ickes for installing a Negro superintendent of nurses in a hospital for Cherokee Indians, "a proud aristocratic people who boast that they never mixed with the negroes. . . . These Cherokees are seeing RED. . . . This will cost the Democratic ticket several thousand votes."

Of course, the obvious aspect of relief in terms of votes was that those who benefited from the programs voted for the administration. But it wasn't quite that simple, and there were plenty of complaints about too many Republicans on the WPA. Paul H. Appleby, chief administrative officer at the Department of Agriculture, explained why you couldn't always hire Democrats. Say the Farm Security Administration wanted to hire a county supervisor in Iowa. You would find that all the candidates had gone to Iowa State College in Ames. The highest Republican vote in Iowa was in Story County where Ames was, and the highest Republican vote in Ames was in the precincts around the college, so if you hired graduates of Iowa State College you hired Republicans. There was no way around it if you wanted qualified people.

The relief programs hummed along, employing between 3 and 4 million people, but in other areas the New Deal seemed to be stalled. In the spring of 1935, FDR was riding at anchor. He did not lift a finger for the Labor Relations Act that Robert Wagner was steering through the Senate. Because of his obligations to southern senators, he did not support the antilynching bill that was suffocated by a filibuster. He had trouble controlling Congress, which had resumed its annual effort to pay the veterans' bonus.

It was impossible to keep up the pace of 1933 and 1934, FDR reflected. You could not ask too much of a people. It was a part of leadership to understand the public psychology. People got tired of seeing the same name in the headlines day after day and hearing the same voice night after night on the radio. If you kept repeating the highest note on the scale they stopped listening.

When the House and the Senate passed a bill in April that called for printing greenbacks to pay off the bonus, FDR was tempted to give it a "veto with a wink," which he would let Congress override. That way the matter would be settled instead of hovering over him in an election year.

Morgenthau, who was set against paying a bonus that would cost the Treasury $2 billion, was distressed to hear FDR say on May 20: "You know, we may have to compromise on this bonus."

"Mr. President, there is nothing like that in your speech" (that FDR was delivering on the twenty-second before both houses of Congress), Morgenthau replied. "You say definitely that you are against the bonus."

"Why yes," FDR said, "but how can I tell what kind of a bill they may pass?"

Morgenthau had a sinking feeling. "If you want me to go on please do not talk that way to me because I am building a bonfire of support for you in your veto message," he said.

"I will not talk to you about any compromise if you will not talk to me about any bonfire," FDR said. "In other words never let your left hand know what your right hand is doing."

Startled at the president's frankness, for Morgenthau knew from experience that this was the way his mind really worked, he asked: "Which hand am I, Mr. President?"

"My right hand," FDR said, "but I keep my left hand under the table."

The president did make his strong antibonus speech two days later. The Senate sustained his veto, and the bonus problem was deferred until 1936.

* * *

In February, for the second year in a row, the man Frances Perkins called "the chief performer on the Hill," Senator Robert Wagner, had introduced his bill for a National Labor Relations Act, which would give labor the right to organize and bargain collectively. Since industry was a large unified force and the worker was isolated, collective bargaining would provide a balance of power. FDR did not support the Wagner bill, still believing that the NRA, for which he had just obtained a two-year extension from Congress, could enforce collective bargaining agreements through Section 7(a). As he had said on numerous occasions, he wanted to use government power to give workers the choice of joining or not joining a union. The Wagner bill, which allowed a majority vote to commit all the workers in a plant, might force unwilling minorities to join unions. FDR did not seem to grasp the political advantage of giving labor a leg up so it could become a force in a Democratic coalition. He was caught between breaking with labor by being against the bill and breaking with business by being for it, so for the time being he did nothing.

Walter Lippmann wrote that "if the bill were passed it could not be made to work. . . . It is preposterous to put such a burden upon mortal men. . . . The bill should be scrapped." But it wasn't scrapped. On May 2, after three weeks of debate, the Senate Labor Committee reported it out without a dissenting vote. Two conservative southern senators, Majority Leader Joe Robinson and Assistant Majority Leader Pat Harrison, seeking to keep the bill from coming to a vote before the end of the session, took Wagner to the White House to convince him that he didn't have a chance.

All Wagner said was "Well, all right, it won't pass. All I want is a vote." FDR said that was fair enough. The vote came on May 16, when the Senate passed the bill 63 to 12. Many senators voted for it even though they did not like it because they did not want to face the opposition of labor in their next election. They figured the Supreme Court would strike it down anyway, and they could win labor support by voting for a law that would never take effect. The act rested on the stratagem that the regulation of local labor conditions would enable interstate commerce to flow more freely; this was intended to circumvent the Tenth Amendment, which reserved jurisdiction over manufacturing and its labor conditions to the states.

It was only after the Senate passed the bill that FDR endorsed it, on May 24. Three days later the Supreme Court axed the NRA, pulling the middle path of cooperation with business out from under him and making the Wagner bill the only measure protecting the workers' right to organize. The Wagner Act passed the House on June 19, the conference report was accepted by both houses on June 27, and on July 5 the president's signature made the National Labor Relations Act the law of the land. It was a triumph, not for FDR, but for Bob Wagner, who had pulled off a 200-to-1 shot, thanks to his doggedness, his reputation in the Senate, and his understanding of his colleagues.

The Wagner Act sparked the "great leap forward" of the unions. John L. Lewis bolted from the AFL later that year and founded the Congress of Industrial Organizations (CIO), which departed from the old idea of craft unions to organize on an industry by industry basis. The day was not far off when he would organize the steel and automobile industries.

Now there would be big labor to oppose big business, and America became a land of great competing forces that fought each other for their shares of power and wealth and political influence. All this came about because of the Wagner Act, which transformed the labor movement and the political process. FDR had said in a press conference as late as May 15 that he had not given the bill "any thought one way or the other." He boarded the train as it was leaving the station, so as not to appear antilabor.

In June 1934, an investigator for the Justice Department named Walter Rice arrived in Brooklyn to look into alleged violations of the NRA live poultry code by the two biggest concerns supplying Jewish customers with kosher chickens, the A. L. A. Schechter Poultry Corporation and its affiliated Schechter Live Poultry Market. In October, the four Schechter brothers were found guilty in district court on nineteen counts, including filing false reports, disregarding wages and hours regulations, and selling unfit and uninspected poultry. The brothers were sentenced to short prison terms. On appeal in 1935, the circuit court sustained conviction on seventeen counts.

The Schechters took the case to the U.S. Supreme Court, and the government consented to the review, in part because the investigating lawyer, Walter Rice, said the 1,500-page record contained material showing how interstate commerce was affected by the Schechters' unfair practices. Donald Richberg, by now the head of NRA, agreed that it looked like the good test case they had been waiting for. Whether to delay or accept a constitutional test of the NRA had been an ongoing argument since its inception eighteen months before. Felix Frankfurter argued that if it was delayed, the NRA would become a familiar part of government machinery and the court would have to accept it. The other school argued that if you tested it quickly you could enforce it, while if you waited and the economic emergency faded, the court would feel free to invalidate it.

The Frankfurter view prevailed, and the Justice Department waited for a case that would illustrate the "flow theory" of interstate commerce, as in the case upholding regulation of a stockyard as the central point in a flow of commerce that began in the states where the cattle were bred and then moved into the stockyards and out through the packing plants to the consumers. They thought they had it in the "sick chicken" case, whereas in fact there was practically nothing in the record that supported the flow theory. There was no flow of commerce since chickens raised in New York were slaughtered and sold in New York. It was not a major industry. Some of the provisions of the live poultry code were among the most outrageous ever

devised by Hugh Johnson and his codifiers. One, for instance, provided that
if a buyer took less than a whole coop, he was not allowed to pick out the
better chickens but had to take a random selection.

The legendary Wall Street firm of Cravath, de Gersdorff, Swaine, and
Wood, which numbered Bethlehem Steel among its clients, took a sudden
interest in the plight of the Schechter brothers and delegated one of its partners, Frederick Wood, to represent them. No one ever discovered who had
paid their fee. But it was the Schechter brothers' own lawyer, Joseph Heller,
who aroused the high court's libertarian instincts by describing how if a cus-
tomer wanted to buy half a coop he had to close his eyes, stick his hand in,
and pull out the first leg he caught hold of. He conveyed a vivid impression
that the code was stupid and unfair and picayune.

James McReynolds, the crusty Tennessee lawyer who had been side-
doored to the Supreme Court after a difficult year as Woodrow Wilson's attorney general, listened incredulously to Heller's account and asked: "And it
is for this that your clients have gone to jail?" "Yes, your Honor," Heller replied. McReynolds stacked up the briefs, snapped a rubber band around
them, dropped them on the floor, leaned back, and closed his eyes. It was all
over.

On May 27, the court in a unanimous decision ruled that the NRA was an
unconstitutional delegation of legislative power and an unwarranted effort
to control interstate commerce. This double-barreled opinion, which seemed
to set a precedent for further tests of New Deal legislation, suggested other
motives than the impartial enforcement of the Constitution. Donald Richberg, who had argued the case for the government with Solicitor General
Stanley Reed, felt the court was dismantling a government experiment that
ran contrary to the political and economic theories of the justices.

Whatever the reason, the NRA, the heart and soul of the recovery program, the system under which the entire economy had been operating for
two years, was null and void.

When FDR heard the news, he asked about the liberals on the bench.
"Where was Brandeis?" "With the majority," he was told. "Where was Cardozo? Where was Stone?" "They too were with the majority."

Four days later his anger boiled over and he told a press conference that
the country had been "relegated to the horse-and-buggy definition of interstate commerce."

In fact, the Supreme Court performed a useful function in eliminating the
NRA, which had become an unmanageable hodgepodge. With the recovery
in hand, business resented such detailed government interference in its operations. Also, it was proving impossible to enforce. Everyone was chiseling.
Its key provision, collective bargaining, had been rescued by the Wagner
Act. The wages and hours provisions could also be saved by legislation. The
truth was that Hugh Johnson's brainchild, with its corporate state overtones
and its suspension of the antitrust laws, was so seriously handicapped that

euthanasia was in order. FDR had mixed feelings, wanting to keep it going while confiding to Frances Perkins that it was "an awful headache."

The Supreme Court jolted him out of his spring lull. If the court struck down New Deal legislation, well, he would simply enact more legislation. He instructed Congress to remain in session into the summer until it had passed his "must" bills—the Wagner Act, Social Security, a bill dismantling holding companies, a soak-the-rich tax bill, and a banking bill.

Much of this new legislation seemed directed against the rich. If the First Hundred Days had comforted the afflicted, the Second Hundred Days would afflict the comforted. It seemed that FDR was responding to a growing chorus of criticism from the business community.

In May, the steel magnate Charles M. Schwab told a meeting of the American Iron and Steel Institute the story of the duke of Wellington before Waterloo. The able-bodied men were already in the army so they rounded up the most nondescript, ragged, and tattered band of recruits they could find, sane and insane, lame, halt, and blind, knowing nothing of tactics, gunnery, or anything. They were paraded before the duke for inspection, and as they passed, one of his generals asked him what he thought, and he said, "Well, I don't know what effect they are going to have on the enemy, but by God! they certainly do scare me." That was the New Deal!

The rich had cause for fright, for on June 19 FDR sent a tax message to Congress in which he said that the transmission of huge fortunes was not consistent with American ideals. He called for an inheritance tax and a tax on corporate income. He was dismayed at the time by the information Morgenthau was providing on the various ways some of the richest men in the country were taking advantage of loopholes in the tax laws. One of the worst offenders was Herbert Hoover's secretary of the Treasury, Andrew Mellon, who had in one case set up his own foundation, given it five paintings, and taken a $3 million tax deduction.

But Congress saw the tax bill as a political ploy to outflank the Share-Our-Wealth movement. The president was only trying to steal Huey's thunder.

At first, when it seemed doubtful that he could get it passed in the session, FDR seemed to lose interest in the bill. Morgenthau had lunch with him on June 26, and asked: "Mr. President, just strictly between the two of us, do you or do you not want your Inheritance Tax program passed at this session?"

"Strictly between the two of us," FDR said, "I do not know, I am on an hourly basis and the situation changes almost momentarily."

The president, who was involved in the passage of five or six major bills at the time, seemed reluctant to throw his personal prestige into what might be a losing battle and let the Treasury officials make the case for the tax bill, which was bitterly attacked in the press. An August 7 memo to Hearst editors said: "The chief instructs that the phrase 'SOAK THE SUCCESSFUL' be used in all references to the administration's Tax Programs instead of the phrase 'SOAK THE THRIFTY' hitherto used, also he wants the words 'RAW DEAL' used instead of 'NEW DEAL.' "

The resulting Revenue Act of 1935, approved on August 30, dumped the inheritance tax, but it did raise the income tax in the upper brackets from 59 percent to 75 percent, and it did pass a graduated corporation tax, which some students of the New Deal consider one of its most important measures.

On August 14, FDR signed the Social Security Act, which helped the elderly and the unemployed, whose benefits would amount to a maximum of $30 a week for twenty-six weeks. "We can never insure one hundred per cent of the population against one hundred per cent of the hazards and vicissitudes of life," he said, "but we have tried to frame a law which will give some measure of protection to the average citizen and his family against the loss of a job and against poverty-ridden old age."

The bill that was hardest to get through was the Public Utility Holding Company Act, for there the president was attacking the utilities giants with their many allies and bottomless resources. FDR knew from his experience as governor that legislators did their bidding. Anyone who wanted to stay in Congress was better off not crossing them.

Still, he was determined to go after these holding companies, which were responsible for high utility rates and milked the operating companies and defrauded their stockholders. The holding company bill was introduced in both houses on February 6, and included the so-called death sentence clause, which would allow the SEC to dissolve any holding company after January 1, 1940.

Two weeks before the bill's introduction, FDR had met with two utilities magnates to see if something could be worked out—Harvey Couch, president of the Arkansas Power & Light Company, and Wendell L. Willkie, president of Commonwealth & Southern. Willkie, a burly, forceful man, took his glasses out of his breast coat pocket and, using them as a pointer, leaned toward FDR and said, "If you will give us a federal incorporation law, we can get rid of the holding companies." He did not say "Mr. President" and he spoke brusquely, as if addressing an employee. The discussion escalated into a real argument, with FDR jutting out his chin as Willkie continued to bark and point his glasses. Finally Willkie said, "Do I understand then that any further efforts to avoid the breaking up of utility holding companies are futile?" FDR gave him a hard look and said: "It is futile." A few weeks later he asked David Lilienthal of the TVA, who had attended the meeting: "Who was that fellow who was in here the other day with Harvey Couch and who leaned over and shook his glasses at me?"

There was a tremendous lobbying effort against the bill. The utilities told their millions of investors that their savings were in jeopardy, to which FDR responded by saying: "I have watched the use of investors' money to make the investors believe that the efforts of the government to protect them are designed to defraud them." Congress was showered with chain letters signed with names taken from phone books. A Senate committee chaired by Hugo Black summoned Howard C. Hopson of the Associated Gas & Electric Company, who was represented by FDR's former law partner, Basil O'Connor, on a $25,000 retainer.

The House rebelled, reporting the bill on June 22 without the "death sentence" clause. One reason for congressional dissatisfaction was the lobbying efforts of two new White House aides. As one congressman said: "The bill was written by Mr. Benjamin Cohen and Mr. Thomas Corcoran, two bright young men brought down from New York to teach Congress how to shoot. Some of us were here when both were yet in short pants." Actually it was Corcoran who did the lobbying, for Cohen was a quiet and retiring fellow from Muncie, Indiana, who stayed out of public view and did the drafting. He was the intellectual, while Corcoran was the mover.

Corcoran was a supercharged Irishman with shrewd blue eyes, dimpled cheeks, tousled hair, and equal parts of charm and self-confidence. Born in Pawtucket, Rhode Island, in 1900, he had made all the right moves—valedictorian at Brown, Junior Phi Beta Kappa, captain of the debating team, Harvard Law School, clerk to Oliver Wendell Holmes, and member of Cotton, Franklin, Wright, and Gordon, a noted Manhattan law firm. He had gone to Washington under Hoover, as a lawyer for the RFC, and had stayed on under FDR. Now, he was on his way to becoming the Artful Dodger of the New Deal, the one who got the tough assignments, in law school jargon an ad hoc man.

Corcoran got the job done, but sometimes it was best not to ask how. Adolf Berle saw him as the symbol of a corrupt progressivism—he had a good deal of the Irish Fenian about him, and the law meant very little. One of the first things Senator Wagner told his new legislative assistant, Leon Keyserling, was: "Don't have anything to do with that fellow Corcoran. I don't want to see him around the office."

More royalist than the king, Corcoran complained to Ray Moley that FDR was soft. "He needs a good, practical person who will keep him down to earth," he said. "He doesn't like hard-boiled people though. For example, I can say to him that if we do so and so we'll get so and so much 'jack' from this district. He immediately shuts up like a clam and looks very mad. I dare say, though, that in the quiet of his library he thinks of all that. He wouldn't be the politician he is. . . . But Heaven help you if you mention it to him."

Corcoran threw his formidable energies into the battle over the holding company bill. He coached Senator Burton K. Wheeler, chairman of the Interstate Commerce Committee, on the bill's intricacies, so he could get it through his committee. He lobbied in hallways, ghostwrote letters, and drafted compromises to proposed amendments. But his arm-twisting got him into serious trouble, for one hot summer day R. Owen Brewster of Maine rose in the House and said:

"During the consideration of the 'death sentence' clause in the holding company bill, Thomas G. Corcoran, Esquire . . . came to me in the lobby of the Capitol and stated to me with what he termed 'brutal frankness' that if I should vote against the death sentence for public utility companies he would find it necessary to stop construction on the Passamaquoddy dam in my district . . . [this was a $36 million work relief project across from the Roosevelt summer residence on Campobello]. Such a suggestion, from such a source, is repugnant to every instinct of decency in legislation and proper regard for our constitutional oath of office. . . . I share with the President his concern at the concentration of economic power. It seems necessary, however, that the membership of this House, without regard to party, shall keep the country alert to the dangers implicit in the concentration of political power."

Concerned that Corcoran's strong-arm tactics would kill the bill's chance in the House, FDR asked him to "please send me as promptly as possible a complete statement of all your dealings on governmental matters with Representative Ralph O. Brewster of Maine."

When the House Rules Committee held hearings, Corcoran talked his way out of it. Brewster had first agreed to vote for the death sentence, he said, and then had changed his mind on discovering a delicate political situation in Maine.

The Public Utility Holding Company Act passed in August, but without the death sentence. It was, however, strong enough to break up most of the utility giants, and whatever companies were left had to register with the SEC.

And so, on August 27, ended the grueling, eight-month-long first session of the Seventy-fourth Congress. It had been exhausting for the president and those around him, involving as it did the WPA, Social Security, the tax bill, the Holding Company Act, and other reform legislation such as the Guffey-Snyder Act, which revived the bituminous coal code killed by the Supreme Court. FDR admitted to Morgenthau that he had maliciously baited him on several occasions out of sheer nervous fatigue. "I was so tired," he said, "that I would have enjoyed seeing you cry or would have gotten pleasure out of sticking pins into people and hurting them."

It was, however, less a carefully thought-out second New Deal than an improvised response to a set of pressures. A way had to be found around the Supreme Court roadblock. Third-party hopefuls had to be outflanked. The filthy rich had to be cut down to size. There were pressures inside and outside the cabinet: Morgenthau wanted tax reforms and Miss Perkins wanted Social Security. Cohen and Corcoran (with Brandeis looking over their shoulders) had pushed the Holding Company Act. Roosevelt patiently rearranged American society, which meant, according to Professor Horace N. Gilbert of the California Institute of Technology, that he had to "drift like a derelict over the charted seas of orthodox and unorthodox economic technique and philosophy." FDR liked that appraisal, since "no two or two thousand economists, businessmen or politicians could possibly agree on a definite policy of permanent reconstruction for more than one year in the future." The trick was not to align himself with any single bloc, and to stay always above ideology. At the "horse and buggy" press conference, he had said, "Don't call it right or left; that is just first-year high school language, just about. It is not right or left. . . ." As a congressman had said during the long session of 1935, the president had more moves than a rocking chair in a roomful of cats.

While FDR was pushing through his domestic program, other leaders in other lands were bent on expansion. Mussolini said he would attack Ethiopia as soon as the rainy season was over in October. The president sent him a personal message on August 18, but it did no good. On August 19 he wrote Senator Key Pittman, chairman of the Foreign Relations Committee, that he wanted a resolution from Congress authorizing him to ban arms exports to one or more belligerents—Ethiopia and Italy in this case—as an emergency measure.

Pittman replied on the same day that "the committee, with few exceptions, was opposed to granting to the President the discretion of determining to which of the warring powers ammunition etc. should be exported and to which it should be unlawful to export. In other words, the committee is almost unanimously opposed to determining in that way the aggressor." The isolationist sentiment that the only way to stop American participation in a war was to keep the president from choosing sides prevailed.

The president did not insist, for there was too much domestic legislation hanging fire. Also, there was a buffoon side to Mussolini. When Ambassador William Phillips sent him a photograph of the Duce goose-stepping in a parade, FDR commented: "It's wonderful what middle-aged men can do when driven to extremes." Who could tell if he meant what he said? FDR took it with a grain of salt, and joked at the August 27 cabinet that the first large order of the Italian troops already in Africa had been for five hundred women of easy virtue.

Pittman introduced a neutrality resolution that would embargo arms shipments against aggressor and victim alike in case of war, and was limited to six months. It passed both houses and FDR signed it on August 31—it was only for six months, while Congress was in recess.

But it kept him from pursuing any kind of vigorous foreign policy, and it tipped off Mussolini that America would stay on the sidelines if he carried out his invasion. As Senator Tom Connally put it, "With the assurance that the United States would not intervene in his aggression, Dictator Mussolini sent his Fascist Italian army and dive bombers into action against Ethiopia in October of that year. Undoubtedly, the so-called Neutrality Act made Mussolini, as well as the other dictators, bolder in planning aggressions on their more peaceful and weaker neighbors. For once fighting began President Roosevelt had no alternative other than to invoke the arms embargo against both Italy and Ethiopia."

America had its own somewhat farcical version of a local dictator in Huey

Long, who had met Mussolini in May 1933, writing FDR that "I was conscious of having been in the presence of a really unusual person." Both men would meet violent deaths, and Long was the first to go, shot in the Baton Rouge state house that September. FDR, who had seen him as a threat in the 1936 election, would have agreed with this assessment of Winston Churchill's: "The Louisiana dictator has met his fate. *'Sic semper tyrannis,'* which means so perish all who do the like again. This was the most clownish of the Dictator tribe. Let us hope that more serious tyrants will also lose their sway." Jim Farley told Harold Ickes that if Huey had lived he would have polled 5 million votes.

In 1936, the reporter Tom Stokes was chatting with the diminutive governor of Wisconsin, Phil La Follette, about the vengeful reaction against the Roosevelt program. It was, Phil said, like the drunk you picked up from the gutter, who ever after bore resentment because you had seen him in a degrading position.

It was odd. The more things improved, the more the anti-Roosevelt crowd barked. Unemployment had dropped from 12 to 4 million. Real estate was up. In New York City, an office building had rented every office before completion, and there were traffic jams again. The stock market was up. Payrolls had doubled. The cash income of farmers had almost doubled. Social Security was operating, financed through payroll taxes. A vast number of people were being helped, and everywhere you went you could see it.

But never had FDR been under such intensely personal attack. The influential Kiplinger newsletter said that some of the words and phrases being heard among Democratic members of Congress and New Dealers were "delusions of power, dictatorial, intoxicated by authority, itch to try new things, surrounded by picked yes-men, out of touch with popular sentiment, it's like Wilson after the war. . . ."

It was the price to be paid for leadership. Roosevelt was the visible target. The New Deal seemed to be the will and intention of a single individual. Businessmen angry at NRA codes or bankers complaining about SEC regulations objected to "that man" interfering in their lives. They went on about socialism, and a planned economy, and Rex the Red, and confiscatory taxes, and the decay of the spirit of self-reliance, and the regimentation of the potato, without stopping to think that the general outline of the program was capitalistic. The purpose of the NRA was to fix prices and assure profits while raising wages and increasing employment. The purpose of the AAA was to limit production and raise farm prices. The SEC was not meant to abolish Wall Street but to save it from its excesses. The purpose of fiddling with the price of gold was to help the farmer. The purpose of deposit insurance was to restore confidence in the banking system. The purpose of RFC purchases of preferred stock in closed banks was to release deposits and new purchasing power.

In this election year of 1936, whoever the Republican candidate was, people would be voting either for or against FDR. Roosevelt accepted that fact, saying "The issue in this campaign is myself and people must either be for me or against me." On January 25, the cream of the Roosevelt-haters convened at the Mayflower Hotel to hear Al Smith, who had bolted the party he had once led and joined the anti-New Deal Liberty League. It was pure personal pique on Al's part—he had made Roosevelt governor and then been denied a second crack at the presidency. The crowd, which included a dozen Du Ponts and disgruntled Democrats like Dean Acheson, cheered as Smith said: "There can only be one capital—Washington or Moscow."

Roosevelt was getting mad. If these people wanted a fight he would give it to them. He knew that Joseph Proskauer, the author of the "Happy Warrior" speech, had helped Al write his Mayflower speech. He asked Morgenthau to use the Treasury Department to find out the sources of Proskauer's income. If, as he suspected, it could be shown that Proskauer was getting a $200,000 or $300,000 retainer from the public utilities, that could be used to expose the reactionary forces behind Smith. Morgenthau finally got him to agree that the way to do it was to let Congress investigate. He got these crazy ideas once in a while, Morgenthau mused, and the best response was to let them slide. FDR also wanted to release the information that General Motors was selling dollars short and buying sterling. Morgenthau had heard it confidentially from a banker, and to announce it would dry up his source. "I constantly stall with him on this sort of thing," he confided to his diary "as his use of this kind of information either openly or surreptitiously is just the kind of thing that makes people call him 'tricky.'"

At the January 24 cabinet meeting, Morgenthau a little after three had whispered something to the president, who, with his eyes on the clock, had said: "I want you to remember that just before half past three on this particular date General Motors was selling the American dollar short." He made a caustic reference to the company's patriotism. Ickes felt there was a link with Al Smith's speech, for Du Pont, which more or less controlled Smith, had heavy interests in GM.

In any case, big business was now identified as unpatriotic and anti-Roosevelt, and the campaign was beginning to shape up as an antibusiness crusade. On a personal level, the treachery of big business was reenacted in FDR's strange association with Ray Moley. Still brooding over his removal from the State Department, Moley had become an Iago-like figure, courting the president and writing speeches for him while harboring a grudge and privately cursing him. He was a disloyal member of FDR's inner circle, drafting campaign material for an administration he did not truly support.

In a meeting they had in May, FDR said he had talked to more businessmen than any other president and that they were generally stupid. The trouble with them was that they had no moral indignation for the sins of other businessmen. "Did they denounce Mitchell and Sinclair [in the Teapot

Dome scandal]? They did not." Moley privately disagreed, and reflected on FDR's utter lack of logic, the scantiness of his precise knowledge, the gross inaccuracies of his statements, the almost pathological lack of sequence in his discussion, the complete rectitude he felt as to his own conduct, and his swollen ego—he had on one occasion said: "I am the Cabinet." Moley had replied that the only alternative to cabinet discussion was dictatorship. "No," said FDR, "it is leadership."

When working on his speeches, he thought the president's ideas were disconnected and fallacious. He was sick of hearing FDR say "my friends" and "you and I know." When FDR told him over lunch that he was going to build a library for his papers in Hyde Park, Moley thought: He will use the money that he has taken away in large gobs from private wealth to build the house to put his junk in. By giving his place to the nation he will relieve himself of taxes for the rest of his life.

At a May 28 dinner at the White House, FDR wondered whether capitalism could be saved. He had told the oil magnate Walter Teagle, "Mr. Teagle, you deal with barrels of oil. I don't know how to sell oil. I deal with votes. I know how to get votes. You don't know how to get votes." FDR said that every time the bankers and businessmen attacked him he gained votes. Moley thought he was dangerous in the extreme, taking less and less advice, telling people less of his purposes.

At another White House dinner about a month later, a few days before the Democratic convention in Philadelphia, the tension between Moley and the president surfaced. FDR baited Moley, telling him that the Republican press quoted his magazine editorials only because he was a former member of the administration. He accused Moley of being in with the businessmen. Bristling, Moley said that was false; he would not allow the statement to go unchallenged. FDR said Moley was acting like a ten-year-old boy. They had further words, until FDR said, "I, the President of the United States, apologize." Pressing his advantage, Moley insisted that the president shake hands on it. FDR said he was mad and would not shake hands. Taking Moley aside, Missy LeHand said that never in the sixteen years she had worked for FDR had she seen him behave so badly. She was dreadfully sorry and could only attribute it to nerves.

The next day, as he went over his acceptance speech with Moley, FDR said: "I was pretty nasty and mean last night, but you were too sensitive." Moley continued to harbor ill will. He felt that FDR was completely irresponsible, unfair to those who disagreed with him, and hostile to criticism. He resented FDR's little digs, such as saying that he thought highly of Tugwell because Tugwell had not changed his views.

The president was also fed up with the press, much of which he saw as in league with big business. Here was a perfect example: The Chicago *Tribune* had run a story with the headline "Moscow Orders Reds in U.S. to Back Roosevelt." This turned out to be based on a speech that Earl Browder had made in Chicago in May, which was reprinted in Russia in an issue of the

Communist International. Still friendly and informal in his press conferences, FDR was upset when the charm didn't work, and he ordered Steve Early to tell offending reporters that they were "cowards" and "cads."

Of course Early did not obey, for he had to remain on cordial terms with the working press. He complained to Ray Moley that each day there was a fresh batch of grievances; he could barely keep from resigning. Under the genial exterior and after more than three years in office, Roosevelt was still sensitive to criticism. At the Gridiron dinner at the Willard Hotel on April 16, he did not miss the chance to stick it to those fellows who had, as he put it, a sense of rumor rather than a sense of humor, the columnists: "For example," he said, "there is Mr. Walter Lippmann, whose English is so limpid and pure that the trigonometry of public affairs is made clear overnight to the kindergartens of America. . . . And there is my friend David Lawrence. There is a nag to take a long shot on. Once in his quarter of a century of writing he was right. He guessed the election of 1916. It must be within the bounds of possibility that he might guess right once more before he dies. And there is Arthur Krock, who will guarantee to give you, more clearly than anyone else, the point of view of the farmer, the laborer, and other members of what he would call the 'lower classes of America.' "

On January 6, the Supreme Court struck again, invalidating the AAA, which paid farmers to produce less out of funds collected from taxes on those who processed the food. This self-financing program had worked fine in the two and a half years it had taken to reach the court. But a food processor, the Hoosac Mills Corporation, challenged its constitutionality and hired a famous lawyer at a six-figure fee, George Wharton Pepper, who wept as he intoned: "I pray almighty God that not in my time may the land of the regimented be accepted as a worthy substitute for the land of the free."

Justice Owen Roberts, once a corporation lawyer with the Philadelphia affiliate of J. P. Morgan as one of his clients, gave the majority decision: The processing tax was not properly a tax but the expropriation of money from one group for the benefit of another as part of a plan to control agricultural production. It was a scheme for imposing federal regulations in a matter reserved to the states. Listening to his rambling arguments, reporter Tom Stokes wondered in amazement how he could wander so many times around the barn, like a stray horse with a bad eye on the wrong side, before he could find the door.

If the AAA was allowed to stand, concluded Roberts, the United States would be "converted into a central government exercising uncontrolled police power in every state of the Union, superseding all local control or regulation of the affairs or concerns of the states."

Far more than the NRA decision, this seemed like a deliberate attempt to destroy the New Deal. How could a state legislature regulate farm production unless other states went along? Any agricultural policy could succeed only on a national scale.

Under the majority reasoning, the federal government could not impose health measures in an epidemic because that would infringe on states' rights, as if the epidemic would not cross state lines. In the NRA decision the court had been unanimous, but this time it was divided 6 to 3. Harlan Stone in his dissent argued that the court was abusing its right of judicial review. "Courts," he said, "are not the only agency of government that must be assumed to have the capacity to govern." It was not the court's function to approve or disapprove social policy, or to throw out laws the justices didn't like.

Solicitor General Stanley Reed, who had been beaten in the NRA case, was beaten again. He wanted to resign, particularly after Attorney General Homer Cummings called him in and said: "Stanley, you're going to make a record that no other Solicitor General ever made. If you don't watch out, you're going to be the only Solicitor General that never won a case." Cummings said in cabinet on February 14 that Chief Justice Charles Evans Hughes had been willing to go either way as long as there was not a 5 to 4 opinion, because the public was getting sick of hairline decisions.

The court in February changed direction, upholding TVA by confining itself to a single issue, the sale of power from the Muscle Shoals dam. Taking a dip in the White House pool with Ray Moley, FDR regretted that the TVA decision made it impossible to raise the question during the campaign of a constitutional amendment to change the court. The justices were frightened by a rising public opinion against its actions, which explained the latest decision.

FDR had misjudged the mood of the court, for on May 18 it struck down the Guffey-Snyder Act, an attempt to rescue the bituminous coal code invalidated in the NRA decision. A test suit had been brought by the Carter Coal Company. The government proved that strikes in the coal industry would affect the railroads and interstate commerce. But Justice George Sutherland in his majority decision ruled that such incidental effects on interstate commerce were not enough to justify federal regulation of labor relations in the coal industry. It did not matter that the court had previously held the coal industry to be deeply enough involved in interstate commerce to require a federal judge to give jail sentences to striking miners. Nor did it matter that every coal-producing state had filed a brief in favor of the act. The court seemed to exist in an abstract, unreal world. The coal industry was still in a state of deep depression, and the Guffey-Snyder Act was an attempt to improve conditions through collective bargaining and wages and hours provisions and price controls. But the court clung to its shopworn laissez-faire gospel. Sutherland gave away his anti-New Deal bias by using words like "obnoxious" and "intolerable."

There was worse to come in June, when the court invalidated New York State's minimum wage law for women. This went back to a 1923 decision that no state law could deprive employer and employee of the equal right to bargain. But this was 1936, when the myth of freedom of contract had been exploded, when anyone who had ever held a job or read a newspaper knew that employees were forced by economic necessity to accept rotten wages and working conditions. How could anyone argue, in the midst of hunger and poverty, that no government could pass laws requiring employers to pay living wages, when one-third of the forty-eight states already had laws like New York's on their books? This was not some eccentric statute hurriedly drafted, it was a carefully written and badly needed law to protect women from being exploited by greedy employers. It was backed by Republicans and Democrats in the nation's most populous state. The Supreme Court decision was an insult to all those who had suffered in the depression and were now hoping for a better life.

To Rex Tugwell, the decision was a perversion of the Fourteenth Amendment, which had been drafted to ban racial discrimination, barring the states from enforcing measures that denied any person "equal protection under the law." An amendment enacted to protect the civil rights of blacks was now being used to prevent the regulation of business, thanks to the contrivance that a corporation was a legal person. There was nothing in the Fourteenth Amendment about minimum wages for women. The court was obviously bent on paralyzing the government, on creating a legal vacuum into which the president could not enter no matter how critical economic and social conditions were.

Anyone doubting the political character of the decision had only to look at the vote. It had been 5 to 4, with Chief Justice Hughes siding with the three liberals, Brandeis, Cardozo, and Stone. Owen Roberts had voted with the four conservatives, McReynolds, Butler, Sutherland, and Van Devanter, giving them the majority. At this time, in the spring of 1936, there was talk that Roberts might be drafted by the Republicans, as Hughes had been drafted from the court to run against Wilson in 1916. As a result, he voted with the conservatives so that he might appear as a foe of the New Deal. But the tactic backfired, because even the Republicans were appalled by the minimum wage decision. The Kansas editor William Allen White wrote that it was tragic, that "no other agency than government can bring justice into the relations of those who work with the machines and those who own the machines." The Republican platform repudiated the decision, pledging to support state laws for minimum wages.

In an election year, it was useful to have an identifiable villain. Roosevelt could campaign against the forces that were trying to dismantle his program, big business abetted by the Supreme Court. Three of the four conservatives had been corporation lawyers and voted as if they were still on retainer. Roosevelt could position himself as the defender of the common good against special interests. They might have the Supreme Court and most of the newspapers on their side, but he had the American people on his side. As he wrote George L. Berry of the Printing Pressmen's Union on August 3:

"During the past three years we have endeavored to correct through legislation certain of the evils in our economic system. We have sought to put a stop to certain economic practices which did not promote the general welfare. Some of the laws which were enacted were declared invalid by the Supreme Court. It is a notable fact that it was not the wage earners who cheered when these laws were declared invalid."

Roosevelt formed an alliance with Congress to circumvent the court decisions. As soon as the Triple A was voided, Congress passed a Soil Conservation Act that found another way of paying farmers to restrict crop acreage—they were given bounties for planting soil-enriching crops like soybeans instead of soil-depleting commercial crops. In June, Congress passed a limited wage and hour bill, the Walsh-Healy Act, which stipulated that goods and services bought by the government had to be made under an eight-hour day, a forty-hour week, and a minimum wage.

Passage of the Walsh-Healy Act illustrated the growing power of labor. In the House, the bill had been stuck in the Judiciary Committee for ten months. William Green, president of the AFL, wired committee members: "Labor is tremendously interested in this bill and firmly expects it to be enacted into law before Congress adjourns. For this reason, I respectfully urge you to be present at the meeting of the Judiciary Committee tomorrow morning. . . . Your absence from this meeting will be construed as opposition to the measure and as being unfriendly to labor. Our representation will be present at tomorrow morning's meeting. Do not fail us. Be present." With the prospect of the union counting heads and reporting absent members to their constituents, the Judiciary Committee reported the bill favorably and the House approved it without a roll call.

Labor became a key element in the New Deal coalition that FDR was assembling. For the first time in a presidential election, the unions formed a nationwide political association, Labor's Nonpartisan League. It was nonpartisan in that it invited support from both the AFL and CIO, not in its choice of candidates. It backed the incumbent, who was doing something for labor, and cemented the alliance of the Roosevelt administration and big labor. John L. Lewis, a lifelong Republican who had backed Hoover in 1932, was the principal contributor, giving FDR about half of the million dollars the league collected. The big bucks now came to the Democratic party from labor rather than business, and labor's voice would have to be heard.

In May, Roosevelt threw his weight behind a new revenue bill, and called in the Democratic senators on the Finance Committee on the twenty-sixth. Pleased with himself, he told Morgenthau: "I do not think you realize the significance of last night's meeting. . . . I had my nerve with me. I tackled the lion in his own den. I went up against the majority members of the Finance Committee knowing that the majority were against me. I told them a thing or two, didn't I?" But Morgenthau did not think the committee would give in, and FDR sulked because he did not sit there at his feet and tell him what a great guy he was. Negotiations went on into June, and finally the Revenue Act of 1936 was passed, with a modest tax on undistributed profits, which would prevent a common form of tax dodging—leaving money in corporate surpluses. Morgenthau thought it was a cornerstone of the new America, the high point of using the taxing power as an instrument of reform.

In an election year, every decision had to be made with an eye on November. Frances Perkins was pressing the president for more wages and hours legislation. "Mr. President, now the Congress will be adjourning [on June 20]," she said. "I think we should get this bill introduced before adjournment, so we can do something with it."

"Mm, well, perhaps, but not too early, Frances, not too early," FDR said.

"What do you mean?"

"If you get it in too early, they forget about what you've done for them when they come to vote."

"Mr. President, what a thing to say!"

"Yes, sure they do. There must be some new, recent benefit that you've given them just at the last minute. . . . We'll pass it next year. It'll be a good talking point. Have it introduced just before adjournment."

This was not cynicism but a fact of life. Voters had to be reminded of what had been done for them. The program heads had to go out and beat the drum or, better yet, find some impartial surrogate to do it. Typical was this Roosevelt request to Henry Wallace: "Will you be thinking over the possibility of a speech on agriculture by an outstanding private citizen, not a member of the Administration, and preferably a city businessman—such a speech to be widely advertised and to have a national hook-up! It is my thought that it should give a review of the Republican agricultural policy from 1921 to 1933, its promises, its mistaken policies, its failures. Go on from there to our own record covering prices, reduction of surpluses, increase of exports, etc."

Conversely, FDR had to protect his flanks. You didn't want a scandal in an election year. The cracks in the system had to be fixed. You didn't want to find dead men on the WPA payroll. Charges of graft and kickbacks had to be vigorously rejected. FDR urged Harry Hopkins to send outside investigators, since people were saying that for the WPA to investigate itself was like asking Baby-Face Nelson to investigate Chicago gangs. Evidence of collusive bidding on public works projects had to be sent at once to the attorney general. A statement had to be issued that WPA workers were free to vote for the candidates of their choice, like any other citizens.

Programs had to be maintained because they translated into votes. "Henry," FDR told Wallace, "through July, August, September, October and up to the fifth of November, I want cotton to sell at 12 cents. I do not care how you do it. That is your problem." When a cutback in relief funds threatened WPA layoffs, FDR advised Morgenthau to "tell Corrington Gill [one of Harry Hopkins's assistants] that I don't give a goddam where he gets the money but not one person is to be laid off on the first of October."

Harold Ickes had never seen such a crowd in his life. There must have been more than 100,000 persons in Philadelphia's Franklin Field on that evening of June 26, waiting to hear FDR make his acceptance speech. The field was completely filled, and the private boxes had been overrun. There were some showers, but they stopped by the time the president went on at ten.

FDR sounded the main theme of his campaign, the attack of the moneyed interests who were trying to cripple reform: "They created a new despotism and wrapped it in the robes of legal sanction. . . . The royalists of the economic order have conceded that political freedom was the business of the Government, but they have maintained that economic slavery was nobody's business. . . . These economic royalists complain that we seek to overthrow the institutions of America. What they really complain of is that we seek to take away their power."

Ickes thought it was the greatest speech he had ever heard. But when Frances Perkins heard the words "economic royalists," she murmured, "This is going to be used against him." Later, when she told FDR that many of her friends were disturbed by the phrase, he laughed and said, "Of course they did not know what I had in mind, but perhaps it was an unlucky choice of words. Anyhow, I don't think people ought to be *too* rich." What was too rich? She wondered if he knew.

Aside from FDR's nomination, the convention made history by discarding the two-thirds rule that had saddled the Democratic party with compromise candidates who invariably lost, like John W. Davis in 1924. Repeal of the two-thirds rule ended the veto that the South had exercised over Democratic presidential candidates for over 100 years.

Running against Roosevelt was the governor of Kansas, Alfred Landon, who had survived the New Deal riptides of 1932 and 1934. He shared the ticket with Frank Knox, the Chicago publisher who had galloped up San Juan Hill with Teddy Roosevelt's Rough Riders.

Landon was an amiable fellow and a sound administrator who had balanced the budget in his state. He had made a modest fortune as an independent oil operator. His slowness of mind and inability to speak in public were elevated into virtues. You felt when you saw his grinning face on posters that you could call him "Alf" and he would not mind. A film director named Ted Bohn was hired to improve his corn-fed image. He taught Landon to thrust out his chin and snap his head up so his pictures did not show too much forehead. Also to button up his smile—a smile was no good unless it was closed, you couldn't just leave it hanging. When in a group, Landon should step out slightly ahead to dominate the picture. When in a car, he should not slump back but sit erect and slightly forward.

Alas, nothing helped. Landon was the captive candidate of the money interests. Still counting on a coalition of business and farmers, the Grand Old Party paid no attention to the labor vote at all. In Des Moines, Landon blew up at the Iowa state chairman and asked, "My God, aren't there any laboring men for me?" The state chairman said there were. "Then why aren't they on the reception committee?" Everywhere he went he was met by local dignitaries.

Landon didn't really have a chance. The third-party, Share-Our-Wealth movement that was supposed to draw votes from FDR was in disarray. Huey Long was six feet under, the Townsend movement had collapsed, and Father Coughlin was on the lunatic fringe with his Jew-baiting and invective. In July in Cleveland he called the president "the great betrayer and liar" and "Franklin Double-Crossing Roosevelt." In September in Cincinnati he called him "anti-God." Ickes complained that "the President is having too much fun sailing and fishing to resent a gross insult or to designate somebody else to resent it."

Why bother, when he knew that he could float into a second term on the current of incumbency. It did not matter that Jack Garner had decided to stay in Uvalde rather than campaign, or that Jim Farley called Landon the governor of "a typical prairie state." There was a huge uproar in the Midwest, and posters appeared of Lincoln with the caption "He Too Came from a Typical Prairie State." "I thought we had decided," FDR admonished, "that any reference to Landon or any other Republican candidate was inadvisable. . . . If the sentence had read 'one of those splendid prairie states' no one would have picked up on it."

That was the strategy—you didn't even mention your opponent or stoop to answering attacks, and you maintained a statesmanlike decorum. Marquis Childs said the president's speeches were like "the friendly sermons of a bishop come to make his quadrennial diocesan call. Bishop Roosevelt reported on the excellent state of health enjoyed throughout this vast diocese, particularly as compared with the miserable state that had prevailed before he took office."

When not speaking himself, the people he had helped would speak for him. In the 1932 campaign, a Colorado dirt farmer named C. E. Luker had gone up to FDR and said, "Mr. Roosevelt, I'm a dirt farmer. If you don't help us we're sunk." He was written up and photographed as typifying the Forgotten Man. Now, during the 1936 campaign, Luker was reported as having just marketed a $16,000 wheat crop. And there were Lukers everywhere, millions of them, from the recently unionized employee to the man on public works who sang:

> "Oh, I'm for you Mr. President,
> I'm for you all the way.
> You can take away the alphabet
> But don't take away this WPA."

Charles M. Schwab, who had compared the New Deal to Wellington's army, had a farm in Pennsylvania with 130 employees. He asked his superintendent to sound them out on the election, and was astonished when the poll showed that they supported FDR 128 to 2.

Foreign policy was not a factor, even though Hitler had reoccupied the Rhineland in March and the Spanish Civil War had broken out in July. The mood of Congress, which had extended the Neutrality Act for another year in February, was deeply isolationist. So was the mood of the country. Ernest Hemingway, who would change his mind once he went to Spain, had written in 1935: "Of the hell broth that is brewing in Europe we have no need to drink." This was the prevailing view, in colleges, among the clergy, in opinion polls. Roosevelt would have been foolish to swim against the current in an election year.

He was, however, concerned, and when Nazi troops marched into the Rhineland, while France did nothing to stop them, he wrote Ambassador Dodd: "Everything seems to have broken loose again in your part of the world. All the experts here, there, and the other places say 'there will be no war.' They said the same thing all through July 1914, when I was in the Navy Department. In those days I believed the experts. Today I have my tongue in my cheek. This does not mean that I am become cynical: but as President I have to be ready just like a Fire Department."

In his famous "I hate war" speech, delivered in August at Chautauqua, the summer encampment that many past American leaders had used as a forum, FDR used a typical left-hand-right-hand-having-it-both-ways approach. To please the isolationists he said: "We shun political commitments which might entangle us in foreign wars. We avoid connection with the political activities of the League of Nations."

Then he added this caveat: "We are not isolationists except in so far as we seek to isolate ourselves completely from war. Yet we must remember that so long as war exists on earth there will be some danger that even the nation which most ardently desires peace may be drawn into war."

Spain was a good example of hands-off policy in an election year. When General Francisco Franco started his uprising in Spanish Morocco and then invaded the Spanish mainland, he was quickly recognized by Hitler and Mussolini. He had rebelled against the legitimate government of Spain, with which the United States had treaty relations. The Neutrality Act did not apply to civil wars, so FDR could have maintained the legal government's right to buy arms in the United States.

But when Senator Tom Connally went to see FDR in Hyde Park to discuss campaign strategy, he asked him whether he planned to discuss the Spanish war, and FDR said he did not. His sympathy was with the established government, he said, although it was far from democratic as we understood the term. Franco controlled the Spanish waters, because the Spanish navy had gone over to his side, and it would be next to impossible to ship them goods. By land the only route was through France, which had a policy of nonintervention, and he saw no reason why we should not amend the Neutrality Act to cover the Spanish situation.

In the meantime, since Congress was not in session, he placed a moral embargo on shipments to Spain on August 11. This had the result of helping Franco, who had all the weapons he wanted from Hitler and Mussolini, while the legal government was hard-pressed. In December, FDR asked Congress to extend the arms embargo to Spain, which it did. This allowed Germany and Italy to interfere in the affairs of Spain with impunity, whereas helping the Loyalists would have discredited the two dictators' adventurism. Stopping a small aggression might have prevented a large one later on.

But FDR showed no interest in saving Spain. He was encouraged in his neutral stand by the State Department, which tended to see the Spanish government as dangerous leftists. On July 23, six days after Franco's revolt, Cordell Hull wired the president, who was cruising off the New England coast, that "one of the most serious factors in this situation lies in the fact that the [Spanish] government has distributed large quantities of arms and ammunition into the hands of irresponsible members of left-wing political organizations." James Clement Dunn, Hull's closest adviser on European affairs, told a reporter: "We here look upon the Spanish Government as a lot of hoodlums." Hull nodded in approval.

Above all, FDR did not want to lose the strongly pro-Franco Catholic vote. Atrocity stories described priests being butchered in Loyalist Spain. A Catholic-inspired "Hands Off Spain" committee had been formed, which denounced the Loyalists as a bunch of Communists and atheists. John L. Lewis said he could not support the Loyalists because there were too many Catholics in the CIO. "I'm not going to get into this problem," he told an aide, "it's too dangerous for me." It was the same for FDR.

It was in this spirit of neutrality that FDR summoned FBI director J. Edgar Hoover on August 24 and asked him to conduct an investigation of subversive activities, particularly by Communists and Fascists. He said the Secret Service had assured him that they had informants in every Communist group, but if that was true it was only to find out about plots on his life, whereas he wanted a broad picture of the activities of these groups.

Hoover pointed out that no government agency was collecting this type of general intelligence, but that the FBI was empowered to investigate any matter referred to it by the Department of State. FDR said he was reluctant to have a formal request come through State, because there were so many leaks. He would put a handwritten memo in his White House safe, instructing the secretary of state to request this information. And so it was that a decision that has affected the national life ever since, the collection of political intelligence by the FBI, was made by FDR in complete secrecy, with only a memo in his safe as written proof.

* * *

By October, FDR was campaigning in earnest. In New York on October 4, he heard a story he found delightful. Subway riders were wearing Roosevelt buttons all the way downtown and then as the Wall Street station approached there was a quick shift to Landon buttons to please the boss. There was a large black turnout, and Senator Wagner told Ickes that in former times Negoes had not come out to see a Democratic candidate.

On his western tour, the president was welcomed as a savior. People in the crowds exclaimed, "He saved my home" and "He gave me a job." There were signs that said "Thank God for Roosevelt." Bystanders said, "I almost touched him." The only ones who were not impressed were the reporters on the campaign train, who had heard it all too many times. When FDR once again gave the sentence about Landon's inconsistencies, "I don't make one speech in the East and another in the West," a reporter blurted out: "No, it's the same old bull everywhere."

Roosevelt in the campaign's final speech at Madison Square Garden on October 31 was at his most rabble-rousing. "Never before in all our history have these forces been so united against one candidate as they stand today," he said. "They are unanimous in their *hate* for me—*and I welcome their hatred.*" The applause, said the *New York Times,* came in "roars which rose and fell like the sound of waves pounding in the surf."

"I should like to have it said of my first administration," he continued, "that in it the forces of selfishness and of lust for power met their *match.* I should like to have it said. . . ." The clamor drowned out his words and he had to shout, "Wait a moment!" Then, "I should like to have it said of my second administration that in it these forces met their *master.*" The din that followed drowned out the promises of cheaper electricity and better working conditions.

Some FDR supporters found the speech divisive. This talk of mastery was undemocratic. The vocabulary was one of class warfare. The singling out of one group as responsible for frustrating the aims of the administration had a troubling resonance. Frances Perkins, for one, felt that he was tarring that minority with too broad a brush. And yet it was not Roosevelt who had created the divisiveness. He had sought an all-class alliance, but the Supreme Court, acting as the agent of big business, was unraveling the New Deal with judicial overkill, almost setting up an antigovernment. He had to show these forces that they did not have the American people behind them.

In his Hyde Park study on the day before the election, FDR told a guest that his guess on the number of electoral votes he would win had been stored away in his personal safe. He told the story of James Monroe's second election in 1820, when he had received all but one vote in the electoral college, and that vote had been withheld so that no man could equal the unanimous election of George Washington. That triumph had been the result of what the history books called the Era of Good Feeling, but no other man since had won such an overwhelming endorsement from the people.

FDR did almost as well as Monroe, winning 523 electoral votes to 8 for Landon, who carried only Maine and Vermont. He won by the biggest popular plurality in history, 27,751,612 to 16,681,913. Congress had so many Democrats that some of them had to sit on the Republican side—334 to 89 in the House, and 75 to 17 in the Senate. It was a complete rout for the Republican party.

Landon said he had been so badly beaten it was like the Kansas cyclone that left the farmer and his wife standing on bare ground. The husband started laughing, and his wife asked him why. "The completeness of it," the husband said.

And yet this was not another Era of Good Feeling. There were hidden dangers in sweeping victories. Without a strong Republican opposition, the Democratic majority would scatter. Labor, which had helped finance the campaign and get out the vote, would call in its debt. There was the danger of complacency, and the danger of loss of momentum.

Finally, there was the danger of the "nine old men," who were above the electoral process. Was there any other democracy in the world that had a court to defeat national legislation? One of the best skits at the Gridiron Club dinner on December 21 was the one on the Supreme Court. Nine men decked out in Santa Claus costumes answered requests for toys. Four Santa Clauses said the request was constitutional, and four said it was not. The Chief Santa Claus said he had been a boy himself once and couldn't vote.

XVI

Life in the White House

When I read the book, the biography famous,
And is this then (said I) what the author calls a man's life?
(As if any man really knew aught of my life,
Why even I myself I often think know little or nothing of my real life,
Only a few hints, a few diffused faint clews and indirections
I seek for my own use to trace out here).

Walt Whitman, *Leaves of Grass*

LOUIS Howe died in April 1936, before he could become an embarrassment to the administration. He had been up to some pretty strange doings. First, there was the toilet kit contract for the CCC camps, which had led to a Senate investigation. Then there was the cash he was collecting for the 1936 campaign, which he kept in his private safe. Bob Bingham, FDR's ambassador in London, had sent him $10,000. Louis then wrote Bingham that he wanted a letter from him that the money was a loan to a friend.

Jim Farley wondered what was going on. He asked Louis for some campaign money for Pennsylvania and Louis refused to give it to him. Louis was collecting money and keeping it for himself. When he went to the Naval Hospital in Bethesda he took the safe with him. Finally FDR had to intervene, writing Louis on March 21: "I think one matter should be made perfectly clear. If your friends make loans to you to be used for education purposes, such as selling publications for public instruction through a nonpartisan organization, all such loans to you should be kept separate and not put into your own personal bank account. For your own protection you should get this straightened out, and if it is a loan it should be made perfectly clear that it is not a contribution."

You had to understand Louis. He was a castoff, a threadbare coat given to charity. One of the New Dealers said he was like the aging first wife in a harem. Younger and prettier wives had claimed the sultan's attention. He had little or nothing to do with policy. He was left out of things. He was in a kind of enforced retirement, losing touch.

He lived in the White House, in the Lincoln Room, a sick man who spent much of his time in bed. His bathroom looked like a drugstore. In August 1935 he had to be moved to the Naval Hospital, where he spent the last months of his life. In earlier years he had seen Franklin through the years as an invalid. Now it was his turn to be read to, and visited, and reassured with hollow good cheer. He asked for a direct phone line to FDR, but did not get it. He told visitors that he was harboring his strength for the '36 campaign. He would be moved to the Biltmore in New York and take charge. On April 11, Harold Ickes came to see him and thought he presented a strange spectacle. On his knees and elbows, with his hair and beard grown out, he looked like a goat. On April 18, he died in his sleep.

No more would the White House halls resound with his cries of "Mein Gott!" and with his orders to the servants to "Tell the President to go to Hell." There was no one left after him who could tell the president that. He had followed Emerson's advice: better be a thorn in the side of your friend than his echo.

Louis was given a state funeral in the East Room of the White House, which Ray Moley did not attend, not wanting to feign a regret he did not feel. Louis had betrayed him during the London Conference of 1933. Missy LeHand told Moley that Louis's unselfish devotion consisted of loafing around, playing politics, and generally making a nuisance of himself.

But he had been the first loyalist. He had believed when no one else did, sticking by Franklin when he was disabled. Louis had literally given up his life to the advancement of FDR, who now wrote a friend with subliminal relief that "we all miss him but he had been getting no pleasure out of life for the past year. He was counting on being in New York at campaign headquarters this summer and the doctors were dreading the day they had to tell him it would not be possible."

One aspect of the presidency was its toll among the faithful. There were people gravitating around Roosevelt who died like soldiers on the battlefield, casualties of the administration (when members of his team fell ill, FDR wrote them that they had been good soldiers). They died of overwork and devotion.

Sometimes the link was not apparent. Livingston Davis, who had served as FDR's assistant in the Navy, killed himself ten years later; perhaps a contributing factor was his sense of the gap between what he and his Harvard classmate had made of their lives.

Helen Reynolds, the leading historian of Dutchess County, with whom FDR maintained a close friendship, often having "nice old chimney-corner talks," was a high-strung woman who had a series of breakdowns caused partly by her loyalty to FDR. She defended him in the company of her Republican neighbors, and the tension of living among the enemies of her dear friend was so great that it affected her health. After the 1940 election she wrote FDR: "I 'broke' in December ... chiefly because as a convalescent from a previous nervous collapse I could not 'take' the election campaign. I was *so* anxious for your success and so beset and worn upon by the fanatical rock-ribs of this community that my nerves snapped again and I had a winter of ups and downs in the nursing home." She died in 1943.

In FDR's immediate circle, aside from Louis Howe, Missy LeHand suffered a stroke from which she never recovered. Removed from the beloved presence, she once tried to set fire to herself. Gus Gennerich, FDR's bodyguard, died in 1936 while accompanying the president on a goodwill visit to South America.

In the cabinet, where, in the early years of the New Deal, they felt as though they were trying to sweep the ocean back, Secretary of the Treasury William Woodin died in 1934, Secretary of War George Dern died in 1936, and Secretaries of the Navy Claude Swanson and Frank Knox died in 1939 and 1944, respectively.

Two of the three principal White House aides died in harness. There was Kentucky-born Marvin McIntyre, tall and cadaverous, who liked to hobnob with the wealthy, and who overcame the tensions of his work with a biting humor. He liked to mimic Eleanor: "Franklin, something has to be done. The Negroes are *not* getting a square deal." He also made fun of his boss, saying: "Yes, you know, the fellow has a lot of the actor in him. Maybe if he had gone on the stage he would have amounted to something." McIntyre died of tuberculosis in December 1943.

Then there was Colonel Edwin "Pa" Watson, born in Eufala, Alabama, who had won a Silver Star for gallantry while commanding an artillery battalion south of Verdun in 1918. He was detailed to FDR in 1933 as military aide, and shared the duties of appointments secretary with McIntyre, but his true responsibility was as court jester and buffoon.

The president loved to tease, and Pa was perfect for ribbing. He used a fragrant after-shave lotion and FDR would say, "Do all army officers smell that pretty in the morning?" and Pa would laugh uproariously. That was his principal asset—the ability to laugh at the president's jokes, particularly when they were on him. Fitting in well with FDR's brand of humor, he was invited for every trip and every poker game. At Bernard Baruch's South Carolina estate in 1935, for instance, Pa was the object of a mock court-martial proceeding for alleging that another member of the party, Admiral Cary Grayson, had shot a turkey tied to a tree. FDR issued humorous memos in the following vein: "Rather than incur the expenses of a Court Martial, it is suggested that General Baruch tie Colonel Watson and Admiral Grayson to convenient trees, distant one hundred paces, that each be armed with a bow and arrow, that each be blindfolded, that each be required to emit turkey calls and that thereafter firing shall begin."

Pa Watson died of a cerebral hemorrhage in March 1945, a month before FDR, as he was returning with the president's party from the Yalta conference. One of the attendants aboard ship was giving him an alcohol rub and,

finding him curiously inert, felt for his pulse. There was none. He continued
to breathe for ten minutes after his heart had stopped beating.

The only survivor of this southern triumvirate was Steve Early, the vola-
tive Virginian. He was also the one who went back the farthest, having met
FDR at the Baltimore convention of 1912, when he was with United Press,
and having gone to work as his advance man in the 1920 campaign. He
served the president during the twelve years and two and a half months of
his administration, and was given high marks by the working press in spite
of (or perhaps because of) his low boiling point and his gift for profanity,
starting with "Jesus Christ on a mountaintop" and working up from there.
He also had a fondness for lewd verse, sending Harry Hopkins one that
began:

> "They kissed and then little Rose cared less
> As gently his hand stole under her dress."

A conventional southern racist of his time, Early did his best to keep the
presidential press conferences lily white, repulsing Eleanor Roosevelt's attempts at integration. On October 28, 1940, a few days before FDR's third-
term election, he created a serious political problem when he kneed a black
New York City policeman in the groin as he tried to board the presidential
train at Pennsylvania Station, causing the policeman to be hospitalized. The
mail was mixed. There were people who said they would switch their vote to
Willkie, but there was also a man from Florida who wrote: "Congratulations
on your handling of the niggers on the New York police force. You must be
a Southerner to know where to hit them where it hurts the most."

Early didn't like Jews any better than niggers. At the 1940 cabinet dinner,
the actor Eddie Dowling gave a speech saying that FDR had helped the
persecuted people of Europe, bringing in as many Jews as he could. When
he had finished, Early came up to him and said: "You would have to say
that, you son of a bitch."

"What did I say, Steve?" Eddie asked.

"Oh, you and your goddamned Jews ... why don't you come down and
tell your jokes and mind your own goddamned business?"

"Go soak your head," Eddie told him. "Who the hell are you but a press
secretary?"

It may, however, have been of some importance that the three men who
controlled access to the president on a daily basis were southerners with the
prejudices of their region more or less deeply ingrained.

Besides those who died on active service, there were those who took advantage of their friendship with the president in ways more or less above-
board. FDR might well have said, "I can take care of my enemies, just save
me from my friends (and relatives)." Basil "Doc" O'Connor made a fortune
thanks to his White House connection. His was one of eight law firms that
handled the reorganization of the Globe & Rutgers Insurance Company as
part of an RFC loan package. When he sent in a bill for $200,000, Jesse

Jones refused to pay, appealing to the White House. But FDR let it be known that he wanted Doc to have a substantial sum, and he finally got $135,000.

Then there was Eleanor's brother, G. Hall Roosevelt, a strapping hearty fellow, who was always applying for RFC loans in letters penned on White House stationery. One of his projects was panning for gold in Alaska. Jesse Jones was about to turn him down when he received a message from FDR to grant the loan in order "to get Hall as far from the White House as possible." When he was involved in a plan for an aluminum plant in Arkansas, FDR wrote Arkansas Senator Joe Robinson on February 15, 1935: "I want to make it clear that G. Hall Roosevelt, even though he is only a distant cousin of mine [not to mention brother-in-law], should have nothing whatsoever to do with this, even though his connection with it is a wholly legitimate business one."

In 1938, Hall was in Paris, trying to arrange for the sale of 150 American planes to the Spanish government, and telling Ambassador William C. Bullitt that the transaction had FDR's entire approval, that they had discussed all the details and the president "had agreed to wink at the evasion of the Neutrality Act because of his interest in maintaining the resistance of the Spanish Government against Franco." This turned out to be an inaccurate rendering of FDR's views, and the deal did not go through.

In 1940, Hall was in Cuba, again on a mission allegedly sponsored by Roosevelt, this time to build airfields with underground hangars. When Hall asked the American ambassador to arrange a meeting with Cuban strongman Fulgencio Batista, FDR wrote that he had "no White House backing. . . . I suggested he place the underground hangars before the Cubans. The rest is bunk."

Hall was a serious drinker. Once at Eleanor's Hyde Park cottage, when her friends Nancy Cook and Marion Dickerman had a turkey in the oven, Hall barged in and told them they didn't know how to cook turkey and pulled it out of the oven and poured whiskey all over it. Another time, on a Labor Day picnic in Hyde Park, he picked up his son Danny and threw him, and Danny winced as he hit the ground. Bernard Baruch, who was there, said, "This boy ought to go to the hospital, I'm afraid his clavicle is broken." "I'll take him right away," Hall said, and promptly drove the car into a ditch. He died at the age of fifty of cirrhosis of the liver.

Then there was Henry Hooker, of Goodale, Hanson, and Hooker, an old family friend whom FDR had retained for his daughter Anna's 1934 divorce. It happened that a group of lawyers in Chicago, who were arguing a tax case in Washington, retained Henry Hooker for $15,000, even though he was not a tax lawyer. Hooker had one unique advantage: when he was in Washington he stayed at the White House. When he called different departments to make appointments the switchboard operator said, "White House calling." That made all the difference.

When Henry Morgenthau, Jr., informed FDR about Henry Hooker's activities, the president was very upset. "What are you going to do?" he asked. "Henry Hooker has been sort of a doormat and house pet all my married life. He sits around on the floor and plays with the children, stays here at the White House. . . . What am I going to do, have somebody watch all of those telephone calls?"

"The great trouble in this world is money and greed," Morgenthau observed.

"It certainly is," FDR replied. "Everyone seems to have it."

One thing was certain. Not since Andrew Jackson, when men with their boots on the sofas flicked their cigar ashes into the flower pots, had there been such informality and ease at the White House. So many people stayed there it was like a boardinghouse. There were so many comings and goings they should have had a revolving door.

On May 16, 1937, the newspaperman Ray Clapper was invited for Virginia reels, with FDR doing the calling. It was a strenuous workout, and afterward a little group of about a dozen gathered in the vast East Room, talking and bantering and horning in, everyone feeling completely relaxed, with the president in a wheelchair and the rest of them sprawled out on cushions on the floor.

George VI had just been crowned in England after the abdication of his brother, and FDR said he had gotten away with something in his coronation delegation. He had sent James Gerard, who was heartily hated in Germany, where he had been ambassador during the World War, General Pershing, who had led the American Expeditionary Force, and Admiral Rodman, who had commanded the naval forces in the North Sea—in other words, three anti-Nazis. "Nobody mentioned it," FDR said, "but don't think Britain didn't get it."

Someone said it was tough on Joe Davies (American ambassador to the Soviet Union), who after renting a house in London didn't get into the Abbey and had to stand in the rain. FDR said it was strange how Joe had made such a hit in Russia—he got around, in contrast to Bill Bullitt, and seemed to find out what the Russians were doing. Joe had been visiting the commissars' country estates, and said they were living in luxury and the mass of the people didn't know it.

Mrs. Roosevelt said the thing that endeared the government to the Russian people was that it was impossible to lose your job. You could be demoted but not fired—the government was your employer.

"Maybe they can't fire you but they can stand you up against the wall and shoot you," Jimmy Roosevelt said. "I'd rather be fired."

"That is *not* part of the theory," Mrs. Roosevelt said.

"It's just a means of creating a vacancy," the president joked.

Then FDR talked about tax dodgers. There was a man who had invented a gadget that brought him a large royalty. Upon retiring from his company on three-fourths pay, he had applied for Canadian citizenship and then asked if he could continue drawing his retirement pay as a foreign national. When told that he couldn't, he dropped the pay and incorporated a company in Bermuda to avoid American income tax. "Talk about your Benedict Arnolds," the president said.

Andrew Mellon's tax return, he went on, showed that he had given $250,-000 in art to the Pittsburgh museum. When a Treasury agent asked the curator if he could see the paintings, the curator said they were not on exhibition. So the agent went to Mellon's home, posing as a plumber, and sure enough, there were the paintings hanging on the walls of Mellon's own home—the artworks that he had listed on his income tax return as having been donated to the museum. Just astounding, Roosevelt exclaimed. He didn't blame the businessmen, he blamed the lawyers.

Another time, there was a party for Tallulah Bankhead, who had just opened in Thornton Wilder's *The Skin of Our Teeth*. Tallulah was late as always, and when the band started playing, Eleanor asked her daughter-in-law Betsy to dance. Betsy was mortified, particularly, she recalled, "when Eleanor raised her arm displaying a thick tuft of armpit hair," but she could not decline. After the first dance, Eleanor said: "Betsy, the boys say you're a very good dancer, but you've stepped on my feet twice." "Oh, no," said Betsy, "I'm not a good dancer at all, but Missy is a very good dancer." Eleanor didn't like to dance as much as she liked to lead, Betsy thought.

The housekeeping in the White House was the worst Betsy had ever seen. Anywhere you put your finger it was black. She wanted to help out, pouring the tea for FDR and going swimming with him and seeing that his feet were up on a stool during a film and taking him to see the doctor about his sinus condition. Betsy was living in Washington because in 1938 her husband, Jimmy, had become his father's secretary. She used to go to FDR's office in the afternoon and have a cocktail with him. Once there was a phone call and FDR said, "Oh yes, Cordell." She pointed at herself and silently mouthed, "Shall I go?" and FDR shook his head. Then he said, "Mama, will you please get off the line—Mama, I can hear you breathing, will you *please* get off the line?"

Betsy's efforts were resented. One evening they had quail for dinner and FDR said, "I'd love to have some quail hash for breakfast." Betsy spoke to the cook, Henrietta Nesbit, who said, "All the quail are gone, eaten by the staff." Then she reported to Eleanor that Betsy was giving her orders.

Mrs. Nesbit was supremely indifferent to the wishes of her employer. The food at the White House was terrible. At the official dinner for the cabinet in December 1934 there were eighty at table, eating ordinary mutton and boiled carrots off solid gold plates with solid gold knives and forks. Mrs. Roosevelt announced that she would serve one glass each of two domestic wines, and kept her word. The champagne, which she said was from New York State and had been recommended by Rex Tugwell, was undrinkable. After dinner, FDR asked Ickes if he had ever tasted worse.

As Harold Ickes put it, social occasions for Eleanor were not something to enjoy but an opportunity to exert a reforming influence. She brought all sorts of people together. At one of her lunches she sat Mrs. Vargas, the wife of the Brazilian dictator, who spoke only Portuguese and French, next to the wife of New York Congressman Sol Bloom, who spoke only Yiddish and Lower East Side English. After several minutes, Mrs. Bloom said loudly, "Anyone that wants this seat can have it for two bits."

Having at first been lukewarm about her husband's election, Eleanor had thrown herself into political activism like no other first lady before her. She had always seen life as a learning experience, constantly using the word. About a woman in Campobello who could not keep her servants because on beach picnics she told them to eat by themselves, she said: "She had never learned that on picnics everyone eats together."

Henry Wallace thought that Eleanor was a psychic casualty who was compensating for the difficulties of her childhood by being enormously active, in an effort to obtain certain rewards that she had long craved, intangible rewards such as appreciation, and the need to mother others than her own children. But it was not only that she hungered for psychic rewards; it was that, because of what she saw as her father's persecution by his own family, she felt strong identification with the underdog.

She identified with Walter White, head of the NAACP, at the time of the Senate filibuster on the antilynching bill in 1935. Steve Early had been complaining that White was a nuisance with his telegrams and letters, and Eleanor wrote him on August 8 that "if I were colored, I think I should have about the same obsession that he has.... The type of thing which would make him get himself arrested in the Senate restaurant is probably an inferiority complex which he tries to combat and which makes him far more aggressive than if he felt equality.... If you ever talked to him and knew him, I think you would feel as I do. He really is a very fine person with the sorrows of his people close to his heart."

The last thing Steve Early wanted was to talk to Walter White and get to know him, but Eleanor had tried, even though her thinking was simplistic, for she was a woman of second-class intelligence and first-class temperament. She had convictions, she had the courage of her convictions, and she did not have the brains to doubt the wisdom of acting on her convictions. Her mind produced banalities the way soap produces suds. Of the Hundred Days she said: "A wonderfully exciting time." Of Churchill she said; "I enjoyed him thoroughly as a human being." Her "My Day" column was a tedious recitation of trivia, such as "Thursday—I have just made the rounds of every room in the White House with Mrs. Nesbit, the housekeeper."

The source of her strength was moral authority. She knew that the downtrodden should be helped, that the poor should have decent housing, that the blacks should be treated fairly, and in pursuit of those indisputably worthy aims she never hesitated to interfere in departmental affairs, arousing a good deal of resentment.

In October 1934, Kiplinger, the author of the newsletter, told Henry Morgenthau that he was fed up with Mrs. Roosevelt. "I have been bursting to say something," he asserted. "What I want to know is, is she first lady of the land or is she Mrs. Roosevelt? A lot of people around town are grumbling. She is constantly throwing monkey-wrenches in the government departments and they are all afraid to say something because she is the wife of the President." Morgenthau begged him to reconsider and not to write anything just yet.

But it was true that she was thought of as a meddler. Harold Ickes, who as head of PWA and various housing programs had to contend often with her reformist zeal, wrote on February 6, 1935: "I wish that Mrs. Roosevelt would stick to her knitting and keep out of the affairs connected with my Department."

Her pet project was the Subsistence Homestead in Reedsville, West Virginia, which turned into nothing but a headache for Ickes. She wanted to build on a lavish scale, and the work was extravagant and wasteful. At the rate they were going, each house would cost $10,000, which was inappropriate to help people in the lowest working classes. "It does seem to me," Ickes wrote, "that she is not doing the President any good. She is becoming altogether too active in public affairs and I think she is harmful rather than helpful. After all, the people did not elect her President, and I don't think the country likes the thought of the wife of the President engaging prominently in public affairs to the extent that she does."

The country would learn to like it, for Eleanor was not going to stop. Indeed, she had to be restrained from some of her whirlwindlike activities that would have been politically embarrassing. In August 1933, Ray Moley asked her not to give a speech in Cleveland that would be seen as an endorsement of one person in a factional fight. In March 1936, Jim Farley asked her not to visit a certain colored school in Florida, which was at the time negotiating for a federal loan; the visit would be "most unfortunate." In December 1937, Steve Early asked her not to express public approval for the cotton industry. She should also ignore the offer of a gift, for "commend cotton and you immediately have wool, flax, rayon and silk manufacturers, stylists and promoters asking your opinion of their products and a merry controversy is certain to ensue." She was forever getting into flaps over people she wanted to endorse or groups she wanted to sponsor, although even her critics in the cabinet admitted that she had a highly developed social sense and was utterly unselfish—in fact, it was her unselfishness that got her into trouble.

Also, no one then realized how useful Eleanor was in drawing some of the fire away from FDR. She was a highly visible decoy that New Deal critics could snipe at. It was like the story about the orator who was holding forth on FDR's wonderful accomplishments. A man in the audience got up and said, "I don't like him." The orator went on and the man got up again and repeated, "I don't like him." The orator then said, "The President in his actions is guided by a power beyond himself, infinite in comprehension." The man in the audience said, "I don't like her either."

The surprising thing is that Eleanor was ambivalent about being first lady. When Franklin was elected, she felt that she had lost her husband, that he now belonged to the nation. During the 1936 campaign, she commented in front of her mother-in-law that it would not break her heart if FDR was not reelected. "Do you think Mother would do anything to defeat Father?" Sara asked Jimmy Roosevelt. "Is that why she stays in politics, just to hurt his chances of re-election?"

That was a dose of Sara's malice, but there was in Eleanor a yearning for a life of intense private emotions, which she at first satisfied in her friendship with the Associated Press reporter Lorena Hickok. Eleanor was passionate without being sexual, and had learned to express her feelings of love openly in her friendships with Nancy Cook and Marion Dickerman. Like them, Lorena Hickok was a lesbian, who had once tried to seduce one of her fellow woman reporters. She was also one of life's casualties, for as a child she had been beaten and raped by her father.

At the time they became close, just after the inauguration, Eleanor needed someone who would love *her,* as an antidote to public life. Inside the mannish and overweight reporter, who knew how to drink with the boys and tell dirty jokes, there was a fluttering romantic who admitted that she had "gone off the deep end" over various women. In her passionate worship, she satisfied Eleanor's need for appreciation. The tone of many of their letters was ardent, with repeated allusions to a physical attachment. If these letters had been written by a man and a woman, there would be little doubt that they were in the midst of a consummated affair. But in the case of Lorena and Eleanor, given the contrast between Eleanor's physical prudishness and her freedom of expression, the likelihood is that it was never more than a loving friendship.

"Hick" gave Eleanor her most precious possession, a sapphire ring, and a few weeks after the 1933 inauguration Eleanor wrote; "Hick darling, all day I've thought of you. . . . Oh, I want to put my arms around you, I ache to hold you close. Your ring is a great comfort. I look at it & think she does love me or I wouldn't be wearing it."

Lorena wrote back: "I remember . . . the feeling of that soft spot just northeast of the corner of your mouth against my lips. . . . I want to put my arms around you and kiss you at the corner of your mouth."

Eleanor reciprocated with assorted expressions of love:

"I couldn't say je t'aime et je t'adore as I longed to do but always remember I am saying it & that I go to sleep thinking of you & repeating our little saying."

"I can't kiss you so I kiss your picture goodnight."

"My dear, if you meet me may I forget there are other people present or must I behave? I shall want to hug you to death. I can hardly wait. . . ."

"Oh dear one, it is all the little things, tones in your voice, the feel of your hair, gestures, these are the things I think about & long for."

"I wish I could lie down beside you tonight & take you in my arms" (this because Lorena was suffering from a stomach disorder on one of her trips to report on the state of the country for Harry Hopkins, a job she took after leaving the AP).

Lorena moved into the White House, where she lived off and on until 1937, sleeping on a daybed in Eleanor's sitting room at the southwest corner. In her diary, she recorded in a code the days when she saw Eleanor and whether it had been a happy meeting. Jealous and bad-tempered, she had a fit when Eleanor promised her an evening and spent it with her daughter instead. Eventually, the passion wound down, and in 1937 Hick moved to New York and took a job working for the World's Fair. The one time in their letters that lesbianism was mentioned was when Hick wrote Eleanor about a friend in New York who had an affair with a married woman, was spurned, and committed suicide. Eleanor replied, in the detached manner of someone who knows nothing about such things: "Poor dear, I hate you to suffer from your friends & thro' your own memories as well."

To the writer Martha Gellhorn, a friend of Eleanor's and an occasional White House guest during the time that Hick was there, the explanation was that Eleanor liked to collect lame ducks. "For sheer unattractiveness," she said, "Lorena Hickok would've been hard to beat. I mean, she looked like a tank, a walking tank; she was a big, heavy, ugly woman who . . . emotionally always seemed to me sort of like the captain of the girls' hockey team—very enthusiastic and friendly. . . . Poor Hick, who was so ugly, so boring, and so unattractive, and really I don't suppose anybody in the world except Mrs. Roosevelt had ever been terribly nice to her. . . . What contemptible stuff [the whispers that Lorena and Eleanor had a lesbian affair]. This poor, good-hearted, heavy, unappealing Hick! It's like having a great St. Bernard dog really. Over and out."

While Eleanor was seeing Lorena Hickok, going on trips with her and putting her up at the White House, FDR started his own friendship with the bright and beautiful Dorothy Schiff, giving rise to the same sort of rumors that plagued the first lady and the reporter. Then married to George Backer, the son of a Tammany contractor, Dorothy first came to Hyde Park in 1936 in connection with some work she was doing for the Democratic State Committee. FDR at once called her by her first name and said he had known her father. He was fascinated by her open-toed shoes, which had just come into fashion.

Dorothy was a woman of the world who knew how to hold a man's attention. She had had an affair with the Canadian press lord, Max Beaverbrook. It did not strike her as unusual when FDR asked to see her again. He told her he was lonely, that no one ever came to Hyde Park, Eleanor was off on her own and the children were scattered.

Missy LeHand always did the calling: "The President is in Hyde Park this week-end and would like to see you." "The President would like you to come to Washington for dinner." These were command performances. She would drop everything, her husband, her activities, and go off to see him. Her husband did not mind, he was flattered that his wife had been picked. Eleanor approved too. "She knew that the relationship was not sexual," Dorothy recalled. "Although if he had said let's go to bed I probably would have."

Dorothy felt that FDR was always more interested in himself than in her. It was not love, it was companionship. He wanted a friendly ear and an attractive presence. She had to listen over and over to the same stories—how once when he was going past the Vanderbilt mansion he saw on a clothesline some black chiffon underwear; stories about how many trees had been planted and about the lapses of Secret Service men. It became less fascinating. Sometimes, if she were to admit her true feelings, even though he *was* the president, she was bored.

She stopped seeing him when she divorced Backer, married Ted Thackrey, and took over the New York *Post*. Her new husband was jealous. Sam Rosenman performed the marriage ceremony and brought her a ribald message from FDR: "She ought to know how by now."

Perhaps the price of a public life was that it made a man insensitive to deep feelings. Politics was based on an exchange of services. Every man was a potential voter, and his vote had to be won through patronage or services rendered. A politician, which FDR was for thirty-five years, was always wooing. Everyone got the same smile and the same handshake, so that there was no differentiation between superficial ties and close ties. To treat everyone like an old friend is to depreciate friendship. The level never changed. It was always the same banter and good cheer, ready for every occasion, whether it was a meeting with congressmen or a family reunion. A man who saw all of life in political terms was bound to suffer a certain amount of emotional undernourishment. In the case of FDR, this was compounded by his arrangement with Eleanor, where there was no intimacy but a politically necessary partnership.

With his children, he produced the same geniality, which effectively concealed that part of himself he gave to no one. By now grown, the children used FDR's eminence in various ways, and were not awed by his office. They had an odd idea of their father, as if a certain dilettantism clung to him, as if what he had done was easy, as if he had inherited the presidency, in the same way they had inherited their situation in life. One night at the White House, according to Betsy, FDR and Eleanor were having dinner with Jimmy and Franklin Jr. and Hall, and the conversation got around to work. The boys and Eleanor ganged up on FDR, and one of the boys said, "You wouldn't know, Pa, because you've never done a day's work in your life." Eleanor nodded in agreement. Betsy was so upset she said, "I think I'm going to have to leave the table," but Hall changed the subject.

For the children, it was a fishbowl existence as members of the most carefully watched family in the country and as focal points for hostile criticism.

Everything from their jobs to their marital lives came under scrutiny.

In 1934, Anna's marriage to the stockbroker Curtis Dall fell apart. Part of the problem was his violent anti-New Deal views. New Dealers were just a bunch of opportunists and hangers-on, he said, who were trekking to Washington with only one idea in their heads, and that was to advance themselves financially. But whatever Dall's faults, it cannot have been easy to be married to a Roosevelt, because when anything went wrong the family closed ranks and ganged up on you. Anna's daughter Sisty recalled that Eleanor "never did like my father, never. Couldn't stand him. And I must say that by the time I was three I couldn't stand him either, because I knew then that my mother was having grave problems. There was something odd about him, even a bit menacing at times."

FDR was given the unpleasant task of informing Curtis Dall that Anna wanted a separation, summoning him to Hyde Park. Dall could see it was not easy for him, and agreed to cooperate in every way possible. Then in May, Anna called him from the White House at his office at Fenner and Beane and said she was going to Reno. Dall asked her to wait, and Anna replied: "Mother and I think you are trying to hold me up." That was what he could never forget, that he had been classified as a fortune hunter. Anna got her divorce on grounds of extreme cruelty, and the two children went to live in the White House. Dall rarely saw them. They did not even write to remember his birthday. He felt he had been "left on a financial and spiritual 'sand-bar' to die." He loved Anna and had been absolutely faithful, but he had been expelled from the charmed circle because the family regarded him as a "small" man. After a day of duck hunting he wrote Anna quite touchingly that "twice I have seen a duck circle the rig after his mate has been shot down, circle it maybe two or three times before he would wing off. That's what I did."

Six months later, Anna married a high-spirited reporter for the Chicago *Tribune,* John Boettiger. "I am frank to say," Harold Ickes commented, "that the President had some reservations about the marriage, but it has been rumored for some time and appeared to be one of those inevitable affairs."

Boettiger left the violently anti-Roosevelt Chicago paper so as not to embarrass the family, and was hired by Hearst as publisher of the Seattle *Post-Intelligencer.* It was hoped that the magic of the Roosevelt connection would generate advertising and circulation.

John Boettiger turned out to be a troubled human being, who sexually molested his teenaged stepdaughter. She thought of him as her father, since she was completely cut off from Curtis Dall. "He used to sneak down to my room," Sisty recalled, "and try to make passes and that sort of thing. And my mother didn't really stop him. She didn't know what to do. . . . I did not try to talk to her about these visits, which occurred fairly frequently, for about a year and a half, for fear she would be hurt and for fear of Popsey's anger and denial and what would be a frightful family explosion. So I coped in my timid little way because, after all, there was never the slightest suggestion of violence. It was all extremely unpleasant and demeaning, however, and I was very happy when I could go off finally to boarding school. . . . Years later my mother told me she'd known about those visits of his to my bedroom where I would be studying at my desk. She tried to counsel him, she said, but he wouldn't listen or scoffed that 'it was time Sis learned a little bit about sex.' Of course, if it had been my kid, and a stepfather was doing what he was attempting to do, I would have kicked him flying, but she couldn't do that."

In 1943, back from the Casablanca Conference, FDR was vividly describing his talks with Churchill to John and Anna, and John said he would give his eyeteeth to go on such a trip. "Well," FDR pointedly said, "you are not in uniform." Boettiger was stung by this reproach from a man he so admired. Although in his forties and too old for the draft, he managed with a little pull to join the Army and was sent to North Africa, writing Anna effusive love letters: "I love and adore you, my Precious One, every single inch of you, more than everything in this world. . . . Most precious, fascinating and incredibly wonderful One."

But John Boettiger, the son-in-law of the man who had said there was nothing to fear but fear itself, was crippled by unnamed and irrational fears. When he was given a task, he felt a dread that he was not up to it, that he would fail. This was what Anna called his "spells," and he began having them in North Africa.

Perhaps moving in the orbit of a certified Great Man made his distress more acute. After the war, the Boettigers moved to Phoenix and started a weekly newspaper, the *Arizona Times*. Again, he was doomed from the start, self-defeated, sure that it would fail, and it did. The strain on the marriage led to separation and divorce in 1949. By this time, Boettiger was working for a public relations firm in New York. He remarried, freeing himself of the Roosevelt tie, which he had come to see was a burden that contributed to his "spells." But the public relations firm failed too. On October 29, 1950, John Boettiger threw himself out a seventh-floor window of the Weylin Hotel in New York City and fell to his death.

John Roosevelt had graduated from Groton in 1934, at the age of eighteen, after collecting six black marks for sending a telegram through a pay station without getting permission from a master. That fall he entered Harvard, and FDR wrote the freshman dean that "he has to study to get things done but knows it . . . he will not be good at assuming or seeking leadership."

John took an interest in politics, writing his father on May 25, 1936: "Why don't you tell Congress to go home and the Supreme Court to go to hell?" He asked for some material on the TVA for a paper he was writing, adding "I almost wish the courts had declared it unconstitutional."

In the summer of 1935 he worked on a TVA forestry project in Knoxville.

Chief Forester Edward C. M. Richards wrote Eleanor on August 8 that, because he was so tall, John stooped and slouched and had bad posture. Also, he smoked too much, hardly stopping to eat his meals. "John apparently has always had everything come easy to him," the chief forester went on, ". . . there is a lack of what might be called 'sufficient iron in the soul'. . . . The astonishing thing to me about it is the truly remarkable way in which John has failed to be spoiled by it. His friendliness, democratic spirit and his entire refusal to be high-hat is a splendid tribute to the basic good stuff that is in him. Nevertheless, it is quite evident that John [believes in] the psychology of making one's way by influence and association rather than by any hard work and personal achievement. . . . Carried to the extreme, it is apt to work out into the development of a perfect snob and parasite."

John did not turn out to be a snob and a parasite. Of the four boys, he was the only one who never ran for office and who refrained from using his father's influence for personal advancement. He abdicated from the family as much as he could, renouncing its advantages and pressures.

John did get into one youthful scrape. On a trip to Europe in the summer of 1937 he found himself in Cannes on the day of the annual "Battle of Flowers," when decorated floats competed for prizes, and was graciously given one of the flower-bedecked carriages so that he could take part in the parade with his friends. Each carriage stopped in front of the Hotel Carlton to be reviewed by the official committee, the *préfet,* the *sous-préfet,* the general in command of the troops, and the mayor of Cannes, Pierre Nouveau. By the time John's carriage reached the Carlton, he had drunk ample quantities of champagne and was three sheets to the wind. When the mayor advanced to present him with a bouquet of flowers, John sprayed him with the contents of a bottle of champagne. A few days later, by way of apology, M. Nouveau received a postcard showing a nude couple in the act of sexual intercourse, on which was written: "To the Mayor of Cannes—*Merde.* John Roosevelt."

All this raised quite a stink in France, which Bill Bullitt, who had been moved from Moscow to Paris as ambassador, helped clear up. On August 19, John wrote his father that the whole thing was "a cheap attempt at publicity by these frogs, but what in hell can you expect from a bunch of people of their caliber. . . . If in the crowded street a man approaches one with a bunch of flowers what is one expected to do especially in a place so overrun with fairies. It's all a bloody lie."

A year later, John married Anne Lindsay Clark, a North Shore debutante whose father was a partner in the investment firm of Scudder Stephens, and was working in Filene's department store in Boston at $18 a week, which he told his father was a job "requiring the mental ability of a child of eight."

Anna, who had a jaundiced view of her dauntless brothers, particularly when it came to their love lives, had hoped that Johnny would be the first member of the family to wait until maturity to get married, but no such luck; he married when he was twenty-two. Knowing what it meant to be married to a Roosevelt, Anna wrote her mother that "Anne may be another one suffering from an inferiority complex and a fear of this awesome family of ours."

Among the much-divorced Roosevelt children, John set the longevity record, remaining married to Anne for twenty-seven years, until 1965, when he obtained a Mexican divorce and married Irene Boyd McAlpin. By that time, he was a Wall Street broker and a Republican who had supported Eisenhower and Rockefeller. In the 1960 campaign he stumped for Nixon, and FDR must have whirled in his grave when he said, "If my father were alive today, he would vote for Nixon."

It was hard to be a Roosevelt, it was something you carried around with you all the time, part crown and part hairshirt. It was a no-win situation: You were expected to do well, and when you did, it was because your father was president. You were lied about and conned and hated and abused, but you couldn't defend yourself.

Franklin Jr. was a good-natured, outgoing lad, with his father's looks. As a boy in Hyde Park, watching a cow have its calf, he had asked, "Do babies come into the world the same way?" Pretty much, he was told. "Gee," he said, "a fellow owes his mother an awful lot, doesn't he?"

When Franklin Jr. entered Harvard in 1933, he made up his mind that he would not trade on his name, that he would lay it aside and start from scratch. He did not grant the usual "Another Roosevelt at Harvard" interview. He worked hard to meet the members of his class, and got to know at least 400 by name. When his name was brought up as the logical candidate for president of the freshman class, he thought at first that it was because he was a Roosevelt, but then he realized that he was really wanted. The proctors, however, wanted the captain of the freshman football team, and told Franklin that if he was elected it would be because of his name and that he should run for vice president. Franklin had tried to make good, but now felt that the cards were stacked against him. He told his roommate and cousin, Bobby Delano, that he wanted to go away where no one knew him, change his name, and start life anew. It was disillusioning that whenever you wanted to do something, your name got in the way.

Known as "Brud," Franklin Jr. was the speed demon of the family, who held the unofficial Cambridge–New York record while at Harvard. In the first three years of driving his La Salle, he piled up a record of two arrests for speeding, two collisions, two civil suits growing out of collisions, a fine for improper plates, and a detention for driving with an expired license. In October 1936, FDR had to pay a Boston law firm $4,500 to settle one of the accident cases. When complaining letters arrived about his sons' driving, FDR replied, "They have been spoken to not once but a thousand times."

Franklin Jr. truly detested the fuss that was made over him as his father's son. While at Harvard he had several run-ins with the press, once knocking a camera out of a photographer's hands. And yet he too sometimes asked for favors, as when he tried to help the homosexual tennis player Gottfried von Cram, who had been convicted on a charge of moral turpitude, get into the United States for a tennis tournament.

Like his brother John, Franklin Jr. was involved in an international incident, while a student at the University of Virginia Law School in Charlottesville. In May 1938, some fraternity house jokers, apparently without his knowledge, placed a transatlantic call to Premier Edouard Daladier of France, person to person from FDR. M. Daladier was not amused, and FDR found a State Department report of the incident on his desk. "It was of course purely a prank," he wrote his son, "but I think it would do no harm for you to let them know at the Fraternity House that that kind of prank can have serious results!"

The previous year, Franklin had married Ethel du Pont, whose father Pierre had spent millions of dollars trying to prevent FDR from becoming president. In New Deal terms, it was a match between a Capulet and a Montague, but FDR had a fine time at the wedding at the Du Pont home in Greenville, Delaware. It appealed to his sense of humor to be feted in the enemy camp, along with such New Deal stalwarts as Harry Hopkins and Frances Perkins. Not everyone saw the humor of the situation, and an anonymous letter from Chicago said that it was "a slap in the face for the millions of American voters who with a curse for the Du Ponts under their breath went to the polls to cast their vote for FDR. . . . To us the Du Ponts represent the most sinister menace in the industrial and capitalist structure of this country. . . . Is the son of FDR to become the chief salesman of munitions?" There it was again, you could not even get married without somebody making a political issue out of it.

Ethel was nervous and overbred. She talked to herself and twisted strands of her hair. FDR called her "our hothouse flower." In May 1938, when she was pregnant, Anna wrote her mother: "My big hope is that he [Franklin] is not hurting Ethel too much. First pregnancy is no cinch anyway, and she has probably had many difficult moods. But to me that does not excuse F. jr. You're right that the wisdom of Solomon is not enough. . . . I'm so afraid with him that too much broad-mindedness and leniency will only lead him to further difficulties."

A year later, when there were marital problems, Anna wrote: "Gee, I'm sorry to hear about Ethel. As a husband, F. jr. would undoubtedly drive me crazy. . . ." Anna and her mother had taken to exchanging chatty letters about the boys' marital woes.

But the main problem of the Roosevelt boys was what to do with their lives. Elliott, for instance, had always been rebellious, objecting while at Groton to being confirmed in the Episcopal church and angry at himself for giving in when his father told him "don't create a problem." He hated Groton and refused to go to Harvard. He went to work for an advertising agency and got married when he was twenty-two to the daughter of a steel magnate, Elizabeth Donner.

In January 1933, Elliott told Ray Moley that he had an offer from the governor of a Mexican province to do some publicity work for a highway they were building—the beauties of travel in Mexico, that sort of thing. Should he take it? Moley told him to be sure that everything was open and aboveboard. To avoid criticism, he should make public who was employing him and for how much.

Elliott got his first glimmer of what life would be like. "I knew when my father became President that it was going to be tough," he said. He quit the ad agency and headed west, where he had a job offer from a small airline in Southern California.

Elliott was driving to California with $32 to his name when FDR closed the banks. "Hey Pop," he said, calling the White House collect, "I don't know how I'm going to make it to California."

"You're better off than I am," FDR said, "I've only got eight dollars." Elliott could hear him over the phone, jiggling the change in his pocket.

"Well, that doesn't help me," Elliott said. "What can I do?"

"I'd drive down the road until I was running out of money," FDR replied, "and then I'd find an agreeable-looking farm and knock on the door and offer to work for my room and board."

"I guess that's all I can do," Elliott said, feeling resentful that his father had not offered to wire him some money.

"What road are you following?" FDR asked.

"Dallas, El Paso, Tucson," Elliott said.

"Just go as far as you can," FDR told him, and went back to running the country.

Just outside Dallas a motorcycle cop stopped Elliott, who protested that he was not speeding. "I know," the cop said. "I was told to look out for you. Isn't your name Roosevelt?" He took Elliott to the Baker Hotel, whose president was waiting on the steps with a key to a room. "How did you hear I was coming through?" the bemused Elliott asked. "Oh, I've got connections," the hotel man said.

It was an amusing way for FDR to demonstrate presidential power to his son. It was also another illustration that, for better or for worse, the president's children would never be treated *normally.*

Favors such as a hotel room had to be balanced against the disadvantages. When Elliott's airline bid on some air mail contracts, Steve Early opened the bid and was horrified that it came from the president's son and turned down Elliott's low bid and gave the contract to Pan American.

Given that sort of treatment, Elliott may have felt that if he could do a friend a favor, why not? In May 1934, he called Henry Morgenthau, Jr., on behalf of Clay Williams of the Reynolds Tobacco Company, to ask if anything could be done to reduce the taxes on tobacco. Morgenthau told him that a reduction would mean a loss in revenue of $75 million, which the Treasury could not afford. "I do wish that the President's family would quit lobbying," he wrote in his diary.

It was hard to resist offers that on the surface seemed innocent enough. When Donald Douglas asked Elliott to be a consultant for his aircraft company, Elliott said, "You'd better not have me on anything to do with the government." But in 1934 Elliott formed a partnership with the Dutch plane designer Anthony Fokker to sell the Russians some Lockheed transports that could be converted to bombers.

The agreement sent by Elliott to Fokker's associate, Herbert Reed, on February 5 said: "It is my understanding that a retainer fee of twenty-five thousand dollars for the services of this corporation will be paid for the year 1934, payable as follows: five thousand to be paid immediately, and the balance as desired."

Fokker testified before the Nye Committee in 1935, and Senator Nye asked for Elliott's 1934 tax returns, on the grounds that he had failed to report the $5,000. "What should we do about it?" FDR asked Morgenthau, who replied, "Frankly I do not know."

But the flap over the Fokker deal died down, and Elliott went to work for Hearst, writing an aviation column, and got into the radio station business in Texas. Again he felt the government was penalizing him and that the FCC was deliberately holding up his licenses. Eleanor wrote FDR on March 9, 1937, that "it does seem as though they had ample time to make up their minds—couldn't you . . . say a word which would hurry them—You know Elliott's disposition, he is beginning to think you are all against him."

FDR was hardly against him, indeed he was instrumental in helping Elliott obtain the financing for his stations. Elliott had been introduced to John A. Hartford, president of the Great Atlantic & Pacific Tea Company. He called the White House from Hartford's office and got his father on the line. Hartford was astonished to hear a hearty greeting. "Hello, John," FDR said, adding: "While any business you have with my son must stand on its own merits, I will appreciate anything you do for him. When you are in Washington come and see me." At that time, Hartford was being sued by the Federal Trade Commission on monopoly charges and the Department of Justice was considering a criminal suit against him.

Hartford bought $200,000 worth of stock in Elliott's company, Texas State Network, Inc. Elliott raised another $50,000 from the New York insurance man David G. Baird, and $25,000 from Judge Charles Harwood.

As a radio commentator, Elliott had an independent slant. In 1939 he was isolationist and anti–third term. Some of the New Dealers were enraged. "Elliott Roosevelt is being insufferable again," Harold Ickes wrote in March 1939. "Over the air the other day he said that Garner was in the driver's seat for the Democratic nomination for President and indicated his approval of Garner's candidacy. . . . I think he is little short of disloyal to his own father, and I cannot understand the President's tolerance. He is certainly working against his father's plans, which are to nominate a liberal ticket in 1940."

But FDR was not about to muzzle one of his sons, and the more his advisers criticized, the more he told Elliott to "go to it." In 1940, however, with the war closing in, Elliott had a change of heart, and decided that if he joined up it might help his father get the Selective Service Act passed.

By this time, Elliott had divorced Elizabeth Donner and married an energetic Texan, Ruth Josephine Googins of Fort Worth, whom he was now having difficulties with. Anna hoped that Ruth and Elliott would stick together, for he needed that balance wheel. He was hard to handle, and had to be managed with subtlety, and Anna was glad it was Ruth's job and not hers. "I am terribly upset about Elliott," she wrote her mother on June 19, 1939. "Of course, there is nothing to do but sit and wait. But I am hoping that that same determination which made Ruth so anxious to marry Elliott without delay will now come to her aid in helping her stiffen Elliott's backbone. I know, because I was with Elliott at the time, that both Ruth and her mother were terribly insistent that the marriage should go through without delay and that they worked on him constantly for this. I am only afraid of one thing and that is that Ruth is so ambitious that she may keep on pushing Elliott to too great an extent with this business of his, without realizing that Elliott does not have the same kind of determination and perseverance that she has."

Elliott's business was in worse shape than his marriage. The radio station company was insolvent. The entire investment capital of $500,000 had gone down the drain, and not a penny had been paid back to investors. Elliott needed a helping hand. In December 1941, after America had entered the war, FDR called up Jesse Jones, chairman of the RFC and self-made Texas millionaire, and said, "Jess, Elliott has a serious financial problem that I wish you would help him straighten out. The radio company he has been running in Texas is in trouble. As you know, Elliott has enlisted in the Army Air Force and will soon be in the combat zone. Of course, we don't know what will happen to him there and for the sake of his wife and three children he would like to adjust matters as much as possible."

FDR asked Jones "as a special favor" to see whether Elliott's creditors were willing to make concessions. Jones called in A&P president John Hartford, who said he was willing "to do anything the President wants me to do about this debt." The money did not mean much to him, since when he died taxes would take 90 percent of it. "Candidly," the chain-store owner said, "I would rather not have Elliott Roosevelt's notes in my estate while I am living or after I am dead." Jones bought the $200,000 in stock that Hartford held as collateral for the loan for $4,000, which he paid out of his own pocket (Elliott paid him back). Hartford destroyed Elliott's notes in his presence, and was allowed a $196,000 bad-debt deduction by the Treasury Department. Jones also obtained a release on the $50,000 Elliott had borrowed from David Baird for $750. But Judge Harwood, who had invested a mere $25,000, refused to settle. He had been promised a federal judgeship or a high military commission, and instead had been made governor of the Virgin Islands, which he felt was not enough.

This was an example of the president using his influence to get one of his sons out of a jam, and it was not the only one.

Jimmy, the oldest boy, was the one who most helped his father, but he was also the biggest liability. He once wrote FDR: "I often fear so greatly of doing something big or small which will bring some hurt to you, and I pray so hard that somehow it may never happen."

And yet it was bound to happen. It started when he was working in Boston in the insurance business, and there were rumors that he obtained commissions from companies that did business with the government. Responding to a critic, Jimmy wrote on September 4, 1934: "I realize of course that rumors are bound to start no matter what business I am in, and that whenever I am successful in securing an account, it will be said that I received it on the basis of political influence.... There is not one single cent of government business on my books, and I have made it a strict policy not to handle anything connected with the government."

When he asked his father to endorse Life Insurance Day, a warning came back from Steve Early: "Washington gossips have been connecting your name, referring to your relationships and to your business, in a way that makes some of your friends uneasy ... some people are always ready to believe the worst of anyone."

As in the case of Elliott's radio stations, FDR felt he had to protect Jimmy when he was in trouble. In September 1937, Senator Burton Wheeler of Montana began investigating a railroad equipment company for which Jimmy had written some insurance, to show that it had been favored by the government. FDR called Morgenthau and asked him to "pick and choose" the information that Wheeler was given. Morgenthau was shocked. He told his aides that he was not about to make an exception so that the president could get his son off the hook. Whatever Senator Wheeler wanted from the Treasury, he would get, and he would tell the president so.

Leaving the insurance business, Jimmy joined the National Grain Yeast Corporation, which also came under investigation on charges that it had done some bootlegging during Prohibition. "I didn't realize," Jimmy later said, "that when you make yeast there is a by-product of alcohol. What did you do with the alcohol?"

One day his father called him in and said that Louis Howe's death had left a big gap, and he needed someone he could trust, and would he consider taking the job. Jimmy served as his father's secretary in 1937 and 1938, and was credited with doing good work as liaison between the White House and the independent agencies. He was proud that only two presidents' sons had worked for their fathers, John Quincy Adams and himself, but he was more of a target than ever. "You were like one of those heads in county fairs that people throw baseballs at whenever they pop up," he recalled.

There was also quite a bit of animosity from the palace guard, who resented Jimmy's closeness and easy access to the president. When he had to take a leave of absence because of illness, Jim Farley asked Morgenthau how he was doing. Morgenthau said it would be awhile before he got back, and Farley said it would be a good thing if he didn't come back at all. Morgenthau said it looked bad with one-third of the nation unemployed to see the president's son getting $10,000 a year plus the money he made outside. Farley said the things he had been doing, such as putting some of his assets in his wife's name so as to minimize his income tax, were just the sort of things the president was opposing.

On one occasion, the president actually broke down and wept with frustration at one of the things that Jimmy had done. A lawyer named Charles Schwartz enlisted Jimmy's help in getting an introduction to William O. Douglas, who had succeeded Joe Kennedy as chairman of the Securities and Exchange Commission. His plan, in the wake of the Public Utility Holding Company Act, was to represent the holding companies before the SEC. He had approached a number of companies and told them that for a retainer of $100,000 a year he would handle and solve all their problems with the agency. Schwartz and Jimmy hoped to get Douglas to endorse or approve of the arrangement.

Douglas was shocked. It would be the biggest scandal since Teapot Dome if it got out that there was a way to fix SEC cases. He wrote the holding companies that they would be foolish to pay Schwartz ten cents, and that "neither Mr. Schwartz nor any other person is the intermediary between the commission and the utility companies."

Jimmy soon showed up in Douglas's office and said that any fool would know that the only time the Democrats could make money was when they were in power. "What chance do we have when the Republicans take over?" he asked. Douglas said he had not accepted public office to make money. He was so upset that he went to the White House with his resignation, and said that he seemed to be standing in the way of ambitious people. Roosevelt cradled his head on his arm and cried like a child for several minutes. Then, wiping away his tears, he said with a faint smile: "Jimmy! What a problem he is. Thanks for telling me. Now get back to your desk. Of course you're not resigning."

The criticism came to a head in 1938 with an article in the *Saturday Evening Post* called "Jimmy's Got It." Written by Alva Johnson, it wildly overstated Jimmy's alleged profiteering, saying that his annual income ranged from $250,000 to $2 million. Jimmy made public his tax returns, which showed his income peaking in 1934 at $49,167.37, and a counterarticle appeared in *Collier's*. But the stress proved too much, and in July he checked into the Mayo Clinic in Rochester, Minnesota, with a perforated ulcer and had two-thirds of his stomach removed.

By this time, his marriage with Betsy Cushing was on the rocks. Betsy recalled Franklin Jr. telling her: "You knew when you married Jimmy you had your fingers crossed." They had two daughters, Sara and Kate, and Jimmy at one point had told brother Johnny that he found pregnant women repulsive, which had gotten back to Betsy.

Jimmy told Betsy he wanted a divorce, and she said, "If you want it that badly just go and get it."

"Gentlemen don't do that," he replied.

But in the hospital he met a nurse named Romelle Schneider, and he filed for divorce and married her. Later, according to Marion Dickerman, Romelle would make him sign a document listing his infidelities, which he agreed to do to avoid a scandal at a time when his father was ill.

When Betsy heard that Jimmy had filed for the divorce, she was invited for dinner at the White House. "Eleanor stared at me all the way through dinner waiting for me to cry because I had just found out, but I wouldn't give her the satisfaction," she recalled.

The family was divided over the divorce. FDR was in Betsy's corner and insisted that Basil O'Connor represent her. But Anna and Eleanor thought that Betsy had deliberately set out to win the president's favor—there were many times when Jimmy was tired out and wanted to go home, but Betsy insisted on waiting for the last minute to have a drink with FDR.

Convalescing in San Benito, California, that September, Jimmy realized that he could no longer work for his father. It was like a blow in the teeth to give it up, for it was such a privilege to watch him make things work, but the doctors told him he was not up to it.

That fall, he was hired by Samuel Goldwyn, who by then had left Metro-Goldwyn-Mayer and founded his own company, and was given the title of vice president and $25,000 a year. He explained to his father that his duties were to dig up historical scenarios and to keep his ears close to the ground and find out why certain stars were unpopular. The word around Hollywood was that Jimmy had been given a job that was the equivalent of PWA leaf raking so that Goldwyn could boast to his friends that the president's son was on the payroll.

It was, however, useful to have an employee with access to government departments and the White House. These were the golden years of the studios. Louis B. Mayer of MGM, for instance, had a salary of $1.3 million in 1937, and was, for that year and the eight years following, the highest salaried man in the United States, earning more than the president of General Motors. New studios formed, and there were complicated stock deals involving millions of dollars that came under the scrutiny of the Treasury Department.

Darryl Zanuck, the boy wonder from Wahoo, Nebraska, had resigned from Warner Brothers in 1933 and founded 20th Century with Joseph Schenck of United Artists. Mayer put up half the money, $375,000, because he wanted them to hire his son-in-law, William Goetz. Schenck's brother, Nicholas, the president of MGM, put up the other half. In 1935, 20th Century merged with Fox, a much bigger but declining studio. Fox had a net worth of $36 million as against $4 million for 20th Century, and there were intricate stock manipulations.

The Treasury Department investigated and found that a revenue agent had been bribed to falsify his reports on the 20th Century-Fox merger. There had been a conspiracy to defraud the government by concealing more than $7 million. Henry Morgenthau, Jr., decided that the evidence of fraudulent intent was strong enough to warrant criminal prosecution, and proceedings were instituted against Darryl Zanuck, Joe Schenck, William Goetz, and a number of others.

It was at about this time that Jimmy Roosevelt was hired by Goldwyn, who was not involved in the merger but who was a defendant in an antitrust case concerning distribution. FDR said to Jimmy in December 1938: "How can you do this with a suit pending?" Jimmy said it was a civil suit. "What is the difference between a civil and a criminal suit?" FDR asked. "All I know is that you are working for a man who is fighting the United States Government."

It was customary for studios to lend their stars and directors to other studios, and in this case Jimmy was loaned to Joe Schenck to help him with his troubles. Another inducement was that Schenck loaned Jimmy $50,000. Morgenthau found out about the loan when he learned that Schenck had used Jimmy's note as collateral to negotiate another loan with the National City Bank.

On May 24, 1939, Jimmy called one of Morgenthau's aides from the White House to inquire about the tax case against Schenck. He wanted to know whether it would be possible to discuss it with Treasury officials before the case went any further. Morgenthau told the aide to write Jimmy not to phone him anymore.

In January 1940, Zanuck was found guilty of tax evasion, and Morgenthau called Attorney General Frank Murphy and said: "Mr. and Mrs.—whatever those people's names are—Zanuck. Well, they got a little bill this morning from me for $870,000. . . . So the next couple of weeks why I think that the movie colony may realize that this is a democracy. . . . I'm sure Mr. and Mrs. Zanuck were surprised when they opened their mail this morning."

Murphy: "Too bad you didn't send it on Christmas Eve."

On February 28, 1940, Jimmy dropped in to see Morgenthau. He said he was just passing by, just wanted to say hello. Then he made a motion to get up, but didn't. "By the way," he said, "does Joe Schenck really stink? Does he smell?"

"Well, what about it?" Morgenthau asked.

"Well, if he does, I don't want to do business with a man like that," Jimmy said.

"Well, I can't advise you," Morgenthau said. "Time will tell. We have a policy in the Treasury that a man is innocent until proven guilty."

"Then your advice to me is to wait."

"That's my advice to you. Wait and see what happens. I don't know the man personally. . . . He's still on the Infantile Paralysis Foundation board, isn't he?"

"I think he's going to resign because it might be embarrassing for father."

Morgenthau had a good laugh over that one. Did Joe Schenck stink? If you tried to say it fast you got tongue-tied.

Schenck's tax evasion trial was set for February, with a separate trial for perjury coming later. Jimmy asked his father whether the tax evasion indictment could be settled before the trial, because "of all the unpleasant dealings into private matters and the tabloid reactions." But this time, FDR stayed out of it. There were limits to what a president could do to help his children. Schenck was indicted for tax evasion and perjury on June 4, 1940, and was convicted in April of the following year on some of the charges. He resigned from 20th Century-Fox and moved to Connecticut—to the Danbury Federal Penitentiary.

The president's children were like chess pieces being pushed around the board of national politics by men who made a business of knowing the guy who knows the guy. They were constantly manipulated by the kind of opportunist who would kill his mother for a profit. As FDR once told Jim Rowe, who succeeded Jimmy as his aide: "One of the worst things in the world is being the child of a president! It's a terrible life they lead!"

That's why the president bent the rules every now and then to help them out. Allowances had to be made for their special situation. You could say of them what was said in defense of England's first governor general of India, Warren Hastings, after he had been cleared of charges of high crimes and misdemeanors: "When you considered his unmatched opportunities, you marveled at his restraint."

It was all a part of life at the White House during the Roosevelt years, which had a zany *Hellzapoppin* quality never seen before or since. You never knew what was going to happen next, whether Louis Howe would be wandering down the hall with nothing on, or Lorena Hickok would be drinking alone in her room, or a daughter-in-law would be pouring out her marital woes to Eleanor, or a friend of the family would be using the White House switchboard to make a business deal.

It was a carnival with sideshows. One night an Italian magician, the Great Giovanni, came to entertain after dinner. He picked Henry Morgenthau's pocket and told him that since he couldn't hang onto his own wallet he wasn't fit to run the Treasury. The president roared. He took the gun out of Colonel Starling's holster—the head of the Secret Service detail, who had been protecting presidents for thirty years. Starling said it wasn't funny, and if he did it again he'd be shot. He threw a pack of cards in the air and the card FDR had chosen stuck to the chandelier. The president said he would give almost anything to learn how to do it. Then, in his thick Italian accent, he said: "Meesta Presidenta, be surea you feexa you watcha tighta." FDR felt his wrist and his watch was gone. "Hey, give it back," he said. The Great Giovanni had turned the tables on them all, giving the president and his aides a lesson in how much of life is illusion.

XVII

Through Me Many Long-Dumb Voices

Through me many long-dumb voices,
Voices of the interminable generations of prisoners and slaves,
Voices of the diseas'd and despairing and of thieves and dwarfs,
Voices of cycles of preparation and accretion,
And of the threads that connect the stars, and of wombs and
of the father-stuff,
And of the rights of them the others are down upon,
Of the deform'd, trivial, flat, foolish, despised,
Fog in the air, beetles rolling balls of dung.

Walt Whitman, *Leave of Grass*

FOR the first time, thanks to the amendment pushed through in 1932 by Senator Norris, the inauguration was held on January 20 instead of in March. It rained on that day, a chilling downpour that at times sluiced down in torrents. Waiting at the Capitol after the service in St. John's Episcopal Church, Cordell Hull told Ickes that Japan was on the verge of economic collapse. She did not have the money to carry out her plans against China. Morgenthau arrived with a flask of Scotch, and he and Ickes took a pull to fortify them against the bad weather.

A bit after noon Roosevelt came out, bareheaded in the driving rain, on the arm of his son Jimmy, and walked to the speaker's stand on a runner of carpet that was like a saturated sponge. He had refused a glass shield—if people had to stand in the wet to hear him, he would stand in the wet to talk.

Then the president faced Chief Justice Charles Evans Hughes—two formidable men who would soon be locked in a battle for which the present ceremony was in fact the opening bell. Hughes asked him, with steadily mounting emphasis whether he would "preserve, protect, and defend the Constitution of the United States." With equal emphasis, and with his voice rising in volume with each word, the president replied that he would. But what was the Constitution, was it what five out of nine justices said it was, or was it what the president and millions of Americans believed it to be? The court was mired in politics. Four justices, with help from the swing vote of the fifth, had crippled the power to govern by striking down New Deal legislation, oblivious of the basic principle enunciated by Justice Bushrod Washington in 1827: "It is but a decent respect due to the wisdom, the integrity, and the patriotism of the legislative body, by which any law is passed, to presume in favor of its validity, until its violation of the Constitution is proved beyond all reasonable doubt."

As he took the oath, FDR knew full well that there was nothing in the Constitution that gave the Supreme Court the right to override the legislative branch. On four separate occasions, the framers of the Constitution had voted against giving judges the right to pass on the constitutionality of acts of Congress. Not until 1803 had Chief Justice Marshall asserted that right, and that was because he hated Jefferson and wanted to block the progress of a new order he resented and distrusted. Now history was being repeated, and Congress had to reclaim the powers that had been filched from it by usurpation.

In his inaugural speech, FDR promised to continue the work of the first term, for "I see one-third of the nation ill-housed, ill-clad, ill-nourished." As he listened, Harold Ickes thought that four years ago the country had been near collapse. Every bank was closed, and now they were prospering. Had there ever been a more striking contrast between two successive inaugurations, unless it was Lincoln's two terms?

The president drove back to the White House, where he was given an alcohol rubdown and some dry clothes. Then he stood in the rain again for the parade. When Steve Early called on him that evening after dinner, FDR said, "You can't guess what I am doing." "Playing with your stamps?" "That's right. Rather a nice contrast to the inaugural evening four years ago." Then everyone had been in a state of panic, but now things were so changed that he could sit alone with nothing more to worry about than his stamp collection. The crisis was over, or so it seemed.

Packing the Supreme Court was not a new idea. On March 6, 1933, Ray Moley had dinner with Huey Long, who asked: "Did it ever occur to you that Congress could increase the membership of the Supreme Court?" Moley thought that was ridiculous, and replied, "Did it ever occur to you that Congress could add its entire membership to the Supreme Court just as well as all members of the United States Army?"

But with the obstruction of the four conservatives, the idea seemed less ridiculous. They would not change and they would not retire. At a cabinet meeting right after the 1936 election, FDR said he expected McReynolds to be on the bench when he was 105 years old. These men were relics of another America, they had started from nothing in pioneer communities, where there was always more land, and those who worked hard prospered, and you did not need help from the government. To have them betray their allegiances to laissez-faire was like asking them to repudiate their own lives. To believe that they were devoid of prejudices and passions was to believe in the tooth fairy. The history of the Supreme Court was political history, with positions changing, and minority views becoming majority views. The danger came when the court pretended otherwise, setting itself up as a super-government.

Roosevelt thought at first of a constitutional amendment adding justices, but that was impractical. It would require a two-thirds vote of both houses, and then submitting it to the states, three-fourths of which had to approve. Supposing thirteen governors refused to submit it, the amendment was dead. It was easy for moneyed interests to buy up enough state legislatures to prevent passage. There were enough gerrymandered states with Republican assemblies, like New York. As Roosevelt put it, "Give me ten million dollars and I can prevent any amendment to the Constitution from being ratified by the necessary number of states." An amendment would take years, and would become an issue in the 1938 elections and cost a number of Democratic congressmen their seats.

No, an amendment was out, there had to be another way, and Attorney General Homer Cummings thought he had found it. Since 1935, he had been incubating a plan to add justices to the court that, ironically enough, was based on a memo Justice McReynolds had drafted in 1913 when he was attorney general. Frances Perkins was sure that Cummings was pushing the plan because he hoped to become a Supreme Court justice himself if it was adopted. He was its author and instigator, and convinced the president that it would work.

It seemed like a cinch. The court's abuses were evident, and the president's electoral triumph was an invitation to remedy the situation. Congress would support him because it was Congress that the court was overruling. After all, there were only eighty-nine Republicans in the House and sixteen in the Senate. The duty of the huge Democratic majority was to have the courage of the president's convictions.

But at the same time that FDR was preparing his assault, there were signs that the court was willing to surrender without a fight. One night at a dinner party, Frances Perkins sat next to McReynolds, who was most gallant, and who said of his colleagues that "some of them would be glad to retire, and I'm sure would accommodate [Roosevelt] if they felt sure they were going to get their salaries for life." That was the sticking point, for in 1932 the Justices could retire with their full salary, $20,000, but the Economy Act of 1933 had cut that in half. When Roosevelt complained that there had not been a single Supreme Court vacancy in his first term, that was the reason. The two oldest of the four conservatives, Van Devanter and Sutherland, wanted to resign but could not afford to. The oldest of the nine was of course Brandeis, who was eighty and voted with the liberal minority. Whenever Frances Perkins saw Charles Burlingham, the president of the New York Bar Association, he would ask, "Why doesn't Isaiah retire and let the President appoint Felix [Frankfurter]?" He didn't like Brandeis, who he thought gave himself airs and was only an average lawyer. Reverent assemblies called on him on Sunday afternoons as though going to an audience with the pope.

In 1936, a bill had been introduced to provide the justices with retirement at full salary for life, and once it was passed the problem would solve itself. It was a better and less divisive solution than enlarging the court to fifteen justices, thought Solicitor General Stanley Reed when Cummings tried to sell him on the plan. How would you get better results out of fifteen than out of nine? You might put judges on to support your program but what would happen fifteen years down the line? What about the long-range validity of their decisions?

Roosevelt had not thought it through. He was forging ahead without his usual wiliness, determined to bulldoze the court into submission. Major New Deal legislation, such as the Wagner and Holding Company acts, and Social Security, were working their way up for court tests, and he felt he could not wait—something had to be done *now*.

On February 3, FDR held the annual White House dinner for the federal judiciary, and not a hint of the court-packing plan was disclosed. On the morning of February 5, he read the message in the cabinet room to congressional leaders and cabinet members. The gist of the plan was that when a Supreme Court justice did not retire six months after reaching the age of seventy, a new judge could be added, up to six.

It was not unusual to change the number of judges, the message said. The Supreme Court had started with six in 1789, was reduced to five in 1801, increased to seven in 1807, to nine in 1837, and to ten in 1863, reduced to seven in 1866, and raised back to nine in 1869.

The message was clothed in concern for the judicial work load. In the past year the court had declined to grant review in 695 out of 803 cases. "Many of the refusals were doubtless warranted," FDR read, "but can it be said that full justice is achieved when a court is forced by the sheer necessity of keeping up with its business to decline, without even an explanation, to hear 87% of the cases presented to it by private litigants."

The tone was gratuitously wounding, in that it equated age with incompetence. "In exceptional cases, of course," it said, "judges, like other men, retain to an advanced age full mental and physical vigor. Those not so fortunate are often unable to perceive their own infirmities. They seem to be tenacious of the appearance of adequacy." Brandeis, the oldest justice, and still a productive member of the liberal minority, was bound to be hurt, and so was the seventy-five-year-old chief justice, Charles Evans Hughes. There had not been such an insult to the court since Theodore Roosevelt had described one of its members as "an old fuzzy-wuzzy with sweetbread brains."

While FDR read his message, most of the cabinet members laughed and nodded in appreciation at his sallies, but the congressional leaders remained strangely silent. They were in fact in various stages of shock. House Majority Leader Sam Rayburn resented the president's method of folding a bill inside a message to Congress instead of permitting the proper committees to draft the legislation. The leaders had not been consulted or informed. They had been summoned to the White House at 10:00 A.M. to hear a message that would be read to both houses of Congress at noon. The message had already been mimeographed and released to the press—there was no chance for discussion or amendment—it was a fait accompli. Then they were supposed to get out the vote for something they knew nothing about. Rayburn thought FDR was turning into a little tin god.

Congressman Hatton Sumners, chairman of the House Judiciary Committee, thought that if FDR had told him about the court-packing plan he could have introduced his retirement bill earlier in the session, and at least two justices would have retired. That would have made court packing unnecessary. Before you decided whether to have lungs or gills on a living creature, you had to make up your mind whether you wanted a man or a fish. If you wanted a republic you had to have an independent judiciary.

Jack Garner did not say a single word throughout the meeting. It was the first time Ickes had seen him sit entirely silent. Garner also thought that if the congressional leaders had been told about the plan in advance they could have talked FDR out of it and in favor of the retirement bill. He saw the court-packing plan as a threat to party harmony.

When the congressional leaders drove back to the Capitol, Hatton Sumner said: "Boys, here's where I cash in my chips."

Speaker of the House William Bankhead told Congressman Lindsay Warren: "Lindsay, wouldn't you have thought that the President would have told his own party leaders what he was going to do? He didn't because he knew that hell would break loose."

All hell did break loose. The president had failed to anticipate public reaction. He had violated his own method of making sure he had support before he went ahead. Court packing was the one great topic, like an American Dreyfus case, and there were acres of editorials.

As Sinclair Lewis told his wife, Dorothy Thompson: "There is one certain remedy for a headache . . . decapitation. . . . The President says the Supreme Court has, and is, a headache. He proposes to cure it, but he is a busy man. It's a long way upstairs to get the aspirin, and the doctors disagree, anyhow, as to just what's wrong with Auntie. So he has jumped into the kitchen for a cleaver. . . . Nice fellow, the President. Can't bear the sight of long drawn out pain." A lot of Americans felt the same way—it was overkill.

Much of the legal profession was against the plan. As Charles C. Burlingham wrote FDR on February 19: "You can't feel more strongly than I about the majority opinions, especially AAA and Minimum Wage. . . . BUT I don't like your method. I suppose you are in a hurry and this is *your* Congress. It's all very well to refer to previous changes in the size of the court. Only one involved a desire to affect decisions of the court—the appointment of Bradley and Strong by President Grant in 1869, and there is still considerable doubt and confusion about that episode which however has always been regarded as more or less scandalous and discreditable to the Court."

FDR still seemed to have the backing of the man (and woman) in the street, who had come to regard the Supreme Court majority as an ally of capitalistic exploitation. A hospital nurse said: "I didn't know whether to be for or against the President's plan until I saw a picture in a magazine showing the Supreme Court's dining room. All the judges had different knives and forks, and special salt and pepper shakers. That settled me. I've had enough experience with crotchety old patients to know that people who insist on all sorts of special favors sometimes aren't up to standard. If those judges can't use regular silverware and dishes, then they're too finicky and peculiar to run the government."

Charles Evans Hughes saw it as his duty to save the court by defeating the plan. Abandoning judicial detachment, he would fight a patently political battle, using every trick he had learned in a career that went back farther than the president's—he had been governor of New York in 1907, had fought a presidential campaign in 1916, and had been secretary of state under Harding and Coolidge.

Meanwhile, FDR was mobilizing his troops. The tireless Joe Robinson, Democratic majority leader in the Senate, who had been promised the first vacant seat on the bench, was drumming up support but finding a lot of backsliding among reliable Roosevelt men.

Tommy Corcoran was on the Hill, making his usual unsubtle offers. Approaching Wheeler of Montana, who up to now had been a teacher's pet of the New Deal, he said that if Wheeler went along on the court plan he could sit in on the naming of some of the new justices. "If you don't go along," Corcoran said, "he'll make a deal with Tammany and the Southerners and he'll put their people on the court." Wheeler said Corcoran was probably right but he was not going along. Pounding the table, Wheeler said, "Well, Tommy, he isn't going to get it!"

Wheeler became the leader of the anti-court-packing bloc in the Senate, which grew from eighteen to thirty. He worked on wavering senators as FDR brought administration pressure to bear through speeches and fireside chats and friendly calls from cabinet members.

On March 1 the Retirement Act passed. It was an escape hatch that FDR could have taken. All sorts of signals were being emitted—Justice Stone told Congressman Emmanuel Celler that two members of the court would retire within a year—but the president did not hear them.

On March 10, the Senate Judiciary Committee opened hearings on the bill, S. 1392. In the meantime, Mrs. Brandeis went to call on Wheeler's daughter living in Alexandria and said as an afterthought: "You tell your obstinate father we think he is making a courageous fight." That was the tip-off that Brandeis was willing to help, and Wheeler went to see him at 2205 California Street, full of misgivings that he might be overstepping the bounds of propriety. Perhaps he should confine his visit to asking questions of fact. Was the court docket really crowded? Brandeis suggested he ask the chief justice, and led Wheeler to a phone. Wheeler was stunned when Hughes offered to write a letter that he could read to the Judiciary Committee.

And so it was that on Monday, March 22, 1937, Wheeler told the Judiciary Committee, which was sitting in the marble-walled caucus room of the Senate Office Building, that "I have a statement from a man who knows more about the court than the President of the United States, than the Attorney-General, than I do or any member of this committee." He then read the letter, which explained in detail that the court was fully abreast of its work, destroying the president's main argument. More judges would only make for inefficiency and delay. There would be "more judges to hear, more judges to confer, more judges to discuss, more judges to be convinced and to decide."

It was a shocking departure from impartiality for a chief justice to give an advisory opinion on a bill affecting the court. Also, the letter left the impression that Hughes's views were endorsed by the entire court, whereas only Brandeis and Van Devanter had cosigned it. Nonetheless, the letter had a tremendous impact, and Bob Jackson, then assistant attorney general, said it did more than any other single thing to turn the tide.

Vacationing in Warm Springs, FDR still thought the bill was in good shape. Tommy Corcoran told him the administration had enough votes in the Senate to carry it.

But on March 29 the Supreme Court in a 5-to-4 decision upheld the minimum wage law of the state of Washington. This was a complete somersault, for six months before the court had voided a New York State minimum wage law for women under the due process clause. Now the justices were saying that due process should not be used for the exploitation of labor and that the states had the right to regulate wages and hours. In his majority decision, Justice Hughes brought the court into the twentieth century when he deplored "the exploitation of a class of workers who are in an unequal position with respect to bargaining power and are thus relatively defenseless against the denial of a living wage."

Sitting at the government table, Bob Jackson thought the explanation was a joke—it was just face-saving. Harold Ickes thought that it was "an admission on the part of the Supreme Court of charges that we have made to the effect that it hasn't been following the Constitution but has been establishing as the law of the land, through Supreme Court decisions, the economic and social beliefs of the judges of that court."

The timing seemed to indicate that the decision was a response to the court-packing plan. The court was saying that it could reform itself, without additional judges. In fact, the Washington case had been argued the previous October and voted on in December, before the plan was announced. Harlan Stone was ill and the court voted 4 to 4, with Owen Roberts reversing the position he had taken against the New York law when he was a presidential hopeful in June 1936. This was the famous switch in time that saved nine. There were technical differences between the two cases, but that was shadowboxing. Stone came back in February and, as expected, cast his vote to uphold, and the decision was announced in March. Thus Hughes could argue that "the President's proposal had not the slightest effect on our decision." And yet the climate of the times, the president's great victory at the polls, and the growing anticourt sentiment must have played a part. As Teddy Roosevelt once said: "I may not know much law, but I do know that one can put the fear of God in judges."

On that same day, March 29, the justices approved a new Frazier-Lemke Act on farm mortgages, which it had previously struck down, as well as the collective bargaining provisions of the Railway Labor Act.

On April 12, lo and behold, they upheld the Wagner Act and provided a new interpretation of the federal commerce power. This involved a case where the National Labor Relations Board had ordered the Jones & Laughlin steel company to reinstate ten employees dismissed for union activity. The circuit court refused to enforce the order, holding that it lay beyond the range of federal power. The Supreme Court ruled that the power to regulate interstate commerce included the power to enact laws "for its protection and advancement." Jones & Laughlin had its headquarters in Pennsylvania but shipped three-fourths of its products to other states and owned mines in Minnesota, steamships on the Great Lakes, and warehouses in four states. Industrial strife in the company would affect interstate commerce. As part of the protection of interstate commerce, the majority decision said, "employees have as clear a right to organize and select their representatives for lawful purposes as the respondent has to organize its business and select its own officers and agents. . . . When industries organize themselves on a national scale, making their relation to interstate commerce the dominant factor in their activities, how can it be maintained that their industrial labor relations constitute a forbidden field into which Congress may not enter?" Thus collective bargaining became the law of the land, and the four dissenters expressed the swan song of their dying gospel.

Reading the morning papers on April 13, FDR thought it was terribly funny. In September 1935, the New York *Herald Tribune* had carried an editorial called "Thumbs Down on Wagner Act." Today's editorial was entitled "A Great Decision." At a press conference later that day, he made it clear that he was not dropping the court-packing plan. One decision was not enough. You could not know how the court would respond in child labor or minimum wage cases. When he asked people what they thought they said, "Lord only knows." "My guess would be," he went on, "the feeling of the average man and woman on the street is 'so far so good but'—and then, perhaps the old phrase 'so what.' That is about as far as we have gotten in 24 hours, 'so what.' "

The situation ripened when Willis Van Devanter, prodded by Senator Borah, who told him it was the patriotic thing to do, retired on May 18 and left for his Maryland farm. It seemed that Roosevelt had everything he wanted without pushing through his plan—a court that was liberalizing its interpretation of the Constitution and upholding New Deal legislation, the removal of an obstructionist judge, and a vacancy on the bench. But one vacancy was not enough, for he had promised the first one to Joe Robinson, a sixty-five-year-old conservative from Arkansas, and to single him out when the whole point was to bring in younger and more liberal judges would make the battle against the court a bad joke. He had to have several vacancies.

Van Devanter's resignation was timed to coincide with the vote of the Judiciary Committee, chaired by Senator Henry Fountain Ashurst of Arizona, born in a covered wagon off the old California Trail, who had been in the Senate since 1912 and who had once said: "Politics is like being on roller skates. Sometimes you go where you want and sometimes you go where the roller skates take you." After hearing eighty-five witnesses and 1.5 million words of testimony, the committee on May 18 voted 10 to 8 that the court bill "do not pass," and adopted a report calling the plan "a measure which should be so emphatically rejected that its parallel will never again be presented to the free representatives of the free people of America." The report was rough, reading like a bill of impeachment, except that it referred to the bill instead of to the president. Six Democrats on the committee had jumped ship.

On May 24, the court upheld the Social Security Act. Bob Jackson had argued the case on May 5 and told Ray Clapper, the columnist on the Washington *Daily News,* that "the whole argument was pointed at Roberts. I was arguing to a one-man court. Instead of speaking for the radical viewpoint, I stressed the arguments that would appeal to conservatives. I emphasized that the act encouraged thrift, it helped workers take care of themselves. . . . The depression had left the thrifty in the same kind of a hole as the shiftless. This was intended to restore security to the man who works." Jackson had argued around Roberts's previous decisions so that he would not feel he was contradicting himself if he voted for the act. After all, Roberts had written the opinion denying railroad workers retirement pay. "Roberts asked no questions at all," Jackson went on. "He has the best poker face on the court. The Chief Justice, when you score a point, you can see his eyes twinkle and can feel it. Sutherland will ask questions to indicate what is in his mind—as in this case—'did the federal government take the state's money?' Butler asked what conditions were imposed on the states. But Roberts gives you no clue at all." Jackson thought the court had cut the ground from under the president. It had gone as far as anyone expected it to go. This was a new interpretation of the federal taxing and spending power.

The chief justice was outsmarting the president. What was the point of chasing a train that was already in the station? But FDR still thought he could win and badly wanted to add to the court six judges to his liking. "We must keep up—and strengthen—the fight," he wrote a congressman. After all, a lot of those renegade Democrats on the Hill had been elected thanks to him. In states whose senators were against the bill he held up judicial appointments.

Roosevelt even brought in the leader of the renegades, Burt Wheeler, for a little friendly persuasion. It was a typical Roosevelt performance, blending the anecdotal and the hortatory. "Burt," he said, "there was a justice of the Supreme Court of Missouri who was visiting in London and was invited to sit on the Appellate Court as a guest. A case was presented where two boys were convicted of a crime in the lower court and had not been permitted to put in the defense of an alibi. When the argument was over, the presiding justice turned to the Missouri judge and said 'what do you think we ought to do about the case?' The Missouri judge said he thought it ought to be reversed, whereupon the presiding judge said 'we do,' and reversed the case and turned the boys loose. This is the sort of thing we ought to have over here."

"That's what we have got here," Wheeler replied. "It is so elementary in our jurisprudence that a party be present at the commission of the crime that no justice of the peace, state judge, or federal judge would think of not allowing the defendant to put in the defense of an alibi."

FDR changed the subject, asking Wheeler to let the Republicans lead the fight against the court bill, for he was splitting the party. Wheeler defiantly said he would carry on as leader. "Well," FDR said, "let's keep the bitterness out."

"The Supreme Court and the Constitution," Wheeler said, "are a religion with a great many people in this country and you can't keep the bitterness out of a religious fight." Wheeler added that the bill was opposed by Brandeis, who had been a liberal before FDR had ever heard the word. "Justice Brandeis was all in favor of it, at first," FDR said, "but the old lady—the nice old lady—kept dropping little drops of water on his head until he changed his mind." Wheeler could not help thinking that FDR had good reason to be suspicious of the influence of wives.

If he dropped the court bill, Wheeler said, he could have at least two resignations on the bench. "How can I be sure?" Roosevelt asked, expressing a flicker of interest. Wheeler assured him that it was so, but FDR insisted he wanted the bill passed. At his June 4 press conference he said that dropping the court fight would be silly. He denounced the court for taking a four months' vacation while important cases such as PWA were pending. Someone asked if he would accept two judges instead of six. "You are talking about trees," he said, "I am talking about the forest."

On June 11, Jack Garner, who as vice president was president of the Senate and a vital part of the administration strategy, left in disgust for Uvalde, not wanting to work for a bill he despised. That left Joe Robinson in the Senate carrying the whole load, using every ounce of personal prestige, pleading not only for the plan but for his own cherished ambition to become a justice.

On July 7, FDR tried to cajole Garner back to Washington. Could he return in time to save the amended bill by trying to head off a filibuster? "Then there is, as you know," FDR wrote, "the really continuing comment on your absence—criticism from papers like the editorial in the Scripps-Howard papers last night. . . . I have consistently said that it was all nonsense and that you were coming back very soon."

On the morning of July 14, Joe Robinson was found dead on the floor of his bathroom, in the little apartment in the Methodist Building where he had lived for many years, a copy of the *Congressional Record* near his right hand. He was the victim of a heart attack. More to the point, the victim of the court-packing plan, for he had succumbed to his exertions at the president's bidding.

Tom Corcoran called Missy LeHand and told her that FDR's phone would soon be ringing with messages to drop the court bill. Bernard Baruch called FDR and urged him to drop the bill and not kill any more senators. Miffed, FDR replied that what was killing senators was the filibuster preventing a vote—it would get through easily if it were allowed to come to the floor. But the opponents were trying to capitalize on Robinson's death. It was ghoulish, thought Harold Ickes, the way Wheeler and the others were fighting over his corpse.

On Monday, July 19, FDR had Hugh Johnson to lunch. When the Wagner Act had been upheld in April, Johnson had written FDR: "I was taken for a ride on a chicken truck in Brooklyn two years ago and dumped out on a deserted highway and left for dead. It seems this was all a mistake. Please advise if I can claim damages and back wages from the Associated Press." Since his ouster from the NRA, Johnson had been writing a sometimes vitriolic column, and over lunch the president read aloud his latest effort, in which he said that it was a good thing Joe Robinson had died before learning of FDR's treachery, for the president had no intention of putting him on the high court.

When he had finished reading, FDR looked at Johnson and said: "Hugh, do you know what fine, loyal old Joe Robinson would have said to you if you had written that while he was alive? He would have said, Hugh, that you are a liar, a coward, and a cad." "Mr. President," Johnson haltingly replied, "I am sorry, I am very sorry." And then, as the president told the story to Harold Ickes, Hugh broke down and cried.

But fine loyal old Joe Robinson was not alive, and the bill's chances died with him. On the train trip back from the funeral in Little Rock, Garner had been counting noses.

"How did you find the court situation, Jack?" FDR asked him when he reported on July 20.

"Do you want it with the bark on or off, Cap'n?"

"The rough way."

"All right. You are beat. You haven't the votes."

On top of everything, at this critical juncture, Governor Herbert Lehman of New York released a letter to Senator Wagner opposing the court plan. He was the only governor to inject himself into the fray. FDR was furious. He had handpicked his lieutenant governor and successor. He had sent him around to dedicate penitentiaries and bridges and to open roads and county fairs. "It was not only bad, it was terribly bad," FDR told Adolf Berle. "It was fifth grade, not even high school." FDR had taken him into legislative conferences and had taught him the business. It was like a student you built up and taught all you knew. And that was how he paid him back, the son of a bitch. The pride of Lucifer himself could hardly have created a more distorted psychology.

FDR was tired and nervous and put out about the court bill, but he would not admit defeat. He thought he could still win, but it was tremendously important that Alben Barkley of Kentucky be elected to succeed Robinson over Pat Harrison of Mississippi. The election of Harrison would be disastrous, not only to the court bill but to his entire program.

To make sure that Barkley won, in a contest in which he was supposed to remain neutral, FDR applied pressure on Harrison's Mississippi colleague, Theodore Bilbo, who hated Harrison, and on Senator William H. Dietrich of Illinois, who was up for reelection and needed the support of Chicago boss Ed Kelly. A telephone call from Kelly, promising him two federal judges, did the trick.

Barkley was elected majority leader on July 20, by one vote, but Garner was shocked by FDR's meddling. There was nothing to be done about the court bill, however, for on July 22 the Senate voted 70 to 20 to recommit it to the Judiciary Committee, which was a polite form of euthanasia. The coup de grace had been the decision of seven freshman senators to vote to recommit. "That this was a terrific defeat for the President cannot be denied," wrote Ickes. Wheeler had told a group of senators who were suggesting a compromise: "Nothing doing. We must teach that man in the White House a lesson. We must show him that the United States Senate has to be consulted and is going to have something to say about how the government is run." Fishing in troubled waters, Tom Corcoran said it was Garner who had betrayed FDR, secretly working against him on the recommittal. The bill would have had a better chance had he stayed in Uvalde overseeing his pecan pickers. Later a substitute measure was enacted, so as, in Garner's words, "not to bloody the President's nose." But there would be no new judges.

The court-packing plan was the worst blunder of Roosevelt's peacetime presidency. Even those closest to him, like Marvin McIntyre, felt that he had not handled it with his usual astuteness. He had a bad case of post-election hubris and was expecting servile acquiescence from the Congress. But this was not the Hundred Days, when legislation could be rubber-stamped without debate because the nation was in crisis; this was an attack on the jewel of the American system.

FDR had offended his own congressional majority by the cavalier way he threw the plan at them. The reaction was an "I hope you choke" feeling. There was no tangible benefit in voting for it, while voting against it would not hurt them in their constituencies. It was much easier to vote against a principle than against a public works program.

It was customary to say that he lost the battle but won the war. But the war did not have to be fought. It was all so unnecessary. Under the leadership of its canny chief justice, the court was changing. The minimum wage decision was proof of that. Also, by 1937 the laws were better drafted. Instead of loose assertions of unlimited federal power, the lawyers had learned how to use the commerce clause as the key to government regulation. Roosevelt was told repeatedly that there would be vacancies, but remained indifferent to the court's dynamics. In his obstinacy, he revealed for all to see the streak of vindictiveness usually masked by the geniality.

The court-packing plan taught him the lesson that electoral victory did not translate into legislative docility. Now he had a court that would uphold the bills but not a Congress that would pass them. It cost him the friendship of powerful senators and the loyalty of his vice president, who for the rest of the second term would be an adversary in the cabinet. It made FDR want to punish those who had opposed the plan, which led to another mistake, the 1938 purge. And finally, it stalled the administration engine, which would continue to cough and sputter until a war emergency started it humming again.

Of course there was the Van Devanter vacancy to fill. On the evening of August 11, FDR saw Alabama Senator Hugo Black, and after the mandatory period of teasing, he came to the point by showing him a blank Supreme Court nomination form. He asked if he might fill it in with his visitor's name. Black was a relatively young fifty-one-year-old from the Deep South, which had been long neglected on the high court. He was that rare bird, a southern senator devoid of the prevailing prejudices below the Mason-Dixon line. Some called him the most radical man in the Senate. Born poor, the last of eight children of a storekeeper father, he put himself through law school and became a trade-union lawyer in Birmingham. FDR picked him because he was right geographically, he was a loyal New Dealer, the Senate would have to confirm one of its own, and he did not want a jurist who might "shrivel the Constitution into a lawyer's contract."

Black had been elected senator in 1926, when the Ku Klux Klan had real clout in Alabama, but he denied that he had been a member. A reporter for the Pittsburgh *Post-Gazette* unearthed his letter of resignation, written in his own hand, and signed in the cabalistic Klan manner, "Yours I.T.S.U.B.," Yours in the Sacred Unfailing Bond. He had been a member, taken the oath, paid his dues, and worn the white robes. When he became a Supreme Court justice, the quip went, he would not have to buy robes, only dye them.

FDR told Joe Kennedy that he could not understand why Black had not come out and admitted he was a Klansman. "If Marlene Dietrich invited you to make love to her," Kennedy said, "would you say you were no good at making love?"

Tom Corcoran went to see Black and advised abject repentance accompanied by a repudiation of the Klan and its members. "I did join the Klan," Black said in a radio broadcast. "I later resigned. I have never rejoined." FDR thought that had done the trick. Why should a man be branded by one mistake? Black was confirmed 63 to 13. Even Cotton Ed Smith of South Carolina, who had goddamned the nomination all over the place, did not have the guts to vote against a fellow senator. One of those who did was Carter Glass, who said of Black: "Whoever he is, his name is Charlie McCarthy."

After Black, there was a cascade of vacancies. The irony of the whole court-packing battle was that four years later seven out of nine justices were FDR appointees. He had packed the court after all. Sutherland resigned in 1938 and was replaced by Solicitor General Stanley Reed. Felix Frankfurter came in for Cardozo and William O. Douglas for Brandeis. Frank Murphy came in for Pierce Butler and James Byrnes and Robert Jackson for Hughes and McReynolds. The only two remaining pre-Roosevelt judges were Harlan Stone and Owen Roberts. Another irony was that most of the important New Deal legislation was upheld by the Hughes court that Roosevelt was trying to pack. Once they had ruled on the scope of the federal commerce power the Roosevelt court had little left to do but continue the swing of the pendulum. For instance, in the New River decision, the Roosevelt court ruled that an upland stream in West Virginia, 100 miles from the main river, affected navigation to the extent that the federal government controlled it. That was when Wendell Willkie said: "Now the toilet water in the men's room is navigable."

The cares of office, particularly after the Supreme Court struggle, were reflected in the president's appearance. During an August cruise aboard the *Potomac,* Ickes observed: "It was clear to me that he has paid a heavy toll during these past four years. His face is heavily lined and inclined to be gaunt as compared with what it was when he took office in 1933, and he is distinctly more nervous. He is punch drunk from the punishment he has suffered recently."

Part of the punishment was a level of abuse in the press that reached a new high in 1937. At his May 18 press conference, FDR read aloud two of the more revolting items, both of them distributed by the McClure Syndicate as confidential "pink sheets" for the information of editors and not for publication.

"Unchecked," the president read. "A New York specialist high in the medical field is authority for the following, which is given in the strictest confidence to editors: Toward the end of the last month Mr. Roosevelt was found in a coma at his desk. Medical examination disclosed the neck rash which is typical of certain disturbing symptoms. Immediate treatment of the most skilled kind was indicated, with complete privacy and detachment from official duties. Hence the trip to southern waters, with no newspaper men on board and a naval convoy which cannot be penetrated."

"Number 2," the president went on. ". . . At a recent private dinner in New York an official of the American Cyanamid expressed in extreme form the bitterness towards the administration which is typical of the personal reactions of many right-wing leaders in business. The gentleman in question asserted in so many words that 'the paranoiac in the White House' is destroying the nation, that a couple of well-placed bullets would be the best thing for the country, and that he for one would buy a bottle of champagne as quick as he could get it to celebrate such news."

Wasn't the second item actionable? a reporter asked.

"You know, that does not make any difference at all," FDR said. "The President of the United States does not sue for libel and the Department of Justice does not proceed for libel." He had no recourse, even for items such as these, the one alleging that he had syphilis, the other repeating a recommendation for his assassination.

Nothing the president did was above suspicion. People seized on the fact that he went fishing aboard Navy ships at the taxpayers' expense. A high school civics class in Augusta, Illinois, wrote him: "Do all the taxes collected in the United States go for the general welfare of the people? If this is so, we would like to know the source of the finances for your fishing trips."

The standard reply was that using the ships for the president's vacations was good for Navy morale—the officers and men were at peak efficiency when the commander in chief was on board.

It was a small thing, but an easy way to get at Roosevelt. On April 28, from the Presidential Special en route to New Orleans, Walter Trohan of the Chicago *Tribune* wrote that FDR in the comfort of his private car was inspecting the fishing tackle he would employ for ten days of plying Gulf waters for the elusive tarpon. "The President flexed the rods, oiled the reels, wound the lines and fondled the lures of a fisherman's outfit, which had cost American taxpayers more than $2,500,000 in the last four years. Tons of the finest fighting craft and thousands of the fighting men of the American Navy have been massed so that one man in a battered hat might find a few hours' escape from official cares."

With the amount of flak the president was taking, it was sometimes hard to believe that this was the same man who had won a landslide victory the previous November. Some of it was close to home. Senator Sherman Minton told FDR in March that he had sat next to his "adoring" cousin Alice Roosevelt Longworth at dinner and that "she has you measured already for your shirt—brown sleeves, black body and red tail." John R. Tunis wrote him in June that he had written a book on the 1911 class at Harvard, to which he belonged, and that statistics showed "that the most disliked person among this body of graduates was F. D. Roosevelt, 1904."

That did not surprise Roosevelt. The last place he expected support from was Harvard. In any event, he had grown a thicker skin to protect him from the daily barbs. His motto now was borrowed from Joe Kennedy: Don't get mad, get even.

A couple of weeks after the 1936 election, John L. Lewis came to the White House, all puffed up from having contributed to the president's victory with his half-million dollars and the vote-getting power of Labor's Nonpartisan League. When you gave substantial money you were entitled to something in return. Lewis told the president that he expected to be consulted often on questions of national policy, and that the office of secretary of labor should be seen as a patronage plum for the CIO wing of the labor movement. It was at this point that FDR realized that the fellow who had agreed to everything he said at their first meeting, with the coal operators, had become a megalomaniac.

John L. Lewis was in the headlines in 1937, the year of the sit-down strike and labor fever. This was the natural outcome of the Wagner Act, which was declared constitutional that April, and which gave every worker the right to join a union. Thus the workers struck the automobile and steel industries to avail themselves of that right.

The sit-down strike proved to be an effective weapon against such open-shop industrial empires as General Motors. You could strike a plant that made one part and cripple the company. In December 1936, in the company town of Flint, Michigan, the GM workers laid down their tools and refused to leave the plant.

This was a shocking thing to many Americans, including two members of the president's cabinet. Jim Farley felt that the strikers had no more right to remain in the factories than his cook had, if she went on strike, to stay in the kitchen and prevent someone else from making the meal. In January, Jack Garner had his hottest argument yet with FDR when he told him that the sit-down strike was a brazen defiance of the law. "I couldn't get those strikers out without bloodshed," FDR said. "Then John L. Lewis is a bigger man than you are if you can't find some way to cope with this," Garner angrily replied. The strikers, coupled with the court-packing plan, permanently soured Garner on FDR.

But the president was farsighted enough to see that it would only make matters worse to call out the troops and battle it out with the strikers. As he told Frances Perkins, "Well, it is illegal, but what law are they breaking? The law of trespass, and that is about the only law that could be invoked. And what do you do when a man trespasses on your property? Sure, you can order him off. You get the sheriff to order him off if he tries to pitch a tent in your field without your permission. If he comes on your place to steal, why you have him for theft, of course. But shooting is out and killing a lot of people because they have violated the law of trespass somehow offends me. I just don't see that as the answer. The punishment doesn't fit the crime. There must be another way."

In Michigan, Governor Frank Murphy felt the same way. As the son and grandson of Irish rebels, and as the former mayor of Detroit, who had seen the ravages of the depression in the working class, he was in sympathy with the strikers and refused to use force. "I'm not going down in history as bloody Murphy," he said.

In February, with both the state and the federal power lukewarm about breaking the strike, General Motors agreed to recognize the United Auto Workers as a bargaining agent. Soon all the other automakers but Ford fell into line, and in March U.S. Steel also agreed to comply. It was perhaps the greatest victory ever won by American labor, and it reinforced John L. Lewis's image as the man who never lost. But it was won only because FDR had the wisdom not to take action against a kind of strike that would later be declared illegal by the Supreme Court, for in 1939 the sit-down strike was outlawed, with Charles Evans Hughes writing the opinion: "The employees have the right to strike but they have no license to commit acts of violence or to seize their employer's plants."

That June, when the CIO was striking the holdout steel companies such as Republic and Youngstown, FDR got fed up with Lewis and made his famous "a plague on both your houses" remark; he sent word to Lewis that he had not meant the CIO but only those industries that would not comply with collective bargaining and those labor groups that engaged in violence. Unappeased, Lewis replied in a Labor Day radio broadcast: "It ill behooves one who has supped at labor's table and who has been sheltered in labor's house to curse with equal fervor and fine impartiality both labor and its adversaries when they become locked in a deadly embrace." By the time he had made that talk, the CIO had reached a membership of 3.7 million, surpassing the AFL. It had a rich treasury of dues and political clout, thanks to the administration of Franklin D. Roosevelt.

In 1937, FDR's thoughts turned on who would follow him. On a beautiful moonlit night in May aboard the *Potomac,* he told Morgenthau: "I cannot help but think who will carry on as my successor after 1940. Take Wallace, he thinks the same as we do but he is a poor administrator."

"He certainly is," Morgenthau chimed in.

"Governor Earle [of Pennsylvania] might do."

"I thought he had a lot of women problems."

"He has, but he's getting over them. His heart is in the right place as far as people go. Take Herbert Lehman, he might do, but he hasn't got a sense of humor. He would just die if he was President, from worry."

"What about Farley," Morgenthau asked, "will he run for governor [of New York]?"

"I don't think so," FDR said, "because I don't think he could be elected.

Nor could he be elected President. The country's not ready for a Catholic."

Morgenthau asked about Hull and FDR said "he is too sick a man," but mentioned Barkley as a possibility. Then he said, "Now I have got somebody who has a good voice on the radio, popular with the people and thinks the way I do." That was Harry Hopkins, the only one the president got enthusiastic about.

Morgenthau was sure that FDR wanted him to say, "Well, of course, Franklin, you are the only person who can succeed yourself," but he did not rise to the bait.

Prodded by Morgenthau, FDR wanted to go after the economic royalists who did not pay their fair share of taxes. There were still too many loopholes in the tax laws, such as sales between husbands and wives and the creation of multiple trusts. The president's old friend Grenville Clark and his wife had sixteen such trusts. Jules S. Bache showed no taxable income for 1936, but his Canadian trust had an income of more than $1 million. Jacob Schick had become a British subject through naturalization in Canada, and had formed a corporation in the Bahamas. Mrs. Du Pont Ross paid her husband a salary for managing her estate, and took a tax deduction as a business expense. Alfred P. Sloan of General Motors had a yacht that was owned by one of his holding companies, and he rented the yacht and deducted the rent as a business expense.

Incensed, the president told Morgenthau on May 17: "I want to name names. I am going on the air and tell this story. I want a list of the people who formed foreign corporations. . . . In the words of Theodore Roosevelt, my spear knows no brother. I don't know who's on this list—I don't care. It may have been Barney Baruch. Who is Incorporated Yacht?"

"Sloan," one of Morgenthau's aides said.

"I didn't know it was Sloan," FDR said. "It might have been Baruch."

A few days later he asked Morgenthau, "What's the name of the young fellow who's doing this investigation up in New York?"

"Do you mean Tom Dewey?"

"Yes, how would he be [to investigate tax evasion]?"

"He'd be magnificent, but I doubt whether you can get him."

"Well, that's the kind of fellow I want."

But as Senator Ashurst had once said, in politics you sometimes went where the roller skates took you, and in the fall of 1937 they took Roosevelt right into a recession. This was after he had decided to cut deficit spending and balance the budget; he had that June made big cuts in work relief programs. On October 19, 17 million shares changed hands on the New York Stock Exchange, and prices skidded. Between September 15 and December 15 about 1.8 million people lost their jobs. It was like 1933 all over again.

Roosevelt was convinced the big money interests were behind the recession rather than his own curtailing of deficit spending. He told Ickes it was an "unconscious conspiracy" to force the hand of the administration. His advisers were split between savers like Morgenthau and spenders like

Tom Corcoran and Harry Hopkins. Marriner Eccles, a governor of the Federal Reserve Bank, advised countercyclical spending, a new idea popularized by the British economist John Maynard Keynes.

Roosevelt didn't know whether to spend or to save, and was as touchy as a man with a bunion. On November 2, when Morgenthau told him they were headed toward another depression, he got "very excited, very dictatorial and very disagreeable." The next day at cabinet he exploded: "I am sick and tired of being told by the Cabinet, by Henry and by everybody else for the last two weeks what's the matter with the country and nobody suggests what I should do."

At lunch with Morgenthau on November 8, he was so despondent that he speculated about a fascist takeover in the United States. Four or five people might get together, talk it over, and decide they had to have their own man in Washington. About two thousand men had decided to go on strike against the government. American industrialists had concluded that they had to get their own man in the White House.

The president called a special session of Congress in November, but it was a shambles, achieving nothing except another filibuster of the antilynching bill.

On December 6, he left for a fishing trip in Florida. He told Ickes that he was going to let Congress alone to find out whether or not it could run the government without his help, and Ickes wondered whether he was going through some kind of spiritual crisis. He was so listless and unlike himself, a man who had given up. Part of it, of course, was an infected jaw, which made them cut the trip short.

The downturn gave economic royalists a chance to snipe. Baruch and others said punitive taxes had broken business confidence. After all the billions spent and all the acronym agencies, after all the rhetoric of renewal, there were still 10 million Americans unemployed, and people were hurting.

At the December 30 cabinet meeting, FDR looked straight at Jack Garner and said, referring to the message he would deliver to Congress in a few days: "Jack, I am going to reassert leadership." Garner asked whether he had ever given it up, and FDR replied that he had put it on the shelf because he was tired.

"You were afraid, Mr. President," Garner retorted.

FDR repeated that it was fatigue.

"Before you went to Florida, Mr. President," Garner persisted, "you were both scared and tired. You were willing to give up on taxation, on holding companies. . . ."

Ickes was stunned. He had never seen anyone talk like that to the president.

The same feeling of powerlessness in the face of economic forces such as the recession extended to foreign affairs. Distant America had little bearing on matters in Europe and the Far East. Roosevelt read the dispatches from his envoys and wondered where the world was heading.

In England, King Edward VIII had abdicated in favor of his brother, George VI, married his paramour, and been given the title of duke of Windsor. Ambassador Bingham saw the change as healthy, writing FDR that "the Duke of Windsor was surrounded by the pro-German cabal and many people here suspected that Mrs. Simpson was actually in German pay. I think that is unlikely and that her strong pro-German attitude was the result of flattering propaganda. However, the whole crowd has been cleared out. The Court has become respectable again, and the situation from the dynastic end is immeasurably improved." (In other words, Bingham had been told that Edward VIII could not have children.)

The news from Germany was disquieting. In Paris, Bill Bullitt reported that "Austria is likely to be left hanging on the bough to be plucked at an appropriate moment." In March, Mayor Fiorello La Guardia of New York City said that the New York World's Fair ought to have an exhibit called the Chamber of Horrors featuring a certain brownshirted fanatic who was trying to embroil the world in war. The German press called La Guardia a Jew Communist whoremonger, and Cordell Hull had to offer formal apologies. At cabinet, FDR turned with a grin to Hull and asked: "What would you say if I should say that I agreed completely with La Guardia?" Hull said it wouldn't be so bad if he hadn't replied to the remarks in the German press. FDR touched his left wrist lightly with the first two fingers of his right hand and said: "We will chastise him like that."

In May, the president signed a new Neutrality Act, with no date of expiration. Goods would be sold to belligerents only on a cash-and-carry basis, and arms could not be carried on American ships.

On the night of July 7, Japanese and Chinese soldiers fought at the Marco Polo bridge, ten miles west of Peiping. It was the start of an undeclared war, with the Japanese pouring troops into China. In Tokyo, Ambassador Joseph Grew saw how popular the war was, how everyone seemed to have the Banzai! spirit, and wondered where the Japanese isolationists were.

FDR helped China by lending it money against the gold and silver it had stockpiled in the United States. While struggling with the recession at home, he was forced to devote more attention to foreign affairs. On October 5 in Chicago, the capital of midwestern isolationism, he gave his celebrated "quarantine" speech: "When an epidemic of physical disease starts to spread, the community approves and joins in quarantine of the patients in order to protect the health of the community against the spread of the disease."

What this meant no one knew. The next day at a press conference, Ernest Lindley asked: "You say there isn't any conflict between what you outline and the Neutrality Act. They seem to be on opposite poles to me and your assertion does not enlighten me."

FDR: "Put your thinking-cap on, Ernest."

Lindley: "I have been for some years. They seem to be at opposite poles. How can you be neutral if you are going to align yourself with one group of nations?"

FDR: "What do you mean, 'aligning'? You mean a treaty? . . . There are a lot of methods in the world that have never been tried yet."

Lindley: "But, at any rate, that is not an indication of neutral attitude— 'quarantine the aggressors' and 'other nations of the world.' "

FDR: "I can't give you any clue to it. You will have to invent one."

Cordell Hull felt the quarantine statement had been a grave mistake, setting their campaign to create an aware public opinion back six months and giving the isolationist a made-to-order target. United against the speech, the isolationist coalition was formed, made up of pacifist groups, labor unions, the clergy, the socialists and other leftists, and sections of Congress. Two members of the House, Fish and Tinkham, threatened to start impeachment proceedings. The AFL resolved that "American labor does not wish to be involved in European or Asiatic wars." A campaign was launched to secure 25 million signatures to a "Keep America Out of War" petition. Magazines featured articles with titles such as "The War Boom Begins" and "We Needn't Go to War." Some New Dealers were themselves isolationists. Jerome Frank, later chairman of the SEC, wrote that it was hopeless to undertake "the task of helping Europe or of promoting world order."

Given the vehemence of isolationist reaction, FDR rode out the storm. There was no use calling the charge to find that no one was following. Privately, he had wanted to draw up an actual quarantine line beyond which Japan would be told she would not be permitted to trade or expand if she continued her conquest of China. On several occasions, he asked Under Secretary of State Sumner Welles to trace on the large map of the Pacific he had on a stand in the rear of his office the various lines he had under consideration. This took place during the summer, before the quarantine speech. Thus the speech was not a trial balloon to test public opinion, or a groping for a new policy, but a definite intention of isolating Japan, which he was unable to carry out owing to the isolationist clamor.

FDR at this point was eager to go further than public opinion would let him. "I am really worried about world affairs," he wrote a friend on November 10. "The dictator nations find their bluffs are not being called and that encourages other nations to play the same game. Perhaps you will be back in uniform yet—and thank the Lord the Navy and incidentally the Army have made a lot of real progress in the past four years."

On December 12, six Japanese planes attacked the U.S. gunboat *Panay* and the three oil tankers it was convoying in the upper Yangtze River. The *Panay* was sunk, and passengers trying to escape in lifeboats were strafed, and strafed again on shore as they tried to hide. Three Americans were killed, and many were wounded. To Ambassador Joseph Grew, it seemed clear that the Japanese government could no longer control its military. He was coming to hate the word "sincerity" because the Tokyo papers said that hostilities in China must continue because China refused to show "sincerity." What this meant was "if I hit you and you hit back, you are obviously insincere."

At the December 17 cabinet meeting, FDR said that the attack had been deliberate. The Japanese had three motives, he said. In the first place, an arrogant and unrebuked assault on the United States would impress the Chinese with the power and strength of Japan. In the second place, Japan wanted to make it uncomfortable for any Western power to stay in the Yangtze or in any other part of China. In the third place, Japan wanted to force all Westerners out of China.

Secretary of the Navy Claude Swanson, reflecting the views of the Navy brass, wanted to go to war at once. It was odd, thought Ickes, to see this most feeble member of the cabinet, his voice so thick it could hardly be understood, taking such a belligerent stance. When he said that if we were going to chastise Japan, this was the time to do it, FDR replied, "Claude, I am a pacifist."

When Ambassador Makoto Saito was received by Hull, he arrived looking downcast and appearing to be humbled, and apologized for "a very grave blunder." On December 23, the Japanese government met Hull's four demands: apologies, indemnities of $2.2 million, the punishment of the officers involved, and assurances for the future.

And yet what could America do by itself? The British were completely inert. When FDR invited British Prime Minister Neville Chamberlain to come to the United States for talks in September, he declined, arguing that there was little prospect of improving the situation in the Far East.

FDR kept trying to involve the British, and in January 1938 he proposed a plan thought up by Sumner Welles to convene the entire diplomatic corps to the White House to hear the president urge upon them world peace, the reduction of armaments, and equal access to raw materials. This message could be delivered on January 22, but only with British support.

Welles informed the British ambassador, Sir Ronald Lindsay, on January 11, and the next day Sir Alexander Cadogan, permanent under secretary of the Foreign Office, recorded in his diary that "Roosevelt has wild ideas of formulating a world settlement! But must know by *Monday* (Jan. 17) whether we agree he should go ahead. . . . This is not the way to transact business!" Horace Wilson (Chamberlain's éminence grise), Cadogan went on, "was very anti-Roosevelt . . . but it is important not to break with R." Chamberlain arrived that evening at six, summoned back from the country. "He hates R's idea," Cadogan wrote, "but I tried to point out that we mustn't snub him."

Chamberlain at once rejected the plan, for he was in the midst of offering Mussolini de jure recognition of the conquest of Ethiopia in return for a pledge that he would contribute to friendly relations. The lineup of democracies that FDR proposed might be used by the dictators as a pretext for a break.

Roosevelt and Hull were shocked to learn to what lengths Chamberlain would go to appease the dictators. On January 15, Hull told Sir Ronald Lindsay that de jure recognition would be "capitalized by desperado nations," and "the repercussions in the Pacific area might be serious in many ways." But in view of Chamberlain's refusal to go along, and of Hull's dislike of a plan drafted by his enemy, Sumner Welles, Roosevelt agreed on January 17 to postpone it, although adding that he was gravely concerned by recognition, which would encourage Japanese aggression and offend American public opinion.

Pressed by his foreign secretary, Anthony Eden, Chamberlain replied on January 21 in a more conciliatory tone that the president's plan would be welcomed, and that recognition would be granted Italy only as part of a general settlement. But by this time, owing to Hull's continued resistance, FDR had lost interest in the plan, and the British lost an early opportunity to involve the United States in a European settlement. Anthony Eden resigned over the Italian policy, but FDR curiously came around to it, which showed his shifting feelings on appeasement. Welles told Sir Ronald Lindsay on January 22 that "the President regarded recognition as an unpleasant pill which we should both have to swallow, and he wished that we should both swallow it together."

When recognition took place in April 1938, in exchange for Italian promises to pull their troops out of Spain, FDR released a statement commending the treaty, on the ground that it showed that peace could be preserved by negotiations. "I very much regret that the President made any such statement," Ickes commented. ". . . These negotiations are contrary to the convictions of the liberals in Great Britian. Chamberlain, the Astors, et al., are more or less profascist in sentiment, and it was this group that particularly wanted to come to terms with Mussolini. I think this was an unnecessary and regrettable act on the President's part."

In midstream, halfway through his second term, FDR appeared to be sinking. Partly, it was the lassitude of office, the feeling that in effect his presidency was over. "The next two years really don't count," he told Morgenthau over lunch on January 16, 1938. "They are over the dam. I think you and I can get by with another three billion deficit in the '40 and '41 [budgets] and then it will be up to whoever succeeds us which will most likely be either a conservative Democrat or a conservative Republican. The thing for us to be thinking about is what will happen after we are out . . . the next Administration will most likely begin to economize and slash expenditures and the chances are we will have chaos as a result. . . . After they have failed they will most likely send for us to come back and solve the problem."

He has made up his mind that he is just going to mark time for the next two years, Morgenthau reflected, and is already beginning to think what he is going to do when he is out and how he is going to plan to get back the way Cleveland did.

Harold Ickes thought FDR was "a beaten man" who had lost all his fight
and courage and was just letting things drift. There seemed to be no third-
term hopes. Jim Farley told anyone who would listen that he couldn't imagine anyone so crazy as to want another term. "I do a lot of little things for
Mrs. Roosevelt," he said, "and she is always saying that she wants this or
that done before Franklin gets out. So I think she is counting on it. Of course
there might be a war that would change the situation but if there isn't I
doubt he would permit himself to be renominated."

In fact, FDR at this point had picked his successor. It was Harry Hopkins,
although that was another problem, because he had been so sick. His wife,
Barbara, had died of cancer in October 1937, and two months later he went
into the Mayo Clinic where doctors removed two-thirds of his stomach to
cut away a cancerous growth. Reporters were told it was ulcers. When he
came back to Washington in the spring of 1938, he had a long talk with the
president, who told him he was disinclined to run again. But who else was
there? Hull was too old, Ickes was too irascible, Farley was a Catholic with
no knowledge of foreign affairs, and he did not want Wallace.

Of course Hopkins had liabilities, FDR went on. He had been divorced,
but so had other candidates, such as Jim Cox in 1920, while Grover Cleveland had survived the scandal of a bastard. There was also his health. The
presidency was a killing job. He himself would have been able to shed the
brace from his left leg had he not been persuaded by Al Smith to return to
public life prematurely in 1928. But FDR thought Harry was the best man
and would make him secretary of commerce and for the moment keep him
back a little.

Privately, Hopkins had his doubts, for even if his health improved, he
knew he couldn't finesse the divorce. Earlier, he had gone to Jerome Frank,
who acted as his personal lawyer, and said: "Look, I want to tell you about
my divorce. My first wife was very vindictive and she wouldn't give me a
divorce except in New York. There was only one ground: adultery. She
wouldn't agree unless my second wife be named as correspondent. That's
the way it was done. Now, that wouldn't look so good, would it?"

"No," Frank agreed. "Talk about an adulterer and a lover in the White
House wouldn't sound so good."

In any event, at the start of 1938, Roosevelt had a sort of "what's the use!"
attitude. He felt misunderstood. He had saved the capitalist system and the
businessmen were down on him. Bernie Baruch had testified before the
Senate Committee on Unemployment that the recession was the New Deal's
fault. FDR felt like reading him out of the party. That kind of criticism reminded him of the doctor who was called into consultation in the case of a
man who was about to die of a large tumor. The doctor's only comment was
"What an extraordinary and wonderful tumor! I must write a paper about
it."

Most businessmen had the intelligence of eighth-grade schoolboys as far
as government was concerned. FDR had asked one of them, "What do you

think should be done about the farm tenancy and sharecropper problem?" The man said he could see no relation between that and business until FDR pointed out that if you had 20 million sharecroppers that was a lot of people with no purchasing power to buy the products of industry.

He had called in Alfred Sloan of General Motors and told him about a system of communal land cultivation that might be adapted to the 3 million inhabitants of the Appalachian Mountains, but Sloan just sat there with his mouth hanging open and said he had never heard of such a thing. He had even given lunch to Henry Ford, who had done his best to wreck the NRA, and gave him a hundred chances to offer suggestions, but all Ford could talk about was the small factories on the River Rouge where the workers had enough land to grow part of their food supply. It was really discouraging to think that when the economic royalists were unrestricted they had brought on the worst crash in history, and had to be lifted out of the slough of despond by the very government they were now condemning.

As if on cue, in mid-March 1938 a scandal in the highest reaches of economic royalty broke to confirm FDR's misgivings. William O. Douglas, chairman of the SEC, told the president that one of his Groton and Harvard classmates, Richard Whitney, was in big trouble. "No, not Dickie Whitney!" FDR exclaimed. He clung to the idea that there were standards, and that if you had gone to Groton and Harvard and if you had wealth and position, you met those standards.

Richard Whitney had been governor, vice president, and president of the New York Stock Exchange. With his lordly presence and ample girth, a Porcellian charm dangling from his gold watchchain, he was the champion of Wall Street's battle against government regulation.

But Richard Whitney was a crook. He lost so much money in Florida peat humus and other equally brilliant investments that he began borrowing. He pledged his customers' securities, without authority, as collateral for bank loans. He embezzled the funds of the New York Stock Exchange pension fund, of which he was a trustee, and of the New York Yacht Club, of which he was treasurer. His fellow stock exchange members and his brother George, a Morgan partner, covered for him, but finally he was expelled from the exchange for misconduct and arrested and charged with grand larceny. He served five years in Sing Sing, where he played on the baseball team.

Who was the real traitor to his class, Roosevelt or Whitney? When J. P. Morgan testified in the subsequent investigation, and was asked, "Do you know Richard Whitney?" he replied: "I knew him." The past tense amounted to exile from polite society. After his arrest, the stock exchange mended its ways, realizing that it was better to work with the law than against it. It accepted a paid president and three members of the stockholding public on its board of governors.

FDR wanted the businessmen to understand that if they continued to attack him he was going to attack back. He remained the champion of the people against entrenched forces. In 1938, with the NRA men like Hugh

Johnson and Donald Richberg gone, who had wanted to work with big business and go easy on monopolistic practices, FDR was listening to the anti-big-business gospel according to Brandeis, which reached him via Tom Corcoran. Thurman Arnold, a maverick lawyer who had been mayor of Laramie, Wyoming, was placed in charge of the antitrust section of the Justice Department and went on a trust-busting spree. He went after the American Medical Association to prevent it from crushing group health experiments. He went after the construction industry and had grand juries handing out indictments almost daily. Businessmen were saying: "Good God, you prosecute us for doing what the NRA prosecuted us for not doing."

Not only were the businessmen against him, but his Democratic majority in Congress was as incapable of mending its splits as Humpty Dumpty. Senator William H. Smathers of New Jersey warned FDR that many of his Democratic colleagues were heading back to conservatism. "They resent, feel hurt, and possibly a little jealous," he said, "that you have not asked their advice on important matters but on the contrary—as they put it—have relied for your advice upon 'two kids, Corcoran and Cohen, who never ran for public office, who are impractical and theorists.' "

In Congress, it was open season on FDR. Burton Wheeler in a speech in Boston that February said: "I do not have a son who was in the insurance business, nor has one of my sons married a Du Pont heiress." In rebuttal, information was leaked to Drew Pearson that one of Wheeler's sons had a good job in the Justice Department, while two others had summer jobs in Glacier National Park, where Wheeler himself had a summer home on federal land; his son-in-law had a job with the SEC, his sister was his congressional secretary, and her son, Wheeler's nephew, was an investigator for the Bituminous Coal Commission; so much for nepotism.

It was with Congress in a pugnacious mood that FDR tried to get his reorganization bill passed that March. The point of the bill was to streamline the federal government in order to limit the influence of Congress on decisions made by administrative agencies. It wasn't only the dangers of the pork barrel, it was that some congressional leaders became fixtures who spent their entire careers watching presidents come and go while they, in reality, conducted the business of government. For these men, who became chairmen of important committees, every administration was no more than a skirmish with a fresh set of troops who had to be fought off but would eventually go away. Thus the bill was in fact a request for Congress to reform itself, which was like asking a riverboat gambler to turn in his marked cards.

The debate on this rather technical and undramatic bill turned into a highly charged test of the New Deal and FDR's prestige. All the pent-up resentments in Congress were unleashed. The bill, said Senator Josiah Bailey of North Carolina, would give FDR "all the powers of a dictator." Carter Glass of Virginia said FDR had conspired with "the CIO social desperados" to foment class hatred.

"So who is going to do it?" Wheeler asked. "Some professor or some clerk in the department is going to do it ... they are going to say to my people in Montana, 'We are going to abolish the Bureau of Indian Affairs.'... Although they have never set foot on an Indian reservation in their lives, they are going to sit down in some office in Washington and tell members of the Senate and of the House what ought to be done."

The Senate passed the bill in late March, 49 to 42, but in a rare political flub FDR hurt his chances in the House. Vacationing in Warm Springs on March 29, he told reporters that the Senate vote "proved that the Senate cannot be purchased by organized telegrams based on direct misrepresentation." As Congressman Clifford Hope of Kansas put it: "The President didn't help his bill any by his remarks about the Senate not having been bought. That really stirred the animals up."

The fight in the House was the hottest in half a century. Farley warned FDR that in spite of a large Democratic majority the vote would be close. If he lost this one, he would lose control of the party.

Specific measures, such as the creation of a Department of Welfare under Harry Hopkins, were denounced. It "would throw our government into a permanent relief business," said Congressman Lyle Boren of Oklahoma. The assurances that presidential power would not increase, said Congressman Dewey Short of Missouri, were "not worth a continental when they come from men who care no more for their word than a tomcat cares for a marriage license in a back alley on a dark night."

On April 8, by a vote of 204 to 196, the bill was recommitted—it was dead. Its opponents had created a successful anti-Roosevelt coalition. April 8, 1938, may well have been the low point of the Roosevelt presidency. He had been beaten on the court plan and on the reorganization bill. It seemed like the end of Rooseveltian reform and of the New Deal.

Another way of attacking the administration in Congress was through committee hearings. In 1938, Texas Congressman Martin Dies cranked up the first committee on un-American activities, which soon became a headline-grabbing anti–New Deal forum. Dies had been a Roosevelt supporter in 1936, but turned against him when a big dam project for his district was turned down. He originated the techniques later brought into full bloom by Senator Joseph McCarthy—unfounded charges, lack of substantial evidence, use of guilt by association, denial of opportunity for the accused to answer the charges, and repeated public assertions of the extreme danger of a largely imaginary threat.

Dies, whom Harold Ickes called "the outstanding zany in our political history," picked mostly New Deal targets. The Federal Theater and Writers projects, he said, were "a hotbed for Communists." Charges that Frances Perkins was protecting West Coast labor leader Harry Bridges from deportation led to an attempt to impeach her. Another accusation was that twelve of the TVA's 3500 employees were members of the Communist party. Congressman J. Parnell Thomas, a member of the Dies Committee, said that "in some respects it [the Fifth Column] is synonymous with the New Deal, so the surest way of removing the Fifth Column from our shores is to remove the New Deal from the seat of government."

The charges were often absurd, such as having belonged to the Committee to Boycott Chinese Silk and Popularize American Cotton, or some equally obscure group. But there was in fact some Communist infiltration of government departments and of the CIO. John P. Frey, the secretary-treasurer of the Metal Trades Department, AFL, a loyal New Dealer and a friend of FDR's going back to the Navy days, provided the Dies Committee with evidence of a Communist cell inside the Department of Agriculture, centered on Nathan Witt and John Abt, who had served as counsel for the Senate Civil Liberties Committee, which exposed labor espionage and union busting—Frey had photostats of their dues payments to the party. Communist infiltration of the CIO was cheerfully acknowledged by John L. Lewis, whose general counsel, the resourceful Lee Pressman, was a party member. Thus there were a few pellets of truth in Dies's buckshot, fired at FDR in an election year.

In spite of these attacks, the New Deal was still kicking, for after the April 8 low point there was an upturn in June when Congress passed a $3.75 billion spending program. Morgenthau had threatened to resign when FDR told him he was going back to public works and deficit spending. "Well, I am going to go ahead and take care of the unemployed, no matter what it costs," FDR said. Morgenthau told him it did not do any good to yell. "The trouble with you," FDR said, "is that you are piqued and sore because you have not been consulted."

"I'm awfully afraid that the cards are stacked against us," Morgenthau told his aides. "They had just stampeded him during the week I was away. He was completely stampeded. They stampeded him like cattle."

On June 14 the Fair Labor Standards Act, the final panel in the great New Deal triptych made up of collective bargaining, Social Security, and wages and hours regulation, was passed, ending a two-year battle. No workers could thenceforth be employed at less than twenty-five cents per hour (to be raised to forty cents over seven years), for more than a forty-four-hour week (to be dropped to forty hours in three years). The provision against employing children under sixteen rewarded the efforts of all those who had long fought to abolish child labor. The bill covered about 12 million workers. Though the twenty-five-cent minimum seemed pitifully low, and was a compromise with the southern bloc, it brought immediate pay increases to 750,000 workers. This was the last great reformist measure of the New Deal, which had now met most of its stated goals.

Late that spring, John M. Carmody, the head of the Rural Electrification Administration, was called to the White House. Lawrence Camp was there, who had been chosen to oppose Senator Walter George in the Democratic primary in Georgia. In the president's office, the map of Georgia had been spread out on an easel, and the town of Barnesville had been marked, where an REA project was nearing completion.

FDR said that if Senator George was in Maine he would vote exactly the way Senator Wallace White of Maine was voting, as a Republican on all the issues the president cared about. He wouldn't mind if Senator George had been elected as a Republican, but he'd been elected as a Democrat, on the platform that the president was putting into action. FDR said he would go down to Barnesville and speak at the dedication of this REA project, just before the primary.

On June 22, Senator Josh Lee of Oklahoma wrote FDR: "What would you think about bearing down on those who voted against your program, who are now patting you on the back in their campaigns, feeling for a soft place to stick a knife after elections? The vote on the Reorganization Bill might be a good one to use as an example or test of loyalty."

Two days later, in a fighting mood for the first time that year, FDR announced his intention to purge the party of conservatives. "Never before have we had so many Copperheads," he said in a fireside chat. "And you will remember that it was the Copperheads who, in the days of the War Between the States, tried their best to make Lincoln and his Congress give up the fight, let the nation remain split in two and return to peace—peace at any price.... As the head of the Democratic Party ... I feel that I have every right to speak in those few instances where there may be a clear issue between candidates for a Democratic nomination.... Do not misunderstand me. I certainly would not indicate a preference in a State primary merely because a candidate, otherwise liberal in outlook, had conscientiously differed with me on any single issue. I should be far more concerned about the general attitude of a candidate toward present day problems and his own inward desire to get practical needs attended to in a practical way."

The message was clear. FDR would inject himself into the primaries, which he did with unfortunate results. Voters resented outside interference in local politics. To use the president's own vocabulary, it wasn't cricket.

In Iowa, Senator Guy Gillette was marked for the ax. Harry Hopkins announced that if he was voting in his home state he would vote for Gillette's opponent. But the proxy fell flat, and Gillette was renominated and reelected.

During the summer, FDR traveled south, striking at entrenched bourbonism in three states. In Georgia he attended the REA ceremonies on the campus of the Barnesville Military Academy, where he publicly humiliated Senator George by lambasting him as he sat one row away. "First," FDR asked, "has the record of the candidate shown, while differing perhaps in details, a constant active fighting attitude in favor of the broad objectives of the party and of the government as they are constituted today; and secondly, does the candidate really, in his heart, deep down in his heart, believe in these objectives? ... I regret that in the case of my friend, Senator George, I cannot answer either of these questions in the affirmative." There were mixed boos and cheers. FDR shook hands with George, who said, "Mr. President, I want you to know that I accept the challenge." "Let's always be friends," replied FDR. In September, FDR's candidate Lawrence Camp ran a very bad third after former Governor Talmadge and Senator George, who was renominated and reelected.

After going fishing in Florida, FDR passed through Greenville, South Carolina, on his train and told a crowd of 15,000: "I like the way you look. You don't impress me as being people willing to work for fifty cents a day, as one of your senators has said." This was a dig at Cotton Ed Smith, but he too was renominated and reelected.

At Denton, on the Maryland Eastern Shore, FDR spoke of Senator Millard E. Tydings as one of "those in public life who quote the golden rule, but take no steps to bring it closer." FDR actually saved Tydings, who in the opinion of Maryland Assemblyman Alan Goldsborough could have been beaten by almost anyone but who won by 60,000 votes.

The purge's sole success was the defeat of House Rules Committee Chairman John O'Connor (Doc's brother) in New York, thanks to Tom Corcoran's string pulling. Instead of liberalizing the party, FDR had further split it. He rationalized his blunder by saying that the candidates had been too entrenched, that it was not the general public that had voted but only the enrolled Democrats, with all their personal and political associations.

In the November elections, the Republican-conservative coalition in both houses was further strengthened, for the Republicans gained eight seats in the Senate and almost doubled their number in the House, from 88 to 170. Still the Democrats kept their majority, and the president took comfort in the fact that he was the first two-term president since James Monroe who had not lost control of Congress before the end of his second term, although that was true in numbers only.

Nineteen thirty-eight saw the dictator powers boldly play the game of grab. In March, Nazi tanks rumbled into Austria. In China, the Japanese stepped up the pace of war. In Ethiopia, the Italians consolidated their gains. Franco was close to final victory in Spain. Russia was a question mark, absorbed in purges a world away from FDR's mild effort.

Ambassador Joseph E. Davies, Bullitt's successor, attended the trials in a state of bewilderment. Some of the high officials in the prisoner's dock had given lunches for him, and among the guests were the men who were now prosecutor and judge. Another defendant was a heart specialist who had treated Davies. It was a gruesome thing to watch. But Davies reported that, regardless of the trials, "these people here are going to wield an increasing and enormous force both in European and world affairs."

FDR was being a bit of a mugwump in foreign affairs. Why should he do more in Europe than the countries directly concerned, Germany's neighbors, who were doing nothing? He had the Wilsonian hatred of embroiling the United States in a war, of being dragged in by Europe once again. He truly did not want to get in.

For the moment he was waiting to see if the appeasement policy would work, and wrote John Cudahy, now the American envoy in Dublin, on March 9 that "if a Chief of Police makes a deal with the leading gangsters and the deal results in no more hold-ups, that Chief of Police will be called a great man—but if the gangsters do not live up to their word the Chief of Police will go to jail."

Also, he was getting no help from Cordell Hull and those around him at the State Department. Hull was inept and passive, tongue-tied at press conferences, incapable of making a reasoned presentation of a subject. He relied on stock responses, such as "We are looking into all phases of the situation," and Tennessee sayings, such as this one on Axis aggression: "When you're in a pissing contest with a skunk make sure you've got plenty of piss." All he really did was sign cables prepared by the country desk officers. Hull's inaction infuriated Harold Ickes. In March, he refused to issue passports to an American ambulance unit that wanted to go to Spain on the Loyalist side. "This makes me ashamed," Ickes wrote.

Roosevelt was constantly prodding Hull. Why didn't he organize a relief program for Chinese civilians? Why didn't he hold the Japanese accountable for their looting of American-owned property in China? There was plenty of Japanese-owned property in the United States that could be held in escrow. "Enough said!" Why didn't Bill Phillips, the American ambassador in Rome, ask Mussolini to explain why eighty Italian planes and fifty pilots had been sent to Japan?

No one at State was making the case for a forceful policy against the dictators, though the case for isolationism was made ad nauseam. Adolf Berle, the brain truster and prodigy, now assistant secretary of state, actually tried to convince FDR that Hitler was Europe's best chance, writing him on September 1: "It is quite possible that this half-mad 'scourge of God' is the only instrument capable of re-establishing a race and economic unit which can survive and leave Europe in balance." Hitler was merely undoing the unsound work of Versailles, Berle said, and America should stay out of it.

FDR had sent Joe Kennedy to London, wanting him out of the country rather than lending his talents to the conservative wing of the party. He told Morgenthau that Kennedy was "a very dangerous man" and that "I have made arrangements to have Joe Kennedy watched hourly and the first time he opens his mouth and criticizes me, I will fire him." At the same time, he said he would miss Joe because of his stories. Right after his confirmation hearings he told FDR: "I was so surrounded by senators at yesterday's committee meeting that it reminded me of the time when I was head of Keith's [theaters]. Sophie Tucker was the headline attraction, but the number before her was a dwarf act. I went backstage just as Sophie was coming on, fighting her way through a storm of midgets. She flung up her arms and screamed at me: 'Mr. Kennedy, how can I perform when I am up to my neck in dwarfs?' I didn't know the answer then, but I do now. Senators are worse than dwarves."

Kennedy quickly placed himself in the front line of appeasers. Three days after getting his credentials he reported that he was "thoroughly convinced" that the United States "would be very foolish to try and mix in." In September he had to be warned by Hull not to give a speech saying that war was unthinkable and that no dispute was worth the life of a son or a brother, which was an appeal to Englishmen over the heads of their government and a tip-off to Hitler that he could go as far as he liked.

Kennedy reported Neville Chamberlain's muddled remarks: "He likened Germany to a boa constrictor that had eaten a good deal and was trying to digest the meal before taking on anything else." "It is easy to get into war but what have we proved after we are in." And, after a trip to Germany to see Hitler: "This really is not as much fun as shooting grouse."

Another factor in the State Department's attitude was that some of the top career men saw Bolshevism as a worse threat than Nazism and were so anti-Semitic that they did not object to Hitler's persecution of the Jews. Breckinridge Long, who would become assistant secretary of state in 1939, wrote in his diary that he was more concerned about a Bolshevik Germany than about Hitler. Jay Pierrepont Moffat, Groton and Harvard, and chief of the division of European affairs, favored a Japanese protectorate of China because the Japanese were anti-Communist. In 1934, when Ernst Hanfstaengl, Harvard 1909 and close to Hitler, was invited to be an aide at the Harvard commencement, Moffat was furious that "all the Jews in Christendom arose in protest" and advised the class marshal not to give in to Jewish pressure. But President Conant did not want Harvard used as a base to spread approval of the Nazi regime, and Hanfstaengl did not attend. Moffat had served in Warsaw, where he had met Soviet Foreign Minister Maxim Litvinov, writing that he had "the malevolent look of an untidy Jew."

Bill Bullitt's crude anti-Semitism was expressed in a letter to a State Department colleague describing Constantine Oumansky, Litvinov's press secretary and later Soviet ambassador to the United States, as "a wretched little kike. . . . It is perhaps only natural that we should find the members of that race more difficult to deal with than the Russians themselves."

Bullitt wrote the president poisonous letters that may have influenced his thinking, such as this one: "Daladier imparted to me a fact so horrifying yesterday that I did not dare put it in a cable. The counter-espionage services of the French Army recently arrested nearly two hundred military spies. Of these spies, more than one-half proved to be genuine Jewish refugees from Germany—men and women who had been persecuted and expelled by Hitler—who for gain had entered his employ while enjoying French hospitality. Daladier personally was utterly horrified. He said that he did not dare publish the list of spy arrests because it would unleash such a fury against the Jews in France that the development of anti-Semitism might go to dreadful limits, and he believed that anti-Semitism was the vehicle for fascism. He finally said sadly, 'it really appears that on earth some races are *maudites* [doomed].' I believe you should instruct our counter-espionage services of all sorts to keep an especially vigilant eye on the Jewish refugees from Germany. Sad, isn't it?"

John Cudahy, the head of legation in Dublin, who had a few years earlier compared the Nazi Brownshirts to an American fraternal order, reported to the State Department that "the handling of the Jews by the present German government, which may be shocking and revolting, is from any realistic or logical approach a purely domestic matter and none of our concern. It is not stretching the analogy too far to say that Germany would have just as much warrant to criticize our handling of the negro minority if a race war between blacks and whites occurred in the United States."

Thus, both from the striped-pants, old-school-tie boys like Moffat and from the businessmen-envoys like Cudahy and Kennedy, FDR was getting the message that the United States should not interfere with Hitler's policies.

Congressman Emmanuel Celler said in February that in the handling of the Jewish refugee question the State Department had a "heartbeat muffled in protocol." Roosevelt at this point wanted to keep the problem off his doorstep, for if he let in a lot of Jewish refugees it would be used against him by the isolationists. He told Rabbi Stephen Wise on January 24 that the German Jews should be moved to some place like West Africa or Venezuela or Mexico. They ought to be given $1,000 a family, which American Jews could raise.

The president commissioned Isaiah Bowman, president of Johns Hopkins University and the author of *Limits of Land Settlement,* to make a study of possible sites. "What I am rather looking for," he wrote, "is the possibility of uninhabited or sparsely inhabited good agricultural lands to which Jewish colonies might be sent. . . . Do you think there is any possibility in Western Venezuela or on the Eastern slope of the Andes? . . . All this is merely for my own information because there are no specific plans on foot." Bowman recommended settlement planning on a world scale, spreading the refugees among Africa, South America, Asia, and Australia—every habitable continent, in fact, except the one they came from and North America. FDR also sent Bill Phillips to ask Mussolini to allow Jews to settle in the plateau region of southern Ethiopia. The Duce said that was impracticable, for the region was inhabited by a people unsympathetic to the Jews.

At the March 18 cabinet, however, FDR had a change of heart, saying that "after all, America has been a place of refuge for so many fine Germans in the period of 1848 and why couldn't we offer them again a place of refuge at this time?" He suggested combining the German and Austrian quotas, since Austria had been swallowed by Germany, which allowed about 27,000 Jews to reach the United States in 1939. Since this was done under existing norms, without legislation, it did not create political problems. He told Morgenthau, however, that to let in any more Jews he needed a good salesman, "a man good enough to sell bed-warming pans to the Indians."

Morgenthau and Ickes were the only two among the president's advisers who wanted to stop Hitler. "You know, Mr. President," Morgenthau told FDR on September 19, "if we don't stop Hitler now he is going on down through the Black Sea—then what? The fate of Europe for the next hundred years is settled. There is no question in my mind that if the countries around Europe would establish a blockade we could choke Germany to her knees and that is our last chance."

Ickes was sure "of the President's desire to avoid any embroilment in European quarrels." But FDR was outraged that France and England were about to let Hitler invade Czechoslovakia, after which they would "wash the blood from their Judas Iscariot hands."

When FDR secretly met British Ambassador Sir Ronald Lindsay on September 20, he told him that the Anglo-French note asking the Czechs to give up their Sudeten provinces was the most terrible, remorseless sacrifice that had ever been demanded of a state, and would provoke a highly unfavorable reaction in America. He did not know what to do to help. If he disapproved of German aggression he might encourage Czechoslovakia to vain resistance. "Several times in the conversation," Lindsay reported to Viscount Halifax, Eden's successor as foreign secretary, "he showed himself quite alive to the possibility that somehow or other in indefinable circumstances the United States might again find themselves involved in a European war. In that case he regarded it as almost inconceivable that it would be possible for him to send any American troops across the Atlantic even if his prestige were as high as it had been just after the 1936 elections. But it was just possible that if Germany were able to invade Great Britain with a considerable force, such a wave of emotion might arise, that an American army might be sent overseas."

At the end of September 1938, Europe was on the edge of war. The French had boxed up the stained glass windows of Chartres Cathedral. In London, gas masks were distributed.

FDR sent an appeal to Hitler, and Ickes thought that might have had some bearing on the Führer's decision to call a conference in Munich with Chamberlain and Daladier. "Good man," FDR wired Chamberlain on September 29. They agreed to the partition of Czechoslovakia, and for the moment war was averted, but Ickes reported that it seemed to be "a totally disgraceful thing and the President may want to dissociate himself from too close a connection."

Then on November 7, after the shooting in Paris of a minor German Foreign Office man by a young Jew whose parents had been deported to Poland, came Crystal Night—a wave of anti-Jewish rioting that left synagogues burned, shops looted, and Jews killed. This government-sponsored barbarism caused a shift in American public opinion. Ambassador

Hans Dieckhoff reported from Washington that "the respectable patriotic circles, which are thoroughly anti-Communist and, for the greater part, anti-Semitic in their outlook, also begin to turn away from us. . . . That men like Dewey, Hoover, Hearst, and many others who have hitherto maintained a cooperative reserve and have even, to some extent, expressed sympathy toward Germany, are now publicly adopting so violent and bitter an attitude against her is a serious matter."

On November 15, the president at his 500th press conference said: "I myself could scarcely believe that such things could occur in a twentieth-century civilization.

"With a view to gaining a first-hand picture of the current situation in Germany I asked the Secretary of State to order our ambassador in Berlin to return at once for report and consultation."

XVIII

When Bad Men Combine

When bad men combine, the good must associate; else they will fall,
one by one, an unpitied sacrifice in a contemptible struggle.

Edmund Burke

In 1939, the Roosevelt administration shifted its priority from domestic to foreign policy, and FDR regained his vigor and sense of purpose. Reform legislation was suspended as FDR sought to have Congress repeal the Neutrality Act. The patient process of weaning public opinion away from isolationism began. FDR had to begin by educating himself, for his thinking did not follow a straight line. To follow his twisting thoughts is like trying to follow a trout in a stream, which disappears under a rock, resurfaces, sends up bubbles, appears as a flash of color, and then glides out of sight. FDR in those months was in slow gestation, indefinite, uncertain, probing, still hoping that America could stay out of war but preparing for the worst.

In his January 4 message to Congress he said: "The world has grown so small and weapons of attack so swift, that no nation can be safe. . . . There are methods short of war, but stronger and more effective than mere words, of bringing home to aggressor governments the aggregate sentiments of our own people."

It did not take long for the public to learn what "methods short of war" were. On January 23, a Douglas twin-engine light bomber spun out of control while performing a low-altitude test and crashed in a parking lot at North American Aviation's plant outside Los Angeles, destroying nine cars and injuring ten bystanders. The pilot was killed trying to parachute out.

Pulled from the wreckage before it caught fire was an injured Frenchman, Paul Chemidlin. What was a Frenchman doing aboard the prototype of a military aircraft? As it happened, he was a member of a secret mission, headed by the financier Jean Monnet, in America to buy planes for the French air force.

FDR had handed this hot potato to Henry Morgenthau, Jr., because the War Department was in open rebellion, refusing to show the French anything. The president wanted them to buy American planes as long as they paid cash, and in January they started testing the various models. After the January 23 crash, it all came into the open and led to an investigation by the Senate Committee on Military Affairs. Morgenthau testified on January 27 and found some hostile senators who thought they were getting the run-around. Isolationists like Gerald Nye and Bennett Clark made it pretty hot for him. Why had the French been allowed to learn U.S. military secrets? Why was the president refusing to release the documents concerning the mission? Morgenthau felt he was taking the rap for the president, although it served a useful purpose, for the French got all the bombers and half the dive bombers they had ordered before September, and the orders woke up the aviation industry, laying the foundation for the great expansion to come.

For the moment, however, FDR had some serious missionary work to do in Congress. He had to engineer a turnabout of major proportions. For among the giants of the Senate and their disciples, isolationism was not a political position but an article of faith. Men like Edgar Borah, Hiram Johnson, Burton Wheeler, Gerald Nye, and Arthur Vandenberg had sat on the old Senate Munitions Committee of 1934–35, which had concluded that American intervention in the World War had made millions for the munitions makers.

Grafted to their distrust of the eastern financial establishment—the conviction that the Morgans and Du Ponts had duped Wilson into entering a European war—was a doctrine composed of various strands: the anti-British strand, the anti-Semitic strand, the "Fortress America" strand, as well as what might be called the "grouchy" strand, like the woman who thought she had rheumatism but could not locate the pain. The one unbudgeable bed-rock article of the doctrine was that American intervention in a European war was not only a mistake but an *evil*. You had to keep your distance from the corrupt Old World, from the boundary-grabbing nations and the leaders who did not keep their word. America had been founded as a breakaway movement from European values, and this was just another chapter in the same story. It was morally wrong to risk the contamination of everything they cherished to bail out bankrupt Europe.

Roosevelt had to convince them that the threat to Britain and France was also a threat to America, and that you could help your friends without getting your feet wet. On January 31 at 12:45 P.M., in the Executive Office at the White House, he met with the Senate Military Affairs Committee and gave them a survey of his world view. It was partly an attempt to patch things up with the Senate, and partly the wish to throw a good scare into them that would shake them from "the doctrine." As an example of the presidential "total view," a mixture of history, political savvy, and common sense, all done in that homely "just a bunch of the boys chewing the fat" style, it was one of FDR's better efforts.

After a prologue in which he linked the passing of the first Embargo Act to the Napoleonic Wars, FDR got down to basics: "About three years ago we got the pretty definite information that there was in the making a policy of world domination between Germany, Italy, and Japan. . . . There are two ways of looking at it. The first . . . is the hope that somebody will assassinate Hitler or that Germany will blow up from within; that somebody will kill Mussolini or he will get a bad cold in the morning and die. . . . The other attitude is that we must try to prevent the domination of the world. . . . Now it may come to you as a shock . . . but what is the first line of defense in the United States? . . . . The first line of defense in the Pacific is a series of islands, with the hope that through the Navy and the Army and the airplanes we can keep the Japanese from dominating the entire Pacific Ocean. . . .On the Atlantic, our first line is the continued independent existence of a very large group of nations. . . .

"But if this wild man . . . who conceives himself to be, as Schuschnigg said after the famous visit to Berchtesgaden, he said that Hitler, walking up and down the room for about eight hours, pounding the table and making speeches, only mentioned two people in his entire conversation, one was Julius Caesar and the other was Jesus Christ. He kept on talking about these people in such manner as to indicate that he believes himself to be a reincarnation of Julius Caesar and Jesus Christ. What can we do about a personality like that? We would call him a 'nut.'

"Now if he insists on going ahead to the westward . . . and the French and the British . . . decide to fight, then you come to a question of arms. . . . It is a fifty-fifty bet that they would be put out of business and that Hitler and Mussolini would win. . . . Then the next step, which Brother Hitler suggested in the speech yesterday, would be Central and South America. . . . Those are things you ought to regard. . . . Do not say it is chimerical; do not say it is just a pipe dream. Would any of you have said six years ago . . . that Germany would dominate Europe. . . . This is the gradual encirclement of the United States by the removal of our first lines of defense. . . ."

Senator Lewis of Illinois expressed the isolationist fear: "Did you intend to leave the impression," he asked, "that it was the duty of this Government to help protect and maintain the independence of these nations . . . by whatever effort may be necessary to do it?"

"No, no," FDR reassured him. "I probably saw more of the war in Europe than any living person. . . . Therefore, you may be quite sure that about the last thing that this country should do is ever to send an army to Europe again."

But Senator Nye, as he listened, wondered. It was shocking that FDR was determined to utterly ignore the neutrality law and consider France our first line of defense. All he could think was "get the uniforms ready for the boys."

Hiram Johnson, the California progressive who had proclaimed himself "happy as a clam at high tide" when FDR was elected, but who broke with him over the World Court, now thought that he cared no more for what would happen to the country in a war than the man in the moon. He had developed a dictator complex, and found in the Jews a class that cheered him on. But there were a very considerable number of others who thought in terms of America and America alone.

One of the senators at the meeting leaked a story quoting FDR as saying that America's frontier was on the Rhine, which was not an unreasonable distillation, although he had not said it in so many words. The story created an uproar, and at his February 3 press conference FDR called it "a deliberate lie." "Some boob got that off," he added. Nye thought FDR meant him, and had yet another reason to resent the president.

FDR was more ambivalent about helping the British than he cared to admit to the senators, for he was fed up with their pessimism and inability to help themselves. On February 10, Roger B. Merriman, the master of Eliot House at Harvard, sent him a letter from the Cambridge historian George Macaulay Trevelyan: "We are prepared to die in the last ditch at worst. . . . In any case nothing will be left of civilization except machinery. . . . The only thing that will stop a war coming pretty soon—since Hitler and Mussolini are both 'rabid' men—would be the United States letting them know that you will take part if they make aggression. But as I gather there is little chance of that, I think the prospects are very black indeed."

"I wish the British would stop this 'we who are about to die, salute thee' attitude," FDR replied. Lord Lothian, the new British ambassador, had recently been to see him, playing the same mournful tune—the British for a thousand years had been the guardians of Anglo-Saxon civilization, but the scepter of the world had dropped from their palsied fingers, and only the United States could snatch it up and save the world. FDR "got mad clear through" and told him that just so long as he and other Britishers like him took that attitude of complete despair, the British would not be worth saving anyway.

But Roosevelt never gave in to the kind of systematic anti-British feeling that obsessed advisers such as Adolf Berle, who said that the history of relations with England "was a history of half truth, broken faith, intrigue behind the back of the State Department, and even the President." At a dinner at the British embassy, the wife of the naval attaché was presiding, Lothian being a bachelor, and persisted in her patronizing way in talking about "out here"—as if she was in Egypt, Berle thought. He finally told her quite bluntly that you should not say "out here" when you were in the American capital. Her conduct reinforced his feeling that the English had learned nothing and forgotten nothing.

In spite of momentary annoyances, FDR continued to respect England. A great people, brought up in a great tradition, he told his doctor, Ross McIntire, one night at dinner at the White House. Often an irritating people by reason of a conviction of superiority so ingrained and perfected by time as to transcend mere egotism, and a shrewd hard-bargaining people, aggressive territorially and in every trade relation; nevertheless a steadfast people, a people kin to us by blood, holding the same ideals, and our assured ally in the event of war.

On March 15, the Germans overran Czechoslovakia, and on the following day FDR asked Senate Majority Leader Tom Connally to come to the White House. Connally found him in a bad mood, cursing the Neutrality Act: "If Germany invades a country and declares war, we'll be on the side of Hitler by invoking the act. If we could get rid of the arms embargo, it wouldn't be so bad."

Key Pittman, chairman of the Senate Foreign Relations Committee, had launched a substitute bill, but it wasn't getting anywhere because he was ill and inactive. "Perhaps I had better start with the House," FDR said. "The King and Queen of England are coming over in a few months to visit us and I'd like to have the arms embargo repealed before their arrival."

In mid-April, following up on his idea that a number of nations in Europe were America's first line of defense, FDR asked Hitler and Mussolini to refrain from attacking those nations, which he listed by name, numbering thirty-one. This attempt at personal diplomacy at a time when Hitler was already on the march may seem naive, but it was part of FDR's plan to educate Americans by proving that you could not negotiate with dictators.

On April 20, FDR saw Charles Lindbergh, who was just back from three years in Europe and had not yet become a leader and symbol of the "Keep America Out of War" movement. The Minnesota farm boy turned pilot was the son of a Swedish-born lawyer who, as a Republican member of the House, had opposed the U.S. entry into the World War and written a tome entitled *Why Is Your Country at War?* Isolationism was part of Lindbergh's heritage. It was in his blood. In his own country, Lindbergh had been both worshiped and victimized. The kidnapping and death of his son, and the outrageous conduct of the press (photographers broke into the morgue to snap the boy's corpse), made fame nauseating.

He and his wife, Anne, fled to Europe, visiting Russia and Germany. In Russia, he found mediocrity everywhere. Why, they let women into their air force! While in Germany, shepherded by the American military attaché, Colonel Truman Smith, they found "a sense of decency and values which in many ways is far ahead of our own." Hitler was "undoubtedly a great man, and I believe he has done much for the German people."

On three separate visits, the Germans showed Lindbergh their air force and let him fly their planes. He became an unpaid but all the more convincing tout for German invincibility in the air. In September 1938 he briefed Joe Kennedy, backing up the ambassador's view that the British would get clobbered. A month later, on October 18, two and a half weeks after Munich, Lindbergh was back in Berlin. Ambassador Hugh R. Wilson, soon to be recalled, gave a stag dinner for him, and invited Goering, who handed Lindbergh a small red box. It was the Service Cross of the Order of the German Eagle with the Star, a high decoration for civilians, awarded to "Lindy" for his service to aviation. Taken aback, he accepted, not wanting to be rude to a high German official while a guest in the American embassy. Also, he was a vain man, protesting that he disliked all the attention, but secretly pleased to be asked to Cliveden by the Astors, to sit for the sculptor Jo Davidson, to be decorated by the head of the Luftwaffe.

The Nazi medal left Lindbergh open to attack. Harold Ickes denounced him for accepting "a decoration at the hands of a brutal dictator who with that same hand is robbing and torturing thousands of fellow human beings," and referred to him as a "Knight of the German Eagle."

And so on April 20 the two men who would become the chief isolationist and the chief interventionist met privately for the first and last time—the man who felt that the values of the "real America" had to be defended against the rabble, and who complained upon arriving at the White House and finding a crowd of well-wishers and press photographers that there would have been more dignity and self-respect among African savages, and the man who saw the interest of all America, both the threat from without and the need to defend the values within. Actually, FDR and Lindbergh had something in common, besides being American heroes, though they did not know it. They both had a sophomoric love of practical jokes, with the fondness for the discomfiture of others that that implies. Lindbergh at a dinner attended by the columnist Dorothy Thompson put Listerine in a decanter of Burgundy. Miss Thompson, who respected good wine, never forgot it.

Seated at his desk, and surrounded by paintings of ships on the walls, FDR leaned forward in his chair as Lindbergh entered. It was only after the meeting that he stopped to think that the president was a cripple. He did not notice it at the time. The charm was based on finding some point in common. "How's Anne?" FDR asked. "She knew my daughter in school, you know."

FDR seemed tired, but with enough energy to carry on for a long time. His face had the gray look of an overworked businessman. His voice had the even tone one gets when the mind is dulled by too much conversation. Roosevelt judged his man quickly and played him cleverly, Lindbergh thought. He left the meeting feeling that "there is something about him I did not trust, something a litle too suave, too pleasant, too easy."

FDR already saw Lindbergh as a potential danger who had to be neutralized, but charm wouldn't do it. Five months later, when he was about to speak on the radio against American involvement in the war, Lindbergh received a curious offer. It came from Secretary of War Harry H. Woodring, via Air Force General "Hap" Arnold, who had asked Truman Smith to pass it on to his friend. If Lindbergh stayed off the radio he would be made air secretary in the cabinet. "So you see," Truman Smith said laughing, "they're worried." Lindbergh was insulted that FDR thought he could be bribed. All he had was his integrity.

FDR was getting nowhere with repeal legislation, no matter how many congressmen he coaxed. It made him bad-tempered. On May 18, Morgenthau unburdened himself to Eleanor. Franklin had been bullying and browbeating him. Eleanor said that when he was not feeling well he liked to take it out on those close to him, who he knew could take it. She would have had a row with him long ago over the festivities for the king and queen because he insisted on passing on each name himself, but because he was sick she let him have his own way.

A few days later, Morgenthau lamented the sorry state of the administration with Tom Corcoran and Ben Cohen, who said that FDR wasn't even able to fire his isolationist secretary of war for fear of losing the Kansas delegation in 1940 (Harry Woodring had been governor of Kansas). They went on a long critique on the complete disorganization in the White House and the way FDR frittered his time away. Steve Early sat on everything and Pa Watson was no more than a doorkeeper. Sam Rosenman had said that FDR still ran the United States as though it was the state of New York, wanting to do it on a personal contact basis—he had never really learned how to run his own office. Corcoran said the trouble was they had a power house without any transmission lines. Morgenthau replied that they had a power house with a cold boiler.

Morgenthau kept trying to fire the boiler. He was the only member of the administration who prodded FDR on the Jewish refugee question. At lunch on June 19, he said: "Now, Mr. President, a year has passed and we have not got anywhere on this Jewish refugee thing. What are we going to do about it?"

"I know we have not," the president replied. "At last even Sam Rosenman has got his eyes open and sees that it isn't so easy. The whole trouble is England. The Jewish Refugee Committee in England isn't getting anywhere."

"Isn't there something that can be done?" Morgenthau asked.

"Well," FDR said, "I talked to the president-elect of Paraguay the other day at lunch, and he said he would take 5,000."

Morgenthau pointed out that the problem was 5 million Jews rather than 5,000, not just in Germany but in Poland, Rumania, and Hungary.

"Absolutely," FDR said. "That's what I have been saying, but I can't make any headway. I am willing to go so far, if necessary, to have them even call it the Roosevelt plan. If you will give me a list of the thousand richest Jews in the United States I am willing to tell them how much they should give. A man like Zemurray, United Fruit, ought to give five million, and a lot more like him."

FDR was quite willing to "spread the Jews thin all over the world," as he put it, but he did not want them entering the United States in large numbers. In any case it was politically unfeasible to change the quota system—all he could do was extend visitors' visas. He refused to support the Wagner-Rogers bill, which would have admitted 20,000 refugee children in 1939 and 1940 outside the quota system. The bill was amended to death in committee.

Roosevelt's feelings about the Jews were complicated. He surrounded himself with Jewish advisers—Morgenthau, Sam Rosenman, Felix Frank-furter, Ben Cohen—whom he liked and admired. One of his reasons, ac-cording to Jerome Frank, was that Jews did not get the presidential bee. Since they knew there could not be a Jewish president, they would not be-come political threats. Rosenman and Frankfurter were Jewish "Uncle Toms." Rosenman never mentioned the refugees, and was against the relax-ation of quotas. Frankfurter, who called Morgenthau "a stupid bootlick," was more interested in New Deal legislation than in the plight of the Jews. Actually Frankfurter, who sent FDR a steady stream of messages telling him what a wonderful job he was doing on foreign policy, was more of a bootlick than Morgenthau, who did not hesitate to come to grips with the president on the refugees.

Roosevelt was outraged by the persecution of the Jews and had the hu-mane reaction that something must be done. But at the same time there lin-gered in him a residue of the social anti-Semitism he had inherited from his mother and other relatives such as his half brother Rosy and his uncle Fred Delano, all three of them anti-Semites.

Thus FDR would sometimes make unflattering references to the Jews, who he felt should be restrained in certain areas. They should, for instance, accept a quota system at Harvard. "Some years ago," he told Henry Mor-genthau, "a third of the entering class at Harvard were Jews and the ques-tion came up as to how it should be handled." As a member of the board of overseers, Roosevelt helped to formulate the decision "that over a period of years the number of Jews should be reduced 1 or 2 percent a year until it was down to 15 percent."

FDR carried on a friendly correspondence with anti-Semites such as Miller Reese Hutchinson, an industrial engineer, who was "Uncle Hutch" to the president's "Marse Franklin," and who wrote him in "Rastus" dialect in 1937: "I dun tuk notiss, arter tryin ter git erlong wid Jews, dat effin yer holds er stik uv candy er mile long fer one uv um ter eat, he gwineter bite yer fin-ger when he's et der las inch. Hitler is rite in one respect."

FDR certainly did not believe Hitler was right, but he might well have laughed heartily over the rest of the letter. When Burton Wheeler came to see him one day to discuss the third term, FDR said, "You know, Jack Gar-ner wants to run for President, but he couldn't get the nigger vote." Wheeler was startled that FDR had used the word "nigger." "Farley wants Hull to run," FDR went on, "because of the fact that he wants to be Vice-President and he thinks Hull might not live and he'd become President. Cardinal Mundelein says that he wants to see a Catholic President some time but he doesn't want to see him come in the back door. You know, Burt, Mrs. Hull is part Jewish and you don't have to go back through your ancestors or mine to find out if there's any Jewish blood in our veins. We're either Dutch or English."

So here, thought Wheeler, was the man who had the Negro vote, the Irish vote, and the Jewish vote in the palm of his hand expressing his true feelings about them all—the blacks were really just "niggers," the Irish Catholics were unworthy of the highest office, and the Jews were not true Americans, in the way that the old families of English and Dutch ancestry were.

Despite FDR's best efforts, the Neutrality Act had not been repealed by the time the king and queen of England visited the United States in June, on a goodwill mission that might quell some of the anti-British sentiment. Roosevelt was amused by their requests for eiderdown comforters and hot water bottles for the ladies-in-waiting—after all, this was not the North Pole but Washington in June.

Bill Bullitt sent him a confidential report on Their Britannic Majesties: "The little Queen is now on her way to you together with the little King. She is a nice girl—eider-down or no eider-down—and you will like her, in spite of the fact that her sister-in-law, the Princess Royal, goes around England talking about 'her cheap public smile.' She resembles so much the female caddies who used to carry my clubs at Pitlochry in Scotland many years ago that I find her pleasant. . . . The little King is beginning to feel his oats, but still remains a rather frightened boy." It was best not to mention the Windsors, since "about a month ago the Duke of Windsor wrote to Queen Mary that Bertie had behaved toward him in such an ungentlemanly way because of 'the influence of that common little woman' the Queen, that he could have no further relations with Bertie. Brotherly love, therefore, not at fever heat."

And so on June 9, half a million people packed Pennsylvania Avenue to see Army planes fly overhead, and the cavalry ride by, while in an open car a mild-looking young man in a fore-and-after with lots of gold braid sat next to a gentleman in top hat and glasses, listening like a schoolboy.

At the end of June, the House voted to maintain the arms embargo. Roosevelt's distress was apparent in this letter to New York Congresswoman Caroline O'Day: "I think it may interest you to tell you in great confidence that two of our embassies abroad tell us this afternoon that the action of the House last night has caused dismay in democratic, peaceful circles. The anti-war nations believe that a definite stimulus has been given to Hitler by the vote of the House, and that if war breaks out in Europe, because of further seeking of territory by Hitler and Mussolini, an important part of the responsibility will rest on last night's action. . . . I honestly believe that the vote last night was a stimulus to war."

FDR had no recourse but to try the Senate again, convening Senate leaders from both parties to his upstairs study on July 18. "I made a terrible blunder signing the Neutrality Act in 1935," he said. "We base our need for changing the present law on the ground that it works in Hitler's favor. War may come at any time."

"But there won't be a war this year, Mr. President," said Senator Borah with finality.

Turning to Hull, FDR asked: "Cordell, what do you think about the possibility of danger ahead?"

"If Senator Borah could only see some of the cables coming to the State Department about the extremely dangerous outlook in the international situation," Hull declared, "I feel satisfied he would modify his views."

Speaking from the vantage point of one who had seen it all before, Borah retorted: "That's what some Secretaries of State said in Wilson's time, but I got up on the Senate floor and showed that I had more information than they had and I say now that there's not going to be a war. You may have information but I have some too—I spent my own money for it." At that, the other senators laughed, for Borah was a notorious skinflint.

It was all Hull could do to keep from exploding. That Borah would give more credit to some two-bit newsletter in London that he subscribed to than to the State Department was a terrible disparagement of his whole service. Hull knew from the cables piled high on his desk that Borah was everlastingly wrong.

At 2:50 A.M. on Friday, September 2, the American ambassador in Warsaw, Anthony J. Drexel Biddle, managed to get through to Bill Bullitt in Paris and, despite the poor connection, give him the news that Germany had invaded Poland. Bullitt called FDR, who by 3:00 A.M. was passing it on to Cordell Hull. Joe Kennedy also called Hull to tell him that it was "all over," and that "the party is on." Was there any question that the British would act, Hull asked. "Oh, unquestionably, none," replied Kennedy.

Roosevelt found that he was enjoying the crisis. Three days earlier at cabinet, he had said, "That is fine, that is fine, things are happening. I like it when something is happening every minute." Now that it had happened, he was startled by a strange feeling of familiarity. In the years of World War I, the telephone at his bedside with a direct wire to the Navy Department had time and again brought him tragic messages in the night, and the lights had switched on in the nerve centers of government. He felt that he was picking up an interrupted routine.

At his press conference that morning, there was some humor at Borah's expense. A reporter said he was in Poland Springs, Maine (taking the cure, for he was unwell, and would die in January 1940), and FDR said, "Oh, I thought you said Poland. That would have been news."

The question the reporters wanted answered was "Can we stay out?" to which the president replied: ". . . I not only sincerely hope so, but I believe we can; and . . . every effort will be made by the Administration to do so."

Two days later, however, despite Joe Kennedy's assurance, the attack on Poland became a world war. The card castle of appeasement tumbled down on that Sunday morning when Chamberlain announced: "I have to tell you that this country is at war with Germany." A month before, Chamberlain had sent FDR a personal plea for the secret Norden bombsight. My God, didn't he read the papers? Didn't he know about the Neutrality Act? FDR replied that his request "could not be granted unless the sight desired by the British Government was made available to all other governments at the same time."

In a fireside chat that evening, FDR said: "This nation will remain a neutral nation, but I cannot ask that every American remain neutral in thought as well. Even a neutral has a right to take account of facts. Even a neutral cannot be asked to close his mind or his conscience."

Hull had objected to the sentence, saying that it would hurt FDR in his fight over the Neutrality Act, that it would strengthen the hand of those who said that he was trying to get America into the war.

In fact, the war gave FDR the leverage he needed to repeal neutrality, and he convened Congress in special session on September 21. The day before, the president met with fifteen House and Senate leaders from both parties for one of his before-the-game pep talks. "The German press," he told them, "if you have been following it day by day as I do, is displaying on the front page—this is in the family, there is no reason for not talking about it—every remark that Bennett Clark makes, that Borah makes, that Hiram Johnson makes, that Hamilton Fish makes . . . and they display those statements . . . as being pro-German. . . . They are assuming that these statements . . . are a definite recognition of the purity of Germany's motives. . . . And the things they are saying about the people that want to repeal the embargo is almost unprintable. We wouldn't put them even in a Hearst paper in this country."

One of the conferees said the public would understand repeal because sentiment was heavily toward France and Britain.

"I am darned glad that you said something that I couldn't say," FDR observed, "and that is without question the overwhelming sentiment in this country is in favor of France and England winning the war."

The Soviets, who had signed a nonaggression pact with the Nazis on August 23, were another thorn through their control of American Communists. "This morning," FDR went on, "I got word that the Soviets sent word to the Communist Party in this country . . . to do everything in their power to prevent the repeal of the embargo. Now that is straight from Moscow." The Communists were now the allies of the isolationists.

FDR was fed up with the Russians, not only because they had invaded Poland to share in the spoils but because of their harassment of American diplomats. In a memo to Hull, he said that "we should match every Soviet annoyance by a similar annoyance here against them." Thus, when the American public health surgeon in Moscow was not allowed to leave Russia because he had refused to submit his personal effects to a customs inspection, a Soviet ship seeking to go through the Panama Canal without a proper bill of health was stopped. When long distance calls from the American embassy could only be made by personal appearance at the Moscow central telephone station, FDR urged that "we might apply the same rules to the Russian Embassy here. . . . What is sauce for the goose might well be sauce for the gander too!"

The campaign to stop repeal, financed partly by German funds, flooded congressmen with letters, many of them paraphrasing the radio talks of Father Coughlin. Lindbergh, now an authority on foreign affairs, spoke against repeal on September 15 and October 13.

It was a month-long fight, with an intense behind-the-scenes effort from the White House, and with Jack Garner for once in the president's camp, managing the strategy.

Here is a typical Garner memo, dated September 21: "Tell Barkley, Sherman Minton and Jim Byrnes to do two things:

"1. To keep their mouths shut and to shut off debate.

"2. Keep the ball going at least six hours a day for a week. If, at the end of a week, a filibuster starts, have night sessions and move the convening hour from noon to 11:00 and run it through to 10:00 or 11:00 every night. Tell them we are going to take care of neutrality first. Such other legislation as might be desired for emergency purposes might be considered after neutrality has been passed but NOT before."

FDR received individual senators daily, to bring them around. The nose counting began. Senator Barbour was going to vote "right" but would not announce it until the voting started. Senator Reynolds would vote against. Senator Glass was too sick to take part in the fight. Senator Bridges had come around to the president's view after his recent visit.

It was touch and go. FDR asked the governor general of Canada, Lord Tweedsmuir, to postpone a visit because "I am almost literally walking on eggs. . . . I am at the moment saying nothing, seeing nothing, and hearing nothing."

The isolationists fought repeal with rhetoric—FDR planned "to send the boys of American mothers to fight on the battlefields of Europe"—and with amendments to bar the sale of flamethrowers and poison gas. But on October 27 the Senate repealed the arms embargo by 63 to 30, with the House following a few days later. Now the allies could buy the hardware they needed, but it would have to be cash and carry.

The battle to regain control of arms sales had taken most of the year. It was a victory roughly equivalent to the passage of major New Deal legislation, the NIRA, or the Wagner Act. FDR was a navigator turning a large ship around in a narrow channel against a stiff current. This was the first turn of the ship—the next two would be Selective Service and Lend-Lease. With repeal, he established the plausible notion that the way to stay out of the war was to help the Allies beat the Germans.

The answer to that line of reasoning was committed to his diary by Senator Arthur Vandenberg of Michigan, who, as it turned out, was endorsed by events: "My quarrel is with this notion that America can be half in and half out of this war. . . . I hate Hitlerism and Naziism and Communism as completely as any person living. But I decline to embrace the opportunist idea—so convenient and so popular at the moment—that we can stop these things in Europe without entering the conflict with everything at our command, including men and money. There is no middle ground. We are either all the way in or all the way out."

The president, however, genuinely believed in 1939 that he could limit American involvement to arms sales. On December 16, Harry Hopkins sent him a poem written in 1775 by Joseph Warren:

> "Lift up your hands, ye heros,
> And swear with proud disdaine;
> The wretch that would ensnare you
> Shall lay his snares in vain.
> Should Europe empty all her force
> We'll meet her in array
> And fight and shout and fight for
> Free Amerikay."

"Interesting," FDR replied, "as showing that a nation of four million people with few resources thought even in those days that they could lick the world. I fear that today altogether too many people in Amerikay want, as they did then, to 'fight and shout and fight.' Some of us believe there would be more shouting than fighting."

Just as important in its far-reaching effects as the repeal of the arms embargo was the connection formed that year between FDR and Einstein. When Hitler came to power in 1933, Einstein gave up his German citizenship and moved to Princeton. He and a number of other scientists who became the architects of the atom bomb (Einstein did not work on the bomb, but his formula for energy had demonstrated its potential destructive capacity) were Hitler's gift to America—Leo Szilard, Edward Teller, Hans Bethe, John von Neumann, and Stanislaw Ulman, all arrived fleeing Nazism.

Invited to stay at the White House in January 1934, Einstein wrote a poem to honor the occasion, which loses something in the translation:

> "In the Capital's proud glory
> Where Destiny unfolds her story,
> Fights a man with happy pride
> Who solution can provide."

Leo Szilard was upset when he heard early in 1939 that two German scientists had accomplished the fission of uranium. He got in touch with Alexander Sachs, a Russian émigré and New Deal economist, who presumably had access to high government officials. Sachs promised that if Einstein wrote a letter to the president he would deliver it personally. Written on August 2, the letter, which was not delivered until October, said in part: "This new phenomenon would also lead to the construction of bombs, and it is conceivable—though much less certain—that extremely powerful bombs of a new type may thus be constructed. A single bomb of this type, carried by boat or exploded in a port, might very well destroy the whole port together with towns of the surrounding territory. However, such bombs might very well prove to be too heavy for transportation by air."

FDR did not even have a scientific adviser at the time, but he had had plenty of experience dealing with inventors, crackpot and otherwise, while assistant secretary of the Navy, like the fellow who had thought up the magnetic firing device for mines. It was part of his optimistic and adventurous nature to try new ideas, even if they sounded preposterous, and he passed Einstein's letter on to Pa Watson with the note that "this requires action."

Within days, a committee was appointed under Lyman J. Briggs, director of the National Bureau of Standards. It met on October 21, 1939, with Szilard, the Budapest physicist Eugene Wigner, and the Italian physicist Enrico Fermi, who had fled Mussolini's Italy for New York, stopping off in Stockholm to pick up a Nobel prize for his demonstration of radioactive elements produced by neutron irradiation.

The physicists said they needed $2,000 to pursue their experiments. But the military were skeptical. Who were these eggheads who came from the wrong side of the pond and spoke broken English? Colonel K. R. Adamson, the Army representative, said that research on atom bombs would be a waste of time. When a new weapon was developed, it usually took two wars to find out whether it was any good. In any case, it was not weapons that won wars, it was the morale of the troops.

If that was the case, Wigner said, perhaps the Army's budget could be cut. Piqued, Adamson said: "Well, as far as those two thousand dollars are concerned, you can have it."

From such humble beginnings the atom bomb was built. The first committee became the Advisory Committee on Uranium in April 1940, and Fermi and Szilard were excluded, for if the government provided funds on the recommendation of a committee two of whose members were aliens, there might be a congressional investigation.

In November 1940, Columbia University was given a contract to develop the Fermi-Szilard system, which was transferred to the University of Chicago in February 1942, and then to Oak Ridge, Tennessee, and Los Alamos, New Mexico. The supreme irony was that Szilard and Fermi could not get their citizenship until their five-year residence period was up. They were entrusted with the greatest secret of the war but, under regulations then in force for aliens, they could not cross a state line after 8:00 P.M., and when they went on a trip they needed the permission of the state attorney general.

And so it was that the greatest scientific figure of the century and the greatest American statesman of the century united in giving birth to the age of nuclear destruction. The German Jewish immigrant and the Hyde Park patrician were partners in bringing to the planet a change in the relation of man to the universe that would have a greater effect on human destiny than the theory of Copernicus or the law of gravity.

Roosevelt did not live to see the atom bomb in action, but Einstein spent the rest of his life regretting that he had helped to launch it, saying: "I made one great mistake in my life—when I signed the letter to President Roosevelt recommending that atom bombs be made . . . but there was some justification—the danger that the Germans would make them."

Whenever talk of a third term came up, FDR said he was not interested. He was prepared to accept Hull in 1940 if there was a progressive in second place such as Harry Hopkins or Bob Jackson. He was afraid that the reactionary South would control the convention and nominate a so-called middle-of-the-roader. The top spot seemed wide open, and although Hull said he didn't want it, two other members of the cabinet, Jim Farley and Jack Garner, had their eyes on it.

Tom Corcoran, however, was trying to launch a "draft Roosevelt for a third term" movement. He told Morgenthau that all the members of the cabinet who were running for president should be ordered to stop it and get behind Roosevelt.

Corcoran had his finger in all sorts of pies. He went to Chicago and immersed himself in Catholic politics, and claimed that he had picked the successor to the influential Cardinal Mundelein. "It was a tough fight but we made it," he told David Lilienthal. "See how important that is for 1940?" he asked with a significant sidelong glance. "See what it means to have the right line-up in Mundelein's place?"

Lilienthal was shocked that Corcoran was mixing the church up in Chicago machine politics. It was hard to believe it had been authorized. Tom at first had been like a campus leader, full of zest and fun, but now he was like a cynical ward leader—he would throw so many knives in your back you'd look like a porcupine. He thought he was the only one who could protect the president from the forces of reaction, and was constantly trying to slip things through rather than be aboveboard.

FDR told Sumner Welles in May that he wanted nothing to do with third term talk. He did not consider it or want it, and was "violently and vividly" opposed to it. A third term movement would make him vulnerable to attacks that everything he had done was to serve his ambition. As Adolf Berle put it, "the Corcoran crowd naturally want a third term, because with anyone else, they would not be allowed within fifty miles of the White House."

As for the three main contenders, they all found reasons to hope. Hull was sure that FDR had picked him. When they discussed a foreign policy point that would not be settled for several years, the president's face would light up and he would say, "Why that's fine. At that time you'll be in my chair, if my efforts succeed, and you'll be in a good position to deal with it."

At a cabinet dinner, Mrs. Hull sat next to the president and told him her husband did not like making speeches. "Well tell him he had better get used to it," FDR replied. "He'll have a lot of it to do soon." Even after the war broke out in September, FDR still said he wanted Hull.

He did not want Farley, whose abilities he held in contempt, but who was trying to get the party machine behind him. Ickes thought Jim would run the country like a ward politician. His ignorance was dumbfounding. He was always coming to FDR with statements like "Why Boss, you know I don't know anything about economics," and "Why Boss, you know I don't know anything about international affairs." One of his remarks on foreign affairs was that a Nazi was a person who hated a Jew more than was necessary. FDR also had a low opinion of Mrs. Farley, whom he called "real shanty Irish," and who spent all her time in New York running around with a cheap crowd and going to nightclubs.

In February, Ickes told FDR that everyone knew Farley was disloyal. "You only have to look at his face at Cabinet to know that," FDR replied.

In August, FDR invited Farley to Hyde Park to try to tell him that if he was nominated he had no chance of winning. "I know perfectly well that you will have enough delegates at the next national convention to hold the balance of power," he said, and then outlined Farley's record, adding: "You don't want to spoil that record. Neither of us wants to nominate a ticket next year of such a sort that as we leave the Convention Hall we will know that that ticket will be defeated. Only liberal candidates on a liberal platform can win next year. I will not support anyone but a liberal. I will not support either a conservative or a straddlebug. I will not support a tweedledummer.... I not only won't support a reactionary on the Democratic ticket, I will not support anyone who apologizes for the New Deal." The message did not get through, for Farley still had visions of the unattainable.

"I've been playing my game too all this time," he told Ray Clapper in February 1940, "and Roosevelt is going to find he has to deal with me and Hull and Garner. If I come out and say I don't think there should be a third term and that I am for Hull, Roosevelt can't run. My name ... is going before that convention as a candidate regardless of what Roosevelt does." Farley could control the convention because as party chairman he could appoint the committee on arrangements, which would pick the keynoter and the permanent chairman. He was confident the convention would nominate a Hull-Farley ticket.

But his confidence was shaken by an Ernest Lindley article in March that quoted FDR as saying: "You know what a lot of people down your way would say if we nominated Jim for Vice President.... They would say we are using Cordell Hull as a stalking-horse for the Pope." Farley felt the president had sidestepped and double-crossed him. He took to dropping into churches at late hours.

For the third man, FDR felt real hatred, which he did his best to conceal. Jack Garner had become the leader of the congressional barons who had fought the president since the court-packing plan. He now used his influence in Congress to sabotage the president's policies (with the exception of the Neutrality Act repeal). He was a cabinet-level enemy, practically a defector, passionately opposed to a third term. As the *Congressional Digest* put it, "It is a case of Franklin D. Roosevelt, epitome of the New Deal ... against John Nance Garner, to whom much of the New Deal is anathema."

Now that he was rich, Garner had little sympathy for the forgotten man. On his pecan farm in Uvalde, he exploited Mexican labor, whom he paid a penny a pound for shelled pecans. He owned a bank, and charged stockmen 10 and 12 percent on loans. Some of the ways he enriched himself were best kept quiet. "I won a lot of money at poker," he once told Jim Farley. "How much?" Farley asked. "About two hundred thousand," Garner said. "Who from?" asked the incredulous Farley. "The Davis, Elkins crowd." These were the owners of Pennsylvania and West Virginia coal mines, and of course, Farley reflected, the winnings were a hidden bribe, helping to explain Garner's virulent antilabor position.

Cabinet meetings had become unpleasant, with FDR and Garner baiting each other. In May, FDR said: "The Vice-President is not here so we can talk freely." On June 16, Garner interrupted the president by saying, "Well, didn't I tell you so?" and "You remember that I brought that up two or three years ago." FDR wanted to help Finland, the only country that had paid its war debt, which Russia had invaded, and was sure that Garner was lobbying on the Hill against Finnish aid. At the January 19, 1940, cabinet, he said that the most reviled person in history was Pontius Pilate, and made a motion of washing his hands, while glowering at Garner.

At the end of July 1939, FDR got an assist from John L. Lewis, who, with the full intention of discrediting Garner's presidential aspirations, said at a congressional hearing on proposed amendments to the wages and hours legislation: "The genesis of this campaign against labor ... is not hard to find. [It] emanates from a labor-baiting, poker-playing, whiskey-drinking, evil old man whose name is Garner." Pounding the table until the ashtrays jumped, Lewis continued: "Some gentlemen may rise in horror and say, 'Why Mr. Lewis has made a personal attack on Mr. Garner.' Yes, I made a personal attack on Mr. Garner for what he is doing, because Garner's knife is searching for the quivering, pulsating heart of labor."

The Texas delegation prepared a rebuttal denying that Garner did any of the things Lewis had charged him with, but one young, pro–New Deal congressman elected to the House from Austin in 1937 refused to sign it—Lyndon Johnson. He did sign a watered-down resolution that was read to a cheering House, but by resisting the original draft he won FDR's sympathy. Johnson had already come to his attention as a partisan of rural electrification who, armed with maps and charts, had made a pitch for dams in his congressional district. After looking at them, FDR called in someone from the Interior Department and said, "I want us to look into working on those dams down there where this new young Congressman from Texas, Lyndon Johnson, is." "Mr. President," the man from Interior replied, "they don't have but five households a mile, there's not enough people down there to meet the criteria." "Don't worry," FDR said with a laugh, "they'll breed fast." Now, following the resolution incident, patronage began flowing

Johnson's way. Alvin J. Wirtz, the attorney for Brown & Root, Texas builders closely identified with Johnson, was made under secretary of the interior, a sign that Johnson had become the key Roosevelt loyalist in Texas.

Those favoring Garner were scratching their heads on the right strategy to make him look like presidential timber. A memo from Texas Congressman Roy Miller said that he had to be built from the ground up. He had no color, he could not speak, he was old and could not be shown. "We have to make an Andrew Jackson without Andrew Jackson's force. We believe the American people are tired and want to sit down. They want one of their own kind to sit in a rocking-chair. On the disloyalty issue we will say 'who made Caesar?' " This of course was a reference to the 1932 convention, when Garner had thrown the Texas delegation to FDR, clinching his nomination. But Frank Murphy, the new attorney general, argued that in the wake of John L. Lewis's remarks the Garner boom was only a ghost walking at night in a graveyard.

When Garner announced in December that he was a candidate, FDR joked at a December 19 cabinet meeting: "I see that the Vice-President has thrown his bottle—I mean his hat—into the ring, and, according to Harold, Dewey has thrown his diaper into the ring." FDR told Steve Early that he wished some cartoonist would draw a picture of Baby Dewey throwing his diaper and Baby Garner throwing a bottle of "red eye" into the ring.

By this time the war was on in Europe, and FDR told Ickes that he could not rule out the possibility of a third term. And yet he continued to act as though nothing was further from his mind. David Lilienthal went to see him on November 2 to ask for more appropriations in case FDR was not reelected in 1940 so that his successor could not sabotage TVA.

That wasn't the way to look at it, FDR said, the program would stand a better chance if they established that the cost would not expand. "Suppose Vandenberg is elected next fall," he said, "or Landon, or say, Hoover." He rubbed his eyes and grinned. "They tell me he wants to be President again. God knows why. The burned child is supposed to fear the fire. If that should happen and I should send in a budget on Jan. 3, 1941, Vandenberg would throw it out, of course. He would cut TVA more mercilessly if you had to go up to 60 million than if you could show continually declining expenditures and ascending revenues; in other words, that you are getting out of the woods."

The war was a reason to seek a third term, as was saving the New Deal from destruction, but there was also a compelling reason not to run, which FDR expressed when Nebraska Senator George Norris urged him in February 1940 to run again.

"Did you ever stop to think," FDR asked, "that if I should run and be elected I would have much more trouble with Congress in my third term and much more bitterness to contend with as a result of my running for a third term than I have ever had before?"

"But if you don't run," Norris asked, "where will all the Liberals go?"

"George," FDR said, "I am chained to this chair from morning till night. People come in here day after day, most of them trying to get something from me, most of them things I can't give them, and wouldn't if I could. You sit in your chair in your office too, but if something goes wrong or you get irritated or tired, you can get up and walk around, or you can go into another room. But I can't, I am tied down to this chair day after day, week after week, and month after month. And I can't stand it any longer. I can't go on with it."

On January 24, 1940, over lunch with Morgenthau, FDR said: "I do not want to run unless between now and the convention things get very, very much worse in Europe."

To find out how bad things were, he sent over Assistant Secretary of State Sumner Welles in February. The British ambassador, Lord Lothian, told FDR that Welles should make it clear to Hitler and Mussolini that the United States would not allow a blitzkrieg or a submarine blockade against England and France. But the president said he could not do that. Not a quarter of Congress would support it. It was an election year. If he raised the issue it would produce a violent isolationist reaction. Only events would compel the American public to face realities.

"Telegram from Roosevelt," wrote Alexander Cadogan of the Foreign Office on February 2, "about his awful half-baked idea of sending Sumner Welles (!) over here with a flourish of trumpets to collect data on which Roosevelt is to proclaim basis of peace!"

At this point, FDR was still hoping to turn back the clock. Welles asked Prime Minister Neville Chamberlain whether he would be willing to negotiate if Hitler moved out of Poland and Czechoslovakia. Chamberlain said he would not because Hitler "personifies a system with which the British government has learned from bitter experience it is impossible to make terms."

Hitler made a good impression on Welles, who reported to FDR that he spoke in a beautiful German of which he (Welles) could follow every word. "He has, in real life, none of the somewhat effeminate appearance of which he has been accused," wrote Welles. "... He was dignified both in speech and movement, and there was not the slightest impression of the comic effect from mustache and hair which one sees in his caricatures."

Mussolini made an even better impression, and Welles, after seeing him, arrived in Paris singing his praise to French leaders, much to their dismay. Premier Daladier told Bill Bullitt that Welles had given the impression that Germany was invincible and that France and England should try to get a compromise peace, which would leave Germany in control of Central and Eastern Europe, by using the offices of that great European, Mussolini. Bullitt wrote FDR that Welles's excursion into personal diplomacy had been damaging to the president's prestige.

The one European statesman of whom Welles disapproved was Winston Churchill, whom he described as a drunk and a windbag. Welles found him smoking a twenty-four-inch cigar and drinking a whiskey and soda, and, he wrote FDR on March 12, "It was quite obvious that he had consumed a good many whiskeys before I arrived." He spoke for an hour and fifty minutes, just a rehash of his recent book, *Step by Step,* and Welles could not get a word in.

Churchill had joined Chamberlain's war cabinet the previous September as first lord of the Admiralty, a position he had already occupied in World War I. Chamberlain's policy of appeasement lay in ruins, and a creeping frustration paralyzed Britain's will in the subsequent months of the "phony war." One evening, Lord Normanbrook, who was private secretary to the home secretary, turned on the radio and heard the voice that would become so familiar say: "The Royal Navy has immediately attacked the U-boats, and is hunting them night and day—I will not say without mercy, because God forbid we should ever part company with that—but at any rate with zeal, and not altogether without relish!" The word "relish," so unexpected, as if he was actually enjoying the job, convinced Normanbrook that Churchill was the man needed to prosecute the war. Chamberlain, the man of peace, could not be a war leader.

It was a generous gesture on Roosevelt's part to initiate a secret correspondence with Churchill a few days after he had been named to the Admiralty, disregarding the fact that Churchill had snubbed him in 1914 when, as assistant secretary of the Navy, he had asked to take a look at Admiralty operations.

Churchill responded eagerly, for he alone among British leaders saw the vital importance of the United States. In May, the "Naval Person" who signed the letters became "Former Naval Person." As prime minister, his historical function would be to involve the United States in the maintenance of the European order, which he did by means both fair and unfair. This was his finest hour, at the age of sixty-five, when most men retire, not what had gone before in a long political career frustrated by failure—the disastrous Dardanelles expedition of 1915, the adherence to the gold standard as chancellor of the Exchequer, the years in the wilderness when he had sought to maintain British rule in India, all of it penance to endure while waiting for the call to greatness.

The pointlessness of the Welles mission became apparent when Hitler invaded Denmark and Norway in April. Denmark fell in days, Norway in weeks. FDR had grave doubts about Britain's ability to fight. "The thing that has made me hopping mad," he told Morgenthau, "is where was the British Fleet when the Germans went up to Bergen and Oslo? It is the most outrageous thing I have ever heard of. I am just hopping mad!"

"I want you to do something for me in the strictest confidence," FDR told Morgenthau on April 29. "I want you to take care of Italy."

"Well, I don't understand what you mean," Morgenthau said.

"Don't let any of their money get out of this country."

"You give me the damnedest assignments I ever received."

"Well, take care of it, and don't let anybody know you are doing it."

Morgenthau reflected that only ten days ago Sumner Welles had asked him to cancel the fine on four Italian steamers caught smuggling narcotics, as a way to increase FDR's influence with Mussolini, and now he was being told to freeze Italian assets. How times changed!

In May came the true shocker when the Germans sliced through France. "The German tanks have crossed the River Meuse as if it did not exist," Bullitt reported on May 14. "They have run through the French anti-tank defenses which consisted of railroad rails sunk deep in concrete and protruding from the ground as if the rails were straw. They have crossed the anti-tank traps and completely demolished the concrete fortifications by which the Maginot Line had been extended." The new premier, Paul Reynaud, told Bullitt that "at this moment there is nothing between those German tanks and Paris."

In the midst of the rout, Reynaud made a formal protest that the American assistant military attaché in Paris, Colonel Sumner Waite, had helped the Germans by discussing operations with his boss in Washington over an open telephone line. The conversation on May 13 with General Sherman Miles, chief of Military Intelligence, went like this:

Waite explained how the Germans broke across the frontier.

Miles: "Now wait a minute. That's all you have to give me? How was the German piercing movement around Maastricht carried out?"

Waite: "What they did was, they landed parachutists on top of the forts. By means of either gas or flame-throwers they forced the garrison to surrender. I was very much surprised because it was supposed to be gas-proof."

Miles: "How about the success in the air? Have the Germans shown strong superiority?"

Waite: "The Germans of course outnumber them pretty much."

Miles: "I think we will have to stop this telephoning. It's too expensive and it's not fair to the French. . . . It might be picked up."

The Germans seemed unstoppable, and FDR had to face the alarming possibility that Britain would be next, and then there would be nothing but the Atlantic between America and the Nazis. As he reflected on the danger, an odd image came into his head. He saw himself in 1918, motoring along Bantry Bay, looking at the beautiful Irish girls along the road. They opened their mouths to curse the British officers who were with him in the car, and when they did, he noticed that their teeth were black and decayed. "Wouldn't you think that one's mind would make different kinds of pictures when things are going fast?" he asked Adolf Berle. But the image of beauty hiding ugliness was an accurate metaphor for America's being drawn into war to save the values of Western civilization.

In the eight years since Roosevelt's election, the military had been ignored. An isolationist from Kansas was secretary of war, whose claim to fame was that in 1938 he had stopped the Boeing B-17s from going into production as an economy measure. The entire Army numbered 227,000 men, as against a German regular army of 850,000. There were only a handful of bombers and employable tanks. The P-40s and other fighters still had machine guns that were synchronized to fire through the propeller, as in 1918.

In a talk to Congress on May 16, FDR proposed a massive military build-up. Explaining how enemy bombers could take off from West Africa and bomb Omaha, he set a production goal of 50,000 planes a year. America could not count on France and England, and had to prepare for aggression. The reasoning seemed to be that a well-armed America could watch the rest of the world go to hell. Thus a largely isolationist Congress had by October 1940 voted $7 billion for defense.

On May 20, Lindbergh gave an antiwar speech, and FDR told Morgenthau: "If I should die tomorrow, I want you to know this. I am convinced that Lindbergh is a Nazi." Already, he was taking the attitude that those who disagreed with him were disloyal. In fact, the isolationists had a valid case, rooted in the feeling that England expected every American to do his duty. The chances of a German attack on the United States were remote, and there were sound reasons not to become involved. But to Roosevelt, the isolationists were helping Hitler, and he took extraordinary measures to combat subversion.

On May 21, he authorized Attorney General Bob Jackson to allow wiretapping, in spite of a 1939 Supreme Court decision that evidence obtained through wiretaps was not admissible in a federal court. J. Edgar Hoover said he needed it desperately. The wiretaps would be used only against suspected spies and subversives, preferably aliens. In fact, wiretaps were also used against FDR's political enemies. On one occasion, FDR called in Hoover and told him that Jim Farley was talking to Ray Tucker, an anti-New Deal newspaper editor in Hartford, Connecticut. "I want you to tap Farley's wire," FDR said. "I couldn't do that to a member of the Cabinet, Mr. President," Hoover said. "However, I will tap Ray Tucker's wire."

Placed in charge of all "subversive" investigations and wiretaps, the FBI greatly increased its power. Hoover set up the Special Intelligence Service, which he built up to 360 agents working overseas, mainly in Latin America, but also in other countries where the FBI was not mandated to operate.

In 1940, for instance, at the request of the State Department, a special agent of the FBI was assigned to the U.S. embassy in Moscow. There was a security problem in the code room. Single men employees were associating with a ring of prostitutes controlled by the GPU (Russian military intelligence). The girls pretended not to know English so the men would discuss their business freely in front of them at parties. At one of these occasions a code room employee had disclosed that an embassy official, Charles Bohlen, had just brought new codes to Moscow, and that an embassy agent was buying Russian currency on the black market in Persia. Other employees who did not associate with the prostitutes, the FBI agent's report said, were engaging in sexual perversion in the code room itself, until one of them had a breakdown and resigned. As a result of the investigation, the entire code room staff was changed. But the incident showed that FDR ordered measures that no previous president would have condoned—sending the FBI to spy on American embassies.

The president received daily reports on Nazi and Communist subversion from the FBI, some of them farfetched, which influenced his thinking. According to Hoover, the National Maritime Union had a Communist on board every boat afloat, possessing sabotage materials. The German espionage system was also infiltrating the labor movement with agitators to hinder the defense program, Hoover said.

On one occasion, an indignant J. Edgar Hoover telephoned Morgenthau to complain that Frances Perkins had appointed the labor leader Walter Reuther to head the Safety Device Board, which investigated safety devices in defense factories. "Now Walter Reuther is one of the Reuther brothers," Hoover said, "C.I.O. Communist he is, who was educated at the propaganda college in Moscow, and was sent over to this country about eight or nine years ago and was very active in the Detroit area. Now, this assignment that he's been given allows him to go into any factory in this country and make his survey and to look over the safety devices."

"Look," Morgenthau said, "why don't you tell Madame Perkins that?"

"Well," Hoover replied, "you know I can't get to first base with her. . . . I mean, she doesn't believe that there is a Communist in this country." Here for once was the great wiretapper tapped, for Morgenthau recorded all his telephone calls.

It was in this climate of twin threats from Communism and Fascism, magnified by Hoover, that FDR signed the Smith Act in July 1940, requiring 3.5 million aliens to register and be fingerprinted, and fined or imprisoned for anything written or spoken that could subvert the armed forces.

At 4:00 P.M. on May 20, 1940, an almost hysterical Bill Bullitt called the president from Paris. There were 3 to 5 million refugees moving south on the roads of France. They had no food, and women and children were literally dying of starvation. German aviators were bombing and strafing the columns of refugees. Frantically, Bullitt asked FDR to send planes and to bring the Atlantic Fleet into the Mediterranean. "I am sorry you keep referring to that Atlantic Fleet," FDR replied in a note on May 31, "because such talk reminds me of Mother Alice who met a rabbit. I cannot of course give you a list of the disposition of our ships but if you knew it you would not continue fantasies."

Bullitt saw a French surrender within days. There was a total disintegration of leadership. The country was run by Paul Reynaud's mistress, the comtesse de Portes. Events now began to bunch up in the worst way. On May 28, the Belgian army surrendered, and the British began their gallant evacuation of Dunkirk. On May 29, an American destroyer removed the French gold reserve of $250 million. Also on May 29, the Neutrality Act was amended to allow American pilots to deliver planes to Canada for shipment to Europe.

But the time for shipping planes to France had passed. On June 9, the French government prepared to ~vacuate to Tours. Bullitt said he was staying in Paris, and ordered twelve Thompson submachine guns in case the Germans attacked the embassy and he had to make a last stand.

On June 10, Italy attacked France. When he heard the news, FDR was leaving for Charlottesville to give the commencement speech at the University of Virginia—Franklin Jr. was graduating from the law school. The sentence everyone seized on was: "On this tenth day of June, the hand that held the dagger has stuck it into the back of its neighbor." But more important, the speech was a turning point in its expression of sympathy for "those nations that are giving their life blood in combat." FDR pledged to extend to England and France "the material resources of this nation." He was moving slowly, step by step, not wanting to get too far ahead of his own people, but taking into account events that America could not ignore.

It was too late to bail out the French, for on June 14 the Germans entered Paris. The French government had fled, but Bullitt was still there, doing his "burning deck" routine. Hull observed that he would have been of more use in Tours, working with the French government during the armistice talks, but then added sadly that had he been in Tours he would have been "spinning around like a goose that's been hit on the head with a corncob." The situation in Europe was hell and sheet lightning. The whole thing was caving in like a rickety house.

Roosevelt called in the French ambassador and asked him what his government was going to do now that the Germans had taken Paris. The ambassador beat his breast and said, "Mr. President, France will live *on* and *on* and *on!*" But what were the army and navy going to do, FDR asked. Again the ambassador beat his breast, repeating: "France will live *on* and *on* and *on!*" The president was disgusted. "*Jee*-sus Christ," he muttered under his breath.

France had caved in, but in England Churchill on June 4 gave his stirring "we shall never surrender" speech. On May 15, five days after becoming prime minister, he had begun his dogged campaign to involve the United States in the war. "The voice and force of the United States may count for nothing if they are withheld too long," he wrote Roosevelt. "You may have a completely subjugated, Nazified Europe established with astounding swiftness, and the weight may be more than we can bear. All I ask now is that you should proclaim non-belligerency, which would mean that you would help us with everything short of actually engaging armed forces. Immediate needs are: first of all, the loan of forty or fifty of your older destroyers to bridge the gap between what we have now and the large new construction we put in hand at the beginning of the war."

Roosevelt's reply was not encouraging. He would need authorization from Congress, and the destroyers might be earmarked for America's own defense requirements. But Churchill kept harping on the destroyers, bringing them up in every letter, exaggerating their importance: "The whole fate of the war may be decided by this minor and easily remediable factor." It was true that the Dunkirk operations had reduced England's destroyer strength from ninety-four to forty-three, but the war that summer was aerial rather than naval.

FDR was in no hurry to wrestle with Congress, which on June 28 decreed that he could not transfer any warships to a belligerent until the chief of naval operations certified they were not essential to the defense of the United States.

But Churchill had found an ally in Harry Hopkins, to whom he wrote separately, also insisting that the need for the destroyers was vital. On June 18, Hopkins sent this memo to FDR: "Unless we do something to give the English additional destroyers, it seems to me it is absolutely hopeless to expect them to keep going." Roosevelt did not act on Hopkins's advice. There were other factors to consider. If he moved too fast, the destroyers could become a divisive issue at the Democratic convention in July.

Besides, he was sore at the British for not following his advice on the way to lick Hitler. "I have been telling them, but they won't listen to me," he confided to Morgenthau. "I know South Germany, because I bicycled over every foot of it when I was a child and there is a town every ten miles. I have suggested to the English again and again if they sent a hundred planes over Germany for military objectives that ten of them should bomb some of these smaller towns that have never been bombed before. There must be some kind of factory in every town. That is the only way to break the German morale." FDR was displaying his ruthless streak, as in World War I, when he had wanted to mine Norwegian waters, which Admiral Beatty had refused to do. At least, thought Morgenthau, you had to hand it to the British, they stuck by their ethical methods of warfare.

Churchill kept plugging away, making the destroyers the test of American intentions. On July 21: "Mr. President, with great respect I must tell you that in the long history of the world this is a thing to do NOW." On August 13: "Each destroyer you can spare to us is measured in rubies." Repeatedly, he raised the specter of invasion. Was it possible? England had not been invaded since 1066.

It was not until August that the device of trading the destroyers for eight British bases was found. Churchill at first balked at giving up a piece of empire and, as FDR recalled it, told him: "How am I going to explain all this to the British people? They will say Americans are taking our territory."

"I told Winston," FDR said, "listen Winston, those places are nothing but a headache to you—you know that. They cost the British Treasury five million pounds—nearly twenty-five million dollars—every year. They are nothing but a headache. If you think I want your headaches you are mistaken. I don't. Furthermore, those places are inhabited by some eight million dark-skinned gentlemen and I don't want them coming to the United States and adding to the problem we already have with our 13 million black men. I tell you, Winston, it's just a headache and you can keep it."

The transfer could be made without Congress, and the deal went through more than three months after Churchill's first request. The destroyers started coming into service in November, and FDR's estimate that they were "on their last legs" proved correct. They were barely seaworthy, and so hard to maneuver that twelve of the fifty collided with friendly ships. Admiral of the Fleet Lord Rovey wrote: "I thought they were the worst destroyers I had ever seen, poor seaboats with appalling armament and accommodation. The price paid for them was scandalous."

Far from deciding the fate of the war, the destroyers were a headache, more garnets than rubies, but that was not the point. The destroyer deal was an act of political commitment, the first link in a chain binding America and England.

With the Democratic convention approaching, FDR remained Sphinxlike about his intentions. There was plenty of circumstantial evidence to support the thesis that he did not want to run. He spoke with great enthusiasm about the removal of his papers to Hyde Park. He planned to take Harry Hopkins with him and get him a job at Vassar. On January 20, he signed a three-year contract with *Collier's* magazine at $75,000 a year for twenty-six articles.

He told Ed Flynn that Cousin Teddy had once said that the United States was "sick and tired of the Roosevelts. They are sick of looking at my grin and they are sick of hearing what Alice had for breakfast. In fact, they want a rest from the Roosevelts." In May, Eleanor told Harry Hopkins that her husband did not have the same zest for administrative detail he once had and that, quite frankly, he was probably bored. She was anxious not to have him run again.

He seemed to be encouraging heirs apparent such as Hull, Hopkins, and Ickes. He had wanted Bob Jackson to run for governor of New York in 1938 as a jumping-off spot, but Farley blocked it, saying that Bob could have walked from the Battery to Buffalo and no one would have recognized him. There were so many hopefuls that the *New Yorker* wrote: "Nominate your friend for President. It makes a charming and inexpensive Christmas gift."

In the spring, John L. Lewis urged FDR to run again. The president said that was a bad idea, against tradition. It didn't give the young men in the party a chance to get ahead. He'd like to be a free man, get his sinuses fixed so he could breathe better. Lewis brought his bristling brows together and said: "I agree there is something in what you say, Mr. President, but I want to make a suggestion. The one way to make the third term popular in this country would be if John L. Lewis stood with you on the ticket as Vice-Presidential candidate. . . . That would make it go over."

"Can you beat it?" FDR asked when he told Frances Perkins about the meeting. Lewis obviously believed that the president would not live through the term and he would succeed him.

On May 28, the two chief anti-third-term plotters discussed the situation over lunch. "Jim, what's the Boss going to do?" Garner asked.

"Your guess is as good as mine," Farley said.

"Hell, he's fixed it so nobody else can run now. . . . Ah well, there's no use watering spilt milk."

"I went along with the assurances he gave me that he wouldn't run. So did you and so did Cordell. And we are all left high and dry. Al Smith warned me never to rely on Roosevelt's word."

On June 15, the Republican convention opened in Philadelphia and Wendell Willkie stole the nomination from under the noses of the party professionals. Until recently a Democrat, who had voted for FDR in 1932, Willkie had endeared himself to Republican businessmen by leading the fight against TVA as president of a powerful utility.

On June 19, Roosevelt appointed Henry Stimson as secretary of war and Frank Knox as secretary of the Navy. This kind of double play was FDR at his best. Both men had fought in France in World War I and were Republican internationalists who believed that America should play a large part in world affairs. Their appointment gave a bipartisan character to the administration, and would cut the ground from under Willkie's attacks on FDR's foreign policy. Knox, a self-made millionaire, had been Landon's running mate in 1936. Stimson, who in his long life had done all the right things, from Yale and Harvard Law School to secretary of war under Taft and secretary of state under Hoover, was a vigorous seventy-two—he still rode and played deck tennis and croquet.

These patently political appointments were a tip-off that FDR was running, although as late as June 20 Hull was told that he was the one. But at lunch with Hull on July 3, by which time France had signed the armistice, FDR suddenly said: "Well now, let's talk politics. You know, there are many people saying to me, 'you can't afford to let us down.' " He had been reading Washington's letter to Madison, in which Washington complained about the criticism against his running for a second term. He wanted to write a letter to someone like George Norris, saying that he wanted to go back to Hyde Park, and then the convention would nominate Hull.

"Of course such a letter would not delay your nomination by a split second," Hull said.

FDR speculated on how he might win. If the war stopped, Willkie might beat him. He then started to point out Hull's weaknesses, such as the feeling in the Farm Belt against his trade agreements. Hull could probably win by taking Wallace or some Farm Belt person as vice president.

Hull protested that he had no intention of running. But he sensed in Roosevelt's tone and language a complete reversal from a few days before, when he had without hesitation advocated his candidacy. Hull knew that he had made up his mind to seek a third term, and although he was opposed to a third term, fearing it would set a precedent, there was a case to be made for it in wartime, for you could not have a leaderless government during the three-month interregnum.

FDR then insisted that Hull should be vice president. Hull was moved—tears came to his eyes—but he said he didn't want it. Roosevelt kept coming back to it, saying: "If you don't take it, I'll have to get Henry Wallace."

Roosevelt's handling of the convention was a lesson in political strategy. He knew that Farley and Garner would place their names in nomination to block him. He knew that the old line conservative wing of the party had control of the convention's temporary organization under the temporary chairman, House Speaker William Bankhead of Alabama. He knew that the conservatives would be allied with what he called the "Haters' Club"—men of various persuasions, such as Burton Wheeler, Millard Tydings, and Carter Glass, united in their aversion to Roosevelt. He had to outmaneuver these groups, avoid all discussion of the propriety of a third term, and win on the first ballot by an overwhelming margin.

He did this by declining to seek the nomination. When the convention opened in Chicago on July 15, Harry Hopkins, the messenger from the throne, carried a penciled note from FDR to Speaker Bankhead, which he asked him to convey to the delegates, and which said: "You and my other close friends have known and understood that I have not today and have never had any wish or purpose to remain in the office of President, indeed anywhere in public office, after next January."

Outwardly, the situation seemed chaotic. Ickes fretted that they were in Chicago without a program, without a floor leader, without knowing who was making the nominating speech—it was all leaderless and planless. When he had mentioned this to FDR, the president had grinned and said he was "trusting in God."

To God and Harry Hopkins, architect of the draft. Harry had suites at three hotels—the Stevens, to keep an eye on Farley, the Blackstone across the street, and the Ambassador East, a few miles up the lakefront, for privacy. Everyone knew he was the man to see—that he slept at the foot of the president's bed. Into Hopkins's suites trooped such Democratic bosses as Frank Hague of New Jersey and Chicago's Mayor Ed Kelly. The message was that Roosevelt would refuse the nomination if more than 150 votes were cast against him on the first ballot.

On the evening of July 16, it was Alben Barkley, as permanent chairman, who read Roosevelt's message that he did not want the nomination. This was followed by a thunderous demonstration orchestrated by Mayor Kelly. From loudspeakers around the hall came the cry: "We want Roosevelt." Delegates started parading in the aisles with their state standards, soon to be joined by hundreds of spectators. It took an hour to restore order.

The next day, July 17, Roosevelt was nominated, and so were Farley, Garner, Tydings, and Hull. Only one ballot was necessary. FDR won 946

votes, while his four opponents totaled 147—seventy-two for Farley, sixty-
one for Garner, nine for Tydings, and five for Hull. In his final task for the
Democratic party, Farley moved to make the nomination by acclamation,
and there was a roar of "Ayes."

Only one speech, that of Carter Glass nominating Farley, had made a specific reference to the third term. "What a pity that poor old Carter made
such a sorry spectacle of himself in Chicago," FDR wrote a friend. ". . . It
lowers my respect for the fundamental integrity of the old man."

Roosevelt had outmaneuvered and effectively muzzled the conservatives
he had tried to purge in 1938. The next morning, July 18, Paul Appleby, the
top Wallace man at the convention, met with Harry Hopkins at his unpub-
licized suite at the Ambassador East. Hopkins had spoken to the boss at 2:30
A.M. He had said flatly, "It's Wallace." "It is our job," Hopkins told Appleby, "to arrange things so that word of the President's choice is spread as
inoffensively and persuasively as possible." All the disappointed hopefuls
had to be tactfully notified. FDR had agreed to call one and only one, and
they would have to see the others.

Appleby marveled at Roosevelt's skill in managing the convention. "His
use of that skill was deeply habitual," he recalled. "It was the source of his
flexibility, and of a kind of opportunism intricately related to democratic
leadership. He was in a high-level political sense a planner, always looking
forward, calculating the future, but seeing the future in terms of a variety of
alternatives always developing out of a set of current alternatives. It was this
quality that enabled him to encourage different men along somewhat different or competitive lines. . . . He was a pluralistic leader of a pluralistic people."

The conservatives rallied against Wallace. He was a mystic, an ex-Re-
publican, a poor campaigner, a man who couldn't even run his own department, much less the country. At least a dozen men thought they had the
green light from the president for the number two spot and were busy cor-
ralling delegates.

But the labors of Hopkins and Appleby paid off, and on the evening of
July 18 all of the candidates opposing Wallace withdrew, except for Senator
Bankhead. Scott Lucas, the New Deal senator from Illinois, withdrew with
the words: "Had this been a free and open convention. . . ." The pro-Wallace speeches were hissed. At one point, an anguished delegate from Missouri climbed to the platform and cried: "Don't teach my boys to scratch the
ticket," meaning that if Wallace was nominated, his "boys" in Missouri
would not vote the Democratic ticket.

In the Oval Study, FDR played solitaire and listened on the radio to the
disputes on the convention floor, and wrote out a statement refusing the
nomination, which he planned to deliver if Wallace was not chosen. He had
told Harry Hopkins that he would not run with anyone else. Wallace was a
liberal who would protect the New Deal legacy if Roosevelt died.

Wallace's name was booed each time it was mentioned, but the convention knew that he came as part of the Roosevelt package, and gave him 627 votes out of 1,100.

The president had won his fight, but hundreds of Democratic delegates went home mad. Some joined Democrats-for-Willkie clubs. Maddest of all was Jim Farley, who could now agree with Al Smith that the time had not come when a man could say his beads in the White House. He resigned as postmaster general and went to work for Coca-Cola. FDR had offered to make him honorary chairman, and when Farley declined and FDR asked him why, Farley said: "I don't like to answer you, because you and I have been very friendly." "I think I'm entitled to an answer," FDR said. "Here it is," Farley replied. "Boss, you've lied to me and I've lost all faith in you." Farley never forgot the expression on FDR's face. He just shrugged. He was a funny fellow that way.

Farley joined the Haters' Club. A report from J. Edgar Hoover to Harry Hopkins on August 9, 1942, said: "At a small dinner party in New York City, Jim Farley and his wife were most vituperative in their criticisms of President Roosevelt. Farley said FDR was using the present war to have himself elected to a fourth term as President. Mrs. Farley said the New Deal program had turned out so disastrously that the war was the only way FDR could keep himself in power. Farley said war could be terminated easily within the next year but that FDR contemplated dragging it out until at least 1945 in order to stay in office for a fourth term."

The 1940 campaign was, as Henry Wallace put it, "under cover, exceedingly dirty." One evening in August, Sam Rosenman was working in the Executive Office when Harry Hopkins phoned and asked him to stop by his room in the White House. Sam found Harry sitting at a bridge table with some photostatic copies of letters spread out before him. He gathered them together and silently passed them over, and went over to lie on the couch as Sam read them.

Sam had a sinking sensation as he read the letters. Some of them were handwritten and signed by Henry Wallace, others were typed. They were composed in a mystical jargon that was rather bizarre coming from a member of the cabinet. You would have to have serious doubts about their author's fitness for serving in an office where he was a heartbeat away from the presidency.

"I have many hard, careful things to do and at the same time I must evoke a new spirit in many quarters," said one of the handwritten letters. "Therefore I must read Agny Yoga and sit by myself once in a while. We are dealing with the first crude beginnings of a new age. May the peace of the Great One descend upon you."

Some of the letters dealt with current events, using some sort of code, as in this example, also handwritten: "The rumor is the Monkeys are seeking friendship with the Rulers so as to divide the land of the Masters between them. The Wandering One thinks this and is very suspicious of Monkeys. . . . He does not like the Rulers and wants adequate preparation for two or three years hence."

Hopkins said the originals were in the possession of the treasurer of the Republican National Committee, locked up in a vault in a bank on Wall Street. The letters would be dynamite if they were released and it was proved that Wallace had written them.

Wallace was out of town, but Hopkins had called his assistant, Paul Appleby, and asked him to check on the letters' authenticity. Appleby reached Wallace, asking him if he had ever written letters fitting Hopkins's description, and Wallace said: "I guess that's right, Paul." Later, when he saw the photostats, Wallace said only the handwritten letters were genuine.

Appleby arrived at the White House at about 11:00 P.M., and Hopkins asked him what the letters were about. Appleby explained that in 1933 Wallace had become involved with a Russian "guru" named Nicholas Roerich. This man, who was also a friend of FDR's mother, was an expert on Central Asia and a painter of naive religious works, which he exhibited in a museum and foundation funded by wealthy patrons on Riverside Drive in New York.

Wallace had told FDR in December 1933 that the Department of Agriculture was interested in importing drought-resistant grasses from Central Asia. He wanted to send Roerich on an expedition to Manchuria, which had been invaded by the Japanese. FDR, who had met Roerich and liked him, approved, and the expedition arrived in the Manchurian city of Harbin in the winter of 1934. Roerich expressed pro-Japanese sentiments and came under the attack of the White Russian colony in Harbin. The State Department, disturbed that an American agricultural mission was mixing in political intrigue, complained to Wallace, who terminated the mission and broke with Roerich in 1936.

The "guru" letters had been written in 1933 and 1934 to Roerich and his son George, and to Frances Grant, the executive director of the Roerich museum in New York, whom Wallace also addressed as "Modra" or "M."

In Wallace's code, FDR was the Wandering One or the Flaming One, the Monkeys were the British, the Rulers were the Japanese, and the land of the Masters was Manchuria. Thus, in the letter previously quoted, Wallace was informing the Roerichs that FDR was suspicious of alleged British plans to divide Manchuria with the Japanese.

When the State Department got curious, Wallace wrote George Roerich on April 17, 1934, that "the Old House [State Department] . . . has learned something and are calling on me Thursday noon. I shall of course take the strongest possible stand which does not violate the law of discretion. If need be I shall take the matter up with the Sour One [Hull] who is under obligation to me." In September 1933, Wallace had invited Hull to attend an organization meeting for the Roerich Banner of Peace conference, which was held in October. Hull prudently declined, but Wallace did prevail upon FDR to accept the Roerich Peace Banner.

Wallace showed a lack of judgment in writing the letters, some of which revealed confidential information, to a man who may have been a Japanese agent and who, a few weeks before Pearl Harbor, wrote an article in a Russian newspaper praising the Japanese conquest of Manchuria. When he broke with the Roerichs, they began to undermine him and sold his letters to the Republicans.

As Rosenman and Hopkins reread the letters and talked about the ridicule and derision that might be heaped on the ticket, they became more and more dejected. "Sam," Hopkins asked, "is there any way that we can get Wallace off the ticket now, or is it too late? When we tell the President about these letters tomorrow, he may want to have Wallace resign as a candidate—and if he does, he will ask us how to go about it. We better be prepared."

In the early morning, as the White House cleaning crews came in with their dusting machines and carpet sweepers, Rosenman looked up the law about declinations of nominations by candidates for the vice presidency. There was no legal way to withdraw even if Wallace wanted to.

Hopkins and Rosenman arrived in Roosevelt's bedroom as he was finishing his breakfast and handed him the photostats. The president's face clouded over as he hurriedly glanced at five or six letters on top of the heap. "Have you any information about how the Republicans expect to use these letters in the campaign?" he asked. They weren't sure they'd be used at all, Hopkins said, they might boomerang.

FDR was stuck with Wallace, whom he wanted to keep in any case, but said that Appleby should go out to Chicago where Wallace was campaigning, and keep him on track. Appleby went, and prepared a statement with Wallace and his lawyer, Morris L. Ernst. When Wallace was asked point-blank about the letters by a reporter for the Pittsburgh *Post-Gazette*, which had come into possession of copies, he said: "Your publisher must know of the rejection of the material by handwriting experts. He must know the story of the disgruntled discharged employee [Roerich]—a tax evader, who dare not re-enter this land—from which all this stems." Wallace said the letters were forgeries.

Appleby felt bad about his role in the whole mess. He had lied for the good of the party. He later wrote Sam Rosenman: "I was responsible for that reply, and it is a sore point on my conscience because it was as nearly a dishonest thing as I remember ever having been a party to."

As it turned out, no newspaper printed the "guru" letters except for the one in Pittsburgh. At Willkie's specific direction, the Republicans did not make use of the damaging material. Perhaps he felt that to use below-the-belt tactics would hurt the accuser more than the accused.

But there was another reason. The Democrats knew that Willkie had a mistress in New York, the writer and editor Irita Van Doren, who was reported to have helped him with some of his speeches. FDR was quite prepared to fight back, scandal for scandal, as he told presidential aide Lowell Mellett, shortly after his meeting with Rosenman and Hopkins:

"[We can] spread it as a word-of-mouth thing, or by some people way, way down the line. We can't have any of our principal speakers refer to it, but the people down the line can get it out. I mean the Congress speakers, and state speakers, and so forth. They can use the raw material. . . . Now, now, if they want to play dirty politics in the end, we've got our own people. . . . Now you'd be amazed at how this story about the gal is spreading around the country. . . . Awful nice gal, writes for the magazines and so forth and so on, a book reviewer. But nevertheless there is the fact. And one very good way of bringing it out is by calling attention to the parallel in conversation. . . . Jimmy Walker, once upon a time, was living openly with this gal all over New York. . . . She was an extremely attractive little tart. . . ."

FDR went on to say that when he was governor, Walker had appeared before him in 1932 in Albany on various charges, and had hired his wife for $10,000 to come with him and attend church on Sunday and put up a good front. "Now Mrs. Willkie may not have been hired," he said, "but in effect she's been hired to return to Wendell and smile and make this campaign with him. Now whether there was a money price behind it, I don't know, but it was the same idea."

In any case, neither scandal was used in the campaign. It was a Mexican standoff, the "guru" letters against the girlfriend in New York. Sam Rosenman always wondered why FDR continued to place Wallace in positions of power and influence. FDR was convinced, Rosenman thought, that Wallace was through with his Roerich connections and had given up mysticism. He saw Wallace as a genuine liberal, with a following, who would keep the New Deal faith.

Of course, there was plenty of material on Willkie that they did use. As Lord Bryce put it, "When political controversy is languid, personal issues come to the front." It was put out that Willkie's hometown, Elwood, Indiana, had signs saying "Nigger, don't let the sun go down on you." Photographs were taken to prove that Willkie's father had been buried in potter's field as a drunkard. Much was made of the groups that backed Willkie, such as the Bund, the Italian Fascists, the American Communist party, and Father Coughlin. Photostatic evidence was released of Willkie's onetime membership in Tammany Hall.

His public record was almost completely the record of his dealings with TVA as president of the Commonwealth & Southern holding company. His utility companies had employed labor spies and bribed state legislators. This was no tousle-haired Hoosier, the Democrats pointed out, but a bare-knuckled Wall Street man.

Willkie was a novice campaigner, who took the gee-whiz tone and the folksy touch as far as it could go. His foot was often to be found in his mouth, as when, in Joliet, he told the crowd that Roosevelt had "telephoned to Hitler and Mussolini and urged them to sell Czechoslovakia down the river." When, in Pittsburgh, he promised to appoint a labor leader as secretary of labor, he added: "And it won't be a woman, either."

"Why didn't he have sense enough to leave well enough alone?" FDR asked Miss Perkins. "Why did he have to insult every woman in the United States? It will make them mad, it will lose votes. . . . He's sure to make other boners as time goes on. . . . If we don't do anything to break the spell, I'm pretty sure he will talk himself out of enough votes to carry me without much effort."

FDR's best weapon was the incumbency. He was the president and commander in chief, and made eight nonpolitical tours of defense installations at government expense. As Ickes put it, "The President cannot adjourn the Battle of Britain in order to ride circuit with Mr. Willkie."

On one of these tours, on the train in early September, FDR was his old self, genial and laughing and full of energy, although older and grayer. "You can't say that everyone who is opposed to Roosevelt is pro-Nazi," he said, sticking out his jaw and flashing his grin, "but you *can* say with truth that everyone who is pro-Hitler in this country is also pro-Willkie."

This sort of thinking was translated at the campaign-worker level into smears connecting Willkie with Nazism, such as a document emanating from the Democratic National Committee that said Willkie had been nominated "by the Hitler formula."

The Republicans fought back with various attacks on FDR, such as the one over Elliott's commission. Elliott had been something of an isolationist in his Texas radio talks, but in September 1940 he joined the Army Air Corps and was made a captain. Favoritism was charged, and Republicans wore buttons saying: "Papa, I Want to Be a Captain."

There was such a flap that FDR stopped in Dayton, Ohio, where Elliott was stationed, on one of his tours, to see his son. Elliott found him with Army Air Corps commander, General Henry "Hap" Arnold. "Bunny," he said, "I think we've got a problem. Hap and I have been talking about it to figure out what to do."

"I think I ought to resign my commission and reenlist as a private," Elliott said.

"No, that would mean admitting you were not entitled to it. Would you mind being assigned to overseas duty?"

"I'd be glad to," said Elliott.

"Fine, list your preferences."

"I want to go to a warm climate, the Philippines, Hawaii, the Panama Canal Zone or Bermuda."

"You put 'em down just the way you want 'em," Hap Arnold said.

Then the sealed orders came—Newfoundland, under three feet of snow. Elliott went cursing up to the White House, but there was nothing his father could do. "There's good fishing up there," he said. "Not this time of year," Elliott replied, "it's frozen solid." Once again, he felt, he had been penalized for being the president's son.

Another problem was the black vote, which had flocked to FDR in 1936 but was now on the fence. The Selective Service Act had passed in mid-September, and black leaders were concerned about segregation in the Army and the small number of black officers. Henry L. Stimson, the secretary of war, although coming from an abolitionist family, had a low opinion of black capabilities. He had seen Woodrow Wilson yield to the same sort of demands and appoint black officers that went over to France "and the poor fellows made perfect fools of themselves," he wrote in his diary, "and one at least of the Divisions behaved very badly. The others were turned into labor battalions. Leadership is not imbedded in the Negro race yet and to try to make commissioned officers to lead the men into battle—colored men—is only to work disaster to both. . . . Colored troops do very well under white officers but every time we try to lift them a little bit beyond where they can go, disaster and confusion follow. . . . We are preparing to give the Negros a fair shot in every service, even to aviation where I doubt very much if they will not produce disaster there. . . . I hope for heavens sake they won't mix the white and the colored troops together in the same units for then we shall certainly have trouble."

Prodded by his wife, Roosevelt called a meeting on September 27 between the secretaries of war and the Navy and three black leaders—A. Philip Randolph of the Brotherhood of Sleeping Car Porters, Walter White of the NAACP, and T. Arnold Hill of the Urban League. Stimson did not deign to attend, but sent one of his assistant secretaries, Robert P. Patterson.

FDR tried to finesse the segregation issue by saying that in combat segregated units would have to mix. "Of course, the main point to get across is," he said, "that we are not (as we did) in the World War, confining the Negro to the non-combat services. We're putting them right in, proportionately, into the combat services. . . . Now suppose you have a Negro regiment . . . here, and right over here on my right in line, would be a white regiment. . . . Now what happens after a while, in case of war? Those people get shifted from one to the other. The thing gets sort of backed into."

Randolph said that since the races could work together in factories, they could work together in the Army.

FDR agreed. "Up on the Hudson River where I come from," he said, "we have a lot of brickwork . . . up around Fishkill . . . and, heavens, they have the same union where the white workers and the Negro workers do most of the brickwork. And they get along; no trouble at all."

Randolph asked Knox about prospects for integrating the Navy. Knox, who in private liked to express his scorn for all other races but the white, bluntly said: "We have a factor in the Navy that is not so in the Army, and that is that these men live aboard ship. And in our history we don't take Negroes into a ship's company."

"If you could have a Northern ship and a Southern ship it would be different," FDR said with a laugh. "But you can't do that."

The Negro leaders left under the impression that FDR was going to do something about segregation in the military. Of course, he could do nothing, since his service secretaries were adamantly against it, not to mention the generals and admirals. They felt betrayed when on October 9 Steve Early called a press conference to announce that, as a result of the conference with Negro leaders, the War Department had determined a policy "not to intermingle colored and white enlisted personnel in the same regimental organizations." The newspapers indicated that the policy had been approved by the Negro leaders. It was the old double cross, they felt, and it did not improve matters when Steve Early kicked a black policeman in the groin just before the election.

But FDR did throw out a few sops to the blacks. In late October, the outstanding black Army officer, Colonel Benjamin O. Davis, was promoted to brigadier general. The first reaction the president received was a telegram from Charleston, West Virginia: "Mr. President, are you crazy, appointing a nigger as general in the United States Army?" Also, on October 10, FDR met again with Frank Knox and suggested that "since we are training a certain number of musicians on board ship—the ship's band—there's no reason why we shouldn't have a colored band on some of these ships, because they're *darned good at it*. . . . Look, to increase the *opportunity*, that's what we're after." In FDR there coexisted the liberal president who wanted to give every citizen a fair shake and the slave-owning ancestry which made him fond of jokes about colored "pussons," jokes that invariably stereotyped the Negro as stupid and lazy, although having a good sense of rhythm.

John L. Lewis was another thorn in the president's side. They had a real personality conflict. Lewis was always complaining that labor was not getting its due, whereas FDR felt he had bent over backward for labor. But FDR kept trying, and asked him to the White House on October 17, saying: "John, sit down over here by my side. . . . John, I want your support." Lewis asked what he was going to do for labor, and his tone irritated the president, who asked: "What do you mean? Haven't I always been friendly to the CIO?"

"Well," said Lewis, "if you are a friend of labor, why is the FBI tapping all my phones, both my home and my office, and why do they have instructions to follow me about?"

"That's a damn lie," FDR said.

"Nobody can call John L. Lewis a liar," Lewis said, "and least of all Franklin Delano Roosevelt." He got his hat and coat, but FDR asked him to come back, and they chatted some more, and Lewis said he had seen the president's orders to tap his phones. Then Lewis stuck out his hand and FDR shook it, looking away.

They had never been friends, but they had been political allies, and now that too was ended, for on October 25 Lewis paid $45,000 for an hour of prime time on all three networks and, with millions of Americans listening, came out for Willkie. The radical labor leader, whose union was riddled with Communists, the originator of the sit-down strike, the organizer of the coal mines and the steel and auto industries, was backing the pure product of Wall Street, the candidate whose power companies had hired labor spies and promoted company unions. It was amazing what spite could make a man do.

Claiming to speak for 10 million union members, and putting his own leadership on the line, Lewis said: "It is obvious that President Roosevelt will not be re-elected to the third term unless he has the overwhelming support of the men and women of labor. If he is, therefore, re-elected, it will mean that the members of the CIO have rejected my advice and recommendation. I will accept the result as being the equivalent of a vote of no-confidence, and will retire." Still hurting at being rebuffed for the vice presidency, Lewis gave his people an ultimatum: it was him or FDR.

If the labor vote switched to Willkie, FDR would lose states like Michigan, Pennsylvania, and Ohio—it could cost him the election. Also, for all his blunders—the wild statements, the paralyzed throat, so that a throat specialist had to travel with him—Willkie was a dogged campaigner, the first candidate to run against Roosevelt who had a chance to win. Hoover had been dumped into the swamp of the Great Depression with the anchor of his years in office tied to his ankles. Landon had been in a David-Goliath situation, and, except in myths, Davids get their heads bashed in. Willkie pledged to get 8 million more Republican voters than Landon's 16 million, and it looked as though he might do it. What he lacked in political know-how he made up in sheer guts, invading the enemy territory of factory towns like Flint and Toledo, where he had the entire produce department flung at him, as well as some dairy products.

With an amateur's energy, not unlike FDR's in 1910, he traveled 19,000 miles in fifty-one days, covering thirty states and giving 500 speeches. The dark-green, twelve-car special flew by prairies, over rusty freight spurs that had never carried a passenger train, flew by towns whose names were the secret poetry of America. What a spectacle it was, of small knots of taut-skinned farmers gathering on station platforms in Missouri, of the rally in Albuquerque, the biggest in New Mexico's history, of the parade in Chicago, where a telephone directory, a bedspread, and a cantaloupe were flung at the candidate, of the return to Coffeyville, Kansas, where he had once taught history, of hecklers in Toledo, to whom he replied: "Boos don't hurt me. . . . All I ask is a square shake." The normally cynical reporters were in awe of his stamina and tenacity. *Time* described the tour as "a fantastic form of political melodrama."

For the first time, the Roosevelt camp had to consider the possibility of losing. Around the middle of October, Will Alexander, who was on Henry Wallace's staff, went to the White House to see Harry Hopkins, whom he found sitting on a canopied bed with two telephones in his lap. "Do you know what's about to happen?" Hopkins said with fury in his voice. "Well, this fellow Willkie is about to beat the Boss, and we damn well better do something about it. . . . We've always had the support of John L. Lewis and his miners. John L. Lewis is going to make a speech next week. . . . He declares that he won't support the President. It means we may lose labor. The President has done more for these negroes in this country than anybody ever did since Abraham Lincoln, and you can't get a word out of any of them. It looks as though they are all going to go against him. You damn well do something about that."

Harold Ickes felt that FDR would lose unless he gave up the inspection trips and made some political speeches. But Missy LeHand told him the president did not want to be put in the position of having people say that Willkie had smoked him out. Such was the liability of incumbency, you had to stick to the statesmanlike stance and avoid climbing into the political arena.

Two weeks before the election, however, FDR agreed to stump, and made his first speech in Philadelphia on October 23, telling Morgenthau that he had the bit in his teeth and was going to let Willkie have it. "This fellow didn't know he was up against a buzzsaw," FDR said.

But in the last two weeks, the party professionals were feeding Willkie another tactic, which was to label FDR a warmonger. In St. Louis on October 25 he shouted: "We do not want to send our boys over there again and we do not intend to."

FDR had to respond, even though he was offended by the redundancy of the term "foreign wars." On October 30 in Boston, in a speech written in part by the playwright Robert Sherwood, an interventionist who had fought in a Canadian regiment in World War I, the president pledged to "stand on the platform of our party: we will not participate in foreign wars and will not send our army, navel, or air forces to fight in foreign lands outside of the Americas except in case of attack."

Thus, in its final days, the campaign boiled down to two catch-all phrases: "A vote for Willkie is a vote for Hitler" against "A vote for Roosevelt is a vote for war." Henry Wallace in New York said that "millions of Americans know from personal observation the extent of Nazi propaganda and Nazi performance for the election of the Republican candidate. Regimented Nazi organizations are marching in the Republican parade."

Willkie kept hitting the theme that if FDR won American boys would soon be on the transports, whereas if he won aid would go to Britain only with the consent of Congress instead of through the president's "slick legal shortcuts." Earlier, he had approved of the destroyer deal, but now he called it "the most dictatorial act ever taken by an American President."

And so the day came, November 5, when more than 49 million Americans went to the polls, the largest turnout ever. One of them was the president, voting in Hyde Park, where someone had put up a sign that said: "Safe on Third."

But was he? What would labor do, and the Catholic vote, which Jim Farley had been undermining, and the Negro vote, and the Italian vote, defecting because of the "stab in the back" speech. He had against him one of the strangest coalitions ever formed in American politics, made up of isolationists, profascists, Communists, Democrats-for-Willkie such as his onetime budget director, Lewis W. Douglas, and his onetime mentor, Al Smith, John L. Lewis, three-quarters of the country's newspaper publishers, and the regular Republicans.

As he sat at the family dining-room table that evening with tally sheets and a row of freshly sharpened pencils in front of him, FDR had a premonition that he might lose and asked his Secret Service bodyguard, Mike Reilly, to make sure that he was left alone. He had broken out in a heavy sweat, and it seemed to Reilly that he had lost his nerve.

But as the results came in, he had reason for good cheer. The big industrial states were for him, his own New York (by only 225,000 votes), and Illinois, Massachusetts, and Pennsylvania. Ohio and Wisconsin swung into the Democratic column. By midnight, he knew that he had won.

The final tally showed 27,244,160 votes for Roosevelt to 22,305,198 for Willkie, who won only 82 electoral votes to FDR's 449. The president won every large city except Cincinnati. Labor and the blacks had stayed loyal.

Willkie had come across as a me-too candidate, in Ickes's words "the rich man's Roosevelt," who wanted only to fine-tune most of the New Deal programs. Nor did he challenge Roosevelt's internationalism until the final days of the campaign; he was not a consistent nor a convincing spokesman for the millions of Americans who wanted nothing to do with the war in Europe. He could not make any serious inroads among the beneficiaries of the New Deal, to whom he appeared as a Wall Street emissary.

There was also the contrast between the tested and the untested in a time of crisis. As Mayor La Guardia put it, "I would rather have FDR with his known faults than Willkie with his unknown qualities."

Finally, there was the people's trust in a leader whose greatness was intuitively acknowledged. In an election eve radio talk, Carl Sandburg called the president "not a perfect man and yet more precious than fine gold."

XIX

*I Dare Not Shirk
Any Part of Myself*

———

*I dare not shirk any part of myself,
Not any part of America good and bad,
Not to build for that which builds for mankind,
Not to balance ranks, complexions, creeds and the sexes,
Not to justify science nor the march of equality,
Not to feed the arrogant blood of the brawn belov'd of time.*

Walt Whitman, *Leaves of Grass*

FDR achieved mastery by surrendering to politics. By 1940, he had been practicing for thirty years. He would serve in the highest office longer than any other president. He knew how to govern the way Casals knew how to play the cello; he knew every shading and modulation.

Roosevelt understood presidential power as the pure derivative of a collective force straining toward a constantly compromised idea of the Common Good. On one hand there were the voters; on the other, a bargain made with heaven. Power in a democratic society did not corrupt, it was virtuous in the dual sense that it came from the collective will of the people as well as from a transcendental moral compact.

The man four times elected president, accused a thousand times of being a dictator, kept always present the awareness that his power was fragile because it came from forces outside himself; it could be maintained only if he made himself the embodiment of both the collective will and the moral compact. If he lost the ability to personify the psyche of his people he would lose his power, because it was derivative.

He alone was in that position—those who shared the power were not. "Wallace and Ickes were in here for an hour," he told a visitor one day, "arguing over who should control a couple of sticks along the Cumberland River." This was a stand of trees that Ickes wanted to bring under the Department of Interior. "And you know, for all the squabbling, neither one of them controls any votes." Because he controlled the votes, he saw how trivial their argument was.

Also, he saw himself as a participant in a process shared by previous presidents. This he had grasped at firsthand, from having personally known five presidents, and from having absorbed the American past as a legume absorbs water. He saw himself as a member of the crew of presidents, all building the same house. In 1925, during his years out of office, he reviewed Claude Bowers's book *Jefferson and Hamilton: The Struggle for Democracy in America,* liking it because it prompted "the constantly recurring thought of parallel or at least analogous situations existing in our own generation." The struggle between Jeffersonian democracy and Hamiltonian aristocracy was going on in a different form, as business interests took over the country in the Republican administrations of the twenties.

In Jefferson the gifted amateur, Roosevelt found a model for the protean man, the man of many gifts and disguises, the man with chameleonlike powers of adaptation, the man whose true self is protected by an essential elusiveness, and who rises through his variously altered shapes to great stature—Proteus in Greek mythology being the keeper of the seals, who would foretell the future if anyone could seize and hold him but who would change into other shapes to escape and avoid having to tell the truth. Roosevelt too adopted a stance of deliberate changeability. It allowed him to hold contradictory views simultaneously, juggling apples and oranges until the time was ripe for a decision.

In Lincoln too he found a model, as having waged war to keep the moral compact. In Theodore Roosevelt and Woodrow Wilson were further models, and he often liked to recall what one or the other had said, as when he sent Arthur Bliss Lane to head the American legation in Riga, reminiscing that Wilson had told him after the Versailles Peace Conference that "St. Peter will deny me entrance to the pearly gates because I have resurrected three dead languages—Latvian, Lithuanian, and Estonian."

Or again, as he was working late on a speech with Tommy Corcoran and Donald Richberg, he read it through, pausing at one passage and saying: "Now, this I must say in the true TR manner," thrusting his chin forward and baring his teeth. "Oh, but Mr. President," interjected Corcoran, "the difference between you and TR is that you never fake." FDR leaned forward and replied: "Oh, but Tommy, at times I do, I do!"

While modeling himself in certain ways on past presidents, FDR developed his own personal style, by which he can be identified. It is in the elements of the "Roosevelt style" that the artistry of this most slippery of presidents can be tracked and studied. Walt Bowie caught it in his remark about the Harvard *Crimson* days: "In his geniality there was a kind of frictionless command." Henry Wallace caught it when he commented in January 1940 on FDR's kidding—he had kidded Morgenthau about being a "kulak," which is what the agriculture people at Cornell were called, and he had kidded Wallace about the Bureau of Nematology (nematodes being wormlike creatures that preyed on sugarbeets), calling it the Bureau of Nepotology and saying "Last year the Bureau of Nepotology was getting $102,000, and this year it wants $107,000." The president was enjoying his ability to artistically modify the truth, Wallace thought. It was a technique of domination, a way of asserting his superiority without abrasiveness. "In that way," Wallace wrote in his diary, "he fills out his artistic sense of the fitness of things."

Kidding and humor were strong elements of the "Roosevelt style." In this aspect of his nature, he fitted the Jungian concept of the "trickster," an archetypal character recurring in diverse societies, such as the medieval jester and the hook-nosed and squeaky-voiced Punch.

FDR liked to boast about the trickster side of his nature. One story was that while at Harvard he had bet a schoolmate that he could hit a golf ball 400 yards. "The other fellow said that was a ridiculous boast," FDR said, "and figured he had easy pickings. Well, unfortunately for him he didn't specify the exact conditions under which I was to hit the ball. I, therefore, took the golf ball down to the lake that was frozen over. Naturally, when I hit the ball it skimmed over the ice for a distance beyond four hundred yards. I won my bet."

In trickster fashion, Roosevelt's stories tended to be at someone else's expense. Once, John C. Reynolds, a heavy contributor to the 1940 campaign, and president of the tobacco company that made Camels, came to see him, and FDR told him they were the only kind of cigarette he smoked.

"Mr. President, can we use that for advertising?" the delighted executive asked.

"Well, perhaps," FDR responded. "How much?"

"If you will give me a signed letter saying that you smoke Camels," Reynolds said excitedly, "and how much you like them, I will give you $50,-000."

"All right," FDR agreed. "Shall we say something like this? Dear Mr. Reynolds: I always smoke Camels cigarettes because I think Mr. Reynolds and myself are the only people in America who can smoke them without getting a sore throat."

Reynolds, who had visions of scoring the greatest coup in advertising history, was let down hard, and walked out, muttering "Oh, go to hell" under his breath.

Sometimes FDR went too far, and his teasing hurt. After the 1940 election, the columnist Dorothy Thompson lost her contract with the Republican New York *Herald Tribune* because she had come out for him. Roosevelt sent her this gratuitously wounding telegram: "At least I kept my job."

Or there was the incident involving James Landis, former dean of Harvard Law School, who was named director of civil defense and was getting out pamphlets on what to do about shelters and blackouts. In the pamphlet on blackouts there was the phrase "when you hear the siren, terminate the illumination." A reporter at a presidential press conference picked up the phrase as an example of bureaucratic jargon, and FDR responded with: "What can you expect of a Harvard professor?" Feeling repentant, he invited Landis to the White House that evening, mixed two old-fashioneds, and said, "I'm awfully sorry about this morning, but I just couldn't help it."

It was true. He just couldn't help it, no matter how hurtful or silly, if it was an occasion for merriment. In October 1943, RFC Chairman Jesse Jones wrote him that War Mobilization Director James F. Byrnes and Democratic National Committee Secretary George Allen each owned a wirehaired terrier, "and great rivalry has developed between their owners as to which dog can piddle the most times in a given walking distance when taken for his evening stroll . . . in order that there may be no skullduggery, the dogs will be taken to the contest by disinterested parties, and it has been suggested that the campus of the Russell Young School of Expression will be the place of demonstration."

"Strictly between ourselves," FDR replied, "you and I can make a lot of money out of that contest. Let the odds on Allen's dog go sky-high. You and I will then bet on Byrnes' dog. Boss McIntyre and I know how to work it."

It bordered on the absurd that in the autumn of 1943, when the Russians were locked in a death struggle with the Germans and Stalin was pleading for a second front, and the Allied armies were stalled in the Italian campaign, FDR could have devoted a few minutes of his precious time to a dog-pissing contest. But it was a measure of his sanity that he found release in humor in the midst of crisis. It was a very American kind of safety valve, like the sign on the office door that says: "Gone Fishin'."

Humor was a tool of government, a way to keep his cabinet members and agency heads in line. When Donald Richberg took over the NRA, some policy disagreement put him in an angry mood and he told associates he was resigning. Word of this reached the president, who called Richberg late one evening and said: "I have just had some bad news, Don. Secretary Hull is threatening to resign. He is very angry because I don't agree with him that we ought to remove the ambassador to Kamchatka and make him third secretary to the embassy at Svodia." It dawned on Richberg that FDR was not talking about Hull at all. His friendly amusement was far more effective than the stern displeasure he might have shown, which would only have made Richberg's hackles rise.

His method with cabinet members was oblique and jesting. He rarely told anyone off, but you knew where you stood. If he was mad at someone, he would freeze him out, as he did Jim Farley. When Farley said something, he would reply, "Really, really, indeed," as if his comments were totally off the point.

It was touching to see how cabinet members sought to be in his good graces, like courtiers given the king's napkin to hold. Ickes and Morgenthau practically had ulcers worrying whether or not they were in the president's favor. Ickes told Bill Douglas in 1942 that he had no affection for the president anymore and what the president thought about him was a matter of indifference. He didn't get all worked up the way he used to. He couldn't stand going through the emotional upsets that he used to have for which the president was almost altogether responsible. But this sour mood sweetened at the first sign of presidential favor, when FDR wrote him that "oil in oil you have done a good job" as petroleum director.

FDR loved to kid Ickes, who was the administration's number one kibbitzer, always sticking his nose into other people's business, while complaining that the other departments were poaching on his preserve; he said there should be a portrait of "Harold stuffed in his underwear, saying 'they have taken everything else away from me.'"

As for Morgenthau, Ickes wrote: "He is the deferential type, and his whole life is wrapt up with the President." Morgenthau did indeed chart his intimacy with FDR in his diary on an almost daily basis. A call from the president would lead to a diary entry such as this: "It certainly is wonderful for me to be on such an intimate footing with him and it is incidents like this which make me feel how close I am to him." In December 1939 Morgenthau broke his toe and asked FDR if he could borrow one of his canes. "You know," he told his secretary, "I am just a baby about it. Part of the reason I sent for the cane was because I wanted the President to know that I had broken my toe."

The knack of always finding a connection with everyone he met was another element of style. It was a stratagem of ingratiation, and yet it was not contrived. It came naturally, like an involuntary reflex. It was a useful instinct, in a pluralistic society, to find what unites rather than what divides, to look for bonds and connections in a sprawling land of strangers.

One time Marion Dickerman heard FDR say something unkind about Norman Davis, a diplomat who headed American delegations to various international conferences. Then she saw Davis come to Hyde Park and work closely with the president for a couple of days. "I think you are an awful hypocrite," she told FDR when Davis had gone. "What do you mean?" he asked. "Well, I know what you said about Mr. Davis, yet you worked like two old cronies."

"Don't you realize," FDR said, "that you very seldom find a person who agrees with you on everything? Don't look for it. It's ridiculous. When you find a person who cares deeply for something which you care about, you work with them on that, and do not bring in causes for differences."

Finding connections was also a way of displaying the breadth of his knowledge, like a singer who can range from bass to tenor. He had a trick of placing himself at the disposition of the other person's interests. He could talk to a botanist about plants, and to an architect about buildings. When he met Churchill's doctor, Sir Charles Wilson, in December 1941, he talked about the burn victims at Pearl Harbor. "He made me feel that I had known him for a long time," Wilson said.

Roosevelt could floor you with these small virtuoso performances. When Anthony Eden, the British foreign secretary, visited Washington in March 1943, FDR told him: "I know where you must speak, in Annapolis, and the State Legislature of Maryland will meet to hear you and we will link you up with all the other State Legislatures across the country."

"Surely they don't want to be reminded of the colonial past," Eden said.

But FDR remembered that in the early seventeenth century George Calvert, the first Lord Baltimore, had been given a charter to colonize Maryland, which his family ruled for 140 years. In the seventh generation Corinne Calvert, the last of the line, had married Sir Robert Eden, the last colonial governor of Maryland, who happened to be Anthony Eden's great-great-grandfather. Having the more subtle mind, FDR had found the connection. What could be better than to have the descendent of a colonial governor return to the scene of the crime, on bended knee, so to speak, pleading for help? The state of Maryland still flew the Eden coat of arms as its flag.

"Don't they just," FDR said. "You'll see."

Calling people by their first names was part of connecting. There were objections that it was phony, since they couldn't reciprocate. But it was done with such geniality that it could not be called condescending.

Once at a cabinet meeting when Harold Ickes was absent, his under secretary, Abe Fortas, took his place. FDR didn't know who he was and passed a note to Attorney General Francis Biddle, who whispered "Fortas," and then another note that said, "Not his last name, his *first* name." When Fortas's turn came, FDR asked, "Well, Abe, what's been going on in Interior?" You couldn't take offense, because it was so ingenuous.

With those he liked and trusted, the president let his hair down and pretended to be one of the boys. There were often poker games with Harold Ickes, Bill Douglas, and Henry Morgenthau. FDR was delighted when he outbluffed Jack Garner, said to be the best poker player in Washington, with sevens and fours against Garner's two pairs king high. They invented a hand called "Bushy," named after the bearded Chief Justice Charles Evans Hughes.

Ickes also gave parties where Tommy Corcoran sang and played the accordion. At one of these, in July 1936, Ickes reported that "the President seemed to enjoy himself hugely and he entered into the fun very naturally and spontaneously. I kept them all supplied with their favorite highballs. The President certainly carries his liquor well. He must have had five highballs after dinner. He drank gin and ginger ale but he never showed the slightest effect."

On another occasion, the president did show the effects of overimbibing. This was in Warm Springs, where he decided to give a party because the good ladies of Georgia had sent him two hampers of quail. Eddie Dowling went foraging, and found some fifteen-year-old corn liquor, pure as champagne. Everyone got to feeling pretty good, but then FDR wanted to go and asked Eddie and Gus to wheel him down to the car. It was raining cats and dogs and they were pushing the chair down a narrow wooden walk and tramping through red clay, and Roosevelt began to tickle them.

"Cut it out, will you," Eddie said.

"Oh you fellows, you like the girls," FDR said. "That's how we used to tell whether you like the girls or not. If you were ticklish, you like the girls. And if you took a buttercup and put it under your chin. . . ."

At this point, the chair tipped over, and Eddie slipped in the mud, and FDR in his chair fell on top of him. The president was laughing hilariously. "Will you please get up," Eddie asked. "My face is in the mud."

"Ha, ha," the president roared, "in the mud, in the mud. Eddie Dowling and Gus Gennerich. Why you rascals, what do you suppose would have happened if you did that to Napoleon?"

This capacity for fun was rather wonderful in a man immobilized from the hips down. Of course, Roosevelt on the job was sometimes peevish and out of sorts, but most of the time he enjoyed himself, content in the exercise of power. He loved to know what was going on, not only affairs of state but gossip, which he encouraged his aides to provide.

But those who thought the president relied on rumor and innuendo were in for a surprise. In May 1939, FDR held up an important list of State Department promotions, and the people at State were frantic, because the delay was affecting the promotion procedure and was bad for morale. Finally, in May, Sumner Welles went to see him with George Messersmith, the head of the Foreign Service Personnel Board.

Roosevelt pulled the list out of a drawer and said, "I haven't done anything about this because there are some names that shouldn't be on it."

Messersmith pointed out how carefully the promotion lists were drawn up. FDR said he knew that but he had some private information about some of the men. He asked Messersmith to go down the list with him—there were about 100 names, among which he objected to five or six. Pointing to the first name, he said: "He is drinking too much, and any man in such a post as he has who drinks too much is not responsible and will talk too much." Messersmith said the man had stopped drinking after a severe reprimand, and was a useful officer who deserved promotion. "As long as he is drinking he is a bad example and I can't approve of his being promoted," FDR said.

Coming to another name, he said: "His wife talks too much and she calls me unspeakable names in front of foreigners, and no Foreign Service officer and no wife of a Foreign Service officer should speak critically in this way and in such terms of the President of the United States and of his superiors. If he is that kind of man, he is not fit for the job he holds."

Messersmith told Roosevelt that he did not think his information was correct. "I have my sources of information too," FDR said, "and in this case I think mine are better than yours."

As they left the president's office, Welles and Messersmith agreed that he had probably been listening to gossip, and was frivolously holding up some important promotions. They decided to have State Department inspectors conduct investigations in the various embassies where FDR had stated objections.

In the meantime, the following memo from the president arrived on Sumner Welles's desk on May 18:

"Please let me know more about Childs's foreign wife and family. I have my doubts.

"I do not think I can go along with Hogdon. His trouble has not been confined to the episode in Washington, and if he were in the Army or the Navy he would not be promoted.

"Gerald A. Crew—I gather that he is best known in the Mayflower and Shoreham bars. Is he honestly the type you want to promote in the Service?

"Frederick P. Latimer: It seems rather definitely known that several years ago while in Helsingfors he talked publicly about this government being in the hands of Communists, headed by the undersigned."

When the results of the investigation arrived, Roosevelt's information turned out to be accurate in every case. The names were eliminated from the promotion list. It dawned on Messersmith that he was one of the best-informed presidents the country had ever had. Messersmith marveled at how wide and correct his sources were.

One of Roosevelt's most notable achievements, and one for which he was the least acclaimed, because it was not apparent, was the way he turned his invalidism into an element of style. It was like sleight of hand, he made you forget that he was a cripple. There were people ready to swear that when they were ushered into the Oval Office the president had risen to greet them. He always dismissed his incapacity with a jest, as when Eleanor asked him how he would receive the guests at the inaugural reception and he said: "I'll tell you what we'll do. We'll arrange to have me carried into the East Room and put up on the mantel where everyone can see me."

David Lilienthal was shocked to see the Secret Service men scoop the president up as one would a child and carry him out the door as he swung his arms over their shoulders, still talking vivaciously. He had never seen such complete unself-consciousness, or anything quite so touching as the contrast between the ghastly invalidism and his indomitable and really gay spirit.

Because he was an invalid, FDR developed special techniques for dealing with people. When they came to see him, usually to ask for something, he was a captive audience, unable to get up or leave the room. As a defense mechanism, he became skillful at verbal diversion, talking around the subject until time was up, reminiscing about his boyhood to a senator who wanted to discuss patronage matters.

It could be a frustrating experience for a public official. A few minutes with the president was a prize much sought, but getting anything out of it took as much advance planning as the D-day landing. When Marriner Eccles, a governor of the Federal Reserve System, came in for lunch one day in 1939, he was followed by FDR's Aberdeen terrier, Fala (named after one of his Scottish relatives, Murray of Fala Hill).

The president opened a desk drawer, took out a ball, and threw it across the room. This game continued for four or five minutes, with Eccles praising Fala's tricks while privately cursing the time lost, which might represent the margin between alternative national policies. Finally FDR said, "That's enough now. I've got to go back to work." Eccles was just getting started presenting his program for cushioning the inflationary inflow of gold from abroad when FDR bellowed: "Well, I'll be God-damned! Marriner, do you see what I see?"

In a corner, Fala was relieving himself on the rug. FDR pushed a button and a guard came in and was told to rub the dog's nose in the mess. All of this, and the postmortem discussion, took five to ten minutes more. Then FDR said, "And now, Marriner, we can talk about our business," as Pa Watson appeared in the door to announce the next visitor.

"The distractions most often arose from the character of the Presidency itself," Eccles reflected. "For each [caller representing one] of the President's multiple roles ... wanted him to concentrate on that one role and no other.... [Those] whose absorbing interest was the farmer, or the laborer, or the big and little businessmen, or the ground forces, the naval forces, the air forces, the Latin Americans, the English, the Russians, the French, the Chinese, the enemy, the neutral powers, and on and on ... through all the list of things that make the globe. And always and forever, when Roosevelt was about to get to the root of the matter, something that followed a law of its own being would foul up the air. The President would have to drop everything while the mess was being attended to."

It was a measure of Roosevelt's artistry that he was able to compose so many different forces, all vying for his attention. Anyone else would have had a nervous breakdown, but his equanimity was rarely ruffled. This too was partly the result of his disability, which had taught him calm and patience. In his Navy days, prior to his illness, he had been far more irritable. His old boss, Josephus Daniels, recognized the change, writing him in April 1935: "One of your sources of strength is your natural and acquired courtesy and freedom from showing irritation even when justified. ... Some people, not knowing the stuff of which you were made, jumped to the conclusion that your uniform courtesy lacked behind it resolve and determination. I rejoice, knowing that there is steel behind the velvet, that you never show the steel unless it is absolutely necessary.... In the respect that you do not brandish the Big Stick you are wiser than your cousin Theodore, and in never showing your temper you are wiser than our chief Woodrow Wilson. The Bible promises high reward for one who keeps his temper ... he is 'greater than one who taketh a city.'...."

What was often taken for weakness was in fact a method of governing that FDR had evolved from his own character traits and from his disability. He had been taught as a child to avoid confrontation and friction. Just as the kid who had to fight for everything developed a scrappy nature, the kid who had everything handed to him learned the benefits of voluntary agreement. Just as the strong and healthy man likes a fight for its own sake, as a test of his muscles, the invalid learns to husband his strength and fight only when other means have been exhausted. This is a successful method for the head of a democratic government, where friction is undesirable. You cannot have government by confrontation, making enemies right and left. You cannot be always shouting at people and knocking heads. Roosevelt knew from the depth of his own nature and experience how to avoid friction and achieve results voluntarily. He could make the hard decisions after exhausting the avenues of compromise.

His much-mentioned deviousness was part of the nonconfrontation technique. You could see it in small things. When he was governor of New York, his lieutenant governor, Herbert Lehman, came to Hyde Park to see him and started pacing up and down the library, which was irritating. The phone rang, and Louis Howe, who was curled up in a corner of the library, started for it. "Louis Howe, can't you sit still?" FDR exclaimed. Howe had not moved until the phone rang. The remark was addressed to Lehman.

Roosevelt operated by indirection, and was quite candid about it. Meeting a group of businessmen in May 1941, he told them: "You know, I am a juggler, and I never let my right hand know what my left hand does. I may have one policy for Europe and one diametrically opposite for North and South America. I may be entirely inconsistent, and furthermore I am perfectly willing to mislead and tell untruths if it will help win the war."

It took a complex and many-sided nature to deal with the shifting surfaces of a pluralistic society, not to mention the crisis of a world at war. Being evasive was not a weakness but a way of governing. FDR was the master of the either/or reply, as in this response to a question on capital punishment at a 1933 press conference: "My own personal belief is that I would like to see capital punishment abolished throughout this country, but on the other hand, every law enforcement officer with whom I have ever spoken ... believes that capital punishment is a definite and distinct deterrent of murder. It is, primarily, a legislative matter."

To attack evasiveness as weakness was an obvious strategy for Roosevelt's critics. Walter Lippmann, who had badly misjudged him in 1932, and thus went to great pains to belittle him in order to justify his initial mistake, recalled: "Roosevelt in the grand perspective of the times was an enormous figure, but Roosevelt up close was always disappointing. Churchill was just as good close and at a distance. Roosevelt was a wonderful finagler, he loved to take a complicated thing that involved a certain amount of deception—hornswoggling of other people—and get it done. He had a technique of government that was like old Joseph Pulitzer's, who thought the only way to find out what was going on was to have two men in each job and have them quarrel. Then he'd hear the quarrel and make up his mind. When anything went wrong, Roosevelt wouldn't change the man, he'd set up another office."

Trapped in his own systematic misappraisal of Roosevelt, Lippmann was unable to see that behind the finagling there was a subtle mind with a grasp of all the strands, and that setting up parallel lines of command was often the best way to get results.

Of course, the heads of the old-line departments were unhappy over the president's "finagling." Secretary of War Henry Stimson, who had served three other presidents, complained that things were terribly disorganized. "The President has created so many of these special agencies with somebody at the head of it who feels perfectly free to go direct to the President," he wrote in November 1941, that "the first thing I know they have been to the President about some matter that infringes on our jurisdiction and which ought to come up from the bottom rather than down from the top and I have to take it and handle it in my office after the President has formed an opinion or prejudice on the subject and do the thing back-end-to, with the difficulty of having to undo a false position sometimes.... This has been the source of at least two-thirds of my difficulty and pressure here for the last year—the topsy-turvy, upside-down system of poor administration with which Mr. Roosevelt runs the government."

Henry Morgenthau got positively frantic when his department was circumvented. "The President," he told his Treasury aides in July 1943, "instead of holding up the old-line departments, he is constantly watering us down.... The President is so harassed at the White House ... they have no administrative organization. They have got Pa Watson ... they have Marvin McIntyre ... Steve Early, who contacts the newspapers, and that is about all.... They are maneuverers, they are finaglers, they are much smarter than I am, they are interested in their personal ambitions.... I don't think Harry Hopkins is competent to be the second man on the war, which he is. I mean every cable, everything—people have no conception.... That is the President ... he is having these great victories in the war [so that] everybody else sinks into insignificance.... That is all he cares about.... I have been here ten years, and your moral fibers begin to weaken after a while. You take a rubber band, you pull it so often and it snaps."

Stimson was too much of a "by the book" man to approve of FDR's methods, and in Morgenthau there was a strong element of personal jealousy; he resented anyone who was closer to the president than he was. Also,

cabinet members seldom saw beyond the concerns of their own departments. Only one man saw the whole picture, and that was the president,
whose nature was pragmatic and whose orientation was toward problem
solving, at the risk of administrative unorthodoxy.

It was his problem-solving instinct that permitted FDR to cut through peripheral issues to get to the heart of a matter. In March 1942 the cabinet was
discussing the barbed-wire dilemma. The Russians, who always asked for
the highest specifications, wanted barbed wire with five barbs, whereas
American barbed wire had three and four barbs. Should they satisfy the
Russian demands? To make five-barbed wire meant changing the machinery and delaying production. As various views were expressed around
the table, FDR spoke up: "Tell Litvinov [the Soviet foreign minister] that it
hurts just as much to sit on a four-barbed wire as on a five."

Now, there was another, nonpragmatic side of FDR in that he sometimes fell for nutty ideas. In his optimism, he thought everything was possible. In 1941 he explained to Averell Harriman that helicopters could be
flown from the decks of merchant ships. They would hover over convoys,
spotting U-boats and dropping depth charges, and if they had trouble landing on the wobbly decks, they could be caught in big nets trailing behind
the base ships. All one could say, thought Harriman, was "Uh-huh,
uh-huh."

Roosevelt told Morgenthau: "I have got something very hush-hush to tell
you. I want three or four million dollars from you." This was for the helicop-
ter project, which would involve building flat decks on ordinary steamers. "I
don't know if it would work," the president said, "but it is new and hasn't
been tried, and it is a good idea." Of course it came to nothing.

"There's something he's got that eludes me," Harry Hopkins told Frances
Perkins one day. "I don't feel the liberty to press for it. I don't feel that I
have any right to pry."

"Why Harry," Miss Perkins replied, "it's clear that he's got a relationship
to God."

"I think that's it," Harry said. "But by gosh, I can't find out what it is nor
how he gets this relationship."

"He's got a perfect trust in God, hasn't he?"

"Yeah, that's it, he has. But why? It seems unreasonable at times, but he
falls back on something that gives him complete assurance that everything is
going to be all right, that he isn't able to share with me, nor to explain to me.
Why should he be so sure that it will be all right?"

It would be all right because FDR had struck his bargain with God. He
had made the moral compact. He was an expression of the collective
American will, and America had God on its side, and he had incorporated
America, was the embodiment of America, and therefore God was with him.

The corollary of this belief was self-righteousness. Those who opposed him, like the senators who had voted against the World Court, would have to be forgiven by God. He was on the side of right, of Jeffersonian democracy versus Hamiltonian aristocracy, of the forgotten man versus the fat cats. And buried just beneath those noble aims was the inherited assumption that America, its ideals and its form of government, had been made by the good Anglo-Saxon and Dutch Protestant stock that had first reached its shores and to which Roosevelt belonged. The others, the immigrants, the Catholics, the Jews, latecomers to an already formed society, were not quite up to snuff.

In January 1942, Leo T. Crowley, a Catholic economist who had been made alien property custodian, witnessed an extraordinary outburst when he had lunch with the president. For no apparent reason, FDR started giving him the following lecture: "Leo, you know this is a Protestant country, and the Catholics and the Jews are here on sufferance. It is up to both of you [Crowley and Morgenthau] to go along with anything that I want at this time."

Crowley told Morgenthau he had never been so shocked in his life. "Something has happened to the President," he said. "He has lost touch with the people."

"What am I killing myself for at this desk if we are just here by sufferance?" Morgenthau asked.

Another side of Roosevelt's self-righteousness was that he had a tendency to take the credit but not the blame. There was an element of self-satisfaction in the way he took responsibility for every success. In May 1938, a young reporter for the New York *Herald Tribune* named Joseph Alsop, who was related to the Oyster Bay branch of the Roosevelts, was invited to dinner at the White House and heard FDR hold forth on the Hoare-Laval deal concerning Ethiopia. A few days ago, FDR said, the British ambassador, Sir Ronald Lindsay, had brought the archbishop of Canterbury to the White House for tea. Roosevelt said he couldn't talk to Lindsay about Ethiopia, but he got the archbishop off in a corner and gave him an earful. A couple of days later, the Hoare-Laval agreement was scrapped. Alsop observed FDR thrust his chin in the air as he spoke, as if to say, "I did it and ain't I smart?" He later told some fellow reporters that he was disgusted with the president's "unmitigated gall and excessive ego."

Nor did Roosevelt like to be upstaged. When Canadian Prime Minister Mackenzie King came to see him in Warm Springs in April 1940, FDR complained that all King could talk about was what a great man he (King) was, and how he had pulled this trick and that trick to get reelected. It had taken three days to get him started on the war. (As a sidelight on the foibles of the great, it's worth mentioning that King was a mystic who held seances and communicated with the dead. FDR after his death appeared to King several times, usually telling him what he wanted to hear. At a seance in 1947, Roosevelt's spirit begged King not to retire, saying: "You have that slow Scotch way with you, you are not clever, you are wise. That is why I want you to hold on." At a 1948 seance, FDR's spirit warned King "not to forget Asia." King kept a diary where he described his psychic experiences in detail.)

The worst side of self-righteousness, however, was not the perfectly human trait of taking credit when he had achieved so much but the habit of equating all forms of opposition with disloyalty. Isolationists were helping Hitler, and some of the Willkie supporters were pro-Nazi.

Roosevelt was the first president to use the taxing power to go after his political enemies. In April 1942, James Rowe, a former FDR aide who had gone to work for the Justice Department, went to see Morgenthau and said: "About Father Coughlin. We'd sort of like a pretty full investigation on the income tax and everything else." Morgenthau didn't like that kind of job and turned Rowe over to one of his assistants. The investigation was averted when a deal was struck with the Catholic hierarchy to take Coughlin off the air.

The president also asked for an investigation of Hamilton Fish, the Republican congressman who represented Dutchess County as part of his district in the House. Fish was a pro-German appeaser who had met with Nazi leaders in August 1939 and had vacationed at Ribbentrop's castle. He was quoted in German newspapers as saying that Germany's claims were just, and headed the National Committee to Keep America Out of Foreign Wars. Fish spoke at a meeting of that committee on October 26, 1939, and asked, "Who made our foreign policy up, where did it originate from?" and the audience roared back, "The Jews, the Yiddles, the kikes!"

FDR wanted to have him indicted for violating the statute that barred a private citizen from conducting foreign affairs, but Cordell Hull advised against it. So FDR asked Morgenthau to study his tax returns and get something on him. What Morgenthau got was that in 1937 Fish had become a close friend of the dictator of the Dominican Republic, Rafael Trujillo. A protégé of Fish's, a White Russian named George Djamaroff, was hired as director of propaganda for the Dominican Republic, at $50,000 a year. The presumption was that Djamaroff split the salary with Fish. But Morgenthau's tax people did not have enough to go on and declined to ask for an indictment.

Another time, FDR used the Secret Service to investigate the source of an unfavorable story in the *Wall Street Journal.* Morgenthau was beside himself. "I will not have the Secret Service used for this purpose," he fumed. "It is an outrageous performance. [Steve] Early knows better than that. If he wants to do that kind of thing, let him use F.B.I."

According to whether one was a political friend or a foe, the treatment one received from the Treasury in tax fraud cases could be markedly different, as can be illustrated from the way the Moe Annenberg and Brown & Root cases were handled.

Moses Annenberg got into the newspaper business through the back door, so to speak. After being the Hearst hatchet man in the Chicago circulation wars, he took over the *Daily Racing Form* in 1922 and later the *Morning Telegraph* and the wire service that the bookmakers and horse parlors used, until he had a monopoly on racetrack information. It was alleged that the Capone mob was on a million-dollar-a-year retainer to protect that monopoly. Whenever a rival racetrack sheet started up, someone wrecked the machinery in their printing plant.

Anyway, the money rolled in, and in 1936 Annenberg bought the Philadelphia *Inquirer* and started attacking the New Deal and flamboyant George Earle, the first Democratic governor of Pennsylvania in forty-four years. Earle was up for reelection in 1938, and FDR sent Harold Ickes to Philadelphia on November 4 to speak against the Annenberg-backed candidate, Arthur H. James. But James won. Annenberg had unseated FDR's man in Pennsylvania.

This would not, however, have been enough to single Annenberg out for Roosevelt's special wrath. The reason for that was revealed in a recently declassified internal FBI memo signed by J. Edgar Hoover and dated November 7, 1938, which said: "The President took up several matters with me, first, the case of Moe Annenberg, publisher of the Philadelphia Inquirer. The President stated that Secretary of the Interior Ickes was to speak at Philadelphia on Friday evening, November 4th, and he, the President, had been in receipt of information that Annenberg's group would not only file a libel suit against Secretary Ickes, but had made threats that the Secretary had better not come to Philadelphia, otherwise they would 'get' the Secretary even though it might take a year. He stated that the report had indicated that the Secretary would know what this meant as he, the Secretary, had come from Chicago. The President concluded that this meant that they intended to do bodily harm to the Secretary at Philadelphia or some time subsequent thereto."

Annenberg had threatened one of his cabinet members, thereby placing himself on the president's hit list. Early in 1939, FDR ordered an all-out investigaton of Annenberg for tax fraud. It was Morgenthau's biggest criminal case, involving thirty-five agents, who went through the records of 5,000 gambling establishments. They would go into Chicago poolrooms and ask to see the books, and there would be no books. Annenberg was said to have the highest earned income in the country, $6 million a year.

On March 2, 1939, Morgenthau met with FDR to discuss pressures to have the case dismissed. An appeal for leniency had come from former Governor Earle, who was under investigation for accepting under-the-table money from a Philadelphia contractor. Perhaps a deal could be struck. "Governor Earle," FDR explained, "was afraid that with this new Republican administration which Annenberg controls, that he would get a Moscow trial on his own case and go to jail and Earle thought that if this administration would settle with Annenberg, that in return for that, Annenberg would see that Earle would not go to jail." But FDR did not want to settle, and told Morgenthau to proceed full steam ahead.

At lunch with Morgenthau on April 10, FDR said: "I want Moe Annenberg for dinner."

"You're going to have him for breakfast—fried," Morgenthau replied.

Annenberg desperately tried to get the matter settled, and saw Attorney General Frank Murphy on April 25, claiming that he was ignorant of what his accountants were doing. But on August 11, the grand jury returned an indictment, and at the end of November FDR told Morgenthau that he wanted him to "collect every dollar and put Annenberg in jail."

Annenberg's son Walter had also been indicted, as a corporate officer, and Annenberg made a deal with the prosecution to plead guilty in exchange for having the charges against his son dropped. Also, a trial would have revealed the protection money he had paid in his racetrack operations. At the hearings in Chicago in June 1940, he was sentenced to three years in jail and ordered to pay $8 million in back taxes and penalties. It was the biggest settlement the Treasury Department had ever obtained.

And so, that July, Moses Annenberg, who had dreamed of ending his life as the gentleman publisher of a respected newspaper, was admitted not to the "main line" society he aspired to but to the federal penitentiary in Lewisburg, Pennsylvania. He had felt the full force of the government's might when applied to an individual, no matter how rich and well connected. At the age of sixty-four, he was a broken man. He served about two-thirds of his sentence, and was paroled on June 11, 1942. But Annenberg was mortally ill and died on July 20 of a brain tumor.

How differently matters were handled in the tax fraud case concerning the 1941 campaign of Lyndon B. Johnson to fill the Senate seat of the deceased Morris Sheppard of Texas. Johnson had become a Roosevelt favorite in the 1940 campaign by being the number one fund raiser for the Democratic Congressional Campaign Committee. Eleanor on November 9 reminded her husband that "Lyndon Johnson raised $100,000 single handed for the Congressional campaign. Will you write him a note of thanks?" Much of the money came from his Texas contractor friends Brown & Root, to whom Johnson had brought millions in contracts for the construction of the Corpus Christi Naval Air Station.

In his 1941 Senate race, Johnson ran in the primary against three better-known Democrats, Governor Wilbert Lee "Pappy" O'Daniel, Attorney General Gerald Mann, and Congressman Martin Dies. He had to find ways to circumvent the Corrupt Practices Act (Hatch Act), which limited the campaign spending of a candidate to Congress to $25,000.

Brown & Root came to the rescue. Bonuses of $30,000 and $40,000 were paid to company vice presidents, who turned the money over to the Johnson campaign. Brown & Root attorneys were paid "legal fees" that were also funneled into the campaign.

Johnson had about $200,000 to spend, but lost the primary to Pappy O'Daniel by a narrow margin. In July 1942, IRS agents followed the twisting trail of the Johnson campaign finances to the disguised contributions, which they saw as a blatant example of criminal tax fraud.

Brown & Root was in big trouble, and so was Lyndon Johnson, who went to see his friend, onetime presidential assistant Jim Rowe, telling him that the investigation was politically inspired by the anti-third-term leaders in Texas, Jack Garner and Jesse Jones.

The next thing you knew, the Brown & Root lawyer, Alvin J. Wirtz, had an appointment with the president. Wirtz was a clever Texas fixer of the avuncular, down-home, I'm-just-a-country-boy sort—an outstanding conniver who knew his way around Washington, having served as under secretary of the interior from 1939 to 1941.

On November 11, 1942, FDR called Morgenthau and implied that he should put a stop to the investigation of Brown & Root. "The President called . . . to tell me that he had been seeing Mr. Wirtz," Morgenthau recorded in his diary, "had seen him twice, and why was I personally going after these people in Texas, and why did I have to go after them personally. I said 'Mr. President, I am not going after them personally.' So he asked if I would see Mr. Wirtz, that the people involved there wanted to pay up."

Not knowing what it was all about, Morgenthau asked two of his assistant secretaries, Elmer Irey and John L. Sullivan, for a briefing. "There is apparently a million and a little less than a quarter thousand dollars involved," Irey informed him. ". . . The principal item is of alleged fraud. . . . It consists of bonuses paid by the corporation to officers and employees and in turn passed over by them to the Johnson campaign, and then deducted by the organization as legitimate deductions."

"Say this slowly," Morgenthau asked.

"They pay these bonuses to their officers and employees," Irey went on, "and deduct them as legitimate expenses. As a corporation, they couldn't make political contributions and deduct them. In turn, the officers turn them over to the campaign fund."

"Of Lyndon Johnson," Morgenthau said. "That is nice. That is the best one I have heard in a long time."

"I will tell you what Wirtz is going to tell you," said Sullivan. "Wirtz will tell you that he is convinced that this income tax investigation is being used as a witch hunt to build up a case of violation of the Hatch Act. . . . He will also plead for a quick disposal of the matter. . . . He will ask that the investigation be closed, and the matter ended. That is what his story is going to be."

"You haven't completed your investigation?" Morgenthau asked.

"No," Irey said.

"How can we stop in the middle?"

"You can't," Sullivan said. "You can merely expedite your investigation."

On November 12, the Texas fixer saw the secretary of the Treasury, who said: "I hear you want to see me about this case in Texas, the contractor down there."

"Mr. Secretary," Wirtz said in his Texas drawl, "the matter came up this way. I had a meeting with the President and in discussing conditions generally in Texas I told him about the situation that I thought perhaps bordered on the political somewhat. I told him that I thought, growing out of the Congressional campaigns of 1940, the impression had got around Texas that these people [Brown & Root] were heavy campaign contributors, they had been supporters of the President all the time; that the talk was going around that they were being investigated; and if they owed taxes they certainly ought to be forced to pay them. I didn't think they should be shown any favors because of any political connections or activities, but I didn't think they should be persecuted. It occurred to us [Wirtz and FDR] that the best thing to do was talk to you about it."

"All of my interest in this case is when somebody stirs something up at the White House," Morgenthau said with annoyance, "and every time they do it, I have got to answer for it."

"I am not saying that your men are, down in Texas," Writz went on, "but I do say that this investigation has been going on for more than a year. They had not confined themselves to the books, they have gone over the state to various banks, various businessmen, in what has been notoriously known down there that they are inquiring about the political activities of these men."

"Are you satisfied yourself as to your client's status?" Morgenthau asked.

"I have satisfied myself as to this," Wirtz said. ". . . That they had an enormous increase in business beginning probably in '38 or '39 when they did a big job, followed by the construction of a naval base at Corpus Christi, which caused quite an increase. It just pyramided up—loomed up. They were construction men; they had their auditing and book-keeping forces all scattered. . . . I have known these men a long time and I can't believe that if they were setting out to defraud the government they would have gone about it in that way. I think they owe something by careless book-keeping. . . . I am not asking . . . that these people be treated any different than any other taxpayer."

"Didn't you ask the President if we would sit down and settle it now?" Morgenthau inquired.

"No sir," Wirtz replied. "My suggestion to the President was that as soon as all of the facts were known that we try to sit down and get the matter settled. . . . I wouldn't ask the President to do anything that wasn't in accord with good departmental practice."

"Well, I am sure he won't ask me," Morgenthau said. "He never has."

"I am too fond of the President to ask him to take any action that would in any way be embarrassing," Wirtz said.

"He has never asked me to do anything," Morgenthau repeated. "He has always left it to me. All I can assure you or your client is the thing is taking its normal course."

And so it did for a while. The agent in charge, E. C. Werner, was told to pursue the investigation. In January 1943, six IRS agents started going through the Brown & Root records. They found evidence of fraudulent bonuses totaling more than $150,000. In addition, Brown & Root had underpaid its taxes by more than $1 million. With the 50 percent penalty, it would owe the government about $1.5 million. There were also criminal penalties and the possibility of jail for Lyndon Johnson and Herman Brown, the millionaire contractor who had started as a two-dollar-a-day rod carrier for surveyors and who now ran one of the state's biggest construction companies. FDR would lose his principal ally in Texas, who had fought the inimical forces of Jack Garner and Jesse Jones, and who had been so helpful in finding funds for impecunious Democratic candidates in the 1940 election.

The investigation went on for a year, accumulating overwhelming evidence of fraud. But on the morning of January 13, 1944, Lyndon Johnson and Alvin Wirtz saw the president. That afternoon, Assistant Secretary of the Treasury Elmer Irey was summoned to the White House. That same day, a new agent with no previous knowledge of the case was sent to Texas. He recommended that the IRS collect the penalty rather than prosecute. The investigators, who were just beginning to question prominent figures in the Johnson campaign, were told to send in their final reports, showing underpayment of $1,099,944 and a penalty of $549,972. This was negotiated down, and Brown & Root paid a total of $372,000. There was no indictment, no trial, and no publicity that would have been embarrassing to the Democrats in an election year.

How do you stop a tax fraud investigation in the middle, Morgenthau had asked. The answer was simple. The president threw his authority in the balance and ordered it stopped.

Moe Annenberg, the Jewish immigrant who made his millions from illegal gambling and mob protection, who attacked the New Deal and threatened to "get" Harold Ickes, was prosecuted to the full extent of the law and sent to jail. He paid not only with imprisonment but with his life. "I want Moe Annenberg for dinner," FDR said, and he got him.

Lyndon Johnson, the New Deal congressman who admired FDR and did his bidding, and whose conviction for tax fraud would have been a blessing for the president's enemies in Texas in an election year, escaped prosecution thanks to his good offices. "Why are you personally going after these people in Texas?" FDR asked Morgenthau, who stopped going after them.

When presidential likes and dislikes came into play, there were two standards of justice. Roosevelt could justify favoritism by telling himself that Annenberg was basically a gangster who had plundered an overlenient society and was being brought to justice, while Johnson was a valuable ally whose political enemies were out to get him.

When you were on the side of the angels, it was all right to help your friends. There was no point in being in politics if you could not defeat your enemies, in and out of the polls. Above all, and with certain exceptions such as the Supreme Court fight, Roosevelt was a *winner.* He won elections, he won wars, and he prevailed over his domestic enemies. Robert W. Wooley, the longtime Kentucky Democrat, said that FDR reminded him of what had been said about Andrew Jackson: "He beat everything that ever went up against him—he beat the Creeks, he beat the British, he beat Dickinson, he beat Webster, he beat Clay, he beat Calhoun, he beat the bank, and in his old age he joined the church and beat the devil."

That was part of the art, the style, of which yet another element was cunning. The president's hand was invisible. No one in the general population saw it destroy Annenberg or rescue Lyndon Johnson. Carl Sandburg wrote FDR in December 1940: "I am glad you are cunning—as Lincoln and Jackson were cunning."

There were times when the hand became visible, when you could watch Roosevelt the artist in action, giving a virtuoso performance.

You could see it in his relations with the press. Roosevelt had revived the moribund institution of the press conference (Hoover had met the press infrequently and answered only written questions submitted twenty-four hours beforehand), and turned it into a distinctly American device for informing the nation. The press conference served the same function as question time in the House of Commons, when ministers had to show their adroitness in responding to embarrassing "supplementaries."

In his regular Tuesday afternoon and Friday morning press conferences, FDR gave a masterful display of his grasp of government. Little was arranged or rehearsed, although there were some planted questions. The reporters fired at will on complicated technical subjects, and the president replied fully and lucidly when he chose to, or used his wit for evasion. It was a friendly but sometimes barbed verbal joust, in which FDR found a substitute for the competitive sports he could no longer practice.

He instinctively understood that the press corps, an outwardly cynical but inwardly supersensitive breed, wanted one thing above all—not to be treated like the help. They wanted respectability, which he granted them by treating them as equals and by using the great leavening agent of laughter. It was a way of softening up the audience, and it worked, even after the reporters caught on that they were being manipulated, that the chumminess and first-name basis were forms of psychological bribery, that the off-the-record remarks they had at first been so eager to get were a way to keep the lid on a story, that the front-row regulars who laughed the loudest and asked the planted questions and supplied the "Thank you, Mr. President" at the end of the conference were a claque.

There was some disillusionment, which, as Leo C. Rosten points out, was the externalization of professional guilt at having been taken in by a master showman, but by and large FDR kept his rapport with the reporters, who could remind themselves that he was a vast improvement over past presidents they had known.

The thing to remember is that FDR could be manipulative and genuine at the same time. He really liked the chaff and the repartee with the press corps. Sometimes he was pushed into dropping the geniality, as when he sharply told a persistent reporter: "This isn't a cross-examination."

Sometimes too he went after particular reporters, such as John O'Donnell of the New York *Daily News*, who often heckled the president and who in June 1943 came out with a story that the Waacs had been issued contraceptives. Secretary of War Henry Stimson said it was a slander on American womanhood, and FDR at his next press conference presented O'Donnell with the Iron Cross for his services to the Führer.

Another time, he got mad at Drew Pearson and took Steve Early aside, saying "Steve, Drew Pearson is a son of a bitch. I have put up with his insolence and his scurrilous column for some time. I want you to pick up his pass." Early said that was not a good idea, but FDR insisted. Early approached him the next morning, hoping he had cooled down, but FDR said: "Pick up Drew Pearson's press pass and bring it to me." Early said he would, and it would be accompanied by his resignation. "Well, if you feel that strongly about it," FDR said, "maybe we'd better wait a few days."

Other columnists also aroused presidential anger. Westbrook Pegler, who called Eleanor "Boca Grande," was described by FDR as "a cad with the hide of a rhinoceros" and had his tax returns audited. Of Arthur Krock, FDR complained that nine times out of ten his stories in the *New York Times* contained false statements. "I am all in favor of chloroforming for certain newspaper men," he wrote a friend. "Not Drew Pearson alone—but some of the more subtle murderers like Arthur Krock." He liked to tell the story that Krock, on visiting Paris for the first time, had asked to be taken to the Louvre to see the Venus de Milo, and upon seeing that masterpiece of Greek sculpture had complained that the lady had halitosis. In a memo dated July 29, 1943, he wrote: "Krock never wrote an article laudatory of anything or any human being without putting a snapper on the end that left a bad taste in your mouth. He never loved anybody or anything. He never patted a dog. He never had a real friend—man, woman, or beast."

That was the other side of FDR's geniality; he was thin-skinned, as most artists are about their work, and he really hated the columnists who wrote unfavorable articles. There was something in Krock's suggestion that the administration was guilty of "more ruthlessness, intelligence, and subtlety in trying to suppress legitimate unfavorable comment than any other I have known."

FDR personally went to inordinate lengths to get back at his enemies in the press. When John T. Flynn wrote an anti-Roosevelt article in the *Yale Review* in July 1939, FDR wrote the editor, Wilbur J. Cross, a former governor of Connecticut, that although he loved controversy, Flynn should be barred from writing in the review because he was destructive rather than constructive. Cross replied on July 19 that "there is no danger of another article by him in this magazine so long as I have any connection with it."

He also got a *New York Times* reporter reassigned by complaining to the publisher about one of his stories. This was John White, who reported in November 1940 that the United States and Uruguay had reached agreement on naval and air bases. FDR wrote Arthur H. Sulzberger on November 13 that this was not the first time the government had been embarrassed by one of White's stories. On December 7, Sulzberger called Pa Watson to say that White would be relieved from duty in Uruguay.

In July 1939, he wanted Morgenthau to investigate the *New York Times* for tax fraud. "I would like you to investigate a couple of companies for me especially," FDR said on July 17. "Now take the *New York Times,* for example. Not that I have got anything against Arthur Sulzberger, but he's just plain stupid."

"What do you want me to do?" Morgenthau asked.

"Well, where did they get the money from to pay their income tax?"

"They got it from the Times Company," Morgenthau explained. "They bought back preferred stock."

Perhaps more than anyone in the press, FDR hated Henry Luce, whom he believed was conducting a systematic anti-administration campaign in *Time* and *Life* magazines. He accused *Time* of "a notable contribution to Nazi propaganda" in printing the "disgusting lie" that the president of Chile was in his cups. Ten days after publication the president died of an alcohol-related illness. He was furious when *Life* published in its December 15, 1941, issue a picture story on Brazilian air bases operated by Pan American Airways from which American bombers were being ferried to Europe. One picture was captioned "A U.S. air field," implying that Brazil had ceded its territory to the United States, and the Brazilian dictator, Getulio Vargas, protested.

It came as no surprise that in 1942, when Luce applied for war correspondent credentials to visit China, he was turned down. He was convinced, correctly, that it was an act of presidential spite. In 1943, FDR opposed giving one of *Time*'s best correspondents, John Hersey, a Silver Star for assisting in the care and removal of wounded under fire on two occasions. This was not heroism, FDR argued, but something that "any man . . . who had red blood in his veins would do."

The president also had in it for Luce's wife, Clare Booth, who was elected to the House in 1942. Mrs. Luce, whom Noel Coward once described as "that fascinating little meat-axe topped by that innocent little bow," irked the president by turning a purely social reply to a 1943 invitation to the White House for 120 freshman congressmen into a political speech, which she released to the press, expressing her disquiet about circumstances on the home front. Steve Early said it reminded him of the Persian quip: "When they came to shoe the Sultan's horse, the louse lifted up his leg."

Roosevelt in cabinet referred to Clearly Loose, and Loose and Wild, and said: "You know, she was Barney Baruch's girl. Yes, he educated her, gave her a yacht, sent her to finishing school, she was his girl."

When, in June 1944, she gave a speech saying that if mothers and wives lost their sons they could blame FDR for his lack of preparedness, there was this telephone conversation on June 28 between Sam Rosenman and Henry Morgenthau:

Rosenman: "Did you hear Clare Luce last night?"

Morgenthau: "I heard enough to turn my stomach."

Rosenman: "She called the President a liar. . . . She could have left that out. . . . It's a lousy thing to make political capital out of dead soldiers."

Morgenthau: ". . . It may boomerang."

Rosenman: ". . . She's a sort of a snake, you know."

When FDR was campaigning in Mrs. Luce's Bridgeport district that fall, Sam Rosenman tried to get him to say that in Scotland, where one of his ancestors came from, they pronounced town as "tune" and louse as "Luce," but he decided not to.

Above all, and more than any other twentieth-century president except perhaps John F. Kennedy, Roosevelt was savvy about the press; he knew how reporters' minds worked. Here he is in 1935 lecturing some of his agency heads on the reporter's trade:

"It is a special art all by itself. They have been doing it all their lives. . . . Unless you have years of experience in handling it you will fall into the traps they have set for you. If some reporter says to you, 'Mr. so-and-so makes such a remark, what do you think of it,' . . . there is a definite reason why you should not comment on it. In the first place, it catches you cold; you haven't studied it. In the second place, the question that is made to you by this member of the press is so phrased in many cases as not to represent what the other department actually said. There are . . . many trick ways of putting things.

"Just for example, last Friday one of the members of the press said, 'Mr. President, what have you got today about the speech made by the American Ambassador in England in which he advocated and suggested a much closer working relationship between Great Britain and the United States?' Obviously he was trying to get me to say, 'Why I am of course in favor of a close relationship between Great Britain and the United States.' If I had said that it would have been expressed the next morning that the President advocates a working alliance between the United States and Great Britain. In the middle of the Naval Conference, when both Great Britain and the United States were having trouble with Japan, it would have become a sensational story—an Anglo-American alliance against Japan. On the other hand, if I had said, 'I have no comment to make on the speech of the American Ambassador,' there would have been a headline intimating that the President had dissented with the remarks of the American ambassador. Either way I answered the question I would have been wrong. I said to the young man, 'I have not read the speech of the American Ambassador. I cannot answer any quotation from it which you give from memory, and there is therefore no comment upon it. . . .'

"Remember that there has always been a great deal of loose talk in Washington. I have met it for years. Remember that when you go out to dinner the lady you are sitting next to is probably a sieve to one to three or more members of the press. Remember, everything you say as head of a department at a dinner or a dance or a night club will, ten to one, get to the press inside of twelve hours. How does Drew Pearson live, at one extreme? How does Arthur Krock live, at the other extreme? By the gossip that he picks up in Washington. . . . There are a large number of people, many of them your close friends, many of them my close friends, who actually get paid for giving information to the public press. I am sorry to have to say that, but I know the names of a dozen people who are getting paid for nice juicy information. You would be surprised if I told you their names.

"There has never been such a thing in the last fifty years as an Executive Session of the Senate of the United States, which is supposed to take up absolutely confidential matters of great public purport so important and so secret that they clear the galleries and put everybody out—I say there has never been an Executive Session that was not full public property of the press within half an hour. It is an unfortunate commentary on the legislative branch. I do not want the executive branch to have that reputation, but today it has that same reputation. I think the time has come to turn the corner. If anything comes up that affects any other department outside of your own, do not answer it. If your toes are being stepped on, come and tell me. I think that covers it."

Another example of "artistry in action" was Roosevelt's meeting with Congressman Martin Dies on November 29, 1940. It was one of the rare times when minutes were kept, because FDR did not trust Dies, a blond, burly, cigar-smoking man who represented the hill people of East Texas and had become the first chairman of the House Committee on Un-American Activities.

Dies used the committee to make a name for himself by throwing out wild charges about Communists in government. He was an unscrupulous, rampaging, headline-hunting embarrassment to the administration. In October 1938, a month before the elections, Dies charged that Frank Murphy, the governor of Michigan, had been guilty of treasonable activity in his settlement of the Flint sit-down strikes of 1936. In his first formal criticism of a congressional committee, FDR called Dies's charges "a flagrantly unfair and un-American attempt to influence an election." But Murphy was one of eleven Democratic governors unseated in the election, and Dies could take part of the credit.

In 1939, Dies charged that 500 government employees were on the mailing list of the "Communist-front" American League for Peace and Democracy. Asked about the accusation in a press conference on October 27, FDR replied: "I have not read enough of the details of that rather sordid procedure to comment."

In January 1940, the Dies Committee claimed it had a list of 1,800 Communists working for the government. Dies kept coming up with new lists that always had the same names, Harold Ickes observed. He was like a man who chewed gum and stuck it under the edge of his desk so he could chew it again.

FDR was increasingly annoyed, not only because the charges were largely unfounded, but because in the cases where they *were* founded Dies was frustrating the work of the Justice Department by premature disclosures. Attorney General Robert Jackson complained to the president in November 1940 that Dies Committee disclosures about Manfred Zapp, a key Nazi in the United States, had ruined FBI efforts to prepare a legal case against him.

Clearly, Dies had to be warned that he was gumming up the real work of apprehending subversives. FDR agreed to see him. Here was the president coming to terms with an enemy, a member of his own party who had shown rank disloyalty, a man he despised but would have to charm and coax into compliance. It was the voice of reason and compromise against the voice of a demagogue who had carved out a power base by seeing subversives everywhere. FDR had to neutralize him so that the proper agencies could get on with their work.

"He doesn't look very vicious, does he?" Dies joked as he was led into the president's office on the morning of November 29, 1940.

Calling him by his first name, although there were other names he would have preferred, FDR said: "Now, Martin, what do you think we should do in relation to your committee and its work with the Attorney-General and the State Department? . . . There is a great deal of feeling, as you know, that we have got to have some kind of demarcation between administrative work and investigatory."

"When you are dealing with organizations that legally exist," Dies said, "that have charters under our state laws, but you know that the organization is a window dressing for espionage and sabotage," there could be no objection to full disclosure.

"Have you got legal proof?" FDR asked.

"No, you don't have it under existing law. Naturally, you can't prosecute the German-American Bund, because it pretends one thing when we know actually it stands for another. But you can expose it and then you practically destroy its effectiveness."

"As long as you are careful not to expose any organizations which are not guilty of subversive activities. At the same time you have to protect innocent people."

"I think that is correct," Dies said. ". . . We had quite a bit of trouble with certain movie actors who were contributing large sums of money to these organizations. At first there was a great deal of resentment against the committee; but later they appeared before the committee, one after another, and confessed to the fact they had been careless and indiscreet in lending their names and prestige without investigating who was in control of the organization."

"Of course almost everybody does that," FDR said, "all make mistakes. They must not be held up to the public as a whole as being sympathizers because of a contribution, where it may be ignorance on their part. . . ."

The president then got down to the basic question: The Dies Committee's disclosures were impeding regular investigations. They were an encroachment by a congressional committee on the investigative functions of the Justice Department. "I will give you a very simple example," he said. "I sent the other day to the F.B.I. some rumors—that's all they were, rumors, reports—about three people in the government. They were in minor positions. Now, the investigation of those three people is an extraordinarily delicate matter, because they would be like quail—if you ever flushed them—they would know they were being investigated, and you would never get anything on them. . . . In catching them we may pick up three or four more names that we haven't got under suspicion at the present time. Now if this investigation were disclosed to a Congressional Committee, how long would it be before Mr. A., Mr. B., and Mr. C. would know about it? Just on the doctrine of experience, you can't tell any Congressional Committee anything in secret. The press has it in 12 hours. I don't know an exception to the case."

Gone was Dies's bluster and extravagance. Before the president he was conciliatory, almost meek. "We certainly do not want to prevent the successful prosecution of any cases," he said, "although . . . how many cases of conviction of espionage and sabotage have there been in the past few months?"

"Very few," FDR acknowledged, turning the implied criticism against Dies. "You can't get those convictions in the normal way of prosecution. You have to have positive evidence. You can't do it through allegations."

Dies said he had suspected subversives in his files who were working in national defense. "Now," he asked, "is our solution to wait until we get them in an act of sabotage, which is the most difficult of all offenses to apprehend?"

"Suppose," FDR said, "you have in a government arsenal 12 people under investigation by the F.B.I.; they are tied up through membership in the Communist Party, which at the time they joined it was a legal party. Out of those 12 people, you investigate further and you find five or six active workers. The government has a right to discharge those people and will probably do so properly. . . . Out of those dozen people there may be three or four who were theoretical Communists. I have in mind a man I know who works in an arsenal [in Roosevelt homilies, the "man I know" made frequent appearances]; he is a nice little man of 55. He has been a theoretical

Socialist, he has been a theoretical Communist, he would not hurt a fly. He is the most inoffensive little man I know of. Now, he might be one of those 12 people; I would not fire him. Why? Because I would trust him with my last dollar."

This was more than Martin Dies could bear. What, trust a Commie? After all, following the signature of the Nazi-Soviet pact, it was Dies who had coined the expression "CommuNazi." Dies owed whatever celebrity he had to his anti-Communist vigilance. "But if his record had been that of an agitator. . . ," Dies protested.

"There is an element of danger because of that past record," FDR replied, "not the mere fact that they have been a member of some organization. If you go through the list of people in this country, what was the Communist vote in 1936? . . . Half a million votes? . . . Now, I would not bar from patriotic defense efforts every one of those people who had voted for a Communist in 1936 or 1938 or 1940. Neither would you."

"I would be suspicious of them," Dies said, unwilling to go along with this whitewashing of the Communist electorate.

"Oh, I would check them," FDR said. "Absolutely. But the mere fact that they voted for a Communist when voting for a Communist was legal doesn't automatically entitle us to say to the public, 'Those people are disloyal.' They may be loyal."

"I doubt if any method you can devise," Dies replied, "any new law—if any method will take the place of the democratic method of exposure. Primarily, you educate innocent people so that they will get out."

The president had hooked a shark, and given him plenty of line, but now the shark was running away with the line. He would have to start pulling in a bit.

"I think education is very necessary, Martin," he said, "just so long as you don't hurt human lives, because it is awfully hard, as I say, for the word of acquittal to catch up with the charge which is not proved."

". . . Let's take [a] real situation," Dies said. "When we obtained the papers on the German house in Los Angeles, we found one list marked 'German sympathizers and friends.' It contained the names and addresses of 1250 people mostly of German descent. Many of them are working in our aircraft industries. We have the names of some of them in the North American and the Douglas. We got 18 of the workers who have come and testified under oath . . . telling of specific acts of sabotage; and you have the testimony of five different acts of sabotage on one airplane, and it finally crashed."

"That of course is a thing which should be taken up by you immediately with the F.B.I.," FDR said. "Give those names and tell them what you have. . . . That is a prosecuting thing which they are far better able to do than you or I."

"The most effective thing is to expose them," Dies repeated. "Most of these organizations are going out of business. The American League folded up, and the German-American Bund has become more or less inactive. We know their plan was to sabotage."

"If you have the evidence, you fire them," FDR said. "You have to act individually, because it is the individual that you fire rather than the organization."

It was at this point that the president brought in his shark, for Dies said: "I am willing to go every way that any man ever can do to cooperate with you in this whole matter."

"If you could go to the Attorney-General," FDR said, relaxing now that he knew he had won, "and make arrangements in regard to your giving out through the committee of lists of names and individuals which might interfere with actual investigation looking to prosecution by the Department of Justice agents."

The fight had gone out of Dies. He was now apologetic, almost maudlin. "I don't want to cross wires," he said, "regardless of anything you might have been told, and I know you have been told a great deal. I have carried on under great pressure. I have been ridiculed. I have been denounced. I have had to pay a pretty high price for what I have done. I want to work with you. I don't want to be at any cross-purpose with the Executive Department. The only thing I ask is that the Department of Justice show some degree of cooperation in return. Here is a case: Mr. Hoover is a very excellent man, but he syndicated an article that was widely printed that was construed as against us."

Magnanimous in victory, FDR said: "You have a talk with Bob [Jackson] and see if you can eliminate that very good example you use of Hoover saying or doing something which you take as a reflection on the committee."

Relations with the Justice Department improved after the meeting. Dies realized it was unproductive to fight the F.B.I., with whom he began to share some of the information collected by his committee. Since FDR did not release the transcript of their talks (indeed, Steve Early told Dies there was no transcript), Dies fabricated his own version, in which FDR told him that Stalin was a great man and the Communists were not a threat to America. With his wild charges, Dies continued to be "a hair shirt for the administration," as Ickes called him, until 1944, when he decided not to seek reelection.

Here is a final (though far from exhaustive) element of style: the art of knowing the limitations of the office, of knowing when to step in and when to step out, when to move and when to abstain from moving, when pressure is useful and when it is not, when to sway heaven and earth and when to leave well enough alone.

In 1942, a twenty-five-year-old black sharecropper in Virginia named Odell Waller shot and killed his white landlord, Oscar Davis, in a dispute over fifty-two sacks of wheat. Waller was owed those sacks of wheat, they were his share of the crop he had sweated to harvest, but Davis would not release them. While Waller was away from the tin-roof shack he called home, his wife and mother were evicted. Returning to find himself cheated and homeless, Odell Waller was filled with rage, got a gun, and shot the landlord four times. An all-white jury found him guilty of murder in the first degree, and he was sentenced to death by electrocution.

The Waller verdict came at a time when American blacks were being told they had to help win the war for democracy and freedom. It became a black Sacco and Vanzetti case, with Odell Waller a symbol of oppression that encompassed the sharecropper system, the poll tax, and the denial of equal rights in every area of life.

Where could Waller carry his grievance—to the white courts of Virginia? What fair-minded person could believe the prosecution's contention that Waller was "habitually armed," and that the landlord had intended in good faith to deliver the wheat? Any black man could imagine the scene, could see Waller asking for his share and hear the landlord reply: "You want that wheat, nigger, try and get it."

The injustice was made more blatant by comparison with a case in the same Virginia county of Pittsylvania, tried before the same judge who had tried Waller. A white farmer named R. G. Siddle had shot and killed an unarmed black sharecropper after a quarrel. It took the jury about fifteen minutes to acquit Siddle, who was free on a $1,000 bond and never saw the inside of a jail.

Struggling with the grammar and spelling he had never learned, Waller made a pathetically eloquent statement: "Have you thought about some people are allowed a chance over and over again then there are other allowed little chance some no chance at all. . . . In my case I worked hard from sun up until sundown trying to make a living for my family and it ended in death for me. You take big people as the President, Governors, judges, their children don't never have to suffer. They has plenty money. Born in a mention [mansion] nothing ever to worry about. I am glad some people are that lucky. The penitentiary all over the United States are full of poeple who was pore tried to work and have something, couldn't so that maid them steel and rob."

Waller also wrote Eleanor Roosevelt, who had, in the ten years that her husband had been in office, earned a reputation for helping the downtrodden. In June 1942, he wrote: "Allow me a chance please you will never regret it. My days is short my time will be up the 19 of this month."

Along with a summary of the case, Eleanor left a memo for FDR: "This pathetic. Couldn't he go in the Army?"

It would have been easy for Roosevelt to stay out of it. This was a matter for the governor of Virginia, Colgate W. Darden, Jr., who held the powers of reprieve, commutation, and pardon. Any federal interference, particularly on the part of the president, was inappropriate.

And yet FDR felt himself compelled to intervene. There was something in his nature, perhaps something that had happened to him as a boy, that made him respond intensely to the injustice of one man bullying and intimidating another. It was not only that, as Henry Wallace once put it, "he thought that justice was written into the eternal order of things," it was that this particular kind of injustice, where a helpless man is pushed to the limit, aroused in him a deep emotional empathy.

It had happened before, when he was assistant secretary of the Navy. There had been the case of a young Georgia boy aboard ship, terrorized by a brutal quartermaster, who was pushed to the breaking point and killed the quartermaster in self-defense. FDR had his sentence commuted from death to life imprisonment. When he was no longer in the Navy, he tried to have the boy pardoned, writing secretaries of the Navy who were his friends, but to no avail. Three days after his inaugural in March 1933, he personally pardoned the boy, now a man.

There was another reason why FDR responded to the plight of Odell Waller. It was a political mistake to carry out his sentence at a time when the black population of America was sensitized to injustice because of its contribution to the war effort. You could not ask black men to fight and be killed in the service of a country that valued them so little. There was enough injustice in the armed services into which they were inducted. Black protests rose in proportion to the effort they were asked to make to win the war. If Odell Waller was executed, there might be race riots, or mutinies in black Army units.

Thus, on June 15, 1942, the president wrote a letter which overruled everything he had ever learned about the Constitution and states' rights:

"I hope you will let me send you this wholly personal and unofficial note," he wrote Colgate W. Darden, Jr., "which it would be very presumptuous for me to send as President. I have only once before written in a similar vein to the governor of a State—for I was a Governor once upon a time myself. I would have resented receiving such a communication from a President of the United States but I would have had no resentment if it had come from an old friend who just happened to be President.

"This relates to Odell Waller, who unfortunately got his case into the public prints in many newspapers throughout the country.

"I had a somewhat similar case when I was Governor of New York [Here FDR was probably updating the case of the boy in the Navy to his years as governor, to better impress the governor of Virginia.] A man shot one of his neighbors. He was a poor ignorant fellow who became thoroughly imbued with the thought that his neighbor would kill him over an argument which had lasted for days. He was without question 'scared' whether rightly so or not is really beside the point. . . . With this in mind he armed himself and when the neighbor advanced against him in a very threatening way he fired. The jury convicted him of murder in the first degree. The two elements of intent to kill and premeditation were accepted by the jury, but I could not accept the two elements because first, I did not think the firing of the gun was with intent to kill but that the intent was to save himself. Similarly, the jury found premeditation, but there again I could not agree because it was, in my mind, premeditation to defend himself and only to shoot in order to preserve his own life. I commuted the man's sentence to life imprisonment. I shall always be glad I did so.

"Will you, therefore, try to think of this note as merely a suggestion from an old friend who has let the death sentence take its course in very many cases, but who really hopes that you will recognize that perhaps the killer element in human nature may not have been present in the case of this unfortunate man who might have just been 'scared for his own life.' "

Three days later Darden replied: ". . . I appreciate the spirit which prompts your interest in this most difficult situation. [Supreme Court] Justice [Harlan] Stone late last night refused to take any action in reference to the case, and counsel for Waller have asked me to hear them on the matter of commutation. This I expect to do within the next few days."

Darden refused commutation. He treated the case in the strict, unheroic spirit of a crossroads magistrate. His final opinion was laden with pious phrases such as a warning against "racial discord at a critical time when every loyal citizen should strive to promote unity."

FDR felt that his ammunition had been spent. There was nothing more he could do. He should not even have sent the letter in the first place. It had not done any good, and to make any further effort would be worse than useless. The only intelligent course of action was to disassociate himself from a lost cause.

Having exhausted all legal appeals, Odell Waller was due to go to the chair on July 2. On July 1, black leaders, including Walter White of the NAACP, held a death vigil. Perhaps they thought of distant lands where American troops were in combat. It was a long way from the Richmond penitentiary to the jungles of the Philippines, which the Japanese had overrun. On that same day, the Japanese announcer in Manila said: "In spite of the clearly benevolent aims of the Imperial Japanese Army in the Philippines, there are still some Filipinos who continue to offer utterly useless and wasteful resistance." Those Filipinos were fighting for the independence that America had guaranteed them before the war, and the promise that they would live in a society where there were no second-class citizens.

A day away from Waller's execution, Eleanor Roosevelt had not given up. Four times on the evening of July 1 she tried to reach the president on the phone, and four times she got Harry Hopkins, who told her that he was unavailable. Although Hopkins thought she was wrong to insist, he could not help admiring her burning determination to see that justice was done.

Eleanor could be more outspoken because she was not president. She appointed herself protector of the helpless, particularly the blacks. She accepted the criticism, like a person who accepts snake bites, drawing the venom. During the war, a fifty-one-year-old major in the Army Reserve, Elmer H. Holland, was arguing about her with a colonel fifteen years younger than he was, who said, "Well, I see Mrs. Roosevelt was in such-and-such a place last night. I suppose she slept again with another buck nigger." Holland hit the colonel twice, knocking him out cold. He was sure he would be court-martialed, but nothing ever came of it.

FDR had thrown his authority in the balance to no avail, and now his sense of timing told him to go no further. It was, as Henry Wallace put it, his sense of the artistic fitness of things. His opponents called him a dictator, but in this instance he was completely powerless.

FDR told Hopkins he did not want to discuss the Waller case with Eleanor. Governor Darden, he said, was acting entirely within his constitutional rights. In addition, he doubted very much whether the governor could have reached any other decision.

When Eleanor called again, Hopkins urged the president to come to the phone. She would not take "No" for an answer. The president did, and told her that under no circumstance would he intervene. He urged her very strongly to say nothing more about it.

On the morning of July 2, Odell Waller was electrocuted.

When FDR's friend Edward Bruce, who was a member of the Commission on Fine Arts, wrote in September 1941 that FDR was a truly great artist who sought perfection and designed his pictures with infinite care, FDR replied on October 2: "There 'ain't no such thing' as a masterpiece of permanence in the art of living or the art of government. That type of art catches a mood, fits the method of expression into the emotions of the day and then mingles oils with water colors and steel engravings with dry point. On Tuesday I conferred with some of the experts on social security. We patted ourselves on the back for all that we had done in eight years. But the reason for our meeting was that only forty million Americans out of one hundred and thirty millions were deriving real benefits from what we had started. And we realize that it had been far easier to help the lives of the forty million than it would be in the next few years to extend those benefits to another ninety million."

XX

The Way to War

I am their leader. I must follow them.

Lord Melbourne

O n January 20, 1941, for the first time in the history of the country, a president was sworn into office not only for a third term but for a third successive term.

As twice before, prior to the inaugural, a special service was held in St. John's Episcopal Church, across Lafayette Square from the White House. This time, however, there were small changes, indicative of the times. Roosevelt was brought in on the arm of a Marine captain rather than of his son James, who had enlisted, as sons all over the country were enlisting or being drafted, the visible expression of a nation preparing for war.

Endicott Peabody, who twice before had conducted the ceremony, his presence representing to Roosevelt the ideal of public service that he had followed, had retired to Arizona at the age of eighty-four. The absence of this figure of moral rectitude seemed to underline the disintegration of the values he had upheld. Frank R. Wilson, rector of St. James's Episcopal Church at Hyde Park, where FDR was a senior warden, took his place, and read the Twentieth Psalm, with the president and the members of his cabinet, including the new vice president, Henry Wallace, responding: "Some trust in chariots, and some in horses; but we will remember the name of the Lord our God. They are brought down and fallen: but we are risen, and stand upright."

Then, under a clear sky, with the sun shining, came the inaugural address, from the east portico of the Senate wing of the Capitol, followed by the parade down Pennsylvania Avenue. But this time the parade did not have the usual circus atmosphere of funny hats and feathered Indians. It was a display of military might before the commander in chief, of tanks and heavy guns, and riflemen marching with fixed bayonets, as 300 military planes passed over the reviewing stand. Only the less-than-martial but uniformed young men of the Civilian Conservation Corps recalled the New Deal.

There was a term in admiralty law, which a young lawyer named Roosevelt had made his specialty, called the agony of collision. This was the interval between the time when collision became inevitable and the actual moment of impact, during which the captain had to prepare for the worst under precarious conditions. In 1941, America lived through the agony of collision.

Roosevelt after his reelection still thought collision was avoidable. His policy was to appease Japan in the Pacific while setting in place the machinery to assist the British. He believed that America could limit its involvement to being the "arsenal of democracy." "Give us the tools and we will finish the job," Churchill promised.

In October 1940, the American ambassador in Japan, Joseph Grew, had with the president's approval told the America-Japan Society that American opinion resented Japanese aggression in China and favored economic retaliation against further violations of American rights.

But there was no economic retaliation. Instead, oil and gasoline and finished steel continued to flow to Japan. In 1939, the United States supplied 93 percent of Japan's petroleum needs, 30 million barrels. The Japanese, who depended on imports for 90 percent of their gasoline, were known to be stockpiling petroleum products. Their navy ran on American fuel oil. Their air force ran on American high-octane aviation gasoline.

In 1940 and during the first half of 1941, as their intentions became manifest, American oil continued to be sold to the Japanese. The arsenal of democracy, as Samuel Grafton put it, was also the filling station of fascism. The hawks in the cabinet, Stimson, Morgenthau, and Ickes, were shocked that Roosevelt allowed this to happen. The day would come when American boys would face Jap battleships propelled by American fuel oil, their drive shafts turning on American grease.

On July 19, 1940, at the British embassy, when the men were separated from the women after dinner, Stimson said: "The only way to treat Japan is not to give in to her on anything." Lord Lothian, the ambassador, was quite upset, because Cordell Hull and the State Department were not taking that line at all. "Well," he said, "after all, you are continuing to ship aviation gasoline to Japan."

"Well," said Morgenthau, "nobody has asked me or even suggested to me that we stop shipping aviation gasoline."

"If you will stop shipping aviation gasoline to Japan," Lothian said, "we will blow up the oil wells in the Dutch East Indies so that the Japanese can't come down and get that, because we have all felt that if we put too much pressure on Japan they would go down there and take those oil wells."

Morgenthau excitedly passed on Lothian's plan to FDR the next day at the White House. They were joined by Under Secretary of State Sumner Welles, who objected that blowing up the wells would provoke Japan into making war on Britain and that peace initiatives would be spoiled.

In frustration, Morgenthau told his aide, Harry Dexter White: "Harry, if you can tell me who is the appeaser over there and who is the buck passer, I would like to know. If you ever heard a more beautiful Chamberlain talk than I listened to Sumner Welles give about Russia and Japan and Russia and China getting together, and then of course ... everything is going to be lovely. And after that then Japan is going to come over and kiss our big toe and say 'we love you, darling.' "

On July 22, Morgenthau asked FDR to add petroleum products and scrap metal to the list of strategic materials subject to embargo. He enlisted Ickes and Stimson to back him up. "Oh hell," Ickes told him, "it ought to have been done then first.... The way they piddle around here!" Stimson informed FDR that the Japanese were trying to corner the aviation gasoline market. Approaches had been made to nearly every American oil company and contracts had been drawn up for 1.2 million barrels.

Roosevelt agreed to place scrap metal and petroleum products on the list, but the State Department pressured him to limit the embargo to high-octane gas and steel scrap. At the July 25 cabinet there was a showdown between Morgenthau and Welles, who went at it until the president told them to go in a corner and settle their differences. The result was that the State Department issued new export control orders limiting the embargo to high-octane gas and steel scrap.

On July 27, Ambassador Grew passed on an odd report he had picked up from the Peruvian minister in Tokyo: "There is a lot of talk around town to the effect that the Japanese, in case of a break with the United States, are planning to go all out in a surprise mass attack on Pearl Harbor. I rather guess that the boys in Hawaii are not precisely asleep."

The State Department took no more notice of this warning than it did of Grew's other dispatches. He kept saying that Japan was preparing for a southward advance, that Japan was openly and unashamedly one of the predatory nations, that there was bound to be a showdown with the United States, that the Japanese army was capable of surprise actions, that a national psychology of desperation would develop into a determination to risk all.

It was like throwing pebbles into a lake at night, thought Grew. You were not even allowed to see the ripples. He could only assume that his recommendations were unwelcome. His British colleague, Sir Robert Craigie, always got a prompt response. His government's policy was constantly made clear to him, whereas Grew was given no indication of administration policies or intentions. Indeed, he sometimes heard Washington news from Craigie.

The president wanted to be his own secretary of state, but the cost was high, because day-to-day affairs were left to the ineffectual Cordell Hull, in whose absence Sumner Welles often acted in an insubordinate manner. FDR did not seem concerned over the power struggle between the two. He too had been insubordinate under Josephus Daniels, and he could use their divisiveness to his own advantage. But to the man in the field, State Department policy, or lack of policy, was a mess.

Morgenthau was at a loss to explain the president's attitude on Japan. After an August 16 meeting at the White House he recorded in his diary: "Much to my surprise the President talked in the same vein as Sumner Welles, namely that we must not push Japan too much at this time as we might push her to take Dutch East Indies."

It was only when Japanese troops marched into Indochina with the agreement of Vichy France, on September 24, 1940, that Hull appeared to agree to a complete embargo. Morgenthau was furious at Hull. "Now they've got into Indo-China," he complained, "and what the hell do they care if we put this or that or the other thing on, I mean the horse has been stolen out of the stable. . . . Hull, that's his responsibility. . . . Will they do anything about oil, the one thing that would stop them, no, they won't touch it. . . . No, Sir! Not until [the Japanese have] taken Indo-China and then they're going to do it the next day."

Hull reneged, saying that he did not want an embargo on scrap or gasoline until Japan had invaded the Dutch East Indies. Stimson, who was sure that sooner or later young American men would be "offering their bodies to the flames," kept working on the president. On October 8, he again urged an embargo on oil. British and Australian ships, he said, would keep the Japs from seizing the oil fields in the Dutch Indies. If they attacked, the wells would be plugged. FDR seemed interested, and asked if the fields were near the coast. Stimson brought the maps to show him.

Even Eleanor, who was supporting the pacifist American Youth Congress with a contribution of $200 a month, joined the hawks, writing her husband on November 12: "Now we've stopped scrap iron, what about oil?"

"The real answer which you *cannot* use," FDR replied the next day, "is that if we forbid oil shipments to Japan, Japan will increase her purchases of Mexican oil and furthermore, may be driven by actual necessity to a descent on the Dutch East Indies. At this writing, we all regard such action on our part as an encouragement to the spread of war in the Far East."

FDR wanted peace in the Pacific in order to pursue bolder policies in the European war. He appeased the Japanese in order to concentrate on helping the British.

And so, in spite of domestic shortages and the demands of the British, gasoline continued to be shipped to Japan in the first six months of 1941. Between July 1940 and June 1941, the United States exported (to Japan and others) 4 million barrels of high-octane gasoline and 10 million barrels of crude oil.

Ickes, who had been made petroleum coordinator, knew that the Japanese were increasing the number of tankers calling at West Coast ports for oil. In one week, they had loaded 400,000 barrels in Los Angeles. The octane content was always 1 percent less than the octane under embargo. Lubricating oil was being shipped to Japan while American plants were going short. Unable to contain himself, Ickes held up 2,000 barrels of oil standing on a wharf in South Philadelphia, waiting to be loaded on a Japanese steamer. But he had not cleared it with State, and FDR wrote him a stinging rebuke.

Sure that he was right, Ickes replied on June 23, 1941, that the full embargo of oil to Japan would be a popular move that would make it "not only possible but easy, to get into this war in an effective way."

"Please let me know," FDR shot back on the same day, "if this would continue to be your judgment if this were to tip the delicate scales and cause Japan to decide either to attack Russia or to attack the Dutch East Indies."

Ickes was so mad he threatened to resign, which led the president on July 1 to explain the true reason for his policy: "It is terribly important for the control of the Atlantic for us to help keep the peace in the Pacific. I simply have not got enough Navy to go round—and every little episode in the Pacific means fewer ships in the Atlantic."

Ickes was in despair. "My God!" he told Morgenthau on July 15, "Chamberlain at his best couldn't appease the way our State Department does."

"We still send out every week the list of the gasoline that goes," Morgenthau said.

"Say . . . isn't it ghastly?" Ickes responded. ". . . You know what they're doing, they're building up a bigger supply so they'll be ready for us. . . . We're just giving, week by week . . . hundreds of thousands of gallons to put away so that when they're ready for us they won't meet any trouble about their oil supply."

"That's right," Morgenthau said. "They don't have to go down to the Dutch East Indies."

It was an odd situation, where the executive, allied with the State Department, was being fought by three other departments, War, Interior, and Treasury, but the Japanese takeover of French Indochina made the president change his mind.

On July 26, Japanese funds were frozen. Japan could no longer pay for American products and was effectively barred from further oil imports. The economic sanctions that Ickes, Morgenthau, and Stimson had been urging for a year were finally in place. A great change had come over Hull. "Nothing will stop them except force," he told Sumner Welles on August 4.

One obstacle to Anglo-American cooperation was removed with the departure from London of Joseph P. Kennedy in October 1940. The British had come to detest Kennedy, who was generous with defeatist advice. Roosevelt had been waiting for the right moment to recall him, telling Morgenthau in October 1939: "Joe always has been an appeaser and always will be an appeaser. If Germany or Italy made a good peace offer tomorrow, Joe would start working on the King and his friend the Queen and from there on down, to get everybody to accept it and he's just a pain in the neck to me."

Kennedy had been named "Man of the Week" in Father Coughlin's magazine, *Social Justice,* in February 1939. There he was on the cover of the Jew-baiting, FDR-hating sheet, with Teddy on his lap dressed in a sailor suit, and John F. standing behind him in a double-breasted pinstripe, and the rest of his children.

Roosevelt didn't like the reports he was getting about his ambassador. An FBI report said that Kennedy and a Wall Street crony, Ben Smith, had met with Goering in Vichy France in 1940, and that they had donated a considerable amount of money to the German cause. Douglas Fairbanks wrote FDR in November 1940 that Kennedy had visited one of the Hollywood studios and told the producers that the Jews were being blamed for the war and that they should stop making anti-Nazi pictures.

The most disturbing report came after Kennedy's recall, in January 1941. FDR passed it on to Harry Hopkins, who was on a mission in London, writing him on January 15: "The following is 'a tale that is told' and that only. Nevertheless, because it has been brought to my attention, I have the official duty of running it down—and that I must ask you to do insofar as it can be done at the London end. The story is: 'Before the Czechoslovak crisis, it is reported that Joe Kennedy sold Czechoslovakian securities short and is supposed to have made a very large sum—whether it was 500,000 dollars or 500,000 pounds, I don't know. The latter is alleged. I do not know whether the time of this alleged short sale was during the crisis before Munich, which was the time that the Sudeten area was taken away from Czechoslovakia, or whether the time was in the spring of 1939. The informant was Alfred Bergman, who is a West Pointer and not a Jew, so I am told. His source is Masaryk in London, who I suppose is Jan, the son of President Masaryk. I hate to think of even the possibility of Joe having made a short sale of this kind while he was Ambassador and therefore in possession of confidential information. However, it must be looked into and I suggest that you see Masaryk, try to run it down and if necessary get the help of the British Government to discover the broker or brokers, if there were any. . . ."

There is no evidence that Hopkins confirmed the charge, but the mere fact that he was in London showed how his fortunes had risen. He was now in fact deputy president, at a time when FDR was relying less on his cabinet and the old-line agencies. It was the Charlemagne system, with counts of the realm who outranked the dukes. Hopkins was eerily attuned to the mental processes of his boss, and he got things done. When someone asked FDR what it was exactly that Hopkins did, he said: "I can answer that with a single illustration. We've just had a cable from the British asking for 325,000 75mm. shells. The Army said 'Sorry, we haven't got any.' I turned the thing over to Harry. He found 100,000 shells at Fort Bragg, left there since 1919, and another 150,000 in Manila. Then he got five manufacturers to produce 25,000 more apiece."

On December 16, 1940, FDR had said to Morgenthau: "I have been thinking very hard about what we should do for England, and it seems to me that the thing to do is to get away from the dollar sign. . . . We will say to England, we will give you the guns and ships that you need, provided that when the war is over you will return to us in kind the guns and the ships that we have loaned to you." Thus was Lend-Lease born, and at his press conference that day FDR used the famous analogy of lending your garden hose to a neighbor whose house was on fire, to keep the fire from spreading. It was enlightened self-interest. Britain could not pay. Lord Lothian had told the press, "Well boys, Britain's broke: it's your money we want."

Now, less than a month later, in January 1941, Hopkins was in London. He thought of himself as "a catalytic agent between two prima donnas." Churchill, he reported, *was* the British government. They became fast friends, although, as Ickes commented, even if the president had sent a man with the bubonic plague, Churchill would have received him with open arms.

With his all-or-nothing nature, Hopkins espoused the British cause. He told Churchill on January 10: "The President is determined that we shall win the war together. Make no mistake about it. He has sent me here to tell you that at all costs and by all means he will carry you through, no matter what happens to him—there is nothing he will not do so far as he has human power."

In laying the basis for the "special relationship," Hopkins went far beyond what he could reasonably pledge, since Congress had not yet approved the Lend-Lease Act, House Resolution 1776, "To Promote the Defense of the United States and for Other Purposes."

"The Dictator Bill" was what its opponents called it, as in this Chicago *Tribune* headline: "Church Groups Wage Fight on Dictator Bill." The CIO opposed it because it would give the president the power to ignore labor legislation. Senator Wheeler said: "It will plow under every fourth American boy," and charged that the Army had ordered 1.5 million caskets. Senator Clark of Montana said it was a war bill.

Claims of British penury were disbelieved by the American public. At a January 17 cabinet, Jack Garner said the British had plenty of money to pay, and Claude Wickard, the new secretary of agriculture, said the farmers in the Midwest believed the British had almost unlimited wealth. FDR said Britain was stripped to the waist and her belt was tightly drawn.

The isolationists feared that Lend-Lease would lead to the convoying of war materials by American ships, which was exactly what Stimson was hoping. But thanks to skillful handling in both houses, and some horse trading (no convoying, a two-year limit on the legislation), Lend-Lease passed in February 1941 in the House by 260 to 165, and in March in the Senate by 60 to 31. The initial appropriation was $7 billion. The total aid from 1941 to 1945 added up to $27 billion.

Lend-Lease *did* bring America closer to war in that, to pursue Roosevelt's analogy, when you lend your neighbor your garden hose, you take a greater interest in the fire. British purchasing missions and military advisers began arriving in Washington. Americans on a day-to-day basis could see their water supply trying to douse the fire.

There was some resistance on the part of the American military, who were apprehensive that the British would grab everything. After meeting with British procurement head Sir Arthur Salter, Emory S. Land, the chairman of the U.S. Maritime Commission, wrote FDR on April 11: "My primary reaction is as follows: If we do not watch our step, we shall find the White House en route to England with the Washington Monument as a steering oar."

"Which would you rather do," Roosevelt replied, "give away the White House and the Washington Monument and save civilization including American independence and the democratic system or have the White House and the Washington Monument taken over by people under a different regime. Think it over."

There were also charges that the British were profiteering from Lend-Lease. Hopkins, its administrator, got reports that they were selling to Latin America steel and aluminum obtained under the program, and that Lend-Lease cheese was being sold unrationed at ninety cents a pound. Oscar Cox of the Office for Emergency Management wrote Hopkins on August 20, 1944: "The damned rumors of our being played as suckers may backwash on the request for more funds. . . . The White House may also want to nail . . . the stories about the British using our tankers for commercial business." The profiteering was minor, however, compared with England's economic exhaustion after the war.

In January 1941, the day the Lend-Lease text was out, newspaper publisher Roy Howard called Wendell Willkie and said: "This is the chance to send that son of a bitch up as a dictator." When Willkie refused to blast Lend-Lease, Howard said: "All the time and effort I have spent on you has been wasted." The Scripps-Howard papers, he promised Willkie, were going to "tear your reputation to shreds." "If Howard weren't such a little pipsqueak," Willkie told friends, "I'd have felt like knocking him down."

You would have to knock a lot of people down if you wanted to get at the isolationists, for they were indeed a formidable array, stretching in political coloration from extreme right to extreme left, across the board. In Congress, there was an odd alliance among old-style progressives like Bob La Follette and Burt Wheeler, new-style jingoists like Martin Dies, and Communist-supported leftists like Vito Marcantonio. They all agreed that international bankers, mostly Jews, were trying to drag America into war.

In the population at large, you had everything from pro-Nazis like Father Coughlin to Socialists like Norman Thomas, antiwar liberals like Robert Hutchins, scholars like Charles Beard, and union leaders like John L. Lewis.

District 2 of the Maritime Federation published a pamphlet called *The*

Yanks Are Not Coming, which sold 300,000 copies. At the Allis-Chalmers plant in Milwaukee, which had a $40 million defense contract for turbines, Communist agitators whipped up a strike and a riot that closed the plant in April. "The strike does not seem to be a legitimate controversy between labor and capital," Henry Stimson reported to FDR on April 5, "but a deliberate attempt by a Communistic leader with a notorious record to foment disturbances."

Concerned, the president asked that FBI powers be broadened in going after subversives in the labor movement. He had no more patience with them than with appeasers, who were merely helping Hitler, no matter how well-meaning. "I am somewhat disturbed by the activities of Mr. Malcolm Read Lovell, Executive Secretary of the Quaker Service Council," he wrote Eleanor in January 1941. "He is definitely working for appeasement. He would do very well in some relief work among the Chinese. Just a hint."

Eleanor, who had been an ardent supporter of the American Youth Congress, broke with the group early in 1941, writing the president, Jack McMichael: "I have reluctantly come to the conclusion that, knowingly or unknowingly, you, like the Newspaper Guild, are controlled or used by the Communists.... This does not mean that I am not interested in all of you whom I know as individuals, but it does mean I cannot be as actively identified."

Isolationism found a natural breeding ground in young people of draft age. At Princeton, the Veterans of Future Wars asked FDR to appoint an Unknown Soldier at once, "so we can know who he is before he gets killed." Vassar students enrolled in an Association of Future Gold Star Mothers and proposed a trip to Europe to select cemetery sites for their future dead sons. At Yale, Robert Douglas Stuart, Jr., the son of a Quaker Oats executive, started a discussion group that blossomed into the America First Committee. Financed at the start by Robert E. Wood, the chairman of Sears, Roebuck, America First became the most powerful vehicle in the country for promoting isolationist goals, mushrooming to 500 chapters and a membership of 800,000 among whom were some impressive names: Henry Ford; Alice Roosevelt Longworth, Teddy Roosevelt's daughter; Chester Bowles, later head of the Office of Price Administration; Kingman Brewster, Jr., later president of Yale; the novelist Kathleen Norris; the actress Lillian Gish; and, of course, the quintessential American hero, Charles A. Lindbergh.

Lindbergh was the star of America First, battling Roosevelt for the soul of America. Would America (in his view) join the corrupt European nations in an absurd war, or would it remain pure and true to its ideals? Here were two charismatic leaders, both inspiring worship and arousing hatred, both with a knowledge of Germany, both wanting to save their country.

Roosevelt moved quickly to discredit Lindbergh, likening him in his April 25 press conference to Clement Laird Vallandigham, an Ohio congressman who had opposed the Civil War and advised Union soldiers to desert. He was arrested, jailed, and eventually banished behind Confederate lines. In plain English, a Vallandigham was a traitor. Three days later, Lindbergh resigned his commission in the Army Air Corps Reserve. He would not take this insult, he wrote in his diary.

But Roosevelt did far less damage to Lindbergh than Lindbergh did to himself. He virtually self-destructed in September, when in a speech in Des Moines he named the Jews as among the "principal war agitators."

"Their greatest danger to this country," he said before a crowd of 8,000, "lies in their large ownership and influence in our motion pictures, our press, our radio, and our Government. I am not attacking either the Jewish or the British people. Both races I admire. But I am saying that the leaders of both the British and the Jewish races, for reasons which are as understandable from their viewpoint as they are inadvisable from ours, for reasons which are not American, wish to involve us in the war."

This was translated in public opinion as: Lindbergh hates what Hitler hates. America First policies and Nazi policies are the same. Had not a Nazi shortwave broadcast in January called America First "truly American and truly patriotic"?

Lindbergh illustrated the axiom that sometimes the most dangerous men are true innocents. He did not realize that every fascist and anti-Semite in the country would applaud him, that he would become a hero to the Bund, the Silver Shirts, the Ku Klux Klan. That was the trouble with America First, it had a core of patriotic members who thought they were defending American values, but it became contaminated by persons and groups connected with the Nazis and the Japanese. It became unclean.

There was something to be said for the view that America should not try to remake the world in its own image, but Lindbergh was brought down by his own political naïveté and his half-baked pro-German views, and the isolationist movement came crashing down with him. After the Des Moines speech, as Samuel Grafton observed, "almost every American in Who's Who has now come to the mourner's bench to testify to his belief in democracy. . . . It was 'count me out on the Lindbergh stuff.' "

After Pearl Harbor, the Lone Eagle tried to get into the Air Force but was blocked by Stimson. Finally, Henry Ford gave him a job at the Willow Run plant, which had converted to planes. There and later at Lockheed he developed liquid-cooled engines and a fuel economy system that increased the cruising distance of bombers, making a contribution to the war effort.

Roosevelt knew from his intelligence sources that isolationist groups were being manipulated and funded by the Axis powers. An FBI report in January 1941 told him that Frau von Lewinsky, the wife of the former German counselor, was working with Burton Wheeler's wife in America First, and was preparing at the request of Senators Tydings and Wheeler an outline of Hitler's peace objectives.

Also Army cryptographers had broken the Japanese diplomatic code, and the intercepts, known as "Magic," provided proof that the Japanese were promoting and funding "peace groups." On November 6, 1941, the Japanese ambassador in Washington, Kichisaburo Nomura, cabled Tokyo that Hidenari Terasaki, ostensibly the second secretary but in fact in charge of espionage, was working on a committee of Japanese-American friends. "This committee," Nomura said, "will be promoted by Americans and will have the appearance of being financed by American money, although a portion of actual expense will be borne by the Japanese Embassy in Washington." Terasaki was also working on a plan for the impeachment of the president. This involved the case of Tyler Kent, a code clerk in the American embassy in London who had been arrested and imprisoned on the Isle of Wight by Churchill after being caught passing embassy documents to a German agent. Terasaki's contact was an America First member named C. K. Armstrong, who told him that "Lindbergh and [Colonel Robert] McCormick [publisher of the Chicago *Tribune*] wanted to use the [Tyler Kent] documents to impeach the President."

As the isolationists were discredited, interventionism began to be seen as the correct position. When Lord Halifax replaced Lord Lothian as British ambassador in Washington (Lothian, a Christian Scientist, died in December 1940 after refusing treatment for an illness), he was subjected to both sides. At the Harvard commencement when Halifax spoke in June, President James Conant asked the question: "How long will the people of the United States think it right to let the British do all the fighting for them?" But in Detroit, he had eggs thrown at him by some isolationist ladies. He commented that Americans were indeed fortunate to be able to throw eggs when the English got an egg a month. "The egg business, " he wrote Churchill, "has been quite useful in the odd way these things work."

The world crisis was one of those moments in history, like the Civil War, when the American system had to redefine itself. It was, on several levels, a test of America ideals. What was the American Way? Was it to remain neutral or help the Allies? Was it to get into the war or stay out?

Another test for American values was the refugee question. In this land of immigrants, should a generous policy be maintained for the victims of war in Europe, many of them Jewish? Or should a more cautious policy be adopted for security reasons, and to soothe the isolationists?

On September 18, 1940, the SS *Quanza* landed in Norfolk with eighty Jewish refugees who had escaped via Portugal. Since they had no visas, they had been turned away in Mexico and Nicaragua. Mrs. Roosevelt took an interest in their plight. Patrick Malin of the President's Advisory Committee on Political Refugees went to Norfolk and arranged for their admission.

It was a generous and humanitarian gesture, but it infuriated the man in the State Department who was in charge of refugee matters, Breckinridge Long. Rich and patrician, Long came from old Anglo-Saxon stock—the

Breckinridges of Kentucky and the Longs of North Carolina. He had grown up in Missouri, and had started in public life under Wilson, when he had made friends with Roosevelt. A floor manager at the 1932 convention, he was rewarded with the post of ambassador to Italy. In 1941, now head of the Special War Problems Division at the State Department, Long was an isolationist who felt that the Soviet Union was a greater threat than Nazi Germany. He also had a visceral dislike of Jews and foreigners that bordered on the xenophobic. He did not want America contaminated by large numbers of Eastern European Jews, whom he saw as lawless, scheming, defiant, in many ways unassimilable. "The general type," he wrote in his diary, "was just the same as the criminal Jews who crowded our police court dockets in New York and who could never become moderately decent American citizens."

When Long heard that the *Quanza* refugees had been admitted, he flew into a rage. This was a violation of the law that he would not be party to. He wanted the president's committee curbed so that immigration laws were carefully observed.

Thus were the lines drawn, with Breckinridge Long waging a crusade to keep refugees out, backed by the weight of his department, and with the president's committee trying to bring more refugees in, backed by Mrs. Roosevelt and Jewish groups. What was the president's position?

Roosevelt had set up the advisory committee in 1938 because he did not want to fight Congress to change the immigration laws. According to polls, 83 percent of Americans were opposed to changing the quota in 1940. He wanted to run around the problem by working within the existing quota system and by looking for a place to put the Jews outside the United States.

He got quite a lot of mail urging him to comply with the spirit of Emma Lazarus's poem: "Give me your tired, your poor, your huddled masses yearning to breathe free. . . ." R. D. Turner, who raised oysters on Similk Beach in Anacortes, Washington, heard some of his customers say they didn't want these people from Europe, which prompted him to write the president. He wasn't a Jew lover, he knew them well, but he wasn't a Jew hater either. He could hear the wail of their babies as if they were next door. If we could help them we should do it. We could take a million of them even if they didn't have a dime.

But no attempt was made to expand the quota and make America a land of asylum. Roosevelt had experts looking at British Guiana and Angola as possible resettlement areas. On March 17, 1939, the Nansen aid group had wired: "Refugee situation extremely critical. For sake of humanity kindly intervene German Government open border for transit through Poland." But the State Department did not intervene. On June 2, Pa Watson memoed: "Caroline O'Day asked me last night at dinner if you would give her an expression of your views on the bill providing for 20,000 refugee children being allowed into America regardless of the quota system." FDR declined to support the bill.

In June he turned down a plan to amend the $50 million Red Cross appropriation so that $1 million could be used at the president's discretion to defray the transportation costs of refugee children from England, France, Belgium, and Holland. The plan was backed by Harry Hopkins and Attorney General Francis Biddle, but FDR did not want to spend his credit with Congress by seeking more discretionary money.

Also in June, the Immigration and Naturalization Service was transferred from the Labor Department to the Justice Department, and the Alien Registration Act, which required the registration and fingerprinting of all aliens over fourteen, began to be enforced.

In Europe, American consulates were besieged by thousands of desperate persons hoping for visas. Obeying the letter of the law, and aware of the attitude of their superiors, the consular staffs sometimes worked with heartbreaking slowness. It took them weeks and months to examine legal documents, allocate quota numbers, and check affidavits of support and other assurances that the refugees would not become public charges.

Breckinridge Long directed the consuls to issue visitor or transit visas only to persons with exit permits. As he wrote Adolf Berle: "We can delay and effectively stop for a temporary period of indefinite length the number of immigrants into the United States. We could do this by simply advising our consuls to put every obstacle in the way ... which would postpone and postpone the granting of the visas."

On July 3, 1940, a writer and teacher named Varian Fry wrote Eleanor urging that someone go to France to help "intended victims of Hitler's chopping-block" leave the country. She relayed Fry's letter to FDR, who replied the same day: "His suggestion may have all the merit in the world but it most certainly cannot be authorized or abetted by the Government of the United States." Fry left for Marseilles and set up the Emergency Rescue Committee, which managed to get about 1,500 refugees out of France with forged passports and other less-than-legal methods before he was arrested and deported in August 1941. It was a notable example of private initiative at a time when the government dragged its feet, though the State Department did announce on July 14 that children under sixteen fleeing war zones would be given visitors' visas.

On September 12, 1940, FDR gave $240 to the U.S. Committee for the Care of European Children, which was intended to cover the cost of transportation for the children of a Jewish family named Klein, whom his cousin Muriel Martineau had brought to his attention. But that was one family. In the overall struggle the refugees were losing ground. The president's committee was prodding the State Department to facilitate visas for intellectuals and political refugees, submitting 567 names, but Long sabotaged their efforts. Fewer than forty were granted visas.

Eleanor intervened on September 28, writing FDR that James G. McDonald, chairman of the advisory committee, was "so wrought up about it. . . . I am thinking of these poor people who may die at any time and who are asking only to come here on transit visas."

FDR agreed to see McDonald, but Long got to him first, on October 3, and used the security gambit on him. Rabbi Stephen Wise, he said, had been urging him to give visas to two officials of the World Jewish Congress, whom Long described as political agitators responsible for the overthrow of a government in Rumania.

The president agreed that such persons were undesirable, and, as Long put it, "expressed himself as in entire accord with the policy which would exclude persons about whom there was any suspicion that they would be inimical to the welfare of the United States no matter who had vouchsafed for them and irrespective of their financial and other standing. I left him with the satisfactory thought that he was whole-heartedly in support of the policy which would resolve any doubts about admissability of any individual."

A few days later, when McDonald's turn came and he began criticizing Long, FDR told him not to "pull any sob stuff." The consuls on the spot should have final say on the visas and pass on each case individually.

With FDR backing up Long's stonewalling, another means had to be found. It came through Harold Ickes, who as secretary of the interior had the Virgin Islands under his jurisdiction. Ickes discovered that nonimmigrant aliens could be admitted to the Virgin Islands without visas. This loophole, designed for vacationers, could be applied to refugees. In November, Ickes had the governor of the Virgin Islands issue a proclamation admitting refugees on their appearance at a port of entry. After a short stay and an affidavit that they were bona fide residents, they could proceed to the United States.

Long was frantic. There were 12,000 refugees in Portugal, among them many German agents, he was sure, and here was a pipeline to siphon them into the United States. He warned the president, who was "a little perturbed" and asked him to talk to Ickes. But Long found Ickes sarcastic and obstinate. When he tried to explain that the consulates were a sieve through which the refugee applicants could be strained, Ickes replied that the holes in the sieve were too small. Long got back to the president, who was, he recorded, "still more provoked and said he would send an order suspending the proclamation."

On December 18, Ickes got the president's "cease and desist" order, with FDR explaining that "the Virgin Islands . . . present to this Government a very serious social and economic problem not yet solved. . . . I cannot . . . do anything which would conceivably hurt the future of present American citizens. The inhabitants of the Virgin Islands are American citizens." In other words, he did not want thousands of refugees competing for jobs with backward islanders.

Thus was another avenue of escape blocked. Thousands of course did reach the United States, but thousands more were shut out. In 1938, for example, when Jews could still leave Germany, there were 150,000 applications for visas, while the annual quota was 27,370. Hull reported that in the six-month period between July and December 1940, which was the time of greatest demand, they had issued a total of 22,508 visas. In addition, from the 1,224 names submitted by the advisory committee, 402 had been accepted. In 1941, the combined German-Austrian quota was 37,000, and, according to Long, refugees were still getting out—the Germans were charging $485 a head, which he called "a sinister traffic."

Doubtless more could have been done. But the plight of the refugees was low on the president's list of priorities. He had to turn around a nation tempted by isolationism. He had to get Lend-Lease and conscription and military appropriations passed. He had to prepare the country for war. He had to deal with the isolationist wing in Congress and the isolationist press. In 1940, he had to get reelected. Refugees did not vote. They had no political clout, except for the private groups that rather timorously spoke up on their behalf. There was no lobby acting on their behalf. Even Jewish leaders in Congress advised FDR that it was not feasible to change the quota.

FDR listened with a receptive ear to the arguments of Breckinridge Long. He was sensitized to subversion, seeing daily evidence in intelligence reports of espionage and sabotage. He tended to believe the argument that among the refugees there would be a proportion of spies. He tended to accept the link Long made between Jews and international Communism. For a number of reasons, he thought, it was better to be cautious than to fling open America's gates to every refugee. To have Breckinridge Long in charge of refugee matters was like putting a right-to-life advocate in charge of family planning, but nothing was done to have him transferred.

In February 1941, appeals were made to FDR to admit Mrs. Leon Trotsky, widow of the Russian revolutionary assassinated in Mexico on Stalin's order, and her fifteen-year-old grandson, to the United States. Emil Ludwig, who had recently published a biography of FDR, wrote him that the widow was cooped up in a guarded house, in constant danger. She was nonpolitical and wanted only to work on her husband's archives. Here was a life worth saving, that of a woman who for thirty-seven years had shared the destiny of a great thinker and leader.

David Dubinsky, the pro-FDR labor leader, also wrote, and on his letter Eleanor added this notation: "FDR—Dubinsky is such a good leader and so loyal I feel like trying, but would like your opinion."

On February 11 he gave it, thinking perhaps of the commotion the Dies Committee could cause if Mrs. Trotsky were admitted: "This is another of those unfortunate cases where public opinion has to be taken into account. I have no doubt that Mrs. Trotsky is wholly non-political, but the public for another year or two could not see that fact. Furthermore, if the GPU is after the grandson, they would probably get him almost as readily here as anywhere else. Frankly, I am inclined to think that she and the boy would be safer in some relatively small town or village in Mexico than anywhere else—some place so small that any stranger would be immediately recognized."

The ever-vigilant Breckinridge Long got into the act, writing Pa Watson on February 12: "I feel strongly that Mrs. Trotsky and her grandson should not be allowed to enter the United States. She is closely associated with a violent faction of the Communist Party and I am convinced that her entry into this country would provoke widespread controversy and possibly might lead to violence."

The next day, FDR responded to Emil Ludwig's plea via Pa Watson: "Will you tell him [Ludwig] that it is being looked into and then forget it?"

In 1941, FDR could almost forget the entire refugee problem. Hitler had taken it off his hands. Many American consulates in occupied Europe had closed their doors. The Jews who had not gotten out were in hiding or were caught and sent to camps. In France, the collaborationist Premier Pierre Laval promised to deliver every Jew into Nazi hands. Four thousand Jewish children were snatched from their parents and deported to Germany. The Nazis boasted that the city of Rouen was now *judenrein,* free of Jews. With every cattle car that rolled eastward, there was less of a refugee problem.

In contrast to his "our hands are tied" policy on refugees, FDR was pushing steadily to involve America in the Atlantic and in Europe. After all, he knew firsthand from his Navy experience that this was the way America had entered World War I—Wilson had gone in after U-boats had sunk three American ships in March 1917.

There was no grand strategy and little rattling of sabers. Much of Roosevelt's action was surreptitious, for he had to contend with a divided public opinion. There was the seen, the half-seen, and the unseen.

The seen was whatever had to go through Congress and got into the papers, like Lend-Lease. The half-seen was a series of measures that could be taken by executive order, or no order at all. For example, during the blitz in the summer and fall of 1940, when England suffered a pilot shortage, FDR encouraged American boys going to Canada, where they could join the RAF, so long as they did not take an oath of allegiance to the king. "Frankly, I think the British have been terribly slow not to act on this before," he complained.

Other discreet actions in the first months of 1941 included allowing (in March) the British carrier *Illustrious* to be repaired in a U.S. shipyard; transferring ten old Coast Guard rumrunner chasers to the British navy; and training 8,000 British pilots in America.

There were also secret moves, such as Harry Hopkins's pledge to Churchill that Roosevelt was in for keeps, whatever he said in public, and the secret meetings in Washington from January to March 1941 between American and British military staffs, which drew up war plans to defeat Germany and her allies.

In his search for further involvement that would not cause tremors at home, Roosevelt hit on the device of couching his actions in terms of security measures for America's defense. In line with this, on April 9 the United States acquired the right to establish bases in Greenland.

In the same way, FDR was publicly against convoys, because that might involve American ships in a shooting war. But patrols were all right, to protect America against the planes and ships of aggressor nations.

It was on one of these patrols, on April 10, that the first clash of the war between American and German forces took place. While rescuing the survivors of a torpedoed Dutch ship, the destroyer USS *Niblack* dropped three depth charges to try to sink the U-boat.

On April 11, FDR secretly advised Churchill that he was extending the patrol area to west longitude 25 degrees, or, as Stimson put it, "midway between the westernmost bulge of Africa and the easternmost bulge of Brazil." This was in effect a form of convoying in the western half of the Atlantic, which would free some British ships for other duties.

Stimson, who was insensitive to the political context, thought the president was disingenuous. He was trying to hide an act that was clearly hostile to the Germans as a reconnaissance. But Roosevelt's problem was that there were not enough ships to effectively patrol the Atlantic. He did not have enough butter to spread over the bread, he said at cabinet on April 24.

Stimson and George Marshall, the courtly and reserved Pennsylvanian who had been sworn in as Army chief of staff on September 1, 1939, urged FDR to move some of the Pacific Fleet based in Hawaii into the Atlantic. Marshall was sure that with our heavy bombers and new pursuit planes, the land force could put up such a defense that the Japanese would not dare attack Hawaii, which was so far from their home base.

But FDR refused to do that, arguing that the fleet had to stay in Hawaii as a striking force to protect the southwestern Pacific, including Singapore. The real reason was that Hull was conducting secret negotiations with Ambassador Nomura, and the fleet's departure would be construed by the Japanese as an admission of weakness.

On April 25 at cabinet, FDR said the Atlantic patrols were a step forward, and Stimson replied: "Well, I hope you will keep on walking, Mr. President. Keep on walking." The whole cabinet burst into a roar of laughter.

When the extension of the American patrol area became known, German admirals Raeder and Dönitz advised striking at U.S. ships, but Hitler said no, still hoping to end the war before America got in. As chief of naval operations Admiral Harold R. ("Betty") Stark informed FDR on May 17: "It is my understanding that German submarines have instructions to 'beat it' just as fast as they can if they see [an American] man-o-war coming over the horizon."

Roosevelt was a man in search of an incident, which Hitler had given orders not to provide. "I am not willing to fire the first shot," he told Ickes. "I am waiting to be pushed into the situation," he told Morgenthau.

"I get so bored," Linda Bradley of El Cajon, California, wrote a friend, "with FDR's attitude of 'push me, Public, late to the war.'"

Like Linda Bradley, Stimson and Ickes were weary of the president's apparent lack of leadership. "He has flashes of genius," wrote Stimson, "but when it comes to working out a hard problem in a short time and with the aid of expert advisers, well, he just doesn't quite connect and it doesn't work."

In addition, FDR was sick in May with an intestinal disturbance. Ickes was so concerned at seeing "an inactive and uninspiring President," that he called a meeting on May 12 with the other malcontents in the cabinet—Stimson, Frank Knox, and Bob Jackson—to see if they would be willing to sign some sort of document saying there was a failure of leadership.

"We all felt that the country was sadly in need of leadership and that only the President himself could supply the want," he wrote in his diary. "We know the defense program is not anywhere near what it ought to be.... We felt that the State Department was a bottleneck.... What we wanted is something dramatic, something that will arrest the attention of the world."

That "something dramatic," that "something to arrest the attention of the world," came in June, not from Roosevelt, but from Hitler, who invaded the Soviet Union.

At dawn on June 22, the German ambassador to Moscow, Count Schulenburg (who would be shot in 1944 for taking part in the plot to kill Hitler), presented himself at the Kremlin before Foreign Minister Molotov with a formal declaration of war. Molotov, the icy bureaucrat who had made a career of impassivity, uttered this strangled and incredulous cry: "Do you believe that we deserved that?"

Faithful to the nonaggression pact, the Russians were supplying Germany with wheat to feed its army, munitions to feed its guns, and oil to feed its war machine (just as the United States was supplying Japan). And now that war machine had turned against them.

Only the Russians were surprised. The British and the Americans had been trying to warn them for months. The British learned of the "Barbarossa" plan from various intelligence sources and from Rudolf Hess, who had parachuted into Scotland in May. As early as March 24, American ambassador in Moscow Laurence A. Steinhardt cabled Cordell Hull that, having abandoned their plan to invade England, and convinced that America would soon enter the war, Germany had decided to invade Russia and seize her main productive areas.

Confirmation came from Magic. The Tokyo-Berlin traffic was cracked in April 1941, and the first message read was one where Goering outlined to the Japanese ambassador in Berlin, Hiroshi Oshima, the German attack on Russia, giving the number of divisions and types of planes.

By June 12, Steinhardt reported, German divisions were massed on the

Soviet border. The Soviets were taking haphazard measures, such as drills against parachute attacks. By June 20, the German embassy was evacuating its personnel, and the attack was expected within days.

Stalin did not believe the warnings, nor did he entirely discount them. That is why in June there were military maneuvers around Kiev. That is why many Soviet divisions were pulled back from the border to prepare a defense in depth. Nonetheless, Stalin was caught by surprise as 130 German divisions in three army groups swept across the border. In all his years as ruler of the Soviet state, this was one of the rare times when he could be accused of wishful thinking. The Russians lost 2,000 planes in the first twenty-four hours, many of them on the ground. Goering would not believe the reports of his pilots until he was driven around the front in a touring car and shown the smoking wrecks of planes.

Appeasement was contagious. In 1936, the Russians had fought in Spain, that dress rehearsal for World War II, while the democracies stayed neutral. In 1939, the Russians had sought an alliance with France and Britain, all committing troops to attack Hitler. The answer was Munich. Litvinov had failed and was succeeded by Molotov, who stalled the Germans with a non-aggression pact. Of course, the Russians went beyond appeasement by sharing in the spoils—half of Poland and the Baltic states—so that when they were invaded it could be said they were reaping what they had sowed.

The invasion of Russia transformed the war. As Harold Macmillan put it, it "determined the character and issue of the war itself and formed the mould into which the life of Europe has since been poured."

Here was the new equation:

Protected on its eastern border by a neutrality pact with Japan signed on April 13, the Soviet Union could concentrate all its resources against Germany. Never, until August 1945, did a Russian soldier fight a Japanese soldier. Each time the Germans asked the Japanese for help, the answer was a polite negative.

Mired in a massive land war on the eastern front, where the Russians fought alone for nearly three years, the "invincible" Wehrmacht learned the lesson of defeat. It was a physical and psychological blow from which it would not recover.

The invasion of Russia dictated the strategy of the second front. With so many German divisions pinned down in the east, the Allies were able to strike in the west, forming one of the two jaws of a great clamp that would squeeze the Nazi war machine into surrender.

In fact, it took Stalin less than a month to ask for a second front, in a July 18 letter to Churchill: "It seems to me that the military situation of the Soviet Union, as well as Great Britain, would be considerably improved if there could be established a front against Hitler in the West—Northern France. . . ." From the initial request to the actual landing, nearly three years would elapse.

Among the diverse reactions to the invasion, Herbert Pell, American minister to Hungary, reported on June 23 "the great joy of many Hungarians, who would like to see them cut each other's throats. They hope to see the Russians beaten and the Germans bogged down and destroyed."

Many Americans felt the same way, that it was like a gang war, and the more gangsters killed each other the better. The question was, how long could the Russians hold out. Stimson conferred with the chief of staff and the men in the War Plans Division, who estimated it would take Germany one to three months to beat Russia. Indeed, that was the way it looked, for Russia was off to a poor start, and no nation had yet withstood a blitzkrieg.

But they were smaller nations. Only Russia with her continent-size 8 million square miles had the advantage of depth. Also, the Russians had kept their industrial capacity a secret. Their steel production was 70 percent that of America. In June 1940, Stalin had 24,000 tanks, 4,000 of which had been built since the pact with Hitler. The Soviets had been making tanks since 1928, according to the Bolshevik dogma that war is normal and peace is abnormal. They had a new model tank each year, just as in America there was a new model car, and some of their tanks were better than the German tanks. So the Russians hung on. Conscripts by the thousands were loaded into freight trains for the front. Generals were shot for cowardice. Peasants with muskets were decorated for gallantry.

Churchill, that archfoe of Bolshevism, urged all-out support of Russia, having announced two days before the invasion that "if Hitler invaded Hell, I would at least make a favorable reference to the Devil in the House of Commons."

Roosevelt saw the invasion as a chance to limit America's involvement to supplying the Russians as well as the British. If the Russians held, perhaps he could remain true to his pledge of not sending "your boys to foreign wars." It was certainly worth the gamble.

His first step was unfreezing $40 million in Russian funds, so they could buy matériel while public opinion developed in favor of Lend-Lease. Then, on July 9, he took over the occupation of Iceland from the British. The German navy saw this as a casus belli, and demanded the right to sink American freighters and warships. Hitler kept his admirals on a leash, ordering on July 19 that "in the extended zone of operations, U.S. merchant ships, whether single or sailing in English or American convoys, and if recognized as such before resort to arms, are not to be attacked."

At the end of July, while the concerned agencies bickered about how to finance Russian purchases, FDR sent Hopkins to Moscow to see Stalin. On July 30 and 31, Hopkins spent six hours with a man he described as five feet six, 190 pounds, built close to the ground, "like a football coach's dream of a tackle." He had the raspy voice of a chain-smoker, and wore stout baggy trousers, a snug-fitting blouse, and boots that shone like mirrors. He was a plain man, blunt and to the point. "It was like talking to a perfectly coordinated machine," he said, "an intelligent machine."

Stalin, who had attended the Frunze military academy in Moscow, hearing a general who had served under the czars lecture on Clausewitz, now gave Hopkins a lecture on a new sort of war. Yes, after six weeks of fighting, the Germans had thrust 400 kilometers into Russia, but that created difficulties for them. There were 400 kilometers between their front lines and their supplies and reserves. They had to haul vast quantities of fuel and other matériel long distances over bad roads. Thousands of troops were immobilized guarding the supply lines against Russian guerrillas, who were more familiar with the terrain and knew how to use the natural cover better.

There was no line in the classical sense. Having your front pierced did not mean defeat when you had depth. "Even the German tanks run out of petrol," Stalin said. Germany at the outset had 30,000 tanks to Russia's 24,000, but "moving mechanized forces through Russia was very different from moving them over the boulevards of Belgium and France."

Stalin did not propose to underrate the enemy, as the British had done, but the Germans would have trouble after the heavy rains. They had no stomach for a winter offensive.

In the meantime, Stalin needed 20,000 antiaircraft guns, thousands of heavy machine guns, a million rifles, high-octane gas, aluminum, 3,000 pursuit planes and 3,000 bombers. The bill would run to $2 billion.

Hopkins liked the way Stalin did business. It was all cleaned up at two sittings. But he also noticed the cringing subordinates in a country where generals who lost battles ended up in front of firing squads, and the secretiveness bordering on paranoia. When he asked General Yakovlev what Russia's heaviest tank weighed, the general replied: "It is a good tank."

On balance, Hopkins thought the Russians would hold, and cabled FDR: "I feel ever so confident about this front. . . . There is unbounded determination to win."

Impressed, FDR wanted to send the Russians what they wanted, and when it did not go out fast enough, he gave vent to a rare outburst. At the August 1 cabinet meeting, he chewed out the white-haired and venerable secretary of war: "The Russians have been given the run-around," he said. "I am sick and tired of hearing that they are going to get this and they are going to get that. Whatever we are going to give them, it has to be over there by the first of October, and the only answer I want to hear is that it is under way." He was particularly incensed by 140 P-40s, sent to England in crates, and now slated for the Russians, and said: "Get the planes right off with a bang next week."

Another group that was getting the runaround was the blacks. They were excluded from defense work. The federal agency in charge of defense contracts, the Office of Production Management, was not helpful. A. Philip Randolph, the head of the Brotherhood of Sleeping Car Porters, pulled the black leadership together for a march on Washington. His union was made up of men who made their living from the tips of well-off whites; they had reversed their "Uncle Tom" image to become a militant force in the black community.

FDR thought he could stall and sweet-talk the blacks, and asked his wife and Mayor La Guardia to coax them out of marching. But Randolph insisted on a meeting with the president, which took place on June 18, 1941, and was attended by, among others, the secretaries of war and of the Navy, William S. Knudsen, head of OPM and former head of General Motors, Mayor La Guardia, and Walter White, head of the NAACP.

A. Philip Randolph came from a poor family in Florida. He had gone to the Cookman Institute in Jacksonville, the first high school for blacks in that state, founded by the Methodists. After graduating, he had gone to work collecting life insurance premiums in black neighborhoods. Fed up with dunning his own people, he moved to New York and became a Pullman porter and a labor organizer.

"Hello, Phil," Roosevelt said as Randolph walked in, "which class were you in at Harvard?"

"I never went to Harvard, Mr. President," Randolph replied.

"I was sure you did. Anyway, you and I share a kinship in our great interest in human and social justice."

FDR went into the reminiscence routine that was part of the sweet talk, but Randolph broke in: "Mr. President, time is running on. You are quite busy, I know. But what we want to talk with you about is the problem of jobs for Negroes in defense industries. Our people are being turned away at factory gates because they are colored. They can't live with this thing. Now, what are you going to do about it?"

"Well, Phil, what do you want me to do?"

"Mr. President, we want you to do something that will enable Negro workers to get work in these plants."

"Why, I surely want them to work too. I'll call up the heads of the various defense plants and have them see to it that Negroes are given the same opportunity to work as any other citizen in the country."

"We want you to do more than that. . . . We want you to issue an executive order making it mandatory that Negroes be permitted to work in these plants."

"Well, Phil, you know I can't do that," FDR said, taken aback. "If I issue an executive order for you, then there'll be no end to other groups coming in here and asking me to issue executive orders for them too. In any event, I couldn't do anything unless you called off this march of yours. Questions like this can't be settled with a sledgehammer." The march was scheduled for July 1.

"I'm sorry, Mr. President, the march cannot be called off."

"How many people do you plan to bring?"

"One hundred thousand, Mr. President."

FDR turned to Walter White, as if calling Randolph's bluff. "Walter, how many people will really march?"

"One hundred thousand, Mr. President."

FDR remembered the Washington race riots in 1919, in which scores had been killed and injured. "You can't bring 100,000 Negroes to Washington," he said. "Someone might get killed. . . . Call it off, and we'll talk again."

Randolph said he had pledged to his people not to leave with anything less than an executive order.

FDR told him to confer with his assistants and find a way to solve the problem with defense contractors.

"Not defense contractors alone," Randolph said. "The government too. The government is the worst offender."

Bristling, FDR told Randolph that the president of the United States was not accustomed to being told what to do with a gun to his head.

"I shall have to stand by the pledge I made to my people," Randolph insisted.

La Guardia broke the impasse: "Gentlemen, it is clear that Mr. Randolph is not going to call off the march, and I suggest we all begin to seek a formula."

A committee of five was appointed to draw up an executive order, which FDR signed on June 25. The order banned discrimination in defense industries and government because of "race, creed, color, or national origin." FDR appointed a Fair Employment Practices Committee to enforce it. The march was called off.

Not since Reconstruction had there been a federal law in favor of equal rights for blacks. For the first time in the twentieth century, the federal government was enforcing civil rights. It was the thin edge of the wedge.

On September 23, Mark Ethridge, chairman of the Fair Employment Practices Committee, wrote FDR that the RAF Ferry Command, which was recruiting American pilots, was turning down black applicants. Was it appropriate for Ferry Command to discriminate in activities supported by U.S. funds?

FDR gave one of his famous either/or replies: "I agree with you that it is not a good thing for the R.A.F. Ferry Command to turn down applications because they do not belong to the white race. Nevertheless, I think it would be not only discourteous but presumptuous for us to interfere with the war procedure of a different nation."

In January 1941, FDR had said to Hopkins: "A lot of this could be settled if Churchill and I could just sit down together for a while."

Hopkins arranged a meeting, which took place from August 9 to 12 in Placentia Bay, at the eastern tip of Newfoundland, about 800 miles northeast of Boston. It was the first face-to-face meeting between the president and the prime minister, establishing the custom of wartime conferences among Allied leaders, of which there would be many.

On August 9, the brand new British battleship *Prince of Wales,* carrying Churchill and his team of military and civilian aides, approached Placentia Bay. The boatswain gave the order "Fall in for entering harbor," and the battleship anchored across from the heavy cruiser USS *Augusta,* which carried the president and his aides.

The two men about to meet had vastly dissimilar natures. Churchill was more leonine, Roosevelt more feline. Roosevelt was serene in the exercise of power, having been president almost nine years. Churchill was domineering and demanding; he had been prime minister a little over a year, after a long career of ups and downs. Roosevelt had greater balance and equanimity. Churchill had moods, fits of depression that could last for weeks. He could not live with his mistakes and keep his balance, said his doctor, Charles Wilson, and the urge to obliterate them grew into a cast of mind where he was incapable of seeing that he was at fault.

The qualities that made Churchill a great wartime leader had their dark side—a colossal egocentricity and contant self-reference: "I can do this. I won't do that," said Churchill when speaking of national policy. Roosevelt was a great leader in both peace and war, the colors of his palette were more varied and muted. While Roosevelt seemed to be responding to the will of the people, Churchill was always pulling his country behind him.

Churchill had greater mastery of language and eloquence, which he trailed behind him like the wake of a ship. Roosevelt was not an orator in the grand manner, he tried to speak simply and colloquially, and to find images from everyday life, such as the garden hose. Roosevelt worked with speech writers, while Churchill wrote his speeches himself.

They also differed greatly as commanders in chief. Roosevelt's experience was in the Navy. When it came to the Army, he was an armchair strategist who loved maps and technical information but usually deferred to the experts. When he overruled his able secretary of war, Henry Stimson, and his able chief of staff, George Marshall, it was for political rather than military reasons.

Churchill thought of himself essentially as a military man. He had gone to military school, taken part in the British cavalry's last great charge, at Omdurman, had fought and been captured in the Boer War. As first lord of the Admiralty he had been in charge of the amphibious landings at the Dardanelles, of which the D-day landings were the direct descendant. In disgrace in 1915, he had gone to France and fought in the trenches. He was a self-professed war lover, who had once called war "delicious."

As minister of defense, he interfered in the day-to-day conduct of operations, driving his generals to distraction. General Alan Brooke, his chief of staff, regretted his urge "to stick his fingers into every pie before it was cooked." He was petulant, unreasonable, bullying, sarcastic, abusive. When Brooke told him it would take twenty-four hours to cover the ground from A to B during the Norway expedition, Churchill asked: "Explain to me exactly how every one of those twenty-four hours will be occupied."

Churchill had this in common with Hitler, that he fired generals as scapegoats for his own mistakes and replaced them with more pliable men. Hitler managed to destroy the brilliant tradition of his general staff, which had been true to its motto, "Be, Not Seem," and Churchill too managed to impair the effectiveness of his armies with his constant meddling.

In contrast, Roosevelt did not second-guess the generals, and did not fire them. American generals tend to be of two types, the whittlers and the *grands seigneurs*. Of the first type, he had to recall Stilwell, who made himself objectionable to Chiang Kai-shek. Of the second type, he kept Patton in place in spite of conduct bordering on the pathological, and he kept MacArthur in command in the Pacific even when he was encouraging feelers for the Republican nomination in 1944.

Churchill came to Placentia Bay as a pleader. His policy in 1941 was to draw the American Navy across the Atlantic so that a clash with Germany was bound to come. Either Hitler would hold back the U-boats from operating in the western Atlantic for fear of sinking U.S. ships, which would ease the pressure on British convoys, or he would risk bringing America into the war.

Churchill saw himself as a suitor, using all his powers of persuasion to get the reluctant American bride to the altar. This was the language he used on December 9, after Pearl Harbor, when someone at a chiefs of staff meeting advised a cautious approach toward America. "Oh!" said Churchill with a wicked grin, "that is the way we talked to her while we were wooing her; now that she is in the harem, we talk to her quite differently." And yet the tone of courtship returned when necessary. On October 29, 1943, Churchill wrote: "I have a great wish and need to see you," and the next day: "I was not aware you had been rushed at the last minute on any occasion and I am very sorry ... if I am to blame." One can chart the decline of Britain as a first-class power in the tone of Churchill's telegrams.

At Placentia Bay, he was able to subdue his naturally overbearing nature and charm the charmer. It was an exercise in humility. You had to see the two of them on the morning of August 10 when they sang hymns—FDR with his head up and his mouth wide open lustily singing "O God Our Help in Ages Past," while Churchill, who thought singing hymns was a waste of time, looked not into his hymnbook but over the top of his spectacles to see who else was singing.

You had to see him, as they broke the ice and fell into easy banter, winning over Roosevelt with self-deprecating humor, as when the president said: "I can't understand primogeniture—I have five children and I would give them all equal shares of my estate."

"No, Mr. President," Churchill replied, "we call it the Spanish curse. We give everything to the oldest and the others strive to duplicate it and found empires. While the oldest, having it all, marries for beauty. Which accounts, Mr. President, for my good looks."

Those close to Churchill marveled at his patience. This was indeed his finest hour. Privately, Churchill described FDR as a "charming country gentleman," which translated as "a bit of a lightweight." In the same vein, Sir Alexander Cadogan said that at dinner on August 9 he conversed charmingly about his country estate at Hyde Park, where he hoped to grow Christmas trees for the market.

There was a certain amount of teeth gnashing from the British, who wanted to discuss global strategy. Churchill wanted an American occupation of the Azores and an attack on French North Africa. He wanted to drag FDR in farther, but the president refused to be dragged, wanting no World War I style secret commitments. "We wish to God there had been!" the British said when asked.

He did agree, according to Cadogan, "that the U.S. Navy would take over the America-Iceland stretch of the Atlantic." But when the military staffs got together, the British found the Americans awfully reticent. Lieutenant Colonel Ian Jacob, who as assistant secretary of the war cabinet took part in the discussions, recorded in his diary on August 11: "Not a single American officer has shown the slightest keenness to be in the war on our side. They are a charming lot of individuals but they appear to be living in a different world from ourselves."

They did come up with a vaporous declaration of principles solemnly called the Atlantic Charter, but the British left Placentia Bay in a gloomy state of mind. "I think the general opinion in our party," Ian Jacob recorded on August 18, "would be that the Americans have a long way to go before they can play any decisive part in the war. . . . Both their Army and their Navy are standing like reluctant brothers on the brink."

The meeting was a success in personal terms, however, the start of a friendship based on Churchill's side on equal parts of dire need and genuine fondness. As for Roosevelt, he came back to Washington admiring Churchill's qualities of mind, stubbornness, and ability as a trader. "But of course, you know," he said at cabinet, "Grandpa's pretty good at trading too." "You want to look out, Mr. President," someone responded, "Churchill may be pulling your leg by letting you win the first round."

When FDR returned from Placentia Bay a sobering piece of news awaited him. On August 13, the House had passed the bill (previously passed by the Senate 45 to 30) to extend the Selective Service Act for six months by a single vote, 203 to 202. Resistance to the bill was one of the isolationists' last large-scale efforts.

Abusing the privilege of the congressional frank, Senator Wheeler mailed a million postcards that said: "Write to President Roosevelt today that you are against our entry into the European war." Parents of drafted boys who had been told their sons would be in uniform for a year, which the bill proposed to extend to eighteen months, were eager to respond. A slogan called OHIO (Over the Hill in October) sprang up. Its very name was practically an appeal to desertion.

There was tremendous pressure on the House, which on the day of the vote was packed with flag-carrying mothers and young men in uniform. Speaker of the House Sam Rayburn had his finest moment that day. He called in his notes: "Do this for me. I won't forget it." He broke the House tradition that members should not be expected to vote against the interests of their constituencies, and appealed to their patriotism: You cannot allow the Army to be disbanded. Four votes switched, and the bill passed by one vote. In a tie, Rayburn would have voted, but it was a close call, showing the depth of antiwar feeling in the American heartland.

FDR was also having trouble getting the country behind aid to Russia. The isolationists found allies in the Catholics, for Pope Pius XI had in a 1938 encyclical condemned any cooperation with Communism. Roosevelt wrote his successor, Pius XII, that it was his understanding that "churches in Russia are open." Finally in October, the archbishop of Cincinnati, John T. McNicholas, said the encyclical was not intended to condemn all forms of aid to the people of Russia. That same month, the Lend-Lease Act was amended to apply to Russia.

Casting about for some way to make the American people see that the war was dangerous to *them,* FDR hit on the Nazi threat to Latin America. This was an old fixation of his, which he had described to Josephus Daniels at dinner at the White House on January 14, 1939, as part of his obligation under the Monroe Doctrine. The first danger would come from Brazil, he said, where there were 1.5 million Germans. The Nazis would send armadas of bombers from Africa—look how Africa jutted out on the map; Dakar was only 1,600 miles away from the coast of Brazil—and a civil war would start in Brazil and German planes would swoop down and Brazil would turn Nazi.

There was some evidence of Nazi penetration in Latin America. On May 30, 1940, the American minister in Montevideo, Edwin C. Wilson, warned Sumner Welles that the Uruguayan authorities had foiled a Nazi coup. FDR ordered the cruisers *Quincy* and *Wichita* off the Uruguayan coast, and on June 13 the local Nazi party was disbanded. There was definite propaganda and economic penetration (such as the growth of German airlines), and the threat of a pro-Nazi coup in Bolivia in 1941. But in Mexico, Ambassador Josephus Daniels said rumors of Nazi penetration were unfounded, and the State Department was divided about its importance.

FDR, however, repeatedly used the Nazi threat to Latin America to drum up support for his policies of aid to England and increasing commitment in the Atlantic. When in a press conference on April 25, 1941, he announced the extension of patrols halfway across the Atlantic, the reason was "for the safety of the Western Hemisphere." When he occupied Greenland, belonging to Denmark, which had signed an armistice with Germany, it was under the Monroe Doctrine's "no transfer" principle—Germany could not acquire a hemispheric colony through the armistice.

FDR saw that anything done in the name of hemispheric defense blunted the isolationist charge that he was leading the country to war. He was eager for any information that could substantiate the Nazi threat. When Hess landed in Scotland, FDR wrote Churchill on May 14 to persuade him to tell "what Hitler has said about the United States, or what Germany's plans are in relation to the United States or to other parts of the Western Hemisphere, including commerce, infiltration, military domination, encirclement of the United States."

Hess was not forthcoming, but FDR continued to press the case, telling the Pan American Union in May that "unless the advance of Hitlerism is forcibly checked now, the Western Hemisphere will be within range of the Nazi weapons of destruction."

After Placentia Bay, however, Churchill had doubts about America's purpose. Giving in to one of his somber moods, he wired Harry Hopkins on August 28: "I don't know what will happen if England is fighting alone when 1942 comes. The Germans have thirty submarines on a line from North Ireland to the eastern point of Iceland and we have lost 50,000 tons in the last two days."

Hopkins talked the cable over with FDR, and they decided that Churchill was pretty depressed, and this was his way of taking it out on them. "I told the President," Hopkins said, "that not only Churchill but all the members of the Cabinet and all the British people I talked to believed that ultimately we will get into the war on some basis or other."

Churchill had told his son Randolph after Placentia Bay that America had to be brought "boldly and honorably" into the war. In the summer of 1941, however, he was so desperate that dishonorable methods were used as well. British intelligence forged documents intended to reinforce Roosevelt's fears of a Nazi attack in Latin America, which were conveniently brought to the president's attention.

This was done by the British Security Coordination (BSC), which had set up shop in New York City under Sir William Stephenson, known as "The Quiet Canadian" or "Intrepid." BSC had an office in Ottawa called Section M, staffed by handwriting and documents experts, which produced high-quality forgeries.

It was only a matter of giving the president a nudge by expanding a bit on a plausible scenario. Major Elias Belmonte, the Bolivian military attaché in Berlin, was known to be pro-Nazi, and was said to be planning a coup to overthrow the Bolivian government of pro-British President Peñaranda and establish a Nazi dictatorship.

BSC operatives were able to get copies of Belmonte letters, which were sent to Section M's handwriting experts. The forged Belmonte letter, dated June 9, 1941, and typewritten in Spanish, was addressed to Dr. Ernest Wendler, the German minister to Bolivia, and said: "The moment is approaching to strike in order to liberate my poor country from a weak government and from capitalistic tendencies. I go much further and believe that the coup should take place in the middle of July since I consider the moment to be propitious."

The letter, which Stephenson said had been intercepted by one of his agents, was passed on to J. Edgar Hoover, who passed it on to Cordell Hull, who showed it to FDR. Here was proof of what he had been saying, that the Nazis were planning to take over Latin America. On September 3, the president conveyed his indignation to the nation at large, stating that he knew of three Nazi plots in Latin America, of which the Belmonte plot was one.

Additional fuel for the president's angry mood was provided when a U-boat fired two torpedoes at the destroyer USS *Greer,* which was on a mail run to Iceland. The torpedoes missed. There had been considerable provocation, for the *Greer* had trailed the sub for three hours, acting as a spotter for a British patrol plane.

Roosevelt was at Hyde Park and at once began working on a speech to make the most of the incident, but was interrupted on September 7 by his mother's death—she was two weeks short of her eighty-seventh birthday—in her corner room. Although an invalid, she had come home from Campobello to enjoy the company of her son. After the funeral on September 10, Eleanor wrote her daughter Anna: "Father has begun to forget all that was ever disagreeable in his relationship to Granny but he was not emotional. . . . I kept being appalled at myself because I couldn't feel any real grief or sense of loss and that seemed terrible after 36 years of close association." On September 25 Eleanor's brother, Hall, died in Walter Reed Hospital. He had been drinking a quart of gin a day. Again Eleanor was unfeeling. "It's such an unattractive death," she wrote Anna. "He's mahogany color, all distended."

The *Greer* was not much of an incident, but it was all FDR had, and he went with it on September 11. A black mourning band circling the arm of his light seersucker suit, he gave his "shoot on sight" fireside chat, in which he compared Hitler to a uniquely American creature: "When you see a rattlesnake poised to strike you do not wait until he has struck you before you crush him. . . . From now on if German or Italian war vessels enter the waters, the protection of which is necessary for American defense, they do so at their own peril."

On September 13, the Atlantic Fleet was issued orders to escort convoys of any nationality and destroy any German or Italian forces they might encounter. This was a undeclared naval war. But Hitler, whose armies could see Moscow's spires forty miles away, hoped for a quick end to the Russian campaign and told his admirals: No incidents.

Yet there were bound to be incidents when ships of different flags were mixed in convoys, particularly at night. On October 16, a forty-ship convoy 400 miles south of Iceland ran into a wolf pack. Three ships were torpedoed, and more were being picked off when a rescue force of five American destroyers out of Reykjavik arrived. By then it was dark, and the USS *Kearny* was hit by a torpedo, but made it back to Iceland. Eleven crewmen were killed. The first American blood had been spilled.

The news arrived in time for the Senate debate on FDR's proposed amendments to the Neutrality Act, which had been passed in the House 259 to 138. FDR wanted to arm American merchantmen and send them all the way to British ports. In the Senate, the isolationists were putting up a stiffer fight. As Senator Robert A. Taft said, the Neutrality Act was the only thing remaining between America and war.

At this point, the British forgery mill made a timely move. One day in his office, Ivar Bryce, a wealthy sportsman who had joined the BSC through his friendship with Ian Fleming, drew a detailed map of Latin America as Hitler might divide it. He showed it to Sir William Stephenson, who saw that it had possibilities. What if a genuine map of this sort were discovered, or captured from the enemy—what a commotion it would cause among the America Firsters who thought they could get along with Hitler.

Stephenson decided to forge the map and turn it over to the FBI. Section M went to work, producing a slightly travel-stained map with the highest German secrecy classification, a map that the German high command would have sworn was one of their own, with Gothic lettering and official seals, and a division of Latin America into areas suspiciously like the old Spanish viceroyalties that the forgers had copied. Handwritten notes in the margins referred to "fuel reserves for transatlantic flights" and the possibility of Mexican participation.

The map found its way to the president in time for his Navy Day speech on October 27, which was broadcast to the nation, and in which he mentioned that "Hitler has often protested that his plans for conquest do not extend beyond the Atlantic Ocean. I have in my possession a secret map, made in Germany by Hitler's Government—by planners of the new world order. It is a map of South America and part of Central America as Hitler proposes to organize it. Today in this area there are fourteen separate countries. The geographical experts of Berlin, however, have ruthlessly obliterated all the existing boundary lines and have divided South America into five vassal states bringing the whole continent under their domination. And they have also arranged it that the territory of one of these new puppet states includes the Republic of Panama and our great life-line, the Panama Canal. This map makes clear the Nazi designs, not only against South America but against the United States itself."

These sinister revelations were the main topic of FDR's press conference the next day. Asked if he would release the map, he said: "No, and for a very good reason. The map has on it—it's in my basket at the present time—it has on it certain manuscript notations, which if they were reproduced would in all probability disclose how—where the map came from. And on account of these manuscript notations it might be exceedingly embarrassing to a number of people. It might also dry up the source of future information."

"Mr. President," a reporter said, "if you have had time to read the German comment—Berlin comment—you may have noticed that they were accusing you of having faked the map. They speak of the map as a fraud, a forgery, a fake. . . . They make that very serious claim."

"Well," said the president, "you know, they made the serious claim about ten days ago that I had torpedoed the *Kearny*. . . . I suppose that is as good an answer as you can make."

"Mr. President, have you had occasion to make that map available to the Latin American nations concerned?"

"No. . . . It would only be done in the strictest confidence. . . . The kind of confidence that would be . . . I suppose so they could not be traced . . . the poor devil that we got it from."

Isolationist senators like Burt Wheeler also thought the map was a fake. It certainly cut the ground from under them in the Neutrality Act debate. With the help of the president's revelations about the Nazi plan to divide Latin America, the amendments passed the Senate in October 50 to 37, and the House passed the Senate bill in mid-November. American vessels could now carry arms to British ports.

Churchill's department of dirty tricks helped bring America closer to war. As Wheeler and others suspected, the Great Debate was fixed. It was fixed on the other side too, for the isolationists were funded by the Germans and the Japanese. But just as the Axis nations manipulated Americans who sincerely wanted to stay out, the British manipulated FDR. As one of the American operatives who had acted as liaison with Stephenson's BSC, in a spirit of cooperation and trust, put it when he learned of the forgeries forty-three years after the event: "I felt as if a member of my club had been passing bad checks."

Roosevelt apparently accepted the forgeries in good faith, but never questioned their authenticity because they suited his own aims so well. In fact, there were no Nazi maps, or secret air bases, or plots to overthrow Latin American governments. The Nazis were too busy fighting the Russians in Europe and the British in Africa (Rommel had arrived there in February 1941) to concern themselves with Latin America. In a way that bordered on violating the public trust, Roosevelt invented a Nazi menace to mobilize American public opinion in favor of war. In so doing, he became the accomplice of British efforts to bring America into the war by all available means.

It's ironic that Roosevelt has been accused of deceit in his Japanese policy, where there was no deceit, and of planning the attack on Pearl Harbor, whereas he was completely and genuinely surprised by it; while in his "Nazi threat in Latin America" policy, he was deceitful and used British forgeries, but was not called to account for it. He invented imaginary threats in Latin America while disregarding real threats in the Pacific.

The revisionist case on Pearl Harbor is that Roosevelt knew the attack would take place and allowed it to take place to push America into the war.

As Harry Elmer Barnes put it: "The net result of revisionist scholarship applied to Pearl Harbor boils down essentially to this: In order to promote Roosevelt's political ambitions and his mendacious foreign policy some three thousand American boys were quite needlessly butchered."

To understand Pearl Harbor you have to understand Magic and how it worked. This might be summed up as "the curse of having the data."

In February 1939 the Japanese began to use an enciphering machine for its diplomatic code between Tokyo and Washington. In its small bureau of cryptanalysis, the Army had a man named William F. Friedman, whose Russian-Jewish immigrant father was a salesman for Singer sewing machines. Friedman, not quite single-handedly, was able to build a replica of the Japanese machine. It took him eighteen months and gave him a nervous breakdown. But in August 1940 the first message in the diplomatic code (dubbed "Purple") was deciphered.

American military intelligence was now tapped into the worldwide Japanese diplomatic network. All the coded radio messages between the Foreign Office in Tokyo and the Japanese embassies in foreign capitals could be picked up by radio intercept stations, deciphered, and sent to Washington for translation. A number of other codes were deciphered as well. This secret weapon, this ability to overhear Japanese plans and intentions, was called Magic. As Rear Admiral Arthur H. McCollum of Naval Intelligence said, "It looked like real gravy."

In Washington, the task of handling Magic was shared by the Army and the Navy. The Army had its Signal Intelligence Service, or SIS, under Colonel Otis K. Sadtler, with a staff of under 400. The Navy had a Communications Security Unit under Commander Lawrence L. Safford, with a staff of about 300.

This was something that had never been done before. They had to make up the procedures as they went along—there were no precedents or existing regulations. As a result, problems arose.

One was the time of processing. One message took fifty-nine days to process. This was the lag between the day of radio interception and the finished product of the translated message. Say a message from the Japanese consul in Honolulu to Tokyo was intercepted by the Honolulu station. The deciphered message was usually sent to Washington by air clipper, a weekly flight often delayed by bad weather.

In Washington, there was a translation bottleneck—too few translators, who sometimes broke down from overwork. You had a couple of dozen persons trying to keep up with thousands of messages from message centers in Japanese embassies, consulates, and legations all over the world. Many times it was impossible to solve a new key until enough traffic had accumulated. Until the messages were converted into English the useful intelligence might just as well have filled a wastebasket. Messages had a priority depending on their place of origin, and Honolulu messages had a low priority because of the bedrock conviction that Pearl Harbor could not be attacked.

The diplomatic messages were framed in a classical Japanese that was tough to translate—you had to know Japanese myths, allegories, allusions, habits of equivocation. A message that arrived shortly before December 7— "Nich-bei kankei wa kitai ni hinsu"—was translated by the Navy as "Japanese-American relations are not up to expectation," whereas a more accurate version would be "have passed the brink of disaster."

For security reasons, the distribution of Magic was so restricted that an overall evaluation of the material was practically impossible. Those who got Magic were the president and the secretary of state; the secretary of war, the Army chief of staff, and the director of Military Intelligence; the secretary of the Navy, the chief of naval operations, the chief of the Navy War Plans Division, and the director of Naval Intelligence. Not even Hap Arnold, commander of the Army Air Corps, was on the list.

The two men in command at Pearl Harbor, Admiral Husband E. Kimmel and General Walter Short, did *not* get Magic after July 1941 because it was felt there were too many spies and Japanese at Pearl Harbor, and in any case the material was more diplomatic than military, and better evaluated in Washington.

But in Washington, evaluation was haphazard. Magic was distributed daily, one month by the Army, one month by the Navy. When it was the Army's turn, SIS delivered the messages to Colonel Rufus Bratton, chief of the Far Eastern section of Military Intelligence, who had gone to Japan as a language student. Bratton screened out the material he thought was valuable and burned the rest. The screened material was sent in locked leather dispatch cases to those who had access, at which time the previous day's output was picked up and burned. When it was the Navy's turn, Lieutenant Commander A. D. Kramer, the head of the Navy translation unit, personally brought the messages in a locked pouch to those who had access, waited while they scanned the messages rapidly, and then took them away. No one was allowed to keep a series of messages. It was like being shown a single frame in a film; you would have to see hundreds of frames to detect any movement or pattern.

No one had the responsibility of studying the entire file as a series of frames telling a story. There was no interservice intelligence staff to evaluate Magic. A joint Army-Navy Intelligence Committee was authorized on October 11, 1941, but did not meet until after December 7. The extent of evaluation was to mark a significant message with an asterisk or a red check.

The signs pointing to Pearl Harbor were raindrops in a squall of messages. So what if the Japanese were asking about ship movements in Honolulu? They were asking about ship movements in a lot of other ports. Magic never told the precise target and the date. It gave hints that seemed relevant only after the event. The tendency to lend prominence to the signals that supported current expectations about enemy behavior prevailed. It was unanimously held that Pearl Harbor was not a target.

Adding to the confusion was the fact that the Japanese were informed in April 1941 that their diplomatic code had been cracked. On April 1, Sumner Welles happened to tell the British ambassador, Lord Halifax, that according to a Magic dispatch from the Japanese ambassador in Berlin, the Germans were planning to attack the Soviet Union. Halifax passed the information on to the Foreign Office, using a code "for telegrams of a less confidential nature."

On April 28, the German chargé d'affaires in Washington, Hans Thomsen, sent this top secret message to Berlin: "As communicated to me by an absolutely reliable source [a term the Germans used for intercepted foreign communications], the State Department is in possession of the key to the Japanese coding system and is therefore able to decipher information telegrams from Tokyo."

On May 3, a German agent called on Ambassador Hiroshi Oshima in Berlin to pass on the news. On May 5, Japanese Foreign Minister Yosuke Matsuoka wired Ambassador Nomura: "According to a fairly reliable source of information it appears almost certain that the United States Government is reading your code messages."

At this point, the whole Magic operation seemed doomed, but incredibly the Japanese did not change their code. They were simply more careful in phrasing their messages, refraining from sending secret policy decisions.

In Washington, however, security was further tightened, to the point where, in May, Magic service to the president was discontinued. This came about because, earlier that spring, Colonel Rufus S. Bratton of Military Intelligence had located a Magic memo in Pa Watson's wastebasket. G-2 decided that since most of the Magic traffic was State Department business anyway, it would furnish the material to State, which could then take it up with the White House.

The Navy also cut off the president, but allowed his naval aide, Captain John R. Beardall, to see selected documents and brief FDR orally. The president made no objection, for he was overwhelmed by the European situation—whether to transfer the Pacific Fleet, whether to help Russia, the August meeting with Churchill, the extension of the Selective Service Act, and the amendments to the Neutrality Act. He left the Far East to Hull.

It was not until November that FDR began pressing Beardall to bring him original Magic material. Beardall told Lieutenant Commander Alwin D. Kramer of Naval Intelligence that FDR grasped things more rapidly visually than orally, and on November 12 the daily service was resumed. But for six crucial months, the president was given only indirect and piecemeal information about intercepted Japanese messages.

It is against this Magic background—its value as a trump card, but a card that was badly played—that the events leading up to Pearl Harbor must be assessed. On February 14, Roosevelt received the new Japanese ambassador, who was not a diplomat but an admiral whom he had known during World War I. Kichisaburo Nomura, a 200-pound six-footer, was said to be pro-American. Referring to their old association, FDR said that he would call Nomura Admiral and that they were friends and could talk candidly: relations were deteriorating; the American people were concerned about Japanese movements to Indochina. It would not do either of them any good to get into a war. Nomura said he would strive to preserve peace.

The beauty of Magic was that it revealed the gap between what the Japanese were saying and what they were thinking. Their deceit could be tracked on a daily basis. When Roosevelt, thanks to Magic, saw Foreign Minister Matsuoka's instructions to Nomura, he wrote Sumner Welles that they "seem to me to be the product of a mind which is deeply disturbed and unable to think quietly or logically."

While Nomura said he was striving for peace, a July 2 Magic message from Tokyo said: "Although every means available shall be resorted to in order to prevent the United States from joining the war, if need be, Japan shall act in accordance with the Three-Power Pact and shall decide when and how force will be employed." It was then that the Japanese advanced into southern Indochina, which led Roosevelt to freeze their assets on July 26.

Roosevelt kept up negotiations to buy time for the Army and the Navy to fortify the Philippines, and because he wanted peace in the Pacific in case an incident in the Atlantic brought America into war. He offered a plan for turning Indochina into a Switzerland-like neutral, on condition that the Japanese withdraw all their forces. Japan countered with a plan for a summit meeting between the president and Prime Minister Fumimaro Konoye.

While these diplomatic exchanges went on, the Magic intercepts showed Japan's intention to pursue southern expansion. "I had brought with me the last magics which gave a very recent example of Japan's duplicity," Stimson wrote in his diary on August 8 after seeing Hull. "[Their] most engaging program of peace . . . is a pure blind . . . and they have already made up their minds to a policy of going south through Indo-China and Thailand. The invitation to the President is merely a blind to try to keep us from taking definite action. The papers show this right on their face."

But Roosevelt took the idea of a meeting with Konoye seriously enough to discuss where it should take place. Hawaii was too far. What about Juneau, Alaska? In Tokyo, Ambassador Grew thought that Konoye, as leader of the peace party, wanted to reach a settlement "almost at any price." On September 6, Konoye invited Grew to dinner—it was unheard of for the prime minister to consort with envoys—and said he had a ship ready to meet the president. He was ready to use the emperor's influence for peace.

On September 10, Eleanor wrote her daughter, who was living in Seattle, that "Father told me this morning to tell you at once that there are still negotiations going on and he might go to Alaska to meet the Japs. You and John [Boettiger] are not to mention this to anyone. If he goes he would leave about Oct. 10 and be returning via Seattle about Oct. 21st."

But the meeting never took place, largely because Cordell Hull was against it. Hull, who saw Nomura almost daily, was shocked by the contrast between his protestations of peaceful intentions and the contents of the Magic messages. He told FDR that to meet with Konoye without having reached a preliminary agreement would be another Munich.

On October 16 the Konoye goverment fell. The war minister, General Hideki Tojo, became prime minister. Hull saw him as stubborn and stupid, with a small-bore, one-track mind—a track that said war was inevitable. Grew felt that FDR's refusal to negotiate had brought down Konoye. Hardened by its reading of Magic, the administration no longer trusted the Japanese. There had been too much trickery, too much bad faith. Japan was like a criminal whose promises to go straight were suspect because of his long record.

Conscious of the low regard in which he was held, Ambassador Nomura offered his resignation on October 22. "I don't want to be the bones of a dead horse," he cabled Tokyo. "I don't want to continue this hypocritical existence, deceiving other people. . . . Please send me your permission to return to Japan." Permission was denied.

On October 29, Hull asked Stimson whether he favored an immediate declaration of war. Stimson said no, he wanted to strengthen the Philippines first.

On November 5, Stimson knew from Magic that the Japanese were sending an envoy who would bring a proposal that was impossible to accept. Also on November 5, the Japanese government made the secret decision to go to war with the United States, England, and Holland, and to attack a number of targets in the Pacific.

On November 6, Stimson saw FDR, who was trying to think of something to say to the Japanese envoy that would buy time. He might propose a truce, he said, in which there would be no movement or armament for six months.

At cabinet on November 6, FDR told how Lincoln had polled his cabinet and found them all saying no and had then said "the Ayes have it." He wanted to conduct a poll on whether the country was ready to back him if he attacked the Japanese navy, or whether he would have to wait for an incident. The cabinet voted unanimously that the country would support him. Attorney General Francis Biddle said it would be a popular move for, in addition to our traditional dislike of the Japanese, everyone would think of it as naval warfare, not requiring an expeditionary force.

On November 17, the carrier fleet that would attack Pearl Harbor left its bases for a secret rendezvous point at Hitokappu Bay in the remote and sparsely inhabited Kuril Islands. The carriers would maintain radio silence until the day of the attack. Dumping garbage off the Kurils was strictly prohibited.

On the same day in Washington, where peace negotiations still went on, Ambassador Nomura, who knew nothing of the attack plans, reported that "the difficulty seems to be . . . the suspicion that the United States harbors of

Japan . . . based on the fear that the German and Japanese military clique will . . . prevail."

A second ambassador, Saburo Kurusu, had arrived two days before to reinforce Nomura. Kurusu was like a cartoon Japanese, short with thick glasses and a pencil mustache, but he spoke idiomatic English because his wife was American.

On November 18, Nomura and Kurusu spent two hours and forty-five minutes with Hull, who knew from the inflamed tone of the Magic intercepts that Japan was preparing for war. One message from Tokyo to the Japanese consul in Hong Kong on November 14 (translated on the twenty-sixth) said that if no agreement was reached "we will completely destroy British and American power in China. We will take over all enemy concessions and important enemy rights and interests in China."

"As long as Japan is tied to Hitler by means of the Tripartite Pact," Hull said, "there shall be great difficulties in adjusting the Japanese-U.S. relations. . . . Unless the fundamental trouble is removed, it will be impossible to expect any progress in our talks."

Kurusu was unyielding. "If something is impossible to do," he said, "it simply can't be done, regardless of what fancy words are used to dress it up. Even if you tell us to abrogate, or at least to make ineffective, the Tripartite Pact at this time, that is something that is impossible for us to do."

On November 19, in one of the strangest episodes of that frantic month, Nomura had one of his agents, a man named Schmitt, call on Supreme Court Justice Felix Frankfurter, who told him that "if Japan makes certain moves, she will be in a war with the United States." Roosevelt was not finding the support he needed for a war against Germany, Frankfurter said, but in a war against Japan the country would be unified. It would be mainly an aerial and naval war, and even if Japan won early victories in places distant from the American mainland, the United States would emerge victorious in the long run.

Schmitt said that a first step toward peace was to make available to Japan gasoline and other embargoed products. "There is a fear that gasoline and like materials would be used to conduct southward and northward aggressions and further invasions of China," Frankfurter said. Japan had to show she could be trusted.

In another, equally strange episode the same day, Nomura was visited by Bishop James E. Walsh, superior general of the Maryknoll Society, a well-meaning but naive priest who had been brainwashed by Japanese intelligence into believing that Japan really wanted peace. Bishop Walsh was accompanied by no less a personage than a member of the cabinet, Postmaster General Frank C. Walker, a prominent Catholic layman. They said that from the president on down, the administration wanted an agreement and would resume oil exports if the Japanese withdrew their troops from Indochina.

In the meantime, a number of ominous Magic signals were coming in, but they did not seem so at the time. On November 15, from Tokyo to Washington: "The following is the order and method of destroying the code machines in the event of an emergency. . . ." War was the obvious emergency, but the message was not translated until November 25.

On November 19, Tokyo to Washington, came the message that the warning for breaking off diplomatic relations would come as the weather broadcast "East winds, rain." This would be the signal for destroying all secret papers. War was the obvious reason for breaking off diplomatic relations, but the message was not translated until November 28.

The military knew Japan was on the march, but believed it would attack Burma or Thailand. They had a mind-set that a small country like Japan would never make a first strike against a big power like the United States. If the Japanese were crazy enough to fight the United States, they would attack the Philippines. They would never attack Pearl Harbor, it was too far away and too well defended. In a May 1941 memo to FDR General Marshall said: "The island of Oahu, due to its fortifications, its garrison and its physical characteristics, is believed to be the strongest fortress in the world." After describing its air defenses, he added: "With this force available a major attack against Oahu is considered impracticable."

The "it can't happen here" attitude existed also at Pearl Harbor. In August 1941, when George C. Dyer, executive officer of the heavy cruiser *Indianapolis,* sought to increase his ship's state of readiness to "modified condition two," which meant crews on duty two days out of four, his wife called to complain that "all the wives have been calling me, asking 'what's the *Indianapolis* trying to do? Fight the war by itself?' Their husbands aren't coming home and they're upset."

On November 22, a Magic intercept from Tokyo to Nomura said that the deadline for negotiations was November 29: "This time we mean it, the deadline absolutely cannot be changed. After that things are automatically going to happen." To Hull, it was unreal. He had to sit there and listen to Nomura and Kurusu for hours, as if they were all good friends, Nomura sometimes giggling, Kurusu baring his teeth in a broad grin, while he knew and they knew that if he did not submit to their demands they would be at war and thousands of men would die.

On November 23, Roosevelt said to Ickes that he wished he knew whether Japan was playing poker or not. He was not sure whether or not Japan had a gun up its sleeve. Ickes, who had long thought that Japan provided the best entrance into the war, replied that sooner or later she would be at our throats. "When I know I am going to be attacked," he said, "I prefer to choose my own time and occasion," But FDR said Japan was too far away to be attacked. "It seemed to me," Ickes reflected, "that the President had not yet reached the state of mind where he is willing to be aggressive as to Japan."

It was on November 25 that Magic brought proof of such obvious and large-scale Japanese treachery that the entire negotiation effort collapsed. When Stimson got back to his office, he found news from G-2 that a Japanese troop convoy of from ten to thirty ships, meaning a force as great as 50,000 men, had left Shanghai bound for Indochina. One ship carried bridge equipment and another landing boats. The convoy had been spotted south of Formosa on its way to Indochina. At the very moment the Japanese envoys in Washington were negotiating the withdrawal of their troops from Indochina, Japan was actually *doubling* the size of its force there.

On November 26, Stimson called FDR to ask if he had seen the paper he had sent over about the new Japanese expedition. When Stimson told him they had started a new troop movement toward Indochina, "he fairly blew up—he jumped into the air, so to speak, and said he hadn't seen it and that that changed the whole situation because it was evidence of bad faith on the part of the Japanese that while they were negotiating for an entire truce—an entire withdrawal—they should be sending this expedition down there to Indo-China. I told him it was a fact that had come to me through G-2 and through the Navy Secret Service and I at once got another copy of the paper."

Stimson also notified Hull, who was so angry that he said: "I have washed my hands of it and it is now in the hands of you and Knox—the Army and the Navy." When Nomura and Kurusu went to see Hull at 4:45 that afternoon they found him a changed man. There was no give at all now in the American position. Hull said that Japan must evacuate all its forces from China and Indochina. Nomura and Kurusu were dumbfounded. They could not even report such an ultimatum back to Tokyo, they said.

"Our failure and humiliation are complete," Nomura reported to Tokyo. He could not understand why Hull was proposing such hard terms. The talks had broken down, and it now seemed that a clash was inevitable.

And yet the talks had not completely broken down, for on November 27 the president agreed to see the Japanese envoys, to make still another try at avoiding a Pacific war. "In the last Great War, Japan and the United States were together on the side of the Allies," FDR said. "At that time, both Japan and the United States were given ample proof that Germany failed to comprehend the way the people of other countries think. . . . I am one of those who still harbors much hope that Japanese-U.S. relations will be settled peacefully."

"Your recent proposals," Nomura said, "will no doubt be the cause of painful disappointment to the Japanese Government."

"To tell you the truth," FDR replied, "I too am very disappointed that the situation has developed in the manner that it has. However, during the several months that these conversations were being conducted, cold water was poured on them when Japan occupied southern French Indo-China. According to recent intelligences, there are fears that a second cold water dousing may become an actuality." FDR was tipping his hand, telling Nomura that he knew about Japan's troop movements.

Nomura said he still hoped for a settlement and had faith in FDR's states-manship. Roosevelt left for Warm Springs, not knowing that "the agony of collision" had begun. For on November 26, the same day he learned of the Japanese ship movements toward Indochina, another Japanese fleet was setting out from Hitokappu Bay—six carriers, two battleships, two heavy cruisers, one light cruiser, nine destroyers, three submarines, and eight tank-ers. Their orders, received the previous day, said: "The task force, keeping its movements strictly secret and maintaining close guard against subma-rines and aircraft, shall advance into Hawaiian waters and upon the very opening of hostilities, shall attack the main force of the United States fleet in Hawaii and deal it a mortal blow."

There was nothing in Magic to indicate the movement of this fleet, but Roosevelt was called back from his vacation on November 30 by a saber-rattling speech of Tojo's charging that the United States was hindering co-operation and "for the honor and pride of mankind, we must purge this sort of practice from East Asia with a vengeance." In Washington, an alarmed Kurusu called the head of the American desk in Tokyo, Kumaichi Yama-moto, to say that "it puts us in a very difficult position. All of you over there must watch out about these ill-advised statements."

In the final week before the attack, the Magic intercepts were like a huge billboard announcing "War Is Coming," but neglecting to specify the time and place. From Berlin, Oshima reported on November 29 that Foreign Minister Ribbentrop had pledged that "should Japan become engaged in a war against the United States, Germany, of course, would join the war im-mediately. There is absolutely no possibility of Germany's entering into a separate peace with the United States under such circumstances. The Führer is determined on that point."

On December 1, the Japanese forces afloat changed their radio call sig-nals, which normally changed every six months, after only one month. The intelligence summary for U.S. military forces said: "The fact that service calls lasted only one month indicates an additional progressive step in pre-paring for active operations on a large scale."

On December 3, Tokyo sent its Washington embassy funds for the return to Japan of the families of its officials. Two days later Tokyo asked for the immediate recall of its spy chief, Hidenari Terasaki. Kurusu, who was kept in the dark about war plans, could not understand why his top intelligence man was being removed, and asked as a personal favor to keep him.

Also, Magic picked up another message that Japanese embassies and con-sulates in Washington and London and various places in Southeast Asia were being ordered to destroy their codes and ciphers. This information was passed on to Pacific commanders, but did not lead to any further defensive measures at Pearl Harbor. General Short assumed the Navy was patrolling the sea lanes leading to the harbor, which it was not. Admiral Kimmel as-sumed that the Army had ordered an all-out alert, which it had not, and that the radar was in full operation, whereas it was on only from 4:00 to 7:00 A.M.

On December 1, Adolf Berle walked into a meeting between Hull and Stanley Hornbeck, the State Department Far East expert. "Come in," said Hull, "you might learn something." An outraged Hornbeck was urging force of arms against Japan, which had taken Formosa, taken Korea, taken Manchuria, taken Peiping and Shanghai and Nanking and Hankow and Canton, which had driven 30 million Chinese from their homes, which had sunk the *Panay* and bombed American missions and hospitals and schools, and killed and injured American men and women and children. And we were still saying "go on with your activities . . . we won't use force to stop you."

Hull pointed out that the Army said it would not be ready for another three weeks and the Navy wanted another three months. Hornbeck said the Navy had asked for six months in February, which Hull had obtained through negotiations. Now they wanted three more. The president ought to stop asking the Navy and tell them.

In the meantime, there was ever heavier Magic traffic between Tokyo and Honolulu. November 28: "Anticipating the possibility of ordinary telegraphic communication being severed when we are about to face the worst of situation." Honolulu to Tokyo, November 28: "Twelve thousand men (mostly marines) are expected to reinforce the troops of Honolulu during December and January. There has usually been one cruiser in the waters about 15,000 feet south of Pearl Harbor and one or two destroyers at the entrance to the harbor." Honolulu to Tokyo, December 5 (translated December 10): "During Friday morning, the 5th, the three battleships mentioned in my message 239 arrived here. The [carrier] *Lexington* and five heavy cruisers left port on the same day. The following ships were in port on the afternoon of the 5th: 8 battleships, 3 light cruisers, 16 destroyers." Because of the translation jam and the low priority given to messages from Honolulu, this and other messages showing a heightened interest in Pearl Harbor ship movements were not made available to the president and other Magic recipients.

At the December 5 cabinet meeting, Hull was denouncing the Japanese as "the worst people I ever saw" when Frank Knox piped up: "Well, you know, Mr. President, we know where the Japanese fleet is."

"I think we ought to tell everybody how ticklish the situation is," FDR said. "We have information, as Knox just mentioned . . . well, you tell them what it is, Frank."

"We have very secret information that mustn't go outside this room," Knox said in his sputtering way, "that the Japanese fleet is out. They're out of the harbor. They're out at sea." He was talking about the various fleet movements off Japan, not the carrier force headed for Pearl Harbor, which had not been detected.

The other members of the cabinet looked as though their eyes would drop out, and the president looked very severe, nodding his head and scowling.

"We haven't got anything like perfect information as to their apparent destination," FDR interjected. "The question is, in the mind of the Navy and in my mind, whether the fleet is going south."

"Singapore?" several cabinet members asked in chorus.

"Probably," FDR agreed. "That's the presumed objective if they go south."

"Every indication is that they are going south," Knox said.

"But it's not absolutely certain that they couldn't be going north," FDR replied. ". . . You haven't got information with regard to direction."

"That's right, we haven't, but it is so unlikely that they would go north."

"Well," said FDR, "there are the Aleutians. There are fishing grounds."

"That might be," said Knox, "but it's most unlikely. . . . I must draw the conclusion that they're going south. I don't think they're out just to maneuver. We in the Navy think they must be going to do something."

Something, but what? Also on December 5, Admiral Yamamoto, commander of the Japanese Combined Fleet, sent this instruction to the South Seas force, which by then was heading south through "the vacant sea" toward the Hawaiian Islands: "The time has come to be loyal to the utmost and put into practice a destructive militarism."

On December 6, the FBI, which was tapping the phone of the Japanese consulate in Honolulu, reported that they had been burning papers for two days. There were more Magic messages, translated too late to be of use. From Honolulu to Tokyo, a list of ships observed at anchor: nine battleships, three light cruisers, three submarine tenders, seventeen destroyers. Also on December 6, from Honolulu, in reply to a query from Tokyo: There were no barrage balloons over Pearl Harbor as a defense against air attack, said Nagao Kita, Japanese consul general in Honolulu, so "I imagine that in all probability there is considerable opportunity left to take advantage for a surprise attack against these places." This direct reference to a surprise attack was not translated until December 8, for it had arrived in PA-K2, not a top-priority code. The decoders could not know until they started working on it what it held.

With the pertinent Magic information unavailable, FDR made one last peace effort, drafting a message to Emperor Hirohito, which he sent to Hull with a covering memo: "Dear Cordell: Shoot this to Grew—I think it can go in gray code—our least secret code—saves time—I don't mind if it gets picked up. FDR." Hull sent it to Grew at 9:00 P.M. on December 6.

At about the same time, a thirteen-part message from Tokyo to Washington had been intercepted and translated and was on its way to the president. Navy Commander Lester R. Schulz arrived at the second-floor study of the White House with a locked pouch. He handed the fifteen typewritten pages to FDR, who was with Harry Hopkins. FDR read it for about ten minutes and passed it to Hopkins, who read it and gave it back. "This means war," Roosevelt said. It was too bad, Hopkins said, that they could strike the first blow and we could not.

"No, we can't do that," the president said. "We are a democracy and a peaceful people. But we have a good record."

At dawn on Sunday, December 7, the Japanese carrier force in two parallel columns advanced toward Oahu Island through choppy seas, having increased its speed to twenty-four knots with the departure of the tankers after the final refueling.

The carriers stopped 180 miles off Oahu. Japanese pilots wearing headbands that said *Hissho* (Certain Victory) climbed into the cockpits of their dive bombers, torpedo bombers, and pursuit planes and flew into the rising sun, emblem of their nation. As the 350 planes approached Pearl Harbor unopposed, they could see the beaches and palm groves in the early morning sunlight, the lush vegetation, the neat rows of barracks and the planes at Hickam Field, the white highway curling through the hills, and the battleships anchored two by two. At 7:53 A.M. (1:23 P.M. Washington time), the code words announcing that they had caught the Pacific Fleet in harbor were sung out: "Tora! Tora! Tora!" (Tiger! Tiger! Tiger!).

Rear Admiral William Rhea Furlong, in command of Battle Forces Pacific, a fleet of service vessels, who lived aboard his ship, the minelayer *Oglala,* saw a bomb explode nearby and thought: What a stupid, careless pilot, not to have secured his releasing gear.

An admiral playing golf looked up from the tee and said: "Jesus Christ, why doesn't anyone tell me anything around here—I didn't know we'd invited the Russians for fleet maneuvers."

Later, at the hearings, the commander of a battleship was asked: "When did you first believe you were under enemy attack?"

"I didn't believe it when I saw the planes," he replied, "and I didn't believe it when I saw the bombs fall. I believed it when I heard obscenities coming down the squawk box—Admiral Kimmel had specifically forbidden that."

When the first shock of bewilderment was over and the Americans fought back, they weren't ready. The Army had been told not to install antiaircraft guns on Diamond Head because they would scare the tourists. On the light cruiser *Phoenix,* the locks on the ammunition boxes had to be hacked off. The fuses on the shells had a minimum peacetime setting to keep them from exploding until they had reached a safe distance from the ship.

In Washington, Cordell Hull went to the office even though it was Sunday, and learned from a Magic intercept that the Japanese ambassadors had been asked to submit the thirteen-part telegram, the one the president had seen the night before, at 1:00 P.M. Hull met with Stimson and Knox, and they agreed that the Japanese were holding the message back in order to accomplish something already under way. "Hull is very certain that the Japs are planning some deviltry and we are all wondering where the blow will strike," Stimson recorded.

At noon, Nomura called Hull to ask for a 1:00 P.M. appointment. Later, he asked for a postponement (it was taking longer than he had expected to decode and type up the long message).

At the White House, Harry Hopkins was having lunch with FDR when Secretary Knox called at about 1:40 P.M. and said an air raid was on in Honolulu and that it was "no drill."

When Nomura arrived at the State Department with Kurusu at 2:05 P.M., they were kept waiting in the gloomy reception room under the portrait of Elihu Root. Hull was on the phone with FDR, who said, "There's a report that the Japanese have attacked Pearl Harbor."

So this was where the months of almost daily negotiations had led. Hull knew what the Japanese envoys wanted, and was inclined not to see them. But then he thought that the attack had not been confirmed, and there was one chance out of a hundred it was wrong. He received them coolly, and did not ask them to sit down. Nomura handed him the note, which he pretended to read, having already seen the intercepts.

And now all of Hull's pent-up rage at having been tricked, at having honestly sought an agreement with these two ambassador-decoys, when all the time the Japanese had been preparing for war, burst out, and he said: "I must say that in all my conversations with you during the last nine months I have never uttered one word of untruth. [But] in all my fifty years of public service I have never seen a document that was more crowded with infamous falsehoods and distortions—on a scale so huge that I never imagined until today that any government on this planet was capable of uttering them." He nodded toward the door, and the two Japanese, the hulking Nomura and the diminutive Kurusu, walked out with their heads bowed. They were supposed to have given Hull the news at 1:00 P.M., a few minutes before the attack, so that it could not be said Japan had attacked without warning, but they had been delayed.

Stimson was having lunch at Woodley, his mansion overlooking Rock Creek Park, when FDR called asking: "Have you heard the news?" "Well," said Stimson, "I have heard about the Japanese advances in the Gulf of Siam." "Oh no, I don't mean that," FDR said. "They have attacked Hawaii. They are now bombing Hawaii." Stimson's first feeling was one of relief. The indecision was over. The Japs had solved the whole thing by attacking, and now the United States could enter the war united.

Lieutenant General Lucius D. Clay was watching the Washington Redskins as a guest of Jesse Jones, when, during the half, the loudspeaker started blaring out messages: "Is Admiral so-and-so here and if he is will he please report to the Navy Department?" After half a dozen such requests everyone was wondering what was going on. Someone said there had been an attack on Pearl Harbor. "The Japs would attack Guam or the Philippines," Clay said, "but Pearl Harbor's impregnable. I just can't believe they would attack Pearl Harbor."

In Omaha, two soldiers stopped to read a radio bulletin outside the *World Herald,* and one whistled and said, "Take your last look at Omaha."

At 8:30 P.M., the cabinet convened in the Blue Room, the big oval room on the second floor of the White House, over the south portico. FDR sat at his desk with his back to the wall as extra chairs were brought in. There were no pleasantries as the cabinet members arrived, Hull seemingly calm, Knox white-faced, Biddle bald and bright-eyed, saying: "I'm just off the plane from Cleveland. For God's sake, what's happened?"

Roosevelt said this was the most important cabinet meeting since 1861. The Japanese had actually bombed Pearl Harbor. Six battleships out of eight had probably been put out of business. Guam had been taken, and there had been an attack on Wake Island and possibly on Midway.

The president's face was gray and drawn as he described the day's events. It seemed to Frances Perkins that his pride in the Navy was such that he was having a difficult time getting out the words describing how it had been caught unawares, how bombs had dropped on ships tied to their moorings.

Twice, he said to Knox: "Find out, for God's sake, why the ships were tied up in rows." "That's the way they berth them," Knox replied. But FDR could not accept the idea that the Navy had been caught off guard. It was the worst naval disaster in American history.

The president then read a message that he planned to deliver the next day to a joint session of Congress, calling for a declaration of war against Japan.

At 9:45, ten congressmen arrived—Senators Alben Barkley, Charles L. McNary, Tom Connally, Warren Austin, and Hiram Johnson, and House members Sam Rayburn, Jere Cooper, Joe Martin, Sol Bloom, and Charles Eaton—and the cabinet members moved back to let them have the chairs. With them, Roosevelt was more debonair and discursive, alluding to his past Navy experience and his expertise in military affairs.

"Nothing about casualties on their side?" a congressman asked.

"It's a little difficult," FDR said. "We think we got some of their submarines but we don't know."

"Well, planes—aircraft?"

"We did get, we think, a number of their planes. We know some Japanese planes were shot down, but there again—I have seen so much of this in the other war. One fellow says he has got fifteen of their planes, and you pick up the telephone and somebody else says five. . . . I should say that by far the greater loss has been sustained by us."

"There is a story coming over the radio that we got one of their airplane carriers."

"I don't know," FDR said. "Don't believe it. . . . I wish it were true. . . . Of course it is a terrible disappointment to be President in time of war, and the circumstances . . . came most unexpectedly."

"I can't help wondering what can we do to do anything."

"The only specific thing to do," FDR replied, "[is that] our ships . . . we don't know what ships . . . are out trying to get the Japs at this moment. . . . They can't send for fear of disclosing their position."

"There are two airplane carriers of the Japanese Navy over there?"

"Probably," FDR said. "In other words, if you take the timing out, those planes—carriers and their attending cruisers, and probably battleships—I don't know—at sundown last night, at about dark, were standing in the dark away from where they launched their planes. Now, let us assume that they launched those planes at a distance of a hundred miles at daylight. That means that they had twelve hours to get to that point in the dark, and running at perhaps 25 knots, that would be 300 miles further away. In other words, at dark, last night, they might very well have been 400 miles away from the island, and therefore out of what might be called a good patrol distance. Patrol out of a given point—300 miles under normal conditions, but 500 miles is a long way for reconnaissance patrol. . . . At dawn they were 100 miles away from their island—they launched their planes—they steamed this way and that, or reversed their course. The planes dropped their bombs and went back."

That was a pretty accurate summary of the Japanese attack, considering that FDR didn't have much to go on. But Tom Connally of Texas, who had recently become chairman of the Senate Foreign Relations Committee, wasn't satisfied with the explanation. Springing to his feet, his face purple, he banged on the president's desk and shouted: "They were supposed to be on the alert, and if they had been on the alert . . . I am amazed at the attack by Japan, but I am still more astounded at what happened to our Navy. They were all asleep. Where were our patrols?"

Turning to Knox, he bellowed: "Didn't you say last month that we could lick the Japs in two weeks? Didn't you say that our Navy was so well prepared and located that the Japanese couldn't hope to hurt us at all? . . . Why did you have all the ships at Pearl Harbor crowded the way you did? And why did you have a long chain across the mouth of the entrance, so that our ships could not get out?"

"To protect us against Japanese submarines," the unhappy Knox replied.

"Well, Mr. President," someone said, "this nation has got a job ahead of it, and what we have got to do is roll up our sleeves and win this war."

The meeting was breaking up, and FDR said as a parting shot: "Remember that out there it is nearly just about dawn. They are doing things and saying things during the daytime out there, while we are all in bed."

"We are in bed too much," one of the departing congressmen said.

The next day, Roosevelt became the second American president in the twentieth century to ask for a declaration of war. From the rostrum of the House of Representatives, he uttered the now-famous words to a joint session of Congress: "Yesterday, December 7, 1941—a date which will live in infamy—the United States of America was suddenly and deliberately attacked by naval and air forces of the Empire of Japan."

After describing in some detail what the Japanese had done, he asked "that the Congress declare that since the unprovoked and dastardly attack by Japan on Sunday December 7, 1941, a state of war has existed between the United States and the Japanese Empire."

The isolationists were silenced. Even Senator Wheeler said we had to lick the hell out of Japan. It took only thirty-three minutes to vote for war, with only one member of the House, the pacifist Jeanette Rankin, dissenting. On the same day in England, both houses of Parliament voted unanimously to declare war on Japan.

In Berlin, Ambassador Oshima demanded that Germany declare war on the United States, as Ribbentrop had promised. Hitler was willing, and did not ask for a Japanese declaration of war on Russia in exchange. He thought he could defeat Russia without the Japanese, for whom he held a racist contempt, calling Emperor Hirohito "a lacquered half-monkey." But he had to hold up the spirit of the Tripartite Pact, and anyway, there was a state of de facto war, since American ships were firing on German U-boats in the Atlantic. Also, he was being true to his principle of total war, against Bolshevism in the east and Jewish capitalism in the west. And so, on December 11, at a time of new reverses in the east, when the attack on Moscow had failed, and the ground around the Russian capital was a snow-covered graveyard for German soldiers, Hitler spoke to the Reichstag in Berlin's Kroll Opera House. In a speech that mocked and insulted Roosevelt—"I consider him mad, just as Wilson was," he said—Hitler declared war on America, saving FDR the trouble of another vote in Congress, where the opposition might have rallied. America was now at war on two sides of the world, far from its shores.

The theory, still peddled, that FDR had advance warning of the Pearl Harbor attack but let it take place to assure United States entry into the war deserves to be laid to rest.

First, there was FDR's own nature, one of the strongest components of which was his love for the Navy. As General Marshall once complained, "I wish you'd stop referring to the Army as 'you' and the Navy as 'we.' " It was unthinkable that he would allow the Navy he cherished to be destroyed with a heavy loss of life. Frances Perkins noted that on December 7 his pride in the Navy was such that he had great difficulty in coming to terms with the defeat.

Second, there was the logic of events. The conspiracy theory argues that advance notice was withheld from Kimmel and Short, who, had they been warned, would have sent out patrols, which might have made the Japanese turn back. Not telling them assured the attack. But such a conspiracy required the connivance of men of unquestioned integrity, men like Henry Stimson and George Marshall, who would never for a moment have agreed to the villainous strategy of sacrificing Pearl Harbor. Nor is it credible that Frank Knox and Betty Stark would have agreed to the destruction of "their" Navy.

The conspiracy theory also requires the complicity of the British, who in January 1941 had been given the Purple machine, so that they were deciphering the same Magic codes as the Americans. Is it conceivable that the

British would have agreed to a conspiracy of silence to destroy the U.S. fleet in the Pacific, which was their principal protection against Japanese aggression in the Far East? If the British had come across any clue about Pearl Harbor, they would have rushed to the White House with it.

Even if FDR had been given advance warning, he obviously would have placed Pearl Harbor on highest alert. A victory at Pearl Harbor would have brought the United States into war just as fast as a defeat, since in either case there had been a surprise attack. With advance notice of the position of the Japanese carrier fleet, he would not have kept eight battleships at their moorings. He would have ordered all the necessary measures to repulse the Japanese force.

Third, there is the questionable evidence presented by the conspiracy theorists, and particularly by John Toland in his 1982 book, *Infamy: Pearl Harbor and Its Aftermath*. Toland based his case largely on information provided by "Seaman Z," who allegedly told him that between December 2 and 6, when he was serving in Naval Intelligence in San Francisco, he had tracked the Japanese carrier force to a position northwest of Hawaii, and that his information had been transmitted to the president, who ignored it.

In 1983, "Seaman Z" was revealed to be Robert D. Ogg, who was interviewed by Commander I. G. Newman, a consultant to the Naval Security Group Command for declassification and historical matters.

In 1941, Ogg was a young man of twenty-four, interested in radio and electronics, who joined the Navy as a seaman first class and was assigned to an intelligence unit in San Francisco commanded by Lieutenant Elsworth A. Hosmer. He did mainly wiretapping work (which, in passing, was illegal), bugging hotel rooms frequented by suspected Japanese agents with the help of the telephone company, bugging the Japanese consulate, and recording transpacific calls when the circuits were open.

On December 2, Lieutenant Hosmer informed Ogg that Press Wireless and Globe Wireless, two commercial telegraph agencies, had picked up some Japanese radio signals on totally new frequencies. He gave Ogg two bearings, one of them San Francisco and the other somewhere that Ogg does not recall, and asked Ogg to plot the position of the signals.

This was an improvised effort, duplicating the far more expert work of the Navy's OP-20-G section, in charge of radio intelligence, which had a West Coast direction-finding station at Dutch Harbor in the Aleutian Islands. Ogg was inexperienced in plotting positions from radio signals. Commander Newman pointed out: "Given the vagaries of a direction finding system, simply two bearings without a cross-bearing, or a series of cross-bearings, makes the fix somewhat suspect." In other words, Ogg and Hosmer were a couple of amateurs trying to outguess the pros.

Press Wireless and Globe Wireless were tuning radio dials and hearing coded signals. How did Ogg know the signals were Japanese, Newman asked. "I never questioned that at the time," Ogg replied. "They just said they were Japanese. . . . But I'm not sure of that either."

Ogg was handed some signals he knew nothing about, passed on by commercial wireless companies, and plotted the position of the sender on a chart, from two bearings. According to Toland, "using a large chart, Z managed to get cross bearings on the mysterious signals. He told Hosmer it could possibly be the missing carrier force."

Commenting on that passage to Commander Newman, Ogg stated: "I never made such a mention to Hosmer whatsoever. I just knew that there was some form of Jap transmission that was on these odd frequencies in that area east of the International Date Line. Certainly no reference that it was a carrier force rather than it was a fishing force."

Ogg confirmed that there was not the slightest evidence of a carrier force on the move. It could have been anything, some fishing boats. "I certainly had no feeling that an entire Jap fleet . . . was involved," Ogg repeated.

Toland further stated that Lieutenant Hosmer reported Ogg's findings to Captain Richard P. McCullough, district chief of intelligence, who said he was a personal friend of the president's and had passed them on to FDR. There is no evidence that FDR knew Captain McCullough, any better than he knew hundreds of officers in the Navy, where he had served for seven years, or that he received any communication from McCullough.

Ogg's boss, Lieutenant Hosmer, did not check Ogg's findings with the Navy's direction-finding station. When Ogg heard that Captain McCullough had passed on information to the White House, he told Commander Newman, he presumed that they were *not his plots,* but that "it must have come from other channels, meaning OP 20 G."

All Japanese sources concur that the carrier fleet kept radio silence. Japanese communications officers aboard the carriers physically removed the tubes from transmitters, or locked the hand keys so they could not be used. Carrier signals were sent out from other ships near Japan to convince American intelligence that the carrier fleet was in home waters.

All the evidence indicates that Pearl Harbor was a real and horrifying surprise to every member of the administration, from the president on down. When Adolf Berle heard the news, he thought that "if there is anyone I would not like to be, it is Chief of Naval Intelligence." And yet were the decipherers of Magic to blame for the lack of intelligence evaluation and the delays in translating the low-priority messages from Honolulu? The low priority was part of a mind-set shared by the Army and the Navy, the service secretaries, and the president himself, that Pearl Harbor could not be attacked—it was out of the question, unimaginable, unthinkable, in the realm of fantasy. It was too far, too well defended, the waters of the harbor were too shallow for torpedo attacks—there were a hundred reasons.

Beyond the shortcomings of individual officers, the mistakes of Admiral Kimmel and General Short, there was a collective resistance to the possibility that America could be attacked; it was the complacency of the peaceful giant, who believes that his great strength will protect him. It was a habit born of not having been at war in the Pacific since 1898, which bred "ho hum," "it can't happen here," "let's not get excited" attitudes. The basic failure of Pearl Harbor was the failure to imagine that it could happen, so that estimates of Japanese behavior were based on the assumption that they would attack somewhere else. When Admiral Theodore Stark Wilkinson, the head of Naval Intelligence, was asked at the Pearl Harbor inquiry, "Was there, Admiral, during the month or so preceding Dec. 7, 1941, any discussion in which you participated concerning the likelihood of a Japanese move toward Pearl Harbor?" he replied: "Unfortunately, no."

Pearl Harbor became embedded in the national psyche as the outstanding example of American vulnerability, as the model of what happened when everything went wrong in a battle. "Remember Pearl Harbor" became the reminder of the worst snafu in American history.

Of course in the first days following the battle it seemed like a disaster. Chester Nimitz, the son of a Texas cowboy, who had gone to Annapolis because there were no openings at West Point, was sent out to succeed Admiral Kimmel on December 16. Nimitz saw oil half an inch thick in the water of the harbor, and docks piled with coffins being taken to a collection point. All the surface ships were sunk, so he took command of the fleet aboard a submarine, hoisting his four-star flag on the conning tower.

Frank Knox's report to FDR on December 14, after a visit to the scene of battle, was pessimistic indeed. General Short, fearful of sabotage, had bunched up his planes on the various air fields, making the Japanese air attack more effective. The Navy, fearful of a submarine attack, had taken no specific measures against an air attack. The Navy patrol bombers had gone south on the morning of December 7, making no contact with enemy craft. The Army carried out no dawn patrol. The state of readiness was "condition three," meaning that about half the guns were manned. At one radar station, an Army officer showed a concentration of planes to the north, which he relayed to the Aircraft Warning Information Center. There, the second lieutenant in charge said the planes were probably from the aircraft carrier *Enterprise,* and neglected to pass the sighting on to headquarters. Antiaircraft guns were unmanned when the Japs made the first of three sweeps. By the third sweep, ten U.S. fighter planes were in the air. The final results left the Army air fields and the naval stations badly damaged and resulted in the immobilization of the majority of the Navy's battle fleet in the Pacific for months to come, the loss of 75 percent of the Army's air strength in the Pacific, and an even greater percentage of the Navy's.

And yet it was not a decisive military victory, for Pearl Harbor was soon back in operation as a naval base and fleet anchorage. The Japanese did not carry out their orders to deal the American fleet "a mortal blow," for the three aircraft carriers, the jewels of the fleet, were out and survived to fight again. Aside from the carriers, the battleships sunk or damaged were with one exception soon back in commission. They were easy to raise in the shallow harbor, and easy to repair because the Japanese did not destroy the dry docks or machine shops, and were later used as monitors to support U.S.

landings on Japanese-held islands. The Japanese attack concentrated on the destruction of ships and planes, but the permanent installations, such as the fuel dumps and the repair facilities, were not destroyed.

Strategically, the attack succeeded in doing what a year of daily efforts on the part of FDR had not done—it brought America into the war, guaranteeing the eventual defeat of the Axis powers. One can search military history in vain for an operation more fatal to the aggressor. The Japanese had attacked the one country they could not defeat, rather than help Germany defeat the Russians.

Pearl Harbor was in the limelight, but two other battles at that time had a greater military importance. On December 6 (December 7, Pacific time), with Moscow encircled, the Russians launched a 100-division counteroffensive on a 200-mile front. Where did Stalin find the troops? Many of them were the Siberian divisions that he had removed from his eastern flank as a result of the neutrality treaty with Japan; only when he learned that Pearl Harbor had been attacked did he release Zhukov's troops in the Moscow area. The Japanese had opted for southern expansion and would leave Russia alone.

It was 36 degrees below zero on the Russian front, but to the Siberian troops that was a normal temperature. Not so to the Germans, who had no winter overcoats—Hitler had forbidden them as a sign of defeatism on the opening of the campaign in June—it would all be over before winter. The oil froze in the German tanks, which had to be started by lighting fires under them. The Germans abandoned Moscow, the amazing advance was stopped, and for the first time during the war the supposedly invincible Wehrmacht retreated all along the front. Like Napoleon, Hitler could have replied, if asked which Russian general had done the most to defeat him: "General Winter." On December 6, he admitted that "victory could no longer be achieved."

More crushing than Pearl Harbor, though never investigated, was the defeat inflicted on General MacArthur in the Philippines. Stimson and Marshall had decided in December 1940 to strengthen the Philippines as a deterrent against Japan. MacArthur was recalled to active duty and took command in July 1941. He was being sent most of the 1941 plane production that was not earmarked for Britain and Russia—four heavy bomber groups (272 planes with 68 in reserve), and two pursuit groups of 130 planes each. The idea was that in case of a Japanese attack, he would bomb Japan and Formosa. There were plans for incendiary attacks to burn up the wood and paper houses of Japanese cities. But only 30 of the bombers had arrived by the time of the Japanese attack.

More than half of MacArthur's aerial force was destroyed on the ground when the Japanese attacked the Philippines nine hours after Pearl Harbor. Unlike Short and Kimmel, MacArthur was getting Magic, and on top of that he had a nine-hour warning, and still nothing was done, proving that even the probability of attack is not enough to instill a spirit of preparedness.

MacArthur had precise orders for the dispersion of his planes, an attack on Formosa, and the defense of Clark Field. But when the Japanese bombers struck at 12:15 on December 8, they found Clark Field undefended, and the B-17 bombers sitting there, wingtip to wingtip, waiting to be destroyed. Three months later, on March 11, 1942, MacArthur retreated to Australia. This was arguably the worst Allied defeat of the war, worse than Pearl Harbor, worse than the early months of the Russian campaign, for it cost the United States the Philippines, the British Malaya and Burma, and the Dutch the oil-rich East Indies. It also helped explain the Pearl Harbor mentality, for even when MacArthur knew that he was going to be attacked, he did not prepare for it. His dereliction was worse than Short's or Kimmel's, who were forcibly retired and threatened with courts-martial while MacArthur was awarded the Medal of Honor. FDR had a curious change of heart regarding Kimmel and Short. Right after Pearl Harbor, when Stimson pointed out that they had merely reflected the apathy of the entire country, he said he did not want them to be severely punished. But in February 1942 he told Stimson that the temper of the people required courts-martial. Short and Kimmel would be told to retire, and advised that court-martial charges were being drawn up against them. Marshall and Stimson were staggered by the unfairness of the procedure. The whole thing looked as though they were being dragooned. But the courts-martial never took place.

The difference between a scapegoat and a hero seemed to be mainly the stature of the individual and the ability to create an image. MacArthur gave press conferences in which he said that he was going to "win or die." He did neither, departing under orders from Corregidor and leaving General Jonathan Wainwright to do the fighting, but announced: "I shall return." When he was told there was no incident that could support giving MacArthur the medal, Roosevelt gave orders to "make an incident."

Roosevelt was now commander in chief rather than president. He was an executive who could commit American power abroad rather than a requester of legislation from a contentious Congress. He could make strategy decisions with the two other commanders in chief, Churchill and Stalin, order American troops into battle, make secret commitments, rule by executive order and the "inherent" powers of the presidency.

He was comfortable in his new role. On December 14, Attorney General Francis Biddle found him having his sinus-plagued nose swabbed by his doctor, Admiral Ross T. McIntire. How many Germans are there in the country? Roosevelt asked. About 60,000, Biddle said. And you're going to intern them all? Roosevelt wanted to know. Well, not quite all, Biddle said. "I don't care so much about the Italians," Roosevelt commented, "there are a lot of opera singers, but the Germans are different, they may be dangerous." "Please," McIntire pleaded, and his patient sank back. The color was back in his cheeks. The prospect of action always made him feel better.

XXI

The Difficult Alliance

I will make a song for the ears of the President,
full of weapons with menacing points,
And behind the weapons countless dissatisfied faces.
Walt Whitman, *Leaves of Grass*

O ne of the first problems Roosevelt faced after Pearl Harbor was the
Japanese population of over 100,000 in California, where some of the
most important airplane factories and naval shipyards were located. California was seized by anti-Japanese hysteria. Every Japanese was seen as an
enemy and a spy. With few exceptions, the entire California political establishment—Governor Culbert Olson, Attorney General Earl Warren, the
California congressmen, and the California press, led by Hearst—spear-
headed the movement to have the Japanese, including the American-born
ones, known as nisei, relocated in camps.

Echoing their views was the military commander in California, Lieutenant General John L. De Witt, commanding general of the Western Defense
Command, who was determined not to repeat the Pearl Harbor mistake of
unpreparedness. As he put it, he was "not going to be a second General
Short." Any rumor of Japanese sabotage or espionage found a willing lis-
tener in General De Witt, who operated on the theory that "a Jap is a Jap."

In January the pressure built up, as all sorts of groups, from the Native
Sons and Daughters of the Golden West to the Grower-Shipper Vegetable
Associates, with whom the Japanese truck farmers competed, clamored for
evacuation. At cabinet on February 1, FDR mentioned a movie actress who
had told him she was afraid the Japanese would poison her vegetables. It
was pure hysteria, thought Ickes, and the removal of the Japanese would be
a cruel and unnecessary step.

J. Edgar Hoover, who had interned 942 Japanese aliens in the days after Pearl Harbor, informed Attorney General Francis Biddle that there was no basis for evacuation in a memo that said: "The necessity for mass evacuation is based primarily upon public and political pressure rather than on factual data. Public hysteria and, in some instances, the comments of the press, and radio announcers, have resulted in a tremendous amount of pressure being brought to bear on Governor Olson and Earl Warren, Attorney-General of the state, and on the military authorities."

In an attempt to calm public fears, Biddle drafted a press release on February 1 that he planned to release jointly with the War Department, which said that the Army had designated eighty-eight prohibited areas in California from which enemy aliens would be evacuated; that the FBI had found no evidence of sabotage but was on the alert; and that the Departments of Justice and War "are in agreement that the present military situation does not at this time require the removal of American citizens of the Japanese race."

At a meeting to discuss the draft with Stimson and several of his aides, Biddle said there was too much hysteria over the Japanese, and that the Department of Justice would have nothing to do with interfering with the rights of American citizens, whether Japanese or not. That was too much for the jingoistic Provost Marshal General, Allen W. Gullion, who said: "Well, listen, Mr. Biddle, do you mean to tell me that if the Army, the men on the ground, determine that it is a military necessity to move citizens, Jap citizens, that you won't help me?" Biddle responded that the Justice Department would be through if they started interfering with the rights of citizens. "General De Witt has told me," General Gullion replied, "that he has traveled up and down the West Coast, he has visited all these sectors, he has talked to all the Governors and other local civil authorities and he has come to this conclusion—it is my understanding that General De Witt does favor mass evacuations."

A year later, in April 1943, General Gullion was under FBI investigation for allegedly forming an organization inside the Army known as the SGs, for Slim (his nickname) Gullion, which aimed, according to an FBI informant, "to save America from FDR, radical labor, the Communists, the Jews, and the colored race." This was the man who made himself the main apologist for the evacuation of the Japanese.

On February 2, General De Witt called Assistant Secretary of War John J. McCloy to say that he had conferred with Governor Olson and they had agreed that all Japanese, whether native or American-born, should be removed from the areas of California designated as combat zones. If something wasn't done soon, De Witt said, people would take matters into their own hands, because "out here, Mr. Secretary, a Jap is a Jap to these people now."

Stimson was undecided. De Witt was clamoring for evacuation and claimed to have evidence that Japanese spies were contacting submarines off the coast. But, he wrote in his diary on February 3, "we cannot discriminate among our citizens on the ground of racial origin."

In the meantime, public pressure mounted. Attorney General Earl Warren and about 100 California sheriffs and district attorneys demanded that all Japanese aliens be removed from the state.

On February 4, the Justice and War departments met again to see whether there were grounds to justify an evacuation, and McCloy said: "You are putting a Wall Street lawyer in a helluva box, but if it is a question of the safety of the country, or the Constitution of the United States, why the Constitution is just a scrap of paper to me."

Biddle had lunch with the president on February 7 and defended the Justice Department position that mass evacuation was inadvisable—the FBI was not staffed to handle it, and it was not a job for the Army. There was the danger of hysteria moving east and affecting the German and Italian populations of Boston and New York. However, Biddle added, the Army should prepare a plan of evacuation in case of an air raid or attempted landing on the West Coast. FDR was receptive to the idea of a plan, mentioning the risk of Fifth Column retaliation in case of a raid. Already the president showed greater concern for the danger of potential Fifth Columnists than for the injuries connected with mass evacuation.

Stimson on February 10 was worrying that evacuation "will make a tremendous hole in our constitutional system." He was waiting for a report from General De Witt, which had not arrived, although he knew that De Witt would ask for the relocation of the entire Japanese population of 120,000, including the Nisei.

On February 11, he spoke to the president: "I took up with him the West Coast matter first and told him the situation and fortunately found that he was very vigorous about it and told me to go ahead on the line that I had myself thought the best." Thus, even before General De Witt's report had arrived, FDR was in favor of evacuation. According to Biddle, he told Stimson to prepare a plan for wholesale evacuation. Here was specific authorization at the highest level, "carte blanche," as McCloy put it. It was dictated by military necessity, FDR said, adding: "Be as reasonable as you can."

On February 12, Walter Lippmann came out with a column headlined "The Fifth Column on the Coast," in favor of evacuation. The West Coast should be made a combat zone open only to those with a reason for being there, he said. Saboteurs could be native-born Nisei as well as aliens, Lippmann warned, adding that "nobody's constitutional rights include the right to reside and do business on a battlefield," a statement that would have been laughable had it not been taken as supporting the evacuation of all Japanese from the West Coast.

Here was a situation where J. Edgar Hoover, later much maligned as a violator of civil rights, was against the evacuation of the Japanese, while Walter Lippmann, the influential liberal pundit, the voice of reason, the conscience of his time, had no qualms about crushing the rights of the Japanese and repeated unfounded hysteria about sabotage.

On February 14, General De Witt finally sent his recommendation for the evacuation of all Japanese from the coastal areas of California, Oregon, and Washington. His only reason was that the Japanese "are organized and ready for concerted action. . . . The very fact that no sabotage has taken place to date is a disturbing and confirming indication that such action will be taken." In other words, because nothing had happened yet, something was going to happen.

Biddle was now the only holdout against evacuation, but he was taking abuse from California congressmen, one of whom, Leland Ford, called his office "and told them to stop fucking around. I gave them 24 hours' notice that unless they would issue a mass evacuation notice I would drag the whole matter out on the floor of the House and of the Senate and give the bastards everything we could with both barrels. . . . I told them . . . that if they would not take immediate action we would clear the goddamned office out in one sweep."

Biddle made one last try, writing the president on February 17 that full-scale evacuation was not only unconstitutional, it would disrupt agricultural production, tie up transportation, and require thousands of troops. "It is extremely dangerous for the columnists," Biddle went on, "acting as 'Armchair Strategists and Junior G-Men,' to suggest that an attack on the West Coast and planned sabotage is imminent when the military authorities and the F.B.I. have indicated that this is not the fact. It comes close to shouting FIRE! in the theater; and if race riots occur, these writers will bear a heavy responsibility. Either Lippmann has information which the War Department and the F.B.I. apparently do not have, or he is acting with dangerous irresponsibility."

But FDR had already decided, and when Stimson and Biddle and their respective aides met on February 18 to discuss the drafting of an executive order, Biddle could not oppose evacuation any further. On February 19, FDR signed Executive Order 9066, which prescribed who had a right to be in military areas. The order did not mention the Japanese but was clearly directed against them.

As a result of the order, directly requested by FDR, against the advice of the Justice Department and the FBI, about 120,000 Japanese on the West Coast were relocated in camps. About half of these were American citizens, who lost their homes and their farms, whose careers and lives were interrupted, who were deprived of liberty and due process and branded as disloyal without trial or proof.

Roosevelt had indicated in an editorial written while at Warm Springs his animosity toward the Japanese, which had not lessened now that he was at war with them. He seemed to agree with the view that all Japanese in the United States were potential enemies. He expressed no sympathy for their plight. Morgenthau reported on March 5 that "I told McCloy about having seen the President this morning, and that he was interested in what happened to the Japanese after they got moved—not in what happened to their property."

Those who opposed the evacuation kept their mouths shut. "I interjected nothing," Ickes said after a cabinet discussion in March, "however I feel that it is both stupid and cruel. At vast expense and with a total disregard of any considerations due any Japanese, these people will be torn from their homes and transported to inland camps there to be maintained by the Government until drum-head court-martials shall decide whether it is safe for them to return. . . . It also stands to reason that the cleverest fifth columnists will be the ones who escape."

Roosevelt also wanted the 140,000 Japanese evacuated from Oahu, where there *had* been espionage, and wrote Frank Knox on February 26: "I do not worry about the constitutional question—first, because of my recent order and second because Hawaii is under martial law. The whole matter is one of immediate and present war emergency." War emergency could cover some questionable decisions, although in the case of Oahu evacuation did not prove feasible, the Army and the Navy fearing a labor shortage.

In July, when the Japanese were in assembly camps in California, waiting to be moved to relocation camps farther inland, Governor Olson asked that they be kept in California until the harvest was over, so they could be used for cheap labor. Stimson, disgusted with his hypocrisy, now wanting to employ the unfortunate people whose evacuation he had demanded, refused.

By the end of 1943, 119,000 Japanese had been relocated in camps in California, Idaho, Utah, Wyoming, Colorado, and Arkansas. About 22,000 had been released to pick up the threads of their lives. The camps, according to a survey by Harry Hopkins, were not like internment camps, they were more like small towns, with churches, hospitals, post offices, stores, schools, gambling, and prostitution. A normal life was possible. But many of the Nisei were resentful—they could not grasp why they, American citizens, had been evacuated while Germans and Italians retained their freedom. Some had sons or brothers in the armed forces. The 15,000 thought to be disloyal had been sent to Tule Lake, California, where in November 1943 there was a mutiny in which 500 Japanese armed with knives and clubs shut up the camp director and his aides in the administration building. The Army had to move in to restore order, and remained until January 15, 1944. At a December 17 cabinet meeting, FDR urged that a strong hand be used "and it did not make any difference what the Japs in Japan thought about it." "Wait a minute, Mr. President," Henry Wallace interjected. "It makes a lot of difference to the Americans whom the Japs have in the camps in the Philippine Islands." The president backed off, and the extent of punishment of the leaders of the riot was isolation in a stockade.

The internment of the Japanese, upheld by two Supreme Court decisions in 1944, lasted until December 1944. Stimson wanted to end it earlier, wondering at a cabinet meeting on May 26 whether it was time to let the Japs go home. There was no longer any military necessity for keeping them. Ickes on June 2 bluntly told FDR that "the continued retention of these innocent people in the relocation centers would be a blot upon the history of this country." One complication was that Stimson at cabinet had passed around two snapshots found on the bodies of dead Japanese soldiers showing American aviators bound hand and foot on their knees with heads forward and Japanese executioners with broad-edged swords raised, ready to strike off their heads. It was a dreadful sight for those who were charged with the responsibility of seeing to it that the Japanese in this country were treated humanely, Ickes thought.

Roosevelt was in no hurry, telling Ickes on June 12 that "the more I think of this problem of suddenly ending the orders excluding Japanese Americans from the West Coast the more I think it would be a mistake to do anything drastic or sudden." He wanted the matter handled gradually. There was no point in upsetting the West Coast in a presidential election year.

Finally, a termination plan was drawn up and presented to FDR by Stimson on December 13. Relocation had been instituted when an attack on the West Coast seemed probable. Now the situation had changed, and many Japanese soldiers had been recruited from relocation camps. On December 17 the exclusion order was rescinded, and the Japanese began to be released. They were, as W. H. Auden wrote in another context,

> "Left alone with their day, and the time is short and
> History to the defeated
> May say Alas but cannot help or pardon."

Making decisions that were shocking in terms of American values such as civil rights or the humane conduct of warfare was a wartime president's terrible responsibility. The idea that a democratic society which lived by a code of ethics must not adopt certain types of weapons was swept aside by the need for victory. Thus Roosevelt agreed to produce the necessary poisons for biological warfare. On April 29, 1942, he told Stimson to take $200,000 out of his Special Fund and launch the production of toxins that would spread anthrax and botulism. By 1944, bomb techniques for the dispersal of the toxins had been developed, four main facilities had been built in Maryland, Mississippi, Utah, and Indiana, the anthrax toxin was in production in mud form, the procurement of a million four-pound bombs had been authorized, and a plant was completed on December 20 that was capable of producing 500,000 filled and fused bombs a month.

The anthrax toxin was never used, but another weapon with similar scourgelike properties was, after the president's death. Roosevelt consistently supported the manufacture and use of the atomic bomb. In March 1942, he turned the development of the bomb over to the War Department, emphasizing "absolute secrecy." Vannevar Bush, the director of the Office of Scientific Research and Development, told him that "the stuff will apparently be more powerful than we then thought." Concerned that the United States was in a race with Germany, FDR said he wanted the program "pushed not only in regard to development, but also with due regard to time. This is very much of the essence."

Aware of the postwar implications of the bomb, FDR signed a secret agreement with Churchill at the first Quebec Conference in August 1943 for collaboration and full exchange of information. He overruled his scientific advisers, who pointed out that Britain had contributed next to nothing to the making of the bomb, in the interest of the "special relationship" that it was desirable to maintain when the war was over. This offer to share the secrets of the bomb was not extended to the Soviet Union. At a conference with Churchill on September 18, 1944, in Hyde Park, it was agreed in a secret aide-mémoire that "when a bomb is finally available, it might perhaps, after mature consideration, be used against the Japanese, who should be warned that this bombardment will be repeated until they surrender."

At a meeting with Stimson on December 30, 1944, FDR approved the production and testing of the bombs, and the training of the crews of the 509th Composite Group. The Japanese cities that would be the targets of the bomb had already been chosen. The Air Force was ordered not to bomb those cities in its B-29 raids so there would be some unspoiled targets for the new weapon. When General Hap Arnold presented the list of target cities to Stimson, the secretary of war struck off Kyoto. Arnold argued that it was an important manufacturing center with a population of 743,000 and should be destroyed. But Stimson said it was one of the holy cities of the world, and had an outstanding religious significance. The four cities chosen for atomic attack were Hiroshima, Niigata, Nagasaki, and Kokura. Thus, when Truman became president in April 1945, he inherited his predecessor's plan for exploding the bomb over Japan. The War Department letter of instructions to Air Force General Carl Spaatz on July 25, 1945, listed the four cities that Stimson had picked, of which two were targeted.

After Pearl Harbor, FDR was not only president of the United States, but leader of a Grand Alliance conducting war on three continents and two oceans. The alliance was an enormously intricate piece of machinery, with countless cogs and shafts and levers and fulcrums, the moving parts of which functioned in alternating harmony and cross-purpose. That this Rube Goldberg contraption worked at all is largely a tribute to FDR's intuitive grasp of coalition warfare.

The key to coalition warfare was giving priority to coalition above national interests. This also meant giving priority to coalition interests over strategy. It was possible, as the Japanese showed in their Pacific operations, to win a campaign and lose the war. The coalition had to stay together in spite of major strategic differences and basic national conflicts. As FDR once told George Marshall: "I am responsible for keeping the grand alliance together. You cannot, in the interest of a more vigorous prosecution of the war, break up the alliance."

In overruling his military advisers for policy reasons, Roosevelt was intuitively following the doctrine of Karl von Clausewitz, the man who is to military thinking what Freud is to psychoanalysis, and who held that strategy was the handmaiden of policy. First he had to resolve the differences with his own military establishment, and then he had to make compromises with his allies.

Roosevelt was also alert to the political nature of the war. Even Stalin had to respond to public opinion. Chiefs of state, like generals in the field, could absorb only a certain number of defeats. Roosevelt and Churchill had to see the war in the context of domestic politics and pressures. Roosevelt was all too aware that Churchill could be challenged and deposed from power at any time by a vote of no confidence in the House of Commons, and wrote him on March 18, 1942: "You have the additional burden which your delightful unwritten Constitution puts your form of government in in war times just as much as in peacetime. Suddenly, the American written Constitution, with its four-year term, saves the unfortunate person at the top a vast number of headaches." Churchill used the threat of loss of office as a bargaining chip, with great effectiveness.

Roosevelt's political mastery made him a successful coalition leader, although there were dangers in applying political wisdom to military situations. Winning a war was in certain ways like winning an election, but an election could be won by a slim margin, whereas a war had to be won by an overwhelming concentration of power. In politics, it was better to do something than to do nothing, but in war it was sometimes better to do nothing. It was Roosevelt's need for action in 1942 that committed him to the North African landing and a Mediterranean strategy.

The riddle of World War II is this: Why did it take the Grand Alliance two and a half years to mount the cross-Channel operation that ended the war in Europe?

The answer begins with the strategy of each ally. The Russians had no choice—it was fight the Germans or be conquered. The British pursued an imperial strategy that lay within the means of their diminished navy and small army (never more than twenty divisions in the field, whereas Stalin in 1943 was fighting 156 German divisions). They could not save the Far East, where they lost Hong Kong and Singapore in the first months of the Japanese offensive, which made them all the more determined to save the Middle East. They fought Rommel in the Libyan desert to defend Egypt and the Suez Canal, the Iraqi oil fields, and the route to India. This was not colonial warfare in the old Kiplingesque Gunga Din sense, but a strategy that was popular with British public opinion and the British military because it satisfied a national bias—it was the traditional British defense of imperial interests. The only trouble with this strategy was that it could not win the war. In

March 1942, Stimson complained to the head of the British shipping mission in Washington, Sir James Arthur Salter, that he had watched for two years with great concern Britain's attempt to defend her outposts in every part of the world without any consideration of their importance, and that he did not wish to have the United States follow that example because if they did the Allies would lose the war.

The way to win the war, as Stimson and Marshall unwaveringly insisted, was to follow the basic Clausewitz doctrine that every war college teaches— to attack the principal force of the principal enemy, that is, to open a second front against the Germans. Churchill himself had described Russia as "the main and principal theater of war." But Churchill, for his own domestic needs and private reasons, sponsored diversionary operations instead of concentrating on the invasion of France. Fortunately for the Allies, Japan had not followed Clausewitz either. Instead of attacking Russia, which would have required Stalin to fight on two fronts, the Japanese chose a peripheral war in the wrong direction. Stalin was saved by the failure of Axis coalition strategy.

The United States had a greater strategic choice, being free to focus its military might on either Japan or Europe. A "Pacific lobby" led by General MacArthur and Admiral Ernest King clamored for a main effort against Japan, but Stimson and Marshall and Roosevelt all recognized the need to relieve Russia, which fighting Japan would not do. The first priority was to beat the Germans, and after that the Japanese would realize that the jig was up.

But Stimson and Marshall, in their support of a second front, had to make compromises—first with the British in the North African landings, and second in the Pacific theater, where American resources were diverted for the island-hopping and leapfrogging strategies, so that American troops fought land battles in the jungle with Japanese soldiers who could live on a bowl of rice a day.

In addition to strategic differences, each ally had its partly open and partly hidden political agenda. Stalin's agenda for Eastern Europe was not yet apparent, but already there were points of friction within the alliance. The United States maintained relations with Vichy France, ostensibly as a listening post and to keep the French fleet out of Hitler's hands, and shunned General Charles de Gaulle's Free French, who had infuriated Cordell Hull by occupying the tiny islands of St. Pierre and Miquelon off the Newfoundland coast, a violation of the Monroe Doctrine. The British supported de Gaulle and considered the Vichy French enemies. One of Churchill's unstated reasons for promoting a North African landing was to install the Free French there and emerge as the protector of France's colonies. Another point of friction was India, where Roosevelt rather clumsily meddled in favor of independence, which was anathema to Churchill.

Roosevelt's hidden agenda was nothing less than a new world order. He wanted an end to the French and British colonial empires, and a world policed by the United States, England, Russia, and China, excluding continental Europe, that seedbed of conflict, which had twice dragged the United States into world wars. Having served under Wilson, the lesson of history for Roosevelt was not to lose the peace after you had won the war.

This hidden agenda, not a stated doctrine but a pattern emerging in the tapestry of events, was in keeping with the Clausewitz principle that war is a mercantile transaction in which the object is to emerge in a better position than the one started in. The object for America was an orderly world in which she would not be pulled into a European war every twenty years. As FDR wrote his Harvard classmate, the class poet Arthur Davison Ficke, on November 9, 1942: "All of the old philosophies which were based on a national horizon have suddenly been thrown into a world kettle. You and I will not live to see the working out of the attendant problems but I often feel that these years represent something very big that is wholly new in the world. If in 1904 you and I had breathed the thought that thirty-eight years later Americans would be fighting in Africa, in China and in the Solomon Islands we would have been considered even more unorthodox than we really were."

One example of Britain's hidden agenda was the unstated reason for repeatedly delaying a cross-Channel operation. It had to do with the touchiest of all wartime matters: who does the dying. Once, when Marshall was arguing for an immediate invasion of France, one of Churchill's aides turned to him and said: "It's no use—you are arguing against the casualties on the Somme." The British had lost 900,000 killed in World War I. An entire generation had been sacrificed in stupid frontal attacks to save the French, and the memory of that fearful slaughter was the unseen participant at every Anglo-American conference. Churchill, who had fought in the trenches, and who, whenever he spoke in the House of Commons, remembered the absent faces, was determined that it would not be repeated. And it was not, for in World War II the British lost 400,000 dead (soldiers and civilians), while the Russians lost a staggering 20 million—about half the total population of England. British strategy was always directed at limiting British casualties.

There was also among the British a suspicion of amphibious exercises, for those they had tried had left a bitter taste, going back to Gallipoli and including, more recently, the landings in Norway and the evacuations from Crete and Dakar. Indeed, Churchill's chief of staff, Field Marshall Sir Alan Brooke, had commanded the Dunkirk evacuation and associated an amphibious landing with retreat.

Finally, it was traditional for Britain, with her small army, to favor "back door" operations. The British had beaten Napoleon by going through Spain, and Gallipoli had been an attempt to end trench warfare by getting at the Germans through Turkey. Churchill was irresistibly drawn to "end runs" in the Mediterranean that would avoid frontal attacks with high casualties.

Of course the gamesmanship of coalition warfare required that reasons be found to justify a Mediterranean strategy, even if the reason was a red herring—that the Germans must be prevented from linking up with the Japanese through the Middle East. The Americans had their own bluff, which was that out of exasperation with the British they would transfer their forces to the Pacific. Another game plan was to use a defeat to bolster your argument, as Churchill had done after Tobruk. You also had to buy support for your position, as when Churchill said that Admiral King's support for the North African landings had been bought by giving him what he wanted in the Pacific.

Another useful tactic was to overlook your ally's more obvious delusions. Churchill did not respond to FDR's questionable assumption that he could handle the Russians, expressed in a March 18 letter: "I hope you will not mind my being brutally frank when I tell you that I can personally handle Stalin better than either your Foreign Office or my State Department. Stalin hates the guts of all your top people. He thinks he likes me better, and I hope he will continue to do so." In the same vein, Anthony Eden thought that "U.S. policy is exaggeratedly moral, at least where non-American interests are concerned," but refrained from repeating that to England's best ally.

Finally, it was a feature of coalition warfare that, because strategy was the result of compromise, the side with the poorest case usually won, as in those Democratic conventions where a lackluster candidate acceptable to all factions was nominated. Thus the British won their case for a North African landing; thus the Americans won their case for landing on the Atlantic shore of Morocco rather than in the Mediterranean. It was like those Broadway angels who have to invest in a couple of flops before the producer will let them invest in a hit; the Allies had to try the wrong strategy before they could agree on the right strategy.

After Pearl Harbor, Churchill lost no time coming to Washington, arriving on December 22, for he was deeply concerned that the Americans would mount an all-out effort against Japan, leaving the British and the Russians to deal with Hitler. At this first summit meeting of the Allies at war, known as Arcadia, the British were not impressed by the president's military expertise. As Ian Jacob, assistant secretary to the war cabinet, recorded in his diary, "The President is a child in military affairs, and evidently has little realization of what can and cannot be done. He doesn't seem to grasp how backward his country is in its war preparations, and how ill-prepared his army is to get involved in large-sale operations."

This was a view shared by some of the president's own people, who thought he was too easily influenced by Churchill. "Besides being a rank amateur in all military matters," wrote General Joseph W. Stilwell on December 29, "FDR is apt to act on sudden impulse. On top of that he has been completely hypnotized by the British, who have sold him a bill of goods. . . . The Limeys have his ear, while we have the hind tit."

When Stilwell, who had been named chief of staff to Chiang Kai-shek, called at the White House on February 9, he found FDR "very pleasant and very unimpressive. As if I were a constituent in to see him. Rambled on about his idea of the war . . . 'a 28,000 mile front is my conception' etc. etc. 'The real strategy is to fight them all,' etc. etc. Just a lot of wind."

Whatever misgivings the British had were kept under wraps, and the Arcadia Conference proceeded in the seasonal spirit of goodwill. At the Christmas Eve dinner, the scene that stood out for FDR's childhood friend Mrs. Bertie Hamlin was the lighting of the tree at the south portico—the two great men standing together in the house that the British had once burned down and expressing words of faith. There was the serenity of the evening on the one hand and the noise of the steam shovel digging the White House air raid shelter on the other.

It was a time of prolonged familiarity between the two leaders. One morning, W. R. Jones, one of the British aides, delivered Churchill's morning paper in the little room off his bedroom while he was having his bath. In the hall, Jones bumped into FDR, who was coming down in his wheelchair and who said: "Good morning. Is your Prime Minister up yet?" "Well, sir," said Jones, who had a stilted, English butlerish way of speaking, "it is within my knowledge that the Prime Minister is at the present moment in his bath." "Good," said FDR, "then open the door." Jones flung open the bathroom door and there was Churchill, standing naked on the bath mat, pink and round. "Don't mind me," FDR said as the prime minister grabbed a towel.

Churchill's fears were soon allayed, for it was agreed at once that Germany was the main enemy and Europe the decisive theater. The next question was how to get at Germany. Churchill had arrived with position papers, an agenda, and a staff geared to produce quick additional papers. The Americans, as Ian Jacob pointed out, "have no 'War Book.' . . . They will get all right, but they have a hell of a lot to learn."

In the face of American unpreparedness, it was fairly simple for Churchill to sell his concept of invading North Africa, while giving lip service to a later cross-Channel operation: "In 1943 the way may be clear for a return to the Continent, across the Mediterranean, from Turkey into the Balkans, or by landing in Western Europe."

There was much grumbling among the president's military advisers. Stimson feared FDR's fondness for "trial balloons," and Marshall worried that the president seemed to agree to everything Churchill said. But the seething discontent was pushed aside by other matters, such as the need for a unified command—a Combined Chiefs of Staff. Churchill had brought his three to Washington, while the Americans had nothing similar. Thus was the U.S. Joint Chiefs of Staff created, holding its first meeting in February. For the first time, the U.S service chiefs—Marshall, Hap Arnold (under Marshall's command, the Air Force still being a part of the Army), and (from March on) Admiral Ernest King, who were joined in July by Admiral William Leahy, named chief of staff to the president—functioned as a corporate body. Stimson for one was gratified, believing as he did that "both Mr. Roosevelt and Mr. Churchill were men whose great talents required the balancing restraint of carefully organized staff advice."

On January 13, the Combined Chiefs of Staff accepted "Gymnast," as the North African operation was called. FDR was pleased, for it would mean fighting German ground forces "face to face as soon as possible." He had finally found that great salesman he had once been looking for, who could sell bed-warming pans to the Indians.

Churchill went home to face a vote of confidence over reversals in Libya, which he won by 464 to 1, but on February 15 there was a worse defeat—Singapore surrendered. Averell Harriman reported to FDR from London on March 7 that "Singapore shook the Prime Minister himself to such an extent that he has not been able to stand up in this adversity with his old vigor. A number of astute people, both friends and opponents, feel it is only a question of a few months before his government falls."

The Americans had been taken by surprise, but after Arcadia they started thinking, and it did not take them long to realize they had bought a pig in a poke. The scattering of Allied forces was, as Stimson put it, the stopping up of ratholes. Marshall agreed. They had to fight in Europe, and concentrate men and resources in England for the final assault. The president had to be brought around. At lunch in the cabinet room on March 25 with Roosevelt, Hopkins, Knox, and Admiral King, Stimson and Marshall made their case. Stimson was staggered by the president's willingness to undertake Middle Eastern and Mediterranean operations—it was the wildest kind of dispersion debauch—but finally he and Marshall brought him back to the Atlantic and held him there.

Roosevelt was receptive, because with the winter over the Germans were on the offensive again in Russia. His greatest fear was a Russian defeat or negotiated peace, as he told Morgenthau on March 11: "I would go out and take the stuff off the shelves of the stores and pay them any price necessary and put it in a truck and rush it to the boat. . . . Nothing could be worse than to have the Russians collapse. I would rather lose New Zealand, Australia or anything else than have the Russians collapse."

Marshall drew up a plan for a cross-Channel operation—a "toehold landing" in 1942, called "Sledgehammer," to be followed by an all-out landing in 1943, called "Roundup"—which the president approved on April 1, directing Marshall and King and Harry Hopkins to take the plan to London and sell it to the British. To show he meant business, he raised landing craft to a higher priority on the Navy's Shipbuilding Precedence List.

It was the April meetings in London that caused much of the trouble and confusion to come, for the British pretended to adopt a plan that they had no intention of carrying out. They were afraid that if they did not agree, the Americans would shift their effort to Japan.

At lunch with Hopkins, Anthony Eden was all for the cross-Channel plan, while thinking that "we could not help the Russians by a landing on the European continent in 1942. It could only be a costly disaster."

At the first meeting with the British chiefs of staff, on April 8, the British made one objection after another to the invasion of France in 1942—lack of air cover, shortage of landing craft, uncertainties of the tide. Admiral Dudley Pound said the Royal Navy could not guarantee the safe passage of troops across the Channel. Admiral King, still hoping for the Pacific option, supported him, saying that "it is pointless to argue against the knowledge of the British Navy, who know the English Channel better than any of us."

The situation was not improved by a lack of sympathy between generals Brooke and Marshall. Alan Brooke, who had led a corps in battle while Marshall had been a staff man, was patronizing—the Americans were raw beginners, his manner conveyed, their ideas were simplistic. It would have been tactless of Marshall to mention that Brooke's field experience had been gained leading retreats—the Flanders campaign of World War I and the Dunkirk evacuation.

On April 14, however, Churchill and his chiefs of staff accepted the plan for a landing in 1943, with the caveat that the 1942 landing, or large-scale raid, would depend on how the Russians did against the Germans. The tone of the meeting, as General Hastings Ismay recalled it, was that "everyone was enthusiastic . . . everyone seemed to agree with the American proposals in their entirety. No doubts were expressed. . . . Perhaps it would have obviated future misunderstandings if the British had expressed their views more frankly. . . . Our American friends went happily homeward under the mistaken impression that we had committed ourselves."

Indeed they had. Hopkins was sure that decisions had been taken that could not be reversed. Surely that impression was not mistaken, for on April 17 Churchill confirmed to FDR that "we wholeheartedly agree with your conception of concentration against the main enemy, and we cordially accept your plan with one broad qualification. . . . It is essential that we should prevent a junction of the Japanese and the Germans. . . ." This, of course, was the number one British red herring, justifying the holding back of British resources, set aside against a projected Japanese attack in India. Churchill did however agree to attacks in Europe in 1942 and 1943. "We are proceeding with plans and preparations on that basis," he said. "Broadly speaking, our agreed programme is a crescendo of activity on the Continent."

All of this was no more than promises. Stimson and Marshall played the game, frustrating MacArthur's attempts to make Australia the main theater of war. On May 2, Marshall had to talk FDR out of sending more men to Australia, saying it would destroy the Channel project. On May 14, Stimson brought up with the president the trouble MacArthur was making.

In the meantime, the Russians were thinking dark thoughts about Allied promises that did not materialize. Beaverbrook informed Hopkins that Stalin believed Britain wanted Russia and Germany to destroy each other. Britain treats the Russians like natives or Negroes, Stalin had said.

Molotov, already famous for his robotlike aloofness, arrived in Washington at the end of May to plead for a second front. Hitler might take Moscow and the Russians would have to withdraw to the Volga, Molotov told the president on May 29. An Anglo-American invasion of the Continent in 1942 could draw off forty German divisions. FDR asked Molotov to bear in mind that he had to reckon with military advisers who were inclined to prefer a sure thing in 1943 to a risky venture in 1942.

The conversation turned to what American public opinion thought of the Soviet Union. Hopkins said the American Communist party, composed largely of disgruntled people, including a comparatively high proportion of distinctly unsympathetic Jews, misled the average American. Roosevelt said that although he was far from anti-Semitic (the usual demurral that precedes an anti-Semitic remark), there was a good deal in Harry's point of view. Molotov admitted, in a remark that verged on the jovial, that there were Communists and Communists and that even in Russia there was a distinction between Jews and kikes.

The next day, they met again, this time with Marshall, and Molotov again pleading for a second front. The troops were ready, Marshall said, the planes and armored divisions were ready, the problem was transport. Roosevelt authorized Molotov to tell Stalin to expect the formation of a second front in 1942, a premature pledge he would later have occasion to regret.

On June 1, when they met for the last time, FDR repeated his pledge, but urged that Stalin give up some of the ships he had been promised to strengthen the second front buildup. The Soviets could not have their cake and eat it, he said. What would happen, Molotov asked with sarcasm, if the Russians cut down their demands and then the second front did not materialize? Again, Roosevelt said he expected it to take place, and that even as they spoke the British and the Americans were in personal consultation on such questions as landing craft.

Aside from the second front, the talks with Molotov were remarkable in that FDR revealed (as he could not to Churchill) his conception of a new world order. He saw the four major Allies acting as the policemen of the world. They would maintain sufficient armed forces to impose peace, and they would have inspection privileges to guard against the sort of clandestine rearmament that Germany had engaged in.

What concerned him, Roosevelt said, was the establishment of a peace that would last twenty-five years, at least the lifetime of the present generation—in other words, peace in our time. Molotov inquired about the reestablishment of France as a great power. In his communications with Vichy, Roosevelt described himself as eager to restore the greatness of France. On January 20, in a message to Marshal Pétain through Ambassador Leahy, he said that "one of his greatest wishes is to see France reconstituted in the postwar period in accordance with its splendid position in history. The word 'France' includes the French Colonial Empire." But to Molotov, he gave away his true feelings: that might perhaps be possible, he replied, within ten or twenty years.

Roosevelt also described his plan for dismantling the colonial empires of England, France, and Holland. After the war, there would be many islands and colonial possessions that would have to be taken away from weak nations. This would mean the abandonment of the mandate system, so that the islands now held by the Japanese would not go to the British or the French. Perhaps the same procedure should apply to the islands now held by the British. They should be placed under international committees of trustees.

For instance, FDR went on, take Indochina, Thailand, the Malay States, and the Dutch East Indies. Each of these areas would require a different lapse of time before achieving readiness for self-government. The white nations could not hope to hold them as colonies in the long run. There was already a palpable surge toward independence (mightily abetted, he could have added, by the Japanese having chased away the colonial powers). It might take twenty years to accomplish what the United States had accomplished in forty-two years in the Philippines—independence.

Here was Roosevelt at his most candid, admitting his long-range plans to reduce the French and the British to second-rate powers by breaking up their empires. In the case of India, he was already actively interfering for independence, but had to pull back once he realized his meddling was endangering the Grand Alliance. On several occasions, Roosevelt told Churchill that he favored independence for India. Churchill always responded angrily—this was one area where he was not open to the advice of his great friend and ally—but FDR kept plugging away.

Roosevelt felt there was so much dissatisfaction among the Indian people that they would cave in if Japan attacked. He suggested forming a temporary government representing different groups and castes that would be given dominion status at once. Churchill received this suggestion with a stream of curses, but replied politely on March 6 that any such form of government "would have a disastrous effect on Indian Army made up of different groups—Moslems would start asking if they would have an army of their own—the question of Pakistan would have a bad effect on the Punjabis. Their minds would be taken off fighting the enemy, recruitment would be imperiled, communal disturbances would break out. . . ."

Roosevelt decided at that point to send Louis Johnson, a former under secretary of war, to India as his personal representative. This the British deeply resented, for they were about to send Sir Stafford Cripps to India with the offer that Britain would grant full independence if it was demanded by a constitutional assembly after the war. The timing of Johnson's arrival would make it appear that he was acting as mediator between Cripps and the Indians. The Cripps offer was refused by the majority Congress party led by Jawaharlal Nehru. Johnson cabled FDR on April 11 that the British had sabotaged the talks by making a warmed-over offer that the Congress party had to refuse. "London wanted a Congress refusal," Johnson said. "Does England prefer to lose India to enemy retaining claim of title at peace table rather than lose it by giving freedom now? . . . The hour has arrived when we should consider a replotting of our policy in this section of the world."

The British, who were almost certainly reading Johnson's cables, had proof of the extent of American meddling. Churchill advised Harry Hopkins that "Louis Johnson recently expressed himself in critical terms about the handling of the Indian negotiations, and has given alarmist reports about the attitude of the Indian population. . . . Frankly we do not think his comments have very much weight."

Dismayed by Johnson's report and the failure of the talks, FDR once again, on April 12, urged Churchill to make "a fair and real offer to the Indian people." That was too much for Churchill. At a time when Japan had invaded Burma and was poised to strike against India, Roosevelt was suggesting constitutional experiments with a period of trial and error. What an act of madness! His mind was back in the American War of Independence, with which he had compared the situation, and he thought of the Indian problem in terms of the thirteen colonies fighting George III. Replying to FDR, Churchill said that "anything like a serious difference between you and me would break my heart, and would surely deeply injure both our countries at the height of this terrible struggle."

The alliance came first, and Roosevelt backtracked. When Mahatma Gandhi that summer urged civil disobedience, which would have the effect of a general strike at a time when Japanese troops were at India's borders, FDR at cabinet on August 7 said that Gandhi might be all right in his way but he did not have any government experience—he was like a man who could take a watch apart and understand every part in the watch but who could not put the watch back together to make it tick. When Ickes on August 10 wrote the president that "we are fighting for freedom and yet Great Britain denies India freedom," he replied on August 12: "You are right about India but it would be playing with fire if the British Empire were to tell me to mind my own business." Churchill already had, and FDR got the message.

That June came the turning point of the Pacific war, when the entire Japanese fast carrier group, the same four carriers that had attacked Pearl Harbor, was sunk at the Battle of Midway. The Japanese were afflicted with "victory disease." They were too stretched out. Thanks to Magic intercepts that gave away their plans to invade Midway, the outermost island of the Hawaiian chain, 1,136 miles northwest of Pearl Harbor, dive-bombers caught the carriers on June 4 as their planes were being refueled and rearmed after a first strike. The very ships that had attacked Pearl, the *Akagi,* the *Kaga,* the *Hiryu,* and the *Soruy,* could now be observed burning and sinking, and the very planes that had bombed Pearl were now destroyed—250 of them, with a loss of 2,200 officers and men, about the same as the losses at Pearl. It was more than a victory, it was a soul-satisfying settlement of scores, which strengthened the hand of those who, like General MacArthur and Admiral King, wanted a more vigorous prosecution of the Pacific war.

Things were not going nearly so well in the Russian campaign, where the Germans had moved into the Crimea and surrounded Sebastopol. "The whole question of whether we win or lose the war depends on the Russians," FDR told Morgenthau on June 16. "If the Russians can hold out this summer and keep three and a half million Germans engaged in war we can definitely win. . . . We know that at the beginning of the war the Japanese fleet was almost as big as ours. However, once we lick the Germans, with the help of England's fleet we can defeat the Japanese in six weeks."

But early in June, Churchill sent the charming Admiral Louis Mountbatten, who in his enthusiasm for adventurous schemes was not unlike the young Roosevelt of Navy days, to make the case against an invasion of France in 1942. The argument was that a landing would not draw troops away from the Russian front because Hitler had twenty-five divisions in France and the Allies did not have enough landing craft to match that strength.

Roosevelt was divided, saying on the one hand that he wanted a footing on the continent in 1942 and on the other that he had been struck by Churchill's remark in a recent telegram: "Do not lose sight of Gymnast." What Roosevelt really wanted was an operation in which American troops were involved prior to the congressional elections in November. He had seen Wilson lose control of Congress in 1918, days before the end of World War I, and had no desire to repeat the experience. He knew that an American victory in the European theater would help bring in the vote.

When Mountbatten brought the happy news that Roosevelt was wavering, Churchill at once decided to leave for Washington to argue the case, in such a hurry this time that he flew instead of going by boat as he had in December.

At the June 17 meeting of the war cabinet, Stimson was distressed to see that FDR was once again "showing dispersion fever." The president took up the case for Gymnast, arguing that a North African landing would take some pressure off Russia. This was another British red herring, for in fact the landings would give Hitler immunity from a real second front. Marshall and Stimson vigorously argued against Gymnast, while King, who was supposed to be so tough he shaved with a blowtorch, "wobbled around in a way that made me rather sick with him," according to Stimson. "He is firm and brave outside the White House but as soon as he gets in the presence of the President he crumbles up. It was a disappointing afternoon."

The next day Churchill arrived, landing in the Potomac in a Boeing flying boat from Bermuda. On June 19 he joined the president at Hyde Park, where they discussed pooling their information on the atom bomb, known by the code name "Tube Alloys." While FDR drove Churchill around the estate in his car with hand controls, and asked Winston to feel his biceps, which a famous prizefighter had envied, Stimson and Marshall fretted that Roosevelt would fall under the prime minister's spell.

They returned to Washington on the evening of the twentieth, and the next morning after breakfast Churchill and General Ismay went to see FDR in his study. Roosevelt handed Winston a telegram that said: "Tobruk surrendered with 25,000 men taken prisoner." Tobruk was the only strong point left in Libya between Rommel and Egypt. In Tobruk were all the stores and installations for the intended British summer offensive. The British had raised the white flag after a ferocious tank battle, and the Twenty-first Panzer, a force far inferior in numbers, had captured the town.

For the first time of the war, Ismay saw Churchill wince. "What can we do to help?" Roosevelt asked. Churchill asked for Sherman tanks, 300 of which were at once dispatched, arriving in time to take part in Montgomery's triumph at El Alamein in October. Ismay saw how vital to Britain the two leaders' friendship was. How long, he wondered, would it have taken to get the tanks by going through channels?

Shocked, but far from speechless, Churchill used the Tobruk defeat to revive interest in Gymnast. The North African strategy was crucial now to save the British in Egypt. The meetings that Sunday, June 21, continued through the day and into the evening, when, out of the blue, FDR proposed that a large American force might be thrown into the Middle East between Alexandria and Teheran. Marshall was so taken aback, it was such a dismissal of everything they had been planning for, that he refused to discuss it and left the room, controlling his fury.

The next day, June 22, there was a bitter struggle between Stimson and Churchill, who said that not one responsible soldier on his staff thought a 1942 invasion of France was feasible. The Germans had dug defenses on the northern coast, and were well-nigh impregnable. The Channel would be a river of blood, recalling the carnage of Passchendaele and the Somme.

Stimson said he did not want to send troops to their death any more than Churchill did, but that the thing to do was prepare for an invasion in 1943, with might and main.

Churchill said the troops might be used more profitably somewhere else.

Stimson reminded him that he had been skimming the defenses of Great Britain to send troops to the Middle East, and that the presence of American divisions in Britain would provide protection against a surprise invasion.

Once again, the president offered to land a big American force between Egypt and Iran. Stimson was grateful that Churchill did not encourage such a strategic absurdity. "The President was in his most irresponsible mood," Stimson recorded in his diary. "He was talking of a most critical situation in the presence of the head of another government with the frivolity and lack of responsibility of a child."

The next two days were days of great anxiety as Stimson and Marshall saw their plans for an invasion of France imperiled. Churchill was pushing for American troops to go at once to Libya, but Stimson bought him off with the promise of 100 105-mm howitzers. When Churchill left on June 25, Stimson felt that his cross-Channel strategy had been saved, but complained that "Marshall and I had Churchill on our necks for three days."

In fact, Roosevelt had been swayed by Churchill's argument that a 1942 invasion of France was doomed, and that they could not afford to stand idle during the whole of 1942. It was in this context that Gymnast looked attractive. Also, headlines in the American papers said "Tobruk Fall May Bring Change of Government" and "Churchill to Be Censured." Churchill needed a victory in Africa to save his government, just as FDR needed American troops in combat against Germans before the election. Gymnast answered both these needs.

Having beaten back a motion of censure on July 1 by a vote of 475 to 25, Churchill wrote FDR a week later that "no responsible British general, admiral, or air marshal is prepared to recommend Sledgehammer as a practicable operation in 1942. . . . I am sure myself that Gymnast is by far the best chance for effective relief to the Russian front in 1942. . . . Here is the true second front of 1942."

When Marshall heard the news he got very stirred up. He was sick of decisions that did not "stay made." Why were the British always reneging? Stimson too was staggered. Marshall urged in a memo to FDR that if the British did not hold to their agreements, American forces should take up the war with Japan. Stimson hoped the threat would work. "If they persist in their fatuous defeatist position," he wrote, ". . . the Pacific operation . . . will be a great deal better . . . than a tepidly operated [invasion of France] in which the British do not put their whole heart."

When Stimson saw the president on July 15, Roosevelt assured him that he was absolutely sound on a second front in France, but disapproved of Marshall's memorandum on the Pacific. It was a little like "taking your dishes and going away," he said. Stimson agreed, but it had to be used as a threat "to get through the hides of the British."

"When you are trying to hold a wild horse," Stimson said, "the way to do it is to get him by the head and not by the heels, and that is the trouble with the British method of trying to hold Hitler in the Mediterranean and the Middle East."

That evening at dinner, Roosevelt confided his true thoughts to Harry Hopkins: "My main point is that I do not believe we can wait until 1943 to strike at Germany. If we cannot strike at Sledgehammer, then we must take the second best—and that is not the Pacific. . . . Gymnast had the great advantage of being a purely American enterprise, it would secure Western Africa and deny the ports to the enemy, it would offer the beginning of what should be the ultimate control of the Mediterranean—it is the shortest route to supply."

The president had already made up his mind on Gymnast. But not wanting to confront Stimson and Marshall, he sent Marshall and Harry Hopkins to London for a "showdown" with the British, the result of which was foreordained, although Marshall still believed the Sledgehammer strategy had a chance. Stimson felt that Marshall, "better than anybody, can put some inspiration into the rather lethargic and jaded minds of the British General Staff."

When Marshall and Hopkins arrived in London on July 20, however,

Sledgehammer was dead, for the simple reason that the invasion season across the English Channel was from May to September 15—after that the waves were too high for landings—and the British had been promised a two-month invasion notice. Marshall was greeted by the far from lethargic British chiefs of staff, who had already approved Gymnast as "the only feasible proposition."

After three meetings with the British, the stalemate was complete, and Hopkins wrote a note, probably to Marshall, that said: "I feel damn depressed." On July 23, having heard the news, Stimson saw the president, who "expressed his deep disappointment in the British attitude, and I told him that it seemed to me to be the result of a fatigued and defeatist government which had lost its initiative, blocking the help of a young and vigorous nation whose strength had not yet been tapped by either war."

Roosevelt now ordered Hopkins to agree to the Gymnast landings, no later than October 30 (the week before the elections). Stimson when informed said it would hold up the cross-Channel invasion, which FDR admitted. "This decision marks what I feel to be a very serious parting of the ways," Stimson recorded. "The more I reflect on it the more clear does the evil of the President's decision appear to me."

Thus, in the first year of the war, Stimson and Marshall were at loggerheads with the president. They distrusted his military judgment and Churchill's ability to lead him down the Mediterranean path, using American forces to defend the British Empire in operations that would delay victory in Europe and the Pacific. "Torch," as the North African landings were now dubbed, they held to be basically unsound.

And yet FDR felt he had to overrule his military advisers, for if there was no operation in 1942 it would be hard to resist the outcry for a main American effort in the Pacific. He had to rescue the "Germany first" concept and repair the cracks in the Grand Alliance. He also had to enhance his chances to keep control of Congress. On July 25, Harry Hopkins, who was loyal to the political needs of his boss rather than to the strategic demands of the military, sent the president a telegram of classic brevity: "Africa. Thank God."

And so the troops that it was impractical to transport twenty miles across the Channel would be carried 1,000 miles across the open sea to land on the northwest hump of Africa, in the high surf of Atlantic beaches.

Marshall thought of resigning, but later acknowledged "the political necessity for action. The public demands it. They must have action. The party opponents utilize the lack of it to attack those in power. It presented a difficult business. The military staff planners, as a rule, do not fully appreciate this phase of the matter, if at all."

On July 30, three days after his return from London, Harry Hopkins was married for the third time, in the Oval Office of the White House. The bride was the beautiful and chic Louise Macy, who had been Paris editor of *Harper's Bazaar*. Ickes wondered what she saw in Harry, who was "just a facile and quick-footed charity worker." The only reason he could see was that she wanted to be the wife of the man who was closest to the president of the United States. Ickes's information was that Louise Macy had feathered her nest with settlements from rich lovers like Bernie Baruch and Jock Whitney, who had set her up in business in New York. Two years earlier, according to Ickes, Hopkins had refused to marry a wealthy widow he was engaged to, Mrs. Dorothy Donovan, who committed suicide by throwing herself out a sixteenth-floor apartment window.

One of the wedding gifts, the press reported, was an emerald from Lord Beaverbrook, who had been on the receiving end of Lend-Lease. When Hopkins was attacked for accepting the gem, there were denials all around. The new Mrs. Hopkins said, "I never owned an emerald and don't own one now." Beaverbrook said that "the story is all fabrication from first to last, but the Germans will like it." Robert Sherwood, in his book *Roosevelt and Hopkins,* spoke of "the fantastic story of the Beaverbrook emeralds." As it happened, Beaverbrook had not given Harry and Louise an emerald but an antique diamond clip that had been in his family. Hopkins sent the clip to Assistant Secretary of the Treasury Herbert E. Gaston to have it appraised as more than 100 years old, and as such not subject to duty.

FDR invited Harry and Louise to live at the White House, which did not please Eleanor, whose friendship with Hopkins was strained. He made himself at home a bit too much. Recently, at an important dinner, he had ordered the servants to change Eleanor's seating arrangement. Eleanor also complained that Harry and "Louie" drank so many cocktails that "they really are quite high sometimes before they sit down to dinner."

The ripples of the change in strategy began to be felt. Combat groups once allocated to the cross-Channel invasion were now sent to the Pacific, where the costly invasion of the Solomon Islands was under way. Hitler had bought a year's deferment of the second front at the cost of 125,000 troops he would have to commit to North Africa—a bargain. In August, as a result of the Canadian commando raid on Dieppe, he ordered that the Atlantic Wall defenses must be finished by May 1943, with first priority to ports and last priority to open beaches.

Russia would get no relief in 1942, which Churchill hastened to Moscow in August to explain. In the meantime, the preparations for Torch were dragging. The British suspected that the Americans were diverting forces to the Pacific theater, and Eisenhower, now the American commander in England, had to reassure them that they were going to land in North Africa "if I have to go alone in a rowboat."

When Marshall informed FDR about the delays, FDR folded his hands as if in prayer and said: "Please make it before Election Day." But when, in September, the landings had to be postponed until November 8, there was not a word of complaint. It was a blow, but he would not interfere with the Army's agenda.

There were other ways to win an election, and one of them was to co-opt the leading Republican, Wendell Willkie, who was sent on his One World tour in September. In China, Madame Chiang "wound him around her little finger," according to embassy counselor John Carter Vincent, and referred to him privately as "a perpetual adolescent." In Russia, he backed a second front, which embarrassed FDR, who told a press conference that he had not read Willkie's remarks. When Willkie was back and making speeches about the "reserv-wharr of goodwill" he had found, FDR mimicked him when he was asked how he would deal with the manpower shortage. "We'll just draw on our reserv-wharr of woman power," he said.

FDR heard from J. Edgar Hoover that Willkie was shooting off his mouth in off-the-record talks. He told the New York Newspaper Guild that the American military censor in Cairo was a homosexual who had gotten his job through society connections in Washington. He told the Young Republicans that Stalin had a harem—"maybe some of us would like to have one too, but ... Stalin likes them middle-aged, fat, and frowsy." After cabinet on October 20, FDR told Henry Wallace that Willkie had been in to see him, and "had obviously been drinking considerably," but when he checked with the newspaper boys, "they said he ... had only had four or five drinks in the 45 minutes before he went in to see the President." Despite his teasing, however, FDR thought the Willkie trip had been useful.

It did not save him at the polls, for on November 3 the Republicans picked up forty-four seats in the House, where they closed in on the Democrats, 209 to 222, and nine seats in the Senate. George Norris, a Senate fixture for so many years, was beaten in Nebraska despite Roosevelt's endorsement. Senators Prentice Brown and Josh Lee lost in Michigan and Oklahoma. Thomas E. Dewey carried New York by 600,000 votes. It was the usual off-year rebuff, with a low voter turnout and local issues taking precedence over global strategy.

The strategy for Torch, in the meantime, was leading to "some of the wildest arrangements outside of Tom Sawyer's famous plans to deliver Jim the Nigger," according to Adolf Berle. The British, concerned that Hitler would strike through Spain, had promised Franco a piece of French Morocco in exchange for neutrality. FDR had insisted that de Gaulle be kept out of the operation, for his involvement would surely mean civil war between the Free French and the Vichy French. Harold Ickes thought the president's policy was "Vichy-Vashy." Each ally had its pet Frenchman, and General Henri Giraud, escaped from a German POW camp, had been brought to Gibraltar, whence Eisenhower planned to transport him to North Africa in the hope that he would take command of French forces. The British had in mid-October received secret messages from Admiral Jean-François Darlan, commander in chief of all French forces, asking for the supreme command of the rumored American expedition and claiming he could rally the French. But there was little enthusiasm in London for Darlan, who had given away British naval secrets to the Germans, helped the anti-British rebellion in Iraq, tried to arrange for French merchantmen to carry supplies to Rommel, and identified himself wholeheartedly with the policy of collaboration.

It was a tragedy that the first fighting done by American ground forces in the European theater was against America's oldest ally, France. Only a quarter of a century before, General Pershing had arrived in France and said, "Lafayette, we are here." Now, Americans and Frenchmen were killing one another as American troops landed in Casablanca, Oran, and Algiers.

But the fighting lasted only a few days. American casualties were less than 1,500. The first landings were on November 8. The next day, General Giraud arrived in Algiers with General Mark Clark. It was hoped that Giraud's prestige would end the fighting, but he was ignored. As it happened, Darlan was also in Algiers, ostensibly to see his polio-stricken son. It soon became clear that Darlan was the only Frenchman in North Africa with the authority to end the fighting, and a deal was struck—Eisenhower left him in command.

At cabinet on November 15, FDR was in high spirits. The conception of Torch had been his own, he said, and he had finally persuaded Churchill to do it. It was remarkable that they could have landed 500 ships with so little loss. The German reconnaissance planes had been sound asleep. It was a magnificent exploit, although, as FDR put it, he now had three Kilkenny cats on his hands in the persons of de Gaulle, Darlan, and Giraud.

Completely surprised by Torch, the Germans were now in a race to reach Tunisia. The Luftwaffe sent 500 planes, most of them from the eastern front. But the Wehrmacht, relieved from the threat of attack in France, moved twenty-seven fresh divisions from Europe to the Russian front, so that Torch, far from providing relief, actually increased the pressure on Stalin. In addition, the shipping required for the African operations in 1943 cut the amount of matériel sent to the Russians by ship to less than one-third the 1942 levels. The principal result of Torch, however, which Stalin had yet to discover, was that there would be no cross-Channel operation in 1943.

One unforeseen dividend for the Allies was that the landings tested the battle-worthiness of the green American troops. Here was large-unit training with live ammunition, on the site of the Third Punic War. As Field Marshal Sir John Dill, head of the British military mission in Washington, wrote a friend: "I have just seen two of our lads who were with Patton at Casablanca. They say that cooperation between the land and the air force was good and that the tank units when once ashore were well handled. But the rest is all muddle and a terrible lack of control and training. . . . If there had been any opposition on the beaches no landing would have taken place. . . . These Casablanca troops are not well trained—at any rate for amphibious operations."

To FDR Darlan was a Kilkenny cat, but to American liberals he was hardly better than a Nazi. The reaction was: If we can make a deal with Darlan in North Africa, we can make a deal with Goering in Germany. Among those most affected was Morgenthau, who almost felt like giving up on the war. At dinner on November 17 at the Stimsons', he said that Darlan was a ruthless person who had sold many thousands of people into slavery, and if we were going to back these fascists, how could you explain it to the American people? Stimson said the arrangement had brought enormous benefits and was only temporary.

Temporary indeed, for Darlan was assassinated on December 24 by a twenty-year-old Frenchman of monarchist persuasion named Bonnier de la Chapelle, who had been manipulated by the British and the Gaullists. British intelligence recruited him and gave him the gun. The Gaullists planted the idea in his head that killing Darlan would help restore the heir to the French throne, the comte de Paris. Both the Gaullists and the British wanted Darlan eliminated. As Churchill put it, his murder "relieved the Allies of their embarrassment at working with him, and at the same time left them with all the advantages he had been able to bestow."

It was just another piece of Roosevelt luck, thought Ickes. Perhaps as a gesture of atonement to the man who, shortly before his assassination, had written that the Allies would squeeze him dry like a lemon and then throw him away, FDR later invited Darlan's son to Warm Springs to be treated for his polio.

On Thanksgiving day, November 26, 1942, in the East Room of the White House, the Roosevelt administration gathered to worship—the cabinet, the Supreme Court, the Army and Navy chiefs, and the heads of the war agencies. There was Felix Frankfurter, a bald spot in the center of his gray thatch, and the storklike Robert Sherwood, and Hap Arnold looking like a somewhat older Eisenhower, and Sumner Welles, with his dignified bearing and the tilt of his chin—no one could look more like a career diplomat; there was Marshall, impressive-looking, with an expression in his eyes of creative intelligence that you rarely saw in professional soldiers, and Ickes, with his pale and red-headed young wife, looking sour as ever.

And there was the president, reading the Thanksgiving Proclamation in a quiet voice. It was less than a year after America's entry into the war, and he had much to be thankful for. In fact, he would have agreed with Count Ciano's remark that "the God of war has now turned from Germany and gone over to the other camp."

In October, with the pyramids almost in sight, Rommel had been forced into a decisive battle with Montgomery and was thrown back with heavy losses at El Alamein. It was his last thrust into Egypt, and the beginning of total defeat in the desert war. As Churchill said, "Before Alamein we never had a victory. After Alamein we never had a defeat."

In the Pacific, the turning point had been reached with the Battle of Guadalcanal in mid-November. The Japanese fleet was beaten back with heavy losses, and the Japanese would soon evacuate the island. There was a shift in American strategy to the offensive.

In Russia, the German Sixth Army was trapped outside Stalingrad at the onset of winter—200,000 of Germany's finest, with 1,800 big guns and 100 tanks and 10,000 vehicles. A great pincer movement had encircled them on November 22, and Hitler had ordered them to stand fast. Hitler, who had fired his chief of staff, General Franz Halder, was described by several persons who had recently seen him as a broken man showing signs of madness, ranting about Roosevelt, that "tortuous, pettifogging Jew," Churchill, that "raddled old whore of journalism," and Stalin, that "half beast, half giant."

In North Africa, Torch had been a magnificent feat. After occupying Morocco and Algeria with light casualties, American and British troops were moving toward Tunisia, which was expected to fall just as easily. The next step was the invasion of Europe.

Roosevelt's voice, that voice so well known on the airwaves of the entire world, made very little sound as he sang the hymns, for he approached them in the diffident way of the ordinary man who isn't accustomed to singing. His face was serene and attentive, and he drew up his eyebrows as he read the words, just as if he were still one of the senior wardens in the little church at Hyde Park.

XXII

Democracy, While Weapons Were Everywhere Aim'd at Your Breast...

Democracy, while weapons were everywhere aim'd at your breast,
I saw you serenely give birth to immortal children; saw in dreams
your dilating form.
Saw you with spreading mantle covering the world.

Walt Whitman, *Leaves of Grass*

On the evening of Saturday, January 9, 1943, Roosevelt (who was three weeks short of his sixty-first birthday) and his party boarded the presidential train at the secret siding near the Bureau of Engraving and Printing for the first of four major conferences he would hold that year on three continents with Churchill (and once with Stalin). He was the first president to leave the country in wartime, and the first since Lincoln to visit an active theater of war.

From Miami, the presidential party took a Pan American flying boat to Trinidad. It was Roosevelt's first flight since the 1932 Democratic convention at Chicago, but the discomfort and fatigue of flying were the same. The first leg of the 6,000-mile flight to Casablanca, from Miami to Trinidad, off the coast of Venezuela, took ten hours at 146 miles per hour—they could go no faster at first because they were carrying 4,600 gallons of gasoline and 900 liters of bottled water.

The second leg, Trinidad to Belém, on the northern coast of Brazil, took nine hours. Since Belém was just south of the equator, there were Crossing the Line ceremonies for first-timers, who were turned from pollywogs into shellbacks. The transatlantic leg from Belém to Bathurst in British Gambia on the west coast of Africa took nineteen hours. In Bathurst, FDR found his preconceptions about colonies confirmed. The British, who had held Gambia since 1620, had exploited the resources and not put anything back in. The natives were half-clothed and undernourished. The life expectancy was twenty-six years, and the prevailing daily wage was fifty cents and a bowl of rice.

From Bathurst it was another eight hours by C-54 to Casablanca. During previous legs they had cruised at 4,000 feet, but now they had to rise to 11,-000 feet in the unpressurized plane to cross the snowcapped peaks of the Atlas Mountains. Roosevelt's doctor, Ross McIntire, was worried about the president's heart; it was dangerous for him to go above 7,500 feet, not to mention the long hours of flying time—Admiral Leahy had to abandon ship in Trinidad because of a fever.

The arrival in Casablanca on January 14 was a happy one, however, for two of FDR's sons, Elliott and Franklin Jr., one in the Air Force and the other in the Navy, were on hand to greet him. The conference was held in Anfa, a resort five miles from the city, on a knoll overlooking the Atlantic— a postcard setting, with the blue of the water, the white of the buildings, the red of the soil, the green of the palm trees, and the lavender of the bougainvillea.

To Harold Macmillan, one of Churchill's political advisers, it was like a meeting of the two emperors in the later period of the Roman Empire, the emperor of the East and the emperor of the West. Their villas were fifty yards apart, and they met late at night to discuss matters with each other's generals. The emperor of the East spent most of the day in bed, ate and drank enormously, settled global problems, and played bezique. The emperor of the West was surrounded by court figures and two sons, and drank highballs and talked by the hour. It was a mixture between a vacation cruise and summer school. Between meetings, the field marshals and admirals went down to the beach and made sand castles.

The difference between the two emperors was that the emperor of the East had a plan. The British had brought along a 6,000-ton liner, a sort of floating map room, stocked with files, a library, and technical equipment. Churchill and his chiefs of staff presented an unshakable front, producing chapter and verse, plans and statistics. The plan was to continue the conquest of North Africa, link up with British troops in Egypt, invade Sicily, and threaten Southern Europe, which it was hoped would bring Turkey into the war.

Behind the plan was the unstated intention to kill the cross-Channel invasion for yet another year. As Stimson put it, it was like the old steamboat on the Mississippi that worked its whistle and its paddle from the same engine—the funnel for the whistle was so big that when it blew it stopped the paddle. If the Allies pursued their Mediterranean strategy, there would not be enough resources for the invasion of France. The British technique was to draw the Americans into the Mediterranean a step at a time—first the landings in North Africa, then the landing in Sicily, and then the invasion of Italy, each step following logically from the one before it.

And so, once again, the Americans were pulled into the British conception of peripheral operations that did not attack the principal enemy and that left the Soviet Union to carry on the war in Europe alone. In five days of talks between the British and American chiefs of staff, from January 14 to 18, the Mediterranean strategy carried the day. This was because there was not the same unity of thought among the Americans. Marshall carried the ball for a cross-Channel invasion in 1943. King was absorbed in his operations in the Pacific. Arnold tended to agree with the British view that the Germans could be beaten by carpet bombing, and was not opposed to an invasion of Italy; where he could use the airfields.

The Americans had painted themselves into a corner by stopping the flow of troops and landing craft to Britain after the North African landings. They said they would not place an army in England just to sit there on spec. The flow would resume when a specific operation was decided on. But now the British were arguing that no operation could be decided on because the forces were too small for a second front in 1943. It was a vicious circle.

As Ian Jacob, the assistant secretary of the war cabinet, recorded in his diary, "Much as they [the Americans] wanted to prosecute the war against Germany, they didn't quite see how it was to be done. They were uncertain of the possibility of an invasion of Northern France, but they had a deep suspicion of the Mediterranean. . . . They regarded the Mediterranean as a kind of dark hole, into which one entered at one's peril. If large forces were committed to the Mediterranean, the door would suddenly and firmly be shut behind one."

The British argument, as Ian Jacob put it, was that "very large allied forces were available in North Africa and the Middle East, forces inured to battle and accustomed to victory." Whereas, as Brooke argued, only twenty-one divisions would be in England by August 1943, too few for an invasion of France. It was better to move into Italy, which would draw Germans away from Russia, while garrisoning England for a 1944 cross-Channel attack.

Marshall fought a stubborn rearguard action for a 1943 invasion, but received no support from FDR, who once again agreed with the British rather than his own military people. On January 15, according to Brooke, FDR "expressed views in favor of operations in the Mediterranean." According to Ian Jacob, "the President was quite of the Prime Minister's way of thinking."

FDR had come to the conference with a disorganized command and no coherent plan for winning the war. Stimson and Leahy, who would have backed up Marshall, were not there. He had given no thought to the invasion of Sicily and Italy, and his mind was preoccupied by the sideshow of

French leadership—how to get "the bride" de Gaulle and "the bridegroom" Giraud together during the conferences.

Even without Roosevelt's support, Marshall continued to oppose "interminable operations" in the Mediterranean. By January 17, which Brooke called "a desperate day," the Combined Chiefs had not reached agreement, and the Americans had again fallen back on the argument that if there were no invasion of France in 1943 they would prefer to give priority to the defeat of Japan—what FDR in 1942 had called "picking up our dishes."

On January 18, a discouraged Brooke told Sir John Dill, the head of the British military mission in the United States, who had given his people advance notice of what the American position would be: "It is no use, we shall never get agreement with them." Dill suggested a compromise—go ahead now with the Mediterranean while preparing for a cross-Channel invasion in 1944. If they brought these unsolved problems to Churchill and Roosevelt, Dill said, "you know as well as I do what a mess they would make of it."

That afternoon the British paper was accepted. It made no mention of the invasion of Italy, in order to obtain American agreement on the next two steps—clearing the African coast and invading Sicily, an operation dubbed "Husky." Churchill had reported to Brooke that Roosevelt "also seems increasingly inclined to Operation 'Husky,' which he suggested to me last night should be called 'Belly.' " Once again, FDR had been captivated by the Churchillian view of easy victories and open-ended operations. Once again, he chose a strategy that would keep American troops engaged, to guard himself against pressures for shifting to an all-out effort against Japan.

The British were much better at winning the conferences than they were at winning the war, and Casablanca was a total British victory. As Ian Jacob wrote, "The remarkable thing about it all was that the gradual education of the Americans to our way of thinking was found to have proceeded even farther than we had thought possible.... Our ideas had prevailed almost throughout.... We came to the Conference with more experience, with a much more complete and competent team, and having much more thoroughly thrashed out the possibilities. They came probably without any serious attempt having been made between Navy and Army to come to an agreed view. Divided, they naturally fell to our combined front."

But the price of following British strategy had eventually to be paid. For one more year, the promise of a second front was delayed. While the Allies fought six German divisions in Africa, Stalin fought 185 German divisions in Russia. His country was devastated, millions of his people were under Nazi occupation, millions more had been killed—it was a land of destroyed cities, maimed soldiers, widows, teenage boys sent to the front after a week's training, and uninterrupted slaughter that dwarfed all the other military operations of the war.

Roosevelt understood Stalin's situation, telling his son-in-law John Boettiger, who had asked why the Russians did not seem interested in discussing postwar problems: "Suppose the Germans held New England and the Atlantic seaboard and we were fighting with everything we had to drive them out. Do you suppose we would take time out to go somewhere else and talk postwar?"

The relief of the second front did not come. Brooding in the Kremlin, Stalin measured the gap between promise and reality. The Allies seemed to be deliberately letting him fight the Germans alone. They had arranged it that way, so that Russia would be bled white, while they picked easy operations with low casualties. His naturally suspicious nature had much to feed on, for he had been put off two years in a row. Soon after Casablanca, he recalled his ambassadors from Washington and London.

The delay in the second front cast a shadow over all of Stalin's subsequent dealings with the Allies. The danger of letting the Soviets do the fighting was that they would come to you at some point with a bill to be paid. The greater their contribution to the war, the more authority they would have behind their demands. The sooner the second front, the stronger the Allied position to resist Soviet claims. By letting the Soviets fight alone for three years, the Allies gave them more of a say in the postwar organization of Europe. Here, not at Yalta, was the original transaction that led to Soviet expansion in the Balkans and the beginning of the Cold War. To the victor the spoils! Stalin came into the Allied conferences with the enormous prestige of being responsible for 75 percent of German casualties.

Such was Churchill's "underbelly" strategy. The prime minister's animal comparisons changed according to the military theater. On his visit to Moscow he drew an alligator and told Stalin the belly could be attacked as well as the snout. But in the Pacific, he likened Japan to an octopus and said the place to strike was the center and not the tentacles.

While alienating his Russian ally, Churchill's strategy played right into the hands of the enemy. If Hitler had been dictating Allied strategy, he could not have asked for anything better. He could always spare small forces to hold up the English and Americans in the Mediterranean while the defenses of the Atlantic Wall were strengthened.

The British saw the war as a chance to seize bits and pieces of territory rather than take the unattractive Channel route, the only one that could establish the Allies in Europe and help Russia. Step by step, Churchill pulled the Americans into the Mediterranean vacuum, never disclosing his full intent. Marshall questioned the British plans. Was an attack on Sicily a means to an end or an end in itself? If the former, it meant that Italy would have to be invaded from the south, a longer and more arduous route.

The other consequence of Casablanca was that, despite Roosevelt's intention, troops and matériel began to be allocated to the Pacific theater on almost a fifty-fifty basis. Of the 80,000 American troops that were to have reached England in the first three months of 1943, only 15,000 arrived, in British ships. The rest, including ships and landing craft, were sent to implement MacArthur's leapfrogging strategy—instead of methodically fighting island by island (it would have taken years to reach Japan that way), some enemy strong points were bypassed to "hit them were they ain't." The bypassed garrisons were left to wither on the vine. In the Pacific, 1943 was the year of the final capture of Guadalcanal, and of the forward thrust into the central Solomons and the Gilbert and Marshall islands. The attack on Tarawa used the latest amphibious tractors and tank-loaded LCMs. It became customary to see in newspapers arrows indicating American advances into Japanese territory.

It remained at Casablanca for the Allied leaders to sort out the French imbroglio. On January 17, Roosevelt met with General Giraud, who told him dramatically that it could be observed that he wore no ribbons or decorations; he had forsworn wearing them until he could march down Unter den Linden at the head of the army that would occupy Germany. Roosevelt saw in Giraud a man of limited capacity, devoid of political astuteness—a "slender reed," he told his son Elliott, "a dud."

On January 22, he saw de Gaulle, whom Churchill had finally dragged to the conference. At this first meeting in Roosevelt's villa, his naval aide, Captain John McCrea, stood behind the door listening. He heard what FDR said, which could not have pleased the general, but de Gaulle replied so meekly that his remarks were indistinct.

"The President stated that he supposed the collaboration on the part of General Eisenhower with Admiral Darlan had been the source of some wonderment to General de Gaulle," said McCrea's report. ". . . The President alluded to the lack of power on the part of the French people at this time to assert their sovereignty. . . . It was therefore necessary to resort to the legal analogy of trusteeship. . . . In other words, the President stated that France is in the position of a little child unable to look out and fend for itself and that in such a case a court would appoint a trustee to do the necessary. . . . The President stated that following the Civil War in our home country, there was a conflict of political thought and that while many mistakes were made nevertheless the people realized that personal pride and personal prejudices must often be subordinated for the good of the country. . . ." De Gaulle swallowed the twenty-minute lecture and the insulting description of France as "a little child" without a murmur.

Two days later, in the sunny garden of Roosevelt's villa, before a swarm of photographers and correspondents, de Gaulle and Giraud shook hands and agreed on a joint statement. In fact they had agreed on nothing, and Giraud would soon disappear from contention as a French leader. Roosevelt, however, formed the impression that de Gaulle was mentally unstable. Discussing the Casablanca Conference with Felix Frankfurter, he tapped his right temple and said, "I think he is a little touched here." De Gaulle's insistence in seeing himself as the man destined to save France, in the line of Joan of Arc, struck FDR as grandiloquent nonsense bordering on megalomania. De Gaulle to him was like a man in a lunatic asylum who thinks he's

Napoleon. He had been created by Churchill, who kept him and fed him, but he claimed to speak for France. Roosevelt, who because he had immense power did not need to assert it, felt ill at ease with a man who had no power but the power of his own intransigent will. Roosevelt had might without majesty, de Gaulle majesty without might. Cordell Hull, who was rabid on the subject, reinforced Roosevelt's dislike of de Gaulle, as did Leahy, the former ambassador to Vichy France. Stimson at first disliked him too, writing on January 3, 1943, that he "gave the impression of a general who had too many press agents and was too occupied with his personal fortunes to do any fighting." De Gaulle wrote of his first meeting with the President: "Beneath his patrician mien of courtesy, Roosevelt looked at me without goodwill." He was right.

It was after the stage-managed handshake of the two French generals that FDR, during a press conference, announced the doctrine of unconditional surrender in an almost casual way: "Some of you Britishers know the old story—we had a General called U. S. Grant. His name was Ulysses Simpson Grant, but in my, and the Prime Minister's early days, he was called 'Unconditional Surrender' Grant. The elimination of German, Japanese and Italian war power means the unconditional surrender by Germany, Italy, and Japan. That means a reasonable assurance of future world peace. It does not mean the destruction of the population of Germany, Italy, or Japan, but it does mean the destruction of the philosophies in those countries which are based on conquest and the subjugation of other people."

Churchill later said in the heat of a House of Commons debate that he had not heard the term "unconditional surrender" until the president uttered the words, whereas in fact, in a report to his own war cabinet on January 20, he had proposed "the firm intention of the United States and the British Empire to continue the war relentlessly until we have brought about the 'unconditional surrender' of Germany and Japan. The omission of Italy would be to encourage a break-up there. The President liked this idea, and it would stimulate our friends in every country." The war cabinet replied that Italy should be included, and Churchill agreed. Thus the announcement of unconditional surrender was not an off-the-cuff impromptu remark, but one that had been decided in concert with Churchill.

For Roosevelt, unconditional surrender was rooted in the determination not to repeat the mistake of Woodrow Wilson, who had lost the peace at Versailles. As Breckinridge Long put it: "We are fighting this war because we did not have an unconditional surrender at the end of the last one."

In 1942, Cordell Hull had set up an Advisory Committee on Postwar Foreign Policy, which had a subcommittee on security problems chaired by Norman H. Davis, chairman of the American Red Cross and an old friend of FDR's. It was this subcommittee that came up with the idea of unconditional surrender. On May 20, Davis discussed it with the president, who adopted it.

There were two other reasons that made unconditional surrender attractive at the start of 1943. One was that it sounded good back home after the Darlan episode and the clamor that FDR was cooperating with fascists. The other was that it would reassure the Russians, whose suspicions were aroused by the delay in the second front, that there could never be a separate Anglo-American peace with the Germans.

The military later said that unconditional surrender was a mistake, that it was unduly rigid and stiffened German resistance. Eisenhower said it prolonged the war by sixty to ninety days. And yet, in Roosevelt's perspective of a lasting peace, not to repeat the escape clauses of the Fourteen Points, it had to be done. When this war was won, Roosevelt and Churchill agreed, it would stay won.

Casablanca took its toll, for Churchill (who was sixty-eight) caught pneumonia, and FDR was bedridden, writing the prime minister that "I think I picked up sleeping sickness or Gambia fever or some kindred bug in that hell-hole of yours called Bathurst. It laid me low—four days in bed—then a lot of sulphadiathole which cured the fever and left me feeling like a wet rag. I was no good after 2 P.M., and, after standing it for a week or so, I went to Hyde Park for five days; got full of health in glorious zero weather—came back here last week and have been feeling like a fighting cock ever since."

While the Casablanca Conference was on, American troops moved toward Tunisia, which was supposed to be a walkover. Marshall had predicted occupation in two or three weeks unless the Axis forces reinforced, which they did. Now a major campaign was required, involving American, British, and French troops fighting together under the command of Eisenhower, who had been given a fourth star.

Captain Harry C. Butcher, Ike's naval aide, recorded on January 27 that a German plane had dropped a note on an American airfield that said: "Why don't the Americans come out and fight?" When they did come out in their first encounter of the war against the Germans, they took a beating. Of the battle at Sidi-bou-Zid in central Tunisia on February 17, Butcher wrote: "It's the worst walloping we have taken in this fight, and perhaps the stiffest setback of our ground forces in the war." A few days later, when the Americans failed to hold Kasserine Pass, Butcher recorded that "the outstanding fact to me is that the proud and cocky Americans today stand humiliated by one of the greatest defeats in our history. This is particularly embarrassing to us with the British."

Indeed, there was a tendency among the British to sneer at the "green" American troops. When General Hugh Wilkinson, who was Churchill's liaison officer with MacArthur in Australia, was back in England that spring he met with Churchill on March 15. Pale and wan after his bout with pneumonia, Churchill said it was a good thing Eisenhower was in command, for if the poor performance of the American ground troops had taken place under a British commander there would have been hell to pay.

How, Churchill wondered, could the Americans have lost 2,000 prisoners while suffering casualties of only about 100? "There is too much of that sort of thing going on," he muttered. Another British general, Brigadier Simpson, told Wilkinson that the American performance in Tunisia had been "distinctly sticky" —in the Maknassy area, 240 Sherman tanks were held up by twenty German tanks. The present slogan in Tunisia was "How Green Was Our Ally." The Tommies were saying "Oh, well, the Germans had the Ities, so we've got the Yanks."

"Eisenhower's neck is in a noose and he knows it," Butcher wrote. But after the February reverses, the Germans began to retreat, caught in a two-sided attack between Allied forces in the west and Montgomery's Eighth Army in the east—they linked up in April. General George S. Patton took command of Second Corps, which had fought badly in February, and the Allies entered Tunis in May. The Americans were learning as they fought. It was the end of the African campaign, with Rommel defeated and 250,000 prisoners taken, half of them German. The stage was set for the invasion of Sicily.

When Stalin learned of the Casablanca decisions, he was not pleased, and cabled Churchill on March 18 that while the Anglo-Americans were twiddling their thumbs in North Africa, Germany had transferred thirty-six divisions (including six armored divisions) to the eastern front. "Now as before I see main task in hastening of second front in France," Stalin said. ". . . Uncertainty of your statements concerning contemplated Anglo-American offensive across channel arouses grave anxiety in me about which I feel I cannot be silent."

FDR somehow still believed there could be a cross-Channel invasion in 1943, telling John Boettiger on April 1: "There definitely will be an attack upon the continent before the year is out. I don't know where it will be, but it must be done." The problem was the Army, FDR said. Whenever he asked the Army, "Can you do this?" they said, "No, we're not ready yet."

In fact, the Army was diverting troops to Pacific operations. As Brooke wrote in his diary on February 25: "Am very worried by the way the Americans are failing to live up to our Casablanca agreements. They are entirely breaking down over promises of American divisions to arrive in this country." And again on April 15: "Their hearts are really in the Pacific and we are trying to run two wars at once, which is quite impossible with our limited resources in shipping."

In order to put a stop to the slippage toward the Pacific, and to reveal to Roosevelt the next step in the Mediterranean campaign—the invasion of Italy—Churchill called for yet another summit conference, this one in Washington, to be called "Trident." Because of his recent bout with pneumonia, air travel was out, and he arrived on May 11 aboard the *Queen Mary*, which was also carrying several thousand German POWs.

This time the Americans were ready. They would not let the British stampede them as they had at Casablanca. Marshall obtained a promise from Roosevelt not to waver from the cross-Channel policy. Still, Stimson worried that "it will be the same story over again. The man from London will arrive with a program of further expansion in the eastern Mediterranean and will have his way with our chief, and the careful and deliberate plans of our staff will be overridden."

The British noticed the change at the first meeting on May 12. When Churchill (who was staying at the British embassy rather than the White House, as if to underline the divergent positions) argued for moving on to Italy and the Balkans, FDR sharply disagreed—the continuing drain of the occupation of Italy would prejudice the buildup for cross-Channel, and though there now seemed no chance in 1943, it would have to be done in the spring of '44. The only sure way to force Germany to fight and help Russia was by striking at once through France.

The British were dismayed. Their views were not prevailing as they had at Casablanca. They saw how much more interested American public opinion was in the Pacific war. It was "lick the Japs first and let Hitler wait." They would have to compromise with the Americans or risk an all-out American war against Japan. Brooke was depressed. The Americans were also urging a land war in Burma, to open up the Burma road and keep China supplied, which, as Churchill told Brooke, was "like munching a porcupine quill by quill."

All was "a tangled mass of confusion," Brooke recorded on May 14 after a meeting with FDR in his study. Brooke was distracted by the "queer collection" of objects on the president's desk, which he tried to memorize: blue bronze lamp, two frames, bronze bust of Mrs. R., bronze ship's-steering-wheel clock, four cloth toy donkeys, one tin toy motorcar, one small donkey made of two hazel nuts, jug of iced water, pile of books, large circular match stand and inkpot ... that was all he could remember, though there were many other items.

By May 17, Stimson saw a deadlock. The British were "holding back dead" from the cross-Channel invasion and the Burma operation "and are trying to divert us off into some more Mediterranean adventures. Fortunately, the President seems to be holding out. FDR told me he was coming to the conclusion that he would have to read the Riot Act to the other side and would have to be stiff."

Trident was the turning point in the Grand Alliance, when Roosevelt stopped rubber-stamping Churchill's strategic views and started backing the strategy of his own military chiefs. Stimson said the British reminded him of what Lincoln had said about one of his generals—that although he couldn't skin the deer he could at least hold the leg. They were trying to arrange the matter so that Britain and America held the leg while Stalin skinned the deer, "and I think that will be a dangerous business for us at the end of the war. Stalin won't have much of an opinion of people who have done that and we will not be able to share much of the postwar world with them."

Prophetic words, but in the meetings of the Combined Chiefs of Staff the deadlock did not break. As they walked together on the way to one meeting,

Marshall told Brooke: "I find it hard even now not to look on your North African strategy with a jaundiced eye." "What strategy would you have preferred?" Brooke asked. "Cross-Channel operations for the liberation of France and advance on Germany," Marshall replied. "We would finish the war quicker." "Yes," Brooke rejoined, "but not the way we hope to finish it," meaning with low British casualties and after waiting for Russia to exhaust the Germans.

The strain was telling on Marshall. It was charged in a Senate debate that the military secretly wanted to give priority to the Pacific theater. His self-control cracking, Marshall blew up, telling Stimson: "This is a personal attack on me. They are trying to destroy my character and reputation."

May 19 was the day of reckoning, when the British agreed to garrison twenty-nine divisions for an invasion of France in May 1944, to be called "Overlord." At the same time, the invasion of Sicily would proceed, followed by an operation "best calculated to eliminate Italy from the war and to contain the maximum number of German forces."

This was not the explicit assurance of an invasion of Italy that Churchill wanted, and he continued to press his case. On May 24, in solitary debate with the president, Stimson reported, "the Prime Minister was as obstinate as a little Dutchman and fought to the end and finally said, 'Well, I will give up my part of this if you will let me have George Marshall to go for a trip to Africa.'" Weary of harangues, FDR agreed. Marshall complained that he was being traded like a piece of luggage. Stimson was sure that Churchill wanted to work on Marshall and convert him to the Italian invasion.

FDR had finally learned to resist Churchill. Stimson reported that even on the morning of his departure, May 26, "Churchill had acted like a spoiled boy when he refused to give up one of the points . . . that was in issue. He persisted and persisted until Roosevelt told him that he wasn't interested in the matter and that he had better shut up. I am very glad that for once the President did stand up to him in the way that he ought to be stood up to."

Trident was a three-week ordeal, a marathon, but it cleared the air. At last, the British had been pinned down to a date for the cross-Channel operation.

It was Franklin D. Roosevelt's destiny to preside over two bloodless revolutions in the United States, one caused by the depression and the other by World War II. War was as powerful an agent of domestic social change as the depression. It transformed the country in deep and lasting ways, in some ways weakening the cause of reform, in others strengthening the hand of government, and in yet others helping disadvantaged groups.

As a wartime president, Roosevelt was able to govern almost without restraint from Congress. It was the "magic wand" theory of government, a broad delegation of powers through the War Powers Act and executive orders.

The Lend-Lease statute was a good example: it allowed the president to "sell, transfer title to, exchange, lease, lend, or otherwise dispose of any defense articles." Congress had in effect abdicated its right to "regulate land and naval forces." It was, as Benjamin Cardozo had said of the NRA, "delegation run riot."

The Second War Powers Act gave the president the right to designate a theater of military operations. This was the device used to ban the Japanese from the West Coast, which was designated a military area. It was a limited example of martial law. The Constitution was set aside for the duration. Mr. New Deal, as Roosevelt himself put it, was replaced by Dr. Win the War.

If Roosevelt wanted to create a new agency, he simply wrote an executive order. It was alarmingly casual. The OSS was created in June 1941 on the basis of a five-page outline from William J. Donovan, on which the president scribbled for the then acting director of the budget, Jack Blandford, "Jack, get together with Bill Donovan and fix this up." The executive order had to be couched in general terms, "to coordinate information of interest to the government"—you could not say you were creating an agency to spy on foreign countries. The Army and the Navy, who knew a poacher when they saw one, fought Donovan down to the wire. At first he was coordinator of information, and only a year later did his agency become the Office of Strategic Services.

The OSS collected millions of dollars in unvouchered money, accountable to no one but the president. Donovan went to FDR, who went to the budget director and asked him to cough up another $5 million. The OSS wasn't even under the authority of the Joint Chiefs of Staff. The military took a jaundiced view of OSS operations, particularly after June 1943, when OSS agents burgled the Japanese consulate in Lisbon and copied the code books. The Japanese discovered the burglary, which compromised Magic. Major General George V. Strong of G-2 wrote Marshall on July 6, 1943: "It appears obvious that the ill-advised and amateurish efforts of OSS representatives in Lisbon have so alarmed the Japanese that it is an even money bet that the codes . . . are in imminent danger of being changed."

The war fostered the notion that there were matters the government was not accountable for, either to Congress or to the public. Habits of secrecy, alien to an open society, were formed. When Harry S. Truman, a Missouri senator who had been rebuffed trying to get defense contracts for small businessmen in his state, formed the Senate Special Committee to Investigate the Defense Program, he insisted on finding out about the supersecret S-1 (atom bomb) project. Stimson wrote on March 13, 1944, that Truman "threatened me with dire consequences. I told him I had to accept the responsibility for those consequences because I had been directed by the President to do just what I did do. Truman is a nuisance and a pretty untrustworthy man. He talks smoothly, but acts meanly."

Actually, Truman's committee was fearless and efficient in exposing corruption and collusion in defense industries. It seemed that Congress, while relinquishing its legislative functions, had made up for it by expanding its investigative functions. Truman's committee was one example, and Martin Dies's committee, which periodically announced that it had discovered Communists in government, was another.

It was also in secrecy and under martial law that eight German saboteurs were convicted in July 1942, on the grounds that they had violated their status as combatants. Tried before a commission of seven officers, they were sentenced on August 3 and within a week six of the eight had been executed. This was close to a kangaroo court, but as a wartime measure it was given the sanction of the attorney general and the Supreme Court.

Decisions that profoundly affected millions of Americans were made by executive order. On December 5, 1942, Executive Order 9279 transferred Selective Service from the War Department to the War Manpower Commission, a new agency headed by former governor of Indiana Paul McNutt, who issued a "work or fight" order—workers had to choose between the draft and transfer to jobs in industries with manpower shortages. It was a denial of the right to work where you wanted, the same kind of labor draft they had in Germany. Of course, the blow was softened by exemptions—for farm workers and fathers, among others.

Wartime government imposed restrictions on both business and labor. The Office of Price Administration turned over the names of more than 3,000 firms that were violating price ceilings to the IRS for audit. The War Labor Board, set up to arbitrate labor disputes, enforced sanctions on businesses as well as unions. When the giant mail-order house of Montgomery Ward refused to allow a union shop, the U.S. Post Office removed the seventy employees it had kept for thirty years on the premises to handle parcelpost shipments to customers. But when 16,000 rubber workers in Akron refused to end a two-week-old strike, they were warned that the Goodyear Company might be released from its obligation to maintain a union shop.

The no-strike pledge of the war's early days was broken because of labor discontent over wage ceilings. In 1943, there were strikes all over the country, from San Francisco shipyards where the machinists walked out to Chrysler employees in Michigan and coal miners in Pennsylvania. John L. Lewis was continuing his feud with FDR, who tried to nail him on tax evasion, but the evidence was thin. As Attorney General Biddle put it, "When you shoot at a king you have to hit him."

Roosevelt wondered what to do. It was a fact that coal could not be mined without the cooperation of 400,000 miners. It was another fact that there had to be coal to make steel, the basic material of national defense. "There are not enough jails in the country to hold these men," Ickes told the president, "and if there were, I must point out that a jailed miner produces no more coal than a striking miner."

Congress lent a hand with the first bill ever passed to curb the activities of trade unions. The Smith-Connally Act gave the president the power to seize plants useful in the war and to act against strikers. Roosevelt vetoed it because it also outlawed union contributions to political campaigns, but the veto was overridden. In this manner he obtained the necessary power to curb Lewis while avoiding the stigma of being antilabor. And yet, even with the Smith-Connally Act, the coal problem was not solved, and miners continued to walk out periodically, even when faced with the threat of losing their draft deferment.

Just as antitrust legislation had once been used against unions, the Smith-Connally Act was used against big business. Montgomery Ward, with 78,-000 employees, and 600 stores in forty-seven states, refused to agree to dues checkoffs and a union shop. In December 1944, FDR ordered the Army to take over the company, in spite of Stimson's objections that Montgomery Ward had nothing to do with the war effort—it stored, sold, and distributed civilian goods. Thus was the power of the federal government affirmed against a business that in fact had prospered during the Roosevelt years, with the revival of purchasing power among the farmers who were its principal customers.

The war also made deficit spending a habit, the government spending nearly twice as much from 1941 to 1945 as it had spent in the previous 150 years. This too was justified as an emergency measure but would become the norm in postwar years. To help pay for the war, the tax structure was changed to include millions of new taxpayers from the middle and lower middle class. Withholding, now taken for granted by every salaried American, was introduced in the 1943 Revenue Act.

The war weakened the cause of reform and liberalism by creating a new set of priorities. Many New Deal measures, such as Social Security and collective bargaining, were too much a part of the social fabric to be touched, but others had either outworn their usefulness or were casualties of the war effort. Rural electrification was cut back because of the military's demands for copper. The manpower shortage made employers ignore child labor laws, and there were millions of teenage workers and high-school dropouts. As Harry Hopkins put it, why get a degree when you could help beat Hitler?

After the 1942 congressional elections, the anti-Roosevelt coalition put riders on appropriations bills (to get around a veto) to kill the National Youth Administration and the Home Owners Loan Corporation. The CCC was terminated, its enrollment having fallen to 100,000, with most able-bodied young men joining the services. With full employment, a work relief program was no longer needed, and the WPA was given an "honorable discharge" in April 1943, when the last relief check was mailed.

In some cases, the remaining New Deal agencies were handed distasteful assignments. The Farm Security Administration supervised the West Coast agricultural property of the relocated Japanese. In the camps, work projects were set up by former WPA employees.

Nowhere was the change from Mr. New Deal to Dr. Win the War so plain as in the government's antitrust policy. At the start of the war, the Justice Department's antitrust chief, Thurman Arnold, was going full throttle, the appropriations for his division having risen from $413,000 in 1938 to $2.3 million in 1942. Arnold merrily continued his pending cases against Standard Oil of New Jersey (which had agreed to stay out of the synthetic rubber market in collusion with I.G. Farben of Germany) and Du Pont (which had pooled patents and restricted competition with American Lead).

These were companies with large defense contracts. Stimson, who thought of Thurman Arnold as "a self-seeking fanatic," could not get the attorney general to call him off, and appealed to FDR on March 4, 1942, writing that the prosecution of antitrust suits was "delaying and confusing the war effort." Stimson had begged Mr. du Pont to go back into the explosives business, and he agreed and built new powder plants at a cost of many millions. Just at that critical moment, Thurman Arnold began to prosecute the entire group of explosives makers. "Mr. Hitler himself could hardly have chosen a surer way to embarrass our munitions makers today," Stimson wrote. "Such a clash between the functions of one department of our government against the defense activities of another in such a crisis as confronts us ought to be susceptible to a remedy."

Indeed it was, and FDR replied on March 20: "If it is true that any substantial slowing up of war production is being occasioned by anti-trust suits, prosecutions or court investigations, then the war effort must come first and everything else must wait. For unless that effort is successful, the anti-trust laws, as indeed all American institutions, will become quite academic."

Thurman Arnold was kicked upstairs to the court of appeals, and antitrust suits were for the time being deferred. But in 1944, with the onset of his fourth presidential campaign, Roosevelt's attitude changed. The Justice Department, under Arnold's successor, Wendell Berge, reopened its suit against Du Pont and the British munitions maker Imperial Chemical.

Stimson was frantic, for by that time Du Pont had built and was operating the uranium separation plant in Oak Ridge, Tennessee. It would be disastrous to distract the key Du Pont executives who were handling our most secret and important project by asking them to defend themselves in an antitrust suit, Stimson wrote FDR on May 22, 1944. Obviously, the attorney general was moving ahead because he had not been informed about the atom bomb project, a closely held secret. The project was on the verge of completion and might be delayed by antitrust people nosing around in the Du Pont files.

But FDR was more interested in the vote-getting potential of antitrust prosecution, and wrote Biddle on August 14: "You are authorized to proceed. . . . Further delay should not occur in the interest of justice and the enforcement of law." Here was another example where political and military needs did not jibe, and the president chose the former. Biddle successfully prosecuted the Du Pont case, while Stimson's fears of delay proved to be unfounded.

Another result of the war was the rehabilitation of the businessman, who had been the villain of the New Deal. The champions of laissez-faire had been in the enemy camp for years. Some had gone to jail, like Richard Whitney, while others, like Henry Ford, had spurned the Blue Eagle and fought the unions with gangs of hired thugs. Now the economic royalists were in demand, for the war was won by the will, the know-how, and the productive capacity of American industry.

Gone were the brain trusters and "campus experts"—Rexford Tugwell had been put out to pasture as governor of Puerto Rico, and Adolf Berle was named ambassador to Brazil in 1944. The new men were businessmen, and the new acronyms were the war agencies they headed, which changed with dizzying speed, for war work in Washington chewed up men faster than the battlefield.

William S. Knudsen of General Motors headed the OPM (Office of Production Management) with labor leader Sidney Hillman. Knudsen brought in other businessmen, such as Jack Biggers, president of the Libby-Owens-Ford company, and Bill Harrison, head of AT&T. When FDR observed that all of Knudsen's men were Republicans, the self-made Scandinavian immigrant replied: "Mr. President, in the field of big business like we are doing, in the war effort, all the executives are Republican—like the men we want." On the next list there was a Democrat, and when FDR told Knudsen he must have made a mistake, he replied: "No, Mr. President, I didn't make no mistake, he is a Democrat but he voted for Villkie."

The OPM gave way to the SPAB (Supply, Priorities, and Allocation Board), which was replaced by the WPB (War Production Board) under Donald Nelson, a Sears, Roebuck vice president. These men were not elected, not in the cabinet, not subject to congressional approval, but they held substantial power.

They turned the country around to a war economy, and brought industrial production in line with military needs. In what other country could a pickle plant have become a pontoon maker, while a firm that made kitchen sinks switched to cartridge casings? Of course the government gave the businessmen sweet deals. They could borrow the money to build their plants and were guaranteed a profit under the cost-plus contracts. The Army and Navy ordnance people ordered the goods from those who could deliver fastest. They didn't want strikes or delays, and they didn't care if the companies loaded up on overtime rather than hire the unemployed, or whether they complied with the new regulations for the hiring of blacks.

When the small businessmen complained that the big boys like General Electric and Du Pont were hogging the defense work, another executive order created the Division of Contract Distribution under the rising millionaire Floyd B. Odlum, so that the little machine shop in Indiana could actually get a defense contract. Odlum leased a couple of trains from the B&O for three months, had them painted red, white, and blue, and routed them around the country filled with a traveling exhibit of small parts necessary for the war effort—nuts and bolts, fuses, compressors. But that didn't do the job, and FDR replaced him with the Smaller War Plants Corporation.

In spite of the head rolling and the constant changes, the wartime production effort worked so well that in 1943 there was a glut. The United States had overproduced Sherman tanks, but after these splendid plants had been built and these thousands of men had been given jobs it was embarrassing politically for FDR to have to shut them down. The British had to be asked to cut down their own production so they could take more American tanks. The Russians did not want them, and there was no other way to unload them. FDR appealed to Churchill to accept 8,300 American tanks in 1943.

The businessman was enshrined as hero when Roosevelt, in September 1942, visited the airplane plant of his archfoe, Henry Ford, in Willow Run, Michigan, as once he had visited such triumphs of the New Deal as TVA. Ford had finally been unionized, and the Air Force had loaned him $200 million to build a bomber plant. The genius of mass production had promised to build 100 planes a day.

The main aisle of the plant was wide enough so that the president, riding in a car, could follow the operations from start to finish. And so it happened that Roosevelt, sitting beside Henry Ford, symbolizing the new alliance between big business and big government that spawned the military-industrial complex, saw the whole miraculous process—the aluminum sheets unloaded from freight cars, the sheets shaped by giant hydraulic presses, the big pieces of stamped metal placed on conveyor belts and moved to the different assembly units, and, at the other end, the finished plane. There was nothing like it in the world.

Roosevelt enjoyed himself immensely, and kept up an uninterrupted monologue, but Ford did not enter into the spirit of the event. He was morose and uncommunicative, being at that time in near dotage, old and worn and paranoid, suspicious of the Air Force officers stationed at the plant, and so obsessed that a government agent would attack him that he made his chauffeur carry a gun. And yet the plant, which produced 8,685 B-24s, was a triumph. As Randolph Churchill said after a visit: "If Hitler could see Willow Run, he'd cut his throat right now."

By the end of 1944, nearly 2 million blacks were employed in munitions and defense industries. This was due more to the manpower shortage than to the Fair Employment Practices Act. But either way, it broke down the time-honored bar to the employment of blacks as skilled workers. The war was a time of considerable advance for blacks. It gave the civil rights movement an urgency and legitimacy it had not had before. Now it was not "we are being mistreated" but "we are fighting too." The black leaders could demand rather than plead.

Roosevelt's position was to support the cause of racial justice whenever it helped the conduct of the war. Thus he prodded Frank Knox to recruit more blacks in the Navy, writing him on January 19, 1942: "I think that with all the Navy activities, the Bureau of Navigation might invent something that colored citizens could do in addition to the rating of messmen." In April, the Navy authorized for the first time the enlistment of blacks for general service, but not aboard ships, where a ban continued on mixed crews. After James V. Forrestal succeeded Knox in 1944, however, the Navy integrated the crews of twenty-five ships.

In the Army, the cause of black combat units suffered a setback when, in the Italian campaign, the Ninety-second Division, made up of black enlisted men and black and white officers, dissolved during a three-day German offensive, abandoning its equipment and even its clothing. But in 1944, by which time 1 million blacks were serving in the Army, the idea of attaching small black groups to white units was accepted under the pressure of battle losses, and 2,500 blacks fought in the Battle of the Bulge.

On the home front, James Landis, the director of civilian defense, insisted on black representation on civil defense councils, and fought the political forces of southern cities to obtain it—after all, he argued, bombs would not discriminate between the races.

In April 1944, the Supreme Court ruled that the white primary, which excluded blacks from the vote in eight southern states, was unconstitutional. By 1946, 75,000 blacks were voting in Texas primaries, and Texas congressmen were shaking hands at black church picnics.

In April 1943, a group of black students from Howard University picketed Thompson's, a segregated restaurant with a convenient location for black government workers. As pickets outside carried signs that said "We Die Together, Let's Eat Together," three of the demonstrators sat down and were refused service; joined by black servicemen, they were eventually served.

Thus did the war create conditions under which the civil rights movement could make important gains. The ideology of racism was discredited by the information that had begun to come out of the Nazi death camps. It was all too apparent that racist theories, including those of white supremacy, led not only to the lyncher's noose but to the gas chamber.

The war was good to big business, big labor, and big government. It was also good to blacks and to women, who joined the work force in large numbers to take jobs previously held by men—Rosie the Riveter became part of the home-front lore. The war was good to most Americans in a time of prosperity and full employment. After the war, 65 percent of those questioned in a poll said that the war years had not been a time of hardship. Indeed, it was a time of elation, with the country unified in a just cause and in the inconvenience of rationing. A common enemy of undisputed villainy did wonders for morale, and as a civic reminder: "Hitler smiles when you waste miles." For a time, it was not only America the Beautiful but America the Just. We were the good guys, fighting to save the world from fascism, and seeking no territorial gain. Much of the self-righteousness of the '50s, and right on to the Vietnam War, where once again we had only come to help, was left over from the moral certainty of World War II.

It's generally accepted that the Roosevelt administration, the longest in the nation's history, was without scandal. In fact, there were several scandals, which, because they did not involve presidential misconduct, were not stains on Roosevelt's reputation as Teapot Dome and Watergate stained Harding and Nixon but which nevertheless shook up the administration.

In July 1943, the Army's inspector general was ordered to investigate Army intelligence activities in the service commands, and particularly the activities of the Counter-Intelligence Corps, which had the mission of investigating subversion, treason, sabotage, and espionage among the military. Military Intelligence, or G-2, was informed that the CIC must be drastically reduced because it had incurred the displeasure of the president. By the time the inspector general's report was submitted to the deputy chief of staff, Lieutenant General Joseph McNarney, on January 1, 1944, there remained 963 agents in the CIC. These were merged with about 900 provost marshals into a new unit called the Security and Intelligence Corps (SIC). February 4, 1944, was set as the day when all CIC offices would close and all CIC functions would cease. For more than two years the CIC did not exist. Only in May 1946 was it authorized again as a separate unit by President Truman.

What had happened to cause the complete dismantling of an important branch of Military Intelligence? The story begins with the friendship formed between Eleanor Roosevelt and Joseph P. Lash, a leader of the American Youth Congress. They met in November 1939, when Eleanor attended a Dies Committee hearing at which Youth Congress leaders, including Lash, testified. Lash was an intense young man with strong antifascist views who had briefly gone to Spain during the civil war, at a time when it seemed to be mainly the Communists who were fighting fascism. He was never a Communist party member, though he was close to the party until the signing of the Nazi-Soviet pact.

Lash was Eleanor's link to the younger generation and its politics. She took him under her wing, as she was apt to do with those she became fond of, lending him money, writing letters of recommendation on his behalf, and becoming involved in his personal life. When Lash fell in love with a married woman named Trude Pratt, Eleanor gave comfort and advice to the lovelorn.

In 1942, she tried to help Lash get into the Navy, which objected to his radical past. On January 9, she asked Attorney General Francis Biddle "to run down for me . . . what they really have on Joe Lash. . . . I am concerned not to see him unjustly treated." But the first lady's intercession did no good, and the Navy turned Lash down.

Eleanor told Lash that since he was thirty-two he might as well remain a civilian, but he was drafted in the Army in April 1942, and in January 1943 he was sent to the Air Force training center at Chanute Field in central Illinois to take the weather observer's course.

The head of Counter-Intelligence at Chanute was a colonel named P. F. Boyer, whose judgment did not match his zeal and who saw in Lash a suitable subject for investigation because of his suspected Communist affiliations. A "mail cover" was placed on him. His foot locker was searched. When he left the base, he was shadowed by CIC agents.

The mail cover revealed that Lash was in correspondence with the first lady, who wrote long and affectionate letters to "dearest Joe" that were signed "all my love, E.R.," discussing not only his turbulent love affair with Trude Pratt but also political events in Washington.

Eleanor had been promising to visit Lash, and arrived on the morning of March 5, 1943, in Urbana, the nearest city to the Chanute air base, with her secretary, Malvina Thompson. They checked into the Hotel Lincoln, taking a room with twin beds and an adjacent room for Lash, who had a weekend pass. Lash arrived in the evening, not realizing he was being tailed.

The CIC agent's report, filed March 7, said that when Lash arrived he was directed to room 330. Mrs. Roosevelt ordered dinner for three sent to her room, 332. The next day, March 6, Mrs. Roosevelt and Lash remained in their rooms, except for lunch in the hotel dining room. Mrs. Roosevelt checked out on the morning of March 7, paying all the bills.

The following weekend, March 12, Lash again went to the Hotel Lincoln, this time to see Trude Pratt, who was planning to leave her husband and marry him. He took a separate room, but spent most of his three-day stay in Mrs. Pratt's room, which the CIC had bugged. According to the March 16 surveillance report, "Subject and Mrs. Pratt appeared to be greatly endeared to each other and engaged in sexual intercourse a number of times during the course of their stay at the Urbana Lincoln Hotel."

Colonel Boyer had planned to arrest Lash at the hotel on a morals charge, but decided to wait until Mrs. Pratt's next visit, at which time the Urbana police could make the arrest. General R. E. O'Neil, the commander at Chanute, was anxious to have Lash removed from the field, and a morals charge would provide grounds for disciplinary action. "Also," as Colonel Boyer wrote his superior in Washington, Colonel John Bissell, chief of Counter-Intelligence Group, G-2, on March 17, "it might be thought advisable to give the arrest sufficient publicity so that E.R. would not care to intervene in the matter."

Boyer was mightily pleased with himself. His investigation of Lash had netted a big fish—the first lady herself. Eagerly hunting for subversion, he saw in the letters from and meeting with Eleanor proof of a far-reaching plot. Passing on to Colonel Bissell the results of his mail cover and surveillance, on March 17, he commented that "the inferences which can be drawn from the evidence of these five enclosures is staggering. They indicate a gigantic conspiracy participated in by not only Subject and Trude Pratt but also E.R., Wallace, Morgenthau, etc." It seemed significant to Colonel Boyer that Mrs. Pratt was actively involved with student organizations—she was executive secretary of the International Student Assembly and general secretary of the International Student Service.

That March, Lash was waiting for a transfer to an Air Force weather forecasting school in Grand Rapids, Michigan. Late in March, however, another opportunity for a meeting with Eleanor arose—she would be passing through Chicago with her secretary, Malvina Thompson, en route to Minneapolis and Seattle. Lash joined her in Chicago at the Hotel Blackstone, and this time the CIC bugged her room.

The, had dinner together, and after dinner Lash was drowsy, and Eleanor stroked his forehead. "I loved just sitting near you while you slept," she later wrote him. The next morning, Eleanor was tipped off by a hotel employee that her room had been bugged by Army agents. She informed Harry Hopkins, who protested to his good friend George Marshall, who took it up with his intelligence people.

At this point, FDR learned that his wife had been placed under electronic surveillance without presidential authority. He knew there were anti-Roosevelt groups in the Army, and right-wing groups who believed that Eleanor and cabinet members such as Wallace were part of a Communist conspiracy, and he must have wondered if this was an attempt to discredit him by going after his wife. In any case, it was improper for the CIC to be carrying out a surveillance of the first lady that was not authorized by the White House.

This was what led to the dismantling of the CIC and to the destruction of CIC files on subversives, so that no mention of the first lady would remain. Presidential disfavor focused on CIC group chief Bissell, who was relieved of his duties and who was told by friends in the War Department that he had been blackballed by the White House and would never be promoted to brigadier general. Colonel Bissell was deeply embittered at the way he had been treated—he was sure his career was ruined.

As for Lash, he arrived in Grand Rapids in early April to take his course at the weather school, only to receive orders on April 21, 1943, for overseas duty. He left for New Caledonia with a group of weather forecasters, feeling that he was the object of special attention, part of the fallout from the president's wrath. As the law of the ocean has it, when a whale becomes agitated, the shrimp are tossed about.

The matter did not end there, for in December 1943 an FBI agent named George C. Burton, who was acting as liaison with G-2, provided, in a memorandum, some rather startling additional information concerning the Lash/first lady surveillance.

At a G-2 social function, Burton reported on December 31, he had a long talk with Colonel Kibler, the head of CIC. Kibler said that "the reason Counter-Intelligence Corps had been wrecked was that Harry Hopkins and the Secret Service had ordered it to be so wrecked. . . . [T]hrough some unknown means Harry Hopkins had learned that the Counter-Intelligence Corps was investigating Joe Lash, former Young Communist leader who is now in the Army, and that in this investigation they had run upon Mrs. Roosevelt who had come to Chicago apparently for the purpose of meeting Lash."

Burton next sought out Colonel Bissell at his home in Washington. Bissell confirmed that he had been told he would never advance any further in the Army and would never be given overseas duty because he had been connected with the Lash/first lady investigation in Chicago.

Bissell then told Burton what he claimed to have heard from his successor, Colonel Forney. Shortly after Forney had taken over, that is to say in April, General George V. Strong, head of G-2, received a call to proceed to the White House with Colonel Forney and the complete records of the Lash/first lady investigation. When they reached the White House, at about 10:00 P.M., they were received by the president, Pa Watson, and Harry Hopkins, and were ordered to produce the entire record of the investigation.

Colonel Forney was highly embarrassed, Bissell told Burton, because the record included a recording of what had transpired between Lash and Mrs. Roosevelt in the hotel room, which had been obtained through planting a microphone in the room, and this recording "indicated quite clearly that Mrs. Roosevelt and Lash engaged in sexual intercourse during their stay in the hotel room."

Still according to Bissell, Colonel Forney stated that after the hotel room recording was played, Mrs. Roosevelt was called into the conference and was confronted with the information, "and this resulted in a terrific fight between the President and Mrs. Roosevelt."

At about 5:00 the next morning, Forney told Bissell, FDR summoned Hap Arnold and ordered him to send Lash on his way to a combat post within ten hours.

It was later learned, Bissell told Burton, "that the President had ordered that anybody who knew anything about this case should be immediately relieved of his duties and sent to the South Pacific for action against the Japs until they were killed. . . . Bissell stated that the only thing that kept these men from being sent to the South Pacific was that it was learned that there were too many of them to be treated in this manner. Col. Bissell stated that the only reason that more was not done to him was that General Watson apparently came to his defense and assured the President that Bissell would not talk about this matter indiscriminately."

Such was the content of FBI agent George Burton's explosive memo, which only came to light years later when it was found in J. Edgar Hoover's confidential file. Much of it is hard to believe, and based on the account of an officer who was admittedly rancorous for the harm done to his career. That Roosevelt, who disliked confrontations, would have summoned his wife and had a "terrific fight" with her in front of four witnesses was completely out of character. That he would have ordered servicemen to be sent to the South Pacific "until they were killed" was not a way the president, with his love of the understated and subtle phrase, would ever have expressed himself.

That the fifty-eight-year-old Eleanor Roosevelt could have had a sexual liaison with the thirty-three-year-old Joseph Lash was equally improbable.

Mrs. Roosevelt had passionate friendships, and expressed herself in loving terms, but according to her own children she was not interested in the physical side of love. That she should have conducted an affair with Mr. Lash, whom she knew to be in love with Trude Pratt, while befriending them both, was wholly out of keeping with her strict moral standards.

In January 1951, in response to various inquiries, the FBI searched its files for material on the Lash/first lady investigation. It found photostats of the CIC records, and it found the Burton memo, but according to a memorandum for J. Edgar Hoover dated January 18, "there were no recordings in the Bureau files between Mrs. Roosevelt and Lash. Obviously, they [the CIC] did have a microphone because there were recordings of conversations between Lash and Mrs. Trudie [sic] W. Pratt which also reflected what transpired in the hotel room."

The possibility arises that Colonel Forney, in his account, mistook the recording of Lash with Mrs. Pratt for a recording of Lash with Mrs. Roosevelt. Surely, however, if such a recording had been played to the president, he would have recognized at once that the voice was not his wife's.

What remains of this rather seamy incident is that the CIC, in its ardor to catch Mr. Lash, went far beyond its authority in its surveillance of the first lady, and made wild and unsubstantiated charges. The president, with understandable fury at having his wife spied on, terminated the unit and sent Lash overseas.

The incident does display, however, a certain lack of judgment on the part of Mrs. Roosevelt. In her position, one may ask, under constant scrutiny, was it wise to spend weekends in hotels in adjoining rooms with a young serviceman? Her supposedly incognito trips to Illinois remind one of the novel where the pope ventures into the streets of Rome in disguise, escaping the restraints of the Vatican, to talk to simple folk.

Repeatedly, Mrs. Roosevelt found herself in embarrassing situations because she did not exercise sufficient caution. She was trusting, gullible, a soft touch. Thus, from 1941 to 1944, she acted as a conduit between Communist leader Earl Browder and FDR. In this case, she was taken in by a crackpot named Josephine Truslow Adams, a Communist whom the party puffed up because she was a direct descendant of John Adams. Miss Adams convinced Browder that she had a pipeline into the White House, repeating to him in detail accounts of meetings with the president that had never taken place.

Eleanor forwarded her letters to FDR, writing her on one occasion: "I think you should know that your letters go directly to the President. What then happens I do not know." Another time, taking at face value one of Miss Adams's picaresque accounts, Eleanor wrote: "I think you are very brave, but I do hope you will do nothing that will endanger you."

In her quest for self-aggrandizement, Miss Adams passed on to her Communist friends remarks that Mrs. Roosevelt supposedly made. Some of these remarks concerned J. Edgar Hoover, and an FBI agent who had infiltrated the party reported them to his boss, further envenoming the already difficult association between the head of the FBI and the first lady.

"Now you see what a bastard Hoover is," Mrs. Roosevelt was reported as saying. "That's how he covers up his fascist attitude. Pretty smug, isn't he?" "You should have seen Franklin," she was also quoted as saying. "He hit the ceiling. He said this was just another proof of the duplicity of that smug would-be Himmler." All of this was a product of Miss Adams's fertile imagination, though to Hoover it may have seemed all too plausible. Eleanor had in January 1941 been angered by an FBI investigation of her secretary, Edith B. Helm, and had written Hoover on January 26 that his efforts "seem to me to smack too much of Gestapo methods."

Eleanor made her position on Communism clear to Miss Adams in a letter dated November 18, 1943, explaining that "I do not like American Communists because they have caused a great deal of trouble here and did all they could to hamper us before Germany went into Russia. Now that it suits their purpose they cooperate. I am all for helping Russia defeat Hitler but nevertheless I do not want American Communists working here against the good of our country at any time."

The Adams connection may have helped Browder, who had in March 1941 started serving a four-year prison sentence for using a passport obtained by a false statement. FDR commuted his sentence in May 1942, wanting to dispel the feeling, at a time when Russia was America's ally, that the unusually long sentence for that offense had been imposed because of his political views.

In December 1943, the Board of Immigration affirmed a deportation order for Browder's Russian-born wife, Mrs. Raissa Berkman Browder, because she had entered the country illegally from Canada in 1933. Once again FDR intervened, writing Attorney General Biddle on January 14, 1944: "I think this Mrs. Browder business is getting into the silly stage. Of course her husband was an American Communist who was for many years very much under the thumb of the Comintern. Of course his wife was in exactly the same position. She was a Russian. That is true. But her husband is an American and they have three children born in this country.... Common sense can, in my judgment, lead to only one conclusion."

Common sense did, and with a little Rooseveltian sleight of hand, Mrs. Browder was deported to Canada, where she was promptly handed a reentry visa for the United States. According to Cordell Hull, FDR wanted it that way so he would not be embarrassed when he met Stalin at the next Big Three conference.

Eleanor forwarded ideas to FDR with a disturbing lack of discernment. In August 1942 she passed on this suggestion from a man in California: "Suppose we collected as many hornets, bees and wasps as we possibly could get. Keep them in their hives and put them in a plane. Have the plane fly as low as possible and drop them on the enemy's lines. I think they will retreat in utter confusion."

FDR was fond of offbeat ideas, and had actually transmitted to OSS chief Bill Donovan a suggestion for using bats in surprise attacks on the Japanese with a note saying "this man is *not* a nut. It sounds like a perfectly wild idea but is worth you looking into." But the insect attack was too wacky even for him, and he replied to Eleanor: "I have heard of bees in his bonnet."

Eleanor saw her role as bringing to the president's attention matters he might otherwise ignore. The railroads had reduced fares for men in uniform but nothing had been done by the bus companies. Could any pressure be brought to bear? The Navy was asking seamen whether they were in favor of Loyalist Spain, and if they answered "yes" they were taken off the ships. What to do? Melvyn Douglas could not get the military assignment he wanted because of his supposed Communist association. Could the president help? A Mr. Tripp had an idea for the camouflage of ships and of entire cities. It was so simple it was incredible no one had thought of it. Would the Navy see him?

Each day her memos piled up on the president's desk, many of them useful. But sometimes FDR was irritated by her constant prodding. One day she wanted something done about the segregated toilets in the Atlanta post office. As if Roosevelt didn't have enough to do, he had to worry about the Georgia toilets. He wished Eleanor would pay more attention to domestic matters such as the White House food. He was eating chicken at least six times a week, and when he complained he got sweetbreads six times a week. "I am getting to the point," he wrote his wife on April 29, 1942, "where my stomach positively rebels and this does not help my relations with foreign powers. I bit two of them today."

The danger of Eleanor as first interceder was that she was used by people with axes to grind to get to the president. Anna Rosenberg, a politically ambitious woman who served as FDR's liaison with Mayor La Guardia, undermined Frances Perkins to Eleanor, probably seeing herself as a likely candidate to replace her. Instead of supporting the only woman in the cabinet, Eleanor echoed Mrs. Rosenberg's viewpoint in this memo to her husband: "I must say that one hears on every side criticism of Frances and doubt expressed as to what she is going to be able to accomplish. . . . I should feel very badly if you removed Frances without giving her something comparable." In this case, her advice was not taken.

And who was it that put her up to bad-mouthing the OSS chief in Switzerland, Allen Dulles, at the time he was conducting delicate peace negotiations with German agents? In a February 1945 memo for FDR, she wrote that "Allen Dulles who is in charge of Bill Donovan's outfit in Paris [sic] has been counsel, closely tied up with the Schroeder Bank, that is likely to be representative of the underground Nazi interests after the war. There seem to be in Paris a great many people who are pretty close to the big business side!" Dulles was not in Paris, but never mind, Roosevelt had Harry Hopkins run it down anyway.

Even though one might pause at Eleanor's occasional wild pitches, one had to admire her courage. She was not afraid to confront men who made their subordinates tremble when she felt that an injustice had been done. In April 1944, she took on Henry Stimson in the case of three second lieutenants who had been stripped of their commissions at hearings before Army reclassification boards. She insisted that Stimson meet with the three, much to his annoyance, but it was hard to say no to the first lady, and on April 7 he "plunged at once into a thankless task that Mrs. Roosevelt has thrown at me," considering it "a sentimental attempt at personal government on her part."

Stimson formed a poor impression of the three—one was a paranoid, the second a police court lawyer, the third not too bright. All three were evidently unfit for command. He lectured them on the errors of their ways in having obtained irregular access through the White House. Honorable officers, he said, would rather have their hands cut off than go through some nonmilitary channel. "I spent nearly two hours and a half with the bunch," he recorded. "A frightful waste of time in a very busy period. . . . I shall now have the task of writing Mrs. Roosevelt and telling her not to do it again."

But Eleanor did not give up that easily, and was in Stimson's office on April 8. The secretary pointed out that officers who lost their commissions could reenter the ranks at the highest noncommissioned grade they had previously held. He reminded her that when he had been at the War Department under Taft, he had often dealt with senators seeking favors for officers. He had told them then that he did not think much of officers who used such methods. If it became known that the three young men could get redress through the back door of the White House, he said, democracy in the United States would be finished.

Eleanor saw that Stimson had a point, and said that if the three young men were her sons she would advise them to go on as noncommissioned officers. In fact, one of the three, Stephen Jaworowsky, did reenlist as a noncom, and was reappointed second lieutenant that August. Pleased at his victory, Stimson recorded that "impulsive as she is, she is a kindly and a good woman. . . . I hope I have stopped this lady's intervention in these things for good."

Although she had the best intentions, Eleanor was a mixed blessing, used as a conduit by special interest groups with dubious motives, and sometimes intervening inappropriately. FDR kept a copy of a poem entitled "The Lady Eleanor," of which the last stanza gives the drift:

> ". . .And despite her global milling,
> Of the voice there is no stilling,
> With its platitudes galore,

As it gushes on, advising,
Criticizing and chastising,
Moralizing, patronizing,
Paralysing—ever more
Advertising Eleanor."

On August 16, 1943, Sumner Welles resigned, ending a brilliant twenty-eight-year career in the State Department. He was at the time acting secretary of state in the absence of FDR and Cordell Hull, who had gone to Canada to attend the first Quebec Conference. What could have prompted this career diplomat, who was the de facto secretary of state thanks to the president's trust and friendship, to resign in wartime?

The chain of events leading up to Welles's resignation begins with the death by heart attack of William Brockman Bankhead, forty-eighth Speaker of the House of Representatives, on September 15, 1940, at the age of sixty-six. FDR, who was grateful to Bankhead for having renounced his vice-presidential aspirations at the Democratic convention three months earlier, decided to attend the funeral in the Speaker's hometown of Jasper, Alabama.

September 1940, less than two months before the election, was a busy time, and cabinet members were reluctant to be away from their desks for two days on a long train ride to Alabama, but as Steve Early explained it to Frances Perkins: "The President insists we owe this to the Speaker. We're in a campaign. We've got to make friends. Many of these Southerners are disaffected. There's a big anti-war crowd in the South. There's nothing like showing respect to one of their own to make them feel favorable to you. The President's got the right idea. It's going to be a full-dress state funeral." Most of the cabinet members went, but Cordell Hull, although a friend and one-time colleague of the Speaker, stayed in Washington to monitor foreign affairs and sent Sumner Welles in his place.

The presidential train carrying Bankhead's coffin arrived in Jasper at 1:30 P.M. on September 17, and the president's party joined the funeral cortege. All the stores were closed, and the town's population lined the streets to do justice to their distinguished son. After the interment, a family affair attended by Bankhead's actress daughter, Tallulah, there was a church service. The church was filled with flowers, and it was so hot and humid that Frances Perkins felt stuck to the back of the pew. The service seemed endless, with speech after speech, and sermon and hymns. It was a great relief when it was all over, and they said good-bye to the mayor and other town officials, and got back on the train at 3:30 for the ride back to Washington. Ties loosened, collars opened, coats were pulled off. Jesse Jones set up whiskey for everyone, saying: "I'll put it in my will that I'll haunt anybody who gives me a state funeral."

There was considerable drinking, and late that evening, when Henry

Wallace went into the diner to eat, he found Sumner Welles sitting with John Carmody of the Maritime Commission. Wallace joined them, noticing that Welles was throwing back one whiskey after the other. He was discussing his trip to Europe earlier that year, and telling of his very high esteem for Mussolini. Wallace was upset. How could the number two man in the State Department praise the fascist conqueror of Ethiopia?

Clearly intoxicated, Welles retired to his sleeping compartment and began ringing his service bell. Several Negro porters answered the call, and to their dismay the drunken Welles greeted them with lewd homosexual advances. None of them accepted, and the next afternoon the train pulled into Union Station, with Welles acting as though nothing had happened.

Such behavior was completely at variance with the image Welles projected of the reserved and proper diplomat. Even to the British, so conscious of the precedence afforded by the right school and the right club, Welles seemed aloof and haughty. "It is a pity that he swallowed a ramrod in his youth," observed Sir Alexander Cadogan upon their first meeting. "I have hobnobbed with him a lot and have tried to get through his reserve."

A distillation of old New England bloodlines, Welles was named for his great-uncle, Charles Sumner, the Massachusetts abolitionist senator. He went to Groton and Harvard (where he was a classmate of Eleanor Roosevelt's brother, Hall), and was a page boy at FDR's wedding, being eleven years his junior. In 1915, Roosevelt wrote then Secretary of State William Jennings Bryan to "commend to your good offices Mr. Sumner Welles, who desires to take the examinations for the Diplomatic Corps this spring. I have known him since he was a small boy and have seen him go through school and college and I would be most glad to see him successful in entering the Diplomatic Corps." At the State Department, his tall and solemn bearing, his correct and formal manner, his Savile Row tailoring and his malacca cane, made him seem the model diplomat. This stately product of the eastern establishment became chief of the Latin American desk in 1921, at the age of twenty-eight. By that time he was married to Esther Slater of Boston, and they had two sons, Benjamin and Arnold. In 1923 they were divorced, and two years later he married Mathilde Townsend, whose grandfather, William Lawrence Scott, had made his millions developing the Pennsylvania Railroad.

In Washington, Welles lived in the great Massachusetts Avenue mansion his wife had inherited, with fifteen servants, where he could entertain on a far grander scale than his superiors. Mrs. Welles had her idiosyncrasies; it was said that every night she turned down the covers on the bed of her long-dead mother. Weekends were spent at Welles's Maryland residence, Oxon Hill Manor, and the family vacationed in Palm Beach and Bar Harbor.

Welles put up a convincing front. Ickes described him as "a man of almost preternatural solemnity and great dignity. If he ever smiles, it has not been in my presence. He conducts himself with portentous gravity and as if he were charged with all the responsibilities of Atlas. Just to look at him one can tell that the world would dissolve into its component parts if only a portion of the weighty state secrets that he carries about were divulged." But behind the facade he was a tormented man, a compulsive alcoholic with a penchant for lower-class male sexual partners, preferably black. His homosexual episodes were known to some of his Foreign Service colleagues. When he was made under secretary of state in 1937, edging out the Virginia gentleman and former congressman and judge R. Walton Moore, ambassador to Germany William E. Dodd commented that it was "distressing news. . . . His conduct [in Cuba] was most embarrassing." Cordell Hull, who detested him, referred to him jocularly as "my fairy."

One of the porters who had been invited to perform homosexual acts upon the drunken Welles filed a complaint with his employer, the Southern Railway Company, which despite its name had its headquarters in Philadelphia. William Christian Bullitt, FDR's ambassador to Paris until the fall of France, and presently not employed by the government, lived in Philadelphia and picked up the story.

Bullitt hated Welles. He felt that his old friend Walton Moore should have been under secretary. Here was proof positive that Welles was unfit for the job. Bullitt was of the "brilliant but erratic" sort, and his scruples were few. He had seduced FDR's secretary, Missy LeHand, whose friendship greatly facilitated access to the president. When Bullitt was ambassador to the Soviet Union, she had visited him in Moscow, only to find that he was involved with a ballet dancer. Now that Missy had been felled by a stroke, Bullitt's access was restricted, although he could, like Sumner Welles, claim a close friendship with the president, going back to 1932, when he had been foreign policy adviser before the election.

Bullitt saw the incident on the train as a way to get rid of Welles. He started spreading the story, until it reached the ears of the White House staff. On January 3, 1941, Pa Watson sent for J. Edgar Hoover and told him that the president wanted to turn over to him a very delicate and confidential matter. Watson then proceeded to tell Hoover what was said to have happened on the train trip coming back from Jasper. The president wanted a thorough investigation.

On January 29, Hoover briefed FDR on the results of the investigation, which included affidavits from the Pullman porters. "I told the President," Hoover said in a memo, "that on the trip to Jasper, Alabama, on Sept. 18 [*sic*], 1940, it had been alleged that Mr. Welles had propositioned a number of the train crew to have immoral relations with them." Hoover then went on to say that, from interviews with the parties concerned, it appeared that the allegations were true.

Hoover also told the president that Bullitt had got hold of the story and had told Senator Burton Wheeler that Welles had "gotten fresh" with a Pullman porter. Bullitt said he did not want to report the story to the president, because anyone who took bad news to the president "would get his own legs cut off." But he would ask his friend Walton Moore to talk to FDR.

Welles learned from a newspaper friend that Bullitt was spreading the story around, Hoover went on, and went to Attorney General Biddle to nip the scandal in the bud, telling him that "he had been drinking rather heavily and was no doubt considerably under the weather." Welles told Biddle that he had been taken sick in the small hours of the morning and had taken a sleeping pill and sent for some coffee from the dining car as he had a bad heart and coffee was the only thing that relieved it. Beyond that, he did not recall anything else happening.

In February 1941, Walton Moore died. Brooding over the death of his best friend in the State Department, with whom he had often discussed how harmful it was to have Welles remaining in his job, Bullitt could contain himself no longer. At a morning meeting on April 23, he told FDR that Moore had sent for him on his deathbed and charged him with a mission he could not evade, however unpleasant it was to carry out. Moore said that he could not die with peace of mind unless he knew that the president was certain to be informed about a very dangerous matter. Moore wanted the president to see certain papers, which Bullitt had brought with him.

Bullitt handed FDR a document, which was apparently an affidavit from the railroad company. The president read the first page, looked over the other pages, and finally said: "I know all about this already. I have had a full report on it. There is truth in the allegations."

Judge Moore, Bullitt said, felt that the maintenance of Welles in public life was a menace to the country, since he was subject to blackmail by foreign powers, which used crimes of this kind to get public officials to spy for them. Moore was also convinced that this matter was of the utmost danger to the president personally—a terrible public scandal might arise at any time that would undermine the country's confidence in the chief executive.

FDR said he did not think any newspaper would touch it. It was too scandalous to print. Bullitt replied that Moore thought the scandal would arise from a demand for criminal prosecution, not from newspaper publication.

FDR said Welles would never behave that way again, for he was having him watched day and night by a guardian, under the guise of his needing a bodyguard as a public official, to make sure there was no repeat performance.

Bullitt replied that it was not a matter of future acts but of past crimes committed. He had discussed the matter with Cordell Hull, who said that he considered Welles worse than a murderer.

FDR said he knew it was a crime and he knew Welles was liable to prosecution but he did not think anyone would initiate prosecution.

Morale in the State Department and the Foreign Service was being ruined by the knowledge that a man of Welles's character was in charge of appointments and transfers, Bullitt argued.

FDR said that to him there was a different question, which he had not decided how to handle. He found it convenient to have Welles in the State

Department. His problem was whether to end the utility of someone he found useful.

Bullitt's next argument was that FDR was asking Americans to die in a crusade for all that was decent in human life; he could not have among the leaders of such a crusade a criminal like Welles. Bullitt then delivered an ultimatum to the president: he wanted to do all he could to prepare for war and beat Hitler, but he would under no circumstances take a position in the State Department or the Foreign Service unless Welles was dismissed.

FDR had heard enough. He pushed the button under his desk, summoning Pa Watson. When Watson appeared, FDR said: "Pa, I don't feel well. Please cancel all my appointments for the rest of the day."

Truly it was sickening that some of his closest friends and advisers were plotting against each other as in an Elizabethan tragedy. Truly it was dispiriting that a president, who could make decisions that affected millions of his people, could not save one man from the character flaw that was his undoing. He could not save Welles, a man who represented everything that was best in the American background, a background similar to his own, from the self-destructiveness of his nature. He could not save Bullitt, another American aristocrat born to wealth and family position, from an obsession to destroy his enemy that was worthy of Iago.

In December 1941 FDR tried to put a stop to Bullitt's troublemaking by sending him on an assignment to Cairo, but he was back in February 1942, again unemployed. Roosevelt found him a job in the Navy Department in the hope that it would keep him quiet.

FDR's fondness for creating parallel lines of command was partly to blame for the situation. He knew that two of his greatest enemies in day-to-day leadership were the inertia of the government departments and their rivalry in protecting their turf. Thus he created alternate lines of command. In the State Department, he relied on Sumner Welles. Together they mixed their international recipes behind Hull's back. Hull was constantly bypassed, with Welles writing FDR outside State Department channels when he traveled abroad. It was like the German general staff, where a staff lieutenant with two red stripes down his pants leg outranked a nonstaff general.

When a foreign diplomat arrived in Washington, he would make a formal call on Hull, then spend two hours with Welles. When a problem arose with State, the other departments went to Welles, knowing he had the president's ear. Hull gradually abdicated his position, and Welles was in charge during the secretary's long absences because of poor health. At the first meeting between Roosevelt and Churchill in Newfoundland in August 1940, it was Welles who represented the State Department.

Hull had practically nothing to do with wartime foreign policy. He did not go to Casablanca, and when he asked to see the minutes he was told they were not available. He was kept in the dark about the president's policy toward the French, which Ickes thought was "one of the most astonishing things that I have heard for a long time."

The escalation from armed neutrality to open warfare between Hull and Welles occurred in January 1942, when Welles went to Rio de Janeiro for a meeting of Latin American nations, who were being asked by the United States to break their ties with the Axis. The pro-Nazi government of Argentina refused, and without consulting Hull, Welles worked out a compromise "recommending rupture." Hull heard about the compromise on a radio news program, and was ready to agree with the commentator's appraisal that Argentina had defeated the United States' main objective. He at once called Welles and gave him a tongue-lashing laced with curses, accusing him of undermining department policy and predicting that his folly would lead to widespread criticism. Hull insisted that Welles substitute "require" for "recommend," but Welles refused. Hull asked FDR to arbitrate, and after hearing both sides he agreed with Welles, making Hull even more furious. In fact, the Rio Conference was a triumph of hemispheric solidarity, for Argentina was isolated when all the other countries broke with the Axis nations.

Ignored by his under secretary and rebuffed by the president, Hull was so low that he penciled out his resignation. But he was a fighter, raised in the Tennessee feuding tradition, and would not quit, leaving the vacancy for Welles to fill. He would see to it that Welles quit first.

Hull knew that Welles was out to replace him, and that FDR was probably agreeable to the plan. Welles cultivated columnists like Drew Pearson, telling them he was the man to approach for favors. He would save up information coming into the department and release it when Hull was out of town. Once, when Arthur Krock went to see Hull, they began talking about disloyalty to superiors, and Hull pointed to the locked door between his office and Welles's and said: "I've got the prime example of disloyalty right in there."

To Hull and Bullitt, who had now joined forces to remove Welles, the incident on the train was providential. It could be used against the man who had belittled Hull and shoved him aside and wormed his way into the president's favor. But the months passed, and nothing was done. The president seemed determined to cover the whole thing up.

Hull could not allow the opportunity to pass, and on October 24, 1942, he took the unusual step of requesting a secret meeting with J. Edgar Hoover in his apartment at the Wardman Park Hotel. Hull told Hoover that Mrs. Hull had heard from the wives of several senators stories about Welles that gave him a great deal of concern. Hull said he understood that Hoover had made an investigation of the matter about a year ago. He asked if he could see the report.

If Hull was given a copy of the report, he could use it to bring pressure on the president to fire Welles. This was perfectly clear to Hoover, who saw no point in getting mixed up in State Department vendettas. Hoover said he could not provide a copy of the report without presidential consent, which he knew would not be granted. Hull said that unless steps were taken, the whole matter could be highly embarrassing, but he was unable to pry the report out of Hoover.

A new tack had to be tried, which Hull and Bullitt were already working on, and this was to take the story to the Hill in the hope that the Truman Committee, the watchdog committee on the war, would investigate it. One of the members of that committee was the old-fashioned Republican senator from Maine, R. Owen Brewster, to whom Bullitt and Hull leaked the story.

Senator Brewster saw Hoover on April 27, 1943, saying that he knew the FBI had investigated "disgraceful actions" of Sumner Welles. Brewster said the information was so shocking that he had not discussed it with anyone but had come straight to Hoover. Brewster demanded to see the report, but Hoover again declined.

Biddle discussed the case with Hoover, who said it was puzzling. Usually, a homosexual's course was clearly charted and his characteristics were well defined, Hoover said. But in the two reported instances concerning Welles, he was dead drunk both times. Perhaps, Hoover said, he had been so drunk that the incident was blotted out of his memory completely.

Brewster then went to Attorney General Biddle and threatened him with a Senate probe of Welles. If hearings were held, how would FDR explain keeping Welles in office for more than two years after learning of his homosexuality? Biddle asked the senator to wait until he had called the matter to the president's attention.

When Biddle saw the president, FDR said he needed Welles, who was the only man in the State Department who really knew what was going on in different parts of the world. Biddle said it would be a good idea to get rid of him. What a nice liability he would be in the '44 campaign, with all the whispering that was going on.

On May 4, Steve Early brought in Bullitt to tell him that it had come to the president's ear that Bullitt had turned some of the Welles documents over to Cissy Patterson, publisher of the Washington *Times Herald*. Bullitt said that was "a damned lie."

Early said he was worried about the Welles case. It looked like it was about to break into the open. Bullitt said he had told FDR that Welles would be his Achilles' heel and had to be dismissed for his good and the good of the country. The president had resented his remarks, and their intimate friendship had ended, Bullitt said.

Early said he respected Bullitt for speaking frankly to FDR, "even though the President got angry." Of course, the president and everyone else in the White House knew the allegations were true, but the president had hoped to keep them quiet.

They could not be kept quiet, and Roosevelt had to make up his mind to ask for Welles's resignation. He had covered up the incident for more than two years, but Bullitt and Hull were relentless. If it came out that the number two man in the State Department in wartime was a homosexual, it would be a crippling blow to the 1944 campaign. The blackmail of homosexuals in high places was a proven fact. Alfred Redl, the intelligence chief of the Austro-Hungarian army, had turned spy for the Russians under threats of disclosure.

FDR had allowed the cover-up because he needed Welles and because he was a loyal friend. Welles was a man of his background and class, a younger man whom he had helped along in his career, and who was close to Eleanor—almost a member of the family. FDR balanced his fondness for Welles against his lack of tolerance of homosexuals in general and of drunkards in the State Department. While in the Navy, he had personally commanded a section assigned to the entrapment of homosexuals in Newport, Rhode Island. In May 1942, when newspaper articles accused Senator David I. Walsh of Massachusetts of engaging in homosexual practices in New York City male brothels and thus exposing himself to blackmail, FDR expressed no sympathy, and told Senator Alben Barkley that the way this sort of thing was handled in the Army was for a fellow officer to leave a loaded revolver with the accused, who would obligingly shoot himself. Also, FDR personally vetoed the promotion of a Foreign Service man who drank too much. But in the case of Welles, their long and close association made the president protective, even when the risk was high.

It was time for Welles to walk the plank, and he wrote his letter of resignation on August 16. The announcement was not made until September 25, and the press speculated that he had resigned because of his rift with Hull or his pro-Russian policy. The true reason was not mentioned, and the Truman Committee probe was called off.

The Welles resignation had a devastating effect on the State Department. In Latin American affairs, Welles's special preserve, it marked the end of Pan-American solidarity and the Good Neighbor policy. Welles was one of the rare career men in the higher echelons who was sympathetic to the Jews, and his continued presence might have made a difference on the refugee question. In terms of morale, there was continued infighting between "Welles men" and "Hull men." Welles, in his own insubordinate way, had provided the leadership that Hull could not, and this too was lost. Edward Stettinius, Jr., Welles's replacement, came from the ranks of business (he had been board chairman of U.S. Steel) and did not command the loyalty of the career men. Hull had survived, getting rid of Welles as he had gotten rid of Ray Moley in 1933, saying at the time: "I cut the sonofabitch's throat from ear to ear." But he lost the president's trust and friendship, and was completely ignored—he was not even informed of major wartime decisions. After Teheran, when Morgenthau told him that the dismemberment of Germany had been agreed upon, Hull said, "Henry, this is the first time I have ever heard this. I have never been permitted to see the minutes of the Conference. I have asked and I have not been allowed to see them."

Bullitt too was out in the cold. He continued to write long position papers on the postwar situation for the president, but they were ignored. Bullitt was the first of the president's advisers to understand the postwar threat that would come from the Soviet Union, and predicted over and over that all of Eastern Europe would fall under Soviet domination. It was unfortunate that because the messenger was non grata his message was also discredited.

Desperate for a wartime job, Bullitt called on Hull on February 1, 1944. Hull said that the day before he had urged FDR to employ Bullitt, but FDR said he had not liked the way Bullitt had acted in the Welles affair. Hull reminded FDR that he had been sitting on a keg of dynamite for two years and that whoever was responsible for getting Welles out had performed a great public service. "I told the President that it was criminal for a man of Welles' habit to hang himself around our necks and hang on when he knew that the exposure of his behavior would blow the administration into the air," Hull told Bullitt. FDR said he would think over what job to give Bullitt.

On March 11, Hull showed FDR a proposal to make Bullitt ambassador-at-large for Africa and the Middle East. FDR took the proposal and wrote on the bottom: "Why not Minister to Saudi Arabia?"—a post he knew Bullitt would refuse. Roosevelt was violent on the subject of Bullitt, telling Henry Wallace on one occasion that "Bill ought to go to hell" for what he had done. Unwanted in his own country, Bullitt joined the Free French in May, was made an aide to General de Lattre de Tassigny, and landed with the French First Army in Southern France in 1944.

Welles, who not that long ago had been the president's emissary to Churchill, Mussolini, and Hitler, and who had with the president designed America's foreign policy, was now a private citizen, active in charity work, author of a foreign affairs column and of books with such portentous titles as *The Time for Decision* and *We Shall Not Fail.* He may have reflected on the nature of his downfall—it was one of those "for want of a nail the shoe was lost" mishaps. If Speaker Bankhead had not died two months before the election, the president would not have gone to Jasper; if Hull had not been mired in fruitless negotiations with the Japanese, he would not have sent Welles in his place; if it had not been so insufferably hot in the Jasper church, he would not have started drinking; and so on. Circumstances seemed to have conspired against him.

Welles lived for another eighteen years, time enough to reflect on past mistakes. On Christmas night 1948 he was found unconscious beside a creek, his toes and fingers frozen, less than a mile from his Oxon Hill estate. The story given to the press was that he had slipped while on one of his customary nocturnal walks.

In May 1952, a Military Intelligence memo from the First Army reported that "John Metcalfe says the National Lecture Management of Washington, of which he is the president, had to drop Sumner Welles from the list of its lecturers; the reason—Welles' drunkenness and homosexuality. Welles is said to have started drinking like a fish. Combined with the homosexuality, the other vice often makes Welles entirely unfit for the lecturing."

Welles died in 1961, and was described as a great man maligned in a farewell column by his friend Drew Pearson, to whom he had regularly leaked information. According to Pearson, when Bullitt called on FDR after the Welles resignation to ask for his support in the race for mayor of Philadelphia, FDR told him: "If I were the Angel Gabriel and you and Sumner Welles should come before me seeking admission into the Gates of Heaven, do you know what I'd say? I would say: 'Bill Bullitt, you have defamed the name of a man who toiled for his fellow men, and you can go to hell.' And that's what I tell you to do now."

But part of the responsibility in the Welles case was the president's, for creating conditions that led to venomous rivalry in the State Department, and for thinking he could cover up a scandal that continued to fester until it was dealt with. In presidential politics, as FDR well knew, it isn't what you've done but what you can be attacked for.

As Sumner Welles was resigning, another summit meeting was under way in Quebec. At stake was the priority of the cross-Channel operation in the spring of 1944, at a time when Allied armies were engaged in the Mediterranean. On July 10, Sicily had been invaded, and on July 25 Mussolini resigned and King Victor Emmanuel III named Marshal Pietro Badoglio prime minister. Peace feelers could be expected from the new Italian government, which would enhance further Mediterranean moves.

This time, when Churchill, as was his habit, spent several days alone with the president to soften him up to the British view, he found FDR unshakable. In fact, in their two days of talks at Hyde Park, it was Churchill who gave in on the issue of Marshall as commander, even though he had promised the job to Brooke.

The conference lasted from August 13 to 24, with the Combined Chiefs of Staff finally agreeing to give priority to the cross-Channel invasion, Overlord, in May 1944. There would be an initial assault of three to five divisions on open beaches in western Normandy. Also, the Americans agreed to an invasion of Italy, where German troops were pouring in. During the conference, on August 17, the news arrived that Patton had captured Messina, in Sicily, and the Germans were fleeing across the straits. In Russia, the Germans were withdrawing along their entire southern front. One sure sign of declining Axis prestige was that the Portuguese now agreed to give naval and air bases in the Azores to the British.

As the military men agreed on Overlord, Cordell Hull (who was attending his first summit conference as a result of Welles's resignation) and Anthony Eden differed on recognition of the French Committee of National Liberation formed in Algiers that June. Giraud was being eased out by a series of clever moves on the part of de Gaulle, though neither Hull nor Eden knew that yet. Churchill had written FDR on July 2 advising recognition: "What does recognition mean? One can recognise a man as an emperor or as a grocer. . . . As you know I have always taken the view that de Gaulle should be made to settle down to honest team work." Roosevelt replied on July 20, vetoing recognition and saying that "the next thing we know the committee would want to exchange ambassadors with us."

This was the matter that Hull and Eden continued to wrangle over in Quebec. Sir Alexander Cadogan, a member of Eden's staff, found Hull "a dreadful old man," vague and wordy, "and rather pig-headed, but quite a nice old thing, I dare say."

Eden said the British had to live twenty miles from France and he wanted to rebuild her as much as he could. Hull accused the British of financing de Gaulle and his anti-American statements to the tune of $60 million a year. The president, he said, did not want to give de Gaulle a white horse on which he could ride into France and make himself the master of a government there. Neither side would budge, and Cadogan said that Hull was "as vindictive as an old woman about whom someone had been spreading scandal."

The Americans held their own, and Brooke left the conference feeling "the inevitable flatness and depression which swamps me after a spell . . . of battling against difficulties, differences of opinion, stubbornness, stupidity, pettiness, and pig-headedness." Churchill had told him off-handedly that he was losing the command of the cross-Channel invasion to Marshall, which was a blow. Marshall at the conference had been unbudging, even threatening to resign if the British pressed their point.

Since 1942, FDR had been hoping for a summit meeting with Stalin. According to Hull, "he had been much impressed by the head-on clash between Stalin and Churchill, but he thought that through the force of his own personality, and with the terrific power behind him that the United States was demonstrating in the Pacific and Europe, he could succeed where the Prime Minister had failed."

FDR had wanted Stalin to come to Casablanca, but Stalin had to stay in Russia, where he was in direct command of the fighting, making such decisions as which targets to bomb and which divisions to deploy. Also, Stalin was wary of the Anglo-American lineup that refused to open a major second front in Europe. In April 1942, FDR proposed a meeting with Stalin on the Alaskan border, but that came to nothing. In May 1943, he sent former ambassador to the Soviet Union Joseph E. Davies to Moscow to suggest that all questions could be settled at a Big Three meeting, but Stalin was skeptical. FDR tried a fourth time by asking Stalin to the Quebec Conference, again in vain.

After Quebec, Stalin proposed a conference of foreign ministers in Moscow. FDR and Churchill eagerly accepted, glad to have him join the team. Cordell Hull, who had been benched since Pearl Harbor by the shift in decision making from diplomatic to military and by the machinations of Sumner Welles, now had his finest moment. The seventy-two-year-old secretary of state, who suffered from claustrophobia and had a horror of flying, made the long trek to Moscow by hops aboard a four-engine plane, arriving on October 18. During the conference, he made a hit with the Soviets by saying, when Eden was arguing that all legal forms should be observed in punishing the Germans, that "if I had my way, I would take Hitler and Mussolini and Tojo and their arch-accomplices and bring them before a drumhead court-martial. And at sunrise on the following day there would occur an historic incident." Molotov and his people uttered loud exclamations of approval.

The conference, however, was used by Churchill to undermine Overlord. To Churchill, a strategic decision arrived at after long and arduous negotiation was no more than a delaying action to allow the situation to ripen so that the decision might be changed.

Churchill's heart was still in the Mediterranean. On September 3, the British Eighth Army had streamed across the Strait of Messina. On September 9, Mark Clark landed south of Naples. With Italy invaded, Churchill wanted to move eastward and attack Rhodes, and then move into the Balkans. But this pet plan was about to be compromised by the transfer of seven battle-hardened divisions and a number of landing craft from the Italian theater back to England for the Overlord buildup. Churchill wired Eden on October 20 about "the dangers of our being committed to a lawyer's bargain for Overlord in May, for the sake of which we may have to ruin the Italian front and Balkan possibilities."

Churchill asked Eden to sound out the Russians on Balkan operations. Eden replied that they were completely and blindly set on the invasion of France.

After a promising start, the Italian campaign had bogged down. On October 21, General Sir Harold Alexander, commander of the campaign, presented a pessimistic summary—the Germans had built up to twenty-four divisions at least in Italy, while the Allies had only eleven divisions and were losing men and matériel to Overlord. Alexander foresaw a long and costly slogging match.

Churchill forwarded Alexander's report to Eden on October 26, asking him to show it to Stalin and commenting: "I will not allow, while I am responsible, the great and fruitful campaign in Italy, which has already drawn heavy German reserves into action, to be cast away and end in a frightful disaster, for the sake of crossing the Channel in May." He would not go ahead with Overlord unless certain conditions were met, he said, and he would not be bound to the date.

When Eden delivered the report, Stalin asked whether this meant a postponement of Overlord. Eden said that was impossible to say, but it had to be faced. Stalin tried to nail him down: would the postponement be one month or two? Eden said he could not tell, but it was desirable for the Big Three to meet. Stalin agreed, seeing that once again the British were trying to weasel out of the cross-Channel commitment. He realized that Churchill was as keen to hurt Hitler as he was, Stalin said, adding with a gust of laughter that

Churchill had a tendency to take the easy road, leaving the hard road to him.

In Washington on October 28, upon learning that Eden had given General Alexander's summary to Stalin, Stimson was beside himself. "Jerusalem!" he exclaimed in his diary, "this made me angry . . . [and] shows how determined Churchill is with all his lip service to stick a knife in the back of Overlord, and I feel more bitterly about it than I ever have before." He could not go to FDR, who was "almost inaccessible. He has been sick three or four days, and . . . it is as difficult to get at him as it would be to get at Mohammed."

Churchill's interference was "dirty baseball," Stimson felt. He was afraid of its effect on the president, "who is wobbling around again making remarks about the Balkans." On October 29, however, Marshall sent a telegram to General John R. Deane, head of the American military mission in Moscow, outlining the views of the Joint Chiefs against any diversions, with which FDR seemed quite in accord. The president told Stimson that he would not think of touching the Balkans until the Russians were so advanced in their invasion of Germany that American troops could act side by side with them. Stimson said it was dangerous to talk about the Balkans at all. As he left the president's office he raised his hand in admonition and said: "Remember, no more Balkans."

The foreign ministers' conference lasted until November 3, and went over most of the war's political problems, from Turkish neutrality to the postwar division of Germany. As Eden noted, it was the high tide of good relations with the Soviets, in whom little of their later intransigence had yet surfaced.

Upon Hull's return, the Senate approved 85 to 5 the Connally Resolution for the establishment of a postwar international organization. Avoiding Woodrow Wilson's mistake, Roosevelt had congressional backing for Hull's prestige in Congress had something to do with the easy passage of the resolution.

Finally it was arranged. Roosevelt and Churchill would go to Teheran for talks with Stalin, stopping first in Cairo for meetings with Chiang Kai-shek. Stalin had an unbeatable reason for staying close to his borders—he was in the midst of a war involving 500 divisions. The British and American leaders would travel halfway around the world as a gesture of appreciation that he had fought alone in Europe for two and a half years. The president was bound by the Constitution to sign or veto bills and return them to Congress within ten days of their passage. But he got around that by saying the ten days began when he got the bill.

Stimson, who was not going, worried that the British would do their utmost to sabotage Overlord. "With all his lip service," he wrote, "Churchill is against the Channel operation and instead is determined to push forward new diversions into the Balkans. . . . The President has been going very straight lately and has stood up to Churchill better than at any time heretofore, but he too has an impulsive nature and a mind which revolts against the dry facts involved in logistics and therefore both Marshall and I are always nervous for fear of the effect of some sudden impulse on his part."

Stimson had "a very long and hard talk" with Marshall, who, since the press had started predicting he would command Overlord, had become so reticent that FDR complained he couldn't get any advice out of him. There was considerable resistance to Marshall's giving up his job as chief of staff. The other joint chiefs lobbied against it, arguing that no one had Marshall's knowledge of global war, or his balanced judgment on the ins and outs of the different theaters. Eisenhower, slated to replace Marshall, was not on cordial terms with MacArthur, and that would be a problem. "We have the winning combination here in Washington," Admiral King said. "Why break it up?"

General Pershing had written FDR on September 14 that he was "deeply disturbed" that Marshall was being transferred to a tactical command in a limited area. In a reply that showed that he had already decided on Marshall two months before Teheran, the president said: "I want George to be the Pershing of the second World War—and he cannot be that if we keep him here." In the meantime, Mrs. Marshall was moving their furniture from Fort Myer to the family home in Leesburg, Virginia, in anticipation of the move to London.

On November 13, Roosevelt and his party sailed from Hampton Roads, Virginia, aboard the battleship *Iowa*, which was commanded by his former naval aide, Captain John McCrea. The passage to the port of Oran in Algeria would take a week, which would be spent drawing up papers to meet Churchill's expected objections to Overlord. In a diary he kept of the trip, FDR wrote on the first day of the crossing: "This will be another Odyssey— much farther afield and afloat than the hardy Trojan whose name I used to take at Groton when I was competing for school prizes. But it too will be filled with surprises."

Oddly, for a conference that would cover political as well as military matters, FDR did not bring anyone from the State Department. He did not want Hull, and Welles was gone—there was no one at State he trusted. Aside from the Joint Chiefs, his main adviser was Harry Hopkins.

On the second day out, FDR was wheeled to the deck after lunch to watch the antiaircraft battery fire at large black balloons. Suddenly an officer on the bridge yelled, "It's the real thing!" The battleship listed from the effect of full rudder and pulsed with flank speed as the general alarm clanged. One of the escorting destroyers, the *William D. Porter,* was conducting a dry run with the *Iowa* as a notional target. A short circuit occurred and a live torpedo was launched. The torpedo exploded with a big thud in the battleship's disturbed wake. Roosevelt, his ears stuffed with cotton, did not realize until later that the U.S. Navy had almost torpedoed its own commander in chief and the Joint Chiefs of Staff. Admiral King wanted to relieve the destroyer's commanding officer but the president told him to forget it.

Arriving in Oran on November 20, FDR was met by Eisenhower and two of his sons, Elliott and Franklin Jr. They flew to Tunis aboard the C-54 *Sacred Cow,* and the next morning the president toured some of the Tunisian battlefields. As they drove to the Medjerda River, Roosevelt explained to Ike, as if still trying to convince himself, why Marshall should have the command that Ike so badly wanted: "Ike, you and I know who was Chief of Staff during the last years of the Civil War but practically no one else knows, although the names of the field generals—Grant, of course, and Lee, and Jackson, Sherman, Sheridan and the others—every schoolboy knows them. I hate to think that 50 years from now practically nobody will know who George Marshall was. That is one of the reasons I want George to have the big command—he is entitled to establish his place in history as a great General." Ike felt like a quarterback who gets benched in the fourth quarter, but did not argue the point. His naval aide, Harry C. Butcher, took it up with Hopkins, saying that Marshall was needed at home to deal with Congress. It would take him six months to get the feel of a combined land, air, and sea command, while Ike had already done it for a year successfully.

Roosevelt left Tunis for Cairo on Sunday, November 21. "We came in the back way," he wrote in his diary, "so as to avoid German planes from the desert. Saw the Nile 100 miles So. of Cairo—an amazing scene—& followed the narrow belt of fertile fields, with many villages, until we came to the big pyramids & my old friend the Sphinx. We all dined (not the Sphinx) at my villa."

Churchill was there with his team, waiting to draw the Americans once again into Mediterranean adventures. He had begun with landings on the coast of Morocco, and pulled them across North Africa into Tunisia, Sicily, and Italy. Now he wanted to proceed 100 miles farther east, to capture the island of Rhodes, off the southern coast of Turkey. Even his own chief of staff, Alan Brooke, thought that his "obsession" with Rhodes was unsound and that Churchill, because he was no longer the predominant partner, was putting forth whimsical proposals "purely to spite the Americans."

Aside from that, Churchill was annoyed that the talks were starting with Chiang and Far Eastern operations. That was putting the cart before the horse. Churchill, the great sidetracker, was afraid of being sidetracked in "minor" China operations that would divert resources from the European theater.

FDR, however, was determined to keep alive the spirit of resistance in China by launching fresh operations there, and conferred with Stilwell, asking him please not to call Chiang "Peanut." In attendance at the first plenary session on November 23 were the generalissimo and madame (whom Stimson called "the Missimo"), Chiang with his shrewd foxy face, the skin stretched taut over the bones, and madame in a clinging black dress with a slit up the side, displaying a shapely pair of legs—a personality in which sexual allure and ambition mingled to achieve her ends.

An amphibious operation in Burma was proposed, which the British stiffly resisted. When Brooke asked if landing craft could be diverted from the Far East for operations in the Mediterranean, American tempers flared. As General Stilwell recalled, "Brooke got nasty and King got good and sore. King almost climbed over the table at Brooke. God, he was mad! I wish he had socked him."

It seemed to the British that Roosevelt was pandering to Chiang, who had done nothing to contribute to the defeat of Germany and very little to the defeat of Japan, at the expense of European operations. The Americans, on the other hand, were weary of arguing the same plans over and over. It was discouraging that Overlord, a plan twice agreed to, at Trident and at Quebec, had to be debated once again. And yet that was what occurred at the plenary session on November 24, when Churchill made the case for changing the date of Overlord to attempt the capture of Rhodes. "His Majesty's Government cannot have its troops standing idle," Churchill intoned. "Muskets must flame."

Marshall could take it no more, and interrupted Churchill's oratory to say: "God forbid that I should try to dictate . . . but not one American soldier is going to die on that goddamned beach." His exasperation was such that he might have questioned Churchill's maxim that the only thing worse than having allies was not having allies.

The British felt the same way, and Cadogan thought the American assessment of Chiang "bordered on the ludicrous" and that the prime minister had to endure much, including American expressions of higher morality. When FDR told Churchill that Chiang had no designs on Indochina, Churchill replied "Nonsense!"—which moved the president to say: "Winston, you have four hundred years of acquisitive instinct in your blood and you just don't understand how a country might not want to acquire land somewhere if they can get it. A new period has opened in the world's history and you will have to adjust to it."

FDR saw himself as a higher authority composing differences, writing Eleanor on November 25: "I have been working hard—acting as a solvent between various people in all three outfits" (American, British, and Chinese).

On November 26, the Combined Chiefs of Staff met again and, according to Brooke, "it was not long before Marshall and I had the father and mother of a row!" That was the final afternoon, and the Cairo Conference ended with almost nothing settled, except that there would be an offensive in Burma, and that Overlord might have to be delayed for a month to assure the success of Mediterranean operations.

That evening, quarrels were set aside as FDR hosted a Thanksgiving dinner where he carved turkey for twenty. Afterward, there was dance music from phonograph records, and the guests were treated to the incongruous spectacle of the sixty-eight-year-old prime minister of England dancing with Pa Watson.

Roosevelt's party of about seventy (including the Filipino mess boys from Shangri-la, his retreat in the Maryland hills), left Cairo on November 27 aboard the *Sacred Cow* for the 1,310-mile hop to Teheran. "We passed over Bethlehem and Jerusalem & the Dead Sea," FDR recorded in his diary. "Everything very bare looking—& I *don't* want Palestine as my homeland. . . . I still don't like flying. This [Teheran] is a very dirty place—great poverty!"

Although the Iranian capital was occupied by Soviet troops, which was one reason Stalin had picked it, the road from the airport to the city was lined with Persian cavalrymen every 500 yards, who advertised the route while offering no protection. Great crowds milled in the streets, and a man with a pistol or a bomb could easily have found his target.

Worried about security when they landed at dusk, FDR's bodyguard, Mike Reilly, approached Staff Sergeant Robert C. "Tiny" Ebaugh of the Counter-Intelligence Corps and said: "How would you like to be a clay pigeon?" Without waiting for an answer, he went on: "You are going to ride in the President's car. You are expendable. The President is not. This is a hat. Try it on. This is the President's cape. Have you got a cigarette holder?"

And so it was that Sergeant Ebaugh, member of a unit that would soon be disbanded on the president's order, rode in the big limousine at the head of the procession, with a full colonel for chauffeur, waving his cigarette holder and tipping his snap-brimmed Panama, and exposing himself to a potential assassin's bullets as the president rode in the Army staff car that was sixth in the procession. They were doing twenty miles per hour, and in traffic jams the crowds pressed up to the window and stared at the anxious double in the hat and cape. Ebaugh was glad when it was over.

The American legation was about half a mile from the Russian compound, where security was enforced by the NKVD. Stalin and Molotov cooked up a story that German agents were plotting to kill the president as he traveled across the city from the legation to the Soviet embassy, where the meetings would be held. Reilly, who was worried about German paratroopers landing on the flat roof of the legation, advised FDR to move to the Russian compound, even though it could be taken for granted that the conversations of the American delegation would be monitored.

"The Russians discovered a plot," FDR wrote in his diary, "to get him [Stalin], & WSC & me as we drove to each other's legations so at Stalin's plea I moved down to the Russian compound where there is an extra house & the danger of driving thro the streets is eliminated as WSC lives next door & there are flocks of guards." For Roosevelt, who was counting on the personal touch to improve relations with Stalin, the move was a way of showing his trust and of facilitating private meetings. He arrived at his new quarters at 3:00 P.M. on November 28, and fifteen minutes later Stalin came to call.

On this mild and sunny Sunday afternoon in Teheran was held the first meeting that had ever taken place between an American president and a Soviet head of state, a practice that would carry into the postwar era.

Sitting in his wheelchair and dressed in a blue suit, Roosevelt warmly greeted the short, stocky man with thick straight graying hair, a bushy mustache, and the pallor known as "Kremlin complexion." The suggestion of advancing age in his physical carriage was corrected by the mustard-colored uniform of a field marshal, with a broad red stripe down the trousers and a jacket that looked as if a tailor had placed a shelf on each shoulder and decorated it with white stars and gold lace.

Roosevelt had been briefed about the Soviet Union over the years by his ambassadors, by Bullitt on how you couldn't trust the Russians and by Davies on the purges of the thirties, but he knew very little about the man who now stood before him. What they had in common was that they both ruled continent-sized land masses, and were both builders of new social systems. Each personified the "soul" of his people—Stalin the peasant shrewdness and endurance, Roosevelt a geniality that masked his cunning, a generosity of spirit, and a love of large conceptions. Each had shown the strength to conquer adversity, Roosevelt by attaining the highest office in spite of his polio, Stalin by coming to power after Siberian exile and imprisonment.

Aside from that, the two men were as different as the language they spoke and the systems they represented: Roosevelt the coddled heir of Hudson River gentry, and Stalin, born Joseph Dzhugashvili three years before the president, the son of a drunken peasant and a laundress. A bright lad, growing up in the small Georgian town of Gori, and sent to Tiflis Theological Seminary when he was fourteen, the religious studies somehow helping to shape the revolutionary that Stalin became at age nineteen.

When FDR was writing editorials in the Harvard *Crimson* chiding the student body for "listless cheering" at football games, Stalin was denouncing the czarist regime in clandestine publications. When FDR was "running for Dickey," Stalin was arrested for leading a riot. When FDR was going to debutante dances, Stalin was robbing a bank to obtain funds for the party. One was formed in opposition, the other in adherence to the system he grew up in.

When FDR was a young lawyer in New York, Stalin was Bolshevik leader of the Caucasus, wanted by the police, living with forged papers. By the time FDR was a state senator, Stalin was a famous public enemy. In 1916, when FDR was fishing off his yacht in Campobello, Stalin was in Siberian exile, and survived by floating logs down the river with 100 hooks on them, towing the caught sturgeon in a rowboat.

When the Bolsheviks came to power in 1917, Stalin was a key figure at thirty-eight. Lenin made him general secretary of the Central Committee in April 1922, a post he kept for thirty years. A month later, Lenin suffered a stroke, and before his death two years later he recommended that his protégé be removed from the Central Committee because "Stalin is too rude." Thus the break with Trotsky, and the struggle for leaderships that the more unscrupulous man won.

As Roosevelt rose through the electoral process, Stalin increased his power through intrigue and maneuver, in a system that could not resolve its internal differences without bloodshed. Compared to the American republic, the Bolshevik regime was still in its infancy when Roosevelt met Stalin—its entire history was condensed in one nightmarish quarter century. Stalin was its second leader—it was as if, all proportions kept, Roosevelt had been the successor of George Washington. Forms of leadership depend on the dangers to be warded off, and the Bolshevik state was plunged at once in civil war, Reds against Whites, with the Whites armed and financed by outside nations, including Britain, where Churchill, then secretary of war, was the most impassioned anti-Bolshevik in the government. (Later, in *Great Contemporaries,* Churchill would describe George Bernard Shaw's 1937 visit to Russia this way: ". . . and Arch Commissar Stalin, 'the man of steel,' flung open the closely-guarded sanctuaries of the Kremlin, and pushing aside his morning's budget of death warrants and *lettres de cachet,* received his guest with smiles of overflowing comradeship.") Then they were attacked by the Poles, who got as far as Kiev—it was a four-year war that bred in Stalin the fear of invasion and the hatred of traitors.

He ruled a nation that was always under threat, from outside enemies and from "deviationists." A Soviet leader could never relax and count on a system that worked, like the American two-party system of fixed elections. He had great power, but also great insecurity, which was conducive to paranoia, to the belief that one is surrounded by enemies and that setbacks are not the product of human error or circumstance but of treason.

While Roosevelt defeated the economic royalists at the polls, Stalin liquidated the entire class of rich peasants, of whom at least 5 million were exiled or imprisoned or killed. Stalin really believed that every kulak was hiding grain. Then came the terror of the thirties, where, in a population of 170 million, an estimated 4 million were arrested. The purge, and the practice of self-incrimination at public trials, became normal methods of government, just as elections every two years for the House and every six years for the Senate were normal methods in the United States. It was a system that institutionalized brutality in the name of social progress.

Now, in 1943, Stalin was devillainized because he was an ally fighting an even greater villain. He had already fought three wars—the war to save Russia against the Whites and the Poles, the war to preserve the Bolshevik system and his own power, and the war against Hitler's armies, which was going well. At Teheran, he was embarking on the fourth, the war to dominate Eastern Europe and establish Russia as a world power.

How could Roosevelt, who knew so little of the forces that had shaped Stalin, guess that this dignified and self-possessed gentleman, so calm and soft-spoken as he puffed on his pipe with the white dot of Dunhill, was the man who had raved at and terrorized his subordinates, once scribbling on an appeal for mercy from a general, "scoundrel and male whore"?

Roosevelt saw a man who might become a useful partner, with whom, as it became clear at this first meeting, he saw eye to eye on key issues. Like FDR, Stalin did not think much of de Gaulle, who acted as though he was the head of a great state while in fact he had little power. The real physical France under Pétain, he said, was helping Germany by providing ports, materials, and machines for the war effort, and this France should be punished for its attitude. The French ruling class should not share in any of the benefits of peace in view of their record of collaboration with Germany.

FDR said that Churchill wanted France quickly reconstructed as a strong nation, while he felt that years of honest labor would be necessary before this was possible. Here was an initial point of agreement between the two leaders, who both wanted a weak postwar Europe to avoid further wars. Russia, like America, had twice been drawn into European wars; both had been attacked by surprise in 1941.

Stalin then said he did not propose to have the Allies shed blood to restore Indochina to colonial rule. FDR said he agreed 100 percent. After 100 years of French rule, the inhabitants of Indochina were worse off than before.

FDR said it would be better not to discuss India with Churchill, who merely proposed to defer the entire question to the end of the war. Stalin agreed it was a sore spot with the British. FDR suggested reform from the bottom, "somewhat on the Soviet line." The young Foreign Service man and Soviet expert who was acting as interpreter, Charles E. Bohlen, thought the president's remark betrayed his ignorance about the Soviet Union, where a clique of revolutionaries had imposed revolution from the top.

Stalin replied that the Indian question was complicated, with different levels of culture and isolated castes. Reform from the bottom, he said, would amount to revolution.

As the two leaders ended their first talk and prepared to go to the 4:00 P.M. plenary session, they could reflect that they shared similar worldviews. They both wanted to neutralize Europe so as not to be drawn by European quarrels into further wars, and they both appeared to favor the dismantling of the colonial empires of France and Britain (though Stalin had been more diffident about India than Roosevelt might have wished), which would end their tenure as world powers. In this they were natural allies against Churchill, with his unreconstructed Tory principles and his determination to maintain the British Empire. At the plenary session, they would find that they were allies on more immediate military matters as well.

Churchill, Roosevelt, and Stalin took their places at the round table with the green baize cover. It was the first time that the three had gathered to discuss the conduct of the war. At the president's insistence, there was no agenda. It was the kind of seat-of-the-pants flying he liked best.

Chairing the first meeting, FDR opened by saying that the English Channel was a disgreeable body of water to cross, unsafe for military operations prior to May 1, which was why Overlord had been set for May.

Churchill had laryngitis. He was in a sour mood because he had practically lost his voice, but he broke in at this point to say that the British had every reason to be thankful that the English Channel was a disagreeable body of water.

FDR had previously mentioned that the United States was bearing the brunt in the Pacific, with most of its Navy and a million men. The distances were so great that a supply ship operating from the West Coast could make only three round-trips a year.

In response, Stalin made what was perhaps the most dramatic statement of the conference—when Germany was defeated, Russia would join the war against Japan. Here was another reason for FDR to court Stalin, to make sure he did not change his mind.

Then they turned to Overlord, with Churchill offering his plan for operations in the Aegean islands, which might bring Turkey into the war.

Stalin came down hard against this dispersal. It was unwise to scatter forces through the eastern Mediterranean, he said. He preferred holding the line in Italy and following Overlord with an invasion of Southern France. In any case, he said, the Turks would not enter the war. Churchill said they would not be "so mad" as to miss the chance of joining the Allies. Stalin replied that some people preferred to stay mad.

The Americans were relieved to have Stalin's help against Churchill's Mediterranean fixation. FDR said he was opposed to any delays for Overlord.

The first meeting ended at 7:30 with Churchill checked by the Roosevelt-Stalin combination. Alan Brooke found himself admiring Stalin's quick grasp of all the strategic implications. He was more farsighted than Churchill, for he made his strategy fit his long-range political aims. When he said that Turkey would not come in, what he was really saying was that he wanted the British and the Americans to stay out of the Balkans. Nor was he in any hurry for the Allies to push up the leg of Italy, which would place them uncomfortably close to Austria and Yugoslavia.

An hour later, FDR was host at a dinner of steak and baked potatoes, and the discussion continued. As the guests assembled, the president mixed martinis, which were mostly vermouth and ice, and offered one to Stalin, asking him how he liked it. "Well, all right," Stalin replied politely, "but it is cold on the stomach."

Perhaps his tongue was loosened by the martinis and the dinner wine, for Stalin became violent on the subject of France. She had no right to retain her former empire, he said, and her entire ruling class was rotten to the core. It would be not only unjust but dangerous to leave in French hands any important strategic points after the war.

FDR said he agreed in part. New Caledonia and Dakar should be placed under United Nations trusteeship.

Churchill said he could not conceive of a civilized world without a flourishing and lively France.

Turning to Germany, FDR said that the very word "Reich" should be stricken from the language.

Stalin replied that it was not enough to eliminate the word, the Reich itself must be made impotent to ever again plunge the world into war. He favored dismemberment of Germany.

Once again, Stalin and FDR had similar views, while Churchill, thinking of the postwar balance of power in a Europe overshadowed by a strong and expansionist Russia, was prepared to be more lenient with the Germans.

At this point, FDR turned green, and beads of sweat appeared on his face. He put his hand to his forehead, and asked to be excused. It turned out to be nothing worse than indigestion, but he was absent for the rest of the evening, as Stalin and Churchill continued to argue about Germany.

Stalin said German industry must be dismantled. Between the wars, watch factories had made fuses for shells, and furniture factories had made toy rifles used to train thousands of soldiers. Churchill said he was not against the toilers but against the leaders. Stalin spoke bitterly of the toilers' blind obedience. In 1907 when he was in Leipzig, he said, 200 German workers had failed to show up at an important mass meeting because there was no controller at the station to punch their tickets, which would permit them to leave the platform.

Churchill suggested they change the subject to Poland. Britain had gone to war on account of Poland. What did Marshal Stalin think about frontiers? Taking three matches, he showed how the Polish border could be moved westward, in the same way that soldiers at drill executed the order "left close," even if that meant stepping on some German toes. The two leaders agreed to try to settle the question of Poland's borders without consulting the Poles. The idea was that Poland could be moved to the west, like a piece of furniture, with the Russians taking some Polish territory in the east, which would be compensated by the Poles taking some German territory in the west.

The next morning, the twenty-ninth, Churchill invited FDR to lunch, but the president declined, not wanting Stalin to think he was hatching private schemes with his British ally. Churchill was put out, telling his doctor, Charles Wilson: "It is not like him."

The British were alarmed by the all too obvious Russo-American entente. "This conference is over when it has only begun," Brooke said. "Stalin has got the President in his pocket." Churchill told Sir Alexander Cadogan that he realized what a small nation Britain was when "I sat with the great Russian bear on one side of me, with paws outstretched, and on the other side the great American buffalo, and between the two sat the poor little English donkey, who was the only one . . . who knew the right way home."

Such was the always present though unstated British assumption: they were right because they had been at it longer, while the Americans were raw beginners and the Russians were barbarians. The British had Cromwell behind them, and Pitt and Disraeli. They had fought Louis XIV and Napoleon. In fact, they were obsessed by the more recent experience of World War I and the sacrifice of an entire generation. Behind all the stated reasons, the fixation on Mediterranean operations was a subliminal attempt to delay and perhaps avoid the heavy casualties of Overlord. As acknowledged by one of their own military experts, Major General Sir John Kennedy, assistant chief of the Imperial General Staff under Brooke: "Had we had our way, I think there can be little doubt that the invasion of France would not have been done in 1944."

Although turning down lunch with Churchill, FDR held a second private meeting with Stalin that afternoon at 2:45, and described his concept of the postwar world: a United Nations Assembly, with an Executive Committee, and a third body, the Four Policemen, the enforcers, ready to meet any threat.

Stalin said the small nations of Europe would object to China, which was not a powerful state. Nor would England be after the war, he might have added, financially drained and shorn of her empire. Already the idea of the Four Policemen was heading in the direction of Two Policemen, two superpowers who would divide Europe into spheres of influence.

At the second plenary session at 3:30, Stalin popped a highly embarrassing question: "Who will command Overlord?" he asked. FDR said it had not been decided. Leaning over to Admiral Leahy, he whispered, "That old Bolshevik is trying to force me to give him the name of our Supreme Commander. I just can't tell him because I have not yet made up my mind."

"Then nothing will come out of these operations," Stalin said. He still thought the Allies were stalling, and asked about the timing of the operation.

FDR said it should not be later than May 15 or 20.

"I don't care if it is the first, the fifteenth, or the twentieth," Stalin said, "but a definite date is important." As he spoke, in a low, almost inflectionless voice, he doodled wolf heads on a pad with a red pencil.

Churchill did not agree. He did not think the many great possibilities in the Mediterranean should be cast aside as valueless merely on the question of a month's delay in Overlord.

Stalin looked across the table at Churchill and said: "I wish to pose a very direct question to the Prime Minister about Overlord. Do the Prime Minister and the British staff really believe in Overlord?"

Churchill had his back to the wall. It was an obvious question, but one that FDR had never been able to ask. Glowering and chomping on his cigar, he said that provided there were not more than twelve German mobile divisions behind the coastal troops, "when the time comes it will be our stern duty to hurl across the Channel against the Germans every sinew of our strength."

"What if there are thirteen divisions?" Stalin asked.

"Naturally," Churchill replied.

Stalin's tenacity had pinned the British down, much to the annoyance of Brooke, who wrote in his diary: "After listening to the arguments put forward during the last two days I feel more like entering a lunatic asylum or nursing-home!"

That evening at the dinner he hosted, Stalin was relentless in his badgering of Churchill, with Roosevelt seeming to enjoy his old friend's discomfiture—trying to be pals with Uncle Joe, thought Bohlen.

"I can't understand you at all," Stalin said. "In 1919 [when Churchill was supporting the anti-Bolsheviks] you were so keen to fight and now you don't seem to be at all. What happened? Is it advancing age? How many divisions do you have in contact with the enemy? What is happening to all those 2 million men you have in India?"

On and on it went. Almost every remark was barbed. Just because the Russians were simple people, Stalin said, it was a mistake to believe they were blind and could not see what was before their eyes. He strongly implied that Churchill nursed a secret affection for the Germans and wanted a soft peace.

In fact, Stalin went on, 50,000 and perhaps 100,000 of the German general staff must be physically liquidated. Churchill took strong exception to what he termed the cold-blooded execution of soldiers who had fought for their country, ignoring frantic signs from Anthony Eden that he was being teased. "I would rather be taken out into the garden here and now and be shot myself," Churchill said, "than sully my own country's honor by such infamy."

Always the arbitrator, FDR said he would put the number to be executed at 49,000, hoping to reduce the matter to ridicule.

The conversation turned to postwar bases, and Churchill said that although Britain did not seek to acquire new territory, no one would take Singapore or Hong Kong away without a war. When Churchill asked Stalin what his territorial interests were, he replied: "There is no need to speak at the present time about any Soviet desires, but when the time comes, we will speak."

The next morning, November 30, Churchill sought a private meeting with Stalin, since Roosevelt had been seeing him and had avoided Churchill in spite of their close friendship and the intertwining of their vital interests. When he once again presented the British case, Stalin warned him that the Red Army was counting on Overlord. The Russians were war weary. A feeling of isolation might develop in the Red Army. Like presidents and prime ministers, authoritarian rulers had to respond to the demands of the governed masses. There was a point beyond which Stalin could not go. He required a second front to remain in effective command of the army.

At the third plenary session that afternoon it was announced that Overlord would definitely be launched in May. The Americans, repeatedly stalemated in their conferences with the British, prevailed when backed by the

Russians. Stalin promised a large-scale offensive in May to keep the Germans pinned down in the east (it actually began on June 23).

That evening was Churchill's sixty-ninth birthday, and he hosted a dinner in the British legation dining room, which was decorated in the Persian style, with the walls covered by a mosaic of small bits of mirror, and curtains of deep red over the windows, and Persian waiters in blue and red liveries with white cotton gloves, the tips of the fingers flapping as they passed the plates. In the center of the table was a large birthday cake. The evening was cordial, and many toasts were drunk. Churchill repaid the teasing of the previous night with high praise, describing Stalin as worthy to stand with the great figures of Russian history and deserving the title "Stalin the Great." He toasted FDR for guiding his country along the "tumultuous stream of party friction and internal politics amidst the violent freedoms of democracy."

In that casual tone that made earthshaking events sound like Sunday outings, Roosevelt recorded that "the conferences have been going well, tho' I found I had to go along with the Russians on military plans. This morning the British came along, too, to my great relief. . . . This trip has been worth every mile of travel."

Political questions had been postponed until December 1, the fourth and final day of the conference, because of the debate on Overlord. Stalin had insisted on a decision before other matters were discussed, and had obtained it without having to give anything away in exchange, except the promise of an offensive in the east. With Overlord a certainty, the Allies were counting on that offensive, which meant that they needed Stalin. He now had some leverage for achieving his goals in Eastern Europe, aside from the claim that he had been fighting alone for so long.

Before the plenary session at 3:20 that afternoon, FDR had his third and most important private meeting with Stalin. He told him that there was an election in 1944, and while personally he did not wish to run again, if the war was still in progress he might have to. Thus Stalin was the first to learn that Roosevelt might seek a fourth term.

Stalin had two things on his mind: First, he wanted the Allies to agree to a border between Poland and the Soviet Union that would correspond to the 1919 Curzon Line, which roughly matched the border drawn by Molotov and Ribbentrop in 1939. With this border, portions of eastern Poland would be annexed by the Soviet Union, which was of course unthinkable to the Poles. Second, he wanted the Allies to agree in writing to the incorporation of the Baltic states as part of the Soviet Union, an annexation of three small, independent states.

As to Poland, the president said, there were between 6 and 7 million Polish-Americans, and as a political man he did not want to lose their votes in 1944. Of course he agreed with Stalin about the westward shift in Poland's borders, but he hoped that Stalin would understand that for political reasons he could not take part in any such arrangement, now or even next winter.

Roosevelt's disclosure that he would stay out of discussions on Poland was not calculated to restrain Stalin, who detected in the American president a willingness to let him have his way in disputed areas bordering on the Soviet Union. Indeed, two months before Teheran, FDR told Cardinal Spellman: "There is no point to oppose these desires of Stalin because he has the power to get them anyhow. So better give them gracefully."

Roosevelt saw that there was no way to stop Stalin in areas occupied by the Red Army. He did not want to disturb the military accords just arrived at by making political demands that would be impossible to enforce. In the long run, a strong Russia and a strong America, along with England and China, were the best safeguards for a postwar peace, with a dismembered Germany and a weakened France and Italy making it unlikely that another war could start in Europe.

As to the Baltic states, Roosevelt said he fully realized that they had through history been part of Russia. Jokingly, he said that when the Red Army reoccupied these areas he did not intend to go to war with the Soviet Union. However, there were in the United States a number of Lithuanians, Latvians, and Estonians. The big issue at home and in world opinion would be the expression of the peoples' will. There should be some sort of referendum, perhaps not right after reoccupation by Soviet forces, but some day, and personally he was confident that the people would vote to join the Soviet Union.

With a wink to Stalin, FDR was in effect saying: "Go ahead and hold your referendum, even though you and I know it's rigged, as long as you satisfy public opinion."

Not understanding the president's offer, Stalin insisted that the Baltic republics had exercised no autonomy under the last czar and he did not see why the question of public opinion was now being raised.

Trying to make his position more obvious, FDR replied that the truth of the matter was that the public neither knew nor understood what was involved here. In other words, public opinion would be easy to manipulate.

Still not getting it, Stalin said there would be plenty of chances under the Soviet constitution to express the will of the people, but that he could not agree to any form of international control.

FDR had not mentioned international control, and now suggested that Stalin make some declaration about future elections. He was sending a clear signal that he had no intention of bargaining over Poland's borders or the annexation of the Baltic states. First the war had to be won, and the Red Army would have to keep killing Germans.

And yet the Allies would never again be in as favorable a position to extract concessions from Stalin, for they still held the biggest bargaining chip—Overlord. But because there was no united British-American position on Overlord, the chance was lost to use it effectively to check Stalin in Eastern Europe. Instead, FDR had to align himself with Stalin to impose Overlord on the British, which made it impossible for him to ask for anything in return for the launching of the invasion.

Later in the day, there was the curious spectacle of Stalin and Churchill rearranging the lives of millions of people as they studied maps of Europe and carved up Poland, which would give up eastern areas to Russia and gain western areas in Germany, its new western borders being the Oder-Neisse line, although no one thought to ask which branch of the Neisse was meant, which would lead to future confusion. Churchill said it did not break his heart to cede parts of Germany to Poland and the Lvov area to Russia. He would try to obtain the agreement of the exiled Polish government in London. FDR stayed out of it, asking only whether the area the Poles were gaining was about equal to the area they were losing. He watched as Stalin drew the new eastern border of Poland on a map with a red crayon, illustrating the powerlessness of the Poles to determine their own fate and the ascendance of the Soviet Union in Eastern Europe.

Nor did Churchill and Roosevelt protest when Stalin accused the London Poles of being pro-German and of sending agents to kill partisans in Poland. Their silence implied that they would not do much to prevent Stalin from installing a puppet government in Warsaw.

The last item on the agenda was Germany, with all three leaders now agreed on some form of dismemberment. Churchill wanted to separate Prussia, "the evil core of German militarism," from the rest of Germany. FDR had a plan to divide Germany in five. To use the American expression, Churchill commented, the president had "said a mouthful." Stalin said it did not matter whether Germany was divided in six states or two, it had to be kept from making combinations with other countries such as Hungary.

Did Stalin contemplate a Europe composed of little states, disjoined, separated, and weak, Churchill asked.

Not Europe, Stalin replied, only Germany. Poland would be strong, France would be strong, Italy would be strong. FDR said Germany had been less dangerous to civilization when divided into 107 principalities. Churchill said he hoped for larger units. At stake once again was the role of Europe in the postwar world, which Churchill sought to maintain in a classic balance-of-power arrangement, while Stalin and Roosevelt wanted a diminished Europe, unable to drag them into future wars.

On this note, the Teheran Conference ended. FDR had courted Stalin, believing that generosity and friendliness would cement their alliance. He promised, for instance, that one-third of the Italian fleet would be turned over to the Soviet Union. But in 1944, the Combined Chiefs of Staff objected to the transfer because the ships were needed for Overlord and the transfer would anger the Italians, whose cooperation was needed. Finally, one American and thirteen British ships were handed over to the Soviet navy on the eve of Overlord.

Roosevelt found himself in agreement with most of Stalin's views—the dismemberment of Germany, the dismantling of colonial empires, the reduced postwar position of France. He was sympathetic to Stalin's desires for warm-water ports, to the annexation of the Baltic states, and to the rearrangement of Poland. A shift in the balance of power from Europe to the Soviet Union seemed at the time like the lesser of two evils, since the war they were now fighting and the war they had fought twenty years before had both originated in Europe. Some of the Soviet Union's demands would have to be met in order to win the war against Germany and Japan and guarantee the peace. FDR believed that Stalin was "getatable" and without hypocrisy, and that the Soviet Union would be cooperative in rebuilding the postwar world.

In Washington, the violently anti-Bolshevik Republican, Henry Stimson, thanked the Lord that Stalin had been at Teheran. He had saved the day. He had been direct and strong and had brushed away Churchill's diversionary attempts with a vigor that rejoiced Stimson's soul. The president had been very haphazard and Marshall, as an interested party, had kept himself aloof. The British had created a vicious circle: First, Overlord could not succeed unless German divisions were drawn away from France. Second, the only way to draw them away was an attack in the eastern Mediterranean. Third, that attack could not be made without taking ships from Overlord. Into this vicious circle, Stalin had burst like a bombshell, and by his blunt speaking deflected Churchill's efforts.

The president left Teheran feeling that the conference had been a great success. Robert Sherwood later wrote that it was "the supreme peak" of his career. Overlord had finally been nailed down, and would not be unnailed. The Soviet Union had promised to fight Japan. The end of the war was in sight, with the three Allies at last coordinating their strategies.

Beneath the surface good feelings, however, suspicions lingered. As Admiral Leahy said to Harry Hopkins when they left for Cairo on the morning of December 2: "Well, Harry, all I can say is, nice friends we have now."

And as Stalin later told Milovan Djilas, when you came down to it, you had to be as much on your guard with Churchill and Roosevelt as you did with a couple of pickpockets. "Churchill is the kind who, if you don't watch him, will slip a kopek out of your pocket! By God, a kopek out of your pocket! And Roosevelt? Roosevelt is not like that. He dips his hand only for bigger coins."

Churchill's reputation as a statesman was founded on tenacity. He never surrendered. If you slammed the door in his face he came in through the window. Even after Teheran, in the four days Roosevelt stayed in Cairo, he kept pushing the capture of Rhodes. At dinner on December 3, he kept the president up until midnight, using "every artifice in his large repertoire," according to Admiral Leahy, to get FDR to drop the Burma operation and use those forces to seize Rhodes. "The President didn't budge," Leahy said. "Roosevelt insisted that promises to Chiang Kai-shek be fully carried out."

But on December 6, at a meeting with Hopkins and Stilwell, FDR asked, "Well, Joe, what do you think of the bad news? We're in an impasse. I've been stubborn as a mule for four days but we can't get anywhere ... the British just won't do the operation."

"I am interested to know how this affects our policy in China," Stilwell said.

"Well now, we've been friends with China for a gre-e-e-at many years. I ascribe a large part of this feeling to the missionaries. You know I have a China history. My grandfather went out there, to Swatow and Canton, in 1829, and even went up to Hankow. He did what was every American's ambition in those days—he made a million dollars, and when he came back he put it into western railroads. And in eight years he lost every dollar. Ha! Ha! Ha! Then in 1856 he went out again and stayed all through the Civil War and made another million. This time he put it into coal mines, and they didn't pay a dividend until two years after he died. Ha! Ha! Ha!"

FDR had big plans for making China a great power and Hong Kong a free port, but he had to renege on the amphibious operation. Ships were needed for Overlord, and something had to give, and it was Burma.

For three days, on December 4, 5, and 6, there were meetings with Turkish President Ismat Inönü and his people, and Churchill pleaded, cajoled, and almost threatened the soldier president of the once-powerful Ottoman state to bring his people into the war, all in vain. Marshall was relieved, for he did not want the Turks to come in and "burn our logistics right down the line."

Marshall—there was another problem FDR had been turning over in his mind. There was sure to be an outcry back home if he was named to command Overlord. The isolationist press would be up in arms. The Joint Chiefs would be upset. He would lose the one man who could control General MacArthur, and who could tame the wild men in Congress.

On December 4, FDR sent Hopkins to tell Marshall he was concerned about the appointment, which was the tip-off that he had changed his mind. On December 5, he asked Marshall to lunch at his villa. Marshall was too much the soldier to ask for the supreme command of the greatest operation of the war, even though it was the dream of his life. After much beating around the bush, FDR asked him what he wanted to do. So, Marshall thought, it would be left up to him to exercise self-denial. Marshall repeated that he wanted the president to feel free to act in the best interest of the country. He would cheerfully go wherever he was needed. That was enough for FDR, who said: "Well, I didn't feel I could sleep at ease if you were out of Washington." Self-denial could be a form of heroism. Marshall gave up the command to Eisenhower, whose path to the presidency was thus set.

Back in Tunis on December 7, FDR told his new commander, "Well, Ike, you'd better start packing." That night he recorded in the diary he kept during the trip: "Tonight I had Elliott and Eisenhower and [Carl] Spaatz & 9 of

Elliott's staff officers to dine—dinner cooked by Elliott's mess—& served by two Italian prisoners who like %10 of all the wops are crazy to come to the U.S. for 'good.' "

Before leaving Cairo, Roosevelt and Churchill had driven across the Nile to Giza on December 6 to see the Sphinx. As the evening shadows fell, the prime minister and the president, who had been pictured as a Sphinx by a cartoonist, stood gazing at the winged lion with the head of a woman, a colossal figure of natural rock 189 feet long. Dwarfed by this wonder of the world, they remained for a long time in silence. Did this half woman, half beast know the answer to the riddle of what the next year would bring? Would the landing in France succeed? Would Stalin roll back Hitler's armies? Would the president run for an unprecedented fourth term? She told them nothing, maintaining her inscrutable smile.

XXIII

We Thought We Were Done with These Things

We thought we were done with these things but we were wrong.
We thought because we had power, we had wisdom.
We thought the long train would run to the end of Time.
We thought the light would increase.
            Stephen Vincent Benét, "Litany for Dictatorships"

War was the word on the lips and on the minds of Americans, from the president on down to the economic royalists, two of whom, J. P. Morgan and his partner, Thomas W. Lamont, were at lunch in early January 1944, wondering what kind of a New Year Hitler was having, with the Allies closing in. Lamont imagined the Führer sitting in his immense glass room at Berchtesgaden on New Year's Eve, gazing out gloomily on the Bavarian Alps.

"Yes," chimed in Jack Morgan, "and I know just what he is saying"—and he rolled off these lines from *Macbeth*:

"I am sick at heart, I have liv'd long enough; my way of life
Is fall'n into the sear, the yellow leaf,
And that which should accompany old age,
As honor, love, obedience, troops of friends,
I must not look to have; but in their stead,
Curses, not loud, but deep."

And yet there was no cause for complacency. The worst fighting still lay ahead for American soldiers, and the daily casualty list did not discriminate between the humble and the mighty. Early in February, Harry Hopkins, who was about to undergo a serious operation at the Mayo Clinic, heard that his eighteen-year-old son, Stephen, had been killed in the Marshall Islands. He died while carrying ammunition to an isolated machine-gun nest on the Kwajalein atoll, a boy not yet out of his teens, who in civilian life would have been starting college. His father was called "Rasputin," and it was said that his illness was "Potomac fever," and that he profited from his association with Roosevelt. If he had, he might have kept his son alive.

Condolences arrived from Churchill in the form of another quotation from *Macbeth:*

> "Your son, my lord, has paid a soldier's debt:
> He only liv'd but till he was a man;
> The which no sooner had his prowess confirm'd
> In the unshrinking station where he fought,
> But like a man he died."

While men were dying in places with obscure names, the president was carrying in his mind a global war, a railroad strike, a threatened steel strike, and a revolt in Congress. Without consulting the chairman of the Ways and Means or Finance committees, he had vetoed a tax bill on the grounds that it favored business interests that were lobbying Congress. For example, cut timber was taxed as a capital gain instead of as a crop liable to pay ordinary rates.

On February 21, FDR met with the Big Four—Vice President Wallace, Senator Majority Leader Alben Barkley, Speaker of the House Sam Rayburn, and House Majority Leader John McCormack. He read extracts from his veto message, dwelling at length on the capital gains provisions for lumbermen. Barkley took sharp issue but, as Wallace noted, Roosevelt didn't seem to listen. He had a habit of taking the ball and running with it. It was like the time when he had received an ambassador just back from five years in Brazil by saying: "Let me tell you about Brazil."

A disgusted Barkley drove back to the Hill with Wallace, saying "What's the use? I am through. I can't get the votes in the Senate under the methods that are being followed." The next day, FDR sent up his veto message, which included the phrase that the bill would "rob the needy to enrich the greedy." It was like waving a red flag in Barkley's face.

On February 23, Barkley resigned as majority leader, repudiating the president whose errand boy in the upper house he had been for seven years. It was the most dramatic session of the Senate that Wallace had ever seen. When Barkley began to speak, the chamber filled up, with people coming over from the House. All the pent-up resentment of Congress came out in the normally courtly man who had always been loyal to Roosevelt. "In his effort to belittle and discredit Congress throughout his veto of this bill," Barkley thundered, "the President says 'this is not a tax bill but a tax relief bill providing relief not for the needy but for the greedy.' That statement, Mr. President, is a calculated and deliberate assault upon the legislative integrity of every member of the Congress of the United States." As he finished, by asking Congress to override the veto "if it has any self-respect yet left," every senator there jumped to his feet and applauded for nearly two minutes.

It was a highly emotional occasion, with the same kind of rapt attention you get around a prize ring, Wallace thought, even though one of the fighters wasn't there. Wallace wished FDR had not come down so heavy on the cut trees. What he was really doing was giving Sam Rayburn an oblique lesson on capital gains for Texas oil, not realizing it would infuriate Barkley.

The president was at Hyde Park, and William D. Hassett, his new press secretary, found him in his little study, examining old documents with his friend and cousin, Margaret Suckley. "Alben must be suffering from shell shock," FDR observed on hearing the news. Hassett thought it was remarkable that there was not a word of anger or recrimination.

For the first time in American history, Congress overrode a veto of a revenue bill, 72 to 14. Barkley's resignation was accepted, and then he was reelected as majority leader. He was now a hero for defying the president.

There was another setback on the soldier vote bill. To assure the passage of a federal ballot for the men in uniform, FDR sent Congress a message that January, which was read to the Senate while it was considering the bill: would 11 million servicemen be denied their vote because there was no federal machinery? This was seen as gross interference in the affairs of the Senate. Also, southern senators saw the bill as an attempt to circumvent the poll tax and allow blacks to vote. As a southern senator put it: "Roosevelt says we're letting the soldiers down. Why, God damn him. The rest of us have boys who got into the Army and Navy as privates and ordinary seamen and dig latrines and swab decks and his scamps go in as lieutenant-colonels and majors and lieutenants and spend their off time getting medals in Hollywood. Letting the soldiers down! Why, that son of a bitch. Who's proposing this thing, anyway?" It was Lucas of Illinois, a product of the Chicago machine, and Guffey of Pennsylvania, and "dear Alben. These three great statesmen are asking us to set aside the Constitution 'because of an emergency.' . . . Why those bastards! Just a bunch of political thimbleriggers, that's what they are, them and that—that man in the White House."

The other objection to the soldier vote was that FDR would be running again, and the soldiers would be marched up en masse to the polls to vote for their commander in chief. "If the Commander-in-Chief would remove himself as a candidate," one senator said, "this bill would pass in a day."

And yet, as Bill Hassett observed, "the Boss is as noncommittal as the statue of Elmer Poughkeepsie" regarding the fourth term. At the White House correspondents' dinner on March 4, some of the boys said this might be the last one FDR would host. Bob Hope was MC, and one of his gags was: "Mr. Roosevelt has been president so long that when I was a boy my father said to me, 'Bob, maybe some day you will grow up to be vice president.'"

Sure that he would run again, Congress watered down the soldier vote bill so that it was under state control. FDR was so annoyed that he did not sign it, though it became law.

Those close to the president saw that he was in poor health, which could have a bearing on fourth term plans. Recovering from post-Teheran bronchitis, his voice was husky and out of pitch. When Hassett asked him how he felt, he said "like hell." On March 26, with a temperature of 104, he decided to go to the Naval Hospital in Bethesda for a checkup.

On March 27, Howard J. Bruenn, a cardiologist in the Naval Reserve, was on duty when the president was wheeled in and lifted to the examining table by attendants. He had a cough that produced yellow sputum and seemed very tired. His complexion was gray. X rays showed an enlargement of the cardiac shadow, mainly of the left ventricle, due to a dilated aorta. The diagnosis was alarming: acute bronchitis, cardiac failure of the left ventricle, high blood pressure, and heart disease.

None of these findings had been suspected by Roosevelt's regular doctor, Ross McIntire. Dr. Bruenn's recommendations were one or two weeks in bed, a reduced salt intake, weight reduction, codeine to control the cough, and sedation to ensure sleep. But these recommendations were rejected because of the demands on the president's time.

In the next few days, half a dozen medical experts discussed the situation. There was definite congestive heart failure. Dr. Frank Lahey, a medical consultant to the Navy, said the situation was serious enough to warrant giving the president the full facts.

On April 1, Dr. Bruenn examined Roosevelt again. His color was poor and he was short of breath. It was agreed that he would take digitalis for his heart, cut his cigarettes to six a day, and eat less. He weighed 188 pounds, all in the chest and abdomen because of the atrophied legs. The president agreed to take a nap in the afternoon. Thereafter, Dr. Bruenn saw him three or four times a week, in the morning after breakfast.

Dr. Bruenn accompanied the presidential party when FDR left in May to spend two weeks at Bernie Baruch's estate in South Carolina, Hobcaw. Hassett, who detested Baruch, felt that he was only inviting the president to make himself seem important. In a remark that was deleted from the published version of his diary, Hassett repeated the anti-Semitic joke about Hitler's Germany, where "after the circumcision, they throw away the Jew."

Roosevelt took a breather at Hobcaw, going over the contents of the pouch, signing papers, and receiving visits from Eleanor, Anna, and Lucy Mercer Rutherfurd, who lived in nearby Aiken.

He had some trouble with what at first he thought was a growth in his colon. Then suddenly it moved to his left side under his heart, and then to his right side. It could not be a growth, moving around like that, but it was very painful. Dr. Bruenn gave him codeine injections to relieve the pain of what was apparently a gallbladder attack. He had gone to Bernie's with a big box of stamps that he never opened, and a stack of detective stories that he didn't read. He just sat around or lay down without trying to do anything, which was most unusual.

Back in Washington on May 18, FDR kept to his new schedule of callers before lunch, lunch alone or with the family, and a nap after lunch, with no afternoon visitors. As he wrote Harry Hopkins, who was recovering from his operation in White Sulphur Springs, "I . . . have cut my drinks down to one and a half cocktails per evening and nothing else—not one complimentary highball or nightcap. Also, I have cut my cigarettes down from twenty or thirty a day to five or six a day. . . . My plans—my medical laboratory work not being finished—are to be here about three days a week and to spend the other four days a week at Hyde Park, Shangri-La or on the Potomac. For later in the summer I have various hens sitting but I don't know when they will hatch out. I had a really grand time down at Bernie's—slept twelve hours out of the twenty-four, sat in the sun, never lost my temper, and decided to let the world go hang. The interesting thing is the world didn't hang. I have a terrific pile in my basket but most of the stuff has answered itself anyway."

Here was a seriously ill president, at a time when methods for hypertension control were still primitive, who would have to decide within weeks whether to run for a fourth term. The true state of his health was kept secret, and Dr. McIntire produced regular announcements that the president's health was excellent in all respects.

Morgenthau, who did not know the true state of his health, sensed that something was wrong at a cabinet meeting on May 18. The president was flippant and uninformed. When Stettinius, who was acting secretary of state, reported on the coup of a group of army officers in Argentina who were favorable to the Axis, the president said: "Well, Ed, you make a bad face at the Argentinians once a week. You have to treat them like children."

Perplexed, Stettinius replied: "Mr. President, I don't think that that is enough. After all, we can win the war in Europe, win it in Asia, and find out we have a strong rich fascist country at our back yard."

When they discussed China, the president said the answer was price controls, which to Morgenthau showed a complete ignorance of the situation. After the cabinet, he said to Wallace: "I have never heard the President have so much misinformation or be so badly informed on any subject."

The president's decline in health coincided with a time of strain in the partnership with England. In many areas the Allies were at odds. Churchill wanted to recognize de Gaulle's committee, but FDR did not. Churchill wanted to keep the Italian king on the throne, while FDR insisted the Italian people should have the sort of government they wanted.

The postwar struggle for the maintenance of empire and the old order in Europe had already begun, and FDR was amusingly critical of the British, pointing out that they had given some Lend-Lease pipe to King Ibn Saud so that he could bring drinking water to his palace.

When Stettinius came to call on March 17 before leaving for London, FDR gave him a lecture on one of his favorite subjects, colonial trusteeships. "Back in 1936," he said, "the Secretary [Hull] and I proposed it for a little island in the Pacific—Canton Island. Pan-American airways needed it for an air base in the hop to New Zealand and Australia. We sent a little group down to establish a base, and the British sent a cruiser down and asked our people to get off because the island was a British possession. The head of our group asked how they figured that one out. The British officer produced a map. 'Well?' our man asked. 'It is shown in red on the map,' the officer replied. Apparently anything shown as red anywhere on a map belongs to the British."

Roosevelt then mimicked the accent of the British ambassador, Sir Ronald Lindsay: "Well now, Mr. President, this is a British island. You simply can't do this." "But Ronnie, I've done it," the president said, still with the accent. The British would take land anywhere in the world even if it were only a rock or a sandbar, the president said. They would not give in on any colony belonging to another country, such as French Indochina, because they were afraid we would ask them to do the same in some of their possessions, such as Burma or the Malay Peninsula.

The British under Churchill would not give up their colonies and, as Stettinius learned in London, would not recognize China as a great power. Churchill referred to the Chinese as "the pigtails," and said "there is no unity, and there is much Communism [in China]. For thirty-five years, we have had in China unstable government and division. It is nonsense to talk about China as a great power." On the other hand, Churchill said, a strong France was needed for a peaceful and happy Europe, even though she might be sensitive and difficult to deal with.

Other British intentions in Europe became clear at the end of May, when Churchill advised FDR that he had proposed an agreement with the Soviets on spheres of influence in Eastern Europe—the Soviets "would take the lead in Rumanian affairs, while we would take the lead in Greek affairs . . . since Rumania falls within the sphere of the Russian armies and Greece within the Allied command."

Still hoping that some degree of self-determination might be possible in Eastern Europe, FDR rejected spheres of influence, which seemed like a blatant carving up of Europe between two conquerors. It would hand all the countries that the Red Army occupied over to Stalin. It was a division of spoils that the president would not accept.

It was also just at the time of the deterioration in his health that Roosevelt was faced with a crisis on the Jewish refugee question. Saving the Jews had not been a high priority on his agenda. It was not even discussed at the summit conferences, absorbed as the Allies were in military plans. Congress was opposed to opening up the quota, and the State Department stalled on all rescue plans.

When FDR first heard about the Final Solution in September 1942, he refused to believe it, telling Felix Frankfurter that the deported Jews were simply being employed on the Soviet border to build fortifications. The first OSS report called information about German extermination plans "a wild rumor inspired by Jewish fears," though later OSS reports described the deportation of Jews to death camps in Poland.

On December 7, Rabbi Wise and other Jewish leaders gave the president a twenty-page paper on the Nazi "Blue Print for Extermination," and FDR assured the group that efforts would be made to save the Jews and punish those who had committed the crimes.

Breckinridge Long wrote in his diary that "Rabbi Wise and others like him might lend color to the charges of Hitler that we were fighting this war on account of and at the instigation and direction of our Jewish citizens."

In April 1943, there was an Anglo-American conference on refugee problems in Bermuda, in which Long played the key role. Not surprisingly, according to a British participant, it was "a facade for inaction."

On May 7, Cordell Hull assured the president that there was plenty of room under existing quotas to accommodate large numbers of Central European refugees. Enlarging the quotas, he said, would only anger Congress, "where there is a prevailing sentiment for even more drastic curtailment of immigration." FDR agreed, replying on May 14 that "I do not think we can do other than comply strictly with the present immigration laws."

In June, the president saw the Zionist leader Chaim Weizmann. Escorting him to the White House on June 12, Sumner Welles was sympathetic, saying that Ibn Saud had been writing letters demanding a stop to immigration in Palestine, "which of course is childish." The British policy was that there should be no more Jewish immigration after March 31, 1944.

Weizmann told FDR that Jews had a right to Palestine. The president said the Arabs had done very badly in this war, and that they had not developed their vast territories. Perhaps the Jews might help with the development. In any case, he believed that the Arabs could be bought. Weizmann said the 500,000 Jews in Palestine felt trapped, and that Jews must be assured they had a future there. In fact, Roosevelt did not intend to take any stand on this question, wanting to remain on good terms with his British ally and Arab leaders.

It was because of State Department obstruction that Morgenthau became active in the refugee question. He was following in the footsteps of his father, who as ambassador to Turkey had tried to help save Armenians from massacre.

In June 1943, the Treasury Department sponsored a plan to evacuate up to 70,000 Jews from Rumania at a cost of $170,000. The money would be held in Switzerland for Rumanian officials to collect after the war. The president was sympathetic, but the State Department scuttled the plan on the ground that it would make foreign exchange available to the enemy.

Morgenthau was shocked when, in August, the State Department announced the formation of a Commission to Save European Art and Monuments, when there was no commission to save the Jews. People were getting killed and months passed and there was a gang in the State Department blocking everything.

On November 26, Breck Long testified before the House Foreign Affairs Committee that in the ten years since the start of the Hitler regime about 580,000 refugees had been taken in, all under the quota. Congressman Emmanuel Celler pointed out that the majority of the 580,000 were not Jews. "Long says that the door to the oppressed is open but that it 'has been carefully screened,' " Celler said. "What he should have said is 'barlocked and bolted.' By the act of 1924 we are permitted to admit about 150,000 immigrants each year. During the last fiscal year only 23,725 came as immigrants. Of these only 4,705 were Jews fleeing Nazi persecution. If men of the temperament and philosophy of Long continue in control of immigration administration, we may as well take down that plaque from the Statue of Liberty and black out the lamp beside the golden door."

At a December 18 meeting at the Treasury Department, one of Morgenthau's assistants, Josiah E. DuBois, said: "The only question we have in our minds in dealing with this Jewish issue is to get this thing out of the State Department into some agency's hands that is willing to deal with it frontally."

Morgenthau worried aloud that people would say he was only getting involved because he was a Jew, adding: "I would say to Mr. Hull, 'After all, if you were a member of the Cabinet in Germany today, you would most likely be in a prison camp, and your wife would be God knows where, because Mrs. Hull is a Jewess, you know. Did you people know that . . . ? Her name is Wirtz. And if he were in Germany today, he couldn't hold the position he has because he is married to a Jewess, even though she changed her name to Whitney.' "

Two days later Morgenthau went to see Hull, telling him that "in simple terms, the British position is that they apparently are prepared to accept the possible—even probable—death of thousands of Jews in enemy territory because of the difficulties of disposing of any considerable number of Jews should they be rescued."

Morgenthau urged immediate action. "The trouble is," Hull said in his bumbling way, "the fellows down the line, there are some of them—I don't get a chance to know everything that is going on." That was the trouble with Hull—he didn't know what was happening on his own doorstep.

Breck Long took Morgenthau aside to say he was not responsible for the delays. "Well, Breck, as long as you raise the question," Morgenthau said, "we might be a little frank. The impression is all around that you particularly are anti-Semitic!"

"I know that is so," Long replied. "I hope that you will use your good offices to correct that impression, because I am not."

Back at the Treasury, Morgenthau complained that FDR would never get rid of people like Long. "What does he want Social Security for, or old-age pensions?" he asked. "As long as you work for the President, you don't need it. He never fired anybody."

The next step was to go to the president, and Morgenthau wanted "the most terrific document of condemnation of these people" to shake up Roosevelt, whose position, he said, "is no different from what the English Foreign Office says, and what everybody else has said. The whole strain is this: 'This whole thing is a damned nuisance.' When you get through with it, the attitude to date is no different from Hitler's attitude."

Randolph Paul, Morgenthau's general counsel, prepared the report "On the Acquiescence of This Government in the Murder of the Jews," which charged the State Department with procrastination and willful failure to act.

On January 16, 1944, Morgenthau saw the president, who agreed that some action should be taken, such as the setting up of a War Refugee Board. He defended Breckinridge Long, however, saying that Long had become soured on the problem when some of the refugees recommended by Rabbi Wise had turned out to be bad people. Morgenthau said only three of the Jews who had come to the United States had turned out to be undesirable. FDR said he had been told the figure was considerably larger.

Under the War Refugee Board, which was headed by John H. Pehle of the Treasury Department, there was a change for the better. Hull notified his embassies and legations that they should facilitate visas for Jews. In early March 1944, there arrived in Istanbul a group of Jewish children from Bulgaria. It was the first tangible saving of lives that could be attributed to Morgenthau's efforts. The board was also instrumental in getting Jews out of France and Rumania that spring.

Roosevelt was coming around to admitting some Jewish refugees outside the quota. Morgenthau recorded on May 16 the president's feeling that "if there was a specific situation involving a small group of people . . . say between five hundred and a thousand, that needed help, he would be willing to bring them in and send a message to Congress saying what he had done."

The question was, where to put them? Ickes proposed Puerto Rico, but FDR pointed out that tent cities would be destroyed during the hurricane season. The matter was turned over to Stimson, who told Morgenthau on May 20 that he had found a military camp. "How many people are they really proposing to bring over?" Stimson asked. "As near as I have it," Morgenthau said, "this is a token that we, the United States Government, aren't high and mighty in asking the rest of the world to do something which we aren't willing to do ourselves. That is what the Germans keep saying. They keep telling the people, 'Look, here the United States is asking the rest of the world to do something which they are not willing to do themselves.' "

By the time Morgenthau and Pehle saw the president, on June 8, the Allies had taken Rome, and 1,800 refugees a week were pouring into Allied-held Italy. The Army, Pehle said, was considering raising from 8,000 to

25,000 the number of refugees to be held in Italy, and from 25,000 to 40,000 those to be cared for in the Middle East. In the meantime, 1,000 refugees in southern Italy would be brought to the United States outside the quota and settled in Fort Ontario, Oswego, New York. "I know the fort very well," FDR said. "It goes back to before the Civil War times and is a very excellent place." He wanted the refugees to have health checks so they would not bring any contagious diseases into the country.

On June 12, FDR informed Congress that 1,000 refugees would be given asylum and sent home at the end of the war. Fort Ontario would be like a free port, for goods not intended for import but held in storage. It was a painless way for the president to show his concern "for the pitiful plight of the persecuted minorities of Europe."

Until Morgenthau became involved, there was no commitment to save Jews in the Roosevelt administration. A group of State Department career officers quietly sabotaged efforts to bring in refugees. Other more pressing matters crowded the subject from the president's mind. Aside from vague humanitarian instincts, he did not have a sense of urgency about the Jews. It was a bothersome marginal matter in which he had to navigate between anti-immigrant nativist sentiments in Congress and conflicting pressures within his own departments. There was a complete lack of cooperation from the British, who did not want tens of thousands of escaped Jews migrating to Palestine. Why, he may have asked himself, should this be a specifically American problem?

Had it not been for Morgenthau, nothing would have been done. The other Jews in Roosevelt's entourage, Rosenman, Frankfurter, and Baruch, took little or no part in rescue efforts. Indeed, Rosenman urged Morgenthau to tone down his report, saying: "I would have one suggestion only . . . that this proposed order applies to Poles and Greeks as well, and to all who are willing to get out. . . . Your report is liable to give him the impression that this is purely Jewish." By February 1944, when the War Refugee Board began its work, the extermination of the Jews had been under way for more than two years. Roosevelt's record on this issue was not what it might have been, but it was better than nothing. When he was forcefully confronted by Morgenthau, he acted.

On Palestine, FDR continued to refuse to side with the Jews, arguing that if the United States took a pro-Jewish position it might trigger a holy war in the Arab nations. In December 1944 he wrote Senator Wagner to oppose a joint resolution on Palestine in Congress, for which Zionist groups had been lobbying. "There are about half a million Jews there," he said. "Another million want to go. They are of all shades—good, bad, and indifferent. On the other side of the picture there are approximately seventy million Mohammedans who want to cut their throats the day they land. The one thing I want to avoid is a massacre or a situation which cannot be resolved by talking things over. Anything said or done here just now would add fuel to the flames."

* * *

A case could be made that a great president must have a ruthless edge. Roosevelt had it. The cordiality was genuine, and so was the dislike of hurting people's feelings, but when he was exercised he could be ruthless and obstinate to the point of obtuseness. This is the way he was about de Gaulle, refusing to listen to advice, refusing to be sensible, stubbornly insisting that the general did not represent the French people. The drama of recognition was played out in the unlikely arena of a currency dispute.

In preparation for the Overlord landing, some sort of money had to be printed that the Allies could use in France. This task fell to Morgenthau, who on January 8, 1944, went to see the president, who was sick in his bedroom, with Assistant Secretary of War John J. McCloy. They proposed that the bills should have the words *République Française* on them, but the president objected strenuously, saying: "How do you know what kind of a government you will have when the war is over? Maybe it will be an empire; maybe we'll have an emperor again. I don't want to do anything to indicate what kind of government it is going to be."

"It seems to me if you put on the words 'République Française' it isn't going to tie your hands at all," Morgenthau said.

"Henry, you talk just like the British Foreign Office," FDR said.

"If you fix it 'République Française,' then there is one less worry that de Gaulle is going to be a dictator," McCloy said.

"I have heard all these arguments," FDR said. "De Gaulle is on the wane." He wanted the bills to say simply *La France,* and to show a French flag supported on either side by British and American flags.

If de Gaulle was on the wane, Morgenthau wondered who was on the wax. "I am completely in the War Department's corner on this question of recognition of the Committee when we go in there," he told McCloy after the meeting, "and I think that every day we are losing means loss of lives, because more and more of the people are going to be antagonistic if and when our troops land there. . . . My God, if we had any justification for Darlan—using him as a means to an end—it seems to me that this group— let's call a spade a spade. After all, I take it what the President is doing—this is all part and parcel of not recognizing de Gaulle."

"The flag has a little *élan,*" McCloy conceded. ". . . Just the French flag waving, waving in the breeze, and *Emis en France.*"

Later that day, they met with the Free French representative Jean Monnet, who insisted that *République Française* was crucial to differentiate the bills from the Vichy currency. "I assure you it is a touchy, very fundamental issue," he said. "If we do not put 'French Republic' we create a confusion in people's minds and they will wonder why the Committee is in fact doing what Vichy has done."

"We will make one more effort," Morgenthau promised. "But supposing . . . we are unsuccessful . . . can we give an order Monday morning to go ahead?"

"That is all right," Monnet said. "But please do everything you can."

"We are all with you," Morgenthau replied. "But we are all subordinates."

The president would not budge. McCloy reflected to Morgenthau that eventually they would have to have come around to recognition. "After all, when our men land in France, they want to be treated like friends and not enemies. I am going to prophesy that in the not too distant future Churchill will make up with de Gaulle . . . and it is going to leave the president high and dry all by himself."

Stimson, who at first had disliked de Gaulle, now wanted to cooperate with him, having heard from Eisenhower that he was easier to work with and no longer anti-American. De Gaulle apparently controlled the resistance movements inside France and would be useful in helping the Allies set up some form of civil administration.

Stimson had a long talk with FDR on January 14, but found him clinging to the notion that de Gaulle would not last, and that other French groups would emerge. Stimson called General Marshall, who was in London, to tell him about the talk, and said: "A little bit at the end I thought I had him and I am going to keep on and try. . . . But I don't have much hope because . . . I have no assistance from the State Department. . . . Mr. Hull has been very strongly of the same view that de Gaulle was not to be trusted. . . . I asked him [FDR] where he got his information about the other parties and he told me it was from General Donovan [head of the OSS]. . . . This morning [January 15] McCloy and I have been talking with Donovan. I find that the President was mistaken in thinking that Donovan believes there were a lot of other groups. . . ."

Marshall reported that Churchill and Eden were disagreeing violently on the matter. Eden wanted to recognize de Gaulle and had most of the cabinet with him. "De Gaulle stands uncompromising," Marshall said, "very much as John L. Lewis. He leads his people the same way as Lewis leads his union. And he doesn't concede one inch. . . . He is implacable."

Anthony Eden felt that the resistance movement in France and the majority of French opinion were overwhelmingly behind de Gaulle. Churchill's attitude was: "Don't ask me to quarrel with the President over de Gaulle." Eden recorded in his diary on March 4: "President's absurd and petty dislike of de Gaulle blinds him. It would be folly for us to follow him in this." It was not only personal dislike on Roosevelt's part, although there was plenty of that, it was the long-range goal to have a weak France in postwar Europe, which the president had revealed to Stalin. De Gaulle was the one man who might be able to restore France, and Roosevelt was not about to help him.

With the exception of Hull, feeling in the cabinet was running in de Gaulle's favor. Ickes on April 2 wondered about "the President's bullheaded obstinacy, based largely on a personal dislike of de Gaulle, to recognize the French Committee," when even Russia had recognized it.

Roosevelt did not want de Gaulle informed about Overlord, cabling

Churchill on April 8 that "I am a good deal concerned by the French National Committee's demands in regard to military matters. The tone of these communications verges on the dictatorial, especially when we consider the simple facts. Personally I do not think that we can give military information to a source which has a bad record in secrecy. The implied threat to stay out of operations in France would if carried out do the Committee and its leaders irreparable harm."

Eisenhower, trying to bring together the hundred strands of Overlord, informed Stimson on May 11 that it was simply not feasible to keep complete secrecy from de Gaulle in an operation that included French naval, air, and airborne units, and where assistance was expected from the French resistance. Information must be divulged to a few French officers at the highest level. "The sum total of these delays and resentments," Ike wrote, "is . . . likely to result in acute embarrassment to the allied forces, and it will be too late, after the event, to correct them all." He had to count on de Gaulle for the initial approach to the French population, who would have to be reconciled to the necessity of allied bombing of their towns.

FDR did not want Eisenhower to get involved with the de Gaulle committee on a political level, writing him on May 12 that "it must always be remembered that the French people are quite naturally shell-shocked from suffering at the hands of the German occupation. . . . Some time will be required for them to think through the matters relating to their political future quietly and normally. As the liberators of France we have no right to color their views or to give any group the sole right to impose on them one side of a case."

Of course what he was really doing was spoiling the chances of the most obvious group. Eisenhower knew that he could not carry out the president's orders, for in practice there was no clear-cut demarcation between military and political matters when you were operating on foreign soil.

With Overlord only days away, Ike wrote FDR on May 26 that his information was "that there exist in France today only two major groups, of which one is the Vichy gang, and the other characterized by unreasoning admiration for de Gaulle." When they turned over liberated areas to local self-government, "it is possible that we then shall find a universal desire to adhere to the de Gaullist group."

This analysis did not please Roosevelt at all, and he replied on May 26 that "I am perfectly willing to have de Gaulle made President, or Emperor, or King or anything else so long as the action comes in an untrammeled and unforced way from the French people themselves." He didn't want any Gaullist "porch-climbing robbers" to be forced on people. How did Eisenhower know there were only two major groups in France? In fact, he had overlooked the biggest group of all, which "consists of those people who do not know what it is all about. . . . They have not made up their minds as to whether they want de Gaulle and his Committee as their rulers. . . . It is awfully easy to be for de Gaulle . . . but I have a moral duty that transcends 'an easy way'. . . . Self-determination is not a word of expediency. It carries with it a very deep principle in human affairs."

Roosevelt had been relying on Donovan's reports to back up his anti-Gaullist policy, but by this time even Donovan was reporting a surge of Gaullist sympathy in France. An April 3 OSS report for the president said: "France overwhelmingly wants de Gaulle. He has promised on his return to surround himself with a truly French government representative of those who stayed in France and resisted the invader." The tortures by the *milice* and the Germans of resistance members and their families had contributed to pro–de Gaulle sentiment.

At the end of May Churchill invited de Gaulle to London. No one would understand the French being cold-shouldered, he told FDR, asking him to send someone over with the rank of Stettinius to join in the talks. Roosevelt refused, wiring Churchill: "All good luck in your talks with prima donna."

In his continued rejection of de Gaulle, Roosevelt was exhibiting a little-noticed Calvinist streak. France had failed, and failure had to be punished. De Gaulle, even though he had dissociated himself from France's surrender by forming the Free French in London, was contaminated in Roosevelt's view. France had fallen from grace, and de Gaulle was French, and therefore he did not count for much.

The great day came, fought over so many times at conferences with the British, and still viewed with misgivings in England. Miss Wilkinson, who served under Home Secretary Herbert Morrison, told Henry Wallace that "opening up a second front is just giving jam to the Russians. We can destroy Germany from the air." With the British, Wallace reflected, it was heads I win tails you lose. If anything went wrong it would be Ike's fault, and if things went right the praise would go to Montgomery, who had postponed the invasion for thirty days. He had put in so many hedges it would not even have taken place had not England been bulging with so many American soldiers they had to be sent somewhere.

Henry Stimson thought of the thousands of young men who were facing death. He felt vindicated, for he had been urging the operation ever since Churchill had come over right after Pearl Harbor, and had also fought for an American command, while the president had wobbled all over the lot.

The armada sailed on the evening of June 5, 5,000 ships steaming out of rivers and bays along the English coast and forming two long lines half a mile apart, barrage balloons anchored by cables swaying over every third or fourth ship. Aboard the battleship HMS *Ramillies,* Captain G. B. Middleton was gloomy about the prospects. He thought it was a desperate venture to land in choppy seas on a defended coast. As he passed his flagship, he made a signal tendering his respects, to which came the reply: "I hope all your shots hit and you make German the court language of Hell."

At about midnight, Middleton heard the buzz of hundreds of planes carrying 24,000 paratroopers and towing gliders filled with soldiers. Arriving at dawn at his station off the crescent-shaped beaches along the Normandy coast, Middleton made contact with his spotter and opened fire on the shore battery that was his main target, scoring a hit on the fourth shot.

In a landing craft carrying 150 men, Colonel Russell P. Reeder, Jr., could see the red and yellow flashes of the Allied ships shelling the coast. Nearing Utah Beach, the boat grated on the sand, its iron gate dropped, and Reeder felt as if he were in the kickoff of some terrible football game. With the infantrymen of the Fourth Division, he walked out in three feet of water, German artillery flying over his head, and then ran 200 yards to the top of the dunes. There they found small white signs with death's-heads in black and the word *Minen!* Moving on, they were soon fighting German infantrymen hidden in hedgerows.

More than 150,000 men landed that day, securing a perimeter that would slowly expand into the long-awaited second front. At his press conference that afternoon, the room was packed and FDR looked well in a white shirt, with a dark blue bow tie with white polka dots, and gray cotton trousers. Once he cupped his hand to the back of his ear to hear a question. Discussing the invasion in detail, he said that Channel weather had postponed it for one day, and Eisenhower alone had determined the actual date and the landing sites. Things were going well, but the war was not over. You didn't just land on a beach and walk to Berlin.

One thing that did not go well was cooperation from de Gaulle. Furious at being left out of the invasion, he allowed only twenty of the 500 French liaison officers to make the crossing, and refused to support the Allied currency.

An angry Stimson called FDR on June 10 and said: "A leader who is supposed to be an ally of ours has virtually stabbed our troops in the back on the beach-head of France. . . . Currency is as much one of our weapons as our guns and to take this action at the moment when we are fighting to save his country puts you in a position where you should not recognize him by receiving him in this country until he has righted that wrong and apologized." FDR was impressed, thought Stimson. There were innumerable incidents that showed de Gaulle to be an egocentric and unreliable man.

Just as angry was Morgenthau, who knew de Gaulle was lying when he said the French had not been consulted on the currency. Monnet had approved the design and the wording, and now de Gaulle was calling it "counterfeit money"—*faux billets.* "If this man de Gaulle throws us down," he told his aides on June 10, "then . . . Jean Monnet . . . should be kicked out of Washington. . . . He was in on every bit of this. . . . And I don't give a God-damn what the State Department or the War Department says."

The currency was being used as the central argument for political recognition, Morgenthau thought. "Now, with our men on the beaches of France," he told McCloy, "this fellow comes along and holds . . ."

"And talks about his personal status," McCloy said. "It's just outrageous."

"Puts a gun to our backs," Morgenthau said.

It wasn't as bad as all that, for Churchill reported on June 14 that the French people seemed to be taking the notes. "I am quite sure," he said, "that if an old woman in Bayeux sells a cow to an American Quartermaster and is paid in these notes, when she presents them at Morgenthau's office in Washington he will have to see that she is not a loser in the transaction."

"This currency issue is being exploited to stampede us into according full recognition to the Committee," FDR replied. ". . . It seems clear that prima donnas do not change their spots."

Upon reflection, Stimson decided that they had to work with de Gaulle, because the situation was paralyzing Eisenhower. Once again, on June 15, he spent an hour with the president to try and convince him that Eisenhower should be able to deal with the de Gaulle committee as the authority responsible for civil administration in France.

"That's all very well," FDR said, "but you can't do that the way we could guarantee a free election to Nicaragua, by putting Mercurochrome on each voter's hand so he wouldn't vote twice and with a Marine at the ballot box."

Stimson said you could give him the authority on condition he would go through with all that, and if he didn't, you had the moral pressure to exert and you could withdraw recognition and crimp him in his supplies. But you couldn't interfere in the elections and beat de Gaulle, who was somebody, with nobody.

Roosevelt was adamant. He still believed de Gaulle would crumble and that his British supporters would be confounded by the progress of events. That was contrary to everything Stimson heard—de Gaulle was gaining strength as the invasion proceeded, he had become the symbol of deliverance to the French people. The president insisted that new parties would spring up and de Gaulle would become a very small figure. He already knew of some such parties. When Stimson asked him how he knew, he said Donovan had told him.

Even as FDR and Stimson spoke, de Gaulle had landed in France, where he was greeted as a savior and began putting in his people as prefects and subprefects in liberated areas, and acting very much like a head of state.

"I don't know why they let de Gaulle set foot in France," Morgenthau said to McCloy on the phone on June 16.

"Well, that was the British, of course, who insisted on that," McCloy said. "I thought it was a mistake because it gave him a build-up. . . . [Churchill] communicated with the President on it and the President said 'all right, provided you make it clear that it's what you want to do. I wouldn't do it, but go ahead and do it."

That same day, Stimson called in Donovan, who trimmed a bit on what FDR had said. He didn't have anybody else in mind, and acknowledged that de Gaulle was the leader of 90 percent of the resistance movement. Donovan did not think de Gaulle should be recognized as head of a provisional government, but that he should be given full recognition as a military leader under Eisenhower. Stimson then called Marshall, who was in London following Overlord, and who said that as soon as the American people learned that the reason their boys were dying was obstruction by the French, there would be a tremendous reaction. Marshall was so incensed that a few days later at a house party at Chequers he turned loose on Eden, saying that if it got out that he was trying to force recognition of de Gaulle there would be such a wave of indignation in the United States it would swamp the whole damn British Foreign Office. Eden's face flushed, and he left the room, containing his anger.

FDR was taking a lot of flak from the press on de Gaulle. Walter Lippmann and most of the other pundits wrote that he was the hope of France and should be recognized as such. With the Democratic convention coming up the last week in July, he decided to invite de Gaulle to Washington. He could stifle the criticism without giving in on policy. It would be a cordial gesture to make up for nonrecognition.

By July 1, FDR was impatient because nothing had been heard from de Gaulle (who says in his memoirs that he accepted on June 26). He asked Hassett to contact the Free French and find out de Gaulle's plans. Hassett said that in an interview in Rome after a private audience with the pope de Gaulle was quoted as saying: "If I go to the United States to present our greeting to Mr. Roosevelt and the American people, I will be very happy and honored." But there was not a word about his plans. FDR shook his head and said: "He's a nut."

While Roosevelt waited for *le grand Charles,* American soldiers celebrated the Fourth of July on French soil. In Bayeux, a Frenchman invited an American officer to come to his house and drink a glass of old brandy. The American saw a calendar on the wall with the date March 11, 1941. "You're a little behind with your calendar, buddy," he said. "But, Captain," the Frenchman asked, "you don't know what is March 11, 1941?" "Nope, can't think of it," the captain replied. "Monsieur," said the Frenchman, "that is the date of the final defeat of Germany. That is the date your President Roosevelt signed the Lend-Lease decree. *Buvons, messieurs, buvons à la santé du Président* Roosevelt." (Let us drink, gentlemen, to the health of President Roosevelt.)

On July 6, Roosevelt sent a plane to Algiers for the general's flight to Washington. De Gaulle had heard that the president liked model boats and he got one of his naval officers to provide him with a working model of a French submarine, about five feet long, battery operated. It submerged and upped periscope and fired little torpedoes and did everything that a submarine is supposed to do. When FDR got it, he gave it to his grandson Curt (Anna's son by Curtis Dall) to take to the naval station outside Washington and see if it worked. Curt reported back that it did, and FDR said, "Curt, you can have it." Eleanor, the conscience of the Western world, said:

"Franklin, you can't give away a gift from a foreign head of state." "He's not a foreign head of state," Roosevelt quickly replied, "he's merely the head of a committee."

On July 9, Ickes had a long talk with the president after lunch. By the time they were finished, it was after three, and FDR said he had not had his nap and was expecting de Gaulle at 4:30. Then, in a rather unfriendly voice, he said: "Just wait and look at de Gaulle's chin." Ickes asked if it was a "Charles Evans Hughes chin." FDR said it receded and that his handshake was flabby. Later, when Ickes met de Gaulle, he took a good look at the chin and saw that it didn't recede. De Gaulle had a high-bridged, typical French nose but his chin was not weak, although it did not jut. His handshake was fine. He was tall, well made, upstanding, and soldierly. All of which showed how a man's prejudices could warp his perception.

For his part, de Gaulle saw Roosevelt as "an artist, a seducer." The president described his new world order—a four-power directorate to settle the world's postwar problems. Of the other three, thought de Gaulle, the United States would control China and Britain, and would have to yield to the Soviets in the Balkans. He warned the president not to give secondary importance to Western Europe, but saw that he could not count on the United States to help France regain her place among nations.

"De Gaulle and I skated pretty roughly on current subjects," FDR wrote Congressman Joseph Clark Baldwin on July 19, "though I talked with him a good deal about the future of France, her colonies, world peace, etc. On future things he seemed quite tractable as long as France is treated on a 'mondiale' basis. He is very touchy about the honor of France but I think he is essentially selfish."

De Gaulle did not leave Washington completely empty-handed, for on July 11 FDR announced that he was granting de facto recognition to the French Committee of National Liberation as "qualified to exercise the administration of France."

But de jure recognition was still months away. As the British diplomat Duff Cooper said of de Gaulle, "There are men whose instinct is to say No whenever ordinary people would say Yes." That was not normally Roosevelt's way, but in this case he was more Gaullist than de Gaulle.

In mid-August, the Allies landed in southern France, assisted by the Free French, and still de Gaulle was not recognized.

On August 25 de Gaulle entered Paris with the Leclerc division and still he was not recognized.

On September 9, de Gaulle formed a provisional government, and still he was not recognized. Even his archfoe, Cordell Hull, recommended recognition on September 17, but FDR replied: "I have had lengthy talks with the Prime Minister in regard to recognition of the Provisional Government of France. He and I are both very much opposed to it at this time. The Provisional Government has no direct authority from the people. It is best to let things go along as they are for the moment."

In early October, Jefferson Caffery arrived in Paris as American ambassador. Roosevelt had named an envoy to a government he did not recognize. De Gaulle refused to see Caffery.

On October 14, Churchill told FDR that events had reached a point where they had to make a decision. There was no doubt the provisional government had the support of a majority of the people.

Eisenhower also urged recognition. If de Gaulle were overthrown, chaos would follow. It was going to be a long, hard winter, with severe coal shortages. Better that a French government be blamed than the Allied command.

FDR at this point decided that recognition would be desirable once Eisenhower set up his "Zone of the Interior" and turned it over to de Gaulle. Then he would have something to administer.

This was done on October 20, and the next day FDR saw Stettinius and gave his approval for recognition, which was jointly announced on October 23 by the United States, Britain, and the Soviet Union. De Gaulle's response was brief: "The French government is satisfied to be called by its name."

The "other parties" that Roosevelt kept referring to had not materialized. He would have preferred almost anyone else, but finally had to accept the reality of de Gaulle. As in the packing of the Supreme Court, he did not act with his usual finesse. In the name of self-determination, he maintained his hostility toward de Gaulle much longer than political wisdom warranted, holding up the political process in France until he was ready to decide what the complexion of postwar Europe should be.

The Democratic convention was coming up on July 19, and in May there were some anti-fourth-term rumblings in Texas when the state Democratic convention refused to instruct its delegates for the president. Roosevelt supporters bolted the convention and held their own meeting and elected their own delegates. Ickes saw the fine hand of Secretary of Commerce Jesse Jones behind the split, telling FDR on June 18 that Jesse was a son of a bitch and he would not believe him under oath. FDR replied that he wouldn't either, and that he was perfectly willing to go back to Hyde Park. In any event, he would have from November 7 to January 20—and he made some throat-cutting gestures.

The real problem, Ickes said, was his running mate. He should drop Wallace. FDR said Wallace would cost the ticket a million votes. Ickes said it would run as high as 3 million. In a close election, it could determine the result.

FDR had sent Wallace on a two-month trip to Russia and China. He mentioned a speech Wallace had made in Siberia, saying that India should be free. "Henry says the wrong thing at the wrong time," the president observed. "I believe the same things but I just don't say so when it is not the right occasion."

About the only supporter Wallace had in the White House was Eleanor Roosevelt. On July 6, FDR told Morgenthau that she was pushing him hard to keep Wallace. Morgenthau said: "If something should happen to you, I certainly wouldn't want Wallace to be President."

That was also the tack being taken by Edwin W. Pauley, a California oilman who was treasurer of the Democratic National Committee, and who had been going around the country for a year mobilizing the opposition to Wallace. His slogan was: "You are not nominating a vice president but a president." Everyone knew that Roosevelt would not live much longer. And Wallace would make a mighty strange president—he was too much the prophet, too unworldly and mystical. Why, one night he had challenged his Russian tutor, Colonel C. M. Paul, to a foot race from the Wardman Park to the Mayflower Hotel. Colonel Paul was loaded down with books and couldn't keep up. "Wallace is only running for fun," he said, "but I'm running for my life. If an FBI man saw me chasing him down the street, he might think I was trying to kill the Vice-President of the United States."

Pauley made a deal with Pa Watson, who was violently anti-Wallace, to arrange appointments with the president for anti-Wallace Democrats and to block the pro-Wallace people. It was like dripping water on a stone. They came day after day and said they didn't want Wallace. Roosevelt began to realize that he could not impose Wallace on the convention, as he had done in 1940.

FDR also knew that Wallace would be a problem because he had been labeled by the FBI as a security risk, manipulated by the Communists. When Wallace went on a Latin American swing in April 1943, he was under FBI surveillance, and after the trip J. Edgar Hoover sent Attorney General Francis Biddle this memo, on May 3: "I wanted to advise you of information which has reached me from a confidential source which indicates the possibility that Vice-President Wallace is being unknowingly influenced by Bolivian Communists. . . . I am informed that some Congressional Committees already have this information and may make an open or public issue of it. . . . It is alleged that the Bolivians have furnished Mr. Wallace with improper information concerning working conditions in the Bolivian mines. . . ."

On another occasion, on February 4, 1944, Wallace spoke in Los Angeles to a union audience. The FBI agent in Los Angeles, R. B. Hood, reported to Hoover that the meeting had been under "the influence of the Communist Party . . . many well-known Communists were in the audience." Edward G. Robinson, the master of ceremonies, "is a well-known follower of the Communist Party line. There was no doubt whatever that the Communist element in the Southern California section had so infiltrated this reception for the Vice-President . . . as to enable them to secure complete control." It seemed like an effort to discredit Wallace in the eyes of the president.

When Wallace got back from his trip on July 10, having traveled 27,000 miles in fifty-one days, he was asked to lunch by Sam Rosenman and Harold Ickes, who had been enlisted by Roosevelt to break the bad news. Ickes told him that he had made a lot of enemies and should not let his name be presented. Rosenman said he would not help the ticket in the fall. Wallace did not want to talk politics, as he was seeing the president that afternoon at 4:30 to report on his mission.

Wallace and the president talked for two hours about his trip and then FDR said: "I am now talking to the ceiling about political matters." Wallace was of course his choice as a running mate, the president asserted, but a lot of people had been in to see him saying he could not be nominated, and that if he was he would cost the ticket 1 to 3 million votes.

"Mr. President," Wallace said, "if you can find anyone who will add more strength to the ticket than I, by all means take him."

FDR said he could not bear the thought of his name being put up and rejected. "You have your family to think of," he said. "Think of the catcalls and jeers and the definiteness of rejection." Wallace was thinking that he was much more worried about the future of the Democratic party than about his family. It was getting late, and the president asked him to come back for lunch the next day, July 11.

At lunch on the eleventh, Wallace brought FDR some stamps and coins from Outer Mongolia and an Uzbek robe that had been given to him in the Central Asian city of Tashkent. He also brought a statement he wanted the president to release that said: "It appears the convention will name me. I trust the name with me will be Henry A. Wallace. He is equipped for the future. We have made a team which pulls together, thinks alike and plans alike." FDR said he had worked out another wording, but would study Wallace's version.

They went over the probable convention vote state by state, and Roosevelt mentioned that many people looked upon Wallace as a Communist or worse, although as a matter of fact there was no one more American than he was, no one more of the American soil. Some referred to Wallace, FDR went on, as that fellow who wanted to give a quart of milk to every Hottentot. "You know, Mr. President, I never said that," Wallace interjected. "That was said for me by the president of the NAM." FDR replied that he had always defended Wallace against his critics.

Roosevelt was being pulled in two directions. He felt loyalty to Wallace, whose "guru" letters he had successfully suppressed in 1940, but he knew he could not buck the convention. That evening, there was a decisive meeting after dinner at the White House with some of the anti-Wallace leaders, including Pauley and Robert E. Hannegan, chairman of the Democratic National Committee.

In the blue oval room on the second floor, they went over the vice-presidential prospects. Sam Rayburn was eliminated because of the split in the Texas delegation, Jimmy Byrnes because he came from the poll tax state of South Carolina and had been born a Catholic, and Alben Barkley because of his recent disloyalty over the tax bill.

Pauley was amazed when FDR proposed Supreme Court Justice William O. Douglas. He would have the following of the liberal wing of the party,

Wallace's people, the president said, plus he had practical experience as a logger, and played a good hand of poker, and looked like a Boy Scout, with hair that fell appealingly into his eyes, which he swept out with a gesture of his hand. This proposal was met with stony silence, and Pauley thought that FDR must have sensed that no one wanted Douglas any more than Wallace.

Truman's name came up, and FDR said he didn't know him too well, but that he had done a good job on his committee investigating the war. Pauley was for Truman, and so was Hannegan, who owed his political rise to the Missouri senator. Hannegan was the son of a policeman who had risen in the St. Louis Democratic machine. Truman got him named collector of internal revenue, and then he was promoted to commissioner.

There was a lot of support for Truman, and finally FDR turned to Hannegan, who was sitting next to him on the divan, and put his hand on Hannegan's knee and said: "Bob, I think you and everyone else want Truman. . . . Bob, if that is the case it is Truman."

Two days later, FDR again had lunch with Wallace, and promised to send a letter to Senator Samuel D. Jackson of Indiana, the permanent chairman of the convention, saying that if he were a delegate he would vote for Wallace. He also mentioned the July 11 dinner with the party bosses, who all thought Wallace would harm the ticket.

"If you think so," Wallace said, "I will withdraw at once."

"I have no basis for a judgment of my own," FDR replied. "The only way I could find out would be to drive among the farmers in Dutchess County."

As Wallace was leaving, he said: "Well, I am looking ahead to the results of next week no matter what the outcome." They shook hands, and Roosevelt drew him close and turned on his full smile and said: "While I cannot put it just that way in public, I hope it will be the same old team." Then he added: "Even though they do beat you out at Chicago, we will have a job for you in world economic affairs," which should have been a tip-off to Wallace, who had ten years of close observation of the president's Machiavellian nature behind him, that his goose was cooked.

The situation was further complicated by James F. Byrnes, who had left the Supreme Court to become director of war mobilization and to whom FDR had also vaguely indicated that he had the green light. Having heard from Hannegan that FDR was for Truman first and Douglas second, Byrnes called the president in Hyde Park on July 14.

"Jimmy, that is all wrong," said FDR. "That is not what I told them. It is what they told me. . . . I had nothing to do with it. . . . I did not express myself. Objections to you came from labor people, both federation and C.I.O."

"I wanted to know," Brynes said, ". . . whether you authorized Hannegan . . . to make the statement that you preferred other candidates."

"After all, Jimmy," FDR said, "you are close to me personally, and Henry is close to me. I hardly know Truman. Douglas is a poker partner. He is good in a poker game and tells good stories."

Thus Byrnes went to the convention in Chicago on July 19 laboring under the impression that he was the president's choice, an impression shared by Wallace, who had it in writing—the president's letter to Senator Jackson that said: "I personally would vote for his [Wallace's] renomination if I were a delegate to the Convention."

To balance this dangerous letter, Hannegan and Pauley intercepted Roosevelt's train, which was passing through Chicago on July 19 on an inspection trip to San Diego, and asked for a letter backing Truman. FDR wrote out the letter by hand and gave it to Grace Tully to type up. "You have written me about Harry Truman and Bill Douglas," the letter said. "I should, of course, be very glad to run with either of them and believe that either one of them would bring real strength to the ticket."

The train was leaving the station by the time Pauley and Hannegan got the letter. As Hannegan scanned it, the color drained from his face. "What does it say?" Pauley asked. "My God, it's got Douglas in it," Hannegan said. They decided not to show the letter, which would encourage the Douglas supporters. As for Truman, he was committed to Jimmy Byrnes.

On the afternoon of July 20, the day that FDR was due to be nominated, the Democratic bosses met with Truman in the Blackstone Hotel. Truman insisted that he did not want the vice presidency. Hannegan put in a call to FDR in San Diego. "Bob," the president said, "have you got that guy lined up yet on that Vice-Presidency?"

"No," Hannegan said. "He's the contrariest goddamn mule from Missouri I ever saw."

"Well," Roosevelt said, "you tell him if he wants to break up the Democratic Party in the middle of the war and maybe lose that war that's up to him."

Truman capitulated, although he was embarrassed, after telling everyone he was not a candidate. That evening, FDR was nominated. Wallace made the seconding speech, after which there was a tremendous demonstration in his honor, with banners and noisemakers and the pipe organ playing "Iowa, That's Where the Tall Corn Grows," over and over.

Roosevelt gave his acceptance speech over the radio from San Diego to the delegates sitting in the Chicago Stadium—he was about to leave for Hawaii for meetings with General MacArthur.

On July 21, Wallace won the first ballot for the vice-presidential nomination, with 429½ votes to 319½ for Truman, and 427 votes scattered among thirteen favorite sons, who held the balance of power. On the second ballot, Pauley and Hannegan lined up the city bosses and the anti-Wallace southerners, and there was a bandwagon effect for Truman, who won by 1,031 to 105.

There were two deeply disappointed men following that vote. One was Jimmy Byrnes, who felt that FDR had deceived him. He had, Byrnes thought, been swayed by warnings that he would lose 200,000 black votes in New York State.

The other was Henry Wallace, who remembered the president pulling him by the hand, with his mouth close to Wallace's ear, and the words that came out of that mouth: "I do hope it will be the same old team." Byrnes had been used as a stalking-horse for Truman, Wallace felt. Hannegan had told labor leader Sidney Hillman on July 17: "We will withdraw Byrnes if you will withdraw Wallace."

Wallace had lost to the machine, and it was a bitter loss. Ambassadorships had been promised, and government jobs, Wallace was sure. The whole panoply of patronage had been used against him. FDR had promised his support while at the same time directing the fight against him. There were two letters in two pockets. FDR had lost control of the party to the fund raisers and city bosses who had put in Truman, and would later get their rewards—Truman would make Hannegan postmaster general and Pauley under secretary of the Navy—and Pauley would go to Ickes during the '44 campaign to tell him that there would be major campaign contributions from oilmen if the government gave up its claim to federal lands in California—shades of Teapot Dome!

Wallace thought the president's behavior was the product of a sick mind. By a sick mind, Wallace meant that he was unwell, and that not enough blood was reaching his brain. If he had been a well man, he would simply have told Wallace: "I don't want you to run." Instead, he vacillated back and forth, completely under the spell of the bosses. He could at the same time be sincerely for Wallace while letting them put Truman over.

Wallace should have known that it was not a sick mind but Roosevelt's customary method of handling problems by sidestepping rather than confronting them. He told everyone what they wanted to hear and let the situation resolve itself. Truman was not his choice, but the convention did not want Wallace, and if he tried to force the issue as he had in 1940, he would have a rebellion on his hands. So he went along with Truman for the sake of party unity, even though he had to betray Byrnes and Wallace—the main thing was to keep the Republicans out of the White House while the war was still on.

Roosevelt left for Pearl Harbor on July 21 aboard the heavy cruiser *Baltimore*. It was a good way to show that he was fit for another term, and there was no better campaign strategy than doing his job as commander in chief. He took Sam Rosenman along, and also Fala, and Sam had to tell the sailors to stop cutting snips of hair off Fala for souvenirs, or the dog would have been bald.

Arriving on the twenty-sixth, FDR threw himself into three hectic days of inspections of shore installations, leaving time for meetings with MacArthur and Nimitz. He had left the Pacific war pretty much up to the two of them. The island-hopping strategy was a success, and the Marines had landed on Saipan in June, precipitating a major air and submarine action where the Japs lost three carriers, known as "The Great Marianas Turkey Shoot."

Summoned from Australia, MacArthur arrived aboard the *Baltimore* in a leather windbreaker and gold-braided cap set at a jaunty angle. There had been a bit of a presidential boomlet for the general, masterminded by Michigan Senator Arthur Vandenberg. MacArthur was willing, and kept in touch with the efforts made on his behalf. He was entered in some primaries early in 1944, and came in second in Wisconsin behind Dewey, picking up three delegates. But in April Congressman Albert L. Miller of Nebraska made public his correspondence with MacArthur. Miller had written that "if this system of left-wingers and New Dealers is continued for another four years, I am certain that this monarchy which is being established in America will destroy the rights of the common people," to which MacArthur had replied that "your description of conditions in the United States is a sobering one indeed and is calculated to arouse the thoughtful consideration of every true patriot.... We must not inadvertently slip into the same condition internally as the one which we fight externally."

Vandenberg commented that "Miller, in one inane moment, crucified the whole MacArthur movement and MacArthur with it." Ickes thought MacArthur should be cashiered for sounding off. It was dirty cricket to criticize the commander in chief. He wasn't a great general or a great man. Drew Pearson had told him that the first Mrs. MacArthur, the Philadelphia society woman Louise Brooks Cromwell, now married to the actor Lionel Atwill, did takeoffs on MacArthur preparing for war in front of a mirror. She would bend her forefinger and hold it out to illustrate MacArthur's virility, and when she had a few drinks she said that Doug didn't think his penis was for anything except to pee with. Roosevelt had encouraged MacArthur to sue Drew Pearson for the unfairness of his column, telling him that anyone with an actionable grievance against the columnist would do the country a service. MacArthur had filed a suit for $1,750,000, but he had a Eurasian mistress in Washington, a former Singapore chorus girl to whom he had written love letters signed "Daddy," and he withdrew his suit when he heard that Pearson had obtained the letters. Admiral William D. Leahy, who accompanied Roosevelt to Pearl Harbor, commented: "He could have won the suit. He was a bachelor at the time. All he had to do was look everybody in the face and say: 'So what? Cunt can make you look awfully silly at times.' "

After dinner on July 27, Sam Rosenman sat on the lawn under palm trees and watched the moonlight on Waikiki's rolling surf, as FDR conferred with MacArthur, Nimitz, and Leahy. Once in a while he looked through the window of the stucco mansion at the conference, thinking that he could not possibly picture Dewey there as commander in chief.

Nimitz wanted to bypass the Philippines and attack Formosa. MacArthur was committed to the Philippines—he had promised to return. He later claimed that he had told the president privately: "I dare say that the American people would be so aroused [if the Philippines were bypassed] that they would register most complete resentment against you at the polls this fall." In any case, Roosevelt agreed to attack the Philippines.

MacArthur was shocked by Roosevelt's appearance. His mind was keen and his voice was as good as ever, but he was obviously in poor health. Actually, FDR was feeling better. He was proud that he had lost weight. On the way back he stopped in Alaska and at the Navy Yard in Bremerton, Washington, where for the first time in months he put the braces on his legs and stood for thirty-five minutes to deliver a speech. Dr. Bruenn, in attendance on the trip, noted that he experienced substernal oppression with radiation to both shoulders.

Back from Hawaii, Roosevelt tried to mend some cracks in the alliance. The Big Four, the mainstay of postwar security, were not acting in unison. Each one seemed to be going off on a tangent, indifferent to Roosevelt's global strategy.

Stalin had his private plans on the Polish question. By August, the Red Army had entered Poland and was on the outskirts of Warsaw. Moscow radio broadcast appeals to the Polish underground to rise up. When they did, the Russians stopped their advance. They were stalled on the Vistula River, but it also suited Stalin's plans to allow the anti-Communist Warsaw underground to be slaughtered by the Germans.

Roosevelt and Churchill asked him to drop supplies and munitions. He replied that the uprising was "a reckless adventure," whose leaders were a handful of "power-seeking criminals." They asked to send planes that could land in Soviet territory after dropping supplies to the Poles. Stalin refused. At this point, Roosevelt, whose first priority was to draw Stalin into the war against Japan, gave up on helping the Poles, cabling Churchill on August 24: "My information points to the practical impossibility of our providing supplies to the Warsaw Poles."

Churchill begged FDR to reconsider, warning that the fall of Warsaw would undermine the position of the London Poles. FDR said there was nothing he could do, but on September 10 the Russians backtracked and agreed to make drops with the Allies. The Red Army was still stalled on the Vistula where they could not get their tanks across because of German shelling. The insurgents were more of a problem than a help, as they were isolated in four parts of Warsaw, intermingled with the Germans, so that it was difficult to shell German positions. On September 13, Allied and Soviet supply planes flew over Warsaw. The U.S. planes dropped from such high altitudes that in some cases the wind landed the supplies twenty miles away, while the Soviets used small training planes that dropped from an altitude of 1,200 feet. In any case, it did no good, and on October 5, General Bor, the leader of the uprising, surrendered. By this time, the Red Army had pushed into Rumania and Bulgaria and had reached the Yugoslav border, but could not or did not cross the Vistula to enter Warsaw. Stalin insisted that the failure to relieve Warsaw had been due to enemy strength, but he could not admit this publicly.

Churchill in the meantime was pressing the London Poles to accept the

Curzon line, which meant the loss of the oil fields of Galicia and of the Polish city of Lvov, an island of Poles in a sea of Ukrainians. Stanislas Mikolajczyk, the head of the London Poles, appealed to Roosevelt, who would not help. Stalin said he was an old man who could not go to his grave under the stigma of betraying the Ukrainians. Mikolajczyk resigned, ending the possibility of compromise between the London Poles and Stalin, who now recognized the Soviet-controlled Lublin Committee as the provisional government of Poland. Allied policy in Poland was a shambles.

Roosevelt advocated self-determination, but was not willing to quarrel with Stalin to back it up. He did not want any American troops involved in the Balkans. The reality of the situation in Europe was that your writ ran just as far as your army of occupation.

In Moscow, Averell Harriman saw a startling change come over the Soviets now that the end of the European war was in sight. They would not exchange weather information or justify their Lend-Lease requests. Everything was a problem, from exit visas for Russian women who had married Americans to Russian help in finding American POWs in Rumania. They seemed to interpret generosity as a sign of weakness. What would Russia do next? Would she seek a separate peace with Germany? Would she declare war on Japan? No one knew. Russia was a closed book.

In China, where there was a three-cornered struggle among the Japanese, the Chinese Communists, and Chiang Kai-shek, the generalissimo was caving in. China was supposed to be a great power, one of the Big Four. In reality it was a fragmented and chaotic mess, as Henry Wallace reported to FDR during his June trip—morale was low, there was little confidence in Chiang, the military situation was terrible.

To Stimson, the situation was confounded by feuding between Stilwell and General Clare Chennault, head of the air force. "And the worst of it is," Stimson recorded, "that the President . . . is always a Chennault man. He hasn't got the real foundation of military knowledge to show the folly of it and worst of all he has got that wretched little grandson of Mrs. Douglas Robinson [Theodore Roosevelt's sister Corinne] whom he insisted on giving a commission to, in China now, and this little devil—Alsop his name is [Joseph Alsop, the columnist]—fills the President and Chiang with violent hostility to Stilwell to whom this Alsop has taken a great dislike."

In July, FDR asked Chiang to put Stilwell in charge of all Chinese forces, and sent his troubleshooter, Major General Patrick J. Hurley, secretary of war under Hoover, to bring a settlement between Chiang and Mao. But Chiang told Hurley that Stilwell must go, and in October he went. "It was a sad ending," thought Stimson, "a sacrifice, due to errors which the President himself had committed in the type of private envoys whom he had sent there and who filled his head with poison on the subject of Stilwell." The president's Chinese strategy was in ruins. There was no reform of the army, no drive against the Japanese, no settlement with the Communists—instead, confusion and inaction.

In the meantime, there were more conferences, at Dumbarton Oaks in Washington, to decide the organization of the United Nations—the Russians wanted a vote for each of the sixteen Soviet republics—and at Quebec, for the second time, from September 11 to 16. On the agenda at Quebec was how to punish Germany, a question to which Henry Morgenthau, Jr., had the answer—turn Germany into an agrarian state by eliminating industry from the Ruhr and Saar basins. Morgenthau felt that in pursuing this tough line he had the blessing of the president, who had told him on August 19: "We have got to be tough with Germany, and I mean the German people, not just the Nazis. We either have to castrate the German people or you have got to treat them in such a manner so they can't just go on reproducing."

Morgenthau appointed among his Treasury aides a Committee on Germany, keeping in mind the additional benefit that if the Ruhr were put out of business the steel and coal mines of England would flourish. On September 2, he showed his plan to FDR, who said he wanted that "Germany should be allowed no aircraft of any kind, not even a glider . . . nobody should be allowed to wear a uniform, and there would be no marching, and that would do more to teach the Germans than anything else that they had been defeated." Morgenthau said that didn't go far enough, he wanted to see the Ruhr dismantled, and the president seemed to like the idea.

Two days later, Morgenthau told his aides that "the only thing . . . I will have any part of, is the complete shut-down of the Ruhr. . . . Just strip it. I don't care what happens to the population. . . . I would take every mine, every mill and factory and wreck it. . . . Steel, coal, everything. Just close it down. . . . I am for destroying first and we will worry about the population second. . . . Why the hell should I worry about what happens to their people?"

The Treasury drafted its "Program to Prevent Germany from Starting a World War III." Morgenthau was surprised when the president asked him to be in Quebec on September 14. He had not been asked to any previous summit conferences, and surmised that he was needed because Hull had begged off and Harry Hopkins was temporarily out of favor, and because his plan had found acceptance.

On September 14 at a state dinner at the Citadel in Quebec, Morgenthau explained his proposal. Almost at once, low mutters and baleful looks came from Churchill, who said: "I am all for disarming Germany, but we ought not to prevent her living decently. There are bonds between the working classes of all countries, and the English people will not stand for the policy you are advocating. I agree with Burke. You cannot indict a whole nation." Churchill became quite incensed, and said he had not come to Quebec to discuss a scheme that would mean "England being chained to a dead body."

Roosevelt did not say much. Morgenthau thought it was his way of managing Churchill, letting him wear himself out in his attack, and then moving in to compose the situation. Watching Roosevelt, Charles Wilson, Churchill's doctor, wondered whether his health was affecting his judgment. He had lost a lot of weight—you could put your fist between his neck and his collar. Men at his time of life did not go thin all of a sudden for nothing.

The next morning, September 15, Morgenthau also had to settle phase two of Lend-Lease. Churchill had told him in August that England was broke and would need postwar help. Morgenthau, who wanted a strong and prosperous English economy, came up with $3 billion of nonmilitary aid for 1945. But according to Treasury aide Harry Dexter White, Roosevelt held out on signing the Lend-Lease package until he had been assured of British cooperation on postwar Germany. At one point Churchill said: "What do you want me to do, stand up and beg like Fala?"

An agreement was reached, and by the noon meeting on the fifteenth, Churchill had reversed himself on the Morgenthau plan. His scientific adviser, Lord Cherwell (F. A. Lindemann), who wore a slide-rule tie clip, had convinced him that the plan would save Britain from bankruptcy by eliminating a dangerous competitor. "Someone must suffer for the war," he said, "and it was surely right that Germany and not Britain should foot the bill." Churchill agreed that "they brought it on themselves."

Not only did Churchill accept the Morgenthau plan, he dictated the memorandum initialed by himself and Roosevelt, which said that "the program for eliminating the war-making industries in the Ruhr and in the Saar is looking forward to converting Germany into a country primarily agricultural and pastoral in its character."

Eden, who rarely lost his temper, was in a state of shock, turning on Churchill to say: "You can't do this. After all, you and I have publicly said quite the opposite." They got quite nasty with each other, until Churchill said: "When I have to choose between my people and the German people, I am going to choose my people," which sounded like an allusion to the linkage between the German issue and Lend-Lease.

Back in Washington, Stimson was just as angry as Eden, and fumed that "I have yet to meet a man who is not horrified at the 'Carthaginian' attitude of the Treasury. It is Semitism gone wild for vengeance and . . . will lay seeds for another war in the next generation." Lord Cherwell was "an old fool who had . . . loudly proclaimed that we could never cross the Channel." How could the president, he wondered, conduct negotiations on matters of concern to the State and War departments with only Morgenthau, his yes-man from the Treasury, present?

Hull was against the plan too, telling FDR that it was bound to lead to last-ditch, bitter-end German resistance that would cost thousands of American lives. He was sure that Britain had gone along with the plan in order to get the dollar credit proposed by the Treasury.

Soon after Quebec, FDR began to backtrack in the face of press criticism. The Republicans were using the Morgenthau plan as a campaign issue. He admitted to Stimson on September 27 that it was a false step. A week later he told Stimson that "Henry Morgenthau pulled a boner" and he had no intention of turning Germany into an agrarian state. Stimson quoted the lines from the memorandum about "converting Germany into a country primarily agricultural and pastoral in character," and Roosevelt "was frankly staggered by this and said he had no idea how he could have initialed this." It was a sign of Roosevelt's declining health that on October 3 he did not recall what he had initialed on September 15. In any case, the Morgenthau plan was dead.

The treatment of postwar Germany was only one of many areas of disagreement between the United States and Britain as the war approached a conclusion. The "special relationship" seemed to be coming apart at the seams. Churchill bitterly opposed "Anvil," the invasion of Southern France that had been promised to Stalin at Teheran. Anvil was "bleak and sterile," and he was "deeply grieved" at the "casting aside" of the Italian campaign, "with all its dazzling possibilities." Stalin would rejoice over Anvil, since Eastern, Central, and Southern Europe would "fall naturally" into his control. "I always think of my early geometry," FDR replied. "A straight line is the shortest distance between two points."

Churchill worked on Eisenhower, on one occasion in August unlimbering his rhetoric for a six-hour session, which included charges that America was bullying the British and threats that if matters did not improve he would "lay down the mantle of my high office." But Anvil took place as scheduled in mid-August, and soon Marseilles and Toulon were in Allied hands.

The British felt that America was dictating to them now that they were financially exhausted by the war. The State Department, wanting to bring down the pro-Nazi regime in Argentina, asked Britain not to renew its contract for Argentine beef. Churchill pleaded with Roosevelt: "Please remember that this community of 46 million imported 66 million tons a year before the war and is now managing on less than 25 million. The stamina of the workmen cannot be maintained on a lesser diet in meat. You would not send your soldiers into battle on the British service meat ration, which is far above what is given to workmen."

Wrangling over postwar air routes was seen as another American attempt at intimidation. Roosevelt warned that Congress would not be in "a generous mood" with further dollar credits if agreement had not been reached over air routes. Churchill said he hoped that FDR would not use "the club of Lend-Lease" to "run us out of the air altogether." The signing of a bilateral air agreement between the United States and Ireland seemed to the British a low blow.

In Italy, when the British vetoed Count Sforza as foreign minister, the State Department issued a communiqué that this matter should be "purely an internal affair," which infuriated Churchill. In Greece, British troops were fighting Communist guerrillas in Athens, a battle that FDR wanted no part of. At a cabinet meeting, his whimsical solution to the crisis was to give every Greek a rifle and let them fight it out, a rather extreme form of self-determination. Churchill pleaded for American support, which did not come.

When Churchill ordered his commanding officer in Greece, General Ronald Scobie, to evacuate Athens "with bloodshed if necessary," the order was leaked to the Washington press, causing further discord.

Churchill knew that FDR would pull American troops out of Europe as soon as he could. They would not remain in France, Italy, or the Balkans, and they would share in the occupation of Germany for only a year or two. Anticipating an American pullout, Churchill had to stay on good terms with Stalin while trying to contain Soviet expansion. He began to think what FDR had thought at Teheran—that he could reach some understanding with Stalin—and went to Moscow in October on his own.

The agreement he made, which he knew FDR would have done his utmost to prevent, was the "sphere of influence" paper, which expressed in percentages Soviet and British areas of control.

"Let us settle about our affairs in the Balkans," Churchill told Stalin. "Your armies are in Rumania and Bulgaria. We have interests, missions, and agents there. Don't let us get at cross-purpose in small ways. So far as Britain and Russia are concerned, how would it do for you to have ninety per cent predominance in Rumania, for us to have ninety per cent of the say in Greece, and go fifty-fifty about Yugoslavia?" It sounded as though Churchill was playing a board game with the Balkans as the board. He wrote it out on a half sheet of paper, adding a fifty-fifty split for Hungary and a seventy-five–twenty-five Russian predominance for Bulgaria.

Thinking of history's verdict, Churchill said: "Might it not be thought rather cynical if it seemed we had disposed of these issues, so fateful to millions of people, in such an offhand manner? Let us burn the paper." "No, you keep it," Stalin said.

The agreement gave the Russians a free hand in Rumania, Hungary, and Bulgaria, and impeded the Allied negotiating position. Churchill was outraged when there was a Communist coup in Rumania the following February, and yet it was a direct result of his policy. Bulgaria and Hungary would soon join Rumania in becoming Soviet satellites. When Churchill made his famous "iron curtain" speech in Fulton, Missouri, in 1946, no one mentioned that he had helped to draw the curtain.

Global strategy was left in abeyance that fall as Roosevelt campaigned for a fourth term. The 1944 campaign was different from the three preceding ones in that it was a wartime election, and FDR was campaigning as commander in chief. It was also a campaign in which a crucial factor was kept from the voters—the true state of the president's health. And it was the only campaign in which FDR came to detest his opponent. He had not minded Landon, whom he called the White Mouse who wanted to live in the White House, and he actually liked Willkie, even though deriding him as an eternal adolescent, but he really had no use for New York Governor Thomas E. Dewey.

Dewey had made his reputation as district attorney when he prosecuted

Legs Diamond and Lucky Luciano. He was a plodding, uninspiring candidate, propelled by the sheer force of his ambition, the walking antithesis of FDR, stiff and uneasy, covering his shyness with arrogance, lacking in political artistry. He had once told a *Daily News* reporter: "Don't you realize that Franklin Roosevelt is the easiest man in the world for me to beat?"

That summer, when further investigation of Pearl Harbor was the order of the day in Congress, Dewey heard opportunity knock. An anti-Roosevelt officer in the Army leaked information to him that at the time of Pearl Harbor the United States had been cracking the Japanese codes. When General Marshall got wind that Dewey was thinking of using the information in his campaign, he was appalled—any disclosure that the Japanese codes had been broken would harm the war effort at a time when MacArthur was about to invade the Philippines.

Marshall sent a letter to Dewey by courier in late September describing the victories gained from having the codes, such as Midway, and "the tragic consequences if the present political debates regarding Pearl Harbor disclose to the enemy . . . any suspicion of the vital sources of information we now possess."

Dewey was furious, saying that "Franklin Roosevelt . . . knew what was happening before Pearl Harbor, and instead of being re-elected he ought to be impeached." But he did not use the information, which might have won him thousands of votes. He may have reasoned that there would be backlash, with the commander in chief accusing him of hurting the war effort.

Another issue he decided not to use was health—he might have said that Roosevelt was on his deathbed, unable to deliver a speech standing up and unfit to run, but that too could create sympathy for the president, who in the last month of the campaign had completely disregarded his regimen of rest and was out on the hustings.

Instead, Dewey focused on the Communism issue, bringing up the pardon of Earl Browder and saying that a Communist was anyone "who supported the fourth term so our form of government may be more easily changed."

Perhaps the true importance of the 1944 election was labor's unprecedented role in coordinating a national effort to get the vote out. It was Sidney Hillman's finest moment. The Lithuanian-born onetime pants presser ran the Political Action Committee as a full-time partner in the Democratic coalition, balancing the influence of the party's conservative wing. Acting like a nationwide Tammany machine, the PAC set up registration booths inside factory gates and took voters to the polls. "Every worker a voter" was the slogan. As Henry Wallace noted, "Sidney Hillman had a payroll of $65,000 a month and a more powerful organization for getting out the vote than the Democratic National Committee." *Time* magazine was coming out with a Hillman cover, to make it appear that Jewish labor was running the Democratic party.

In Martin Dies's Texas district, Jefferson County, where the poll tax restricted voting, thousands of shipyard and oil-field workers in Port Arthur and Beaumont were given money by the PAC to pay their poll tax and register for the primaries. In May 1944, Dies withdrew from the primary contest. Hillman had actually succeeded in getting rid of a man who had been a major annoyance to the president for years. Two other members of the House Un-American Activities Committee, Joe Starnes of Alabama and John Costello of California, were defeated in primary contests.

Hillman became one of Dewey's prime targets. "Now . . . with the aid of Sidney Hillman," he said in Boston on November 1, "the Communists are seizing control of the New Deal . . . to control the Government of the United States." Clare Booth Luce complained that the PAC was spending money "like confetti" in her district and said: "If my head is to roll in a basket, at least it's a more American head than Sidney Hillman's."

Harold Ickes was incensed. It was the dirtiest campaign he had ever seen. Dewey was appealing to race and religious prejudice. He had the mind of a shyster lawyer. FDR agreed that it was the meanest campaign ever. Dewey had hit him below the belt several times, quite deliberately and viciously. Harry Hopkins passed on a letter from a woman who had been raised in Dewey's hometown, Owasso, Michigan. She said he was a nasty, bad-tempered bully who had split his lip in a fistfight at the University of Michigan—that was why he wore a mustache. "It has come to my attention that a gentleman with a mustache would like to shave it but does not dare find out what is underneath," FDR commented. "It would be a pity to have him go through life not knowing what is underneath."

The president was so mad at Dewey that at the end of the campaign he would not use his name "because I think I'm a Christian." On October 21, he drove through the streets of New York in a rainstorm, bareheaded and without his cape, to give the lie, as Hassett put it, "to the cowardly skunks who have carried on unremittingly a whispering campaign . . . against his health."

The thrust of the president's campaign was the obvious one that Sinclair Lewis embroidered upon in a radio talk on November 1: "Suppose you are a surgeon. Would you care for the idea, if as you started a crucial operation, for which you have been prepared by weeks of clinical tests, you were told to quit? The operation will be finished by a bright young intern, who has never done anything more serious than remove a wart, but who has read a lot of books and talked with a lot of his fellow apprentices, and who is young and bouncing and would just love to do a major operation. Let's hope the patient won't pass out in the process."

November 7 at Hyde Park was bright and clear and cold. Stalin had just announced that Japan, like Germany, was an aggressor nation. FDR sat at a table in the dining room that night, getting the returns with Admiral Leahy from two ticker-tape machines in a corner, with the radio on. The returns were posted on a large board at one end of the room. Adding up some New York returns, Roosevelt leaned over and said: "Bill, see those returns? Everything is all right now. We can forget about New York State." There was a midnight supper, and afterward FDR stopped filling out returns. "It's all over," he said, "so what's the use of putting down the figures." Dewey conceded at 3:45 A.M., but the president was miffed that he hadn't sent the traditional telegram of congratulations. As he took the converted dumbwaiter to his second-floor bedroom, he told Hassett: "I still think he is a son of a bitch."

The PAC had done its work well. A near record 48 million voters had gone to the polls. But it was Roosevelt's most slender victory—he won 53.4 percent of the popular vote, compared with 54.7 percent in 1940. The Democrats picked up twenty-two seats in the House and lost one in the Senate.

A Republican victory, Roosevelt felt, would have meant a return to isolationism and the end of American involvement in the postwar organization of the world. Now he had a mandate to continue his efforts for a new world order that would guarantee peace for a good long time—say a couple of generations; more than that one could not hope for. No one was omniscient. One could not, as Wilson had done, promise the war to end all wars, but one could to some extent rearrange the planet to prevent another European war.

XXIV

Hush'd Be the Camps Today

Hush'd be the camps today;
And soldiers let us drape our war-worn weapons,
And each with musing soul retire to celebrate
Our dear commander's death.

Walt Whitman, *Leaves of Grass*

Saturday, January 20, 1945, the fourth inauguration: the president had learned that in the early days of the republic the oath of office had often been taken elsewhere than on the steps of the Capitol. This time he would do it in the White House and there would be no parade—it saved money and time, and would be easier on him.

The day was cold and gray, and there was an inch of snow on the ground. When Roosevelt appeared on the south porch of the White House, the Marine band in their red uniforms played the opening bars of "Hail to the Chief." Jimmy Roosevelt and a big Secret Service man leaned down, and he wrapped his arms around their necks and was raised, stiff-legged from the braces, until he could grasp the edge of the lectern. He shook hands with Truman and faced Chief Justice Harlan Stone.

You could see that it was hard on him, Truman thought, and he wore no overcoat or hat, only a thin suit. Henry Wallace saw his body shake, especially the right arm as he grasped the rail. He seemed to have lost about twenty pounds. He was a gallant but pitiable figure, summoning his precious strength. He would probably never again give a speech standing. He was in fact standing for the first time since his August speech at the Bremerton Navy Yard. His weight was down to 165 pounds, and when he had gone to Warm Springs to rest after the election he had lost his appetite. "I can't eat," he had complained, "I can't taste food."

Among the many old friends standing on the snow-crusted White House lawn, veterans of past inaugurations, was Mildred Thompson, dean of Vassar College, who thought of all that had been said by Roosevelt's enemies about his being a dictator. No, this was not the way a dictator would do it. There was no Sportspalast. There were no shouting throngs before a Palazzo Venezia, and no goose-stepping soldiers. This was a man in visible pain, consuming himself before their eyes, not for himself but for his country. He could not stand unassisted, but there he stood, for those outside as well as inside the gate.

The speech took no more than five minutes. "We have learned," the president said, "to be citizens of the world, members of the human community. We have learned the simple truth, as Emerson said, that 'the only way to have a friend is to be one.' " The oath administered and the speech concluded, he was helped by his son back to his chair, walking with the lock-knee motion that, no matter how many times one had seen it, was always a demonstration of courage.

Frances Perkins could not keep the tears from her eyes. Woodrow Wilson's widow came up to her and said: "I feel terrible. I feel dreadful. Oh, it frightened me. He looks exactly as my husband looked when he went into his decline. Don't say that to another human soul."

Senator Ed Johnson of Colorado, who had been against a fourth term, thought the inauguration was grim. "There wasn't any smiling," he said. "It was all solemnity this time. Very solemn." The fourth term was beginning in a mournful mood.

And yet there was cause for rejoicing. The dictators were at bay. Berlin was in ruins from round-the-clock bombing, while to the east 180 Soviet divisions were closing in. Tokyo was on fire from the bombs of the B-29s that made daily runs from the Marianas.

With the enemy virtually beaten, the problems that now arose concerned the Allies—Britain and Russia were playing power politics in Europe. FDR was fed up with the British, he had told Stettinius, who had replaced the sick and exhausted Hull as secretary of state, on January 2. They were undermining American policy in China, not wanting to see a strong postwar China challenging their Asian supremacy.

He was going to Yalta, a health resort on the Black Sea, for another meeting with Churchill and Stalin, and he also hoped to meet with King Ibn Saud to discuss the Arab question. Stettinius said that sooner or later they would have to take a definite position on Palestine. FDR planned to take a map of the Near East with him to show Ibn Saud what a tiny area Palestine occupied. Giving a portion to the Jews would not harm Arab interests, he said, as long as they did not move into adjacent parts. It would also be a good idea to take Djibouti away from France and turn it over to Ethiopia.

On January 11, FDR had met with Senate leaders of both parties, and had been more candid than ever before about the limits of American power. "The Russians have the power in Eastern Europe," he said. It was obviously impossible to have a break with them, and therefore the only practicable course was to use what influence we had to improve the situation. Bob La Follette argued that the Russians would try to settle everything by force of arms before the United Nations machinery was set up, so that it would be too late to respond.

There were other changes in the cabinet besides Hull. Frank Knox had died in 1944 and been replaced by James V. Forrestal, and a spot had to be found for Henry Wallace. The first thing Roosevelt did after his inauguration was fire Jesse H. Jones as secretary of commerce and federal loan administrator. He was convinced that "Jesus H. Jones," as he called him, had conspired against him in the election, first by splitting the Texas delegation and then by secret intrigues with Dewey.

Roosevelt usually shrank from firing people, but this time he did it with relish, writing Jones on the day of the inaugural that Henry Wallace "has told me that he thought he could do the greatest amount of good in the Department of Commerce" and that he wanted Jones to think about an ambassadorship.

Jones felt grievously wronged. In 1940 he had rescued Elliott Roosevelt by arranging to have canceled $275,000 in loans for his bankrupt radio stations. And now he was getting the ax. Jones insisted on seeing the president, and there was an emotional confrontation on Sunday, January 21, at 12:30 P.M. Jones said he knew what the president had against him, but that he had had no part in the Texas convention revolt, which had been led by George Butler, who was married to one of his many nieces. He had no more control over George Butler than FDR had over some members of his family, an allusion to Elliott's bad debts.

Jones recalled that at the Chicago convention in 1940 Jim Farley had wanted him for vice president, and Elliott had insisted on seconding the nomination, saying that his father was crazy to have picked Wallace, and he had told them both that he would respect the president's choice and did not want his name presented.

FDR said he knew that, but those were bygones. He wanted Jones to go to France or Italy and help reconstruct either of those countries. Jones said he wasn't interested, and in any case he was out of sympathy with the plan to give those people everything to the point of bankrupting ourselves. FDR then asked Jones to take over the Federal Reserve Board. Jones said no, he would be in continuous clash with Morgenthau, who didn't know anything about finance, and the president would side with Morgenthau against him.

Jones asked if he could stay on as loan administrator, separating the job from the Department of Commerce. FDR turned him down. "I'm an old man," Jones later told Frances Perkins, "and I've done everything I could for the President and saved him from many many troubles and fished him out of all kinds of hot water. And now they throw me overboard in this rough way. It is just terrible."

Having been ousted, Jones decided to make it as difficult as possible for Wallace to be confirmed in both jobs. He had strength on the Hill, and the business community and the press were behind him. Wallace knew he was in trouble—Jones had bought votes on the Hill with his RFC loans, and had built up a political empire by making it possible for his friends to make money legally but not always properly.

For all his mysticism, Wallace was a fighter, and he wanted to stay in the administration despite his ambivalence about Roosevelt, who had betrayed him at the convention. He had loved Roosevelt—he used to dream that he was walking with him, and it made him so happy that Roosevelt could walk. Roosevelt tried to soft-soap him on January 19 by saying he had put on a magnificent fight at Chicago but was missing the reserve strength. That was too much, and Wallace said: "I would have won if your Postmaster-General Frank Walker had not called up the chairman of every delegation on Wednesday night." FDR said it had been done without his knowledge or consent. Wallace wanted to say "Bullshit" but restrained himself.

You had to go back to this, Wallace reflected: Roosevelt had become a Democratic state senator in a Republican district by following a strictly opportunistic political course. Later on, he was the Democratic governor of a Republican state and had to follow the same technique. He was like the man in the rowboat who looks in one direction and rows in the other, with a smile on his face, joy in his heart, and trust in God.

Wallace had to fight for confirmation before the Senate Commerce Committee. In the meantime, Senator Walter George of Georgia introduced a bill to sever the lending agencies from the Department of Commerce. Jesse Jones testified before the Commerce Committee that Wallace was not qualified to run both jobs. The George bill passed, and Wallace was confirmed as secretary of commerce on March 1. The loan administration job went to Fred W. Vinson, the former congressman who had taken over from James Byrnes as economic stabilization director.

On January 22, two days after the inauguration, FDR left Washington for the Norfolk Navy Yard to board the cruiser *Quincy.* Unlike the Teheran Conference, when Hopkins had been his only civilian adviser, this time he brought along a full team—Hopkins, Stettinius, Byrnes, Pa Watson, Steve Early, and Ed Flynn, the boss of the Bronx, who was going to Russia to study how Catholics were treated. The Joint Chiefs also came, with the exception of Hap Arnold.

On January 30 he celebrated his sixty-third birthday aboard ship, with five cakes on the table, one from his Filipino chef, one from the enlisted men, one from the warrant officers, one from the commissioned officers, and one from his advisers. He watched the transfer of mail and dispatches from the *Quincy* to an escorting destroyer. The mail was thrown off the *Quincy*'s stern in a powder can and recovered by the destroyer, a method that probably went back to the days of Columbus.

When FDR arrived in Malta on February 2, Churchill and Harriman were waiting. It was like a family outing, for they had all brought daughters, Anna and Sarah and Kathleen. The next day, the president flew from Malta to Yalta in the *Sacred Cow,* which was equipped with an elevator.

The *Sacred Cow* landed on the icy runway of Saki airfield, ninety miles from Yalta, and Roosevelt was lowered to the ground in his wheelchair. A cape covered his shoulders, and he looked thin and drawn, staring ahead with his mouth open, as if not taking things in. Harriman was shocked by his appearance. Charles Wilson, Churchill's doctor, recorded in his diary that "the President appears to be a very sick man. He has all the symptoms of hardening of the arteries of the brain in an advanced stage, so that I give him only a few months to live." Churchill walked over to the *Sacred Cow* and stood at the president's side, as an Indian attendant might have accompanied Queen Victoria's phaeton, thought Wilson.

A dying president had traveled more than 6,000 miles, from the coast of Virginia to the coast of the Crimea, because Stalin had insisted that on the advice of his doctors *he* could not travel. FDR had overruled his advisers, who did not see why he had to cart himself all over the world to meet Stalin.

He had made this great and final effort because, as Churchill put it, "the whole shape and structure of post-war Europe clamored for review." The Red Army had occupied Poland, Bulgaria, Rumania, and parts of Hungary and Yugoslavia. Russian military prestige was at its highest. The Russians were moving west faster than the Allied armies, stalled in northern Italy and in the Battle of the Bulge, were moving east. The Red Army was fifty miles from Berlin.

Roosevelt had told Stimson before leaving that Stalin seemed to be imitating Britain's policy of having a *cordon sanitaire* of friendly nations around it, and was planning to surround himself with buffer states he could control. Roosevelt had observed during the Warsaw uprising how abruptly Stalin could divorce himself from coalition strategy to pursue his own ends. His blunt refusal to facilitate air drops to the underground was a clear message that the Allies would have no part in determining the affairs of Poland.

Russia in February 1945 was the only great power left on the Eurasian land mass, and Roosevelt had become Stalin's accomplice in making a strong Russia the alternative to the fulcrum Europe system which had drawn the United States into two world wars. Their common program was the dismantling of Germany, a defeated Italy, and a diminished England and France through the loss of their colonial empires. FDR was not averse to the *cordon sanitaire* so long as the formalities of self-determination were respected in terms of elections and referendums. As he had told the Senate leaders in January, the Russians had the power in Eastern Europe and the Allies did not have much leverage, particularly since Churchill had poisoned the well with his spheres-of-influence deal.

Roosevelt's top priority at Yalta was not to keep the Russians out of Eastern Europe, where their presence was already an accomplished fact, but to enlist the Soviet Union's early entry in the war against Japan. The atom bomb was still in the testing stage. No one knew whether and when it would become operational. The Joint Chiefs were planning an invasion of the Japanese home islands, the conquest of which they estimated would take eighteen months. The war would drag on into 1946, with Americans doing most of the fighting. Soviet participation would create a second front, with the Red Army moving into Manchuria and containing the 2 million highly rated Japanese troops that were stationed there, who might continue to fight after the home islands surrendered. Stalin could also allow U.S. bombers to operate from airfields in eastern Siberia.

The Joint Chiefs had spelled it out to FDR in a memo dated January 23, when he was already aboard the *Quincy:* "Russia's entry at as early a date as possible consistent with her ability to engage in offensive operations is necessary to provide maximum support possible without interfering with our main effort against Japan. The objective of Russia's military effort against Japan in the Far East should be the defeat of the Japanese forces in Manchuria, air operations against Japan proper in collaboration with U.S. air forces based in Eastern Siberia, and maximum interference with Japanese sea traffic between Japan and the mainland of Asia."

Such were the considerations that were uppermost in the president's mind at Yalta. Roosevelt thought that Stalin was a man of his word. He had promised a major offensive timed with D-day to tie down the German divisions on the eastern front, and he had honored that vital military commitment.

Of course, trust in Stalin had to be balanced against the warning messages that Harriman had been sending since the spring of 1944. Poland, the first test of Stalin's intentions toward small border states, had revealed a Soviet policy of "aggressiveness, determination and readiness to take independent action." In August, Harriman described Stalin, Foreign Minster Vyacheslav Molotov, and Deputy Foreign Minister Andrey Vyshinsky as "men bloated with power [who] expect that they can force acceptance of their decisions without question upon us and all countries."

Roosevelt also knew from Stimson that the Russians were spying on the atom bomb project, although the secretary of war assured him that they had not yet gained any real knowledge of it. Stimson had told the president that he "believed it was essential not to take them into our confidence until we were sure to get a real quid pro quo for our frankness." FDR agreed.

The true quid pro quo was that, once Stalin knew he would not be allowed to share in the secrets of the atom bomb, he felt justified in taking whatever unilateral actions he felt were necessary in Eastern Europe. Coalition strategy was corroded by the elemental forces of national interest. Churchill led the way in his insistence on a Mediterranean strategy that would safeguard British interests and limit British casualties, delaying the second front for three years. The United States, so generous in supplying its allies with the machinery of war, drew the line at sharing the atom bomb with Russia. Stalin, who was willing to continue the war against Japan, did not tolerate Allied interference in Eastern Europe. Each ally had a restricted zone with a "Keep Off" sign on it.

Roosevelt's ability to get tough with "unaccountable Joe," as the British called him, was limited because he had come to Yalta as a pleader, desperately needing the Soviet pledge to fight Japan that would save thousands of American lives and shorten the war.

Stalin arrived at Yalta on February 4, and that afternoon he and Molotov came to call on FDR in his study at Livadia Palace, which had been built of white granite 150 feet above the Black Sea shore as a vacation home for the czars. As at Teheran, the Soviet and American leaders met privately, excluding Churchill. "The President," Anthony Eden later wrote, "mistakenly, as I believe, moved out of step with us, influenced by his conviction that he could get better results with Stalin direct than could the three countries negotiating together."

Turning on the charm, FDR said he had been struck by the extent of German destruction in the Crimea and was thus more bloodthirsty in regard to the Germans than he had been a year ago. He hoped Stalin would again propose a toast to the execution of 50,000 German officers.

Stalin replied that the destruction in the Crimea was nothing compared to the Ukraine, where the Germans had time to act with method and calculation. They were savages, and seemed to hate with a sadistic hatred the creative work of human beings.

Stalin had recently met de Gaulle, and FDR asked him how he had got on with that difficult fellow. Stalin said he had not found him a very complicated person, but that he was unrealistic in the sense that France had not done very much fighting in this war, and yet he demanded full rights with the Americans and the British and the Russians, who had borne the burden of the fighting. The French contribution was very small. In 1940 they had not fought at all.

Implied in Stalin's view of de Gaulle was the principle that whoever had fought the most and suffered the most casualties should have the biggest plate at the negotiating table. Stalin had fought alone in Europe, and the Red Army was responsible for three out of four German soldiers killed. The message was clear. If the second front had started sooner, the Allies would have been in a better position to curb his appetite.

FDR said he had something indiscreet to tell Stalin, which he would not want to say in front of Churchill. This was another technique of ingratiation, making Stalin his confidant while distancing himself from Churchill. For two years, FDR said, the British had been artificially building up France into a strong power that would garrison 200,000 troops on its eastern border to hold the line for the period required to assemble a strong British army. The British were a peculiar people who wanted to have their cake and eat it too.

Germany would be divided into zones of occupation, and FDR wondered aloud whether France should have a zone.

Why should they, Stalin asked.

Only out of kindness, the president said.

Kindness was the only reason, Stalin and Molotov replied in chorus, *con brio.*

It was a little before five, and they moved to the grand ballroom for the first formal conference. Harry Hopkins, still Roosevelt's chief adviser, was absent; he had taken sick on the boat and had been put to bed when they got to Livadia. "He looked ghastly," wrote Charles Wilson. "His skin was a yellow-white membrane stretched tight over the bones." He was surviving on paregoric, plasma, and liver extract.

The first meeting was devoted to military matters, with FDR remarking that soon American and Russian troops would join up somewhere in Germany. Later the president was host to dinner and cocktails, which he did not mix, as he had at Teheran. There was something unreal about these three elderly men sitting around a table at a Black Sea resort, eating ten-course meals interrupted by multiple toasts, alternately chaffing and praising each other, and enjoying the warm glow of camaraderie that came from their high positions and the knowledge that their place in history was secure, and, as they ate and drank and joked and waited for the interpreters to finish, deciding the fate of hundreds of millions of people. It was Lewis Carroll country, and sometimes it made as much sense as when the White King said: "Mind the Volcano." Things got "curiouser and curiouser" in this Looking-Glass world, "with cats in the coffee and mice in the tea." Churchill and Stalin deciding the geographical position of Poland were like the Walrus and the Carpenter taking the oysters for a walk. The Yalta Conference sometimes seemed to be the product of an overly inventive mind.

And yet this was the real world, a world at war, and there were ominous implications when Stalin said that small powers had no right to dictate to big powers. It was ridiculous to believe that Albania should have an equal vote with the great powers who had won the war. Roosevelt tended to agree that the big powers should write the peace, but Churchill quoted the verse: "The eagle should permit the small birds to sing and care not wherefore they sang."

The reason behind the small powers talk became clear at the second meeting, at 4:00 P.M. on February 5, when Stalin refused to agree to an American proposal limiting the veto in the Security Council of the United Nations in cases when one of the members was a party to a dispute.

Roosevelt embarked on a long and tortuous monologue on Germany, which he wanted divided into five or seven states. Churchill toyed with his cigar and Eden stared at the ceiling as the president rambled on about the Germany he had known in 1886. Even Stalin, usually the picture of calm, seemed impatient. The question of whether to fragment Germany was adjourned for further study.

Churchill then spoke up to support a French zone of occupation. Britain did not want to bear the whole weight of an attack by Germany in the future, and thus wanted to see a strong France in possession of a large army.

The French zone would be taken from the British and American areas, not affecting the Soviet zone, Churchill said.

It was at this point that, to underline the importance of French participation, Churchill questioned how long the United States would keep troops in Europe.

It was one of the decisive moments of the conference, for FDR admitted that American troops would not stay in Europe much more than two years. He could obtain support in Congress for any reasonable measures designed to safeguard the future peace, but he did not believe this would extend to the maintenance of an appreciable American force in Europe. To Stalin, it meant that he could go along with the president's Boy Scout ideas on free elections in Eastern Europe, since in two years the U.S. troops would be packing up.

Stalin conceded that France could have an occupation zone—it was a small price to pay for the withdrawal of American troops—but he could not accept that France should be placed on the same footing as the Big Three by being given a seat on the Allied Control Commission. He could not destroy the truth, he said, which was that France had opened the gate to the enemy.

Churchill, in an allusion to the Nazi-Soviet pact, said that every nation at the start of the war had made mistakes. It was the duty of the Allies to provide for France.

Roosevelt sided with Stalin because he too did not wish France to be treated as an equal, and because it was useful to agree with him in anticipation of the secret negotiations soon to take place on the Pacific. France should have a zone but not take part in the control machinery, FDR said. Otherwise, other nations, such as the Dutch, whose farmland had been flooded with salt water when the Germans destroyed the dikes, might claim a voice on the Control Commission.

Churchill made the point that the French could not administer an occupation zone without being on the Control Commission, and a final decision was deferred to another time.

The final question to come up on February 5 was reparations from Nazi Germany. The Russians presented a plan for taking $20 billion from Germany by confiscating industrial equipment and production over a ten-year period, of which the Soviet Union would get half.

Roosevelt and Churchill agreed that the Soviet Union was entitled to the lion's share, having suffered the most, but they also remembered the problems reparations had created after World War I, the chaos of the Weimar Republic, the embitterment of Germany that led to the rise of Hitler, and the burden on the United States, which financed the reparations through loans.

Stalin argued that by taking reparations in goods rather than cash, the World War I problems would be avoided.

But Churchill said the $20 billion figure was fantastic. The total of World War I reparations had been only $2 billion. The British too had suffered, selling off their overseas assets to finance the war, yet Britain would not demand large reparations. It was bad policy to bleed the Germans white. If you wanted a horse to pull your wagon you had to feed him. That was right, Stalin retorted, but you had to take care that the horse did not turn around and kick you.

FDR said he would support Soviet claims, since he did not want the German standard of living to be higher than the Russian. At the same time, the Germans should not be allowed to become a burden on the world. This question too was put off to further study.

For the next three days, February 6, 7, and 8, the Allies grappled with the question of Poland. Of all the matters discussed at Yalta, this one took up the most time. What should its borders be? Should it, as proposed at Teheran, be displaced to the west, giving Stalin the region populated by Ukrainians, which included the city of Lvov? Should it be governed by the London Poles or the Soviet-controlled Lublin Poles?

In fact, as Harriman pointed out, events were in the saddle. If possession was nine-tenths of the law, Stalin had won, for the Red Army occupied Poland and the Lublin Committee was in Poland issuing decrees, whereas the other group was in distant London. It was hard to argue with this de facto situation. Nonetheless, Roosevelt tried, with the only leverage he had—the 6 million Polish-Americans, who would like to see Lvov and the oil fields assigned to Poland. Would Stalin make a gesture, and also install a more representative government?

Stalin would not, for, as he presented it, it was still a matter of military necessity. "As a military man," he said, "I demand from a country liberated by the Red Army that there be no civil war in the rear. The men in the Red Army are indifferent to the type of government as long as it will maintain order and they will not be shot in the back." The London Poles, in his view, were inciting disorder, while the Lublin Poles were preserving order. Further, Poland had always been the corridor of attack against Russia, and that corridor had to be plugged. The Curzon line on which the new boundaries would be based had been drawn by Lord Curzon and Clemenceau over Lenin's protests. "Should we then be less Russian than Curzon and Clemenceau?" Stalin asked. "You would drive us into shame. I could not take such a position and return to Moscow with an open face."

There was no give in Stalin on Poland, but Roosevelt kept trying, writing him on the evening of February 6 that he was "greatly disturbed" about the situation, since it would put them all in a bad light to have Stalin recognizing one government while Roosevelt and Churchill recognized another. "We cannot recognize the Lublin Government as now composed," he went on, proposing a more broadly based lineup pledged to holding free elections.

To avoid a collision on Poland, Stalin on February 7 adroitly detoured by making an important concession on voting in the Security Council, which made it seem that the Russians were willing to bend to preserve Allied unity, and which carried the message that the United States and Britain should do the same with regard to Poland. Stalin accepted the American proposal limiting the Security Council veto and cut his demands for multiple votes in the General Assembly from sixteen to three. Roosevelt called this "a great step forward," although he later insisted on parity for the United States, and Churchill expressed his "heartfelt thanks."

Then Stalin presented a new plan on Poland with token concessions that the Allies could accept without losing face. There were a few small bites in the Curzon line, and an offer to enlarge the Lublin Committee with "some democratic leaders from Polish émigré circles." Both FDR and Churchill protested the use of the word "émigré," saying it was preferable to think of the London Poles as "temporarily abroad." But neither challenged the main point, the retention of the Lublin Committee as the government of Poland.

On the frontier question, Churchill wondered about Polish expansion to the west. It would be a pity, he said, to stuff the Polish goose so full of German food that it got indigestion. British opinion would be shocked at the forcible expulsion of a large German population. When Stalin was at his most reassuring he could also be at his most deceitful, and he said that most Germans in those areas had already fled the Red Army, which was untrue. Churchill said that simplified the problem—with regard to space for the refugees, there must be plenty, since Germany had suffered 6 to 7 million casualties and would probably suffer a million more. Possibly 2 million more, Stalin added. Such was the callousness of wartime leaders accustomed to death on a large scale.

Another major Soviet concession came that day on France. Roosevelt announced his conversion to Churchill's view that France should have a seat on the Control Commission. Stalin extended both arms above his head and said: *Sdaiyous*—"I surrender." He was outnumbered, and it was another weight thrown on the scales to obtain agreement on Poland.

The wall was up on Poland, but Roosevelt and Churchill with their weak battering ram kept trying to break through, coming back on February 8 with a proposal for a Polish government drawn from Warsaw, London, and "other democratic elements inside Poland." Churchill argued, as had Roosevelt before him, that the conference would be a failure if it ended with the Big Three recognizing separate Polish governments. England had gone to war over Poland, and could not betray the London Poles and the 150,000 Polish troops fighting in France and Italy.

Stalin repeated that the Polish provisional government was just as legitimate as de Gaulle's in Paris, where no elections had yet been held. Elections would be held in Poland soon. How soon, FDR asked. In a month, Stalin replied, if there were no disasters on the front (in fact the election, by no means free, was held nearly two years later, on January 19, 1947). Roosevelt then proposed that the Polish question be referred to the foreign ministers, who drafted an agreement that was approved on February 9.

The agreement seemed in line with the American proposal—the Polish provisional government would include democratic leaders from Poland itself and Poles abroad. This provisional government would hold "free and unfettered elections as soon as possible on the basis of universal suffrage and secret ballot."

Roosevelt and Churchill felt that they had done their best for a free Poland, but to Harriman the language was much too vague. At the embassy, it was often said that in trading with the Russians you had to buy the same horse twice. It would all have to be argued over again, and the machinery for including the London Poles and holding free elections would have to be nailed down, for as things stood Stalin could implement the agreement any way he liked.

Accompanying the agreement on Poland was a declaration calling for free elections in all liberated areas of Europe, which Stalin had approved. "I want the election in Poland to be beyond question," FDR had said. "I did not know Caesar's wife, but she was believed to be pure."

"It was said so about Caesar's wife," Stalin had replied, "but in fact she had certain sins." Fewer sins, Jimmy Byrnes later reflected, than this declaration had violations. It was useful mainly in showing how the Soviets broke their word.

For Roosevelt the crucial meeting of the conference was a second private meeting with Stalin on February 8. Stalin presented his bill for Soviet entry in the war against Japan, and it was a stiff one:

- The return of the southern half of Sakhalin, a big island off the coast of Siberia, which had been seized by Japan in the 1904 war against Russia;
- The return of the Kurils, a group of thirty-one volcanic islands north of Japan, which had been ceded to Japan in an 1875 treaty of commerce and navigation;
- The use of Dairen, the fine harbor in southern Manchuria and the terminus of the Manchurian railway, as a warm-water port;
- The use of Port Arthur, next door to Dairen, as a naval base;
- Soviet control of the Chinese-Eastern Railroad and the South Manchurian Railroad, which would give them a foothold in Manchuria.

Roosevelt was in a fix. He was being asked to make concessions on property that did not belong to him. Self-determination was a farce, with Poland being moved around without asking the Poles, and with the Russians moving into Manchuria without asking the Chinese. There might be other equally valid claims on the Kuril Islands, which had not been taken in warfare but given to Japan by treaty.

When FDR reminded Stalin that he had not had a chance to discuss these matters with Chiang Kai-shek, the Soviet leader fell back on one of the most common ploys of coalition strategy, used often by Churchill and Roosevelt, as when Churchill said he could not go along with this or that measure because the war cabinet or the House of Commons would oppose it, and FDR invoked Congress in the same way. Stalin too, it turned out, had to respond to the wishes of his people, who would not understand why Russia was going to war against Japan. Germany had invaded Russia, but Japan had until now remained neutral. If the benefits were obvious, however, the people would see the national interests involved, and it would be easier to explain the decision to the Supreme Soviet, which Stalin for the sake of argument was equating with the legislative bodies of Britain and America, whereas in fact it merely rubber-stamped his decisions.

Roosevelt's embarrassment was acute, and he repeated that he had not hand a chance to talk to Chiang, and that in any case it was difficult to speak frankly to the Chinese, who did not keep secrets. Stalin was insistent—the proposals should be put in writing and agreed on before the conference ended.

And so it was that the agreement was signed behind the backs of the Chinese, although Stalin accepted the requirement of Chiang's eventual concurrence. Stalin agreed to go to war against Japan two or three months after Germany's surrender. This was the period required to move Soviet divisions from the European front to Siberia. Sakhalin and the Kurils would be returned to the Soviet Union; Dairen would be an international free port and Port Arthur would be leased, and the railroads would be operated by a joint Chinese-Soviet company, "it being understood that the preeminent interests of the Soviet Union shall be safeguarded." Harriman did not like the term "preeminent interests," but FDR did not see the point of arguing over two words. The main thing was that the Soviets were now committed to fight Japan. The Joint Chiefs were pleased. Admiral Leahy said: "This makes the trip worthwhile."

To some of the senior diplomats who attended Yalta, the honors for negotiating skill went to Stalin. "I must say I think Uncle Joe much the most impressive of the three men," wrote Alexander Cadogan. "He is very quiet and restrained. . . . The President flapped about and the P.M. boomed, but Joe just sat taking it all in and being rather amused. When he did chip in . . . he spoke very much to the point."

Gladwyn Jebb could not help admiring Stalin's ability. Of the three, "he had the greatest natural authority, and while recognizing him for the appalling tyrant that he certainly was, one was bound to admit that it was not only his unparalleled ferocity but also his sheer political ability that enabled him for thirty years to be the undisputed Tsar of all the Russias."

The British were saying that the president had gone to bits physically and that it was affecting the conference. Churchill said he didn't seem to read the briefing papers. But as Harriman believed, the president's health did not make that much difference. It was not possible to obtain a better agreement on Poland with the Red Army in control of the country, or to get Stalin to fight Japan with fewer concessions.

As if the human drama being acted out at Yalta needed climactic scenes, the final two days of the conference, February 9 and 10, saw outbursts from Churchill and Stalin. If there was one word certain to make Churchill lose his temper, that word was "trusteeship," with its connotation that Britain should relinquish India and Hong Kong. When Stettinius uttered the word on February 9 in a harmless aside, Churchill reacted like one of Pavlov's dogs: "I will not have one scrap of British territory flung into that area," he proclaimed, going on in the same vein until FDR brought him to order by saying: "I want Mr. Stettinius to finish the sentence he was reading because it does not refer to the matter you have been speaking about."

"If we are out I have nothing to say," Churchill went on. "As long as every bit of land over which the British flag flies is to be brought into the dock, I shall object so long as I live."

Stettinius observed that all he had in mind was taking away the mandated islands from Japan. "We have had nothing in mind with reference to the British Empire," he said.

On February 10, Churchill read a telegram from the war cabinet saying that the $20 billion figure for German reparations was too high. Stalin rose, always an ominous sign, and gripped the back of his chair with such force that his brown hands went white at the knuckles. Spitting out his words, he said that great stretches of his country had been laid waste, and the peasants had been put to the sword. Reparations would have to be paid to the countries who had suffered the most.

Sensing a crisis, Harry Hopkins, risen from his sickbed, passed this note to FDR: "The Russians have given in so much at this conference that I don't think we should let them down. Let the British disagree if they want to—and continue their disagreement at Moscow. Simply say it is all referred to the Reparation Commission with the minutes to show the British disagree about any mention of the 20 billion." And so it was put off, with the Soviets later insisting, at the Potsdam Conference, that FDR had supported their claim for $20 billion in reparations, while in fact he had only agreed to the figure as a basis for discussion.

February 10 was the last night of the conference. The next day the three leaders would disperse, back to their respective capitals, to finish the war and carry their nations into another era. At the final dinner, hosted by Churchill, they were relaxed, exchanging shoptalk as in any profession. Churchill was facing difficult elections and did not know what the left would do. Stalin said that left and right were parliamentary terms. In France, Daladier, who was supposed to be on the left, had dissolved the trade unions, while Churchill, who was supposed to be on the right, had never molested them. Stalin asked FDR if there was a labor party in the United States, and the president replied that although labor was powerful there was no specific party.

After dinner, FDR asked Stalin if he was for the Zionists, and Stalin said he was in principle, although he saw the difficulties of the Jewish problem. The Soviet attempt to establish a Jewish home in the Birobidzhan area of Siberia had failed because the Jews scattered to the cities after two or three years.

FDR said he was going to see King Ibn Saud, and Stalin asked what concessions he intended to make. Roosevelt said there was only one concession he might offer and that would be to give Ibn Saud the 6 million Jews in the

United States. Stalin responded that the Jews were "middlemen, profiteers and parasites," and repeated a Russian saying that "no Jew could live in Yaroslav," a city known for sharp traders. Roosevelt smiled but did not reply.

At lunch on February 11 the final communiqué was signed, with FDR suggesting that Stalin sign first, as the host, and Churchill jocularly arguing that he should sign first because of his age and the alphabetical order. After lunch, FDR drove to Sebastopol to spend the night aboard the code ship USS *Catoctin,* which was moored there, as a gesture to his old friend Vice Admiral Wilson Brown. Harriman thought it was an unnecessary trip that affected the president's health, with a three-hour drive over twisting roads and unbearable heat aboard ship. On the morning of the twelfth, the president left for Saki airfield, where he took the *Sacred Cow* to Cairo for his meetings with three kings of mid-Orient, Farouk of Egypt, Haile Selassie of Ethiopia, and Ibn Saud. Churchill sought out Harry Hopkins to ask him what Roosevelt's intentions were in Cairo, and Hopkins said it sounded like "a lot of horse-play," but Churchill thought it was a deep-laid plot to undermine the British Empire in the Mediterranean.

In the years to come, Yalta would be described as a sellout to Stalin and the root of our subsequent difficulties with the Soviet Union. In fact, the Americans and the British left Yalta feeling that they had scored an impressive victory. The Soviets had wanted a firm commitment on German reparations and did not get it. They had wanted to exclude France from the control machinery of a defeated Germany, but France was included. They had wanted a statement in the Declaration on Liberated Areas that would exclude governments-in-exile from the new governments formed in those areas. They did not get their way. Even on Poland, which was overrun by the Red Army, the agreement on the new government and free elections represented a major concession to the Americans and the British.

Yalta was a defeat for the Soviets, and they so regarded it. What they won at the negotiating table their armies already possessed. Their post-Yalta conclusion was that there was no point in cooperating with the West. Stalin did not honor his commitments. He broke his word repeatedly. If Yalta was a sellout, why did he go to such lengths to violate the agreement? The postwar problems did not result from Yalta but from Stalin's violations.

A War Department memo on Yalta, dated April 3, 1945, and marked "very important" in Stimson's handwriting, said: "The State Department feels that Stalin made very big concessions at Yalta in granting the United States and Britain tri-partite interests in liberated areas adjacent to Russia, particularly with respect to the Balkans and the new Polish government. They believe that he did so when he had it in his power to merely sit tight and force the Lublin Government down our throat."

Roosevelt had won Stalin's pledge to support Chiang Kai-shek and enter the war against Japan. As it turned out, Soviet participation was not a factor in the defeat of Japan, which offered to surrender on August 10, the day after the second atom bomb was dropped on Nagasaki, but how could Roosevelt have known that in February 1945? Nothing done at Yalta contributed to the loss of China by Chiang Kai-shek. In Europe, only by the maintaining of British and American forces after the German surrender could the Soviet Union have been made to withdraw from the territory it controlled and live up to its commitments, but the British and American people were in no mood for such an undertaking and demanded a rapid demobilization.

In dealing with the Soviets at Yalta, there was the American assumption that the other fellow is a good guy who will respond with decency if he is treated right. Roosevelt came to feel that Stalin viewed the world in somewhat the same light as he did, and even the arch anti-Bolshevik Churchill returned from Yalta thinking what Roosevelt had thought at Teheran—that he could reach a lasting understanding with the Soviet dictator. He told his junior ministers on February 23: "Poor Neville Chamberlain believed he could trust Hitler. He was wrong. But I don't think I'm wrong about Stalin." This euphoria was the result of Yalta, because Stalin had been so reasonable and conceded so much.

On the morning of February 14, FDR awaited the arrival of King Ibn Saud aboard the USS *Quincy,* on Great Bitter Lake in the Suez Canal. He had been briefed that the king was a tall, heavy man in his sixties, with a beard dyed black. He was lame and his vision was impaired by cataracts. His pleasures were prayer, perfume, and women—he had many wives, and forty-two sons. He had a good sense of humor—to visitors of ministerial rank, he often made the facetious offer of a wife. In deference to his religious beliefs, there should be no smoking in his presence.

At 10:00 A.M., the destroyer USS *Murphy* was sighted, its forecastle covered with Oriental rugs. Dressed in flowing robes, Ibn Saud sat in a large Louis XV chair, surrounded by armed guards. The gangway was thrown over, and the king came on board, followed by sons, brothers, the royal taster, the royal astrologer, the leader of the prayers, the purse bearer, two coffee servers, a herd of sheep and, in the words of the memorandum, "miscellaneous slaves."

When he saw the president, Ibn Saud remarked how fine it was to proceed in a wheelchair and not have to use up energy. FDR had one of his wheelchairs transferred to the *Murphy,* and later had three more shipped to Saudi Arabia, so the king could roll around the palace, saving his feet.

When they got down to discussing Palestine, Ibn Saud said the Jews should go back to the lands from which they had been driven. FDR agreed that Poland was a case in point. The Germans appeared to have killed 3 million Polish Jews, by which count there should be enough space there to resettle many homeless Jews.

Ibn Saud then said that the Arabs and the Jews could never cooperate, neither in Palestine nor in any other country, and that the Arabs would choose to die rather than yield their lands to the Jews.

According to Hopkins, Roosevelt was shocked by Ibn Saud's intransigence, because more Jews in Palestine represented such a small percentage of the total population of the Arab world. But he was also impressed by the king's determination and promised to do nothing to assist the Jews against the Arabs and to make no move hostile to the Arab people. Of course, he added, it was impossible to prevent resolutions in Congress and articles in the press.

Ibn Saud emphasized that the Jews had made the countryside bloom only because millions of dollars in British and American capital had been poured into Palestine. If those same millions had been given to the Arabs they would have done quite as well. There was also a Palestine army of Jews armed to the teeth, he said, who did not seem to be fighting Germans.

The king convinced FDR that the Arabs meant business. The president seemed to be won over to the Arab cause, and later said in a press conference that he had learned more about Palestine in five minutes from Ibn Saud than in the rest of his lifetime. The only thing he learned, Hopkins reflected, was what everyone already knew—that the Arabs didn't want any more Jews in Palestine.

The *Quincy* put into Newport News on February 27, and FDR went straight to the White House. Pa Watson had died of a cerebral hemorrhage on the return trip, Harry Hopkins was sick, Steve Early was leaving—it seemed like the end of an era. But on February 29, Jonathan Daniels, son of Josephus and recently appointed administrative assistant, heard laughter coming from the president's bedroom. He was sitting up in bed in his pajamas and a bed cape, and Daniels wondered how he could sit so upright with nothing to support him. Senator Barkley was there, telling him how mistaken the rumors of his illness were, and FDR told the story about the drunk who was refused a drink and undertook to prove he was sober. "Why you see that cat there coming in the door," the drunk said, "he has got two eyes and if I was drunk I would see four." "Hell man," the bartender replied, "you are drunker than I thought. That cat isn't coming in the door, it is going out."

Despite the good cheer, Anna thought her father was failing, and she took Daniels aside and told him she was going to restrict his activities and reduce the strain of personal contacts. There was the suggestion of a regency, Daniels thought, in which Anna and her husband, John Boettiger, would protect the president from the outside world. Shades of Mrs. Wilson and Dr. Cary Grayson!

On March 1, Roosevelt addressed a joint session of Congress in the House of Representatives. Senator Thomas C. Hart of Connecticut was surprised to see him appear in a wheelchair, something he had never done before. He was rolled to the well of the chamber and transferred to a red plush chair. "I hope that you will pardon me for the unusual posture of sitting down during the presentation of what I want to say," Roosevelt began, "but I know you will realize that it makes it a lot easier for me in not having to carry about ten pounds of steel around on the bottom of my legs, and also because of the fact that I have just completed a 14,000 mile trip."

As he started to read his speech, Senator Bourke Hickenlooper told Senator Hart: "Watch his hands." He was having trouble turning the pages in the loose-leaf binder. His right hand was not working, and he had to use his left hand. He rambled on, ad libbing when he lost his place. Obviously he was a very sick man.

But toward the end, his voice rose as he expressed his confidence in the arrangements made with Stalin and outlined his hope for the future: "The Crimea Conference . . . ought to spell the end of a system of unilateral action, the exclusive alliances, the spheres of influence, the balances of power, and all the other expedients that have been tried for centuries—and have always failed. We propose to substitute for all these, a universal organization in which all peace-loving nations will finally have a chance to join."

Those around Roosevelt continued to maintain the illusion that he was fine. Bill Hassett said on March 12 that he was in the pink of condition, and had plunged into an accumulation of work with old-time zest, taking on a full calendar of visitors.

One of the visitors was General Lucius D. Clay, who had been named Eisenhower's deputy in occupied Germany. Jimmy Byrnes took Clay in, warning him that "he's going to ask you some trick question, like what would you do if in Heidelberg during the night the Germans rose up and attacked and killed a field of soldiers." Instead, the president started to reminisce about his trips to Germany as a boy. Then he said he had heard that Clay was an Army engineer who had built a large dam in Texas, and that he ought to consider a great power development in Central Europe, along the lines of TVA. The president never gave Clay a chance to get a word in, and as they left Byrnes kidded: "General, you talked too much." "I was so shocked watching him," Clay replied, "that I don't know whether I could have made sense of a reply. Mr. Byrnes, we've been talking to a dying man." "Oh, you're crazy," Byrnes replied. "He's been like this for a long time."

On the evening of March 22, Roosevelt attended the annual dinner of the White House correspondents in the Presidential Room of the Statler Hotel. Curtains were drawn, the conductor of the Navy Band raised his baton, and the blare of "Hail to the Chief" swept across the room as FDR appeared in his wheelchair, looking thin and tired. He shifted into his seat and gave a little wave in response to the applause, as if to say "that isn't necessary."

Sprinkled in the audience were Harry Truman, in a dark suit with a breast-pocket handkerchief folded so that the four corners showed, and Ickes the sourpuss, and Morgenthau looking owlish behind his glasses, and the balding Biddle with his pencil mustache.

The show began with Danny Kaye asking the audience to shout out gibberish as background for his rendition of "Minnie the Moocher," followed by Jimmy Durante in his beat-up hat and cigar, saying indignantly: "What a stinker that General Marshall gave me . . . what a stinker," and Fanny Brice singing "I'm a secondhand Rose, with secondhand clothes . . ."

The four-time president seemed to be enjoying himself as he chain-smoked and sipped wine, the man who had faced thousands of audiences and was impervious to the interest he generated: "The Old Man is getting a kick out of it, all right. . . . He takes everything in his stride, doesn't he? . . . How does he look? Looks pretty thin, doesn't he? Looking pretty old. . . ."

Suffering from a cold, FDR said: "I want to give you a word, the word Humanity. We all love Humanity, you love Humanity, I love Humanity. Humanity's with me all the time. I go to bed and I dream of Humanity. I get up and I eat breakfast and there's Humanity, Humanity follows me around all day. So with that in mind, with that word Humanity, here's your headline and here's your story—I am calling off the press conference for tomorrow morning."

They all laughed and applauded and stood up to watch him being wheeled out, and as he went out the door they saw the toss of the head, the smile, and the hand uplifted and waved in the old familiar way.

There were good reasons to smile, for the military situation was encouraging. In the Pacific, Iwo Jima had been attacked in February, and on April 1 came the boldest move of the campaign, the attack on Okinawa, which was about 300 miles from the southern tip of Japan. The fighting was savage, with heavy American losses. It was a taste of what would come if the Japanese home islands had to be invaded. These people fought with irrational fury, sinking ships by crashing planes into them.

And yet, as the Marines fought their way across the East China Sea, FDR pursued a bankrupt China policy in his continued support of Chiang Kai-shek. He saw no alternative to Chiang, and still hoped to build China up as one of the Big Four, to support his postwar policies of trusteeships in French and British colonies. On February 23, aboard the *Quincy,* he had told reporters that Chiang did not want Indochina, but that it was better not to talk about a trusteeship, which would only make the British mad.

"Is that Churchill's idea on all territory out there," a reporter asked, "he wants them all back just like they were?"

"Yes, he is mid-Victorian on all things like that," FDR replied. Back in Washington, he told advisers that he would do all he could to get independence for Indochina.

In Europe, Allied forces were on the Rhine, and the Russians had crossed the Oder, the future eastern frontier of Poland. On March 7 the U.S. First Army captured Cologne. The Remagen bridge had been left intact for the Rhine crossing.

Politically, however, the good spirit of Yalta was breaking down in a climate of mutual suspicion. With thousands of American POWs liberated in areas occupied by the Red Army, the Soviets were violating the Yalta agreement that American teams should have immediate access to them.

Harriman cabled FDR that he was "outraged" at Soviet stalling. For the first time, FDR adopted a stern tone with Stalin, cabling him on March 17: "Frankly I cannot understand your reluctance to permit American officers and men to assist their own people in this matter. This Government has done everything to meet each of your requests. I now request you to meet mine in this particular matter."

It did no good, and Harriman reported on March 24 that American POWs were being kept in Soviet camps in "unbelievable" conditions. "Our men were mixed with civilian refugees of all kinds, sleeping on floors with utterly no sanitary or washing facilities. Food was served twice a day at irregular intervals and consisted of barley soup, bread, potatoes, or kasha and tea or coffee. There were no delousing facilities." In the meantime, Eisenhower was giving Soviet contact officers complete freedom of movement.

Harriman was sure the Soviets were using the POW issue as a club to win concessions on Poland, where they had violated the Yalta agreement by installing the Lublin Poles as the provisional government. For the first time, FDR could see the Soviet police state at work. The Sovietization of Poland was advancing daily. Soviet troops were hunting down members of the anti-Communist Home Army. The prisons were filling. There were mass arrests. The possession of an old German newspaper was considered proof of collaboration.

On April 1, FDR expressed his concern to Stalin. "So far," he said, "there has been a discouraging lack of progress made in the carrying out, which the world expects, of the political decisions which we reached at the conference, particularly those relating to the Polish question. I am frankly puzzled as to why this should be, and I must tell you that I do not fully understand in many respects the apparent indifferent attitude of your government." On April 7, Stalin replied that the Polish discussions had reached "a dead end."

Also in violation of Yalta, King Michael of Rumania was bullied into naming a Soviet-backed premier on March 6. Two days later, Churchill cabled FDR that "we have been hampered in our protests against these developments by the fact that in order to have the freedom to save Greece, Eden and I at Moscow in October recognized that Russia should have a largely preponderant voice in Rumania and Bulgaria while we took the lead in Greece." Although Soviet actions in Rumania clearly violated the principles of Yalta, there was not much Churchill could say, for Stalin would reply: "I did not interfere with your action in Greece, why do you not give me the same latitude in Rumania?"

FDR agreed on March 11 that "Rumania is not a good place for a test case. The Russians have been in undisputed control from the beginning and with Rumania lying athwart the Russian lines of communications it is more difficult to contest the plea of military necessity and security which they are using to justify their action."

Thus, through a combination of Red Army occupation and spheres-of-influence deals, Roosevelt and Churchill found themselves powerless to implement the Yalta agreements.

Stalin suspected that the Allies were negotiating for a separate peace in Germany. Hitler had moved divisions to the eastern front until there were less than thirty divisions facing the British and the Americans, and 150 divisions facing the Russians. General Karl Wolff, the SS commander in Italy, had sent emissaries to meet in Zurich in March with Allen Dulles, the OSS chief in Switzerland. Dulles said his terms were unconditional surrender, and Wolff said he would do his best to convince the German commander in chief in Italy, Field Marshal Albert Kesselring, that surrender was the best course. Sir Harold Alexander, the Allied chief in Italy, decided to follow up the contacts.

When Stalin was informed, he was furious that a German surrender was being arranged without the Soviet Union. He was alert to any signs of a separate peace, the Bolsheviks having negotiated one with the Germans in 1917.

There followed a flurry of messages between FDR and Stalin, the one explaining that there was nothing underhanded in the meetings with the Germans, the other insisting that the Allied actions were engendering distrust. The contacts with Wolff, in fact, led to nothing, but Stalin was misinformed by his intelligence people and sent to FDR on April 3 one of the most insulting communications ever addressed by one chief of state to another, in which he accused the president of being a liar or a dupe of his aides.

Stalin said that he had been informed that negotiations had taken place in which the Germans had agreed to let the British and Americans advance unopposed to the east in exchange for easier peace terms. "Why was it necessary to conceal this from the Russians?" he asked.

Stung, FDR replied on April 5: "Frankly, I cannot avoid a feeling of bitter resentment toward your informers, whoever they are, for such vile misrepresentations of my actions or those of my trusted subordinates."

Stalin shot back a cable defending his suspicions. Why was it, he asked, that the Germans "continue to fight savagely with the Russians for some unknown [railroad] junction in . . . Czechoslovakia, which they need as much as a dead man needs poultices, but surrender without resistance . . . important towns in Central Germany. . . . Don't you agree that such behavior of the Germans is more than strange and incomprehensible?"

It was up to Roosevelt to be the peacemaker, and in his last message to Stalin he thanked him for his "frank explanation" of the Swiss incident, which had now faded into the past. "There must not, in any event," he added, "be mutual mistrust, and misunderstandings of this character should not arise in the future. I feel sure that when our armies make contact in Germany and join in a fully coordinate offensive the Nazi armies will disintegrate." The date of this message was April 12.

Privately, however, FDR was himself full of mistrust of the Russians. On March 29, the day he left for a period of rest in Warm Springs, he saw the

New York Times columnist Anne O'Hare McCormick, and told her that he no longer believed what he had told Congress about his confidence in the arrangements made with Stalin at Yalta. He said that either Stalin was not a man of his word or else he did not have the control of the Soviet government that FDR had thought he had.

On March 24, FDR had gone to Hyde Park for a few days, returning to Washington on March 28 and leaving on the afternoon of the following day for Warm Springs, where he arrived March 30. He was so tired that he could only sit in a chair with a book in his hands. But after a couple of days he picked up, signing papers and answering mail, particularly his troublesome correspondence with Stalin. When he accepted Jimmy Byrnes's resignation as director of war mobilization, he said: "It's too bad some people are so prima-donnaish." In the afternoons he went on drives through peach orchards, under blue skies.

He was pleased with the news that the Japanese cabinet had fallen in the wake of the invasion of Okinawa, and on April 5 he had a visit from President Sergio Osmeña of the Philippines, who described the destruction of Manila. After lunch, he gave a press conference, his 998th, in which he pledged that independence would be granted to the Philippines as soon as the Japanese were out.

He was looking forward to attending the opening session of the San Francisco Conference on April 25, when the charter for the United Nations would be drawn up. On April 6, in the living room of his cottage, he worked on a design for the UN stamp. "What do you think of this?" he asked two visiting cousins, Margaret Suckley and Laura Delano. "A simple new stamp without an engraving—on the top line '3 cents 3,' on the bottom line 'United States Postage,' and in the middle 'April 25, 1945.' "

On April 9, Lucy Rutherfurd arrived from Aiken with her friend, the society portraitist Elizabeth ("Mopsy") Shoumatoff, whom she had commissioned for a portrait of the president, telling her: "He's so thin and frail, but having lost so much weight, his face looks the way it did when he was younger." Roosevelt spent the last days of his life with the woman he might have married had he followed the inclinations of his heart.

On April 11, he worked on his Jefferson Day speech, which he planned to deliver on the thirteenth, bent over the table, with Grace Tully by his side in case he wanted to dictate, and Fala lying with his head on his master's foot. "Well," he said after he had finished, "I've written much of that speech in my own hand."

That evening Henry Morgenthau, Jr., came to dinner, and was shocked at the president's haggard appearance. His hands shook as he mixed cocktails, and he started knocking the glasses over when he poured. His memory was bad—he was constantly confusing names. He had great trouble transferring himself from his wheelchair to the dinner table. They had veal and noodles, and a delicious waffle with whipped cream and a chocolate sauce. Miss Delano's Irish setter threw up, and she picked up the vomit with her handkerchief, which didn't seem to upset the president at all. Morgenthau discussed his plans for Germany, and the difficulties he was having with the State Department crowd, and FDR said: "Henry, I am with you 100 percent."

On the morning of April 12, Mopsy Shoumatoff set up her easel, and FDR emerged at noon wearing a double-breasted gray suit and a crimson tie, looking like a contented man. Hassett had brought two bills to sign, the war news was good, and he was looking forward to his favorite Georgia dish, Brunswick stew, at a barbecue that evening. "Mr. President," Mopsy said, "you look so much better than yesterday that I am glad I did not start work until today." She had been sketching since her arrival, and Bill Hassett thought that she was altogether too pushy, interrupting the paperwork constantly, measuring the president's nose, asking him to turn this way and that. Hassett resolved to ask Dr. Bruenn to put an end to this hounding of a sick man.

Documents were spread around the room, with the president's signature drying on them. "My laundry," he said, laughing heartily at his own joke. He sat at the card table near the fireplace, in the leather chair he liked, with his back to the windows that overlooked the pine trees, and went to work signing papers. Mopsy Shoumatoff got started, placing the eyes, as Lucy and Margaret Suckley watched, chatting on a sofa, and Laura Delano came in with her dog. Signing a bill to increase the borrowing power of the Commodity Credit Corporation, he told Laura Delano: "Here's where I make a law." At twenty minutes to one, his butler, Arthur Prettyman, brought a tray with gruel and cream and what Roosevelt called his "green cocktail," which he drank.

Mopsy Shoumatoff went over the shadows with Windsor blue, and the face came to life. The Filipino boy came in and started setting the table, and FDR said: "We have fifteen more minutes to work." Margaret Suckley sat on the sofa crocheting, Laura Delano poured fresh water into a bowl of roses, and Lucy sat watching near the window.

As Mopsy painted the upper part of the president's face, near the hairline, he suddenly raised his hand and passed it over his head several times in a strange, jerky way. "I have a terrific headache," he said. Without a sound, he slumped forward in his armchair. Margaret Suckley thought he was looking for something and asked: "Have you dropped your cigarette?"

Roosevelt's brow was furrowed with pain. He tried to smile and put his left hand to the back of his neck, saying: "I have a terrific pain in the back of my head." Margaret Suckley and Laura Delano tilted his chair back as Mopsy Shoumatoff and Lucy Rutherfurd ran out to find Dr. Bruenn, who was having lunch. Lucy said they had better leave. It would not do for the press to find them there.

Arthur Prettyman and the Filipino boy, Irineo Esperancilla, carried the president to his bed. He was a completely dead weight. By the time Dr. Bruenn arrived, he was unconscious and covered with a cold sweat, but s breathing. He had voided involuntarily. Hot water and blankets had b applied. It was apparent to Bruenn that the president had suffered a massive cerebral hemorrhage.

Dr. Bruenn administered amyl nitrate to relieve the intense vasoconstriction. At 3:15, his pupils were dilated, and there was an occasional spasm of rigidity and a marked slowing of respiration. As Dr. Bruenn watched, the president's face turned bluish-purple, a condition common to cerebral hemorrhages, when an excessive amount of hemoglobin (the iron-containing protein in red blood cells) in the capillaries of the face discolors the skin.

At 3:31 P.M., the breathing turned to gasps. Dr. Bruenn injected Adrenalin into the heart muscle, but no heartbeat was audible. At 3:35 P.M. Central War Time, Dr. Bruenn pronounced the president dead.

Franklin Delano Roosevelt died a soldier's death. He died, like the young men who were shot in caves on Okinawa or who were hit by shell fragments while crossing the Rhine, in combat. His form of combat was convincing his people that America must join the war against the Axis, and leading the Allied coalition, and traveling many thousands of miles in difficult conditions to hold the necessary meetings that would win the war. The long and unrelenting effort had killed him as surely as a bullet.

It was only the death of one man, and yet it was more, for "the whole earth is the sepulcher of famous men; and their story is not graven only on stone over their native earth, but lives on far away, without visible symbol, woven into the stuff of other men's lives." There would be no more fireside chats, no more Hundred Days, no more brain trust, no more New Deal, no more third and fourth terms, no more Grand Alliance, no more cross-country campaigns with eager upturned faces seen from back platforms. But one thing was sure: No president would ever look at the office again as had presidents before him.

Not long before his death, the American ambassador to London, John G. Winant, had given him George Washington's walking stick, the one with the thirteen stars on it that Washington had given to Jerome Bonaparte. Winant recalled Sir James Barrie's rectoral address to the students of St. Andrews, when he had told them that he could not provide them with a staff for the journey in the world that lay before them, but perhaps he could tell them "how to use it and lose it and find it again, and cling to it more than ever. You shall cut it, as is ordained, every one of you for himself, and its name is courage."

At 5:05 that afternoon, Harry Truman was in Sam Rayburn's office when Steve Early called and asked him to come to the White House. Truman thought it was about Bishop Atwood, the Episcopal bishop of Arizona, a friend of FDR's who had been buried that day. He told Rayburn he'd be back in a few minutes. He was ushered into Mrs. Roosevelt's study on the second floor. She put her arm around his shoulder and said: "The president is dead." Truman went home to his apartment at 4701 Connecticut Avenue in a state of shock. How would he deal with the war effort, with the armed forces, with Churchill and Stalin?

At 7:09 he took the oath of office, this onetime farm boy, soldier, haberdasher, protégé of Pendergast, senator, vice president, and now president. Back in Missouri, his former business partner, Spencer Salisbury, said: "Harry Truman's the luckiest man I ever knew. He's as lucky as a bull with two pricks."

In his office, Sam Rayburn looked out at the dwindling afternoon light, his right hand in a half fist, and tears welled in the shrewd eyes set like marbles in the round face. "Now the sons of bitches will start trying to dance all over his grave," he said. "Well, by God, let them try."

David Lilienthal felt physically ill when he heard the news. Then he felt consternation at the thought of that Throttlebottom, Truman, taking Roosevelt's place. "The country and the world don't deserve to be left this way," he thought, "with Truman at the head of the country at such a time." Never again would he see the waving hand and that sense of great vitality and joy of living. How he would have enjoyed himself as ex-president, just having fun, writing memoirs.

At his desk in the Office of Economic Stabilization, Thomas Emerson heard five bells ring on the ticker, which meant a flash—my God, FDR was dead. It was a shock. He was a father figure. There was no one to take his place. Who would hold together the Democratic party? Who would shield the government from attacks by the lunatic fringe of Congress, the McKellars and the Bilbos? Their points of view would now carry more weight.

In Poughkeepsie, a five-year-old girl named Renee Adriance was taken by her banker father to dinner at a private club, a bastion of the Hudson River Republican establishment. In the middle of dinner, the radio was turned on to announce the president's death. Everyone in the dining room stood up and cheered. The little girl wondered why they were applauding the death of the president, which should have been an occasion for sadness. She wondered in later years how a man whose greatness was established could have been so hated.

Vacationing in La Jolla, California, Breckinridge Long remembered the days when they were both assistant secretaries and their offices had been close together in the east corridor of the old State, War, and Navy building. They would often meet on the way to lunch or after golf or tennis in the locker room of the Chevy Chase Club. Long had gone to Warm Springs in the summer of 1932 and watched him demonstrate how both ankles and one knee had mended to the point where they could hold his weight standing— only the other knee would not lock, it would pop out under pressure. He was confident that one day he would walk unaided, but alas it had never happened. Long wondered what had estranged him from the White House, unless it was Harry Hopkins and his subsurface hostility. In any case, Roosevelt was a remarkable person, and Long wished his memory well.

In Berlin, encircled by the Red Army, Goebbels called Hitler and said: "My Führer, I congratulate you! Roosevelt is dead. It is written in the stars that the second half of April will be the turning-point for us. This is Friday 13 April. It is the turning-point." Goebbels called for champagne, seeing in Roosevelt's death the sign that a change of fortune would occur, just as it had in the Seven Years War with the miracle of the House of Brandenburg. Seventeen days later, on April 30, with the Russians closing in on his bunker, Hitler shot himself with his Walther pistol, a reviled and unlamented suicide.

At 1:00 A.M. on April 13, during a farewell party at the embassy, Harriman heard the news in Moscow and arranged an appointment with Stalin, who was clearly moved. He held Harriman's hand for thirty seconds saying nothing, before asking him to sit down, and then questioned him closely about the circumstances of the president's death. Harriman said it was a tragedy for international relations, and that Soviet cooperation was more important now than ever. Stalin wanted to know all about Truman. Harriman said he was a middle-of-the-road New Dealer, on good terms with the Senate, determined to carry out Roosevelt's policies. Although inexperienced in foreign affairs, he would choose good advisers and listen to them. Stalin later became convinced that Roosevelt had been poisoned. There was no autopsy, and his ambassador in Washington was denied permission to view the body, for FDR's face was badly disfigured. That was not a good enough reason for Stalin, whose own paranoia about assassination plots made him skeptical about natural deaths in other leaders.

On the morning of Friday, April 13, Professor Paul H. Buck's class, "The Making of Modern America, 1865 to the Present," met as usual at nine in Harvard Hall. The class had reached the years before World War I, and two main questions emerged: how to solve economic problems to obtain a more equitable society, and how to secure a peaceful world. That morning, Professor Buck planned to talk on Woodrow Wilson.

In his class were returned veterans with the experience of war as well as civilian undergraduates. It was not a normal peacetime class, and it was no ordinary morning. Buck faced the class and thought for a moment of what had happened, and of the young men before him, most of whom had been seven or eight or nine when Roosevelt had first entered the White House. He had been the only president of their generation. What could one say?

Lincoln had died on April 15, 1865, and Roosevelt had died on April 12, 1945. The similarity did not need to be underlined, but it was a start, and he started by quoting Whitman:

> "Hush'd be the camps today;
> And soldiers let us drape our war-worn weapons,
> And each with musing soul retire to celebrate
> Our dear commander's death."

"As one studies history," Buck went on, "the stature of a man is judged by what he does to build or destroy the faith by which men live. . . . Mr. Roosevelt was great because he, like Lincoln, restored men's faith. . . ."

He tried to explain the poignancy of the situation to someone who, like himself, had seen two wars and the failure that had followed the first. The class was transfixed, hearing their own thoughts and hopes made articulate. It was one of those rare communions for which all teachers wait and all students hope.

At the American embassy in Rio de Janeiro on the evening of April 12, there was a strange occurrence. People began converging on the embassy, people from all classes of Brazilian society, people from the slums and the fine beachfront houses of Copacabana, who had never seen Roosevelt, who had never heard him speak, who knew nothing about the American system, but who had some dim awareness that his death was a loss not only to his own people but to them, because he had thought of the little man, because his message of a fair society had extended beyond the borders of his own country. A beggar stood in the street and wept. An old man stopped an American to tell of his sorrow. Barefoot peasants stood in front of the embassy for a long moment, then moved on in silence. Hundreds of students from the law school gathered in front of the embassy gate. More people came, little people, almost apologetic, saying they were of no importance but wanted to express their grief. They came unasked to pay homage to a man they knew only remotely, through the newspapers or the radio, but who had in some way touched their lives.

On the morning of April 13, a hearse carrying a flag-draped bronze coffin drove from the Little White House to the Warm Springs railroad station. Steve Early thought that the undertaker, Mr. Lesene of the Patterson Funeral Home, was "a chiseling son of a bitch. His bill was $3100 and he wanted to be giving interviews to the newspaper." Outside Georgia Hall, the main building of the Warm Springs Foundation, patients in wheelchairs and on crutches watched the hearse go by. The streets were lined with troops from nearby Fort Benning, standing shoulder to shoulder at present arms. The hearse was followed by the Fort Benning Army Band and 100 infantrymen armed with carbines, the colors of each company carrying black streamers.

At 9:55, the hearse reached the train siding, and eight enlisted men loaded it into the last car. Crossing the Georgia countryside, the train passed four black women at the edge of a cotton field, kneeling with their hands clasped. In his drawing room, too drained to dictate, United Press correspondent Merriman Smith thought of Roosevelt's D-day prayer: "Some will never return. Embrace these, Father, and receive them, Thy heroic servants, into Thy kingdom."

Roosevelt was crossing the land for the last time, the land he had governed longer than any other president, the land he had loved and changed, in ways that could not be changed back. He was crossing the cotton fields of Georgia and the tobacco farms of the Carolinas, and at every whistle-stop station crowds formed, farmers and sharecroppers and shopkeepers, school-children who had grown up with his picture on the classroom wall, and men in overalls with sunburned faces who stood with their arms around their wives' shoulders. At a country depot in South Carolina, a few Boy Scouts sang "Onward Christian Soldiers," and folks gathered around and joined in, and then people a block away took it up, and soon it seemed as if the whole town was singing, and that the singing would spread from town to town across the land until all of America would join in, millions of voices rising in unison to honor their dead president.

On the morning of April 14, the train crossed the Potomac and backed into Union Station, and a small, black-draped caisson drawn by six white horses carried the coffin to the White House with full military honors—muffled drums, the crack of hands on rifle stocks, the clip-clop of horses' hooves. Under a muggy April sky, the caisson proceeded down Delaware and Constitution avenues, right on 15th Street, left on Pennsylvania, and through the northwest gate, into the White House grounds. The crowds had to be held back by soldiers. Bill Hassett saw people kneeling on the sidewalk in prayer.

As she watched the funeral procession, Vassar Dean Mildred Thompson thought that he had died at the right time. How bitter would Lincoln's end have been had he lived through Reconstruction, and how sad for Wilson that he had not died on the trip back from Versailles.

Thomas Emerson could feel the current of emotion passing through the crowd. When he was alive we were critical, he thought, we felt that he didn't know what he was doing, or wasn't energetic enough in settling disputes between agencies, we were always complaining, but now that he was dead you could already sense the process of deification at work, of a man who had operated beyond reproach and could have solved all the future problems of the country had he lived.

The invitation in black Gothic print said: "Funeral services for Franklin Delano Roosevelt, Late President of the United States." The Tennessee driver taking David Lilienthal to his Washington-bound plane recalled the years before the New Deal when he had worked in a Knoxville spinning mill: "They didn't even treat us like humans," he said. "Sixteen cents an hour.... If you asked to get off on a Sunday, the foreman would say 'All right, you stay away Sunday, but when you come back Monday someone else will have your job.... No sir, I won't forget what he done for us."

In the East Room, the casket, kept closed because the cerebral hemorrhage had turned the president's face purple, lay between the tall portraits of George and Martha Washington. Six servicemen stood at attention. Looking even taller in black, Eleanor Roosevelt walked in on her son Elliott's arm—her other three sons were overseas. So many members of the previous and present administrations, more than 200, crowded the East Room for the

4:00 P.M. service by Episcopal Bishop Angus Dun that they spilled over into the Blue and Green rooms. When it was over, Sidney Hillman tottered across Pennsylvania Avenue and sat on a bench in Jackson Park. He sat there alone for hours, and it seemed to him that he would never be able to get up and walk again.

Later, Eleanor confronted her daughter. She had heard from Laura Delano that Lucy Rutherfurd had been in Warm Springs, and had also come to the White House when Anna was hostess. Why hadn't she been told? Why had her daughter been an accomplice to her husband's final deceit? Eleanor willed herself to control her feelings. She knew that Franklin might have been happier with a different wife. But they had stayed together. They had endured.

Conspicuous by his absence from the president's funeral was Winston Churchill, who, while the president was alive, had always been eager to come to Washington. He had made great professions of friendship, writing as recently as March 18 that "our friendship is the rock on which I build," and that he would never forget how Roosevelt had comforted him over the loss of Tobruk by giving him 300 Sherman tanks. But now he would not cross the Atlantic to mourn his ally. Churchill was a man of action and decision, not of funerals. When he wanted something from Roosevelt, the trip was worth it. For a ceremonial function, it was not. "When P.M. woke up about 6" on April 13, Cadogan recorded, "there were hectic telephone conversations betweeen Anthony [Eden] and him. P.M. of course wanted to go. A. thought they oughtn't both be away together. P.M. says he'll go and A. can stay. I told A. that if P.M. goes, he must stay. A. due to leave at 7.45. At that hour, no decision reached. P.M. said he would decide at Aerodrome . . . Discovered P.M. had not gone."

That night, the presidential train, seventeen cars filled with politicians and officials, pulled out of Union Station, bound for Hyde Park. The train was so heavy that at first it would not start—a coupling broke three times. It rolled on through the night, passing through Maryland, Delaware, Pennsylvania, New Jersey, and into his home state, following the Hudson River and reaching Hyde Park on the clear Sunday morning of April 15.

Close to 300, they assembled in the rose garden enclosed by a high hemlock hedge planted by the president's mother many years ago to hide a kitchen garden, which was later changed to flowers.

Here the president had often said that he wanted to be buried, thought Bill Hassett as he looked at the open grave. It was the anniversary of Lincoln's death, and Hassett had spotted a lilac bush in flower beyond the hedge, which reminded him of the opening line of Whitman's tribute: "When lilacs last in the dooryard bloomed."

On three sides of the garden, soldiers, sailors, and marines were lined up, wearing ribbons that meant Cassino, and the Solomons Slot, and Iwo Jima, and Normandy. On the fourth side stood a detachment of West Point cadets. The evenly spaced shots of twenty-one guns going off echoed across the

Hudson, announcing the procession's arrival. Through the opening in the hemlock hedge came a youthful crucifer, followed by the Reverend Anthony of St. James's Church, who was nearing eighty, his surplice fluttering in the April breeze. Then came eight servicemen straining under the weight of the bronze coffin, so that two officers jumped to their aid, followed by Eleanor and other members of the family.

Dr. Anthony read the committal words from the Book of Common Prayer, and the coffin was lowered into the ground. Hassett thought of the president's enemies, those who said he bought votes with relief money. He thought of a line in a prayer: "That they may find fellowship with Lazarus, who once was poor." Then he thought, not of the president who had saved the country from economic despair, not of the commander in chief who had saved the free world from dictators, but of the man he had worked with, from whom he had never heard an angry or impatient word, or a complaint of any kind.

Standing behind Bob Hannegan and Ed Pauley, Henry Wallace was reminded of the skunk cabbage in bloom he had seen from the train window. Roosevelt had had a genuine spiritual power to lift people, but now the Pauleys and the Hannegans were in the saddle. He saw Eleanor cross herself as she turned away from the grave and say "God rest his soul." He could tell from the way she said it that she believed his soul had been caught up in many conflicts, often uncertain as to its real course, and would now find peace.

Standing next to Mackenzie King, Henry Stimson thought of the Constitutional Convention of 1789, when Benjamin Franklin had said, referring to the carved image of the sun on the back of George Washington's chair: "Throughout this Convention I have been watching that image of the sun and wondering whether it portrayed a setting or a rising sun. Now I am certain that it is a rising sun." Was it now, he wondered, a rising sun?

West Point cadets fired three volleys, and then came the saddest sound in the world, the sound of a bugler playing taps. The president was at rest, his grave a short distance from the room where his wicker basket had swung.

Epilogue:
The Transformation

Roosevelt's commitment to public service was formed by the example of his distant cousin and the sermons of his headmaster. The strong sense of who he was and what he represented, which often stifles ambition among the privileged, in his case nurtured it. History to him was a living force that shaped the present. The past was filled with heroes whose lessons could be learned. America had no Caesar, no Charlemagne, no Napoleon, but America had Washington, who, like the barons at Runnymede, had acted not only for a class but for a people. America had Jefferson, who had established the young republic as a real democracy based on universal suffrage. America had Jackson, who had prepared the nation for its westward expansion. America had Lincoln, who had saved the Union. At each crisis, the right man was waiting to emerge, not designated by birth, but from behind any door of any hamlet or city—any man who was big enough to do the job.

As a young man, Roosevelt was not big enough. There was something constricted and self-limiting in his nature. He was unpopular among his fellow state senators, and as assistant secretary of the Navy he chafed at being in a subordinate position and had an exalted opinion of himself. His comeuppance came when it was revealed that he had commanded a secret unit that employed young sailors to entrap homosexuals in Newport.

It was then that he contracted polio and went through the transformation that made him big enough. The stricken prince, "seeing through a glass darkly," suffered the trauma of near defeat. He learned the hard lesson that man's first duty is not to give in.

His illness made it possible for him to identify with the humiliations and defeats of depression America. It was a suffering land, but it had the capacity to change and to grow, as he did. Indeed, this capacity for growth became the core of his character.

A man who could not walk became president of a country that had lost hope. With a simple set of beliefs—a belief that things could be improved, a belief in the democratic process—he transmitted his own confidence to the nation. "Your Constitution is all sail and no anchor," Macaulay had written in 1857, to which Roosevelt replied: "Mine is a different anchor . . . my anchor is democracy—and more democracy."

The country we are living in today is to a great extent of his making. He transformed America. The New Deal lives on in a hundred ways, from Social Security to the TVA, from subsidies to tobacco farmers to the alliance of labor with the Democratic party. Instead of a government run by big business, we have the competing forces of big government, big labor, and big business—government by pressure point, the most intricate in the world.

The Democratic party as we know it, a coalition of labor, the urban and ethnic vote, the black vote, and the less and less solid South, which no longer nominates candidates by a two-thirds vote, is his making. Roosevelt truly believed that the Democratic party was the party of the people, while the Republicans represented business elites. The Republican principle, as he saw it, had come down from Alexander Hamilton in a straight line, holding that the common people were not capable of wise government. This meant gigantic combinations of wealth, protected by favorable legislation.

Roosevelt had "instinctive wisdom," said Francis Biddle, "rooted in his own physical suffering." There was a kind of fusion between his personal condition and the process of government. Sometimes, in the emergencies of the Hundred Days and the war, you could get things done in a hurry, but usually it required the same kind of patience that he demonstrated in such small daily tasks as getting from place to place. The patience necessary in the democratic process was built into his own condition. One of the mistakes of his peacetime administration, the packing of the Supreme Court, took place because he had lost patience.

Those who worked closely with him attested to the brilliance of his mind and the breadth of his knowledge. Nothing human was alien to him, said Adolf Berle. He could tell you about naval construction, constitutional law, the history of coins, the ability of white men to live in the tropics—he could tell you about *anything*. Recent studies that measure managerial skills seem to be describing Roosevelt when they stress "multidimensional thinking" and such other desirable attributes as "getting groups to collaborate well," "being able to spot hidden patterns in an array of facts," "using forms of influence to build alliances," "the ability to acquire information without being overwhelmed." On "socialized power," as it is called today, Roosevelt wrote the book.

The other side of that political intelligence was a lack of frankness, a passion for manipulation, a mental and emotional shallowness, and a streak of vindictiveness. He liked to keep the strings in his hand by using confidential agents, sometimes with disastrous results, as in the demise of Sumner

Welles. Although the president of an open society, he often operated in secrecy.

Roosevelt had an amazing serenity of being, a self-control he had learned during his illness. Usually he was unruffled and cheerful, and one has to look very hard to find any neurotic tendency, such as the sleepwalking of his youth. Robert Sherwood, while admitting that he had never understood the president's "heavily forested interior," found him "spiritually the healthiest man I have ever known. He was gloriously and happily free of the various forms of psychic maladjustment which are called by such names as inhibition, complex, phobia." In contrast to the other leaders of his time, he was never posturing or vainglorious like Mussolini, never enraged like Hitler, never haughty and aloof like de Gaulle, never brutal and ruthless like Stalin, never hectoring like Churchill. He seemed to draw on an inexhaustible reservoir of goodwill, and to act on the admonition in the Reverend Peabody's favorite prayer: "Let unconquerable gladness dwell."

Finally, he transformed the world we live in. He sponsored and supported the manufacture and use of the atom bomb, ushering in the nuclear age. He sought a new international order, an alternative to the European balance of power. Both world wars had started in Europe, and he saw a way to reduce the mischief-making capacities of the European powers by accepting Russia's expanded role in world affairs. He was not, as some have said, duped by the Russians. He deliberately supported a great Soviet role in the postwar world, both in Europe and the Far East. He made concessions, giving Stalin multiple votes in the United Nations and a sphere of influence in Manchuria through control of the railroads and harbors.

He did not live to see the result, which was largely in accord with his plans. Europe was neutralized, divided into Atlantic Pact and Warsaw Pact nations. France and England, Germany and Italy, were reduced to small-power rank. France lost Indochina and Algeria, not through trusteeships but through war, and the rest of her colonial empire. England lost India and Malaya and the Middle East.

It was all pretty much as Roosevelt intended: the dismantling of the colonial empires, which never put back into a country what they took out, and a Europe that no longer had the initiative in world affairs. Germany was divided in two, whereas he had proposed further fragmentation. The Four Policemen became two, since China and England were unable to claim great-power status. The United Nations was in place, and the world was dominated by two superpowers.

Except that they were not friends as he had hoped, they were adversaries, "two scorpions in a bottle," as Robert Oppenheimer once called them. The balance of terror replaced the balance of power, creating deterrence through the threat of potential extinction. What this led to was the elimination of war on the territory of the combatants. Instead of countries with common borders invading one another, as had been the practice in Europe for centuries, two superpowers on opposite sides of the planet now exported wars to designated battlegrounds in distant lands, preferably the Third World, where life was cheap and conventional weapons could be used.

Thus the post-Roosevelt era saw a series of proxy wars in which the superpowers confronted one another on a third country's territory. There was never any fighting in the Soviet Union or in the United States, and no nuclear weapons were used. Sometimes, as in Vietnam, American troops were engaged, and sometimes, as in Afghanistan, Soviet troops were engaged; but American troops never fought Soviet troops.

Such was the new order that Roosevelt brought in, at the cost of the subjugation of Eastern Europe and of virtually continuous Third World wars, called by some "the Third World War." Can we say the system is a success? All that Roosevelt wanted, as he said repeatedly, was to make a peace more lasting than Wilson's, a peace that would last several generations, through the lifetimes of the young men who had fought in World War II.

Between the end of World War I and the start of World War II, twenty-one years elapsed. It has now been forty years since the end of World War II, and a thriving doomsday industry has told us what would happen in the event of a nuclear war, an event that has yet to occur. As Churchill predicted in one of his last speeches, "Peace may become the sturdy child of terror."

ACKNOWLEDGMENTS
AND SOURCES

I am very much indebted to the people at the Franklin D. Roosevelt Library in Hyde Park, in particular to its director, William R. Emerson, and to all the members of the staff, who make the FDRL a pleasure to work in; also to the people at the Hoover Institution, the Yale University Library, the Manuscript Room of the Butler Library at Columbia University; also to George Caldwell at the Library of Congress, and to John Taylor at the National Archives, who gave me the benefit of his long experience.

I would like to thank the following for interviews, advice, and/or letters: Samuel H. Beer, Mrs. Jonathan Bingham, Blanche Cook, Ernest Cuneo for his wit and wisdom, Allen Drury, Thomas I. Emerson, Doris Faber, Nona Ferdon, Irwin F. Gellman, James K. Hall, Chief of the FOIA section, FBI, Montgomery Hare, Averell Harriman, Trumbull Higgins for his military expertise, H. Montgomery Hyde, Ian Jacob, David Kahn, Leon H. Keyserling, Warren Moscow, Jeffrey Potter, Dr. Herman Roiphe, Elliott Roosevelt, James Roosevelt, Dorothy Rosenman, James H. Rowe, Dorothy Schiff, Jordan Schwarz, Richard Norton Smith, and Mrs. John Hay Whitney.

I would also like to pay tribute to the six important works on Franklin D. Roosevelt from which every other writer on FDR benefits: John Morton Blum, *From the Morgenthau Diaries,* 3 vols. (Boston: Houghton Mifflin, 1959–65); James MacGregor Burns, *Roosevelt: The Lion and the Fox* (New York: Harcourt, Brace, 1956) and *Roosevelt: The Soldier of Freedom* (New York: Harcourt Brace Jovanovich, 1970); Frank B. Friedel, *Franklin D. Roosevelt,* 4 vols. (Boston: Little, Brown, 1952–73); William E. Leuchtenburg, *Franklin D. Roosevelt and the New Deal, 1932-1940* (New York: Harper & Row, 1963); and Arthur M. Schlesinger, *The Age of Roosevelt,* 3 vols. (Boston: Houghton Mifflin, 1957–60).

ABBREVIATED TITLES OF SOURCES FREQUENTLY CITED

COHP: Columbia Oral History Project, Butler Library, Columbia University

FBI: Federal Bureau of Investigation documents obtained under the Freedom of Information Act

FDRL: Franklin Delano Roosevelt Library:

ER: Eleanor Roosevelt Papers

EROH: Eleanor Roosevelt Oral History Project

HM: Morgenthau Diaries

OF: Official File

PPF: President's Personal File

PSF: President's Secretary's File

HI: Hoover Institution for War, Revolution, and Peace, Stanford, Calif.

LC: Library of Congress, Washington, D.C.

NA: National Archives, Washington, D.C.

PP: *The Public Papers and Addresses of Franklin D. Roosevelt, 1932-1945.* 13 vols. New York: Random House, 1938-50.

YU: Yale University Library, New Haven, Conn.

OTHER SOURCES CITED

Acheson, Dean. *Morning and Noon.* Boston: Houghton Mifflin, 1965.

Adams, Henry H. *Harry Hopkins: A Biography.* New York: Putnam, 1977.

Ader, Robert, ed. *Psychoneuroimmunology.* New York: Academic Press, 1981.

Alinsky, Saul. *John L. Lewis: An Unauthorized Biography.* New York: Putnam, 1949.

Altman, O. R. "Second Session of the Seventy-fourth Congress." *American Political Sciences Review* 30 (December 1936): 1086-1107.

Anderson, Jervis. *A. Philip Randolph: A Biographical Portrait.* New York: Harcourt Brace Jovanovich, 1973.

Arlow, Jacob A. "The Only Child." *Psychoanalytic Quarterly* 41 (October 1972): 507-536.

Arnold, Henry H. *Global Mission.* New York: Harper, 1949.

Ashburn, Frank D. *Peabody of Groton: A Portrait.* New York: Coward McCann, 1944.

Bagby, Wesley M. "Progressivism's Debacle: The Election of 1920." Columbia University thesis, 1953.

Baker, Leonard. *Roosevelt and Pearl Harbor.* New York: Macmillan, 1970.

Balog, C. E. "Adolf A. Berle, Jr.: The Intellectual as Modern Priest." University of Illinois thesis, 1973.

Barker, Elisabeth. *Churchill and Eden at War.* London: Macmillan, 1978.

Barkley, Alben W. *That Reminds Me.* Garden City, N.Y.: Doubleday, 1954.

Barnes, Harry E. "Pearl Harbor after a Quarter of a Century." *Left and Right* 4 (1968).

Bellow, Saul. "In the Days of Mr. Roosevelt." *Esquire* 100 (December 1983): 530-532.

Bellush, Bernard. *Franklin D. Roosevelt as Governor of New York.* New York: Columbia University Press, 1955.

Berg, Roland H. *The Challenge of Polio: The Crusade Against Infantile Paralysis.* New York: Dial Press, 1946.

Berle, Adolf A. *The Adolf A. Berle Diary, 1937-1971.* Hyde Park, N.Y.: Franklin D. Roosevelt Library, National Archives and Records Service, General Services Administration, 1978. Microfilm.

Berle, Adolf A. *Navigating the Rapids, 1918-1971: From the Papers of Adolf A. Berle.* Edited by Beatrice Bishop Berle and Travis Beal Jacobs. New York: Harcourt Brace Jovanovich, 1973.

Bernstein, Irving. *Turbulent Years: A History of the American Worker, 1933-1941.* Boston: Houghton Mifflin, 1970.

Beschloss, Michael R. *Kennedy and Roosevelt: The Uneasy Alliance.* New York: Norton, 1980.

Binkley, Wilfred E. *President and Congress.* New York; Knopf, 1947.

Birkenhead, Earl of. *Halifax: The Life of Lord Halifax.* Boston: Houghton Mifflin, 1966.

Black, Theodore Milton. *Democratic Party Publicity in the 1940 Campaign.* New York: Plymouth, 1941.

Blum, John Morton. *V Was for Victory: Politics and American Culture During World War II.* New York: Harcourt Brace Jovanovich, 1976.

Boettiger, John R. *A Love in Shadow.* New York: Norton, 1978.

Bohlen, Charles E. *Witness to History, 1929-1969.* New York: Norton, 1973.

Bottome, Phyllis. *From the Life.* London: Faber & Faber, 1946.

Braden, Spruille. *Diplomats and Demagogues: The Memoirs of Spruille Braden.* New Rochelle, N.Y.: Arlington House, 1971.

Brand, Donald R. "Corporatism, the NRA, and the Oil Industry." *Political Science Quarterly* 98 (Spring 1983): 99–118.

Broughton, Roger J. "Sleep Disorders." *Science* 159 (March 8, 1968): 1070–1078.

Bruenn, Howard J. "Clinical Notes on the Illness and Death of President Franklin D. Roosevelt." *Annals of Internal Medicine* 72 (April 1970).

Bryant, Arthur. *Triumph in the West: A History of the War Years Based on the Diaries of Field-Marshal Lord Alanbrooke.* Garden City, N.Y.: Doubleday, 1959.

Bryant, Arthur. *The Turn of the Tide: A History of the War Years Based on the Diaries of Field-Marshal Lord Alanbrooke.* Garden City, N.Y.: Doubleday, 1957.

Bullitt, William C. *For the President, Personal and Secret: Correspondence Between Franklin D. Roosevelt and William C. Bullitt.* Edited by Orville H. Bullitt. Boston: Houghton Mifflin, 1972.

Bullock, Alan. *Hitler, a Study in Tyranny.* New York: Harper & Row, 1962.

Burner, David. *Herbert Hoover: A Public Life.* New York: Knopf, 1978.

Butcher, Harry C. *My Three Years with Eisenhower: The Personal Diary of Captain Harry C. Butcher, USNR, Naval Aide to General Eisenhower, 1942 to 1945.* New York: Simon & Schuster, 1946.

Byrnes, James F. *Speaking Frankly.* New York: Harper, 1947.

Cadogan, Sir Alexander. *The Diaries of Sir Alexander Cadogan, O.M., 1938-1945.* Edited by David Dilks. New York: Putnam, 1972.

Canfield, Cass. *Up and Down and Around: A Publisher Recollects the Time of His Life.* New York: Harper's Magazine Press, 1971.

Carlson, Earland Irving. *Franklin D. Roosevelt's Fight for the Presidential Nomination, 1928-1932.* Ann Arbor: University Microfilms, 1956. Microfilm.

Carmichael, Donald Scott, ed. *F.D.R. Columnist: The Uncollected Columns of Franklin D. Roosevelt.* Chicago: Pellegrini & Cudahy, 1947.

Caro, Robert A. *The Path to Power.* New York: Knopf, 1982.

Caro, Robert A. *The Power Broker: Robert Moses and the Fall of New York.* New York: Knopf, 1974.

Chalmers, William S. *The Life and Letters of David, Earl Beatty.* London: Hodder & Stoughton, 1951.

Chandler, Alfred D., Jr., and Salsbury, Stephen. *Pierre S. Du Pont and the Making of the Modern Corporation.* New York: Harper & Row, 1971.

Churchill, Allen. *The Roosevelts: American Aristocrats.* New York: Harper & Row, 1965.

Churchill, Winston S. *Closing the Ring.* Boston: Houghton Mifflin, 1951.

Clark, R. A., and Capparell, H. V. "The Psychiatry of the Adult Only Child." *American Journal of Psychiatry* 8 (1954): 487–499.

Cole, Wayne S. *Charles A. Lindbergh and the Battle Against Intervention in World War II.* New York: Harcourt Brace Jovanovich, 1974.

Cole, Wayne S. *Roosevelt and the Isolationists, 1932–1945.* Lincoln: University of Nebraska Press, 1983.

Connally, Tom. *My Name Is Tom Connally.* New York, Crowell, 1954.

Cooney, John. *The Annenbergs: The Salvaging of a Tainted Dynasty.* New York: Simon & Schuster, 1982.

Costello, John. "Remembering Pearl Harbor." *Naval Institute Proceedings,* September 1983.

Cox, James M. *Journey Through My Years.* New York: Simon & Schuster, 1946.

Creel, George. *Rebel at Large: Recollections of Fifty Crowded Years.* New York: Putnam, 1947.

Dall, Curtis B. *FDR, My Exploited Father-in-Law.* Tulsa: Christian Crusade, 1968.

Dalton, Hugh. *Fateful Years: Memoirs.* London: Muller, 1957.

Daniels, Jonathan. *The End of Innocence.* Philadelphia: Lippincott, 1954.

Daniels, Jonathan. *White House Witness, 1942–1945.* Garden City, N.Y.: Doubleday, 1975.

Daniels, Josephus. *The Cabinet Diaries of Josephus Daniels, 1913–1921.* Edited by E. David Cronon. Lincoln: University of Nebraska Press, 1963.

Daniels, Josephus. *The Wilson Era: Years of Peace, 1910–1917.* Chapel Hill: University of North Carolina Press, 1944.

Davis, Kenneth S. *Invincible Summer: An Intimate Portrait of the Roosevelts, Based on the Recollections of Marion Dickerman.* New York: Atheneum, 1974.

Delano, Daniel W., Jr. *Franklin Roosevelt and the Delano Influence.* Pittsburgh: Nudi, 1946.

Dizikes, John. *Britain, Roosevelt, and the New Deal: British Opinion, 1932–1938.* New York: Garland, 1979.

Djilas, Milovan. *Conversations with*

Stalin. Translated by Michael B. Petrovich. New York: Harcourt, Brace & World, 1962.

Dodd, William E. *Ambassador Dodd's Diary, 1933-1938.* Edited by William E. Dodd, Jr., and Martha Dodd. New York: Harcourt, Brace, 1941.

Douglas, William O. *Go East, Young Man: The Early Years: The Autobiography of William O. Douglas.* New York: Random House, 1974.

Drury, Allen. *A Senate Journal, 1943-1945.* New York: McGraw-Hill, 1963.

Dunne, Gerald T. *Hugo Black and the Judicial Revolution.* New York: Simon & Schuster, 1977.

Eccles, Marriner. *Beckoning Frontiers: Public and Personal Recollections.* New York: Knopf, 1951.

Eden, Anthony. *The Reckoning: The Memoirs of Anthony Eden, Earl of Avon.* Boston: Houghton Mifflin, 1965.

Ekirch, Arthur A., Jr. *Ideologies and Utopias: The Impact of the New Deal on American Thought.* Chicago: Quadrangle Books, 1969.

Erikson, Erik H. *Childhood and Society.* New York: Norton, 1950.

Erikson, Joan M. "Nothing to Fear: Notes on the Life of Eleanor Roosevelt." In *The Woman in America,* edited by Robert Jay Lifton. Boston: Houghton Mifflin, 1965.

Eubank, Keith. "The Teheran Conference: An American View," unpublished paper.

Faber, Doris. *The Life of Lorena Hickok: E.R.'s Friend.* New York: Morrow, 1980.

Farley, James A. *Behind the Ballots: The Personal History of a Politician.* New York: Harcourt, Brace, 1938.

Feingold, Henry L. *The Politics of Rescue: The Roosevelt Administration and the Holocaust, 1938-1945.* New Brunswick, N.J.: Rutgers University Press, 1970.

Feis, Herbert. *1933: Characters in Crisis.* Boston: Little, Brown, 1966.

Ferdon, Nora Stinson. "FDR, A Psychological Interpretation of His Childhood and Youth." University of Hawaii thesis, 1971.

Flynn, Edward J. *You're the Boss.* New York: Viking, 1947.

Frankfurter, Felix. *From the Diaries of Felix Frankfurter.* Edited by Joseph P. Lash. New York: Norton, 1975.

Freedman, Max, ed. *Roosevelt and Frankfurter: Their Correspondence, 1928-1945.* Boston: Little, Brown, 1967.

Garraty, John A. *The New Commonwealth, 1877-1890.* New York: Harper & Row, 1968.

Gellman, Irwin F. *Good Neighbor Diplomacy: United States Policies in Latin America, 1933-1945.* Baltimore: Johns Hopkins University Press, 1979.

Gellman, Irwin F. "The New Deal's Use of Nazism in Latin America." In *Perspectives in American Diplomacy.* New York, 1976.

George, Alexander L., and George, Juliette L. *Woodrow Wilson and Colonel House: A Personality Study.* New York: J. Day, 1956.

Gilbert, Martin. *Winston S. Churchill: The Wilderness Years.* London: Macmillan, 1981.

Gladwyn, Lord. *The Memoirs of Lord Gladwyn.* London: Weidenfeld & Nicolson, 1972.

Goldberg, Richard Thayer. *The Making of Franklin D. Roosevelt: Triumph Over Disability.* Cambridge, Mass.: Abt Books, 1981.

Goodhart, Philip. *Fifty Ships that Saved the World: The Foundations of the Anglo-American Alliance.* Garden City, N.Y.: Doubleday, 1965.

Goodman, Walter. *The Committee: The Extraordinary Career of the House Committee on Un-American Activities.* New York: Farrar, Straus & Giroux, 1968.

Gosnell, Harold F. *Champion Campaigner: Franklin D. Roosevelt,* New York: Macmillan, 1952.

Gould, Jean. *A Good Fight: The Story of F.D.R.'s Conquest of Polio.* New York: Dodd, Mead, 1960.

Grafton, Samuel. *An American Diary.* Garden City, N.Y.: Doubleday, 1943.

Gravlee, Grady. "A Rhetorical Study of FDR's 1920 Campaign." Louisiana State University thesis, 1963.

Grew, Joseph. *Turbulent Era: A Diplomatic Record of Fifty Years, 1904–1945.* Edited by Walter Johnson. Boston: Houghton Mifflin, 1952.

Gunther, John. *Roosevelt in Retrospects: A Profile in History.* New York: Harper, 1950.

Halsey, William F., and Bryan, J. III. *Admiral Halsey's Story.* New York: Whittlesey House, 1947.

Harbaugh, William H. *Lawyer's Lawyer: The Life of John W. Davis.* New York: Oxford University Press, 1973.

Harriman, Averell, and Abel, Elie. *Special Envoy to Churchill and Stalin, 1941–1946.* New York: Random House, 1975.

Harris, Ruth R. "The Magic Leak of 1941 and Japanese-American Relations." *Pacific Historical Review* 50 (February 1981): 77–96.

Harvard Alumni Bulletin, Roosevelt Memorial Issue, April 28, 1945.

Hassett, William D. *Off the Record with F.D.R., 1942–1945.* New Brunswick, N.J.: Rutgers University Press, 1958.

Hawkins, Hugh. *Between Harvard and America: The Educational Leadership of Charles W. Eliot.* New York: Oxford University Press, 1972.

Hawley, Ellis W. *The New Deal and the Problem of Monopoly: A Study in Economic Ambivalence.* Princeton: Princeton University Press, 1966.

Herring, E. Pendleton. "First Session of the Seventy-third Congress." *American Political Science Review* 28 (February 1934): 65–83.

Herring, E. Pendleton. *Presidential Leadership: The Political Relations of Congress and the Chief Executive.* New York: Farrar & Rinehart, 1940.

Herring, E. Pendleton. "Second Session of the Seventy-third Congress." *American Political Science Review* 28 (October 1934): 852–866.

Higgins, Trumbull. *Winston Churchill and the Second Front, 1940-1943.* New York: Oxford University Press, 1957.

History of the Counter-Intelligence Corps. Vol. 6. Washington, D.C., 1961.

Hull, Cordell. *The Memoirs of Cordell Hull.* New York: Macmillan, 1948.

Huthmacher, J. Joseph. *Senator Robert F. Wagner and the Rise of Urban Liberalism.* New York: Atheneum, 1968.

Ickes, Harold L. *The Secret Diaries of Harold L. Ickes,* 3 vols. New York: Simon & Schuster, 1953-54.

Ismay, Lord. *Memoirs.* New York: Viking, 1960.

Johnson, Alvin Page. *Franklin D. Roosevelt's Colonial Ancestors: Their Part in the Making of American History.* Boston: Lothrop, Lee & Shepard, 1933.

Johnson, Hugh S. *The Blue Eagle, from Egg to Earth.* Garden City, N.Y.: Doubleday, Doran, 1935.

Jones, Alfred Haworth. *Roosevelt's Image Brokers: Poets, Playwrights, and the Use of the Lincoln Symbol.* Port Washington, N.Y.: Kennikat Press, 1974.

Josephson, Matthew. *Sidney Hillman, Statesman of American Labor.* Garden City, N.Y.: Doubleday, 1952.

Josephson, Matthew, and Josephson, Hannah. *Al Smith, Hero of the Cities: A Political Portrait*

Drawing on the Papers of Frances Perkins. Boston: Houghton Mifflin, 1969.

Joslin, Theodore G. *Hoover Off the Record.* Garden City, N.Y.: Doubleday, Doran, 1934.

Jung, C. G. *Collected Works,* vol. 9, pt. 1. Princeton: Princeton University Press, 1959.

Karl, Barry D. *Charles E. Merriam and the Study of Politics.* Chicago: University of Chicago Press, 1974.

Keller, John. " 'Franklin's On His Own Now'—The Last Days of Louis McHenry Howe." *Saturday Evening Post,* Oct. 12, 1940, pp. 42, 47, 131–140.

Kilpatrick, Carroll, ed. *Roosevelt and Daniels: A Friendship in Politics.* Chapel Hill: University of North Carolina Press, 1952.

King, Ernest J., and Whitehall, Walter Muir. *Fleet Admiral King: A Naval Record.* New York: Norton, 1952.

Kleeman, Rita Halle. *Gracious Lady: The Life of Sara Delano Roosevelt.* New York: Appleton-Century, 1935.

Kleeman, Rita Halle. *Young Franklin Roosevelt.* New York: Messner, 1946.

Koenig, Louis W. *The Invisible Presidency.* New York: Rinehart, 1960.

Krock, Arthur. *Memoirs: Sixty Years on the Firing Line.* New York: Funk & Wagnalls, 1968.

Lash, Joseph P. *Eleanor and Franklin: The Story of Their Relationship.* New York: Norton, 1971.

Lash, Joseph P. *Love, Eleanor: Eleanor Roosevelt and Her*

Friends. Garden City, N.Y.: Doubleday, 1982.

Leahy, William D. *I Was There: The Personal Story of the Chief of Staff to Presidents Roosevelt and Truman.* New York: Whittlesey House, 1950.

Lee, Raymond E. *The London Journal of General Raymond E. Lee, 1940-1941.* Edited by James Leutze. Boston: Little, Brown, 1971.

Levy, David M. *Maternal Overprotection.* New York: Columbia University Press, 1943.

Lewin, Ronald. *The American Magic: Codes, Ciphers and the Defeat of Japan.* New York: Farrar, Straus & Giroux, 1982.

Lewis, David L. *The Public Image of Henry Ford: An American Folk Hero and His Company.* Detroit: Wayne State University Press, 1976.

Lilienthal, David E. *The Journals of David E. Lilienthal.* Vol. 1. New York: Harper & Row, 1964.

Lindbergh, Charles A. *The Wartime Journals of Charles A. Lindbergh.* New York: Harcourt Brace Jovanovich, 1970.

Lindley, Ernest K. *Half Way with Roosevelt.* New York: Viking, 1936.

Lippman, Theo, Jr. *The Squire of Warm Springs: F.D.R. in Georgia, 1924-1945.* New York: Simon & Schuster, 1977.

Looker, Earle. *This Man Roosevelt.* New York: Brewer, Warren & Putnam, 1932.

Louchheim, Katie, ed. *The Making of the New Deal: The Insiders Speak.* Cambridge: Harvard University Press, 1983.

Lowenheim, Francis L.; Langley, Harold D.; and Jonas, Manfred, eds. *Roosevelt and Churchill: Their Secret Wartime Correspondence.* New York: Saturday Review Press, 1975.

MacArthur, Douglas. *Reminiscences.* New York: McGraw-Hill, 1964.

MacCracken, Henry Noble. *Blithe Dutchess: The Flowering of an American County from 1812.* New York: Hastings House, 1958.

Macmillan, Harold. *The Blast of War, 1939-1945.* New York: Harper & Row, 1968.

Marder, Arthur J. *From the Dreadnought to Scapa Flow: The Royal Navy in the Fisher Era, 1904-1919.* Vol. 5. New York: Oxford University Press, 1970.

Martin, George. *Madam Secretary, Frances Perkins.* Boston: Houghton Mifflin, 1976.

Mason, Alpheus Thomas. *Harlan Fiske Stone: Pillar of the Law.* New York: Viking, 1956.

May, Ernest R., ed. *The Ultimate Decision: The President as Commander in Chief.* New York: Braziller, 1960.

Miller, Merle. *Plain Speaking: An Oral Biography of Harry S. Truman.* New York: Putnam, 1974.

Mitgang, Herbert. *The Man Who Rode the Tiger: The Life and Times of Judge Samuel Seabury.* Philadelphia: Lippincott, 1963.

Moley, Raymond. *After Seven Years.* New York: Harper, 1939.

Moody, F. Kennon. "FDR and His

Neighbors." State University of New York at Albany thesis, 1981.

Moran, Lord. *Churchill: The Struggle for Survival, 1940–1965: Taken from the Diaries of Lord Moran.* Boston: Houghton Mifflin, 1966.

Morison, Elting E. *Admiral Sims and the Modern American Navy.* Boston: Houghton Mifflin, 1942.

Morison, Samuel Eliot. *Three Centuries of Harvard, 1636–1936.* Cambridge: Harvard University Press, 1936.

Morris, Edmund. *The Rise of Theodore Roosevelt.* New York: Coward, McCann & Geoghegan, 1979.

Morrison, Joseph L. *Josephus Daniels: The Small-d Democrat.* Chapel Hill: University of North Carolina Press, 1966.

Moscow, Warren. *Roosevelt and Willkie.* Englewood Cliffs, N.J.: Prentice-Hall, 1968.

Moses, Robert. *Public Works: A Dangerous Trade.* New York: McGraw-Hill, 1970.

Mosley, Leonard. *Blood Relations: The Rise and Fall of the du Ponts of Delaware.* New York: Atheneum, 1980.

Mosley, Sir Oswald. *My Life.* New Rochelle, N.Y.: Arlington House, 1968.

Murray, Robert K. *The 103d Ballot: Democrats and the Disaster in Madison Square Garden.* New York: Harper & Row, 1976.

Nicolson, Harold. *Diaries and Letters, 1930–1939.* New York: Atheneum, 1966.

Normanbrook, Lord, et al. *Action*

This Day: Working with Churchill. Edited by Sir John Wheeler-Bennett. New York: St. Martin's Press, 1969.

O'Connor, Raymond G. *Diplomacy for Victory: FDR and Unconditional Surrender.* New York: Norton, 1971.

O'Keane, Josephine. *Thomas J. Walsh, a Senator from Montana.* Francestown, N.H.: M. Jones, 1955.

Paone, Rocco M. "The Presidential Election of 1920." Georgetown University thesis, 1950.

Paul, John R. *A History of Poliomyelitis.* New Haven: Yale University Press, 1971.

Pecora, Ferdinand. *Wall Street Under Oath: The Story of Our Modern Money Changers.* New York: Simon & Schuster, 1939.

Perkins, Frances. *The Roosevelt I Knew.* New York: Viking, 1946.

Pilat, Oliver. *Drew Pearson: An Unauthorized Biography.* New York: Harper's Magazine Press, 1973.

Pogue, Forrest C. *George C. Marshall: Ordeal and Hope, 1939–1942.* New York: Viking, 1966.

Polenberg, Richard. *Reorganizing Roosevelt's Government: The Controversy over Executive Reorganization, 1936–1939.* Cambridge: Harvard University Press, 1966.

Polenberg, Richard. *War and Society: The United States, 1941–1945.* Philadelphia: Lippincott, 1972.

Prange, Gordon W. *At Dawn We Slept: The Untold Story of Pearl*

Harbor. New York: McGraw-Hill, 1981.

Pritchett, C. Herman. *The Roosevelt Court: A Study in Judicial Politics and Values, 1937–1947.* New York: Macmillan, 1948.

Pusey, Merlo J. *Charles Evans Hughes.* 2 vols. New York: Macmillan, 1951.

Richberg, Donald. *My Hero: The Indiscreet Memoirs of an Eventful but Unheroic Life.* New York: Putnam, 1954.

Richberg, Donald. *The Rainbow: After the Sunshine of Prosperity, the Deluge of the Depression, the Rainbow of the NRA, What Have We Learned? Where Are We Going?* Garden City, N.Y.: Doubleday, Doran, 1936.

Rollins, Alfred B., Jr. "The Political Education of FDR." Thesis, FDRL.

Rollins, Alfred B., Jr. *Roosevelt and Howe.* New York: Knopf, 1962.

Rollins, Alfred B., Jr. "Young Franklin D. Roosevelt as the Farmer's Friend." *New York History* 43 (April 1962): 186–198.

Roosevelt, Anna. "First My Father . . . Then My Son." *McCall's,* January 1949, pp. 4, 60.

Roosevelt, Eleanor. *The Autobiography of Eleanor Roosevelt.* New York: Harper, 1961.

Roosevelt, Eleanor. *This Is My Story.* New York: Harper, 1937.

Roosevelt, Elliott. *Hunting Big Game in the Eighties: The Letters of Elliott Roosevelt, Sportsman.* Edited by Anna Eleanor Roosevelt. New York: Scribner's, 1933.

Roosevelt, Elliott, and Brough, James. *An Untold Story: The Roosevelts of Hyde Park.* New York: Putnam, 1973.

Roosevelt, Franklin D. *F.D.R.: His Personal Letters.* Edited by Elliott Roosevelt. 4 vols. New York: Duell, Sloan & Pearce, 1947–50.

Roosevelt, James, and Schalett, Sidney. *Affectionately, F.D.R.: A Son's Story of a Lonely Man.* New York: Harcourt, Brace, 1959.

Roosevelt, James, with Libby, Bill. *My Parents: A Differing View.* Chicago: Playboy Press, 1976.

Roosevelt, Nicholas. *A Front Row Seat.* Norman: University of Oklahoma Press, 1953.

Roosevelt, Sara. *My Boy Franklin.* As told to Isabel Leighton and Gabrielle Forbush. New York: Long & Smith, 1933.

Rosen, Elliot A. *Hoover, Roosevelt, and the Brains Trust: From Depression to New Deal.* New York: Columbia University Press, 1977.

Rosenman, Samuel I. *Working with Roosevelt.* New York: Harper, 1952.

Rosten, Leo C. "President Roosevelt and the Washington Correspondents." *Public Opinion Quarterly.*

Schriftgiesser, Karl. *The Amazing Roosevelt Family, 1613–1942.* New York: Funk, 1942.

Schwarz, Jordan A. *The Speculator: Bernard M. Baruch in Washington, 1917–1965.* Chapel Hill: University of North Carolina Press, 1981.

Shannon, Fred A. *The Centennial Years: A Political and Economic*

History of America from the Late 1870s to the Early 1890s. Garden City, N.Y.: Doubleday, 1967.

Sherwin, Martin J. *A World Destroyed: The Atom Bomb and the Grand Alliance.* New York: Knopf, 1977.

Sherwood, Robert E. *Roosevelt and Hopkins: An Intimate History.* New York: Harper, 1948.

Shoumatoff, Alex. "Personal History." *New Yorker,* May 3, 1982.

Simon, James F. *Independent Journey: The Life of William O. Douglas.* New York: Harper & Row, 1980.

Smith, Alfred E. *Up to Now: An Autobiography.* New York: Viking, 1929.

Smith, A. Merriman. *Thank You, Mr. President: A White House Notebook.* New York: Harper, 1946.

Smith, Richard Norton. *Thomas E. Dewey and His Times.* New York: Simon & Schuster, 1982.

Sours, John A.; Frumkin, Paul; and Indermill, Richard R. "Somnambulism." *Archives of General Psychiatry* 9 (October 1963): 400–413.

Stacey, C. P. *A Very Double Life: The Private World of Mackenzie King.* Toronto: Macmillan, 1976.

Steeholm, Clara, and Steeholm, Hardy. *The House at Hyde Park.* New York: Viking, 1950.

Steel, Ronald. *Walter Lippmann and the American Century.* Boston: Little, Brown, 1980.

Sternsher, Bernard. *Rexford Tugwell and the New Deal.* New Brunswick, N.J.: Rutgers University Press, 1964.

Stettinius, Edward R. *The Diaries of Edward R. Stettinius, Jr., 1943–46.* Edited by Thomas M. Campbell and George C. Herring. New York: New Viewpoints, 1975.

Stevens, Ruth. *"Hi-ya, Neighbor."* New York: Tupper & Love, 1947.

Stiles, Lela. *The Man Behind Roosevelt: The Story of Louis McHenry Howe.* Cleveland: World, 1954.

Stilwell, Joseph W. *The Stilwell Papers.* Edited by Theodore H. White. New York: Sloane, 1948.

Stokes, Thomas L. *Chip Off My Shoulder.* Princeton: Princeton University Press, 1940.

Sulzberger, C. L. *A Long Row of Candles: Memoirs and Diaries, 1934–1954.* New York: Macmillan, 1969.

Timmons, Bascom N. *Garner of Texas: A Personal History.* New York: Harper, 1948.

Timmons, Bascom N. *Jesse H. Jones: The Man and the Statesman.* New York: Holt, 1956.

Tugwell, Rexford G. *The Democratic Roosevelt: A Biography of Franklin D. Roosevelt.* Garden City, N.Y.: Doubleday, 1957.

Tugwell, Rexford G. *To the Lesser Heights of Morningside: A Memoir.* Philadelphia: University of Pennsylvania Press, 1982.

Ulam, Adam B. *Stalin: The Man and His Era.* New York: Viking, 1973.

Ungar, Sanford J. *FBI.* Boston: Little, Brown, 1976.

U.S. Commission on Wartime Relocation and Internment of Civilians. *Personal Justice Denied.* Washington: GPO, 1982.

U.S. Congress. Joint Commission on the Investigation of the Pearl Harbor Attack. *Report.* Washington: GPO, 1946.

U.S. Congress, Senate. Committee on Naval Affairs. *Report . . . relative to alleged immoral conditions and practices at the naval training station, Newport, R.I.* Washington: GPO, 1921.

Vandenberg, Arthur H. *The Private Papers of Senator Vandenberg.* Edited by Arthur E. Vandenberg, Jr. Boston: Houghton Mifflin, 1952.

Vogel, Nancy. "Change in Hyde Park." Vassar College senior thesis, 1979.

Walker, Turnley. *Roosevelt and the Warm Springs Story.* New York: Wyn, 1953.

Wallace, Henry A. *The Price of Vision: The Diary of Henry A. Wallace, 1942-1946.* Edited by John Morton Blum. Boston: Houghton Mufflin, 1973.

Warner, Emily Smith, and Daniel, Hawthorne. *The Happy Warrior: A Biography of My Father, Alfred E. Smith.* Garden City, N.Y.: Doubleday, 1956.

Wehle, Louis B. *Hidden Threads of History, Wilson Through Roosevelt.* New York: Macmillan, 1953.

Weil, Martin. *A Pretty Good Club: The Founding Fathers of the U.S. Foreign Service.* New York: Norton, 1978.

Weiss, Nancy J. *Charles Francis Murphy, 1858-1924: Respectability and Responsibility in Tammany Politics.* Northampton, Mass.: Smith College, 1968.

Werner, M. R. *Bryan.* New York: Harcourt, Brace, 1929.

Wheeler, Burton K. *Yankee from the West.* Garden City, N.Y.: Doubleday, 1962.

Williams, T. Harry. *Huey Long.* New York: Knopf, 1969.

Wilson, Edmund. *The American Earthquake: A Documentary of the Twenties and Thirties.* Garden City, N.Y.: Doubleday, 1958.

Zilg, G. C. *Behind the Nylon Curtain.* New York: Prentice-Hall, 1974.

NOTES

PROLOGUE

Harvard class of 1904 25th reunion: 25th anniversary report, Harvard University Archives, Houghton Library. • **FDR at class reunion:** FDRL, Group 12, Box 74. • **Beede and Roosevelt:** FDRL, PPF 369, and Group 12, Box 10.

CHAPTER I. THE FIRST FOURTEEN YEARS

Description of America in 1882: *Harper's Magazine* for 1882; Shannon, *Centennial Years;* Garraty, *New Commonwealth.* • **Birth of Franklin:** FDRL, Sara Roosevelt diary. • **Delano family:** FDRL, PPF 73 and 490; Delano, *Franklin Roosevelt;* Churchill, *Roosevelts.* • **Sara's marriage:** FDRL, Sara Roosevelt diary; Kleeman, *Gracious Lady;* Steeholm, *House at Hyde Park.* • **Sara as social presence:** Bottome, *From the Life;* Herbert Claiborne Pell, COHP. • **Sara's anti-Semitism:** FDRL, EROH, Justice Wise Polier. • **Sara at wedding:** Mrs John Hay Whitney to author. • **Letters to Franklin:** FDRL, Papers Donated by Children, Box 9. • **Isaac to James:** FDRL, Papers Donated by Children, Box 52. • **Roosevelt family:** Churchill, *Roosevelts;* Johnson, *Roosevelt's Colonial Ancestors;* Schriftgiesser, *Amazing Roosevelt Family.* • **FDR's colonial ancestors:** Johnson, *Roosevelt's Colonial Ancestors;* Schriftgiesser, *Amazing Roosevelt Family.* • **FDR to Delgado:** FDRL, PPF 73. • **FDR pride in Isaac:** see for example FDRL, radio address from Washington, Sept. 17, 1938. • **Ingham diary:** FDRL, PPF 5327. • **James and Sam Houston:** FDRL, PPF 2324. • **FDR and white oaks:** FDRL, PPF

234. • **James and Vanderbilts:** Hassett, *Off the Record.* • **Hyde Park history:** FDRL, PPF 234; speech at Methodist Episcopal church, Sept. 29, 1933. • **FDR and British cannon balls:** FDRL, PPF 234. • **Life on the Hyde Park estates:** FDRL; Vogel, "Change in Hyde Park"; Moody, "FDR and His Neighbors." • **FDR and Rogers and Vanderbilt estates:** Carl Hamilton, COHP. • **Passion for trees, dislike of city, relations with neighbors, love of farming:** Moody, "FDR and His Neighbors." • **FDR and winter wheat:** FDRL, address to farm groups, May 14, 1935. • **FDR and Clinton:** FDRL, remarks at Hyde Park, Aug. 30, 1934. • **FDR boyhood:** Kleeman, *Young Franklin Roosevelt;* Sara Roosevelt, *My Boy Franklin.* • **"Who is your tree-climbing tutor?":** Herbert Claiborne Pell, COHP. • **FDR in Germany:** FDRL, PPF 1a. • **FDR and "filthy" Germans:** FDRL, Papers Pertaining to Family, Business, and Personal Affairs, 1882–1945. • **FDR and Moses Brown:** FDRL, Group 21A, Box 7. • **FDR and smuggling Chinese:** FDRL, PSF 115. • **Nature of FDR's childhood:** FDRL; Ferdon, "FDR, A Psychological Interpretation." • **FDR and manners:** FDRL, PPF 26. • **Rosy**

Roosevelt's anti-Semitism: FDRL, Papers Donated by Children, Box 20. • **Rosy Roosevelt and boundary dispute:** FDRL, Group 17, Box 25. • **FDR only child:** Arlow, "Only Child"; Clark and Capparell, "Psychiatry of the Adult Only Child"; Levy, *Maternal Overprotection.* • **FDR and torchlight parade:** FDRL, PPF 1072 and PP, remarks at Hyde Park, Nov. 7, 1944. • **Letters signed backward:** FDR, *Personal Letters.* • **FDR and English children in Bad Nauheim:** FDRL, PPF 5612. • **FDR and Huibertje Pruyn:** FDRL, "Some Memories of FDR by Mrs. Charles Hamlin."** • **FDR and Mlle Sandoz:** Ferdon, "FDR, A Psychological Interpretation"; PPF 199. • **FDR to George Van Slyke:** FDRL, PPF 914. • **FDR and "long-haired Polish Jew":** FDR, *Personal Letters.* • **FDR departure for Groton:** FDRL, Sara Roosevelt diary.

CHAPTER II. GROTON

Endicott Peabody and founding of Groton: Ashburn, *Peabody.* • **Fuller Potter doing his best:** Jeffrey Potter to author. • **FDR to Peabody:** FDRL, PPF 398. • **The old boy at the rector's funeral:** Montgomery Hare to author. • **Failure of Groton boys to enter public life:** Herbert Claiborne Pell, COHP. • **James to FDR at Groton:** FDRL, Papers Donated by Children, Box 3. • **Sara to FDR at Groton:** FDRL, Papers Donated by Children, Box 7. • **FDR to parents from Groton:** FDR, *Personal Letters.* • **Theodore Roosevelt at Groton:** FDRL, *The Grotonian,* June 1900. • **FDR boxing with Fuller Potter:** Jeffrey Potter to author. • **Sara on Boers:** FDRL, Papers Donated by Children, Box 7. • **FDR and servant problem:** FDR, *Personal Letters.* • **FDR and Taddy:** FDRL, Papers Donated by Children. • **FDR comments about girls:** FDR, *Personal Letters.* • **English IV exam:** FDRL, Group 14, Box 34. • **George Martin to FDR:** FDRL, PPF 2004. • **Fuller Potter comment:** Jeffrey Potter to author.

CHAPTER III. HARVARD

FDR at Harvard: *Harvard Alumni Bulletin.* • **Elective system and President Eliot:** Hawkins, *Between Harvard and America;* Morison, *Three Centuries.* • **Franklin and Taddy:** FDRL, Papers Donated by Children. • **FDR's fake scoop:** FDRL, Group 10, scrapbooks, and Group 12, Box 76. • **James Curtis comment:** James Curtis, COHP. • **FDR on the *Crimson:*** Walter Sachs, COHP. • **FDR aboard *Deutschland:*** Podell collection, Butler Library, Columbia University. • **FDR and Dickey:** *Harvard Alumni Bulletin;* FDRL, PPF 1954. • **Description of Porcellian:** Canfield, *Up and Down.* • **Greatest disappointment of his life:** Lash, *Love, Eleanor.* • **Franklin was pushy:** Sean Scully to author. • **FDR diary covering 1901–03:** FDRL, Papers Pertaining to Family, Business, and Personal Affairs. • **FDR to Washburn:** FDRL, Group 17, Box 10. • **Darling to FDR:** FDRL, Group 12, Box 40. • **Robert Ruhl on FDR as president of *Crimson:*** FDRL, Group 13, Box 38. • **FDR trip to England:** diary and *Personal Letters.* • **Christmas at Hyde Park:** FDRL, recollections of Anne Rogers Webb.

CHAPTER IV. GETTING MARRIED

Theodore and Elliott Roosevelt: Morris, *Rise.* • **Eleanor and the fantasy father:** Elliott Roosevelt, *Hunting.* • **Eleanor childhood:** Lash, *Eleanor and Franklin;* Eleanor Roosevelt, *Autobiography.* • **She believed the whale really swallowed Jonah":** FDRL, EROH, Justine Wise Polier. • **Marie Souvestre:** Lash, *Love, Eleanor.* • **Franklin and Eleanor courtship:** FDRL, ER; Sara Roosevelt diary; Lash, *Eleanor and Franklin.* • **Caribbean cruise:** FDRL,

PPF 2094. • **Fly Club letters:** FDRL, ER, Box 4937. • **Letter from Mrs. Lyman:** FDRL, PSF 155. • **Sara letters:** FDRL, Papers Donated by Children, Box 7. • **Sleepwalking episodes:** Henry Wallace, COHP. • **Sleepwalking:** Sours et al., "Somnambulism"; Broughton, "Sleep Disorders." • **Honeymoon:** FDR, *Personal Letters.* • **Baylies letter:** FDRL, Group 14, Box 48. • **"When I was a full-fledged lawyer":** FDRL, remarks at Hyde Park, Nov. 3, 1941. • **"Everyone loafs but Milburn":** FDRL, Group 14, Box 48. • **FDR to John Lytle:** FDRL, Group 10, Box 108. • **Mock advertisement:** FDRL, Group 14, Box 48. • **Grenville Clark remarks:** *Harvard Alumni Bulletin.* • **"I haven't invited you into my room":** Mrs. John Hay Whitney to author.

CHAPTER V. STATE SENATE

Political situation upstate: FDRL, Howe papers, Box 46. • **Dutchess county:** MacCracken, *Blithe Dutchess;* Moody, "FDR and His Neighbors." • **Ed Perkins and Newbold:** Mac-Cracken, *Blithe Dutchess.* • **Ed Perkins and FDR:** MacCracken, *Blithe Dutchess;* FDRL, George Palmer interviews with John E. Mack, Feb. 1, 1949, and Thomas Leonard, Jan. 11, 1949. • **FDR and Leonard:** FDRL, Mack interview. • **Hoyt and Forrestal conversation:** FDRL; PPF 990. • **1910 campaign:** FDRL, PPF 990; FDRL, newspaper clips; Rollins, *Roosevelt and Howe;* Gosnell, *Champion Campaigner;* FDRL, State Senate papers, Group 16, Box 16; Harry Hawkey reminiscences: FDRL, PSF 153. • **Pendell and FDR:** FDRL, PPF 338. • **Republican request for contribution:** FDRL, State Senate papers, Group 9, file 3. • **"I think he has a political future":** Gunther, *Roosevelt in Retrospect.* • **Albany diary:** FDRL, State Senate papers, File 1. • **Sheehan fight:** FDRL, State Senate papers and newspaper clips. • **Al Smith called FDR a "damned fool":** Josephson, *Al Smith.* • **Murphy and Tammany:** Weiss, *Murphy;* Huthmacher, *Wagner.* • **St. Patrick's day incident:** FDRL, newspaper clips. • **FDR as young legislator:** FDRL, State Senate papers; Rollins, "Young FDR." • **Efforts to organize the insurgents:** FDRL, State Senate papers. • **Bridge incident:** FDRL, newspaper clips. • **FDR deals with Tammany:** Lawrence Tanzer and Robert S. Binkerd, COHP. • **Osborne letter:** FDRL, State Senate papers. • **1911 campaign:** FDRL, State Senate papers. • **Triangle fire:** Frances Perkins, COHP. • **FDR letter to Putnam:** FDRL, State Senate papers. • **FDR disdain for 54-hour bill:** Frances Perkins, COHP. • **FDR conservation bill:** FDRL, State Senate papers, and remarks at 50th anniversary of State Conservation at Lake Placid, Sept. 14, 1935. • **FDR absent at 54-hour bill vote:** Frances Perkins, COHP; Martin, *Madam Secretary.* • **FDR to Eleanor:** FDRL, ER. • **Trip to Panama:** FDR, *Personal Letters.* • **Louis Howe:** Rollins, *Roosevelt and Howe;* Stiles, *Man Behind Roosevelt.* • **"Beloved and Revered Future President":** FDRL, State Senate papers, Group 9, File 178. • **Dinner party with Krock:** FDRL, Howe papers, Box 35. • **FDR teasing Howe and Howe cursing FDR:** Stiles, *Man Behind Roosevelt.* • **Talk at Columbia:** Rollins, *Roosevelt and Howe.* • **Warburg on Howe:** James P. Warburg, COHP. • **Campaign of 1912:** FDRL, State Senate papers, Group 9, File 178. • **Baltimore convention:** Daniels, *Wilson Era;* Gosnell, *Champion Campaigner;* Werner, *Bryan;* Josephson, *Al Smith;* FDR, *Personal Letters.* • **Letter to Burlingham:** FDRL, Group 17, Box 2. • **Daniels offered secretary of Navy:** Daniels, *Wilson Era.* • **Daniels picks FDR as assistant secretary:** Daniels, *Cabinet Diaries;* Morrison, *Daniels;* Daniels, *End of Innocence.* • **"Conditions at Albany":** FDRL, State Senate papers, Group 9. • **Unpopular with colleagues:** Frances Perkins, COHP. • **"Wonder of the worlds":** FDR, *Personal Letters.*

CHAPTER VI. ASSISTANT SECRETARY OF THE NAVY

FDR to Sara: FDR, *Personal Letters.* • **Sara to FDR:** FDRL, Papers Donated by Children, Box 9. • **"Dear Ludwig":** FDRL, Howe papers, Box 35. • **"I must have signed" and "a most interesting day":** FDR, *Personal Letters.* • **Daniels:** Morrison, *Daniels;* Daniels, *Cabinet Diaries;* Kilpatrick, *Roosevelt and Daniels.* • **"Hearty half hour" with Wilson:** FDRL, Asst. Sec. of Navy papers, Group 10, Box 2. • **FDR and Halsey:** Halsey, *Admiral Halsey's Story.* • **Miller and FDR:** FDRL, Group 21A, Box 8. • **Phillips and FDR:** William Phillips, COHP. • **Adams and FDR:** Eleanor Roosevelt, *This Is My Story.* • **"There's another Roosevelt on the job":** FDRL, Asst. Sec. of Navy papers, scrapbooks. • **"ASTNAV—SECNAV":** Kilpatrick, *Roosevelt and Daniels.* • **"Worked like niggers":** FDR, *Personal Letters.* • **Taft letter:** Morrison, *Daniels.* • **FDR reaction to Mexican crisis:** FDRL, Asst. Sec. of Navy papers, scrapbooks. • **"Huerta's out":** Werner, *Bryan.* • **"Mr. Daniels feeling chiefly very sad":** FDR, *Personal Letters.* • **"Running the real work":** FDR, *Personal Letters.* • **McCarthy to Howe:** FDRL, Howe papers, Box 34. • **FDR releases Sharkey:** FDRL, PPF 3089. • **Louis Howe re Clapham:** FDRL, Asst. Sec. of Navy papers, Group 10, Box 2. • **FDR and Burleson:** FDRL, Asst. Sec. of Navy papers, Group 10, Box 20. • **FDR and post office patronage:** FDRL; Rollins, "Political Education." • **FDR mentioned for governor:** Rollins, "Political Education." • **FDR and 1914 Senate race:** FDRL, Group 10, Box 133; Group 10, scrapbooks. • **FDRL and preparedness:** FDRL, Asst. Sec. of Navy papers, scrapbooks. • **Hearings "really great fun":** FDR, *Personal Letters.* • **Greene to Symington:** FDRL, Asst. Sec. of Navy papers, Group 10, Box 35; Symington to FDR:** Group 10, Box 128. •

Trip to San Francisco: FDRL, Asst. Sec. of Navy papers, Group 10, Box 43; PSF, Box 115. • **Statue of girl:** FDRL, PPF 8393, PPF 5477. • **House prediction:** George, *Wilson and House.* • **"These are hectic days":** FDR, *Personal Letters.* • **Lunch with Daniels:** Morrison, *Daniels.* • **"Baby is a little fussy":** FDRL, Papers Donated by Children, Box 9. • **Emory S. Land on Daniels:** FDRL, Group 21A, Box 7. • **"It seems very hard to wait":** FDR, *Personal Letters.* • **"Tomorrow the inventors come":** FDR, *Personal Letters.* • **Col. House on Daniels:** George, *Wilson and House.* • **FDR and Tammany:** FDRL, scrapbooks. • **Favors to congressmen:** FDRL, Asst. Sec. of Navy papers, Group 10, Box 98. • **FDR's chauffeur:** FDRL, Asst. Sec. of Navy papers, Group 10, Box 98. • **FDR removes officer:** FDRL, Asst. Sec. of Navy papers, Group 10, Box 84. • **Sara on polio:** FDRL, Papers Donated by Children, Box 9. • **Polio epidemic of 1916:** Lippman, *Squire;* Berg, *Challenge;* Paul, *History.* • **Daniels to FDR on yacht:** Kilpatrick, *Roosevelt and Daniels.* • **"Most extraordinary day of my life":** FDR, *Personal Letters.* • **Wilson to Daniels:** Daniels, *Cabinet Diaries.* • **Trip to Haiti:** FDRL, Asst. Sec. of Navy papers, Group 10, Boxes 83, 32, 103. • **Livy Davis and risqué show:** FDRL, Asst. Sec. of Navy papers, Group 10, Box 92. • **Haitian secretary of agriculture:** FDRL, Asst. Sec. of Navy papers, Group 10, Box 83. • **FDR to House:** George, *Wilson and House.* • **Sims appointment:** Morison, *Sims;* FDRL, PPF 3946. • **FDR and Pat Homer:** FDRL, Group 14, Box 97; Group 16, Box 20; Group 10, Boxes 33, 102, 128; Group 12, Box 79; PPF 1309. • **FDR to *Transcript:*** FDRL, Asst. Sec. of Navy papers, scrapbooks. • **Admiral to Daniels:** Morison, *Sims.* • **Declaration of war:** Daniels, *Cabinet Diaries.*

CHAPTER VII. THE NAVY AT WAR

Navy under Daniels: Daniels, *Cabinet Diaries.* • **"I get my fingers into everything":** Kilpatrick, *Roosevelt and Dan-* iels. • **"Do please get through":** FDRL, Asst. Sec. of Navy papers, Group 10, Box 93. • **Brooklyn cantonment:** Lindley, *Half Way.* • **FDR and war risk insurance:** FDRL, Asst. Sec. of Navy papers, Group 10, Box 103; PPF 3125. • **FDR and mine barrage:** Lindley, *Half Way;* Kilpatrick, *Roosevelt and Daniels;* FDRL, Asst. Sec. of Navy papers, Group 10, Box 57. • **Daniels's second thoughts:** Daniels, *Cabinet Diaries.* • **Appraisal of mine laying and German comments:** Marder, *From the Dreadnought.* • **Beatty refusal to mine Norwegian waters:** Chalmers, *Beatty.* • **"I dislike exaggeration":** FDRL, Asst. Sec. of Navy papers, Group 10, Box 93. • **"Do you remember":** Lowenheim et al., *Roosevelt and Churchill.* • **FDR and Kennedy:** Beschloss, *Kennedy and Roosevelt.* • **FDR and Walter Camp:** FDRL, Asst. Sec. of Navy papers, Group 10, Boxes 89, 106. • **"My cold is gone":** FDRL, Asst. Sec. of Navy papers, Group 10, Box 122. • **Winston Churchill report:** FDRL, Asst. Sec. of Navy papers, Group 10, Box 2. • **"The more I think":** FDR, *Personal Letters.* • **FDR and crooked contracts:** Kilpatrick, *Roosevelt and Daniels.* • **FDR as Tammany candidate for governor:** FDRL, Asst. Sec. of Navy papers, Group 10, Box 96. • **Ornsteen letter:** FDRL, Group 10, Box 96. • **1918 trip to Europe:** FDRL, Asst. Sec. of Navy papers, Group 10, Boxes 45, 96, 108, 191; visit with Foch: FDRL, FDR to graduating class at West Point, June 12, 1935. • **"It would be wonderful to be war President":** William Castle papers, HI. • **FDR oversteps himself:** Daniels, *Cabinet Diaries.* • **Howe to Eleanor:** FDRL, Howe papers, Box 35. • **FDR meeting with Belgian king:** FDRL, PPF 234. • **FDR to McCarthy:** FDRL, Asst. Sec. of Navy papers, Group 10, Box 107. • **FDR to Lathrop Brown:** Group 10, Box 107. • **"Miss Mercer is here":**

FDRL, Papers Donated by Children, Box 8. • **"His face is long and firmly shaped":** FDRL, Asst. Sec. of Navy papers, scrapbooks. • **Cowles to FDR:** Lash, *Eleanor and Franklin.* • **Livy Davis and "the ladies of Washington":** FDRL, ER, Box 4937. • **FDR and Lucy Mercer:** FDRL, ER, Box 15. • **"He deserves a good time":** Lash, *Eleanor and Franklin.* • **Motel in Virginia Beach:** James Roosevelt, *My Parents.* • **Anna thought they were Victorian:** FDRL, EROH, Eleanor Seagraves interview. • **Affair consummated:** Mrs. John Hay Whitney to author. • **FDR and divorce:** Elliott Roosevelt to author. • **Lucy Rutherfurd letters to FDR:** FDRL, Family, Business, and Personal Papers, Box 21, Folder 10. • **Lucy to Anna:** FDRL, Halsted papers. • **1919 trip to Europe:** FDRL, Asst. Sec. of Navy papers, Group 10, Box 92. • **FDR to McIlhenny:** FDRL, Asst. Sec. of Navy papers, Group 10, Box 111. • **FDR to Robinson:** FDRL, Asst. Sec. of Navy papers, Group 10, Box 86. • **FDR and Laski:** FDRL, Asst. Sec. of Navy papers, Group 10, Box 129. • **FDR to Robbins:** FDRL, Asst. Sec. of Navy papers, Group 10, Box 121. • **Sims flap:** Morison, *Sims.* • **Brooklyn speech:** FDRL, speeches, 113. • **Daniels feels betrayed:** Daniels, *Cabinet Diaries.* • **FDR and Wehle:** Wehle, *Hidden Threads.* • **Wehle sees Hoover:** Wehle, *Hidden Threads.* • **FDR and Thomas Mott Osborne:** FDRL, Asst. Sec. of Navy papers, Group 14, Box 60; Group 10, Box 116. • **Taussig flap:** FDRL, Asst. Sec. of Navy papers, Group 10, Box 48. • **FDR to Hamlen:** FDRL, Asst. Sec. of Navy papers, Group 10, Box 100. • **"Rex, this is the man":** Tugwell, *Democratic Roosevelt.*

CHAPTER VIII. ON THE NATIONAL TICKET

FDR to Marvin: FDRL, Asst. Sec. of Navy papers, Group 10, Box 110. • **Cox chooses FDR:** Cox, *Journey;* FDRL, PPF 3125. • **Nomination for vice presidency:** Gosnell, *Champion Campaigner;* Lindley, *Half Way.* • **Meeting** with Wilson: Cox, *Journey.* • **Sedgwick and FDR:** FDRL, Group 15, Box 21. • **1920 campaign:** Gravlee: "Rhetorical Study"; Paone, "Election of 1920"; Bagby, "Progressivism's Debacle"; FDRL. • **Butte flap:** FDRL, Group 15,

Boxes 7, 19. • **FDR and Wobblies:** FDRL, speeches. • **Alabama lumberman:** Gravlee, "Rhetorical Study." • **Lynch to FDR:** Gravlee, "Rhetorical Study." • **FDR to Marvin:** FDRL, Group 15, Box 17. • **"Ex V.P., Canned":** FDRL, Group 15, Box 21.

CHAPTER IX. THE NEWPORT SCANDAL

FDR and Section A: Transcript of Court of Inquiry 10821, Military Field Branch of Library of Congress, Suitland, Md.; U.S. Senate Committee on Naval Affairs, *Report.* • **"Damn it, Steve":** Gould, *Good Fight.* • **FDR to Daniels,** "in the long run": FDRL, Group 14, Box 80. • **FDR to Keyes:** FDRL, Group 14, Box 80.

CHAPTER X. THE STRICKEN PRINCE

Polio attack: Gould, *Good Fight.* • **"Thanks to a severe chill":** FDRL, Group 14. • **"You have been a rare wife":** Lash, *Eleanor and Franklin.* • **Delano to Eleanor:** Goldberg, *Making.* • **Stress and illness:** Ader, *Psychoneuroimmunology;* Dr. Herman Roiphe to author. • **Bennett to Lovett:** Lovett papers, Francis A. Countway Library of Medicine, Boston. • **Draper to Lovett:** Lovett papers. • **FDR to Daniels:** FDRL, Group 14. • **Lake to Lovett:** Lovett papers. • **Eleanor at end of her tether:** Lovett papers. • **"If only his wife":** Lovett papers. • **"Mr. R. cheerful":** Lovett papers. • **Lovett to FDR and FDR to Lovett:** Lovett papers. • **FDR to Draper:** FDRL, Group 12. • **Florida and the *Weona:*** FDRL, Group 14. • **Lovett examination:** Lovett papers. • **"I saw FDR":** Lovett papers. • **Girlfriends:** Goldberg, *Making.* • **"The French way":** Dorothy Schiff to author. • **Affair with Missy:** Elliott Roosevelt to author. • **Frankfurter on Missy LeHand:** Frankfurter, *From the Diaries.* • **Missy LeHand and movie camera:** FDRL, HM, Apr. 15, 1935. **Mahoney to FDR:** FDRL, Papers Donated by Children, miscellaneous file. • **Pining for Franklin:** FDRL, Papers Donated by Children, Box 21. • **FDR will:** James Roosevelt to author. • **FDR crawling across floor:** FDRL, Group 16. • **FDR to Wehle:** FDRL, Wehle papers. • **"Pa, how do you get to sleep":** Mrs. John Hay Whitney to author. • **"Polio did that for Franklin":** FDRL, EROH. • **Lehman:** FDRL, EROH. • **Perkins:** Frances Perkins, COHP. • **Adolph C. Miller:** FDRL, Group 21A, Box 8. • **The superego:** Erikson, *Childhood and Society.* • **"Removes the sadness by showing us his legs":** Anna Roosevelt, "First My Father." • **Fabienne Pellerini:** FDRL, PPF 1877. • **Adolph C. Miller and the model boat:** FDRL, Group 21A, Box 8.

CHAPTER XI. THE SEVEN LEAN YEARS

Appeals for sympathy, union business, Brooklyn congressman: FDRL, Group 14, Box 44. • **Griffin to FDR:** FDRL, Group 14, Box 44. • **FDR to Hall Roosevelt:** FDRL, Group 14, Box 101. • **FDR business ventures:** FDRL, Group 14, Boxes 53, 61, 78. • **American Construction Council:** FDRL, Group 14, Box 44. • **FDR a poor lawyer:** Frances Perkins, COHP. • **FDR to Al Smith:** FDRL, Group 11, Box 4. • **FDR to Murphy:** Weiss, *Murphy.* • **Proskauer on FDR:** Joseph Proskauer, COHP. • **FDR to Babe Ruth:** FDRL, Group 16, Box 27. • **1924 Democratic convention:** Murray, *103d Ballot.* • **Jedediah Tingle:** FDRL, Group 16, Box 27. • **FDR to McAdoo:** FDRL, Group 16, Box 22. • **Kansas delegates:** Henry Wallace, COHP. • **John W. Davis:** Harbaugh, *Lawyer's Lawyer.* • **McCarthy to FDR:** FDRL, Group 16, Box 18. • **Meredith to FDR and reply:** FDRL, Group 11, Box 4. • ***Larooco:*** FDRL, Group 14, Box 87. • **Mosley visit:** Mosley, *My Life.* • **Elliott visit:** Elliott Roosevelt to author. •

Warm Springs: Lippman, *Squire;* Walker, *Roosevelt;* Stevens, *"Hi-ya, Neighbor."* • **FDR to Livy Davis:** FDRL, Group 12, Box 40. • **FDR columns:** Carmichael, *F.D.R. Columnist.* • **FDR to Hasbrouck:** FDRL, Hasbrouck papers. • **FDR to Sara:** FDR, *Personal Letters.* • *Polio Chronicle:* FDRL. • **Segregation at Warm Springs:** FDRL, PPF 30. • **Howe ridiculing Al Smith:** FDRL, Howe papers. • **FDR to Al Smith:** FDRL, Group 11, Box 4. • **FDR to Berres:** FDRL, Group 11, Box 1. • **FDR and Moses flap over Howe:** Moses, *Public Works.* • **FDR to Rice:** FDRL, Group 14, Box 62. • **Moses frustrates FDR on budget:** FDRL, Group 14, Box 62. • **FDR to MacDonald, FDR to Smith:** FDRL, Group 14, Box 62. • **Eleanor changing:** Erikson, *"Nothing to Fear."* • **Eleanor to Marion Dickerman:** FDRL, Dickerman papers. • **Dickerman to Cook:** Davis, *Invincible Summer.* • **Elliott on Eleanor and lesbians:** Elliott Roosevelt, *Untold Story.* • **Nancy Cook as lesbian:** Dorothy Schiff to author. • **Esther Lape:** Lash, *Love, Eleanor.* • **Eleanor to FDR:** FDRL, ER. • **Anna to Eleanor:** FDRL, Halsted papers. • **Poor old Sis":** FDRL, Dickerman papers, Box 5. • **Dall meets FDR:** Dall, *FDR.* • **Eleanor asks Dall to return money:** Dall, *FDR.* • **James Roosevelt:** James Roosevelt, *Affectionately, F.D.R.* and *My Parents* • **Marriage to Betsy Cushing:** Mrs. John Hay Whitney to author. • **"I do very much hope you will make law school":** FDRL, Group 12, Box 147. • **James leaves law school:** James Roosevelt to author. • **FDR re de Gerard:** FDRL, Group 12, Box 147. • **Elliott Roosevelt:** Elliott Roosevelt, *Untold Story.* • **Elliott refuses to go to Harvard:** Elliott Roosevelt to author. • **Plan to fly produce:** FDRL, Group 12, Box 147. • **FDR-Wehle exchange:** FDRL, Wehle papers. • **Kimball to FDR and reply:** FDRL, Group 11, Box 4. • **FDR to Lippmann:** FDRL, Group 17, Box 15. • **Eleven minutes after:** FDRL, Group 17, Box 19. • **Roosevelt stunned:** FDRL, Group 17, Box 3. • **Raskob:** Mosley, *Blood Relations;* Zilg, *Behind the Nylon Curtain;* Chandler, *Du Pont.* • **Feeling on Raskob appointment:** FDRL, Group 17, Box 3. • **Howe to FDR:** FDRL, Howe papers. • **Smith parochialism:** Smith, *Up to Now.* • **"Please let me know":** FDRL, Howe papers. • **FDR to Sara:** FDR, *Personal Letters.* • **Raskob offers to fund the Warm Springs Foundation:** FDRL, PPF 226. • **Smith-FDR:** Josephson, *Al Smith.* • **"They are killing the best friend I ever had":** FDRL, PPF 5872. • **Sara to FDR:** FDRL, Papers Donated by Children. • **"A governor does not have to be an acrobat":** Rollins, *Roosevelt and Howe.* • **"He won't live a year" and FDR reply:** FDRL, PPF 5872. • **Moses attacks:** Frances Perkins, COHP; Warner, *Happy Warrior.* • **FDR campaign:** Rosenman, *Working.* • **"Rare good fun":** FDRL, Group 17, Box 10. • **Changes in FDR:** Frances Perkins, COHP. • **"People have been so mean":** Frances Perkins, COHP. • **New York returns:** Rosenman, *Working.* • **"It was only this week":** FDRL, Group 17, Box 11. • **Louis Howe breakfast:** Eddie Dowling, COHP. • **Mrs. Long to FDR:** FDRL, Group 17, Box 22. • **George White to FDR:** FDRL, Group 17, Box 24.

CHAPTER XII. GOVERNOR ROOSEVELT

Moses on inauguration: FDRL, Group 18, Box 87. • **"He rubs me the wrong way":** Caro, *Power Broker.* • **Getting rid of Mrs. Moskowitz:** Frances Perkins, COHP. • **Roosevelt as governor:** Bellush, *Roosevelt.* • **Budget fight:** FDRL, Group 12, Box 147; Group 18, Boxes 36 to 38. • **"This family is going":** FDR, *Personal Letters.* • **Frankfurter to FDR:** FDRL, Group 12, Box 61. • **Prisons:** FDRL, Group 18, Box 59. • **Commutations:** FDRL, Group 12, Box 71; Looker, *This Man.* • **Frankfurter to FDR on pardoning power:** FDRL, Group 12, Box 61. • **Labor:** Perkins, *Roosevelt;* Martin, *Madam Secretary;* Frances Perkins, COHP. • **Investigation of banks:** FDRL, Group 18, Box

14. • **Clark Bros. failure:** FDRL, Group 18, Box 11. • **Roosevelt and the bankers:** FDRL, Group 18, Boxes 11 to 13. • **"I reached out":** Eddie Dowling, COHP. • **FDR testifies for Broderick:** Bellush, *Roosevelt.* • **Moses and Northern State Parkway:** FDRL, Group 18, Boxes 37, 203. • **FDR to Clark:** FDRL, Group 18, Box 203. • **Walbridge flap:** FDRL, Group 18, Box 203. • **Torrey flap:** FDRL, Group 18, Box 203. • **Favor for Buckley:** FDRL, Group 18, Box 203. • **"You're a goddamned liar":** Caro, *Power Broker.* • **Triborough flap:** Ickes, *Secret Diaries;* Frances Perkins, COHP; FDRL, PPF 3650 and OF 25, Box 4. • **Utilities:** FDRL, Group 12, Boxes 65, 153; Group 18, Box 158. • **St. Lawrence:** FDRL, Group 18, Box 59. • **FDR knowledge of history:** Frances Perkins, COHP. • **Requests from citizens:** FDRL, Group 18, Box 1. • **FDR family life:** Samuel I. Rosenman, COHP. • **Keller to FDR:** FDRL, Group 12, Box 94. • **FDR to Howe:** FDRL, Howe Papers. • **Reynolds and Hoover:** Jackson E. Reynolds, COHP. • **FDR to Wagner:** FDRL, Group 18, Box 6. • **Hoover:** Joslin, *Hoover;* Burner, *Hoover.* • **Shafer:** FDRL, Group 12. • **FDR and Mellon:** FDRL, Group 12. •

"What is the state?': PP • **Pound to FDR:** FDRL, Group 12, Box 140. • **Hart to FDR and reply:** FDRL, Group 12, Box 82. • **FDR request for TERA:** PP • **Beer taking bus:** Samuel Beer to author. • **FDR to Dashwood:** FDRL, Group 12. • **FDR to Wehle:** FDRL, Wehle papers. • **Cermak to FDR:** FDRL, Group 12. • **FDR to Shouse:** FDRL, Group 12. • **Governors' conference:** FDRL, Group 12. • **Wheeler and FDR:** Wheeler, *Yankee.* • **Cooke to FDR:** FDRL, Group 12. • **FDR and carpetbaggers:** PP • **FDR to Smith:** FDRL, Group 14, Box 102. • **"Things here" and "I got it":** FDRL, Group 12. • **Meeting with Cox that led to break with Smith:** FDRL, Berle diary (document), Mar. 9, 1938. • **Farley tour:** Farley papers, LC; Farley, *Behind the Ballots.* • **Farley miscalculations:** Rosen, *Hoover, Roosevelt.* • **"He's so wishy-washy":** FDRL, Group 21A, Box 4. • **Baruch to FDR and reply:** FDRL, Group 12, Box 9. • **Lippmann to Baker:** Steel, *Lippmann.* • **FDR to Shouse:** FDRL, Group 12. • **"Oddly enough":** FDRL, Howe papers. • **FDR to Daniels:** Kilpatrick, *Roosevelt and Daniels.* •

CHAPTER XIII. WHO ARE YOU INDEED WHO WOULD TALK OR SING TO AMERICA . . .

FDR to McLean: FDRL, Group 12. • **FDR to Nicholas Roosevelt:** FDRL, Group 12. • **Astrology chart:** FDRL, PPF 1A. • **50th birthday:** FDRL, Group 12. • **Livy Davis suicide:** FDRL, Group 12. • **Anonymous circular:** Carlson, *Roosevelt's Fight.* • **Samuel Lambert disapproval:** Krock, *Memoirs.* • **Smith and Jackson:** Rosen, *Hoover, Roosevelt.* • **Smith and Pendergast:** Carlson, *Roosevelt's Fight.* • **Frankfurter to Lippmann:** Freedman, *Roosevelt and Frankfurter.* • **Lippmann insisting:** Walter Lippmann, COHP. • **FDR reaction:** Rollins, *Roosevelt and Howe.* • **Stern interview:** J. David Stern, COHP • **Grange speech:** PP. • **Test of strength on arrangements:** Rosen, *Hoover, Roosevelt.* • **Howe memos:** FDRL, Howe

papers. • **Brain trust:** Rosenman, *Working.* • **Moley:** Moley, *After Seven Years.* • **Rosenman critical of Moley:** Samuel I. Rosenman, COHP. • **Warburg on Moley:** James P. Warburg, COHP. • **Tugwell:** Tugwell, *To the Lesser Heights;* Sternsher, *Tugwell.* • **Berle:** Balog, "Berle"; Berle, *Navigating.* • **FDR and Angell:** Adolf A Berle, COHP. • **FDR campaign speeches:** PP. • **FDR and Hoover:** Lash, *Eleanor and Franklin.* • **Kroll to FDR:** FDRL, Group 18, Box 71. • **Smith and McAdoo lunch:** Rosen, *Harvard, Roosevelt.* • **Democratic convention:** Farley, *Behind the Ballots;* Rollins, *Roosevelt and Howe;* Rosen, *Hoover, Roosevelt;* Carlson, *Roosevelt's Fight.* • **Kennedy role:** Beschloss, *Kennedy and Roosevelt.* •

Garner role: Timmons, *Garner.* • Texas caucus: Connally, *My Name.* • Raskob to Shouse: FDRL, Group 12. • Ward Smith to FDR: FDRL, Group 12. • Baruch after convention: Schwarz, *Speculator.* • Moley distress: Moley, *After Seven Years.* • FDR and bonus march: Tugwell, *The Democratic Roosevelt* • Two most dangerous men in America: Tugwell, *The Democratic Roosevelt* • Walker hearings: Mitgang, *Man Who Rode.* • Evening in Albany:

Moley, *After Seven Years.* • Lippmann column: FDRL, Group 12, Box 71. • "I have a long memory": FDRL, Rosenman papers. • FDR campaign: FDRL, Group 12. • Mary Roosevelt to FDR and reply: FDRL, Group 12. • Hoover campaign: Stokes, *Chip.* • Frankfurter two-faced: Frankfurter, *From the Diaries.* • "If you are elected": Jackson E. Reynolds, COHP. • FDR in Boston: Moley, *After Seven Years* • Responses to election: FDRL, Group 12.

CHAPTER XIV. THE PEACEFUL REVOLUTION

Roosevelt cheerfulness: Tugwell, *The Democratic Roosevelt* • Ribbing Moley: Moley, *After Seven Years.* • Hanging onto Roosevelt's coattails: Stimson diary, Dec. 21, 1932, YU. • Stimson visit: Stimson diary, Jan. 9, 1933, YU. • Cermak and Paddy Bauler: Bellow, "In the Days of Mr. Roosevelt." • Assassination attempt: Moley, *After Seven Years.* • Eleanor to FDR re Morgenthau: FDRL, Papers Donated by Children, Box 16. • Wallace meets FDR: Henry Wallace, COHP. • Howe to FDR re Glass: FDRL, Howe papers. • Moley wire: Moley papers, HI. • Hull: Hull, *Memoirs.* • Perkins: Frances Perkins, COHP. • Howe comment on Ickes: Rollins, *Roosevelt and Howe.* • Walsh: O'Keane, *Walsh.* • Tugwell thinking about banks: Tugwell, *The Democratic Roosevelt* • Perkins at inauguration: Frances Perkins, COHP. • 1933 inauguration: FDRL, PSF 155. • Aymar Johnson: FDRL, PPF 157. • Pell: Herbert Claiborne Pell, COHP. • Broadcaster Ed Hill: FDRL, PSF 155. • Perkins response: Frances Perkins, COHP. • Edmund Wilson response: Wilson, *American Earthquake.* • Harold Nicolson response: Nicolson, *Diaries.* • Thomas Beck: FDRL, Group 21A. • FDR visit to Holmes: Louchheim, *Making.* • Special session of Congress: Herring, "First Session." • Wadsworth: James W. Wadsworth, COHP. • MacArthur and FDR: MacArthur, *Reminiscences.* • Perkins on CCC: Frances Perkins, COHP. • CCC: FDRL, OF 268. • Howe and toilet kits: FDRL, Howe papers,

Box 71. • Howe getting evidence: Eddie Dowling, COHP. • Nicholas Roosevelt meeting: Nicholas Roosevelt, *Front Row Seat.* • Going off the gold standard: James P. Warburg, COHP. • Wadsworth against AAA: James W. Wadsworth, COHP. • Start of relief operations: Adams, *Hopkins.* • TVA: Lilienthal, *Journals.* • Stock market hearings: Pecora, *Wall Street.* • Woodin at cabinet: Ickes, *Secret Diaries.* • NRA: Keyserling to author; Frances Perkins, COHP; Louchheim, *Making;* Hawley, *New Deal;* Ekirch, *Ideologies;* Brand, "Corporatism"; Richberg, *Rainbow;* Stokes, *Chip;* FDRL, OF 463. • Section 7(a): Keyserling to author; Huthmacher, *Wagner;* Louchheim, *Making;* Frances Perkins, COHP. • Congressional hearings on NRA: Herring, "First Session." • Hugh Johnson: Johnson, *Blue Eagle.* • FDR and Johnson: Frances Perkins, COHP. • Johnson at cabinet meeting: Frances Perkins, COHP. • Ickes and the PWA: Karl, *Merriam.* • New Deal and mule: Ernest Cuneo to author. • Lunch with Stimson: Stimson diary, Mar. 28, 1933, YU. • Amish woman: FDRL, OF 268. • Phillips flabbergasted: William Phillips, COHP. • Jedel diary: Moley papers, HI. • London Conference: Feis, *1933;* James P. Warburg, COHP. • FDR willing to stabilize: Moley, *After Seven Years.* • Moley explanation of FDR's behavior: Moley diary, HI. • British reaction: Dizikes, *Britain.* • Sonofabitch Bingham: Moley diary, HI. • "That pissant Moley": James P. Warburg, COHP.

• **Need to get Moley out:** FDRL, Morgenthau diary, July 1933. • **Moley sent to Hawaii:** Moley dairy, HI. • **"I cut the sonofabitch's throat":** Braden, *Diplomats.* • **Dodd:** Dodd, *Diary.* • **"The Hitler regime":** FDRL, PSF 45. • **"There is a unity":** FDRL, PPF 1193. • **FDR favors Mussolini:** FDRL, PPF 5763. • **New Deal seen as analogue of National Socialism:** Dizikes, *Britain.* • **FDR to Ickes:** Ickes, *Secret Diary.* • **Moley to FDR on Russia:** Moley papers, HI. • **Hull response:** Hull, *Memoirs.* • **Garner response:** Timmons, *Garner.* • **Recognition of Russia:** Bullit, *For the President;* FDRL, PSF 115. • **Gold policy:** Acheson, *Morning and Noon.* • **Warburg on Morgenthau:** James P. Warburg, COHP. • **British reaction to gold policy:** Dizikes, *Britain.* • **Lindsay to Churchill:** Gilbert, *Churchill.* • **Mrs. Lippincott:** FDRL, OF 447. • **"In chemistry":** FDRL, George Biddle, Group 21A. • **Lincoln story:** FDRL, PPF 215. • **FDR to House:** FDRL, PPF 222. • **"Where the owls fuck the chickens":** Raymond Clapper diary, July 13, 1933, LC. • **Ford and the NRA:** Lewis, *Public Image.* • **FDR meeting with coal operators:** Freedman, *Roosevelt and Frankfurter.* • **NRA and the unions:** Bernstein, *Turbulent Years.* • **Creel on NRA:** Creel, *Rebel.* • **Problems with Hugh Johnson:** Frances Perkins, COHP. • **Wagner bill:** Keyserling to author. • **"This might just as well":** Bernstein, *Turbulent Years.* • **Johnson is fired:** Frances Perkins, COHP. • **Second session of Congress:** Herring, "Second Session." • **Air mail contracts:** Cole, *Lindbergh.* • **FDR to Frankfurter:** Freedman, *Roosevelt and Frankfurter.* • **FDR and Hopkins:** Adams, *Hopkins.* • **FDR to Council:** FDRL, Minutes of the National Emergency Council. • **Kennedy appointment:** Beschloss, *Kennedy and Roosevelt;* Ickes, *Secret Diaries;* Louchheim, *Making.* • **FDR to Long:** FDRL, PPF 2337. • **Bahret to FDR** FDRL, PPF 1853. • **FDR to Fred Delano:** Karl, *Merriam.* • **Dart game target:** Dall, *FDR.* • **"The Nightmare of 1934":** FDRL, PPF 457.

CHAPTER XV. STUMBLING IN THE RIGHT DIRECTION

FDR and World Court: Herring, *Presidential Leadership.* • **Dodd in Washington:** Dodd, *Diary.* • **"I can take him":** Williams, *Long.* • **February 5 meeting:** FDRL, Minutes of National Emergency Council. • **FDR to House:** FDRL, PPF 222. • **FDR and Tugwell:** FDRL, Tugwell diary, Mar. 14, 1935. • **Tugwell supporting Olson:** FDRL HM, Mar. 18, 1935. • **Tugwell in Resettlement Administration:** Sternsher, *Tugwell.* • **Hopkins diary:** Adams, *Hopkins.* • **FDR dedicating Boulder Dam:** PP. • **FDR and Talmadge:** FDRL, Hopkins papers, Box 36. • **Disney damning Ickes:** FDRL, Hopkins papers, Box 36. • **WPA hiring:** Paul H. Appleby, COHP. • **FDR and bonus:** FDRL, HM, May 20, 1935. • **Wagner bill:** Huthmacher, *Wagner;* Keyserling to author. • **Schechter case:** Stanley Reed, COHP; Pusey, *Hughes;* Richberg, *My Hero;* Louchheim, *Making.* • **Schwab story:** FDRL, PPF 5067. • **FDR tax bill:** FDRL, HM, June 26, 1935. • **Social Security Act:** Frances Perkins, COHP. • **Meeting with Willkie:** Lilienthal, *Journals.* • **Wagner to Keyserling:** Keyserling to author. • **Corcoran saying FDR was soft:** Moley papers, HI. • **Brewster complaint:** Koenig, *Invisible Presidency.* • **FDR to Corcoran:** FDRL, PSF 141. • **"I would have enjoyed seeing you cry":** FDRL, HM, Dec. 2, 1935. • **FDR to Phillips:** FDRL, OF 2314; **Women of easy virtue:** Ickes, *Secret Diaries.* • **Connally on Mussolini:** Connally, *My Name.* • **Long on Mussolini:** FDRL, PPF 434. • **"The Louisiana dictator has met his fate":** Gilbert, *Churchill.* • **Stokes and La Follette:** Stokes, *Chip.* • **FDR wants to investigate Proskauer, and General Motors sells short:** FDRL, HM, Jan. 27, 1936. • **FDR and Moley:** Moley papers, HI. • **FDR fed up with press:** FDRL, Early papers. • **Stanley Reed beaten again:** Stanley Reed, COHP. • **Supreme Court decisions:**

Mason, *Stone.* • **FDR to Berry:** FDRL, PPF 1523. • **Green to committee members:** Altman, "Second Session." • **Labor a key element:** Bernstein, *Turbulent Years.* • **"I tackled the lion in his den":** FDRL, HM, May 27, 1936. • **Perkins to FDR:** Frances Perkins, COHP. • **FDR to Wallace:** FDRL, Wallace papers. • **Franklin Field:** Ickes, *Secret Diaries.* • **"Economic royalists";** Frances Perkins, COHP. • **Landon and Ted Bohn:** Clapper diary, Sept. 13, 1936, LC. • **"Typical prairie state":** Farley papers, LC. • **Colorado dirt farmer:** FDRL, PPF 4310. • **FDR to Dodd:** FDRL, PPF 1043. • **Spain:** Connally, *My Name;* Hull, *Memoirs.* • **FDR summons Hoover:** FBI memos, Aug. 25 and Sept. 10, 1936. • **Subway riders changing buttons:** FDRL, PSF Box 34. • **FDR on election eve:** FDRL, PPF 2993. • **"The completeness of it":** Clapper diary, Dec. 1936, LC. • **Gridiron dinner:** FDRL, Early papers.

CHAPTER XVI. LIFE IN THE WHITE HOUSE

Bingham sent Howe $10,000, and FDR memo to Howe: FDRL, PSF Box 52. • **Death of Howe:** Keller, " 'Franklin's On His Own Now.' " • **Moley does not attend funeral:** Moley papers, HI. • **"We all miss him":** FDRL, PPF 1524. • **Helen Reynolds to FDR:** FDRL, PPF 234. • **McIntyre:** Daniels, *White House Witness.* • **Pa Watson:** FDRL, McCrea papers, Early papers, Hopkins papers, Box 121; PPF 3684. • **Early:** FDRL, Early papers; "You would have to say that": Eddie Dowling, COHP. • **O'Connor bill for $200,000:** Jesse Jones papers, LC. • **Hall Roosevelt and aluminum plant:** FDRL, OF 598; wants to send planes to Spain: Bullitt, *For the President;* serious drinker, Marion Dickerman, COHP. • **Henry Hooker tax case:** FDRL, HM, Dec. 19, 1935. • **Evening at the White House:** Clapper diary, May 1937, LC. • **Party for Tallulah and housekeeping at the White House:** Mrs. John Hay Whitney to author. • **"Anyone that wants this seat":** Hugh Gibson papers, HI. • **Wallace on Eleanor:** Henry Wallace, COHP. • **FDR to Eleanor:** FDRL, Early papers. • **Kiplinger to Morgenthau:** FDRL, HM, Oct. 19, 1934. • **Ickes critical of Eleanor:** Ickes, *Secret Diaries.* • **Eleanor and Lorena Hickok:** Faber, *Hickok.* • **Martha Gellhorn on Hickok:** FDRL, EROH. • **Dorothy Schiff and FDR:** Schiff to author. • **"You wouldn't know, Pa":** Mrs. John Hay Whitney to author. • **Anna and Curtis Dall:** FDRL, Halsted papers; FDRL, Eleanor Seagraves, EROH. • **Boettiger molesting his stepdaughter:** FDRL, Eleanor Seagraves, EROH. • **Anna and Boettiger:** FDRL, Halsted papers. • **Death of Boettiger:** Boettiger, *Love in Shadow.* • **John Roosevelt to FDR:** FDRL, Papers Donated by Children, Box 20. • **Anna to Eleanor:** FDRL, Halsted papers. • **"Do babies come into the world":** FDRL, Marion Dickerman, EROH. • **Franklin Jr. at Harvard:** FDRL, PPF 2115 • **FDR paying law firm:** FDRL, PPF 4039 • **Daladier prank and Du Pont wedding:** FDRL, PPF 3. • **Anna on Franklin Jr. and Ethel:** FDRL, Halsted papers. • **Elliott to Moley:** Moley papers, HI. • **"I knew it was going to be tough" and drive to California:** Elliott Roosevelt to author. • **"I do wish":** FDRL, HM, May 1, 1934. • **Elliott agreement with Fokker:** FDRL, PPF 3. • **Elliott and radio stations:** Jesse Jones papers, LC; Timmons, *Jones.* • **Anna on Elliott:** FDRL, Halsted papers. • **FDR asks Jones to help Elliott:** Jesse Jones papers, LC; Timmons, *Jones.* • **"I often fear":** FDRL, PPF 3. • **Jimmy and Wheeler investigation:** FDRL, HM, Sept. 21, 1937. • **Jimmy and National Yeast:** James Roosevelt to author. • **"You were like one of those heads":** James Roosevelt to author. • **Jimmy and Charles Schwartz:** Douglas, *Go East.* • **Jimmy and Betsy divorce:** Mrs. John Hay Whitney to author. • **Jimmy hired by Goldwyn:** FDRL, HM, Dec. 6, 1938. • **Schenck-Zanuck investigation:** FDRL, HM, Apr. 11, 1939. • **"How can you do this with a suit pending?":** FDRL, HM, Dec. 6, 1938. • **Schenck loaned Jimmy $50,000:** FDRL, HM, Apr. 4, 1939;

Jimmy calls to inquire: May 25, 1939; Zanuck found guilty; Jan. 8, 1940; Jimmy drops in to see Morgenthau: Feb. 28, 1940. • "One of the worst things": James Rowe to author. • The Great Giovanni: Eddie Dowling, COHP.

CHAPTER XVII. THROUGH ME MANY LONG-DUMB VOICES

"Playing with your stamps": FDRL, Early papers. • Ray Moley and Huey Long: Moley papers, HI. • McReynolds and Brandeis: Frances Perkins, COHP. • Reed on court packing: Stanley Reed, COHP. • Burlingham to FDR: FDRL, PPF 196. • Wheeler opposes plan and contacts Brandeis: Wheeler, *Yankee.* • Bob Jackson argument: Clapper dairy, LC. • FDR and Wheeler: Wheeler, *Yankee.* • Garner and FDR: FDRL, PPF 1416; Timmons, *Garner.* • FDR lunch with Hugh Johnson: Ickes, *Secret Diaries.* • "That was how he paid him back": Henry Wallace, COHP. • FDR picks Black: Dunne, *Black.* • Black and KKK: Dunne, *Black.* • "If Marlene Dietrich": Beschloss, *Kennedy and Roosevelt.* • Court after Black: Pritchett, *Roosevelt Court.* • Cruise aboard *Potomac:* Ickes, *Secret Diaries.* • "Pink sheets": FDRL, complete press conferences. • High school civics class: FDRL, PPF 1A. • *Tribune* story: FDRL, Early papers. • Minton to FDR: FDRL, PSF 188. • Tunis to FDR: FDRL, PPF 4663. • Lewis to White House: Alinksy, *Lewis.* • Farley on sit-down strike: James A. Farley, COHP. • Garner on sit-down strike: Timmons, *Garner.* • FDR to Perkins: Frances Perkins, COHP. • Cruise aboard *Potomac:* FDRL, HM, May 24, 1937. • "Jack, I am going to reassert leadership": Ickes, *Secret Diaries.* • Bingham to FDR: FDRL, PSF 46. • Bullitt to FDR: Bullitt, *For the President.* • FDR and La Guardia: Ickes, *Secret Diaries.* • Grew in Tokyo: Grew, *Turbulent Era.* • October 6 press conference: FDRL, complete press conferences. • Welles tracing line: FDRL, Welles to Rosenman, Rosenman papers. • "I am really worried": FDRL, PPF 1524. • December 17 cabinet meeting: Ickes, *Secret Diaries.* • Japanese meet demands: Hull, *Memoirs.* • FDR peace plan: Cadogan, *Diaries.* • Ickes regrets: Ickes, *Secret Diaries.* • "The next two years": FDRL, HM, Jan. 16, 1938. • FDR picks Hopkins: Sherwood, *Roosevelt and Hopkins.* • Hopkins to Frank: Jerome Frank, COHP. • "What a wonderful tumor": FDRL, PSF 155. • "What do you think": FDRL, PSF 155. • Whitney scandal: Simon, *Independent Journey.* • Smathers to FDR, and Wheeler in Boston: FDRL, PSF 188. • Reorganization bill: Polenberg, *Reorganizing.* • Dies Committee: Goodman, *Committee.* • Morgenthau threatens to resign: FDRL, HM, Apr. 12, 1938. • Carmody to White House: John M. Carmody, COHP. • Lee to FDR: FDRL, PSF 188. • Purge: Stokes, *Chip;* failure of: FDRL, PPF 7459. • Davies in Moscow: FDRL, Early papers. • FDR and Hull: FDRL, PSF 93; Weil, *Pretty Good Club.* • Berle to FDR: FDRL, PSF 93. • Kennedy a dangerous man: Beschloss, *Kennedy and Roosevelt.* • "Surrounded by senators": FDRL, OF 4069. • Kennedy to FDR: FDRL, PSF 53. • Long more concerned about Bolsheviks: Breckinridge Long diary, LC. • Moffat: Weil, *Pretty Good Club.* • Bullitt on Oumansky: FDRL, Walton Moore papers, Group 55, Box 3. • Bullitt to FDR: FDRL, PSF 43. • Cudahy to State Department: FDRL, Walton Moore papers, Group 55, Box 4. • FDR and Bowman: FDRL, PPF 5575. • "America has been a place of refuge": FDRL, HM, Mar. 18, 1938. • FDR meeting with Lindsay: Cadogan, *Diaries.* • "Totally disgraceful": Ickes *Secret Diaries.*

CHAPTER XVIII. WHEN BAD MEN COMBINE

Planes to the French: FDRL, HM, January 1939. • FDR confers with senators: FDRL, PSF 188. • FDR and Merriman: FDRL, PSF 46. • "History of half truths": FDRL, Berle diary, Sept. 13, 1939. • Dinner at Lothian's: FDRL,

Berle diary, Sept. 22, 1939. • **FDR and Connally:** Connally, *My Name.* • **FDR personal diplomacy:** FDRL, HM, Apr. 15, 1939. • **FDR sees Lindbergh:** Lindbergh, *Wartime Journals.* • **Jews did not get the presidential bee:** Jerome Frank, COHP. • **FDR and Hutchinson:** FDRL, PPF 118. • **Wheeler and FDR:** Burton K. Wheeler, COHP. • **Bullitt to FDR:** FDRL, PSF 43. • **FDR to O'Day:** FDRL, PSF 140. • **Hull and Borah:** Hull, *Memoirs.* • **"I like it when something happens every minute":** FDRL, HM, Aug. 29, 1939. • **FDR fed up with Russians:** FDRL, PSF 68. • **Joseph Warren poem and FDR reply:** FDRL, PPF 4096. • **Einstein and FDR:** FDRL, PPF 7177. • **Corcoran in all sorts of pies:** Lilienthal, *Journals.* • **Corcoran crowd wants a third team:** FDRL, Berle diary, Mar. 21, 1940. • **FDR to Mrs. Hull:** Hull, *Memoirs.* • **FDR on Farley:** Frances Perkins, COHP. • **Farley disloyal:** Ickes, *Secret Diaries.* • **Farley and FDR:** Farley papers, LC. • **Farley to Clapper:** Clapper diary, LC. • **Garner won at poker:** Ernest Cuneo to author. • **Cabinet meetings unpleasant:** Ickes, *Secret Diaries.* • **Lewis attacks Garner:** Alinsky, *Lewis.* • **Johnson wants dams:** Louchheim, *Making.* • **"Thrown his bottle into the ring":** Ickes, *Secret Diaries.* • **TVA:** Lilienthal, *Journals.* • **Sumner Welles trip to Europe:** FDRL, PSF 9, 43. • **Normanbrook on Churchill:** Normanbrook, *Action.* • **"I want you to do something":** FDRL, HM, Apr. 29, 1940. • **Waite-Miles conversation:** FDRL, PSF 103. • **FDR motoring along Bantry Bay:** FDRL, Berle diary, May 16, 1940. • **FBI wiretaps:** Ungar, *FBI;* FDRL, HM, May 20, 1940. • **FBI infiltrated U.S. embassy in Moscow:** FDRL, OF 1OB, Dec. 13, 1940. • **Hoover to Morgenthau:** FDRL, HM, May 24, 1941. • **Bullitt to FDR:** FDRL, PSF 2. • **Hull on Bullitt:** Hull, *Memoirs.* • **FDR and**

French ambassador: Eccles, *Beckoning Frontiers.* • **Churchill to FDR:** Lowenheim et al., *Roosevelt and Churchill.* • **Churchill to Hopkins:** FDRL, Hopkins papers. • **FDR to Morgenthau:** FDRL, HM, Apr. 29, 1940. • **Destroyer deal:** Goodhart, *Fifty Ships.* • **FDR contract with** *Collier's:* FDRL, Thomas Beck, Group 21A. • **"Sick and tired of the Roosevelts":** Flynn, *You're the Boss.* • **Wants Bob Jackson for governor:** Ernest Cuneo to author. • **Lewis wants to be vice president:** Frances Perkins, COHP. • **FDR and Hull:** Hull, *Memoirs.* • **1940 convention:** Paul Appleby, COHP; Grafton, *American Diary;* FDRL, PSF 189: Hopkins papers, PPF 104. • **Farley and FDR:** Farley papers, LC. • **FBI report on Farley:** FDRL, OF 10b, Aug. 9, 1942. • **1940 campaign "exceedingly dirty":** Henry Wallace, COHP. • **Hopkins shows Rosenman letters:** FDRL, Rosenman papers. • **Guru letters:** FDRL, Rosenman papers, Box 18. • **Appleby reaches Wallace:** Paul Appleby, COHP. • **Wallace and Roerich:** Wallace, *Price.* • **Rosenman and Hopkins show FDR guru letters:** FDRL, Rosenman papers. • **Wallace denies:** Paul Appleby, COHP; Appleby to Rosenman, FDRL, Rosenman papers. • **FDR to Mellett:** FDRL, FDR tapes. • **1940 campaign:** Black, *Democratic Party Publicity;* Moscow, *Roosevelt and Willkie.* • **FDR to Perkins:** Frances Perkins, COHP. • **FDR and Elliott:** FDRL, FDR tapes; Elliott Roosevelt to author. • **Stimson on black troops:** Stimson diary, Sept. 27, 1940, YU. • **FDR meets with three black leaders:** FDRL, FDR tapes. • **Black leaders feel betrayed:** Anderson, *Randolph.* • **FDR meets with Frank Knox:** FDRL, FDR tapes. • **FDR and Lewis:** Alinsky, *Lewis.* • **Hopkins worried:** Will Alexander, COHP.

CHAPTER XIX. I DARE NOT SHIRK ANY PART OF MYSELF

Wallace and Ickes: FDRL, Charles E. Merriam, Group 21A. • **FDR and Bowers book, and letter to Bowers on Lincoln:** Jones, *Roosevelt's Image Bro-* **kers.** • **"Now, this I must say in the TR manner":** Richberg, *My Hero.* • **Wallace and the Nematodes:** Henry Wallace, COHP. • **Trickster figure:** Jung,

Collected Works. • **Hit a golf ball 400 yards:** Eccles, *Beckoning Frontiers.* • **FDR and Landis:** James Landis, COHP. • **FDR and dog pissing contest:** Jesse Jones papers, LC. • **FDR and Richberg:** Richberg, *My Hero.* • **Ickes has no affection for FDR:** Ickes diary, June 7, 1942, LC. • **"It certainly is wonderful":** FDRL, HM, Aug. 20, 1934. • **FDR and Norman Davis:** FDRL, Marion Dickerman, EROH. • **FDR and Sir Charles Wilson:** Moran, *Churchill.* • **FDR and Eden:** Eden, *Reckoning.* • **FDR and Fortas:** FDRL, Biddle papers. • **Ickes party:** Ickes diary, July 10, 1936, LC. • **FDR in Warm Springs:** Eddie Dowling, COHP. • **State Department promotions:** George Messersmith papers, University of Delaware: FDR memo to Welles: FDRL, PSF 95. • **FDR and Eccles:** Eccles, *Beckoning Frontiers.* • **Daniels to FDR:** FDRL, PPF 86. • **FDR and Lehman:** FDRL, EROH. • **Lippmann on FDR:** Walter Lippmann, COHP. • **Stimson complaint:** Stimson diary, Nov. 12, 1941, YU. • **Morgenthau complaint:** FDRL, HM, July 9, 1943. • **Barbed wire:** Ickes diary, Mar. 7, 1942, LC. • **FDR to Harriman:** Harriman, *Special Envoy.* • **Perkins to Hopkins:** Frances Perkins, COHP. • **Crowley to Morgenthau:** FDRL, HM, Jan. 27, 1942. • **Alsop criticizes FDR:** Clapper diary, May 2, 1938, LC. • **FDR and Mackenzie King:** Stacey, *Double Life.* • **Cough-**

lin investigation: Rowe to author. • **Fish investigation:** FDRL, PSF 93. • **Annenberg career:** Cooney, *Annenbergs.* • **Hoover memo:** FBI, Nov. 7, 1938. • **FDR sees Morgenthau:** FDRL, HM Mar. 2, 1939. • **"I want Moe Annenberg for dinner":** FDRL, HM Apr. 10, 1939. • **"Collect every dollar":** FDRL, HM, Nov. 30, 1939. • **Lyndon Johnson Senate race:** Caro, *Path.* • **FDR calls Morgenthau:** FDRL, HM, Nov. 12, 1943. • **Morgenthau sees Wirtz:** FDRL, HM, Nov. 12, 1943. • **Johnson investigation ended:** Caro, *Path.* • **Wooley reminded of Andrew Jackson:** FDRL, PPF 3506. • **Relations with press:** Rosten, "President Roosevelt." • **"Drew Pearson is a son of a bitch":** FDRL, McCrea papers. • **Pegler a cad:** FDRL, PSF 189. • **FDR and Krock:** FDRL, PSF 178. • **Krock suggestion:** FDRL, PPF 675. • *Times* reporter reassigned: FDRL, Early papers. • **FDR wants *Times* investigated:** FDRL, HM, July 17, 1939. • **FDR and Luce:** FDRL, Early papers. • **Steve Early quip:** FDRL, Early papers. • **Morgenthau and Rosenman on Clare Luce:** FDRL, HM, June 28, 1944. • **FDR campaigning:** FDRL, Rosenman papers. • **FDR on reporter's trade:** FDRL, Minutes of National Emergency Council. • **FDR meets with Dies:** FDRL, PPF 3458. • **FDR and Waller case:** FDRL, PSF 143. • **FDR to Bruce:** FDRL, PPF 2577.

CHAPTER XX. THE WAY TO WAR

1941 Inaugural: Baker, *Roosevelt and Pearl Harbor.* • **Dinner at British embassy:** FDRL, HM, July 19, 1940. • **Morgenthau to White:** FDRL, HM, July 19, 1940. • **Morgenthau to Ickes:** FDRL, HM, July 22, 1940. • **Grew report:** Grew, *Turbulent Era.* • **Morgenthau furious at Hull:** FDRL, HM, Sept. 24, 1940. • **Stimson urges embargo:** Stimson diary, Oct. 8, 1940, YU. • **Eleanor to FDR and reply:** FDRL, PSF 177. • **FDR to Ickes and reply:** FDRL, PSF 175. • **Ickes to Morgenthau:** FDRL, HM, July 15, 1940. • **FDR on Kennedy:** FDRL, HM, Oct. 3, 1940. • **Kennedy named man of the year:** FDRL, OF 3060. • **FBI**

report on Kennedy seeing Goering: FDRL, OF 10b, Box 31. • **Report on Kennedy selling short:** FDRL, Hopkins papers. • **What exactly Hopkins did:** Adams, *Hopkins.* • **"I have been thinking very hard":** FDRL, HM, Dec. 17, 1940. • **Hopkins visit to London:** Sherwood, *Roosevelt and Hopkins.* • **British penury disbelieved:** Claude Wickard, COHP. • **Emery Land to FDR and reply:** FDRL, PPF 7492. • **British profiteering:** FDRL, Hopkins papers. • **Roy Howard calls Willkie:** FDRL, PSF, 194. • **FDR on Quaker:** FDRL, PSF 177. • **Eleanor and Youth Congress:** FBI. • **Isolationism:** Cole, *Roosevelt and Isolationists.* • **FBI** reports on Wheeler: FDRL, OF 10b, Box 12. • **Japanese ambassador on funding isolationists and contacts with America First:** Magic intercepts, SRDJ 16307 to 16567, NA. • **Halifax:** Birkenhead, *Halifax.* • **Landing of Quanza and Long reaction:** Breckinridge Long diary, LC. • **R. D. Turner to FDR:** FDRL, OF 3186. • **FDR and refugees:** FDRL, OF 3186. • **Long to Berle:** Feingold, *Politics.* • **Eleanor and Fry:** FDRL, PSF 117. • **FDR gives $240:** FDRL, OF 3186. • **Appeal to admit Mrs. Trotsky:** FDRL, OF 4295. • **FDR and pilots for RAF:** FDRL, PPF 576. • **Niblack incident:** FDRL, PSF 5. • **"Keep on walking":** Stimson diary, Apr. 25, 1941, YU. • **"It is my understanding":** FDRL, PSF 5. • **Linda Bradley:** FDRL, PPF 707. • **"Flashes of genius":** Stimson diary, Apr. 2, 1941, YU. • **Meeting of malcontents:** Ickes diary, May 12, 1941, LC. • **British learned from Hess:** Lee, *London Journal.* • **Steinhardt to Hull:** FDRL, PSF 31. • **Magic confirmation of attack on Russia:** "Examples of Intelligence Obtained from Cryptanalysis," SRH 066, NA. • **Macmillan:** Macmillan, *Blast.* • **Pell to FDR:** FDRL, OF 2670. • **Situation of Russia:** Trumbull Higgins to author. • **Hopkins in Moscow:** Sherwood, *Roosevelt and Hopkins.* • **FDR meeting with Randolph:** Anderson, *Randolph.* • **Ethridge to FDR and reply:** FDRL, PSF 175. • **Placentia Bay meeting:** Ian Jacob to author. • **Churchill to Brooke:** Bryant, *Turn.* • **"That is the way we talked to her":** Cadogan, *Diaries.* • **Churchill singing hymns:** Frances Perkins, COHP. • **"I can't understand primogeniture":** Ernest Cuneo to author. • **"A charming country gentleman":** Cadogan, *Diaries.* • **"Grandpa's pretty good":** Henry Wallace, COHP. • **Nazi threat to Latin America:** FDRL, PPF 86. • **Nazi penetration of Latin America:** Gellman, "New Deal's Use." • **FDR to Churchill on Hess landing:** FDRL, Map Room papers. • **Churchill to Hopkins:** FDRL, Hopkins papers. • **Churchill told Randolph:** Gilbert, *Churchill.* • **Eleanor on deaths of Sara and Hall:** FDRL, Halsted papers. • **Bryce forgery:** H. Montgom-

ery Hyde to author; Ernest Cuneo to author. • **October 28 press conference:** FDRL, complete press conferences. • **"I felt as if":** Ernest Cuneo to author. • **Pearl Harbor revisionism:** Barnes, "Pearl Harbor." • **Magic background:** Ralph T. Briggs interview, SRH 051, NA; "Magic reports for the attention of the President," SRH 111, NA; "Collection of papers related to the Winds Execute Message," SRH 210, NA; A. D. Kramer interview, SRH 154, NA; "Certain Aspects of Magic in the Cryptological Background of the Various Official Investigations into the Pearl Harbor Attacks," by William F. Friedman, declassified May 22, 1981, SRH 125, NA; "Examples of Intelligence Obtained from Cryptanalysis," SRH 066, NA; "A Version of the Japanese Problem in the Signal Intelligence Service," by John B. Burt, SRH 252, NA. • **Magic leak:** Harris, "Magic Leak." • **"Father told me this morning":** FDRL, Halstead papers. • **"I don't want to be the bones of a dead horse":** SRDJ, NA. • **November 6 cabinet:** FDRL, Biddle papers. • **November 18 Hull meeting:** SRDJ, 16307 to 16567, NA. • **November 19 meetings with Frankfurter and Walker:** SRDJ, 16307 to 16567, NA. • **Marshall to FDR:** Pogue, *Marshall.* • **Dyer increasing readiness:** Lewin, *American Magic.* • **November 22 Magic intercept:** SRDJ, 16307 to 16567, NA. • **FDR and Ickes:** Ickes diary, Nov. 23, 1941, LC. • **"He fairly blew up":** Stimson diary, Nov. 26, 1941, YU. • **"Our failure and humiliation are complete":** SRDJ, 16567 to 17293, NA. • **FDR sees envoys on November 27:** SRDJ, 16567 to 17293, NA. • **More Magic intercepts, and Tokyo recalls its spy chief:** SRDJ, 17293 to 17662, NA. • **"You might learn something":** FDRL, Berle diary, Dec. 1, 1941. • **December 5 cabinet:** Frances Perkins, COHP. • **Pearl Harbor attack:** U.S. Congress Joint Committee, *Report;* Prange, *At Dawn.* • **Hull to the office:** Hull, *Memoirs.* • **Stimson having lunch:** Stimson diary, Dec. 7, 1941, YU. • **Clay watching Redskins:** Lucius D. Clay, COHP. • **FDR at cabinet meeting and with congressmen:** FDRL, OF 4675.

• **"I wish you'd stop referring"**: Pogue, *Marshall.* • **Seaman Z**: Commander I. G. Newman interview with Robert D. Ogg, SRH 255, NA; "Historical Review of OP-20-G," SRH 152, NA. • **Nimitz arrives**: Chester Nimitz, COHP. • **Knox report**: FDRL, PSF 106. • **MacArthur and Philippines**: Costello, "Remembering." • **FDR comfortable in new role**: FDRL, Biddle papers.

CHAPTER XXI. THE DIFFICULT ALLIANCE

Internment of Japanese: U.S. Commission on Wartime Relation, *Personal Justice Denied;* FDRL, Biddle papers. • **FDR and biological warfare**: Stimson "Safe File," NA. • **FDR and atom bomb**: Sherwin, *World Destroyed;* Arnold, *Global Mission.* • **FDR to Ficke**: FDRL, PPF 5522. • **Stilwell on FDR**: Stilwell, *Papers.* • **Christmas eve dinner**: FDRL, PPF 2904. • **FDR and Jones**: Ian Jacob to author. • **Harriman from London**: FDRL, PSF 52. • **"I would go out and take the stuff"**: FDRL, HM, Mar. 11, 1942. • **April meeting with British**: Pogue, *Marshall;* FDRL, Hopkins papers. • **Ismay**: Ismay, *Memoirs.* • **Conversations with Molotov**: FDRL, Hopkins papers. • **Louis Johnson to FDR**: FDRL, PSF 4. • **Churchill to Hopkins**: FDRL, Hopkins papers. • **FDR on Gandhi**: Ickes diary, Aug. 8, 1942, LC. • **King "wobbled around"**: Stimson diary, June 17, 1942, YU. • **Fall of Tobruk**: Ismay, *Memoirs.* • **Struggle with Churchill**: Stimson diary, June 1942, YU. • **"Taking your dishes"**: Stimson diary, July 15, 1942, YU. •

FDR to Hopkins: Sherwood, *Roosevelt and Hopkins.* • **Hopkins and Marshall to London**: Sherwood, *Roosevelt and Hopkins.* • **Marshall thought of resigning**: Pogue, *Marshall.* • **Hopkins wedding**: Ickes diary, Aug. 1, 1942, LC. • **Clip from Beaverbrook**: Daniels, *White House Witness.* • **Eleanor not pleased**: Daniels, *White House Witness.* • **FDR to Marshall**: Pogue, *Marshall.* • **Willkie trip to China**: FDRL, PSF 194. • **FDR mimicking Willkie**: FDRL, PPF 7023. • **Hoover report on Willkie**: FDRL, PSF 194. • **"Some of the wildest arrangements"**: FDRL, Berle diary, Nov. 9, 1942. • **British had secret messages from Darlan**: Cadogan, *Diaries.* • **FDR in high spirits**: FDRL, Biddle papers. • **Torch increasing pressure on Stalin**: Higgins, *Churchill.* • **Dill to friend**: Cunningham papers, British Museum. • **Morgenthau affected**: FDRL, HM, Nov. 17, 1942. • **Darlan assassin recruited by British**: Barley Alison to Don Cook, relayed to author. • **Thanksgiving at White House**: Lilienthal, *Journals.*

CHAPTER XXII. DEMOCRACY, WHILE WEAPONS WERE EVERYWHERE
AIM'D AT YOUR BREAST

Trip to Casablanca: FDRL, Hopkins papers. • **Macmillan and the emperors**: Macmillan, *Blast.* • **Stimson and the old steamboat**: Stimson diary, Nov. 17, 1942, YU. • **Casablanca**: FDRL, Map Room papers, Box 165; Ian Jacob to author; Bryant, *Turn.* • **FDR to Boettiger**: FDRL, Halsted papers. • **Churchill likened Japan to an octopus**: Wilkinson papers, Churchill College, Cambridge. • **Troops and matériel allocated to the Pacific**: Higgins, *Churchill.* • **FDR sees Giraud and de Gaulle**: FDRL, Map Room papers, Box 165. • **Unconditional surrender**: O'Connor,

Diplomacy. • **Americans in Tunisia**: Butcher, *My Three Years.* • **American green troops**: Wilkinson papers, Churchill College, Cambridge. • **"There definitely will be an attack"**: FDRL, Halsted papers. • **"The man from London"**: Stimson diary, May 10, 1943, YU • **Trident Conference**: Bryant, *Turn,* Stimson diary, YU; Pogue, *Marshall.* • **Creation of OSS**: Bernard Gladieux COHP. • **FDR as wartime president**: Binkley, *President;* Blum, *V;* Polenberg, *War;* May, *Ultimate Decision.* • **Strong to Marshall**: Selected Documents Concerning OSS Operations in

Lisbon, Spring 1943, SRH 113, NA. • **Wartime restrictions:** Bernard Gladieux, COHP. • **Strikes:** Bernstein, *Turbulent Years.* • **Antitrust policies:** FDRL, Biddle papers; Stimson "Safe File," NA. • **Rehabilitation of businessmen:** Bernard Gladieux, COHP. • **FDR visits Ford plant:** Lewis, *Public Image.* • **FDR to Knox:** FDRL, PSF 11. • **Dismantling of CIC:** *History of the Counter Intelligence Corps.* • **Friendship between Eleanor and Lash:** Lash, *Love, Eleanor.* • **Eleanor to Biddle:** FBI. • **Mail cover and surveillance reports:** FBI. • **Boyer to Bissell:** FBI. • **Eleanor's room bugged:** FBI. • **Burton memo, Dec. 31, 1943:** FBI. • **1951 memo:** FBI. • **Eleanor and Josephine Adams:** FBI. • **FDR to Biddle:** FDRL, PSF 118. • **Eleanor and the hornets:** FDRL, ER, Box 1660. • **FDR and bats:** FDRL, PSF 12. • **Eleanor and railroads:** FDRL, OF 25 • **Eleanor and Loyalist Spain:** FDRL, PSF 82 • **Eleanor and Douglas:** FDRL, PSF 144. • **FDR irritated:** Jonathan Daniels oral history, Truman Library, Independence, Mo. • **FDR eating chicken six times a week:** FDRL, PSF 177. • **Eleanor on Frances Perkins:** FDRL, PSF 177. • **Eleanor on Allen Dulles:** FDRL, Map Room papers, Box 165. • **Eleanor and Stimson:** Stimson Diary, April 1944, YU. • **"And despite her global milling":** FDRL, PSF 177. • **Bankhead funeral:** Frances Perkins, COHP. • **Wallace finds Welles drinking:** Wallace, *Price.* • **Welles making advances to porters:** Hoover memo, Jan. 30, 1941, FBI. • **Dodd comment:** Dodd, *Diary.* • **Bullitt had seduced Missy LeHand:** Dorothy Rosenman to author. • **Pa Watson sends for Hoover:** FBI. •

Hoover briefs president: FBI. • **April meeting between Bullitt and president:** Bullitt, *For the President.* • **Hull not given Casablanca minutes:** Stimson diary, May 1943, YU. • **Welles in Rio:** Gellman, *Good Neighbor Diplomacy.* • **"I've got the prime example":** Arthur Krock, COHP. • **Hull sees Hoover:** Hoover memo, Oct. 29, 1942, FBI. • **Brewster sees Hoover:** Hoover memo, May 3, 1943, FBI. • **Early sees Bullitt:** Bullitt, *For the President.* • **Bullitt in the cold:** Bullitt, *For the President.* • **"Bill ought to go to hell":** Wallace, *Price.* • **"John Metcalf says":** First Army headquarters memo, May 8, 1952, obtained through Freedom of Information Act. • **"If I were the angel Gabriel":** Pilat, *Pearson.* • **Cadogan:** Cadogan, *Diaries.* • **Eden:** Eden, *Reckoning.* • **Brooke:** Bryant, *Turn.* • **Hull in Moscow:** Hull, *Memoirs;* Eden in Moscow: Barker, *Churchill and Eden.* • **"With all his lip service":** Stimson diary, Nov. 4, 1943, YU. • **Pershing to FDR:** FDRL, PSF 104. • **FDR Teheran diary:** FDRL, OF 200 3-N. • **Incident at sea:** King, *Fleet Admiral.* • **FDR to Eisenhower:** Butcher, *My Three Years.* • **"Brooke got nasty":** Stilwell, *Papers.* • **"Not one American soldier":** Pogue, *Marshall.* • **"How would you like to be a clay pigeon":** Weatherholt papers, HI. • **Teheran Conference:** FDRL, Hopkins papers; Eubank, "Teheran Conference"; Bohlen, *Witness;* Harriman, *Special Envoy;* Moran, *Churchill.* • **Stalin:** Ulam, *Stalin;* Djilas, *Conversations.* • **FDR and Stilwell:** Stilwell, *Papers.* • **FDR and Marshall:** Pogue, *Marshall.* • **Visit to the Sphinx:** Churchill, *Closing the Ring.*

CHAPTER XXIII. WE THOUGHT WE WERE DONE WITH THESE THINGS

Lamont and Morgan: FDRL, PPF 70. • **Stephen Hopkins death:** Sherwood, *Roosevelt and Hopkins.* • **Flap with Barkley:** Drury, *Senate Journal;* Barkley, *That Reminds Me;* Henry Wallace, COHP. • **Soldier vote bill:** Drury, *Senate Journal.* • **"The boss is noncommittal":** Hassett, *Off the Record.* • **Bruenn examination:** Bruenn, "Clinical Notes." •

"After the circumcision": FDRL, manuscript of Hassett book. • **FDR to Hopkins:** FDRL, Hopkins papers. • **FDR to Stettinius:** Stettinius, *Diaries.* • **"I have never heard the president":** FDRL, HM, May 18, 1944. • **FDR on trusteeships:** Stettinius, *Diaries.* • **Spheres of influence:** Lowenheim et al., *Roosevelt and Churchill.* • **"Rabbi Wise and others":**

Breckinridge Long Diary, LC. • **Weizmann sees FDR:** FDRL, HM, June 12, 1943. • **Morgenthau plan to evacuate Jews:** FDRL, HM, July and August, 1943. • **Setting up War Refugee Board:** FDRL, HM, Jan. 16, 1944. • **FDR agrees to let in 1,000 refugees:** FDRL, HM, June 12, 1944. • **FDR and French currency:** FDRL, HM, Jan. 8, 1944. • **Morgenthau and McCloy, and meeting with Monnet:** FDRL, HM, Jan. 8, 1944. • **Stimson to Marshall:** Stimson "Safe File," NA. • **FDR to Churchill re de Gaulle:** Lowenheim et al., *Roosevelt and Churchill.* • **FDR to Eisenhower:** FDRL, Map Room papers, Box 30. • **OSS report:** FDRL, PSF 6. • **"Jam for the Russians":** Henry Wallace, COHP. • **Capt. Middleton:** Middleton papers, Churchill College, Cambridge; Col. Reeder, *New York Times,* June 6, 1984. • **Stimson calls FDR:** Stimson "Safe File," NA. • **"He's a nut":** Hassett, *Off the Record.* • **Americans in Bayeux:** FDRL, PPF 7365. • **De Gaulle gives FDR model submarine:** William R. Emerson to author. • **"Just wait and look at de Gaulle's chin":** Ickes diary, July 9, 1944, LC. • **Recognition of de Gaulle:** FDRL, Map Room papers. • **Jesse Jones a son of a bitch:** Ickes diary, June 18, 1944, LC. • **Pauley working against Wallace:** Edwin W. Pauley, oral history, Truman Library, Independence, Mo. • **Wallace a security risk:** FBI. • **Hoover to Biddle, and Wallace in Los Angeles:** FBI. • **Wallace talks to FDR:** Henry Wallace, COHP. •

July 10 meeting with Democratic chiefs: Edwin W. Pauley, oral history, Truman Library, Independence, Mo. • **Wallace lunch with FDR:** Henry Wallace, COHP. • **FDR letter to Hannegan and Pauley:** Edwin W. Pauley, oral history, Truman Library, Independence, Mo. • **FDR to Truman:** Miller, *Plain Speaking.* • **Wallace had lost, and president's behavior:** Henry Wallace, COHP. • **MacArthur boomlet:** Vandenberg, *Papers.* • **MacArthur's virility:** Ickes diary, Sept. 25, 1943, LC. • **"He could have won that suit":** Pilat, *Pearson.* • **Waikiki conference:** FDRL, Rosenman papers. • **Russia and Polish uprising:** FDRL, Map Room papers; Harriman, *Special Envoy.* • **Feuding in China:** Stimson diary, May 26, 1944, YU. • **Morgenthau plan:** FDRL, HM, September 1944. • **Agreement with Churchill:** FDRL, HM, Sept. 15, 1944. • **"I have yet to meet":** Stimson diary, Sept. 16, 1944, YU. • **"Henry pulled a boner":** Stimson diary, Oct. 3, 1944, YU. • **Special relationship coming apart:** FDRL, Map Room papers. • **Spheres of influence:** FDRL, Map Room papers. • **Dewey:** Smith, *Dewey.* • **Dewey and Magic:** Smith, *Dewey;* Pogue, *Marshall.* • **Sidney Hillman and the PACs:** Josephson, *Hillman.* • **Dewey a bully:** FDRL, PSF 115. • **Sinclair Lewis radio talk:** FDRL, Rosenman papers. • **Election night at Hyde Park:** Leahy, *I Was There.* • **FDR mandate for new world order:** FDRL, PPF, 1169.

CHAPTER XXIV. HUSH'D BE THE CAMPS TONIGHT

Innauguration: Miller, *Plain Speaking;* Henry Wallace, COHP; Bruenn, "Clinical Notes"; Thompson, FDRL, Group 21A; Frances Perkins, COHP; Drury, *Senate Journal.* • **FDR on Ibn Saud and meeting with Senate leaders:** Stettinius, *Diaries.* • **Firing Jesse Jones:** Jesse Jones papers, LC; Timmons, *Jones;* Frances Perkins, COHP. • **Wallace and FDR:** Henry Wallace, COHP. • **Trip to Yalta:** Leahy, *I Was There.* • **Yalta:** Moran, *Churchill;* Bohlen, *Witness;* Harriman, *Special Envoy;* Byrnes,

Speaking Frankly; Sherwood, *Roosevelt and Hopkins;* Yalta Conference minutes: FDRL, Hopkins papers. • **"Uncle Joe the most impressive":** Cadogan, *Diaries.* • **Gladwyn Jebb admired:** Gladwyn, *Memoirs.* • **Yalta a victory:** FDRL, Bohlen, Group 21A; PPF 6207—August 1951 statement by Averell Harriman to the Armed Services and Foreign Relations committees. • **War Department memo:** Stimson "Safe File," NA. • **"I don't think I'm wrong about Stalin":** Hugh Dalton,

Fateful Years. • **Visit with Ibn Saud:** FDRL, Map Room papers, Box 163; PSF 68. • **Daniels hears laughter:** Daniels, *White House Witness.* • **Suggestion of a regency:** Jonathan Daniels, oral history, Truman Library, Independence, Mo. • **FDR addresses joint session:** Thomas C. Hart, COHP. • **Clay visit:** Lucius Clay, COHP. • **Correspondents' dinner:** Drury, *Senate Journal.* • **February 23 press conference:** FDRL, complete press conferences. • **Harriman reports:** FDRL, Map Room papers. • **FDR-Stalin correspondence:** FDRL, Map Room papers. • **FDR no longer believed the Russians:** FDRL, memorandum dictated by Averell Harriman, Jan. 25, 1954. • **FDR in Warm Springs:** Hassett, *Off the Record;* Margaret Suckley, FDRL, Group 21A. • **Morgenthau to dinner:** FDRL, HM Apr. 11, 1945. • **Elizabeth Shoumatoff in Warm Springs:** Shoumatoff, "Personal History"; Hassett, *Off the Record.* • **Death of FDR:** Bruenn, "Clinical Notes"; Shoumatoff, "Personal History"; Margaret Suckley, FDRL, Group 21A; Hassett, *Off the Record.* • **Washington's walking stick:** FDRL, PSF 49. • **Reactions:** Miller, *Plain Speaking;* Lilienthal, *Journals;* Thomas Emerson, COHP; Renee Adriance Simon to author; Breckinridge Long diary, LC; Bullock, *Hitler;* Sulzberger, *Long Row; Harvard Alumni Bulletin.* • **American embassy in Rio:** FDRL, Berle diary, Apr. 12, 1945. • **Crossing the land:** Smith, *Thank You.* • **In Washington:** FDRL, Thompson, Group 21A; Thomas Emerson, COHP; Lilienthal, *Journals;* Josephson, *Hillman.* • **Casket kept closed:** Elliott Roosevelt to author. • **Churchill absent:** Cadogan, *Diaries.* • **Funeral service:** Hassett, *Off the Record;* Henry Wallace, COHP; Stimson diary, Apr. 15, 1945, YU.

INDEX

314, 328; and the depression, 317–22,
346, 348, 354, 379; and governors' con-
ference, 347; renominated, 348; and
Bonus Army, 356–57; campaign and
defeat of, 361–63; and FDR's election,
363, 368–69, 377
Hoover, J. Edgar, 439, 523–24, 568, 601;
reports on Farley, 531; and Annenberg
case, 555; opposes Japanese evacuation,
626, 627; reports on Willkie, 647; and
Mrs. Roosevelt, 672, 673, 674; and
Welles case, 679–80, 682–83; and Wallace surveillance, 726
Hope, Bob, 709
Hope, Clifford, 493
Hopkins, Barbara Duncan, 384, 490
Hopkins, Ethel Gross, 384
Hopkins, Harry, 495, 552, 571, 572, 616,
664, 671, 672, 676, 765; conducts state
relief projects, 322, 333; heads FERA,
384; defeat, 538–39; and "guru" letters,
531–33; at 1940 convention, 529–30;
urges destroyers for British, 526; illnesses of, 490, 707, 711, 748, 757;
picked by FDR as successor, 484, 490;
advises on recession, 484–85; runs
WPA, 417, 435; conflicts with Ickes,
411, 417; heads CWA, 408–9; on NRA
codes, 404; mission to Stalin, 592–93;
and refugee children, 585; administers
Lend-Lease, 580; as FDR–Churchill
liaison, 578–79, 595, 600; FDR's second
in command, 551, 578; surveys internment camps, 629; and son's death,
707–8; and second-front debate,
637–39, 644–45; wedding of, 645–46;
FDR adviser at Teheran, 690, 704; and
Overlord command, 691; at Cairo meet-
ings, 705, 755; and Yalta, 744, 754
Hopkins, Louise Macy, 645–46
Hopkins, Stephen, 707–8
Hopson, Howard C., 425
Hosmer, Elsworth A., 620–21
House, Edward M., 163, 166, 170, 175,
179, 218, 340, 347, 401, 415
House Committee on Un-American Ac-
tivities, *see* Dies Committee
Housewell, Minna Lyman, 102
Houston, David F., 224
Houston, Sam, 30
Howard, Roy, 580
Howatt, D. E., 49
Howe, Edward, 132
Howe, Grace Hartley, 132
Howe, Louis, 129, 131–36, 263, 316; as
FDR aide in Navy years, 147, 153,
158–59, 161, 162, 171, 181, 199, 208,
213; and FDR's polio, 255, 259; and
Smith, 277, 288; and Moses, 278–79; as
gubernatorial-campaign aide, 289–91,
294, 295; has to share FDR, 299; as

aide in presidency bid, 323, 329, 332,
340–42, 346, 354–55, 363–64; and cab-
inet appointments, 370, 372; "toilet-kit
scandal," 381–82; and Moley's ouster,
394; death of, 442–43, 462
Howell, Clark, 330
Howes, William H., 330
Hoyt, Ferdinand A., 114
Hoyt, Julia and Lydig, 68
Hoyt, Morgan, 114
Hubbard, Leroy W., 256, 276
Hudson, Erastus Mead, 234–39, 242, 243
Huerta, Victoriano, 153, 154
Hughes, Charles Evans, 120, 170, 174–75,
374, 375, 467–68; and AAA decision,
432; and minimum-wage decision, 433,
473; and Court-packing attempt,
470–75 *passim*, 479, 480; sit-down-strike
opinion, 483
Hughes, Stanley C., 238
Hull, Cordell, 139, 328, 341, 382, 395,
554, 601, 674; appointment of, 371–73;
and Moley, 391–94, 684; and recognition of U.S.S.R., 397; and Spanish Civil
War, 439, 497; and quarantine speech,
487; misjudges Japan, 467; apologizes
for La Guardia, 486; and *Panay* incident, 488; opposes appeasement, 489;
feuds with Welles, 489, 576, 679,
680–85, 687; and Neutrality Act, 511,
512; as possible candidate, 516–17,
528–29; and fall of France, 525; and oil
embargo, 576–77; negotiations with
Japanese, 589, 606–15; and Pearl Harbor attack, 616–17; and de Gaulle, 633,
657, 686–87, 718, 724; and postwar pol-
icies, 657, 735; at Moscow, 687–89; and
refugee problem, 713, 714; retires, 742
Hull, Mrs. Cordell, 509, 516, 682, 714
Hulten, Eve, 51
Hundred Days, 377–91, 409, 413, 472
Hungary, 737, 745
Hunt, George W. P., 324
Hurley, Frank, 311
Hurley, Patrick J., 327, 733
Hutchins, Robert M., 580
Hutchinson, Miller Reese, 509
Hyde, Alexander, 28, 29
Hyde, Edward, 33
Hylan, John F., 264
Hyneman, Henry L., 240

Ibn Saud, King, 711, 713, 742, 754,
756–57
Iceland, occupation of, 592
Ickes, Harold I., 373, 376, 386, 443, 448,
467, 468, 546, 649, 758; as PWA head,
311–12, 389–90, 409, 417, 450; appointed as interior secretary, 372; and
CCC, 380; conflicts with Hopkins, 411,
417; and equality for blacks, 418; con-